A Dictionary of

World History

D1284549

Edmund Wright graduated from Oxford University in 1985 with a doctorate in history and entered publishing as a reference-book editor. Since 2004 he has been a self-employed contractor. Work has included updating the content of OUP's *Dictionary of World History* (2nd edition 2006 and 3rd edition 2014) and *Dictionary of Computing* (6th edition 2008); proofreading work on the *Shorter Oxford English Dictionary* (6th edition 2007) and the *Historical Thesaurus of the Oxford English Dictionary* (2009).

SEE WEB LINKS

For recommended web links for this title, visit www.oxfordreference.com/page/worldhist when you see this sign.

The most authoritative and up-to-date reference books for both students and the general reader.

Many of these titles are also available online at www.oxfordreference.com

A Dictionary of

World History

THIRD EDITION

OXFORD
UNIVERSITY PRESS

OXFORD
UNIVERSITY PRESS

Great Clarendon Street, Oxford, OX2 6DP,
United Kingdom

Oxford University Press is a department of the University of Oxford.
It furthers the University's objective of excellence in research, scholarship,
and education by publishing worldwide. Oxford is a registered trade mark of
Oxford University Press in the UK and in certain other countries

© Oxford University Press 2000, 2001, 2006, 2015

The moral rights of the author have been asserted

First edition 2000
Reprinted with corrections 2001
Second edition 2006
Third edition 2015

Impression: 2

Published in the United States of America by Oxford University Press
198 Madison Avenue, New York, NY 10016, United States of America

British Library Cataloguing in Publication Data
Data available

Library of Congress Control Number: 2014954275

ISBN 978-0-19-968569-1

Printed in Great Britain by
Clays Ltd, St Ives plc

Contents

Preface

A Dictionary of World History is an alphabetical dictionary in the Oxford Quick Reference series. The book is derived ultimately from the two volumes devoted to the history of the world in the *Oxford Illustrated Encyclopedia*. From this base, the editors of Market House Books Ltd. produced a new history text, making use of their adaptations of this material for the *Encyclopedia of World History* and the history entries in the *Oxford Paperback Encyclopedia*. The entry for each country includes statistical information to supplement descriptions of the country's location, economy, and history.

For this new edition, entries on contemporary subjects, including the biographies of living people as well as countries and conflicts, have been considerably updated. In addition, a number of entirely new entries have been added on events of recent history.

The dictionary is illustrated by spot maps of all the countries and some 25 historical maps. There is also a network of cross-references between related entries. Small capital letters or asterisks are used to indicate cross-references to other articles.

E.W. 2014

Credits

Editor
Edmund Wright

Market House Editors
Anne Kerr
Jonathan Law

Maps
Margaret Tuthill
Linda Wells

Maps on pages 7, 16, 298, 313, 621, and 689 prepared using MAPS IN MINUTES™ © RH PUBLICATIONS (1997).

Abbas I (or **Abbas the Great**) (1557–1628) Shah of Persia (1588–1628). He ended an inherited war with the Ottomans by conceding territory (1590) in order to free himself from the Uzbek Turks from north-eastern Persia (1598). By 1618 he had strengthened his army by curbing the Turcoman chiefs who supplied his recruits, and by using foreign advisers, and had reconquered the lands ceded to the Ottomans, but he died before the end of a further war over Mesopotamia (1623–29).

Abbasid A dynasty of caliphs ruling in Baghdad from 750 to 1258, claiming descent from Abbas, uncle of the prophet Muhammad. Some were outstanding patrons of culture, such as Mamun (813–33). The dynasty ended with the fall of Baghdad to the Mongols in 1258.

Abbott, Sir John (Joseph Caldwell) (1821–93) Canadian politician, Conservative Prime Minister of Canada (1891–92). Abbott was a compromise choice as Prime Minister after the death of Sir John *Macdonald, but resigned the following year due to ill health.

Abbott, Tony (Anthony John Abbott) (1957–) Australian politician, Prime Minister of Australia (2013–). After graduating from Sydney and Oxford universities, Abbott trained for the Roman Catholic priesthood (1984–87), but left to become a journalist. He was press secretary (1990–93) to John Hewson, leader of the Liberal Party, before entering parliament in 1994 as a Liberal MP. A cabinet minister (2001–07) under John *Howard, he became Liberal Party leader in 2009 and Prime Minister following the Liberal–National coalition's victory in the 2013 election. He is noted for his conservative views on social issues and his scepticism on *climate change.

Abd-al Aziz ibn Saud *See* SAUD.

Abd el-Krim (1881–1963) Moroccan Berber resistance leader. In 1921 he roused the Rif Berbers, and defeated a Spanish army of 20,000.

He held out until 1925, when a joint Franco-Spanish force took him prisoner. He was exiled to Réunion until 1947, when he was given permission to go to France. On the way he escaped to Cairo, where he set up the Maghrib Bureau, or Liberation Committee of the Arab West. After Moroccan independence (1956), he refused to return as long as French troops remained on African soil.

Abdication crisis *See* EDWARD VIII.

Abdul Hamid II (known as **'the Great Assassin'**) (1842–1918) Sultan of Turkey (1876–1909). An autocratic ruler, he suspended Parliament and the constitution and is remembered for the brutal massacres of Christian Armenians in 1894–96. In 1909 he was deposed after the revolt in the previous year of the *Young Turks.

Abdullah II (1962–) King of Jordan (1999–). The eldest son of King *Hussein by his second wife, Abdullah was named as heir in place of his uncle (Prince Hassan) in the last days of his father's life. He continued his father's policies, including cautious engagement with Israel.

Abdullah, Sheikh Muhammad (known as **'the Lion of Kashmir'**) (1905–82) Kashmiri Muslim leader. In the 1930s he actively opposed the rule of the Hindu maharajah of Kashmir. After accepting Indian sovereignty (1947), he eventually won for Kashmir a form of autonomy within India, although he was imprisoned for much of the time between 1953 and 1968 on suspicion of seeking its full independence.

Abdullah ibn Abd al-Aziz (1924–) King of Saudi Arabia (2005–). As crown prince (1982–2005) during the reign of his brother Fahd, he was effectively ruler of Saudi Arabia following Fahd's stroke in 1995. His rule has seen cautious social and economic liberalization coupled with stringent internal security measures to combat terrorism.

Abdullah ibn Hussein (1882–1951) King of Jordan (1946–51). He served as emir of Transjordan (1921–46), becoming Jordan's first king on independence in 1946. He was assassinated.

Abdul Rahman, Tunku (1903–90) Malayan statesman, Prime Minister of Malaya (1957–63) and of Malaysia (1963–70). A skilled negotiator, he secured Malayan independence from Britain (1957) and was one of the architects of modern Malaysia (1963).

Abelard, Peter (1079–1142) French scholar, theologian, and philosopher. His independence of mind brought him into frequent conflict with the authorities and led to his being twice condemned for heresy. He lectured in Paris until 1118. While in Paris he began a tragic love affair with one of his pupils, Héloïse, who was a niece of Fulbert, a canon of Notre-Dame. At Fulbert's instigation Abelard was subsequently castrated. Abelard then entered a monastery and made Héloïse become a nun. Abelard continued his controversial teaching, applying reason to questions of faith, notably to the doctrine of the Trinity. In the early 1130s he and Héloïse put together a collection of their love letters and other correspondence, which was published in 1616. Abelard and Héloïse are buried together in Paris.

Aberdeen, George Hamilton Gordon, 4th Earl of (1784–1860) British statesman. He was Foreign Secretary during 1828–30 and again from 1841 to 1846, when he concluded the Webster–Ashburton and Oregon Boundary treaties, which settled boundary disputes between the USA and Canada. As a leader of those Conservatives who campaigned for free trade, he supported Sir Robert Peel in repealing the *Corn Laws (1846). As Prime Minister (1852–55) of the 'Aberdeen Coalition', he reluctantly involved his country in the *Crimean War and was subsequently blamed for its mismanagement. He resigned in 1855.

abolitionists Militant opponents of slavery in 19th-century USA. In the first two decades of the 19th century, there was only a handful of individual abolitionists, but thereafter, fired by religious revivalism, the abolition movement became a strong political force. Prominent as writers and orators were the Boston newspaper-owner William Lloyd Garrison, the author Harriet Beecher Stowe (whose anti-slavery novel *Uncle Tom's Cabin* sold 1.5 million copies within a year of its publication in 1852), and the ex-slave Frederick Douglass. The abolitionist cause at first found little support in Congress or the main political parties, except among a few individuals such as Charles Sumner, but it played an increasing part in precipitating the political division that led to the *American Civil War.

abolition of slavery *See* SLAVE TRADE, ABOLITION OF.

Aborigine An original inhabitant of Australia. The Aborigines comprise several physically distinct groups of dark-skinned hunter-gatherers who arrived in prehistoric times and brought with them the dingo. Before the arrival of Europeans they were scattered through the whole continent, including Tasmania. In 1788 the Aboriginal population was estimated to stand at around 250,000–300,000 and was divided into more than 500 linguistic groups. Today about 1.5% of the people of Australia are Aborigines. Although over 65% now live in towns and cities, the cultural heritage of the Aborigines has been protected in recent years by changes in Australian federal and state laws that have established land rights, community development programmes, and educational assistance. The Australian parliament apologized for past injustices to Aborigines in 2008.

Aboukir Bay (or Abukir, Abu Qir) A bay on the Mediterranean coast of Egypt, lying between Alexandria and the Rosetta mouth of the Nile. Nelson defeated the French fleet under Brueys at the Battle of the *Nile which was fought in the bay on 1–2 August 1798. Sir Ralph Abercromby's expedition landed near the village of Aboukir and defeated the French in 1801.

Abraham, Plains of *See* PLAINS OF ABRAHAM, BATTLE OF THE.

Absaroke *See* CROW AND HIDATSA.

absentee landlord A landowner not normally resident on the estate from which he derived income and which was generally managed through an agent. While some landlords cared for the welfare of their tenants, others engaged in such practices as the issue of very short leases, which gave unscrupulous agents opportunities to raise rents frequently and evict anyone unable to pay. Abuses were common in pre-revolutionary France and in Ireland, where successive confiscations had led to Irish estates falling into English hands.

Abu Bakr (c.573–634) First *caliph of Islam (632–34). He was one of the earliest converts to Islam and a close companion of the Prophet *Muhammad, who married his daughter Aisha.

When he succeeded to Muhammad's position as temporal leader of the Muslim community, this pious and gentle man was chiefly concerned to reaffirm the allegiance of those Arabian tribes who had withdrawn it at the time of the Prophet's death. These 'wars of apostasy' initiated the *Arab conquests.

Abushiri Revolt (August 1888–89) An Arab revolt against German traders on the East African coast north of Zanzibar. The Arab leader Abushiri (**Abu Bashir ibn Salim al-Harthi**) united local hostility to German colonization at Pangani when in August 1888 the Germans hauled down the Sultan of Zanzibar's flag and hoisted their own. British and German interference in the slave, ivory, and rubber trades, and their conduct in mosques, had already caused resentment. Abushiri's resistance spread inland to the Usambara mountains, and to Lake Victoria. The revolt was crushed by the German explorer and administrator Hermann von Wissmann in 1889.

Abydos 1. A town of ancient Mysia in Asia Minor, situated on a hill overlooking the Dardanelles, north-east of the modern Turkish city of Çanakkale. Abydos was the scene of the story of Hero and Leander and the place where the Persian King Xerxes constructed his bridge of boats over the Hellespont in 480 BC.

2. A town in ancient Egypt and burial place of the first pharaohs, situated on the left bank of the Nile near modern El Balyana.

Abyssinia A former name of *Ethiopia.

Abyssinian Campaigns (1935–41) A series of conflicts between Italy, Abyssinia (*Ethiopia), and later Britain. War broke out as a result of Italy's unfulfilled ambition of 1894–96 to link *Eritrea with *Somalia, and *Mussolini's aim to provide colonies to absorb Italy's surplus unemployed population. In 1934 and 1935 incidents, which were possibly contrived, took place at Walwal and elsewhere. On 3 October 1935 an Italian army attacked the Ethiopian forces from the north and east. Eventually the Ethiopians mustered 40,000 men, but they were helpless against the highly trained troops and modern weapons of the Italians. Fighting continued during the Italian occupation (1936–41). In 1940 the Italians occupied British Somaliland, but in 1941 British troops evicted the Italians entirely from Eritrea, Ethiopia, and Somalia in a four-month campaign with support from Ethiopian nationalists.

Academy The school established at Athens by *Plato in the 380s BC, probably intended to prepare men to serve the city-state. It was as a philosophical centre that it became celebrated, its students including the philosophers *Aristotle, *Epicurus, and Zeno of Citium. Much of its history is obscure, but it survived until its closure by *Justinian I in 529 AD.

Achaean League A confederacy of Achaean and other Peloponnesian states in ancient *Greece. Its name derived from the region of Achaea in the northern Peloponnese. In the 4th century BC an alliance was forged that was dissolved in 338 BC. The League was refounded in 280 BC, under the leadership of Aratus of Sicyon. It became involved in wars with Macedonia and Sparta, before allying itself with Rome in 198. However, war with Rome in 146 led to defeat and the dissolution of the League.

Achaemenid The dynasty established by *Cyrus II (the Great) in the 6th century BC and named after his ancestor Achaemenes. Cyrus' predecessors ruled Parsumash, a vassal state of the Median empire, but he overthrew their king Astyages and incorporated the *Medes within his Persian empire, which by his death in 530 BC extended from Asia Minor to the River Indus. His successor Cambyses II (529–521 BC) added Egypt. *Darius I instituted a major reorganization of the administration and finances of the empire, establishing twenty provinces ruled by Satraps. Both he and *Xerxes failed in their attempts to conquer Greece in the early 5th century. By the time *Alexander III (the Great) invaded with his Macedonian army (334 BC) the empire was much weakened. Darius III, defeated at Issus and Gaugamela and killed by his own men in 330 BC, was the last Achaemenid king; the empire subsequently passed to Alexander and his successors. Achaemenid rule was tolerant of local customs, religions, and forms of government. The construction of a major road system, centred on Susa, facilitated trade and administration. The magnificent remains of *Persepolis provide a glimpse of Achaemenid wealth and power.

Acheh War (1873–1903) A conflict in north Sumatra between the Dutch and the people of Acheh, a sultanate on the northern coast of Sumatra, claimed to be the first Muslim state in south-east Asia. After the fall of Malacca to the Portuguese in 1511 many Muslim traders moved there. By the late 16th century Acheh had reduced the power of Johore and controlled much of Sumatra and Malaya, deriving its wealth from pepper and tin. After the Dutch took Malacca in 1641, Acheh consolidated its rule in Sumatra. Trade rivalry and attempts by the sultan of Acheh to obtain foreign assistance against Dutch domination of north Sumatra caused the dispatch of an abortive Dutch expeditionary force in 1871. Although a larger force, sent later in the year, captured the sultan's capital, the Dutch met with fierce resistance in the interior, organized by the local religious leaders (*ulama*). The war was brought to an end between 1898 and January 1903 by military 'pacification' and concessions to the *ulama*, who were permitted to carry on their religious duties.

Acheson, Dean (Gooderham) (1893–1971) US politician. He served as Assistant Secretary of State, Under-Secretary, and Secretary of State (1949–53), urging international control of nuclear power in the Acheson–Lilienthal Report of 1946, formulating plans for NATO (*North Atlantic Treaty Organization), implementing the *Marshall Plan, and upholding the *Truman Doctrine of US support for nations threatened by communism.

Acheulian *See* PALAEOLITHIC.

acropolis The citadel of an ancient Greek city, most notably of Athens. The Athenian citadel was destroyed by the invading Persians in 480 BC, but *Pericles instituted a rebuilding programme. The Parthenon, built 447–432, was a Doric temple containing a gold and ivory statue of Athena. This was followed by the gateway or Propylaea, the temple of Athena Nike (commemorating victory over the Persians), and the Erectheum, which housed the shrines of various cults. *See also* ELGIN, THOMAS BRUCE, 7TH EARL OF.

Action Française An extreme right-wing group in France during the first half of the 20th century, and also the name of the newspaper published to promote its views. Founded by the poet and political journalist Charles Maurras, it aimed at overthrowing the parliamentary republic and sought to restore the monarchy. Strongly nationalist, it became discredited for its overt *fascism and association with the *Vichy government in 1940–44.

Actium, Battle of The naval battle in 31 BC off north-west Acarnania in western Greece at which Octavian defeated Mark Antony to become ruler of Rome.

Act of Union *See* UNION, ACTS OF.

Adams, John (1735–1826) US Federalist statesman, 2nd President of the USA (1797–1801). He was a key figure in the drafting of the Declaration of Independence (1776), and was minister to Britain (1785–88).

Adams, John Quincy (1767–1848) US Republican statesman, 6th President of the USA (1825–29). The eldest son of President John Adams, he was minister to Britain (1809–14). As Secretary of State (1817–24) he helped to shape the Monroe Doctrine, the principle of US foreign policy that any intervention by external powers in the politics of the Americas is a potentially hostile act against the USA. After leaving office he was prominent in the campaign against slavery.

Adams, Samuel (1722–1803) American patriot, the leader of resistance to Britain in Massachusetts between 1763 and 1776. He founded the Sons of Liberty in Boston and organized riots, propaganda, and boycotts against tax-raising. He attended the *Continental Congress and signed the *Declaration of Independence. He later served as governor of Massachusetts and was drafter of its constitution (1780).

Addams, Jane (1860–1935) US social worker and reformer. With her friend Ellen Grates Starr, she opened Hull House in Chicago in 1889, a pioneer settlement house for workers and immigrants. A pioneer of the new discipline of sociology, she had considerable influence over the planning of neighbourhood welfare institutions throughout the country. She was a leader of the *women's suffrage movement and an active pacifist.

Addington, Henry, 1st Viscount Sidmouth (1757–1844) British Tory statesman, Prime Minister (1801–04). As Home Secretary (1812–22), he introduced harsh legislation to suppress the Luddites and other protest groups.

Addled Parliament (5 April–7 June 1614) The nickname given to *James I of England's second Parliament. In the absence of effective guidance from crown or councillors, those opposed to the king's policies were able to divert the House of Commons to discussion of grievances, including church reform, import duties, and court interference at the elections. The king dissolved the Parliament before it had passed any legislation—hence the term 'addled' meaning empty or muddled—and ruled without one until 1621.

Adenauer, Konrad (1876–1967) German statesman, first Chancellor of the Federal Republic of Germany (1949–63). He co-founded the Christian Democratic Union in 1945. As

Chancellor, he is remembered for the political and economic transformation of his country. He secured the friendship of the USA and was an advocate of strengthening political and economic ties with Western countries.

Adowa, Battle of (1 March 1896) A decisive defeat of the Italians by the Ethiopian Emperor Menelik II. Italy had established a protectorate in Ethiopia in 1889. In 1895 there was a rebellion and at Adowa an Italian force of 10,000 was routed, losing 4500 dead and 300 prisoners. In the resulting Treaty of Addis Ababa the Italians recognized the independence of Ethiopia and restricted themselves to the colony of Eritrea. The battle ensured Ethiopian survival as an independent kingdom in Africa.

Adrian IV (born **Nicholas Breakspear**) (*c.*1100–59) Pope (1154–59). The only Englishman to have held this office, he opposed Frederick I's (Barbarossa's) claims to power.

Adrianople, Battle of (9 August 378 AD) The Roman city of Adrianople, 480 km (300 miles) west of Constantinople, was the scene of the defeat of the Roman forces by the *Visigoths. Emperor Valens, who had hoped to prevent the Gothic invasion of the Roman empire, was killed.

Adrianople, Treaty of (1829) A peace treaty negotiated between Russia and the Ottoman empire. It terminated the war between them (1828–29) and gave Russia minor territorial gains in Europe, including access to the mouth of the Danube, and substantial gains in the Caucasus. The treaty also confirmed the autonomy of Serbia, promised autonomy for Greece, and guaranteed free passage for merchant ships through the Dardanelles.

Aegean civilization *See* MYCENAEAN CIVILIZATION.

Aegospotami, Battle of The naval battle (405 BC) fought in the Hellespont, the strait between the Aegean Sea and the Sea of Marmara, that sealed the defeat of Athens in the *Peloponnesian War. For five days the Athenian fleet attempted to draw *Lysander and the Spartan fleet into battle. As the Athenians were disembarking after the fifth attempt, Lysander launched a surprise attack and captured 160 out of 180 *triremes. He executed all the Athenians whom he took prisoner.

Afars and Issas *See* DJIBOUTI.

Afghani, Jamal al-Din al- (1839–97) Muslim revivalist of Iranian origin. He advocated social and political reforms within Muslim countries and Pan-Islamism. Afghani was active as a teacher in Egypt during the 1870s, edited a newspaper (*al-Urwa al-Wuthqa*, 'the Unbreakable Link') in Paris during the 1880s, and played a part in the protest in Iran in 1891–92.

Afghanistan

Capital:	Kabul
Area:	652,225 sq km (251,825 sq miles)
Population:	30,419,928 (2013 est)
Currency:	1 afghani = 100 puls
Religions:	Sunni Muslim 80.0%; Shiite Muslim 19.0%
Ethnic Groups:	Pathan (Pashto) 42.0%; Tajik 27.0%; Uzbek 9.0%; Hazara 9.0%
Languages:	Pashto, Dari (Persian) (both official); minority languages
International Organizations:	UN; Colombo Plan; Non-Aligned Movement

A mountainous and landlocked country in south-central Asia, bounded on the west by Iran, on the south and east by Pakistan, on the east by China, and on the north by Turkmenistan, Uzbekistan, and Tajikistan.

Physical Afghanistan's eastern region is dominated by the vast mountain range of the Hindu Kush and most of the country is high plateau. In winter much of it is under snow; in spring grass appears, which is scorched dry and swept by the dust storms of summer.

Economy Agriculture, mainly sheep-raising and subsistence farming, is the mainstay of the economy, which has been devastated by nearly 30 years of civil war. The illegal cultivation of opium poppies is now the country's main source of income.

History Afghanistan was conquered by Alexander the Great, and after his death became part of the Bactrian state. A succession of foreign overlords was followed by Arab conquest from the 7th century. The territory was converted to Islam and the most important Muslim ruler was Mahmud of Ghazna. The country was overrun by Mongols in 1222, only becoming united under an Afghan leader in 1747, when

Ahmad Shah founded the Durrani dynasty at Kandahar. In the 19th and early 20th centuries Afghanistan was the focal point of conflicting Russian and British interests. A British attempt to replace the Kabul ruler Dost Muhammad was repulsed in the First *Anglo-Afghan War, but Afghan foreign policy came under British control in 1879 by the Treaty of Gandamak, when Britain gained control of the Khyber Pass. In 1880 Abdurrahman Khan became amir, establishing a strong central government; Afghanistan achieved independence from Britain under his heir, Amanollah Khan, in 1919. In 1953 General Mohammad Daoud Khan seized power and was Prime Minister until 1963, during which time he obtained economic and military assistance from the Soviet Union. There were border disputes with Pakistan, but it was Daoud's policy to maintain 'non-alignment' between the two superpower blocs. In 1964 Afghanistan became a parliamentary democracy, but a military coup in 1973 overthrew the monarchy and Daoud reasserted control. In 1977 he issued a constitution for a one-party state. Within a year, however, he had been assassinated and the Democratic Republic of Afghanistan proclaimed, headed by a revolutionary council, whose first President was Nur Mohammad Taraki. The new regime embarked on reforms, causing some rural unrest. In February 1979 the US ambassador was killed and one month later Taraki was assassinated by supporters of the deputy Prime Minister, Ha'zullah Amin, who sought US support. In December 1979 Soviet troops entered the country. Amin was killed and replaced by Babrak Karmal. Guerrilla Mujahidin forces, equipped with US arms, then waged a *jihad* or holy war against government troops armed and supported by Soviet forces. Some six million refugees fled to Iran and Pakistan. In 1987 the Soviet Union began to disengage, all troops being withdrawn by 1989, when the pro-Soviet government of Mohammad Najibullah was replaced by an Islamic state. However, civil conflict between both rival Mujahidin factions and other militant groups continued. In 1995–96 the Taliban militia, an army of young Islamic militants, gained control of southern Afghanistan, including Kabul, and imposed strict Islamic law. By 1999 they had effectively defeated their rivals in the north (the Northern Alliance) and controlled some 90% of the country. In late 2001 Afghanistan came under heavy air attack from the USA after the Taliban refused to hand over Osama *Bin Laden, whose Afghan-based *al-Qaeda organization was held responsible for the terrorist attacks on the USA on *September 11,

2001. The Taliban regime collapsed and the Northern Alliance occupied Kabul and other cities. An interim government was established that relied on US and (from 2003) NATO forces to maintain security. Hamid Karzai became President in 2002. A democratic constitution was adopted in January 2004, and in October Karzai was victorious in the country's first direct presidential election; he was re-elected in 2009. The country's first parliament in over 30 years met in late 2005. However, Taliban resistance had not been quelled and guerrilla activity revived in the mid-2000s, especially in southern Afghanistan. Increased NATO troop deployments recovered some territory but failed to defeat the Taliban. In 2011 NATO began to transfer security responsibilities to the Afghan army with the aim of withdrawing all NATO forces within three years. Ashraf Ghani was elected President in 2014.

Afghan Wars *See* ANGLO-AFGHAN WARS.

Africa The second largest continent, extending south from the Mediterranean Sea and bounded by the Atlantic and Indian oceans and the Red Sea.

Physical The Equator passes through the middle of Africa, so that all but the very north and south are tropical, although regional differences in climate and landscape are vast. Most of northern Africa is desert, the only significant waterway being the Nile. The west, watered by the Niger and other rivers, is rich in tropical forests, though in many coastal regions there is only swamp. Inland, the ground rises first to savannahs and then to hilly, wooded plateaux in the centre of the continent. Here are some of the largest copper deposits in the world, and also deposits of gold, diamonds, uranium, cobalt, and other minerals. East Africa is a temperate region of great lakes, mountains, and high plateaux. It is split from north to south by the Great Rift Valley. South of the Zambezi River are more highlands, giving way in the south-west to the Kalahari Desert. Then the land rises again, to the temperate veld. This good farming country is very rich in minerals. The southernmost coastal plain is ideal for fruit and plantation crops.

History Evidence suggests that Africa was the birthplace of the human race, as shown by finds at Olduvai Gorge and other sites. By the late Stone Age Proto-Berbers inhabited the north, Ethiopians the Nile valley, while *Negroid peoples moved southwards. Pygmies occupied the central forest, and San and Khoikhoi (called Bushmen and Hottentots by White colonists) roamed the south.

By the 4th millennium BC, one of the world's oldest civilizations had developed in *Egypt. In the north *Phoenicians, and then *Carthaginians, organized sea-borne empires which fell, with Egypt, to Rome in the last centuries BC. Indigenous kingdoms arose in *Nubia and *Aksum. In the 7th century the Arabs seized the north, bringing to it the religion and culture of *Islam.

In Cameroon *c.*500 BC a population explosion sent the Bantu eastwards. They slowly occupied most of southern and central Africa, overwhelming the San people. There and in West Africa chieftainships developed, and some

empires with sophisticated cultures, especially in Islamic states such as *Mali and in Christian *Ethiopia. Their intricate system of commerce reached from the Mediterranean to Indonesia and China. The Portuguese arrival in the 15th century heralded European intervention in Africa, stimulating trade in the west and centre, but interrupting it in the east. In the 16th century the north fell to the Ottomans, while south of the Sahara Europeans began the *slave trade to the Americas. From the 16th to the 18th century in the present Democratic Republic of the Congo (formerly Zaïre) and in central Africa Bantu states developed, some of them sizeable

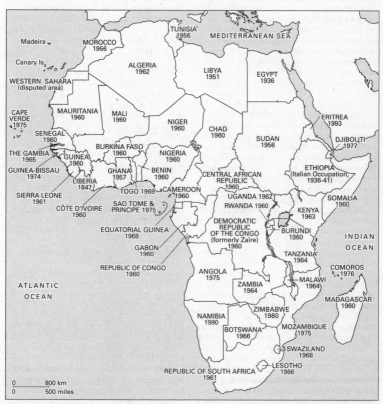

African decolonization. Agitation for political independence was strong in Islamic North Africa before World War II, but south of the Sahara the first Black African independent state to emerge was Ghana (1957). Within decades, White minority rule was confined to South Africa and Namibia. The map shows the years in which the modern African states became independent and gives their modern, rather than colonial-era, names.

empires. During this period the Bantu were pushing their way southwards, but it was not until the 19th century that they began to form recognizable states in the present South Africa. While each tribe or state developed its individual pattern of constitution, some more sophisticated than others, power was generally concentrated in the hands of chieftains and regulated both by tribal conventions and by free public discussion in tribal assemblies.

During the 19th century the interior was gradually opened up to European explorers, traders, and missionaries in an extensive programme of colonization. Imperialist sentiments and the desire to exploit the continent's natural resources produced a series of military campaigns against the local states and tribes. By 1914 almost all Africa was ruled as colonies by European states. After World War I Germany's former colonial empire was divided among the victorious Allies. After 1945 the rise of African nationalism accelerated the process of decolonization, most of the Black countries becoming independent between 1957 and 1980, sometimes as a result of peaceful negotiation and sometimes through armed rebellion. In Namibia (until 1990) and South Africa (until 1994), small White élites held on to political power, but elsewhere the descendants of the original inhabitants assumed responsibility for their own government. The artificial boundaries imposed by colonialism, the rapidity of the transition to home rule, and the underdeveloped state of many of the local economies produced political, social, and economic problems of varying severity all over the continent. Many of the new nations remained unstable and politically impoverished, while drought in the 1980s and early 1990s in both East and Southern Africa caused terrible suffering. Multiparty democracies, which replaced single-party regimes in many African countries in the early 1990s, inherited vast burdens of World Bank and IMF debt. By the early 21st century an AIDS pandemic threatened a population catastrophe in sub-Saharan Africa: about 10% of the adult population has HIV or AIDS, rising to over 20% in southern Africa, and average life expectancy is decreasing.

African Charter on Human and Peoples' Rights A charter adopted by the Organization of African Unity (now the *African Union) in 1981 and ratified by all of its members except South Sudan. The Charter reaffirms the duty of African states to eliminate colonialism, apartheid, and *Zionism, and stresses that civil and political rights cannot be dissociated from

economic, social, and cultural rights. The Charter concurs with the Universal Declaration of Human Rights, and emphasizes the rights of 'peoples'. It established the African Commission on Human and Peoples' Rights, now based in Banjul, the Gambia, a body intended to promote human rights, as well as to investigate complaints from individuals. A protocol to create an African Court on Human and Peoples' Rights was adopted in 1998 and came into force in 2005. However, in many African countries habitual abuse of human rights continues.

African National Congress (ANC) A South African political party. It was established in Bloemfontein in 1912 as the South African Native National Congress by a Zulu Methodist minister, J. W. Dube. In 1914 he led a deputation to Britain protesting against the Native Land Act (1913), which restricted the purchase of land by Black Africans. In 1926 the ANC established a united front with representatives of the Indian community, which aimed to create a racially integrated, democratic southern Africa. It sought to achieve racial equality by nonviolent means, as practised by Mahatma *Gandhi in India, and from 1952 until 1967 was led by the Natal chieftain Albert *Luthuli. Together with the more militant break-away movement, the Pan-Africanist Congress (PAC), it was declared illegal by the South African government in 1960. Confronted by Afrikaner intransigence on racial issues, the ANC saw itself forced into a campaign of violence. Maintaining that *apartheid should be abolished, and every South African have the vote, it formed a liberation army, 'Umkhonto Wesizwe' (Spear of the Nation). In 1962 its vice-president, Nelson *Mandela, and some of his colleagues were convicted of sabotage and jailed for life. The exiled wing of the ANC maintained a campaign of violence during the 1980s, but following the election of President *de Klerk (1989) the party was legalized and Mandela was released from prison in 1990. The ANC subsequently entered into talks with the government and participated in the drafting of a new constitution, which gave the vote to all South African adults. The first multiracial elections, held in 1994, were won by the ANC and Mandela became President. The ANC has been re-elected in all subsequent elections, in 1999, 2004, and 2009.

African Union (AU) An association of African states founded in 2001. It succeeded the **Organization of African Unity**, which was founded in 1963 for mutual cooperation and the elimination of colonialism. The AU extended these aims to encompass eventual political and economic union. Comprising (2013) all African states except Morocco, it has its headquarters in Addis Ababa, Ethiopia.

Afrikaner (or **Boer**) A member of the White Afrikaans-speaking population of South Africa. The term is used particularly to refer to the descendants of the families that emigrated from the Netherlands, Germany, and France before 1806, that is, before Britain seized the Cape Colony. Most Afrikaners follow the Christian Calvinist tradition, which, through the belief that salvation is only possible for a predetermined group of people and cannot be gained by any other individual, even by leading a religious life, contributed to the concept of *apartheid.

Agade *See* AKKAD.

Aga Khan The title of the imam or leader of the Nizari sect of Ismaili Muslims. The first Aga Khan was given his title in 1818 by the shah of Persia, subsequently moving with the majority of the Nizaris to the Indian subcontinent. The present (4th) Aga Khan (Karim Al-Hussain Shah; 1936–) inherited the title from his grandfather in 1957. The title of Aga Khan (which comes from the Turkish words for master and ruler) carries with it responsibility for various services and welfare provisions for members of the Nizari community.

Agincourt, Battle of (25 October 1415) The village of Agincourt in northern France was the scene of the defeat of a large French force by an English army led by *Henry V. Henry's force invaded Normandy in 1415, captured Harfleur, but was intercepted by a large French army after a long march north towards Calais. The English troops, mainly archers and foot soldiers, dug in behind wooden stakes between thickly wooded ground. The next day the French cavalry advanced on a narrow front across muddy ground only to be killed by English archers and infantry. A dozen French notables, including the Constable of France, died, together with perhaps 1,500 knights and 4,500 men-at-arms. English casualties were light but included the Duke of York and the Earl of Suffolk. The battle was fought on St Crispin's day.

Agricola, Gnaeus Julius (40–93 AD) Governor of Roman Britain 78–84. He served with Paulinus against the Iceni queen *Boudicca (61) and commanded the Twentieth Legion in the north-west (70–73). As governor he subjugated the Ordovices of north Wales and extended the frontier north to the rivers Forth and Clyde,

defeating the Caledonians in the process. His successes irritated Emperor Domitian who recalled him to Rome in 84. His career is described in his *Life* by *Tacitus, his son-in-law.

Agricultural Revolution The agricultural changes that occurred in Britain during the 18th century. Some historians stress that agriculture was already undergoing evolutionary change, but that this was speeded up by *enclosure, particularly the parliamentary enclosures of the 18th century. The medieval economy rested on the manorial system and open-field cultivation in strips which hampered change. The Agricultural Revolution saw this replaced by large-scale farming in consolidated units, the extension of arable farming over heaths and commons, the adoption of intensive livestock husbandry, the conversion of a largely self-subsistent peasantry into a community of agricultural labourers, and considerable attention to the improvement of agricultural techniques like *crop rotation, new crops, for example turnips and potatoes, and improved grasses. Viscount *Townshend (1674–1738) and Thomas Coke, Earl of Leicester (1752–1842) were notable for their adoption and promotion of crop rotation; Jethro Tull (1674–1741) for his seed drills; and Robert Bakewell (1725–95) was the most famous of the livestock improvers.

agriculture Cultivation of the soil, including the allied pursuits of gathering crops and rearing livestock. The 'Neolithic revolution', the change from an economy based on hunting and gathering to one based on settled agriculture, is thought to have begun in many independent centres around the world, at very roughly the same time (c.9000 BC): changes in climate and population growth may have stimulated this process. Archaeological evidence suggests at least three independent centres of origin for agriculture based on grain crops (the Near East, the Far East, and meso-America), plus other sites (for example, Peru and Indonesia) where root vegetables formed the main crops. The most complete evidence has come from the Near East, where domesticated barley and emmer wheat strains have been found which date from about 8000 BC. Domesticated animals (e.g. sheep and goats) were reared in large numbers from at least 7000 BC, and there is evidence for the use of the ox-drawn wooden plough from 5000 BC. In the early civilizations of Babylonia, Egypt, the Indus Valley, and China (from c.3000 BC), large-scale irrigation systems were developed.

Agricultural practices spread gradually from the different centres to other parts of the world, and were adapted to local conditions; many different field systems evolved. In Europe and the Mediterranean, practices, once established, remained basically unchanged for many years. Roman farmers used an ox-drawn, wheelless plough with iron shares or blades. They sowed seed by hand, harvested using a curved sickle, threshed grain with a hand flail, and winnowed it by throwing it into the air and letting the wind carry away the chaff. By the 4th century AD, high labour input, the transplanting of seedlings, and use of fertilizers were producing cereal yields in China not matched elsewhere until the 19th century. In the Americas, maize was the main crop in some areas, the potato in others. The llama was domesticated as a beast of burden, while the alpaca was kept for its wool, and the guinea-pig for meat. In medieval Europe, slow improvements were made in agricultural practice, particularly in northern areas. From the 5th to the 12th centuries, agricultural land was created by forest clearance, or was reclaimed from marshland and the sea. From the late 13th to the early 15th centuries, much arable land fell into disuse due to the effects of floods, famine, plague, and wars. Recovery began slowly in the 15th century. In the 17th and 18th centuries several different developments led to improvements in crop yields and in livestock production. In particular, the *Agricultural Revolution of 18th-century Britain introduced new, more efficient practices into farming. Principal among these was the Norfolk four-course system, in which grain and fodder or grazing crops were grown in a four-year rotation. The effects of this system were cumulative: grazing animals manured the land and increased its fertility, while the growing of winter fodder and summer grazing crops meant that animals were better fed, and more productive. In the 18th century selective breeding was introduced, and the Rotherham plough (the forerunner of the modern plough) was developed, along with a variety of simple machines for threshing, chopping animal feed, hoeing, and seed drilling. However, it was not until the mid-19th century that agricultural machinery, for example the reaper and the traction-engine, began to be adopted by farmers. The 19th century also saw the development of agricultural science, with the introduction of the earliest chemical and synthetic fertilizers, and the opening of agricultural research stations in several countries. During this period large areas of the USA, Canada, South America, and Australia were settled: huge sheep and cattle ranches were established, and large areas were given over to wheat farming. In colonial countries, plantation farming of beverage crops, rubber, and sugar cane expanded tremendously, although these developments had little effect on indigenous agricultural practices. Much of the cheap food generated by the opening up of these new areas was exported to Europe. The 20th century has seen far-reaching changes in farming practices. The internal-combustion engine has replaced steam-power for agricultural machinery, and improved transport has led to the development of a world market for some agricultural products. The green revolution saw increased crop production in developing countries. From 1965 to the early 1990s, world cereal production increased by over 70%. Thus India, for example, which formerly suffered regularly from famine and was forced to spend scarce foreign exchange on food imports is now self-sufficient in food although its population has doubled since independence in 1947. Agrochemicals were being used in huge quantities by the 1960s, but since that time the hazards of indiscriminate pesticide use have led to the development of other strategies such as the breeding of disease-resistant plant strains and the use of biological methods of pest control favoured by organic farmers. Genetic development of plant strains and intensive animal breeding have greatly increased the productivity of croplands and livestock in developed countries while the production of genetically modified food has proved controversial. In the UK genetically modified food is generally not sold because of public opposition.

Agrippa, Marcus Vipsanius (63–12 BC) Roman general. Augustus' adviser and son-in-law, he played an important part in the naval victories over Mark Antony, and held commands in both western and eastern provinces of the empire.

Aguinaldo, Emilio (1869–1964) Filipino nationalist leader. He became active in the nationalist movement in the early 1890s and led an armed uprising against Spanish rule (1895–96). He returned during the Spanish–American War (1898) and organized another guerrilla campaign, but, after the US victory, his nationalist aspirations resulted in war with American forces (1899–1901). Finally accepting US rule, he waged a peaceful campaign for independence for the next four decades before collaborating with the Japanese during World War II. Briefly imprisoned by the Americans in 1945, he retired from active politics after his release.

Ahern, Bertie (Patrick Bartholomew Ahern) (1951–) Irish politician, Prime Minister of the Republic of Ireland (1997–2008). The leader of

Fianna Fáil (1994–2008), Ahern was an architect of the Good Friday Agreement of 1998 (*see* NORTHERN IRELAND). He resigned following allegations of corruption.

Aidan, St (died 651) Irish missionary. While a monk in the monastery at Iona, he was assigned the mission of Christianizing Northumbria by the Northumbrian king Oswald (*c.*604–42). Aidan founded a church and monastery at Lindisfarne in 635 and became its first bishop; he also established a school for training missionaries of the Celtic Church. He later founded further churches and monasteries in Northumbria.

air force The armed service concerned with attack and defence in the air. Aircraft were first used in World War I to locate targets for artillery on the Western Front, but from 1916 onwards they were developed for bombing, while rival fighter aircraft engaged in aerial dogfights both in France and in the Mesopotamian Campaign, where aircraft were also invaluable for reconnaissance. Airships were also constructed, especially by Germany, which used Zeppelin airships for bombing attacks against civilian targets. After disastrous crashes in the 1930s, however, airships lost popularity. Very rapid development in aircraft design between the wars meant that World War II began with both sides possessing formidable bomber and fighter capability. During the war dive-bombing techniques as well as heavily armed bombers for massed high altitude air raids (*bombing offensives) were developed, while the invention of radar assisted defenders in locating attacking aircraft. Large troop-carrying planes were also introduced, together with the helicopter, which became a key weapon in later wars in Korea, Vietnam, and Afghanistan. The Cold War, from the late 1940s to 1990, saw the deployment by the superpowers of strategic nuclear bombers and intercontinental ballistic missiles (ICBMs). With the advent of supersonic flight, the high costs of increasingly sophisticated aircraft since World War II have led to the design of aircraft that each fulfil several roles, often jointly developed by a consortium of nations. Air power was decisive in the *Gulf War of 1991. This saw the first large-scale use of several innovations, such as laser-guided bombs and computer-guided cruise missiles, that were able to pinpoint and destroy specific targets. A further development was the use of the Stealth bomber, which was designed to evade and destroy radar defences. Since the late 2000s the USA has used unmanned aircraft, known as 'drones', in *Afghanistan and elsewhere. Some drones are controlled by computers; others still have human pilots, but these are located remotely, often thousands of miles away in the USA.

Aix-la-Chapelle, Treaty of (1748) The treaty that concluded the War of the *Austrian Succession. It restored conquered territory to its original owners, with a few exceptions. The terms were drawn up by the British and French and reluctantly accepted by Empress *Maria Theresa of Austria, who had to abandon Silesia to *Frederick II of Prussia. In Italy Don Philip, the younger son of Philip V of Spain, received Parma. This treaty was a temporary truce in the Anglo-French conflict in India and North America. In North America colonists unwillingly ceded the French fortress of Louisburg, in order to secure the return of Madras to Britain. Prussia's rise to the rank of a great power was strongly resented by Austria. The treaty left many issues of conflict unresolved and war (the *Seven Years War) broke out again eight years later.

Akbar, Jalaludin Muhammad (or **Akbar the Great**) (1542–1605) Mogul emperor of India (1556–1605). Akbar expanded the Mogul empire to incorporate northern India, and established administrative efficiency and a coherent commercial system. He was the first ruler of India to promote religious and racial toleration. Akbar abolished slavery, prohibited the practice of suttee, legitimized the remarriage of widows, and banned polygamy except in cases of infertility.

Akhenaten (or **Akhenaton, Ikhnaton**) (14th century BC) Egyptian pharaoh of the 18th dynasty (1379–1362 BC). The husband of Nefertiti, he came to the throne as Amenhotep IV, and after six years introduced the monotheistic solar cult of Aten, the Sun disc, with the king as sole intermediary, changing his name to Akhenaten. The capital of Egypt was moved from Thebes to his newly built city of Akhetaten (now Tell el-Amarna). He was succeeded by his son-in-law, Tutankhamen, who abandoned the new religion early in his reign.

Akkad (or **Agade**) A city on the Euphrates (as yet undiscovered) which gave its name to an ancient northern Semitic kingdom, traditionally founded by Sargon (2334–2279 BC) in north-central Mesopotamia (modern Iraq). Its power extended over Babylonia, Assyria, and Syria, and even penetrated into Asia Minor, until it was overwhelmed by invading tribes from the east *c.*2150 BC. The Akkadian language, used in Mesopotamia from about 3000 BC and known from cuneiform inscriptions, is the oldest recorded Hamito-Semitic language. Two dialects of Akkadian, Assyrian and Babylonian, were spoken in the Middle East for the next 2000 years before they gave way to Aramaic.

Aksum (or **Axum**) A town in the province of Tigré in northern Ethiopia. It was a religious centre and the capital of a powerful kingdom during the 1st–6th centuries AD. According to ancient Aksumite tradition their kings were descended from Menelik (legendary son of Solomon and Sheba) who brought to the country the Ark of the Covenant containing the original Tablets of the Law given to Moses.

Alamein, El, Battle of (October–November 1942) A critical battle in Egypt in World War II. In June 1942, the British took up a defensive position in Egypt. One flank rested on the Mediterranean at El Alamein and the other on the salt marshes of the Qattara Depression. In August, General *Montgomery was appointed to command the defending 8th Army. He launched an offensive in which, after a heavy artillery preparation, about 1200 tanks advanced, followed by infantry, against the German Afrika Korps commanded by General *Rommel. Rommel was handicapped by a grave fuel shortage and had only about 500 tanks. The outnumbered Germans never regained the initiative. Rommel managed to withdraw most of his men back into Libya, but this battle marked the beginning of the end of the *North African Campaign for Germany.

Alamo, the A mission fort in San Antonio, Texas, and scene of a siege during the Texas Revolution against Mexico of 1836. A Mexican army of 3000 led by Santa Anna besieged the fort held by fewer than 200 men, under the joint command of William B. Travis and James Bowie. The siege lasted from 24 February to 6 March, when the Mexicans finally breached the walls. Travis, Bowie, Davy *Crockett, and all their men were killed. The defence of the Alamo became the symbol of Texan resistance.

Alanbrooke, Alan Francis Brooke, 1st Viscount (1883–1963) British field-marshal. He served with distinction during World War I, and in the 1930s was noted as an artillery expert. In World War II he was a corps commander during the withdrawal from *Dunkirk. Later, as Chief of the Imperial General Staff and Chairman of the Chiefs of Staff Committee (1941–46), he represented the service chiefs in discussions with Churchill. As Churchill's chief adviser on military strategy, he accompanied him to all his conferences with Roosevelt and Stalin.

Alaric I (c.370–410) King of the *Visigoths. He commanded *Theodosius' Gothic allies and helped put down the Western usurper emperor Eugenius. On Theodosius' death the Eastern and Western Roman empires were formally divided. Alaric revolted against the rule of Constantinople (now *Istanbul) and moved with his people in search of homelands. He invaded Italy in 401. Twice defeated by Stilicho, the Roman general, he entered a treaty of alliance with him. After the execution of Stilicho by Emperor Honorius, Alaric repudiated the pact and ravaged Italy, laying siege to Rome three times. The city fell in 410. That same year he planned invasions of Sicily and Africa, but his fleet was destroyed by storms. He died at Cosenza.

Alaska Purchase (1867) The purchase by the USA of Alaska from Russia for $7.2 million (less than two cents an acre) arranged by William H. Seward. It remained an unorganized territory until 1884. Despite extensive copper and gold discoveries there was little population growth.

Alba, Fernando Alvarez de Toledo, Duke of (c.1507–82) Spanish statesman and general. He rose to prominence in the armies of Emperor Charles V. A stickler for discipline and a master of logistics, he contributed significantly to the defeat of the German Protestants at the battle of Mühlberg (1547). Philip II sent him as governor-general to deal with unrest in the Netherlands in 1567, but his notorious 'Council of Blood' executed or banished over a thousand men, and was responsible for sparking off the Dutch Revolts against Spanish rule. He was recalled to Spain at his own request in 1573, and in 1580 Philip gave him command of the forces which conquered Portugal.

Albania

Capital:	Tirana
Area:	28,748 sq km (11,100 sq miles)
Population:	3,002,859 (2012 est)
Currency:	1 lek = 100 qindars
Religions:	Muslim 58.8%; Roman Catholic 10.0%; Eastern Orthodox 6.8%
Ethnic Groups:	Albanian 82.6%; Greek and other minorities
Languages:	Albanian (official); Greek; Macedonian; Romany
International Organizations:	UN; OSCE; Council of Europe; WTO; NATO

A small country in south-eastern Europe, on the Adriatic coast of the Balkan Peninsula, with Montenegro, Kosovo, and Macedonia to its north and east, and Greece to its south.

Physical Its coastal plain is marshy in the north but mostly fertile. Inland are rugged mountains, forested hills, and fast-flowing rivers. It also has the shores of three large lakes within its frontiers.

Economy Formerly a centrally planned economy under communism, since 1992 Albania has undertaken economic reforms, which include the privatization of farmland, state enterprises, and housing; the abolition of price subsidies; and the liberalization of trade. The economy is primarily agricultural, but crude oil is exported. Industry, which is limited, is in great need of modernization.

History As part of the Ottoman empire from the 15th century, Albania was noted for the military dictatorship of Ali Pasha (*c*.1744–1822), whose court was described by the English poet Byron in *Childe Harold*. Nationalist resistance was crushed in 1831, but discontent persisted and a national league was created during the Russo-Turkish War of 1877–78. It became an independent state as a result of the *Balkan Wars in 1912, and after a brief period as a republic became a monarchy under King *Zog in 1928. Invaded by Italy in 1939, it became a Communist state under Enver Hoxha after World War II. Under the strong influence of the Soviet Union until a rift in 1958, it became closely aligned with China until *Mao Zedong's death in 1976. Albania was expelled from the *Warsaw Pact in 1968, but remained Stalinist in policy and outlook until the death of Hoxha in 1985. From then on its isolationism began to ease, with cautious steps to restore democracy in 1990. The Communists (renamed the Socialist Party) held power in the first free elections in 1991, but were defeated by the Democratic Party in 1992. Early in 1997 the collapse of several companies involved in pyramid investment schemes triggered anti-government protests and rioting. A state of emergency was declared, the government resigned, and a Socialist-led coalition came to power after elections in July 1997. Further rioting broke out in 1998 and a new constitution was established. In 1999 thousands of refugees from Kosovo arrived in the country, putting further pressure on the government. Following elections in 2005, the Socialist-led government was replaced by a coalition led by the Democratic Party. The Socialists returned to power in 2013.

Albany Congress (1754) A congress of seven colonies convened by the British Board of Trade at Albany, a town in New York State, to concert defence against the French and pacify the Iroquois. It was at Albany that Benjamin *Franklin presented his "Plan of Union" for a Grand Council elected by the 13 colonies to control defence and Indian relations, but this first step towards American unity was rejected by the individual colonies.

Albemarle, George, 1st Duke of *See* MONCK, GEORGE, 1ST DUKE OF ALBEMARLE.

Alberoni, Giulio (1664–1752) Italian cardinal and statesman. In 1713 he arranged the marriage of the Duke of Parma's niece Elizabeth Farnese with Philip V of Spain. He became effective ruler of Spain in 1715 and strengthened royal power in Spain at the expense of the nobles. His chief aims were to strengthen Spain, nullify the Peace of *Utrecht, and crush *Habsburg power in Italy. He was doubtful about the wisdom of declaring war on Austria in July 1717 and it proved to be a disastrous decision, mainly because of British and French intervention against Spain, and resulted in his dismissal by Philip in 1719. He retired to Rome.

Albert, Prince (1819–61) Consort to Queen Victoria. First cousin of the queen and prince of Saxe-Coburg-Gotha, he revitalized the British court in the first twenty years of his wife's reign. He was one of the driving forces behind the Great Exhibition of 1851; its profits allowed the construction of the Royal Albert Hall (1871) and of museum buildings in South Kensington. In 1861, just before his premature death from typhoid fever, his moderating influence was crucial in keeping Britain out of the American Civil War.

Albigensians (or **Albigenses**) Followers of a form of the *Cathar heresy; they took their name from the town of Albi in Languedoc in southern France. There and in northern Italy the sect acquired immense popularity. The movement was condemned at the Council of Toulouse in 1119 and by the Third and Fourth *Lateran councils in 1179 and 1215, which opposed it not only as heretical but because it threatened the family and the state. St *Bernard and St *Dominic were its vigorous opponents. Between 1209 and 1228 the wars known as the **Albigensian Crusade** were mounted, led principally by Simon de *Montfort. By 1229 the heretics were largely crushed and the Treaty of Meaux delivered most of their territory to France.

Albuquerque, Alfonso de (or **Albuquerque the Great**) (1453–1515) Portuguese colonial statesman. He first travelled east in 1502, and, after being appointed viceroy of the Portuguese Indies four years later, conquered Goa and made it the capital of the Portuguese empire in the east. Albuquerque made further conquests in Ceylon, Malacca, Ormuz, the Sunda Islands, and the Malabar Coast, but was relieved of office as a result of a court intrigue at home and died on the passage back to Portugal.

alcázar (Arabic *al-kasr*, 'the palace') A type of fortress in Spain, built by the Christians during their 14th- and 15th-century wars against the *Moors. It was usually rectangular with great corner towers, and contained an open space or patio, surrounded by chapels, hospitals, and salons. The most renowned is the Alcázar of Seville, built by King Pedro the Cruel (1334–69). The most splendid Muslim fortress-palace in Spain is the Alhambra ('the red'), built by the Moorish monarchs of Granada, chiefly between 1238 and 1358.

Alcazarquivir (locally called **al-Kasr al-Kabir**) A city in northern *Morocco, famous for the battle of the Three Kings (1578). From the 15th century it suffered attacks from Portuguese coastal ports, and became an advanced post of the *mujahidin*, "warriors for the faith", in retaliation. In 1578 Sebastian I of Portugal attacked with 20,000 men, but the Moroccans, mustering 50,000, defeated them utterly. Sebastian himself perished, with 8,000 men, and in 1580 Portugal fell into the hands of Spain.

alchemy A pseudo-science originating independently in China, Greece, and India in about the 3rd century BC, concerned with the possible transmutation of all matter, most famously the transmutation of base metals, such as lead, into gold. The transmutation was variously an end in itself, a means by which to make an elixir of life, and a route to the creation of a panacea, or universal medicine. Early alchemy degenerated into superstition and mysticism, but the art flourished once again in the 8th century AD in Arab countries. Translations of Arabic alchemical texts led in the 12th century to a second revival of alchemy in Europe, notably in Prague. It attracted such medieval scholars as Roger Bacon (*c.*1219–*c.*92) and St Albertus Magnus (*c.*1200–80), and was patronized by princes and emperors. The influential Swiss writer Paracelsus (16th century) was primarily concerned with its medical application to his search for a chemical therapy for disease; his followers developed specialized chemical medicines and sought a universal elixir, which they dreamed would prolong life and restore youth. During the Renaissance alchemy fell into disrepute, but the chemical experience accumulated by alchemists over many centuries became the basis upon which the modern science of chemistry was built.

Alcibiades (*c.*450–404 BC) Athenian general and statesman. Educated in the household of Pericles, he became the pupil and friend of Socrates. In the *Peloponnesian War he sponsored the unsuccessful Athenian expedition against Sicily, but fled to Sparta after being recalled for trial on a charge of sacrilege. He later held commands for Athens against Sparta and Persia, before his enemies finally forced him from Athens and had him murdered in Phrygia.

Alcuin (*c.*735–804) English scholar and theologian. In 782 was employed by Emperor *Charlemagne as head of his palace school at Aachen, where his pupils included many of the outstanding figures in the 'Carolingian Renaissance'. Alcuin played a central role in fostering this cultural revival. In 796 he became abbot of St Martin at Tours, where he continued his work until his death.

alderman (Old English *ealdorman*, 'elderman') A title dating from the Anglo-Saxon period when ealdormen, nobles by birth, exercised considerable powers. They were initially appointed by the crown to administer the shire system (particularly the shire moot or assembly and fyrd). By the 10th century their influence extended beyond the shire, and in the early 11th century their title evolved into 'earl'. Under the Norman kings the senior shire official was the sheriff, and the title alderman later came to apply to those who held municipal office.

Aldermaston A village in Berkshire, England, site of an atomic weapons research establishment. The Campaign for Nuclear Disarmament (CND) held an anti-nuclear protest march (the Aldermaston March) from London to Aldermaston and back each year at Easter from 1958 to 1963.

Alessandri, Arturo (1868–1950) Chilean statesman. In 1920 he was elected President on a liberal policy, but, finding his attempts at reform blocked, he went into voluntary exile in 1924. The following year he was brought back by the army when a new constitution was adopted. He extended the suffrage, separated church and state while guaranteeing religious liberty, and made primary education compulsory. He resigned again in October 1925 and went to Italy. On his return he was re-elected President (1932–38). He reorganized the nitrate industry, developed schools, and improved conditions in agriculture and industry.

Alexander I (c.1078–1124) King of Scotland (1107–24). He succeeded his brother Edgar although the regions of Strathclyde, Lothian, and Cumbria were ruled with Anglo-Norman support by his younger brother (later *David I). Educated in England, Alexander encouraged the feudalization of his country while still retaining its independence of England. After crushing a Celtic revolt (c.1115) he was styled "the Fierce" although he was a pious man, founding Augustinian houses at Scone (1115) and Inchcolm. He refused the Bishop of St Andrews (1120, 1124) leave to acknowledge the ecclesiastical authority of York or Canterbury.

Alexander I (1777–1825) Emperor of Russia (1801–25). The son of Paul I (in whose murder he may indirectly have assisted), he set out to reform Russia and correct many of the injustices of the preceding reign. His private committee (Neglasny Komitet) introduced plans for public education, but his reliance on the nobility made it impossible for him to abolish serfdom. At first a supporter of the coalition against *Napoleon, his defeats by the latter at the Battle of *Austerlitz (1805) and at Friedland (1807) resulted in the Treaties of Tilsit (1807) with France and in his support of the *Continental System against the British. His wars with Persia (1804–13) and Turkey (1806–12) brought territorial gains, including the acquisition of Georgia. His armies helped to defeat Napoleon's *grande armée* at *Leipzig, after its retreat from Moscow (1812). In an effort to uphold Christian morality in Europe he formed a *Holy Alliance of European monarchs. He supported *Metternich in suppressing liberal and national movements, and gave no help to the Greeks during their rebellion against the Ottoman Turks, although they were Orthodox Christians like himself. He was reported to have become a hermit.

Alexander I (1888–1934) King of Yugoslavia (1921–34). Of the Karageorgević dynasty of Serbia, he tried to overcome the ethnic, religious, and regional rivalries in his country by means of a personal dictatorship (1929), supported by the army. In the interest of greater unity, he changed the name of his kingdom, which consisted of Serbs, Croats, and Slovenes, to *Yugo-

slavia in 1929. In 1931 some civil rights were restored, but they proved insufficient to quell rising political and separatist dissent. He was assassinated by a Croatian terrorist.

Alexander II (1198–1249) King of Scotland (1214–49). He succeeded William the Lion. After supporting the English barons in the first Barons' War against King *John he had to suppress revolts in Moray (1221), Argyll (1222), Caithness (1222), and Galloway (1224). His campaigns against England and the Norse in the Western Isles (1249) were motivated by territorial ambitions.

Alexander II (1818–81) Emperor of Russia (1855–81). Known as the 'Tsar Liberator', he was the eldest son of *Nicholas I and succeeded to the throne when the *Crimean War had revealed Russia's backwardness. His Emancipation Act of 1861 freed millions of serfs and led to an overhaul of Russia's archaic administrative institutions. Measures of reform, however, did not disguise his belief in the need to maintain autocratic rule and his commitment to military strength, as witnessed by the introduction of universal conscription in 1874. His reign saw great territorial gains in the Caucasus, Central Asia, and the Far East, to offset the sale of Alaska to the USA (1867). The growth of secret revolutionary societies, such as the nihilists and Populists, culminating in an assassination attempt in 1862, completed his conversion to conservatism. After further assassination attempts, he was mortally wounded (1881) by a bomb, thrown by a member of the People's Will Movement.

Alexander III (or **Alexander the Great**) (356–323 BC) King of Macedon (336–323), the son of Philip II. He was a pupil of Aristotle. After his succession he invaded *Achaemenid Persia, liberating the Greek cities in Asia Minor, and then defeating the Persians in Egypt, Syria, and Mesopotamia. While in Egypt he founded Alexandria (332 BC), his first and best-known city. He decided to rule the Persian empire in cooperation with the Persian nobles, some of whom he appointed as his governors. He went on to extend his conquests eastwards, taking Bactria and the Punjab. He died of a fever at Babylon, and his empire quickly fell apart after his death. Regarded as a god in his lifetime, he became a model for many subsequent imperialist conquerors of antiquity, and the subject of many legends.

Alexander III (1241–86) King of Scotland (1249–86). He defeated Haakon of Norway at

Alexander the Great. Alexander's victorious progress through Asia Minor against the Persians culminated in the defeat of King Darius at Issus (333 BC). Advancing through Phoenicia, where he met resistance from Tyre and Gaza, he reached Egypt in 332 and was welcomed as a liberator. After founding Alexandria he turned eastwards and won a decisive battle at Gaugamela (331). Babylonia offered no serious resistance and he advanced through Batria to the Jaxartes, founding Alexandria-the-Furthest as a defence against nomadic Scythians. His defeat of the Indian ruler Porus on the Hydaspes (326) took him into new territory, but his weary soldiers persuaded him to turn back. On the return journey he sailed down the Hydaspes to the Indus delta, as he was anxious both to conquer Sind and to see 'Ocean', the great river that was believed to encircle the world. After a gruelling desert march he reached Susa in 324. Alexander died at Babylon in 323, in his 33rd year.

the Battle of Largs (1263) and received the Hebrides by the Treaty of Perth. Despite close ties with England (his father-in-law was *Henry III), Alexander resisted English claims to the Scottish kingdom. The early death of his children left the succession to his granddaughter Margaret of Norway.

Alexander III (1845–94) Emperor of Russia (1881–94). Following the assassination of his father *Alexander II he rejected all plans of liberal reform, suppressing Russian nihilists and Populists, extending the powers of nominated landed proprietors over the peasantry, and strengthening the role of landowners in local government. Autocratic in attitude, he was, however, genuinely interested in the principles of administration and his reign saw the abolition of the poll tax, the creation of a Peasant Land Bank, and tentative moves towards legalization of trade unions. Alexander's concept of *naradnost* (belief in the Russian people) led to the Russian language being imposed as the single language of education throughout the empire. Although he resented the loss of the Russian Balkans imposed by the Congress of *Berlin, he nevertheless continued to support

Bismarck's League of the Three Emperors, the Dreikaiserbund, until 1890, when the aggressive attitudes of the new German emperor *William II led to its replacement by an alliance with France.

Alexander Nevsky (*c.*1220–63) Russian soldier, Grand Duke of Vladimir (1252–63). Born in Vladimir, son of the Grand Duke Jaroslav II of Novgorod, he acquired his second name after his defeat of the Swedish army on the banks of the River Neva in 1240. Wars against the Germans and Lithuanians culminated in a battle with the *Teutonic Knights on the frozen Lake Peipus which he won decisively. After his death he was canonized as a saint of the Russian Orthodox Church.

Alexander of Tunis, Harold, 1st Earl (Harold Rupert Leofric George Alexander) (1891–1969) British Field Marshal and Conservative statesman. In World War II he supervised the evacuation from *Dunkirk, the withdrawal from Burma, and the victorious campaigns in North Africa (1943), Sicily, and Italy (1943–45). After the war he became Governor-General of Canada (1946–52) and British Minister of Defence (1952–54).

Alexander the Great *See* ALEXANDER III (ALEXANDER THE GREAT).

Alexandria (Arabic **El Iskandarîya**) The chief port and second-largest city of Egypt, on the Mediterranean coast, northwest of Cairo. Founded in 332 BC by Alexander the Great, after whom it is named, it became a major centre of Hellenistic and Jewish culture, with renowned libraries, and was the capital city until the Arab invasions *c.*641 AD. On an island off the coast was the Pharos lighthouse (3rd century BC), often considered one of the Seven Wonders of the World.

Alfonso V (known as **'the Magnanimous'**) (1396–1458) King of Aragon (1416–58) and of Naples (1443–58). He pursued a foreign policy committed to territorial expansion, particularly in Italy. Joanna II, Queen of Naples, adopted him as her heir and on her death he transferred his court to Naples in 1443, which he developed as a centre of *Renaissance culture. His patronage earned the admiration of contemporary humanists.

Alfonso X (known as **'the Wise'**) (1221–84) King of Castile and León (1252–84). His reign was a contrast between the failure of his political ambitions and his scholarly success as a law-giver. He spent fruitless years trying to become Holy Roman Emperor and failed to complete his father's Crusade against the *Moors in southern Spain. His indecision caused his son, Sancho IV, to rebel and isolate him in Seville. Of real importance was his *Siete Partidas* (1256), a collection of constitutional, civil, and criminal law, the first such work to be written in Spanish.

Alfonso XIII (1886–1941) King of Spain (1886–1931). Alfonso ruled under the regency of his mother until 1902, during which time Spain lost her colonial possessions in the Philippines and Cuba to the USA. In 1923 he supported Miguel Primo de Rivera's assumption of dictatorial powers, but by 1931 Alfonso had agreed to elections. When these indicated the Spanish electorate's clear preference for a republic, the king was forced to abdicate.

Alfred (or **Alfred the Great**) (849–99) King of Wessex (871–99). Alfred's military resistance saved south-west England from Viking occupation. He negotiated the treaty giving the Danelaw to the Norsemen (886). A great reformer, he reorganized his land-based garrisons, founded the English navy, issued a new code of laws, introduced administrative and financial changes, revived learning, and promoted the use of English for literature and education.

Algeciras Conference (1906) An international meeting in Algeciras, Spain, held at Germany's request. Its treaty regulated French and Spanish intervention in Moroccan internal affairs and reaffirmed the authority of the sultan. It was a humiliation for Germany, which failed to obtain support for its hardline attitude towards France except from Austria-Hungary. Britain, Russia, Italy, and the USA took the side of France.

Algeria

Capital:	Algiers
Area:	2,381,741 sq km (919,595 sq miles)
Population:	37,367,226 (2012 est)
Currency:	1 Algerian dinar = 100 centimes
Religions:	Sunni Muslim 99.0%
Ethnic Groups:	Arab and Berber 99.0%
Languages:	Arabic (official); Berber; French
International Organizations:	UN; Arab League; OAPEC; OPEC; Maghreb Union; Non-Aligned Movement; AU

A country extending from the North African coast southward across a large part of the Sahara. Algeria's narrow coastal strip is bounded by Morocco on the west and by Tunisia on the east.

Physical The coast has an equable Mediterranean climate well suited to agriculture. Inland the ground rises until it is mountainous, though here also the valleys are fertile. Plains and plateaux provide grazing, while many of the mountain slopes are forested. South is the desert and further south-east are more mountains with desolate plateaux and volcanic cones and craters.

Economy Algerian industry, mainly state-owned, is based on oil-refining, but cement and steel are also produced. The country's main exports are crude oil, petroleum products, and natural gas (which is now piped to Spain). Agriculture is limited: the northern mountainous region is suited only to grazing and timber, and the south of the country is the Sahara Desert. Algeria imports much of its food, the EU being the major trading partner.

History The indigenous population of Algeria were Berbers, but the coast was colonized by the Phoenicians in the 9th century BC. In the 2nd century BC the Romans incorporated the whole region into the province of Africa. In the 7th century AD the Romanized Berbers resisted the Arab invasion fiercely. Once conquered they were converted to Islam, and became members of the extreme Kharijite sect. From the 11th century they were repeatedly ravaged by the Banu Hilal and other Arabs, and ruled by a series of dynasties until conquest by the Ottoman empire in the 16th century. Throughout the 18th century, Algeria was notorious as a base for pirates raiding Mediterranean shipping. Conquered by France in the 1830s (when its present boundaries were established) and formally annexed in 1842, Algeria was 'attached' to metropolitan France and heavily settled by European Christians. The refusal of the European settlers to grant equal rights to the native population led to increasing instability, and in 1954 a war of national independence broke out which was characterized by atrocities on both sides. In 1962, in spite of considerable resistance in both France and white Algeria, President *de Gaulle negotiated an end to hostilities in the Evian Agreement, and Algeria was granted independence as the result of a referendum. In 1965 a coup established a left-wing government under Colonel Houari *Boumédienne and afterwards serious border disputes broke out with Tunisia, Morocco, and Mauritania. After Boumédienne's death in 1978, his successor Chadli Bendjedid relaxed his repressive domestic policies and began to normalize Algeria's external relations. Algeria was a one-party state, ruled by the FLN (Front de Libération Nationale), from 1976 until 1989, when other political parties were legalized. The fundamentalist FIS (Front Islamique du Salut) party rapidly gained popular support. In 1992 the FIS seemed poised to win a general election but Bendjedid dissolved the government and resigned. A transitional military regime took over and cancelled the election. FIS supporters continued to wage a campaign of violence and terrorism; an estimated 76,000 people were killed in the years 1992–97. A new constitution was adopted in 1996, and in 1999 Abdelaziz Bouteflika was elected president. Disaffection by Islamists and Berber separatists has continued. Bouteflika was re-elected in 2004 and announced plans for a general amnesty, which were subsequently

backed in a referendum. He was again re-elected in 2009. In 2011 Algeria saw demonstrations influenced by the *Arab Spring; in response the government lifted the state of emergency that had been in force since 1992.

Ali Pasha, Mehmed Emin (1815–71) Ottoman statesman and reformer. After service in the Foreign Ministry he became Grand Vizier in 1852. He became one of the leading statesmen of the Tanzimat reform movement, and was responsible for the Hatt-i Humayun reform edict of 1856. This guaranteed Christians security of life and property, opened civil offices to all subjects, abolished torture, and allowed acquisition of property by foreigners. He believed in autocratic rule and opposed the granting of a parliamentary constitution.

Allen, Ethan (1738–89) American soldier. He tried to obtain independence for the state of Vermont, commanding the irregular force the Green Mountain Boys (1770–75). In 1775, during the War of Independence, he seized the British Fort Ticonderoga, but the same year was captured at Montreal. On his release in 1778 he presented to Congress Vermont's claims to independence, which was achieved the following year.

Allenby, Edmund Henry Hynman, 1st Viscount (1861–1936) British soldier. A veteran of the Boer War, during World War I he commanded the First Cavalry Division and later the Third Army on the Western Front. In 1917 he led the Egyptian Expeditionary Force. Having captured Jerusalem in December 1917, he went on to defeat the Turkish forces in Palestine in 1918. He was promoted to Field Marshal and later served as High Commissioner in Egypt (1919–25).

Allende, Salvador (Salvador Allende Gossens) (1908–73) Chilean statesman. As President of Chile (1970–73), he was the first avowed Marxist to win a Latin American presidency in a free election. Having bid for the office unsuccessfully on two previous occasions (1958 and 1964), Allende's 1970 victory was brought about by a coalition of leftist parties. During his brief tenure he set the country on a socialist path, incurring the antipathy of the Chilean military establishment. Under General *Pinochet, a military coup (which enjoyed some indirect support from the USA) overthrew him in 1973. Allende died during the fighting, probably by suicide; he was given a state funeral in 1990.

Allied Intervention, War of See RUSSIAN CIVIL WAR.

Almohad An Islamic dynasty that ruled in Morocco and Spain during the 12th and 13th centuries. The Almohads built many of the defensive monasteries or *ribats* of North Africa. They were defeated by the Portuguese and Spanish on the Iberian peninsula in 1228 and superseded by the Merenid dynasty in Morocco in 1269.

Almoravid An Islamic dynasty that ruled in Morocco and Spain in the 11th and 12th centuries until overthrown by the Almohads in 1147. It founded the city of Marrakesh.

almshouse A sanctuary for the reception and succour of the poor. Almshouses were originally those sections of medieval monasteries in which alms (food and money) were distributed. Most medieval foundations were made by clergymen. Privately financed dwellings, usually for the support of the old and infirm, have also been called almshouses. From the 16th century the charitable relief supplied by almshouses was supplemented by a series of *Poor Laws.

al-Qaeda The international terrorist network that is thought to have carried out the attacks on America on *September 11, 2001. It was founded in about 1991 by Osama *Bin Laden to wage an Islamic holy war against the USA. A series of bomb attacks on US targets in Africa and the Middle East followed. In 1996 Bin Laden transferred his operations from Sudan to Afghanistan, where he enjoyed the support of the *Taliban regime. Following September 11, the USA destroyed al-Qaeda's Afghan operation in its so-called *war on terrorism. However, cells with al-Qaeda links remain active around the world and have been held responsible for bombings in Bali (2002); Saudi Arabia, Morocco, and Istanbul (2003); Madrid (2004); Sharm el-Sheikh and Amman (2005); and Pakistan (2008). The perpetrators of the London suicide bombings of 2005 are thought to have been inspired by al-Qaeda but to have had no formal links with the organization. Two attempted bombings of aircraft were foiled in 2009 and 2010. The network was also active in the opposition to the military presence of Western powers in Iraq following the *Iraq War, and to the democratic Iraqi government established with their support. Bin Laden was killed by US special forces in 2011; he was succeeded as leader by *Ayman al-Zawahiri. From 2011 al-Qaeda participated in the Syrian civil war (*see* SYRIA), in opposition to the Alawite Assad regime.

Elements of al-Qaeda in Iraq formed the core of the militant jihadist group *Islamic State, which took control of large parts of western Iraq and northern Syria in 2013–14.

Alva, Duke of See ALBA.

Ambedkar, Bhimrao Ramji (1893–1956) Indian leader of the Untouchables (the lowest group in the caste system). He led the agitation for their constitutional rights in the 1930s and when Mahatma *Gandhi went on a fast against the provision of separate electorates for the Untouchables, agreed to the Poona Pact (1934) providing reserved seats for them in the legislatures. As the leader and founder of the Scheduled Castes Federation, he opposed the Indian National *Congress, but joined that party after independence. As a leading constitutional lawyer, he played a major role in formulating and drafting the Indian constitution.

Ambrose, St (*c.*339–97) Doctor of the Church. He was a Roman governor at Milan and a converted Christian, though not yet baptized, when he was elected bishop of Milan (374) and became a champion of orthodoxy. He was partly responsible for the conversion of St *Augustine of Hippo. His knowledge of Greek enabled him to introduce much Eastern theology and liturgical practice into the West; Ambrosian (antiphonal) plainsong is associated with his name, and the Athanasian Creed has been attributed to him.

Amenhotep (Greek **Amenophis**) Four Egyptian pharaohs of the 18th dynasty. **Amenhotep I** (16th century BC), son of Ahmose I (founder of the 18th dynasty), reigned 1546–1526. He fought wars in Nubia and raided Libya. **Amenhotep II** (15th century BC), son of Hatshepsut and Tuthmosis III, reigned 1450–1425. Brought up as a warrior, he fought successful campaigns in Syria and the Middle East; he completed some of the buildings begun by his father. **Amenhotep III** (15th–14th century BC), son of Tuthmosis IV, reigned 1417–1379. After early military campaigns, his reign was generally peaceful and prosperous; he embarked on an extensive building programme centred on his capital, Thebes, including the colossi of Memnon and the Luxor temple. **Amenhotep IV** changed his name to *Akhenaten.

American Civil War (1861–65) A war between the Northern (Union) and Southern (*Confederacy) states of the USA. It was officially known as the War of the Rebellion and usually called the War between the States in the

South. Economic divergence between the industrialized North and the agricultural, slave-based economy of the South was transformed into political rivalry by the *abolitionists, and by the dispute over the expansion of slavery into the western territories. By the late 1850s, all efforts at compromise had failed and violence had begun with John *Brown's armed descent on Harper's Ferry (1859). South Carolina seceded from the Union in December 1860 in the wake of Abraham *Lincoln's victory in the presidential election of that year. When the war began with the bombardment of *Fort Sumter (1861), the newly established Southern Confederacy increased to eleven states under the presidency of Jefferson *Davis.

The war itself is best considered as three simultaneous campaigns. At sea, the North held the upper hand, but the blockade imposed in 1861 took a long time to become effective. Virtually no cotton was exported. Massive naval expansion produced a blockade which helped to cripple the Confederate war effort. On land a series of engagements took place in the Virginia Campaigns, where the close proximity of the Union and Confederacy capitals, Washington and Richmond, and the military genius of General *Lee enabled the Confederacy to keep superior Union forces at bay for much of the war. In the more spacious western regions, after a series of abortive starts, the North managed to split the Confederacy in the Vicksburg Campaign, by gaining control of the Mississippi. From here General *Grant moved through Tennessee in the Chattanooga Campaign, opening the way for the drive by *Sherman through Georgia to the sea. This ruthless strategy, together with Lee's surrender to Grant at *Appomattox, brought the war to an end in April 1865. Over 600,000 soldiers died in the Civil War. While the immediate results were the salvation of the union and the abolition of slavery, the challenges of revitalizing the South and promoting racial justice and equality persisted.

American Colonization Society Founded in the USA in 1817 in order to resettle in Africa free-born Africans and emancipated slaves. In 1821 the society bought the site of the future Monrovia, *Liberia, which it controlled until Liberia declared its independence in 1847. After 1840 the society declined and was dissolved in 1912.

American Federation of Labor (AFL) A federation of North American trade unions, mainly of skilled workers, founded in 1886. From its formation until his retirement in 1924,

it was decisively shaped by its President, Samuel Gompers. After mass disorders culminating in the *Haymarket Square riot and the subsequent eclipse of the *Knights of Labor, Gompers wanted a cohesive non-radical organization of skilled workers committed to collective bargaining for better wages and conditions. However, growing numbers of semi-skilled workers in mass-production industries found their champion in John L. Lewis, leader of the more militant United Mine Workers. When he failed to convince the AFL of the need to promote industry-wide unions in steel, automobiles, and chemicals, Lewis formed (1935) the Committee (later the Congress) of Industrial Organizations (CIO), its members seceding from the AFL. In 1955 the rival organizations were reconciled as the AFL–CIO under George Meany and Walter Reuther with a total of 15 million members. This body remained the recognized voice of organized labour in the USA and Canada. The 21st century saw renewed splits, with seven major unions, including the Teamsters, forming the Change to Win alliance in 2005.

American Indians *See* NATIVE AMERICANS.

American Revolution *See* INDEPENDENCE, AMERICAN WAR OF.

Amerindian An indigenous person of Central and South America; the indigenous people of North America are sometimes called Amerindians, but are usually referred to as *Native Americans. Amerindians were formerly classified as a major branch of the *Mongoloid peoples but are now described as a distinct racial group. They were the inhabitants of the New World at the time of the first European exploration in the late 15th century. Their forebears came from north-eastern Asia, most probably taking advantage of low sea levels during the last Ice Age to cross the Bering Strait on land. The earliest certain evidence suggests that people were in the Americas by 15,000 years ago but an earlier date seems increasingly likely. Recent controversial archaeological finds in Mexico, Chile, Brazil, and elsewhere suggest a human presence as early as 30,000 or more years ago. There could have been several separate colonizations; the Inuits (Eskimos) and Aleuts (inhabitants of the Aleutian Islands) are the descendants of the most recent one, within the past 10,000 years. The first colonizers brought little more than simple stone tools and perhaps domesticated dogs for hunting. As hunters and gatherers they spread quickly south; hunting the plentiful game using fine stone projectile points such as those of the *Clovis tradition.

The cultural development of Amerindians provides an interesting comparison with the Old World. Agriculture, which started developing 7000 or more years ago, was based on maize, squash, and beans, with manioc being grown in tropical forest regions. With no suitable animals to domesticate, apart from the llama and the guinea-pig, and no draught animals to pull the plough, the development of more mixed farming was gradual. In the Andes, an advanced metallurgical technology developed from 1000 BC. Complex societies developed in many areas, which grew into sophisticated civilizations, for example, the *Aztecs and *Incas, but most collapsed after the arrival of the *conquistadores and other European explorers in the 16th century.

Amherst, Jeffrey, Baron (1717–97) British general. He commanded the combined operation which captured Louisburg in 1758. On his appointment as commander-in-chief in America, he applied widespread pressure on the French. His own army advanced northward up the Hudson Valley, taking Ticonderoga and Crown Point in 1759 and Montreal in 1760, thus ending French control of Canada. He was then made governor of Virginia, but failed to contain *Pontiac's Native American Rebellion in 1763 and was recalled. He refused to fight against Americans in 1775, but advised on strategy.

Amin Idi (**Idi Amin Dada**) (c.1925–2003) Ugandan head of state (1971–79). Possessed of only rudimentary education, Amin rose through the ranks of the army to become its commander. In 1971 he overthrew President *Obote and seized power. His rule was characterized by the advancing of narrow tribal interests, the expulsion of non-Africans (most notably Ugandan Asians), and violence on a huge scale. He was overthrown with Tanzanian assistance in 1979 and went into exile in Saudi Arabia until his death.

Amritsar massacre (13 April 1919) A massacre of unarmed supporters of Indian self-government by British troops in the city of Amritsar, Punjab. Indian discontent against the British had been mounting as a result of the *Rowlatt Act. The massacre in Amritsar followed the killing, three days before, of five Englishmen and the beating of an Englishwoman. Gurkha troops under the command of Brigadier R. H. Dyer fired on a crowd gathered in the Jallianwala Bagh, an enclosed park, killing 379 and wounding over 1200. Mounting agitation throughout India followed, and Dyer was given an official, if belated, censure.

In 1984 Indian government troops stormed the Golden Temple of Amritsar and killed 400 members of a Sikh separatist group, in revenge for which Indira *Gandhi was assassinated.

Amundsen, Roald (1872–1928) Norwegian explorer. Amundsen made his name as a polar explorer when he became the first to navigate the North-west Passage in the small sailing vessel *Gjöa* (1903–06), during which expedition he also travelled over the ice by sledge and located the site of the magnetic North Pole. In 1911 he beat the British explorer Robert F. Scott in the race to be the first to reach the South Pole. In the 1920s Amundsen devoted himself to aerial exploration of the polar regions, eventually disappearing on a search for the missing Italian airship expedition led by Umberto Nobile (1885–1978).

anarchism The belief that government and law should be abolished and society organized by voluntary means without resort to force or compulsion. The French social theorist Pierre Joseph *Proudhon first expounded the theory that equality and justice should be achieved through the abolition of the state and the substitution of free agreements between individuals. Other anarchist visions of the society of the future include the economic individualism, outlined in the American writer Benjamin Tucker's *Instead of a Book* (1893) and the communism envisaged by the Russian émigré Peter Kropotkin's work *The Conquest of Bread* (1906).

Groups of anarchists tried to find popular support in many European states in the 1860s and 1870s. They were hostile to *Marxism on the grounds that a seizure of state-power by the workers would only perpetuate oppression. The Russian anarchist Mikhail *Bakunin founded a Social Democratic Alliance (1868), which attempted to wrest control of the workers International from *Marx. Anarchists switched between strategies of spontaneous mutual association and violent acts against representatives of the state. The Presidents of France and Italy, the King of Italy, and the Empress of Austria were killed by anarchists between 1894 and 1901. Subsequently they tried to mobilize mass working-class support behind the Russian General Strike, which was a central feature of the *Russian Revolutions of 1905 and 1917. Their influence in Europe declined after the rise of totalitarian states elsewhere. They were active in the *Spanish Civil War, and in the latter half of the 20th century anarchism attracted urban terrorists.

Anasazi A Native American culture centred in the "four corners" region of modern Utah, Colorado, Arizona, and New Mexico, USA. It began *c.*500 BC when a variant, called San Jose (*c.*500–100 BC), of the hunter-gatherer desert cultures took the first steps towards agriculture and village life. Their abundant basketry has given the name 'basket makers' to their early stages. By 450 AD they were making pottery, and by 700–900 great kivas (round ceremonial chambers) were being built. In the 13th to 15th centuries droughts, crop failures, and the influx of Athapascan tribes (*Navaho and *Apache) led to the abandonment of many of their settlements and the building of cliff-dwellings, or pueblos, for defence. They were visited by Francisco Vasquez de Coronado's expedition of 1540–42, by which time they had begun to resettle some of their old territory. Initial relations were friendly, but a shortage of food led to resistance, ended by Coronado's mass execution of Native Americans. Spanish missions came in the 17th century, and attempts were made to expel the missionaries in the 1680s, followed by severe Spanish reprisals from 1692. They became known as the Pueblo Indians.

ancien régime The political and administrative systems in France in the 17th and 18th centuries under the Bourbon kings, before the *French Revolution; it is also applied more widely to much of the rest of Europe. The monarch had (in theory) unlimited authority, including the right to imprison individuals without trial. There was no representative assembly. Privilege, above all, was the hallmark of the *ancien régime*: the nobility were privileged before the law, in matters of taxation, and in the holding of high offices. The French Revolution was an uprising by the underprivileged.

Andean Community A regional economic grouping comprising Colombia, Peru, Bolivia, and Ecuador; Chile withdrew in 1976 and Venezuela in 2006. Formally established by the Cartagena Agreement of 1969—hence its official name, *Acuerdo de Cartagena*—it was an attempt to enhance the competitive edge of the member states in their economic relations with the more developed economies of the Latin American region. A customs union was established in 1995, a free trade area was completed in 2006, and the Community operates a common foreign policy in many areas. In 2004 the Andean Community concluded a cooperation agreement with *Mercosur that aimed to merge the two organizations into a South American Community of Nations. As a result, the members of Mercosur—Argentina, Brazil, Paraguay, and

Uruguay—became associate members of the Andean Community, as did Chile in 2006.

Anderson, Elizabeth Garrett (1836–1917) British physician. Debarred from entry to medical courses because of her sex, she studied privately and in 1865 obtained a licence to practise from the Society of Apothecaries. In 1866 she opened a dispensary for women and children in London, which later became a hospital; it was renamed the Elizabeth Garrett Anderson Hospital in 1918. In 1870 she received the degree of MD from Paris University, and in 1873 she became the first woman to be elected to the BMA. Her influence was considerable in securing the admission of women to professional medical bodies.

Andersonville Prison A prisoner-of-war camp used by the *Confederacy during the *American Civil War. Notorious for the high death rate among its inmates, it had been established in 1864 and suffered from shortage of food, clothing, and medical supplies in the war-stricken South. By the time of its capture by Union (Northern) forces, nearly half the prisoners had died from disease, and as a result of the ensuing outcry the ex-commandant, Captain Henry Wirz, was tried and executed for murder. Subsequent investigation revealed the catastrophe to have been the product less of deliberate barbarity than of the collapse of the Confederate military machine.

Andorra

Capital:	Andorra la Vella
Area:	468 sq km (181 sq miles)
Population:	85,082 (2012 est)
Currency:	1 euro = 100 cents
Religions:	Roman Catholic
Ethnic Groups:	Spanish 43.0%; Andorran 33.0%; Portuguese 11.0%; French 7.0%
Languages:	Catalan (official); French; Spanish
International Organizations:	UN, OSCE, Council of Europe

A small co-principality in the Pyrennes, between France and Spain.

Physical Andorra has a landscape of valleys at around 900 m (3000 feet) which rise to peaks at 2900 m

(9600 feet). The attractive mountain scenery is snow-covered for several months of the year.

Economy Tourism is the main industry, employing 37% of the labour-force, with commerce, forestry, and the construction industry also of importance.

History According to tradition, Charlemagne granted independence to Andorra in 803 AD. Andorra came under the control of the Counts of Urgel and subsequently the Bishops of the diocese of Urgel. A dispute between the French and Spanish heirs of the Bishops and Counts in the late 13th century was resolved by making Andorra a co-principality, jointly ruled by a French and a Spanish prince. In 1993 Andorra adopted a democratic constitution, which legalized political parties and reduced the powers of the co-princes (who are now the President of France and the Spanish Bishop of Urgel), making them constitutional heads of state only.

Andover scandal An event leading to improvement in workhouse conditions in Britain in the 1840s. The *Poor Law of 1834 had resulted in a worsening of conditions in workhouses to discourage all but the really needy from applying for admission. In 1845 able-bodied labourers at the workhouse at Andover, Hampshire, were found to be eating the gristle and marrow from bones they were crushing to make manure. A committee was set up to investigate and the result was the establishment of a new Poor Law Board, responsible to Parliament, and some improvement in workhouse conditions.

Andrada e Silva, José Bonifacio (1763–1838) Brazilian scientist and statesman. In 1821 he gave his support to the regent Pedro, who was left in charge when his father *John VI returned to Portugal. By mid-1822 leading Brazilians were determined that their country should become independent and in December *Pedro I was crowned Emperor of Brazil, with Andrada appointed as Prime Minister. With his two brothers he drew up a draft constitution, but antagonism developed with the emperor, and Andrada was exiled. In 1831 he was invited to return to Brazil by the emperor to become the tutor of his son. When Pedro I abdicated in April 1831 in favour of the boy, Pedro II, Andrada was confirmed as tutor by the council of regency. He was later arrested for "political intrigue" and again left the country.

Andrassy, Julius, Count (1823–90) Hungarian statesman. One of the radical nationalist leaders of the unsuccessful Hungarian Revolution of 1848, he rose to prominence with Francis Deák (1803–76) in the negotiations leading up to the *Ausgleich (Compromise) of 1867. By now a moderate, he served as Hungary's first Prime Minister (1867–71). From 1871 to 1879 he was Foreign Minister of the Austro-Hungarian empire, during which time he limited Russian influence in the *Balkan States.

Andrewes, Lancelot (1555–1626) English prelate, successively Bishop of Chichester (1605), Ely (1609), and Winchester (1619). A celebrated scholar and famous preacher, he was prominent at the courts of *Elizabeth I and *James I. He was a key figure at the *Hampton Court Conference (1603–04) and was closely involved in producing the Authorized Version of the English Bible (1611). He played an important part in developing the theology of the Anglican Communion.

Andropov, Yuri (Vladimirovich) (1914–84) Soviet statesman, General Secretary of the Communist Party of the USSR (1982–84) and President (1983–84). Born in Russia, he served as ambassador to Hungary (1954–57), playing a significant role in the crushing of that country's uprising in 1956. He was appointed chairman of the KGB in 1967; its suppression of dissidents enhanced Andropov's standing within the Communist Party, and he gained the presidency on Brezhnev's death. While in office, he initiated the reform process carried through by Mikhail *Gorbachev, his chosen successor.

Angevin The dynasty of the counts of Anjou in France which began with Fulk I (the "Red"), under the Carolingian emperors of the 9th century. Their badge, a sprig of the broom plant *Genista*, gave rise later to the name of *Plantagenet. Geoffrey of Anjou married *Matilda, the daughter of Henry I of England, in 1128, and their son, as *Henry II of England, was the first of an English royal dynasty. The power of the Angevins under Henry was formidable, overshadowing the *Capetian kings of France. Anjou remained in English hands until 1203 when Philip Augustus wrested it from John. Louis gave the Angevin title to his brother Charles who, as King of Naples and the Two Sicilies, established the second Angevin dynasty. In 1328 *Philip IV inherited it together with Maine from his mother and thus it passed directly to the French crown.

Angkor The capital of the ancient Khmer kingdom in north-west Cambodia, famous for its temples, especially Angkor Thom and Angkor Wat (early 12th century), decorated with relief sculptures. Abandoned in 1443, the site was overgrown with jungle when it was rediscovered in 1860.

Angle A member of a Germanic tribe closely linked to the *Jutes and *Saxons, thought to have originated in Schleswig-Holstein or Denmark. In the 5th century they settled in eastern Britain in East Anglia and *Northumbria. Because of their presence, the land of the *Anglo-Saxons later became known as 'Englaland' and thereby England.

Anglican Church *See* PROTESTANT.

Anglo-Afghan Wars A series of wars between Afghan rulers and British India. The first occurred (1838–42) when Britain, concerned about Russian influence in *Afghanistan, sent an army to replace Dost Muhammad with a pro-British king, Shah Shuja al-Mulk. Resistance to Shuja's rule culminated in an uprising (1841), which led to the destruction of the British Indian forces in Kabul during their withdrawal to Jalalabad (1842). Kabul was reoccupied the same year, but British forces were withdrawn from Afghanistan. The second (1878–80) was also fought to exclude Russian influence. By the Treaty of Gandamak (1879) Britain acquired territory and the right to maintain a Resident in Kabul, but in September of the same year the Resident, Sir Louis Cavagnari, was killed in Kabul and further campaigns were fought before the British withdrawal. The third war was fought in 1919, when the new amir of Afghanistan, Amanullah, attacked British India and, although repulsed, secured the independence of Afghanistan through the Treaty of Rawalpindi (1919).

Anglo-Burmese Wars (1824–26; 1852–53; 1885) Conflicts between British India and Burma. In 1824 a threatened Burmese invasion of Bengal led to a British counter-invasion, which captured Rangoon and forced the cession to Britain of Arakan and Tenasserim, the payment of a large indemnity, and the renunciation of Burmese claims to Assam. After a period of relative harmony, hostile treatment of British traders led to a second invasion in 1852, as a result of which Rangoon and the Irrawaddy delta was annexed. In 1885, the alleged francophile tendencies of King Thibaw (1878–85) provoked a third invasion which captured the royal capital at Mandalay and led to Thibaw's exile. Upper Burma became a province of British India, although guerrilla resistance to British rule was not suppressed for another five years.

Anglo-Dutch Wars Three maritime wars (1652–54; 1665–67; 1672–74) fought between

the United Provinces and Britain on grounds of commercial and naval rivalry. The Dutch navy was commanded by able admirals but the prevailing westerly winds gave the English sailors a significant advantage.

The first war began when the Dutch carrying-trade was undermined by the English Navigation Acts of 1651, and the Dutch refused to salute the English flag in the English Channel. Maarten Tromp defeated *Blake off Dungeness in December 1652, but convoying Dutch merchant ships through the Channel proved difficult and the Dutch chief minister, Johan de Witt, settled for reasonable peace terms from Cromwell in 1654. The Dutch recognized English sovereignty in the English Channel, gave compensation for the massacre at Amboina, and promised not to assist the exiled Charles II. An encounter off the African coast began the second war, followed by the fall of New Amsterdam (renamed New York) to the English, who also defeated the Dutch off Lowestoft in June 1665. However in 1666 Charles II was in financial difficulties, Cornelius Tromp and Michiel de Ruyter won the Four Days War, and Ruyter made his celebrated raid on the English dockyards at Chatham. Peace was made at Breda in 1667. The Navigation Acts were modified in favour of the Dutch and territories gained during the war were retained, the Dutch keeping Surinam and the British, Delaware and New England. In 1672 Charles II, dependent on French subsidies, supported Louis XIV against the Dutch. The Dutch admirals had the advantage and the Treaty of Westminster signed in 1674 renewed the terms of Breda.

Anglo-Japanese Alliance (1902) A diplomatic agreement between Britain and Japan. It improved Britain's international position and consolidated Japan's position in north-east Asia at a time of increasing rivalry with Russia. The two powers agreed to remain neutral in any war fought by the other to preserve the *status quo* and to join the other in any war fought against two powers. Britain and Japan began to drift apart after World War I, and when the Washington Conference was summoned in 1921, Britain decided not to renew the alliance, which ended in 1923.

Anglo-Maori Wars A complex series of conflicts following the colonization of New Zealand. In the mid-1840s there were rebellions under the Maori chiefs Hone Heke and Te Rauparaha. In 1860 the Taranaki Wars began, but Wiremu Tamihana, a leader of the *Kingitanga unity movement, negotiated an uneasy truce in 1861.

Governor Browne was replaced by Sir George *Grey in an attempt to secure peace. Grey and his advisers were reluctant to see the Kingitanga consolidated, for fear that British authority could not be asserted throughout New Zealand, and that land purchases would be halted. Fighting resumed in Taranaki in May 1863 and in July the Waikato was invaded. Fighting with the Kingitanga stopped in 1865 but was sustained by resistance from the Pai Marire (1864–65) and from Titokowaru in Taranaki and Te Kooti on the east coast (1868). London recalled Grey and the British regiments that year, but the pursuit of Titokowaru and Te Kooti, masters of guerrilla warfare, was carried on by settler militia and Maori auxiliaries. The last engagement was in 1872, after which Maori resistance gradually subsided.

Anglo-Saxon A person or language of the English Saxons, distinct from the Old Saxons and the Angles, a group of Germanic peoples who invaded and settled in Britain between the 5th and 7th centuries.

Anglo-Saxon Chronicle A collection of seven manuscripts written in Anglo-Saxon (Old English) that together provide a history of England from the beginning of the conversion to Christianity up to 1154. The major text (known as the *Parker Chronicle*) appears to have been written by one clerk until 891. Most of the copies end in the 11th century; after 1079 only the *Peterborough Chronicle* continued, breaking off abruptly with an unfinished entry for 1154. The *Chronicle* probably originated as notes inserted in the tables used by the Christian Church when calculating the date of Easter.

Angola (formerly **Portuguese West Africa**)

Capital:	Luanda
Area:	1,246,700 sq km (481,354 sq miles)
Population:	18,056,072 (2012 est)
Currency:	1 kwanza = 100 centimos
Religions:	traditional beliefs 47.0%; Roman Catholic 38.0%; Protestant 15.0%
Ethnic Groups:	Ovimbundu 37.0%; Mbundu 25.0%; Kongo 13.0%
Languages:	Portuguese (official); Umbundu; African Bantu languages
International Organizations:	UN; AU; Non-Aligned Movement; SADC; WTO; OPEC

A country of south-central Africa bounded by the Atlantic on the west, the Democratic Republic of Congo (formerly Zaïre) and Zambia on the north and east, and Namibia on the south. While most of Angola lies south of the Congo River, the Cabinda province lies north of the Congo and is separated from the rest of Angola by a section of Congo.

Physical Most of the country lies on a high plateau; but there is a coastal plain which, starting near the mouth of the River Congo, is broad and fertile until, southward, it becomes drier and narrower as it approaches the Namib desert.

Economy Potentially Africa's richest country, Angola has a wealth of mineral deposits, including the oil produced offshore from Cabinda, on which the economy is heavily dependent, diamonds, and iron ore. Exports include crude oil, petroleum products, coffee, diamonds, and mahogany hardwoods. Agricultural crops include sugar cane, bananas, palm oil, and tobacco. Industry is limited to food processing and metal refining. Electricity is generated mainly from hydroelectric dams. The economy suffered major disruption from the civil war, which caused widespread migration, famine, and destitution; however, growth since the war's end has been strong.

History The kingdoms of Kongo and Ndongo were flourishing when the coastal strip was colonized by the Portuguese in the 16th century. Increasing Portuguese involvement in the slave trade led to conflict and the Ndongo kingdom was destroyed. In the 19th century, following wars with the Ovimbundu, Ambo, Humbo, and Kuvale, the Portuguese began to exploit the mineral reserves of the hinterland. In 1951 Angola became an Overseas Province of Portugal. In 1954 a nationalist movement emerged, demanding independence. The Portuguese at first refused, but finally agreed in 1975 after a protracted guerrilla war, and 400,000 Portuguese were repatriated. Almost total economic collapse followed. Internal fighting continued between guerrilla factions. The ruling Marxist party, the Popular Movement for the Liberation of Angola (MPLA), was supported by Cuba, the Soviet Union, and East Germany, and its opponent, the National Union for the Total Independence of Angola (UNITA), by *South Africa and the USA. Punitive South African raids took place from time to time, aimed at Namibian resistance forces operating from Angola. In 1988 a Geneva Accord proposed a solution to the conflict. UNITA leader Jonas Savimbi at first refused to accept its terms, but the MPLA's adoption of more democratic policies, together with the withdrawal of South African aid, led to a peace treaty in 1991 and multiparty elections in 1992. The MPLA won the elections but UNITA disputed the results and fighting broke out again. In 1997 UNITA agreed to participate in a government of national reconciliation, but negotiations collapsed in 1999 and fighting resumed. Savimbi was killed in 2002, and shortly afterwards a ceasefire ended Angola's 27-year civil war. In 2008 the first multiparty elections since 1992 were won by the MPLA, and a new constitution was adopted in 2010. The MPLA retained power in the 2012 elections.

Anguilla The most northerly of the Leeward Islands in the Caribbean. A British colony since 1650, Anguilla formed part of the Federation of the West Indies (1958–62) and subsequently received associated state status with St Kitts and Nevis. Anguilla declared independence in 1967 and two years later was occupied by British troops, who reduced the island to colonial status once again. In 1980 it became a British dependency with full self-government.

annals (from Latin *annus,* 'year') The yearly records kept by the priests in Rome from the earliest times. They noted ceremonies, state enactments, and the holders of office. The high priest (Pontifex Maximus) was responsible for maintaining the records in his official residence. The accumulated material (mainly dating from after 300 BC) was published in eighty books known as the *Annales Maximi c.*123 BC. The name came to be applied generally to the writing of history in strict chronological order.

Annam A former kingdom on the east coast of Indochina now lying largely in Vietnam. After driving out the Chinese in 939 AD, the Annamese maintained an independence that lasted until 1883 when the French established a protectorate. Its last ruler was deposed in 1955.

Annan, Kofi (1938–) Ghanaian diplomat, Secretary General of the United Nations (1997–2006). He was appointed UN Secretary General after the USA had vetoed a second term of office for his predecessor, Boutros *Boutros-Ghali. In February 1998 his intervention helped to prevent renewed war between the USA and Saddam *Hussein's Iraq. He was re-appointed for a second term in 2001. A supporter of the US *war on terrorism in 2001, he subsequently broke

with the USA over the 2003 *Iraq War. He shared the 2001 Nobel Peace Prize with the UN. After retiring from the UN he continued to work for global peace and human rights. He has been a member of The *Elders since 2007 and its Chair since 2013.

Anne (1665–1714) Queen of England and Scotland (known as Great Britain from 1707) and Ireland 1702–14. The last of the Stuart monarchs, daughter of the Catholic James II (but herself a Protestant), she succeeded her brother-in-law William III to the throne, there presiding over the Act of Union, which completed the unification of Scotland and England. None of her five children born alive survived childhood, and by the Act of Settlement (1701) the throne passed to the House of Hanover on her death.

Anne, St Traditionally the mother of the Virgin Mary, first mentioned by name in the apocryphal gospel of James (2nd century). The extreme veneration of St Anne in the late Middle Ages was attacked by Martin Luther and other reformers. She is the patron saint of Brittany and the province of Quebec in Canada.

Anne of Austria (1601–66) Wife of Louis XIII of France, whom she married in 1615. She was the daughter of Philip III of Spain. Her friend Madame de Chevreuse was involved in plots against *Richelieu, and she was accused of encouraging the advances of the Duke of *Buckingham. When her 4-year-old son succeeded to the throne as *Louis XIV in 1643 she was declared regent and gave her full support to *Mazarin during the *Fronde. She influenced her son until her death, though her regency ended in 1651.

Anne of Cleves (1515–57) Fourth wife of Henry VIII. Henry's marriage to her (1540) was the product of his minister Thomas Cromwell's attempt to forge a dynastic alliance with one of the Protestant German states. Henry, initially deceived by a flattering portrait of Anne painted by Holbein, took an instant dislike to his new wife and dissolved the marriage after six months. Subsequently a friendship developed between Anne and Henry, and Anne lived in England for the rest of her life.

Anschluss (German, 'connection') Hitler's annexation of Austria. The *German Second empire did not include Austrian Germans, who remained in Austria-Hungary. In 1934 a coup by Austrian Nazis failed to achieve union with Germany. In February 1938 Hitler summoned

Kurt von Schuschnigg, the Austrian Chancellor, to Berchtesgaden and demanded the admission of Nazis into his cabinet. Schuschnigg attempted to call a plebiscite on Austrian independence, failed, and was forced to resign. German troops entered Vienna and on 13 March 1938 the Anschluss was proclaimed. The majority of Austrians welcomed the union. The ban on an Anschluss, laid down in the *Versailles Peace Settlement and St Germain (1919), was reiterated when the Allied Powers recognized the second Austrian republic in 1946.

Anselm, St (*c*.1033–1109) Italian-born philosopher and theologian, Archbishop of Canterbury (1093–1109). A distinguished theologian and reformer who worked to free the Church from secular control, he preferred to defend the faith by intellectual reasoning rather than by basing arguments on scriptural and other written authorities.

Anson, George, Baron (1697–1762) British admiral, remembered for his circumnavigation of the world (1740–44). Due to shipwreck and scurvy among his crew he returned with only one of his original six ships though with almost £500,000 worth of Spanish treasure. In 1747, off Cape Finisterre, he captured six French enemy warships during the War of the *Austrian Succession. Later, at the Board of Admiralty, he created the corps of marines, and by his reforms and effective planning, played a major part in securing Britain's naval successes in the *Seven Years War.

Antarctica A continent centred on the South Pole, situated mainly within the Antarctic Circle and almost entirely covered by an ice sheet. Exploration at first concentrated on establishing the existence of a continent. Bransfield, Biscoe, Foster, Wilkes, Ross, and Dumont D'Urville all explored the coastline of Antarctica between 1820 and 1840. Later explorers concentrated on reaching the South Pole. *Scott pioneered the way in 1902, followed by *Shackleton in 1908; in 1911 *Amundsen was the first to reach the Pole, and Scott reached it a month later. The American aviator Richard Byrd flew over the South Pole in 1929. Although there is no permanent human habitation, Norway, Australia, France, New Zealand, and the UK claim sectors of the continent (Argentina and Chile claim parts of the British sector); its exploration and exploitation are governed by an

international treaty (Antarctic Treaty) of 1959 renewed in 1991.

Anthracite strike A strike by the United Mine Workers of America, called in 1902 in a bid for higher wages, shorter hours, and union recognition. The employers refused to arbitrate and President Theodore *Roosevelt appointed a commission to mediate, which led the union to call off the strike. In 1903 the commission gave the miners a 10% wage increase but refused to recognize the union. The intransigent behaviour of the employers created public support for the federal government's intervention and the strike signalled an important extension of federal economic responsibilities.

Anti-Comintern Pact (25 November 1936) An agreement between Germany and Japan ostensibly to collaborate against international communism (the *Comintern). Italy signed the pact (1937), followed by other nations in 1941.

Anti-Corn Law League A movement to bring about the repeal of the duties on imported grain in Britain known as the *Corn Laws. Founded in Manchester in 1839 under Richard *Cobden and John *Bright, the League conducted a remarkably successful campaign. A combination of bad harvests, trade depression, and the *Irish Famine strengthened the League's position and in 1846 the Prime Minister, Sir Robert *Peel, was persuaded to abolish the Corn Laws. The expected slump in agriculture did not take place.

Antietam, Battle of (or Battle of Sharpsburg) (17 September 1862) A battle in the *American Civil War, fought in Maryland. After his victory at the second battle of Bull Run, General *Lee invaded the North, but with only 30,000 men under his immediate command was attacked by a Union (Northern) army under General George McClellan at Sharpsburg on the Antietam Creek. Although the Confederates were badly mauled, they held their positions and made an orderly retreat on the following day. The casualties of 23,000 (divided almost equally between the two sides) were the worst of any single day of the war.

Antigonus I (known as the 'One-eyed') (*c*.382–301 BC) An officer in the army of *Alexander III (the Great). After the latter's death (323), and that of the Macedonian regent, Antipater (319), he attempted to re-establish Alexander's empire under his own sole leadership, declaring himself king (306). His considerable success induced his rivals—Ptolemy, Seleucus, Cassander,

a

and Lysimachus—to combine, defeat, and kill him at the 'battle of the kings' at Ipsus.

Antigua and Barbuda

Capital:	Saint John's
Area:	441.6 sq km (170.5 sq miles)
Population:	89,018 (2012 est)
Currency:	1 East Caribbean dollar = 100 cents
Religions:	Anglican 25.7%; other Protestant (mainly Moravian, Methodist, Pentecostal, and Seventh-day Adventist) 50.7%; Roman Catholic 10.4%; other Christian 5.4%
Ethnic Groups:	Black 91.0%; Mixed 4.4%
Languages:	English (official); English creole
International Organizations:	UN; Commonwealth; CARICOM; OAS; WTO; Non-Aligned Movement

A country in the Leeward Island group of the Caribbean, comprising the islands of Antigua, Barbuda, and Redonda (uninhabited).

Physical The main island, Antigua, comprises 280 sq km (108 sq miles) of fairly bare scrubland. Formed of volcanic rock in the south-west and coral in the north and east, it is moderately hilly, rising to 405 m (1329 feet). The coastline is indented. Water is scarce.

Economy The mainstay of the economy is upmarket tourism. Manufacturing industry includes bedding, handicrafts, and the assembly of electrical components for re-export. There is little agriculture.

History Antigua and Barbuda were colonized from the 17th century by the British, who brought slaves from Africa to work on the islands. From 1871 until 1956 the islands were part of the British colony of the Leeward Islands. Antigua and Barbuda joined the West Indian Federation, and in 1967 became an Associated State of Britain, gaining internal autonomy. The country became fully independent in 1981. The Antiguan Labour Party (ALP) held power from 1976 until 2004, when it was defeated in a general election by the United Progressive Party (UPP). The UPP was re-elected in 2009.

Anti-Masonic Party A US political party of the 1820s and 1830s opposed to Freemasons. Formed in 1826 in the wake of the disappearance of William Morgan, a New York bricklayer alleged to have divulged lodge secrets, the Anti-Masonic Party was the product of hysteria, cleverly played upon by local politicians. It played an influential part in the politics of New York and surrounding states, and drew sufficient *Whig support away from Henry *Clay in the 1832 presidential election to help sweep President Andrew *Jackson back into office.

Antiochus Eight Seleucid kings, notably Antiochus III and Antiochus IV. **Antiochus III** (known as 'Antiochus the Great') (c.242–187 BC) reigned from 223 to 187 BC. He restored and expanded the Seleucid empire, regaining the vassal kingdoms of Parthia and Bactria and conquering Armenia, Syria, and Palestine. When he invaded Europe he came into conflict with the Romans, who defeated him on land and sea and severely limited his power. **Antiochus IV Epiphanes** (c.215–163 BC), son of Antiochus III, reigned from 175 to 163 BC. His firm control of Judaea and his attempt to Hellenize the Jews resulted in the revival of Jewish nationalism and the Maccabean revolt.

antipope A person who claims or exercises the office of pope (*papacy) in opposition to the true pope of the time. There have been about 35 antipopes in the history of the Catholic Church, the last being Felix V (1439–49). There have been two main causes. First, a disputed election, in which there was disagreement among the electors or other interested parties as to which person was elected pope. Secondly, the desire of various Holy Roman Emperors to have a more pliable person as pope, and their setting up of antipopes for this purpose. In some cases, especially during the *Great Schism of 1378–1417, it is very difficult to say which person was the true pope and which was the antipope.

anti-Semitism Hostility towards and discrimination against *Jewish people (although there are other Semitic peoples, notably the Arabs, anti-Semitism is only used to refer to prejudice against Jewish people). In the late 19th and early 20th centuries it was strongly evident in France, Germany, Poland, Russia, and elsewhere, many Jewish emigrants fleeing from persecution or *pogroms in south-east Europe to Britain and the USA. After World War I early Nazi propaganda in Germany encouraged anti-Semitism, alleging Jewish responsibility for the nation's defeat. By 1933 Jewish persecution was active throughout the country.

The 'final solution' which Hitler worked for was to be a *Holocaust or extermination of the entire Jewish race; some six million Jews were killed in *concentration camps before the defeat of Nazism in 1945. Anti-Semitism was a strong feature of society within the former Soviet Union, especially after World War II, and remains a problem in eastern Europe and in the former Soviet republics. There is some evidence that anti-Semitism has increased in the 21st century, notably in the Arab world.

Anti-Trust laws US laws restricting business monopolies. After twenty-five years' agitation against monopolies, the *Congress passed the Sherman Anti-Trust Act (1890) that declared illegal 'every contract, combination, or conspiracy in restraint of trade'. The Clayton Anti-Trust Act (1914), amended by the Robinson–Patman Act (1936), prohibited discrimination among customers and mergers of firms that would lessen competition. After World War II there was a further growth in giant multinational corporations and the Celler–Kefauver Antimerger Act (1950) was intended to prevent oligarchic tactics, such as elimination of price competition, as being against the public interest.

Antonescu, Ion (1882–1946) Romanian military leader and fascist dictator. In 1940 he assumed dictatorial powers. He forced the abdication of King *Carol II, and supported the Axis Powers. His participation in the Nazi invasion of the Soviet Union resulted, in 1944, in the fall of his regime as the Red Army entered Romania. In 1946 he was executed as a war criminal.

Antonines A Roman imperial dynasty beginning with Titus Aurelius Antoninus (86–161AD). He succeeded *Hadrian in 137 and was entitled 'Pius' (Latin, 'the Devout') by the *Roman Senate. His reign was peaceful, by virtue of his respect for the traditional role of the Senate. The remains of a column and temple to his memory still exist in Rome. His nephew and son-in-law Marcus *Aurelius was named his adopted son and heir. Aurelius' son, Commodus, was technically the last of the dynasty; but Lucius Septimius *Severus adopted himself into the line. Severus' son 'Caracalla' and great-nephew Elagabalus continued to use the name and the title 'Pius'.

Antonine Wall A defensive fortification about 59 km (37 miles) long, built across the narrowest part of central Scotland between the Firth of Forth and the Firth of Clyde *c.*140 AD, in the time of Antoninus Pius. It was intended to mark the frontier of the Roman province of Britain, and consisted of a turf wall with a broad ditch in front and a counterscarp bank on the outer edge, with 29 small forts linked by a military road. The Romans, however, were unable to consolidate their position and in *c.*181 the wall was breached and the northern tribes forced a retreat from the Forth–Clyde frontier, eventually to that established earlier at Hadrian's Wall.

Antony, Mark *See* MARK ANTONY.

ANZAC An acronym derived from the initials of the Australian and New Zealand Army Corps, which fought during World War I. Originally it was applied to those members of the Corps who took part in the *Gallipoli Campaign. The name came to be applied to all Australian and New Zealand servicemen. Anzac Day (25 April), commemorating the Gallipoli landing (and later contributions to other campaigns), has been observed since 1916.

ANZUS An acronym given to a tripartite Pacific security treaty between Australia, New Zealand, and the USA, signed at San Francisco in 1951. Known also as the Pacific Security Treaty, it recognizes that an armed attack in the Pacific Area on any of the parties would be dangerous to peace and safety, and declares that it would act to meet the common danger, in accordance with its constitutional processes. Following New Zealand's anti-nuclear policy, which included the banning of nuclear-armed ships from its ports, the USA suspended its security obligations to New Zealand in 1986. ANZUS continues to govern security relations between Australia and the USA, and between Australia and New Zealand.

Apache A group of Plains Peoples of the south-western USA. Traditionally, the Apache practised subsistence farming and hunting, and a system of matrilocal (at the home of the wife) residence. Their nomadic existence, using the dog-travois (sledge) in the central and southern Great Plains, gradually led them southwards into semi-desert regions during the 9th to the 15th centuries. They had a reputation as fierce fighters; they and the *Navaho raided towns of the Anasazi as early as *c.*1275. Spanish explorers found them well established in Arizona, New Mexico, Texas, and northern Mexico in the late 16th century and regular contact with Spanish settlements was developed by the early 17th century. As they, and numerous other tribes on the eastern edges of the plains, acquired horses, competition for buffalo hunting became fierce and the *Comanche eventually drove them off the Great Plains into the deserts by the mid-18th century. The Apache resisted domination by the Spanish and Mexicans until the mid-19th century, when their territory was incorporated into the USA. They were not finally subjugated, however, until the end of the 19th century, and many of their chiefs, such as Geronimo, entered into American folklore. They now live in the state of Arizona.

apartheid (Afrikaans, 'separateness') A racial policy in South Africa. It depended on the Population Registration Act (1950) that assigned every person to initially three racial groups, Bantu (Black), White, and Coloured (mixed race); a fourth category, Asian, was added later. These groups were kept separate regarding land ownership, residence, marriage and other social intercourse, work, education, religion, and sport. The word apartheid was first used politically in 1943, but as a concept it goes back to the rigid segregation practised by the settlers since the 17th century. From 1948 onwards, it was expressed in statutes, in job reservation and trade union separation, and in the denial of the vote and parliamentary representation for Black people. In accordance with it *Bantu homelands were created, mostly in areas of poor land and scant resoures, depriving the Bantu-speaking peoples of South African citizenship in return for an illusory and unworkable independence.

From 1985 certain restrictions began to be mitigated by creating subordinate parliamentary chambers for Asians and Coloureds, by relaxation of rules for sport and leisure, by modifying the Group Areas Act that restricted particular areas to certain races, and by abolishing the Pass Laws that forced non-Whites to carry documentation to allow them to move through restricted areas. Increasing internal unrest along with international pressure for its abolition eventually swayed the government and in July 1991 President *de Klerk repealed all remaining apartheid legislation, including the Population Registration Act. In December 1991 a Convention for a Democratic South Africa (CODESA) was established, comprising the government and 18 political groups, including the *African National Congress and the *Inkatha Freedom Party. In 1993 a new transitional constitution, drafted by CODESA, was ratified by the government. The constitution gave the vote to all South African adults and the first multiracial elections were held in 1994.

Apollo programme The US space programme conducted by NASA, announced by President John F. Kennedy in 1961, aimed at 'landing a man on the Moon and returning him safely to Earth'. After a number of ground tests and three unmanned flights, the first manned mission (*Apollo 7*) flew in 1968, powered by a *Saturn V* launch vehicle. Three further *Apollo* flights tested the equipment and techniques to be used in the Moon landing. Then in 1969 *Apollo 11* was launched to make the first manned Moon landing. The three astronauts travelled in the command module, which was docked during flight to both the lunar module and the service module, the latter carrying fuel and supplies. On reaching the Moon, the command and service modules remained in orbit with Michael Collins on board, while Neil Armstrong and Edwin ('Buzz') Aldrin landed on the Moon's surface in the lunar module. There, they set up the Apollo Lunar Surface Experiments Package (ALSEP). When they had completed their tasks, Armstrong and Aldrin took off from the Moon in the upper half of the lunar module and docked with the command module, which took the three astronauts safely back to Earth. Parachutes were used to land the command module in the ocean for recovery by ships and helicopters. There were five more successful missions to the Moon; for the last three the astronauts had a wheeled lunar roving vehicle to help them explore further. In all, *Apollo* astronauts took about fifty experiments to the Moon and brought over 380 kg (840 pounds) of rock back to Earth. Since the last Apollo mission in 1972, there have been no further manned flights to the Moon.

apparitor *See* SUMMONER.

appeasement The efforts by the British Prime Minister, Neville *Chamberlain, and his French counterpart, Édouard Daladier, to satisfy the demands (1936–39) of the *Axis powers. Their policy of appeasement enabled Hitler to occupy the Rhineland, to annex Austria, and to acquire the Sudetenland in Czechoslovakia after the *Munich Pact of 1938. Appeasement ended when Hitler, in direct contravention of assurances given at Munich, invaded the rest of Czechoslovakia in March 1939. A policy of 'guarantees' was then instituted, by which Britain and France pledged themselves to protect Romania, Greece, and Poland should they be attacked by Germany or Italy. The German invasion of Poland five months later signalled the outbreak of World War II.

Appian Way (Latin **Via Appia**) The principal southward road from Rome in classical times, named after the censor Appius Claudius Caecus who began it in 312 BC. It originally stretched to

Capua (*c.*210 km, 132 miles), but was later extended to Brindisi in Apulia.

Appomattox A village in Virginia, USA, scene of the surrender of the *Confederacy Army of Northern Virginia to the Union Army of the Potomac on 9 April 1865. The surrender terminated Confederate resistance in the east and marked the effective end of the *American Civil War.

Aquinas, St Thomas (known as 'the Angelic Doctor') (1225–74) Italian philosopher, theologian, and Dominican friar. Regarded as the greatest figure of scholasticism, he also devised the official Roman Catholic tenets as declared by Pope Leo XIII. His works include many commentaries on Aristotle as well as the *Summa Contra Gentiles* (intended as a manual for those disputing with Spanish Muslims and Jews). His principal achievement was to make the work of Aristotle acceptable in Christian western Europe; his own metaphysics, his account of the human mind, and his moral philosophy were a development of Aristotle's, and in his famous arguments for the existence of God ('the Five Ways') he was indebted to Aristotle and to Arabic philosophers.

Aquino, Cory (Maria Corazón Aquino) (1933–2009) Philippine stateswoman, President (1986–92). Her husband, **Benigno S. Aquino** (1933–83), was the leader of the opposition to the corrupt government of Ferdinand *Marcos. She succeeded her husband as leader of the opposition when he was assassinated and became President following the overthrow of Marcos, surviving several attempted military coups.

Aquitaine An ancient province of south-west France, comprising at some periods the whole country from the Loire to the Pyrenees. As a result of the marriage of Eleanor of Aquitaine to the future Henry II in 1152, from 1154 kings of England were also dukes of Aquitaine. This situation continued until 1453 when Charles VII took Bordeaux and united the region with France as the province of Aquitaine.

Aquitaine, Eleanor of *See* ELEANOR OF AQUITAINE.

Arab conquests Wars which, in the century after the death of *Muhammad in 632, created an empire stretching from Spain to the Indus valley. Beginning as a jihad (holy war) against the apostasy of the Arabian tribes that had renounced *Islam they acquired a momentum of their own as the Arabs, inspired by the prospect of vast booty and the belief that death in battle would gain them instant admission to paradise, confronted the waning power of Byzantium and Persia.

In Syria and Egypt the conquerors allowed both Christians and Jews to keep their faiths as *dhimmi* (protected peoples) upon payment of a discriminatory tax. Local resistance in Persia and North Africa made the conquests there slower. After the first civil war (656–61) the Arab capital was moved from Medina to Damascus by the *Umayyads, and under the *Abbasids to the new city of Baghdad where, with the encouragement of the caliphs *Harun al-Rashid and al-Mamun (786–833 AD), Islamic culture flowered. The political unity of this empire was short-lived—rival caliphates appeared in North Africa and Spain in the 9th and 10th centuries—but cultural coherence was maintained by the universality of the Arabic language and Islamic law (*shariah*), and by the traffic of traders, scholars, and pilgrims which these made possible.

Arabi Pasha (Egyptian name **Ahmad Urabi Pasha al-Misri**) (1839–1911) Egyptian nationalist leader. A conscript in the Egyptian army, he rose to the rank of colonel in the Egyptian–Ethiopian War (1875–76). In 1879 he took part in an officers' revolt against the Turkish governor of Egypt and led a further revolt in 1881. In 1882, when Britain and France intervened at the request of Khedive Tawfiq, by bombarding the city of Alexandria, he organized a nationalist resistance movement. The British defeated him at *Tel-el-Kebir and exiled him to Sri Lanka. He returned to Egypt in 1901.

Arab League (or **League of Arab States**) An organization of Arab states, founded in Cairo, Egypt in 1945. The principal aims of the League are to protect the independence and sovereignty of its members and to strengthen the ties between them by encouraging cooperation in different fields. Opposition to the state of Israel and the demand for the establishment of a *Palestinian state have been central to the policies of the League. In 1989 a mediation committee consisting of three of the members of the Arab League helped to negotiate a ceasefire in Lebanon. In 1990 the League narrowly approved a proposal to dispatch Arab forces to support the US-led coalition against Saddam Hussein's invasion of Kuwait, but the conflict exposed serious divisions among members. The League supported the peace accord between Israel and the PLO (1993) but decided to uphold the boycott of Israel until it withdrew from all the occupied territories. It strongly opposed the 2003 *Iraq War.

Arab Spring (2010–11) A series of popular uprisings against authoritarian regimes in North Africa and the Middle East. Each uprising took inspiration from its predecessors as details spread via *social media, and they shared some common characteristics: in each case initial popular protests were met with attempts at repression, which only increased the protests. Thereafter the fate of each uprising varied. The first, in *Tunisia at the end of 2010, quickly led to the flight of President Ben Ali and democratic elections in late 2011. Protests followed in *Egypt, but here the rapid deposition of President *Mubarak still left the army unchallenged as the power behind the state. In *Libya the struggle was more protracted, with tribal tensions defining the pro- and anti-government forces. Foreign military aid to the rebels was crucial to the eventual overthrow of President *Gaddafi. Protests in *Yemen initiated political manoeuvres that eventually led to the replacement of President Saleh by his vice president and a promise of political reform. In *Syria mass protests against President Bashar al-Assad developed into a civil war that is still (2014) unresolved. In other states, such as Algeria, Jordan, Morocco, and Oman, protests led to some reforms but no change of regime; and in Bahrain the protests were violently crushed.

Arafat, Yasser (1929–2004) Palestinian leader, chairman of the Palestine Liberation Organization (PLO) from 1968. In 1956 he co-founded Al Fatah, the Arab group that came to dominate the PLO from 1967. In 1974 he became the first representative of a non-governmental organization to address the United Nations General Assembly. Despite challenges to his authority within the PLO, he remained its leader until his death. After the signing of a PLO–Israeli peace accord providing for limited Palestinian autonomy in the West Bank and the Gaza Strip, Arafat became leader of the new Palestine National Authority in July 1994. The same year he shared the Nobel Peace Prize with Yitzhak *Rabin and Shimon *Peres. Arafat won a landslide victory in the first Palestinian presidential elections (1996). However, from 2000 Israel held Arafat's regime responsible for failing to curb the second *intifada and, except for a short period in 2002, kept him a virtual prisoner in his Ramallah headquarters from 2001 until shortly before his death.

Aragon, Catherine of *See* CATHERINE OF ARAGON.

Arapaho An Uto-Aztecan-speaking Native American tribe of the Great Plains and prairies of eastern North Dakota and western Minnesota. In 1870 with the founding of the Arapaho Agency most settled on a reservation in Oklahoma.

Arbenz Guzmán, Jacobo (1913–71) Guatemalan statesman. A member of the Revolutionary Action Party, he served as President (1951–54). His comprehensive agrarian reforms made possible the expropriation by the government of large estates owned by Guatemalans and US conglomerates. His administration was considered to be communist by the Roman Catholic Church and the US government and so the *Eisenhower administration sent arms to Guatemala's neighbours enabling Carlos Castillo Armas to depose Arbenz in 1954.

archaeology The study of the past of humankind, especially in the prehistoric period, and usually by excavation. Archaeological research includes four stages. The most obvious is recovery of material by excavation, chance find, surface survey, and observation from the air. Digging remains crucial because it alone can recover the precise context of finds, without which they lose much of their significance. It can take a wide variety of forms depending on the nature of the site—an isolated grave, a long-occupied cave, a wreck on the sea-bed, a standing building, a modern construction site, and many more. Then, finds have to be turned into evidence by analysis. Their form, composition, date, and associations all have information to impart. Typology (study of changes in forms) can link finds from different sites. A whole battery of scientific and mathematical aids can be brought to bear at this stage. Thirdly, the results have to be built into a coherent story to give an account of what happened when. Finally, and often the most difficult task, reasons must be sought for the processes of cultural change.

archer A soldier armed with bow and arrows. Archers have practised their deadly skill since prehistory in most parts of the world, for example, the Romans employed Scythian archers on horseback. In the Middle Ages the cumbrous but powerful crossbow was widely used in continental Europe, despite being forbidden against all except infidels by the Lateran Council of 1139. In England the potential of the longbow was discovered in the time of Edward I, but it was in Edward III's reign that full use was first made of it; nearly 2 m (6 feet) long, and made of yew, oak, or maple, it enabled accurate firing of arrows at a range of up to about 320 m (350 yards), and it gave England such victories as *Crécy in 1346 and *Poitiers in 1356. Archery became the English national sport; Roger Ascham, tutor to the future *Elizabeth I, published *Toxophilus*, a treatise on archery (1545). The musketeer superseded the archer in Europe from the 16th century, but in 19th-century North America the Native Americans proved how devastating the mounted archer could be, even against men armed with rifles.

Arctic exploration Exploration of the ice-covered ocean around the North Pole. The search for a north-west and a north-east passage from Europe to the Orient gave impetus to Arctic explorations from the 16th century onwards. The British geographer Sir John Barrow promoted explorations in the early 19th century, while an attempt by Sir John Franklin (1845) to find the north-west passage led to his disappearance and ultimate confirmation of his death. The 40 or more search parties sent out after him brought back valuable information about the Arctic regions. In 1850 the British Arctic explorer Robert McClure completed a west–east crossing, but the first continuous voyage remained unachieved. In 1878–79 the Swedish Baron Nordenskjöld undertook the first traverse of the north-east passage from Norway to the Bering Strait, but the north-west passage was not completed until the voyage of the Norwegian Roald *Amundsen in 1903–06. During the 20th century there have been many Arctic expeditions made by Soviet, US, and European scientists seeking ways to develop and exploit the region; a number of drifting observation stations have also been set up on ice floes. In 1968 oil was discovered in northern Alaska, and exploration for further Arctic oilfields has continued. The first vessel to cross the North Pole underwater was a US nuclear submarine, the *Nautilus*, in 1958 and in 1977 the Soviet icebreaker *Arktika* was the first surface ship to reach the Pole.

Ardennes Campaign (also called **Battle of the Bulge**) (16–26 December 1944) The last serious German counter offensive against Allied armies advancing into Germany in World War II (*Normandy Campaign). It resulted from a decision by Hitler to make an attack through hilly, wooded country and thereby take the US forces by surprise. Last-ditch resistance at several points, notably at Bastogne, held the Germans up long enough for the Allies to recover and prevent the Germans reaching their objective of Antwerp.

Areopagus A council that met on the hill of that name in ancient *Athens. Drawn in the beginning from the richest class, the Eupatridae, it was originally an advisory body to the kings, but by the 7th century BC virtually ruled Athens. Its influence was still considerable in the early 5th century. Ephialtes' removal of its "guardianship of the laws" in 462–61 marked the beginning of the radical *Athenian democracy. It continued to judge some criminal and religious cases, but power thereafter lay with the popular assembly and the lawcourts.

Argentina

Capital:	Buenos Aires
Area:	2,780,092 sq km (1,073,399 sq miles)
Population:	42,192,494 (2012 est)
Currency:	1 peso = 100 centavos
Religions:	Roman Catholic 92.0%: Protestant 2.0%; Jewish 2.0%
Ethnic Groups:	White, mainly Spanish and Italian extraction 97.0%; Mestizo, Amerindian, and other 3.0%
Languages:	Spanish (official); Italian; Amerindian languages
International Organizations:	UN; OAS; Mercosur; WTO

The second largest country of South America, which occupies nearly the whole of the south-east of the continent, from the Andes to the Atlantic Ocean and from tropical Bolivia to the Southern Ocean.

Physical In the west the cordillera, some of it volcanic, contains deposits of many minerals. The foothills are wooded, except in the south, and shelter valleys with vineyards and orchards. In the extreme north is the Gran Chaco, an area of subtropical forest and swamp, from which run tributaries of the Paraná. The Chaco yields hardwoods, and its southern part opens into land suitable for plantation crops. Southward, in the centre of the country, lie the pampas—a vast region of high plains which supports some of the best agricultural and livestock farming in the world. Further south is Patagonia, a series of cold, infertile plateaux which are suitable only for sheep grazing.

Economy Argentina's principal exports are agricultural products such as cereals, soya beans, and meat, but there is also a broad range of manufacturing industry, and petroleum products and motor vehicles are significant exports. A high percentage of agricultural land is taken up by large cattle-raising estates. Argentina has important oil and natural gas deposits (notably in Patagonia) and these have played a major role in the development of industry. An economic crisis in 2001–02, during which Argentina defaulted on its debts, was a severe setback, but strong growth resumed in 2003. High levels of inflation and external debt continue to pose problems.

History The Inca empire extended into northwest Argentina, further south the indigenous people were nomadic hunters. The country was colonized by the Spanish from 1515 onwards, with settlers dedicating themselves to stock raising on the fertile pampas and agriculture in the areas of Salta, Jujuy, and Cordoba. In 1776 Argentina was incorporated into the viceroyalty of La Plata, with its capital in Buenos Aires; in addition to Argentina, the viceroyalty of La Plata comprised Uruguay, Paraguay, and Bolivia. The independence of the country, as the 'United Provinces of South America', was declared at the Congress of Tucuman in 1816. Divisional differences produced a series of conflicts between unitarios (centralists) and federales (federalists) which characterized much of the 19th century. The lack of political or constitutional legitimacy saw the emergence of the age of the *caudillos until the promulgation of the National Constitution in 1853. The second half of the 19th century witnessed a demographic and agricultural revolution. The fertile plains (pampas) in the interior were transformed by means of foreign and domestic capital, while immigrant workers (principally from Spain and Italy), an extensive railway network, and the introduction of steamships and refrigeration vastly increased the export of cattle and grain. The influx of immigrants between 1870 and 1914 contributed to an increase in the national population from 1.2 million in 1852 to 8 million in 1914. Argentina's export-orientated economy proved vulnerable to the fluctuations of the international market, and the Great *Depression saw a drop of 40% in the nation's exports. The military coup of 1930 saw the emergence of the armed forces as the arbiter of Argentinian politics. The failure of civilian democratic government and of achieving sustained economic growth has led to frequent military intervention. This was true even in the case of Peronism, the populist movement created with the support of trade unions by Juan Domingo *Perón (1946–55). Perón was re-elected as President in 1973 after an 18-year exile. His death in 1974 was followed by another period of military dictatorship (1976–83) in a particularly bitter and tragic period of authoritarian rule, as a result of which an estimated 20,000 Argentinians lost their lives in the 'dirty war' waged by the junta against opposition groups. In 1982 the armed forces suffered a humiliating defeat in the *Falklands (Malvinas) War with Britain, and in 1983 a civilian administration was elected under President Raul Alfonsin of the Radical Party. The process of redemocratization in Argentina faced severe problems, most notably a virtually bankrupt economy and the political sensitivity of the armed forces to reform. The Perónist Justicialist Party came to power in 1989 with Carlos Menem as President. Diplomatic relations with Britain were restored and the economy deregulated. The constitution was amended in 1994, allowing the President to hold office for two terms, and Menem triumphed again in presidential elections in 1995. Menem was succeeded in 1999 by Fernando de la Rua, but an economic crisis caused him to resign in December 2001. Following a chaotic few days in which three Presidents served briefly, Eduardo Duhalde took office in January 2002. He took emergency powers to rescue the economy. Duhalde was succeeded by Nestor Kirchner following presidential elections in 2003. Kirchner did not stand for re-election in 2007, instead supporting the successful candidacy of his wife, Cristina Fernández de Kirchner. She was re-elected in 2011.

Arianism The teaching of Arius (250–336 AD), a Libyan priest living in Alexandria, who preached a Christian heresy. He declared *Jesus Christ was not divine, simply an exceptional human being. In 325 the Council of *Nicaea excommunicated and banished him. After *Constantine's death the Roman empire was divided on the issue and another condemnation was issued at Constantinople in 381. Germanic invaders of the empire generally adopted Arianism as it was simpler than orthodox Christianity. It spread throughout western Europe and persisted in places until the 8th century.

Aristides (or **Aristides the Just**) (5th century BC) Athenian statesman and general. In the Persian Wars he commanded the Athenian army at the battle of Plataea in 479 BC, and was subsequently prominent in founding the Delian League, an alliance of Greek city-states that joined against Persians in 478–447 BC and constituted the Athenian empire.

Aristotle (384–322 BC) Greek philosopher and scientist. A pupil of Plato and tutor to Alexander the Great, in 335 BC he founded a school and library (the Lyceum) outside Athens. His surviving written works constitute a vast system of analysis, including logic, physical science, zoology, psychology, metaphysics, ethics, politics, and rhetoric. He established the inductive method of reasoning and proposed a system for the classification of plants and animals.

Arkwright, Sir Richard (1732–92) British inventor and industrialist. A pioneer of mechanical cotton-spinning, in 1767 he patented a water-powered spinning machine (known as a 'water frame'), the first such machine to produce yarn strong enough to be used as warp. He also improved the preparatory processes, including carding. He established spinning mills in Lancashire, Derbyshire, and Scotland, and became rich and powerful, despite disputes with rivals over patents and opposition to his mechanization of the industry.

Armenia A region south of the Caucasus in Asia Minor, comprising the Republic of Armenia (*see* ARMENIA, REPUBLIC OF) but also parts of eastern Turkey and northern Iran. Armenian culture dates from the 6th century BC, when people who referred to themselves as the Hay and were descended from the ancient Phrygians founded a civilization on the ruins of the ancient kingdom of Urartu. After successive annexation over 500 years by the Persians, Macedonians (Alexander the Great), and Romans, the kingdom of Armenia reached its height under Tigranes II (95–55 BC). Further subjugation by Rome, the Byzantine Empire, Persia, and the Mongol Empire culminated in over two centuries of rule by the Turks, from the early 16th century onwards. In 1828 north-east Armenia was ceded by the *Ottoman Turks to Russia. Agitation for independence developed in both Russian and Turkish Armenia, leading to a series of large-scale massacres that culminated in the deportation by the *Young Turk government of all Turkish Armenians to Syria and Palestine (1915), in which over one million died. A short-lived independent Transcaucasian Federal Republic, comprising Armenia, Azerbaijan, and Georgia, was created in 1917 but collapsed a year later. The separate republic of Armenia lasted from 1918 until 1920 when, following the Battle of Kars, Turkey captured some more Armenian territory. The remainder of Armenia proclaimed itself independent, but was again attacked by Turkey. It then became a Soviet Republic, and joined the Soviet Union. The Transcaucasian Republic was recreated as a Soviet Socialist Republic in 1922, but split in 1936. In Turkish Armenia, Turkish massacres and mass deportations continued until the Treaty of Lausanne (1923) confirmed incorporation of the region into the new republic of Turkey.

Armenia, Republic of

Capital:	Yerevan
Area:	29,766 sq km (11,490 sq miles)
Population:	2,970,495 (2012 est)
Currency:	1 dram = 100 lumas
Religions:	Armenian Orthodox 94.7%; other Christian 4.0%
Ethnic Groups:	Armenian 97.9%; Russian and Kurdish minorities
Languages:	Armenian (official); Russian; minority languages
International Organizations:	UN; Commonwealth of Independent States; OSCE; Council of Europe; Euro-Atlantic Partnership Council; WTO

A country in west Asia, formerly a constituent republic of the Soviet Union.

Physical The Republic of Armenia comprises the north-eastern part of the historic kingdom of Armenia, the rest of this region forming part of Turkey.

Economy Mineral resources include copper, lead, and zinc, and there has been rapid industrial expansion, particularly in diamond processing and jewellery, mechanical engineering, clothing and textiles, chemicals, motor vehicles, food processing, microelectronics and software, and mining. Agriculture remains important as a source of employment. There is considerable hydroelectric potential, but Armenia is dependent on imports for its other energy requirements.

History An independent Armenian republic was proclaimed in 1920, but in 1922 this was reunited with its former partners, Georgia and Azerbaijan, as the Transcaucasian Soviet Socialist Republic. This split in 1936 and the Soviet

Socialist Republic of Armenia was proclaimed. In 1989 ethnic violence erupted over the status of the Armenian region of Nagorno Karabagh (Christian) within Azerbaijan (Shiite Muslim). Armenia became independent in 1991, having declared itself no longer part of the Soviet Union. Sporadic violence in Nagorno Karabakh has continued, despite a ceasefire agreement (1994), and Armenia temporarily withdrew from peace talks in 1995. In 1996 the region unilaterally declared independence. Attempts to broker a permanent peace settlement have continued. Armenia's first parliamentary elections since independence were held in 1995 and a new constitution was approved by a referendum. The nationalist Robert Korch-aryan was elected President in 1998 and 2003. He was succeeded by Serzh Sarsyan in 2008.

Arminius (*c.*18 BC–19 AD) Leader of the Germanic resistance to Roman colonization. Born into a noble family, he served as an officer in the Roman auxiliary forces and became a Roman citizen. However, he turned against Rome and in 9 AD annihilated Quinctilius Varus and his three legions, thereby wrecking *Augustus' German policy; in 16 he thwarted the attempt of *Tiberius' nephew Germanicus to renew the conquest. Nevertheless, he failed to unite the fragmented Germanic tribes; in 19 his own aspirations to kingship encountered popular opposition and he was murdered.

Arminius, Jacobus (born **Jakob Harmensen**) (1560–1609) Dutch theologian, the founder of the theological movement known as Arminianism. He studied at Utrecht, Leiden, Basle, and Geneva before being ordained in 1588. The last six years of his life were spent as professor of theology at Leiden University. Arminianism subsequently gave rise to the Dutch Remonstrant movement and in England it influenced Archbishop *Laud.

arms and armour Personal weapons and protective clothing used in combat or for ceremonial purposes, regarded as objects of beauty as well as of practical use. In Europe armourers have invariably been workers in metal, but in other parts of the world materials such as wickerwork, bone, and coconut fibre have been used. Outside Europe, the richest traditions of arms and armour have been in the Japanese and Indo-Persian cultures, in which metal (in the form of both mail and plate) is combined with leather and padded and studded textiles. European armour reached its highest peak of development in the 15th and 16th centuries,

when plate armour, which had gradually replaced mail, encased the whole body in an ingeniously articulated suit. The finest armours were made in Germany and Milan; the main English centre of production was Greenwich, where Henry VIII established workshops. Henry's own armours were intended more for the tournament than the battlefield, because by the 16th century firearms were becoming so effective that armour could not be made proof against bullets without being excessively heavy. Cavalry continued to wear breast and back plates until the early 18th century, however. Among weapons, the sword occupies pride of place as the symbol of knighthood, justice, and power. Certain towns—notably Toledo in Spain in the 16th and 17th centuries—have been famous for their production and in Japan the blades of the great swordsmiths are regarded with an almost religious veneration.

arms race A process in which two or more states, feeling themselves to be insecure or threatened, acquire armaments, each side responding to the acquisition of arms by the other with a further build-up of its own. This action-reaction mechanism may acquire a momentum of its own, fuelling perceptions of insecurity, threat, and the need for more armaments. This is particularly so during times of rapid technological innovation, as in the "naval race" between Britain and Germany to build Dread-noughts before World War I. A more recent example was the US–Soviet arms race, especially their competition for strategic nuclear weaponry, which started after World War II (*see* COLD WAR). Some believe arms races to be a cause of conflict; to others they are a reflection of underlying political distrust, not a cause of it. One theory on arms races is that, if controlled at a key stability point, they may contribute to some kind of strategic stability, akin to a balance of power.

army An organized force of people armed for fighting on land. Armies came into existence with the earliest states and underpinned the great empires of antiquity: Egypt, Babylon, and Assyria. The essential components of armies in early history were infantry, with some chariots, and cavalry. In ancient Greece the tendency towards greater professionalism reached its climax with the Macedonian army of Alexander the Great. From this time on, the development of siege techniques was an important part of military practice. The generals of Carthage, especially *Hannibal, hired mercenaries to great effect in their forces, but it was the armies of

Rome, gradually evolving into fully professional standing forces, which dominated Europe from the 2nd century BC to the 5th century AD. Less organized but swiftly moving armies then came to the fore in the *Dark Ages, from those of *Attila the Hun to the Mongols. In Europe in the Middle Ages the limitations of the heavily armoured mounted knight were finally exposed by Swiss infantry armed with pikes or halberds and English infantry armed with longbows. The use of mercenaries (see CONDOTTIERE) again became commonplace.

The major advances of the 15th and 16th centuries were the invention of gunpowder and the development of cannon. Organization, discipline, and further advances in weaponry led to the creation of highly efficient armies, most notably those of *Frederick II (the Great) of Prussia. In the late 18th century, European armies were mainly of mercenaries recruited (often under pressure) and trained by a professional officer class. The first conscript armies were recruited in France to fight the *Revolutionary and *Napoleonic Wars. During the 19th century most European countries adopted a system of conscription of young men to train and serve for about two years. (Britain only enforced conscription in 1916–18 and again between 1939 and 1959.) European armies played an essential role in 19th- and early 20th-century *imperialism, their superior fire-power enabling them to dominate the peoples of Africa and Asia. The *American Civil War (1861–65) saw large armies of the Union (the North) and the Confederacy (the South) engaged in a struggle in which railways were crucial for movement of troops, and new infantry weapons, such as the breech-loading rifle and the repeating carbine, were developed. By the time of the *Franco-Prussian War in 1870–71 heavy artillery was developing, but infantry and cavalry tactics remained little changed until World War I, when motor transport and heavier artillery developed. Even then, armies were slow to adapt to armoured vehicles and the massed infantry attacks of its battles still used rifle, bayonet, and hand-grenade as their basic weapons, now pitched against machine guns. By World War II armies were fully motorized and tanks played a major part in the *North African Campaign and at the Eastern Front. This mobility required large back-up fuel and maintenance services. Basic infantry tactics still remained essential (even though the rifle was being replaced by the semiautomatic or automatic submachine gun), especially in the jungle warfare of the *Burma Campaign. They remained so for later campaigns in Korea, Vietnam, and the Falklands. In the *Cold War balance of power, large armies of *NATO and the *Warsaw Pact continued to face one another in Europe, armed with both conventional weapons and missiles. Allied victory in the *Gulf War was achieved through massive tank deployment. Since the end of the Cold War the armies of UN member nations have increasingly been combined to form multinational peace-keeping and 'rapid reaction' forces.

Arnhem, Battle of (September 1944) Battle in Holland in World War II. Parachutists of the 1st Allied Airborne Division (British, US, Polish) were dropped in an attempt to capture key bridges over the Lower Rhine to enable the Allied armies to advance more rapidly into Germany. The attempt failed, and resulted in 7,000 Allied casualties. German units blocked the path of Allied divisions, which were attempting to reach and reinforce the airborne troops.

Arnold, Benedict (1741–1801) American soldier and traitor. He was a hero of the early stages of the War of *Independence, serving with conspicuous valour at Ticonderoga, the invasion of Canada, and Saratoga Springs. After 1778, possibly persuaded by his loyalist wife, he began plotting with Clinton to deliver West Point to the British. When his courier, Major André, was captured, he fled to the British, for whom he fought thereafter. He died, neglected, in England.

Artaxerxes II (c.436–358 BC) King of Persia 404–358, the son of Darius II. He crushed the rebellion of his younger brother *Cyrus the Younger at Cunaxa in 401. By the peace of Antalcidas, made with the Spartans in 386, he recovered the Greek cities of Asia Minor, but he was unsuccessful in his attempts to repossess Egypt, and he put down the satraps' revolt of 366–358 only with difficulty. His son, Artaxerxes III, killed his brothers and crushed two rebellious satraps in order to establish his power. In 343 he finally forced Egypt back into the empire, but his reign was one of terror and he was murdered by his minister Bagoas in 338.

Arthur Traditionally king of Britain, historically perhaps a 5th- or 6th-century Romano-British chieftain or general. His life and court have become the focus for many romantic legends in various languages, including the exploits of adventurous knights and the quest for the Holy Grail. The stories were developed and recounted by Malory, Chrétien de Troyes, and others; the Norman writer Wace (12th century) mentions the 'Round Table', which enabled the knights to be seated in such a way that none had precedence. Arthur's court was at Camelot, a place variously located by writers and historians in Wales, Somerset, Cornwall, and Winchester.

Arthur, Chester Alan (1830–86) US Republican statesman, 21st President of the USA (1881–85). He was appointed Garfield's Vice-President in 1881 and became President after Garfield's assassination. During his term of office, he was responsible for improving the strength of the US navy.

Artigas, José Gervasio (1764–1850) National hero of Uruguay. He led the Uruguay-an movement for independence from Spain during the years 1811–13 and maintained this in the face of the territorial ambitions of Argentina in 1814. Uruguay also had to contend with Por-tuguese expansionists from Brazil, and Portu-guese troops captured Montevideo in 1817. Artigas was unable to dislodge them. He con-ducted guerrilla warfare against them for three years, but in 1820 was forced to retreat to Argentina and never returned to Uruguay.

artillery War engines or firearms too large to be managed by a single soldier. Ballistas, on-agers, and catapults were early examples of artillery. Their use was largely restricted to siege warfare and it was in such operations that the cannon came to replace them. Modern artillery functions in the same way as all firearms, but fires larger projectiles over longer distances. Muzzle-loaders, common from the 15th to the 19th century, had their explosive charge and ammunition loaded from the front of the barrel. Breech-loaders, used in the 15th and 16th cen-turies and reintroduced on a large scale in the mid-19th century, have the charge and shot loaded at the rear. Modern categories of artillery fire solid shot, shrapnel, or explosive shells. They include field guns, which fire with a flat trajectory, howitzers and mortars, which have arching trajectories, antitank guns, firing high-velocity shot, and self-propelled guns. Since 1918 there has been a decline in the importance of heavy artillery as missiles, bomber aircraft, and armed helicopters have taken over many of their roles, while mortars have taken over many light artillery roles.

Artois, Charles, Comte d' *See* CHARLES X.

Arusha Declaration (1967) A major policy statement by President Nyerere of *Tanzania. The text was agreed by the executive of the political party TANU (Tanganyika African National Union) and proposed that TANU

implement a socialist programme by which the major means of production would be placed under the collective ownership of the farmers and workers of the country. No party member would be allowed more than one salary or to own more than one house, nor any capitalist stocks and shares. Banks were nationalized, followed by large industrial and insurance companies, as well as the larger trading firms. Nyerere was deeply committed to the concept of *ujamaa*, which saw all land and natural re-sources as belonging to the people within their village communities, and following the declar-ation there emerged many farm collectives. The policy was moderated after 1977 to allow some private investment, and largely abandoned after 1987.

Aryan A member of the peoples (not to be regarded as a race) speaking any of the lan-guages of the Indo-European (especially Indo-Iranian) family. The idea current in the 19th century of an Aryan race corresponding to a definite Aryan language was taken up by na-tionalistic, historical, and romantic writers. It was given especial currency by the French writer and social theorist Joseph-Arthur, Comte de Gobineau (1816–82), who linked it with the theory of the essential inferiority of certain races. The term 'Aryan race' was later revived and used for purposes of political propaganda in Nazi Germany.

Arya Samaj A Hindu reform movement. Founded in 1875 by Swami Dayananda Saras-wati (*c.*1825–83), it appealed to the authority of the Vedas (sacred texts) in support of pro-grammes of social reform and education. Its supporters, such as Lala Rajpat Rai, were prominent in political movements opposed to British rule, and their activities aggravated Hindu relations with Sikhs and Muslims.

Asante (or **Ashanti**) The largest and most prestigious of the chiefdoms of Ghana, in West Africa. It emerged, under the Asantehene (king) Osei Tutu in the 1670s, as a powerful kingdom, the Asante Confederacy, ruled by the Asante-hene from Kumasi (now in Ghana). The wealth of the confederacy was based on the control of trade, particularly of cola nuts, and of gold mines, and by selling slaves for European goods to the European trading stations established along the Gold Coast of West Africa. In 1807 the Asante occupied Fanti coastal territory. Follow-ing the British abolition of the slave trade they fought the British between 1824 and 1831, and again in 1874, when field-marshal Viscount Wolseley (1833–1913) took and burned Kumasi, the Asante capital. Further troubles (1895–96) ended in the establishment of a Protectorate and the exile of Asantehene *Prempeh I, and in 1901 Britain annexed the country. In 1924 Prempeh was allowed to return and an Asante Confederacy Council was set up in 1935 as an organ of local government, the Asantehene being head. In that year the Golden Stool, symbolizing the soul of the Asante people, was restored to Kumasi.

The people of the southern tropical forest of Ghana, who are also known as Asante, are a primarily agricultural people who farm crops for local consumption and produce cocoa as an important export crop. Asante society is organized on the principle of matrilineal descent (from men to men, via their mothers and sisters), but the Asante also recognize spiritual characteristics inherited from the father. The office of lineage head is symbolized by a lineage stool.

Ascham, Roger (c.1515–68) English humanist scholar and writer. His posts included that of tutor to the future Elizabeth I and Latin secretary to Queen Mary and later to Elizabeth. He is noted for his treatise on archery, *Toxophilus* (1545), and *The Scholemaster* (1570), a practical and influential treatise on education.

Ashikaga (also called **Muromachi**, from the district in Kyoto where, after 1392, the shoguns lived) The *shogunate in Japan from 1339 to 1573. In 1333 Ashikaga Takanju (1305–58) overthrew the *Hojo, who had acted as regents for the *Kamakura shoguns. Soon after he drove the emperor Go-Daigo from the capital of Kyoto. In the ensuing dynastic dispute he installed Koyo as emperor and in return the emperor appointed him shogun in succession to the Kamakura shogunate, which had become ineffectual. He moved the shogunate from Kamakura to Kyoto. The Ashikaga shoguns never exercised great power as the shogunate witnessed much fighting between rival *daimyo and their *samurai armies. The increasing disorder of the Ashikaga shogunate ended in 1573 when *Oda Nobunaga and his army drove the shogun from Kyoto.

Ashley Cooper, Anthony *See* SHAFTESBURY.

Ashurbanipal King of Assyria (c.668–627 BC). The grandson of Sennacherib, he was responsible for the sacking of the Elamite capital Susa and the suppression of a revolt in Babylon. However, he is chiefly recognized for his patronage of the arts; he established a library of more than 20,000 clay tablets at Nineveh, which included literary, religious, scientific, and administrative documents.

Asia The largest continent in the world, occupying a third of its land surface. Asia stretches from the Arctic to the Equator and from the Ural Mountains to the Pacific Ocean. Asia includes the Indian sub-continent, the peninsula of Asia Minor, and numerous islands, including *Japan, the *Philippines, and *Indonesia.

Physical The extreme north is mainly tundra, which gives way to the vast expanse of Siberia. The land rises to the south and central Asia is mountainous, containing the Himalayas, the highest mountains in the world. Major rivers, including the Indus, the Ganges, the Mekong, and the Yangtze provide water and sediment for large areas of India and China. The volcanic and earthquake zone at the edge of the Eurasian plate runs from Japan, across the south of the continent to Turkey in the west.

History The ancient civilizations of *Sumeria, *Babylon, *Assyria, Media, and Persia, as well as those of *China and *India arose in Asia. The world's major religions originated in Asia, Judaism and Christianity expanding westwards. Population movements have been affected by the topography, many cultures surviving in isolation in the mountains while conquerors, such as the *Huns, *Mongols and *Cossacks, created vast empires. European trade with China was taking place via the *Silk Road as early as the 2nd century BC. In the 15th century sea routes, discovered by such explorers as Vasco *da Gama led to the creation of companies, including the *East India Companies that were keen to exploit new resources. The European colonial powers acquired lands in Asia and it was not until the mid-20th century that European influence began to wane as former colonies gained independence. The 20th century also saw the rise of communism in the form of the Soviet Union and the People's Republic of China. The USA became involved in the *Korean War and the *Vietnam War and its fears of a major communist alliance were only averted by the ideological divergence of the Soviet Union and China after 1960. Japan led an economic boom, the 'tiger economies' of south-east Asian countries in particular growing rapidly in the 1980s and 1990s. The early 21st century saw the emergence of China and India as major economic powers. The Middle East has continued to be troubled by violent unrest.

Asia Minor (or **Anatolia**) The westernmost part of Asia now comprising Asiatic Turkey. The first major civilization established there was that of the Hittites in the 2nd millennium BC. The Greeks colonized the western coast, while the kingdoms of Lydia and Phrygia developed independently. The land was subjugated by various invaders, including Cyrus of Persia (546 BC) and Alexander the Great (333 BC). It was subsequently the Roman province of Asia and then part of the Byzantine empire. Conquered by the Turks, it became part of the Ottoman empire from the end of the 13th century until the establishment of modern Turkey after World War I.

asiento de negros A contract made between Britain and Spain in 1713 for the sale of slaves to the Spanish American colonies. In the Peace of *Utrecht (1713) Spain granted Britain a monopoly of the supply of slaves to the Spanish American colonies of 144,000 slaves at 4,800 a year for thirty years, with other privileges. They were the origin of the speculation that resulted in the *South Sea Bubble and led to endless disputes, including the War of *Jenkins's Ear between England and Spain in 1739. The treaty was ended by agreement in 1750.

Askia Muhammad I (died 1528) Emperor of *Songhay in West Africa (1493–1528). Originally named Muhammad Turé, he was *Sonni Ali's best general. He usurped Songhay from Ali's son in 1493, thus founding a new dynasty, and took the title Askia. He was a convert to Islam, but tolerant towards pagans, and made the pilgrimage to *Mecca, meeting many notable men, especially the great Muslim teacher al-Maghili. He had close political and commercial relationships with Morocco and Egypt, organized an efficient administration and an army and a navy on the River Niger, and made Timbuktu the capital of the Songhay empire, developing it as an intellectual and religious centre.

Asoka (died c.232 BC) Emperor of India (c.269–c.232 BC). He embarked on a campaign of conquest, but after his conversion to Buddhism (which he established as the state religion) he renounced war and sent out missionaries as far afield as Syria and Ceylon to spread his new faith.

Asquith, Herbert Henry, 1st Earl of Oxford and Asquith (1852–1928) British Liberal statesman, Prime Minister (1908–16). In the years before World War I he introduced the third bill for Irish Home Rule, while also contending with the challenge posed by the women's suffrage movement and outrage from the House of Lords over *Lloyd George's People's Budget (1909). In 1915 Asquith brought the Conservatives into a coalition government, but his failure to consult his colleagues divided the Liberals; he was displaced as Prime Minister by Lloyd George the following year, but retained the party leadership.

Assad, Hafiz al- (1928–2000) Syrian Baath statesman, President (1971–2000). While in office he ensured the strengthening of Syria's oil-based economy and suppressed political opposition such as the uprising of Muslim extremists (1979–82). He supported the coalition forces during the 1991 *Gulf War. He was succeeded by his son, Bashar al-Assad (1965–).

assassin (from the Arabic *hashishiyun*, 'smoker of hashish') A member of a secret sect of the Ismaili branch of Shiite Islam. It was founded by Hasan ibn al-Sabbah in 1078 to support the claim of Nizar to the *Fatimid caliphate and a headquarters was established at Alamut in north-west Persia. The assassins wielded influence through suicide squads of political murderers, convinced that they would earn a place in paradise if they died while obeying orders.

assizes A procedure introduced into English law in the later 12th century by *Henry II. The Assize of Clarendon (1166), which dealt with criminal trials, and the Assize of Arms (1181), which reorganized local defence and police measures, were enactments made at sessions of the king's council. The assizes of novel disseisin and mort d'ancestor (both relating to tenancy), and the Grand Assize (to determine titles to disputed lands) were introduced by sessions of Henry II's council (1166, 1176, and the late 1170s); these procedures remained important throughout the Middle Ages.

Travelling justices were established in the 13th century; these justices came to be called justices of assize and their sessions were called assizes. A system of such judicial sessions was regularized (1293–1328) and judicial circuits were established that remained in force until a new system of Crown Courts was set up in 1971.

Association of Caribbean States An association of 25 Caribbean basin countries formed in 1994 for the purpose of promoting regional integration, economic cooperation, and a common approach to regional political problems.

Association of South-East Asian Nations (ASEAN) A regional organization formed by Indonesia, Malaysia, the Philippines, Singapore, and Thailand through the Bangkok Declaration of 1967. Brunei joined in 1984,

Vietnam in 1995, Myanmar (Burma) and Laos in 1997, and Cambodia in 1999. ASEAN aims to accelerate and to promote regional stability. In 1992 it agreed to create the ASEAN Free Trade Area (AFTA) as the first step towards the creation of an ASEAN common market. Progress towards internal free trade is ongoing, and ASEAN is also working towards free trade with regional trading partners. The ASEAN-Australia-New Zealand Free Trade Area was created in 2009.

Assyria An ancient country in what is now northern Iraq. It was originally centred on Ashur, a city-state on the west bank of the Tigris, which first became prominent and expanded its borders in the 14th century BC. From the 8th to the late 7th century BC Assyria was the dominant Near-Eastern power and created an empire which stretched from the Persian Gulf to Egypt. Its capital city was Nineveh near modern Mosul, Iraq. The state fell in 612 BC, defeated by a coalition of Medes and Chaldeans.

Astor, John Jacob (1763–1848) US fur trader and financier. He entered the American fur trade and by 1800 had established the beginnings of a commercial empire, with chartered ships plying both the Atlantic and the Pacific. His American Fur Company, formed in 1808, dominated the fur trade in the prairies and mountains within a decade. In 1834 he sold his interest in the fur trade and spent his remaining years managing his highly profitable property holdings.

Astor, Nancy Witcher Langhorne, Viscountess (1879–1964) US-born British Conservative politician. She became the first woman to sit in the House of Commons when she succeeded her husband as MP for Plymouth in 1919. She supported causes about which she had deep convictions, such as temperance and women's rights, rather than following the party line.

Atahualpa (died 1533) The last ruler of the *Inca empire, son of Huayna Capac. Ruling from 1525 in Quito (now in Ecuador), he defeated Huáscar, his half-brother and co-ruler in Cuzco, whom he killed after the battle of Huancavelica in 1530. In 1532 he marched against Francisco *Pizarro and remnants of the Huáscar faction, who had allied themselves to the Spaniards; at Cajamarca he was drawn into an ambush, captured, and held for ransom. He ordered a room to be filled with gold and silver objects while another army secretly marched to free him, but was murdered when Pizarro learned of the plan. Shortly thereafter Pizarro captured Cuzco and within a few years Spain ruled the lands of the Incas.

Atatürk, Kemal (or **Kemal Pasha Atatürk**; born **Mustafa Kemal Atatürk**) (1881–1938) Turkish general and statesman, President (1923–38). Leader of the postwar Turkish Nationalist Party, he was elected President of a provisional government in 1920. With the official establishment of the Turkish republic in 1923, he was elected its first President, taking the name of Atatürk (Turkish for 'father of the Turks') in 1934. During his presidency he introduced many political and social reforms, including the abolition of the caliphate, the adoption of the Roman alphabet for writing Turkish, and other policies designed to make Turkey a modern secular state.

Athanasius, St (*c.*296–373) Greek theologian. As bishop of Alexandria he was a consistent upholder of Christian orthodoxy, especially against Arianism. He aided the ascetic movement in Egypt and introduced knowledge of monasticism to the West.

Athelstan (893/4–939) King of England (925–39). Effectively the first king of all England, Athelstan came to the thrones of Wessex and Mercia in 924 before becoming king of all England a year later. He successfully invaded both Scotland and Wales and inflicted a heavy defeat on an invading Danish army.

Athenian democracy A form of popular government established in Athens by Cleisthenes (died 508 BC) in the last decade of the 6th century BC. The principal organ of democracy was the popular assembly (*ekklesia*), which was open to Athenian male citizens aged over 18. All members had the right to speak and it was the assembly that decided all legislative and policy matters. The council (*boule*) of 500, elected by lot for a year from Athenian male citizens over the age of 30, was an executive body which prepared business for the assembly and then saw that its decisions were carried out. *Pericles dominated the democracy until his death in 429, but none of the 'demagogues' who followed him achieved the same level of influence.

Athenian empire The cities and islands mainly in the Aegean area that paid tribute to Athens in the 5th century BC. It developed out of the *Delian League as Athens, by virtue of its great naval superiority, imposed its will on its allies. A significant step was the transference of the League's treasury from Delos to Athens probably in 454 BC, since this ensured for Athens absolute control of the tribute. Inscriptions and literary sources reveal the means by which Athens controlled its subjects: the installation of garrisons; the establishment of clenruchies (colonies) of Athenian citizens in important or rebellious areas; the encouragement of local democracies; the referral of important judicial cases to Athens; the imposition of Athenian weights and measures throughout the empire; and officials to keep an eye on subject cities.

As long as it had a strong navy, Athens could crush revolts and enforce its will throughout the Aegean, but the empire died with Athens' final defeat in the *Peloponnesian War. Nevertheless it did establish the Second Athenian Confederacy in 377 BC, trying to avoid the mistakes of the 5th century.

Athens The capital of modern Greece, historically an ancient Greek city-state. It was formed as a result of the unification of a number of small villages of the surrounding region of Attica. It was first under the rule of hereditary kings, and monarchy was followed by a longlived aristocracy, first successfully challenged by *Solon in 594 BC. Tyranny was established by *Pisistratus, temporarily in 561 and more permanently in 546, until his son Hippias was driven out in 510. Within a few years Cleisthenes had put the *Athenian democracy on to a firm footing.

In 490 BC and 480–479 the city-state enjoyed success in the *Greek-Persian Wars. Subsequently its rulers transformed the *Delian League into the *Athenian empire. The city supported brilliant artistic activity, attracting artists from throughout the Mediterranean. However, it was defeated by Sparta in the *Peloponnesian War, losing by 404 the empire, almost all its fleet, and the city walls. It recovered remarkably in the 4th century BC and led the resistance to *Philip II of Macedonia. The city was a centre of philosophy, science, and the arts, centred on the *Academy.

Athens was prey to the successors of Alexander the Great, losing its independence in 262 BC, though regaining it in 228. After supporting *Mithridates VI, King of Pontus, (120–63 BC) against Rome, it was successfully besieged by his antagonist, *Sulla, and sacked (87–86). From then on its importance was as a university town which attracted many young men, particularly Romans. This apart, the city underwent a prolonged period of historical obscurity and economic decline. It was captured by the Turks in 1456, and suffered during the Venetian siege of 1687.

Atkinson, Sir Harry (Albert) (1831–92) New Zealand statesman, Prime Minister (1876–77; 1883–84; 1887–91). Born in Britain, he emigrated to New Zealand in 1853 and became a member of the House of Representatives in 1861, also serving as a commander in the Maori Wars in the early 1860s. During his first term as Prime Minister he passed a bill abolishing the colony's provincial governments. He later served as colonial treasurer (1879–82; 1882–83) and is chiefly remembered for the austere economic policy that he pursued throughout the 1880s to boost New Zealand's recovery from economic depression.

Atlantic, Battle of the The name given to a succession of sea-operations in World War II. They took place in the Atlantic, the Caribbean, and northern European waters and involved both submarine blockades and attacks on Allied shipping. German U-boats, sometimes assisted by Italian submarines, were the main weapon of attack, but aircraft and surface raiders also participated. About 2800 Allied, mainly British, merchant ships were lost, placing the Allies in a critical situation. After summer 1943, with the introduction of better radar, the provision of long-distance aircraft and of escort carriers, and the breaking of German codes, the situation eased, although technical innovations subsequently increased the U-boats' effectiveness. It was only the capture of their bases by Allied land forces that finally put an end to the threat.

Atlantic Charter A joint declaration of principles to guide a post-World War II peace settlement. It resulted from a meeting at sea between *Churchill and F. D. *Roosevelt on 14 August 1941. It stipulated freely chosen governments, free trade, freedom of the seas, and disarmament of current aggressor states, and it condemned territorial changes made against the wishes of local populations. A renunciation of territorial ambitions on the part of Britain and the USA was also prominent. In the following month other states fighting the *Axis powers, including the USSR, declared their support for these principles. The Atlantic Charter provided the ideological base for the *United Nations Organization.

Atlantis A legendary island said to have been submerged following an earthquake nearly 12,000 years ago. *Plato describes Atlantis in a myth, leading some people to suggest it was the Minoan civilization on Crete, destroyed by the volcanic eruption of Thera (Santorini) in 1500 BC.

attainder The extinction of civil rights and powers when judgement of death or outlawry was recorded against a person convicted of treason or felony. It was the severest English common law penalty, for an attainted person lost all his goods and lands to the crown. Procedure by Act of Attainder became common in the Wars of the *Roses, when because it was reversible it could be used as a powerful threat. Of the 397 people condemned by process in Parliament between 1453 and 1509, over 250 ultimately had their attainders reversed. Acts of Attainder came to be disapproved of because an opportunity for defence was not necessarily given; they became rare in the 18th century and ceased after 1798.

Attila (406–53) King of the Huns (434–53). From his base in Hungary he ravaged vast areas between the Rhine and the Caspian Sea between 445 and 450, inflicting great devastation on the Eastern Roman Empire. Attila then invaded the Western Empire but was defeated by the joint forces of the Roman army and the Visigoths at Châlons in 451. He and his army were the terror of Europe during his lifetime, and he earned the nickname 'Scourge of God'.

Attila Line (or **Sahin Line**) The frontier line dividing Greek from Turkish Cyprus following the Turkish invasion of 1974. The invasion, which was likened to the action of Attila the Hun, put into effect Turkey's scheme for the partition of Cyprus (the Attila Plan). It stretches from Morphou Bay in the west to Famagusta in the east.

Attlee, Clement Richard, 1st Earl Attlee (1883–1967) British Labour statesman, Prime Minister (1945–51). He became Labour Party leader in 1935, and deputy Prime Minister in 1942 in Churchill's coalition government. Following his party's landslide election victory in 1945, Attlee became the first Labour Prime Minister to command an absolute majority in the House of Commons. His term saw the creation of the modern welfare state and a wide programme of nationalization of major industries (including coal, gas, and electricity). Foreign policy initiatives included a progressive withdrawal from colonies and support for NATO.

AU See AFRICAN UNION.

Aubrey, John (1626–97) English antiquarian and author. He was a pioneer of field archaeology, most of his researches being centred on the earthworks and monuments in Wiltshire (particularly Avebury and Stonehenge) and became one of the first Fellows of the Royal Society in 1663. As an author, he is chiefly remembered for the lively and anecdotal collection of biographies of eminent persons, such as John Milton and Francis Bacon, known as

Brief Lives, a bowdlerized edition of which was first published in 1813.

Auchinleck, Sir Claude John Eyre (1884–1981) British field-marshal. He served with distinction in World War I. He commanded the land forces at Narvik in the ineffectual Norwegian campaign in April–May 1940, was commander-in-chief in India (1940–41) and from mid-1941 he commanded in North Africa. He led the advance in Libya, but was driven back by stronger German forces in 1942. When *Tobruk surrendered, he took personal command of the troops, establishing the key defensive line at El *Alamein. Churchill then replaced him with *Montgomery and he returned to India as commander-in-chief.

Augsburg, League of An alliance formed between Emperor Leopold and some German princes in 1686 to resist *Louis XIV's advance into the Rhineland. The Holy Roman Emperor, the Dutch, Spain, and Sweden joined and a Grand Alliance was established when the French invaded the *Palatinate.

Augsburg, Peace of An agreement to accept the existence of both Lutheranism and Catholicism in Germany, decided in 1555 by the Diet of the Holy Roman Empire at Augsburg, in south Germany. Although the agreement had many flaws and satisfied neither side completely it averted serious religious conflict within the empire for over 50 years.

Augsburg, War of the League of See NINE YEARS WAR.

Augsburg Confession A statement of the Lutheran position approved by *Luther that was presented to Charles V at the German city of Augsburg on 25 June 1535.

augur An official diviner or soothsayer in ancient Rome. The augur's task was to watch for indications of the attitude of the gods towards proposed activities of the state or its officers. They played a key role in choosing or "inaugurating" successive non-hereditary kings of early Rome. The name was thought to be linked with birds (Latin, *aves*), since they scrutinized the activities of birds, besides other animals, as well as accidents, and dreams, particularly on the eve of military expeditions and at the moment of important births. All political assemblies of the Roman people were preceded by the taking of "auspices".

Augustine of Canterbury, St (died *c.*605) The first Archbishop of Canterbury. He was chosen (596) by Pope Gregory the Great to convert the English to Christianity. With forty monks Augustine came first to Kent (597) and converted King Ethelbert, whose wife was already a Christian. Consecrated archbishop (597), Augustine organized the church into twelve dioceses (598) but failed at a meeting with the Celtic bishops in 603 to resolve the differences between the Roman and Celtic churches, although these differences were resolved at the Synod of *Whitby (664). Augustine's work was instrumental in the re-establishment of Christianity in England.

Augustine of Hippo, St (354–430) Doctor of the Church. Born in North Africa of a pagan father and a Christian mother, he underwent a series of spiritual crises in his early life, described in his *Confessions*. While in Milan he was influenced by the bishop, Ambrose, adopting his Neoplatonic understanding of Christianity and being baptized by him in 386. Augustine henceforth lived a monastic life, becoming bishop of Hippo in North Africa in 396. His episcopate was marked by his continual opposition to the heresies of the Pelagians, Donatists, and Manichees. Of his extensive writings, perhaps his best-known work is the *City of God*. His theology has dominated all later Western theology, with its psychological insight, its sense of man's utter dependence on grace (expressed in his doctrine of predestination), and its conception of the Church and the sacraments.

Augustus (known until 27 BC as **Octavian**) (63 BC–14 AD) The first Roman emperor. Originally called Gaius Octavius, he took the name Gaius Julius Caesar Octavianus when he was adopted by the will of his great-uncle Julius Caesar in 44 BC. He established his position as one of the triumvirate of 43 BC, gaining supreme power by his defeat of Antony in 31 BC. A constitutional settlement in 27 BC in theory restored the republic but in practice regularized his sovereignty; in the same year he was given the title Augustus (Latin for 'venerable'). His rule was marked abroad by a series of expansionist military campaigns and at home by moral and religious reforms intended to restore earlier Roman values disrupted during previous civil wars.

Augustus II (or **Augustus the Strong**) (1670–1733) King of Poland (1696–1733). He was Elector of Saxony from 1694 and succeeded *John III (John Sobieski) as King of Poland in 1696. He joined Russia and Denmark against *Charles XII of Sweden without Polish support but was defeated. Charles had him banished and Stanislaus Leszczynski elected king in his place. Augustus recovered his position after Charles's defeat at Poltava (1709) and for the rest of his reign brought some economic prosperity to Saxony and Poland, although renewed war with Sweden lasted until 1718. A ruler of considerable extravagance, supposed to be the most dissolute monarch in Europe, he was a patron of the arts and gave special support to the Dresden and Meissen china factories.

Aung San (1914–47) Burmese nationalist leader. A leader of the radicals from his student days, during World War II he accepted Japanese assistance and secret military training for his supporters. Returning to Burma in 1942 he became leader of the Japanese-sponsored Burma National Army, which defected to the Allies in the closing weeks of the war in the Pacific. As leader of the postwar Council of Ministers, in January 1947 he negotiated a promise of full self-government from the British; in July of that year he and six of his colleagues were assassinated by political rivals during a meeting of the Council.

Aung San Suu Kyi (1945–) Burmese political leader. Daughter of Aung San, she became the co-founder and leader of the National League for Democracy (NLD), the country's main opposition party, in 1988. Although she was placed under house arrest in 1989 and not allowed to stand as a candidate, the NLD won 80% of the seats in the democratic elections of 1990; the ruling military government refused to recognize the NLD's victory. A supporter of political reform through non-violent public protest and democratic processes, she was awarded the Nobel Peace Prize in 1991. She was released from house arrest in 1995, rearrested in 2000, released in 2002, and again rearrested in 2003. Finally released in 2010, she was elected an NLD member of parliament in 2012.

Aurangzeb (1618–1707) Mogul emperor of Hindustan (1658–1707). Having usurped the throne from his father, Aurangzeb assumed the title Alamgir (Conqueror of the World). His expansionist policies increased the Mogul empire to its widest extent, and it experienced a period of great wealth and splendour, but constant rebellions and wars greatly weakened the empire and it declined sharply after his death.

Aurelian (full name **Lucius Domitius Aurelianus**) (c.215–75) Roman emperor (270–75). Originally a common soldier, he rose through the ranks and was elected emperor by the army.

By a series of military campaigns, including the defeat of Queen Zenobia at Palmyra (272), he successfully quelled rebellions and repelled barbarian invaders; he also built new walls round Rome, and established the state worship of the Sun. He was assassinated by his own army officers.

Aurelius, Marcus (full name **Caesar Marcus Aurelius Antoninus Augustus**) (121–80) Roman emperor (161–80). The adopted successor of Antoninus Pius, he was occupied for much of his reign with wars against Germanic tribes invading the empire from the north. He was by nature a philosophical contemplative; his *Meditations* are a collection of aphorisms and reflections based on a Stoic outlook and written down for his own guidance.

Aurignacian *See* PALAEOLITHIC.

Ausgleich (1867; German, 'compromise') A constitutional compromise between Hungary and the *Austrian empire following the defeat of Austria in Italy and Germany. It was drawn up by Francis Deák, and ratified by the Austrian emperor *Francis Joseph, granting Hungary its own parliament and constitution but retaining Francis Joseph as King of Hungary. A dual monarchy, *Austria-Hungary, was created, in which the *Magyars were permitted to dominate their subject peoples and the Austrians the remaining seventeen provinces of the empire.

Austerlitz, Battle of (2 December 1805) A battle fought by Austria and Russia against France, near the town of Austerlitz in Moravia. Alexander I of Russia persuaded *Francis I of Austria to attack before reinforcements arrived. Their complicated plan to encircle the French allowed *Napoleon to split their army and defeat each half. It was a decisive battle; the Russian army was forced to withdraw from Austria, and Austria signed the Treaty of Pressburg (1805), in which it recognized Napoleon as King of Italy, and ceded territories in northern Italy, the Alpine regions, and on the Adriatic coast.

Australia

Capital:	Canberra
Area:	7,682,300 sq km (2,966,200 sq miles)
Population:	22,015,576 (2012 est)
Currency:	1 Australian dollar = 100 cents
Religions:	Roman Catholic 25.3%; Anglican 17.1%; other Protestant 11.7%; other Christian 7.1%
Ethnic Groups:	White 92.0%; Asian 7.0%; Aboriginal and other 1.0%
Languages:	English (official); minority and Aboriginal languages
International Organizations:	UN; OECD; Colombo Plan; ANZUS Pact; Secretariat of the Pacific Community; Pacific Islands Forum; Commonwealth; WTO

An island country and continent in the Southern Hemisphere in the south-west Pacific Ocean. Surrounding it are numerous islands, the largest being Tasmania, and off its east coast lies the Great Barrier Reef.

Physical Much of the continent has a hot, dry climate, and a large part of the central area is desert or semi-desert; the most fertile areas are on the eastern coastal plains and in the south-west corner of Western Australia.

Economy Australia's economy is based on mining, agriculture, and industry. Agricultural land, which is periodically devastated by drought, accounts for 64% of Australia's territory, almost all of this being devoted to cattle and sheep. Australia is a leading world producer and exporter of wool, beef, wheat, coal, iron ore, aluminium, and other metals. Manufacturing industry is aimed principally at domestic markets. There is also a large service sector.

History Australia was first inhabited by *Aborigines thought to have migrated from south-east Asia 50,000–40,000 years ago. Although the first known European discoveries of the continent were those made in the early 17th century, there may have been earlier Portuguese discoveries. It was visited by an Englishman, William Dampier, in 1688 and 1699. Captain James Cook claimed British possession of the eastern part of the continent in 1770, naming it New South Wales. The British penal colony of New South Wales was founded in 1788. Immigration of free settlers from 1820 onwards aided the colony's development, as did exploration, which opened pastures for the wool industry. Squatter settlement of much of eastern

Australia led to conflict with the Aborigines, resulting in events such as the Myall Creek Massacre (1838). Van Diemen's Land (from 1855 Tasmania), settled in 1803, became a separate colony in 1825. Moreton Bay, founded as a penal settlement in 1824, became the colony of Queensland in 1859. The colony of Western Australia was founded in 1829. The Port Phillip District, settled illegally in 1834, became the colony of Victoria in 1851. South Australia, founded as a province in 1834, became a crown colony in 1842. All of the colonies except Western Australia were granted responsible government during the 1850s. The *gold rushes of the 1850s and 1860s brought many changes. The White Australia Policy can be traced back to that period. Demands for land to be opened for selectors increased. Western Australia, granted responsible government in 1890, developed more slowly than the other colonies. In 1901 the six colonies were federated as self-governing states to form the Commonwealth of Australia. Powers were distributed between the Commonwealth and state governments, and with the crown through its representative, the governor-general, retaining (until 1931) overall responsibility for defence and foreign affairs. State legislators would have full responsibility for internal state affairs. Sir Edmund *Barton, who had been prominent in the federation movement, was the first Prime Minister. The Northern Territory was transferred from South Australia to the Commonwealth in 1911. In the same year land was transferred to the Commonwealth from New South Wales, for the creation of the Australian Capital Territory, Canberra. (Jervis Bay was added to the Australian Capital Territory in 1915.) The Commonwealth Parliament met in Melbourne until 1927, when it was transferred to Canberra. In the 1930s reserves were established for the *Aborigines, and in 1981 the Pitjantjara Aborigines were granted freehold titles to land in Southern Australia. Australia fought with the Allies in both World Wars and with the USA in *Vietnam. After World War II ties with Britain diminished, and Australia joined the *ANZUS and *South-East Asia Treaty Organization powers. The Labor governments of the 1970s and 1980s, led by Gough *Whitlam and Bob *Hawke, strengthened trade ties with the non-communist Far East, but a deteriorating economy in the 1980s led to labour unrest and in 1991 to the replacement of Hawke by his deputy, Paul *Keating. In response to increasing support for Australia becoming a republic, Queen Elizabeth II announced (1993) that she would agree to such a constitutional change if the Australian people

wanted it. A referendum motion to replace the Queen with a President was defeated in 1999. Following the Labor Party's heavy electoral defeat by a Liberal-National Party coalition in 1996, Liberal leader John *Howard was appointed Prime Minister; his party was re-elected in 1998, 2001, and 2004. Australia participated in the 2003 *Iraq War and in subsequent military operations until 2009. Labor returned to power in 2007 under Kevin *Rudd. Shortly before the 2010 election rivalry within the Labor party led to his replacement by Julia *Gillard; however, Rudd regained the leadership in 2013. This infighting contributed to Labor's defeat in the 2013 election by the Liberal-National Party Coalition under Tony *Abbott; other factors were economic problems and an unpopular immigration policy.

Australian Federation Movement
(1890–1900) A movement to seek federation of the six Australian colonies and (initially) New Zealand. Two pressure groups for federation were the Australian Natives' Association and the Australasian Federation League. In 1889 the six Australian colonies and New Zealand agreed to send delegates to a federal conference in Melbourne in 1890. It was decided to hold a full convention the following year in Parliament House, Sydney, at which a draft constitution was drawn up. A second convention was held in 1893 in the small New South Wales town of Corowa convened by the Australian Natives' Association, at which it was proposed that a national referendum be held. By now indifference had increased in New Zealand as its trade shifted to Britain with the invention of refrigeration. In Australia too, opposition to New Zealand's participation was growing, and plans for the federation were dropped. In 1895 the Premiers of the six Australian colonies met to reconsider the draft constitution drawn up in 1891. New Zealand was now excluded. Ten delegates from each colony were chosen (elected by the people, except in the case of Western Australia) and the Australian Federation Convention first met in Adelaide (March 1897). It was agreed that a referendum should be held. It met again in January 1898, when after much compromise a proposed constitution was agreed. The first referendum failed. The second (held in 1899 after amendments were made) passed in all colonies and was given royal assent in 1900, the Commonwealth of *Australia coming into being on 1 January 1901.

Australoid See ABORIGINE.

australopithecines See EARLY HUMANS.

Austria

Capital:	Vienna
Area:	83,857 sq km (32,377 sq miles)
Population:	8,219,743 (2012 est)
Currency:	1 euro = 100 cents
Religions:	Roman Catholic 73.6%; Protestant 4.7%; Muslim 4.2%
Ethnic Groups:	Austrian 91.1%; Croat, Slovene, Serb, and Bosniak 4.0%; Turkish 1.6%
Languages:	German (official) and other minority languages
International Organizations:	UN; OECD; EU; Council of Europe; OSCE; Euro-Atlantic Partnership Council; WTO

A country in central Europe, bounded by Italy, Slovenia, and Croatia to the south, Hungary and Slovakia to the east, the Czech Republic and Germany to the north, and Liechtenstein and Switzerland to the west.

Physical Much of Austria is mountainous, with the River Danube flowing through the north-east of the country. Austria is the most densely forested nation in central Europe, with 40% of its land covered by trees. In the Alpine regions, south-facing mountain slopes have been cleared for pasture land and crops. In the Danube valley, arable land is characterized by very fertile soils.

Economy The economy has large service and industrial sectors, with agriculture contributing only 1.6% of GDP. Industries include construction, manufacturing, food processing, timber, wood processing, paper, cardboard, metals, chemicals, and communications equipment. Tourism is also important. Trade is largely with western Europe, especially Germany. A large portion of the Austrian economy was placed in public hands after World War II, but most of this has now been privatized.

History The Celtic tribes which had settled in the area from about 500 to 200 BC were conquered by the Romans in 14 BC, and the region remained part of the *Roman empire, with the Danube as its frontier. A succession of Germanic invaders (Vandals, Goths, Huns, Lombards, and Avars) in the 5th century AD ended with a short period of stability under *Charlemagne. *Magyar invaders then followed, but these were decisively defeated by *Otto I (the Great) at the Battle of Lechfeld in 955. Otto invested Leopold of Babenberg with the title of Margrave of Austria, and the Babenberg dynasty lasted until 1246. In 1282 Rudolf I, Count of *Habsburg invested his two sons jointly as Dukes of Austria, the older son Albert (Duke of Austria 1282–1308) founding a dynasty which survived into the 20th century. The first Habsburg Holy Roman Emperor was Frederick III (1452–93) and perhaps the greatest *Charles V (1530–56). From Vienna, the Habsburgs ruled the vast empire which, before its dissolution in 1918, included Hungary, Bohemia, Moravia, Burgundy, Tuscany, Piedmont, Croatia, Bosnia and Herzegovina, Bukovina, Slovenia, parts of Serbia, of Romania, and of Spanish America, Silesia, Spain, Luxembourg, The Netherlands, Venetia, and Naples. In 1575 the court moved from Vienna to Prague, where it remained until 1621. Vienna withstood a Muslim siege in 1529 and again in 1683, when the *Polish army forced the *Ottoman retreat. The War of the *Austrian Succession brought the conflict over supremacy in the German orbit to a head, and the *Seven Years' War confirmed Prussia as a power of equal weight. The end of the 18th century saw almost continuous conflict, with Austrians fighting against the French revolutionary armies in The Netherlands, the Rhineland, and northern Italy. The unification of Germany by Prussia in 1866–71 excluded the *Austrian empire from German affairs and destroyed hopes for the creation of a union of all the German-speaking peoples. Austria was forced to make concessions to the Hungarians by forming *Austria-Hungary. Austrian diplomats, however, retained links with the new *German Second empire, and tried to gain German support for their ambitions against Russia in the Balkans through an alliance system. During World War I the Austrian Imperial Army was virtually under German military control. Defeat and revolution destroyed the monarchy in 1918, and the first Austrian republic which followed it was only a rump of the former state. This was destabilized by the Nazis, who in 1934 murdered *Dollfuss and staged an abortive coup. They were more successful in achieving *Anschluss in 1938, when Hitler's army invaded the country without opposition. Defeated in World War II, Austria was invaded by Soviet troops, and divided into separate occupation zones, each controlled by an Allied Power. In 1955 a treaty between the Allies and Austria restored full sovereignty to the country. The treaty prohibited the possession of major offensive weapons and required Austria to pay heavy reparations to the USSR, as well as to give assurances that it would ally itself with neither East nor West Germany, nor restore the Habsburgs. It remained neutral, democratic, and increasingly prosperous under a series of socialist regimes. The socialists were re-elected in general elections in 1995, the year in which Austria joined the *European Union. In 2000, the participation of the extreme right-wing Freedom Party in a new governing coalition led to temporary diplomatic sanctions by the EU and some other countries. Austria adopted the *euro as its currency in 1999–2002.

Austria-Hungary (or **Austro-Hungarian Empire**) The 'Dual Monarchy', established by the Austrian emperor Francis Joseph after Austria's defeat by Prussia in 1866 in which Austria and Hungary became autonomous states under a common sovereign. The dualist system came under increasing pressure from the other subject nations, including Croatians, Serbs, Slovaks, Romanians, and Czechs, and failure to resolve these nationalistic aspirations was one of the causes of World War I. After their victory the

Allies gave support to the emergent nations, and the Austro-Hungarian Empire was dissolved by the Versailles peace settlement (1919).

Austrian empire (1806–67) Those territories and peoples from whom the Habsburg emperors in Vienna demanded allegiance. Following the dissolution of the Holy Roman Empire (1806), Emperor Francis II continued to rule as *Francis I (1804–35), Emperor of Austria and of the hereditary Habsburg lands of Bohemia, Hungary, Croatia and Transylvania, Galicia (once a province of Poland), and much of northern Italy (Venetia and Lombardy). He ruled by means of a large bureaucracy, a loyal army, the Roman Catholic Church, and an elaborate police force. His chief minister was Chancellor *Metternich. Nationalist feelings were emerging, and during the reign of his successor Ferdinand I (1835–48), liberal agitation for reform developed. Vienna was becoming rapidly industrialized and in March 1848, at a time of economic depression, riots in the capital led to Metternich's resignation. The emperor abolished censorship and promised a constitution. This, published in April, was not democratic enough for radical leaders, who

Austria-Hungary. The empire and its successor states. Austria-Hungary was doomed to collapse because of the ethnic tensions between its subject peoples.

organized a popular protest on 15 May 1848. The emperor fled to Innsbruck and later abdicated. His 18-year-old nephew *Francis Joseph succeeded. There were movements for independence among all the peoples of the empire, including the Hungarians led by *Kossuth, the Czechs, Slovaks, Serbs, Croats, Romanians, and Italians. A Pan-Slav conference met (1848) in Prague. But the opposition to the government in Vienna was divided and the Prime Minister, Felix Schwarzenberg and Francis Joseph were able to regain control. The army crushed the reform movements in Prague and Vienna and with the help of Russia, subjugated Budapest. Alexander Bach, the new Minister of the Interior, greatly strengthened the centralized bureaucracy, and the empire regained some stability, until its defeat by France and Piedmont at *Magenta and Solferino, which ended Austrian rule in Italy. In an effort to appease nationalist feeling the emperor proposed a new federal constitution, but it came too late and after a further defeat at Sadowa he agreed to the *Ausgleich (Compromise) of 1867 and the creation of *Austria-Hungary.

Austrian Succession, War of the (1740–48) A complicated European conflict in which the key issues were the right of *Maria Theresa of Austria to succeed to the lands of her father, Emperor Charles VI, and the right of her husband Francis of Lorraine to succeed to the imperial title. Francis's claims (in spite of the Pragmatic Sanction) were disputed by Charles Albert, Elector of Bavaria, supported by Frederick II of Prussia and Louis XV of France. Additionally Philip V of Spain and Maria Theresa were in dispute over who should have control of Italy, and Britain was challenging France and Spain's domination of the Mediterranean (War of *Jenkins's Ear), and fighting for control of India and America (King George's War).

After the death of Charles VI in 1740 war was precipitated by Frederick II of Prussia, who seized Silesia. The war began badly for Austria: the French seized Prague, a Spanish army landed in north Italy, Charles Albert was elected Holy Roman Emperor, and Silesia was ceded by treaty to Frederick II in 1742. Britain now supported Austria by organizing the so-called Pragmatic Army (Britain, Austria, Hanover, and Hesse) and under the personal command of George II it defeated the French at *Dettingen in 1743. Savoy joined Austria and Britain (Treaty of Worms, September 1743) and the tide of war began to turn in Austria's favour. In 1744–45 Frederick II re-entered the war, determined to

retain Silesia. Meanwhile Charles Albert died and Francis was elected Holy Roman Emperor in exchange for the return of the lands of Bavaria to the Elector's heir. Frederick II won a series of victories against Austria, and the Treaty of Dresden (1745) confirmed his possession of Silesia. The struggle between France and Britain intensified. The French supported the Jacobite invasion of Britain (the *Forty-Five) and in India the French captured the British town of Madras (1746). The British won major victories at sea: off Cape Finisterre, Spain and Belle-Ile, France in 1747. By 1748 all participants were ready for peace, which was concluded at *Aix-la-Chapelle. The war had been a long and costly effort by Maria Theresa to keep her Habsburg inheritance intact and in this she largely succeeded. But Austria was weakened and Prussia, which held Silesia, consolidated its position as a significant European power.

Austro-Prussian War (or **Seven Weeks War**) (June–August 1866) A war fought between Prussia, allied with Italy, and Austria, allied with Bavaria and other, smaller German states. War had become inevitable after *Bismarck challenged Austria's supremacy in the German Confederation. Hostilities finally broke out when Bismarck, having gained France's neutrality and the support of Italy, proposed that the German Confederation should be abolished. Prussian troops forced the Austrians out of Schleswig-Holstein, but the Austrians defeated the Italian army at Custozza. However, the Prussian army, better trained and equipped, crushed the main Austrian army at Sadowa. Seven weeks later the Austrians signed the Treaty of Prague, by which the German Confederation was dissolved. Austria ceded Venetia to Italy, while Prussia annexed the smaller states into the new North German Confederation. Austria, excluded from its territories in the south and from political influence to the north, turned towards the east, accepting the Hungarian *Ausgleich and forming *Austria-Hungary.

automation The use of automatic machinery and systems, particularly those manufacturing or data-processing systems which require little or no human intervention in their normal operation. During the 19th century a number of machines such as looms and lathes became increasingly self-regulating. At the same time transfer-machines were developed, whereby a series of machine-tools, each doing one operation automatically, became linked in a continuous production line by pneumatic or hydraulic devices transferring components from one operation to the next. In addition to these technological advances in automation, the theory of 'scientific management', which was based on the early time-and-motion studies of Frederick Winslow Taylor in Philadelphia, USA, in the 1880s was designed by Taylor to enhance the efficiency and productivity of workers and machines. In the early 20th century, with the development of electrical devices and time-switches, more processes became automatically controlled, and a number of basic industries such as oil-refining, chemicals, and food-processing were increasingly automated. The development of computers after World War II enabled more sophisticated automation to be used in manufacturing industries, for example iron and steel.

The most familiar example of a highly automated system is perhaps an assembly plant for automobiles or other complex products. Over the last few decades automation has evolved from the comparatively straightforward mechanization of tasks traditionally carried out by hand, through the introduction of complex automatic control systems, to the widespread automation of information collection and processing.

Averroës (Arabic name **ibn-Rushd**) (*c.*1126–98) Spanish-born Islamic philosopher, judge, and physician. His extensive body of work includes writings on jurisprudence, science, philosophy, and religion. His most significant works were his commentaries on Aristotle, which, through a reliance on Neoplatonism, interpreted Aristotle's writings in such a way as to make them consistent with Plato's, and sought to reconcile the Greek and Arabic philosophical traditions.

Axis Powers An alliance of fascist states fighting with Germany during *World War II. The term was used in an agreement (October 1936) between Hitler and Mussolini proclaiming the creation of a Rome–Berlin 'axis round which all European states can also assemble'. Japan joined the coalition on signing the *Anti-Comintern Pact (November 1936). A full military and political alliance between Germany and Italy (the Pact of Steel) followed in 1939. The Tripartite Pact between the three powers in 1940 cemented the alliance, and, by subsequently joining it, Hungary, Romania, and Bulgaria, as well as the Nazi-created states of Slovakia and Croatia, became members.

Axum *See* AKSUM.

Ayman al-Zawahiri (1951–) Egyptian-born leader of the *al-Qaeda terrorist network (2011–). He studied medicine at Cairo University and then served in the Egyptian army. Involved in militant Islamist activity since his teenage years, he was imprisoned (1981–84) following the assassination of Anwar al-*Sadat. He then travelled to Saudi Arabia, Pakistan, and Afghanistan, where he met Osama *Bin Laden. In the early 1990s al-Zawahiri became leader of the Islamic Jihad militant group, which merged with al-Qaeda in 2001. He was closely involved in the *September 11 attacks on the USA and in the following years gradually assumed the practical leadership of al-Qaeda as Bin Laden was forced into hiding. He became the formal leader after Bin Laden's death in 2011.

Ayub Khan, Muhammad (1907–74) Pakistani soldier and statesman, President (1958–69). After independence he became the first Commander-in-Chief of the country's army (1951–58) and served as Minister of Defence (1954–55), taking over the presidency shortly after the declaration of martial law. His term of office saw the introduction of a new constitution and the lifting of martial law in 1962, but civil liberties were curtailed. Opposition to his foreign policy with regard to India and his increasingly repressive style of government led to widespread disorder and he was ultimately forced to resign.

Ayuthia *See* SIAM.

Azerbaijan, Republic of

Capital:	Baku
Area:	86,600 sq km (33,430 sq miles)
Population:	9,493,600 (2012 est)
Currency:	1 manat = 100 gopik
Religions:	Muslim 93.4%; Eastern Orthodox 4.8%
Ethnic Groups:	Azeri 90.3%; Lezgian 2.0%; Russian 1.3%; Armenian 1.3%; Talysh 1.3%
Languages:	Azeri Turkish (official); Armenian, Russian, and other minority languages
International Organizations:	UN; Commonwealth of Independent States; OSCE; Euro-Atlantic Partnership Council; Council of Europe; Non-Aligned Movement

A country in western Asia, in the Caucasus. Situated on the west coast of the Caspian Sea, Azerbaijan is bordered by Armenia to the west, Georgia and Russia to the north, and Iraq to the south.

Physical The Apsheron Peninsula in the north contains the long-established Baku oilfields. The hot and arid Kura valley runs towards the south-east below the Caucasian foothills. The Caspian coastal plain with a subtropical climate is more naturally fertile; round it lie well-wooded hills with deep valleys. The mountainous south-west contains the large and scenic Lake Gyoygyol as well as numerous deposits of copper, iron, and lead.

Economy Azerbaijan was the world's leader in petroleum production at the beginning of the 20th century, and has rich mineral resources, including petroleum, gas, and metal ores. Other industries include manufacturing and chemicals. Agriculture provides 40% of employment, with products including cotton and food crops; viticulture is also important.

History The country comprises the part of the Azerbaijan area that was conquered by Russia in the 18th and 19th centuries (the remainder of the traditional Azerbaijan area is now incorporated in Iran). By 1914 it was the largest oil-producing area in the world, centred on Baku. After the Bolshevik Revolution in Russia of 1917, it declared its independence, but in 1920 was conquered by the Red Army. The Azerbaijan Soviet Socialist Republic was created, which in 1922 was linked with Armenia and Georgia as the Transcaucasian Soviet Federated Socialist Republic. This split in 1936 into three separate republics as members of the Soviet Union. The autonomous region of Nakhichevan formed an exclave within Armenia, while a second area, that of Nagorno Karabagh, inhabited by Christian Armenians and claimed by Armenia, lay within the Republic. Severe violence erupted over the latter, with military intervention by the Soviet Union in 1989. In 1991 Azerbaijan declared its independence, as a Shi'ite Muslim state, and the Nakhichevan region declared its own independence in 1992. Fighting in Nagorno Karabagh and Nakhichevan has continued sporadically, despite several ceasefire agreements. Nagorno Karabagh declared itself to be independent in 1996. In 1993 President Elchibey was ousted in a military coup; President Geidar Aliyev took over, his position being ratified in elections. Parliamentary elections in 1995 were won by Aliyev's party and he was re-elected in 1998 amidst violent protests and allegations of fraud. He was succeeded by his son, Ilham Aliyev, at the 2003 presidential elections. Ilham was re-elected in 2008.

Azikiwe, Nnamdi (Benjamin Nnamdi Azikiwe) (1904–96) Nigerian statesman, President (1963–66). Azikiwe founded (1944) the anti-colonial National Council of Nigeria and the Cameroons, a gathering of forty political, labour, and educational groups. He was the first Governor-General of an independent Nigeria (1960–63) and its first President when it became a republic. When his civilian government was ousted by a military coup in 1966, Azikiwe joined the Biafran secessionist government. In 1978, after the reunification of Nigeria, he founded the Nigerian People's Party and was its leader until 1983.

Aztec The indigenous people dominant in Mexico before the Spanish conquest of the 16th century (also called *Mexica* or *Tenochca*) who arrived in the central valley of Mexico after the collapse of the Toltec civilization in the 12th century. By the early 15th century they had risen to dominance of the area and a century later commanded a territory that covered most of the central and southern part of present-day Mexico, exacting tribute from their subjects. They were a warring people who slew captives as human sacrifices to their chief god, but their lifestyle was comfortable and (for the rulers) luxurious, and the Spaniards under Cortés arrived to find a rich and elaborate civilization centred on the city of Tenochtitlán, which boasted vast pyramids, temples, and palaces.

B

Baader-Meinhof gang Byname of the West German anarchist terrorist group, Red Army Faction. Its leaders were Andreas Baader (1943–77) and Ulrike Meinhof (1934–76). The group opposed and attacked the capitalist organization of German society and the presence of US armed forces by engaging in murders, bombings, and kidnappings. The leaders were arrested in 1972 and their trial and deaths (by suicide) received considerable publicity. The group continued its terrorist activities until 1998, forming a number of splinter cells.

Babeuf, François Noël (1760–97) French Revolutionary who called himself 'Caius-*Gracchus, tribune of the people'. A domestic servant before the French Revolution, he moved to Paris in 1794. There he started to publish the *Journal de la liberté de la presse*, in which he argued that the Revolution should go further than establishing political equality. He formed a small group (the Equals) of discontented artisans and soldiers and campaigned for the equal ownership of property by all. This idea thrived in the turmoil following *Robespierre's execution but secret agents learnt of his plans for an armed rising on 11 May 1796. He was captured and executed.

Babington Plot (1586) A conspiracy to coordinate a Spanish invasion of England with a rising of English Catholics, to assassinate *Elizabeth I, and to replace her on the throne with *Mary, Queen of Scots. Anthony Babington (1561–86) was the go-between in the secret preparations. *Walsingham monitored Babington's correspondence with the captive Queen Mary until he had enough evidence of her treasonable intentions to have her tried and executed in 1587, Babington having been executed at Tyburn after torture.

Bábism The doctrines of a Muslim messianic Shiite sect. Founded in 1844 by the Persian Sayyid Ali Muhammad of Shiraz (1819–50) known as the *Báb ed-Din* (the gate or intermediary between man and God), who declared himself to be the long-awaited Mahdi. For inciting insurrection the Báb was arrested in 1848 by the government and executed in 1850, his remains being interred (1909) on Mt Carmel, Palestine. In 1863 Baha'ullah and his son Abdul Baha declared themselves the new leaders, and their followers became known as the *Baha'is.

Babur (1483–1530) The first *Mogul Emperor of India (1526–30). He was born in Ferghana, Central Asia, in a princely family of mixed Mongol and Turkish blood. Failure to recover his father's lands caused him to turn reluctantly south-east, for India seemed to present the last hope for his ambitions. Defeat of Ibrahim Lodi, the Afghan ruler of Delhi, at the Battle of Panipat in 1526 initiated 200 years of strong Mogul rule in India. Having conquered much of northern India, Babur ruled by force, lacking any civil administration. In addition to his military genius, he possessed a love of learning and wrote his own memoirs.

Babylon An ancient city in Mesopotamia, first prominent under Hammurabi who made it capital of the kingdom of *Babylonia. The city (now in ruins) lay on the Euphrates 88 km (55 miles) south of present-day Baghdad and was noted for its luxury, its fortifications, and particularly for the 'Hanging Gardens', which were one of the Seven Wonders of the World.

Babylonia The ancient name for southern Mesopotamia (earlier called Sumer), which first became a political entity when an Amorite dynasty united Sumer and Akkad in the first half of the 2nd millennium BC. At this period its power extended over Assyria and part of Syria. After c.1530 BC first the Hittites then other invaders, the Kassites, dominated the land, and it became part of the Assyrian empire. With the latter's decline Babylonia again became prominent under the Chaldeans (625–538 BC), only to fall to Cyrus the Great, whose entry into *Babylon ended its power for ever.

Bacon, Francis, 1st Baron Verulam, Viscount St Albans (1561–1626) English statesman and philosopher. He became a barrister in 1582 and entered Parliament two years later. In the 1590s he prospered as a member of the *Essex faction at court, and published his first edition of witty, aphoristic *Essays* (1597). Under James I Bacon rose to be Lord Chancellor (1618). In 1621 he was impeached by Parliament for accepting bribes and his political career was ruined. In retirement he devoted himself to literary and philosophical work and contributed significantly to the European Scientific Revolution and to the *Enlightenment.

Bacon's Rebellion (1676) An uprising in Virginia, North America, led by an English immigrant, Nathaniel Bacon. Dissident county leaders and landless ex-servants followed his opposition to the governor, Sir William Berkeley (1606–77). Though he was initially successful, Bacon died soon after the passage of reforms in the Virginian Assembly. Underlying the rebellion were problems caused by depressed tobacco prices and lack of colonial autonomy.

Baden-Powell, Robert, 1st Baron Baden-Powell of Gilwell (Robert Stephenson Smyth Baden-Powell) (1857–1941) British soldier and founder of the Boy Scout movement. He became a national hero after his successful defence of Mafeking (1899–1900) in the Boer War. The Boy Scout movement, which he founded in 1908, and the Girl Guide movement, which he founded together with his sister Agnes and his wife Olave in 1910, grew to become important international youth movements.

Badoglio, Pietro (1871–1956) Italian general and Prime Minister. By 1925 he was chief of staff; Mussolini appointed him governor of Libya (1929) and sent him (1935) to rescue the faltering Italian campaign in *Ethiopia. He captured Addis Ababa and became governor. When Mussolini was deposed in 1943, he was chosen to head the new non-fascist government. He made peace with the advancing Allies, declared war against Germany, but resigned soon afterwards.

Badon, Mount *See* GILDAS.

Bagehot, Walter (1826–77) British economist and journalist. He worked as a banker before becoming editor of the *Economist* in 1860, a post which he held until his death. His insight into economic and political questions is shown in his books *The English Constitution* (1867), *Lombard Street* (1873), and *Economic Studies* (1880).

Baha'i A monotheistic religion founded in Persia in the 19th century by Baha'ullah (1817–92) and his son Abdul Baha (1844–1921). The seat of its governing body, the Universal House of Justice, is in Haifa, Israel, adjacent to the golden-domed shrine of the Báb where his bones were buried in 1909 after freedom was granted to religious minorities in the Ottoman empire.

Bahamas, Commonwealth of the

Capital:	Nassau
Area:	13,939 sq km (5,382 sq miles)
Population:	319,031 (2012 est)
Currency:	1 Bahamian dollar = 100 cents
Religions:	Baptist 35.4%; Anglican 15.1%; Roman Catholic 13.5%; Pentecostal 8.1%
Ethnic Groups:	Black 85.0%; White 12.0%
Languages:	English (official); English creole; French (Haitian) creole
International Organizations:	UN; OAS; Commonwealth; CARICOM; Non-Aligned Movement

A country in the Caribbean, consisting of a group of islands in the western Atlantic Ocean, set between Florida and Hispaniola.

Physical Of the 700 mainly coral islands some thirty are large enough to live on, the largest being the Grand Bahama and New Providence islands.

Economy Tourism makes a large contribution to the economy, while a favourable system of taxation has led to the Bahamas becoming an important centre for offshore financial services. There is some industry and agriculture.

History The earliest known inhabitants of the Bahamas were Arawak Indians. According to most historians, Guanahani was the site of Columbus's first landing in the Americas in 1492. The Spanish subsequently raided the islands, attacking and enslaving the Arawaks, but did not settle there. In 1629 the Bahamas were included in the British Carolina colonies, but actual settlement did not begin until 1648, with settlers from Bermuda. By this time all the Arawaks had died out. Possession was disputed by Spain, but was acknowledged in 1670 under the Treaty of Madrid. The Bahamas became a British Crown Colony in 1717. Of major strategic importance, they were captured by the Spanish in 1782, but returned to Britain in 1783. There were also frequent raids by pirates. Many Africans were brought to the islands to work as slaves in the sugar plantations. A civil-rights movement led to the creation of the Progressive Liberal Party (PLP) in 1953. The PLP advocated parliamentary representation for the Black majority, and independence for the Bahamas. Internal self-government was achieved in 1964, the PLP was elected in 1967, and independence was gained in 1973. In 1992 the Free National Movement (FNM) won elections, ending 25 years of PLP government. The PLP was returned to power in elections in 2002, but was again defeated by the FNM in 2007.

Bahmani A dynasty of sultans who controlled the Deccan plateau in central India from 1347 to 1518. The dynasty was founded by Ala-ud-din Bahman Shah, who in 1347 rebelled against his Delhi suzerain. His successors expanded over the west-central Deccan, reaching a peak in the late 15th century under Mahmud Gawan, who successfully held encroaching Hindu and Muslim powers at bay. During the early 16th century the Hindu empire of Vijayanagar to the south expanded at the Bahmanis' expense, and between 1490 and 1518 the sultanate gradually dissolved into five successor Muslim states, Bijapur, Ahmadnagar, Golconda, Berar, and Bidar.

Bahrain

Capital:	Manama
Area:	760 sq km (293 sq miles)
Population:	1,281,332 (2012 est)
Currency:	1 Bahrain dinar = 1000 fils
Religions:	Muslim 81.2%; Christian 9.0%
Ethnic Groups:	Bahraini Arab 46.0%; Iranian, Indian, Pakistani, other Arab, European minorities
Languages:	Arabic (official) and minority languages
International Organizations:	UN; Arab League; OAPEC; GCC; Non-Aligned Movement; WTO

A sheikhdom in the Arabian Gulf.

Physical Bahrain consists of a group of islands some 32 km (20 miles) off the Arabian coast. The largest island is some 16 km (10 miles) wide and three times as long.

Economy The country's exports are dominated by crude oil and petroleum products from a large oil refinery on Bahrain Island. There is also a large financial and business sector, and tourism, shipbuilding, and ship repair are also significant.

History Iran, which ruled Bahrain from 1602 to 1783, was expelled by the al-Khalifas, who still reign. British political control dates from 1820. Oil was discovered in 1932, when the Bahrain National Oil Company was formed. After the withdrawal of Britain in 1971 and the abandonment by Iran of its claims, the country joined the Arab League. Tension between Shiite and Sunni communities increased, leading to the suspension of the National Assembly in 1975. Together with other members of the Gulf Cooperation Council (Saudi Arabia, Kuwait, Qatar, and Oman), Bahrain repeatedly called for an end to the *Iran–Iraq war (1980–88), while retaining its neutrality then and in the *Gulf war (1991). Its economy became increasingly diversified as oil reserves dwindled. Increasing opposition to the government and demands for the restoration of the National Assembly led to rising civil unrest in the mid-1990s. A new constitution was adopted in 2002 and Bahrain became a democratic constitutional monarchy. In 2011 demonstrations inspired by the *Arab Spring were violently crushed.

bailiff The estate manager of the lord of the manor in England from the 11th century. The word 'bailiff' gradually shifted its meaning and in the later Middle Ages, when lords more commonly let out their manors to farmers, the bailiff was one of the lesser officials of the sheriff. Farmers and urban landlords also employed him as a rent-collector, knowing that his legal skills could be drawn on in cases of non-payment.

Baker, Sir Samuel White (1821–93) British explorer who traced the Nile tributaries in Ethiopia (1861–62). In 1864, despite the opposition of Arab slave traders, he located the Nile source in Lake Albert Nyanza.

Bakunin, Mikhail (1814–76) Russian revolutionary, leading exponent of *anarchism and founder-member of the Russian Populist movement. He served in the emperor's army until his dismissal in 1835. After taking part in the *Revolutions of 1848 he was exiled to Siberia. He escaped in 1861 and went to London, which was used as a headquarters for militant anarchists and communists. The first International Workingmen's Association, founded in 1864, was marred by the conflict between *Marx and Bakunin.

Balaklava, Battle of (25 October 1854) An inconclusive battle during the *Crimean War. Following their defeat on the River Alma, the Russians retreated to Sevastopol, which was then besieged by British, French, and Turkish troops, supplied from the small port of Balaklava. Russian forces moved down into the Balaklava plain, where they were met by the British cavalry division under Lord Lucan. Lord Raglan, British commander-in-chief, sent orders to the Light Brigade under Lord Cardigan to "prevent the enemy carrying away the guns". It is assumed this order referred to guns on the Vorontsov Heights, but Cardigan understood it to require a direct frontal charge down the valley. Fired on by guns from both flanks and to the front, he and a few dragoons reached the Russian line before retreating. In this "Charge of the Light Brigade" 247 men were killed out of a force of 673. The Russians failed to capture Balaklava, but they held on to the Vorontsov Heights and thus cut the paved supply-road from the port to the besieging allied forces above Sevastopol.

Balboa, Vasco Núñez de (1475–1519) Spanish explorer. Having settled in the new Spanish colony of Hispaniola in 1501, in 1511 Balboa joined an expedition to Darien (in Panama) as a stowaway, but rose to command it after a mutiny. He founded a colony in Darien and continued to make expeditions into the surrounding areas. In 1513 he reached the western coast of the isthmus after an epic twenty-five-day march, thereby becoming the first European to see the Pacific Ocean.

Baldwin, Robert (1804–58) Canadian statesman. Born in York (renamed Toronto in 1834), he was elected to the Assembly of Upper Canada in 1829 and became one of the leaders of the campaign for reformed government that would give more say to elected representatives. After the Act of Union (1840) he was elected for Canada West and in 1842–43 led a reformist ministry with Sir Louis-Hippolyte La Fontaine.

Baldwin, Stanley, 1st Earl Baldwin of Bewdley (1867–1947) British statesman. A Conservative Member of Parliament (1908–37), he was a member of *Lloyd George's coalition (1918–22) but led the Conservative rebellion against him. He was Chancellor of the Exchequer under Bonar *Law and was chosen as Prime Minister in preference to Curzon when Law resigned in 1923. He lost the 1923 election in an attempt to introduce tariffs but returned to office in 1924. His premiership was marked by the return to the gold standard, the *General Strike, Neville *Chamberlain's social legislation, and the Trades Dispute Act of 1927. He lost the 1929 election, but served under Ramsay *Macdonald in the coalition caused by the 1931 crisis, succeeding him as Prime Minister in 1935. His last ministry had to deal with the Abdication crisis (*see* EDWARD VIII), which he handled skilfully. In 1935 he approved the Hoare-Laval pact which allowed fascist Italy to annex Ethiopia. Although international relations continued to deteriorate with the German occupation of the Rhineland and the outbreak of the *Spanish Civil War, Baldwin opposed rearmament, believing that the public would not support it.

Baldwin I (*c.*1058–1118) King of Jerusalem (1100–18). On the death of his brother, Godfrey of Bouillon, he was crowned first King of Jerusalem. He foiled the ambitions of the Patriarch Daimbert and ensured that Jerusalem would become a secular kingdom with himself as its first monarch. His control of the Levantine ports secured vital sea communications with Europe, and by asserting his suzerainty over other Crusader principalities he consolidated the primacy of the Latin Kingdom of Jerusalem.

Balewa, Alhaji Sir Abubakar Tafawa (1912–66) Nigerian statesman. He entered politics in 1946, and became a member of the Central Legislative Council in 1947. The first Prime Minister of the Federation of Nigeria, he retained his office when the country became independent (1960) until he was killed in an army coup.

Balfour, Arthur James, 1st Earl (1848–1930) British statesman, nephew of Lord *Salisbury. As Chief Secretary of Ireland (1887–91) he was an opponent of *Home Rule and earned from the Irish the nickname "Bloody Balfour". He served as Prime Minister (1902–05) but his government was undermined by his vacillation over tariff reform. His Education Act (1902) established a national system of secondary education. He created a Committee of Imperial Defence (1904), and helped to establish the *entente cordiale (1904) with France. The Conservatives were crushingly defeated in the 1906 general election. Balfour then used the House of Lords, described by Lloyd George as "Mr Balfour's poodle", to attempt to block contentious Liberal legislation. He resigned the leadership of the Conservative Party in 1911. As Foreign Secretary in Lloyd George's war cabinet, he is associated with the *Balfour Declaration (1917) promising the Jews a national home in Palestine. The Statute of *Westminster owed much to his inspiration.

Balfour Declaration (2 November 1917) A declaration by Britain in favour of a Jewish national home in Palestine. It took the form of a letter from Lord *Balfour (British Foreign Secretary) to Lord Rothschild, a prominent *Zionist, announcing the support of the British government for the establishment of a national home for the Jewish people in Palestine without prejudice to the civil and religious rights of the non-Jewish peoples of Palestine or the rights and political status of Jews in other countries. The Declaration subsequently formed the basis of the mandate given to Britain for Palestine and of British policy in that country until 1947.

Balkans (or **Balkan States**) The countries occupying the Balkan peninsula of southeastern Europe, lying south of the Danube and Sava rivers, between the Adriatic and Ionian seas in the west, the Aegean and Black seas in the east, and the Mediterranean in the south. It is the home of various peoples including Albanians, Vlachs, Greeks, Serbs, Bulgars, and Turks. From the 3rd to 7th century the Balkan peninsula, nominally ruled by the Byzantine emperors, was invaded by successive migrations of Slavs; later, parts of it were conquered by Venice and other states. In 1356 the Ottoman invasion began. Constantinople fell to the Turks in 1453, and by 1478 most of the peninsula was in their power; the subject nations, though largely retaining their languages and religions, did not recover independence until the 19th century. In 1912-13 Turkey was attacked and defeated by other Balkan peoples in alliance, then the former allies fought over their gains. After World War I the peninsula was divided between Greece, Albania, Bulgaria, and Yugoslavia, with Turkey retaining only Constantinople and the surrounding land. The area was in turmoil from 1991 to 1995 as Yugoslavia disintegrated into its constituent republics, and a savage ethnic conflict developed in Bosnia and Herzegovina.

Balkan Wars (1912-13) Two short wars, fought between Serbia, Montenegro, Greece,

Romania, Turkey, and Bulgaria for the possession of remaining European territories of the *Ottoman empire. In 1912 Greece, Serbia, Bulgaria, and Montenegro formed the Balkan League. In October 1912 the League armies captured all but Constantinople (now Istanbul). European ambassadors intervened to re-draw the Balkans map to the advantage of Bulgaria and detriment of Serbia in the Treaty of London (May 1913). A month later, Bulgaria launched a pre-emptive attack on the Serbs and Greeks, who coveted Bulgaria's gains, but was defeated. In the Treaty of Bucharest (August 1913) Greece and Serbia partitioned Macedonia, and Romania gained part of Bulgaria. Albania, which had been under Turkish suzerainty, was made an independent Muslim principality. A 'big Serbia' now presented a considerable threat to Austria-Hungary. Russia promised to support Serbia in its nationalist struggle and Germany offered military aid to Austria-Hungary. The assassination of the Austrian heir apparent, Archduke Francis Ferdinand, at Sarajevo (1914) gave Austria-Hungary the pretext to invade Serbia, leading to the outbreak of World War I six weeks later.

Ball, John (died 1381) English rebel. Ball was a Wycliffite priest who preached an egalitarian social message. He was excommunicated and imprisoned for heresy, but released in June 1381 during the Peasants' Revolt. He was later captured, tried, and hanged as a traitor.

Ballance, John (1839-93) New Zealand statesman. In the 1890 elections the Liberals emerged as the first party in New Zealand politics, broadly united on a programme of radical reform, and Ballance became Premier (1891-93). Ballance and his Liberal successors established the tradition of using the state to regulate the economy and protect poorer groups, laying the foundations of basic stability in New Zealand society.

Balliol, Edward (died c.1364) King of Scotland (1332-56), son of John Balliol. In 1332 he landed in Fife to reclaim the throne his father had given up. He defeated the Scots at Dupplin and was crowned at Scone. Within three months he was forced to flee but returned with the help of *Edward III of England after his victory at Halidon Hill. In 1341 Balliol was again expelled from Scotland and in 1356 he resigned his claim to the Scottish throne.

Balliol, John (c.1250-1313) King of Scotland (1292-96). He was descended through his maternal grandmother from *David I of Scotland

and in 1291–92 his claim to the crown was upheld in a trial between him and Robert Bruce,
Lord of Annandale. The trial was arranged by
*Edward I of England and less than a month
after his coronation (30 November 1292) Balliol
grudgingly did homage to Edward as his superior.
In 1295 he attempted to ally with France, which
resulted in an English invasion of Scotland.
Balliol was forced to give up his kingdom to
Edward and was taken as a captive to England,
before retiring to his estates in France.

Balmaceda, José Manuel (1840–91) Chilean statesman and liberal reformer. He was first
elected to the Chilean Congress as a Liberal in
1864. As leader of the anti-clerical group he was
sent to Argentina in 1878 to persuade that
country not to enter the War of the Pacific. He
became a member of the cabinet of President
Santa Maria (1881–86) and was himself then
elected President (1886–91). Despite national
prosperity, tension arose between President
and Congress, which Balmaceda increasingly
ignored. In January 1891 this resulted in civil
war. Balmaceda took refuge in the Argentinian
Embassy, where, rather than face trial, he shot
himself.

Baltic Entente (1934) A mutual defence pact
between Estonia, Latvia, and Lithuania. Soon
after World War I there were negotiations for an
alliance between all the countries which had
recently broken away from the Russian empire,
that is, Poland, Finland, Estonia, Latvia, and
Lithuania, but these collapsed. Latvia and Estonia did however make an agreement in 1923,
which Lithuania joined in 1934.

Bancroft, Edward (1744–1821) US traitor.
Born in Massachusetts, he studied medicine in
London. He met Benjamin *Franklin, and during the War of Independence was a friend of
Arthur Lee and Silas Dean. Bancroft was actually an agent for England at an annual fee of
£500 and a life pension and it was almost a
century before his activities as a British agent
were discovered.

Banda, Hastings Kamuzu (1906–97) Ma-
lawian statesman, Prime Minister (1964–94) and
President (1966–94). He studied medicine in the
USA and practised in Britain before returning to
lead his country (formerly Nyasaland) to independence. As the first President of the Republic
of Malawi he created an autocratic and paternalistic one-party state; a pragmatist, he was the
first Black African leader to visit South Africa
(1970) and later established trading links with it.
Banda was defeated in Malawi's first multiparty

elections in 1994; the following year he was
acquitted on charges of murdering four political
opponents.

Bandaranaike, S. W. R. D. (Solomon West
Ridgeway Dias Bandaranaike) (1899–1959)
Sinhalese statesman. He formed the Maha Sin-
hala Party in the 1920s. In 1931 he was elected
to the new State Council and after independence he assumed ministerial power. In 1952 he
founded the Sri Lanka Freedom Party (SLFP),
which was the leading partner in the coalition
which won the 1956 elections, attracting left-
wing and Buddhist support. As Prime Minister
(1956–59) Bandaranaike pursued a policy of
promoting the Sinhalese language, Buddhism,
socialism, and neutrality. His policy alienated
the Tamils. After his assassination in September
1959 by a dissident Buddhist monk, his widow,
Mrs Sirimavo *Bandaranaike, succeeded him as
Prime Minister.

Bandaranaike, Sirimavo Ratwatte Dias
(1916–2000) Sinhalese stateswoman, Prime
Minister of Sri Lanka (1960–65; 1970–77; 1994–
2000). The world's first woman Prime Minister,
she succeeded her husband, S. W. R. D. *Bandaranaike, after his assassination. Opposition to
her policies and continuing ethnic conflict resulted in an overwhelming defeat in the 1977
elections. She was charged with misuse of
power in 1980, stripped of her civil rights for six
years, and expelled from Parliament. Her
daughter, Chandrika Bandaranaike Kumaratunga (1945–), became Prime Minister and
then President in 1994, whereupon Bandaranaike resumed the post of Prime Minister.
Kumaratunga served as President until 2005,
being narrowly re-elected in 1999.

bandkeramik *See* NEOLITHIC.

Bandung Conference (1955) A conference
of Asian and African states at Bandung in Java,
Indonesia. Organized on the initiative of President *Sukarno and other leaders of the Non-
Aligned Movement, the Bandung Conference
brought together twenty-nine states in an attempt to form a non-aligned bloc opposed to
colonialism and the 'imperialism' of the superpowers. The five principles of non-aggression,
respect for sovereignty, non-interference in
internal affairs, equality, and peaceful co-
existence were adopted, but the subsequent
emergence of the non-aligned movement was
hamstrung by the deterioration of relations between India and China, and by the conflicting
forces set loose by decolonization.

Bangladesh

Capital:	Dhaka
Area:	143,998 sq km (55,598 sq miles)
Population:	163,654,860 (2012 est)
Currency:	1 Bangladesh taka = 100 paisa
Religions:	Muslim 89.5%; Hindu 9.6%
Ethnic Groups:	Bengali 98.0%; Bihari and other minorities
Languages:	Bengali (official); English
International Organizations:	UN; Commonwealth; Colombo Plan; Non-Aligned Movement; WTO

A tropical low-lying country of the Indian subcontinent.

Physical Situated at the head of the Bay of Bengal, Bangladesh is mainly occupied by the deltas of the Ganges and the Brahmaputra. It is a land of rivers, which flood regularly in the monsoon season, leaving fertile soil on their banks. The south-west delta area, the Sundarbans, is mainly swamp and jungle; the region is subject to frequent cyclones which are funnelled up the Bay of Bengal and exacerbated by large-scale deforestation, thus causing immense damage and loss of life and crops. Some of the worst floods in the country's history left 25 million people homeless in 1998.

Economy The country remains one of the world's poorest, despite rapid economic growth in the 2000s. Clothing exports and remittances from expatriates working abroad provide 12% of GDP. The country grows most of the world's supply of jute, and jute products are an important export. Other exports include clothing, shrimp, and leather goods. Industry is limited and the main source of employment is agriculture, with rice the most important food crop. There are substantial undeveloped reserves of oil, coal, and natural gas.

History Bangladesh was established in 1971 from territories which had previously formed the eastern part of Pakistan. Evidence of discontent in East Pakistan first appeared in the 1952 Bengali-language agitation and became much stronger after the 1965 *Indo-Pakistan War. In 1966 the Awami League put forward a demand for greater autonomy which it proposed to implement after its victory in the 1970 elections. In March 1971, when this demand was rejected by the military government of Pakistan, civil war began, leading to a massive exodus of refugees to India. India sent help to the East Pakistan guerrillas (the Mukti Bahini). In the war of December 1971, Indian troops defeated the Pakistan forces in East Pakistan. The independence of Bangladesh was proclaimed in 1971 and recognized by Pakistan in 1974. The first Prime Minister, Mujibur Rahman, was murdered in 1975 and a period of political chaos, ethnic riots, floods, and famine followed, Bangladesh being declared the world's poorest country in 1987. In 1990 the military leader President Ershad was forced to resign, was arrested, and imprisoned for corruption. Elections in 1991 restored civilian rule under Prime Minister Begum Zia and a new constitution was adopted. From 1995 Zia's government was troubled by strikes and mass protests against privatization and other policies. Following two elections in June 1996 Sheikha Hasina Wajed became the head of a coalition government, but Zia was returned to power in 2001. In both 1998 and 2004 severe floods affected over half of the country and left many millions of people homeless. Zia resigned in 2006, but elections were postponed amid unrest and a caretaker government ruled Bangladesh with military support until 2009. Hasina won elections in December 2008 and became Prime Minister in January.

Ban Ki-moon (1944–) South Korean diplomat and politician, Secretary General of the United Nations (2007–). After leaving university in 1970, he mainly served in South Korea's diplomatic service but had spells in government, notably as Minister of Foreign Affairs and Trade (2004–06). He was elected to succeed Kofi *Annan as Secretary General of the United Nations in 2006 and took office on 1 January 2007; he was elected for a second term in 2011.

Bank of England The British central bank, popularly known as the 'Old Lady of Threadneedle Street', where its London office stands. It was founded in 1694 as an undertaking by 1268 shareholders to lend £1,200,000 to the government of William III to finance his wars against France. In return it received 8% interest and the right to issue notes against the security of the loan. These privileges were confirmed in 1708 when its capital was doubled, and it was given a monopoly of joint-stock banking which lasted until 1826, thus preventing rival banks from having large numbers of shareholders.

The bank is controlled by the Governor of the Bank of England and a court of 16 directors, appointed by the Crown. Its responsibilities include acting as banker to the government and as its agent in the issue of treasury bills; functioning as lender of last resort to the clearing banks, enabling it to control the amount of money in circulation; issuing the country's stock of money as supplied by the Royal Mint; acting as registrar for government stocks; managing, on behalf of the Treasury, the money market and exchange equalization account; and determining the interest-rate structure of the economy.

Bannockburn, Battle of (24 June 1314) A major battle fought between *Edward II of England and *Robert I (the Bruce) at Bannockburn, about 4.5 km (2 miles) from Stirling in Scotland. Edward's large invading army, perhaps 20,000 strong, was outmanoevred and forced into the Bannock burn (or river) and adjacent marshes; it was a disastrous defeat for the English, and Edward was lucky to be able to flee to safety.

Bantu homelands (informal name **Bantustans**) The former "homelands" reserved for Black Africans in the Republic of South Africa, regarded by many as the clearest manifestation of *apartheid. Ten Bantu homelands were created by the Bantu Self-Government Act of 1959. The Black population was assigned to a homeland according to ethnic or linguistic group despite the fact that only 40% actually lived in these areas. The Bantu Homelands Constitution Act (1971) established them as Separate Development Self-Governing Areas and envisaged eventual "independence". This was in fact granted to four of the homelands: Transkei, chiefly Xhosa people, in 1976; Bophuthatswana, chiefly Tswana, in 1977; Venda in 1979; and Ciskei in 1981. The populations of these homelands automatically lost their South African citizenship, becoming citizens of the new states. Most of these states were made up of scattered areas of poor-quality land and were not viable as independent countries; for this reason, and because most of their citizens were South African residents, they were only recognized by South Africa itself. Each of the four began with a democratic constitution, but were inherently unstable. There were military coups and counter-coups in all of them during the 1980s. The Bantu homelands were abolished following South Africa's adoption of a multiracial constitution in 1994 and South African nationality was restored to all their citizens.

Bao Dai (1913–97) Emperor of Vietnam (1926–45). His initial aim to reform Vietnam did not receive French colonial support. During World War II he collaborated with the Japanese and in 1945 he was forced to abdicate by the *Vietminh. In 1949 he renounced his title and returned to Saigon as head of the state of Vietnam within the French Union. In 1955, after the partition of Vietnam at the Geneva Conference, he was once again deposed when power in the new republic of South Vietnam passed to Ngo Dinh Diem. He then went into exile, living mainly in France.

Barak, Ehud (1942–) Israeli Labour politician and soldier; Prime Minister from 1999, when he defeated Binyamin *Netanyahu in elections, until 2001. He tried, but failed, to negotiate a final peace with the Palestinians. His authority was undermined by the beginning of the second *intifada in 2000 and he retired from politics after losing the 2001 general election to Ariel *Sharon. He returned to public life in 2005, and in 2007 became Labour leader and then Minister of Defence in Ehud *Olmert's coalition government. He retained this post in Netanyahu's Likud-led government from 2009; but in 2011 Labour discontent at government policy caused him to leave Labour and form the Independence Party, which remained part of the government. He left the government in 2013.

Barbados

Capital:	Bridgetown
Area:	430 sq km (166 sq miles)
Population:	288,725 (2012 est)
Currency:	1 Barbados dollar = 100 cents
Religions:	Anglican 28.3%; Pentecostal 18.7%; Methodist 5.1%; Roman Catholic 4.2%
Ethnic Groups:	Black 93.0%; White 3.2%; Mixed 2.6%
Languages:	English (official)
International Organizations:	UN; OAS; CARICOM; Commonwealth; Non-Aligned Movement; WTO

An island country in the south-east Caribbean.

Physical Barbados is the most easterly of the Windward Islands in the Caribbean Sea. Of coral formation, it is about 34 km (21 miles)

long by 22 km (14 miles) wide and rises in gentle stages to some 336 m (1100 feet).

Economy Barbados was historically dependent on sugar cane and its products, but the principal economic activities are now tourism, financial services, and information services. These industries were severely affected by the 2009 global recession.

History Barbados may have been visited by the conquistador Rodrigo de Bastidas in 1501; however the island that he called Isla Verde (because of its luxuriant vegetation) could have been Grenada rather than Barbados. The earliest inhabitants were thought to have been Arawak Indians, and later also some Carib Indians, but they had disappeared by the time British settlers began to colonize the island in 1627. Barbados became a British Crown colony in 1652. The British brought a large number of Africans to Barbados to work as slaves on sugar plantations. When slavery was abolished in 1834 six-sevenths of the population was Black. Cane sugar remained the principal product of the island throughout the 17th, 18th, and 19th centuries. Barbados was also a strategic port for the British navy. In 1958 Barbados joined the West Indies Federation and in 1966 became fully independent within the Commonwealth. The Democratic Labour Party (DLP) was in power from 1961 until 1976 and from 1986 until 1994, when the Barbados Labour Party (BLP) won general elections. The BLP was re-elected in 1999 and 2003, but the DLP was victorious in 2008 and 2013.

Barbarossa (Turkish **Khayr ad-Din Pasha**) (*c.*1483–1546) A famous *corsair and later grand admiral of the *Ottoman fleet. He and his brother Aruj first came to fame for their success against Christian vessels in the eastern Mediterranean. Aruj was killed fighting in 1518 and his brother Khayr ad-Din diplomatically ceded Algiers and its territory to the Ottoman sultan. He served as viceroy until 1533, when he was made grand admiral. In 1534 he took Tunis, but Charles V expelled him in 1535. After a number of minor engagements he retired in 1544.

Barbarossa, Frederick *See* FREDERICK I.

Barbary Wars *See* TRIPOLITAN WAR.

Bar Cochba (or, in Jewish sources, **Simeon bar Kosiba**) Jewish leader of a rebellion in 132 AD against the Roman emperor Hadrian's intention to rebuild Jerusalem as a non-Jewish city. His claim to be the Messiah was accepted by some. A number of letters in his handwriting

have been found in archaeological excavations near the Dead Sea in Israel.

Barebones Parliament The assembly summoned by Oliver *Cromwell in July 1653, after he had dissolved the *Rump Parliament. It consisted of 140 members chosen partly by the army leaders and partly by congregations of 'godly men'. Known initially as the Parliament of Saints, it was later nicknamed after 'Praise-God' Barbon, or Barebones (*c.*1596–1679), one of its excessively pious leaders. Its attacks on the Court of Chancery and on the Church of England alarmed both Cromwell and its more moderate members. The dissolution of this Parliament was followed by the Instrument of Government and the proclamation of *Cromwell as Lord Protector.

Barents, Willem (*c.*1550–97) Dutch explorer and leader of several expeditions in search of a *North-east Passage to Asia, south of the Arctic Ocean. He discovered Spitsbergen and reached the Novaya Zemlya archipelago north of European Russia. His accurate charting and valuable meteorological data make him one of the most important of the early Arctic explorers. The Barents Sea, north of Russia, is named after him.

Baring crisis (July 1890) A financial crisis in *Argentina. The London merchant bank of Baring Brothers was the country's financial agent in Europe, where a crisis of confidence occurred over the inflationary policy of President Juarez Celman (1886–90). The President gave way to his deputy Carlos Pellegrini, who had to stabilize the currency and adopt the gold standard before London would give any more credit. One result was heavy urban unemployment, although the refrigerated beef and corn industries continued to expand. Approximately a century later (1995) Barings Bank collapsed as a result of unmonitored loss-making speculation by a futures dealer, Nick Leeson, on the Singapore markets.

Barnardo, Thomas John (1845–1905) Irish-born doctor and philanthropist. He went to London in 1866 and while still a student of medicine, he founded the East End Mission for destitute children (1867), the first of many such homes. Now known as Dr Barnardo's Homes, they cater chiefly for those with physical and mental disabilities.

Barnet, Battle of (14 April 1471) A battle in the Wars of the *Roses fought between the Lancastrian forces, led by Richard Neville, Earl of *Warwick ('the Kingmaker') and the Yorkist troops of *Edward IV. Both sides suffered heavy losses, but Warwick was slain and Edward's recovery of his throne was made almost certain.

baron A member of the lowest rank of the English peerage. The title was introduced in England with the Norman Conquest and signified the vassal of a lord. Its limitation to those who held land directly from the king in return for military service occurred early. *Magna Carta (1215) made the distinction between the lesser baronage, summoned to the Great Council (Parliament) by general writ, and the greater baronage, called by personal writ, which was regarded as having conferred a hereditary peerage on the recipient.

Barons' Wars (1215–17; 1264–67) Two civil wars fought in England between the King and the barons. The first began in June 1215 at Runnymede, King *John, faced by the concerted opposition of the barons and Church, conceded *Magna Carta. He failed to honour his promise and thereby provoked the barons to offer the crown to Louis, Dauphin of France, who landed in Kent in May 1216. John's death (October 1216) and the reissue of Magna Carta by the regent of his son *Henry III prevented a major civil war. With his defeat at Lincoln and the capture of his supply ships off Sandwich, Louis accepted the Treaty of Kingston-upon-Thames in September 1217.

The second arose from baronial opposition to the incompetent Henry III and led to his accepting a programme of reform, the Provisions of Oxford (1258). Henry's renunciation of those reforms led to civil war in 1264, the baronial forces being led by Simon de *Montfort. The king's capture at the Battle of Lewes (May 1264) began a brief period of baronial control when de Montfort sought to broaden his support by extending parliamentary franchise to the shires and towns (1265). After his defeat and death at Evesham (August 1265), the struggle was continued unsuccessfully until 1267 by his supporters.

barrow (or **tumulus**) An earthen mound raised over a grave (if of stone, 'cairn' is the usual term). Grave-mounds of this type were characteristic throughout Europe and parts of central and southern Asia during the *Neolithic and *Bronze Ages, and in places much later. They occurred less frequently in other parts of the world.

Barth, Heinrich (1821–65) German explorer and geographer. The most influential of 19th-century European observers of West African life, Barth was a member of a British-sponsored expedition which left Tripoli in 1850 to explore the hinterland to the south. His five-volume account of his explorations, *Travels and Discoveries in North and Central Africa* (1857–58), contains much valuable anthropological, historical, and linguistic data.

Barton, Sir Edmund (1849–1920) Australian statesman and jurist, first Prime Minister of Australia (1901–03). He helped to draft the proposed Commonwealth constitution and went to England in 1900 (accompanied by Alfred Deakin) to see the bill through Parliament. He resigned as Prime Minister in 1903 to become a senior judge in the High Court of Australia, serving until 1920.

Baruch, Bernard (Mannes) (1870–1965) US industrialist and financier, the respected adviser of presidents from Wilson to Eisenhower. In World War I he served on the Council of National Defense and was the successful Chairman of the War Industries Board. In the 1940s he acted as special adviser on war mobilization and post-war planning. He was appointed to the UN Atomic Energy Commission, which proposed (1946) a World Atomic Authority.

basket-makers A group of Native Americans in Colorado and neighbouring areas who developed out of the desert cultures in the last centuries BC. They adopted farming from *Mexico. The baskets they used instead of pottery have been preserved in the dry climatic conditions of their territory.

Basque A member of an ethnic group inhabiting the western Pyrenees on both sides of the French-Spanish border; this region in known as the Basque Country. The Basques possess a distinctive culture and language, perhaps the result of their relative isolation from the rest of Europe until comparatively recently. It has been suggested that their ancestors migrated to Europe from the Caucasus about 12,000 years ago and about 5000 years ago moved to the Basque country. Although he Basque country is divided between France and Spain, the Basques have maintained an identity separate from both states. From the 14th century onwards the Basques were renowned for their fishing and whaling skills. Basque culture underwent a revival in the late 19th century, which ensured its continuance into the 20th century. During the *Spanish Civil War, the Basques supported the Republic; in reprisal, German aircraft acting on behalf of *Franco's Nationalists destroyed the Basque town of Guernica in 1937. Under Franco's regime, concerted attempts were made to suppress the Basque culture and language.

In recent decades many Basques in Spain have campaigned for an independent Basque state, some through the nationalist party *Herri Batasuna* or its violent military wing ETA (Basque Fatherland and Liberty). In 2011, after several abortive ceasefires, ETA declared 'a definitive cessation of armed activity'.

Bastille A fortified prison built on the city wall of Paris, France, between 1370 and 1382 in the reign of Charles V. Used by Cardinal Richelieu, Louis XIII's Minister, it became an infamous state prison in the 17th century. During the French Revolution it was completely demolished after being stormed on 14 July 1789. The prison is remembered in the name of a huge square, the Place de la Bastille, and a national holiday (Bastille Day) held annually on 14 July.

Batavia The former name (until 1949) of Jakarta in *Indonesia.

Batavian Republic The name given to the Netherlands by the French who occupied that country from 1795 until 1806 when Napoleon installed his brother Louis as King of Holland.

Batistá y Zaldívar, Fulgencio (1901–73) Cuban statesman. He was President of Cuba (1933–44; 1952–58), having come to national prominence in 1933 when, as a sergeant in the army, he led a successful revolt against President Gerardo Machado y Morales. He established a strong, efficient government, but increasingly used terrorist methods to achieve his aims. He amassed fortunes for himself and his associates and the dictatorial excesses of his second term contributed to his overthrow in *Castro's revolution in December 1958.

Batlle y Ordóñez, José (1856–1929) Uruguayan statesman. He was President of Uruguay (1903–07; 1911–15) and initiated legislation to increase public welfare. He believed that the Swiss Bundesrat or federal council was well suited to his own country's needs and during his second term he tried to have the office of president eliminated altogether. His political opponents compromised by agreeing to an executive branch in which power was shared between a president and a nine-man council. This decentralization of power placed Uruguay on a unique path in the 20th century.

Battenberg, Prince Louis (1854–1921) British admiral. Of Polish-German descent, he became a naturalized British subject in 1868 and joined the navy, becoming First Sea Lord in 1912 in the critical period before the outbreak of World War I. His decision, criticized by some,

not to disperse the naval squadrons gathered for exercises at Portsmouth at the time of the assassination of the Archduke *Francis Ferdinand at Sarajevo in 1914, assisted Britain's readiness for war. Anti-German hysteria in the early months of the war forced his resignation in October 1914. He became a marquis in 1917, giving up his German titles, and adopting the equivalent English name of Mountbatten. He married Princess Alice, granddaughter of Queen Victoria, in 1884. The younger of their two sons was Lord Louis Mountbatten, later Earl *Mountbatten of Burma, and one grandson became Prince Philip, Duke of Edinburgh.

Bavarian Succession, War of the (1778–79) A war between Austria and Prussia resulting from *Joseph II's ambition to add Bavaria to the *Habsburg dominions. The childless Maximilian Joseph of Bavaria (died 1777) had designated Karl Theodore, Elector Palatine, as his heir. He was a weak man with illegitimate sons to provide for and in January 1778 he agreed to sell a third of Bavaria to Joseph. *Frederick II headed the opposition to this and the "Potato War" (so called because the Prussian troops occupied their time by picking potatoes) took place in Bohemia: no battles were fought. Russia advanced into Poland, France offered mediation, and the Peace of Teschen was signed, under which Austria gained only the very small area of Innviertel.

Baxter, Richard (1615–91) English Puritan minister. He was ordained as an Anglican clergyman, but rejected belief in episcopacy and became a *Nonconformist. In 1645 he became chaplain to a *Roundhead regiment. He published the first of some 150 pamphlets in 1649 and in 1650 *The Saints' Everlasting Rest*, an important devotional work. During the Commonwealth period, his appeals for tolerance did not succeed. At the Restoration he became a royal chaplain but refused a bishopric. The 1662 Act of Uniformity forced his resignation, and in about 1673 he took out a licence as a Nonconformist minister. In 1685 he was imprisoned and fined by Judge *Jeffreys for 'libelling the Church'.

Bayard, Pierre du Terrail, Chevalier de (1473–1524) French soldier. He served under several French monarchs, including Louis XII, and became known as the knight 'sans peur et sans reproche' (fearless and above reproach).

Bayeux Tapestry A celebrated piece of embroidered linen fabric (not a tapestry) depicting the Norman Conquest of England in 1066. It is about 70 m (231 feet) long—the last section is lost—and 50 cm (19½ inches) wide, and is arranged with one episode succeeding another in more than seventy scenes. Perhaps made to the order of William the Conqueror's half-brother, Bishop Odo of Bayeux in Normandy, it was displayed for centuries in the cathedral at Bayeux and is now housed in the former Bishop's Palace there.

Bayezid I (known as **Yildirim 'Thunderbolt'**) (1347–1403) Ottoman sultan (1389–1402). He succeeded his father Murad I and absorbed rival Turkish principalities in western Asia Minor, took Trnovo in Bulgaria (1393), and Thessaloniki in Greece (1394), blockaded Constantinople (1394–1401), and defeated a Christian army at Nicopolis in 1396. His thrust into eastern Asia Minor, however, brought him to disaster at Ankara in 1402, and he died a captive of his conqueror, *Tamerlane.

Bayezid II (c.1447–1512) Ottoman sultan (1481–1512). He wrested the throne from his brother Jem on the death of their father Mehmed, fought inconclusively with the *Mamelukes (1485–91), gained Greek and Adriatic territories from Venice, and was faced with the emerging power of Ismail Safavi. He abdicated a month before his death in favour of his youngest son, Selim.

Bay of Pigs (or **Cochinos Bay**) A bay on the southern coast of the island of Cuba in the Caribbean Sea, the scene of an unsuccessful invasion attempt in April 1961 by US-backed Cuban exiles seeking to oust the Communist government of Fidel Castro.

Bazaine, Achille François (1811–88) French general. During the *Franco-Prussian War he was appointed commander-in-chief, but was reluctant to give battle. He withdrew to Metz with 176,000 French troops and capitulated to *Bismarck on 27 October 1870. Convicted of treason (1873), he was sentenced to death, but this was commuted to 20 years' imprisonment. After one year he escaped to Italy and then Spain, where he died.

Beaker cultures The people in many parts of western Europe at the end of the *Neolithic period (c.2600–2200 BC) who made and used a particular type of decorated pottery drinking-vessel. It was shaped like an inverted bell, with or without handles, and ornamented with zones of stamped impressions. These pots were valuable to their owners, and are often found as grave-goods in male burials, along with weapons such as a copper dagger or the remains of archery equipment. Their wide distribution, from the western Mediterranean to northern Germany, led earlier investigators to postulate a 'Beaker Folk' spreading northwards from Portugal, or perhaps from central Europe. They are now seen more simply as part of a general trend to ostentatious display of personal wealth, introduced at that time from central Europe.

Beale, Dorothea (1831–1906) Pioneer in higher education for women in Britain, together with her friend Frances Mary Buss (1827–94), the headmistress of the North London Collegiate School for Ladies. In 1858 she was appointed principal of the recently established Cheltenham Ladies' College, a position she was to hold until her death. She founded (1885) St Hilda's College, Cheltenham, for women teachers and lent her support to the establishment of St Hilda's Hall (later College), Oxford, in 1893. She was also an enthusiastic advocate of women's suffrage.

Beaufort An English family descended from three illegitimate sons of *John of Gaunt (fourth son of Edward III) and Katherine Swynford. The children were legitimated in 1407 but with the exclusion of any claim to the crown. Their father and their half-brother *Henry IV made them powerful and wealthy: Thomas (died 1426) became Duke of Exeter, John (c.1371–1410) was made Lord High Admiral and Earl of Somerset, and Henry (died 1447) was Bishop of Winchester and later a cardinal. As a court politician he led the so-called constitutional party against Humphrey, Duke of Gloucester. The *Yorkists had no love for the Beauforts, and by 1471 all three of the Earl of Somerset's grandsons had been killed in battle or executed. The male line thus ended, but their niece Margaret Beaufort (1443–1509), daughter of John, Duke of Somerset, who married Edmund *Tudor, enjoyed a life of charity and patronage of learning after her son became king as *Henry VII.

Beauregard, Pierre Gustave Toutant (1818–93) US general. He served as an engineer during the *Mexican-American War and was appointed superintendent of West Point in 1860, but he resigned at the outbreak of the *American Civil War to join the *Confederacy. As commander at Charleston, he ordered the first shot of the war against the Union-held *Fort Sumter. Beauregard was the field commander in the Confederate victory at the first battle of Bull Run (1861) before being promoted to full general and sent to the western theatre, where, after the battle of Shiloh (1862), he commanded the Army of Tennessee.

Beaverbrook, William Maxwell Aitken, Baron (1879–1964) British financier, statesman, and newspaper owner. In 1910 he became a Conservative Member of Parliament and in 1916 took an important part in overthrowing *Asquith and manoeuvring *Lloyd George into the premiership. By 1918 he owned the *Evening Standard*, the *Sunday Express*, and *Daily Express*, with a record world circulation. Through these newspapers he supported the Hoare–*Laval pact and Chamberlain's *appeasement of Hitler by the *Munich Pact (1938). In 1940 he became Minister of Aircraft Production and a member of Churchill's war cabinet and his efforts in producing fighter aircraft were significant in ensuring that the Battle of *Britain was won.

Bechuanaland The former name (until 1966) of *Botswana.

Becket, St Thomas à (*c.*1118–70) English prelate and statesman. A close and influential friend of Henry II, he served as his Chancellor and in 1162 became Archbishop of Canterbury, a position Becket accepted with reluctance, foreseeing the inevitable conflict of interests between the king and the Church. He soon found himself in open opposition to Henry, first on a matter of taxation and later over the coronation of Henry's son. The king in anger uttered words that motivated four knights to assassinate Becket in his cathedral on 29 December. The murder aroused indignation throughout Europe, miracles were soon reported at his tomb, and Henry was obliged to do public penance there. The shrine became a major centre of pilgrimage until its destruction under Henry VIII (1538).

Bede, St (or **the Venerable Bede**) (*c.*673–735) English monk, theologian, and historian. He lived and worked at the monastery in Jarrow, on Tyneside. Often regarded as 'the Father of English History', he wrote a number of historical works including *The Ecclesiastical History of the English People* (completed in 731). This is considered a primary source for early English history; it has vivid descriptions and is based on careful research, separating fact from hearsay and tradition.

Beecher, Lyman (1775–1863) US temperance reformer and Presbyterian clergyman. In 1832 he was appointed First President of the Lane Theological Seminary in Cincinnati, where his daughter, Harriet Beecher, author of *Uncle Tom's Cabin* (1852), married Calvin Ellis Stowe, professor of biblical literature. Lane Seminary students were among the first *abolitionists. Beecher became a target for attack by conservative Presbyterians and had to face charges, of which he was finally acquitted, of slander, heresy, and hypocrisy.

Begin, Menachem (Wolfovitch) (1913–92) Israeli statesman. Active in the *Zionist movement throughout the 1930s, he was sent with the Polish army-in-exile to Palestine (1942), where he joined the militant *Irgun. On the creation of *Israel (1948) the Irgun regrouped as the Herut (Freedom) Party and elected Begin as its head. He was leader of the Opposition in the Knesset (Parliament) until 1967, when he joined the National Unity government. In 1970 he served as joint chairman of the Likud (Unity) coalition, and after its electoral victory in 1977 became Prime Minister (1977–83). He negotiated a peace treaty with President *Sadat of Egypt at *Camp David, but remained opposed to the establishment of a Palestinian state.

Beit, Sir Alfred (1853–1906) South African financier and philanthropist. Of German origin, he settled in Kimberley as a diamond merchant in 1875 and became a close friend of Cecil *Rhodes. His interest in gold greatly contributed to the development of the Rand and the British South African Company, and later of *Rhodesia. He made benefactions to scholarship and the arts.

Belarus, Republic of

Capital:	Minsk
Area:	207,600 sq km (80,134 sq miles)
Population:	9,625,888 (2012 est)
Currency:	1 rouble = 100 kopeks
Religions:	Eastern Orthodox Church 80%; Roman Catholic, Protestant, Jewish, and Muslim minorities
Ethnic Groups:	Belorussian 83.7%; Russian 8.3%; Polish 3.1%
Languages:	Belorussian (official); Russian (official); minority languages
International Organizations:	UN; Commonwealth of Independent States; OSCE; Euro-Atlantic Partnership Council; Non-Aligned Movement

A landlocked country in eastern Europe, formerly a constituent republic of the Soviet Union. It is bounded on the west by Poland, on the north-west by Latvia and Lithuania, on the north and east by Russia, and on the south by Ukraine.

Physical Gentle hills run through a series of low plains which are forested with conifer, oak, lime, and ash. Many rivers drain the land into the vast area of the Pripet Marshes.

Economy Under the Soviet Union most industry in Belarus was dependent on processing raw materials from other parts of the country and after independence the country's inability to pay market prices for supplies led to severe recession. In 1994 Belarus entered into monetary union with Russia, which enabled it to obtain cheap Russian raw materials, and Russian control of Belarus's economy has continued to grow. Principal industries include oil refining and the manufacture of machinery, vehicles, and consumer goods. An important export is oil, imported from Russia at a discounted cost and sold on at the world market price.

History Belarus (once referred to as White Russia) had been part of Lithuania and later Poland until conquered by Russia under Catherine the Great. Heavy fighting took place during and after World War I, before the Treaty of Riga (1921) which divided the area between Poland and the newly declared Soviet Socialist Republic of Belorussia, which joined the Soviet Union. In 1939 the latter occupied all the area as far as the River Bug, and heavy fighting took place after the German invasion in 1941. In 1945 the Belorussian SSR was granted a seat in the UN National Assembly, and Poland abandoned its claim to western Belorussia, its Polish population being transferred to Poland. The rich steppe lands in the south of the republic suffered heavy pollution from the Chernobyl disaster of 1986. In April 1991 the Belorussian SSR declared its independence from the Soviet Union, renaming itself the Republic of Belarus. Multiparty politics were adopted, but the communists have continued to dominate politics and the centrally planned economy has been maintained. A presidential constitution was adopted in 1994 and Aleksander Lukashenko (1954–) was elected President later that year. In four referendums in 1995 Belarussians voted in favour of establishing even greater political, economic, and cultural links with Russia than had existed during the Soviet era. A union treaty establishing joint economic, foreign, and defence policies between the two countries was signed in 1996 and further areas of cooperation were agreed in subsequent years. Also in 1996, Lukashenko greatly increased the President's powers, his plans being opposed by parliament but supported in a referendum. He was re-elected in 2001, 2006, and 2010 in polls widely regarded as flawed. His dictatorial style of government and Belarus's poor record on human rights led to strained relations with other European countries. A foreign-exchange crisis in 2011 required large international loans, mainly from Russia, to stabilize the economy.

Belau *See* PALAU.

Belaúnde, Terry Fernando (1912–2002) Peruvian statesman. He was elected to the Chamber of Deputies (1945–48). In 1956 he helped to found the moderate Popular Action Party and in 1963 was elected President with the support of both Popular Action and Christian Democrats in opposition to Haya de la Torre, the candidate for APRA (Alianja Popular Revolucionaria Americana). His first term of office (1963–68) is remembered for its social, educational, and land reforms, as well as for industrial development and the construction of a vast highway system across the Andes. He was a strong supporter of the US Alliance for Progress programme, but his economic policies resulted in high inflation. He was deposed by the army and fled to the USA. He returned briefly to *Peru in 1970, but was deported. He returned again in 1976 and was again President (1980–85). During his second term inflation grew worse and he was unable to counter the terrorist activities of the Sendero Luminoso (the Shining Path organization).

Belgae An Iron Age Celtic people of north-west Europe occupying part of ancient Gaul to the north of the Seine and Marne rivers. They were defeated by Julius Caesar in 57 BC.

Belgium

Capital:	Brussels
Area:	30,518 sq km (11,783 sq miles)
Population:	10,444,268 (2012 est)
Currency:	1 euro = 100 cents
Religions:	Roman Catholic 75.0%
Ethnic Groups:	Fleming 58.0%; Walloon 31.0%

Languages:	Flemish, French, German (all official); Italian
International Organizations:	UN; EU; NATO; OECD; Council of Europe; OSCE; WTO

A country in north-west Europe on the North Sea. It is bounded inland by The Netherlands, Germany, Luxembourg, and France.

Physical The coastal area comprises broad, sandy beaches backed by dunes. Inland, most of the rivers run across the flat, fertile Flanders Plain, north-eastward to The Netherlands. In the south-east the land rises from the Sambre–Meuse valley to the highlands of the Ardennes. Here the soil is poor, and the land generally forested. The Campine coalfield is in the east.

Economy Service industries are of great importance, partly because of the location in Brussels of the headquarters of the EU, NATO, and other international institutions. Industries include engineering, metal products, vehicle assembly, and transportation equipment. Other than coal, Belgium has no natural resources and processes imported raw materials. Major exports include machinery, chemicals, finished diamonds, and metal products. Agriculture is limited to production for the domestic market.

History Belgium takes its name from the *Belgae, one of the peoples of ancient Gaul, but by the 5th century immigrations from the north had resulted in a large settled German population. After several centuries under the Franks the region split into independent duchies and, especially in Flanders, free merchant cities. In the 15th century all of what is now Belgium became part of the duchy of *Burgundy, but the Low Countries (which included Belgium) in 1477 passed by marriage to the Habsburg empire of Maximilian I. They were later absorbed into the Spanish empire, and in 1713 passed to *Austria. Belgium was occupied by France in 1795 during the French Revolutionary wars.

Following the defeat of Napoleon, Belgium became one of the provinces of the kingdom of The *Netherlands in 1815. However, in 1830 it separated from The Netherlands following a national revolution, and Prince Leopold of Saxe-Coburg was elected king. After an unsuccessful Dutch invasion, an international treaty was drawn up guaranteeing Belgian neutrality in 1839. In the later 19th century Belgium's King Leopold II (1865–1909) headed an international Association of the Congo (1876), following the exploration of the River Congo by H. M. *Stanley. This association was recognized at the Berlin Conference (1884) as the Congo Free State, with Leopold as its unrestrained sovereign. As the Congo was opened for trade, appalling atrocities against Africans were committed, leading to its transfer from Leopold's personal control to the Belgian Parliament (1908). Independence was granted to the Congo in June 1960, but was immediately followed by violence and bloodshed.

In 1914 Germany's invasion of Belgium precipitated Britain's entry into World War I. The country was occupied by the Germans, against whom Albert I (1908–34) led the Belgian army on the Western Front. When Germany invaded again in 1940 Leopold III (1901–83) at once surrendered. However, a government-in-exile in London continued the war, organizing a strong resistance movement. After the war Leopold was forced to abdicate (1951) in favour of his son Baudouin (1930–93). After World War II the main task for Belgium was to unite the Flemish-speaking northerners with the French-speaking Walloons of the south. In 1977 the Pact of Egmont, introduced by the Prime Minister, Leo Tindemans, recognized three semi-autonomous regions: that of the Flemings in the north, the Walloons in the south, and Brussels. The regions of Flanders, Wallonia, and Brussels were given greater autonomy by a constitution, adopted in 1993, that defines Belgium as a federal nation. Wilifried Martens (1936–2013) was Prime Minister from 1979 to 1992. Following his death in 1993, King Baudouin was succeeded by his younger brother, Albert II (1934–). Belgium adopted the *euro as its currency in 1999–2002. In the 2000s Flemish–Walloon political tensions led to political instability and increasing difficulty in forming governments. King Albert II abdicated in 2013 and was succeeded by his son Phillippe (1960–).

Belisarius (505–65 AD) Roman general under *Justinian. He was instrumental in halting the collapse of the Roman empire, if only temporarily. In 530 he defeated the Persians in the east, although they quickly reasserted themselves in Syria. Six years later he conquered Vandal North Africa, capturing its king. In 535–40 he took back Italy from the *Ostrogoths, advancing as far north as Ravenna, taking their king prisoner, and followed it with a second Italian campaign a few years later. He took Rome in 549 but was dismissed and even charged with conspiracy by a jealous Justinian, though reinstated in 564.

Belize

Capital:	Belmopan
Area:	22,965 sq km (8,867 sq miles)
Population:	334,297 (2012 est)
Currency:	1 Belize dollar = 100 cents
Religions:	Roman Catholic 39.3%; Pentecostal 8.3%; Seventh Day Adventist 5.3%; Anglican 4.5%
Ethnic Groups:	Mestizo (Mayo-Spanish) 48.7%; Creole (predominantly Black) 24.9%; Maya 10.6%; Garifuna 6.1%
Languages:	English (official); English creole; Spanish; Mayan; Garifuna
International Organizations:	UN; Commonwealth; CARICOM; OAS; Non-Aligned Movement; WTO

A small tropical country lying at the south of the Yucatán Peninsula in Central America. It is bounded by Guatemala to the west and the Caribbean Sea to the east.

Physical Belize is mainly low-lying and covered with rainforest; only in the south does it rise to pine forest and savannah. It is near an earthquake belt and is occasionally subject to hurricanes.

Economy Tourism is the principal source of foreign exchange and oil reserves have been exploited since their discovery in 2006. Other industry is limited mainly to food processing and clothing, and the chief exports are processed sugar and other agricultural products, clothing, and crude oil.

History The British settled Belize in the 17th century, proclaiming the area (as British Honduras) a crown colony in 1862. Subject to the jurisdiction of the governor of Jamaica, the colony sustained itself with little direct support from the British government. Grudging acceptance by its Latin American neighbours in the 19th century led to treaties recognizing its permanent boundaries. In 1964 the colony gained complete internal self-government. It adopted

the name Belize in 1973, and in 1981 became an independent state within the *Commonwealth of Nations. However, Guatemala continued its long-standing claim to the territory on the basis of old Spanish treaties. In 1991 Guatemala recognized Belize's independence, the two countries having reached a provisional agreement on mutual fishing rights. In 1998 the country was devastated by Hurricane Mitch. In 2012 Belize defaulted on an interest payment on its public debt, which was restructured in 2013.

Bell, Alexander Graham (1847–1922) Scottish-born US scientist and inventor. Bell studied sound waves, the mechanics of speech, and speech therapy. Having moved to the USA in the early 1870s, he developed his ideas for transmitting speech electrically, and gave the first public demonstration of the telephone in 1876; he founded the Bell Telephone Company the following year. He also invented the gramophone (1897) as a successful rival to Thomas Edison's phonograph. He later carried out research in a number of other areas, including hydrofoil speedboats and aeronautics.

Bello, Alhaji Sir Ahmadu (1906–66) Nigerian statesman. He became leader of the Northern People's Congress, and, in 1952, the first elected minister in Northern Nigeria, and in 1954 Premier. When Nigeria became independent in 1960, his party combined with *Azikiwe's National Council of Nigeria and the Cameroons (NCNC) to control the federal Parliament. Bello's deputy in the NPC, Abubakar Tafawa *Balewa, became federal Prime Minister, while Bello himself remained to lead the party in the north. In 1966, when the army seized power, Bello was among the political leaders who were assassinated.

Belshazzar (6th century BC) Son of Nebuchadnezzar and last king of Babylon. According to the Bible (Dan. 5), he was killed in the sack of the city and his doom was foretold by writing which appeared on the walls of his palace at a great banquet. In inscriptions and documents from Ur, however, he was perhaps the grandson of Nebuchadnezzar and the son of Nabonidos, last king of Babylon, and did not himself reign.

Ben Bella, Ahmed (Muhammad Ahmed Ben Bella) (1916–2012) Algerian statesman, Prime Minister (1962–63) and President (1963–65). In 1952 he founded the Front de Libération Nationale (FLN), which instigated the Algerian War of Independence (1954–62). He was elected Prime Minister of a provisional government shortly before the end of the war, becoming the first President of an independent Algeria the following year. As President he initiated social and economic reform and encouraged closer links with other Arab nations. Overthrown in a military coup, he was kept under house arrest until 1979 and lived in exile until 1990, when he returned to Algeria to lead the opposition to the ruling regime.

Benbow, John (1653–1702) English admiral. He was prominent in sea battles against the French for control of the English Channel during the early 1690s. He served in the West Indies for most of the period 1698–1702, where in his last engagement his daring plans for pursuing the retreating French were defied by his own captains. He died of his wounds in Jamaica, leaving a reputation for vigour, toughness, and bravery.

Benedict, St (c.480–c.550 AD) Italian hermit. A hermit from the age of 14, he attracted many followers by his piety; of these he chose the most devoted to form twelve small monastic communities, ultimately establishing a monastery at Monte Cassino (c.540). His *Regula Monachorum* (known as the Rule of St Benedict), austere but tempered by moderation, formed the basis of Western monasticism.

Benedict XVI (born **Joseph Alois Ratzinger**) (1927–) Pope (2005–13). After teaching theology at the universities of Bonn, Münster, and Tübingen, he was appointed Archbishop of Munich and Freising and created a cardinal in 1977. Pope John Paul II appointed him Prefect of the Congregation of the Doctrine of the Faith—formerly the Inquisition—in 1981, in which post Ratzinger gained a reputation as a conservative enforcer of doctrinal uniformity. He became dean of the College of Cardinals in 2002 and so played a prominent part in the funeral of John Paul II in 2005; he was quickly elected to succeed him. Seeing himself as John Paul's heir, Benedict largely continued his predecessor's policies, but did not seek to emulate his flamboyant style. In 2013 he resigned the papacy and assumed the title 'Pope Emeritus', becoming the first pope since 1415 not to die in office.

Benedictine A monk or nun of an order following the rule of St *Benedict. From the original Benedictine foundations at Subiaco and Monte Cassino in Italy the number of monastic houses in Europe grew to many thousands. The order reached its peak of prestige and influence in the 10th and 11th centuries, with the abbey of *Cluny in Burgundy its most prestigious foundation. The basic concept of Benedictine monasticism was that it should encourage a way of life separated from the world, within which monks could achieve a life devoted to prayer.

benefit of clergy The privilege entitling a cleric, on being accused of a crime, to be exempted from trial by a secular court, and to be subject only to the church courts, which usually dealt with him more leniently. It was a system open to abuse, especially when clerics were numerous and difficult to identify with certainty, as was the case in the Middle Ages. Indeed the mere ability to read was often accepted as proof of clerical status. In England it was a principal issue in the controversy between Archbishop Thomas à *Becket and *Henry II and the privilege was largely conceded by the crown in the aftermath of Becket's murder in 1170; later its application was limited by various Acts of Parliament and it was finally abolished in 1827.

Beneš, Edvard (1884–1948) Czechoslovak statesman, Prime Minister (1921–22), President (1935–38; 1945–48). A founder (with Tomáš Masaryk) of modern Czechoslovakia, he served as Masaryk's Minister of Foreign Affairs 1919–35, during which time he championed the League of Nations (he served as its chairman six times) and established close ties with France and the Soviet Union. He resigned as President over the Munich Agreement, and during World War II came to London as head of the Czechoslovakian government in exile (1941–45). In 1945 he returned to his country to regain the presidency, but resigned after the 1948 Communist coup.

Ben-Gurion, David (1886–1973) Israeli statesman, Prime Minister (1948–53; 1955–63). Born in Poland, he emigrated to Palestine in 1906, where he became an active Zionist. He was elected leader of the predominant socialist faction (the Mapai Party) of the Zionist movement in 1930. When the state of Israel was established in 1948, he became the country's first Prime Minister and Minister of Defence. After expulsion from the Labour Party in 1965 he formed a new party with Moshe Dayan.

Benin, Kingdom of West African kingdom based on Benin City, now in southern Nigeria, probably founded in about the 13th century. Its iron work and bronze and ivory sculptures rank with the finest art of Africa. It developed by trading in ivory, pepper, cloth, metals, and, from the 15th century, slaves. The kingdom achieved its greatest power under Oba Equare, who ruled from about 1440 to 1481. With his powerful army he conquered Yoruba lands to the west and Lower Niger to the east. He initiated administrative reforms, established a sophisticated bureaucracy, and ensured that the Portuguese, who arrived on the coast in 1472, did not establish control over Benin. The kingdom expanded further in the 16th century but by the 18th century its power waned with the growing strength of Oyo and other Yoruba states. Its extent declined further in the 19th century. Continuing slave-trading and the use of human sacrifice in religious rituals precipitated a British military expedition in 1897, which was massacred, whereupon a British force razed Benin city. The kingdom of Benin was incorporated into the new protectorate of southern *Nigeria in 1900. The republic of *Dahomey subsequently took the name Benin.

Benin, Republic of

Capital:	Porto Novo
Area:	112,622 sq km (43,484 sq miles)
Population:	9,877,292 (2013 est)
Currency:	1 CFA franc = 100 centimes
Religions:	Roman Catholic 27.1%; Muslim 24.4%; Vodun 17.3%; Protestant 10.4%
Ethnic Groups:	Fon 39.2%; Adja 15.2%; Yoruba 12.3%; Bariba 9.2%; Peulh 7.0%; Ottamari 6.1%; Yoa-Lokpa 4%; Dendi 2.5%
Languages:	French (official); Fon; Yoruba; other tribal languages
International Organizations:	UN; AU; Non-Aligned Movement; ECOWAS; Franc Zone; WTO

A West African country lying between Togo and Nigeria on the Gulf of Guinea.

Physical Benin has a southern coastline of only 125 km (78 miles) but extends inland for 700 km (460 miles) to Niger. The coast is sandy with large lagoons and is hot and wet. Inland there is a fertile clay plain with thick tropical forest that rises to a sandy plateau with savannah vegetation. In the north the land falls away to the middle Niger River valley.

Economy Benin has a primarily agricultural economy, with exports of cotton, foodstuffs, and textiles. There is some light industry, which includes textiles and food processing. Privatization of state-owned industries began in 2001 and has aided economic growth.

History Formerly known as Dahomey, this region was ruled by kings of Yoruba origin until the French occupied it in 1892. It was constituted a territory of French West Africa in 1904. As Dahomey, it became an independent republic within the *French Community in 1960, after which periods of civilian government alternated with military rule. In 1972 it was declared a Marxist–Leninist state, and its name was altered (1975) to Benin. Under the leadership of Mathieu Kérékou (President 1972–91), Benin achieved greater domestic stability and international standing. In the country's first free elections, held in 1991, Kérékou was defeated by his Prime Minister Nicéphore Soglo, whose government moved towards a free-market economy with the support of the IMF. Legislative elections in 1995 were indecisive and a coalition government was formed. However, presidential elections held in 1996 saw a surprise victory for the former dictator Kérékou, who was re-elected in 2001. He was succeeded in 2006 by Thomas Yayi Boni, who was re-elected in 2011.

Bennett, Richard Bedford, Viscount (Viscount Bennett of Mickleham and of Calgary and Hopewell) (1870–1947) Canadian statesman, Conservative Prime Minister (1930–35). Having failed to counter the effects of the Great Depression, Bennett proposed bold reforms in 1935. These reforms provoked distrust within his party and failed to inspire the public and the Conservatives were defeated in the general election later that year.

Bennington, Battle of (16 August 1777) A battle of the American War of *Independence in which 1600 *Green Mountain Boys under General John Stark overwhelmed 1200 German mercenaries of *Burgoyne's army. Encouraged by this success, the Americans forced Burgoyne to surrender after the defeat at *Saratoga.

Bentham, Jeremy (1748–1832) British philosopher, the founder of the Utilitarian school of ethics and political thought. He promoted the idea that the morality of an action could be measured by its effects on people: the greatest happiness of the greatest number should be the goal, and human institutions judged by the extent to which they contributed to that happiness. He supported much humanitarian reform and provided the inspiration for the founding of London University.

Bentinck, Lord William Cavendish

(1774–1839) British statesman. After serving in Flanders and Italy, he was posted to India as governor of Madras (1803–07). He was recalled to Britain after a mutiny at Velore for which, by his prohibition of sepoy beards and turbans, he was held responsible. After serving in the *Peninsular War he returned to India as governor-general of Bengal (1827–33) and effectively was the first governor-general of all India (1833–35). His administration substituted English for Persian and Sanskrit in the courts, brought about educational reforms, suppressed the practice of ritual strangling (*see* THUG), and abolished suttee, in which a widow was burned on her dead husband's pyre.

Bentinck, William Henry Cavendish, 3rd Duke of Portland (1738–1809) British

statesman. As leader of the Whig Party he was briefly Prime Minister at the end of the American War of Independence in 1783. Later he supported the government of William *Pitt (the Younger) in its opposition to the French Revolution. After Pitt's death (January 1806) and the failure of the so-called "Ministry of All the Talents" (1806–07), he was persuaded (1807) to take office again as Prime Minister. Then an old man, he failed to prevent internal dissension in his government, which led to the duel between *Canning and *Castlereagh, on news of which he resigned.

Berber An indigenous person of northern and north-western Africa. Traditionally, the Berbers speak Berber languages, although most literate Berbers also speak Arabic. The Berbers are Sunni Muslims, and their local tribal groups are often led by a hereditary religious leader. The Berber peoples include several distinct groups: settled farmers living in the Atlas mountains; transhumance farmers (who move their livestock seasonally from region to region); and the nomadic Tuareg of the Sahara.

History The Berbers have occupied the mountains and deserts of northern Africa since prehistoric times. *Herodotus recorded that they were found in various tribes. They do not seem commonly to have formed kingdoms, although they cooperated on occasions, for example against Roman rule. Their extreme independence and austerity were exemplified by the *Donatist *circumcelliones* (violent bands of

marauders) of the 4th and 5th centuries, by the Kharijite sect of early Islam, and by the cults of *marabouts*, Islamic holy men of ascetic devotion and organizers of fraternities. In this way they both resisted the *Arab conquest and transformed Islam to suit their own tastes. They supported the *Umayyads in Spain, and the *Fatimids in Morocco, and then set up several dynasties of their own, of whom the *Almohads and the *Almoravids were the most important.

Beria, Lavrenti (Pavlovich) (1899–1953)

Soviet politician and head of the secret police (NKVD and MVD) (1938–53). Born in Georgia, he rose to prominence within the Soviet Communist Party under Stalin's patronage. As head of the secret police Beria was directly involved in the infamous 'purge trials' in which Stalin's opponents were eliminated; he was also responsible for the deportation of thousands to forced labour camps. After Stalin's death he was rumoured to be planning to seize power; feared by rival politicians, he was arrested. Although his fate is not certain, it was officially announced that he had been tried and shot as a traitor.

Berlin, Congress of (1878) A conference of

European powers. It revised the Treaty of San Stefano (1878) which had ended the war between the *Ottoman empire and Russia (1877–78). Under the chairmanship of the German chancellor, Otto von *Bismarck, the congress limited Russian naval expansion; gave Montenegro, Serbia, and Romania independence; allowed Austria-Hungary to occupy Bosnia and Herzegovina; reduced *Bulgaria to one-third of its size; and placed Cyprus under temporary occupation by the British. The congress left Russian nationalists and *Pan-Slavs dissatisfied, and the aspirations of Greece, Serbia, and Bulgaria unfulfilled. Bismarck's handling of the congress antagonized Russia, and the claim of *Disraeli, that it had achieved "peace with honour", proved unfounded.

Berlin Airlift (1948–49) A measure under-

taken by the US and British governments to counter the Soviet blockade of Berlin. In June 1948 the USA, Britain, and France announced a currency reform in their zones of occupied Germany. The Soviet Union, fearing this was a prelude to the unification of these zones, retaliated by closing all land and water communication routes from the western zones to Berlin. The western Allies in turn responded by supplying their sectors of Berlin with all necessities by cargo aircraft. The siege lasted until May 1949, when the Russians reopened the surface routes. The blockade confirmed the division of

Berlin, and ultimately of Germany, into two administrative units.

Berlin Wall A barrier between East and West Berlin. It was built by the *German Democratic Republic in August 1961 in order to stem the flow of refugees from East Germany to the West: over three million had emigrated between 1945 and 1961. The Wall was heavily guarded and many people, especially in the 1960s, were killed or wounded while attempting to cross. As a result of popular protests, it was demolished in 1989.

Berlusconi, Silvio (1936–) Italian businessman and statesman; Prime Minister (1994–95; 2001–06; 2008–11). From the 1970s he built up a media-based business empire that came to dominate Italian television and made him Italy's wealthiest person. He entered politics in 1993 with the foundation of the conservative populist Forza Italia party and became Prime Minister following the 1994 elections. However, his coalition collapsed after only seven months. Berlusconi remained the leading figure on the right wing of Italian politics for the rest of the 1990s but was increasingly dogged by accusations of corruption. Although convicted on several occasions, he managed to avoid imprisonment. Re-elected in 2001, he became the first Italian Prime Minister since World War II to serve an entire parliamentary term, until he was narrowly defeated in the 2006 elections. This government undertook an ambitious programme of liberalizing economic reform—which was largely unsuccessful—and strongly supported the US *war on terrorism and the *Iraq War of 2003. Berlusconi's third term as Prime Minister was overshadowed by conflict with the courts over corruption charges and by allegations of sexual misconduct; and in 2011 a growing financial crisis (*see* EUROZONE CRISIS) led to his resignation. In 2013 he was convicted of tax fraud and barred from public office.

Bernadotte, Folke, Count (1895–1948) Swedish international mediator. The nephew of Gustav V, he entered the Swedish army as a young man. During World War II he worked for the Swedish Red Cross and in 1948 was appointed as UN mediator to supervise the implementation of the partition of *Palestine and the creation of *Israel. He was murdered by Israeli terrorists.

Bernard of Clairvaux, St (1090–1153) French theologian and abbot. He was the first abbot of Clairvaux in France; his monastery there became one of the chief centres of the Cistercian order. He was noted for his asceticism, severity, and eloquence; his preaching at the council of Vézelay in 1146 instigated the Second Crusade; he had the French theologian Peter Abelard condemned for heresy.

Berwick, Treaty of Three treaties were named after Berwick-upon-Tweed, a town in Northumberland, sited on the border between England and Scotland. The first (3 October 1357) was to release from captivity of David II of Scotland in return for a large ransom to be paid to Edward III of England, but this debt was never fully discharged. The second (27 February 1560) committed the English to send the Scottish Protestants military aid to help overthrow the Roman Catholic regent Mary of Guise. The third (18 June 1639) ended the first *Bishops' War between Charles I and Scottish Covenanters, although it did not fully resolve the conflict and was regarded as unsatisfactory by both parties.

Besant, Annie (1847–1933) British social reformer and theosophist. She became a Fabian, a trade-union organizer (including the match girls' strike of 1888), and a propagandist for birth control. She became a leading exponent of the religious movement of theosophy, and founded the Hindu University in India, helping to form, in 1916, the All India Home Rule League. She was President of the Indian National *Congress 1918–19, one of only three Britons to have held this office.

Betancourt, Rómulo (1908–81) Venezuelan statesman. An avowed democrat, he served as President from 1959 to 1964, presiding over a period of redemocratization following a long period of military juntas. He initiated a modest programme of agrarian reform, increased the taxes paid by the foreign oil companies, and secured a series of benefits for organized labour. Attacked by the right-wing supporters of his predecessor and by the radical socialists, he turned the presidential office over to a freely elected successor in 1964.

Bevan, Aneurin (known as '**Nye**') (1897–1960) British Labour politician. A brilliant though often abrasive orator, he was MP for Ebbw Vale 1929–60. His most notable contribution was the creation of the National Health Service (1948) during his time as Minister of Health (1945–51). He resigned from the government in protest against the introduction of health-service charges. The leader of the left wing of the Labour Party, he was defeated by

Hugh Gaitskell in the contest for the party leadership in 1955.

Beveridge, William Henry, 1st Baron
(1879–1963) British economist and social reformer. At the invitation of Winston *Churchill he entered (1908) the Board of Trade and published his notable report, *Unemployment*, in 1909. In it he argued that the regulation of society by an interventionist state would strengthen rather than weaken the free market economy. He was instrumental in drafting the Labour Exchanges Act (1909) and the National Insurance Act (1911). In 1941 he was commissioned by the government to chair an inquiry into the social services and produced the report *Social Insurance and Allied Services* (1942). This was to become the foundation of the British *welfare state and the blueprint for much social legislation from 1944 to 1948.

Bevin, Ernest (1881–1951) British Labour statesman and trade unionist. He was one of the founders of the Transport and General Workers' Union, serving as its first General Secretary (1921–40), and was a leading organizer of the General Strike (1926). He later entered Parliament, serving as Minister of Labour in Churchill's war Cabinet. As Foreign Secretary (1945–51), he helped form the Organization for European Economic Cooperation (1948) and NATO (1949). Unable to find a solution to the problem of Palestine, he surrendered the British mandate to the United Nations in 1947.

Bhagavadgita (Sanskrit, 'Song of the Lord') A Hindu philosophical poem inserted into the sixth book of the Mahabharata. The poem, which is the most famous religious text of *Hinduism, consists of 700 Sanskrit verses divided into 18 chapters. It was probably written in the 1st or 2nd century AD. The Pandava prince Arjuna, revolted by the prospect of killing his kinsmen in battle, seeks guidance from Krishna, disguised as his charioteer. Krishna urges Arjuna to fulfil his caste duties as a warrior selflessly and, revealing his divinity, preaches absolute devotion (*bhakti*) to the all-loving Supreme Being incarnated from age to age to save mankind. This is the first clear presentation of this doctrine in Hindu texts, and represents a move away from the priestly sacrificial cult of the Vedas to a devotional Hinduism open to all.

Bhave, Vinoba (1895–1982) Indian leader. A follower of Mahatma *Gandhi from 1916, he was active in attempts to revitalize Indian village life. Imprisoned by the British (1940–44) for defying wartime regulations, Bhave was, after Gandhi's assassination (1948), widely regarded as the leading exponent of Gandhism. He founded (1948) the Sarvodaya Samaj to work among refugees. In 1951 he began the *Bhoodan or land-gift movement, and led the Shanti Sena movement for peace and economic and social reform.

Bhoodan A movement in India begun in 1951 by Vinoba *Bhave with the object of acquiring land for redistribution to landless villagers. At first the object was to acquire individual plots, but from the late 1950s an attempt was made to transfer ownership of entire villages to village councils. The movement had a measure of success in Bihar state.

Bhopal An industrial city in central India, the capital of the state of Madhya Pradesh. The city is said to have derived its name from its 11th-century founder Raja Bhoj who created lakes by building dams or *pals*. In December 1984 leakage of poisonous gas from a US-owned pesticide factory caused the death of about 2500 people and thousands suffered injury in the world's worst industrial disaster.

Bhutan, Kingdom of

Capital:	Thimphu
Area:	38,394 sq km (14,824 sq miles)
Population:	725,296 (2012 est)
Currency:	1 ngultrum = 100 chetrum (Indian rupee also legal tender)
Religions:	Buddhist 75.0%; Hindu 25.0%
Ethnic Groups:	Bhutia 50.0%; Nepalese 35.0%
Languages:	Dzongkha (a Tibetan dialect) (official); Sharchhopka; Lhotshamkha
International Organizations:	UN; Colombo Plan; Non-Aligned Movement

A small country in south Asia, lying in the Himalayas between China in the north and India in the south.

Physical The northern part of Bhutan is entirely mountainous with spectacular peaks rising to 7300 m (nearly 24,000 feet). Deep valleys with fast-flowing rivers lead to warmer and lower land in the south, which is forested and offers soil for cultivation.

Economy Tourism is significant in a largely agricultural economy with some light industry. Only about 9% of Bhutan's territory is cultivated; the chief crops are rice, maize, and fruit. Principal exports are electricity and metals. India, the major export destination, provides an annual subsidy.

History Bhutan existed as a political unit by the end of the 17th century. The country is referred to in earlier monastic texts, but its early history is not clear. The first rulers of Bhutan were religious and political leaders, but the functions were later divided between a spiritual leader, the Dharma Raja, and an administrator, the Deb Raja. The Deb Raja was in theory elected by the regional governors, but in practice the strongest governor claimed the position. During the 19th century there were frequent wars between rival governors. The Dharma Raja was succeeded by a person traditionally regarded as a reincarnation of him. The office ceased to exist in the early 20th century when no reincarnation of the last Dharma Raja could be agreed. In 1907 a powerful regional governor was elected as the first hereditary maharaja, or king, who is called the Druk Gyalpo. His great-grandson Jigme Singye Wangchuk became king in 1972.

In 1774 Bhutan and the *East India Company signed a treaty of cooperation. This was replaced in 1865 by a treaty with Britain, which allowed Britain to supervise Bhutan's external affairs. This role was transferred to British India in 1910, and to the newly independent Indian government in 1949. During the 1950s and 1960s the king liberalized Bhutanese customs, abolishing slavery and the caste system and improving the status of women. He established a National Assembly in 1953 and a Council of Ministers in 1968; however, political parties remain illegal. The country has received large numbers of Tibetan refugees and Nepalese immigrants. In 1990 ethnic conflict broke out in southern Bhutan, with many Nepalese demanding greater recognition and protesting against government measures aimed at preserving Bhutanese culture and language. Thousands of refugees fled to Nepal, and their right to return is an unresolved issue. In 1998 King Jigme Singye Wangchuk devolved much executive authority to the Council of Ministers, and a fully democratic constitution was implemented between 2005 and 2008. Jigme Singye Wangchuk abdicated in 2006 in favour of his son, Jigme Khesar Namgyel Wangchuck.

Bhutto, Benazir (1953–2007) Pakistani stateswoman, Prime Minister (1988–90; 1993–96). The daughter of Zulfikar Ali *Bhutto and an opponent of the existing regime, she became joint leader in exile of the Pakistan People's Party (1984), returning to Pakistan in 1986 to campaign for open democratic elections. Following President Zia ul-Haq's death she became the first woman Prime Minister of a Muslim country. She took her country back into the Commonwealth and promised radical social reform, but failed to win widespread support from other parties. She was dismissed as Prime Minister and defeated in the ensuing election, re-elected as head of a coalition government in 1993, and dismissed again in 1996. In 1997 she was defeated in the elections. Tried in absentia for corruption, she was sentenced to five years' imprisonment in 1999; a retrial was ordered in 2001, but Bhutto failed to attend and was sentenced (2002) to three years' imprisonment. She was granted an amnesty and returned to Pakistan to fight elections called for January 2008, but was assassinated in a suicide bombing in Rawalipindi whilst campaigning in December 2007.

Bhutto, Zulfikar Ali (1928–79) Pakistani statesman, President (1971–73) and Prime Minister (1973–77). As Pakistan's Foreign Minister (1963–66) he instigated a rapprochement with China and became known as an outspoken defender of his country's interests. He formed the Pakistan People's Party in 1967, coming to power as Pakistan's first civilian President in 1971 and later (after constitutional changes) serving as Prime Minister. While in office, he did much to strengthen national morale and introduced social, constitutional, and economic reforms. He was ousted by a military coup and executed for conspiring to murder a political rival.

Biafra A state proclaimed in 1967 when part of eastern Nigeria, inhabited chiefly by the Ibo people, sought independence from the rest of the country. In the ensuing civil war the new state's troops were overwhelmed by numerically superior forces, and by 1970 it had ceased to exist.

Bible The sacred book of Christianity. All Christian Churches accept two sections of the Bible: the Hebrew scriptures, known as the Old Testament, and specifically Christian writings, known as the New Testament. In addition, some Churches, including the Roman Catholic Church, accept a third section called the Apocrypha, found in the Greek version of the Old Testament (Septuagint). Each section consists of a number of separate books, written at different times by different authors. However, most Christians consider them to be endowed with unique divine authority.

The Old Testament contains 39 books. The first five books ('the Law', the Torah, or Pentateuch) describe the origins of the Jewish people. 'The Prophets' give a history of the settlement in *Canaan, the period of the kingdom of *Israel, and prophetic commentaries. 'The Writings' consist of the remainder of the books including the Psalms, Job, and Daniel. The final content of the Hebrew Old Testament was probably agreed c.100 AD. The New Testament consists of 27 books. The four Gospels (meaning 'good news'), attributed to Matthew, Mark, Luke, and John, record the life, death, and resurrection of *Jesus Christ. The Acts of the Apostles traces the development of the early Christian Church and the Epistles (or Letters), notably those of St Paul, contain advice on worship, conduct, and organization for the first Christian communities. The Book of Revelation gives a prophetic description of the end of the world. Most of these books were acknowledged as canonical (accepted as sacred and genuine) by the middle of the 2nd century. The Apocrypha (Greek, 'hidden things') is the name given to a collection of 12 books written between 300 BC and 100 AD. They were included in the Septuagint, a Greek translation of the Old Testament of the 3rd and 2nd centuries BC that was used by the early Christian Church. These books do not appear in the Hebrew Old Testament and are not accepted by all Christian Churches.

The Bible was originally written in Hebrew, Aramaic, and Greek. The first translation of the whole book was the Vulgate (405 AD) of St *Jerome. The first translation into English was undertaken by John *Wyclif and his followers (1382–88). The development of printing stimulated the production of vernacular editions. Martin *Luther translated the New Testament into German in 1522 and William *Tyndale into English in 1525–26. William Coverdale's edition of the Bible, drawing heavily on Tyndale's work, was first published in 1535 and revised as the Great Bible in 1539. The Authorized or King James Version (1611), named after *James I who agreed to a new translation at the *Hampton Court Conference, was produced by about 50 scholars and remained for centuries the Bible of every English-speaking country. There are now translations of all or part of the Bible in over 1760 languages.

Bidault, Georges (1899–1982) French statesman and journalist. After serving in World War I he became professor of history in Paris. During World War II he became a distinguished leader of the French *resistance movement. He was a founder-member and leader (1949) of the Mouvement Républicaine Populaire. Bidault was Foreign Minister in several administrations of the Fourth Republic (1944, 1947, 1953–54) and Prime Minister (1946, 1949–50, 1958). He subsequently became bitterly opposed to Algerian independence: he became President of the National Resistance Council in 1962, was charged with plotting against the state, and went into exile in Brazil. He returned to France in 1968.

Bihar A region in India comprising the middle Ganges plains and the Chota Nagpur plateau in north-eastern India. The region had its 'golden age' during the evolution of early Indian civilization. Among its ancient kingdoms was Magadha, where both Gautama *Buddha and the Jain Seer, Mahavira, preached. Its capital, Pataliputra (now Patna), was adopted by several notable empire builders, including the Mauryas and the *Guptas. About 1200 it came under Muslim influence and remained subservient to the Delhi sultans until becoming a province of the *Mogul empire in the 16th century. In 1765 British victories resulted in its amalgamation with Bengal and the introduction of indigo plantations.

Bijapur A city and former state on the Deccan plateau, south-western India. It was the capital of a Muslim kingdom, founded by the Yadava dynasty in the 12th century. It fell under the control of the *Bahmani Muslims in the 14th century. Its era of independent splendour was from 1489 to 1686 when the Adil Shahi sultans made it their capital and were responsible for Islamic architecture of outstanding quality. In 1686 the Mogul emperor *Aurangzeb defeated Bijapur, but was unable to exert firm control and the region soon fell under *Maratha sway, from which it passed into East India Company hands in the early 19th century.

Bikini Atoll An atoll in the *Marshall Islands, west central Pacific. It was the site for 23 US nuclear bomb tests (1946–58). Despite expectations that it would be fit again for human habitation in 1968, the atoll remains too contaminated for the return of the Bikinians, who have been relocated on surrounding islands. In 1985 the USA agreed to decontaminate the atoll, a process that would take 10–15 years. By 1996 radiation levels were considered low enough for tourism to be permitted.

Biko, Steve (Stephen Bantu Biko) (1946–77) South African civil rights activist and student leader. A medical student at the University of Natal, he was co-founder and President of the all-Black South African Students Association, whose aim was to raise Black consciousness. Active in the Black People's Convention, he was banned and then arrested on numerous occasions (1973–76). His death in custody, by falling from a window at police headquarters in Pretoria (officially suicide but widely regarded as murder), made him a hero and martyr. Following disclosures about his maltreatment in prison, the South African government prohibited numerous Black organizations and detained newspaper editors, thus provoking international anger. In post-apartheid South Africa, police officers giving evidence before the Truth and Reconciliation Commission in 1997 confessed to assaulting Biko but continued to maintain that his death was accidental. The Commission refused to grant them amnesty, but they have not been prosecuted.

Bill of Rights (1689) A declaration and Act of Parliament stating the conditions upon which *William III and Mary were to become joint sovereigns of England, Scotland, and Ireland. Its major provisions were that the king could not levy taxes without the consent of Parliament, that he no longer had the power to suspend or dispense with the laws, and that there was to be no peacetime standing army without Parliament's consent. These terms dealt with issues that had been raised by the actions of *James II and were seen as a guarantee of Englishmen's liberties, helping to justify the name *Glorious Revolution for the events of 1688–89. American patriots often referred to the Bill of Rights when claiming, in the dispute with Britain in the late 18th century, that their liberties had been undermined.

Bill of Rights (1791) The first ten amendments to the *Constitution of the USA. The constitutional arrangements of 1787 were assumed to guarantee human and civil rights, but omission of specific rights led to criticism. To prevent this issue jeopardizing ratification, a Bill of Rights was adopted in 1791. Based on features of the English *Bill of Rights (1689) and common law principles, it guaranteed freedom of speech, press, worship, assembly, and petition (the first amendment). US citizens had the right to speedy and fair trial, reasonable bail, and to bear arms. They could not be forced to incriminate themselves (the fifth amendment) or suffer unwarranted search and seizure or cruel and unusual punishments.

Billy the Kid (born **William H. Bonney**) (1859–81) US outlaw. He arrived in New Mexico in 1868. A frequenter of saloons, he moved effortlessly into robbery and murder. In 1878 he became prominent in a cattle war, killing the local sheriff, Jim Brady. The territorial governor, Lew Wallace, was unable to persuade Billy to cease his activities. Sheriff Pat Garrett captured him in 1880, but he escaped, only to be shot by Garrett at Fort Sumner, New Mexico.

Bin Laden, Osama (1957–2011) Leader and founder of the *al-Qaeda terrorist network. Born in Saudi Arabia, he inherited a fortune from his father's construction business, which he has used to further his militant Islamic politics. In the late 1990s his guerrilla organization helped to thwart the Soviet invasion of Afghanistan, making him a hero to many Muslims. His followers then carried out a series of attacks on overseas US targets (from 1992). However, it was the terrorist outrage of *September 11, 2001, that brought him worldwide notoriety and made him the prime target of the USA's *war on terrorism. Although he survived the US attack on al-Qaeda's command centre in Afghanistan, his whereabouts for many years were unknown. He was killed in a US military raid on a secure compound in the Pakistani town of Abbottabad.

Birla Indian commercial and industrial family of the Marwari or Hindu merchant caste. The best known member of the family was Ghanshyam Das Birla, who became Mahatma *Gandhi's principal financial backer, paying most of the cost of the *ashram* (retreat), the Harijan organizations, the peasant uplift campaign, and the national language movement, as well as supporting many other Gandhian welfare projects. It was at Birla House, New Delhi, that Gandhi was killed. The Birla family has continued to manage a successful business empire.

Bishops' Wars (1639–40) Two brief conflicts over Charles I's attempt to impose Anglicanism on the Scots, and important as a factor leading to the outbreak of the *English Civil War. Since 1625 the king had been trying to take back former church lands from Scottish noblemen, provoking great bitterness. In 1637, a modified version of the English Prayer Book was introduced in Scotland. This spurred the *Covenanters into abolishing the episcopacy. The first war (May–June 1639) was a bloodless fiasco. Charles had refused to call a Parliament to vote funds and, acknowledging that his new recruits were no match for the Covenanters, he made peace at Berwick. For the second war (August–September 1640), refused supplies by the

English 'Short Parliament', he obtained money from the Irish Parliament, but his army was routed by the Covenanters at Newburn, near Newcastle upon Tyne. With the Scots occupying Northumberland and Durham, Charles was forced to make peace at Ripon, and to call the *Long Parliament.

Bismarck, Otto von, Prince of Bismarck, Duke of Lauenburg (Otto Eduard Leopold von Bismarck) (known as 'the Iron Chancellor') (1815–98) German statesman.

As Minister-President and Foreign Minister of Prussia under Wilhelm I from 1862, Bismarck was the driving force behind the unification of Germany, orchestrating wars with Denmark (1864), Austria (1866), and France (1870–71) in order to achieve this end. As Chancellor of the new German Empire (1871–90), he continued to dominate the political scene, passing legislation intended to break the influence of the Catholic Church at home and consolidating Germany's position as a European power by creating a system of alliances. Bismarck was forced to resign in 1890 after a policy disagreement with Wilhelm II.

Black-and-Tans An auxiliary force of the Royal Irish Constabulary. The demands of the Irish Republicans for a free *Ireland led in 1919 to violence by the Irish Republican Army against the Royal Irish Constabulary, an armed police force. Many of the policemen resigned, so the British government in 1920 reinforced the RIC with British ex-soldiers. Their distinctive temporary uniforms gave them their nickname of Black-and-Tans. They adopted a policy of harsh reprisals against republicans, many people being killed in raids and property destroyed. Public opinion in Britain and the USA was shocked and the Black-and-Tans were withdrawn after the Anglo-Irish truce in 1921.

Black Death (1347–50) The most virulent epidemic of bubonic and pneumonic plague ever recorded. It reached Europe from the *Tartar armies, fresh from campaigning in the Crimea, who besieged the port of Caffa (1347). Rats carrying infected fleas swarmed aboard trading vessels, thus transmitting the plague to southern Europe. By 1348 it reached France, Spain, and England; a year later Germany, Russia, and Scandinavia. Numbers of dead

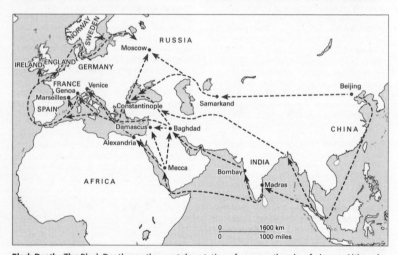

Black Death. The Black Death was the most devastating of many outbreaks of plague. Although its origins are uncertain, it is believed to have come from the Far East and to have been carried westward to Europe by merchants, pilgrims, and other travellers. It spread especially fast along sea trade routes, transmitted by the fleas of rats on board ship. The particular virulence of this epidemic may have been due to the presence of the more deadly pneumonic variety of plague, the only form that can be directly transmitted from one human to another (by sneezing, for example). It is estimated that as much as one-third of the population of Europe and the Near East died as a result of this outbreak in less than 20 years.

cannot be exact but up to 25,000,000 may have died in Europe, including perhaps one-third of the population in England.

Blackfoot A Native American tribe of the Great Plains and prairies of northern Montana and southern Alberta. Divided into Blackfoot Proper, Blood Blackfoot, and Piegan subgroups, the Blackfoot are among the westernmost of the Algonquian-speaking peoples. They were formerly almost entirely dependent on buffalo and other large game. The principal Blackfoot city is Browning, Montana, which is home to the Museum of the Plains Indians.

Black Hand Symbol and name for a number of secret societies that flourished in the 19th and early 20th centuries. It was the name adopted by a Serbian terrorist organization, founded in 1911 by Colonel Dimitrijevic largely from army officers, to liberate Serbs still under Habsburg or Turkish rule. It organized the assassination at Sarajevo of Archduke *Francis Ferdinand (1914), an event that contributed to the outbreak of World War I. The name and symbol were adopted by organizations controlled by the *Mafia in the USA and Italy, which used intimidation and murder to gain their ends.

Black Hawk War (1832) A war against the Sauk and Fox Native Americans. Between the *Louisiana Purchase and the 1830s, there was steady pressure from White settlers to remove the remaining Native Americans east of the Mississippi to the new territory, and Native American land rights were eaten away by a series of enforced treaties. In 1831, the Sauk and Fox Native Americans, led by Chief Black Hawk, were forced by the local militia to retreat across the Mississippi into Missouri. In the following year, threatened by famine and hostile Sioux, the Sauk and Fox recrossed the river to plant corn. When they refused to comply with the local military commander's order to leave, a brief war broke out in which the starving Sauk and Fox were gradually driven back, before being trapped and massacred near the mouth of the Red Axe River in early August. Black Hawk's defeat and death allowed the final loss of Native American land rights east of the Mississippi in favour of the White settlers.

Black Hole of Calcutta A prison room at Fort William, Calcutta, India, so called after the alleged suffocation there in 1756 of some English prisoners. They had been incarcerated by the nawab, Siraj ud-Daula, in retaliation for extending the fort against previous agreements. The incident has an important place in British imperial mythology, for British accounts grossly exaggerated both the smallness of the room and the number of prisoners, thus suggesting an act of barbarism on the nawab's part.

Black Muslim Movement An Islamic organization in the USA. It was founded in 1930 and led by Elijah Muhammad from 1934 until his death in 1975. The Movement expanded greatly in the 1950s when *Malcolm X became one of its spokesmen; by the 1960s, at the height of the *Black Power Movement, it probably had over 100,000 members. With the suspension of Malcolm X from the Movement and his assassination in 1965, it lost some of its influence to the militant Black Panthers, but continued to establish separate Black enterprises and to provide a source of inspiration for thousands of Black Americans. Elijah Muhammad was succeeded in 1975 by his son, Wallace D. Muhammad, who advocated a more moderate form of Islam and racial integration. This led to disagreements within the Movement and in 1976 it split into the American Muslim Mission and the radical Nation of Islam, led by Louis Farrakhan.

Black Power Movement A term used among Black people in the USA in the mid-1960s. The movement aimed at a more militant approach towards securing *civil rights, and stressed the need for action by Black people alone, rather than in alliance with White liberals. Many Black Americans felt that the civil rights movement had done little to alter their lives, and under such leaders as Stokeley Carmichael they proposed that Black Americans should concentrate in their own communities to establish their own political and economic power. In 1966 a Student Non-Violent Coordinating Committee (SNCC) was formed by Carmichael to activate Black college students, and at the same time the *Black Muslim Movement was advocating Islam as the Black salvation. Others, like the Black Panthers, emphasized violence and militancy, but all were concerned to stress the value of Black culture and heritage. The riots in the cities in the middle and late 1960s seemed to herald new waves of Black militancy, but the intensity of the Black Power Movement tended to decline in the early 1970s, when many Black people began cooperating with White organizations against the *Vietnam War.

Black Prince *See* EDWARD THE BLACK PRINCE.

Black September Palestinian terrorist organization. It emerged after the defeat of the Palestinian guerrilla organizations in Jordan in

September 1970, from which event it took its name. It was claimed to be an independent organization, but was apparently a cover for al-Fatah operations, the most infamous of which was the massacre of Israeli athletes at the Munich Olympics in September 1972. Shortly after that event the organization became inactive.

Blackshirt The colloquial name given to the *Squadre d'Azione* (Action Squads), the national combat groups, founded in Italy in 1919. Organized along paramilitary lines, they wore black shirts and patrolled cities to fight socialism and communism by violent means. In 1921 they were incorporated into the Fascist Party (*see* FASCISM) as a national militia. The *SS in Nazi Germany and the followers of Oswald *Mosley's British Union of Fascists in the 1930s were also known as Blackshirts.

Blackwell, Elizabeth (1821–1910) US physician. She was the first woman to gain a degree in medicine in the USA. Born in Bristol, England, she emigrated with her family to the USA in 1832. After her father's death she supported her family by teaching, and began studying medicine privately. Rejected by various medical schools, she was finally accepted by the Geneva Medical College, New York, graduating in 1849. She practised in New York but later lived in England, becoming professor of gynaecology at the London School of Medicine for Women (1875–1907).

Blaine, James Gillespie (1830–93) US politician. He was Secretary of State to President *Garfield (1881), and to President Benjamin *Harrison (1889–93). As leader of the so-called 'Half Breeds' Republicans (those committed to a conciliatory policy towards the South and to civil-service reform), he helped three lesser men (Rutherford Hayes, Garfield, Harrison) attain the presidency but was denied the prize himself in the 1884 election against *Cleveland.

Blair, Tony (Anthony Charles Lynton Blair) (1953–) British Labour politician, Prime Minister 1997–2007. Blair, a lawyer before entering politics, was elected as a Labour Member of Parliament in 1983 and became a member of the shadow cabinet in 1984. A 'modernizer', he took part in negotiations to end the 'closed shop' *trade union monopoly over certain jobs, and insisted that the *Labour Party should support private enterprise. As shadow spokesman for Home Affairs (1992–94) he emphasized the need to tackle the underlying social causes of crime. He became Leader of the Opposition following the death of John Smith in 1994 and led 'New Labour' to an overwhelming victory in the general election of 1997. In government he promoted major constitutional changes, including devolution in Scotland and Wales and a new settlement in Northern Ireland. A sweeping victory in the general election of 2001 gave him a second term. Following the events of *September 11, 2001, Blair pledged the UK's full support for President *Bush's *war on terrorism and committed British troops to the conflict. In 2003 Blair involved British troops in the *Iraq War, on the grounds that Iraq's weapons of mass destruction posed an imminent threat. When no such weapons were found, Blair faced mounting criticism but continued to justify the UK's participation. Domestically, after 2001 he concentrated on reform of the public services, especially health and education. He was returned for a third term in 2005, albeit with a much reduced parliamentary majority. He resigned in 2007 and immediately left parliament; he subsequently served as an international envoy to the Middle East as well as lecturing and pursuing business and charitable interests.

Blake, Robert (1599–1657) English admiral. He was a member of the *Long Parliament and fought for the *Roundheads during the *English Civil War. He achieved successes against the Royalists (1649–51), the Dutch (1652–54), and Spain (1656–57). His involvement in the preparation of the *Fighting Instructions* and *Articles of War* was crucial to the developing professionalism of the English navy, as was his association with the building of large, heavily armed vessels.

Blanc, Louis (1811–82) French politician and historian. In 1839 he published *The Organization of Labour* in which he outlined his ideal of a new social order based on the principle 'from each according to his abilities, to each according to his needs'. In 1848 he headed a commission of workers' delegates to find solutions to problems of exploitation and unemployment. The suppression of the workers' revolt later that year forced him to flee to Britain and he did not return until 1871.

Blanco, Antonio Guzmán *See* GUZMÁN BLANCO.

Blanqui, Louis Auguste (1805–81) French radical thinker and revolutionary leader. He launched an attack on the Paris Hotel de Ville in 1839. Sentenced to death, his sentence was later commuted to life imprisonment. A brief period of freedom allowed him to lead the republicans in the *Revolution of 1848. He remained in prison until 1859, was re-arrested in 1861, and escaped to Belgium in 1865, where he organized the extremist republican opposition to *Napoleon III. He was imprisoned in 1871, after attempting to overthrow the French provisional government. His influence over the Commune of Paris was considerable. He died in 1881, two years after being finally released from prison.

Blenheim, Battle of (13 August 1704) A major battle of the War of the *Spanish Succession that took place in the Bavarian village of Blenheim on the north bank of the River Danube. John Churchill, 1st Duke of Marlborough, commanded a British and Austrian army that defeated the French forces of Louis XIV. **Blenheim Palace**, the Duke's seat at Woodstock in Oxfordshire, England, was named after this victory. Begun in 1705, the building was designed by the English architects Sir John Vanbrugh and Nicholas Hawksmoor. The park was laid out by 'Capability' Brown.

Bligh, William (1754–1817) British admiral. He accompanied Captain Cook on his second voyage (1772–75). On a further visit to the South Pacific islands in 1788, his irascible temper and overbearing conduct provoked the *Bounty mutiny. Returning to Britain, he served under Nelson at Copenhagen (1801) and in 1805 was appointed governor of New South Wales. Conflict with the New South Wales Corps culminated in the *Rum Rebellion of 1808. He settled in England in 1810.

Blitzkrieg (German, 'lightning war') A military tactic employed by the Germans in World War II, which was especially successful in campaigns against Poland, France, Greece, and the Soviet Union. It employed fast-moving tanks and motorized infantry, supported by dive-bombers, to throw superior but slower enemy forces off balance and thereby win crushing victories rapidly and with small expenditure of men and materials. In Britain, where it was known as 'the Blitz', it consisted of an air assault on British cities in 1940. After 1941, Germany's enemies were better prepared and new battlefields in the Soviet Union and Africa were less suited to the technique.

Blood, Thomas (*c.*1618–80) Irish colonel and adventurer. He lost his estates at the *Restoration in 1660 and hoped to persuade the authorities to return them by his attack on Dublin castle in 1663. His most famous exploit was the theft of the English crown jewels from the Tower of London in 1671. Charles II, who examined Blood personally after his arrest, was so impressed with his audacity that he was pardoned and his estates restored.

Blood River, Battle of (16 December 1838) A battle fought between Voortrekkers (Afrikaners) and *Zulus, led by *Dingaan, near a tributary of the Buffalo River. The river became known as Blood River after its waters were reddened with the blood of some 3000 Zulus, killed to avenge the slaughter of about 500 Afrikaners earlier in the year. The Zulu defeat enabled the Afrikaners to establish the Republic of Natal.

Bloody Assizes A series of trials held in 1685 to punish those who took part in *Monmouth's Rebellion, conducted by Judge *Jeffreys, the Lord Chief Justice, in those centres of western England most affected by the rebellion. Of 1400 prisoners brought before him, 300 were hanged and 800 more were sold as slaves in the colonies. The severity of the sentences helped to mobilize support for William of Orange in the West Country in 1688.

Blücher, Gebhard Leberecht von (1742–1819) Prussian field-marshal, whose victories were due more to dash and energy than to military tactics. Forced to surrender to the French in 1806, he helped to re-create his country's opposition to *Napoleon, and was commander-in-chief of the armies in their victory at *Leipzig in 1813. The following year he led the invasion of France, gaining a major victory at Laon, which led to the overthrow of Napoleon. He retired to Silesia, only to be recalled when Napoleon returned. His intervention at a late stage of the battle of *Waterloo was decisive.

Blum, Léon (1872–1950) French statesman, Prime Minister (1936–37; 1938; 1946–47). A lawyer and literary critic, he was drawn into politics by the Dreyfus affair of 1894; he joined the Socialist Party in 1902 and became its leader in opposition in 1925. During the 1930s he led the Popular Front, being elected France's first socialist and Jewish Prime Minister in 1936. He introduced significant labour reforms, but was forced to resign the following year. Interned in Germany during World War II, he returned to France to head a socialist caretaker Cabinet, and retained the party leadership until his death.

Boadicea See BOUDICCA.

Boer (from Dutch, 'farmer') A South African of Dutch descent. See AFRIKANER.

Boer Wars (or **South African Wars, Anglo-Boer Wars, First and Second Wars of**

Freedom) (1880–81; 1899–1902) Wars fought between Britain and Transvaal and between Britain and Transvaal and the Orange Free State. The first arose from the British annexation of the Transvaal in 1877 and the incompetent administration that followed. In 1880 it was thought that the *Gladstone government would grant independence, or at least self-government; when hopes were dashed, *Kruger, Joubert, and *Pretorius took power as a triumvirate. British disasters at the battles of Laing's Nek, Ingogo, and Majuba Hill forced peace upon Gladstone, who granted self-government. The second Boer War (1899–1902) was caused by multiple grievances. The Boers, under the leadership of Kruger, resented the imperialist policies of Joseph *Chamberlain, which they feared would deprive the Transvaal of its independence. The refusal of political rights to uitlanders aggravated the situation, as did the aggressive attitude of Lord Milner, British High Commissioner. For Britain, control of the Rand goldfield was all-important. In 1896 the Transvaal and the Orange Free State formed a military alliance. The Boers, equipped by Germany, never mustered more than 88,000 men, but defeated Britain in numerous initial engagements, for example, Spion Kop. British garrisons were besieged in Ladysmith, Kimberley, and Mafeking. In 1900 the British, under *Kitchener and Roberts, landed with reinforcements. The Boers were gradually defeated, despite the brilliant defence of the commandos. Kitchener adopted a scorched-earth policy, interning the civil population in *concentration camps, and systematically destroying farms. Peace was offered in 1901, but terms that included the loss of Boer independence were not agreed until the Peace of Vereeniging in 1902.

Boethius, Anicius Manlius Severinus

(c.480–524 AD) Roman statesman and philosopher. He is best known for *The Consolation of Philosophy*, a work written in a mixture of prose and verse while he was in prison for treason. In this he argued that the soul can attain happiness in affliction by realizing the value of goodness and meditating on the reality of God. While drawing upon Stoicism and Neoplatonism, his work echoed Christian sentiments and exercised considerable influence throughout the Middle Ages.

Bohemond I (c.1056–1111) Norman Prince of Antioch, the eldest son of Robert Guiscard. He fought for Guiscard against the Byzantine emperor, Alexius *Comnenus; after his father's death he joined the First *Crusade and played a prominent part in the capture of the Syrian city of Antioch. He established himself as prince in Antioch but was captured by the *Turks and imprisoned for two years. In 1107 he led an expedition against the *Byzantine empire and was defeated by Alexius, making peace at the Treaty of Devol (1108).

Bokassa, Jean-Bédel (1921–96) President of the Central African Republic (1966–76); emperor of the Central African Empire (1976–79). After a distinguished career in the French Army, Bokassa became commander-in-chief of the forces of his newly independent country in 1964 and seized power in a coup two years later. Bokassa's rule became increasingly arbitrary and authoritarian and he was implicated in the massacre of civilians. He proclaimed himself President for life in 1972 and was named Emperor in a lavish investiture ceremony in 1976. In one of the poorest countries of Africa, he spent huge sums on maintaining a luxurious lifestyle modelled on that of Napoleon I. He was deposed, with French support, in 1979. After spending seven years in exile, Bokassa was condemned to death on his return, but this sentence was commuted to one of life imprisonment. He was given amnesty and freed in 1993.

Boleyn, Anne (1501–36) Second wife of Henry VIII and mother of Elizabeth I. Although the king had fallen in love with Anne, and had divorced Catherine of Aragon in order to marry her (1533), she fell from favour when she failed to provide him with a male heir. She was eventually executed because of alleged infidelities.

Bolger, James Brendan (1935–) New Zealand statesman, Prime Minister (1990–97). He was leader of the National Party, which won elections in 1990 and 1993. He formed a coalition government after the elections of 1996 but resigned the following year.

Bolingbroke, Henry of See HENRY IV.

Bolingbroke, Henry St John, 1st Viscount

(1678–1751) English politician. He entered Parliament as a Tory in 1701, became Secretary of State following the Tory triumph of 1710, and was responsible for negotiating the Peace of *Utrecht in 1713. Dismissed by George I in 1714, and impeached by the Whig Parliament of 1715, he fled to France, where he joined James Edward Stuart, but soon became disillusioned with the *Pretender's cause. In 1723 he was pardoned by George I and allowed back into England.

Bolívar, Simón (known as **'the Liberator'**) (1783–1830) Venezuelan patriot and statesman. Bolívar was active in the Latin-American independence movement from 1808 onwards. Although his military career was not without its failures, he succeeded in driving the Spanish from Venezuela, Colombia, Peru, and Ecuador; Upper Peru was named Bolivia in his honour.

Bolivia

Capital:	La Paz (administrative); Sucre (judicial)
Area:	1,098,581 sq km (424,164 sq miles)
Population:	10,461,053 (2012 est)
Currency:	1 boliviano = 100 centavos
Religions:	Roman Catholic 95.0%; Protestant 5.0%
Ethnic Groups:	Quechua 30.0%; Mestizo 30.0%; Aymara 25.0%; White (mainly Spanish extraction) 15.0%
Languages:	Spanish, Aymara, Quechua, and 34 other indigenous languages (all official)
International Organizations:	UN; OAS; Andean Community; Non-Aligned Movement; WTO

A landlocked country of central South America. It is bounded by Brazil and Paraguay to the north and east, Argentina to the south, and Peru and Chile to the west.

Physical In the southwest is a great plateau, the Altiplano, some 800 km (500 miles) long and 3,660 m (12,000 feet) high, set between two even loftier ranges of the Andes. At its northern end is the southern shore of a huge mountain lake, Titicaca, while in the south there are vast salt pans. The north-east by contrast has low plains with hot, wet rainforest and several navigable rivers. Southward the ground rises to plains which are covered with woodland and grass.

Economy The mountains of Bolivia offer large deposits of minerals: mining and smelting are the principal industries. Other industry includes natural gas and oil production, textiles, and food processing. Natural gas and tin, of which Bolivia is one of the world's largest producers, are major exports. Principal agricultural crops include soya beans, coffee, and coca; the last is processed into cocaine, of which Bolivia is the world's third largest producer. Bolivia's economy has suffered from protracted political instability, fluctuating commodity prices, a large external debt, high inflation, and lack of investment.

History The area became an important Ayamará Indian state between 600 and 1000 AD but was conquered by the growing *Inca state c.1200. Some Ayamará continued to resist, however, and were not completely subdued until the late 15th century, Spanish conquest followed six years after Francisco *Pizarro's landing in Peru in 1532, and in 1539 the capital at Charcas (modern Sucre) was founded. The discovery of silver deposits in the Potosí mountains in 1545 led to the establishment of the Audiencia (a high court with a political role) of Charcas, under the viceroyalty of Peru. Revolutionary movements against Spain occurred here earlier than anywhere else in South America—at La Paz in 1661, Cochabamba in 1730, Charcas, Cochabamba, La Paz, and Oruro in 1776–80—but all failed.

Independence was finally won under José de Sucre, at the battle of Ayacucho (1824). A National Assembly declared Upper Peru independent, and named it Bolivia after Simón *Bolívar. A short-lived Peru-Bolivian Confederation was formed (1825–39). Control of the Atacama coast region, where rich guano nitrate deposits were found, was challenged by Chile in 1842 and finally lost in 1884 in the disastrous War of the Pacific. A series of military dictatorships (1839–80) was succeeded by more liberal regimes, with Liberal and Republican Parties alternating. In 1930 a popular revolution elected a reforming President, Daniel Salamanca. In 1936, following the disastrous *Chaco War, military rule returned. In 1952 the Bolivian National Revolution overthrew the dictatorship of the junta, and Paz Estenssoro, leader of the MNR (Movimiento Nacionalista Revolucionario) Party returned from exile and was installed as President. Tin mines were nationalized, adult suffrage introduced, and a bold programme of social reforms begun. Paz was re-elected in 1960 but overthrown in 1964 by a military coup. In 1967 a communist revolutionary movement, led by Ché *Guevara, was defeated. Military regimes followed each other quickly. Not all were right-wing, and that of General Juan José Torres (1970–71) sought to replace Congress by workers' soviets. Democratic elections were restored in 1978, but there was another military coup in 1980 and a state of political tension continued until 1982, when civilian rule was restored. A succession of Presidents—including the return of Paz Estenssoro (1985–89) and a former military dictator, Hugo Banzer (1997–2001)—struggled with economic problems and the unrest caused by attempts to resolve them. Free-market reforms led to economic growth in the 1990s and vigorous action was taken against the cultivation of coca. However, progress stalled thereafter: economic growth slowed from 1999, and coca production increased in the early 21st century. In 2006 Juan Evo Morales became Bolivia's first indigenous President. His programme of nationalization and wealth redistribution caused political divisions and unrest; but it was popular with the poor indigenous majority and Morales was re-elected in 2009 and 2014.

Bolshevik (Russian, 'a member of the majority') The wing of the Social Democratic Party in Russia which, from 1903, and under the leadership of *Lenin, favoured revolutionary tactics. Their opponents, the Mensheviks ('members of the minority'), led by Martov and Georgi Plekhanov, favoured a loosely organized mass labour party, in which workers had more influence, and which was prepared to collaborate with the liberal bourgeoisie against the Tsarist autocracy. After the abortive *Russian Revolution of 1905 Bolshevik leaders fled abroad, having made little appeal to the peasantry, and it was the Mensheviks led by *Kerensky who joined the Provisional Government, following the February *Russian Revolution in 1917. The infiltration by Bolsheviks into soviets and factory committees contributed to the success of the October Revolution. During the *Russian Civil War the Bolsheviks succeeded in seizing control of the country from other revolutionary groups. In 1918 they changed their name to the Russian Communist Party. The Mensheviks were formally suppressed in 1922.

bombing offensives (in World War II) Attacks by bomber aircraft on military and civilian targets. As part of his *Blitzkrieg tactics, Hitler deployed dive-bombers in the offensives in Poland (1939) and western Europe (1940). In August 1940 the first major German offensive was launched against Britain, a series of daylight attacks by bombers, many of which were destroyed by fighter aircraft of the Royal Air Force in the Battle of *Britain. A German night-bombing offensive on civilian targets then began which lasted until May 1941. The Allied air offensive against Germany and the occupied countries grew in intensity throughout the war. The development of radar to intercept aircraft and direct gunfire revolutionized the Allied bombing offensive. Increasing resources were made available to the British Bomber Command under Air Marshal Sir Arthur Harris, and daylight raids by the US Air Force, combined with British night-bombing, endeavoured to obliterate key German cities. Meanwhile the bulk of German bombing power was turned to the Eastern Front, where fighter-bombers supported the army, attacking besieged cities, such as Leningrad and Stalingrad. Pilotless flying bombs (V1s) and rocket missiles (V2s), launched against southern England during 1944 and 1945, did relatively little damage. In the Far East a massive bombing offensive was launched by US forces against Japanese cities in October 1944. On 6 and 9 August 1945 respectively, US aircraft dropped the world's first atomic bombs on the Japanese cities of *Hiroshima and *Nagasaki, bringing the war against Japan to a close.

Bonhoeffer, Dietrich (1906–45) German Lutheran theologian. An active opponent of Nazism, he signed (1934) the Barmen Declaration in protest against attempts by German Christians to synthesize Nazism with Christianity. He was forbidden by the government to teach, and in 1937 his seminary at Finkenwalde was closed. In 1942 he tried to form a link between the Germans opposed to Hitler and the British government. Arrested in 1943, he was sent to Buchenwald concentration camp, where he was hanged in 1945.

Boniface VIII (1235–1303) Pope (1294–1303). He was a papal diplomat and lawyer who travelled widely. He quarrelled disastrously with *Philip IV of France when he asserted papal authority to challenge Philip's right to tax the clergy. In response Philip had him seized in 1303. The shock hastened the pope's death and contributed towards the transfer of the papacy from Italy to Avignon in France.

Bonner, Yelena *See* SAKHAROV, ANDREI.

Bonnie Prince Charlie *See* STUART, CHARLES EDWARD.

Boone, Daniel (*c*.1734–1820) US pioneer. Moving west from his native Pennsylvania, Boone made trips into the unexplored area of Kentucky from 1767 onwards, organizing settlements and successfully defending them against hostile Native Americans. He later moved further west to Missouri, being granted land there in 1799. As a hunter, trail-blazer, and fighter against the Native Americans he became a legend in his own lifetime.

Booth, Charles (1840–1916) British social researcher. As the author of *Life and Labour of the People in London* (1891–1903) he presented an exhaustive study of poverty in London, showing its extent, causes, and location. Aided by Beatrice *Webb, his methods, based on observation and on searches into public records, pioneered an approach to social studies which has been influential ever since. His special interest in the problems of old age accelerated the Old Age Pensions Act (1908).

Booth, John Wilkes (1838–65) US assassin of President *Lincoln. Brother of the tragic actor Edwin Booth, and sympathizer with the *Confederacy, he participated during the closing stages of the *American Civil War in a small conspiracy to overthrow the victorious Lincoln government. On 14 April 1865 he mortally wounded Lincoln in Ford's Theatre in Washington and escaped to Virginia, but was discovered and killed on 26 April. Four of his fellow conspirators were hanged.

Booth, William (1829–1912) British religious leader and founder of the Salvation Army (1878). Originally a Methodist preacher, Booth, assisted by his wife, Catherine, preached in the streets, and made singing, uniforms, and bands a part of his evangelical mission. He used his organizational gifts to inspire similar missions in other parts of the world.

Borden, Sir Robert Laird (1854–1937) Canadian statesman. He was chosen as leader of the Conservative Party in 1901. In the general election of 1911 he defeated the Liberals and succeeded *Laurier as Prime Minister of Canada. Knighted in 1914, he remained in office throughout World War I, leading a coalition government after 1917 and joining the imperial war cabinet. He retired from political life in 1920.

Borgia, Cesare (*c.*1476–1507) Italian statesman. The illegitimate son of Cardinal Rodrigo Borgia (later Pope Alexander VI) and brother of Lucrezia *Borgia, he became a cardinal in 1493. He succeeded his brother Juan, possibly through murder, as captain-general of the papal army in 1499. Through two campaigns he became master of a large portion of central Italy, but after the death of his father (1502) his enemies rallied and he was defeated at Naples in 1504.

Borgia, Lucrezia (1480–1519) Italian noblewoman. The illegitimate daughter of Cardinal Rodrigo Borgia (later Pope Alexander VI), she married three times, according to the political alliances useful to her father and to her brother, Cesare *Borgia. Always associated with the scandals of her birth and marriages, after her third marriage in 1501 she established herself as a patron of the arts and became increasingly religious.

Boris Godunov (*c.*1551–1605) Tsar of Russia (1598–1605). He began his career of court service under *Ivan IV (the Terrible), became virtual ruler of Muscovy during the reign of his imbecile son Fyodor (1584–98) and engineered his own elevation to the Tsardom. He conducted a successful war against Sweden (1590–95), promoted foreign trade, and dealt ruthlessly with those *boyar families which opposed him. In 1604 boyar animosity combined with popular dissatisfaction ushered in the 'Time of Troubles'—a confused eight-year dynastic and political crisis, Boris having died suddenly in 1605.

Bormann, Martin (1900–*c.*45) German politician. Bormann was appointed to Hitler's personal staff in 1928 and succeeded Hess as Party chancellor in 1941. Bormann was considered to be Hitler's closest collaborator, but remained the most obscure of the top Nazis and disappeared at the end of World War II. He was sentenced to death *in absentia* at the Nuremberg trials in 1945 and was formally pronounced dead in 1973 after identification of a skeleton exhumed in Berlin.

Bornu See KANEM-BORNU.

Borodino, Battle of (7 September 1812) A battle fought between Russia and France, about 110 km (70 miles) west of Moscow. Here *Kutuzov chose to take his stand against *Napoleon's army. The Russian position was centred upon a well-fortified hill. After twelve hours of fierce combat, a terrific artillery bombardment and a decisive cavalry charge split the Russian forces. They were forced to withdraw and Napoleon, claiming victory, marched on an undefended Moscow. Over 80,000 men were lost in the most bloody battle of the *Napoleonic Wars.

borough A town in England, enjoying particular privileges. The boroughs evolved from the Anglo-Saxon *burhs* and from the 12th century benefited from royal and noble grants of charters. Their representatives attended Parliament regularly from the 14th century, having first

been summoned in 1265 when Simon de
*Montfort called two representatives from each
city and borough. The Scottish equivalent of the
English borough was the burgh.

Boscawen, Edward (1711–61) British admiral, known as 'Old Dreadnought'. He served
in the West Indies during the War of *Jenkins's
Ear and the War of the *Austrian Succession,
and was in charge of naval operations at the
siege of Louisburg, Nova Scotia, in 1758, where
his success opened the way for the conquest of
Canada. His most famous exploit was the destruction of the French Mediterranean fleet off
the Portuguese coast at Lagos in 1759, which
helped to establish British naval supremacy in
the *Seven Years War.

Bosch, Juan (1909–2001) Dominican statesman. He founded the leftist Partido Revolucionario Dominicano (PRD) in 1939 and was exiled
during the dictatorship of Rafael *Trujillo. After
the latter's assassination he returned (1961) to
the Dominican Republic and was elected President (1962–63) in the first free elections for
nearly forty years. He introduced sweeping liberal and democratic reforms, but after nine
months in office was overthrown by rightist
military leaders with the backing of the Church,
of landowners, and of industrialists. His supporters launched their revolt in 1965, a movement which prompted a military intervention by
the USA. In 1966 he was defeated for the presidency by Joaquin Balaguer, who had heavy US
backing.

Bose, Subhas Chandra (1897–1945) Indian
nationalist politician. With Jawaharlal *Nehru
he founded the Indian Independence League
in 1928. He became President of the Indian
National *Congress Party (1938–39) but quarrelled with other leaders. He escaped from virtual house arrest (1941), went to Germany but
failed to secure Nazi support and in 1943 went
to Japan and Singapore. There he assumed
command of the Indian National Army, recruited from Indian prisoners-of-war, and
formed a provisional Indian government.

Bosnia and Herzegovina

Capital:	Sarajevo
Area:	51,197 sq km (19,767 sq miles)
Population:	3,875,723 (2012 est)
Currency:	1 marka = 100 feninga

Religions:	Muslim 40.0%; Eastern Orthodox 31.0%; Roman Catholic 15.0%
Ethnic Groups:	Bosniak 48.0%; Serb 37.1%; Croat 14.3%
Languages:	Bosnian, Croatian, Serbian (all official)
International Organizations:	UN; OSCE; Council of Europe; Euro-Atlantic Partnership Council

A country in south-east
Europe, in the Balkan
Peninsula. It is bordered
by Croatia to the north and
west, Serbia to the east,
and Montenegro to the
south-east.

Physical The country is
mostly mountainous and wooded. It has a short
Adriatic coastline.

Economy The poorest of the former Yugoslav
republics, Bosnia and Herzegovina suffered severe economic disruption from the civil war
(1992–95). It has a variety of mineral resources,
including coal, iron, copper, chrome, manganese, cinnabar, zinc, and mercury. Livestock
are raised, and the principal crops are cereals,
fruits, and vegetables. Industries include mining,
steel, vehicle assembly, and textiles. Many Bosnians are migrant workers in Western Europe.

History First inhabited by the Illyrians, the
region became part of the Roman province of
Illyricum. *Slavs settled in the 7th century and,
in 1137, it came under Hungarian rule. The
Ottomans invaded in 1386 and after much resistance made it a province in 1463. They governed through Bosnian nobles, many of whom
became Muslim, though much of the population became rebellious as Ottoman power declined. During the early 18th century Austrian
forces began to push the Turks back. The rise of
*Pan-Slavism provoked revolts in 1821, 1831,
and 1837. A revolt in 1875 brought Austrian
occupation, which was consolidated by formal
annexation into *Austria-Hungary in 1908. This
provoked protest from Serbia and Russia. An
international crisis only subsided when Germany
threatened to intervene. Serbs continued to protest and to indulge in terrorist activity, culminating in the assassination of the Archduke
*Francis Ferdinand and his wife in the capital
Sarajevo in 1914. This sparked off World War I,
after which Bosnia was integrated into the new
Kingdom of Serbs, Croats, and Slovenes, later

renamed *Yugoslavia. During World War II the two provinces were incorporated into the German puppet state of Croatia, and were the scene of much fighting by the Yugoslav partisans. After the war they were integrated into *Tito's communist Yugoslavia.

Alija *Izetbegović became President in 1990. In 1992, as Yugoslavia disintegrated, the mainly Muslim population of Bosnia and Herzegovina voted to become an independent country in a referendum. Although most Western countries recognized this decision, areas occupied mainly by the Serb and Croat minorities proclaimed themselves independent of the Muslim-dominated government and all three groups began fighting for territory. Attempts by the UN and the European Community to mediate in the ensuing ferocious civil war made little headway. The three main factions agreed in principle to Bosnia and Herzegovina being a federal nation with regions based on ethnic groupings but failed to agree on the borders of the proposed regions.

In April 1992 the Serbs besieged Sarajevo; by the end of that year, with backing from the Serb-led Yugoslav army, they had taken possession of over two-thirds of the country. Although a UN peacekeeping force intervened to defend Muslims and others fleeing from "ethnic cleansing", it was unable to prevent thousands of civilians from being massacred. In 1994 NATO shot down Serb fighter planes that were flying in the UN-established "no-fly zone" and bombed Serb ground targets. That same year Bosnian Muslims (Bosniaks) and Bosnian Croats formed an alliance, and by mid-1995, with support from the Croatian army, they had recaptured a large amount of territory from the Serbs. Further NATO air strikes led to the lifting of the siege of Sarajevo in September 1995. In December 1995 a US-brokered peace deal, the *Dayton Accord, was signed. This stated that although Bosnia and Herzegovina would remain a single state with unchanged borders, it would henceforth be divided into a Bosnian–Croat Federation in the west and a Bosnian Serb Republic in the north and east. Although there has been no resumption of full-scale violence, a number of serious problems remain—notably the resettlement of many thousands of refugees and the capture and prosecution of war criminals on all sides. In 1996 Izetbegović was re-elected as the chairman of a new tripartite rotating presidency, serving alongside a Serb and a Croat. The implementation of the non-military aspects of the Dayton Accord lies with an internationally appointed High Representative, who is effectively the supreme civilian authority in Bosnia and Herzegovina. NATO was responsible for military peacekeeping operations until December 2005, when it was replaced by an EU force. High unemployment led to violent anti-government demonstrations in 2014.

Boston The state capital of Massachusetts, USA, on Boston Bay. Founded *c*.1630 as the principal settlement of the Massachusetts Bay Company, Boston was an early centre of New England Puritanism. Faneuil Hall Marketplace, bequeathed to the city as a public meeting-hall and market place in 1742, is known as the 'Cradle of Liberty'. Bostonians took the lead in resisting British attempts at taxation with the *Stamp Act Riots (1765). In 1770 troops threatened by a mob opened fire, killing five people in the Boston massacre. When tea ships from England in 1773 threatened other tea importers and clandestine revenue-raising under the *Townshend Acts, the *Sons of Liberty threw the cargo overboard in what was known as the **Boston Tea Party**. The city, having been evacuated by the British, was entered by George *Washington in 1776, and was a *Federalist stronghold in the early republic.

Bosworth Field, Battle of (22 August 1485) A battle fought close to the English town of Bosworth in Leicestershire, its outcome was to establish *Henry VII and the Tudor dynasty on the English throne. Just over a fortnight after Henry had landed on the Welsh coast, he and his army of Welsh followers were met in battle by *Richard III's larger army. The issue was uncertain when Lord Stanley arrived and with his followers went over to Henry's side; Henry was victorious, Richard was killed, and at the end of the day Stanley placed Richard's crown on Henry's head.

Botany Bay An inlet of the Tasman Sea on the coast of New South Wales, south-east Australia, just south of Sydney. In 1770 Captain James *Cook landed here naming the bay after the large variety of plants collected by the naturalist on the voyage, Sir Joseph Banks (1743–1820). Chosen as the site for a penal settlement in 1787, it proved to be unsuitable and a location at nearby Sydney Cove was selected.

Botha, Louis (1862–1919) South African soldier and statesman, first Prime Minister of the Union of South Africa (1910–19). One of the most successful Boer leaders in the Boer War, Botha became commander-in-chief in 1900 and waged guerrilla warfare against the British forces. As Transvaal's first Prime Minister he played a leading role in the National Convention (1908–09), which was responsible for drafting the constitution for the Union of South

Africa; he became its Prime Minister a year later. Botha supported the Allies in World War I, gaining recognition for his annexation of German South West Africa in 1915.

Botha, P. W. (Pieter Willem Botha) (1916–2006) South African statesman, Prime Minister (1978–84), State President (1984–89). He joined the National Party in 1936 and was involved in party organization, particularly in Cape Province, until his election as Prime Minister. An authoritarian leader, he continued to enforce apartheid, but in response to pressure introduced limited reforms, including a new constitution (1984) giving certain classes of non-Whites a degree of political representation. His resistance to more radical change ultimately led to his fall from power.

Bothwell, James Hepburn, 4th Earl of (1536–78) Scottish Protestant nobleman, the third husband of *Mary, Queen of Scots. He was a supporter and adviser of Mary, while she was married to *Darnley. In 1567 he was acquitted of Darnley's murder but then his swift divorce, promotion to the dukedom of Orkney and Shetland, and marriage to Mary caused the Scottish lords to rise against him. He fled from Scotland after the Battle of Carberry Hill (June 1567), when Mary's forces were defeated. He turned to piracy, but was captured in Norway, and died in a Danish prison.

Botswana

Capital:	Gaborone
Area:	581,730 sq km (224,607 sq miles)
Population:	2,127,825 (2012 est)
Currency:	1 pula = 100 thebe
Religions:	Christian 71.6%; traditional beliefs 6.0%
Ethnic Groups:	Tswana 79.0%; Kalanga 11.0%; Basarwa 3.0%
Languages:	Setswana, English (official); local languages
International Organizations:	UN; AU; SADC; Non-Aligned Movement; Commonwealth; WTO

A landlocked country in southern Africa. It is bordered by Namibia to the west and north, Zimbabwe to the east, and South Africa to the south.

Physical Botswana lies in the hot, dry central region of southern Africa. The north-west, which has 600 mm (24 inches) of rain a year, drains into a swampy basin, the Okavango, the only surface water in the country. The centre and west is covered by the Kalahari Desert, while in the east is a large salt-pan, the Makgadikgadi.

Economy Diamonds are the chief export, producing revenues that have supported a high growth rate, although Botswana was hit hard when demand for diamonds slumped in the 2009 global recession. It is thought that further mineral wealth awaits discovery; other exports are copper, nickel, soda ash, and beef. Agriculture is mainly pastoral. The government is attempting to use Botswana's diamond wealth to diversify the economy, and tourism and financial services are increasingly important.

History Botswana was formerly known as Bechuanaland. British missionaries visited the southern Tswana people in 1801, and in 1817 the London Missionary Society settled at Kuruman. David *Livingstone and other missionaries operated from here during the second quarter of the 19th century. In 1885 the British protectorate of Bechuanaland was declared, to be administered from Mafeking. The success of the cattle industry led the Union of South Africa to seek to incorporate Botswana, along with Basutoland (Lesotho) and Swaziland, but this was rejected by the British government in 1935; no transfer would be tolerated until the inhabitants had been consulted and an agreement reached. The dominant tribe was the Ngwato, whose chief Seretse *Khama was banned from the country from 1948 until 1956 for marrying an Englishwoman. By now a nationalist movement had begun, which culminated in a democratic constitution in 1965 followed by independence on 30 September 1966, as the republic of Botswana, with Seretse Khama as President. He was succeeded on his death in 1980 by the vice-president Quett Masire, who was re-elected in 1989 and again in 1994. In 1998 Masire retired and Festus Mogae became President; in 2008 Mogae was in turn succeeded by Ian Khama, Seretse Khama's eldest son and a former commander of the Botswana Defence Force. AIDS was a major challenge in the early 21st century, with over 35% of the adult population being infected with HIV or AIDS. However, unlike many other developing countries, Botswana was able to afford comprehensive medical treatment.

Boudicca (or **Boadicea**) (died 62 AD) A queen of the Britons, ruler of the Iceni tribe in eastern

England. When Rome broke the treaty made with King Prasutagus (her husband) after his death in 60 AD, Boudicca led her forces in revolt against the Romans and sacked Colchester, St Albans, and London before being completely defeated by the Roman governor Suetonius Paulinus. She committed suicide soon after her defeat, but her name became a symbol of native resistance to the Roman occupation.

Bougainville, Louis Antoine de (1729–1811) French explorer. Between 1766 and 1769 he led the first successful French circumnavigation of the globe, visiting many of the islands of the South Pacific and compiling a scientific record of his findings. The largest of the Solomon Islands is named after him.

Boulanger, Georges Ernest (1837–91) French general and politician. He won increasing popular support for his campaign for revenge on Germany after the *Franco-Prussian War (1870–71). In 1886 he became Minister of War but forfeited the support of moderate republicans who feared that he might provoke another war with Germany. Forced from his ministry in 1887, he became the focus of opposition to the government and won a series of by-elections. He failed to seize this opportunity to make himself President, and his popularity waned. The government prepared to have him tried for treason but he fled into exile.

Boumédienne, Houari (1925–78) Algerian statesman. In the early 1950s he joined a group of expatriate Algerian nationalists in Cairo that included *Ben Bella and in 1955 he joined resistance forces in *Algeria operating against the French. He became chief-of-staff of the exiled National Liberation Front in Tunisia (1960–62). In March 1962 his forces occupied Algiers for Ben Bella after which a peace treaty was signed with France. He displaced Ben Bella in a coup in 1965, ruling until his death in 1978.

Bounty mutiny (1789) A British mutiny that occurred near the Tongan Islands on HMS *Bounty*, under the command of Captain *Bligh. Some of the crew, resenting Bligh's harsh authority, rebelled under the leadership of Fletcher Christian. Bligh and 18 others were cast off in a small, open boat with no chart. Thanks to Bligh's navigational skill and resourcefulness, they covered a distance of 5822 km (3618 miles), arriving in Timor about six weeks later. Some of the mutineers surrendered and others were captured and court martialled in England. Fletcher Christian and some of the other mutineers, with a number of Tahitian men and women, settled on Pitcairn Island in 1790. Their descendants moved to Norfolk Island in 1856.

Bourbon A great European ruling dynasty, founded when Robert of Clermont (1256–1317), the sixth son of Louis IX of France, married the heiress to the lordship of Bourbon. The first duke was their son, Louis I (1279–1341). In 1503 the title passed to the Montpensier branch of the family, but in 1527 headship of the house of Bourbon passed to the line of Marche-Vendôme. Antoine de Bourbon (1518–62), Duc de Vendôme, became King Consort of Navarre, while his brother Louis (1530–69) was made Prince of *Condé. On the death of the last *Valois king in 1589, Antoine's son became King of France as *Henry IV (ruled 1589–1610). His heirs ruled France uninterruptedly until 1792: Louis XIII (ruled 1610–43), Louis XIV (ruled 1643–1715), Louis XV (ruled 1715–74) and Louis XVI (ruled 1774–92). The latter was overthrown during the *French Revolution, and Louis XVII (titular king 1793–95) died without reigning; Louis XVI's brothers Louis XVIII (ruled 1814–24) and Charles X (ruled 1824–30) both reigned after the Bourbon restoration. Louis-Philippe (ruled 1830–48), the last Bourbon King of France, was a member of the cadet Orléans branch of the family.

In 1700 Louis XIV's second grandson became Philip V (ruled 1700–46) of Spain, thus setting in train the War of the *Spanish Succession. His successors have held the Spanish throne ever since (excepting the republican period, 1931–75).

Bourguiba, Habib ibn Ali (1903–2000) Tunisian nationalist and statesman, President (1957–87). Having negotiated the settlement that led to his country's autonomy, he was its first Prime Minister after independence in 1956 and was chosen as its first President when the country became a republic in 1957. A moderate socialist, he embarked on a reform programme intended to improve Tunisia's economy and to establish democratic government. He was deposed following continuing political unrest.

Boutros-Ghali, Boutros (1922–) Egyptian diplomat and politician, Secretary-General of the United Nations 1992–96. He served as Egyptian minister of state for foreign affairs from 1971 to 1991.

Bowell, Sir Mackenzie (1823–1917) Canadian Conservative politician, Prime Minister (1894–96). His party was bitterly divided from the start of his ministry and when half his ministers resigned in 1896, he resigned himself.

bowl cultures *See* NEOLITHIC.

Bow Street Runners The first organized police force, based at Bow Street Magistrates' Court in London, recruited by the magistrate (and novelist) Henry Fielding from the 1740s to augment the forces at his disposal. Their functions included serving writs and acting as detectives. They gained a reputation for efficiency and were much feared and respected by criminals. The formation of the London Metropolitan Police Force in 1829 brought their separate existence to an end.

Boxer Rising (1899–1900) A popular anti-western movement in China. The secret society of Righteous and Harmonious Fists, which was opposed to foreign expansion and the Manchu court, claimed that by training (including ritual boxing) its members could become immune to bullets. The movement began in Shandong province and had its roots in rural poverty and unemployment, blamed partly on western imports. It was pushed westwards and missionaries, Chinese Christians, and people handling foreign goods were attacked. The movement was backed by the empress dowager *Cixi and some provincial governors. In 1900 the Boxers besieged the foreign legations in Beijing for two months until they were relieved by an international force which occupied and looted the capital; Cixi and the emperor fled in disguise. The foreign powers launched punitive raids in the Beijing region and negotiated heavy reparations in the Boxer Protocol (1901). The rising greatly increased foreign interference in China, and further reduced the authority of the *Qing dynasty.

boyar A member of the highest non-princely class of medieval Russian society. In the 10th to 12th centuries the boyars formed the senior levels of the princes' retinues. They received large grants of land and exercised considerable independent power during the period of decentralization after the 13th-century Mongol conquest. However, as the grand princes of Muscovy consolidated their own power, they managed to curb boyar independence.

From the 15th to the 17th centuries Muscovite boyars formed a closed aristocratic class drawn from about 200 families. They retained a stake in princely affairs through their membership of the boyar *duma* or council. *Ivan IV (the Terrible) (ruled 1547–84) reduced their power significantly by relying on favourites and locally elected officials. Their social and political importance continued to decline throughout the 17th century and *Peter I eventually abolished the rank and title.

Boycott, Charles Cunningham (1832–97) British land agent in Ireland. When, at the direction of the Land League, Irish tenants on the estate of Lord Erne in County Mayo asked for rent reductions and refused to pay their full rents, Boycott ordered their eviction (1880). *Parnell urged everyone to refuse all communication with Boycott and to ostracize his family. The policy was successful and Boycott was forced to leave. The practice of non-communication became known as boycotting.

Boyne, Battle of the (1 July 1690) A major defeat for the Stuart cause which confirmed *William III's control over Ireland. It took place near Drogheda, where the recently deposed *James II and his Irish and French forces were greatly outnumbered by the Protestant army led by William III. When William attacked across the River Boyne James's troops broke and fled. He returned to exile in France, and William's position as King of England, Scotland, and Ireland was immeasurably strengthened. The victory is still commemorated annually by the Orange Order, a political society founded in 1795 to support Protestantism in Ireland.

Bradford, William (1590–1657) Pilgrim leader. He was born in Yorkshire and escaped to Holland with the Scrooby separatists. After the *Mayflower* reached Plymouth, the first permanent colony in New England, he was elected governor and guided the colony until his death. He pacified the Native Americans, achieved financial independence from the London merchants, and wrote his *History of Plimmoth Plantation*.

Bradlaugh, Charles (1833–91) British social reformer. A republican and keen supporter of reform movements, he was tried, with Annie *Besant, in 1877–78 for printing a pamphlet on birth control. The charge failed and contraceptives could thereafter be openly advertised.

Bradley, Omar Nelson (1893–1981) US general. In *World War II he commanded a corps in the North African and Sicilian campaign. He commanded US land forces in the *Normandy Campaign, and later, following the *Ardennes Campaign, went beyond Eisenhower's orders to link up with the Soviet forces on the Elbe in 1945. He was instrumental in building up *NATO, formulating US global defence strategy in the post-war years, and in committing US troops to fight in the *Korean War.

Braganza The ruling dynasty of Portugal (1640–1910). Alfonso, an illegitimate son of John I of Portugal, was made first Duke of Braganza (1442). His descendants became the wealthiest nobles in the kingdom and, by marriage into the royal family, had a claim to the Portuguese throne before the Spaniards took control of the country in 1580. When the Portuguese threw off Spanish rule in 1640, the 8th Duke of Braganza ascended the throne as John IV. The title of Duke of Braganza was thenceforth borne by the heir to the throne.

Brandenburg A German state, the nucleus of the kingdom of *Prussia. German conquest of its Slavic population began in the early 12th century. The margravate (established *c.*1157) took its name from the town of Brandenburg, west of Berlin. In 1356 the *margrave's status as an imperial *Elector was confirmed by the Golden Bull of *Charles V.

Strong central government began with the advent of the *Hohenzollern dynasty in 1415. Brandenburg accepted the Lutheran *Reformation after 1540, and in the early 17th century it acquired further territories in western Germany and also Prussia (1618). After an initial period of neutrality during the *Thirty Years War, *Frederick William (the Great Elector) (1620–88) entered the fighting and secured excellent terms at the Treaty of *Westphalia (1648). He subsequently achieved full sovereignty in Prussia (1660) and turned Brandenburg-Prussia into a centralized European power with a highly effective army and bureaucracy. He used the opportunity offered him by Louis XIV's persecution of the *Huguenots to develop his country's industry and trade. In 1701 Elector Frederick III (1657–1713) was granted the title of King in Prussia, and from that time Brandenburg was a province of the Prussian kingdom.

Brandenburg Gate The only one of the city gates of Berlin to survive. It was built in 1788–91 by Carl Langhans (1732–1808), chief architect to Frederick William II of Prussia, in neoclassical style, and surmounted by the Quadriga of Victory, a chariot drawn by four horses. After the construction of the Berlin Wall (1961) it stood in East Berlin, a conspicuous symbol of a divided city; it was reopened on 21 December 1989.

Brandreth, Jeremiah *See* PENTRICH RISING.

Brandt, Willy (born **Karl Herbert Frahm**) (1913–92) German statesman, Chancellor of West Germany (1969–74). He was mayor of West Berlin (1957–66) and in 1964 he became chairman of the West German Social Democratic Party. He achieved international recognition for his policy of détente and the opening of relations with the former Communist countries of the Eastern bloc in the 1960s. A pragmatist, he encouraged the negotiation of joint economic projects and a policy of non-aggression. He also chaired the Brandt Commission on the state of the world economy, the report on which was published in 1980 (*see* BRANDT REPORT). He was awarded the Nobel Peace Prize in 1971.

Brandt Report A report, entitled *North–South: A Programme for Survival* (1980), by an international commission on the state of the world economy. Convened by the United Nations, it met from 1977 to 1979 under the chairmanship of Willy *Brandt. It recommended urgent improvement in the trade relations between the rich Northern Hemisphere and poor Southern for the sake of both. Governments in the north were reluctant to accept the recommendations. Members of the commission therefore reconvened to produce a second report, *Common Crisis North–South: Cooperation for World Recovery* (1983), which perceived 'far greater dangers than three years ago', forecasting 'conflict and catastrophe' unless the imbalances in international finance could be solved.

Brandywine, Battle of (11 September 1777) An engagement in the American War of *Independence when British forces were attacking Philadelphia. Washington was outmanoeuvred by Sir William Howe and was forced to retreat with heavy losses. The British occupied Philadelphia on 27 September, but this victory was offset by *Saratoga less than a month later.

Brauchitsch, Walter von (1881–1948) German field-marshal. As commander-in-chief of the German army (1938–41), he carried out the occupation of Austria (*see* ANSCHLUSS) and Czechoslovakia (*see* SUDETENLAND) and conducted the successful campaigns against Poland, the Netherlands, and France. He was relieved of his command by Hitler as a scapegoat for the German failure to capture Moscow.

Brazil

Capital:	Brasília
Area:	8,514,877 sq km (3,287,612 sq miles)
Population:	201,009,622 (2012 est)
Currency:	1 real = 100 centavos

Religions:	Roman Catholic 73.6%; Protestant 15.4%
Ethnic Groups:	White 53.7%; Mulatto 38.5%; Black 6.2%
Languages:	Portuguese (official); German; Japanese; Italian; Amerindian languages
International Organizations:	UN; OAS; Mercosur; WTO

The largest country in South America. Brazil borders ten countries, has a coastline 7400 km (4600 miles) long, and straddles the equator from latitude 4° N to past latitude 33° S.

Physical The whole of the northern region lies in the vast Amazon basin with its tributary rivers. South of this are the Mato Grosso with its grassland plateau and the *campos*, mountain plateaux intersected by deep river valleys. In the region of great lakes the climate becomes suited to coffee-growing. Southward the land drops away to a vast plain suitable for livestock and plantation farming. The destruction in recent decades of up to 12% of the vast Amazonian rainforest is a cause for world-wide concern.

Economy A huge newly industrialized country, Brazil has the seventh largest economy in the world. Industry is concentrated in the centre and south, while the drought-prone north and north-east remain undeveloped. Only about 7% of Brazil's land area is considered arable; coffee, soya beans, cereals, and rice are important crops. Brazil is rich in minerals: it has the third largest reserves of bauxite in the world, the largest reserves of columbium, high-grade iron ore, one of the largest reserves of beryllium, as well as gold, manganese and tin in large quantities. Industries include textiles, shoes, chemicals, and cement. Brazil also has one of the world's largest capacities for hydroelectric power production. Although high inflation, foreign debt, and extreme inequalities in wealth distribution have led to severe social problems, Brazil has one of the fastest-growing economies in the world.

History Brazil is the only South American country originally established as a Portuguese colony, having been awarded to the Portuguese crown by the Treaty of Tordesillas (1494). Settlement began in 1532 with the foundation of São Vicente by Martim Afonso de *Sousa. During the first half of the 16th century twelve captaincies were established. No centralized government was established until 1549 when Thomé de Sousa was named governor-general and a capital was established at Salvador (Bahia). The north-eastern coast was lost to the Dutch briefly in the 17th century but was regained.

By 1800 the prosperity of the colony had outstripped that of Portugal. As a result of the *Napoleonic Wars, the Portuguese court was transferred to Rio de Janeiro, which was transformed into the centre of the Portuguese empire. When John VI returned to Lisbon in 1821, his son Pedro remained behind as regent. In 1822 he became Emperor Pedro I of Brazil in an almost bloodless coup and established an independent empire that lasted until the abdication of his son Pedro II in 1889. Brazil's neo-colonial economy based upon agricultural exports, such as coffee and wild rubber produced upon the fazenda (estate), and dependent on slave labour, remained virtually intact until the downfall of the country's two predominant institutions—slavery (1888) and the monarchy (1889). In 1891 Brazil became a republic with a federal constitution. The fraudulent elections of 1930 and the effects of the Great *Depression prompted the intervention of the military and the appointment of Getúlio *Vargas as provisional President. Vargas was to remain in power until he was deposed in 1945. He remained a powerful force in international politics until his suicide in 1954. Vargas' successor, Juscelino Kubitschek (1956–61) embarked upon an ambitious expansion of the economy, including the construction of a futuristic capital city at Brasília, intended to encourage development of the interior. President João Goulart (1961–64) had to face the consequent inflation and severe balance-of-payments deficit. In rural areas peasant leagues mobilized behind the cause of radical land reform. Faced with these threats, Brazil's landowners and industrialists backed the military coup of 1964 and the creation of a series of authoritarian regimes which sought to attract foreign investment. President Figueiredo (1978–84) re-established civilian rule and democracy, and under his successor José Sarne (1985–89) a new constitution was approved. Rapid industrialization, together with urbanization, had greatly increased inequalities of income. In the early 1990s very high inflation, together with an economic recession, challenged the government of President Collor de Mello, who resigned in 1992 following allegations of corruption. Itamar Franco then served as President until 1995, when Fernando Cardoso succeeded him. Cardoso pursued privatization policies that slowly strengthened the economy. He was succeeded in 2003 by Luis Ignacio Lula da Silva, the first left-wing President since the 1964 coup. Re-elected in 2006, he was succeeded in 2011 by Dilma Rousseff, his chosen candidate, who became Brazil's first woman President.

Breakspear, Nicholas *See* ADRIAN IV.

Breckinridge, John Cabell (1821–75) US politician and general. He served as a Democrat member of the House of Representatives (1851–55), before being elected as *Buchanan's Vice-President in 1856. When the Democratic Party split in 1860, he ran for President against Abraham *Lincoln as the candidate of the Southern Democrats. From November 1861, he saw extensive service as a major-general in the army of the Confederacy Party before becoming Secretary of State for War under Jefferson *Davis in 1865.

Breda A Dutch city in North Brabant, historically an important frontier town close to the Belgian border. The **Compromise of Breda** in 1566 was a league formed by Protestant and Catholic nobles and burghers to fight against *Philip II's policies in the Netherlands. The most dramatic event in its history was its surrender to the Spanish commander Spinola in 1625; it was retaken by the Dutch in 1636 and finally became part of the Netherlands in 1648. The **Declaration of Breda** was made by *Charles II in 1660 just before his Restoration, promising an amnesty, religious toleration, and payment of arrears to the army. The **Treaty of Breda** (1667) ended the second *Anglo-Dutch War.

Breitenfeld, Battles of Two battles during the *Thirty Years War, which take their name from a village near Leipzig. The first was fought on 17 September 1631, between Count Johannes Tilly's Catholic forces and the Protestant army of *Gustavus II (Adolphus) of Sweden. Despite an early advantage, Tilly's traditional infantry squares were overwhelmed by the Swedes' flexible linear tactics. Gustavus's victory was the first major Protestant success of the war, and it announced the arrival of Sweden as a power on the European stage. The second battle, on 2 November 1642, ended in another Swedish victory.

Brendan, St (*c.*486–*c.*575) Irish abbot. The legend of the 'Navigation of St Brendan' (*c.*1050), describing his voyage with a band of monks to a promised land (possibly Orkney or the Hebrides), was widely popular in the Middle Ages.

Brest-Litovsk, Treaty of (1918) An agreement between Soviet Russia, Germany, and Austria-Hungary, signed in the town of that name in Poland. The conference opened in December 1917 in order to end Soviet participation in World War I. *Trotsky skilfully prolonged discussions in the hope of Allied help for the *Russian Revolution or of a socialist uprising of German and Austro-Hungarian workers. Neither happened. *Lenin capitulated and ordered his delegates to accept the German terms. By the treaty, Russia surrendered nearly half of its European territory: Finland, the Baltic provinces, Belorussia (now Belarus), Poland, the Ukraine, and parts of the Caucasus. The German armistice in the west (November 1918) annulled the treaty, but in the *Versailles Peace Settlement Russia only regained the Ukraine.

Brétigny, Treaty of (1360) Treaty concluded between Edward III of England, and John II of France following John's defeat and capture at *Poitiers. It released John on payment of a ransom of three million crowns, brought the *Hundred Years War temporarily to a halt, and saw the English renounce claims to Anjou and Normandy while retaining Gascony and Guyenne. It was never fully implemented, and Anglo-French hostilities broke out again in 1369.

Bretton Woods Conference (1944) A United Nations monetary and financial conference. Representatives from 44 nations met at Bretton Woods, New Hampshire, USA, to consider the stabilization of world currencies and the establishment of credit for international trade in the post-war world. They drew up a project for an International Bank for Reconstruction and Development (*World Bank) which would make long-term capital available to states urgently needing such aid, and a plan for an International Monetary Fund (IMF) to finance short-term imbalances in international trade and payments. The Bank and the Fund continue as specialized agencies of the United Nations.

Brezhnev, Leonid Ilyich (1906–82) Soviet statesman. He was President of the Praesidium of the Supreme Soviet (i.e. titular head of state) (1960–64). As First Secretary of the Communist Party, he replaced *Khrushchev (1964). Through these two offices he came to exercise effective control over Soviet policy, though initially he shared power with *Kosygin. Brezhnev's period in power was marked by economic and social stagnation, the intensified persecution of dissidents, and attempted *détente, followed by renewed *Cold War, in foreign affairs. He was largely responsible for the decision to invade *Czechoslovakia in 1968, maintaining the doctrine that one socialist state may interfere in the affairs of another if the continuance of socialism is at risk.

Brian Boru (c.926–1014) The last High King of Ireland (1011). He had previously made himself ruler of Munster and Limerick in southern Ireland. In doing so Brian, ruler of the Dal Cais dynasty of Munster, overcame the influence of the powerful Uú Néill dynasty which had dominated Ireland for three centuries. In 1012 the men of Leinster, supported by the Norse settlers of Dublin, rose in revolt. The Battle of Clontarf brought victory to Brian's forces, though he was killed in the fighting.

Briand, Aristide (1862–1932) French statesman. He was 11 times Premier, and Foreign Minister in 14 successive governments. He entered Parliament in 1903, a strong socialist and an impressive orator. In 1905 he took a leading part in the separation of Church from state and by 1909 had become Premier. In the 1920s he was a powerful advocate of peace and international cooperation, and supported the League of Nations. The cabinet he headed in 1921 fell because of his criticism of France's harsh treatment of Germany after the *Versailles Peace Settlement. Working closely with Austen *Chamberlain and Gustav Stresemann, the British and German Foreign Ministers, his greatest achievements were the *Locarno Pact (1925) and the *Kellogg–Briand pact (1928).

BRIC An acronym for 'Brazil, Russia, India, China': the four states regarded as the developing countries most likely to become leading world economies in the early 21st century. The term was coined in 2001 by the economist Jim O'Neill.

Brigantes The Celtic inhabitants of northern Britain between the Humber and the Tyne, known as the 'mountain folk'. After the Roman invasion in 43 AD, Emperor Claudius formed an alliance with their queen Cartimandua. Roman troops helped suppress at least three revolts against her; she also handed over the refugee *Caratacus. During the *Roman civil wars (68–69) she was expelled by her anti-Roman husband, Venutius. Petillius Cerialis was made governor (legatus) of Britain by Vespasian; he

advanced north c.71–74 AD, and established Eboracum (York) as a permanent legionary fortress for the Ninth Legion in this former tribal territory.

Bright, John (1811–89) British Liberal politician and reformer. A noted orator, Bright was the leader, along with Richard Cobden, of the campaign to repeal the Corn Laws. He was also a vociferous opponent of the Crimean War (1854) and was closely identified with the 1867 Reform Act.

Britain (in full **Great Britain**) The island containing England, Wales, and Scotland, and including the small adjacent islands. After the Old English period 'Britain' was used only as an historical term until about the time of Henry VIII and Edward VI, when it came into practical politics in connection with the efforts made to unite England and Scotland. In 1604 James I was proclaimed 'King of Great Britain', and this name was adopted for the United Kingdom at the Union of 1707, after which 'South Britain' and 'North Britain' were frequent in Acts of Parliament for England and Scotland respectively. *See also* UNITED KINGDOM.

Britain, Battle of (August–October 1940) A series of air battles between Britain and Germany fought over Britain. After the fall of France, German aircraft launched a *bombing offensive against British coastal shipping with the aim of attracting and then destroying British fighter aircraft, as a prelude to a general invasion of Britain. This action (July–August 1940) resulted in heavy German dive-bomber losses. Attacks were then made on southern England, but German losses were again heavy. In late August and early September mass bombing raids took place on British aircraft factories, radar installations, and fighter airfields; these caused heavy British losses, but Hitler ordered the offensive to be diverted to British cities just as RAF Fighter Command was exhausting its reserves of machines and pilots. Hitler's priority of the day-bombing of London gave time for Fighter Command to recover. On 1 October day-bombing of major cities was replaced by night-bombing, but by this time it was clear that the major German objective, to destroy British air power, had failed. On 12 October Hitler postponed indefinitely his plan to invade Britain. Though heavily outnumbered by the Germans, the British lost 900 aircraft against 1,700 German losses. Radar, used by the British for the first time in battle, made a significant contribution.

British empire A network of colonies, protectorates, and other territories that for about 300 years were subject to the British crown and administration. It was superseded by the British Commonwealth, a free association of mainly self-governing nations.

The first British overseas settlements were established in the 16th century and by 1670 there were colonies in America, in New England, Virginia and Maryland. Britain had conquered Jamaica and there were British communities throughout the Caribbean. British colonization was driven by trade, with the *Hudson's Bay Company making inroads into Canada and the *East India Company setting up trading stations in India. The slave trade brought British merchants to west Africa. The empire was maintained by a strong navy and trade restrictions that kept the empire a closed economic system.

In 1800, although Britain had lost its 13 American colonies, it still retained Newfoundland, thinly populated parts of Canada, many West Indian islands, and other islands useful for trading purposes. It held Gibraltar from Spain and in 1788 had created a convict settlement in New South Wales, Australia. During the *Napoleonic Wars Britain acquired further islands, for example Malta, Mauritius, the Maldives, and also Ceylon and Cape Colony, which was particularly valuable for fresh food supplies for ships on the way to the East. Most of these belonged to the East India Company, which was steadily developing and exploiting its trade monopoly in India and beyond. All such acquisitions were seen as part of the development of British commerce, as was to be the seizure of Hong Kong in 1841. From the 1820s, a new colonial movement began, with British families taking passages abroad to develop British settlements. In 1857 the *Indian Mutiny obliged the British government to take over from the East India Company the administration of that vast sub-continent; in January 1877 Queen Victoria was proclaimed Empress of India. New tropical colonies were competed for in the "Scramble for Africa" and in the Pacific. In 1884 an Imperial Federation League was formed, seeking some form of political federation between Britain and its colonies. The scheme soon foundered, being rejected by the colonial Premiers when they gathered in London for the two Colonial Conferences of 1887 and 1897. Strategically, the key area was seen to be southern Africa, and it was the dream of Cecil *Rhodes and Alfred Milner to create a single Cape-to-Cairo British dominion, linked by a railway, and acting as the pivot of the whole

empire, a dream which faded with the Second *Boer War. Another result of the Boer War was the creation of the permanent Committee of Imperial Defence (1902), whose function was to be the coordination of the defence of the empire, and which was to continue until 1938. The empire reached its zenith after World War I, when German and Ottoman *mandates were acquired, and over 600 million people were ruled from London. In the later 19th century movements for home-rule had begun in all the White colonies. Starting in Canada, but spreading to Australasia and South Africa, such moves resulted in 1931 in *dominion status for these lands. Although the Indian National *Congress had been founded in 1885, attempts by the indigenous peoples of the empire to secure similar self-government proved more difficult. It was only after 1945 that the process of decolonization began, which by 1964 was largely complete. Most former colonies remained members of the *Commonwealth of Nations after becoming independent. Fifteen Commonwealth members (other than Britain) recognize the British monarch as head of state; the others recognize the monarch as head of the Commonwealth. Queen *Elizabeth II consented to the ending of constitutional links between Britain and Canada in 1982 and between Britain and Australia in 1986. Republican movements in Australia and New Zealand gained support during the 1980s and 1990s. Britain has 14 remaining dependent territories including Gibraltar, the Falkland Islands, and Bermuda, which rejected independence in a referendum in 1995: Hong Kong was handed back to China in 1997.

British Expeditionary Force (BEF) British army contingents sent to France at the outbreak of *World War I. Following the army reforms of Richard *Haldane a territorial reserve army had been created. This was immediately mobilized when war was declared on 4 August 1914 and, together with regular troops, sent to France under Sir John French. An expeditionary force was again mobilized and sent to France in September 1939 but, after failing to halt the German advance across the Low Countries and France, had to be rescued in the *Dunkirk evacuation.

British Honduras The former name (until 1973) of *Belize in Central America.

British North America Act (1867) A British Act of Parliament establishing the Dominion of *Canada. As the *American Civil War drew to a close there were increasing fears in British North America of US expansionist ambitions. In 1864 representatives from United Canada

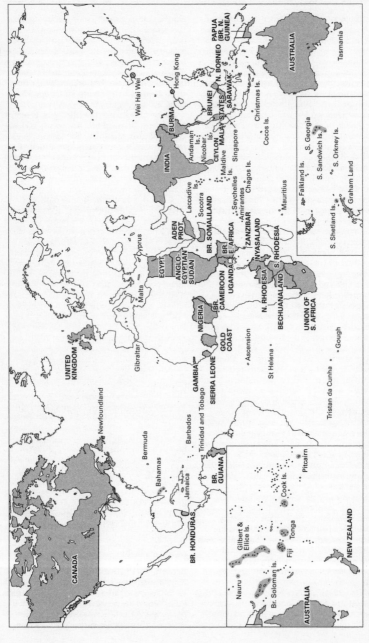

British empire. This map shows the extent of the British empire in 1914.

joined others from New Brunswick, Prince Edward Island, Nova Scotia, and Newfoundland to discuss federation. In 1867 proposals were agreed, although Prince Edward Island and Newfoundland would not ratify them. The British Parliament passed an Act in July 1867 uniting the colonies of New Brunswick and Nova Scotia with the province of Canada, which itself was to be divided into the two provinces of Quebec (Canada East) and Ontario (Canada West), thus creating 'one Dominion under the name of Canada'.

British Raj (Hindi, 'rule') The British government in India, particularly during the period from 1858 to 1947. Created gradually and haphazardly as a by-product of the *East India Company's trading objectives, the Raj's heyday was the half-century following the *Indian Mutiny (1857), which had abruptly ended Company rule. It was an age of *imperialism, symbolized by the proclamation of Queen Victoria as Empress of India (January 1877), and the viceroyalty of Lord *Curzon (1899–1905) over an empire 'on which the Sun never sets'. The Indian National *Congress, which initiated nationalist criticism of the Raj, and eventually succeeded it, was founded in 1885. The Raj ended in 1947 when Britain transferred power to the new states of India and Pakistan. British personnel withdrew, but Western modes of thought, especially through the educational system and the army, have made a continuing contribution to the character and administration of the independent countries (India, Pakistan, and Bangladesh) of the subcontinent.

Bronze Age The prehistoric period during which bronze was the principal material used for tools and weapons. The transition from the *Copper Age is difficult to fix, as is that to the *Iron Age which followed. It is now accepted that the technological advance to bronze was made on several separate occasions between 3500 and 3000 BC in the Near East, the Balkans, and south-east Asia, and not until the 15th century AD among the Aztecs of Mexico. Knowledge of the new alloy spread slowly, mainly because of the scarcity of tin, so the Bronze Age tends to have widely different dates in different parts of the world. Indeed sub-Saharan Africa and Australasia, nearly all of America, and much of Asia never experienced a Bronze Age at all.

Although much more metal came into circulation in Bronze Age cultures, the high cost of tin led to two significant results. International trade increased greatly in order to secure supplies, and greater emphasis on social stratification is noticeable practically everywhere following the introduction of bronze, as those able to produce or obtain it strengthened their power over those without it. In the Middle East the Bronze Age developed into the Iron Age from about 1200 BC, in southern Europe from about 1000 BC, and in northern Europe from about 500 BC.

The Urnfield cultures were a group of central European Bronze Age cultures associated with the Celts. Their origins are first identifiable in Hungary and Romania, dating from about the 15th century BC. They cremated their dead and placed urns of their ashes in flat graves in cemeteries.

Brooke, Sir James (1803–68) British adventurer and ruler of Sarawak (now in Malaysia) (1841–68). Arriving in Borneo in 1839 he helped one of the Brunei princes to put down a revolt and was rewarded with the governorship of Kuching in 1841. He established himself as an independent ruler (the 'White Raja') governing as a benevolent autocrat and extending his rule over much of Sarawak. Renowned for his legal reforms (which successfully adapted local custom) he resisted external attacks by Chinese opponents in 1857. Sarawak was effectively ruled by the Brooke family until the Japanese occupation of 1942–45.

Brown, Gordon (James Gordon Brown) (1951–) British politician, Prime Minister (2007–10). Born in Glasgow, he became a Labour MP in 1983. As Shadow Chancellor (1992–97), he achieved a reputation for economic competence that was important in Labour's election victory in 1997. He then became Chancellor of the Exchequer (1997–2007) and presided over almost continuous economic growth despite increased taxation. This was combined from 2001 with increased spending on education and health care. The longest-serving Chancellor for almost 200 years, Brown exercised considerable power outside his department and became Prime Minister when Tony *Blair resigned in 2007. His premiership was dominated by the *Credit Crunch and its consequences. Brown lost the general election in 2010 and immediately resigned as leader of the Labour party.

Brown, John (1800–59) US *abolitionist. Fired by a mixture of religious fanaticism and a violent hatred of slavery, Brown was responsible for the Pottawatomie massacre, in which five pro-slavery men were murdered. He rapidly emerged as one of the leading figures in the violent local struggle that was making "Bleeding Kansas" into a national issue. His most dramatic gesture came in October 1859 when, at the head of a party of about 20, he seized the federal arsenal at Harper's Ferry, Virginia, in the belief that he could precipitate a slave uprising. The arsenal was recaptured by soldiers two days later, and Brown was hanged for treason and murder.

Browne, Robert (c.1550–1633) English Protestant Nonconformist, founder of a religious sect, the 'Brownists'. His followers were the first to separate from the Anglican Church after the Reformation. His treatise *Reformation without Tarrying for Any* (1582) called for immediate separatism and doctrinal reform. Mental instability undermined his leadership and by 1591 he was reconciled to the Anglican Church. He is seen by English and American *Congregationalists as the founder of their principles of church government.

Brownshirt Member of an early Nazi paramilitary organization, the *Sturmabteilung* or SA ('assault division'). The Brownshirts, recruited from various rough elements of society, were founded by Adolf *Hitler in Munich in 1921. Fitted out in brown uniforms reminiscent of Mussolini's *Blackshirts, they figured prominently in organized marches and rallies. Their violent intimidation of political opponents and of Jews played a key role in Hitler's rise to power. From 1931 the SA was led by a radical anti-capitalist, Ernst Röhm. By 1933 it numbered some two million, double the size of the army, which was hostile to them. Röhm's ambition was that the SA should achieve parity with the army and the Nazi Party, and serve as the vehicle for a Nazi revolution in state and society. For Hitler the main consideration was to ensure the loyalty to his regime of the German establishment, and in particular of the German officer corps. Consequently, he had more than 70 members of the SA, including Röhm, summarily executed by the *SS in the 'Night of the Long Knives', after which the revolutionary period of Nazism may be said to have ended.

Bruce, Robert *See* ROBERT I (THE BRUCE).

Bruce, Stanley Melbourne, Viscount Bruce of Melbourne (1883–1967) Australian statesman. A member of the House of Representatives, he represented the Nationalists and the United Australia Party. He became Prime Minister and Minister for External Affairs in the so-called Bruce–Page government. His government's policies were summed up in the

slogan "Men, Money, and Markets". He served in the British War Cabinet and Pacific War Council (1942–45). He chaired the World Food Council (1947–51) and the British Finance Corporation for Industry (1947–57).

Brundtland, Gro Harlem (1939–) Norwegian Labour politician. After serving as Environment Minister in the Labour government, in February 1981 she became Norway's first woman Prime Minister, but only held office until October of that year. During her second premiership (1986–89) she chaired the World Commission on Environment and Development (known as the Brundtland Commission), which produced the report *Our Common Future* in 1987. In 1992, during her third term of office (1990–96), Norway's application to join the EU was accepted by Europe but voted down in a referendum (1994). Brundtland retired from politics in 1996 and was subsequently Director-General of the World Health Organization (1998–2003), a UN special envoy for climate change (2007–), and an active member of The *Elders.

Brunei

Capital:	Bandar Seri Begawan
Area:	5,765 sq km (2,226 sq miles)
Population:	415,717 (2012 est)
Currency:	1 Brunei dollar = 100 cents
Religions:	Muslim 67.0%; Buddhist 13.0%; Christian 10.0%
Ethnic Groups:	Malay 66.3%; Chinese 11.2%; indigenous 3.4%
Languages:	Malay (official); English; Chinese; minority languages
International Organizations:	UN; Commonwealth; ASEAN; Non-Aligned Movement; WTO; Colombo Plan

A small country on the north-west coast of Borneo, comprising two enclaves surrounded by Sarawak Malaysia.

Physical A narrow coastal plain of alluvium and peat changes inland to rugged hill country of infertile lateritic soils, the highest point being Bukit Belalong at 913 m (2997 feet) in the south-east. The coast is noted for its oil and natural gas, found both on shore and offshore. The climate is tropical.

Economy The economy is almost entirely dependent on oil and natural gas, but Brunei is attempting to diversify into such areas as tourism and financial services.

History By 1800 the Brunei sultanate, which had once controlled all of Borneo, had been reduced to the regions of Sarawak and Sabah. Control of Sarawak was lost to Sir James *Brooke and his successors after 1841, and in 1888 further incursions drove the sultan to accept a British protectorate, which in 1906 was extended through the appointment of a British resident. The Brunei economy was revolutionized by the discovery of substantial onshore oil deposits in 1929 and offshore oil and gas fields in the early 1960s. The sultanate was put under pressure to join the newly formed Federation of *Malaysia, provoking a brief rebellion in 1962 of Bruneians opposed to joining Malaysia. Brunei did not join, however, partly because of its natural resources. It achieved internal self-government in 1971 and de facto independence from Britain in 1983 but did not become formally independent until 1994. A state of emergency has been in force since 1962, allowing the sultan to rule by decree. During the 1990s the level of unemployment and social unrest rose. In 1991 the sultan banned the import of alcohol and the celebration of Christmas, measures designed to encourage the population to adopt strict Islamic codes of behaviour. In 2004 the Legislative Council, all of whose members were appointed by the sultan, met for the first time since 1984. In 2009 Brunei and Malaysia resolved their territorial disputes.

Brunhilda (c. 534–613) Visigothic queen of the *Merovingian kingdom of Austrasia. After her husband's assassination she tried to rule in the name of her son Childebert II but, faced with internal revolts and the opposition of the King of Neustria, she fled to Burgundy. In old age she claimed Burgundy and Austrasia in the name of her great-grandson, but Chlothar of Neustria defeated her. She is alleged to have been executed by being dragged to death by wild horses.

Brüning, Heinrich (1885–1970) German statesman. As leader of the Weimar Republic's Catholic Centre Party, he was Chancellor and Foreign Minister, 1930–32. He attempted to solve Germany's economic problems by unpopular deflationary measures, such as higher taxation, cuts in government expenditure, and

by trying to reduce *reparation payments. But after the elections of 1930 he lost support in the Reichstag and ruled by emergency decrees. He was forced to resign in 1932 by President Hindenburg, whose confidence he had lost. He escaped the 1934 purge and emigrated to the USA.

Bruno, Giordano (1548–1600) Italian philosopher. After a period in the Dominican order, he became a follower of the magical tradition of Hermes Trismegistus. He was a supporter of the heliocentric Copernican view of the solar system, envisaging an infinite universe of numerous worlds moving in space. He was tried by the Inquisition for heresy and later burned at the stake.

Bruno, St (c.1032–1101) German-born French churchman. After withdrawing to the mountains of Chartreuse in 1084, he founded the Carthusian order at La Grande Chartreuse in SE France in the same year.

Brusilov, Aleksky (1853–1926) Russian general. He won a brilliant campaign against Austria-Hungary (1916) in south-west Russia, which, although it cost Russia at least a million lives, forced Germany to divert troops from the *Somme and encouraged Romania to join the Allies. After the fall of the Russian emperor he sided with the *Bolsheviks and directed the war against Poland.

Bruton, John (Gerard) (1947–) Irish Fine Gael statesman, Prime Minister of the Republic of Ireland (1994–97).

Brutus, Marcus Junius (85–42 BC) Roman senator. With Cassius he was a leader of the conspirators who assassinated Julius Caesar in the name of the Republic in 44 BC. He and Cassius were defeated by Caesar's supporters Antony and Octavian at the Battle of Philippi in 42 BC, after which he committed suicide.

buccaneer A pirate or privateer who preyed on Spanish shipping and settlements in the Caribbean and South America in the 17th century. Mainly of British, French, and Dutch stock, buccaneers made their headquarters first on Tortuga Island off Haiti and then on Jamaica. In wartime they formed a mercenary navy for Spain's enemies, fighting with reckless bravery. Their triumphs included the sackings of Porto Bello, Panama, Chagres, New Segovia, and Maracaibo. Henry *Morgan was their most famous commander. After 1680 they penetrated to the Pacific coast of South America. Their power and prosperity rapidly declined in the early 18th century.

Buchanan, James (1791–1868) US Democratic statesman, 15th President of the USA (1857–61). He consistently leaned towards the pro-slavery side in the developing dispute over slavery. Towards the end of his term the issue grew more fraught and he retired from politics in 1861.

Buckingham, George Villiers, 1st Duke of (1592–1628) English statesman, favourite of *James I and Charles I. In 1615 James appointed Villiers, a young man of no distinction but attractive to the king, to the office of Gentleman of the Bedchamber. Thereafter he amassed fortune and power for himself and his followers by distributing offices and favours. His personal extravagance, promotion of Archbishop *Laud, and political incompetence combined to tarnish the reputation of the court. After Charles's accession in 1625 Buckingham remained the king's policy-maker, ignored Parliament's hostility towards war, and insisted on a costly campaign against Spain, which ended in a disastrous expedition to Cadiz in 1625. Parliament attempted to impeach him, charging him with corruption and financial mismanagement, but the king dissolved Parliament and Buckingham pursued campaigns against both France and Spain, personally leading an unsuccessful expedition to the relief of the *Huguenots at La Rochelle. In 1628 he was murdered by a soldier aggrieved by the mismanagement of the war.

Buddha A title given to successive teachers (past and future) of Buddhism, although it usually denotes the founder of Buddhism, Siddhartha Gautama (*c*.563 BC–*c*.480 BC). Although born an Indian prince (in what is now Nepal), he renounced his kingdom, wife, and child to become an ascetic, taking religious instruction until he attained enlightenment (nirvana) through meditation beneath a bo tree in the village of Bodhgaya. He then taught all who wanted to learn, regardless of sex, class, or caste, until his death. 'Buddha' means 'enlightened' in Sanskrit.

Buddhism A major world religion numbering over 300 million followers (exact estimates are impossible since Buddhism does not preclude other religious beliefs). Early Buddhism developed from *Hinduism through the teaching of Siddhartha Gautama (the *Buddha) and his disciples, around the 5th century BC in northern India. Under leaders such as the emperor *Asoka, who converted to Buddhism and en-

couraged its spread, the religion provided a stabilizing political structure throughout India. Offering a way to salvation that did not depend on caste or the ritualism of the Brahmin priesthood of Hinduism, and strengthened by a large, disciplined monastic order (the *sangha*), it made a very great impact; but by the end of the 1st millennium AD it had lost ground to a resurgent Hinduism, and the subsequent Muslim invasions virtually extinguished it in India. Meanwhile however, monks had taken the faith all over Asia, to central and northern areas now in Afghanistan, Mongolia, China, Japan, Korea and Vietnam; and in south and south-east Asia to Sri Lanka, Myanmar (Burma), Thailand, Cambodia, and Laos. The final phase of Buddhist expansion, after the 7th century, saw the emergence of Tantric and Tibetan Buddhism.

Owing to its linguistic diversity and geographical extent, Buddhist teaching, scriptures, and observance are complex and varied, but certain main doctrines are characteristic. Buddhism asserts that all phenomena are linked together in an endless chain of dependency. Buddhism teaches that the suffering of the world is caused by desire conditioned by ignorance, but that by following the path of the Buddha, release from the cycle of rebirth can be achieved.

Mahayana Buddhism arose in the 1st century AD and spread mainly throughout northern Asia. It uses supplementary texts written in Sanskrit and emphasizes the value of seeking enlightenment for the sake of others, rather than as a purely personal goal. **Theravada** Buddhism is based on the *tripitaka*, original teachings of the Buddha, written in Pali. Theravada emphasizes individual enlightenment. **Zen** Buddhism was influenced by Daoism and originated in China in the 7th century, taking hold in Japan in the 12th century. Zen Buddhists believe in *satori*, sudden enlightenment that is achieved under the guidance of a teacher by practising meditation, intellectual exercises, and physical endurance tests.

The last two centuries have demonstrated the resilience of Buddhism and its ability to communicate across cultural barriers. Despite communist revolutions, Western technology, and commercialism, its teaching and its ancient meditation techniques have maintained their appeal. Attempts to revive Buddhism in India are indebted to the impetus of the Theosophical Society, the spread of neo-Buddhism, particularly among the outcastes by *Ambedkar and, in recent times, the presence of Tibetan Buddhist refugees. In Thailand, Buddhism continues to enjoy royal patronage, and the work of the

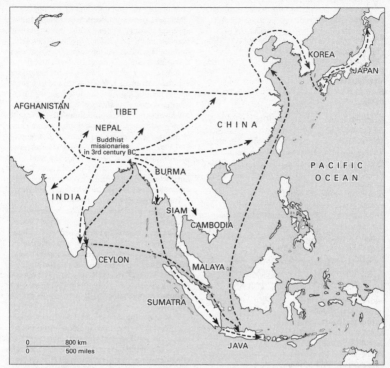

Buddhism. This map shows the extent of Buddhism in about 1000 AD. The expansion of Buddhism beyond India can be traced to the reign of Asoka (273–232 BC), a convert to the religion. He sent out missions, notably to Anuradhapura, capital of Ceylon (Sri Lanka), where Buddhism was established by a relative, perhaps a son. The adoption of Buddhism in other countries was gradual. By the 1st century AD it was spreading throughout central Asia along the SILK ROAD and was known in China, although it did not become widely popular there for another four centuries. From China it reached Korea in the 4th century and Japan in the 6th century, challenging Shinto for a time. It was established in Sumatra and Java in the 5th century and had also spread to Siam (Thailand), Cambodia, and Tibet by the 7th century. Meanwhile Buddhism was in decline in India, where Hinduism was becoming the dominant religion.

sangha is seen as an important factor in social development in the region. Buddhism has survived even in communist China, while in Japan the Pure Land sects of Mahayana Buddhism remain popular. Like Zen, they are also represented in the USA and Europe.

Buganda *See* UGANDA.

Bugis Muslim mercenaries and traders of south-east Asia. They were enterprising seamen and traders living in villages in Sulawesi (Celebes). When Macassar fell to the Dutch (1667)

they lost their livelihood. Thereafter they sought employment as mercenaries and engaged in piracy in Borneo, Java, Sumatra, and Malaya. They fought for and against the Dutch. They suffered a reverse when their leader Raja Haji was killed while assaulting Malacca (1784), but went on to found states, such as Selangor and Riao, on the Malay peninsula.

Bulganin, Nikolai (Aleksandrovich)
(1895–1975) Soviet statesman, Chairman of the Council of Ministers (Premier) (1955–58). Born

in Russia, he succeeded Stalin as Minister of Defence in 1946, and was appointed Vice-Premier in the government of Georgi Malenkov in 1953. Following Malenkov's resignation in 1955, Bulganin became Premier, sharing power with Nikita Khrushchev, who replaced him.

Bulgaria

Capital:	Sofia
Area:	110,879 sq km (42,811 sq miles)
Population:	6,981,642 (2012 est)
Currency:	1 lev = 100 stotinki
Religions:	Eastern Orthodox 59.4%; Muslim 7.8%
Ethnic Groups:	Bulgarian 76.9%; Turkish 8.0%; Roma 4.4%
Languages:	Bulgarian (official); Turkish; Romany; Macedonian; minority languages
International Organizations:	UN; OSCE; NATO; Council of Europe; WTO; EU

A country of the Balkan Peninsula in south-east Europe. It is bordered by Romania to the north, Serbia and Macedonia to the west, Greece and Turkey to the south, and the Black Sea.

Physical The northern boundary of Bulgaria is formed by the River Danube, except in the north-east; about 80 km (50 miles) to the south the long Planina range of Balkan Mountains runs parallel to the river, dividing the country laterally.

Economy Until 1989 Bulgaria was a communist republic closely allied to the Soviet Union. An economic reform programme was introduced in 1991 with the support of the IMF; this involved the return of collectivized land to former owners and the privatization of small businesses. The removal of subsidies from food and other basic commodities caused considerable hardship and further reform stalled until 1994, when a mass privatization programme was launched. In 1996 the country was engulfed by an acute financial crisis when the national currency, the lev, collapsed. Following significant reforms, the mid-2000s saw fast economic growth. This ended with the global recession of 2009, and recovery has been slow. Bulgaria's mineral resources include coal, iron ore, cop-

per, lead, zinc, and petroleum from the Black Sea. Agricultural products include fruit and vegetables, tobacco, and wine, and important industries include electricity generation, gas production, and food processing. Tourism is a growing source of revenue.

History Bulgaria was settled by central Asian tribesmen in the 5th century, colonized by the Romans, and then invaded by Slav Bulgars. They killed Emperor Nicephorus in 811 AD, and captured *Adrianople in 813. Christianity was introduced in the 9th century. Greek and *Magyar threats were repulsed but rebellion, and incursions by Greeks, Russians, and Serbs resulted in the kingdom being divided into three in the 11th century. It was annexed by the *Ottoman empire in 1396 and ruled by the Turks for nearly five centuries.

In the 19th century Bulgarian nationalism led to a series of insurrections against the Ottoman Turks culminating in 1876, when several thousand Bulgars were massacred. Russia gave its support to Bulgaria, and war between Russia and Turkey followed. This was ended by the Treaty of San Stefano (March 1878) which created a practically independent Bulgaria covering three-fifths of the Balkan Peninsula. Britain, however, now feared that the new state would become a puppet of Russia. The Congress of *Berlin (1878) therefore split the country into Bulgaria and Eastern Roumelia, which remained nominally under Turkish rule. In 1879 a democratic constituent assembly elected the German Prince, Alexander of Battenburg, as ruling prince and in 1885 Alexander incorporated Eastern Roumelia into Bulgaria. For this he was kidnapped by Russian officers and forced to abdicate. His successor was another German prince, Ferdinand of Saxe-Coburg (1887–1918). Taking advantage of the *Young Turk movement Ferdinand formally proclaimed full independence from Turkish rule in 1908, and was crowned king. Participation in World War I on the side of Germany led to invasion by the Allies (1916), and the loss of territory through the *Versailles peace settlement. Between 1919 and 1923 Bulgaria was virtually a peasant-dictatorship under Alexander Stamboliyski, the leader of the Agrarian Union. He was murdered and an attempt by communists under *Dimitrov to seize power followed. Military and political instability persisted until 1935, when an authoritarian government was set up by Boris III (1918–43). World War II saw cooperation with Nazi Germany, followed by invasion by the Soviet Union. In 1946 the monarchy was abolished and a communist state proclaimed,

Bulgaria becoming the most consistently pro-Soviet member of the *Warsaw pact countries. In 1989 the communist leader Todor Zhivkov, who had been in office since 1954, was ousted from power. Free elections followed, with a new constitution in 1990. The introduction of privatization and other economic reforms has proved particularly painful in Bulgaria. After elections in 1994 a coalition government was formed (1995), led by the former Communist Party (renamed the Bulgarian Socialist Party, BSP). The BSP was defeated by the Union of Democratic Forces in elections in 1997. In 2001 the former king, Simeon II, became Prime Minister. He was replaced in 2005 by Sergei Stanishev, at the head of a BSP-led coalition. Bulgaria joined NATO in 2004 and the EU in 2007. Following the 2009 election the Citizens for European Development of Bulgaria, a new centre-right party, formed a minority government under Boiko Borisov. He resigned in 2013 in response to popular protests. After the subsequent election a BSP-led coalition was formed with the independent Plamen Oresharski as Prime Minister.

Bulge, Battle of the See ARDENNES CAMPAIGN.

Bülow, Bernard, Prince von (1849–1920) German statesman. He served in the *Franco–Prussian War and the German Foreign Service before becoming German Foreign Minister (1897–1900) and then Chancellor (1900–09) under *William II. In domestic policies he was a cautious conservative, but in foreign affairs his policies were to support the emperor's wish for German imperial expansion. Following the *Boer War, when William openly supported the Boers, von Bülow improved relations with Britain, who suggested in 1900 that Germany might assist to support the decaying regime of Abdul Aziz in Morocco. France was also interested and following the *entente* with Britain (1904) the latter supported its claim. At first von Bülow retaliated by sending the emperor on a provocative visit to Tangier (1905), when Franco-German tension developed. He then, however, helped to convene the *Algeciras Conference (1906) and in 1909 agreed that France be the protector of *Morocco. He supported the Austrian annexation of *Bosnia and Herzegovina, a move that helped precipitate *World War I. Von Bülow retired when he lost the support of the Reichstag in 1909.

Bunche, Ralph (1904–71) US administrator and diplomat. During World War II, he served with the joint chiefs-of-staff and the State De-partment. In 1946 he joined the secretariat of the United Nations and served on the UN Palestine Commission in 1947. After Count *Bernadotte was assassinated in 1948, he carried on negotiations between the warring Arabs and Jews with such skill that he was able to arrange an armistice between them. For this achievement he was awarded (1950) the Nobel Peace Prize, the first awarded to a Black American.

Bunker Hill, Battle of (17 June 1775) A battle in the American War of *Independence ending in a British victory. Thomas *Gage, the British commander besieged in Boston, sent 2400 troops (redcoats) to take the heights occupied by 1600 Americans under William Prescott. Only after three bloody uphill assaults, costing 1000 British against 400 American casualties, were they successful.

Burger, Warren E. (1907–95) Chief Justice of the US Supreme Court (1969–86). In 1955 he was appointed judge in the Court of Appeal in the District of Columbia. A conservative republican, he was appointed by President Nixon as Chief Justice of the Supreme Court in May 1969, to succeed Chief Justice *Warren. He did not, however, seek to reverse all the liberal judgements of his predecessor, especially when civil rights were concerned. In 1971 the Court supported a policy of *busing to lessen racial segregation in schools, but in 1974 its judgement on *Milliken* v. *Bradley* accepted the reality of racial segregation by housing. In the 1978 Bakke case it supported "positive discrimination" in favour of disadvantaged candidates for university admission, i.e. Black or Hispanic students, even though it also ruled that in this particular case a rejected White candidate, Allan Bakke, be admitted. Burger also voted in favour of the right to have an abortion (*Roe* v. *Wade*; 1973). In 1974 Burger wrote a judgement for the case of *United States* v. *Richard M. Nixon*, in which he confirmed that the Supreme Court and not the President was the final arbiter of the US Constitution.

Burghley, Lord See CECIL, WILLIAM.

Burgoyne, John (known as 'Gentleman Johnny Burgoyne') (1722–92) British general and dramatist. He is largely remembered for surrendering to the Americans at Saratoga (1777) in the War of American Independence. His plays include the comedies *The Maid of the Oaks* (1774) and *The Heiress* (1786).

Burgundy A former duchy in south-central France. The Burgundii, a Germanic tribe, settled there in the 5th century. It was under Merovingian control and then absorbed into the *Carolingian empire. Thereafter it was divided between France and the Holy Roman Empire, with the 'duchy of Burgundy' being confined to the part under French rule. From the late 14th century French and imperial Burgundy (Franche-Comté) were reunited under a series of strong dukes. *Philip the Bold also acquired Flanders and *Philip the Good the Netherlands. Geographically the separation of these territories made government difficult and *Charles the Bold tried, but failed, to unite his northern and southern lands by annexing Lorraine. He was killed in 1477, leaving no son to succeed. Louis XI of France seized the duchy of Burgundy and Picardy, but Franche-Comté, Flanders, and the Netherlands passed by marriage to the Habsburg *Maximilian I. The final subjection of Burgundy to France occurred when Louis XIV seized Franche-Comté in 1674.

During its history the duchy had achieved great power and influence, its court in the 15th century being the most splendid in Europe. Certainly some of its dukes were more powerful than many kings of France and when they allied themselves with the English, as they did during the *Hundred Years War, they posed a real threat to the security of the French monarch. The court of the dukes of Burgundy was renowned for its artistic patronage; the name Burgundian School is applied to a group of Flemish panel painters and miniaturists working for them between 1390 and 1420.

Burke, Edmund (1729–97) British man of letters and Whig politician. Burke was a prolific writer on the issues of political emancipation and moderation, supporting proposals for relaxing the laws against Roman Catholics in Britain and protesting against the harsh handling of the American colonies. He was a fierce opponent of the radical excesses of the French Revolution, calling on European leaders to resist the new regime in the influential *Reflections on the Revolution in France* (1790).

Burkina Faso

Capital:	Ouagadougou
Area:	274,200 sq km (105,869 sq miles)
Population:	17,812,961 (2012 est)
Currency:	1 CFA franc = 100 centimes
Religions:	Muslim 60.5%; Roman Catholic 19.0%; traditional beliefs 15.3%
Ethnic Groups:	Mossi: over 40%; Mande, Fulani, Lobi, Bobo, Senufo, Grunshi, and other minorities
Languages:	French (official); Mossi; Dyula; Fulani; Lobi; local languages
International Organizations:	UN; AU; Non-Aligned Movement; Franc Zone; ECOWAS; WTO

A landlocked country in West Africa surrounded by Mali, Niger, Benin, Togo, Ghana, and Côte d'Ivoire.

Physical Burkina Faso lies on a plateau, rising highest in the west and cut in the centre by the north–south route of the Volta River. The soils are mostly coarse and sandy, based on hard rock; the climate is hot and arid, and the natural vegetation except in the river valleys is thornscrub and thin savannah.

Economy Burkina Faso is one of the poorest countries in the world, heavily dependent on western aid. The economy is mainly agricultural and vulnerable to drought, with most of the population engaged in subsistence agriculture. The major exports are gold and cotton. There is some industry, with largely unexploited mineral deposits of manganese and zinc. Many Burkinabé seek employment abroad.

History Before French colonization in the 19th century the region was ruled by a number of Mossi states. It was a French protectorate from 1898, originally as part of French Sudan (now Mali) and later as Haute Volta (Upper Volta). It became an autonomous republic within the *French Community in 1958 and independent in 1960. Following a military coup in 1970, a new constitution was adopted in 1977. A series of military governments followed, including those of Captain Thomas Sankara, who was assassinated in 1987, and Blaise Compaore. The latter ended military rule in June 1991 and held multiparty elections. Compaore's Popular Front won these, and he became President. However, the opposition parties had withdrawn their candidates and there was a widespread boycott of the elections because of alleged corruption. Legislative elections, held in 1992, were won by Compaore's supporters. Compaore and his party (now called the Congress for Democracy and Progress Party) have held power since then, with the opposition continuing to boycott elections until 2002. In 2011 popular and military unrest over rising prices and unpaid salaries challenged Campaore's authority, but his regime survived. He was deposed by a military coup in 2014.

Burma See MYANMAR.

Burma Campaigns (January 1942–August 1945) In 1942 two Japanese divisions advanced into Burma (now *Myanmar), accompanied by the Burma National Army of *Aung San, capturing Rangoon, and forcing the British garrison to begin the long evacuation west. The Japanese reached Lashio at the southern end of the 'Burma Road', thus cutting off the supply link from India to Nationalist China. They captured Mandalay (May 1942) and the British forces under General *Alexander withdrew to the Indian frontier. During 1943 there were attempts to reassert control over the Arakan, but these failed, although General *Wingate with his Chindit units organized effective guerrilla activity behind Japanese lines, where an originally pro-Japanese population was becoming increasingly disillusioned. Early in the spring of 1944 heavy fighting took place in defence of Imphal, when an attempted Japanese invasion of Assam/Northern India was deflected in a series of bloody battles, of which Kohima was the most important. In October a three-pronged offensive was launched by British, Commonwealth, US, and Chinese Nationalist troops, and in January 1945 the Burma Road was re-opened. By now a discontented Aung San had contacted *Mountbatten and in March his troops joined the Allies. Rangoon was finally captured on 1 May 1945.

Burnet, Gilbert (1643–1715) Scottish churchman and historian. He sought advancement in England from 1674, but moved to the Continent on the accession of James II. He became adviser to William of Orange, accompanying him to England in 1688, and was rewarded with the bishopric of Salisbury in 1689. His greatest work was *The History of My Own Times*, published after his death.

Burns, John Elliott (1858–1943) British trade union leader and politician. He had been a factory worker as a child, and was largely self-educated, becoming a radical socialist. The 1889 *London Dockers' strike owed much of its success to his leadership. Burns was one of the first Labour representatives to be elected to

Parliament (1892), but he fell out with Keir *Hardie and turned his back on socialism. As a supporter of the Liberal Party he became President of the Local Government Board (1905–14) and introduced the first Town Planning Act (1909). He was President of the Board of Trade in 1914 but resigned from the cabinet in protest against Britain's entry into World War I.

Burr, Aaron (1756–1836) US Democratic Republican statesman. After losing the presidential election to *Jefferson in 1800, Burr was elected Vice-President. He was defeated in the contest for the governorship of New York in 1804, largely through the campaign of his rival Alexander *Hamilton. Later the same year Burr killed Hamilton in a duel.

Burton, Sir Richard Francis (1821–90) Anglo-Irish scholar and explorer. He joined the Indian Army in 1842 and while employed in military intelligence, he claimed to have learnt 35 languages. He travelled widely; in 1853, disguised as a Pathan, he went on a pilgrimage to Mecca. In 1857–59 he led an expedition into uncharted east central Africa to discover the source of the White *Nile. It reached the great lakes of East Africa, but it was Burton's companion John *Speke who made the final discovery. Later Burton explored West Africa and South America.

He drafted over 80 volumes on the sociology and anthropology of the countries he visited, most of which were published. He also published over 20 volumes of translations, including an unexpurgated translation of *The Arabian Nights*.

Burundi

Capital:	Bujumbura
Area:	27,834 sq km (10,747 sq miles)
Population:	10,888,321 (2012 est)
Currency:	1 Burundi franc = 100 centimes
Religions:	Roman Catholic 61.4%; Protestant 21.4%
Ethnic Groups:	Hutu 85.0%; Tutsi 14.0%; Twa Pygmy 1.0%
Languages:	Rundi, French (both official); Swahili
International Organizations:	UN; AU; Non-Aligned Movement; WTO

A small landlocked country on the east side of Lake Tanganyika in east central Africa. It is bounded to the north by Rwanda, to the east and south by Tanzania and to the west by the Democratic Republic of Congo.

Physical Burundi straddles the watershed of the Congo and the Nile rivers, while the Ruzizi River in the west flows along the Great Rift Valley.

Economy Burundi's economy depends heavily on foreign aid. The main exports are coffee and tea, with cotton and sugar as subsidiary exports. The biggest sector of employment is subsistence agriculture. There are large unexploited nickel deposits, and uranium, vanadium, and gold. Industry is limited. From the late 1980s until the 2000s the economy was disrupted by endemic ethnic violence and an acute refugee problem.

History Burundi was ruled as a monarchy in the 19th century by *Bami* (kings) of the Tutsi tribe, who dominated a population of Hutu. Germany annexed it as part of German East Africa in the 1890s and from 1914 it was administered by Belgium, which obtained a League of Nations mandate and ruled it as a part of Ruanda-Urundi. In 1962 it became independent and in 1964 its union with Ruanda (now Rwanda) was dissolved. Burundi became a republic after a coup in 1966, but tribal rivalries and violence obstructed the evolution of central government. There were military coups in 1976 and 1987, and renewed ethnic violence in 1988 that left 5000 Hutu dead. In 1991 a referendum voted to restore the constitution with 'democracy within the single party'. President Pierre Buyoya (a Tutsi) increased the Hutu membership of his Council of Ministers, but violence continued with many seeking refuge in Zaire and Rwanda. In 1992 a multiparty constitution was adopted. The first Hutu head of state, Melchior Ndadaye, was elected in 1993, along with a Hutu majority in the National Assembly, ending political dominance by the Tutsi. Tutsi army officers staged an unsuccessful coup six days after Ndadaye's election, but in a second coup a few months later killed Ndadaye and many other Hutu politicians. The coup triggered fierce ethnic violence and massacres throughout Burundi and over a million refugees fled their homes, many going to neighbouring countries. Ndadaye's successor, another Hutu, was killed in a plane crash in 1994. Violence and instability continued, with ethnic killings

reaching an average of 1,000 a month in 1996. In July of that year a Tutsi-led military coup ousted President Sylvestre Ntibantunganya and installed Pierre Buyoya in his place. A power-sharing agreement in 2001 gradually restored stability, and a new constitution in 2005 paved the way for the peaceful election of Pierre Nkurunziza as President later that year. Difficulties remain, however: all opposition parties boycotted the 2010 presidential and legislative elections, which resulted in Nkurunziza's unopposed re-election; and some rebel groups remain active.

Bush, George (Herbert Walker) (1924–) US Republican statesman, 41st President of the USA (1989–93). He was director of the CIA from 1976 to 1977, and President Reagan's Vice-President from 1981 to 1988. As President, he negotiated further arms reductions with the Soviet Union and organized international action to liberate Kuwait following the Iraqi invasion in 1990 (*see* GULF WAR).

Bush, George W. (George Walker Bush) (1946–) US Republican statesman, 43rd President of the USA (2001–9). The son of George (Herbert Walker) *Bush, he worked in the oil industry before becoming Governor of Texas in 1995. The presidential election of 2000, in which he stood against Vice-President Al Gore, produced a disputed result and Bush was only declared the winner after a protracted legal battle. Bush responded to the outrage of *September 11, 2001, by announcing a *war on terrorism and ordering military action against Afghanistan. In collaboration with the UK, but without explicit authorization from the UN, Bush instigated the *Iraq War of 2003 on the grounds that Saddam *Hussein was producing weapons of mass destruction. Hussein and his regime were crushed but no such weapons were found. Bush was elected for a second term in 2004, but his popularity subsequently declined, in part because of increasing dissatisfaction with the USA's continuing role in Iraq. He was criticized for his administration's response to *Hurricane Katrina, and measures to counteract the effects of the *Credit Crunch were also controversial.

bushranger Law-breaker who lived in the Australian bush. The term came into use in the early 19th century and the first bushrangers were escaped convicts such as John Donahoe. They often operated in well-organized gangs and attacked both White settlers and *Aborigines.

busing (or **bussing**) An educational policy introduced in the USA in the 1960s. Children were taken by bus from Black, White, or Hispanic neighbourhoods, usually to suburban schools, in order to secure racially integrated schooling. The desegregation movement had mainly affected the southern states, where busing was first introduced, against strong opposition from White families. *De facto* segregation also existed in many northern cities, since the central areas were often inhabited entirely by Black families. In 1971 the Supreme Court approved the principle of busing. In 1972 Congress ordered that further schemes should be delayed. Busing remained a controversial issue and its use steadily declined as a means of racial integration.

Bustamante, Sir Alexander (William Alexander Bustamante) (1884–1977) Jamaican statesman. He was a labour leader and founder of the Jamaican Labour Party, and became his country's first Prime Minister (1962–65) after independence from Britain in 1962. During this time he initiated an ambitious five-year plan which embraced major public works projects, agrarian reform, and social welfare.

Bute, John Stuart, 3rd Earl of (1713–92) Scottish courtier and Tory statesman, Prime Minister (1762–63). His influence with George III ensured his appointment as Premier, but he was widely disliked and soon fell out of favour with the king.

Buthelezi, Chief Mangosuthu (Gatsha) (1928–) South African politician. In 1953 he was appointed assistant to the Zulu king Cyprian, a position he held until 1968. He was elected leader of Zululand (later KwaZulu) in 1970 and was responsible for the revival of the Inkatha movement, of which he became leader in 1975. He was appointed Minister of Home Affairs in Nelson Mandela's Cabinet (1994), but was dismissed by Thabo Mbeki following the 2004 elections.

Butler, Richard Austen, Baron Butler of Saffron Walden (1902–82) British politician. He was President of the Board of Education (1941–45) and was responsible for the Education Act of 1944, which inaugurated universal free secondary education in England and Wales. He was an important influence in persuading the Conservative Party to accept the principles of the *welfare state. Butler held several ministerial posts between 1951 and 1964, including Chancellor of the Exchequer (1951–55), but was defeated in the contest for the leadership of the Conservative Party by

Harold *Macmillan in 1957 and again by Sir Alec *Douglas-Home in 1963.

Buxar, Battle of (22 October 1764) A decisive battle at the town of Buxar in north-east India, which confirmed the *East India Company's control of Bengal and Bihar. Facing the Company were the combined forces of the *Mogul emperor (Shah Alam), the governor of Oudh (Shuja ad-Daula), and the dispossessed governor of Bengal (Mir Qasim). The Company's victory achieved recognition of its predominance in the region, demonstrated by the transfer of the *diwani* (revenue collecting powers) to the Company's agents in 1765.

Byng, George, Viscount Torrington (1663–1733) English admiral. He received promotion for his loyalty to William of Orange, and gained a great reputation for his successes in the War of the *Spanish Succession. His most famous battle was in 1718 at Cape Passaro, when he sank a Spanish fleet which was attempting to take Sicily. His son John (1704–57) owed his rapid and somewhat undeserved promotion to his father's influence. He was sent with an inadequate force in 1756 to save Minorca, then under siege by the French, and to protect Gibraltar, but returned to England having failed to do either. He was court-martialled for negligence and shot.

Byzantine empire The eastern half of the Roman empire. Emperor *Constantine (306–34) had reunited the two halves, divided by Diocletian (284–305), and had refounded the Greek city of Byzantium as his eastern capital, calling it Constantinople (now *Istanbul) (330). At his death in 395 Emperor *Theodosius divided the empire between his sons. After the fall of Rome to the *Ostrogoths (476) Constantinople was the capital of the empire and was famous for its art, architecture, and wealth. While barbarian invaders overran the Western empire, the Byzantine emperors always hoped to defeat them and reunite the empire. Emperor *Justinian reconquered North Africa and part of Italy, making Ravenna the western capital, but his success was shortlived.

After *Muhammad's death (632) Muslim Arab forces swept through Persia and the Middle East, across North Africa, and into Spain. By 750 only the Balkans and Asia Minor remained unconquered. From the 9th century *Charlemagne's Frankish empire dominated the West. In the 8th and 9th centuries religious disunity, notably the *Iconoclastic controversy, weakened the empire. Theological and political differences between Rome and Constantinople led to the *East–West Schism between Latin and Orthodox Christianity. (1054). The vigorous emperor Alexius *Comnenus (1081–1118) defeated barbarian attacks from the north and appealed to the Franks for help against the *Seljuk Turks. In the 12th century, some reconquests were made in Asia Minor and the period was one of achievement in literature and art, only brought to an end by the Frankish sack of Constantinople in 1204. The failure to achieve any united Christian opposition to the Turks and the growing independence of the Balkan princedoms weakened the empire. Ottoman incursions in the 14th and 15th centuries culminated in the capture of Constantinople in 1453 and the end of the empire.

Byzantium *See* ISTANBUL.

cabal A group or association of political intriguers; any political group that pursues its aims by underhand methods. In 17th-century England the word was used somewhat misleadingly of *Charles II's ministers, who did not form a united group, but the initials of whose names, Clifford, Ashley, Buckingham, Arlington, and Lauderdale, happened to spell *cabal*.

Cabeza de Vaca, Alvar Núñez (*c*.1490–*c*.1557) Spanish soldier. He pursued a military career, serving in Europe before joining Pánfilo de *Narváez in an expedition to Florida in 1527. When it failed, he and three other survivors spent ten years trekking 6000 miles through the south of North America and back to New Spain. He hoped to command another expedition, but delays in returning to Spain lost him the opportunity. Instead he was made governor of Rio de La Plata, and led two 1000-mile expeditions through the jungles and up the Rio Paraguay in 1541 and 1542. Arrested in 1543 by jealous colleagues, whom he had prohibited from looting and enslaving the local Indians, he was returned to Spain in chains. His sentence of eight years' exile in Africa was annulled, however, and a royal pension enabled him to write his *Commentarios* on his South American treks.

cabinet The group of ministers responsible for implementing government policy. The cabinet may make collective decisions, as it does in the UK and most European democracies, or it may have only an advisory status, as in the case of the President's cabinet in the USA. The size and membership of cabinets vary, but the holders of the major offices of state, such as the ministers responsible for finance, defence, and foreign affairs, are always included. The monarchs of England always had advisers, but it was not until the *Restoration in 1660 that a cabinet (or cabinet council) developed, consisting of the major office-bearers, and the most trusted members of the Privy Council, meeting as a committee in a private room (the cabinet, whence its name) and taking decisions without consulting the full Privy Council. In the time of Queen *Anne it became the main machinery of executive government and the Privy Council became formal. From about 1717 the monarch *George I ceased to attend and from that time the cabinet met independently. *George III became obliged, through insanity and age, to leave more and more to his ministers, but it was not until after the Reform Act of 1832 that the royal power diminished and cabinets came to depend, for their existence and policies, upon the support of the majority in the House of Commons.

Cabot, John (Italian name **Giovanni Caboto**) (*c*.1450–*c*.1498) Italian explorer and navigator. He and his son **Sebastian** (*c*.1475–1557) sailed from Bristol in 1497 with letters patent from Henry VII of England in search of Asia, but in fact discovered the mainland of North America. The site of their arrival is uncertain (it may have been Cape Breton Island, Newfoundland, or Labrador). John Cabot returned to Bristol and undertook a second expedition in 1498. Sebastian made further voyages of exploration after his father's death, most notably to Brazil and the River Plate (1526).

Cabral, Amilcar (1924–73) Guinean revolutionary. He founded a clandestine liberation organization against Portuguese rule. From 1963–1973 he led a successful guerrilla campaign which had gained control of much of the interior before he was assassinated, supposedly by a Portuguese agent. In the following year Portuguese Guinea became independent as *Guinea-Bissau.

CACM *See* CENTRAL AMERICAN COMMON MARKET.

Cadbury, George (1839–1922) British cocoa and chocolate manufacturer and social reformer. He and his brother Richard (1835–99) took over their father's business in 1861 and established Cadbury Brothers. Committed Quakers, they greatly improved working conditions and in 1879 George Cadbury moved the works to a new factory on a rural site (which he called Bournville) outside Birmingham, where he subsequently built a housing estate intended primarily for his workers.

Cade, John (known as **'Jack'**) (died 1450) Irish rebel. In 1450 he assumed the name of Mortimer and led the Kentish rebels against Henry VI. They occupied London for three days and executed both the treasurer of England and the sheriff of Kent. When many of the rebels accepted an offer of pardon, Cade fled, but died of a wound received in an attempt to capture him.

Cadwallon (or **Cadwalader**) (died 633) King of Gwynedd, north Wales. His hatred of the Anglo-Saxon kingdom of *Northumbria intensified when his attempts at invasion (629) failed and he was forced to flee to Ireland. Although a Christian, he next allied with the heathen King Penda of Mercia. Their victory at Hatfield Chase (632) over Edwin of Northumbria was followed by the devastation of Northumbria. Thereafter Northumbrian fortunes recovered and Cadwallon was killed in battle by Edwin's nephew Oswald at Heavenfield, near Hexham.

Caesar, Julius (Gaius Julius Caesar) (100–44 BC) Roman general and dictator. Born into a Patrician family, he became Pontifex Maximus (High Priest) in 63 BC as part of a deal with *Pompey and *Crassus, the so-called 'First Triumvirate'; as consul in 59 he obtained the provinces of Illyricum and Cisalpine and Transalpine *Gaul. A superb general, able to inspire loyalty in his soldiers, he subjugated Gaul, crossed the River Rhine, and made two expeditions to Britain. He refused to surrender command until he had secured a second consulship for 48 BC, which would render him immune from prosecution by his enemies, by now including Pompey. When the Senate delivered an ultimatum in January 49, he crossed the *Rubicon, took Rome, and defeated Pompey at Pharsalus in 48. He demonstrated clemency by permitting those who wished to do so to return to Italy. After campaigns in Asia Minor, Egypt, Africa, and Spain he returned to Rome in 45.

He governed Rome as dictator, finally as 'perpetual' dictator. His wide-ranging programme of reform, which included the institution of the Julian *calendar, reveals his breadth of vision, but he flaunted his ascendancy and ignored republican traditions. A conspiracy was formed, led by *Brutus and Cassius, and he was assassinated on the Ides (15th) of March 44.

Caesars A branch of the aristocratic Roman Julia clan, the name of which passed from its most famous member Julius *Caesar to become an imperial title. All succeeding Roman emperors adopted it, conferring the title on their designated heirs so that it came to signify a 'prince'. The name and title was used in the Eastern empire as 'Kaisaros'. From this were later derived the imperial Russian and German titles Tsar and Kaiser.

Caetano, Marcello José das Neves Alves (1904–81) Portuguese statesman. He was Prime Minister from 1968–1974. He was ousted from power by General Spinola in 1974 in a *putsch* which brought to an end half a century of dictatorship in Portugal, established by Caetano's predecessor, *Salazar.

Cairo Conference (22–26 November 1943) A World War II meeting, attended by *Roosevelt, *Churchill, and *Chiang Kai-shek, to decide on post-war policy for the Far East. Unconditional surrender by Japan was its prerequisite; Manchuria was to be returned to China and Korea to its own people. At a second conference Roosevelt and Churchill met President Inönü of Turkey and confirmed that country's independence. The *Teheran Conference was held immediately afterwards.

Caledonii The ancestors of the *Picts, the inhabitants of Scotland, known to the Romans as Caledonia.

calendar Any system for fixing the beginning, length, order, and subdivisions of the year. Calendrical systems have been used by societies since the earliest times, nearly all of them based on one of two astronomical cycles: the cycle of the phases of the Moon (the synodic month or lunation), often of major ritual and religious significance, and the cycle of the seasons (the period of the Earth's orbit around the Sun), of importance in agriculture. The two cycles are incompatible in that the synodic month has a period of about 29.5 days, giving a lunar year (12 months) of just over 354 days, over 11 days shorter than the mean solar year of 365.2422 days.

The **Julian calendar** was introduced to the Roman Empire by Julius *Caesar in 46 BC. It was developed from the traditional Roman lunar calendar, as is evident from its division into 12 months. However, the months no longer corresponded to lunations, as days were added to give a total year length of 365 days. Almost exact correspondence with the mean solar year was maintained by the intercalation of a **leap year** containing an extra day, on 29 February, every four years. The average length of the year was therefore 365.25 days which is only slightly longer than the length of the mean solar year. The **Gregorian calendar**, first introduced in 1582 by Pope Gregory XIII and in almost universal civil use today, superseded, with only slight modification, the Julian calendar. The Gregorian reform of 1582 omitted ten days from the calendar that year, the day after 4 October becoming 15 October. This restored the vernal equinox to 21 March and, to maintain this, three leap years are now suppressed every 400 years, centurial years ceasing to be leap years unless they are divisible by 400. The average length of the calendar year is now reduced to 365.2425 days, so close to the mean solar year that no adjustment will be required before AD 5000.

Other calendrical systems continue to be used, particularly for religious purposes, alongside the Gregorian system. The present **Jewish calendar** uses the 19-year Metonic cycle made up of 12 common years and 7 leap years. The common years have 12 months, each of 29 or 30 days, while the leap years have an additional month. The rules governing the detailed construction of the calendar are very complicated but the year begins on the first day of Tishri, an autumn month. Years are reckoned from the era of creation (*anno mundi*) for which the epoch adopted is 7 October 3761 BC. The **Islamic calendar** is wholly lunar, the year always containing 12 months without intercalation. This means that the Muslim New Year occurs seasonally about 11 days earlier each year. The months have alternately 30 and 29 days and are fixed in length, except for the twelfth month (Dulheggia) which has one intercalatory day in 11 years out of a cycle of 30 calendar years.

Caligula (born **Gaius Julius Caesar Germanicus**) (12–41 AD) Roman emperor (37–41). Brought up in a military camp, he gained the nickname Caligula (Latin for 'little boot') as an infant on account of the miniature military boots he wore. Caligula's brief reign as emperor, which began when he succeeded Tiberius and ended with his assassination, became notorious for its tyrannical and cruel excesses.

caliphate Formerly, the central ruling office of Islam. The first caliph (Arabic, *khalifa*, "deputy of God" or "successor of his Prophet") after the Prophet Muhammad's death in 632 was his father-in-law *Abu Bakr; he was followed by *Umar ibn al-Khattab, *Uthman, and Ali: these four are called the Rashidun (rightly guided) caliphs. When Ali died in 661 *Shiite Muslims

recognized his successors, the imams, as rightful possessors of the Prophet's authority, the rest of Islam accepting the *Umayyad dynasty. They were overthrown in 750 by the *Abbasids, but within two centuries they were virtually puppet rulers under Turkish control. Meanwhile an Umayyad refugee had established an independent emirate in Spain in 756, which survived for 250 years, and in North Africa a Shiite caliphate arose under the *Fatimids, the imams of the Ismailis (909–1171). After the Mongols sacked Baghdad in 1258 the caliphate, now only a name, passed to the *Mameluke rulers of Egypt and from the *Ottoman conquest of Egypt in 1517 the title was assumed by the Turkish sultans, until its abolition in 1924. From the late 20th century several radical groups, including *al-Qaeda, advocated the re-establishment of the caliphate. In 2014 the jihadist group *Islamic State declared a caliphate in the territories it controlled in Iraq and Syria, with its leader Abu Bakr al-Baghdadi as caliph.

Callaghan, James, Baron Callaghan of Cardiff (Leonard James Callaghan) (1912–2005) British Labour statesman, Prime Minister (1976–79). He became Prime Minister following Harold Wilson's resignation; the leader of a minority government, he was forced in 1977 to negotiate an agreement with the Liberal Party (the Lib–Lab Pact) to stay in power. After widespread strikes in the so-called 'winter of discontent' (1978–79), Callaghan's government received a vote of no confidence on the issue of Scottish devolution; the Labour Party lost to Margaret Thatcher's Conservatives in the ensuing election.

Calles, Plutarco Elías (1877–1945) Mexican statesman. He achieved prominence as a military leader during the Mexican Revolution (1910–40). As President of Mexico (1924–28), Calles implemented Mexico's constitution (1917) by supporting agrarian reform, organized labour, economic nationalism, and education.

Calvin, John (1509–64) French Protestant theologian and reformer. He began his theological career in France, but was forced to flee to Basle in Switzerland after embracing Protestantism in the early 1530s. He attempted a re-ordering of society on reformed Christian principles, with strong and sometimes ruthless control over the private lives of citizens. From 1541 he lived in Geneva, where he established the first Presbyterian government. He exerted an important influence on the development of

Protestant thought; his theological system, Calvinism, was further developed by his followers, notably Theodore Beza (1519–1605).

Cambodia

Capital:	Phnom Penh
Area:	181,035 sq km (69,898 sq miles)
Population:	15,205,539 (2012 est)
Currency:	1 riel = 100 sen
Religions:	Buddhist 96.4%; Muslim 2.4%
Ethnic Groups:	Khmer 90.0%; Vietnamese 5.0%; Chinese 1.0%
Languages:	Khmer (official); French; English
International Organizations:	UN; ASEAN; Non-Aligned Movement; WTO

A tropical country in south-east Asia flanked by Thailand, Laos, and Vietnam.

Physical Through it from the north flows the Mekong, while westward is a large lake, the Tonlé Sap.

The climate is tropical monsoon, and most of the land marshy or forested. A short coastline faces south-west on the Gulf of Thailand.

Economy The prolonged civil war and the Khmer Rouge regime's policies of resettlement decimated the economy but there has since been a significant recovery, with considerable growth in the 21st century. Clothing is the principal export, and tourism is growing rapidly. Offshore oil reserves were discovered in 2005 but have yet to be exploited. Agriculture remains the principal employer and poverty remains widespread.

History Cambodia was occupied from the 1st to the 6th century AD by the Hindu kingdoms of Funan, and subsequently Chenla. The *Khmer people overthrew the Hindu rulers of Chenla and established a Buddhist empire, centred around the region of *Angkor. The classical, or Angkorean, period lasted from 802 to 1432, with the Khmer empire reaching its peak during the 12th century. After 1432 the empire went into decline and suffered frequent invasions from Vietnam and Thailand. Continuing foreign domination forced Cambodia to seek French protection in 1863, and from 1884 it was treated as part of *French Indo-

China, although allowed to retain its royal dynasty. After Japanese occupation in World War II, King Norodom *Sihanouk achieved independence within the French Union (1949) and full independence in 1953. Sihanouk abdicated in 1955 to form a broad-based coalition government. Cambodia was drawn into the *Vietnam War in the 1960s, and US suspicions of Sihanouk's relations with communist forces led to his overthrow by the army under Lon Nol in 1970, following a US bombing offensive (1969–70) and invasion. The Lon Nol regime renamed Cambodia the Khmer Republic. The regime soon came under heavy pressure from the communist *Khmer Rouge. Following the fall of Phnom Penh in 1975, the Khmer Rouge under *Pol Pot renamed the country Democratic Kampuchea and launched a bloody reign of terror, which is estimated to have resulted in as many as two million deaths, or nearly a third of the population. Border tensions led to an invasion of the country by Vietnam in 1978, and the overthrow of the Pol Pot regime two weeks later. The Vietnamese installed a client regime under an ex-Khmer Rouge member, Heng Samrin, who proclaimed a new People's Republic of Kampuchea, but conflict with Khmer Rouge and other guerrilla groups continued until 1987, when peace talks began in Paris. In 1990 a peace agreement ended 13 years of civil strife. A UN Transitional Authority enforced a ceasefire and installed an interim Supreme Council, under Prince Norodom Sihanouk as head of state. The Council included representatives of the former government—the Cambodian People's Party (CPP) led by Hun Sen—and the former guerrilla movements. Multiparty elections were held in 1993. No party won a clear majority of seats, but a democratic monarchist constitution was adopted; Sihanouk became king and a coalition government was formed with Hun Sen and Norodom Ranariddh, son of Norodom Sihanouk and leader of the National United Front (NUF), becoming co-premiers. The Khmer Rouge refused to participate in the elections and continued to launch guerrilla attacks for some years; by 1999 it was effectively quiescent. In 1997 Prince Ranariddh was ousted by Hun Sen's followers, who were victorious in elections the following year. Hun Sen remained Prime Minister following the elections of 2003, 2008 and 2013. In 2004 Sihanouk abdicated and was succeeded by his son Norodom Sihamoni. The first trial of Khmer Rouge leaders was held in 2010, when Kaing Guek Eav was convicted of war crimes and crimes against humanity.

Cambrai, League of (1508) An alliance of the *papacy, the *Holy Roman Empire, France, and Spain against Venice. Venetian power received a severe check.

Camden, Battle of (16 August 1780) A battle of the American War of *Independence in which some 2000 American militiamen under Horatio *Gates were defeated when attacked by *Cornwallis's army 193 km (120 miles) north-north-west of Charleston, South Carolina. Gates was replaced by Nathanael *Greene as commander of the Southern Army, which revenged itself at the Battle of King's Mountain in October that year.

Cameron, David (William Donald) (1966–) British Conservative politician and Prime Minister (2010–). After graduating from Oxford (1988), Cameron worked for the Conservative Party, first in the research department (1988–92) and then as an adviser to members of the cabinet (1992–94). He then worked for the media company Carlton Communications before entering parliament in 2001. Following the Conservatives' defeat in the 2005 election, Cameron was elected leader and attempted to soften the party's image and broaden its appeal to centrist voters. In the 2010 election the Conservatives emerged as the largest party but without an absolute majority, and Cameron became Prime Minister of a Conservative–Liberal Democrat coalition government. His government focused on cutting the budget deficit, which was widely believed to have reached unsustainable levels following measures taken to counteract the *Credit Crunch. It also initiated reforms in education, social security, and health care.

Cameroon

Capital:	Yaoundé
Area:	475,440 sq km (183,568 sq miles)
Population:	20,549,221 (2012 est)
Currency:	1 CFA franc = 100 centimes
Religions:	traditional religions 40.0%; Christian 40.0%; Muslim 20.0%
Ethnic Groups:	Cameroon Highlanders 31.0%; Equatorial Bantu 19.0%; Kirdi 11.0%; Fulani 10.0%; Northwestern Bantu 8.0%; Eastern Nigritic 7.0%
Languages:	French, English (both official); over two hundred African languages and dialects
International Organizations:	UN; AU; Commonwealth; Non-Aligned Movement; Franc Zone; WTO

A country in West Africa, with Nigeria and Chad to its west and north, the Central African Republic to its east, and Gabon and Congo to the south.

Physical Most of the coastline is low, with creeks, lagoons, and swamps, although near Mount Cameroon, an active volcano, there are steep cliffs. The coastal plain is hot and very wet and covered with thick rainforest. Inland the ground rises to the plateau that makes up most of the country.

Economy Crude oil and oil products are the largest exports, and their revenue has assisted agricultural and industrial development. Other industries include aluminium smelting (from imported bauxite and alumina), food processing, and consumer goods. Apart from oil, mineral deposits include natural gas, gold, uranium, bauxite, nickel, and cobalt. Over two-thirds of the population are engaged in agriculture, with coffee, cocoa, and cotton being exported.

History The Portuguese and other Europeans who explored Cameroon in the 15th and 16th centuries found that it was mainly uninhabited, but it was believed to be the original home of the Bantu peoples. About 1810 King Mbwé-Mbwé walled his capital, Fomban, against the *Fulani empire of Sokoto. Other peoples set up small kingdoms. Germans began trading c.1860, and signed protectorate treaties in 1884. The German Protectorate of Kamerun was confirmed by the Franco-German Treaty of 1911, but in 1916 Anglo-French forces occupied it. From 1919 it was administered under *League of Nations (later UN) trusteeship, having been divided into British and French mandates. In 1960 the French Cameroons became an independent republic, to be joined in 1961 by part of the British Cameroons, the remainder becoming part of Nigeria. The French and British territories in 1972 merged as the United Republic of Cameroon, later renamed the Republic of Cameroon. It was from 1972 a one-party republic ruled by the Cameroon People's

Democratic Movement, from 1982 under President Paul Biya. Legislation providing for multi-party government was adopted in 1990 and, following strikes, demonstrations, and unrest through 1991, President Biya finally held elections in 1992. Biya was re-elected in presidential elections (also held in 1992) but the result was rejected by opponents, who alleged that fraud had taken place. He was again re-elected in 1997—when the opposition boycotted the poll—2004, and 2011. Cameroon joined the *Commonwealth of Nations in 1995. In 2008 the Bakassi Peninsula, with possibly significant oil reserves, was transferred from Nigeria to Cameroon.

Camisards French Protestants, who in 1702 defied *Louis XIV in the Cévennes, a mountainous region of southern France with a strong tradition of independence. The loss of their leaders in 1704 was followed by a period of savage persecution, but the rebels were bought off rather than defeated.

Campaign for Nuclear Disarmament (CND) A British pressure group pledged to nuclear disarmament and to the abandonment of British nuclear weapons. CND was created in 1958 with the philosopher Bertrand Russell as President. Frustration at the lack of progress led to the creation of a splinter-group, the Committee of 100, led by Russell and pledged to civil disobedience. From 1963–1980 CND was in eclipse. It revived in 1980–84 mainly as a protest against the deployment of US cruise missiles at Greenham Common. In 1980 European Nuclear Disarmament (END) was formed, linking closely with dissident groups in Eastern Europe. Similar movements developed in France, Germany, Australasia, and the USA, campaigning after the Cold War against nuclear proliferation.

Campbell, Kim (1947–) Canadian Progressive Conservative politician, the first female Prime Minister of Canada (1993). Campbell replaced Brian *Mulroney as Prime Minister in June 1993 but the Progressive Conservatives were defeated in the general election in October 1993. Campbell lost her seat and resigned as party leader.

Campbell-Bannerman, Sir Henry (1836–1908) British Liberal statesman, Prime Minister (1905–08). He was first elected to Parliament as MP for the Stirling burghs in 1868 and became leader of his party in 1899. His premiership, which ended with his resignation only a few days before his death, saw the grant of self-government to the defeated Boer republics of Transvaal (1906) and the Orange River Colony

(1907), the passing of the important Trade Disputes Act (1906), which exempted trade unions from certain liabilities in connection with strikes, and the entente with Russia (1907).

Camp David Accord (1978) A Middle East peace agreement. It was named after the official country house of the US President in Maryland, where President *Carter met President *Sadat of Egypt and Prime Minister *Begin of Israel to negotiate a settlement of the disputes between the two countries. Peace was made between Egypt and Israel after some 30 years of conflict, and provisions were agreed for an Israeli withdrawal from Egyptian territory. This agreement did not bring about peace with the other Arab countries; rather, it led increasingly to Egypt being isolated from its Arab neighbours.

Camperdown, Battle of (11 October 1797) A naval battle fought off the coast of Holland in which the British fleet destroyed the Dutch fleet. The Dutch tried to lure the British commander on to the shoals, but he accepted the risk, chased them, and captured nine ships.

Campion, St Edmund (1540–81) English Jesuit scholar and Catholic martyr. He was ordained in the Church of England in 1568. In 1571 he left England for Douai in the Low Countries, where he joined the Roman Catholic Church; in Rome, two years later, he became a Jesuit. In 1580 he participated in the first secret Jesuit mission to England. Although he claimed that he came only to teach and minister to the Catholic community, he was arrested, tortured, tried, and executed for treason.

Canaanites The inhabitants of ancient Palestine, but more specifically the land lying between the River Jordan and the Mediterranean. The Canaanites occupied the area in the 3rd millennium BC but it was conquered and occupied during the latter part of the 2nd millennium BC by the Israelites who described it as their 'Promised Land' (Exodus 3:8).

Canada

Capital:	Ottawa
Area:	9,984,670 sq km (3,855,103 sq miles)
Population:	34,568,211 (2012 est)
Currency:	1 Canadian dollar = 100 cents
Religions:	Roman Catholic 42.6%; Protestant 23.3%; other Christian 4.4%

Ethnic Groups:	(by origin) British and Irish 28.0%%; mixed 26.0%; French 23.0%; other European 15.0%; Amerindian 2.0%
Languages:	English, French (both official)
International Organizations:	UN; Commonwealth; OECD; NATO; OAS; OSCE; NAFTA; WTO

The second largest country of the world, occupying the whole of the northern part of North America except for Alaska and bounded by three oceans: the Pacific on the west, the Arctic on the north, and the Atlantic on the east. Canada is a federation of ten North American provinces (Alberta, British Columbia, Manitoba, New Brunswick, Newfoundland, Nova Scotia, Ontario, Prince Edward Island, Quebec, Saskatchewan), the Yukon Territory, the Northwest Territories, and the semiautonomous region of Nunavut.

Physical Canada's southern boundary crosses the Rocky Mountains and continues eastward on latitude 49° N. to the Great Lakes and the Saint Lawrence, and then crosses the northern Appalachian Mountains to join the sea along the Saint Croix River. While the Saint Lawrence is Canada's most important river, the Mackenzie in the north-west is the longest. Northern Canada is a land of lakes, wide and winding rivers, low tundra vegetation, and dark coniferous forests. The heart of the country is a vast grain-growing region, despite a harsh climate of very cold winters and very warm but short summers. The land becomes more hilly in Quebec and the easternmost maritime provinces, and farmers concentrate on orchard crops. Canada has huge deposits of iron ore, zinc, nickel, uranium, and other minerals.

Economy A leading industrial nation, Canada depends on the neighbouring USA, with whom it signed a free-trade agreement in 1989, for about 75% of its trade. Major exports include motor vehicles (assembled from imported components), machinery, crude oil, timber, natural gas, non-ferrous metals, chemicals, and newsprint. With the world's third-largest oil reserves, oil production is of growing importance; however, Canada's plans to exploit Arctic oil and gas reserves are currently hampered by diplomatic issues. Canadian agriculture is diverse, with extensive grain, dairy, and fruit-farming as well as ranching and fur-farming.

History Originally inhabited by *Native Americans and by Inuit in the far north, in the 10th century *Vikings established a settlement at L'Anse aux Meadows. John *Cabot landed in Labrador, Newfoundland, or Cape Breton Island, in 1497 and in 1534 Jacques *Cartier claimed the land for France. The first French settlement was begun by fur traders in Acadia in 1604. In 1608 Samuel de *Champlain founded Quebec on the St Lawrence River. Governor Frontenac defended Quebec against Sir William Phips (1691) and led a successful campaign against the hostile *Iroquois (1696). Explorers followed the routes of the Great Lakes and the Mississippi Valley—*La Salle reached the mouth of the Mississippi in 1682—and the name Canada came to be used interchangeably with that of *New France, which referred to all French possessions in North America. Conflict between Britain and France was mirrored in Canada in the *French and Indian wars. By the Peace of *Utrecht (1713) France gave up most of Acadia, Newfoundland, and Hudson Bay. The remainder of New France was conquered by Britain and ceded in 1763. During or immediately after the American War of *Independence some 40,000 United Empire Loyalists arrived in Nova Scotia (formerly Acadia) and present-day Ontario. St John's Island was renamed Prince Edward Island in 1799 and Cape Breton Island was joined to Nova Scotia in 1820. In 1791 Quebec was divided into Upper and Lower Canada, but following the Act of Union of 1840 the two were reunited to form the Province of Canada. Two frontier agreements were made with the USA: the Webster–Ashburton Treaty (1842) and a treaty ending the Oregon Boundary dispute (1846). Fears of US expansion led to the British North America Act (1867), creating the Dominion of Canada. The new dominion acquired full responsibility for home affairs. In 1870 the Hudson's Bay Company's lands around the Red River were formed into the Province of Manitoba, while the Northwest Territories passed from control of the Company to the federal government. In 1873 Prince Edward Island joined the Confederation, British Columbia, including Vancouver Island, having done so in 1871. This had been on the promise of a Canadian Pacific Railway, which was completed in 1885, enabling prairie wheat to flow east for export. Britain gave Canada title to the arctic islands in 1880. In 1896 the Yukon boomed briefly with the Klondike *gold rush. In

C

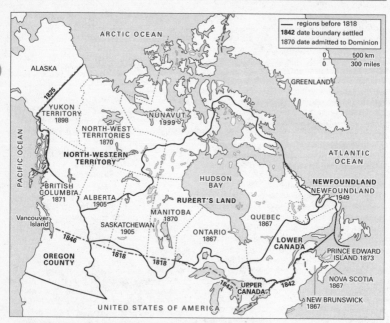

Canada. Following the American War of Independence (1775–83) many loyalists to the British crown moved north into the British colonies of Quebec and Nova Scotia. As the 19th century progressed, Canada evolved from colonial to dominion status (1867), establishing complete national sovereignty in 1982. The 20th century has seen an influx of immigrants from central and southern Europe to add to the earlier settlers of mainly French and British descent, the majority of residents of Quebec remaining Roman Catholic and French-speaking. Those descendants of the country's earlier inhabitants, the Indians and Inuits (Eskimos) who have not been attracted to the industrial south live in scattered settlements.

1905 Alberta and Saskatchewan became federated provinces. Newfoundland joined the dominion in 1949. The Hudson's Bay Company gradually ceded all the lands for which it was responsible, but as a corporation it has retained a significant place in the Canadian economy. As the provinces developed, so did their strength *vis-à-vis* the central federal government, a strongly centralized political system being resisted. In 1982 the British Parliament accepted the complete national sovereignty of Canada, although it retained allegiance to the British crown as well as membership of the *Commonwealth of Nations. Constitutional disputes continued through the 1980s and 1990s, with Newfoundland, Manitoba, and Quebec all rejecting proposed solutions, the last insisting on 'distinct society' status, but rejecting independence in provincial referendums in 1980 and

1995. In 1992 Canada signed the *North American Free Trade Agreement. The semiautonomous region of Nunavut was created in 1999 as a territory for the Inuit people. Following elections in 2006 Stephen Harper became Canada's first right-of-centre Prime Minister in 13 years, at the head of a minority Conservative government. The 2008 election produced the same result, but a convincing victory in 2011 enabled the Conservatives to form a majority government.

Canadian Indians *See* INUIT.

Cannae, Battle of (216 BC) A battle fought at the village of Cannae in southern Italy, which was one of the classic victories in military history. The Carthaginian general *Hannibal, his infantry considerably outnumbered, but stronger in cavalry, stationed his troops in a shallow crescent formation. The densely packed Roman legionaries, under the consuls Aemilius Paullus and Terentius Varro, charged Hannibal's centre, forced it back, but failed to break it. As it slowly and deliberately gave ground, and the Romans pushed deeper, Hannibal effected his brilliant double-encirclement: his cavalry, having defeated the opposing right and left wings, closed the trap and assaulted the Romans from flanks and rear. Out of some 50,000 men the Romans lost 35,000 killed or captured, Hannibal only 5700. Rome's hold on Italy was imperilled, and many of its allies in central and southern Italy defected to Hannibal.

Canning, Charles John, 1st Earl Canning (1812-62) British statesman. The son of George *Canning, he was governor-general of India at the time of the *Indian Mutiny and played a notable part in the work of reconciliation which followed it. He was subsequently first viceroy of India (1858-62) and was known as "Clemency Canning" for his policy of no retribution.

Canning, George (1770-1827) British Tory statesman, Prime Minister in 1827. Foreign Secretary from 1807, he resigned in 1809 after a disagreement with his rival *Castlereagh over a disastrous expedition in the Napoleonic Wars, but returned to office following Castlereagh's suicide in 1822. During this ministry he presided over a reversal of Britain's hitherto conservative foreign policy, being particularly responsible for the support of nationalist movements in various parts of Europe. He succeeded Lord Liverpool as Prime Minister in 1827, but died shortly afterwards.

Canossa A castle in the Apennines, in Italy, where, in the winter of 1077, the German emperor *Henry IV waited for three days until Pope *Gregory VII granted absolution and removed a ban of excommunication from him. Henry had been at odds with the papacy over ultimate control within the Holy Roman Empire. His penance greatly strengthened his hand against the German princes who threatened him, for they had been allies of the pope and when Henry was absolved the princes withdrew their support for Gregory.

Canute (or **Cnut, Knut**) (died 1035) Son of Sweyn I, Danish king of England (1017-35), Denmark (1018-35), and Norway (1028-35). After Edmund Ironside's murder in 1016, Canute became king of England, ending a prolonged struggle for the throne. As king,

he presided over a period of relative peace. He is most commonly remembered for demonstrating to his fawning courtiers that, contrary to their expectations, he was unable to command the tide to stop rising.

Cao Cao (or **Ts'ao Ts'ao**) (155-220) Chinese general. One of China's greatest soldiers, he unified much of northern China after the collapse of the Han dynasty. His conquests enabled his son to found the Wei kingdom, one of the Three Kingdoms. His campaigns and adventures are recorded in one of the classics of Chinese literature, *The Romance of the Three Kingdoms*.

Cape St Vincent, Battle of (14 February 1797) A naval battle off the south-west coast of Portugal in which *Nelson and *Jervis defeated a combined French and Spanish fleet of 27 ships. The British were outnumbered almost two to one, but the disorder of the Spanish fleet cancelled out its advantage in numbers. After this victory the British fleet was able to continue its blockade of Cadiz and to re-enter the Mediterranean in pursuit of Napoleon in Egypt.

Capetian (987-1328) The dynasty of French kings who succeeded the *Carolingians. It was not until the reign of Louis VI (1108-1137) that the dynasty established firm control over its own territories around Paris and began the slow process of gaining real power in France. Philip Augustus (1180-1223) seized Normandy and recovered many other areas which had been occupied by, or were under the influence of, the English crown. This effectively doubled the size of the country. Paris became the true centre of government. By the end of the reign of Philip IV (1285-1314) France had achieved a great degree of stability and acquired many of the legal and governmental systems which were to survive up to the French Revolution. On the death of Charles IV in 1328 the throne passed to the House of *Valois who, together with the later *Bourbons, could claim indirect descent from Hugh Capet (ruled 987-96), the first of the line.

Cape Verde

Capital:	Praia
Area:	4033 sq km (1557 sq miles)
Population:	531,046 (2013 est)
Currency:	Escudo Caboverdiano = 100 centavos
Religions:	Roman Catholic; Protestant

Ethnic Groups:	Creole (mulatto) 71.0%; African 28.0%; European 1.0%
Languages:	Portuguese (official); Portuguese creole (crioulo)
International Organizations:	UN; AU; ECOWAS; Non-Aligned Movement; WTO

A country comprising an archipelago of volcanic islands in the Atlantic Ocean, 563 km (350 miles) west of Cape Verde Peninsula, Senegal, the most westerly point of Africa.

Physical The archipelago is in two groups, Windward and Leeward, and consists in all of ten islands and five islets. Sheer cliffs rise from the sea, and the inland slopes present a jagged landscape as a result of erosion by wind-blown sand.

Economy Agriculture and industry are limited, and commerce, transport, tourism, and public services are the main economic activities. The domestic economy relies heavily on remittances from Cape Verdeans working overseas.

History The islands were uninhabited until they were colonized by the Portuguese from 1462, and were used as a base for the Portuguese slave trade. In 1951 Cape Verde became an overseas province of Portugal and its residents were given Portuguese citizenship in 1961. An independence movement for Cape Verde and *Guinea-Bissau gained strength during the 1950s and 1960s, and later became the African Party for the Independence of Cape Verde and Guinea-Bissau (PAICVGB). Cape Verde gained full independence in 1975, but remained linked with Guinea-Bissau as the PAICVGB was the only legal political party in both countries. In 1980 the PAICVGB in Guinea-Bissau was ousted in a coup and the party in Cape Verde dropped the reference to Guinea-Bissau from its name. A multiparty constitution was adopted in 1991, and elections that same year were won by the newly created Movement for Democracy Party. The PAICV was returned to power in the 2001 elections and again in 2006 and 2011.

capitalism A system of economic organization, based on market competition, under which the means of production, distribution, and exchange are privately owned and directed by individuals or corporations. All human production requires both labour and capital. In a capitalist system, capital is supplied either by the single owner of a firm, or by shareholders in the case of a joint-stock company. Labour is supplied separately by employees who receive a wage or salary. The residual profit of the firm after wages and costs have been paid accrues to the owners of the capital. Firms compete with one another to sell to customers in what is primarily a free market. In its most developed form capitalism, which is based on the principle that economic decisions should be taken by private individuals, restricts the role of the state in economic policy to the minimum. It thus stands for *free trade. During the 20th century capitalist societies were modified in various ways: often a capitalist economy was accompanied by the development of a *welfare state, as in western Europe. Another development was the mixed economy, in which the production of certain goods or services was nationalized, while the rest of the economy remained in private ownership. However, the late 20th century saw a reduction of state involvement in and regulation of the economy, with state-owned industries being privatized and a renewed emphasis on the primacy of the market. Recent decades have also seen the growth of multinational companies operating across national frontiers (*see* GLOBALIZATION), often controlling greater economic resources than small- or medium-sized states.

Capone, Al (Alphonse Capone) (1899–1947) Italian-American gangster. Also known as "Scarface", he was the most flamboyant and widely publicized criminal of the *Prohibition era. In 1925 he took over Chicago's south side gang from Johnny Torrio, and dominated the city's underworld, dealing in bootleg liquor, extortion, prostitution, and other rackets, and controlling the corrupt administration of Major Bill Thompson. His war on other syndicates, culminating in the St Valentine's Day Massacre of 1929 against Bugs Moran's gang, went unchecked until his indictment for federal income tax evasion in 1931 led to a prison sentence. Physically and mentally broken by syphilis, he was released in 1939.

Caporetto, Battle of (24 October 1917) A battle fought north of Trieste when Austro-Hungarian and German forces overwhelmed the Italian army. General Cadorna withdrew his demoralized troops north of Venice, where his new line held, eventually strengthened by British and French reinforcements. Some 300,000 Italian prisoners-of-war were taken, which removed Italy temporarily from the war; this enabled a German offensive for March 1918 on the Western Front to be planned.

Caratacus (or **Caractacus**) (1st century AD) British chieftain, son of Cunobelinus. He took part in the resistance to the Roman invasion of AD 43, and when defeated fled to Yorkshire, where he was handed over to the Romans in 51 AD.

Carbonari (Italian, 'charcoal burners') A secret revolutionary society formed in Italy that was active in France and the Iberian Peninsula. It was formed in the kingdom of Naples during the reign of Joachim Murat (1808–15) and its members plotted to free the country from foreign rule. The society was influential in the revolt in Naples in 1820 that resulted in the granting of a constitution to the Kingdom of the Two Sicilies. Similar revolts took place in Spain and Portugal (1820), Piedmont (1821), Romagna and Parma (1831), all in turn being suppressed. It was supplanted in Italy by the more broadly based *Young Italy movement. Meanwhile the French movement, after mutinies in 1821–22, also declined.

Cárdenas, Lázaro (1895–1970) Mexican statesman. As President of Mexico (1934–40), he carried the *Mexican Revolution to the left during his administration. He redistributed land, encouraged organized labour through support of the Confederación de Trabajadores de Mexico (CTM), and nationalized the property of the foreign-owned oil companies in 1938. Himself a mestizo (of mixed American Indian and European descent), he won the support of the Indian and Mexican working classes.

Cardwell, Edward, Viscount (1813–86) British statesman. A supporter of Sir Robert *Peel, he served as Secretary to the Treasury (1845–46) and as Secretary for War in *Gladstone's ministry of 1868–74. British incompetence in the *Crimean War (1853–56) and the efficiency of the German army in the European wars of the 1860s were the background to Cardwell's military reforms.

Caribbean Community and Common Market (CARICOM) An organization formed in 1973 to promote unity among the many small nations of the Caribbean. The main purpose of the organization is to promote the economic integration of its 15 members by means of a Caribbean Common Market, replacing the former body, the Caribbean Free Trade Association (CARIFTA). Member nations also cooperate on other projects in areas such as health, education, and agricultural develop-

ment. A summit meeting in 1984 agreed to create a single market, but many issues were unresolved. At subsequent annual summit meetings disagreements were gradually settled and in 1995 the members decided to remove all internal trade tariffs by the end of the year. The **CARICOM Single Market and Economy** (CSME) was established in 2006, although not all CARICOM members joined. Its headquarters are in Georgetown, Guyana.

Caribs A people of South American origin, who migrated to the islands of the Lesser Antilles from c.1000 AD. There they replaced the agricultural Arawak culture, killing off most of the men and capturing their women. Many Arawak men were eaten in ritual cannibalism. The Caribs were the first "Indians" discovered by Columbus.

Carlist A conservative who supported the claims of Don Carlos (1788–1855) and his descendants to the throne of Spain. Don Carlos's religious orthodoxy and belief in the divine right of kings made him the natural leader of these traditionalists. After unsuccessful claims to the throne for nearly a century, the Carlists emerged as a strong force with popular support after the establishment of a republic in 1931. In the *Spanish Civil War the Carlists sided with the nationalists and for many years obstructed Franco's aim to restore the Bourbon dynasty. In 1969 Franco overcame Carlist objections and named the grandson of Alfonso XIII, Juan Carlos, as his successor.

Carlyle, Thomas (1795–1881) Scottish historian and political philosopher. He worked as a teacher before starting to write articles for the *Edinburgh Encyclopedia* and critical works on German literature in the 1820s. His first major philosophical work was *Sartor Resartus* (1833–34), which dealt with social values and is written in a mannered prose style. He established his reputation as a historian with his *History of the French Revolution* (1837). Carlyle's influence on the development of social and political ideas in Britain during the 19th century was considerable.

Carmelite A monk or nun who is a follower of the Order of Our Lady of Mount Carmel. Carmelites obey the strict monastic 'rule' of St Albert of Jerusalem. They originated in *Palestine c.1154 but came to western Europe when Palestine was conquered by the Muslims. Their order was approved by Pope Honorius III in 1226. In 1452 the Carmelite Sisters was formed. In 1594 a reformed group of the order was established, the Discalced Carmelites, but it remained essentially similar in organization and objectives.

Carnegie, Andrew (1835–1919) Scottish-born US industrialist and philanthropist. He built up a considerable fortune in the steel industry in the USA, then retired from business in 1901 and devoted his wealth to charitable purposes on both sides of the Atlantic, supporting many educational institutions, libraries, and the arts. One of his most notable achievements was the creation of the Carnegie Peace Fund to promote international peace.

Carnot, Lazare Nicolas Marguerite (1753–1823) French general and military tactician. He entered the French army in 1784 and two years later published his influential *Essay on the Use of Machines in Warfare*. He was a member of the *Committee of Public Safety, was in charge of the war department, and between 1795 and 1797 was a member of the *Directory. He fled to Germany, falsely accused of treason in 1797, following the royalist victory in the elections. He returned to become Minister of War (1800) and continued with his administrative reforms for a year under *Napoleon I, but resigned in 1801.

Caro, Joseph (1488–1575) Jewish scholar and mystic, who wrote the last great codification of Jewish law.

Carol I (1839–1914) First King of Romania (1881–1914). A German-born prince and Prussian officer, he was elected in 1866 to succeed Alexander John Cuza as Prince of Romania. His pro-German sympathies made him unpopular during the *Franco–Prussian War, but skill in manipulating politicians and elections saved him from abdication. As a result of his military leadership in the Russo–Turkish War, he gained full independence for Romania at the Congress of *Berlin and declared a Romanian kingdom in 1881.

Carol II (1893–1953) King of Romania (1930–40). The great-nephew of *Carol I, he was exiled in 1925 for his scandalous domestic life. In 1930 he returned as king, and established a royal dictatorship inspired by intense admiration of *Mussolini. In 1940 he was forced to cede large parts of his kingdom to the *Axis Powers, and to abdicate in favour of his son, Michael.

Caroline of Ansbach (1683–1737) German princess, Queen consort of *George II, whom she married in 1705. She was a popular queen, and during the king's absences in Hanover, she

was four times appointed 'Guardian of the Realm'. She was responsible for enclosing 121 ha. (300 acres) of London's Hyde Park to form Kensington Gardens.

Carolingian empire The collection of territories in Western Europe ruled by the family of *Charlemagne (768–814 AD) from whom the dynasty took its name. Charlemagne's ancestors, Frankish aristocrats, fought their way to supreme power under the *Merovingian kings, the last of whom was deposed by Charlemagne's father *Pepin III in 751. Under Charlemagne, the empire covered modern-day France, part of Spain, Germany to the River Elbe, and much of Italy. Charlemagne was crowned Emperor of the West by Pope Leo III in 800 and made his court a centre of learning (the "Carolingian Renaissance"). After the division of the empire by the Treaty of *Verdun in 843, civil war among the Carolingians, *Viking raids, and the ambitions of rival families subjected the empire to intolerable strains. Nevertheless, Carolingians reigned in Germany till 911 and in France till 987 and they left behind a prestige which later kings of the Middle Ages sought to emulate.

carpetbagger (in the USA) A northerner who moved into the post-Civil War American South. In the wake of the *Reconstruction Acts of 1867, large numbers of Northern entrepreneurs, educators, and missionaries arrived in the South to share in the rebuilding of the former states of the *Confederacy. Some carpetbaggers (so called because it was said that they could transport their entire assets in a carpetbag) hoped to help the Black ex-slave population, but others were interested only in making a quick profit.

Carranza, Venustiano (1859–1920) Mexican statesman. As President of Mexico (1917–20), he played a minor role in the revolution against Porfirio *Díaz but a major role in shaping the course of the Mexican Revolution from 1913–1920. A voice for moderation during the violent decade of revolutionary politics, he defeated his rival Pancho *Villa and reluctantly accepted the leftist constitution of 1917. Driven from office before his presidential term expired, he was assassinated in the village of Tlaxcalantongo on his way into exile.

Carson, Edward Henry, Baron (1854–1935) Anglo-Irish statesman. Elected to the British Parliament in 1892, he opposed the third *Home Rule Bill (1912) and organized a private army of *Ulster Volunteers, threatening that

Ulster would set up a separate provisional government if the Bill proceeded. In 1914 he reluctantly agreed to Home Rule for southern Ireland but insisted that *Northern Ireland, including the predominantly Catholic counties of Tyrone and Fermanagh, should remain under the British crown.

Carson, Kit (1809–68) US frontiersman and guide born in Kentucky, who established headquarters at Taos, New Mexico. He worked with *Frémont along the Oregon Trail in 1842–46, played an important role in the seizure of California from Mexico in 1847, and guided many groups of settlers west during the *gold rush of 1849. He served as a US Indian agent and, during the *American Civil War, was responsible for Union (Northern) scouts in the western theatre. One of the most accomplished of the *Mountain Men, Carson was the subject of many of the legends of the early days of the American West.

Carter, James Earl (known as **'Jimmy'**) (1924–) US Democratic statesman, 39th President of the USA (1977–81). A progressive and reformist governor of Georgia (1970–74), he was elected President on a manifesto of civil rights and economic reform. Although his administration was notable for achieving the Panama Canal Treaty (1977) and the Camp David agreements (1978), he failed to resolve the crisis caused by the seizure of US hostages in Iran. After leaving office, he worked internationally for peace and human rights; he was awarded the Nobel Peace Prize in 2002. Since 2007 he has been an active member of The *Elders.

Carthage The ruins of an ancient city on the north coast of Africa in Tunisia, situated to the west of Tunis. Traditionally founded by Phoenicians from Tyre (in modern Lebanon) in 814 BC, it became a major centre of the Mediterranean, with interests in North Africa, Spain, and Sicily which brought it into conflict with Greece until the 3rd century BC and then with Rome in the Punic Wars, until the Romans destroyed it in 146 BC. It was refounded as a Roman city and prospered. It was a centre of Christianity and *Genseric made it his capital in 439. In 533–34 it was captured by *Belisarius and was part of the Byzantine empire until its destruction by the Arabs in 697.

Cartier, Sir George-Etienne (1814–73) French-Canadian statesman. His involvement in 1837 in the Papineau Rebellion forced him into brief exile in the USA. In 1848 he was elected as a Conservative to the Canadian Legislative Assembly, holding a seat there, and later in the Canadian House of Commons, until his death.

Carver, John (c.1576–1621) Pilgrim leader. He had been deacon of the separatist church in Leiden and led the migration in the *Mayflower* in 1620. Elected first governor of Plymouth Plantation, he died shortly afterwards and was succeeded by William *Bradford.

Casablanca Conference (14–24 January 1943) A meeting in Morocco between *Churchill and F. D. *Roosevelt to determine Allied strategy for the continuation of World War II. Plans were made to increase bombing of Germany, invade Sicily, and transfer British forces to the Far East after the collapse of Germany.

Casanova, Giovanni Giacomo (1725–98) Italian adventurer. He is famous for his memoirs (first published in French 1828–38), describing his adventures in Europe and especially his sexual encounters.

Casement, Roger David (1864–1916) Irish patriot. As a British consular official, he won respect for exposing cases of ill-treatment of native labour in Africa, particularly the Upper Congo, and in South America, and was awarded a knighthood by the British government. He retired from the consular service in 1913. An Ulster Protestant, he supported Irish independence and went to the USA and to Germany in 1914 to seek help for an Irish uprising. His attempt to recruit Irish prisoners-of-war in Germany to fight against the British in Ireland failed, nor would the Germans provide him with troops. Casement, however, was landed on the Irish coast in County Kerry from a German submarine in 1916, hoping to secure a postponement of the *Easter Rising. He was arrested, tried, and executed for treason. His request to be buried in Ireland, rejected at the time, was fulfilled in 1965.

Casey, Richard Gardiner, Baron (1890–1976) Australian diplomat and statesman. He was a United Australia Party Member of the House of Representatives (1931–40). He was Australia's first Minister to the USA (1940–42), joined the British war cabinet (1942–43), and was governor of Bengal (1944–46). On returning to the House of Representatives (1949–60), representing the Liberal Party, Casey held various portfolios including that of External Affairs (1951–60). He was governor-general of the Commonwealth of Australia (1965–69).

Casimir III (or **Casimir the Great**) (1310–70) King of Poland (1333–70). He consolidated the achievements of his predecessor, Władysław I, reorganizing the country's administration, codifying the law, and acquiring territory through diplomacy. Links with Lithuania, Hesse, Silesia, Brandenburg, and the Holy Roman Empire were forged through marriage. He successfully fought against *Russia, the *Teutonic Knights, and the Bohemians of east central Europe.

Castilla, Ramón (1797–1867) Peruvian statesman. As President (1845–51, 1855–62), he encouraged railway development and telegraphic communication, and supported the commercial use of the guano (the nitrogen-rich droppings of fish-eating seabirds) as a fertilizer. He developed the nitrate industries by establishing government monopolies and leasing them to private individuals. He abolished slavery, and freed the Peruvian Indian from tribute payments.

castle A fortified building for the defence of a town or district, doubling as the private residence of a baron in the Middle Ages. Although also called 'castles', Celtic hill-forts, Roman camps, and Saxon burhs were designed to provide refuge for whole populations; archaeological evidence suggests that in England fortified private residences date from the 9th century. The 'motte and bailey' design of the 11th century comprised a palisaded 'motte' (a steep-sided earthen mound) and a 'bailey' (an enclosure or courtyard) separated from the motte by a ditch. Both were surrounded by a second ditch. Initially timber-built, and often prefabricated for rapid assembly, many were later rebuilt in stone. Design modifications in the 12th century included stone tower keeps to replace the motte. The keep (the rounded form was called a shell keep) combined strong defence with domestic quarters. The need to extend these quarters meant that the courtyard had to be protected by a line of towers joined by 'curtain' walls. In the 12th century the concentric castle (one ring of defences enclosing another) was developed from the model of the castles built by the Crusaders, who themselves had copied the Saracens. At the end of the 13th century, *Edward I of England, following a policy of subduing north Wales, built a series of castles, including those at Caernarvon, Conway, Harlech, and Beaumaris. Design improvements saw the further development of rounded towers, which were more difficult to undermine, machicolations, which enabled objects to be dropped or poured on the besiegers, massive

gatehouses, and refinements to the battlements, or crenellations, along the walls. The invention of cannon had made castles obsolete for defensive purposes by the middle of the 16th century.

Castle Hill Uprising (1804) A convict rebellion at Castle Hill, a settlement in New South Wales, Australia. Several hundred convicts, many of them Irish nationalists, captured Castle Hill as part of a plan to gain control over other settlements. The rebellion was crushed by the New South Wales Corps, martial law was proclaimed, and the ringleaders hanged, flogged, or deported.

Castlereagh, Robert Stewart, Viscount (1769–1822) British Tory statesman. Born in Ulster, he began his political career as a Whig in the Irish Parliament and continued to concern himself with Irish affairs, especially *Catholic emancipation, after becoming a Tory in 1795. He was Secretary for War (1807–09) but an attack on his policies by George *Canning led to a duel between them. He became Foreign Secretary in 1812, and in this capacity represented his country at the Congress of Vienna (1814–15), playing a central part in reviving the Quadruple Alliance (whereby Britain, Russia, Austria, and Prussia united to defeat Napoleon). He committed suicide, apparently as a result of mental strain owing to pressure of work.

Castro, Fidel (Fidel Castro Ruz) (1927–) Cuban revolutionary and statesman. Son of an immigrant sugar planter, he joined the Cuban People's Party in 1947 and led a revolution in Santiago in 1953, for which he was imprisoned. His self-defence at this trial, known by its concluding words, *History Will Absolve Me*, was to become his major policy statement at the time. Exiled in 1955 he went to Mexico and in 1956 landed on the Cuban coast with 82 men, including Ché *Guevara, but only 12 men survived the landing. He conducted successful guerrilla operations from the Sierra Maestra mountains and in December 1958 led a march on Havana. The ruthless and corrupt dictator, General *Batista, fled, and on 1 January 1959 Castro proclaimed the Cuban Revolution, ordering the arrest and execution of many of Batista's supporters. Castro declared himself Prime Minister and, unable to establish diplomatic or commercial agreements with the USA, negotiated credit, arms, and food supplies with the former Soviet Union. He expropriated foreign industry and collectivized agriculture. The USA cancelled all trade agreements (1960) and from 1961 Castro was openly aligned with the Soviet Union, emerging more and more strongly as a

Marxist. The abortive US and Cuban invasion (April 1961) of the *Bay of Pigs boosted his popularity, as did his successful survival of the *Cuban Missile Crisis (October 1962) and of several assassination plots. A keen promoter of revolution in other Latin American countries and of liberation movements in Africa, he achieved considerable status in developing countries through his leadership of the *Non-Aligned Movement. With the collapse of the Soviet Union and of *COMECON in 1990, his government faced severe problems. He introduced economic austerity measures in 1991 and some degree of liberalization of Cuba's economy; however, he remained committed to the principle of a planned economy. In 2006 ill health led Castro to transfer his powers to his brother Raúl; although this was intended as a temporary measure, Fidel never resumed his role and retired formally as President in 2008 and as leader of the Communist Party in 2011. He nevertheless remained an influential figure in Cuban and regional affairs.

catacomb An underground burial gallery, especially in early Christian Rome. Catacombs were named after the best known example, St Sebastian in the Hollow (*ad Catacumbas*). Forty such subterranean chambers are known in Rome, tunnelled through soft rock outside the ancient city boundaries. The anniversaries of martyrs were celebrated at the graves. Looted by barbarians and subject to collapse, they were virtually forgotten until their accidental rediscovery in the 16th century. Similar ones are also found as far apart as Salzburg and Malta.

Catalaunian Fields (or **Plains**) The site of a major battle in 451 AD, reputedly near Châlons-sur-Marne in France, but placed by some nearer Troyes. The Roman general Aetius with a combined force of Romans, Goths, and Burgundians defeated *Attila the Hun, forcing his retreat from Gaul. He was expelled from Italy the following year.

Çatal Hüyük See NEOLITHIC.

Cathar (from Greek *katharos*, 'pure') A member of a medieval sect seeking to achieve a life of great purity. Cathars believed in a 'dualist' heresy. Their basic belief was that if God, being wholly good, had alone created the world it would have been impossible for evil to exist within it, and that another, diabolical, creative force must have taken part. They held that the material world and all within it were irredeemably evil. The heresy originated in Bulgaria and appeared in western Europe in the 1140s. In

southern France the followers of this Christian heresy were called *Albigensians.

Catherine I (*c*.1684–1727) Empress of Russia (1725–27). She was a Lithuanian servant girl who was first the mistress and then the second wife of *Peter I. On his death she was proclaimed ruler with the support of her husband's favourite, Menshikov, and the guards regiments. Menshikov became the effective head of government, working through the newly established Privy Council, but fell from power on Catherine's death. Her daughter *Elizabeth Petrovna became empress (1741–62).

Catherine II (or **Catherine the Great**) (1729–96) Empress of Russia (1762–96). A German princess, she was made empress following a plot that deposed her husband Peter III (1728–62). Her attempted social and political reforms were impeded by entrenched aristocratic interests and in later years her reign became increasingly conservative. Under Catherine's rule, Russia played an important part in European affairs, participating in the three partitions of Poland and forming close links with Prussia and Austria, while to the south and east further territorial advances were made at the expense of the Turks and Tartars.

Catherine of Aragon (1485–1536) Spanish princess, the first wife of *Henry VIII of England to whom she was married in 1509. She bore him a daughter, the future *Mary I, but no male heir survived; the importance of the Spanish alliance diminished, and by 1527 Henry, infatuated with Anne *Boleyn, sought a papal annulment, claiming that Catherine's marriage in 1501 to his elder brother Arthur rendered his own marriage invalid. The pope was uncooperative, so *Cranmer annulled the king's marriage in 1533. Thereafter Catherine lived in seclusion in England.

Catherine of Braganza (1638–1705) Portuguese princess and Queen consort of Charles II of England, whom she married in 1662, bringing Tangier and Bombay as part of her dowry. The marriage was childless and she had to tolerate the king's infidelities. As a Roman Catholic, she was unpopular and there were attempts to implicate her in the *Popish Plot. In 1692, as a widow, she returned to Portugal, where she died.

Catholic emancipation The granting of full political and civil liberties to British and Irish Roman Catholics. Partial religious toleration had been achieved in Britain by the late 17th century, but the *Test Acts limited holders of public office to communicant Anglicans and placed additional disabilities on members of other churches. Until 1745 the *Jacobite threat seemed to justify continued discrimination against Roman Catholics and fears of Catholic emancipation led to the *Gordon riots in 1780. By the late 18th century many reformists were agitating for total religious freedom. In Ireland, where a majority were Catholics, concessions were made from 1778 onwards, culminating in the Relief Act of 1793, passed by the Irish Parliament and giving liberty of religious practice and the right to vote in elections, but not to sit in Parliament or hold public office. William *Pitt had become convinced of the need for full Catholic emancipation by 1798 and promises were made to the Irish Parliament when it agreed to the Act of *Union in 1800. Protestant landlords, as well as George III, resisted emancipation and Pitt resigned. Daniel *O'Connell took up the cause for emancipation and founded the Catholic Association in 1823, dedicated to peaceful agitation. In 1828 O'Connell won a parliamentary election for County Clare, but as a Catholic could not take his seat. The Prime Minister, *Wellington, reluctantly introduced a Relief Bill to avoid civil war. The 1829 Act removed most civil restrictions; the only one to survive to the present is that no British monarch may be a Roman Catholic (a ban on the monarch marrying a Catholic was abolished in 2013).

Catholicism See ROMAN CATHOLIC CHURCH.

Catholic League See HOLY LEAGUE.

Cato, Marcus Porcius (or **Cato the Elder**) (*c.*234–149 BC) Roman statesman. As consul in 195 Cato suppressed revolt in former Carthaginian Spain with severity; as censor in 184 he was equally severe against private extravagance. Cato prosecuted *Scipio Africanus for corruption.

Cato, Marcus Porcius (or **Cato the Younger**) (95–46 BC) The great-grandson of Cato the Elder. He was known posthumously as 'Uticensis' after the place of his death. A conservative republican, he long opposed *Pompey, but finally sided with him against Julius *Caesar. He committed suicide at Utica in northern Africa after Caesar's victory at Thapsus, rather than seek Caesar's pardon.

Cato Street Conspiracy (1820) A plot to assassinate members of the British government. Under the leadership of Arthur Thistlewood, a revolutionary extremist, the conspirators planned to murder Lord *Castlereagh and other ministers while they were at dinner, as a prelude to a general uprising. However, government spies revealed the plot and possibly also provoked the conspirators to take action. They were arrested at a house in Cato Street, off the Edgware Road, in London. Convicted of high treason, Thistlewood and four others were executed, the rest being sentenced to transportation for life.

Caucasoids The fair-skinned 'European' people, named after the Caucasus Mountains between the Black and Caspian seas. They occupy Europe, Africa as far south as the Sahara, the Middle East, and the Indian subcontinent; in the past five centuries they have spread worldwide. In parts of Central Asia they were replaced in historic times by *Mongoloids. There was always admixture with, and incomplete differentiation from, neighbouring races.

caudillo (Spanish, 'leader', 'hero') Military dictator in a Spanish-speaking country. In Latin American politics caudillos have tended to circumvent constitutions, and rule by military force.

Cavalier Parliament (or **Long Parliament of the Restoration**) (1661–79) The first Parliament in Charles II's reign to be elected by royal writ. Strongly Royalist and Anglican in composition, it contained 100 members from the *Long Parliament of Charles I. Its long duration enabled the Commons to claim a large part in affairs, despite being in session for only 60 months of the 18 years. Its early years were marked by harsh laws against Roman Catholics and Protestant Dissenters. As its membership changed it became increasingly critical of royal policy.

Cavaliers (from French *chevalier*, 'horseman') The name of the Royalist party before, during, and after the *English Civil War. Opponents used the word from about 1641 as a term of abuse: later it acquired a romantic aura in contrast to the image of puritanical *Roundheads. The party, made up of all social classes, but dominated by the country gentry and landowners, was defined by loyalty to the crown and the Anglican Church. The Restoration brought the Royalists back to power—the Parliament of 1661–79 is called the *Cavalier Parliament.

cave-dwellers See PALAEOLITHIC.

Cavell, Edith (Louisa) (1865–1915) British nurse. In charge of the Berkendael

Medical Institute in Brussels during World War I, she helped many Allied soldiers to escape from occupied Belgium. She was arrested by the Germans and brought before a military tribunal, where she openly admitted her actions and was sentenced to death. Her execution provoked widespread condemnation and she became famous as a heroine of the Allied cause.

Cavour, Camillo Benso, Conte di (1810–61) Italian statesman. He was the driving force behind the unification of Italy under Victor Emmanuel II, king of the kingdom of Sardinia. In 1847 Cavour founded the newspaper *Il Risorgimento* to further the cause of unification. As Premier of Piedmont (1852–59; 1860–61), he obtained international support by forming an alliance with France and participating in the Crimean and Franco-Austrian wars. In 1861 he saw Victor Emmanuel crowned king of a united Italy, and became Italy's first Premier.

Caxton, William (*c.*1422–91) The first English printer. Having learned the art of printing on the Continent, Caxton printed his first English text in 1474, when living in Bruges, and after returning to London in 1476 went on to produce about 80 other texts, including editions of Malory's *Le Morte d'Arthur*, Chaucer's *Canterbury Tales*, and his own translations of French romances.

Ceaușescu, Nicolae (1918–89) Romanian Communist statesman, first President of the Socialist Republic of Romania (1974–89). Noted for his independence of the USSR, for many years he fostered his own personality cult, making his wife Elena his deputy and appointing many other members of his family to high office. His regime became increasingly totalitarian, repressive, and corrupt; a popular uprising in December 1989 resulted in its downfall and in the arrest, summary trial, and execution of Ceaușescu and his wife.

Cecil, Robert, 1st Earl of Salisbury and 1st Viscount Cranborne (1563–1612) English statesman. The son of William Cecil, Lord Burghley, he succeeded his father as *Elizabeth I's chief minister in 1598. He was responsible for ensuring the succession of *James I in 1603. He was created Viscount Cranborne (1604) and Earl of Salisbury (1605). He was made Lord Treasurer in 1608 and was faced with crown debts of nearly a million pounds. He increased the king's income by introducing additional customs duties (impositions) and various other unpopular means.

Cecil, William, 1st Baron Burghley (1520–98) English statesman. He trained as a lawyer and held office under *Henry VIII, *Edward VI, and finally as *Elizabeth I's Secretary of State from 1558. Politically adept, he formulated the queen's policy at home and abroad and was rewarded by the offices of Master of the Courts of Wards and Liveries (1561) and Lord Treasurer (1572). He was created Lord Burghley in 1571.

For 40 years he ensured the stability of the Elizabethan regime. More Protestant in sympathy than the queen, he persuaded her to aid the French Huguenots (1567) and the Dutch Calvinists (1585). He exercised control of appointments to the universities of Oxford and Cambridge and was responsible for ordering the execution of *Mary, Queen of Scots, whose existence he perceived as a threat to the state. He encouraged new industries, particularly glass-making, and introduced financial reforms.

Celt (or **Kelt**) A member of a group of west European peoples, including the pre-Roman inhabitants of Britain and Gaul and their descendants, especially in Ireland, Scotland, Wales, Cornwall, Brittany, and the Isle of Man. The Celtic language is a sub-group of the Indo-European language group, divided into two groups, Goidelic (consisting of Irish, Scots Gaelic, and Manx) and Brythonic (consisting of Welsh, Cornish, and Breton).

The Celts occupied a large part of Europe in the Iron Age. Their unity is recognizable by common speech and common artistic tradition, but they did not constitute one race or group of tribes ethnologically. The origins of their culture can be traced back to the Bronze Age of the upper Danube in the 13th century BC, with successive stages represented by the urnfield and Hallstatt cultures. Spreading over western and central Europe from perhaps as early as 900 BC, they reached the height of their power in the La Tène period of the 5th–1st centuries BC. The ancients knew them as fierce fighters and superb horsemen, with savage religious rites conducted by the *Druid priesthood. They were farmers, who cultivated fields on a regular basis and had developed ox-drawn ploughs to use in place of manual implements, a revolutionary advance that permanently affected people's way of life. But Celtic political sense was weak and the numerous tribes, continually warring against each other, were crushed between the migratory Germans and the power of Rome, and were ejected or assimilated by the former or conquered outright by the latter.

CENTO *See* CENTRAL TREATY ORGANIZATION.

Central African Federation (1953–63)

A short-lived African federation, comprising the self-governing colony of Southern Rhodesia (*Zimbabwe) and the British protectorates of Northern Rhodesia (*Zambia) and Nyasaland (*Malawi). In the 1920s and 1930s Europeans in both Rhodesias had pressed for union, but Britain had rejected the proposal because of its responsibilities towards Africans in Northern Rhodesia and Nyasaland. In 1953 the Conservative government in Britain allowed economic arguments to prevail and a federal constitution was devised by which the federal government handled external affairs, defence, currency, intercolonial relations, and federal taxes. Riots and demonstrations by African nationalists followed (1960–61) and in 1962 Britain accepted in principle Nyasaland's right to secede. A meeting of the four concerned governments at the Victoria Falls Conference agreed to dissolve the Federation.

Central African Republic

Capital:	Bangui
Area:	622,984 sq km (240,535 sq miles)
Population:	5,166,510 (2012 est)
Currency:	1 CFA franc = 100 centimes
Religions:	traditional beliefs 35.0%; Protestant 25.0%; Roman Catholic 25.0%; Muslim 15.0%
Ethnic Groups:	Baya 33.0%; Banda 27.0%; Mandjia 13.0%; Sara 10%; Mboum 7%
Languages:	French (official); Sango; Baya; Banda; local languages
International Organizations:	UN; AU; Non-Aligned Movement; Franc Zone; WTO

A landlocked country in Africa stretching west-to-east from Cameroon to the Sudan and south-to-north from humid equatorial forests bordering the Democratic Republic of Congo to the savannah plains of the Chad basin.

Physical The country mainly comprises low plateaux, with the highest point at 1420 m (4660

feet) in the west. The Oubangi River forms the southern boundary and is an important channel of communication.

Economy The Central African Republic is one of Africa's poorer countries, with a largely agricultural economy. There are export crops of coffee, cotton, and hardwood timber. Diamonds, followed by timber and cotton, constitute the largest export commodity; some gold is mined.

History Archaeological finds have shown that the area was inhabited from palaeolithic times (from about three million years ago), but there are no documentary records until the 19th century. The Central African Republic is thought to have been part of the empire of Gaoga, which flourished in the 16th century, and the region was raided for slaves during the 16th, 17th, and 18th centuries. The French began exploring the country in 1889 and by 1911 had taken full control of it. As the French colony of Ubangi Shari, it formed part of *French Equatorial Africa. In 1958 it became a republic within the *French Community, and fully independent in 1960. In 1976 its President, Jean Bedel Bokassa, declared it an empire, and himself Emperor. Following allegations of atrocities, he was deposed in 1979, and the country reverted to a republic. Political instability persisted, and in 1981 General Kolingba seized power from the civilian government. This was restored in 1986 with Kolingba still President. There were demands for multiparty politics, and a new constitution was adopted in 1992. Elections were held in 1993: Ange-Félix Patassé became President and a coalition government was formed. Patassé was re-elected in 1999. A military coup in 2003 installed General François Bozizé as President. Elections held in 2005 confirmed Bozizé in office and he was re-elected in 2011. His term of office saw conflict with domestic rebel forces and incursions arising from conflicts in neighbouring countries. A ceasefire between government and mainly Muslim rebel forces in 2013 quickly broke down. The rebels occupied the capital, Bozizé fled, and a rebel leader, Michel Djotodia, became President. However, Djotodia could not control his forces, which continued to terrorize the predominantly Christian population. Christian militia groups were formed and, as the government lost control, a savage conflict developed between the Muslim and Christian populations. International pressure forced Djotodia to resign in 2014; he was succeeded by Catherine Samba-Panza.

Central American Common Market

(CACM or ODECA) An economic organization comprising Guatemala, Honduras, El Salvador, Nicaragua, and Costa Rica. Beginning with a treaty signed by all five countries in 1960 the CACM sought to reduce trade barriers, stimulate exports, and encourage industrialization by means of regional cooperation. With a permanent secretariat at Guatemala City, its aim was cooperation with the member countries of the Latin American Free Trade Association (now called the Latin American Integration Association). During the 1970s, it somewhat lost impetus, owing to war, upheaval, international recession, and ideological differences among member states. A new tariff and customs agreement came into effect in 1986, when regional trade improved. In 1993 CACM was superseded by the Central American Integration System.

Central Intelligence Agency

(CIA) *See* INTELLIGENCE SERVICES.

Central Treaty Organization

(CENTO) (1955–79) A mutual security organization composed of representatives of Britain, Turkey, Iran, Pakistan, and Iraq. In 1956 the USA became an associate member. Formed as a result of the Baghdad Pact (1955), it was designed in part as a defence against the former Soviet Union and to consolidate the influence of Britain in the Arab world. Following the withdrawal of Iraq (1958), its headquarters were moved to Ankara. It became inactive after the withdrawal of Turkey, Pakistan, and Iran in 1979.

centurion A professional middle-ranking officer of the Roman army. The title means 'leader of a hundred'. The rigorous discipline, leadership and experience of the centurions made them a vital factor in the success of the professional army.

ceorl A free peasant farmer of Anglo-Saxon England. In status ceorls were above the *serfs but below the *thanes (noblemen), with a *Wergild of usually 200 shillings. They were liable to military service in the *fyrd and to taxation. Although they could own land, they were often forced by economic pressures and by reasons of security to place themselves in the control of the richer landowners. After the Norman Conquest their status diminished rapidly and the term 'churl' came to mean an ill-bred serf.

Cetshwayo (or **Cetewayo**) (*c.*1826–84) Zulu king. Cetshwayo became ruler of Zululand in 1873. He increased his army to defend his territory against the Boers and defeated the British at Isandhlwana in 1879. His capital, Ulundi, was captured eight months later, whereupon he was deposed and sent to London. In 1883 British efforts to restore him failed and he was driven out by an anti-royalist faction. *See also* ZULU WAR.

Ceylon The former name (until 1972) of *Sri Lanka.

Chaco War (1932–35) A conflict between Paraguay and Bolivia. The Gran Chaco, an extensive lowland plain, had been an object of dispute between the two countries since the early 19th century, but Bolivia's final loss of its Pacific coast in 1929 (the Tacna–Arica settlement) prompted it to push its claims to the Chaco. Border clashes in the late 1920s led to outright war in 1932. Bolivia had the larger army and superior military equipment, but the Aymará and Quechua Indian conscripts from the Andean highlands did not fare well in the low, humid Chaco. The Paraguayan colonel José Félix Estigarribia drove the Bolivians west across the Chaco and forced his enemies to sue for peace in 1935. Paraguay gained most of the disputed territory, but the price was immense for both countries. More than 50,000 Bolivians and 35,000 Paraguayans had lost their lives. Economic stagnation was to plague both combatants for years to come.

Chad

Capital:	Ndjamena
Area:	1,284,000 sq km (495,755 sq miles)
Population:	11,193,452 (2012 est)
Currency:	1 CFA franc = 100 centimes
Religions:	Muslim 53.1%; Roman Catholic 20.1%; Protestant 14.2%; traditional beliefs 7.3%
Ethnic Groups:	Sara 27.7%; Arab 12.3%; Mayo-Kebbi 11.5%; Kanem-Bornou 9.0%; Ouaddai 8.7%; Hadjarai 6.7%; Tandjile 6.5%; Gorane 6.3%
Languages:	Arabic, French (both official); Sara; Nilotic; Saharan
International Organizations:	UN; AU; Non-Aligned Movement; Franc Zone; WTO

A landlocked country in north-Central Africa surrounded by Libya to the north, Sudan to the east, the Central African Republic to the south, and Niger, Nigeria, and Cameroon to the west.

Physical Out of the Sahara in its northern half rise the volcanic Tibesti Mountains, with reserves of tungsten, while in the east is the great depression surrounding Lake Chad, with deposits of natron (hydrated sodium carbonate).

Economy Chad is one of the poorest countries in Africa, with a mainly agricultural economy. However, oil production, which began in 2003, has recently driven significant economic growth. The non-oil industrial sector is still small, mostly comprising textiles and food processing. Major exports are oil, cotton, and livestock products.

History Northern Chad has been inhabited for about 10,000 years and southern Chad since about 500 BC. During the 8th century *Berber peoples moved into the area and founded the empire of Kanem. This empire expanded and in the 13th century merged with the kingdom of Bornu. The neighbouring kingdoms of Baguirmi and Ouaddaï grew more powerful during the 16th century. The three kingdoms fought during the 17th century until in the early 1890s all fell under the control of the Sudanese conqueror, Rabeh. French expeditions advanced into the region, and French sovereignty was recognized by the European powers. After confrontation with the British at Fashoda (1898) France declared a protectorate, and in 1908 Chad became part of French Equatorial Africa, though control was complete only in 1912. In 1920 Chad became a colony under French administration, its rich mineral deposits being rapidly exploited. In 1940 Chad was the first colony to declare for the *Free French. It became autonomous within the *French Community in 1958, and a fully independent republic in 1960, with François Tombalbaye as the first President. Since then the country has struggled to maintain unity between the Arabic-speaking Muslim peoples of the north and the more economically developed south and west. In 1980 Libya invaded, proposing union between the two countries. Civil war lasted until 1987, when French and US intervention led to Libya's withdrawal and the installation of Hissène Habré as President. Habré was deposed in 1990 by his one-time military commander Idriss Déby. A democratization process was agreed upon, and a transitional legislature was installed in 1993. In 1994 Libya agreed to hand back to Chad the Aouzou Strip, an area rich in minerals occupied by Libya since 1973. Armed rebels, based in the south of the country, agreed to a ceasefire in 1996 and a constitutional referendum, which had been postponed several times, was held. A new constitution was approved, establishing Chad as a unitary state. Déby and his supporters were victorious in elections in 1996, 1997, 2001, 2002, and 2006. A civil war was fought against northern rebels from 1999–2002. In 2004 unrest in the Darfur region of Sudan spread to eastern Chad, and in 2006 Chad accused Sudan of supporting a rebellion that almost toppled the Déby regime. In 2008 rebel forces again reached Ndjamena, but again withdrew.

Chadwick, Sir Edwin (1800–90) British public health reformer. A friend and disciple of Jeremy *Bentham, he was the architect of the *Poor Law Amendment Act (1834). His report for the royal commission set up in 1833 to investigate the conditions of work of factory children resulted in the passing of the Ten Hours Act. During his term of office as Commissioner of the Board of Health (1848–54), he persuaded urban authorities to undertake major water, drainage, and slum clearance schemes to reduce disease.

Chaeronea The northernmost city of Boeotia, ancient Greece, the scene of two important battles. In 338 BC *Philip II of Macedonia crushed the Thebans, Athenians, and their allies there, and so brought mainland Greece under his control. An enormous stone lion, commemorating the site of the fighting, can still be seen.

In 86 BC two armies of *Mithridates VI, King of Pontus, combined there against the Roman forces of *Sulla, but were defeated despite a considerable numerical superiority. A further Roman victory at Orchomenus ensured the ejection of the Pontic forces from Greece.

Chaka *See* SHAKA.

Chalcedon, Council of (451) The fourth ecumenical council of the Christian Church, held at the city of Chalcedon in Greece. This rejected the view expressed by a meeting—convened without papal approval—at Ephesus in 449 that declared *Jesus Christ to have a single nature, asserting instead that Christ's nature was both human and divine.

Chaldean An inhabitant of Chaldea, the southern part of Babylonia. The Chaldeans were a Semitic people originating from Arabia, who settled in the neighbourhood of Ur *c*.800 BC and ruled Babylonia 625–538 BC. They were famous as astronomers.

Chamberlain, Neville (Arthur Neville Chamberlain) (1869–1940) British Conservative statesman, Prime Minister (1937–40). The son of the politician Joseph Chamberlain, he pursued a policy of appeasement towards Germany, Italy, and Japan as Prime Minister of a coalition government; in 1938 he signed the Munich Agreement ceding the Sudetenland to Germany, which he claimed would mean 'peace in our time'. Although the policy was primarily intended to postpone war until Britain had rearmed, it caused increasing discontent in his own party; he was forced to abandon it and prepare for war when Hitler invaded the rest of Czechoslovakia in 1939. He declared war on Germany in 1939 when Hitler invaded Poland. Chamberlain's leadership in World War II proved inadequate and he was replaced by Winston Churchill.

Champa The kingdom of the Chams, a Malay people, said to have been founded in the 2nd century AD in Vietnam. It was frequently at war with the *Khmers to its west and succumbed in the 15th century to *Annam to the north. Its people are commemorated in *Angkor: in a bas-relief of a battle against the Khmers they are distinguished by their flat hats, each one decorated with a flower.

Champlain, Samuel de (1567–1635) French explorer and colonial statesman. He made his first voyage to Canada in 1603, and between 1604 and 1607 explored the eastern coast of North America. In 1608 he was sent to establish a settlement at Quebec, where he developed alliances with the native peoples for trade and defence. He was appointed Lieutenant-Governor in 1612; much of his subsequent career was spent exploring the Canadian interior. After capture and imprisonment by the English (1629–32), he returned to Canada for a final spell as governor (1633–35).

chancery (from the Latin *cancella*, 'screen', hence a screened-off place, or office) The writing-office attached to the court of a ruler, pope, etc. In England, since it supplied the writ necessary for a lawsuit to be heard by the king's judges, it came to be a law court itself, presided over by its head, the Chancellor.

Chandragupta Maurya (*c*.325–297 BC) Indian emperor. He founded the Mauryan

empire, the first empire in India to extend over most of the subcontinent. From his capital at Paliputra he expanded westwards across the River Indus, annexing provinces deep into Afghanistan from Alexander's Greek successors. The empire continued to expand after his death, but ended in 185 BC.

Changamire (*fl. c*.1500) East African ruler, the name taken by Changa, son of Mwene Mutapa Matope, by adding the Arabic title *amir* (commander) to his given name. On his father's death he killed Nyahuma, the lawful successor. His own son fought Chikuyo, Nyahuma's son, until 1502. He began the dismemberment of the Rozvi empire. His kingdom was known also as Butwa and lasted until the early 19th century, when the Nguni destroyed it. His successors built a number of stone monuments and added to the Great *Zimbabwe.

Channel Tunnel A rail tunnel beneath the English Channel providing a fixed link between the UK and France. Several schemes were proposed from the early 19th century onwards. Work actually started twice, in 1882 and 1974, though it was soon abandoned. The present tunnel, which runs between Folkestone and Sangatte, was begun in 1986 and completed in 1994.

Chapultepec Conference (1945) An Inter-American conference, held in Mexico City. The Act of Chapultepec (1945), adopted by 20 republics, resolved to undertake joint action in repelling any aggression against an American state. This was formalized by the Inter-American Treaty of Reciprocal Assistance (the Rio Treaty, 1947) and constituted a significant step in the history of *Pan-Americanism.

chariot A fast, two-wheeled, horse-drawn vehicle. They were originally designed for use in war, and developed from the battle-wagons used by the *Sumerians *c*.2500 BC, which had four wheels, were drawn by onagers (wild asses), and served as mobile fighting platforms. The use of horses, and light two-wheeled vehicles adapted to them, was introduced to the Near East from the region between the Black Sea and the Caspian *c*.2000 BC. (Horses, which were only the size of ponies, were rarely used for riding.) Their crews consisted of two or three people, who were generally armed with bows or javelins. In northern Europe, however, the chariot was used to carry into battle soldiers who fought on foot. A popular tactic was to equip chariot wheels with scythe blades to hack at the legs of enemy soldiers.

Charlemagne (Latin *Carolus Magnus*, Charles the Great) (742–814) King of the Franks (768–814) and Holy Roman emperor (as Charles I) (800–14). He created an empire by conquering and Christianizing the Saxons (772–77; 782–85), Lombards (774), and Avars (791–99), and restoring areas of Italy to the pope. His coronation by Pope Leo III in Rome on Christmas Day, 800, is taken as having inaugurated the Holy Roman Empire. He gave government new moral drive and religious responsibility, and encouraged commerce and agriculture. A well-educated man, he promoted the arts and education and under Alcuin his principal court at Aachen became a major centre of learning. The political cohesion of his empire did not last, but the influence of his scholars persisted in the Carolingian Renaissance.

Charles I (1600–49) King of Great Britain and Ireland (1625–49). He was the second son of *James I and Anne of Denmark. He was neglected by his father in favour of his favourite, *Buckingham, who also dominated Charles in the opening years of his reign. A disastrous foreign policy, Charles's illegal levying of tunnage and poundage, and the mildness of his policy towards Roman Catholics (*recusants) culminated in the forcing through by a hostile Parliament of the *Petition of Right (1628). From 1629 he ruled without a Parliament.

Charles was a man of strong religious conviction: he was also stubborn and politically naïve. During the 'Eleven Year Tyranny' (1629–40) he relied increasingly on *Laud, *Strafford, and his French Catholic queen, *Henrietta Maria; their influence, and the king's use of unconstitutional measures, deepened the widespread antagonism to the court, especially after the *ship money crisis (1637). The fiasco of the *Bishops' Wars drove him to recall Parliament in 1640. The *Long Parliament forced him to sacrifice Laud and Strafford, who were impeached and executed. He had to accept severe limitations of his powers, but an open breach came in January 1642, when he tried to arrest *five members of the House of Commons, a blunder which united the Lords and Commons against the king and made the *English Civil War inevitable.

The royal standard was raised at Nottingham in August. Charles was soundly beaten at *Marston Moor (1644) and *Naseby (1645) and in 1646 surrendered to the Scots near Newark, was handed over to Parliament the following year, and subsequently captured by the Parliamentary army. After escaping to Carisbrooke Castle, Isle of Wight, he signed the 'Engagement' with the Scots (1647) that enabled him to renew the war with their help, but with little success. He was recaptured in 1648, tried, and publicly executed in London.

Charles I of Anjou (1226–85) King of Naples and Sicily (1266–85), son of Louis VIII of France. He acquired Provence by marriage in 1246. Pope Urban IV was under severe threat from the *Hohenstaufens and gave him the kingdom of Sicily in order to curtail their power. He defeated and killed *Manfred at Benevento, effectively ending Hohenstaufen influence, but then went on to take Naples as well as most of northern Italy, himself becoming a real threat to papal interests. His ambitions were ended by the uprising known as the *Sicilian Vespers in which he was assassinated and the French expelled.

Charles II (or **Charles the Bald**) (823–77) King of the West Franks (843–77), Emperor of Germany (875–77). He was the son of Emperor Louis the Pious. After the death of their father he and his brother, Louis the German, made war on their eldest brother Lothair, who had inherited the title of King of the West Franks. By the Treaty of Verdun in 843 Charles gained that kingdom. He and Louis divided Lothair's central kingdom between them in 870 by the Treaty of Mersen and Charles gained the imperial title in 875. The internal conflicts of his reign were further complicated by *Viking incursions. He was a noted patron of scholarship and the arts.

Charles II (1630–85) King of England, Scotland, and Ireland (1660–85) son of Charles I. After his father's execution in 1649 Charles was declared king in Scotland and then crowned there in 1651, but was forced into exile the same year, when his army attempted to invade England and was defeated by Cromwell's forces at Worcester. He remained in exile on the Continent for nine years before he was restored after the collapse of Cromwell's regime. Charles displayed considerable adroitness in handling the difficult constitutional situation, but continuing religious and political strife dogged his reign. Although he failed to produce a legitimate heir, he moved to ensure the Protestant succession by arranging the marriage of his niece Mary to William of Orange.

Charles II (1661–1700) King of Spain (1665–1700). The last Habsburg to be king of Spain, the childless Charles named Philip of Anjou as his successor. This led ultimately to the War of the Spanish Succession.

Charles III (or **Charles the Fat**) (839–88) King of the Franks (884–87), Emperor of Germany (882–88). He was the youngest son of Louis the German. He inherited Swabia and acquired both east and west Frankish kingdoms by 884 after his older brothers died. He was unsuccessful in repelling *Saracen invaders and was obliged to buy a respite from attacks by the *Vikings and so was deposed in 887. His death marked the end of the Carolingian monopoly of kingship over the Franks.

Charles III (1716–88) King of Spain (1759–88) and of Naples and Sicily (1734–59). His enlightened policies met with opposition in Spain. He tried to improve agriculture and industry, reformed the judicial system, and reduced the *Inquisition's powers. His foreign policy was dominated by alliance with France (the Family Compact, 1761). He lost Florida in 1763 but regained it with Minorca in 1783. In 1779 he began a three-year siege of Gibraltar but failed to retake it from Britain.

Charles IV (1316–78) King of Bohemia (1346–78), Holy Roman Emperor (1347–78). He acquired authority over Austria and Hungary in 1364, and received the imperial crown from the pope, in Rome, in 1355. The Golden Bull (1356) issued in his reign formed the imperial constitution, regulating the duties of the seven *Electors. He was an intellectual, interested in the development of the German language, and founded the University of Prague in 1348.

Charles V (or **Charles the Wise**) (1337–80) King of France (1364–80). He earned his nickname from his intellectual pursuits which included book-collecting and artistic patronage, his religious piety, and his cautious adoption of delaying and 'scorched-earth' tactics in fighting the English during the *Hundred Years War. Assuming responsibility as Regent of France in 1356 when his father, John II was captured at *Poitiers, he quelled revolt in Paris and from the Jacquerie and, aided by the Constable of France, Bertrand du Guesclin, was able to recover most of France from the invading English forces.

Charles V (1500–58) Holy Roman Emperor (1519–56) and (as Charles I) King of Spain (1516–56). The son of *Philip I (the Handsome) and Joanna of Spain, and grandson of Emperor *Maximilian I, Charles came to the throne of Spain in 1516 and united it with that of the empire when he inherited the latter in 1519. Tied down by such wide responsibilities, and hampered by the fact that his authority in his separate territories was established on different bases, Charles was never able to give proper attention to national and international problems. His achievements were none the less considerable. In Spain he survived an early revolt and laid the foundations of the strong government which underpinned Spanish greatness in the century after his death, while in Italy he overcame papal resistance to the establishment of Spanish hegemony. While his long war with *Francis I of France was not decisive, it did weaken France to the extent that it was unable to challenge Spain again before the outbreak of the *Thirty Years War. He blunted the *Ottoman offensive against Christian Europe, and maintained his authority under difficult circumstances in the Netherlands. His greatest failure was in Germany, where he was unable either to check the spread of Protestantism or curb the independence of the local princes. Charles handed Naples (1554), the Netherlands (1555), and Spain (1556) over to his son *Philip II, and the imperial crown (1556) to his brother Ferdinand, and retired to a monastery in Spain.

Charles VII (1403–61) King of France (1422–61). During his youth France was badly ruled by his father Charles the Mad and much territory was lost. Internal quarrels and war with England dominated his reign. At the time of his accession to the throne, much of northern France was under English occupation, including Reims, where he should have been crowned. After the intervention of *Joan of Arc, however, the French experienced a dramatic military revival and Charles was crowned at Reims in 1429. He established greater control over the Church in the Pragmatic Sanction of Bourges of 1438, which upheld the right of the French Church to administer its property and nominate clergy to benefices, independently of the papacy. His reign eventually saw the defeat of the English and the end of the *Hundred Years War. Having recovered most of the land his country had lost to the English, he modernized the administration of the army and did much to lay the foundations of French power in the following decades.

Charles X (1757–1836) King of France (1824–30). As the Comte d'Artois, the dissolute and reactionary brother of Louis XVI, he was ordered by the king to leave France in 1789 and became the leader of the exiled royalists. He returned to France in 1814 and during the reign of his next brother, *Louis XVIII, led the ultra-royalist party. His proclamation to rule by divine right and his choice of ministers who did not reflect liberal majorities in Parliament led to unrest. The defeat of an unpopular ministry in June 1830 prompted him to issue the July Ordinances, which established rigid control of the press, dissolved the newly elected chamber, and restricted suffrage. These measures enraged the populace and he was forced, in the *July Revolution, to abdicate. After the succession of *Louis Philippe, he returned to Britain.

Charles XII (or **Karl XII**) (1682–1718) King of Sweden (1697–1718). Three years after his succession, he embarked on the Great Northern War against the encircling powers of Denmark, Poland-Saxony, and Russia. In the early years he won a series of victories, but in 1709 he embarked on an expedition deep into Russia that ended in the destruction of his army at Poltava and the internment of Charles until 1715. He resumed his military career after his return but was killed while besieging a fortress in Norway.

Charles XIV (born **Jean Baptiste Jules Bernadotte**) (1763–1844) King of Sweden and Norway (1818–44). An active supporter of the French Revolution, he served brilliantly under *Napoleon I in the Italian Campaign. At one time a rival to Napoleon, he nevertheless supported the latter when he proclaimed the empire in 1804. He fought at Austerlitz and Wagram and became governor of Hanover before being invited (1810) by the Swedish Riksdag (Parliament) to succeed the senile, childless Charles XIII. He accepted, becoming a member of the Lutheran Church. As crown prince he allied Sweden with Britain and Russia and played an important part in the defeat of Napoleon at the battle of Leipzig (1813). Having invaded Denmark, he obtained Danish agreement at the Treaty of Kiel (1814) for the transfer of *Norway to Sweden. He succeeded Charles XIII in 1818. Autocratic in style and opposed to demands for a free press and more liberal government, he nevertheless maintained popular support throughout his reign. He was the founder of the present Swedish dynasty.

Charles, Prince (full name **Charles Philip Arthur George, Prince of Wales**) (1948–) Heir apparent to Elizabeth II. Invested as Prince of Wales in 1969, he served in the Royal Navy (1971–76), and married Lady Diana Spencer (*see* DIANA, PRINCESS OF WALES) in 1981. They had two children, Prince *William Arthur Philip Louis (born 1982) and Prince Henry Charles Albert David ('Harry', born 1984). The couple publicly announced their separation in 1993 and divorced in 1996. Charles married Camilla Parker-Bowles in 2005.

Charles Martel (*c.*688–741) (French, *martel*, 'hammer') Frankish leader. He was the son of Pepin II, 'mayor of the palace' under *Merovingian rule. He gained control of the Austrasian province and defeated the Neustrian mayor. Burgundy and Aquitaine were also acquired. His greatest achievement, and the one which made him a traditional French hero, was his defeat of the Muslim forces between Poitiers and Tours in 732, which signalled the end of their northward expansion.

Charles the Bold (1433–77) Duke of *Burgundy (1467–77). He was the greatest of the dukes of Burgundy, and almost succeeded in creating a kingdom independent of France. He tried to persuade the *Holy Roman Emperor to grant him the title of king in 1473. He supported the League of the Public Weal against the French king, Louis XI, and, after 1467, concentrated with successful results on expansion into the Rhineland and Alsace. After 1475, war with the Swiss culminated in his own death in battle. His realm was absorbed by the French and by *Maximilian I.

Charlie, Bonnie Prince *See* PRETENDER.

charter (Latin, *carta*, "written document") A legal document from a ruler or government, conferring rights or laying down a constitution. Charters in England date from the 7th century, when they were used to confirm grants of land, usually recorded in Latin. Borough charters granting towns specific privileges, which could include self-government and freedom from certain fiscal burdens, were regularly awarded by English kings between 1066 and 1216 (over 300 were issued). *Magna Carta (1215) was a charter which sought to regularize the feudal contract between the crown and its *barons.

The commercial and colonial expansion of England from the 16th century led to the use of charters to authorize the trading ventures of companies (*chartered company) and to form the first constitutions of the English colonies in America. Such colonial charters were in the form of a grant to a company (Virginia Company 1606), or gave recognition to the self-governing status of existing colonies (as with Connecticut in 1662). The importance of these charters was recognized by the Americans during the War of *Independence.

chartered company A form of trading company that developed from the European medieval trading guilds and was prominent in the late 16th and 17th centuries. The discovery by explorers of India and America stimulated individual merchants into forming groups, safeguarded by royal charter in order to monopolize trade. Governments awarded exclusive trading rights in a particular area to a few rich merchants. Such companies were easy to control and, with their specially granted diplomatic, legislative, and military authority, they acted as virtual representatives of the crown. Since the companies were so restrictive, they could arouse considerable domestic opposition.

Chartism A popular movement in Britain for electoral and social reform (1836–48). The *Reform Act of 1832 had left the mass of the population without any voice in the country's affairs and widespread discontent was fuelled by a slump in the economy. The Chartist movement began with the formation of the London Working Men's Association, led by William Lovett and Francis Place, who drew up a programme of reform for the common people. In 1838 *The People's Charter* was launched at a meeting in Birmingham: it called for universal male suffrage, annual parliaments, vote by ballot, abolition of the property qualification for Members of Parliament, payment of Members of Parliament, and equal electoral districts. In 1839, the Chartists, now strongly influenced by the Irish radical Feargus *O'Connor, met in London to prepare a petition to the House of Commons. The meeting revealed deep differences of opinion and after Parliament had rejected the petition, there was uncertainty about the movement's future. During that year there were riots in Birmingham and throughout the north of England; the Newport Rising took place in Monmouthshire, and several Chartist leaders were arrested and imprisoned. Reorganizing themselves, in 1842 the Chartists presented a second petition, signed by three million supporters, to Parliament, which again refused to listen to their claims. The plan for a final demonstration, to be held in London in 1848 for the purpose of presenting yet another petition, was called off after the government threatened military resistance, and the movement faded into insignificance, though many Chartists were later active in radical politics.

Chatham, 1st Earl of *See* PITT, WILLIAM, 1ST EARL OF CHATHAM.

Chattanooga Campaign (1863) A campaign during the *American Civil War. On 9 September a Federal army under General W. Rosecrans occupied Chattanooga, a strategic communication centre for the *Confederacy and pushed on south-eastwards. Rosecrans's forces were attacked by a Confederate army under General Bragg, who successfully drove Rosecrans back to Chattanooga, where the Union army was besieged for several weeks. General Ulysses *Grant assumed direct command, broke the siege and counter-attacked, winning the Battle of Chattanooga and opening the way for the advance on Atlanta (1864) and later for the march of General William *Sherman to the sea.

Chavín culture A civilization that flourished in Peru 1000–200 BC. The culture was based on the ceremonial centre of Chavín de Huantar, high in the Andes 280 km (175 miles) north of Lima and spread for hundreds of miles along the Peruvian coast. United more by religion than politics, the Chavín people's most characteristic artefacts are figures, presumably gods, with jaguar fangs projecting from their lips. Notable advances made by the Chavín included improved maize, the back-strap loom, and metallurgy. As Chavín religious authority waned, regional groups appeared that dominated Peru for the next thousand years.

Chechnya *See* RUSSIA.

CHEKA Soviet secret police. An acronym for the All-Russian Extraordinary Commission for the Suppression of Counter-revolution and Sabotage, it was instituted by *Lenin (1917) and run by Dzerzhinski, a Pole. Lenin envisaged the need for a regime of terror to protect his revolution and this was its purpose. Its headquarters, the Lubyanka prison in Moscow, contained offices and places for torture and execution. In 1922 the CHEKA became the GPU or secret police and later the OGPU (United State Political Administration). The OGPU was replaced in 1934 by the *NKVD.

chemical and biological warfare (CBW) The use of synthetic poisonous substances, or organisms such as disease germs, to kill or injure the enemy. They include chlorine, phosgene, and mustard gas (first used in World War I), various nerve gases, defoliant agents, and viruses and bacteria (for example, anthrax). The use of chemical and biological weapons is prohibited by the *Geneva Convention, but their production, possession, or transfer are not. Unlike their World War I counterparts, modern chemical weapons are sophisticated and may be delivered by long-range artillery, missile, or sprayed from aircraft. To be effective, the chemicals must be inhaled or come into contact with skin. The main defence against them is protective clothing—gas masks and special suits made of rubber or treated synthetic cloth.

Biological weapons were banned under the Biological Weapons Convention of 1972, but research production was permitted for defensive purposes. Agreement regarding the limitation of chemical and biological weapons stands high on the agenda of the United Nations Conference on Disarmament, but many states, particularly in the developing world, are reluctant to give up possession of such weapons because they consider them to be a form of deterrence. Iraq's chemical and biological weapons programmes were a prominent issue in the 1990s following the *Gulf War and were used to justify the *Iraq War of 2003. However, no such weapons were found after Iraq's defeat. In 2013 chemical weapons were used in the Syrian civil war (*see* SYRIA).

Cheng Ho *See* ZHENG HE.

Chernobyl A nuclear power-station near Kiev in Ukraine, the site in 1986 of the worst nuclear accident in the world to date. 31 people died trying to fight subsequent fires, and many more received radiation burns or suffered from associated diseases. The accident was the result of unauthorized experiments by the operators of one of the four reactors, in which safety systems were deliberately circumvented in order to learn more about the plant's operation. Fallout from the explosions, containing the radioactive isotope caesium-137, affected large areas of Europe. In particular, livestock in high-rainfall areas received unacceptable doses of radiation. In the mid-1990s large areas of land in Ukraine, Belarus, and south-west Russia were still contaminated and high levels of cancer (especially leukaemia in children) were reported. The power-station was closed when its last nuclear reactor was shut down in 2000.

Cherokee A Native American people (*Plains Peoples) who traditionally inhabited a region stretching across western Virginia and the Carolinas, eastern Kentucky and Tennessee, and northern Georgia and Alabama. Their prehistoric ancestors built ancient Etowah (Georgia), an important ceremonial centre of the eastern Mississippi cultures, visited by Hernando *De Soto in his explorations of 1540–42. The Cherokee lived in towns of longhouses, and were at first easily assimilated into the expanding USA. Smallpox and other European-introduced diseases had greatly reduced their population by the 17th century, when French and English traders made contact. Conflict with White settlers moving westwards led to several wars, which reduced their lands. However, they adopted European methods of farming and

government, including a bill of rights and a written constitution. The Cherokee also developed a distinct and original written language in the early 19th century, which gave rise to an indigenous literature and, later, a Cherokee-language newspaper.

The Cherokee had supported the British in 18th-century wars against the French and during the American War of *Independence. American forces attacked them and by the end of the war their population and territories had been greatly reduced, so in 1827 they established the **Cherokee Nation** in north-west Georgia through a series of treaties with the US federal government. The discovery of gold on their land resulted in pressure from the White settlers to encroach further onto Cherokee territory. Although their treaty rights and tribal autonomy were upheld in the Supreme Court, they fell foul of both the state authorities and Jackson's policy of removal of Native American tribes to land west of the Mississippi. In 1838 President Van Buren ordered the deportation of the remaining Cherokee to the *Oklahoma Indian Territory (*see* TRAIL OF TEARS). In 1906 the Cherokee finally gave up their tribal allegiance and in 1924 they gained the vote as US citizens.

Chiang Kai-shek (or **Jiang Jie Shi**) (1887–1975) Chinese statesman and general, President of China (1928–31; 1943–49) and of Taiwan (1950–75). A prominent general in the army of Sun Yat-sen, in 1925 he became leader of the Kuomintang when Sun Yat-sen died, and launched a military campaign to unite China. In the 1930s he concentrated more on defeating the Chinese Communists than on resisting the invading Japanese, but he proved unable to establish order and was defeated by the Communists after the end of World War II. Forced to abandon mainland China in 1949, he set up a separate Nationalist Chinese State in Taiwan.

Chickasaw A Native American people that inhabited the region of modern northern Alabama and Mississippi, and southern Tennessee, and were descendants of the late prehistoric *Mississippi cultures. They sided with the British in the 18th century and were attacked by the French and French Native American allies. They were forcibly moved to the *Oklahoma Indian Territory in the 1830s.

Chien-lung *See* QIANLONG.

Chifley, Joseph Benedict (1885–1951) Australian Labor statesman, Prime Minister (1945–49). He entered Parliament in 1928; after

World War II he became Prime Minister on the death of John Curtin. During his term of office he continued to fulfil Labor's nationalization and welfare programme; he also initiated Australia's immigration policy and the Snowy Mountains hydroelectric scheme. He was defeated in the 1949 election but remained leader of the Labor Party until his death.

Children's Crusade (1212) A pathetic episode in the *Crusades, growing out of simple faith and fanatical zeal for the recapture of *Palestine from the Saracens. Some 50,000 children, mainly from France and Germany, are said to have taken part in the expedition which probably included poor adults. They believed they could conquer the Saracens by love, not force. About 30,000 reached Marseilles but were tricked by merchants and sold as slaves in North Africa. The rest were dispersed and many were sold as slaves in the east. Very few ever returned to their homes.

Chile

Capital:	Santiago
Area:	756,102 sq km (291,933 sq miles)
Population:	17,216,945 (2012 est)
Currency:	1 peso = 100 centavos
Religions:	Roman Catholic 70.0%; Evangelical 15.1%
Ethnic Groups:	White and Mestizo 95.4%; Mapuche 4.0%
Languages:	Spanish (official); also Amerindian languages (mostly Araucanian)
International Organizations:	UN; OAS; Non-Aligned Movement; WTO; OECD

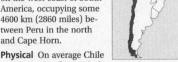

A long and narrow country on the west coast of South America, occupying some 4600 km (2860 miles) between Peru in the north and Cape Horn.

Physical On average Chile is only 160 km (100 miles) in width from the Pacific to the high Andes, along which run the boundaries with Bolivia and Argentina. In the north is the arid Atacama Desert, while in the centre the climate is mild and conducive to most forms of agriculture. Tierra del Fuego, in the extreme south is cold, very wet, and relatively barren, suitable only for sheep grazing. Inland, along the whole length of the country, stretch mountains.

Economy Chile's economy is based largely on the exploitation of substantial mineral reserves, and agriculture. Copper, of which Chile is the world's largest producer, is the major export and provides about 20% of government revenue; fruit, fishmeal, timber products, and wine are also important. Besides copper mining, industries include the production of other metals, food processing, and wood products. In 2010 Chile became the first South American country to join the OECD.

History At the time of the first Spanish contact in 1536 the dominant Indian group, the Araucanians, were theoretically subject to the *Inca empire, but in practice they retained considerable independence within the Inca realm. Though they resisted Spanish encroachments, the Araucanians were gradually pushed south of the Bío Bío River where they were more or less kept under control. Spanish colonization began with the foundation of Santiago in 1541. The colony grew moderately but did not prosper for the next two centuries as it was overshadowed by wealthier Peru. Politically Chile became part of the Spanish viceroyalty of Peru. Chilean independence from Spain was proclaimed in 1810 by *O'Higgins; it was achieved after the South American liberator José de *San Martín crossed the Andes with an army of 3200 men and defeated Spanish troops at the battles of Chacabuco (1817), and Maipo (1818). The discovery of rich copper deposits in the northern Atacama desert had a dramatic impact on economic life, with a railway system developing from 1851. Following war with *Bolivia and *Peru (1879–83), rich natural nitrate deposits were annexed in the north, leading to a 50-year economic boom. By the 1920s synthetic nitrates were replacing saltpetre and dependence on copper exports placed Chile at the mercy of the world market. Political experiments after World War II failed to cope with a series of burgeoning social problems and prompted the election in 1970 of the Marxist democrat Salvador *Allende, the first avowed Marxist in world history to be elected President by popular vote. As the head of the Unidad Popular (a coalition of communists and socialists), Allende was faced with a majority opposition in Congress, and the hostility of the USA. He was increasingly frustrated in his attempts to implement his radical programme of nationalization and agrarian reform. Inflation, capital flight, and a balance-of-payments deficit contributed to an economic crisis in 1973. In September the army commander-in-chief *Pinochet led the military coup which cost Allende and 15,000 Chileans their lives, and prompted one-tenth of the population to emigrate. The military regime which replaced Chile's democracy brutally suppressed all labour unions and opposition groups, and pursued a free-market economy. Although inflation was dramatically reduced, so was demand, output, and employment. The economy continued on a downward spiral in the 1980s with the world's highest per-capita level of external debt. In 1988 Pinochet accepted a plebiscite decision for the 're-establishment' of 'workable democracy', and stepped down. In 1989 Patricio Aylwin was elected President and civilian rule was restored. Aylwin was succeeded in 1994 by Edúardo Frei Ruiz-Tagle. Richard Lagos was elected President in 2000, and in 2006 Michelle Bachelet became Chile's first woman President. Although her government's social reforms were popular, the constitution prevented her contesting the 2009 election; this was won by the conservative Sebastián Piñera after a run-off in early 2010. Bachelet returned to power in 2014.

Chilembwe, John (*c.*1871–1915) *Malawi nationalist. A servant of the missionary Joseph Booth, who sent him to a Negro theological college in the USA, he became a church minister and in 1900 established the Providence Industrial Mission in Nyasaland (now Malawi). Chilembwe protested against the injustices of colonial rule. In 1915 he started a rebellion but it did not gain enough African support and he was shot by the police.

Chimú The most powerful state of the north coast of Peru between *c.*AD 1000 and 1476, when it was conquered by the *Incas. Its capital was Chan Chan, a vast city near modern Trujillo.

China

Capital:	Beijing
Area:	9,596,961 sq km (3,705,407 sq miles)
Population:	1,349,585,838 (2012 est)
Currency:	1 yuan = 10 jiao = 100 fen
Religions:	China is officially atheist, but Daoism, Buddhism, Christianity, and Islam are permitted.
Ethnic Groups:	Han (Chinese) 91.5%; over 50 minorities including Chuang, Hui, Uighur, Yi, Miao, Manchu, Tibetan, Mongolian, Tuchia, Puyi, Korean, Tung, Yao, Pai, Hani, Kazakh, Tai, and Li
Languages:	Mandarin Chinese (official); six other dialects of Chinese; at least 41 other minority languages
International Organizations:	UN; WTO

The third-largest country in the world, occupying most of eastern Asia and bounded by North Korea, Kazakhstan and Mongolia on the north, Russia on the west, Afghanistan, Pakistan, India, Nepal and Bhutan on the south-west and Myanmar (Burma), Laos, and Vietnam on the south-east.

Physical China's coastline adjoins the South and East China Seas and the Yellow Sea. In the north-west lies Xinjiang (Sinkiang), an area of mountains and desert, and in the south-west is the mountainous region of Tibet. The remainder of China is divided laterally by the Yangtze (Chang) River. In the north-east lies Manchuria, on higher ground and with many rivers and lakes. In the west are the mountains and plateaux surrounding the red clay basin of Sichuan, which is well watered and supports a mass of paddy fields. Huge lakes occupy low-lying land to the south of the Yangtze, while southward the terrain rises to many ranges of high hills. Here the climate is subtropical. The plateaux support tea plantations, many of the slopes are terraced for rice, and the deep valleys are full of natural forests of bamboo. The province of Gansu in the north-west region is the principal centre of earthquakes in China, where major earthquakes take place on an average of once every 65 years.

Economy In the late 1970s China adopted pragmatic policies of liberalizing the economy, which accelerated over subsequent decades and made China the world's second-largest economy by 2010. Four Special Economic Zones were established to attract foreign investment, direct state control of factories was loosened, stock markets set up, and responsibility for agriculture switched from collective farms to individual households. Industry saw rapid expansion, which made China the world's leader measured by output; a wide range of major industries includes metals, machinery, armaments, textiles and clothing, oil, cement, chemicals and fertilizers, consumer goods, food processing, transport equipment, telecommunications, and space technology. Mineral extraction of oil, coal, and such metals as iron, aluminium, tin, and tungsten is important. Agriculture continues to employ about one-third of the population, with rice, cereals, and potatoes the main products.

History China has a recorded history beginning nearly 4000 years ago, with the *Shang who settled in the Huang He (Yellow River) valley. Under the Eastern *Zhou, from the 6th century BC, *Confucius and Mencius formulated ideas that became the framework of Chinese society. Daoism, founded by *Laozi, appeared during the 3rd century BC. Gradually Chinese culture spread out from the Huang He valley. A form of writing with characters representing meanings rather than sounds—and required by Shi Huangdi, the first ruler of a unified China, to be written in a uniform style—bound together people divided by geography and different spoken dialects. From the *Qin the concept of a unified empire prevailed, surviving periods of fragmentation and rule by non-Chinese dynasties such as the *Yuan. Under strong dynasties such as the *Han and the *Tang China's power extended far west into Turkistan and south into *Annam. On its neighbours, particularly *Korea and Annam, it exercised a powerful influence. Barbarian invaders and dynasties usually adopted Chinese cultural traditions.

The ideas of *Buddhism began to reach China from the 1st century AD and were gradually changed and assimilated into Chinese culture. The Chinese people, showing remarkable inventiveness, were ahead of the West in technology until about the end of the *Song dynasty. However, after the *Mongol conquest the country drew in on itself. Learning, in high esteem from early times, became rooted in the stereotyped study of the Confucian classics, for success in examinations based on the classics was for centuries the means to promotion in the civil service. In time, study of the classics had a deadening intellectual influence.

Throughout history, China, the 'Middle Kingdom', as it is called by the Chinese, regarded itself as superior to all others—a view shared by philosophers of the *Enlightenment. After the Manchu invasion of 1644, China was ruled by the *Qing dynasty, which was at its most powerful and prosperous in the 18th century. Western countries attempted to establish trading links with the Qing dynasty but with little success. As the power of the Qing dynasty weakened towards the end of the 18th century, Western pressure for change built up, leading to direct European involvement in China. Contact with the West precipitated crisis and decline. After the *Opium Wars, treaty ports became the

focus for both Western expansion and demands for modernization. Rebellions during the 19th century, such as the *Taiping Rebellion, devastated the country and undermined imperial rule in spite of the Self-Strengthening Movement and the abortive Hundred Days Reform. Defeat in the *Sino-Japanese War (1894–95) and the *Boxer Rising stimulated reforms, but the dynasty ended in the *Chinese Revolution of 1911. The Republic that followed *Sun Yat-sen's brief presidency degenerated into *warlord regimes after Yuan Shikai's attempt to restore the monarchy. *Chiang Kai-shek united much of China after the Northern Expedition and ruled from Nanjing with his nationalist *Kuomintang, but his Republic of China collapsed in the face of the Japanese invasion of 1937 and the civil war with the communists, and continued only on the island of *Taiwan after his retreat there in 1949. The *Chinese Communist Party under *Mao Zedong won the civil war, established the People's Republic of China on the mainland, and set about revolutionizing and developing China's economy and society. In the 1950s, land reform led to the *communes and the *Great Leap Forward, and urban industry was expanded and nationalized. Relations with the Soviet Union worsened and during 1966–76 the country was torn apart by the *Cultural Revolution, which ended only with Mao's death. During the 1980s *Deng Xiaoping remained committed to economic reform and to improving relations with the Soviet Union. Pressures for democratization grew, however, and a student demonstration in Beijing in June 1989 was suppressed when the army massacred thousands in **Tiananmen Square**. Gradual moves towards a controlled market economy continued. In 1994 the USA decided to maintain special trade links with China despite its continued violations of human rights. Jiang Zemin (1926–), President since 1993, assumed the role of the country's leader after Deng's death in 1997. Hong Kong reverted to China from British rule in 1997 and Macao from Portuguese rule in 1999. Between 2002 and 2004 Jiang Zemin progressively relinquished his posts to *Hu Jintao; he in turn was succeeded by *Xi Jinping in 2012–13. By the early 21st century the economic reforms of the previous quarter of a century had turned China into a major global power.

China-Japan Peace and Friendship Treaty (1978) An agreement between China and Japan aimed at closer political and economic cooperation. Post-war Japanese foreign policy was characterized by a tension between

dependence on the USA and popular pressure for closer relations with China. The growing western inclination of Chinese policy, the thaw in US–Chinese relations following the Nixon visit of 1972, and increasing Japanese dependence on Asia for its foreign trade improved Sino-Japanese contact, leading to the signing of the Treaty in 1978, one of the major aims of which was the establishment of closer trading links.

Chin dynasty See JIN.

Ch'in dynasty See QIN.

Chinese Civil War (1927–37; 1946–49) Conflicts between nationalist and communist Chinese forces. Hostilities broke out in 1927 during *Chiang Kai-shek's Northern Expedition, with anti-leftist purges of the *Kuomintang and a series of abortive communist urban uprisings. Communist strength was thereafter most successfully established in rural areas and its supporters were able to utilize guerrilla tactics to neutralize superior nationalist strength. After a three-year campaign, Chiang finally managed to destroy the Jiangxi Soviet established by *Mao Zedong, but after the *Long March (1934–35), the communists were able to re-establish themselves in Yan'an, in the north of the country. Hostilities between the two sides were reduced by the Japanese invasion of 1937 and, until the end of World War II in 1945, an uneasy truce was maintained as largely separate campaigns were fought against the common enemy. Violence broke out briefly immediately the war ended, resuming on a widespread basis in April 1946 after the US general George *Marshall had failed to arrange a lasting compromise settlement. During the first year of the renewed conflict, numerically superior nationalist troops made large territorial gains, including the communist capital of Yan'an. Thereafter Kuomintang morale began to crumble in the face of successful military operations by the communists and decreasing confidence in their administration, so that by the end of 1947 a successful communist counter-offensive was well under way. In November 1948 *Lin Biao completed his conquest of Manchuria, where the nationalists lost half a million men, many of whom defected to the communists. In Central China the nationalists lost Shandong and in January 1949 were defeated at the battle of Huai-Hai (near Xuzhou). Beijing fell in January, Nanjing and Shanghai in April. The People's Republic of China was proclaimed (1 October 1949) and the communist victory was complete

when the nationalist government fled from Chongqing to *Taiwan in December.

Chinese Communist Party (CCP) Chinese political party. Interest in communism was stimulated by the *Russian Revolution (1917) and the May Fourth Movement and promoted by Li Dazhao, librarian of Beijing University, and Chen Duxiu. They were co-founders of the Chinese Communist Party at its First Congress in Shanghai in July 1921. Under *Comintern instructions, CCP members joined the *Kuomintang and worked in it for national liberation. Early activities concentrated on trade union organization in Shanghai and other large cities, but a peasant movement was already being developed by Peng Pai. Purged by the Kuomintang in 1927 and forced out of the cities, the CCP had to rely on China's massive peasant population as its revolutionary base. It set up the Jiangxi Soviet in southern China in 1931 and moved north under the leadership of *Mao Zedong in the *Long March (1934–35). Temporarily at peace with the Kuomintang after the Xi'an Incident in 1936, the communists proved an effective resistance force when the Japanese invaded the country in 1937. After the end of World War II, the party's military strength and rural organization allowed it to triumph over the nationalists in the renewed civil war and to proclaim a People's Republic in 1949. It has ruled China since 1949. Internal arguments over economic reform and political doctrine and organization led to the chaos of the *Cultural Revolution (1966–76), during which the CCP appeared to turn on itself. After the death of Mao Zedong and the purge of the *Gang of Four the CCP pursued a more stable political direction under the leadership of *Deng Xiaoping; but allegations of corruption and demands for more open government led to a prolonged crisis in 1987–89, culminating in the Tiananmen Square massacre of an estimated 2000 protesters in June 1989. Despite economic liberalization in China, the CCP retains its monopoly of political power.

Chinese Revolution of 1911 The overthrow of the Manchu *Qing dynasty and the establishment of a Chinese republic. After half a century of anti-Manchu risings, the imperial government began a reform movement that gave limited authority to provincial assemblies, and these became power bases for constitutional reformers and republicans. Weakened by provincial opposition to the nationalization of some major railways, the government was unable to suppress the republican Wuchang

Uprising (10 October 1911). By the end of November 15 provinces had seceded and on 29 December 1911 provincial delegates proclaimed a republic, with *Sun Yat-sen as provisional President. In February 1912, the last Qing emperor *Puyi was forced to abdicate and Sun stepped down to allow Yuan Shikai to become President. The Provisional Constitution of March 1912 allowed for the institution of a democratically elected parliament, but this was ignored and eventually dissolved by Yuan Shikai after the abortive Second Revolution of 1913, which challenged his authority. Yuan had himself proclaimed emperor in 1915, but by that time central government was ineffective and China was controlled by provincial *warlords.

Chinese technology China has the longest unbroken history of progress in science and technology (over 4000 years) of any nation in the world. Four inventions that had a major impact on Western culture were paper, printing from movable type, gunpowder, and the magnetic compass. Paper-making began in China around 50 BC and by the 7th century AD had spread to Korea, Japan, and the Arab world. Wood-block printing was well established in China by 1000 AD, while movable type came about a century later. Gunpowder was first used in China early in the 12th century. It reached Europe less than a century later, where it almost overnight transformed the art of warfare. A form of magnetic compass was probably used in China as early as the 5th century BC, but it was not used for navigation until the 12th century, almost the same time as in Europe. An enormous number of other inventions have their origins in China. Examples include the stern rudder and compartmentalized hulls for ships, the horse-collar harness, paddle-wheel propulsion, and the seismograph. The Great Wall of China and the Grand Canal are outstanding Chinese civil engineering projects.

Ch'ing dynasty See QING.

Chirac, Jacques (René) (1932–) French statesman, Prime Minister (1974–76; 1986–88) and President 1995–2007. He was elected mayor of Paris in 1977, a position he held for 18 years. The founder and leader of the right-wing RPR (Rally for the Republic) Party, Chirac headed the right's coalition in the National Assembly during the socialist government of 1981–86. When his coalition was victorious in the 1986 National Assembly elections, he was appointed Prime Minister by the socialist President François Mitterrand. After an unsuccessful bid for the presidency in 1988, Chirac was elected to succeed Mitterrand in 1995 and re-elected with a landslide in 2002, but he did not contest the 2007 election. In 2011 he was convicted of corruption while mayor of Paris.

chivalry The code of behaviour practised in the Middle Ages, especially in the 12th and 13th centuries, by the mounted soldier or knight. The chivalric ethic represented the fusion of Christian and military concepts of conduct. A knight was to be brave, loyal to his lord, and the protector of women. The songs of the *troubadours celebrated these virtues.

It was a system of apprenticeship: as boys, knights' sons became pages in the castles of other knights; from the age of 14 they learnt horsemanship and military skills, and were themselves knighted at the age of 21. The *Crusades saw the apogee of the chivalric ideal, as new Christian orders of knights (*Knights Templars; *Knights Hospitallers), waged war in *Palestine against the Muslims. During times of peace, the tournament was the setting for displays of military and equestrian skill. The 15th century saw a decline in the real value of chivalry, and though new orders, such as the Order of the Golden Fleece (Burgundy) were created, tournaments survived merely as ritualized ceremonies.

Choctaw An Algonquian-speaking Native American tribe originally inhabiting the lower Mississippi and known as the 'okla homa' ('red people'). They allied with the French and fought the Chickasaw. In the 1830s they were driven off their land and into the *Oklahoma Indian Territory.

Choiseul, Étienne François, duc de (1719–85) French statesman, Secretary of State for Foreign Affairs (1758–70). He concluded the Family Compact of 1761 with *Charles III of Spain and, considering the weakness of the French position, was a successful negotiator at the Treaty of *Paris in 1763. He then tried to reform the army and navy, but was dismissed in December 1770 when he tried to persuade *Louis XV to support Spain against Britain over the Falkland Islands. Lorraine and Corsica were both annexed during his period in office.

Chola A Tamil Hindu dynasty dominant in south India from the 9th to the 13th century. Their origins are uncertain, but they were influential from at least the 3rd century AD, becoming an imperial power on the overthrow of their Pallava neighbours in the late 9th century. Victory over the Pandyas followed, and then expansion into the Deccan, Orissa, and

Sri Lanka. Their peak was during the reigns of Rajaraja I (985–1014) and Rajendra I (1014–44), when Chola armies reached the Ganges and the Malay archipelago. The dynasty remained the paramount power in south India until the mid-13th century, when *Hoysala and Pandya incursions and the rise of Vijayanagar eventually destroyed its claims.

Chou dynasty *See* ZHOU.

Chou En-lai *See* ZHOU ENLAI.

Chrétien, Jean (Joseph-Jacques Jean Chrétien) (1934–) French-Canadian statesman. Before he entered politics in 1963, Chrétien had been a lawyer. He was appointed to nine successive cabinet posts, including Minister of Finance (1977–79), being the first French-Canadian to hold that post. As Minister of Justice (1980–82) he handled negotiations with Britain over revising Canada's constitution. In 1984 Chrétien became Deputy Prime Minister but resigned in 1986, returning to his law practice. In 1990 he resumed his political career and was elected leader of the Liberal Party; he served as Prime Minister from 1993–2003.

Christ *See* JESUS CHRIST.

Christian I (1426–81) King of Denmark and Norway (1448–81) and Sweden (1457–64), who founded the Oldenburg dynasty. Elected to power by the Danish Rigstad and confirming his status by marriage to his predecessor's widow, he gained the Swedish throne after the war of 1451–57, but lost control to the Swedish nobility later. He also gained Schleswig and Holstein and was at war with England (1469–74). Strongly Catholic, he founded the Catholic University of Copenhagen in 1479.

Christian, Fletcher (c.1764–c.1793) British seaman and mutineer. In 1787 he became master's mate under Captain William Bligh on HMS *Bounty*, a ship sailing for the Pacific. In April 1789 Christian seized the ship and cast Bligh adrift on account of his alleged tyranny. In 1790 the crew settled on Pitcairn Island, where Christian was probably killed by Tahitians.

Christianity A religion whose adherents believe in or follow the religion of *Jesus Christ. At first Christianity was simply a Jewish sect which believed that Jesus of Nazareth was the Messiah (or 'Christ', 'anointed one'). Largely owing to the former Pharisee, Saul of Tarsus (later St Paul) it quickly became an independent, mainly gentile, organization. In the early centuries Christians experienced intermittent persecution

by the state, though there was no clear legal basis for this until the reign of the Emperor Decius (AD 250). By the 3rd century, Christianity was widespread throughout the Roman Empire; in 313 Constantine ended persecution and in 380 Theodosius recognized it as the state religion. There were frequent disputes amongst Christians mainly over the status of Christ and the nature of the Trinity, and later over grace and Church organization. Division between East and West, in origin largely cultural and linguistic, intensified, culminating in the Schism of 1054, sealed by the Crusades. In the West the organization of the Church, focused on the Roman papacy, was fragmented by the *Reformation of the 16th century. In the 20th century the ecumenical movement sought to heal these ancient rifts. The *Protestant and *Roman Catholic Churches are the main Christian denominations.

Christian fundamentalism is a Protestant religious movement that stresses traditional Christian doctrines, especially the literal truth of the Bible. Fundamentalism developed in the 1920s in opposition to modern techniques of biblical criticism; its adherents have been particularly powerful in the USA, especially among the various Baptist groups. Fundamentalists were and are particularly noted for their hostility to Charles Darwin's theory of evolution, as shown by the prosecution of J. T. *Scopes in Tennessee. Fundamentalism is associated with evangelicalism, and has re-emerged in recent years as an influential movement, particularly in the USA, where fundamentalist views reach a wide audience through religious broadcasting. Fundamentalists often have an uncompromising social agenda, which they see as traditionalist. This usually includes support for the criminalization of abortion and homosexuality, and insistence on the teaching of creationism (that is, the biblical account of the creation) rather than evolutionary theories in schools. Millenarian ideas rooted in biblical prophecies of the Second Coming have led to support for the state of Israel and for a strongly armed USA. US fundamentalists have been active missionaries, vigorously seeking to convert both non-religious people and adherents of other faiths. Similar movements are now found worldwide, among them the 'House Church' movement in Britain.

Christina (1626–89) Queen of Sweden (1632–54). She was the daughter and successor of *Gustavus II (Adolphus). During her minority, the kingdom was governed mainly by Chancellor Axel Oxenstierna. When she assumed power in 1644, she showed herself to be clever, restless, and headstrong. She attracted many foreign artists and scholars (including *Descartes) to her court, but after a serious constitutional crisis in 1650, she abdicated in favour of her cousin, Charles X.

Chulalongkorn (1853–1910) King Rama V of Siam (Thailand) (1868–1910). Only 15 when his father Rama IV (Mongkut) died, Chulalongkorn was represented by a regent until he reached his majority in 1873 and used the intervening years to travel and study administrative practices abroad. He then continued his father's reformist policies, undertaking a massive modernization of his country.

Church, Benjamin (1639–1718) American soldier, a Rhode Island militia captain in *King Philip's War (1675–76). He cornered Philip in the Great Swamp near Kingston, destroying the remnant of his force. In 1705 he joined a New England expedition against the French in Nova Scotia. His *Entertaining Passages Relating to King Philip's War* appeared in 1716.

His grandson, **Benjamin** (1734–76), was a leading Boston doctor and patriot who in 1775 betrayed the American cause to the British. Paroled from life imprisonment, he died en route to the West Indies.

Churchill, Lord Randolph Henry Spencer (1849–95) British politician. Younger son of the Duke of Marlborough and father of Winston *Churchill, he was elected as Conservative MP in 1874. He became prominent in the 1880–85 Parliament, when he and a group of young Tories became known in opposition to the Liberals as 'the Fourth Party'. A gifted rhetorician, his comment in 1886 that 'Ulster will fight and Ulster will be right' became a slogan for those resisting *Home Rule for Ireland.

Churchill, Sir Winston (Leonard Spencer) (1874–1965) British statesman, Prime Minister (1940–45; 1951–55). Originally a Conservative MP, he changed to the Liberal Party in 1904, serving as Home Secretary (1910–11) under the Liberals and First Lord of the Admiralty (1911–15), but lost this post after the unsuccessful Allied attack on the Turks in the Dardanelles. He returned to the Conservatives in 1924 and was Chancellor of the Exchequer (1924–29). In 1939, under Neville Chamberlain, he became First Lord of the Admiralty again, replacing Chamberlain as Prime Minister in May 1940. Serving as war leader of a coalition government until 1945, Churchill demonstrated rare qualities of leadership and outstanding gifts as an orator. Part of his contribution to victory was to maintain morale at home and to forge and maintain the Alliance, especially with the USA, which defeated the Axis Powers. After the victory he was defeated in the general election of 1945; elected Prime Minister for a second term in 1951, he retired from the premiership in 1955, but remained an MP until 1964. His writings include *The Second World War* (1948–53) and *A History of the English-Speaking Peoples* (1956–58); he was awarded the Nobel Prize for literature in 1953.

Church of England See PROTESTANT.

churl See CEORL.

Chu Teh See ZHU DE.

Ciano, Count Galeazzo (1903–44) Italian politician. A leading fascist, he married *Mussolini's daughter and from 1936–1943 was Foreign Minister. He was among those leaders who voted for the deposition of Mussolini and for this he was tried and shot in Verona by the puppet government established by Mussolini in northern Italy.

Cicero, Marcus Tullius (106–43 BC) Roman statesman, orator, and writer. A supporter of Pompey against Julius Caesar, in the *Philippics* (43 BC) he attacked Mark Antony, who had him put to death. As an orator and writer, Cicero established a model for Latin prose.

Cid Campeador See EL CID (CAMPEADOR).

Cilicia An ancient country, now part of southeastern Turkey. Geographically, it fell into two distinct parts: the western area was mountainous, while the eastern consisted of a fertile plain with Tarsus as its main city. It came under the control of the *Hittites, the *Assyrians, the *Achaemenids, and *Alexander III (the Great) and was fought over by the *Seleucids and *Ptolemies. In the 2nd century BC it became a haven for pirates, who were finally crushed by the Roman general Pompey in 67 BC, and by the end of the century it was part of the *Roman empire. It was occupied by migrating Armenians in 1080. In 1375 it was conquered by the Mamelukes of Egypt and in 1515 by the *Ottoman Turks.

Cincinnatus, Lucius Quinctius (*c.*519–438 BC) Roman republican hero famous for his devotion to the republic in times of crisis. Appointed dictator in 458 when a Roman army was trapped in battle by the Aequi tribe, he won a crushing victory and rescued the beleaguered troops. After this success, he resigned his command and returned to farm his small estate.

Cinque Ports A group of medieval ports in south-east England (originally five: Dover, Hastings, Hythe, Romney, and Sandwich; Rye and Winchelsea were added later) formerly allowed various trading privileges in exchange for providing the bulk of England's navy. Most of the old privileges were abolished in the 19th century and the Wardenship of the Cinque Ports is now a purely honorary post, currently held by Admiral Lord Boyce.

CIS *See* COMMONWEALTH OF INDEPENDENT STATES.

citadel A key feature of a Greek city, being the stronghold around which large communities originally developed. When a city expanded, and a protective encircling wall was built to protect the citizens' houses, the citadel lessened in importance, though it often became a religious centre and housed the public treasury. The *acropolis of Athens is the most famous example.

Civil Rights Acts (1866, 1875, 1957, 1964) Legislation aimed at extending the legal and civil rights of the US Black population. The first Civil Rights Act of 1866 reversed the doctrine laid down by the *Dred Scott decision of 1857 and bestowed citizenship on all persons born in the USA (except tribal Native Americans, not so treated until 1924). It also extended the principle of equal protection of the laws to all citizens. The provisions of the Act were reinforced by the *Fourteenth Amendment to the Constitution, but later decisions of the Supreme Court and lack of will on the part of administrators rendered them largely ineffective. For almost a century thereafter there were few effective federal attempts to protect the Black population against discrimination, and in the South in particular Black people remained persecuted second-class citizens. It was only a series of legislative acts commencing with the Civil Rights Act of 1957 and culminating in the Civil Rights Act of 1964 and the Voting Rights Act of 1965 that finally gave federal agencies effective power to enforce the rights of Black Americans.

Civil War, English *See* ENGLISH CIVIL WAR.

civil wars, French *See* WARS OF RELIGION, FRENCH.

civil wars, Roman *See* ROMAN CIVIL WARS.

Cixi (or **Tz'u-his**) (*c*.1834–1908) Empress dowager of China (1862–1908). A Manchu, she became a concubine of the emperor Xianfeng (ruled 1851–61), giving birth to a son in 1856 who came to the throne in 1862 as the emperor Tongzhi. Cixi acted as Regent for twelve years and, after Tongzhi's death, resumed her position after the elevation of the latter's four-year-old cousin to the throne as the emperor Guangxu. She maintained her power through a combination of ruthlessness and corruption, until the last decade of the century, when the emperor attempted to reverse her conservative policies (Hundred Days Reform). Cixi responded by imprisoning Guangxu and encouraging the *Boxer Rising. Forced by foreign military forces to flee the capital, she returned in 1902, conceding some reforms, but still tried to delay the establishment of a constitutional monarchy.

Clare election (1828) An event in Ireland that led to the passing of the Roman Catholic Relief Act by the British government in 1829. In 1828 Daniel *O'Connell, an Irish lawyer, stood for election to Parliament in the County Clare constituency, winning a resounding victory over his opponent. However, O'Connell, as a Roman Catholic, could not take his seat. The Prime Minister, the Duke of Wellington, felt that if O'Connell were excluded there would be violent disorder in Ireland. Accordingly, despite furious opposition, the government pushed through a *Catholic emancipation measure allowing Catholics to sit in Parliament and hold public office.

Clarence, George Plantagenet, Duke of (1449–78) One of *Edward IV of England's younger brothers. He intrigued with the Burgundians and fell out with both Edward and his other brother, Richard, Duke of Gloucester (*Richard III of England); he was found guilty of high treason and is supposed to have been drowned in a butt of malmsey wine.

Clarence, Lionel, 1st Duke of (1338–68) The second surviving son of *Edward III of England and Philippa of Hainault, known as Lionel of Antwerp from his birth in Antwerp. From about 1341 it was arranged that he would marry the Anglo-Irish heiress Elizabeth de Burgh (1332–63); he was created Earl of Ulster and in 1361 was sent to Ireland as governor, to reassert English rule there. In 1362 he was created Duke of Clarence, the title being derived from his wife's inheritance of the lordship of Clare in Suffolk. After her death another rich marriage was arranged for him, to Violante, the only daughter of Galeazzo Visconti, Lord of Pavia; he died only a few months after this wedding.

The title of Clarence was revived in 1412 for **Thomas of Lancaster** (1389–1421), second son of *Henry IV and Mary de Bohun; it lapsed again after his death.

Clarendon, Constitutions of A document presented by *Henry II of England to a council convened at Clarendon, near Salisbury, in 1166. The king sought to define certain relationships between the state and the Church according to established usage. Churchmen, in particular Thomas à *Becket, saw it as state interference. The most controversial issue, *benefit of clergy, concerned Henry's claim to try in his law courts clerics who had already been convicted in the ecclesiastical courts. After Becket's murder in 1170 Henry conceded the benefit of clergy, but not other points at issue.

Clarendon, Edward Hyde, 1st Earl of (1609–74) English statesman and historian. He began his political career in the Short and Long Parliaments as an opponent of royal authority, but in 1641 he refused to support the Grand Remonstrance, changed sides, and became a trusted adviser of Charles I, and later of Charles II, with whom he shared exile. At the *Restoration Charles II made him Lord Chancellor; he helped to carry out the king's conciliatory policies, and his influence reached its peak when his daughter Anne married the heir apparent, James, Duke of York. Clarendon had little sympathy with the so-called Clarendon Code (1661–65), a series of laws aimed at Roman Catholics and dissenters, but he enforced them against the king's wishes. He was popularly blamed for the naval disasters of the second *Anglo-Dutch War. He fell from power in 1667 and fled to France to avoid impeachment. His *History of the Rebellion* (published 1702–04) is a masterly account of the English Civil War, written from a royalist standpoint but with a considerable degree of objectivity.

Clark, Helen (Elizabeth) (1950–) New Zealand stateswoman; Prime Minister (1999–2008). After lecturing in political studies at Auckland University, she was elected to parliament in 1981 as a Labour MP. She served in the cabinet from 1987–1990, was leader of the opposition from 1993–1999, and was three times (1999, 2002, and 2005) Prime Minister at the head of various Labour-led coalitions. Her government presided over a period of economic growth while enacting social and welfare reforms. From 2009 she was Administrator of the United Nations Development Programme.

Clark, Joe (**Charles Joseph Clark**) (1939–) Canadian politician, Prime Minister of Canada (1979–80). Clark was active in the Progressive Conservative party from 1957 and led the student wing of the party. He became head of a minority government in 1979 but his party fell on a budget question and was defeated in the subsequent elections. He was later minister for constitutional affairs (1991–93) and was again leader of the Progressive Conservatives from 1998–2003. However, he left the party after its 2003 merger with the Canadian Alliance.

Clarkson, Thomas (1760–1846) British philanthropist. A strong opponent of slavery, he became a founder member of the Committee for the Suppression of the Slave Trade. He collected much information about the trade and conditions on slave ships, which was published in a pamphlet and used by William *Wilberforce in his parliamentary campaign for abolition. In 1807 an Act was passed prohibiting British participation in the *slave trade. In 1823 Clarkson became a leading member of the Anti-Slavery Society, which saw its efforts rewarded with the 1833 Act abolishing slavery in the British empire.

Claudius (full name **Tiberius Claudius Drusus Nero Germanicus**) (10 BC–54 AD) Roman emperor (41–54 AD). He spent his early life engaged in historical study, prevented from entering public life by his physical infirmity; he was proclaimed emperor after the murder of Caligula. His reign was noted for its restoration of order after Caligula's decadence and for its expansion of the Roman Empire, in particular the invasion of Britain in the year 43, in which he personally took part. His fourth wife, Agrippina (15–59 AD), is said to have killed him with a dish of poisoned mushrooms.

Clausewitz, Karl von (1780–1831) Prussian general and military theorist. A Chief of Staff in the Prussian army (1815) and later a general (1818), he went on to write the detailed study *On War* (1833), which had a marked influence on strategic studies in the 19th and 20th centuries.

Clay, Henry (1777–1852) US statesman and orator. As Speaker of the House of Representatives (1811–14) he played a central role in the agitation leading to the *War of 1812, and was one of the commissioners responsible for the negotiation of the Treaty of *Ghent that ended it. He was one of the architects of the Missouri Compromise and won support for his American System, a policy to improve national unity through a programme of economic legislation. His final political achievement lay in helping the passage of the Compromise of 1850 between the opposing Free-Soil and pro-slavery interests. His role in arranging major sectional compromises between North and South (1820, 1833, and 1850) earned him the title of 'the Great Compromiser'.

Clegg, Nick (Nicholas Peter William Clegg) (1967–) British politician, Deputy Prime Minister (2010–). Having entered parliament in 2005, he became leader of the Liberal Democrat Party in 2007. After the inconclusive 2010 election he led the party to its first participation in government since 1945, when it formed a coalition with the Conservative Party.

Clemenceau, Georges (Eugène Benjamin) (1841–1929) French statesman, Prime Minister (1906–09; 1917–20). A radical politician and journalist, he persistently opposed the government during the early years of World War I, before becoming Premier and seeing France through to victory in 1918. He presided at the Versailles peace talks, where he pushed hard for a punitive settlement with Germany, but failed to obtain all that he demanded (notably the River Rhine as a frontier). He founded the newspaper *L'Aurore*.

Cleopatra VII (69–30 BC) The last of the *Ptolemies. She became co-ruler of Egypt with Ptolemy XIII in 51, but was driven out in 48. She was restored by Julius *Caesar and in 47 bore a son whom she said was his. In 46 they both accompanied him to Rome. After his assassination in 44 she returned to Egypt, and in 41 met *Mark Antony at Tarsus. He spent the following winter with her in Alexandria and she in due course gave birth to twins. In 37 Antony acknowledged these children and restored the territories of Cyrene and elsewhere to her; she pledged Egypt's support to him. In 34 they formally announced the division of Alexander the Great's former empire between Cleopatra and her children. In 32 Octavian (*Augustus) declared war on her and in the following year the Battle of *Actium resulted in the collapse of her fortunes. In 30 she committed suicide and Egypt passed into Roman hands.

Cleveland, Grover (Stephen Grover Cleveland) (1837–1908) US Democratic statesman, 22nd and 24th President of the USA (1885–89; 1893–97). His first term was marked by efforts to reverse the heavily protective import tariff, and his second by his application of the Monroe doctrine to Britain's border dispute with Venezuela (1895).

climate change The change in world climate patterns over time. Such change has always occurred, both on a large scale since the formation of the earth and on a smaller scale within the span of human history. For example, there is evidence that the period between 900 and 1300 (the **Medieval Warm Period**) saw generally high average temperatures and a benign climate, with wine being produced in southern England and the colonization by the Vikings of such northern lands as Greenland; and that this was followed between *c*.1350 and *c*.1850 by the **Little Ice Age**, with generally cooler average temperatures and extreme weather marked by harsh winters, more frequent famines, and advancing glaciers. However, three factors led to climate change becoming an important issue in the late 20th and early 21st centuries: a body of scientific evidence suggesting that the average world temperature was increasing rapidly; a concern that human activity was in part causing this change; and a fear that, if unchecked, it would lead to massive physical, economic, social, and political disruption within a few human lifetimes. The extent to which these fears and concerns are justified is disputed. It is generally agreed that global average temperature increased by about 0.6 °C over the 20th century—a rapid change—with an acceleration after 1975. The majority of scientific opinion holds that this change was too great and too rapid to be natural: human activity has caused this **global warming** and, unless positive action is taken, it will accelerate with disastrous consequences. These might include: a rise in sea-level, due to thermal expansion of the oceans that will flood coastal areas and perhaps obliterate low-lying countries entirely; altered weather patterns that will affect agriculture and water supply; increasingly extreme weather conditions; and, possibly, an alteration in the ocean currents. The principal human contribution is held to be the emission of large quantities of carbon dioxide and other **greenhouse gases**, which increase the atmosphere's ability to retain heat and thus upset the balance between the energy received from the Sun and that radiated into space. However, other scientific opinions hold that the threat of global warming either does not exist at all, on the grounds that the observed temperature rise is probably a natural fluctuation that is not caused by human actions and will not continue in the long term, or is not serious enough to warrant urgent countermeasures. This range of scientific opinions is mirrored in the political stances adopted on the issue. For many countries and non-governmental organizations, climate change is an urgent threat that requires actions to restrict carbon emissions, such as those embodied in the *Kyoto Protocol. For others, this view is either unnecessarily alarmist or even a political attempt to restrict their economic growth to the benefit of others. The USA, for example, has declined to ratify the Kyoto Protocol, which it considers would penalize US industry excessively compared with that of some developing countries.

Clinton, Bill (William Jefferson Clinton) (1946–) US politician, 42nd President of the USA (1993–2001). A Democrat, he was elected on a programme of reducing the federal deficit by cutting military spending and reforming taxation, while increasing investment in education, training, and infrastructure. He appointed his wife Hillary to head the administration's health-care taskforce; her plans to provide health insurance for all Americans were rejected by Congress in 1994. Abroad, he sought to underpin Russia's reform economy and to maintain trade links with China, despite its poor human rights record. During 1994 Clinton agreed with Russian leader Boris *Yeltsin not to keep their nuclear weapons constantly aimed at each other's countries. He lifted the trade embargo on Vietnam and pledged to work towards the creation of a trans-Pacific free-trade zone. Following mid-term elections in 1994, Clinton's position was weakened as the Republicans gained control of the Senate. In 1996 he authorized the bombing of strategic targets in Iraq in response to Iraqi violations of a UN-imposed no-fly zone above Kurdish areas. He was re-elected in 1996. In 1999 he was impeached on counts of perjury and obstruction of justice for lying about his sexual relationship with a young White House trainee, but was found not guilty by the Senate.

His wife, **Hillary (Diane) Rodham Clinton** (1947–), was a Democratic senator for New York (2001–09) and Secretary of State (2009–13). She ran for President in 2008, narrowly losing the Democratic nomination to Barack *Obama.

Clinton, George (1739–1812) American patriot leader. He controlled the popular anti-British faction in New York City from 1768. After attending the second *Continental Congress (1775–76) he helped draft the state's constitution and served as governor for 15 years. An opponent of Alexander *Hamilton, he joined Thomas *Jefferson in founding the Democratic-Republican party, and was Vice-President (1805–12) to both Jefferson and James Madison.

Clive, Robert, 1st Baron Clive of Plassey (known as **'Clive of India'**) (1725–74) British general and colonial administrator. In 1743 he joined the East India Company in Madras, becoming governor of Fort St David in 1755. Following the Black Hole of Calcutta incident, he commanded the forces that recaptured Calcutta from Siraj-ud-Dawlah (c.1729–57), nawab of Bengal, in 1757. Clive's victory at Plassey later that year made him virtual ruler of Bengal, helping the British to gain an important foothold in India. After a period in Britain 1760–65, he served as governor of Bengal until 1767, restructuring the administration of the colony and restoring discipline to the East India Company, whose reputation had been called into question. Clive was subsequently implicated in the company's corruption scandals; although officially exonerated, he committed suicide.

Clovis (465–511) King of the Franks (481–511). He succeeded his father Childeric (died 481) as king of the Salian Franks at Tournai, and extended Merovingian rule to Gaul and Germany after victories at Soissons (486) and Cologne (496). After his conversion to Christianity, he championed orthodoxy against the Arian Visigoths, finally defeating them in the battle of Poitiers (507). He made Paris his capital.

Clovis culture A prehistoric culture in North America, characterized by lance-shaped stone points, 7–12 cm (3–5 inches) long, fluted near the base. The tools are often found in association with bones of large mammals, such as bison and extinct mammoth, and are assumed to have been used as spear heads. Named after a town in western New Mexico, they are found at sites throughout the mid-west and southwest, USA from a period between 12,000 and 10,000 years ago. At one time, Clovis hunters were regarded as typifying the first Americans, but it has been suggested that people were in the Americas long before, perhaps even by 30,000 years ago.

Cluny, Order of A reformed Benedictine monastic order, whose mother house was the abbey of Cluny in France, founded by Duke William of Aquitaine in 909. Under Abbot Odilo (994–1048) Cluny became the head of a system of dependent "daughter houses" throughout western Europe. In the 11th and 12th centuries Cluny became a spiritual and cultural centre of vast influence; four of its members became popes and it inspired the zealous reforming innovations of Pope *Gregory VII from 1073. The monastery church at Cluny was a model for much ecclesiastical building in Europe. By the 13th century the period of greatest achievement was over, as the monastic ideal suffered from too close an involvement with the secular world and too great a share of its wealth and worldly power.

Cnut *See* CANUTE.

Coates, Joseph Gordon (1878–1943) New Zealand statesman. He represented the interests of the rural poor, including the *Maori. Though he was a member of the conservative Reform Party, he advanced the New Zealand tradition of state action for the public good, developing roads and railways, the state hydroelectricity programme, afforestation, and aiding Maori farming schemes. In coalition with *Forbes during the *Depression he broke the authority of the private banks, established the Reserve Bank, and laid the foundation for economic recovery.

Cobbett, William (1763–1835) British writer and political reformer. He started his political life as a Tory, but later became a radical; the change is reflected in *Cobbett's Political Register*, a periodical that he founded in 1802 and continued for the rest of his life. Cobbett was one of the leaders of the campaign for political and social reform after 1815, although he had already spent two years in prison for his outspoken criticism of flogging in the army (1810–12).

Cobden, Richard (1804–65) British political reformer. A Manchester industrialist, Cobden was one of the leading spokesmen of the free-trade movement in Britain. From 1838, together with John Bright, he led the Anti-Corn Law League in its successful campaign for the repeal of the *Corn Laws (1846).

Cochin China The southern region of Vietnam, centred on the Mekong delta. It was so called to distinguish it from Cochin in India. The home of people akin to the *Khmers, it was not fully absorbed by the Vietnamese until the 18th century. It was the base from which Gia-Long, as emperor of *Annam, unified Vietnam in 1802.

Cochinos Bay *See* BAY OF PIGS.

Cochise (*c.*1815–74) Apache Indian chief. Noted for his courage and military prowess, he gave his word in 1860 that he would not molest US mail riders passing through his Arizona territory in spite of war. In 1872 he made a peace treaty with the US government. He maintained both agreements, despite hostile acts from White people and Native Americans.

Code Napoléon (or **Code Civil**) The first modern codification of French civil law, issued between 1804 and 1810, which sought, under the direction of J. J. Cambacérès, to reorganize the French legal system. Napoleon himself presided over the commission drafting the laws, which drew deeply on the philosophical heritage of the 18th-century Enlightenment, the articles of the laws representing a compromise between revolutionary principles and the ancient Roman (i.e. civil) law upon which much European law was based. The code enshrines the principles of equality, the separation of civil and ecclesiastical jurisdictions, and the freedom of the individual. With its compressed legislative style (the entire law of tort is set out in five articles), the *Code* represents perhaps the pinnacle of the codification achievement; versions of it were adopted in various European countries, and later spread through colonization to Latin America and parts of Africa. It was revised in 1904, and has remained the basis of French private law.

Cod War (1972–76) A period of antagonism between Britain and Iceland over fishing rights. The cause was Iceland's unilateral extension of its fishing limits to protect against over-fishing. Icelandic warships harassed British trawlers fishing within this new limit (1975–76), prompting protective action by British warships. A compromise agreement was reached in 1976 which allowed 24 British trawlers within a 320-km (200-mile) limit. This hastened the decline of many British fishing ports, including Hull and Grimsby.

Coercive Acts (1774) Legislation passed by the British Parliament as a punishment for the *Boston Tea Party. They closed the port of Boston pending compensation, amended Massachusetts's charter, allowed trials to be transferred to other colonies, and troops to be quartered at Boston's expense. Though Lord *North's aim was to isolate Massachusetts, the "Intolerable Acts", as they became known, stiffened American resistance and precipitated the *Continental Congress.

Coke, Sir Edward (1552–1634) English lawyer and politician. He rose to the position of Lord Chief Justice (1613), prosecuting such defendants as *Essex (1601) and the *Gunpowder Plot conspirators (1606). In 1616 James I dismissed him, since, at first a supporter of the royal prerogative, Coke had become a defender of the common law against church and crown: as a Member of Parliament he led opposition to James I and Charles I. He was largely responsible for drafting the *Petition of Right (1628) and wrote commentaries on medieval and contemporary English law.

Colbert, Jean Baptiste (1619–83) French statesman, chief minister to Louis XIV (1665–83). A vigorous reformer, he put order back into the country's finances, boosted industry and commerce, and established the French navy as one of the most formidable in Europe.

Cold War The struggle between the Soviet bloc countries and the Western countries from 1945–1990. The Soviet Union, the USA, and Britain had been wartime allies against Nazi Germany, but even before Germany was defeated they began to differ about the future of Germany and of Eastern Europe. Wartime summit meetings at *Yalta and *Potsdam had laid down certain agreements, but as communist governments seized exclusive power in Eastern Europe, and Greece and Turkey were threatened with similar takeovers, the Western Powers became increasingly alarmed. From 1946 onwards popular usage spoke of a 'Cold War' (as opposed to an atomic 'hot war') between the two sides. The Western allies took steps to defend their position with the formation of the *Truman Doctrine (1947) and the *Marshall Plan (1947) to bolster the economies of Western Europe. In 1949 *NATO was formed as a defence against possible attack. The communist bloc countered with the establishment of the Council for Mutual Aid and Assistance (*COMECON, 1949) and the *Warsaw Pact (1955). Over the following decades, the Cold War spread to every part of the world, and the USA sought containment of Soviet advances by forming alliances in the Pacific and south-east Asia. There were repeated crises (including the *Korean War, the *Cuban Missile Crisis, and the *Vietnam War), but there were also occasions when tension was reduced as both sides sought *détente. The development of a nuclear arms race from the 1950s, only slightly modified by a *Nuclear Test-Ban Treaty in 1963 and *Strategic Arms Limitation Talks (1969–79), maintained tension at a very high level. Senator Joseph *McCarthy capitalized on anti-Russian feeling when alleging a communist plot to take over the US government, which led to a political witch-hunt. Tension intensified in the early 1980s with the installation of US Cruise missiles in Europe and the announcement of the experimental US Strategic Defense Initiative plan to shoot down

missiles in mid-flight and receded with an agreement in 1987 for limited arms control. It began to recede in 1985 with a resumption of START talks, followed by the INF Treaty (1987). Soviet forces withdrew from Afghanistan in 1989 and pacification in such troubled areas as Nicaragua and Angola followed. In December 1989 Presidents Bush and Gorbachev, at a summit meeting in Malta, declared the Cold War officially ended. By then the communist regimes of the Warsaw Pact countries were collapsing and NATO began to change its role. NATO invited the former Soviet countries, including Russia, to join a 'partnership for peace' (inaugurated in 1994) as a first step towards granting them full NATO membership. In 1997 a Russian-NATO Joint Permanent Council was established to reinforce cooperation. Between 1999 and 2009 12 former communist countries joined NATO.

collectivization The creation of collective or communal farms. The policy was ruthlessly enforced in the Soviet Union by *Stalin between 1929 and 1933 in an effort to overcome an acute grain shortage in the towns. The industrialization of the Soviet Union depended on cheap food and abundant labour. Bitter peasant resistance was overcome with brutality, but the liquidation of the Kulaks and slaughter by peasants of their own livestock resulted in famine (1932–33). Gradually more moderate methods were substituted with the development of state farms. In the early 1990s collective farms accounted for about 67% of the area of cultivated land, state farms about 30%, and privately owned farms about 1.6%. Private ownership of land was encouraged by *Gorbachev as part of his economic reforms. After 1945 a policy of collectivization was adopted in a number of socialist countries, but was generally reversed after the collapse of communism in eastern Europe after 1989. The Soviet example was followed in China by *Mao Zedong in his First Five Year Plan of 1953, but was only enforced by stages. China did not copy the ruthless subordination of agriculture to industry, preferring the peasant *commune.

Collins, Michael (1890–1922) Irish nationalist leader and politician. He took part in the *Easter Rising in 1916. Elected to Parliament as a member of *Sinn Fein in 1919, he became Minister of Finance in the self-declared Irish government, at the same time directing the *Irish Republican Army's guerrilla campaign against the British. He was one of the negotiators of the Anglo-Irish Treaty of 1921 and commanded the Irish Free State forces in the civil war that followed partition. On the death of Arthur *Griffith in 1922, he became head of the government, but was shot in an ambush ten days later.

Colombia

Capital:	Bogotá
Area:	1,138,910 sq km (439,736 sq miles)
Population:	45,745,783 (2012 est)
Currency:	1 peso = 100 centavos
Religions:	Roman Catholic 90.0%
Ethnic Groups:	Mestizo 58.0%; White 20.0%; Mulatto 14.0%; Black 4.0%
Languages:	Spanish (official); Amerindian languages
International Organizations:	UN; OAS; Andean Community; Non-Aligned Movement; WTO

A country in the extreme north-west of the South American continent, the only South American country with coasts on both the Pacific and the Atlantic oceans, separated by the isthmus of Panama. To the east is Venezuela, and to the south Brazil, Peru, and Ecuador.

Physical The northern end of the Andes occupies the north-western half of the country, breaking into three great cordilleras which enclose high, cool plateaux. Running from them are several large rivers to water the hot northern coastal plains. South-east of the Andes, plains of rich pasture stretch away to the east and to the south, where the land falls in forested terraces towards the headstreams of the Amazon.

Economy Oil exports are crucial to Colombia's economy, but other industries are being developed, including textiles, clothing, and food processing. As well as crude oil, Colombia has large reserves of coal, natural gas, gold, precious stones, platinum, bauxite, and copper. About 5% of Colombia's total area is arable, while 30% is permanent pastureland; coffee, flowers, and bananas are the most important crops. However, cannabis and coca are also cultivated illicitly on a vast scale for the manufacture of illegal drugs.

History Colombia was occupied by the Chibcha Indians before the Spanish conquest. The first permanent European settlements were made on the Caribbean coast, Santa Marta being founded in 1525 and Cartagena eight years later. Colonization of the interior was led by Gonzalo Jiménez de Quesada, who defeated the Chibchas and founded the city of Bogotá in 1538. The region was initially part of the viceroyalty of Peru, but a different political status came with the establishment of the viceroyalty of New Granada in the first half of the 18th century. The viceroy sitting in Bogotá was given jurisdiction over Colombia, but also over Venezuela, Ecuador, and Panama. Colombia remained a viceroyalty of Spain until the battle of Boyacá (1819) during the *Spanish–South American Wars of Independence, when, joined with Venezuela, it was named by Simón *Bolívar the United States of Colombia. In 1822 under his leadership New Granada, Panama, Venezuela, and Ecuador were united as the Republic of Gran Colombia, which collapsed in 1830. In 1832 a constitution for New Granada was promulgated by Francisco Santander, which was amended in 1858 to allow a confederation of nine states within the central republic, which is now known as the Granadine Confederation. In 1863 the country was renamed the United States of Colombia. The constitution of 1886 abolished the sovereignty of the states and the presidential system of the newly named Republic of Colombia was established. The War of the Thousand Days (1899–1902), encouraged by the USA, led to the separation of Panama from Colombia (1903). Violence broke out again in 1948 and moved from urban to rural areas, precipitating a military government between 1953 and 1958. A semi-representative democracy was restored that achieved a degree of political stability. During the 1980s Colombia achieved sustained economic growth and a successful record of external debt management, but the drug trade increasingly dominated both internal affairs and its relations with the USA. At the same time numerous extremist guerrilla groups, of both Left and Right, resorted to violence. In 1990 the ruling Liberal Party convened a Constitutional Assembly, which produced a new constitution, followed by an agreement by some guerrillas to demobilize and take part in the political process, while several drug traffickers surrendered. However, violence by such left-wing groups as the FARC (Revolutionary Armed Forces of Colombia) and ELN (National Liberation Army), financed largely by the production of and trade in drugs, continued to be a major disruptive force in the 21st century. Peace talks began in 2012, during the presidency of Juan Manuel Santos.

Colombian Independence War *See*
SPANISH–SOUTH AMERICAN WARS OF INDE-
PENDENCE.

Colombo Plan (for Cooperative Economic
Development in South and South-East Asia) An
international organization of 27 countries, established to assist the development of member
countries in the Asian and Pacific regions. Based
on an Australian initiative at the meeting of
*Commonwealth ministers in Colombo in
January 1950 and with seven founder members,
it was originally intended to serve Commonwealth countries of the region. The scheme was
later extended, with the USA and Japan as major
donors; Britain and Canada left in 1991 and
1992 respectively. In 1977 its title was changed
to the 'Colombo Plan for Cooperative Economic
and Social Development in Asia and the Pacific'.

colonialism *See* IMPERIALISM.

Colosseum The medieval name for the
Amphitheatre Flavium, a vast amphitheatre in
Rome begun by the emperor Vespasian *c.*75 AD
and continued and completed by Titus and
Domitian. It was capable of holding *c.*50,000
people, with seating in three tiers and standing
room above; an elaborate system of staircases
served all parts. The arena, floored with timber
and surrounded by a fence, was the scene of
gladiatorial combats, fights between men and
animals, and large-scale mock battles.

Columba, St (*c.*521–97) Irish abbot and missionary. After founding several churches and
monasteries in his own country, he established
the monastery at Iona in *c.*563, led a number of
missions to mainland Scotland from there, and
converted the Picts to Christianity. He is considered one of the leading figures of the Celtic
missionary tradition in the British Isles and
contributed significantly to the literature of
Celtic Christianity.

Columbanus, St (*c.*543–615) Abbot and
missionary, from his youth a monk at Bangor,
Ireland. In about 590 he left for France and
founded monasteries at Annegray and Luxeuil.
His support for the practices of the Celtic
Church, and especially for the Irish dating
of Easter, upset Pope Gregory I and he was
ordered back to Ireland (610). He promptly
crossed the Alps to Lombardy in Italy and established an abbey at Bobbio (614). However,
his austere monasticism lost its appeal before
the more practical provisions of St *Benedict.

Columbus, Christopher (*c.*1451–1506)
Genoese navigator and explorer, celebrated as
the first European to discover America. His
great interest was in what he called his "Enterprise to the Indies", the search for a westward
route to the Orient for trade in spices. For over a
decade he tried to get financial support for his
"Enterprise", and at last in 1492 persuaded
*Ferdinand V and Isabella of Spain to sponsor
an expedition. He set out in the *Santa Maria*,
with two other small ships, expecting to reach
Japan, and when he came upon the islands of
the Caribbean he named them the West Indies,
and the native Arawak people Indians. On Cuba
(which he thought was China) tobacco was
discovered. His published record was the first
documentary evidence in Europe of the existence of the New World. For his second voyage a
year later he was provided with 17 ships and
expected to trade for gold and establish colonies. He surveyed much of the Caribbean archipelago during the next three years, but then,
with no gold forthcoming, he was recalled to
Spain in disgrace. After months of lobbying,
however, he was allowed again to search for
Asia; this time he took a more southerly route,
discovering Trinidad and the mouth of the
Orinoco River, but the colony he had left on
Hispaniola was seething with rebellion.
Ferdinand and Isabella sent a new governor to
control it and paid off Columbus by allowing
him to fit out a fourth voyage (1502–04) at their
expense. He explored much of the coast of
Central America vainly seeking at Panama a
strait that would lead him to Japan, until his
poorly equipped ships became worm-eaten
and unfit for the voyage home. He chartered
another vessel and reached Spain ill and
discredited, and died in obscurity.

Comanche A Native American Uto-Aztecan
people of the plains and prairies of Texas and
Oklahoma. An offshoot of the Shoshone, they
migrated to the plains from the Rocky Mountains to hunt buffalo. Their name is derived
from the Spanish *camino ancho* ('wide trail').

Combination Acts Laws passed by the
British Parliament in 1799 and 1800 in order to
prevent the meeting ('combining together') of
two or more people to obtain improvements in
their working conditions. Flouting the law resulted in trial before a magistrate, and *trade
unions were thus effectively made illegal. The
Combination Acts were repealed in 1824 as a
result of the skilful campaign by Francis Place
and Joseph Hume, and were followed by an
outbreak of strikes. In 1825 another Act was
passed that allowed trade union activity but
limited the right to strike.

COMECON (Council for Mutual Economic Assistance) The English name for an economic organization of Soviet-bloc countries. It was established by Stalin among the communist countries of eastern Europe in 1949 to encourage interdependence in trade and production as the second pillar, with the *Warsaw Pact, of Soviet influence in Europe. It achieved little until 1962, when agreements restricting the satellite countries to limited production and to economic dependency on the Soviet Union were enforced. Its members were: Bulgaria, Cuba, Czechoslovakia, German Democratic Republic, Hungary, Mongolian People's Republic, Poland, Romania, the Soviet Union, and Vietnam (Yugoslavia had associate status). Albania was expelled in 1961. In 1987 it began to discuss cooperation with the *European Community, and it was dissolved in 1990, following the collapse of communist regimes in eastern Europe.

Cominform (Communist Information Bureau) An international communist organization formed to coordinate Party activities throughout Europe. Created in 1947, it assumed some of the functions of the *Internationals, which had lapsed with the dissolution of the *Comintern in 1943. After the dispute between *Tito and *Stalin in 1948 Yugoslavia was expelled. The Cominform was abolished in 1956, partly as a gesture of renewed friendship with Yugoslavia and partly to improve relations with the West.

Comintern (Communist International) Organization of national communist parties for the propagation of communist doctrine with the aim of bringing about a world revolution. It was established by *Lenin (1919) in Moscow at the Congress of the Third International with *Zinoviev as its chairman. At its second meeting in Moscow (1920), delegates from 37 countries attended, and Lenin established the Twenty-One Points, which required all parties to model their structure on disciplined lines in conformity with the Soviet pattern, and to expel moderate ideologies. In 1943 *Stalin dissolved the Comintern, though in 1947 it was revived in a modified form as the *Cominform, to coordinate the activities of European communism. This, in turn, was dissolved in 1956.

comitia Assemblies of Roman citizens meeting for elections or legislation. The oldest assembly, the "Curiata", consisted of representatives of religious groups based on kinship: it survived later as a body which sanctioned adoptions and ratified wills. The creation of the "Centuriata" as the assembly of the people in arms was attributed to King Servius Tullius. It originally elected magistrates and legislated. The citizens were organized in "centuries" according to census rating and military equipment and function, and voting power was weighted in favour of wealth and age. It remained the electoral assembly for consuls and praetors.

The "Tributa" was the meeting of the people in the 35 tribes, based on domicile, in which votes were equal, irrespective of property, but it was the tribal and not the individual vote that counted. Like the "Centuriata" it was convened by consuls or praetors and became the main legislative body and elected most of the lower magistrates. It was perhaps modelled on the "Concilium Plebis", under the presidency of the tribunes of the *plebs. This was established early in the conflict between patricians and plebeians. It consisted of plebeians only and was convened by the tribunes. Bills carried here were "plebiscita"; but after 287 BC "plebiscita" were accorded the same form as laws of the whole Roman people, and were generally also called "leges".

Commines, Philippe de (or **Philippe de Commynes**) (c.1447–1511) French historian. Born in Flanders, the son of a noble Burgundian commander, he was raised at the Burgundian court, joined Louis XI of France in 1472, and was later disgraced for plotting against Charles VIII in 1486. Restored to favour, he joined Charles's invasion of Italy in 1494. He wrote his *Memoires*, six books on Louis and two on Charles during 1489–98.

Committee of Public Safety An emergency body set up in France in April 1793. It was the first effective executive government of the Revolutionary period and governed France during the most critical year of the Revolution. Its nine members (later twelve) were chiefly drawn from the *Jacobins and it contained some of the ablest men in France, dominated at first by *Danton and then by *Robespierre. It successfully defeated France's external enemies but was largely responsible for the Reign of Terror, and its ruthless methods, at a time of growing economic distress, led to increasing opposition. In March 1794 an attempt to overthrow it, led by Hébert, was quashed, but four months later the reaction which overthrew Robespierre marked the end of the Committee's power. It was restricted to foreign affairs until its influence was finally ended in October 1795.

common land (or **common**) Land that is subject to rights of common. These are rights to take the produce from land of which the right-holder is not the owner, for example a right of pasture. They are private rights, and need not be open to all. The right may be restricted, for example, to a portion of the year. The first commons were usually woodland or rough pasture for the villagers' animals in medieval England. By the Statute of Merton (1236) the lord of the manor or other owner of a village was allowed to enclose waste land for his own use only if he left adequate pasture for the villagers. *Enclosure of common land started in the 12th century, and increased dramatically in the second half of the 18th century, often arousing opposition and claims of theft.

In colonial America many village communities had large areas of common land, partly for defensive purposes as well as for pasturage. These areas sometimes survived to be used for recreation, the best known being Boston Common, today a public park but bought by the town for pasturage in 1634.

Commons, House of *See* HOUSE OF COMMONS.

Commonwealth The republican government of England between the execution of Charles I in 1649 and the restoration of Charles II in 1660. The *Rump Parliament claimed to 'have the supreme power in this nation', and ruled through a nominated 40-man Council of State. In 1650 an 'Engagement' to be faithful to the Commonwealth was imposed on all adult males. While Oliver *Cromwell was eliminating Royalist resistance in Ireland and then Scotland (1649–51), the Rump disappointed expectations of radical reform. Unpopular taxes were raised to finance the army's expeditions. Furthermore, the Navigation Acts sparked off the much-resented *Anglo-Dutch War of 1652–54.

Cromwell expelled the Rump in April 1653. He hoped to reach a political and religious settlement through the *Barebones Parliament (July–December 1653), but in December he accepted the necessity of taking the headship of state himself. The period of Cromwellian rule is usually known as the *Protectorate.

Commonwealth, British *See* COMMONWEALTH OF NATIONS.

Commonwealth of Independent States (CIS) A confederation of independent states, formerly among the constituent republics of the Soviet Union, established in 1991 following a summit in the Belorussian city of

Brest at which the USSR was dissolved. The 11 member-states are Armenia, Azerbaijan, Belarus (Belorussia), Kazakhstan, Kyrgyzstan, Moldova (Moldavia), Russia, Tajikistan, Turkmenistan, Ukraine, and Uzbekistan. The administrative headquarters of the CIS is in the Belarussian city of Minsk.

Commonwealth of Nations An international group of 53 nations. Its origins lie with the *British empire: its members are the United Kingdom and, mostly, former British colonies, and its head is the British monarch. The term British Commonwealth began to be used after World War I when the military help given by the *dominions to Britain had enhanced their status. Their independence, apart from the formal link of allegiance to the crown, was asserted at the Imperial Conference of 1926, and given legal authority by the Statute of *Westminster (1931). The power of independent decision by Commonwealth countries was evident in 1936 over the abdication of *Edward VIII, and in 1939 when they decided whether or not they wished to support Britain in World War II. In 1945 the British Commonwealth consisted of countries where the White population was dominant. Beginning with the granting of independence to India and Pakistan in 1947 and Sri Lanka in 1948, its composition changed. In 1949 it adopted the title of Commonwealth of Nations and the requirement for a formal link of allegiance to the British crown was dropped. Thereafter nearly all British colonies have joined the Commonwealth on achieving independence. A minority of countries have withdrawn. The Republic of Ireland (left 1949), Zimbabwe (2003), and The Gambia (2013) have not rejoined; Pakistan left in 1972 but rejoined in 1989; *South Africa withdrew in 1961 because of hostility to its apartheid policy, but was readmitted in 1995; and Fiji withdrew in 1987 because of racist elements in its constitution but rejoined when these were removed in 1997. Other members have been temporarily suspended. In 1995 Cameroon became the first country that has never been wholly ruled by Britain to become a member of the Commonwealth. Mozambique, which has no historical links with Britain, was also admitted in 1995, setting a precedent that was followed by Rwanda in 2009.

Initially the Commonwealth had no specific aims or organization. The Commonwealth Secretariat was established in 1965, and the organization's activities have steadily expanded since then. The Singapore Declaration of Commonwealth Principles (1971) was the first statement of Commonwealth aims, although some, such as personal liberty and rejection of coercion, were at that time widely ignored by member states. In 2012 the Charter of the Commonwealth affirmed the commitment of members to free and democratic societies and the promotion of peace and prosperity.

commune (in China) A small district of local government; in China the basic unit of agricultural organization and rural local government from 1958 to about 1978. Cooperatives were formed when the mutual aid teams that emerged during the land reform of the early 1950s were merged as part of the 'high tide of socialism' of 1955–56. During the *Great Leap Forward these cooperatives were themselves combined to form large units known as communes which were responsible for planning local farming and for running public services. Commune power was gradually devolved to production brigades after the disastrous harvests of 1959–61. In the Four Modernizations movement communes were virtually abolished.

commune (in Europe) A medieval western European town which had acquired specific privileges by purchase or force. The privileges might include a charter of liberties, freedom to elect councils, responsibility for regulating local order, justice, and trade, and powers to raise taxes and tolls. The burghers initially swore an oath binding themselves together. The communes often pursued their own diplomatic policies as political alliances shifted. They flourished where central government was weak and became bastions of local power, and after the Reformation, of religious loyalties. The growth of strong national monarchies reduced them in the 16th and 17th centuries.

Commune of Paris *See* PARIS, COMMUNE OF.

communism A social and political ideology advocating that authority and property be vested in the community, each member working for the common benefit according to capacity and receiving according to needs.

The ideal of communism has been embraced by many thinkers, including *Plato, the early Christians and the 16th-century humanist Thomas More, who saw it as expressing man's social nature to the highest degree. It became the basis of a revolutionary movement through the work of Karl *Marx, who saw communism as the final outcome of the proletarian revolution that would overthrow *capitalism. According to the theories of Marx, a communist society will emerge after the transitional

period of the dictatorship of the proletariat and the preparatory stage of *socialism. In a fully communist society the state will, according to Marx, 'wither away' and all distinctions between social classes will disappear. Marx's theories were influential in 19th-century *Social Democrat parties, and were the moving force behind *Lenin and the *Bolsheviks and the establishment of the political system in the *Soviet Union.

In the hands of *Lenin and his successors in the Soviet Union, *Marxism was transformed into a doctrine justifying state control of all aspects of society. The doctrine had two main elements. The first was the leading role of the Communist Party, seen as representing the true interests of the working class. The party was to control the organs of the state, and was itself to be organized according to the principles of 'democratic centralism'. The second major element in communist doctrine was the social ownership of property and central planning of the economy. In principle, all private ownership of the means of production and all elements of the market economy were to be abolished, and economic life was to be controlled by planning ministries, which would set production targets for factories and collective farms. Although this principle was never fully implemented, Soviet communism was a society whose every aspect was controlled by a small political élite (during the Stalinist period, 1928–53, by a single individual), and was thus the leading example of *totalitarianism. Its economic and military achievements nevertheless inspired revolutionary movements in many other countries, and in some developing countries, such as China, Vietnam, North Korea, and Cuba, communist parties came to power and established regimes based more or less closely on the Soviet model. In eastern Europe, communist governments were installed under Soviet influence at the end of World War II. But the communist model was increasingly criticized in the West, even by those sympathetic to Marxism, for its economic inefficiency, its lack of genuine democracy, and its denial of basic human freedoms. During the 1980s this questioning of Soviet communism spread to eastern Europe and the Soviet Union, culminating in a remarkable series of largely peaceful revolutions, which removed communist parties from power and opened the way to liberal democracy and the market economy.

Following the collapse of the Soviet Union in 1991, the communist countries of eastern Europe mostly adopted pluralist, democratic systems. Similar reforms were introduced in the Marxist-Leninist States of Africa. In the early

21st century there are only five remaining communist states: China, Cuba, Vietnam, Laos, and North Korea. Of these all save North Korea and Laos have introduced some elements of private enterprise and the free market. Such reforms have brought increased prosperity—spectacularly so in China—but the communist party retains a monopoly of political power. Only North Korea continues to practise unreformed Stalinism; and it is thought to be one of the poorest countries in the world.

Communist Manifesto The primary source of the social and economic doctrine of *communism. It was written as *Das Manifest der Kommunistischen Partei* in 1848 by Karl *Marx and Friedrich *Engels to provide a political programme that would establish a common tactic for the working-class movement. The manuscript was adopted by the German Socialist League of the Just as its manifesto. It proposed that all history had hitherto been a development of class struggles, and asserted that the industrialized proletariat would eventually establish a classless society safeguarded by social ownership. It linked *socialism directly with *communism and set out measures by which the latter could be achieved. It had no immediate impact and Marx suggested it should be shelved when the *Revolutions of 1848 failed. Nevertheless, it continued to influence worldwide communist movements throughout the 20th century.

Comnena, Anna (*c.*1083–1148) Historian, daughter of the Byzantine emperor Alexius *Comnenus. She nurtured ambitions that her husband would usurp her brother as emperor but when she was widowed in 1137, she retired to a monastery. She wrote the *Alexiad*, a history in 15 books which was largely an account of the First *Crusade and panegyric of her father's life.

Comnenus, Alexius (1048–1118) Byzantine emperor (1081–1118). In the mid-11th century Byzantine politics were dominated by a military aristocracy and court officials; Alexius Comnenus was an army general who forged an alliance between his military supporters and a number of court officials and so won the throne for himself. He succeeded in checking the challenge from the *Normans under Guiscard in the Mediterranean but was continually harassed by the threat of barbarian invasions. In 1095 he approached Pope Urban II for help in recruiting mercenaries, a call that led to the First *Crusade, which the pope hoped would save the empire from the Seljuk *Turks. The Crusade was to Alexius's advantage and he was able to leave his son John to inherit the Byzantine empire on his death.

Comoros, Federal Islamic Republic of the

Capital:	Moroni
Area:	1,862 sq km (719 sq miles)
Population:	752,288 (2012 est)
Currency:	1 Comorian franc = 100 centimes
Religions:	Sunni Muslim 98.0%; Roman Catholic 2.0%
Ethnic Groups:	Antalote, Cafre, Makoa, Oimatsaha, Sakalava
Languages:	Arabic, French, Comoran (all official)
International Organizations:	UN; Non-Aligned Movement; Arab League; Franc Zone; AU

A country made up of three main islands and several islets in the Indian Ocean.

Physical The Comoro Islands are volcanic. They lie in the Mozambique Channel of the Indian Ocean, between the mainland of Africa and northern Madagascar. The chief islands are Great Comoro, Anjouan, and Mohéli. Great Comoro is well forested. Mayotte, geographically part of the archipelago, is a French dependency.

Economy Exports are dominated by cloves, vanilla, and essential oils for perfume. Most foodstuffs are imported and there is little industry. There is high unemployment and the country suffers from lack of energy resources.

History Arab peoples were living on the islands when the first Europeans encountered them in the 16th century. Since the 17th century the islands have been occupied by many different peoples, including Arab traders, Africans, Indonesians, and Madagascans. The islands became a French protectorate in 1886, a French overseas territory in 1947, and gained internal autonomy in 1961. In 1974 all the islanders voted for independence, except for those living on Mayotte, who voted to remain under French rule. The Comorian government declared the whole archipelago be independent (1975) but France gave Mayotte the status of a 'special collectivity'. In 1978 European mercenaries, led by Bob Denard, overthrew the government and ruled until 1984 when democracy was restored.

Denard returned from exile in 1995 to attempt another coup but French troops invaded and restored democracy. In 1997 Anjouan and Mohéli declared independence from Comoros and demanded to return to French rule. This led the president, Mohammed Taki to assume dictatorial powers. Following his death, Colonel Azali Assoumani seized power in a bloodless coup (1999). A federal constitution was approved in 2001, under which the presidency would be held in rotation by natives of the three main islands. Assoumani, from Great Comoro, was victorious in presidential elections the next year; he was succeeded in 2006 by Ahmed Abdallah Mohamed Sambi, from Anjouan; and in 2011 by Ikiliou Dhoinine, from Mohéli. In 2008 Comoran and African Union troops invaded Anjouan to remove the illegal island government.

Compromise of 1850 A political compromise between the North and South of the USA. Initiated by Henry *Clay, it became law in September 1850. In an attempt to resolve problems arising from slavery it provided for the admission of California as a free state, the organization of the Utah and New Mexico territories with no mention of slavery, the abolition of the slave trade in the District of Columbia (Washington), and a stricter fugitive slave law. Hopes that these measures would provide an enduring solution to North–South antagonism were dashed by the passage of the *Kansas-Nebraska Act (1854) and other issues, including persistent popular resistance to the return of fugitive slaves.

concentration camp Originally a place in which non-combatants were accommodated, as instituted by Lord *Kitchener during the Second Boer War (1899–1902). The Boers, mainly women and children, were placed there officially for their own protection from Kitchener's 'scorched earth policy' in the Transvaal and Cape Colony, but actually to prevent them from aiding the guerrillas. Some 20,000 detainees died, largely as a result of disease arising from unhygienic conditions.

During the *Nazi regime in Germany (1933–45) concentration camps became places in which to intern unwanted persons, specifically *Jewish people, but also Protestant and Catholic dissidents, communists, gypsies, trade unionists, homosexuals, and people with disabilities. Described by *Goebbels in August 1934 as 'camps to turn anti-social members of society into useful members by the most humane means possible', they in fact came to witness

depraved acts of torture, slave labour, horror, and mass murder on a scale unprecedented in any country in any century. Some 200,000 had been through the camps before World War II began, when they were increased in size and number. The camps (Konzetrazionslager, or KZ), administered by the *SS, were categorized into *Arbeitslager*, where prisoners were organized into labour battalions, and *Vernichtungslager*, set up for the extermination and incineration of men, women, and children. In eastern Europe prisoners were used initially in labour battalions or in the tasks of genocide, until they too were exterminated. In such camps as Auschwitz, gas chambers could kill and incinerate 12,000 people daily. In the west, Belsen, Dachau, and Buchenwald (a forced labour camp where doctors conducted medical research on prisoners) were notorious. An estimated six million Jews died in the camps (the *Holocaust), as well as some half million gypsies; in addition, millions of Poles, Soviet prisoners-of-war, and other civilians perished. After the war many camp officials were tried and punished, but others escaped. Maidanek was the first camp to be liberated (by the Red Army, in July 1944). After 1953 West Germany paid $37 billion in reparations to the surviving Jewish victims of Nazism.

In the Soviet Union, Lenin greatly enlarged (1919) the Tsarist forced labour camps, which were renamed Gulags (Russian acronym for the Main Administration of Corrective Labour Camps) in 1930. An estimated 15 million prisoners were confined to the Gulags during Stalin's purges, of whom many succumbed to disease, famine, or the firing squad.

Conciliar Movement (1409–49) A Church movement centred on the three general (or ecumenical) councils of Pisa (1409), *Constance (1414–18), and Basle (1431–49). Its original purpose was to heal the papal schism caused by there being two, and later three, popes at the same time (*see* ANTIPOPE). The movement was successful, deposing or accepting the resignation of the popes concerned. It declared the superiority of a general council of the Church over the papacy, formulated in the decree *Haec Sancta* (sometimes called *Sacrosancta*) of 1415, and tried to make general councils a regular feature of the Western Church. It also dealt with various heresies, the council of Constance burning John *Huss and condemning John *Wyclif in 1415, and it initiated some reforms. The movement, in so far as it challenged papal authority, was eventually defeated by the papacy, but its long-term influence upon Christian Churches was considerable.

Concord *See* INDEPENDENCE, AMERICAN WAR OF; LEXINGTON AND CONCORD, BATTLE OF.

Concordat Agreement between the Roman Catholic Church and a secular power. One of the most important was the Concordat of 1801 between Pius VII and Napoleon I which re-established the Catholic Church in France. Another concordat, in the form of the *Lateran Treaties of 1929, regulated the status of the papacy in Italy, which had been a source of contention since the temporal power of the pope was abolished by unification in 1870. It gave the pope sovereignty over *Vatican City and restored the influence of the Catholic Church in Italy.

Condé A junior branch of the French royal House of *Bourbon. The name was first borne by Louis I de Bourbon (1530–69), prince de Condé, a military leader of the *Huguenots during the first phase of the *French Wars of Religion. A bitter enemy of the *Guise faction, he was killed at the battle of Jarnac. Henry I de Bourbon (1552–88) took over his father's leadership of the Huguenots. He briefly renounced his faith at the time of the *St Bartholomew's Day Massacre (1572), but subsequently embarrassed his cousin, the future *Henry IV, with his Protestant fanaticism.

Henry II de Bourbon (1588–1646) was brought up as a Catholic; he plotted during the regency of Marie de Medici, and distinguished himself only by fathering Louis II de Bourbon, his successor, known as the Great Condé. The latter married a niece of Cardinal *Richelieu, and excelled as a military commander in the last phase of the *Thirty Years War. During the first *Fronde he sided with the court party; disagreements with *Mazarin led to his arrest and imprisonment (1650), and on the failure of his insurrection against the government (1651–52), he fled and took service in the Spanish armies in the Netherlands. When he was allowed to return to France in 1660, he conquered Franche-Comté for *Louis XIV (1668), and held high command in the war against the United Provinces of the Netherlands (1672); but Louis never really forgave him for his part in the Fronde, and his treasonable defection to the Spaniards.

Condorcet, Antoine Nicolas, Marquis de (1743–94) French philosopher and politician. He was the only prominent French *philosophe* to play any real part in the events of the Revolution. As a *Girondin and a friend of the leading revolutionaries Emmanuel Sieyès (1748–1836) and Jacques-Pierre Brissot (1754–93) he was elected to the National Convention. In October 1793 he was condemned by the Revolutionary Tribunal and eventually poisoned himself to avoid the guillotine.

Condor Legion A unit of the German air force sent by *Hitler to aid *Franco in the *Spanish Civil War (1936) on condition that it remained under German command. It aided Franco in transporting troops from Morocco in the early days of the war, and played a major role in the bombing of rebel lines and civilian centres, notably the city of Guernica on 27 April 1937.

condottiere (Italian *condotta*, 'contract') The leader of a medieval mercenary band of soldiers. Mercenaries flourished in the climate of economic prosperity and inter-municipal warfare of 14th- and 15th-century Italy. The earliest such mercenaries were recruited from the unemployed mercenary 'free companies' of the 1360s and included Catalans, the Germans and Hungarians of the so-called Grand Company, and the English Sir John Hawkwood, leader of the White Company in the 14th century. The system was refined in the 15th century by the *Sforzas, although the condottieri were always motivated by self-interest, and changing of sides and loyalties was frequent. The system died out as a result of the Habsburg-Valois wars of the 16th century, which led to changes in the financing and organization of armies.

Confederacy The 11 southern US states that seceded from the Union of the United States in 1860–61. Seven states (Alabama, Florida, Georgia, Louisiana, Mississippi, South Carolina, and Texas) formed themselves into the Confederate States of America on 8 February 1861 at Montgomery, Alabama, with a constitution modelled on the US document but incorporating guarantees of states' rights and the institution of slavery. Jefferson *Davis and Alexander H. Stephens were elected President and Vice-President. After the bombardment of *Fort Sumter, four further states joined the Confederacy (Arkansas, North Carolina, Tennessee, and Virginia). Although the Confederate flag contained thirteen stars, two represented Kentucky and Missouri, border states which in fact remained largely under federal control. Despite the relative weakness of its central government based at Richmond, Virginia, the Confederacy managed to sustain the civil war until its collapse in April 1865 after four years of war with most of its territory occupied, its armies defeated, and its economy in ruins. *See* AMERICAN CIVIL WAR.

Confederation of the Rhine (1806–13) A grouping of middle and south German states. After Napoleon's victory at Austerlitz (1805) he announced the creation of a Confederation of the Rhine, whose members were obliged to abdicate from the old Holy Roman Empire, which was then declared dissolved. After the defeat of Prussia at Jena (1806) other princely states and cities joined. Napoleon had annexed for France all the left bank of the Rhine, but the new Confederation gradually extended from the Rhine to the Elbe. It was at first welcomed by the German people as a step towards unity, but it was really a barrier against Prussian and Austrian power, and as the *Continental System began to result in economic hardship, it became less popular. It contributed a contingent to Napoleon's campaigns of 1813. After his defeat at Leipzig, however, the Confederation broke up; one by one the German states and cities made peace and supported the *Quadruple Alliance of Prussia, Britain, Russia, and Austria. A new *German Confederation was to emerge from the Congress of *Vienna.

Conference on Security and Cooperation in Europe *See* HELSINKI CONFERENCE.

Confucianism A system of philosophical and ethical teachings founded by the most celebrated Chinese philosopher **Confucius** (Kongzi, K'ung Fu Tzu) (*c*.551–479 BC) in the 6th century BC and developed by **Mencius** (Meng-tzu) (*c*.371–*c*.289 BC) in the 4th century BC, one of the two major Chinese ideologies. The basic concepts are ethical ones: love for one's fellows, filial piety, decorum, virtue, and the ideal of the superior man. The publication in 1190 AD of the four great Confucian texts revitalized Confucianism throughout China. A second series of texts, the 'five classics', includes the *I Ching*. There are an estimated 5,800,000 followers of Confucianism in the world.

Congo, Belgian *See* CONGO, DEMOCRATIC REPUBLIC OF.

Congo, Democratic Republic of

Capital:	Kinshasa
Area:	2,344,858 sq km (905,355 sq miles)
Population:	75,507,308 (2012 est)
Currency:	1 Congo franc = 100 centimes
Religions:	Roman Catholic 50.0%; Protestant 20.0%; indigenous Christian 10.0%; Muslim 10.0%
Ethnic groups:	Luba, Kongo, Mongo, and Mangbetu-Azande: about 45%; over 200 other groups, including Rwanda, Bangi, Ngale, Rundi, Teke, Boa, Chokwe, Lugbara, and Banda
Languages:	French (official); Lingala; Kingwana; Kikongo; Tshiluba; local languages
International Organizations:	UN; AU; Non-Aligned Movement; Franc Zone; SADC; WTO

(name from 1971–1997 **Zaïre**) The largest country in equatorial Africa; it is bounded by nine other countries and has an outlet to the Atlantic Ocean at the mouth of the Congo.

Physical Thick forests cover the central districts and there is much swamp. In the south, however, are open highlands. The eastern boundary runs down the Great Rift Valley and includes the western shore of Lake Tanganyika.

Economy The country has substantial agricultural, mineral, and energy resources, whose development has been impeded by corruption, smuggling, lack of infrastructure and investment, as well as civil war (1996–2003) and subsequent instability. The main exports are diamonds, copper, gold, cobalt, wood products, crude petroleum, and coffee. Other than coffee, agriculture includes sugar, palm oil, tea, cocoa, and rubber. Industry includes mining and mineral processing, consumer goods, and metal products.

History The pre-colonial 19th-century history of the country was dominated by the Arab slave trade. *Livingstone was the first European explorer of the country. In 1871 *Stanley undertook to sail down the River Congo. His reports prompted King *Leopold II of Belgium to found the International Association of the Congo (called the Congo Free State from 1885). Stanley began to open up its resources. Maladministration by Leopold's agents obliged him to hand the state over to the Belgian Parliament (1908), and it was renamed the Belgian Congo, but in the next 50 years little was done, except by Catholic mission schools, to prepare the country for self-government. The outbreak of unrest in 1959 led to the hasty granting of independence in the following year, but the regime of Patrice *Lumumba was undermined by civil war, and disorder in the newly named Democratic Republic of Congo remained endemic until the coup of General *Mobutu Sese Seko in 1965. In 1967 the Union Minière, the largest copper-mining company, was nationalized and Mobutu achieved some measure of economic recovery. In 1971 the name of the country was changed to Zaïre. Falling copper prices and centralized policies undermined foreign business confidence, and two revolts followed in 1977 and 1978 in the province of Shaba (formerly Katanga), only put down with French military assistance. The 1980 constitution only recognized one political party, the Movement Populaire de la Révolution (MPR), and Mobutu was re-elected as sole candidate in 1977 and 1984. Multiparty elections were promised for 1991, during which the five main opposition parties all refused to support the President's nominated Prime Minister. Near economic collapse provoked riots, looting, and arson. In a confused situation, Mobutu cancelled elections for a renewal of his term of office in December 1991. During 1992 a national constitutional conference was convened and this replaced the government with a High Council of the Republic. Political instability continued with the President and the High Council appointing rival cabinets. An agreement was reached in 1994, when both cabinets were replaced by a new transitional legislature. The country's social and economic problems were, however, increased with the influx of over 1 million refugees from the civil war in neighbouring Rwanda. In August 1995, Zaïrean troops began the forcible repatriation of Rwandan refugees; however, after international condemnation, this policy was halted the following month. In April 1996 Hutu militiamen and Zaïrean soldiers launched a pogrom against Tutsis in Zaïre, driving hundreds of refugees into Rwanda. This led to civil war, with Zaïrean Tutsi rebels attacking government troops and gradually taking over more of the country. By June 1997 Mobutu fled, the rebels' leader, Laurent Kabila, became president, and the country reverted to its former name. The civil war continued during Kabila's rule; he was killed during an abortive coup in 2001 and succeeded by his son, Joseph Kabila. A transitional government that included the main rebel groups as well as the Kabila regime was established in 2003. The legislature approved a new constitution in 2005 and this was subsequently backed in a referendum; it came into force in 2006 and Kabila was elected President. An

agreement to bring peace to the eastern Congo was signed in 2008. Despite military operations by Congolese and Rwandan forces, unrest continues in the east. Kabila was re-elected as President in 2011 in a disputed election.

Congo, Republic of

Capital:	Brazzaville
Area:	342,000 sq km (132,047 sq miles)
Population:	2,492,689 (2012 est)
Currency:	1 CFA franc = 100 centimes
Religions:	Christian 50.0%; traditional religions 48.0%
Ethnic Groups:	Kongo 48.0%; Sanga 20.0%; Teke 17.0%; Mboshi 12.0%
Languages:	French (official); Lingala; Monokutuba; Kongo; local languages
International Organizations:	UN; AU; Non-Aligned Movement; Franc Zone; WTO

A country in western Africa, whose eastern boundary is the Congo River; it is bounded by Cameroon and the Central African Republic on the north and Gabon on the west.

Physical On its short stretch of Atlantic Ocean coast there are lagoons, large deposits of potash and oil. A small plain rises inland to a forest-covered escarpment, while most of the country comprises savannah-covered plateaux.

Economy Crude oil is the principal export, and oil revenues have funded a growing manufacturing base, which includes cement, food processing, and forestry. Lead, copper, zinc, and gold ore are mined. Cassava, sugar cane, and rice are the chief agricultural crops, and timber is an important export.

History The Congo area is thought to have been uninhabited before the 15th century when Pygmies moved into the area from the north and Kongo (or Vili) people from the east. The two main kingdoms that flourished in pre-colonial times were the kingdoms of Loango and Teke, both of which prospered by supporting the slave trade. De Brazza began exploring the region in 1875 and he made the first of the series of treaties that brought it under French control in 1880. In 1888 it was united with Gabon, but was later separated from it as the Moyen Congo (Middle Congo). It was absorbed with Chad into French Equatorial Africa (1910–58). It became a member of the French Community as a constituent republic in 1958, and fully independent in 1960. In the 1960s and 1970s it suffered much from unstable governments, which alternated between civilian and military rule. Some measure of stability was achieved by the regime of Colonel Denis Sassou-Nguesso, who came to power in 1979 and was re-elected in 1989. Although a one-party Marxist state from 1970, Congo maintained links with Western nations, particularly France, from whom it gained economic assistance. In September 1990 it was agreed to adopt a multiparty political system. A new constitution was devised and accepted in a referendum in 1992. Elections held later that year produced no clear winner and a coalition was formed. The coalition collapsed and fresh elections were held in 1993. However, the results were disputed and fraud was alleged. A campaign of protest about the electoral process and results was launched by one political faction but it rapidly degenerated into fierce fighting between rival militias. Several ceasefire agreements were made and broken between 1994 and 1997, when rebel forces succeeded in re-establishing Sassou-Nguesso as President. He won elections in 2002, but fighting continued; peace was finally secured in 2003. Sassou-Nguesso was re-elected as President in 2009 in an election boycotted by most opposition candidates.

Congo crisis (1960–65) A series of political disturbances in the Democratic Republic of the *Congo following its independence from Belgium. The sudden decision by Belgium to grant independence to its vast colony along the Congo was taken in January 1960. A single state was to be created, governed from Léopoldville (Kinshasa). Fighting began between tribes during parliamentary elections in May and further fighting occurred at independence (30 June). The Congolese troops of the Force Publique (armed police) mutinied against their Belgian officers. Europeans and their property were attacked, and Belgian refugees fled. In the rich mining province of Katanga, Moïse *Tshombe, supported by Belgian troops and White mercenaries, proclaimed an independent republic. The government appealed to the United Nations for troops to restore order, and the UN Secretary-General *Hammarskjöld despatched a peacekeeping force to replace the Belgians. A military coup brought the army commander,

Colonel *Mobutu, to power with a government which excluded the radical Prime Minister, Patrice *Lumumba. In 1961 Lumumba was killed, allegedly by "hostile tribesmen", and Hammarskjöld died in an air crash on a visit to the Congo. The fighting continued and independent regimes were established at different times in Katanga, Stanleyville, and Kasai. In November 1965 the Congolese army under Mobutu staged a second coup, and Mobutu declared himself President.

Congregationalism *Protestant churches based on local autonomy and the equality of all believers. Baptism and the Lord's Supper are the only sacraments accepted. As in other reformed Churches, there are ministers who carry out pastoral and liturgical duties. Their ordination rests with the congregation they serve; there is no formal hierarchy, though in practice senior ministers exercise oversight in particular areas. The Congregational Church in England and Wales merged with the Presbyterian Church of England in 1972 to form the United Reformed Church; in the USA the Congregational Christian Churches merged with the Evangelical and Reformed Church in 1957 to form the United Church of Christ.

Congress, Indian National The principal Indian political party. It was founded in 1885 as an annual meeting of educated Indians desiring a greater share in government in cooperation with Britain. Later, divisions emerged between moderates and extremists, led by B. G. Tilak, and Congress split temporarily in 1907. Tilak died in 1920 and under the leadership of M. K. Gandhi Congress developed a powerful central organization, an elaborate branch organization in provinces and districts, and acquired a mass membership. It began to conduct major political campaigns for self-rule and independence. In 1937 it easily won the elections held under the Government of India Act (1935) in a majority of provinces. In 1939 it withdrew from government, and many of its leaders were imprisoned during the 1941 'Quit India' campaign. In 1945–47 Congress negotiated with Britain for Indian independence. Under Jawaharlal *Nehru it continued to dominate independent *India. After his death a struggle ensued between the Congress Old Guard (the Syndicate) and younger, more radical elements of whom Mrs Indira *Gandhi assumed the leadership. In 1969 it split between these two factions but was quickly rebuilt under Mrs Gandhi's leadership. In 1977 it was heavily defeated by the Janata (People's) Alliance Party, led by Morarji *Desai, who became Prime Minister (1977–79). In 1978 Mrs Gandhi formed a new party, the 'real' Indian National Congress, or **Congress (I)** (for Indira). In 1979 she led this faction to victory in elections and again became Prime Minister in 1980. After her assassination in October 1984 the splits between factions largely healed and leadership of the Congress (I) Party passed to her son Rajiv Gandhi (1944–91), who became Prime Minister (1984–89). He was assassinated in May 1991, during the run-up to a general election. The Congress (I) Party was re-elected under the leadership of P. V. Narasimha Rao, who became Prime Minister until 1996, when the Party lost the general election. Rao resigned as leader of the party later that year and was replaced by Sitaram Kesri. In 1998 Sonia Gandhi, widow of Rajiv *Gandhi, became party leader. Congress (I) won most seats, but not a majority, in the 2004 election. Gandhi declined the post of Prime Minister, although she remained party leader; Manmohan Singh formed a Congress (I)-led coalition government, which was re-elected in 2009. However, the general election of 2014 saw Congress (I) lose power in its worst-ever defeat.

Congress of the USA The legislative branch of the US federal government. Provided for in Article I of the US Constitution, Congress is divided into two constituent houses: the lower, the *House of Representatives, in which membership is based on the population of each state; and the upper, the *Senate, in which each state has two members. Representatives serve a two-year term and Senators a six-year term. Congressional powers include the collection of taxes and duties, the provision for common defence, general welfare, the regulation of commerce, patents and copyrights, the declaration of war, raising of armies, and maintenance of a navy, and the establishment of the post offices and federal courts. Originally, Congress was expected to hold the initiative in the federal government, but the emergence of the President as a national party leader has resulted in the continuous fluctuation in the balance of power between legislature and executive. Much of the effective work of Congress is now done in powerful standing committees dealing with major areas of policy.

conquistadores Spanish soldiers and adventurers in the 16th century. The most famous conquistadores were Hernando *Cortés, the conqueror of Aztec Mexico, and Francisco *Pizarro, the conqueror of Inca Peru; but there were many others. Their discoveries and conquests included the Caribbean, Latin America, southern and south-western USA, and the Philippines. Many would-be conquistadores explored immense areas but conquered nothing and founded no permanent settlements. As proper colonial administrations were established their activity diminished.

conservatism A political outlook that values and supports established institutions and is critical of proposals for radical social change. Conservatism first took shape as an ideology at the time of the French Revolution, when thinkers such as Edmund *Burke (*Reflections on the Revolution in France*, 1790) and Joseph de Maistre (*Considerations on France*, 1796) denounced the revolutionary changes taking place in France as destructive of much that is valuable in society. Since then, conservatism has chiefly been opposed to *liberalism and *socialism. Conservatives have a pessimistic view of human nature. They see people as standing in need of discipline and restraint, and are fearful of the consequences when authority is destroyed and individuals are left to their own devices. They respect tradition as embodying the accumulated wisdom of the ages, and are correspondingly sceptical about untested plans and policies put forward by would-be reformers. Conservatives typically favour: constitutional government as a way of preserving authority without concentrating it in the hands of a despot or dictator; an ordered or ranked society in which people know their proper place and defer to those placed above them in the hierarchy; established religion, in order to integrate people into the fabric of society; and the family, the primary source of moral values and the place where responsible citizens are formed. Conservative economic attitudes have varied with time. Originally conservatives tended to support protectionist policies in contrast to the laissez-faire policies advocated by liberals, but in the 20th century they have increasingly turned to the free market as the best means of organizing economic activity. This synthesis of conservative and classical liberal beliefs can be seen especially in the thinking of the *New Right. Political parties are rarely wholeheartedly conservative in outlook, but politicians of a conservative disposition can be found in the Christian Democratic parties of Europe, in the US Republican Party, and in the *Conservative (Tory) Party in the UK.

Conservative Party (Britain) A major political party in Britain. In 1830 it was suggested in the *Quarterly Review*, a *Tory journal, that a better name for the old Tory Party might be

Conservative since the Party stood for the preservation of existing institutions. The idea was favoured by Sir Robert *Peel's *Tamworth Manifesto, which set out a programme of reforming Conservatism, brought him briefly to the premiership in 1834–35. Although Peel was re-elected in 1841, his conversion to *free trade in 1846 split the Party. Peel's followers after a time joined the Liberals. The majority of the Party under Lord Derby and *Disraeli gradually adopted the title Conservative, though Tory continued to be used also. Between 1846 and 1874 the Conservatives were a minority party though they were in office in 1867 and passed a *Reform Act. In 1867 they were the first party to create a national organization with the formation of the Central Office. Disraeli described the aims of the Party as: "the preservation of our institutions, the maintenance of our Empire and the amelioration of the condition of the people". In 1874, his government embarked on a programme of social reforms and increased the powers of central government. In 1886 those Liberals, led by Joseph *Chamberlain, who rejected Gladstone's *Home Rule policy for Ireland, allied with the Party, whose full title then became the National Union of Conservative and Unionist Associations. The Party was strongly imperialist throughout the first half of the 20th century, although splitting in 1903 over the issue of free trade or empire preference. From 1915 until 1945 the Party either formed the government, except for 1924 and 1929–31, or governed in coalition with the Labour Party (1931–35; 1939–45). Since World War II it has again been in office for long periods (1951–64; 1970–74; 1979–97; from 2010, in coalition). With the growing crisis in *Northern Ireland after 1968 the *Ulster Unionists dissociated themselves from the Party. Until the later 1970s the Party's policies tended to be pragmatic, accepting the basic philosophy of the *welfare state and being prepared to adjust in response to a consensus of public opinion. Under the leadership of Margaret *Thatcher, however, it seemed to reassert the 19th-century liberal emphasis on individual free enterprise, challenging the need for state support and subsidy, while combining this with a strong assertion of state power against local authorities, a trend that continued under the leadership of John *Major. Many publicly owned companies, including British Airways, British Aerospace, British Gas, British Telecom, and British Rail were privatized by the Thatcher and Major governments. By the mid-1990s, however, the popularity of privatization was waning as criticism of the management of many of the newly privatized companies increased. In the General Election of May 1997, the Conservative Party suffered a devastating defeat, recording their lowest proportion of the vote (31%) since 1832 and winning their fewest seats (165) since 1906. Further defeats followed in 2001 and 2005. In the 2010 General Election, with David *Cameron as leader, the party won most seats but not an absolute majority. Cameron became Prime Minister of a Conservative–Liberal Democrat coalition government.

Constance, Council of (1414–18) An ecclesiastical council held at Constance in Germany to deal with reform and heresy within the Christian Church. It resolved the *Great Schism, decreed the regular calling of councils, and presided over the trial and burning of John *Huss. It failed, however, to produce effective reform of outstanding abuses in clerical finance and conduct, or to curb papal independence.

Constantine I (the Great) (full name Flavius Valerius Aurelius Constantinus) (c.274–337) Roman emperor (324–37). On the death of his father Constantius I in 306 at Eboracum (York) the army proclaimed him emperor. After a period of political complications, with several emperors competing for power, Constantine and Licinius divided the empire between them, East and West. War was fought between the two rulers (314) and Constantine defeated and killed Licinius (323) and he became sole emperor, founding a new second capital at Byzantium, which he named Constantinople (now *Istanbul).

He adopted Christian symbols for his battle standards in 312 prompted by a "vision" of the sign of the cross in the rays of the sun. In the following year he proclaimed tolerance and recognition of Christianity in the "Edict" of Milan. Although his own beliefs are uncertain he supported orthodox Christianity in an attempt to maintain the unity of the vast *Roman empire. Sunday was declared a holiday in 326. He and his mother Helena took great interest in the Christian sites of Rome and *Palestine. Basilicas were built on the site of the stable-cave in Bethlehem, where Jesus Christ was supposed to have been born, his alleged tomb in Jerusalem, and St Peter's grave on the Vatican hill in Rome, and at Constantinople (St Sophia). The Eastern Church lists him as a saint.

Constantinople See ISTANBUL.

Constitution of the USA The fundamental written instrument of the US government. It replaced the Articles of Confederation (1781–87), a league of sovereign states, with an effective central, national, federal government. Three months' secret debate among the *Founding Fathers at the Federal Constitutional Convention in Philadelphia in 1787 produced a series of modifications to *Madison's original Virginia Plan. The Great Compromise, between large and small states, gave equal representation in the Senate but by population in the House of Representatives. North and South finally agreed to slaves being counted as three-fifths of a person in representation and taxation, continuation of the slave trade until at least 1808, and no taxes on exports. Conflict between state and central power was reconciled by enumerating areas of federal concern. The principle of popular sovereignty with direct biennial election of congressmen was balanced by indirect election of senators and presidents for renewable six- and four-year terms. Within the federal system of executive (President, Vice-President, cabinet, and civil service), legislature (Senate and House of Representatives), and judiciary (Supreme and other federal courts), a series of checks and balances sought to share and divide power between these three components of government. Thus, for instance, the Supreme Court, appointed by the President with Senatorial approval, may declare actions of the executive or legislature unconstitutional, but may not initiate suits or legislation. The 1787 draft required ratification by nine state conventions. Major opposition in Virginia, Massachusetts, and New York came from the anti-Federalist, states' rights advocates like Patrick Henry or George *Clinton. The constitution was defended in the *Federalist Papers* by James *Madison, Alexander *Hamilton, and John *Jay and came into operation in 1789. Major shortcomings included failure to foresee political parties, initial absence of a *Bill of Rights, complexity of electoral arrangements, and frustration of executive initiative. The loose definition of congressional powers and the persuasive influence of federal grants tipped the balance from state to central supremacy. This flexible guide for government has been amended 27 times, most notably to abolish slavery, to add a Bill of Rights, and to establish Black and female enfranchisement.

Continental Congress (1774; 1775–89) The assembly that first met in Philadelphia to concert a colonial response to the 'Intolerable' Coercive Acts. At its first session, the radicals, led by delegates from Massachusetts, Virginia, and South Carolina, outmanoeuvred the moderates from New York and Pennsylvania and adopted the Suffolk County (Massachusetts)

Resolves, rejecting the Acts as 'the attempts of a wicked administration to enslave America'. The second Congress, convened in the wake of Lexington and Concord, created a Continental Army under George *Washington and, as a result of British intransigence and radical pressure, moved gradually towards the *Declaration of Independence (1776). The Congress undertook the central direction of the War of *Independence, and, under the Articles of Confederation (1781), the government of the USA.

Continental System Economic strategy in Europe, intended to cripple Britain's economy. It was based upon the Berlin (1806) and Milan (1807) decrees of *Napoleon, which declared Britain to be in a state of blockade and forbade either neutral countries or French allies to trade with it or its colonies. At Tilsit (1807) Russia agreed to the system and in 1808 Spain was obliged to join it. Britain responded by issuing Orders in Council that blockaded the ports of France and its allies and allowed them to trade with each other and neutral countries only if they did so via Britain. The restrictions contributed to the *War of 1812 with the USA over the right of neutral ships to trade with Europe. It gradually resulted in Napoleon losing support at home and being challenged abroad. His unsuccessful invasion of Russia in 1812 was provoked by Russian refusal to continue the system and it marked the beginning of his downfall.

Control Commissions Allied administrations established in Germany after both World Wars. After World War I the Commission supervised German demilitarization. During World War II it was agreed by the US, British, and Soviet leaders that, after its defeat, Germany should be divided. Four zones of occupation were created in 1945, administered until 1948 by these Allies and France, the four military commanders acting as a supreme Control Council. Their responsibility was to deal with matters relating to the whole of Germany. In practice the occupying powers administered their zones independently, while the British and US zones merged at the start of 1947. However, the Control Commission undertook significant work especially in the process of removing members of the Nazi Party from important positions. Tension between the Soviet and Western representatives led to the collapse of the system.

convoy system A system used in wartime to arrange for merchant vessels to sail in groups under the protection of an armed naval escort. In 1917 Germany's policy of unrestricted submarine (U-boat) warfare nearly defeated Britain. One ship in four leaving British ports was sunk; new construction only replaced one-tenth of lost tonnage. In the face of this crisis *Lloyd George overruled the Admiralty's refusal to organize convoys, and by November 1918, 80% of shipping, including foreign vessels, came in convoy. In World War II transatlantic convoys were immediately instituted in spite of a shortage of destroyers, using long-range aircraft for protection. During 1942 they were extended to the USA as the Allies were losing an average of 96 ships a month.

Cook, James (1728–79) British naval captain, navigator, and explorer. Cook charted the coasts and seaways of Canada (1759; 1763–7), the St Lawrence Channel and the coasts of Nova Scotia and Newfoundland. He then commanded an expedition in HMS *Endeavour* (1768–71) to Tahiti and continued to chart the coasts of New Zealand and eastern Australia. On a second voyage (1772–5) he became the first navigator to cross the Antarctic Circle but was then driven back by ice. However, he explored vast areas of the Pacific. His third voyage (begun in 1776) was to find the North-West Passage. He sought it backwards, by entering the Pacific and sailing up the west coast of North America. He reached the Bering Strait before a wall of ice forced him to retreat. On the way he had discovered Hawaii, a perfect place for refitting his ships. Returning to Hawaii his crew became engaged in a fight with the islanders over the stealing of a cutter and he was stabbed to death.

Cook set new standards in the sea care of men exposed to lengthy voyages: in order to protect his crews from scurvy (a lethal disease caused by lack of ascorbic acid), he pioneered a diet that included cabbage, cress, and a kind of orange extract. His *Journals* give a detailed account of his three voyages to the Pacific.

Cook, Sir Joseph (1860–1947) Australian politician, Prime Minister (1913–14). Cook was elected Prime Minister in 1913, but he lacked support and was voted out of office the following year.

Coolidge, Calvin (John Calvin Coolidge) (1872–1933) US Republican statesman, 30th President of the USA (1923–29),. Highly popular personally, he was seen as an embodiment of thrift, caution, and honesty in a decade when corruption in public life was common, even in his own administration. He was committed to reducing income taxes and the national debt, and was noted for his policy of non-interference

in foreign affairs, which culminated in the signing of the Kellogg Pact in 1928.

Cooper, Anthony Ashley *See* SHAFTES-BURY.

Cooperative Movement An organization owned by and run for the benefit of its members. First developed in many of the new industrial towns in Britain at the end of the 18th century, the Cooperative Movement was largely an attempt to offer an alternative to competitive *capitalism. In the early 19th century the social reformer Robert *Owen made several attempts to set up his own cooperative communities, but it was with the founding of the Rochdale Pioneers in 1844 that the cooperative movement in Britain really got under way. In 1864 these came together in a federation known as the Cooperative Wholesale Society. In 1869 the Cooperative Union, an advisory and educational body, was formed. The Cooperative Wholesale Society developed as a manufacturer and wholesale trader, opening its first factories and developing its own farms. The Cooperative Party was established in 1917 to represent its members' interests in Parliament, and subsequently contested elections in alliance with the Labour Party. The movement spread rapidly to northern Europe. In the USA the first cooperatives were established at the end of the 18th and the beginning of the 19th centuries. In India and other developing countries, particularly in Africa after World War II, cooperatives have been an important factor in the growth of the economy.

Copenhagen, First Battle of (1801) A naval engagement between the British and Danish fleets. The northern powers (Russia, Prussia, Denmark, and Sweden) formed a league of armed neutrality to resist the British right of search at sea. Without declaring war, a British fleet, commanded by Admiral Sir Hyde Parker, was sent to destroy the Danish fleet, anchored in Copenhagen. The British divided their fleet, *Nelson attacking the Danes from the more protected south whilst Parker attacked from the north. Despite bad weather and the loss of three ships Nelson, ignoring Parker's signal to discontinue action by fixing the telescope to his blind eye, was able to sink or take all but three of the Danish ships. The Danes agreed to an armistice and the league was disbanded.

Copenhagen, Second Battle of (1807) A hostile incident between Denmark and Britain. The news that Denmark was about to join Napoleon's *Continental System and to declare war on Britain, led the British government to challenge Denmark. When the Danes refused to surrender, the British landed troops and shelled Copenhagen.

Copper Age The stage of technological development between the introduction of copper and the manufacture of bronze (an alloy of copper and tin) in the *Bronze Age. As copper was initially very scarce, the impact of metallurgy was often slight, and it was used only for ornaments and rare daggers or flat axes.

Copper appeared at very different dates in various parts of the world. In some cases there was no separate stage before the adoption of true bronze or even iron: in others, Andean South America for example, it was in use for very much longer.

Corday d'Armont, Charlotte (1768–93) French noblewoman, the murderess of *Marat. After a lonely childhood in Normandy she began to attend the meetings of the *Girondins, where she heard of Marat as a tyrant and conceived the idea of assassinating him. She arrived in Paris in 1793 and on 13 July murdered Marat in his bath. A plea of insanity was overruled and she was sentenced to death on the guillotine.

Corfu incident (31 August 1923) The naval bombardment and occupation of the Greek island of Corfu by Italian troops. An Italian general and four members of his staff, engaged under international authority in determining the boundary between Greece and *Albania, had been murdered three days before. Following the bombardment by Italy in which 16 people were killed, *Mussolini issued an ultimatum, demanding a heavy indemnity. Greece appealed to the *League of Nations, which referred the dispute to the Council of Ambassadors. The Council ordered Greece to pay 50 million lire. Under pressure from Britain and France, Italian troops withdrew. The outcome of the dispute raised serious doubts about the strength and efficiency of the League.

Corn Laws Regulations applied in Britain to the import and export of grain (mainly wheat) in order to control its supply and price. In 1815, following the end of the Napoleonic Wars, Parliament passed a law permitting the import of foreign wheat free of duty only when the domestic price reached 80 shillings per quarter (8 bushels). A sliding scale of duties was introduced in 1828 in order to alleviate the distress being caused to poorer people by the rise in the price of bread. A slump in trade in the late 1830s and a succession of bad harvests made conditions worse and strengthened the hand of the

*Anti-Corn Law League. In 1846 the Corn Laws were repealed save for a nominal shilling. This split the Conservative Party, but agriculture in Britain did not suffer as had been predicted. The repeal of the Corn Laws came to symbolize the success of *free trade and liberal political economy.

Cornwallis, Charles, 1st Marquis (1738–1805) British general, who fought in the War of *Independence at Long Island and *Brandywine. He took command of the southern campaign in 1780, defeating the Americans at *Camden and Guildford Court House, but by his relentless pursuit into the interior he lost contact with Sir Henry Clinton and exhausted his troops. His choice of *Yorktown as a base proved disastrous, and he was forced to surrender (1781). Later reinstated, he served as governor-general of Bengal (1786–93, 1805) where he defeated *Tipu Sultan and his Cornwallis Code reformed land tenure. He was also viceroy of Ireland (1798–1801) and negotiator of the Treaty of Amiens (1802).

corsair A privateer of the Barbary Coast of North Africa, and especially Algiers. Piracy existed here in Roman times, but, after the Moorish expulsion from Spain, individuals (with government connivance) began attacks on Christian shipping. The early 17th century was the peak of their activity. Privateering ceased with the French occupation of Algiers in 1830.

Cortés, Hernando (or **Hernando Cortez**) (1485–1547) First of the Spanish conquistadores. Cortés was believed by the Aztecs to be the god-king Quetzalcóatl and was able to overthrow the Aztec empire with a comparatively small army of adventurers. In 1521 he destroyed the Aztec capital Tenochtitlán completely and established Mexico City as the new capital of Mexico (then called New Spain), serving briefly as governor of the colony.

Cosgrave, William Thomas (1880–1965) Irish statesman. Determined to gain Irish independence from Britain, he took part in the *Easter Rising (1916). Elected to the British Parliament in 1918 as a *Sinn Fein member, he became Minister for Local Government in the self-declared government of the Dáil Éireann in 1919. He reluctantly accepted the Anglo-Irish Treaty creating the *Irish Free State. He was President of the Executive Council of the Free State from 1922–1932, during which time the international standing of the new state was greatly enhanced. He was leader of the opposition Fine Gael party in the Dáil Eireann

(1933–44). He was the father of **Liam Cosgrave** (1920–), who in turn became leader of Fine Gael (1965–77) and later Taoiseach (Prime Minister) of the Republic of Ireland (1973–77).

Cossack (from Turkish, 'adventurer' or 'guerrilla') A people in south Russia. They were descended from refugees from religious persecution in *Poland and Muscovy, and from peasants fleeing the taxes and obligations of the feudal system. Settling in mainly autonomous tribal groups around the rivers Don and Dnieper, they played an important role in the history of the Ukraine. A frontier lifestyle encouraged military prowess and horsemanship, males aged 16–60 years being obliged to bear arms. They were democratic, directly electing their leaders or *hetmen*. Their relations with Russia included military service and military alliance, especially against the Turks, but there were rebellions against Russia under the leaderships of Stenka Razin (1667–69), Iran Mazeppa (1709), and Yemelyan Pugachev (1773–74). Ukrainian Cossackdom experienced a revival following the breakup of the Soviet Union in 1991.

Costa Rica

Capital:	San José
Area:	51,100 sq km (19,730 sq miles)
Population:	4,695,942 (2012 est)
Currency:	1 Costa Rican colón = 100 céntimos
Religions:	Roman Catholic 76.3%; Evangelical 13.7%
Ethnic Groups:	White and Mestizo 94.0%; Black 3.0%; Amerindian 1.0%; Chinese 1.0%
Languages:	Spanish (official); English
International Organizations:	UN; OAS; WTO

A small country on the Central American isthmus, between Nicaragua and Panama.

Physical It has a Caribbean coast on its north-east and a Pacific coast on its south-west. While the coastal lowlands have a tropical climate, a range of volcanic mountains occupies the centre of the country, providing plateaux which have a mild climate. There are several peaks over 3350 m (11,000 feet).

Economy The soil is very fertile and supports livestock farming, fruit, sugar, and some of the finest coffee in the world. Bananas are the principal export. Industries include microprocessors, food processing, and medical equipment.

History Costa Rica was discovered by *Columbus during his fourth voyage to the New World in 1502. Permanent settlement did not occur until 1564 when Juan Vásquez de Coronado, with settlers from Nicaragua, founded Cartago on the Meseta Central. The small Indian population fell victim to disease, leaving the ethnic make-up of the area mostly European. Costa Rica formed part of the captaincy-general of Guatemala until 1821, when it joined the independent Mexican empire (1821–23) and then the United Provinces of Central America (1823–38). In 1838 it became an independent republic. A policy of isolation and stability, together with agricultural fertility, brought considerable British and US investment in the 19th century. Apart from the brief dictatorship of Federico Tinoco Granados (1917–19), Costa Rica was remarkable in the late 19th and early 20th centuries for its democratic tradition. After World War II left-wing parties emerged, including the communist. The socialist Presidents Otilio Ulate (1948–53) and José Figueres (1953–58; 1970–74), tried to disband the army, nationalize banks, and curb US investment. A new constitution, granting universal suffrage and abolishing the armed forces, was introduced in 1949. Political tensions in the 1970s were aggravated by economic problems and by the arrival of many fugitives from neighbouring states. President Luis Alberto Monge (1982–86) had to impose severe economic restraint. In 1987 President Oscar Arias Sánchez (1986–90) put forward a peace-plan for Central America, to which President Reagan reacted by reducing US aid to the country. Severe economic difficulties continued, with an IMF-imposed austerity programme and widespread industrial unrest in the early 1990s. However, the economic position improved from the late 1990s. In 2010 Costa Rica elected Laura Chincilla as its first woman President.

Costello, John A. (John Aloysius Costello) (1891–1976) Irish Fine Gael politician, Prime Minister of the Republic of Ireland (1948–51; 1954–57).

Côte d'Ivoire (formerly Ivory Coast)

Capital:	Yamoussoukro (Abidjan, the former capital, remains the seat of government)
Area:	322,463 sq km (124,471 sq miles)
Population:	22,400,835 (2012 est)
Currency:	1 CFA franc = 100 centimes
Religions:	Muslim 38.6%; Christian 32.8%; traditional beliefs 11.9%
Ethnic Groups:	Akan 42.1%; Voltaiques or Gur 17.6%; Northern Mande 16.5%; Kru 11.0%; Southern Mande 10.0%
Languages:	French (official); local languages
International Organizations:	ECOWAS; Non-Aligned Movement; AU; UN; Franc Zone; WTO

A tropical West African country, bounded on the west by Liberia and Guinea, on the north by Mali and Burkina Faso, and on the east by Ghana.

Physical Its south-facing coastline is rocky in the west but elsewhere has sand-bars and lagoons. Three rivers run through the hot, rain-forested lowlands. In the central belt coffee is grown. The Nimba Mountains in the west contain minerals, including iron.

Economy The economy is primarily agricultural, with main exports including cocoa, coffee, and palm oil. Industries include food processing, wood products, oil refining, and gold mining, and there is a well-developed system of hydraulic electricity production from dams. Mineral deposits include iron, cobalt, bauxite, nickel, manganese, and diamonds. Political instability from 1999 to 2011 greatly harmed the economy.

History There were scattered and isolated coastal settlements in the region when European slave traders arrived in the 15th century. The French had established trading posts in the area by the end of the 17th century and in the 19th century made treaties with local chiefs. France obtained rights on the coast in 1842, establishing a colony in 1893, which in 1904 became a territory of French West Africa. In 1933 most of the territory of Upper Volta was added to the Côte d'Ivoire, but in 1948 this area was returned to the reconstituted Upper Volta, today *Burkina

Faso. The Côte d'Ivoire became an autonomous republic within the *French Community in 1958, and achieved full independence in 1960, becoming a one-party republic governed by the moderate Democratic Party of the Côte d'Ivoire and with Félix Houphouët-Boigny its President. The country has large petroleum deposits and a developing industrial sector, but falling cocoa and coffee prices adversely affected the economy during the late 1980s. The resulting policy of economic austerity caused unrest and demonstrations. In the first multiparty elections in November 1990, the President's Democratic Party won all but 10 seats in the National Assembly. Following Houphouët-Boigny's death in 1993, Henri Konan Bedie (1934–) was elected President in 1995. His overthrow by a military coup in 1999 began a period of instability that led to civil war in 2002–03 and the effective division of the country between the rebel-controlled north and the government-controlled south. In 2007 a power-sharing agreement was reached between government and rebels and a provisional government formed; Laurent Gbagbo, President since 2000, remained in office. However, the result of the 2010 presidential election was disputed, with both Gbagbo and Alassane Ouattara claiming victory and forming rival governments. A brief civil war in 2011 ended in victory for Ouattara.

Council of Europe

An association of 47 European states, independent of the European Community. It meets in Strasbourg. Founded in 1949, it is committed to the principles of freedom and the rule of law, and to safeguarding the political and cultural heritage of Europe. Its executive organ is the Committee of Ministers, and most of its conclusions take the form of international agreements (known as *European Conventions*) or recommendations to governments. One of the Council's principal achievements is the European Convention of Human Rights (1950) under which was established the European Commission and the European Court of Human Rights.

Counter-Reformation

A revival in the *Roman Catholic Church between the mid-16th and mid-17th centuries. It had its origins in reform movements which were independent of the Protestant *Reformation, but it increasingly became identified with, and took its name from, efforts to 'counter' the Protestant Reformation. There were three main ecclesiastical aspects. First a reformed papacy, with a succession of popes who had a notably more spiritual outlook than their immediate predecessors, and a number of reforms in the church's central government initiated by them. Secondly, the foundation of new religious orders, notably the Oratorians and in 1540 the Society of Jesus (Jesuits), and the reform of older orders, notably the Capuchin reform of the Franciscans. Thirdly, the Council of *Trent (1545–63), which defined and clarified Catholic doctrine on most points in dispute with Protestants and instituted important moral and disciplinary reforms within the Catholic Church, including the provision of a better education for the clergy through theological colleges called seminaries. All this led to a flowering of Catholic spirituality at the popular level, but also to an increasingly anti-Protestant mentality. The movement became political through its links with Catholic rulers, notably *Philip II of Spain, who sought to re-establish Roman Catholicism by force. The stalemate between Catholics and Protestants was effectively recognized by the Treaty of *Westphalia in 1648, which brought to an end the Thirty Years War and in a sense concluded the Counter-Reformation period.

Courtrai, Battle of (11 July 1302) Sometimes known as the 'Battle of the Golden Spurs'. Philip IV of France had attempted to overrun Flanders but Flemish troops fought the French at Courtrai. Flemish burghers defeated the French nobility, and, in celebration of victory, hung their spurs in the churches of Bruges. The Battle of Courtrai was one of the most significant defeats suffered by France in the 14th century. Charles VI of France responded by sacking Courtrai in 1382.

Covenanter Originally a Scot who opposed the ecclesiastical innovations of Charles I of England. Drawn from all parts of Scotland and all sections of society, Covenanters subscribed to the National Covenant of 1638. This was a revised version of a previous covenant (1581), which had been signed by James VI of Scotland. They swore to resist 'episcopal' (the church governed by bishops) religious changes, and, in the event of such changes, they set up a full Presbyterian system and defended it in the *Bishops' Wars. They hoped to impose their system on England in 1643, by drawing up the *Solemn League and Covenant with the *Long Parliament. Disappointed in this, they turned in 1650 to Charles II, who signed the Covenant, but then abjured it at his *Restoration (1660), condemning it as an unlawful oath. In Scotland in 1661 the episcopacy was re-established, and Covenanters were badly treated. In 1690, the

Presbyterian Church of Scotland was established.

Coverdale, Miles (1488–1568) English biblical scholar. He translated the first complete printed English Bible (1535), published in Zurich while he was in exile for preaching against confession and images. He also edited the Great Bible, brought out in 1539 by the printer Richard Grafton (c.1513–c.1572).

cowboy Originally, a lawless marauder. The name was first applied to some pro-British gangs in the USA during the American War of Independence, who roamed the neutral ground of Westchester county in New York state (their Revolutionary counterparts were 'skinners'). By the 1870s, a cowboy described a herder of cattle on the Great Plains. The cattle industry spread across the Great Plains from Texas to Canada and westward to the Rocky Mountains. The introduction of barbed wire to fence in ranches rapidly encroached on the open ranges, and by 1895 railway expansion had made trail-driving uneconomical, and cowboys settled to work on the cattle ranches.

Cowen, Brian (1960–) Irish Fianna Fáil politician, Prime Minister of the Republic of Ireland (2008–11). He was appointed Prime Minister on the resignation of Bertie *Ahern and his term was dominated by the disastrous effects of the *Credit Crunch and *Eurozone Crisis on Ireland.

Cranmer, Thomas (1489–1556) English cleric, a founding father of the English Protestant Church. He served *Henry VIII on diplomatic missions before becoming Archbishop of Canterbury in 1532. He annulled Henry's marriages to Catherine of Aragon, Anne Boleyn, and Anne of Cleves. During *Edward VI's reign, he was chiefly responsible for liturgical reform including the First and Second English Prayer Books (1549 and 1552) and the Forty-Two Articles (1553). He supported Lady Jane *Grey's succession in 1553; after Queen Mary's accession he was tried for high treason, then for heresy, and finally burnt at the stake in Oxford.

Crassus, Marcus Licinius (known as 'Dives') (c.115–53 BC) Roman politician. He defeated Spartacus in 71 BC, though Pompey claimed credit for the victory. Crassus joined Caesar and Pompey in the First Triumvirate in 60. In 55 he was made consul and given a special command in Syria, where he hoped to regain a military reputation equal to that of his allies by a victory over the Parthians, but after some successes he was defeated and killed.

Crazy Horse (Sioux name **Ta-Sunko-Witko**) (*c.*1849–77) Sioux chief. In 1876 he led a successful rearguard action of Sioux and Cheyenne warriors against invading US army forces in Montana. Shortly afterwards he and his men joined *Sitting Bull at Little Bighorn, where Crazy Horse played an important strategic and military role in the massacre of US forces under General Custer. He surrendered in 1877 and was killed in custody in Nebraska a few months later.

Crécy, Battle of (26 August 1346) The village of Crécy in northern France was the site for the defeat of the French under Philip VI by the *archers of the English king, Edward III. Edward's raiding army, anxious to avoid pitched battle, was trapped by a numerically superior French force. The English bowmen dug pits to impede advancing cavalry, while the knights dismounted and formed three supporting divisions, their right commanded by Edward's son and heir, *Edward the Black Prince. Over 1,500 of the French died, including the cream of the nobility, as against some 40 English dead. Edward was able to march north and besiege Calais. This was a decisive English victory at the outset of the *Hundred Years War.

Credit Crunch The banking and financial crisis that began in 2007, so-called because a principal characteristic was a catastrophic sudden tightening in the availability of credit. From the 1980s onwards, new techniques for risk management and the loosening of regulations led to a huge growth in the global financial services industry. There was a massive expansion in the availability of cheap credit, and loans at relatively low interest rates were offered to customers previously considered bad credit risks. In the mid-2000s concerns grew about the resulting levels of debt and the security of a financial system increasingly reliant on the repackaging of this debt in complex derivatives products; but the trigger for the crisis was 'subprime' mortgages in the USA. Many mortgages had been sold, sometimes fraudulently to unsuitable borrowers, on the assumption that house prices would continue to rise. This assumption proved false when the resulting US house-price bubble burst in 2006. Sophisticated financial products based in part on these 'toxic' loans had been widely traded in world financial markets, and questions were now asked about their precise value. In many cases these questions proved impossible to answer: the original loans had been subdivided and repackaged in such complex ways that the resulting composite products could not be valued accurately. There were also cases of fraud, where high-risk products had been knowingly sold as low-risk. Faced with this uncertainty, the financial markets assumed the worst case, and many banks had to write down the value of their assets and sustain huge losses. In September 2007 concerns about the solvency of Northern Rock, a British bank, led to the first run on a bank in the UK since the 1860s. In order to maintain confidence in the banking system, the British government nationalized Northern Rock rather than allow it to go bankrupt. By contrast, Lehman Brothers of New York collapsed on September 15, 2008 after the US government refused to support it. Faced with this precedent and still unsure about the value of their assets, finance companies lost confidence in each other's creditworthiness and became suddenly much more cautious about risk. Credit became harder to obtain, which led to a sharp global recession in 2008–09. Some countries suffered very severely: *Iceland (2008), *Ireland (2008), and *Cyprus (2012) were almost overwhelmed when their oversized banking sectors failed; and the concerns about creditworthiness spread to states, which led in particular to the *Eurozone Crisis.

By the mid-2010s the worst consequences of the Credit Crunch seemed to have passed. However, credit was still only available on cautious terms, which slowed economic recovery; some finance companies were still burdened with toxic assets; some countries were still in recession; and others had not yet recovered their 2008 levels of GDP. Debate on the lessons of the Credit Crunch and how to prevent a similar occurrence in future has continued.

Cree An Algonquian-speaking Native American people. Traditionally dependent on caribou and moose, they are the southernmost of the major subarctic tribes of Manitoba and Saskatchewan in Canada.

Creek A Muskogean Native American confederacy, originally one of the dominant groups of the mid-south. In the 18th century they were pushed westwards from the coasts of Carolina and Georgia, eventually settling in Indian Territory in Oklahoma where they number 50,000.

Crimean War (1853–56) A war fought by Russia against Turkey, Britain, France, and Piedmont. The immediate cause was the dispute between France and Russia over the Palestinian holy places. War became inevitable after the Russians, having failed to obtain equal rights with the French, occupied territories of the *Ottoman empire in July 1853. In a bid to prevent Russian expansion in the Black Sea area and to ensure existing trade routes, a conference was convened in Vienna. Turkey was pressed by the Powers to make some concessions to placate Russia, but it refused, and declared war. In November 1853 the Russians destroyed the Turkish fleet at Sinope, in the Black Sea. This forced the hand of Britain and France, who in March 1854 declared war, expecting, with their naval supremacy, a quick victory. Austria did not join the Allies but, by mobilizing its army, obliged the Russians to evacuate the provinces of Wallachia and Moldavia which they had occupied. The Allied forces were at first mustered at Varma, but in August 1854 they were transported to Eupatoria on the Crimea with Lord *Raglan, commander-in-chief of an ill-prepared army which had been ravaged by cholera. They were able to defeat the Russian army, skilfully led by Menschikov, at the battle of the River Alma (20 September 1854) and began bombarding the strongly armed fort of Sevastopol. Following the Battle of *Balaklava, a long winter of siege warfare ensued, aggravated by lack of fuel, clothing, and supplies for the Allied armies. Public opinion in Britain became critical of the war after reading eyewitness reports in *The Times*, sent back by the Irishman W. H. Russell, the first journalist in history to write as a war correspondent using the telegraph. Florence *Nightingale received permission to take nurses to the Crimea. Sevastopol fell on 8 September 1855; by that time the Russians, with a new emperor, *Alexander II, were already seeking peace. This was concluded at the Congress of *Paris in 1856.

Cripps, Sir Stafford (Richard Stafford Cripps)

(1889–1952) British politician. During 1945–50 he served in *Attlee's government successively as President of the Board of Trade and Chancellor of the Exchequer. In these posts he was responsible for the policy of austerity—a programme of rationing and controls introduced to adjust Britain to its reduced economy following the withdrawal of US lend-lease. He also directed a notable expansion of exports, especially after devaluation of the pound in 1949.

Crispi, Francesco

(1819–1901) Italian politician. He began as a Sicilian revolutionary republican supporting *Garibaldi's invasion (1860) and ended as a monarchist, a friend of *Bismarck, and twice a dictatorial Premier. During his first ministry (1887–91) a colonial administration was formally established (1889)

in the Ethiopian province of Eritrea. Italy's economic distress was aggravated by his tariff war against France, and he brutally suppressed a socialist uprising in Sicily. His foreign policy was based on friendship with Germany and adherence to Bismarck's *Triple Alliance. His second ministry (1893–96) witnessed the rout of the Italians by the Ethiopians at *Adowa (1896). Italy was obliged to sue for peace and Crispi was forced from office.

Croatia

Capital:	Zagreb
Area:	56,594 sq km (21,851 sq miles)
Population:	4,475,611 (2012 est)
Currency:	1 kuna = 100 lipa
Religions:	Roman Catholic 87.8%; Eastern Orthodox 4.4%; Muslim 1.3%
Ethnic Groups:	Croat 89.6%; Serb 4.5%
Languages:	Croatian (official)
International Organizations:	UN; OSCE; Council of Europe; WTO; NATO; EU

A country in south-eastern Europe, formerly a constituent republic of Yugoslavia.

Physical Croatia is bounded by Slovenia, Hungary, Bosnia and Herzegovina, Serbia, and the Adriatic Sea. In the south-west, the Dinaric Alps form a rugged chain, while the north-eastern part is mostly flat and fertile and well suited to agriculture.

Economy Croatia has an industrialized economy in which chemicals and plastics, machine tools, metals, and other heavy industry are important. Mineral resources include bauxite, petroleum, and natural gas. Tourism is an important source of foreign exchange. The main agricultural products are grains, sugar beet, and potatoes. Grapes are grown mainly on the offshore islands.

History Once the Roman province of Illyricum, the area suffered successive barbarian invasions, with the Slavs becoming the majority population. Conquered by *Charlemagne, the first Croatian state was formed with its own knezes or princes when the Carolingian empire collapsed. With papal support Kneze Tomislav became the first king. Struggles between

*Hungary, Venice, and the *Byzantine empire resulted in rule by the Hungarian crown until 1301, when the House of Anjou took control. From 1381 there was a long period of civil war. The Battle of Mohács in 1526 brought most of the country under *Ottoman rule with the remainder governed by the *Habsburgs. From 1809–1813 Croatia was part of Napoleon's Illyrian province, during which time Croatian nationalism emerged, strongly resisting both Habsburg imperialism and Hungarian control. In 1848 a revolution reasserted Croatian independence, ending serfdom, and proclaiming all citizens equal. In the following year Austria countered by proclaiming the nation an Austrian crownland. In 1868, following the establishment of *Austria-Hungary, the territory was pronounced to be the autonomous Hungarian crownland of Croatia-Slovenia, apart from the coastline of Dalmatia, which was to remain an Austrian province. The Hungarian authorities tried to crush all manifestations of Croatian nationalism, with little success, and in October 1918 an independent Croatia was again proclaimed. This then joined the Kingdom of the Serbs, Croats, and Slovenes (1921), later renamed Yugoslavia. In 1941 it was once again declared an independent state under the fascist leader Ante Pavelič, whose brutal government provoked a guerrilla war. Croatia joined the new Federal Republic of Yugoslavia in 1945. A movement for Croatian independence re-emerged in the late 1980s and a non-communist government was formed in May 1990. By the end of the year anti-Serbian partisans were attacking enclaves of Serbian residents, who were then supported by units of the Serbian-dominated Yugoslav army. A confused military situation developed through 1991 with the ancient city of Dubrovnik being bombarded by Serbian artillery. Croatia was recognized as an independent country by the European Community in 1992, with Franjo *Tudjman as President. Fighting continued in the region of Krajina, which had declared itself to be a Serbian republic, and UN peacekeepers were sent in (1992). Croatian forces attacked Krajina in 1993, and in 1995 launched an offensive that enabled them to regain possession of much of the region. From 1992 Croatian forces were involved in the civil war in *Bosnia and Herzegovina, fighting Bosnian Serbs and, in some areas, Bosnian Muslims. Some Bosnian Croat nationalists even proclaimed themselves to be a separate republic. In 1994, however, the Croatians and the Bosnian government agreed to cooperate. Fighting with the Bosnian Serbs continued until late 1995, when the governments of Cro-

atia, Serbia, and Bosnia accepted a US-brokered peace plan for the region. Tudjman died in office in 1999; his party was defeated in the 2000 elections but regained power in 2003, holding it until 2011 when the centre-left Kukuriku coalition was victorious under Zoran Milanović. Croatia joined NATO in 2009 and the EU in 2013.

Crockett, David (known as **'Davy'**) (1786–1836) US frontiersman, soldier, and politician. He was a member of the House of Representatives 1827–35 and cultivated the image of a rough backwoods legislator. On leaving politics he returned to the frontier, where he took up the cause of Texan independence and was killed at the siege of the Alamo.

Croesus King of Lydia (c.560–546 BC). He expanded his domains to include all the Greek cities on the coast of Asia Minor, and the stories of his wealth indicate the extent of his power. However, he was unable to withstand *Cyrus II (the Great), and after his defeat Lydia entered the Persian empire of the Achaemenids.

Cromwell, Oliver (1599–1658) English general and statesman. He was the driving force in the revolutionary opposition to Charles I in the English Civil War, and was the leader of the Parliamentary forces (or Roundheads), winning decisive battles at Marston Moor and Naseby. After the trial and execution of Charles I, he returned to military command to suppress resistance to the Commonwealth in Ireland and Scotland, finally defeating a Scottish army at Worcester (1651) led by the future Charles II. With the establishment of the *Protectorate, Cromwell became Lord Protector of the Commonwealth (1653–58); although he called and dissolved a succession of Parliaments, he refused Parliament's offer of the crown in 1657. His rule was notable for its puritan reforms in the Church of England.

Cromwell, Richard (1626–1712) Son of Oliver *Cromwell, whom he succeeded as Lord Protector of the Commonwealth of England 1658–59. He was more interested in country life than in politics and, incapable of reconciling the military and civilian factions in Parliament, he retired after a few months. At the *Restoration he fled to the Continent, returning c.1680 to spend the rest of his life quietly in Hampshire.

Cromwell, Thomas (c.1485–1540) English statesman, chief minister to Henry VIII (1531–40). After serving Cardinal Wolsey from 1514, he succeeded him as the king's chief adviser. He presided over the king's divorce from Catherine of Aragon (1533) and his break with the Roman Catholic Church, as well as the dissolution of the monasteries and a series of administrative measures, such as the Act of Supremacy (1534), designed to strengthen the Crown. He fell from favour over Henry's marriage to Anne of Cleves and was executed on a charge of treason.

crop rotation The practice of growing different crops in different years on the same land, in order to prevent the soil's nutrients from being exhausted and to reduce the risk of a build-up of diseases and pests specific to one crop. Crop rotation was widespread in Europe from the time of the *Roman empire. Two-field rotation was practised by the ancient Greeks: one half of a farmer's land was planted in the spring or autumn of each year, while the other half was left fallow (i.e. not planted with crops), to allow the soil to 'rest'. The Romans developed the three-course rotation, which was in use from the Middle Ages until the 18th century. A three-year cycle was followed on each of three fields, with an autumn-sown crop such as rye or winter wheat, a spring-sown crop such as oats or beans, and a year of lying fallow. Two out of three fields were thus in cultivation every year. The three-field system succeeded only in countries with mild climates, such as England. With the *Agricultural Revolution and the acceleration of *enclosures in the 18th century, more scientific methods were applied to crop rotation. A four-course rotation was adopted based on turnips, clover, barley, and wheat. The introduction of root-crops (such as turnips) improved the soil and hence the quality of harvest and livestock; they also smother the weeds that have grown between plants of the previous crop. The replacement of the fallow with a leguminous crop, such as clover, peas, beans, or lentils, boosts the fertility of the soil since leguminous plants are able to 'fix' atmospheric nitrogen, which enriches the soil when they die. From the mid-20th century the increased use of artificial fertilizers reduced the importance of crop rotation.

Crosland, Anthony (Charles Anthony Raven Crosland) (1918–77) British politician. He served as a Labour MP (1950–55; 1959–77). As Secretary of State for Education and Science (1964–67) his strongly held libertarian and egalitarian principles led to the closure of grammar schools, the establishment of a comprehensive state school system, and the growth of polytechnics. During 1965–70 and 1974–77 he

held several cabinet posts, and was Foreign Secretary before his early death.

Crossman, Richard Howard Stafford (1907–74) British politician. He was assistant chief of the Psychological Warfare Division during World War II. He entered Parliament as a Labour MP in 1945. During the Harold *Wilson administrations he was successively Minister of Housing and Local Government, Leader of the House of Commons, and Secretary of State for Social Services. His posthumous *Diaries* (1975–77) provided revealing insights into the working of government.

Crow and Hidatsa (or **Absaroke**) Native Americans who inhabited Montana and northern Wyoming. In prehistoric times they lived in permanent villages and practised a well-balanced agricultural economy with seasonal buffalo hunts. When they acquired horses in the 18th century, the Crow abandoned their villages for a nomadic life of full-time buffalo-hunting, trading meat for some of the crops of the farmer Hidatsa.

crucifixion A form of capital punishment used by various ancient peoples including the Persians, Carthaginians, and Romans for criminals, usually applicable only to slaves and other persons with no civil rights. The victim, nailed or roped to a crossbar, was hoisted on to an upright to form a 'T' or cross. *Spartacus, with 6000 rebels, was crucified in 71 BC, as was *Jesus Christ (c.30 AD). Romans regarded the cross with horror. Only after the emperor Constantine abolished this form of penalty did Christians adopt the cross as a symbol.

Crusades A series of expeditions (11th–14th century) to secure Christian rule over the Muslim-controlled holy places of *Palestine. The wealthy powerful orders of *Knights Hospitallers and *Knights Templar were created by the Crusades. The First Crusade was called by Pope Urban II, and was provoked by the rise to power of the *Seljuk Turks, which interfered with traditional pilgrimage to Palestine. The pope promised spiritual benefits to warriors willing to fight under Christian banners. The Crusaders captured *Jerusalem in 1099 and massacred its inhabitants, establishing a kingdom there under Godfrey of Bouillon. The Second Crusade (1147–49) succeeded only in souring relations between the Crusader kingdoms, the Byzantines, and friendly Muslim rulers. The Third Crusade (1189–92), prompted by *Saladin's capture of Jerusalem, recaptured Acre but achieved little more. The Fourth Crusade

(1202–04) was diverted by Venetian interests to Constantinople, which was sacked, making the gulf between Eastern and Western Churches unbridgeable, though some Crusaders benefited from the division of Byzantine territories known as the Latin empire of the East (1204–61). This briefly replaced the Greek empire at Constantinople until Michael VIII retook the city. Later expeditions concentrated on North Africa, but to little purpose. The fall of Acre in 1291 ended the Crusader presence in the Levant. All, except the peaceful Sixth Crusade (1228–29), were marred by greed and brutality: Jews and Christians in Europe were slaughtered by rabble armies on their way to the Holy Land. The papacy was incapable of controlling the immense forces at its disposal. However, the Crusades attracted such leaders as *Richard I and *Louis IX, greatly affected European *chivalry, and for centuries, its literature. While deepening the hostility between Christianity and Islam, they also stimulated economic and cultural contacts of lasting benefit to European civilization. *See also* CHILDREN'S CRUSADE.

CSCE *See* HELSINKI CONFERENCE.

Cuba

Capital:	Havana
Area:	110,860 sq km (42,803 sq miles)
Population:	11,061,886 (2012 est)
Currency:	1 Cuban peso = 100 centavos
Religions:	Roman Catholic 60.0%; Protestant 5.0%
Ethnic Groups:	White 65.1%; Mixed 24.8%; Black 10.1%
Languages:	Spanish (official)
International Organizations:	UN; Non-Aligned Movement; OAS; WTO

An island country, the largest of the Caribbean Islands.

Physical Cuba is long and narrow—about 1280 km (795 miles) from west to east yet rarely more than 160 km (100 miles) from north to south. Most of it is flat, with plains rising southward to heights seldom greater than 90 m (295 feet), except in the south-east, where the Sierra Maestra reaches 2000 m (6560 feet) and more. The climate is tropical, with heavy rain and easterly winds which often become hurricanes.

Economy Until 1991 Cuba had a centrally planned socialist economy heavily reliant on support from the Soviet Union. This support ended with the Soviet Union's collapse, and the period since has seen a gradual liberalization of Cuba's economy to allow limited private enterprise. The main industries include oil, nickel, pharmaceuticals, and tobacco. These products are all significant exports, together with sugar, the principal agricultural crop and once the mainstay of the economy. Tourism is increasingly important.

History Cuba was first settled by migrating hunter-gatherer-fisher people, the Ciboney from South America, by c.3000 BC. Migrations of agriculturist, pottery-making Arawak Indians from northern South America began to displace them in eastern Cuba after c.1000 BC, but the Ciboney remained in the west. Cuba was discovered by Columbus in 1492 but it was not realized that it was an island until it was circumnavigated in 1508. Spanish settlement began in 1511 when Diego Velásquez founded Havana and several other towns. The Arawak became virtually extinct by the end of the century from exploitation and European-introduced diseases. Black slaves were imported for the plantations (especially sugar and tobacco) from 1526. Britain seized the island in 1762–63 but immediately exchanged it with the Spanish for Florida. Slave importation ended in 1865, but slavery was not abolished until 1886. Various attempts were made by US interests to acquire the island and many Americans fought in the unsuccessful first War of Independence (1868–78). Large US investments were maintained in the sugar industry, which by now was producing one-third of the world's sugar. The second War of Independence (1895–1901) was joined by the USA (1898) after a well-orchestrated press campaign, and Cuba was occupied by US troops (1899–1901). In 1902 the Republic of Cuba was proclaimed. A series of corrupt and socially insensitive governments followed, culminating in the brutal, authoritarian regime of Gerardo Machado (1925–33), which prompted the abortive revolution of 1933–34, the island remaining under US 'protection' until 1934. Fulengio *Batista was President 1940–44 and 1952–59. Although supported by the USA, his second government was notoriously corrupt and ruthless. In 1956 Fidel *Castro initiated a guerrilla war which led to the establishment of a socialist regime (1959) under his leadership. He repulsed the invasion by Cuban exiles at

Cochinos Bay, the *Bay of Pigs (April 1961), and survived the *Cuban Missile Crisis of October 1962. Although his one-party regime could claim considerable achievements in public health, education, and housing, its record on human rights remained poor. Castro maintained a high profile abroad and although the espousal of world revolution was tempered under pressure from Moscow, Cuban assistance to liberation movements in Latin America and Africa was consistent. At home, after the political turbulence of the 1960s, the revolution stabilized with the establishment of more broadly based representative assemblies at municipal, provincial, and national levels. In economic terms, the initial hopes of diversification and industrialization were not realized, and Cuba continued to rely on the export of sugar as well as on substantial financial subsidy from the Soviet Union. Agricultural production in the socialist state was generally poor, and shortages and rationing continued. Yet the regime survived when COMECON and the Soviet Union collapsed in 1990 and 1991 respectively, and the country found itself faced with a grave economic situation. In October 1991 the fourth Congress of the Communist Party endorsed the policy of centralized control, but this policy has since been gradually eroded through necessity: as early as 1993 small-scale private businesses were legalized. In 2006 Castro temporarily transferred power to his brother, Raúl Castro, because of illness; but he never resumed it and Raúl formally became President of Cuba in 2008. His rule has seen accelerated economic liberalization, including further encouragement of private enterprise and the reintroduction of private property in 2011. In late 2014 the USA announced a relaxation of its trade embargo on Cuba, which had been in place since 1961.

Cuban Missile Crisis (1962) An international crisis involving the USA and the Soviet Union. It was precipitated when US leaders learned that Soviet missiles with nuclear warheads capable of reaching the USA were being secretly installed in Cuba. President *Kennedy reinforced the US naval base at Guantanamo, ordered a naval blockade against Soviet military shipments to Cuba, and demanded that the Soviet Union remove its missiles and bases from the island. There seemed a real danger of nuclear war as the rival forces were placed on full alert, and the crisis sharpened as Soviet merchant vessels thought to be carrying missiles approached the island and the blockading US forces. However, the Soviet ships were ordered by *Khrushchev to turn back, and the Soviet

Union agreed to US demands to dismantle the rocket bases in return for a US pledge not to attack Cuba. An outcome of the crisis was the establishment of a direct, exclusive line of communication (the 'hot line') to be used in an emergency, between the President of the USA and the leader of the Soviet Union.

Culloden, Battle of (16 April 1746) A battle, fought on a bleak moor in Scotland to the east of Inverness, in which the *Jacobite forces of Charles Edward Stuart, largely drawn from the Highland clans, were routed during a sleet storm by the English and German troops led by the Duke of *Cumberland. The battle was followed by ruthless slaughter of the Jacobite wounded and prisoners, with survivors hunted down and killed, earning Cumberland the nickname 'Butcher'. Culloden ended the *Forty-Five Rebellion and virtually destroyed the Jacobite cause. It was the last land battle fought in Britain.

Culpeper's Rebellion (1677) A demonstration of local antagonism to the syndicate of proprietors who administered the new colony of North Carolina. It was brought to a head by attempts to enforce the *Navigation Acts on tobacco and to collect land taxes, and by the example of *Bacon's Rebellion in Virginia in 1676. A "parliament" of 18 proclaimed one of the ringleaders, John Culpeper, governor and he ruled until replaced by a proprietorial nominee in 1679. The factionalism and insubordination of North Carolina continued until 1714, with further rebellions in 1689 and 1711.

Cultural Revolution (1966-76) A decade of chaos and political upheaval in China with its roots in a factional dispute over the future of Chinese socialism. Oblique criticisms of *Mao Zedong in the early 1960s prompted him to retaliate against this threat to his ideology-led position from more pragmatic and bureaucratic modernizers with ideas closer to the Soviet Union. Unable to do so in the Communist Party, he utilized discontented students and young workers as his *Red Guards to attack local and central party officials, who were then replaced by his own supporters and often had army backing. *Liu Shaoqi, State Chairman of China since 1959 and Mao's heir-apparent, lost all his government and party posts and *Lin Biao became the designated successor. The most violent phase of the Cultural Revolution came to an end with the Ninth Party Congress in 1969, but its radical policies continued until Mao's death in 1976.

Cumberland, William Augustus, Duke of (1721-65) Third son of George II, British military commander. He gained great notoriety (and his nickname 'the Butcher') for the severity of his suppression of the Jacobite clans in the aftermath of his victory at the Battle of *Culloden.

Cunard, Sir Samuel (1787–1865) Canadian-born British shipowner. One of the pioneers of the regular transatlantic passenger service, he founded the steamship company which still bears his name with the aid of a contract to carry the mail between Britain and Canada. The first such voyage for the company was made in 1840.

Cunningham, Andrew Browne, Viscount Cunningham of Hyndhope (1883–1963) British admiral. At the beginning of World War II he was commander-in-chief in the Mediterranean. Here he was faced with an Italian fleet that was numerically superior to his own. However, he asserted British domination by his air attack on the Italian base of Taranto in 1940, and at Cape Matapan in 1941, where his victory effectually neutralized the Italian fleet for the rest of the war. As First Sea Lord from 1943 he was responsible for naval strategy and attended the meetings of Allied heads of government.

Cunobelinus See CYMBELINE.

Curragh incident A mutiny at the British military centre on the Curragh plain near Dublin. In 1914 the British commander there, General Sir Arthur Paget, on the instructions of Colonel Seely, the Secretary of State for War, informed his officers that military action might be necessary against private armies in Ulster. Officers with Ulster connections were to be allowed to "disappear" or resign. Such an action, threatening army discipline, brought about the resignation of many British army officers, as well as of Colonel Seely.

Cursus Honorum The name given to the ladder of (annual) offices that would-be Roman politicians had to climb. After a prescribed period of military service (though this requirement lapsed in the very late republic), or the tenure of certain minor magistracies, the first major rung was the quaestorship, which before *Sulla effectively, and after Sulla statutorily, gave membership of the *Roman Senate. Thereafter came praetorship and consulship (though not all achieved these offices), and finally the quinquennial office of censor, the crown of a republican politician's career. Other magistracies, the aedileship and the tribunate of the plebs, might be held between quaestorship and praetorship, but were not obligatory. In the middle and late republic, specific minimum ages and intervals between offices were established by statute. Quaestors, praetors, and consuls were often employed after their year of office at Rome as "pro-magistrates" to administer the provinces of the Roman empire.

Curtin, John (Joseph Ambrose) (1885–1945) Australian Labor statesman, Prime Minister (1941–45). He led the Labor party from 1935–1945. As Premier during World War II, he mobilized Australian resources to meet the danger of Japanese invasion, laid down the groundwork for the postwar economy, and introduced various welfare measures. Curtin died while in office.

Curzon, George Nathaniel, 1st Marquis Curzon of Kedleston (1859–1925) British statesman. As viceroy of India (1899–1905) he achieved reforms in administration, education, and currency, and set up the North-West Frontier province (1901). He was instrumental in the partitioning of Bengal in 1901, incurring thereby the ill-feeling of the Hindus. A strong supporter of imperialism, he resigned in 1905 in a dispute with *Kitchener. *Lloyd George included him in his coalition war cabinet (1916–18). He became Foreign Secretary in 1919. Lloyd George's tendency to conduct foreign affairs himself irritated Curzon, who joined the Conservative rebellion in 1922 against the coalition government. Bonar *Law became Prime Minister and made Curzon his Foreign Secretary in 1922. As Foreign Secretary he gave his name to the frontier line proposed (1920) by Lloyd George, between Poland and Russia. The broad outline of the frontier became (1939) the boundary between the Soviet and German spheres of occupied Poland. It was imposed (1945) on Poland by the Allies as the definitive frontier between itself and the Soviet Union.

Cush See NUBIANS.

Custer, George (Armstrong) (1839–76) US cavalry general. He served with distinction in the American Civil War but led his men to their deaths in a clash (popularly known as Custer's Last Stand) with the Sioux at Little Bighorn in Montana. Controversy over his conduct in the final battle still continues.

customs and excise Duties charged on goods (both home-produced and imported) to raise revenue for governments. In England customs date from the reign of *Edward I, when duties were raised on wool and leather.

Tunnage and poundage was introduced under *Edward II. Excise was first levied in 1643 to finance the parliamentary armies in the *English Civil War and was a tax on alcoholic beverages, mainly beer and ale. At the *Restoration Charles II was granted excise duties for life by Parliament. Customs duties are tariffs paid on goods entering (or occasionally leaving) a country. Customs duties between members of the European Union were abolished in 1992. Excise duties are paid on the domestic sale of certain goods and activities, such as alcohol, tobacco, motor fuel, and betting.

Cymbeline (or **Cunobelinus**) (died *c.*42 AD) British chieftain. He was a powerful ruler whose tribe occupied a wide area from Northamptonshire to south-east England. He made Camulodunum (Colchester) his capital, and established a mint there.

Cynics A sect of ancient Greek philosophers popularly thought to have been established by *Diogenes, though his mentor, Antisthenes of Athens, should perhaps be accorded the title of founder. Since the Cynics were never a formal school, with no fully defined philosophy, considerable differences emerged amongst Diogenes' disciples, who adopted only those ideas which appealed to them. Crates of Thebes was his most faithful follower: he demonstrated how in troubled times happiness was possible for the man who gave up material possessions, kept his needs to an absolute minimum, and maintained his independence.

The Cynic philosophy flourished through the 3rd century BC, and the beggar-philosopher, knapsack on his back and stick in hand, became a familiar sight in Greece. A steady decline thereafter was reversed by a temporary revival in the 1st century AD, though the Cynics' readiness to criticize the conduct of the emperors led to many expulsions from Rome. The last recorded beggar-philosopher lived at the end of the 5th century.

Cyprus

Capital:	Nicosia
Area:	9251 sq km (3572 sq miles) (south: 5896 sq km (2276 sq miles); north: 3355 sq km (1295 sq miles))
Population:	1,155,403 (combined; 2012 est)
Currency:	south: 1 euro = 100 cents; north: 1 Turkish lira = 100 kurush
Religions:	Greek Orthodox 78.0% (predominantly in the south); Muslim 18.0% (predominantly in the north)
Ethnic Groups:	Greek 77.0% (predominantly in the south); Turkish 18.0% (predominantly in the north)
Languages:	Greek, Turkish (both official)
International Organizations:	south: Council of Europe; UN; Commonwealth; Non-Aligned Movement; OSCE; EU; WTO; the north is recognized only by Turkey

An island country in the north-east corner of the Mediterranean Sea, with Turkey to the north and Syria to the east.

Physical Cyprus is 225 km (140 miles) long and 97 km (60 miles) in breadth at its widest point. The Kyrenia coast on the north has a range of steep limestone mountains along most of its length. South of that is a treeless plain, hot and arid in summer, while further south still are igneous mountains rising to 1950 m (6400 feet).

Economy In the south, such service industries as tourism, property, and financial services are important. The banking sector became overlarge in the 2000s, which caused an economic crisis in 2012 (see EUROZONE CRISIS). Other important industries are food processing, cement, ship repair, and textiles. Cyprus (Greek, 'copper') still has some copper, as well as iron pyrites and asbestos. The north, by contrast, is primarily agricultural and is dependent on Turkish aid.

History A Mycenaean colony in the 14th century BC, it was ruled successively by the Assyrian, Persian, Roman, and Byzantine empires. *Richard I of England conquered it in 1191 and sold it to the French Crusader Guy de Lusignan under whom it became a feudal monarchy. An important base for the *Crusades, it eventually came under the control of Italian trading states, until in 1571 it fell to the *Ottoman empire. It remained part of the Ottoman empire until 1879, when it was placed under British administration. It was formally annexed by Britain in 1914 and in 1925 declared a crown colony. From the outset there was rivalry between Greek- and Turkish-speaking communities, the former, the majority, desiring union (enosis) with Greece. After World War II there was much civil violence in which the Greek Cypriot terrorist organization *EOKA played the leading role. In 1959 independence within the Commonwealth was granted under the presidency of Archbishop *Makarios, but by 1964 the government was in chaos and a United Nations peacekeeping force intervened. In 1974 a Greek Cypriot coup overthrew the President and Turkish forces invaded, gaining virtual control over most of the island. The Greek national government which had backed the revolt, collapsed. Talks in Geneva between Britain, Turkey, Greece, and the two Cypriot communities failed, and, although Makarios was able to resume the presidency in 1975, the Turkish Federated State of Cyprus was formed in northern Cyprus, comprising some 35% of the island, with its own President. In 1983 it proclaimed itself the **Turkish Republic of Northern Cyprus**. Britain retained an important RAF base, which was also a key intelligence centre. In the early 1990s the presidents of the two communities held talks on uniting the island, but no agreement was reached. Cyprus—in practice, the Greek south—joined the *European Union in 2004. That same year a UN reunification plan was backed by Turkish Cypriots in a referendum but rejected by Greek Cypriots. Following the *Credit Crunch, Cypriot banks came under financial pressure because of their large holdings of bad Greek debt. The international money markets lost confidence in Cyprus's ability to support its over-large banking sector, and in June 2012 Cyprus requested assistance from the EU. A €10 billion loan was agreed in 2013 in return for a radical restructuring of the Cypriot banking sector involving large losses to investors.

Cyril, St (826–69) Greek missionary. The invention of the Cyrillic alphabet is ascribed to him. He and his brother St Methodius (c.815–85) became known as the 'Apostles to the Slavs'. Sent to Moravia, they taught in the vernacular, which they adopted also for the liturgy, and circulated a Slavonic version of the Scriptures.

Cyrus II (the Great) (died 530 BC) King of Persia (539–530 BC), who founded the *Achaemenid Persian empire when he overthrew Astyages, King of Media, and took possession of his capital Ecbatana in c.500. In 546 he defeated *Croesus to take control of Asia Minor and Nabonidus (the last of the Chaldean kings) to add Babylonia, Assyria, Syria, and Palestine to his domains. His policies towards his subjects were tolerant: the Medians had access to important administrative posts and the Jews were freed from their Babylonian *Exile and allowed to start rebuilding the Temple (their main religious centre) at Jerusalem. He was probably killed in battle and was buried at Pasargadae, where his tomb can still be seen.

Cyrus the Younger (died 401 BC) Persian prince, second son of Darius II. On the death of his father (405 BC), Cyrus led an army of mercenaries against his elder brother, who had succeeded to the throne as Artaxerxes II; his campaign is recounted by the historian *Xenophon, who had enlisted in his army. Cyrus was killed in battle north of Babylon.

Czartoryski, Adam Jerzy, Prince (1770–1861) Polish statesman and nationalist leader. A cousin of the last independent king of *Poland, he worked unfailingly at the restoration of his country when Russia, Prussia, and Austria had partitioned it between them. He became the trusted adviser of the Russian Prince Alexander, who became emperor in 1801. The latter appointed him Russian Foreign Minister (1804–05). After the Battle of *Leipzig (1813) he sought the re-creation of Poland from the Grand Duchy of Warsaw, formed by Napoleon. In this he was partially successful as the Polish representative at the Congress of *Vienna, which restored the kingdom of Poland, but with the Russian emperor as king. He was proclaimed President of the Provisional Government of Poland at the time of the Polish revolt of 1830–31, for which he was condemned to death but then escaped to Paris. He became known as the "Polish king in exile" and helped to plan the two unsuccessful Polish rebellions of 1846–49 and 1863.

Czechoslovakia (Czech **Ceskoslovensko**) A former state of central Europe comprising the Czech Republic and Slovakia, which separated and became independent republics in 1993. Czechoslovakia was created out of the northern part of the old Austro-Hungarian empire after the latter's collapse at the end of World War I. It incorporated the Czechs (who had enjoyed freedom within their own state of Bohemia until the rise of Habsburg power in the 16th and 17th centuries) of Bohemia and Moravia with the Slovaks of Slovakia. Czech history between the two World Wars represents a brave and enlightened attempt at integration, undermined by economic trouble and eventually crushed by the Nazi takeover of first the Sudetenland (1938) and then the rest of Bohemia and Moravia

(1939). After World War II power was seized by the Communists and Czechoslovakia remained under Soviet domination, an attempt at liberalization being crushed by Soviet military intervention in 1968, until Communist supremacy was overthrown in a peaceful revolution in December 1989, followed by the introduction of democratic reforms and the eventual separation of Slovakia and the Czech Republic into independent states in 1993.

Czech Republic

Capital:	Prague
Area:	78,867 sq km (30,451 sq miles)
Population:	10,177,300 (2012 est)
Currency:	1 koruna = 100 haléřů
Religions:	Roman Catholic 10.4%; Protestant 1.1%
Ethnic Groups:	Czech 64.3%; Moravian 5.0%; Slovak 1.4%
Languages:	Czech (official); Slovak
International Organizations:	UN; OSCE; Council of Europe; EU; NATO; OECD; WTO

A landlocked country in central Europe, formerly part of *Czechoslovakia.

Physical The Czech Republic comprises Bohemia and Moravia. It is bordered on the west by Germany, on the south by Austria, on the east by Slovakia, and on the north and east by Silesian Poland. The country lies in the headwater area of the main European watershed; the Labe–Vlatava (Moldau–Elba) river system flows in the Bohemian basin towards the North Sea, and the Odra (Oder) flows northwards towards the Baltic. Rich alluvial soils alongside river courses are characteristic.

Economy The principal industry is vehicle manufacture, followed by metals, machinery, glass, and armaments. The main mineral resources are brown coal, lignite, copper, and zinc, and large gold deposits have been found. Wheat, potatoes, sugar beet, and hops are grown. The Czech Republic has benefited from economic reforms and EU membership, which have transformed a Soviet-era centrally planned economy into a successful market economy.

History The Czech Republic came into existence on 1 January 1993; it was, until then, part of Czechoslovakia, but an increasingly strong Slovakian independence movement led to plans to separate the two states. The separation process was set in motion in June 1992 and went so smoothly that it was referred to as the 'velvet divorce'. Václav *Havel, formerly President of Czechoslovakia, was elected President of the Czech Republic (1993). Economic progress was slower than expected, despite the implementation of free-market reforms. The Czech Republic joined NATO in 1999 and the *European Union in 2004.

Dacian wars Campaigns fought by successive Roman emperors over territory corresponding roughly to modern Romania and part of Hungary. The Dacians threatened the lands south of the River Danube which Rome regarded as a natural frontier. Under Emperor Domitian peace was agreed and considerable financial aid given to the Dacians. Then Emperor *Trajan stopped payments, crossed the Lower Danube, and fought two campaigns AD 101 and 105–6 that were commemorated on Trajan's column in Rome, which is still standing today. Dacia became a Roman province, until Emperor Aurelian abandoned it to the Goths in 270.

da Gama, Vasco (*c.*1469–1524) Portuguese explorer. He led the first European expedition round the Cape of Good Hope in 1497, sighting and naming Natal on Christmas Day before crossing the Indian Ocean and arriving in Calicut in 1498. The Portuguese king Manuel I (1469–1521) chose him to lead a second expedition to Calicut in 1502. Da Gama forced the raja of Calicut (who had massacred Portuguese settlers from an earlier expedition) to make peace, also establishing colonies on the coast of Mozambique.

Dahomey A former kingdom in West Africa. In the 16th century the kingdom of Allada, with which the Portuguese had commercial relations, was founded. Two further kingdoms of Abomey and Adjatché (now Porto Novo), were founded *c.*1625. These were united by conquest by Ouegbadja of Abomey between 1645 and 1685, and renamed Dahomey. The kingdom had a special notoriety with travellers from Europe for its 'customs': the 'grand customs' on the death of a king, and the biennial 'minor customs', at both of which captured slaves were sacrificed in numbers to provide the deceased king with attendants in the spirit world. Women soldiers were first trained by King Agadja (1708–32). French trading forts were established in the 18th and 19th centuries, but the rulers of Dahomey succeeded in limiting their influence and restricting the slave trade. Under French rule from 1892, it became independent in 1960, and changed its name in 1975 to the Republic of *Benin.

daimyo (Japanese, 'great names') Japan's feudal lords. They expanded their *samurai armies during the confusion of the *Ashikaga period, and territorial disputes between daimyo threatened Japan's unity. A reallocation of fiefs under *Hideyoshi had reduced their power by 1591. The *Tokugawa controlled much of their activity, although during this *shogunate (1600–1878) the daimyo continued to exercise local control over domains comprising two-thirds of Japan. The new national government at the time of the *Meiji Restoration persuaded the daimyo to surrender their titles, powers, and privileges as feudal landowners, compensating them by payment of a portion of their former revenues. This, along with the dismantling of the *samurai class of warriors who served the daimyo, helped transform Japan from a feudal to a centralized state.

Dakota The largest division of a Native American group of seven related tribes, commonly known as the Sioux, who inhabit areas of Nebraska, Montana, the woodlands of Minnesota, and the eastern Dakotas on the fringe of the northern Great Plains. During the mid-18th century they lost much of their lands to the *Ojibwa. As French and English fur trade increased, so did intertribal warfare, exterminating some tribes and driving others, including the Dakota, on to the plains. They raided the tribes of the Missouri River to the south-east, and also acted as middlemen, exchanging European goods, especially firearms, for corn, tobacco, and other produce. Traditional enemies and trade rivals were the *Cree and Ojibwa to the north and east. In common with other *Plains Peoples, the Dakota were nomadic buffalo hunters, who gathered in tribes during the summer, and dispersed into family groups during the winter. Before they acquired horses, buffalo hunting had been ecologically balanced; seasonal migrations were aided by the travois (sledge), pulled by dogs but later adapted for horses, and the tipi (Dakota for "they dwell"). Over-hunting with horses began to deplete the herds, further exacerbated by White people moving on to tribal lands and systematically devastating the herds.

Daladier, Édouard (1884–1970) French statesman. With Neville *Chamberlain he yielded to Hitler's demands to annex the *Sudetenland of Czechoslovakia in the *Munich Pact (1938). He had served as a Radical Socialist in various ministries and was Premier in 1933 and 1934 and again in 1938–40. Arrested by the *Vichy government in 1940, he was tried at Riom, together with other democratic leaders, accused of responsibility for France's military disasters. Although acquitted, he remained imprisoned in France and Germany. He was elected to the national assembly (1945–58) during the Fourth Republic.

Dalhousie, James Ramsay, 1st Marquess of (1812–60) British statesman and colonial administrator. A Conservative Member of Parliament (1837), he became governor-general of India (1848–56), when he oversaw the extension of British rule through the annexation of the Punjab (1849), of Lower Burma (1852), of Oudh (1856), and of several smaller Indian states, through the use of the so-called Doctrine of Lapse. According to this Britain annexed those states where there was no heir who was recognized by Britain. Dalhousie initiated major developments in communications, including the railway (1853), the telegraph and postal system, the opening of the Ganges canal, and in public works and industry. He removed internal trade barriers, promoted social reform through legislation against female infanticide and the suppression of human sacrifice, and fostered the development of a popular educational system in India. He introduced improved training of the Indian civil service, which was opened to all British subjects of any race.

Dalriads *See* SCOTS.

Dampier, William (1652–1715) English explorer and adventurer. In 1683 he set out on a privateering expedition from Panama, crossing the Pacific to the Philippines, China, and Australia before eventually reaching England again in 1691. In 1699 he was commissioned by the British government to explore the NW coast of Australia and circumnavigated the globe again,

despite being shipwrecked on Ascension Island on the way home.

Danby, Thomas Osborne, 1st Earl of (1632–1712) English statesman. He entered Parliament in 1665 as a supporter of the restored *Charles II. He received rapid promotion, becoming Secretary of the Navy in 1671 and Lord Treasurer in 1673. His reluctant negotiations with *Louis XIV of France to supply Charles II with money led in 1678 to accusations by Parliament of corruption and he was imprisoned until 1684. In 1688 he signed the invitation to *William III of Orange to come to England, regained royal favour, and became Duke of Leeds in 1694, but following further accusations of corruption he retired from public life after 1695.

Dandolo, Enrico (*c.*1108–1205) Member of a Venetian family important in the Middle Ages, and *doge of Venice. He established military and naval power by personally directing the Fourth *Crusade to attack Dalmatia and sack Constantinople. Under him, Venice was victorious against Pisa, secured important treaties with Armenia and the *Holy Roman Empire, and reformed its laws.

Danegeld The tribute paid in silver by *Ethelred II of England to buy peace from the invading Danes. It was raised by a tax levied on land. The first payment (991) was 10,000 pounds in weight of silver (1 pound equals 0.54 kg); later payments were greater—16,000 pounds (994), 24,000 pounds (1002), 36,000 pounds (1007), and a massive 158,000 pounds (1012). Later (1012–51) it was levied to maintain a navy and the royal bodyguard (housecarls), when it was known as 'heregeld'; when raised by the *Norman kings the levy was used for general as well as military purposes.

Danelaw The part of north and east England occupied or administered by Danes from the late 9th century and administered according to their laws until the Norman Conquest.

Danton, Georges (Jacques) (1759–94) French revolutionary. A noted orator, he won great popularity in the early days of the French Revolution. He served as Minister of Justice (1792–94) in the new republic and was a founder member of the governing body, the Committee of Public Safety (1793). Initially an ally of Robespierre and the Jacobins, he later revolted against their radicalism and the severity of the Revolutionary Tribunal, only to be arrested and executed on Robespierre's orders.

Darius I (or **Darius the Great**) (*c.*550–486 BC) King of Persia (521–486 BC). His reign divided the empire into provinces governed by satraps, allowing each province its own government while maintaining some centralizing authority. He developed commerce, building a network of roads, exploring the Indus valley, and connecting the Nile with the Red Sea by canal. After suppressing a revolt of the Greek cities in Ionia (499–494 BC), he invaded Greece to punish the mainland Greeks for their interference, but was defeated at Marathon (490 BC).

Dark Ages The 5th to the 8th centuries in Europe. Following the collapse of the Roman empire, many Germanic tribes crossed through Italy, Germany, France, Spain, and North Africa, often attacking and destroying towns. Rome was sacked on three successive occasions. Many tribes formed their own kingdoms (for example, Vandals in North Africa; Visigoths in Spain; Ostrogoths and Lombards in northern Italy; *Franks in France and western Germany; *Anglo-Saxons in England). The Visigoths helped the Romans defeat the Huns of *Attila at Châlons in 451. The Ostrogoth *Theodoric the Great ruled in Italy (493–526) as the representative of the *Byzantine empire, retaining Rome's administrative system.

The period of the Dark Ages saw cultural and economic decline though in the past this has been exaggerated. The period saw the foundation of Christian monasteries, which kept scholarship alive. The 7th and 8th centuries saw relative stability and during the 9th century learning was encouraged at the courts of *Charlemagne and *Alfred the Great.

Darlan, François (Jean Louis Xavier François Darlan) (1881–1942) French admiral. He became Minister of Marine in the *Vichy government in 1940 and was regarded by the British as pro-fascist. His secret order to his commanders to scuttle their vessels should the Germans attempt to take them over was not known to the British. When the Allies invaded North Africa in 1942 he was in Algiers, where he began negotiations with the Americans. He ordered the Vichy French forces to cease fire and was proclaimed Head of State in French Africa. A month later he was assassinated.

Darling, Sir Ralph (1775–1858) British military commander and colonial administrator. He was the governor of New South Wales from 1825 until 1831. A rigid disciplinarian, he faced many difficulties, largely because of continuing conflict between *emancipists and *exclusionists in the colony. In the controversial Sudds and

Thompson affair (1826) Darling's harsh punishment of these two soldiers was, in popular opinion, responsible for the death of Sudds. The continued agitation over instances of alleged misgovernment resulted in a British House of Commons select committee of inquiry (1835), which exonerated him.

Darnley, Henry Stuart, Lord (1545–67) Anglo-Scottish aristocrat, second husband of *Mary, Queen of Scots. After their union in 1565, Mary produced a son, the future James VI of Scotland and *James I of England. Mary's reliance on her secretary David *Rizzio (who may have been her lover) led Darnley to murder him. Darnley was subsequently murdered in a conspiracy involving the Earl of *Bothwell.

Darrow, Clarence (Seward) (1857–1938) US lawyer. Known as the "attorney for the damned", in 1894 he defended the railway leader Eugene *Debs for his part in the *Pullman strike; although he lost, he earned a reputation for taking on controversial cases. This flair for controversy brought him to the verge of bankruptcy (1911), when he was tried, but acquitted, of conspiring to bribe jurors. He defended over 50 people charged with murder, but only once did he lose a client to the executioner. In 1925 he defended the evolutionist biology teacher in the *Scopes Trial but lost the case.

dauphin The title of the heir to the French throne. Dauphiné was a province in south-east France. It was conquered by the Romans, Burgundians, and Franks. Once a fief of the *Holy Roman Empire, it passed to the kingdom of Arles, and, in 1029 to the counts of D'Albon who, from 1133, took the title of Dauphin of Vienne. By 1282, it had acquired its regional name and it was sold to the future *Charles V of France in 1346. Thereafter heirs to the French throne assumed the title of dauphin. The province acquired a *Parlement in 1453, but was annexed to the crown in 1457 and lost its local privileges, especially during the *French Wars of Religion.

David (died *c.*962 BC) King of Judah and Israel (*c.*1000–*c.*962 BC). In the biblical account he was the youngest son of Jesse, and was made a military commander by Saul after slaying the Philistine Goliath. On Saul's death he became king of Judah and later of the whole of Israel, making Jerusalem his capital. He is traditionally regarded as the author of the Psalms, but it is unlikely that more than a fraction of the psalter is his work.

David, St (or **Dewi**) (6th century) Welsh monk. Since the 12th century he has been regarded as the patron saint of Wales. Little is known of his life, but it is generally accepted that he transferred the centre of Welsh ecclesiastical administration from Caerleon to Mynyw, now St David's. He also established a number of monasteries in England and Wales and many churches in South Wales.

David I (c.1084–1153) King of Scotland (1124–53), sixth son of Malcolm III. Much of his youth was spent at the English court, after his sister Matilda (1080–1118) married King Henry I of England in 1100. After succeeding his brother *Alexander I as king of Scotland, David established a strong administration on the Norman model, bringing many retainers with him from England, encouraging the development of trade, and introducing legal reforms. In 1136, after Henry's death, David invaded England in support of his niece Matilda's claim to the throne, but was decisively defeated at the Battle of the Standard in Yorkshire in 1138.

David II (1324–71) King of Scotland (1329–71), son of Robert the Bruce. His long reign witnessed a renewal of fighting between England and Scotland, with Edward III taking advantage of the Scottish king's minority to introduce Edward *Balliol as an English puppet in his place. After returning from exile in France (1334–41), David was defeated by the English at Neville's Cross (1346) and spent eleven years in prison. His death without issue in 1371 left the throne to the Stuarts.

Davis, Jefferson (1808–89) US statesman and President of the Southern *Confederacy (1861–65). He served in the *Black Hawk War before leaving the army in 1835 to become a Mississippi planter. He commanded the Mississippi Rifles in the *Mexican-American War. Davis served two terms in the Senate (1847–51, 1857–61) and was Secretary of War in the administration of President *Pierce (1853–57). He left the Senate when Mississippi seceded from the Union, and in 1861 was named provisional President of the Confederacy. A year later he was elected to a six-year term. After the defeat of the Confederacy he was imprisoned (1865–67), but treason charges were not pursued. He wrote *The Rise and Fall of the Confederate Government* (1881) and *A Short History of the Confederate States of America* (1890).

Davitt, Michael (1846–1906) Irish nationalist and land reformer. The son of an Irish farmer who had been evicted from his holding, he opposed the British-imposed land-holding system in Ireland. In 1865 he joined the *Irish Republican Brotherhood, a movement committed to the establishment of an independent republic of Ireland. He was sentenced to 15 years' penal servitude in 1870 for smuggling weapons for the *Fenians. Released in 1877 he helped found the Irish Land League in 1879, an organization formed to achieve land reform. With Charles Sewart *Parnell, he sought to protect Irish peasants against evictions and high rents. He was elected a Member of Parliament in 1882 while in prison, and again in 1892 and 1895. The agitation that he led influenced Gladstone to introduce the 1881 Irish Land Act, guaranteeing fair rents, fixity of tenure, and freedom to sell (the Three Fs) to tenants.

Davout, Louis Nicolas, Duke of Auerstädt (1770–1823) Marshal of France. He was made a general by Napoleon after the Battle of Marengo (1800) and marshal in 1804. One of Napoleon's ablest generals, his third corps played a major part at *Austerlitz, Auerstädt, Friedland (1807), and *Wagram (1809). He was responsible for organizing the army that invaded Russia in 1812. During the *Hundred Days, Davout was Minister of War. After the restoration of Louis XVIII he was deprived of his rank and title, but was reinstated two years later.

Dawes Plan (1924) An arrangement for collecting *reparations from Germany after World War I. Following the collapse of the Deutschmark and the inability of the *Weimar Republic to pay reparations, an Allied payments commission chaired by the US financier Charles G. Dawes put forward a plan whereby Germany would pay according to its abilities, on a sliding scale. To avoid a clash with France (which demanded heavy reparations and had occupied the Ruhr to ensure collections) the experts evaded the question of determining the grand total of reparations, and scheduled annual payments instead. Germany's failure to meet these led to the Plan's collapse and its replacement by the *Young Plan.

Dayton Accord The peace agreement, negotiated in Dayton, Ohio and signed in Paris in 1995, that marked the end of the three-year war in Bosnia and Herzegovina. The accord stated that the country would remain a single state within its existing borders but would comprise a Muslim-Croat federation and a Serb republic. A rotating tripartite presidency was established.

Dead Sea Scrolls A collection of Hebrew and Aramaic manuscripts, the first of which were found in 1947 by shepherds in a cave near the north-western shore of the Dead Sea. They belonged to the library of the Jewish (perhaps Essene) community at nearby Qumran, and were probably hidden shortly before the Roman destruction of 68 AD. The scrolls include fragments of nearly every book of the Hebrew Bible.

Deakin, Alfred (1856–1919) Australian Liberal statesman and Prime Minister (1903–04; 1905–08; 1909–10). He accompanied Sir Edmund *Barton to London to steer the Commonwealth Bill through Parliament (1900) and as Attorney-General (1901–03) introduced legislation that created the Australian high court. In his second term as Prime Minister he introduced far-reaching legislation, including protectionist tariffs and commercial laws.

Debs, Eugene Victor (1855–1926) US labour leader. In 1893 he founded the American Railway Union and led it in a secondary strike on behalf of the Pullman workers in 1894 (*see* PULLMAN STRIKE). The strike was broken by the intervention of federal troops and Debs was imprisoned in 1895 for conspiracy. Together with Victor Berger, Morris Hillquit, and others, he formed the Socialist Party of America (1901) and stood as its presidential candidate. A leading pacifist, he was briefly imprisoned for discouraging recruitment to the US armed services in World War I.

Decatur, Stephen (1779–1820) US naval commander. He was promoted captain following his daring recapture of the frigate *Philadelphia* in the *Tripolitan War (1801–05). After the *War of 1812 he became a national hero by forcing the Bey (ruler) of Algiers to sign the treaty (1815) that ended US tribute to the Barbary pirates. He was killed in a duel with a suspended naval officer.

Decembrists Members of a Russian revolutionary society, the Northern Society. A group of Russian army officers, influenced by French liberal ideas, combined to lead a revolt against the accession of *Nicholas I in 1825. Some of their supporters proclaimed their preference for a republic, others for Nicholas's eldest brother Constantine, in the hope that he would be in favour of constitutional reform and modernization. A few Guards regiments in St Petersburg refused to take an oath of allegiance to Nicholas and marched to the Senate House, where they were met by artillery fire. Betrayed by police spies, five of their leaders were executed, and 120 exiled to Siberia. The Decembrists' revolt profoundly affected Russia, leading to increased police terrorism and to the spread of revolutionary societies among the intellectuals.

Declaration of Independence The foundation document of the United States of America, which proclaimed American separation from Britain and was adopted by the *Continental Congress on 4 July 1776. Its principal author was Thomas *Jefferson, who based its arguments on John *Locke's ideas of contractual government. Its celebrated preamble declared that all men are created equal and have inalienable rights to life, liberty, and the pursuit of happiness. There followed a detailed list of acts of tyranny committed by George III, his ministers, and Parliament against the American people, similar in tone to those in the English *Bill of Rights (1689). The original document had 56 signatories whose names were initially kept secret for fear of British reprisals in the event of American defeat.

Declarations of Indulgence Four proclamations issued by Charles II and James II of England in an attempt to achieve religious toleration. Charles II issued Declarations in 1662 and 1672, stating that the penal laws against Roman Catholics and Protestant dissenters were to be suspended, but protests by Parliament caused both attempts to be abandoned. James II issued similar Declarations in 1687 and 1688, the latter leading to the trial of the Seven Bishops. James II insisted that the Declaration should be read in all churches; a Tory High Churchman, Archbishop Sancroft and six bishops who refused to do so were tried on a charge of seditious libel and were acquitted. The verdict was a popular one and widespread protest and defiance followed during the months leading up to the *Glorious Revolution of 1688.

Defence of the Realm Acts (DORA) Legislation (1914, 1915, 1916) by the British Parliament during World War I. Under the Acts government took powers to commandeer factories and directly control all aspects of war production, making it unlawful for war-workers to move elsewhere. Left-wing agitators, especially on Clydeside, were "deported" to other parts of the country. Strict press censorship was imposed. All Germans had already been interned but war hysteria led tribunals to harass anyone with a German name or connection (for example, the writer D. H. Lawrence) and to imprison or fine pacifists (for example, Bertrand Russell). The Act of May 1915 gave wide powers over the supply and sale of intoxicating liquor, powers which were widely resented but which nevertheless survived the war. An Emergency

Powers Act of 1920 confirmed the government's power to issue regulations in times of emergency and in 1939 many such regulations were reintroduced.

de Gasperi, Alcide (1881–1954) Italian statesman. He was elected to the Austro-Hungarian Parliament in 1911, and became Secretary-General of the Italian People's Party (1919–25). From 1929 to 1943 he was given refuge from *Mussolini's regime by the Vatican. He played an important part in creating the Christian Democrat Party as a focus for moderate opinion after the fascist era. De Gasperi was Prime Minister from 1945 to 1953, during which time he adopted a strong stand against communism and in favour of European cooperation.

de Gaulle, Charles (André Joseph Marie) (1890–1970) French general and statesman, head of government (1944–46), President (1959–69). He served in the French army during World War I, and during World War II was a member of the Cabinet at the time of France's surrender in June 1940. He escaped to Britain, where he was an instigator of the resistance and organized the Free French movement. Following the war he became interim President of the new French Republic, but later resigned. Having been asked to form a government, he became President in 1959 and went on to establish the presidency as a democratically elected office (1962). He resigned in 1969 after proposed constitutional changes were rejected by the electorate. In addition to extricating France from the Algerian crisis and strengthening the French economy, he is remembered for his assertive foreign policy (including withdrawing French forces from NATO and blocking Britain's entry to the EEC) and for quelling the student uprisings and strikes of May 1968.

de Klerk, Frederik Willem (1936–) South African statesman. Son of a distinguished Afrikaner family, he was born in Johannesburg and practised law until entering politics in 1972. In 1982 he became Minister of Internal Affairs under President P. W. Botha. At that time he became leader of the National Party of Transvaal and pressed the concept of "limited power-sharing" between the races. On becoming President in September 1989 he appeared to move steadily towards the position of accepting universal suffrage, while being threatened from the right by conservative and extremist groups, many of whom were clearly influencing his police force. In 1990 he opened discussion with Nelson *Mandela and the *African National

Congress, and his government began to dismantle *apartheid legislation. He established an all-party Convention for a Democratic South Africa (CODESA) and in 1992 won a referendum to continue the reform process. In 1993 a new (transitional) constitution was adopted, which gave all South African adults the right to vote. De Klerk was awarded the Nobel Peace Prize, jointly with Mandela, in 1993. He served as Second Deputy President of South Africa from 1994, following the country's first multiracial elections, until 1996, when he withdrew his party from the governing coalition. De Klerk stood down as leader of the National Party in 1997.

Delaware An Algonquian-speaking tribe of Native Americans whose original homelands lay along the Atlantic coast where they cultivated maize. They traded with the first European arrivals in the 17th century but were eventually driven off their lands as more colonists arrived. During the 19th century they moved to Kansas and Oklahoma and today others live in Wisconsin and Ontario.

Delcassé, Théophile (1852–1923) French statesman. As Foreign Minister in six successive governments between 1898 and 1905, he was the principal architect of the pre-1914 European alliances. He was the key figure in negotiations which resulted in the *entente cordiale with Britain (1904) and he paved the way for the Triple Entente with Britain and Russia (1907). In 1911 as Minister of Marine he arranged for cooperation between British and French fleets in the event of war. In 1914 he was again Foreign Minister and helped to negotiate the secret Treaty of London (1915), which persuaded Italy to fight on the side of the Allies in World War I by guaranteeing the retention of the Dodecanese Islands.

Delian League A voluntary alliance formed by the Greek city-states in 478–447 BC to seek revenge for losses suffered during the *Greek-Persian wars. All members paid tribute in the form of ships or money, the latter being stored on the sacred island of Delos, the League's nominal base. At first, under the leadership of Athens, the League actively sought to drive Persian garrisons out of Europe and to liberate the Greek cities of Asia Minor. *Pericles encouraged the conversion of the alliance into the beginnings of the *Athenian empire.

Delphi See ORACLE.

demesne In the Middle Ages, the lands retained by a lord under his direct control. The medieval lord, whether a king or *vassal, needed land to provide food and all other necessities for himself and his own household. Demesnes were the site of his residences which could be manors, palaces, or castles, and possibly all three.

Democratic Party A major political party in the USA. Known in its initial form as the Democratic-Republican Party, it emerged under Thomas *Jefferson in the 1790s in opposition to the Federalist Party, drawing its support from Southern planters and Northern yeoman farmers. In 1828, after a split with the National Republicans (soon called *Whigs) led by John Quincy *Adams and Henry *Clay, a new Democratic Party was formed under the leadership of Andrew *Jackson and John C. Calhoun. Its strong organization and popular appeal kept it in power for all but two presidential terms between then and 1860, when it divided over slavery. It only returned as a major national party in the last decades of the 19th century. By then, while retaining the loyalty of the deep South, it was gaining support from the ever expanding West and from the immigrant working classes of the industrialized north-east. In the early 20th century it adopted many of the policies of the Progressive Movement and its candidate for President, Woodrow *Wilson, was elected for two terms (1913–21). Although in eclipse in the 1920s, it re-emerged in the years of the Great *Depression, capturing Congress and the presidency: its candidate, Franklin D. *Roosevelt, is the only President to have been re-elected three times. From then until the 1990s it tended to dominate the House of Representatives, and generally held the Senate as well. The Democratic candidate Bill *Clinton won presidential elections in late 1992, but in mid-term elections in 1994 the Democrats suffered devastating losses, the Republicans gaining control of both Houses of Congress for the first time since 1954. Clinton was re-elected in 1996, but the Democrats lost the presidency to the Republican George W. *Bush in 2000. They regained the presidency in 2008 with Barack *Obama, the first African American to hold office. In 2010 the Democrats lost control of the House of Representatives to an increasingly right-wing Republican Party. With Democratic supporters disillusioned over what Obama had been able to achieve, the campaign for his re-election in 2012 against the Republican, Mitt Romney, was closely fought. He won more easily than expected, however, to give him a second term as president, although the Democrats were unable to take back the House of Representatives.

Demosthenes (384–322 BC) Athenian orator and statesman. He is best known for his political speeches on the need to defend Athens against the pretensions of Philip II of Macedon, which are known as the *Philippics*. Demosthenes was at the forefront of the campaign to unite the Greek city-states militarily against Macedon; the Greeks were defeated at the battle of Chaeronea in 338 BC, and Demosthenes committed suicide after the failure of an Athenian revolt against Macedon.

Deng Xiaoping (or **Teng Hsiao-p'ing**) (1904–97) Chinese Communist statesman. Offices he held included Vice-Premier (1973–76; 1977–80) and Chairman of the Central Military Commission (1981–89), but his power far exceeded their scope and he was regarded as China's paramount leader from about 1978. Discredited during the Cultural Revolution, he was reinstated in 1977, becoming the most prominent exponent of economic modernization, improving relations with the West, and taking a firm stance in relation to the Soviet Union. In 1989 his orders led to the massacre of some 2000 pro-democracy demonstrators in Beijing's Tiananmen Square. Despite the announcement of his retirement in 1989, he continued to be regarded as the effective leader of China until the end of his life.

Denikin, Anton Ivanovich (1872–1947) Russian general and counter-revolutionary. The son of a serf, he served the Provisional Government as commander of the *Western Front in 1917. After the October Revolution (*see* RUSSIAN REVOLUTION (1917)) he assumed command of a "white" army, the "Armed Forces of the South", gaining control of a large part of southern Russia. In May 1919 Denikin launched an offensive against Moscow which the *Red Army repulsed at Orel. He retreated to the Caucasus, where in 1920 his army disintegrated and he fled to France.

Denmark

Capital:	Copenhagen
Area:	43,094 sq km (16,639 sq miles)
Population:	5,556,452 (2012 est)
Currency:	1 krone = 100 øre;
Religions:	Evangelical Lutheran 95.0%; other Christian 3.0%; Muslim 2.0%

Ethnic Groups:	Scandinavian 95.0%, Inuit, Faroese, German, Turkish, Iranian, Somali
Languages:	Danish (official); Faroese; Greenlandic; German
International Organizations:	UN; NATO; OECD; EU; Council of Europe; OSCE; WTO

A Scandinavian country in northern Europe, situated between the North and Baltic Seas and comprising most of the peninsula of Jutland together with many islands, the largest of which are Sjaelland (Zealand), Fyn (Funen), Lolland, and Bornholm. Since the 14th century Greenland and the Faroe Islands have been Danish sovereign territories. The northern end of the peninsula has coasts on the Skagerrak and Kattegat channels, while to the south there is a land boundary with Schleswig-Holstein in Germany. A bridge linking Denmark to Sweden was opened in 2000.

Physical Denmark is a flat and low-lying country, the sea twisting into it at many points and outwash sand forming much of the subsoil. The climate is temperate with abundant rainfall.

Economy Both industry and agriculture are important in the Danish economy. The agricultural sector is small but highly efficient and meat, meat products, and dairy products are important exports. Important industries include metals, chemicals, food processing, machinery and transportation equipment, and pharmaceuticals. Machinery and pharmaceuticals are exported. In the Faeroe Islands and Greenland fishing and fish processing are the primary economic activities.

History There was active Danish participation in the *Viking explorations and conquests after c.800. King *Canute ruled over a great 11th-century empire comprising Denmark, England, Norway, southern Sweden, and parts of Finland. His reign was notable for the spread of Christianity, initially introduced in the 9th century.

After a period of internal disunity, Denmark re-emerged as the leading Scandinavian nation in the 13th century. Civil warfare and constitutional troubles continued, however, until Christopher II (1320–32) made major concessions to the nobles and clergy at the expense of royal authority. His son, Waldemar IV

(1340–75), re-established royal power, and his daughter, Margaret I (1387–1412), succeeded in creating the Pan-Scandinavian Union of *Kalmar (1397–1523). In 1448 the House of Oldenburg became the ruling dynasty. The 16th-century Protestant Reformation brought a national Lutheran church, and Christian IV (1588–1648) intervened in the *Thirty Years War as a champion of Protestantism. A sequence of 17th-century wars with Sweden resulted in Denmark's eclipse as the leading Baltic power. *Enlightenment ideas reached Denmark in the late 18th century, leading to major land reforms in favour of the peasants.

Denmark supported France during the Napoleonic Wars and in 1814 was forced to cede Norway to Sweden. In 1849 a new constitution ended absolute monarchy and introduced a more representative form of government under a constitutional monarch. In 1863 Denmark annexed *Schleswig-Holstein, which its king ruled personally as a duke, but this was opposed by Prussia and Austria, whose troops invaded in 1864. Schleswig was then absorbed into the *German Second empire. After World War I north Schleswig voted to return to Denmark, which had remained neutral during the war. Despite another declaration of neutrality at the start of World War II, the Germans occupied the country from 1940 to 1945 when all Schleswig-Holstein passed to the new German Federal Republic. After World War II Denmark joined NATO and in 1960 the newly formed European Free Trade Association. Like Britain, it later joined the European Community (1973), its farming community gaining considerably from membership. A close referendum decision in 1992 rejected the draft *Maastricht Treaty but in a subsequent referendum in 1993 the Danes voted to ratify the treaty. Similarly, in 2000 a referendum rejected the adoption of the euro. Denmark was the centre of international controversy in 2006 when a set of newspaper cartoons depicting the Prophet *Muhammad caused widespread anger in the Muslim world.

Depression, the Great (1929–33) A world economic crisis that began in October 1929, when the New York Stock Exchange collapsed, in the so-called Stock Market Crash. As a result US banks began to call in international loans and were unwilling to continue loans to Germany for *reparations and industrial development. Throughout the USA and Germany members of the public began a 'run on the banks', withdrawing their personal savings, and more and more banks had to close. Farmers could not sell crops, factories and industrial concerns could not borrow and had to close, workers were thrown out of work, retail shops went bankrupt, and governments could not afford to continue unemployment benefits even where these had been available. Unemployment in Germany rose to 6 million, in Britain to 3 million, and in the USA to 14 million; in the USA by 1932 nearly every bank was closed. In 1932 Franklin D. *Roosevelt was elected President of the USA, and gradually financial confidence there was restored, but not before the *Third Reich in Germany had established itself as a means for the revitalization of the German economy.

Derby, Edward George Geoffrey Smith Stanley, 14th Earl of (1799–1869) British statesman. Entering Parliament in 1822 as a Whig, he served as Chief Secretary for Ireland (1830–33) and subsequently as Colonial Secretary (1833–34), when he introduced the successful proposals to abolish slavery in the British empire. In the later 1830s he left the Whigs and joined Sir Robert Peel's Conservative government of 1841, but resigned over the repeal of the *Corn Laws. Together with Benjamin *Disraeli he led the Conservative opposition to the succeeding Whig administration. He was Prime Minister in 1852, in 1858–59, and again from 1866 to 1868, when he carried the *Reform Act of 1867 through Parliament. This act, which redistributed the parliamentary seats and more than doubled the electorate, gave the vote to many working men in the towns.

Dermot McMurrough (or **Diarmuid MacMurragh**) (c.1110–71) King of Leinster in Ireland (1126–71). In 1166, after feuding with his neighbours, he was defeated and banished by the Irish High King. He sought support from *Henry II of England and obtained the aid of Richard de Clare, Earl of Pembroke ('Strongbow'), offering him his daughter in marriage and the succession of Leinster. Dermot regained his kingdom in 1170 and after his death Leinster became an English fief and Henry II began to establish English dominance in Ireland.

Desai, Morarji (Ranchhodji) (1896–1995) Indian statesman and nationalist leader. After the death of Jawaharlal Nehru, he was a strong contender for the post of Prime Minister, but his austere and autocratic style made him too many enemies within the Congress Party. In 1977 he was the obvious candidate to lead the Janata opposition to Mrs Gandhi and led his party to victory in the election of that year. As Prime Minister (1977–79) his inflexible style handicapped him in dealing with the economic and

factional problems which confronted him and he resigned in 1979.

Descartes, René (1596–1650) French philosopher, mathematician, and man of science, often called the father of modern philosophy. Aiming to reach totally secure foundations for knowledge, he began by attacking all his beliefs with sceptical doubts, and considered all that was certain was his own conciousness and therefore existence ('cogito, ergo sum' I think, therefore I am).

desegregation In the USA, the movement to end discrimination against its Black citizens. Many segregation laws were passed in the Southern states after the *American Civil War, and they were supported by a Supreme Court decision in 1896 that accepted as constitutional a Louisiana law requiring separate but equal facilities for White and Black people in trains. For the next 50 years, many Southern states continued to use the "separate but equal" rule as an excuse for requiring segregated facilities. With the founding of the National Association for the Advancement of Colored People (NAACP) in 1909 Black and White Americans began making efforts to end segregation, but they met with fierce resistance from state authorities and White organizations, especially in the South. When World War II saw over one million Black people in active military service change was inevitable, and in 1948 President Truman issued a directive calling for an end to segregation in the forces. It was only with the *civil rights movement of the 1950s and 1960s that real social reforms were made. The Supreme Court decision in 1954 that segregation in state schools was illegal as it violated the *Fourteenth Amendment (*Brown v. Board of Education of Topeka*) was a landmark. The efforts of Martin Luther *King, the *Freedom Riders and others ended segregation and led to the passing of the Civil Rights Act of 1964 and the Voting Rights Act of 1965, which effectively outlawed legal segregation and ended literacy tests. There were still Black ghettos in the northern cities, but the purely legal obstacles to the equality of the races had essentially been removed.

Desmoulins, Camille (1760–94) French journalist and Revolutionary. He became an advocate in the Paris *Parlement in 1785, and four years later, after the dismissal of *Necker, he summoned the crowd outside the Palais Royal 'to arms'. On 14 July, the mob stormed the *Bastille. Soon afterwards he began to publish his famous journal *Les Révolutions de France et* *de Brabant*, attacking the *ancien régime. He married Lucile Duplessis in 1790 and began a close association with *Danton. He voted for the execution of *Louis XVI and campaigned against the *Girondins and the journalist Jacques Brissot de Warville. His support of Danton's policies of clemency angered *Robespierre and led to his arrest and execution by guillotine on 5 April 1794. A week later his wife was executed.

De Soto, Hernando (*c*.1500–42) Spanish conquistador and explorer. De Soto took part in the conquest of Central America, before joining Francisco Pizarro's expedition in Peru; he returned to Spain when the Inca King Atahualpa, whom he had befriended, was executed by Pizarro. De Soto was then made governor of Cuba by Emperor Charles V, with the right to conquer the mainland of America. He landed on the Florida coast in 1539 and reached North Carolina before crossing the Appalachian Mountains and returning through Tennessee and Alabama. In 1541 he led another expedition, crossing the Mississippi (which he was probably the first White man to see) and going up the Arkansas River into Oklahoma. They were seeking gold, silver, and other treasure, but returned disappointed. De Soto died on reaching the banks of the Mississippi.

Dessalines, Jean Jacques (1758–1806) Black emperor of Haiti. A former slave, he served under *Toussaint L'Ouverture in the wars that liberated Haiti from France. Although illiterate, he had a declaration of independence written in his name in 1804. With the defeat of the French in a war of extermination he became governor-general of Haiti, and in late 1804 had himself crowned Emperor Jacques I. The ferocity of his rule precipitated a revolt of mulattos in 1805. Dessalines was killed while trying to put down this rebellion.

Destroyer-Bases Deal (1940) A World War II agreement between F. D. Roosevelt and Churchill. Known as the Destroyer Transfer Agreement, it ensured the US transfer to Britain of 50 much-needed destroyers in exchange for leases of bases in British possessions in the West Indies, Newfoundland, and British Guiana. Being of World War I design, the destroyers became surplus to British requirements during the war, but in the early and critical stage of World War II they were an invaluable supplement to available escort vessels.

détente (French, 'relaxation') The easing of strained relations, especially between states. It was first employed in this sense in 1908. The word is particularly associated with the 'thaw' in the *Cold War in the early 1970s and the policies of Richard *Nixon as President and Henry *Kissinger as National Security Adviser (1969–75) and Secretary of State (1973–77).

Dettingen, Battle of (27 June 1743) An important victory for the British over the French in the War of the *Austrian Succession. *George II at the head of 40,000 British, Hanoverian, and Austrian troops marched from the Austrian Netherlands to the banks of the River Main. He was attacked by a larger French army under Noailles, but forced them back across the Main and finally across the River Rhine. George II was the last reigning British sovereign to take command on the battlefield.

de Valera, Eamon (1882–1975) Irish statesman. A fervent nationalist, de Valera was one of the leaders of the Easter Rising in 1916 and was sentenced to death by the British, but was released a year later. He served as leader of Sinn Fein (1917–26) and President of the self-declared Irish government (1919–22), but as an opponent of the Anglo-Irish Treaty headed the militant republicans in the ensuing civil war. In 1926 he founded the Fianna Fáil Party, which he led in the Dáil. In 1932 de Valera became President of the Irish Free State, and was largely responsible for the new constitution of 1937, which created the sovereign state of Eire. He served as Taoiseach (Prime Minister) (1937–48; 1951–54; 1957–59) and President (1959–73).

Deve Gowda, H. D. (1933–) Indian politician, Prime Minister from June 1996 to April 1997 as head of a fragile United Front coalition. Congress (I) refused to support the coalition with Deve Gowda as Prime Minister and so he resigned within a year of taking office.

developing countries (or **less developed countries, underdeveloped countries**) The poorer countries of the world. The term's definition is imprecise, but it usually refers to those countries that have not achieved the level of industrialization necessary for self-sustained economic growth. It thus includes most of Africa and much of Asia and Latin America. The growing differences between developing countries, in which some, such as the prosperous newly industrializing countries (NICs), have become richer and others, such as Somalia (sometimes called the 'least developed countries'), have stagnant or even falling incomes, make it an inadequate term.

Devolution, War of An attempt by *Louis XIV of France to seize the Spanish Netherlands. In 1665, on the death of his father-in-law, Philip IV of Spain, he invoked dubious laws based on local customs by which a child of a first wife (as was his queen Maria Theresa) inherited titles and territory, rather than the son of a second wife. A campaign under the Vicomte de Turenne alarmed Europe, a defensive Triple Alliance was formed by the United Provinces, England, and Sweden to check the French advance, and Louis made peace. He restored most of his conquests, hoping to obtain part of the Spanish empire peacefully on the death of Charles II.

Devonshire, William Cavendish, 4th Duke of (1720–64) British politician, nominal Prime Minister for six months (1756–57), while the effective leader, William *Pitt, had refused to hold the post due to a dispute with the Duke of *Newcastle.

Dewey, George (1837–1917) US admiral. He served in the Union (Northern) navy under Farragut during the *American Civil War. He was granted naval command of the Pacific (1897). His victory over the Spanish fleet at *Manila Bay on 1 May 1898 was not only decisive for the outcome of the *Spanish-American War but also for the future of US imperialism in the Pacific. In 1899 he made a triumphal progress through New York and was created the first ever US admiral.

Diana, Princess of Wales (born **Lady Diana Frances Spencer**) (1961–97) Former wife of Prince Charles. The daughter of the 8th Earl Spencer, she married Charles, Prince of Wales, in 1981. The couple publicly announced their separation in 1993 and divorced in 1996. She and her companion Dodi Al Fayed were killed in a car accident in Paris, causing an unprecedented response throughout Britain (thousands of bunches of flowers laid outside royal palaces and a funeral procession witnessed by a crowd estimated at 2 million).

Diane de Poitiers, duchesse de Valentinois (1499–1566) Mistress of *Henry II of France. She came to court during the reign of Francis I (1515–47) and Prince Henry, 20 years her junior, fell passionately in love with her. On his accession she became queen in all but name displacing Henry's wife, Catherine de Medici. A beautiful and cultured woman, she was friend and patron of poets and artists. She played little part in politics, contenting herself with augmenting her income and providing for her family. On Henry's death (1559) Catherine forced her to surrender the crown jewels and banished her to Chaumont.

diaspora (from Greek, 'dispersion') Jewish communities that have dispersed outside Israel. The process began with Assyrian and Babylonian expulsions in 721 and 597 BC, was continued by voluntary migration, and accelerated by the Roman destruction of the Temple in Jerusalem in 70 AD. By the 1st century AD there were Jewish communities from the Levant to Italy and notably in Babylon and Egypt.

By the early Middle Ages Spain was the main centre of Jewish scholarship, which it remained until the *Inquisition expelled all Jews in 1492. Distinguished Jewish scholars were also found in France and Germany, but from the time of the Crusaders, *anti-Semitism began to develop, many cities confining Jews to ghettos. Poland and Lithuania welcomed Jewish victims of persecution, and by the 17th century Eastern Europe had become the diaspora's centre of gravity until the pogroms of the 1880s drove many westwards, via Germany and Britain, to the USA. The German *Holocaust, during World War II, destroyed many Jewish communities that remained in Europe. The main centre of the diaspora is now the USA, with some 6 million Jews.

Díaz, Porfirio (1830–1915) Mexican general and statesman, President (1877–80; 1884–1911). He led a military coup in 1876 and was elected President the following year. During his second term of office he introduced a highly centralized government, backed by loyal mestizos and landowners, which removed powers from rural workers and American Indians. Díaz promoted the development of Mexico's infrastructure and industry, using foreign capital and engineers to build railways, bridges, and mines. Eventually the poor performance of Mexico's economy and the rise of a democratic movement under Francisco Madero (1873–1913) contributed to Díaz's forced resignation and exile in 1911.

Diaz de Novaes, Bartholomew (c.1455–1500) Portuguese explorer who led the first European expedition (1488) to round the Cape of Good Hope, thus opening the sea route to Asia via the Atlantic and Indian Oceans. On a voyage surveying the West African coast he had sailed to latitude 26° S, off Namibia, when his ships were caught in a storm and swept further south for 13 days. His landfall (1488) was near the southernmost tip of Africa: coasting eastwards, he found that the land turned north. He is attributed with having named it variously as the Cape of Storms and the Cape of Good Hope; he perished just off the Cape in 1500, on a later voyage during which Brazil had been discovered.

Diefenbaker, John George (1895–1979) Canadian statesman. He served as leader of the Progressive Conservative Party (1956–67) and Prime Minister of Canada (1957–63). He introduced some important measures of social reform and sought to encourage economic development, but as Canada experienced increasing economic difficulties in the early 1960s he was forced to devalue the Canadian dollar. In foreign affairs Diefenbaker wished to reduce Canada's dependence on the USA, but his party lost the election of 1963 when he took issue with the USA over the arming with atomic warheads of missiles supplied to Canada.

Dienbienphu (1954) The decisive military engagement in the *French Indo-China War. In an attempt to defeat the *Vietminh guerrilla forces, French airborne troops seized and fortified the village of Dienbienphu overlooking the strategic route between Hanoi and the Laotian border in November 1953. Contrary to expectations, the Vietnamese commander General *Giap was able to establish an effective siege with Chinese-supplied heavy artillery, denying the garrison of 16,500 men supply by air, and subjecting it to eight weeks of constant bombardment between March and May 1954, which finally forced its surrender. The ensuing armistice ended French rule in Indo-China within two months.

Dieppe raid (18–19 August 1942) An amphibious raid by the Allies on Dieppe, Normandy, in World War II. Its aim was to destroy the German port, airfield, and radar installations and to gain experience in amphibious operations. Some 1000 British commando and 5000 Canadian infantry troops were involved. There was considerable confusion as landing-craft approached the two landing beaches, where they met heavy fire. The assault was a failure and the order to withdraw was given. Not only were over two-thirds of the troops lost, but German shore guns sank one destroyer and 33 landing-craft, and shot down 106 aircraft. Although in itself a disaster, the raid taught many lessons for later landings in North Africa and Italy, and the *Normandy Campaign of June 1944—not least the need for careful planning.

Diet (from medieval Latin, 'a meeting for a single day') A meeting of estates or representatives, or even a legislative assembly. The representatives of the German States in the Holy Roman Empire (and the Emperor) met at the Imperial Diet (Reichstag) until 1806. *See also* WORMS, DIET OF.

Digger A member of a radical group that flourished briefly in 1649–50, when England's political future was uncertain. Led by Gerrard *Winstanley, the Diggers began seizing common land and sharing it out. They called themselves the True Levellers, but were opposed and denounced by the *Levellers, who disliked their communistic attitude towards property. Although they themselves rejected the use of force, their settlements in Surrey were dispersed by the authorities in March 1650.

Dimitrov, Georgi (1882–1949) Bulgarian communist leader. From 1929 he was head of the Bulgarian sector of the *Comintern in Berlin. When the *Reichstag was burned (1933) he was accused with other communists of complicity. His powerful defence at his trial forced the Nazis to release him and he settled in Moscow. In 1945 he was appointed head of the communist government in *Bulgaria, which led to the setting up of the Bulgarian People's Republic (1946) under his premiership, a period marked by ruthless Sovietization.

Dingaan (died 1843) Zulu king (1828–40). He was half-brother to *Shaka, whom he murdered. At first friendly to European settlers, missionaries, and the Voortrekkers, he treacherously killed their leader Piet Retief and his followers. He attacked a White settlement near what is now Durban, but was defeated (1838) at the Battle of *Blood River. He then fled, and was succeeded in 1840 by his brother Mpande. Driven into *Swaziland, he was assassinated there three years later.

Dingiswayo (died 1817) Founder of the *Zulu kingdom. In 1807 he became chief of the Mthethwa in the present northern Natal. By conquering neighbouring Nguni peoples he made himself paramount over all surrounding groups and established a rudimentary military state, developing trade with Mozambique. He had already designated *Shaka as his successor when he was assassinated by Zwide, chief of the Ndurande clan of the Zulu, in a rebellion against his rule.

Diocletian (full name **Gaius Aurelius Valerius Diocletianus**) (245–313) Roman emperor (284–305). Faced with military problems on many frontiers and insurrection in the provinces, in 286 he divided the empire between himself in the east and Maximian (died 310) in the west. In 293 he further divided the empire, giving Galerius (died 311) control of Illyricum and the valley of the River Danube, with Constantius Chlorus (died 306) ruling Gaul, Spain, and Britain. An enthusiast for the old Roman religion, tradition, and discipline, Diocletian insisted on the maintenance of Roman law in the provinces and launched the final harsh persecution of the Christians (303). He abdicated in 305.

Diogenes (*c.*400–*c.*325 BC) Greek philosopher. He was the most famous of the Cynics and the pupil of Antisthenes (*c.*445–*c.*365 BC). He lived a life of extreme poverty and asceticism in Athens (according to legend, he lived in a tub) and was nicknamed *Kuōn* ('the dog'), from which the Cynics derived their name. He emphasized self-sufficiency and the need for natural, uninhibited behaviour, regardless of social conventions. Among the many stories told of him is that he took a lantern in daylight, saying that he was seeking an honest man.

Diponegoro (or **Dipanagara**) (1785–1855) Javanese prince, leader of the *Java War (1825–30) against the Dutch. This struggle gained the support of central Javanese society, many of whom saw the prince as a latter-day messiah, a Javanese "Just King" (*Ratu Adil*), who would liberate Java from foreign influence. Fired by a mixture of Javanese mysticism and Islam, Diponegoro demanded recognition from the Dutch as protector of Islam in Java, but successful Dutch military tactics, in particular their use of mobile columns and fortified outposts (*bèntèng*), eventually forced him to the conference table, where he was treacherously arrested and exiled.

Directory, French (1795–99) The government of France in the difficult years between the *Jacobin dictatorship and the Consulate. It was composed of two legislative houses, a Council of Five Hundred and a Council of Ancients, and an executive (elected by the councils) of five Directors. It was dominated by moderates and sought to stabilize the country by overcoming the economic and financial problems at home and ending the war abroad. In 1796 it introduced measures to combat inflation and the monetary crisis, but popular distress increased and opposition grew as the Jacobins reassembled. A conspiracy, led by François *Babeuf, was successfully crushed but it persuaded the Directory to seek support from the royalists. In the elections the next year, supported by *Napoleon, it decided to resort to force.

This second Directory implemented an authoritarian domestic policy ('Directorial Terror'), which for a time established relative stability as financial and fiscal reforms met with some success. By 1798, however, economic difficulties in agriculture and industry led to renewed opposition which, after the defeats abroad in 1799, became a crisis. The Directors, fearing a foreign invasion and a Jacobin coup, turned to Napoleon who took this opportunity to seize power.

disarmament A policy aimed at the banning of armaments, or their reduction to the lowest level possible. It is different from **arms control**, which seeks to manage the arms race by maintaining a balance between the capabilities of both sides. Disarmament, on the other hand, envisages a dramatic reduction in arms in order to achieve peace. Attempts to achieve disarmament by international agreement began before World War I and in 1932 there was a World Disarmament Conference. In 1952 a permanent United Nations Disarmament Commission was established in Geneva. National disarmament pressure groups have tended to seek unilateral disarmament, for example the *Campaign for Nuclear Disarmament. Bilateral agreements are negotiated between two governments, while multilateral agreements are arranged via international conferences or the UN Commission. Important arms limitation talks include the *Strategic Arms Limitation Talks (SALT) and the *Strategic Arms Reduction Talks (START). In the START II Treaty ratified in 1992 the USA and Russia agreed to reduce their nuclear arsenals by two thirds by 2003. However, ratification and implementation stalled, and START II was superseded in 2002 by an agreement for a two-thirds reduction within 10 years. This was in turn replaced by the 'New START' treaty of 2010, which imposed further reductions in deployed warheads and delivery systems.

disciple Pupil or learner, used specifically to describe an original follower of *Jesus Christ. In the Jewish society of Jesus' time many religious teachers attracted disciples who came to be taught their master's interpretation of scriptures. Jesus' followers differed from such groups in several respects. For example, he actively sought out disciples and found many of them among people judged socially or morally as outcasts. The Apostles were the twelve chief disciples: *Peter (the leader), Andrew, James, John, Philip, Bartholomew, Thomas, Matthew, James (the Less), Thaddeus, Simon, and Judas Iscariot. After the suicide of Judas, who betrayed Jesus, his place was taken by Matthias. *Paul and his original companion Barnabas are also considered as Apostles.

Disestablishment Acts Legislation in Britain to remove the financial and other privileges of the Anglican Church. The Anglican Church had been 'established' in the reign of Elizabeth I as the only church allowed within the state, with large endowments and privileges. These came to be strongly resented by Non-Conformists in Victorian England; but proposals that all financial and other state support should be withdrawn failed. In Ireland, however, it came to be accepted as unjust that the Anglican Church should be the established church in a predominantly Roman Catholic population. It lost its privileges by Gladstone's Irish Church Disestablishment Act (1869). The Welsh also pressed for the disestablishment of the Anglican Church in Wales. Heated arguments over the financial implications of Welsh disestablishment arose in the years just before World War I, the Welsh Church Disestablishment Bill eventually becoming law in 1920.

Disraeli, Benjamin, 1st Earl of Beaconsfield (1804–81) British Tory statesman, of Italian Jewish descent; Prime Minister (1868; 1874–80). He played a dominant role in the reconstruction of the Tory Party after Sir Robert Peel, guiding it away from protectionism and generating enthusiasm for the British Empire. He was largely responsible for the introduction of the second Reform Act (1867), which doubled the electorate. In his second term as Prime Minister he ensured that Britain bought a controlling interest in the Suez Canal (1875) and also made Queen Victoria Empress of India. At home his government passed much useful social legislation, including measures to improve public health and working conditions in factories. He wrote a number of novels, including *Coningsby* (1844) and *Sybil* (1845), which drew on his experience of political life.

Dissolution of the Monasteries *See* MONASTERIES, DISSOLUTION OF THE.

Divine Right of Kings A European doctrine teaching that monarchy was a divinely ordained institution, that hereditary right could not be abolished, that kings were answerable only to God, and that it was therefore sinful for their subjects to resist them actively. It evolved during the Middle Ages, in part as a reaction to papal intrusions into secular affairs. The extension of the principle, to justify absolute rule and illegal taxation, aroused controversy. *James I of England upheld the doctrine in his speeches and writings and his son *Charles I was executed for refusing to accept parliamentary control of his policies. After the *Glorious Revolution the

doctrine was far less influential, yielding to anti-absolutist arguments like those of John *Locke. In late 17th-century France *Louis XIV's monarchy was based on the principle of Divine Right.

Dix, Dorothea Lynde (1802–87) US humanitarian and medical reformer. She campaigned for prison reform and also for improvement in the treatment of the mentally ill. During the *American Civil War Dix served as superintendent of nursing for the Union. Perhaps her greatest achievement was in persuading many states to assume direct responsibility for care of the mentally ill.

Dixiecrat Popular name for a US Democrat in a Southern state opposed to desegregation. In 1948 the *States' Rights Democratic Party was founded by diehard Southern Democrats ("Dixiecrats"), opposed to President Truman's renomination as Democratic candidate for President on account of his stand on civil rights (*see* CIVIL RIGHTS ACTS). Its members wished each state to be able to nominate its own presidential candidate without losing the label "Democratic". After Truman's victory they abandoned their presidential efforts but continued to resist the civil rights programme in Congress. Many Dixiecrats moved to support the Republican Party in the 1960s and 1970s.

Djibouti

Capital:	Djibouti
Area:	23,200 sq km (8950 sq miles)
Population:	792,198 (2012 est)
Currency:	1 Djibouti franc = 100 centimes
Religions:	Muslim 94.0%; Christian 6.0%
Ethnic Groups:	Somali 60.0%; Afar 35.0%
Languages:	Arabic, French (both official); Somali; Afar
International Organizations:	UN; AU; Arab League; Non-Aligned Movement; WTO

A small country of northeast Africa, formerly part of French Somaliland, on the south coast of the Gulf of Aden at the narrow entrance to the Red Sea, opposite Yemen.

Physical It lies on the Great Rift Valley: Lake Assal lies at 155 m (509 feet) below sea-level. The climate is harsh and much of the country is semi-arid desert.

Economy Trade is the mainstay of the economy; Djibouti City, the capital, is a free port and through its rail link to Addis Ababa handles trade for Ethiopia and other neighbouring African states.

History The small enclave of Djibouti was created as a port c.1888 by the French and became the capital of French Somaliland (1892). Its importance results from its strategic position on the Gulf of Aden. In 1958 it was declared by France to be the Territory of the Afars and Issas, but in 1977 it was granted total independence as the Republic of Djibouti under President Hassan Gouled Aptidon (re-elected in 1981 and 1987), leading the Popular Rally for Progress (RPP) party. Famine and wars in neighbouring countries have produced many economic problems, with refugees arriving in large numbers from Ethiopia and Somalia. In November 1991 the Front pour la Restauration de la Unité et la Démocratie (FRUD) was formed, mostly of Afar opposition groups opposed to the one-party rule of Gouled Aptidon. There was fighting in the west and south until French mediation in February 1992. Later that year a multiparty constitution was adopted and elections were held. Only one opposition party was allowed to contest the elections; less than half the population voted and the RPP won all the seats. A ceasefire was agreed in 1993 but sporadic fighting continued until 2001. Genuinely multiparty elections were held in 2003. There were border skirmishes with Eritrea in 2008; although UN sanctions were imposed on Eritrea in 2009, its troops did not finally leave Djibouti until 2010.

doge The title of the holder of the highest civil office in Venice, Genoa, and Amalfi from the 7th century until the 18th century. The office originated in Venice; in 1032 hereditary succession was formally banned and election was made increasingly complicated to prevent domination by particular factions, although the Participazio and Candiano families provided most candidates in the 9th and 10th centuries, and the Tiepolo and Dandolo in the 13th and 14th. The system ended with the Napoleonic conquest of 1797. The Genoese introduced a similar system after 1339. Democratic until 1515, it became an aristocratic office thereafter and also succumbed to *Napoleon. The first doge's palace in Venice was built in 814 and destroyed in 976.

The present gothic building was begun in the early 14th century.

dollar diplomacy A term used to describe foreign policies designed to subserve US business interests. It was first applied to the policy of President *Taft, whereby investments and loans, supported and secured by federal action, financed the building of railways in China after 1909. It spread to Haiti, Honduras, and Nicaragua, where US loans were underpinned by US forces and where a US collector of customs was installed in 1911. Although the policy was disavowed by President Woodrow *Wilson, comparable acts of intervention in support of US business interests, particularly in Latin America, remained a recurrent feature of US foreign policy.

Dollfuss, Engelbert (1892–1934) Austrian statesman, Chancellor of Austria (1932–34). He was elected leader of the Christian Socialist Party and Chancellor in 1932. From 1933 Dollfuss attempted to govern without Parliament in order better to oppose Austrian Nazi moves to force the *Anschluss* (the union of Austria and Germany). Five months after promulgating a new Fascist constitution in 1934, he was assassinated by Austrian Nazis in an abortive coup.

Domesday Book A survey of property in England conducted in 1086. Conceived by *William I, but probably to some extent based on pre-Conquest administrative records, it was the most comprehensive assessment of property and land ever undertaken in medieval Europe. Its purpose was to maximize the revenues from the land tax and it caused resentment and even riots. It was given its name on account of its definitive nature; today its volumes are housed in the Public Record Office, London.

Dominic, St (1170–1221) Founder of the **Dominican** order of friars. He was born in Spain, of noble family, but as a young man adopted an austere life, becoming a priest and canon of Osma Cathedral. In 1215 he attended the Fourth *Lateran Council. In that year he founded the Dominicans or 'Black Friars' because they wear a white tunic with a black mantle. The order became very popular in the 13th century, being used by several popes for preaching crusades and for the *Inquisition.

Dominica, Commonwealth of

Capital:	Roseau
Area:	751 sq km (290 sq miles)
Population:	73,286 (2012 est)

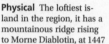

Currency:	1 East Caribbean dollar = 100 cents
Religions:	Roman Catholic 61.4%; Protestant 20.6%; other Christian 8.9%
Ethnic Groups:	Black 86.8%; mixed 8.9%; Amerindian 2.9%
Languages:	English (official); French creole
International Organizations:	UN; OAS; CARICOM; Commonwealth; WTO; Non-Aligned Movement

Dominican Republic

Capital:	Santo Domingo
Area:	48,670 sq km (18,792 sq miles)
Population:	10,219,630 (2012 est)
Currency:	1 Dominican peso = 100 centavos
Religions:	Roman Catholic 95.0%
Ethnic Groups:	mixed 73.0%; White 16.0%; Black 11.0%
Languages:	Spanish (official)
International Organizations:	UN; OAS; Non-Aligned Movement; WTO

An island country, the second largest of the Windward group of the Caribbean Islands.

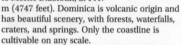

Physical The loftiest island in the region, it has a mountainous ridge rising to Morne Diablotin, at 1447 m (4747 feet). Dominica is volcanic origin and has beautiful scenery, with forests, waterfalls, craters, and springs. Only the coastline is cultivable on any scale.

Economy Dominica's economy was formerly dependent on agriculture, with bananas the leading crop, but tourism is increasingly important and the government hopes to develop an offshore financial sector. Bananas are still the principal export, followed by soap, bay oil, and fruit and vegetables.

History When Europeans first arrived Dominica was inhabited by Carib Indians, who had driven out the earlier inhabitants, the Arawaks. During the 18th century the French and British fought with each other, and with the Caribs, for control of the island. Britain was in possession of the island in 1805, when the French made their last attempt to capture Dominica but were driven out by the British. In 1958 Dominica joined the West Indian Federation and it became an autonomous British Associated State in 1967. It gained full independence in 1978.

Dominica was devastated by hurricanes in 1979 and 1980, and there were two attempted coups in 1981. The Dominican Freedom Party (DFP), under Dame Eugenia Charles (1919–2005), governed the country from 1980 until 1995, when the United Workers' Party (DUWP) won elections. Since 2000 the Dominica Labour Party (DLP) has held power, in coalition until 2005 and alone thereafter.

A country in the Caribbean, the eastern part of the island of Hispaniola.

Economy Telecommunications, duty-free industrial zones, and tourism have been fostered and have now overtaken the formerly dominant agricultural sector. Nickel is the chief export, and sugar, gold, and silver are also important.

History The island of Hispaniola was divided between France and Spain, with France gaining control of the entire island in 1795. *Toussaint L'Ouverture took over the island soon after but the Spanish regained control of the eastern part of the island in 1809. The Dominican Republic declared its independence from Spain in 1821, although in the following year it was again annexed by Haiti. In 1843 the Dominicans revolted from Haitian domination, winning their second independence in 1844. Between 1861 and 1865 the Dominican Republic was re-annexed to Spain and fought a third war for independence (1865) under Buenaventura Báez. Anarchy, revolutions, and dictatorships followed, and by 1905 the country was bankrupt. The USA assumed fiscal control, but disorder continued and the country was occupied (1916–24) by US marines. A constitutional government was established (1924), but this was overthrown by Rafael *Trujillo, whose military dictatorship lasted from 1930 to 1961. On his assassination, President Juan Bosch established (1962–63) a democratic government, until he was deposed by a military junta. Civil war and fear of a communist take-over brought renewed US intervention (1965), and a new constitution was introduced in 1966. Since then redemocratization has steadily advanced, the Partido

Reformista being returned to power in the 1986 elections. The country occupies a strategic position on major sea routes leading from Europe and the USA to the Panama Canal. The Partido Reformista remained in power after the 1990 elections with Joaquín Balaguer as President. The latter resigned as party leader in 1991, but remained President. An IMF austerity programme in 1991 sharply reduced inflation and there were successful efforts to diversify the economy. In 1994 Balaguer was re-elected, but the result was contested. Fresh elections were promised and these resulted in the election as President of Leonel Fernández, leader of the centrist Liberation Party (in 1996). He was defeated in 2000 by Hipólito Mejía, but was elected again in 2004 and 2008. Constitutionally forbidden to run for a third term, he supported the election of Danilo Medina in 2012.

dominion A country in the *British empire that, between 1867 and 1947, had achieved a degree of autonomy but still owed allegiance to the British crown. The first country to call itself a dominion was Canada (1867), followed in 1907 by New Zealand. Australia called itself a Commonwealth (1901), South Africa a Union (1910). After World War II the concept became obsolete as the *Commonwealth of Nations included countries that were republics and did not owe allegiance to the crown, though accepting the monarch as symbolic head of the Commonwealth.

Donahoe, John (c.1806–30) Australian *bushranger. Born in Dublin, he was sentenced to transportation for life. He and two companions went bushranging in New South Wales from 1827 to 1830, when he was killed in a fight in the Bringelly scrub near Campbelltown. He, together with Ned Kelly (1855–80), inspired the glorification and cult of bushranging in Australian society.

Donatist A member of a Christian sect that arose in North Africa in 311 AD out of a dispute about the election of the bishop of Carthage, and which maintained that it was the only true and pure Church and that the ordinations of others were invalid.

Dönitz, Karl (1891–1981) German admiral and U-boat commander. He developed the "pack" system of submarine attack in the early years of World War II. He was appointed grand admiral (1943), commander in chief of the navy, and, after Hitler's death, chancellor of Germany. He was imprisoned for war crimes (1946–56).

Don Pacifico affair An international incident provoked by the actions of a Greek mob, who in 1847 ransacked and burnt the house of Don Pacifico, a Portuguese moneylender who was also a Jew, injuring his wife and children. Pacifico, who had been born in Gibraltar and could therefore claim British nationality, demanded compensation from the Greek government. Insisting on Pacifico's rights as a British subject, the British Foreign Secretary, Lord *Palmerston, took up the case in 1850 and decided to reinforce his entitlement to compensation by blockading Greece with the British fleet. He defended his action, which almost precipitated a war with France, with a masterly speech in Parliament.

Doria, Andrea (1466–1560) *doge of Venice (1528–60), an outstanding soldier and admiral. He fought for Francis I and Charles V, expelled the French from Genoa in 1528, and took power himself, creating the aristocratic republic. His descendants contributed six doges and numerous officials to the state.

Dorians The tribes speaking the Doric dialect of Greek who probably entered Greece from the north c.1100–1000 BC and by the 8th century BC had settled most of the Peloponnese, the southernmost Aegean islands, and the southwest corner of Asia Minor. While culturally distinct in architecture and dialect, the Dorians retained their political system only in Sparta and Crete where the ruling military class subjected the local peoples as serfs and dependants. The Dorians were responsible for the oldest and simplest orders of Greek architecture, known as the Doric order.

Dost Muhammad (c.1798–1863) Amir of Afghanistan. He was ruler of Kabul and Afghanistan (1826–39; 1843–63). Defeated in the first *Anglo-Afghan War, he regained power in 1843 and consolidated his rule in Afghanistan through control of Kandahar (1855), northern Afghanistan (1850–59), and Herat (1863), so establishing the territorial outlines of modern Afghanistan.

dotcom bubble A global speculative rise in share prices between c.1997 and 2000 driven by the alleged opportunities for profit presented by the *Internet. Access to the Internet, and especially to the World Wide Web, became widespread in the mid-1990s, and many new companies proposed utilizing it in various ways. (These companies generally had websites with names ending in ".com", whence the term "dotcom".) Because the Internet was a new medium, new business models that ignored the "old" economic rules were accepted uncritically. Most Internet start-up companies did not expect to make money in the short term, but rather emphasized the scope for major long-term growth. Financed by stock-exchange flotations or venture capital, they sought to build market share by offering free services, with the expectation that they could begin charging when they were securely established; in the meantime, the rise in their share prices fuelled by this expectation of future success would satisfy their investors. A classic stock-market "bubble" developed, with euphoria at rising share values spreading to non-Internet shares. The bubble burst in 2000: Internet start-up companies began to exhaust their start-up capital and go bankrupt, confidence collapsed, and share prices began a long decline.

Douglas, Clifford (1879–1952) British engineer and economist. Before and during World War I he developed his theory of *social credit, arguing that in every productive establishment the total cash issued in wages, salaries, and dividends was less than the collective price of the product. To remedy deficiencies of purchasing power, either subsidies should be paid to producers or additional moneys go to consumers. His ideas became fashionable in Britain (1921–22) and in the dominions, particularly in Canada and New Zealand.

Douglas-Home, Sir Alec, Baron Home of the Hirsel of Coldstream (1903–95) British Conservative statesman, Prime Minister (1963–64). He served as private secretary to Neville Chamberlain in the negotiations with Hitler from 1937 to 1940. Various ministerial offices followed before his appointment as Foreign Secretary under Harold Macmillan in 1960. When Macmillan resigned in 1963, Douglas-Home became Prime Minister, relinquishing his hereditary peerage as 14th Earl of Home (to which he had succeeded in 1951). His government was defeated by the Labour Party in the 1964 elections. Douglas-Home later served as Foreign Secretary under Edward Heath (1970–74).

Douglass, Frederick (c.1817–95) US Black *abolitionist. Born in slavery in Maryland, he made his escape to the free states in 1838. In 1841 he became an agent for the Massachusetts Anti-Slavery Society and a prominent advocate of abolition. An adviser of *Lincoln during the *American Civil War, he remained throughout his life an advocate of full civil rights for all.

Dowding, Hugh Baron (Hugh Caswall Tremenheere Dowding) (1882–1970) British Air Chief Marshal. As Commander-in-Chief of Fighter Command (1936–40) Dowding organized the air defence that defeated the Luftwaffe during the Battle of Britain in 1940. He was relieved of his post the same year in controversial circumstances and retired in 1942.

Downing Street Declaration A document, signed on 15 December 1993 by the British Prime Minister, John *Major, and the Prime Minister of the Irish Republic, Albert Reynolds, declaring their principles and conditions for the conduct of negotiations to achieve peace in *Northern Ireland. The declaration restated the existing positions of both governments, confirming that they would seek the agreement of the people of both Northern Ireland and the Irish Republic to any change to the status of Northern Ireland and would uphold all existing guarantees to Northern Ireland.

Draconian laws The first written code of laws drawn up at *Athens, believed to have been introduced in 621 or 620 BC by a statesman named Draco. Although their details are obscure, they apparently covered a number of offences. The modern adjective "Draconian" (excessively harsh) reflects the fact that penalties laid down in the code were extremely severe: pilfering received the same punishment as murder—death. A 4th-century BC politician quipped that Draco wrote his laws not in ink, but in blood.

Drago, Luis Maria (1859–1921) Argentine statesman, jurist, and writer on international law. The Drago Doctrine, enunciated in 1902 and intended as a corollary to the *Monroe Doctrine, states that no country has the right to intervene militarily in a sovereign American state for the purpose of collecting debts. Drafted in response to a naval blockade (1902) of Venezuela by Britain, Italy, and Germany, the principles of the doctrine were accepted internationally by the Second Hague Conference in 1907.

dragoon A mounted infantry soldier, named in 16th-century France after the short musket called the "dragon". Originally trained to fight on foot, dragoons were organized in infantry companies, not cavalry squadrons, but were progressively trained to cavalry standard. Thus by the early 18th century they were known as medium cavalry in the Prussian army, and light cavalry in the British army.

Drake, Sir Francis (c.1540–96) English sailor and explorer. He spent his early career privateering in Spanish seas. He was the first Englishman to circumnavigate the globe; he set off in 1577 with five ships under the sponsorship of Elizabeth I to investigate the Strait of Magellan, tried unsuccessfully to find the North-West Passage, and finally returned to England via the Cape of Good Hope with only his own ship, the *Golden Hind*, in 1580. He was knighted the following year. Drake's raid on Cadiz in 1587 delayed the sailing of the Armada for a year by destroying its supply-ships, and the next year he played an important part in its defeat in the English Channel.

Dred Scott decision (1857) A US Supreme Court decision regarding slave status. Dred Scott, a slave, had in 1834 been taken by his master into Illinois (a non-slave state) and later into territory in which slavery had been forbidden. Years later, his then owner sued for Scott's freedom in a Missouri (slave state) court, claiming that because of his earlier stay in free territory he should be free. In 1857 the case was decided by the US Supreme Court. The majority of the court held that Scott, as a slave and as a Black person, was not a citizen of the USA, nor was he entitled to use the Missouri courts. He was not free since his status was determined by the state in which he lived when the case was brought, i.e. Missouri. In the highly tense political atmosphere of the 1850s, the Dred Scott decision immediately deepened divisions over slavery, in particular because it declared unconstitutional the *Missouri Compromise of 1820, which had banned slavery from all territory north of the 36° 30′ line of latitude.

Dreikaiserbund See THREE EMPERORS' LEAGUE.

Dresden raid (February 1945) One of the heaviest air-raids on Germany in World War II. The main raid was on the night of 13–14 February 1945 by Britain's Bomber Command; 805 bombers attacked the city, which, because of its cultural significance and lack of strategic importance, had until then been safe. The main raid was followed by three more in daylight by the US 8th Air Force. The Allied commander-in-chief General *Eisenhower was anxious to link up with the advancing *Red Army in south Germany, and Dresden came to be regarded as strategically important as a communications centre. The city was known to be overcrowded with some 200,000 refugees, but it was felt that the inevitably high casualties might in the end help to shorten the war. Over 30,000 buildings were flattened. The numbers of those who died in the bombing and the ensuing firestorm are still in dispute; although early estimates varied from 40,000 to 140,000, a lower figure of 18,000 to 25,000 is now more often cited.

Dreyfus, Alfred (1859–1935) French army officer, of Jewish descent. In 1894 he was falsely accused of providing military secrets to the Germans; his trial, imprisonment, and eventual rehabilitation in 1906 caused a major political crisis in France, polarizing deep-set anti-militarist and anti-Semitic trends in a society still coming to terms with defeat and revolution in 1870–71. Notable among his supporters was the novelist Émile Zola, whose open letter, *J'accuse*, published in 1898, accused the judges at the trial of having convicted Dreyfus at the behest of the War Office.

Drogheda, Siege of See CROMWELL, OLIVER.

Druid A member of the ruling caste of the Gallic *Celts. Knowledge of the Druids is derived chiefly from the hostile accounts of them in the Roman authors Julius *Caesar and *Tacitus. Caesar reports that they exercised judicial and priestly functions, worshipped in groves (clearings in forests), and cut mistletoe from the oak tree (sacred to them) with a golden sickle. The religion was stamped out by the Romans, to prevent its resistance to Roman rule.

Druse (or **Druze**) A member of a political and religious sect of Muslim origin, concentrated in Lebanon, with smaller groups in Syria and Israel. The sect broke away from Ismaili Shiite Islam in the 11th century over a disagreement about the succession to the imamate (leadership), a position in which spiritual and political leadership were and are indissolubly linked. The Druses followed the seventh caliph of the Fatimid dynasty, al-Hakim b'illah (996–1021), who is claimed to have disappeared and whose return is expected. They regard al-Hakim as a deity, and thus are considered heretics by the Muslim community at large.

Dual Monarchy See AUSTRIA-HUNGARY.

du Barry, Marie Jeanne, comtesse (1743–93) Favourite of *Louis XV of France. She was a great beauty who in 1769 became the king's mistress and influenced him until his death in 1774. *Choiseul criticized her and she may have helped to bring about his dismissal. During the *French Revolution she was arrested by the Revolutionary Tribunal and guillotined.

Dubček, Alexander (1921–92) Czechoslovak statesman, First Secretary of the Czechoslovak Communist Party (1968–69). He is generally regarded as the driving force behind the attempted democratization of Czech political life in 1968 that became known as the Prague Spring. At this time he and other liberal members of the government made plans for a new constitution as well as legislation for civil liberties and began to pursue a foreign policy independent of the Soviet Union. In response, Warsaw Pact forces invaded Czechoslovakia in August 1968 and Dubček was removed from office the following year. After the abandonment of Communism at the end of 1989 he returned to public life and was elected speaker of the Federal Assembly in a new democratic regime.

Du Bois, William Edward Burghardt (1868–1963) US Black *civil rights leader and author. Seeking a self-sufficient Black society, he was a co-founder of the National Association for the Advancement of Colored People (NAACP, 1909). His enrolment in the Communist Party earned him the Lenin Peace Prize (1961); this followed federal indictment (and acquittal) during the years of the *McCarthy witch-hunts.

Dudley, Robert, Earl of Leicester (c.1532–88) English nobleman. He became a favourite of Elizabeth I soon after her accession in 1558. Following the mysterious death of Dudley's wife, Amy Robsart, in 1560 it was rumoured that he would marry the queen; this did not happen, although Dudley remained in favour with Elizabeth throughout his life and in 1564 was created Earl of Leicester. He was later given the command of the military campaign in the Netherlands (1585–87) and of the forces preparing to resist the Armada (1588).

Dulles, John Foster (1888–1959) US Republican statesman and international lawyer. He was adviser to the US delegation at the conference which set up the United Nations in 1945 and negotiated the Peace Treaty with Japan in 1951. As Secretary of State under President Eisenhower (1953–59) he strove to improve the position of the USA in the Cold War, to which end he strengthened NATO and urged that the USA should stockpile nuclear arms as a deterrent against Soviet aggression.

Duma An elective legislative assembly introduced in Russia by *Nicholas II in 1906 in response to popular unrest. Boycotted by the socialist parties, its efforts to introduce taxation and agrarian reforms were nullified by the reactionary groups at court which persuaded the emperor to dissolve three successive Dumas. The fourth Duma (1912–17) refused an imperial decree in February 1917 ordering its dissolution and established a provisional government. Three days later it accepted the emperor's abdication, but soon began to disintegrate.

The lower house of the legislature established by the Russian Federation's post-communist 1993 constitution is called the "State Duma".

Dumas, Alexandre (or **Dumas père**) (1802–70) French novelist and dramatist. A pioneer of the romantic theatre in France, he achieved fame with his historical dramas, such as *Henry III et sa cour* (1829). His reputation now rests on his adventure novels, especially *The Three Musketeers* (1844–45) and *The Count of Monte Cristo* (1844–45).

Dumas, Alexandre (or **Dumas fils**) (1824–95) French dramatist. He became one of the most successful dramatists of the Second Empire. His play *La Dame aux camélias* (1852) was based on Dumas's own novel (1848) and inspired Verdi's opera *La Traviata* (1853).

Dumbarton Oaks Conference (1944) An international conference at Dumbarton Oaks in Washington, DC, when representatives of the USA, Britain, the Soviet Union, and China drew up proposals that served as the basis for the charter of the *United Nations Organization formulated at the San Francisco Conference the following year. Attention at Dumbarton Oaks was focused on measures to secure 'the maintenance of international peace and security', and one of its main achievements was the planning of a United Nations Security Council.

Dunant, Jean-Henri *See* RED CROSS.

Dunbar, Battle of (3 September 1650) A battle near the port of Dunbar in Scotland, in which Oliver *Cromwell's force of 14,000 men won a victory over 27,000 Scots, and enormous numbers were taken prisoner together with all the Scottish guns. Cromwell's victory destroyed the *Stuart cause in Scotland for a decade.

Duncan I (c.1010–40) King of Scotland (1034–40). He was ruler of Strathclyde which was added to the Scottish kingdom inherited from his grandfather Malcolm II. His accession was unpopular with the northern tribes and twice he was defeated by the Earl of Orkney before being killed in battle by the Earl of Moray, *Macbeth.

Duncan II (*c.*1060–94) King of Scotland 1094. He gained the throne through the support of William II of England, who provided the army with which Duncan defeated his uncle and rival Donald Bane. However, Duncan's English alliance was resented and he was murdered at his uncle's instigation.

Dunkirk evacuation A seaborne rescue of British and French troops in World War II (26 May–4 June 1940). German forces advancing into northern France cut off large numbers of British and French troops. General Gort, commanding the British Expeditionary Force, organized a withdrawal to the port and beaches of Dunkirk, where warships, aided by small private boats, carried off some 330,000 men—most, but not all, of the troops.

Duns Scotus, John (known as **'the Subtle Doctor'**) (*c.*1265–1308) Scottish theologian and scholar. In opposition to the teaching of St Thomas Aquinas he argued that faith was a matter of will, not dependent on logical proofs. He was also the first major theologian to defend the theory of the Immaculate Conception. His system was accepted by the Franciscans as their doctrinal basis and exercised a profound influence in the Middle Ages. In the Renaissance his followers were ridiculed for their conservatism and abused as enemies of learning, which gave rise to the word *dunce*.

Dunstan, St (*c.*909–88) Anglo-Saxon prelate. During his tenure as abbot at Glastonbury the monastery became a centre of religious teaching. He was appointed Archbishop of Canterbury by King Edgar in 960, and together they carried through a reform of Church and state. He introduced the strict Benedictine rule into England and succeeded in restoring monastic life; a keen supporter of education, he was also known as a musician, illuminator, and metalworker.

Durbar (Persian and Urdu, 'court') Originally a public audience given by a Mogul emperor of India. Under British rule it was a ceremonial gathering usually connected with some royal event. The most magnificent was George V's Durbar in Delhi (1911).

Dutch East India Company A *chartered company established (1602) under the aegis of Prince Maurice of Nassau to coordinate the activities of companies competing for trade in the East Indies and to act as an arm of the Dutch state in its struggle against Spain. It was involved in attacks on the Portuguese (then part of the *Spanish empire), and warfare with native rulers, and created a virtual monopoly in trade in fine spices (for example cloves, nutmeg, and mace) grown under its supervision in the Moluccas and the Banda Islands. In 1619 it made Batavia its headquarters. It ousted the Portuguese from Ceylon, set up trading posts in India, Persia, and Nagasaki, and made the Cape of Good Hope a base for Dutch ships *en route* to and from the East. In 1799 it was liquidated, its debts, possessions, and responsibilities being taken over by the Dutch state.

Dutch East Indies The former name (until 1949) of *Indonesia under Dutch colonial rule.

Dutch empire The overseas territories of the United Provinces of the Netherlands. Dutch wealth rested on the fishing and shipping industries, assisted by Holland's position on the chief European trade routes. Amsterdam became the principal warehouse and trading centre for all Europe. Modern banking methods developed from Amsterdam's exchange bank (1609). Overseas trade with Asia, America, and Africa grew steadily even during war. Spain and Portugal's attempt to exclude the Dutch from the 'New World' prompted them to found the *Dutch East India Company (1602). Growing rivalry with Britain led to loss of maritime supremacy and of all Dutch colonies except in south-east Asia.

Dutch Republic *See* UNITED PROVINCES OF THE NETHERLANDS.

Dutch Revolts (1567–1648) The struggle by the *Netherlands for independence from Spain. The Low Countries formed part of the Spanish empire but the tactlessness of the Council of Regency for Philip II alienated the local nobles, who were excluded from government. High taxation, unemployment, and Calvinist fears of Catholic persecution aroused dangerous opposition which the Duke of *Alba came to crush (1567) with a reign of terror and punitive taxation. Open revolt led by *William I (the Silent) followed. He avoided pitched battles with the superior Spanish forces and exploited his local knowledge, saving besieged cities like Leiden (1573–74) by opening the dykes and flooding the countryside. The sack of Antwerp (1576) led to a temporary union of the whole Netherlands in the Pacification of Ghent. Calvinist excesses soon caused the southern provinces to form the Union of Arras (1579) and make peace with Spain. The northern provinces formed the Union of Utrecht and the war became a

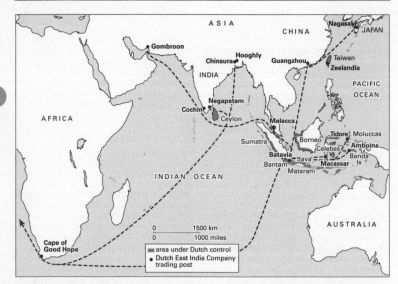

Dutch East India Company. 1602–1799 The Dutch East India Company had two important strategic advantages in the cut-throat competition for trade and constant naval skirmishing among European powers in south-east Asia in the 17th century. Its base at Batavia was ideally placed to defend the company's interests in the Spice Islands, and the acquisition of the Cape of Good Hope in South Africa in 1652 provided a vital staging post for Dutch captains, who followed a direct route to Batavia, taking advantage of the prevailing westerlies. Dutch dominance in the area was largely secured at the expense of the Portuguese.

religious struggle for independence. William held out with foreign aid until assassinated (1584), when the leadership passed to Maurice of Nassau and the politician *Oldenbarneveldt. The United Provinces were saved by Spain's commitment to wars against France, England, and Turkey. A truce (1609) was followed by recognition of full independence at the Peace of *Westphalia (1648).

Dutra, Eurico Gaspar (1885–1974) Brazilian statesman. He served as Minister of War before becoming President of Brazil (1946–51). Winning the presidency as the candidate of the Partido Social Democratico, Dutra had a new constitution adopted during his first year in office and promoted economic nationalism and industrialization. A conservative, he did not repudiate the idea of state participation in the economy.

Duvalier, François (known as 'Papa Doc') (1907–71) Haitian statesman, President (1957–71). His regime was noted for being authoritarian and oppressive; many of his opponents were either assassinated or forced into exile by his security force, known as the Tontons Macoutes. He proclaimed himself President for life in 1964 and was succeeded on his death by his son Jean-Claude Duvalier (known as 'Baby Doc', 1951–2014); the Duvalier regime ended in 1986 when a mass uprising forced Jean-Claude to flee the country.

earl A British nobleman ranking between marquis and viscount, ranked third in the peerage. From Alfred's time *aldermen had charge of shires, but during the 10th century they became more important, with overall control of several shires. King *Canute's dependence on his Scandinavian jarls (earls) gave them territorial power in England over the regions of Northumbria, East Anglia, and Wessex. They presided over the shire court, commanded its fyrd, and retained one-third of the profits of justice (replaced later by King John with a fixed sum). Under the Norman kings in the 11th century shire administration passed to the sheriffs but the hereditary title of earl survived.

early humans Members of the family *Hominidae*, including our own species *Homo sapiens*, our presumed forebears *Homo erectus* and *Homo habilis*, and forms believed to be closely related called collectively the *australopithecines*. Many scientists now also include the African great apes—the two chimpanzees and gorilla—in the human family, rather than grouping them with the more distantly related Asian apes. The traditional way of grouping the large apes (chimpanzees, gorilla, and orang-utan) is in their own family, Pongidae. Estimates of the date of divergence of the ape and human lineages vary. The Asian apes probably branched off 8–12 million years ago and the African apes 10–5 million years ago. The stages of development in which humans diverged from ape-like ancestors and took on their present form took at least five million years. Many details remain uncertain, particularly of the relationship between the australopithecines and the *Homo* lineage, and the position of such remains as those found at Broken Hill, in central Zambia. Here, skeletal material, once called Rhodesian Man, is now usually referred to as Kabwe or Broken Hill Man. These finds are believed to represent a population in Africa 400,000–200,000 years ago that is transitional between late *Homo erectus* and early or 'archaic' *Homo sapiens*.

The first australopithecine fossil was discovered at Taung in southern Africa in 1924 and named *Australopithecus africanus* (southern ape of Africa). Since then, australopithecine fossils have been found in southern and eastern Africa but the relationships between the different forms are still far from clear.

Current opinion divides them into two, or perhaps three main groups that date from over 4 million to nearly 1 million years ago. One of the oldest (4–3 million years ago) and most ape-like is *Australopithecus afarensis*, now known from eastern African sites. This species is often linked closely to *Australopithecus africanus* (3–2 million years ago), best represented at Sterkfontein and Makapansgat in southern Africa. Some authorities consider both these species are human ancestors; others rule out *A. africanus*, some even discount both from being human ancestors. Australopithecines were clearly capable of walking upright but their brains were still ape-like. It is uncertain if they made tools.

Homo habilis ('handy man') refers to a group of human fossil remains found at Olduvai Gorge in Tanzania in the early 1960s; they are now known from other eastern African sites, and perhaps also from southern Africa. They date from about 2.5 million to 1.6 million years ago. Although similar in size to the contemporary australopithecines, their brains were larger, their faces more human-like, and they may have evolved into *Homo erectus*. They were probably the first makers of stone tools, such as the simple pebble and flake artefacts collectively called the Oldowan industry.

Homo erectus ('upright man'), who may have been the predecessor of our own species, *Homo sapiens*, lived in Africa and Asia and possibly in Europe. This hominid was larger than the australopithecines and *Homo habilis*, with a brain approaching the size of a modern human brain. However, the facial bones remained relatively massive and the skull was long and low. One of the hallmarks of this species was a teardrop-shaped stone tool flaked on both sides, the Acheulian handaxe, which was more specialized than the Oldowan tools of *Homo habilis. Homo erectus* was the first member of the human lineage to control and use fire, which with its use of clothing, may have contributed to its spreading from its place of origin in tropical East Africa. It may have evolved from *Homo habilis*, by 1.6 million years ago. By around 1 million years ago or not long before these hominids are presumed to have begun the travels that took them as far as China (Peking Man) and Indonesia (Java Man). The last representatives disappeared 400,000–200,000 years ago.

Homo sapiens ('wise man'), our own species, appeared about 400,000–200,000 years ago. By this stage the brain had enlarged to the modern size, the skull bones had become less heavy, and the back of the head was rounded. The next development is obscure as the *Homo sapiens* lineage apparently split into two main lines, one leading to the **Neanderthals** (*Homo sapiens neanderthalensis*), the other to fully modern people (*Homo sapiens sapiens*). The latter development took place gradually during the past 125,000 years. Anatomical and genetic evidence support the idea that this happened in Africa, but it is possible that there was at least one parallel development in the Far East. In the Middle East, anatomically modern humans had appeared by around 50,000 years ago; in Europe, they came slightly later, and more abruptly around 35,000 years ago. The earliest modern Europeans are often called **Cro-Magnons**. It is not known what part, if any, the Neanderthals played in these Middle Eastern and European developments. Very likely they were not our direct ancestors but they may have interbred with modern people entering Europe from Africa via the Middle East.

With the evolution of modern people came marked advances in tool technology, rapid increase in population, the grouping of social activities in dwellings, and the first appearance of art; the cultural period called the Upper Palaeolithic had begun. These Upper Palaeolithic people almost certainly had a spoken language. With population growth came the colonization of new territories, which seems to have begun soon after the origin of fully modern humans. People had reached New Guinea and Australia from Indonesia by at least 40,000 years ago; there they developed Australoid characteristics in isolation. The timing of the first settlement of the New World is more controversial. It was probably before 15,000 years ago but there is little firm archaeological evidence so far for an earlier colonization. Genetic, linguistic, and

anatomical evidence of modern Amerindians, however, is increasingly suggesting that the first entry into North America occurred between 40,000 and 30,000 years ago.

Neanderthals lived in Europe, the Near East, and Central Asia from about 130,000 to 30,000 years ago. No traces of people with characteristic ('classic') Neanderthal features are known from Africa or the Far East. They are named after the Neander valley near Düsseldorf in Germany where part of a characteristic skeleton was discovered in 1856. Neanderthals flourished particularly during the last Ice Age and were adapted for living in cold environments. Called *Homo sapiens neanderthalensis* to distinguish them from fully modern people *Homo sapiens sapiens*, their features included heavy bones, strong musculature, large brow ridges across a sloping forehead, and larger brains than those of fully modern people. Neanderthals were probably the first people to have burial rites. Flint tools of Mousterian type are usually found with their remains and characterize the Middle Palaeolithic period.

The part played by Neanderthals in later human evolution is controversial. One widely held view is that none were our direct ancestors. A study of DNA undertaken in 1996 indicated that the Neanderthals were a separate species and neither evolved into modern humans nor interbred with other early humans before they became extinct. An alternative opinion is that some Neanderthal groups evolved into fully modern people or that at least some interbreeding between Neanderthals and modern humans took place.

If they were an evolutionary dead end, the reason for their extinction 50,000–30,000 years ago remains a mystery (the date varies according to geographical locality). It is possible that they became too specialized and were supplanted by modern people migrating into Europe from elsewhere, probably Africa via the Middle East.

*Palaeolithic peoples included **hunter gatherers** who subsisted from the natural environment, without involvement in agriculture of animal husbandry. They survived by gathering wild fruit and vegetables, and by hunting. Theirs is the earliest and simplest form of human organization, and has been found all over the world: Australian *Aborigines, the Arctic Inuit, and the Kung-San in southern Africa are all examples of modern hunter-gatherers. They have a nomadic way of life, following seasonal food supplies. They are organized in bands consisting of close kin, but these bands fluctuate in size as members move in and out, according to food availability. Marriage is a very loose institution, and lineage is not considered of great importance. Hunter-gatherer society is egalitarian: leadership is usually based on individual ability and is not hereditary. Relations between men and women are also more egalitarian than in many sedentary societies, though there is a basic division of labour, the men hunting game while the women do most of the gathering. **Cro-Magnons** are early modern people (*Homo sapiens*), found in Europe until about 10,000 years ago. They were generally more heavily built than humans today but otherwise had the same anatomical characteristics. They appeared around 35,000 years ago and are named after a rock shelter in the Dordogne, France, where four adult skeletons, an infant's skeleton, and other remains were found in 1868. With the skeletons were Upper Palaeolithic flint tools of Aurignacian type and signs of decorative art in the form of pierced sea shells. The ancestry of Cro-Magnons is unclear. It was once believed these people were the direct descendants of Neanderthals, but it is now thought that they evolved elsewhere, probably in Africa, replacing the Neanderthals within a few thousand years of reaching Europe. The **cave-dwellers** first used caves as shelters. This became widespread during the Middle and Upper Palaeolithic periods, when humans penetrated for the first time into the northern tundra environments in front of the ice-sheets of the last glaciation. Since the remains of open-air campsites, such as wind-breaks or tents, are generally less well preserved and less likely to be discovered than bones and tools incorporated in cave sediments, early investigators imagined that *Stone Age people lived entirely in caves. This has now been refuted by the excavation of huts and tent-foundations preserved under wind-blown sediments in the Ukraine, central Europe, and France.

East African Community (1967–77; 2000–) An economic association of East African countries. It began with a declaration of intent (June 1963) between Kenya, Tanzania, and Uganda to improve trade, communications, and economic development. This was the East African Common Services Organization and provided for common currency, common market, and customs. This was developed by the Treaty of Kampala (1967) into the East African Community with headquarters in Arusha, Tanzania. It made considerable economic headway before 1971 when Uganda came under Idi *Amin's regime. The Community broke up in 1977, but was revived in 2000; Rwanda and

Burundi joined in 2009. A customs union was established in 2005, and in 2010 members agreed to move towards the free movement of goods, labour, services, and capital in a common market.

Eastern Front Campaigns (World War II, 1939–45) A series of military campaigns fought in eastern Europe. The first campaign (September 1939) followed the *Nazi-Soviet pact (1939), when Germany invaded Poland. Soviet forces entered from the east, and Poland collapsed. Finland was defeated in the *Finnish-Russian War. In June 1941 Hitler launched a surprise offensive against his one-time ally, the Soviet Union. Italy, Romania, Hungary, Finland, and Slovakia joined in the invasion. By the end of 1941 Germany had overrun Belorussia and most of the Ukraine, had besieged Leningrad, and was converging on Moscow. The Russian winter halted the German offensive, and the attack on Moscow was foiled by a Soviet counter-offensive. Britain, now allied with the Soviet Union, launched a joint British-Soviet occupation of Iran (1941), thus providing a route for British and US supplies to the Red Army, as an alternative to ice-bound Murmansk. During 1942 *Leningrad continued to be besieged, while a massive German offensive was launched towards *Stalingrad and the oil-fields of the Caucasus. *Kursk, Kharkov, and Rostov all fell, as did the Crimea, and the oil centre of Maikop was reached. Here the Soviet line consolidated and forces were built up for a counter-offensive which began in December 1942, the relief of Stalingrad following in February 1943. The surrender of 330,000 German troops there marked a turning point in the war. A new German offensive recaptured Kharkov, but lost the massive Battle of Kursk in July. The Red Army now resumed its advance and by the winter of 1943–44 it was back on the River Dnieper. In November 1943 Hitler ordered forces to be recalled from the Eastern Front to defend the Atlantic. Soviet offensives from January to May 1944 relieved Leningrad, recaptured the Crimea and Odessa, and re-entered Poland. Through the rest of the year and into 1945 the Red Army continued its advance, finally entering Germany in January 1945. By April it was linking up with advance troops of the Allied armies from the west, and on 2 May Berlin surrendered to Soviet troops. Victory on the Eastern Front had been obtained at the cost of at least 20 million lives.

Eastern Orthodox Churches *See* CHRISTIANITY.

Easter Rising (April 1916) An insurrection in Dublin when some 2000 members of the Irish Volunteers and the Irish Citizen Army took up arms against British rule in Ireland. The *Irish Republican Brotherhood had planned the uprising, supported by the *Sinn Fein Party. A ship carrying a large consignment of arms from Germany was intercepted by the British navy. Roger *Casement of the IRB, acting as a link with Germany, was arrested soon after landing from a German U-boat. The military leaders, Pádraic Pearse and James Connolly, decided nevertheless to continue with the rebellion. The General Post Office in Dublin was seized along with other strategic buildings in the city. The Irish Republic was proclaimed on 24 April, Easter Monday, and a provisional government set up with Pearse as President. British troops forced their opponents to surrender by 29 April. The rising had little public support at first. Many Irishmen were serving in British forces during World War I. 16 leaders of the rebellion were executed and over 2000 men and women imprisoned. The executions led to a change of feeling in Ireland and in the 1918 general election Sinn Fein won the majority vote.

East Germany See GERMAN DEMOCRATIC REPUBLIC.

East India Company, English A *chartered company of London merchants that gradually transformed trading privileges in Asia into a territorial empire centred on India. Chartered in 1600, the Company soon lost the Spice Islands (Moluccas) to the Dutch, but by 1700 had secured important trading ports in India, notably Madras, Bombay, and Calcutta. In the mid-18th century Anglo-French hostility in Europe was reflected in a struggle for supremacy with the *French East India Company. The English commander *Clive outmanoeuvred the French governor Dupleix in south India, then intervened in the rich north-eastern province of Bengal. Victory over the Bengal ruler in 1757 initiated a century of expansion, the East India Company emerging as the greatest European trader in India, though with strong French competition. Increasingly the company acted as an instrument of colonial government; having lost its commercial monopolies by 1833, it served as Britain's administrative agent in India. Widespread risings in 1857 during the *Indian Mutiny determined, through the India Acts, the transfer of India from company to British government control in 1858, and the company was finally dissolved in 1873. See also DUTCH EAST INDIA COMPANY.

East Timor See TIMOR-LESTE.

East–West relations The relationship existing from the end of World War II between the USA and its allies on one side (the West) and the former Soviet Union and its allies on the other (the East). After the war the USA and the Soviet Union emerged as superpowers based on opposing ideologies, with global interests. The USA had a stake in the security of Western Europe, while the Soviet Union extended its influence over the countries of the Eastern bloc, despite Eastern European discontent, leading to the Yugoslav break with Stalin in 1948 and Soviet repression of dissidents in Poland, Czechoslovakia, and elsewhere. Both sides possessed increasing nuclear capabilities. The bipolar split in world politics became evident in the alliance systems of *NATO and the *Warsaw Pact. The period of mutual distrust and rivalry that ensued, characterized by ideological differences, the dissemination of *propaganda, the build-up of arms, military threat, and occasional misunderstandings and crises, became known as the *Cold War. Each side built up its nuclear arsenals (see ARMS RACE) and attempted to extend its sphere of influence in the developing world. However, the rigid polarization of the first period of the Cold War was broken down in the early 1960s by an ideological split between the communist regimes of China and the Soviet Union, and the formation of the *Non-Aligned Movement, an attempt to remain independent from both East and West. During the 1970s there was a period of *détente when relations improved, only to deteriorate because of the Soviet invasion of Afghanistan (1979), which triggered what many called the second Cold War. However, the later 1980s saw the rise of *glasnost and perestroika in the Soviet Union, progress in arms agreements, the withdrawal of the Soviet army from Afghanistan (1989), the demise of communism in the Eastern bloc, the reunification of Germany in 1990, and the disbanding of the Warsaw Pact in the same year. In 1991 the Soviet Union itself ceased to exist, as the constituent republics asserted their independence. In 1997 a formal alliance between Russia and NATO was signed. However, Russia continued to express dismay at certain aspects of NATO policy and criticized international actions in the former Yugoslavia. Nevertheless, with the demilitarization of East–West relations and prospects of greater cooperation between the two sides, the East–West balance of power has ceased to be an overriding factor in shaping international relations.

East–West Schism The schism between the Eastern Orthodox Church and the Western (or Roman) Church, which became definitive in the year 1054. Tension between the two Churches dated back at least to the division of the *Roman empire into an Eastern and a Western part, and the transferral of the capital city from Rome to Constantinople in the 4th century. An increasingly different mental outlook between the two Churches resulted from the occupation of the West by formerly barbarian invaders, while the East remained the heirs of the classical world. This was exacerbated when the popes turned for support to the *Holy Roman Empire in the West rather than to the *Byzantine empire in the East, especially from the time of *Charlemagne onwards. There were also doctrinal disputes, and arguments over the nature of papal authority. Matters came to a head in 1054 when the two Churches, through their official representatives, excommunicated and anathematized (formally denounced) each other. The breach was deepened in 1204 when the Fourth *Crusade was diverted to Constantinople and sacked the city and a Latin (Western) Empire was established there for some time. There were various attempts to heal the schism, notably at the ecclesiastical councils of Lyons II (1274) and Florence (1439), but the reunions proved fleeting. These attempts were effectively brought to an end when the *Ottoman Turks captured Constantinople in 1453 and occupied almost all of the former Byzantine empire for many centuries. It is only in recent years that the dialogue between the two Churches to heal the schism has been effectively re-opened.

Ecgbert *See* EGBERT.

Economic Community of West African States (ECOWAS) An economic grouping constituted largely on the initiative of General *Gowon at Lagos in 1975 by 15 West African countries, and later (1977) joined by Cape Verde; Mauritania left in 2000. Its object was to provide a programme of liberalization of trade and to bring about an eventual customs union. A common fund was established to promote development projects, with specialized commissions for trade, industry, transport, and social and cultural affairs. A new treaty was signed in 1993, designating the creation of a free-trade zone and a single currency as specific objectives. A parliament and court of justice were established in 2000 and 2001 respectively. The organization contributed significantly to resolving West Africa's armed conflicts in the 1990s.

Ecuador

Capital:	Quito
Area:	283,561 sq km (103,484 sq miles)
Population:	15,439,429 (2012 est)
Currency:	1 US dollar = 100 cents
Religions:	Roman Catholic 95.0%
Ethnic Groups:	Mestizo 71.9%; Montubio 7.4%; Afroecuadorian 7.2%; Amerindian 7.0%; White 6.1%
Languages:	Spanish (official); Quechua; Shuar
International Organizations:	UN; OAS; Andean Community; Non-Aligned Movement; WTO; OPEC

A country on the north-west coast of South America.

Physical Ecuador is bounded by Colombia on the north-east and Peru on the east and south. The Andes run north to south through the middle of the country and between the peaks are high but fertile valleys where the climate is temperate.

Economy The oil industry, nationalized since 1988, produces over half the country's export earnings, but otherwise the economy is primarily agricultural with exports including bananas (of which Ecuador is the world's leading exporter), coffee, and cut flowers. Oil revenues have been invested to develop some manufacturing industry. There are plentiful supplies of natural gas and hydroelectric power to meet domestic energy requirements, and also mineral deposits of lignite, gold, and silver.

History By c.500 AD independent kingdoms had developed with two cultural regions—a coastal one, adapted to the open sea, and one adapted to the interior environment. The Incas conquered the central valley in the 15th century, and their communications network included a road from Cuzco to Quito, which they set up as their regional capital. The Spaniard *Pizarro united the region to his Peruvian conquests in 1535 and installed his brother, Gonzalo, as governor. Internal dissensions led to a take-over by the Spanish crown and the establishment of

Quito as an Audiencia (a high court with a political role) under the viceroy of Peru.

With the victory at Pichincha (1822) by Antonio Sucre Ecuador gained independence, joining Gran *Colombia. When this broke up (1830) it became a separate republic, whose politics reflected the tension between the conservative landowners of the interior and the more liberal, business community of the coastal plain. This led to an almost total breakdown in government (1845–60). Garcia Moreno ruthlessly re-established order as President (1860–75) and, on his assassination, there was a period of stable government under anti-clerical liberal governments. After World War I increasing poverty of the masses led to political turbulence. Although US military bases in World War II brought some economic gain, a disastrous war with Peru (1941) forced Ecuador to abandon claims on the Upper Amazon. Between 1944 and 1972 the caudillo José Maria Velasco Ibarra alternated with the military as ruler, being elected President five times. The discovery of oil in the 1970s might have brought new prosperity, but in fact the mass of the population remained poor and illiterate, with the great haciendas surviving intact. Democratic government was restored in 1979 with the election of the social democrat Jaimé Roldos Aquilera as President (1979–81). He had promised reform but died in a mysterious air-crash. His successor, Osvaldo Hurtado Larrea (1981–84), was accused of embezzlement, and President Febres Cordero (1984–88) faced military intervention, a major crisis of external indebtedness, trade union unrest, and a decline in the oil price. The Democratic Left Party under Rodrigo Borja Cevallos came to power in 1988. It took over management of the oil companies, but still faced grave economic problems. Following elections in 1992 a coalition government was formed under President Sixto Durán Ballén. He introduced free-market reforms and cut public spending, provoking popular unrest, and was replaced in 1996 by Abdala Bucaram (known as 'El Loco', the madman). In 1995 a recurrent border dispute with Peru flared up again, but was settled after several days of fighting. In 1997 Bucaram was ousted on grounds of insanity and Jamil Mahuad was elected President in 1998. An economic crisis in 2000 led to a military coup, which installed Vice President Gustavo Noboa as President. However, in 2002 the coup leader, Lucio Gutiérrez, was elected President. He was dismissed by Congress in 2005 and replaced by Alfredo Palacio. The left-wing Rafael Correa was elected President in 2006. Ecuador defaulted on its public debt in 2008 and a new constitution that strengthened presidential power came into effect that same year. The power of the presidency was again increased in 2011, following police and military unrest in 2010. Correa was re-elected in 2009 and 2013.

Eden, Anthony, 1st Earl of Avon (**Robert Anthony Eden**) (1897–1977) British statesman; Conservative Prime Minister (1955–57). As Foreign Secretary from 1935 to 1938, he was noted for his support for the *League of Nations: he resigned over his opposition to *appeasement but was again Foreign Secretary from 1940 to 1945 and from 1951 to 1955. He was also deputy leader of the Conservatives (1945–55) under *Churchill, whom he succeeded as Prime Minister. Eden's premiership was dominated by the *Suez War. Owing to his experience of appeasement, he was determined to stand up to President *Nasser of Egypt, whom he perceived as a potential aggressor. Widespread opposition to Britain's role in the Suez Crisis, together with his own failing health, led to his resignation.

Edgar (947–75) King of England (959–75). He became king of Northumbria and Mercia in 957 when these regions renounced their allegiance to his elder brother Edwy, succeeding to the throne of England on Edwy's death. Edgar worked closely with St Dunstan during his reign and was renowned for his support of organized religion.

Edgar the Aetheling (from Anglo-Saxon *aetheline*, 'prince') (*c*.1052–*c*.1125) The grandson of Edmund Ironside. His father's death (1057) in exile left Edgar as the heir to *Edward the Confessor in 1066, but because of his youth he was rejected in favour of *Harold II. On Harold's death at the Battle of *Hastings the Witan chose Edgar as king but, despite his involvement in a rebellion against *William I (1069), he was unable to organize any further resistance and became a member of William's court (1074). He was captured by *Henry I at Tinchebrai (1106) for supporting Henry's older brother Robert of Normandy (Curthose), but was later released.

Edgehill, Battle of (23 October 1642) The first battle of the *English Civil War. Charles I's Royalists, marching south from Shrewsbury, with the eventual aim of recapturing London, clashed with the Parliamentarians under the 3rd Earl of *Essex, at Edgehill, near Banbury. Prince *Rupert and his Royalist cavalry gained an early advantage, but the brunt of the fighting was borne by both infantries. Darkness, and the exhaustion of the troops ended the struggle, with no clear victor and heavy losses on both sides.

Edmund I (921–46) King of England (939–46). He succeeded his brother Athelstan as king. In his brief reign he defended Athelstan's territorial gains and reconquered (944) Danish-occupied Mercia. He sought to stabilize his north-west border against Danish raids from Ireland by presenting (945) the region of Strathclyde to his ally the King of Scotland, Malcolm I. Edmund appointed *Dunstan as abbot of Glastonbury and supported his reform of organized monasticism. He was murdered by a convicted robber in a banquet brawl.

Edmund II (Ironside) (c.993–1016) King of Wessex. He was the son of *Ethelred II, who had temporarily (1013–14) lost his throne to Sweyn I of Denmark. Edmund's succession was challenged by Sweyn's son *Canute. Over a period of eight months (1016) they fought six major battles. Defeated at Ashingdon in Essex (October 1016), Edmund agreed to rule southern England and Canute the remainder, either survivor succeeding to the whole country. Edmund died in the following month and Canute became overall ruler.

Edo, Treaty of (1858) Treaty between Japan and the USA. It extended the rights granted to the USA four years earlier by the Treaty of *Kanagawa, establishing diplomatic relations, accepting a conventional tariff, and granting US citizens extra-territorial rights in five treaty ports. Along with treaties signed with other foreign powers, this agreement opened the way to the westernization of Japan, but exposed the *shogunate to nationalist hostility which was to play an important role in its downfall in 1868.

Edward I (1239–1307) King of England (1272–1307), in succession to his father *Henry III. He was married to Eleanor of Castile (1254), then to Margaret of France (1299). Edward's reputation as a successful ruler rests on his military and legal skills (for which he was called "the English *Justinian"). His military achievements, which were motivated by a determination to extend royal power, included the defeat of Simon de *Montfort (1265), the conquest of Wales (1277–82), the suppression of rebellions in Wales (1294–95) and Scotland (1296–1305), and the defence of his lands in Gascony against the French crown (1294–99). His legal reforms covered such matters as feudal administration (Statute of Westminster, 1275), crown lands (Quo Warranto, 1278), and law and order (Statute of Winchester, 1285), and he summoned the *Model Parliament in 1295. He died during a vain expedition to subdue the Scots and was succeeded by *Edward II.

Edward II (1284–1327) The first English Prince of Wales (1301–07) and King of England (1307–27). The fourth (but eldest surviving) son of *Edward I and Eleanor of Castile, he was notorious in his own lifetime for his inordinate affection for Piers *Gaveston and for his unhappy marriage with *Isabella of France, daughter of Philip IV of France. Gaveston dominated Edward by 1304 and helped alienate him from his barons; the barons, led by Edward's cousin, Thomas of Lancaster, hemmed Edward in by a set of Ordinances (1310) and had Gaveston killed in 1312. The king's prestige fell further when he was defeated by *Robert I (the Bruce) at *Bannockburn in 1314, and although he attempted to reassert his royal authority and annulled the Ordinances (1322), his own wife and her lover, Roger *Mortimer, imprisoned him in 1326 and finally had him murdered.

Edward III (1312–77) King of England, Ireland, and France (1327–77). He succeeded his father, *Edward II, though the throne was at first his in little more than name, power remaining in the hands of his mother, *Isabella of France, and her lover Roger *Mortimer; but in 1330 Edward had Mortimer arrested and began his personal rule. He secured the Scottish frontier with relative ease by the victory of *Halidon Hill (1333); but his initial French strategy was less successful, for although he prudently bought up the allegiance of France's neighbours the cost proved excessive. By 1341 Edward was virtually bankrupt. In 1346 he sought to justify his claim to the French throne by the more direct means of leading a vast army to France, and victories at *Crécy (1346) and in Brittany made him effectively king in France. The English by now were gaining a taste for foreign warfare and booty, and the truce of 1354 was ended by a fresh invasion of France two years later, crowned by the epic victory that Edward's son, *Edward the Black Prince, won at *Poitiers.

The rest of Edward's long reign was less successful—there were failures in France between 1369 and 1375, and after the death of his wife, Philippa of Hainault in 1369, his health and mind began to deteriorate; he fell under the influence of his mistress, Alice Perrers. Edward left his successor, *Richard II, with a legacy of social discontent in England as well as the possession of vast tracts of France.

Edward IV (1442–83) King of England (1461–70; 1471–83). He was the eldest son of Richard, Duke of *York and so had a clear hereditary right to the throne by descent from Edward III. He gained the throne at the age of 19 with the help of his cousin Richard Neville, Earl of *Warwick, while the Lancastrians hesitated after their victory of St Albans, and he then defeated them at *Towton. His marriage to Elizabeth Woodville and alliance with Burgundy alienated Warwick, who in October 1470 invaded England from France and secured *Henry VI's nominal restoration, but Edward won back the throne by victories at *Barnet and *Tewkesbury (1471). Thereafter he was a strong ruler and promoter of English commerce, but his dissolute lifestyle probably caused his early death, which left England with a 12-year-old king, *Edward V.

Edward V (1470–83) King of England (1483), the eldest son of *Edward IV and Elizabeth Woodville. His short reign, which began on 9 April 1483, was little more than a power struggle between the Woodvilles and his paternal uncle Richard, Duke of Gloucester. In June, Richard assumed royal dignity as *Richard III, and it was at some time between then and August of the same year that Edward and his brother were murdered in the Tower of London, probably at the instigation of Richard.

Edward VI (1537–53) King of England (1547–53). He was the son of *Henry VIII and Jane Seymour. During his minority effective power was exercised by Edward *Seymour, Duke of Somerset until 1549, and subsequently by John Dudley, Duke of *Northumberland. He favoured the Protestant religion, endorsing Archbishop *Cranmer's English Prayer Books (1549 and 1552). Contemporaries noted his studious, unemotional nature, and a callous streak reminiscent of his father. Always a sickly child, he died of tuberculosis aged 16.

Edward VII (1841–1910) King of Great Britain and Ireland and dependencies overseas, Emperor of India (1901–10). The eldest son of Queen *Victoria and Prince Albert, he was 59 before he succeeded to the throne on the death of his mother. As Prince of Wales he served on the Royal Commission on working-class housing (1884–85), but in general the queen excluded him from public affairs, denying him access to reports of cabinet meetings until 1892. As monarch his state visit to Paris in 1903 improved relations between Britain and France, and promoted public acceptance of the *entente cordiale. In domestic politics he was influential in 1910 through his insistence that his approval for the Parliament Bill to reform the House of *Lords must be preceded by a general election. He was succeeded in 1910 by his second son, *George V.

Edward VIII (1894–1972) King of Great Britain and Northern Ireland and of dependencies overseas, Emperor of India (1936). The eldest son of King *George V, he abandoned the crown in the **Abdication crisis**. The king let it be known that he wished to marry Mrs Wallis Simpson, a twice-divorced American, which would have required legislative sanction from the British Parliament and from all the dominions. The British government under Stanley Baldwin, reflecting public opinion and strong opposition from the Church of England under the Archbishop of Canterbury (Cosmo Lang), opposed the king's wish, as did representatives of the dominions. Edward chose to abdicate, making a farewell broadcast to the nation, and commending his brother, the Duke of York, who succeeded him as *George VI. Created Duke of Windsor, he was governor of the Bahamas during World War II but took no subsequent public role. He settled in France, but was buried at Windsor, together with the duchess after her death in 1986.

Edward the Black Prince (1330–76) Prince of Wales (1343–76), the eldest son of *Edward III. He was an outstanding example of the chivalric ideal, a military leader who helped restore national pride to the English by a series of victories in the *Hundred Years War. He commanded part of his father's army at *Crécy (1346), and in 1356 won the Battle of *Poitiers, capturing John II. In 1367 he restored King Pedro to the throne of Castile, but the campaign in Spain ruined his health. By his love match to Joan, the 'Fair Maid of Kent', he left one son, the future *Richard II.

Edward the Confessor, St (c.1003–66) King of England (1042–66). He succeeded King *Canute's Danish heirs as king, temporarily re-establishing the West Saxon monarchy, although he had favoured the Normans, among whom he had been brought up. In 1045 he married the daughter of Earl Godwin of Wessex and six years later put down a rebellion by the earl. It will never be known for certain whether, as the Normans claimed, he promised the crown to Duke William before his death; the succession after his death of Harold, Earl Godwin's son, caused the Normans to take England by conquest. Edward was the founder of Westminster Abbey (1045), and had a great reputation for piety. He was canonized in 1161.

Edward the Elder (died 924) King of Wessex (899–924). He was the eldest son of King *Alfred, whom he succeeded in 899. He continued his father's policy of repossessing the *Danelaw.

A system of fortified towns was developed. A series of victories (909–18) secured the Midlands and the important towns of Derby, Leicester, Lincoln, Stamford, and Nottingham and convinced the Danes of the need to recognize English rule south of the Humber. Edward's authority was also acknowledged in southern Scotland.

Edward the Martyr, St (c.963–78) King of England (975–78). He succeeded his father Edgar as king, but his accession was disputed by his stepbrother *Ethelred II, and while visiting him and his stepmother Alfrida at Corfe Castle in Dorset, Edward was murdered. Miracles were reported at his tomb at Shaftesbury and Ethelred had to pronounce the date of Edward's death (18 March) a solemn festival. He was canonized and became the focus of a considerable medieval cult.

Egbert (died 839) King of Wessex (802–39). In 825 he won a decisive victory near Swindon, bringing Mercian supremacy to an end, and annexed Kent, Essex, Surrey, and Sussex. In 829 Mercia itself fell to Egbert and Northumbria acknowledged his rule. By the time of his death, Mercia had become independent again, but his reign foreshadowed the supremacy that Wessex later secured over all England.

Egmont, Lamoral, Count of, Prince of Gavre (1522–68) Flemish statesman and soldier. He was made stadholder (governor) of Flanders and Artois in 1559. Although he was a member of *Philip II of Spain's regency council, he opposed his sovereign's policy of imposing Catholicism and Spanish government on the Netherlands, and helped to oust Cardinal Granvelle from his pre-eminent position in the government of the Netherlands (1564). In 1565 he withdrew from the council with *Horn, but during the first phase of the *Dutch Revolts he vacillated, and refused to join *William I (the Silent) in armed resistance. He was seized by *Alba in 1567, and beheaded on a charge of treason.

Egypt

Capital:	Cairo
Area:	1,001,450 sq km (386,662 sq miles)
Population:	95,294,388 (2012 est)
Currency:	1 Egyptian pound = 100 piastres
Religions:	Muslim 90.0%; Coptic 9.0%
Ethnic Groups:	Egyptian 99.6%
Languages:	Arabic (official)
International Organizations:	UN; AU; Arab League; OAPEC; Non-Aligned Movement; WTO

A country in the north-east corner of Africa, bounded by its Mediterranean and Red Sea coasts, Israel in the north-east, Sudan in the south, and Libya in the west.

Physical It is generally hot and arid—the south experiences some years with no rain at all—and civilization depends on the waters of the Nile, which are regulated by the Aswan Dam. To the west of the Nile valley is a desert of rock, sand, and gravel, with a few oases, and the great Qattara Depression. To the east is a range of hills with limestone and sandstone plateaux, and on the east bank of the Gulf of Suez is the Sinai desert. The fan-shaped Nile delta in the north, where the climate is wetter, is very fertile.

Economy Egypt's main exports are of crude oil, petroleum products, and cotton. Other agricultural products include rice, cereals, and fruit and vegetables; industries include textiles, food processing, and tourism. Foreign-exchange earnings from the Suez Canal, from Egyptians working abroad, and from tourism make an important contribution to the economy. The political instability since 2011 has slowed economic growth.

History Egypt is the site of one of the first civilizations, together with Mesopotamia, of the Old World. Agriculture and metallurgy were both introduced from western Asia and the great fertility of the Nile floodplain allowed the growth of a highly distinctive cultural tradition. Two kingdoms, one in the Delta (Lower Egypt) and one centred upstream round Thebes (Upper Egypt), were in existence during the 4th millennium BC. These were unified by the conquest of Lower Egypt some time shortly before 3000 BC, initiating the Protodynastic period. The shift of the capital to Memphis, near the head of the Delta, in the Old Kingdom (2700–2200 BC) perhaps indicates the importance of sea-borne trade with the Levant. The major pyramids were constructed here on the desert edge overlooking the river. A period of fragmentation (the first of two 'intermediate' periods) separated the Old from the Middle Kingdom (c.2050–1750), when some expansion into Palestine took place and the Nubian frontier was fortified. After a period of domination by foreign rulers (the *Hyksos), the New Kingdom (1550–1050) marked an age of imperial expansion when Egypt fought the Asiatic powers for control of Palestine. It was punctuated by the Amarna Period when *Akhenaten founded a new capital and religion. Egypt suffered from attacks of marauding *Sea Peoples in the 12th century BC, but maintained continuity of tradition into the Late Period (c.650–332). However, its independence came to an end with its successive incorporation into Assyrian, Persian, and Hellenistic empires. When the Romans took it, Egypt was virtually self-governing. It was a granary for Rome, and its capital, Alexandria, became the world's chief commercial centre, when the sea route to India was opened in about 106 AD.

Until 451 Alexandria had been the intellectual centre of the Christian Church. When the Arab armies reached Egypt in 639, they had little difficulty in taking the country. Under Arab rule taxes were lighter, administration remained in local hands, and there was little pressure for conversion to Islam. The new capital of Misr, now Old Cairo, was the military base for the Arab conquest of North Africa. In the 9th century the caliphate gradually weakened, and Ibn Tulun, a Turk, made it independent for a time. In 969 the *Fatimids seized the country and built a new capital named al-Qahira, Cairo. Local administration continued with little change, and the country's prosperity is reflected in the richness of Fatimid art and architecture. The Fatimid dynasty of Saladin came to power in 1171, followed by the *Mamelukes, foreign slave rulers under whom Egypt had the most prosperous period in her history (1250–1517). Then, with the rest of North Africa and the Middle East, Egypt fell to *Ottoman Turkey, although Mamelukes still maintained much local power. In 1798 Napoleon invaded Egypt in an attempt to restrict British trade with the east, but was driven out by the Turkish and British armies in 1801.

Egypt was restored to the Ottoman empire in 1802 but enjoyed almost total independence under the rule of pashas (descendants of Mehemet Ali) in Cairo. The construction of the Suez Canal in the 1860s made Egypt strategically important and in 1882 the British occupied the country in the wake of a nationalist revolt led by *Arabi Pasha. They ruled the country in all but name through the Agent and Consul-General Lord Cromer. Egypt became a British protectorate in 1914 and received nominal independence in 1922 when Britain established a constitutional monarchy, with Sultan Ahmed as

King Fuad I. Britain retained control of defence and imperial communications. In 1936 an Anglo-Egyptian treaty of alliance was signed, providing for a British garrison for 20 years, but for a gradual British withdrawal. This was interrupted by World War II. In 1948 Egyptian forces failed to defeat the emerging state of Israel and in 1952 King *Farouk was overthrown by a group of army officers, one of whom, Colonel *Nasser, emerged as the head of the new republic. Nasser's nationalization of the *Suez Canal in 1956 provoked abortive Anglo-French military intervention and in the same year he embarked on another unsuccessful war against Israel. Helped by Soviet military and economic aid, Nasser dominated the Arab world, although he suffered another heavy defeat at Israeli hands in the *Six-Day War of 1967. His successor, Anwar *Sadat, continued his confrontationalist policies, but after defeat in the *Yom Kippur War of 1973, he turned his back on the Soviet alliance, sought an accommodation with Israel, and strengthened his contacts with the West. This change of policy damaged Egypt's standing in the Arab world and in 1981 Sadat was assassinated by Islamic fundamentalists. His successor, President *Mubarak, has followed a policy of moderation and reconciliation. Egypt was formally re-admitted to the Arab League in 1989. In 1991 Egypt sent troops to support the US-led alliance in the *Gulf War and in return had its debts to the USA reduced. During the 1990s militant Islamic fundamentalists grew increasingly violent. In 2005 Mubarak was re-elected for a fifth term in Egypt's first multi-candidate presidential election. However, in 2011 huge popular protests against repression, corruption, and poverty—part of the *Arab Spring—led to Mubarak's resignation. A military government liberalized the constitution, but preserved its own position as the power behind the state. In 2012 Mohammed Morsi, the Muslim Brotherhood candidate, was elected President. However his pro-Islamist rule polarized the country and he was deposed in 2013 following more popular protests; military rule was restored. A new constitution was approved in 2014 and the military leader Abdel-Fattah el-Sisi was elected President.

Egyptian and Mesopotamian technology Technology of the early civilizations in Egypt and in Mesopotamia, both of which arose in about 3000 BC. The early civilizations of Mesopotamia included the Sumerian, Assyrian, and Babylonian empires. These two areas provide the earliest known examples of many basic technologies—pottery and glass-making, the extraction and working of metals, textiles, woodworking, and building techniques—which were firmly established long before the Christian era. Both had highly developed agricultural systems in which strictly controlled irrigation played a critical role. They were skilled at astronomical observation and computation and devised intricate *calendars, important for observing the annual cycle of sowing, growth, and harvesting. Systems of pictographic writing were developed in both areas, and standardized weights and measures were introduced. Both civilizations had highly organized urban communities and established trading relationships with distant countries, facilitated by the development of shipbuilding and of road systems.

Eichmann, Adolf (Karl Adolf Eichmann) (1906–62) German administrator. He was responsible for carrying out Hitler's final solution and for administering the concentration camps, in which 6 million Jews perished. After the war he went into hiding in Argentina, but in 1960 he was traced by Israeli agents, abducted, tried, and subsequently executed.

Eighteen-Twelve, War of *See* WAR OF 1812.

Einstein, Albert (1879–1955) German-born US theoretical physicist, founder of the theory of relativity, often regarded as the greatest scientist of the 20th century. In 1905 he published three outstanding papers dealing with the photoelectric effect, Brownian motion, and his special theory of relativity. Relativity abandons the idea of absolute space and time as a reference framework for all bodies; instead a distinction is made between the framework of the observer and that of the object. Among the theory's most important conclusions is that mass and energy are interconvertible, expressed by the equation $e = mc^2$ (c being the speed of light). In 1915 Einstein published the general theory of relativity. This extended his ideas to gravitation, which he treated as a curvature of the space–time continuum. The general theory was vindicated when the predicted deflection of light rays passing through a substantial gravitational field was confirmed by observations during the solar eclipse of 1919. As a Jew, Einstein decided to live in the USA when Hitler came to power in 1933. For the remainder of his life he sought without success a unified field theory embracing electromagnetism, gravitation, and quantum mechanics. In 1939 he wrote to President Roosevelt about the military potential of nuclear energy, greatly influencing the decision to build an atom bomb. After the war he spoke out passionately against nuclear weapons.

Eisenhower, Dwight David (known as **'Ike'**) (1890–1969) US general and Republican statesman, 34th President of the USA (1953–61). In World War II he was Commander-in-Chief of Allied forces in North Africa and Italy (1942–43) and Supreme Commander of Allied Expeditionary Forces in western Europe (1943–45). As President, he adopted a hard line towards Communism both in his domestic and foreign policy; in the USA an extreme version of this was reflected in McCarthyism.

Eisenhower Doctrine A statement of US foreign policy issued by President *Eisenhower after the *Suez War and approved by Congress in 1957. It proposed to offer economic aid and military advice to governments in the Middle East who felt their independence threatened and led to the USA sending 10,000 troops to Lebanon (1958) when its government, fearing a Muslim revolution, asked for assistance. Britain had also sent troops (1957) to protect Jordan, and despite Soviet protests US and British forces remained in the Middle East for some months. The Doctrine, whose assumption that Arab nationalism was Soviet-inspired came to be seen as fallacious, lapsed with the death (1959) of the US Secretary of State, John *Dulles.

El Alamein *See* ALAMEIN, EL, BATTLE OF.

ELAS A communist-dominated guerrilla army in Greece. The initials stand for the Greek words meaning National People's Liberation Army. It was created during World War II by the communist-controlled National Liberation Front (EAM) to fight against German occupation forces. By the time of the German defeat and withdrawal (1944–45) EAM/ELAS controlled much of Greece and opposed the restoration of the monarchy, aiming to replace it with a communist regime. A bitter civil war broke out (1946–49), which prompted US promise of support in the *Truman Doctrine (1947). Stalin's unwillingness to support the Greek communists contributed to their defeat.

El Cid (Campeador) (*c.*1040–99) (Arabic *al-Said*, 'the lord' and Spanish *campeador*, 'champion') Spanish hero. He was Rodrigo Díaz de Bivar, a Castilian nobleman, who was exiled after the war between the brothers Sancho II of Castile and Alfonso VI of León, becoming a mercenary captain fighting mainly for the *Moors. He captured Valencia on his own behalf but was expelled in 1099, dying shortly afterwards. Many of the legends concerning him bear little relation to historical facts.

Elders, The A group of former global states-men and stateswomen who use their experience to work for peace and human rights. Brought together by Nelson *Mandela in 2007, members include Kofi *Annan, Gro Harlem *Brundtland, Jimmy *Carter, Mary *Robinson, and Desmond *Tutu.

El Dorado A fictitious country (according to some, a city) abounding in gold, believed by the Spanish and by Sir Walter Raleigh to exist upon the Amazon. The origin of the belief, which led Spanish conquistadors to converge on the area in search of treasure, appears to have been rumours of an Indian ruler, in what is now Colombia, who ritually coated his body with gold dust and then plunged into a sacred lake while his subjects threw in gold and jewels.

Eleanor of Aquitaine (c.1122–1204) Daughter of the Duke of Aquitaine, queen of France (1137–52) and of England (1154–89). She was married to Louis VII of France from 1137; in 1152, with the annulment of their marriage, she married the future Henry II of England. Her ten children included the monarchs *Richard I (the Lionheart) and *John, whose accession she strove to secure. She acted as regent (1190–94) while Richard was away on the Crusades.

Eleanor of Castile (c.1244–90) Queen of England (1272–90). She was the daughter of Ferdinand III of Castile in Spain and married *Edward I of England in 1254. Eleanor bore 13 children and accompanied her husband on Crusade (1270–73). After her death at Harby in Nottinghamshire, her body was embalmed and taken to Westminster Abbey. At each of the ten overnight stopping places Edward ordered a stone cross to be erected to her memory, the 'Eleanor crosses'.

Elector A prince of the *Holy Roman Empire who had the right to elect the emperor. Although the monarchy was elective by the 12th century, it was not until the contested election of 1257 that the number of Electors was fixed at seven. The office of Elector disappeared when Napoleon abolished the empire in 1806.

Electoral College A group of people chosen to elect a candidate to an office. Probably the oldest College is that which meets in Rome to elect a new pope, consisting of the cardinals of the Church. The idea was adapted by the framers of the American Constitution in 1787, each state appointing as many electors as it had members of Congress, these electors then meeting to choose the President of the USA. As

states extended their franchise these electors came to be chosen by direct election. With the emergence of organized political parties, the holding of a national party convention to select presidential candidates developed. Candidates in each state are all now chosen beforehand by party associations and their vote is decided by their party's convention. Thus, for each state (except Maine since 1972 and Nebraska since 1996), following a presidential election, the candidate who has won a majority of the popular vote in that state will gain all that state's electoral votes. In the event of a tied election the President is chosen by a vote in the House of Representatives.

Elgin, James Bruce, Earl of (1811–63) British statesman and colonial administrator. As governor-general of British North America (1847–54) he was given the task of carrying out the recommendations made by the Durham Report. In 1848 he implemented "responsible" government with the formation of the Baldwin-La Fontaine ministry to be responsible to the elected legislative assembly. He introduced measures to improve education in Canada and to stabilize the economy, which was depressed by the new British policy of *free trade. After leaving Canada, he jointly led an Anglo-French force that marched into Beijing in 1860 to secure ratification of the Treaty of Tianjin. In 1862 he was appointed viceroy of India, dying in office a year later.

Elgin, Thomas Bruce, 7th Earl of (1766–1841) British diplomat and art connoisseur. When envoy at Constantinople (1799–1803) he feared the destruction of Greek antiquities in the conflict between Turks and Greeks and ob-tained permission from the Turks to remove them. Between 1803 and 1812 he transported a number of sculptures to England, many from the Parthenon in Athens (which was under Turkish control). The British government vin-dicated Elgin's actions and purchased the 'Elgin Marbles' from him in 1816 for £35,000 to exhibit them in the British Museum, where they can still be seen, in spite of Greek claims for their return.

Elizabeth I (1533–1603) Daughter of Henry VIII, queen of England and Ireland (1558–1603). Succeeding her Catholic sister Mary I, Elizabeth re-established a moderate form of Protestant-ism as the religion of the state. None the less, her reign was dominated by the threat of a Catholic restoration (eventually leading to the execution of Mary, Queen of Scots) and by war with Spain, during which the country was saved from invasion by the defeat of the Armada in 1588. Her reign was characterized by a flowering of national culture, particularly in the field of literature, in which Shakespeare, Marlowe, and Spenser were all active. Although frequently courted, she never married.

Elizabeth II (born **Princess Elizabeth Alexandra Mary**) (1926–) Daughter of George VI, queen of the United Kingdom since 1952. She has always shown a strong personal commitment to the Commonwealth, and is one of the most travelled present-day monarchs, having made extensive overseas tours and many public appearances at home.

Elizabeth Petrovna (1709–62) Empress of Russia (1741–62). She was the unmarried daughter of *Peter I (the Great), a beautiful and extravagant woman who seized the throne from the infant Ivan VI. She was more interested in social life and the arts than in affairs of state and government was conducted mainly by her ministers. Russia increased its hold on Poland in the War of the Polish Succession and the *Seven Years War. On her death Peter III immediately changed sides, thus making *Frederick II's ultimate victory possible.

El Salvador

Capital:	San Salvador
Area:	21,041 sq km (8,124 sq miles)
Population:	6,108,590 (2013 est)
Currency:	1 US dollar = 100 cents
Religions:	Roman Catholic 57.1%; Protestant 21.2%
Ethnic Groups:	Mestizo 86.3%; White 12.7%; Amerindian 1.0%
Languages:	Spanish (official), Nahua
International Organizations:	UN; OAS; WTO

The smallest Central American country, situated on the Pacific coast. Only some 80 km (50 miles) wide, it is bounded on three sides by Guatemala, Honduras, and Nicaragua and has a 258-km (160-mile) southward-facing coastline.

Physical It comprises a hot, very wet coastal plain with wooded inland slopes, above which rise volcanic mountains with cratered lakes; as the country is at a junction of two crustal plates, earthquakes occasionally occur.

Economy Products assembled from imported parts, coffee, and sugar are the principal exports. Other industries include food processing, oil, and chemicals. Tourism, financial services, and remittances from expatriates are important.

History After it was conquered by Pedro de Alvarado, a lieutenant of Hernan *Cortés, El Salvador formed part of the viceroyalty of New Spain, but was subject to the jurisdiction of the captain-general sitting in Guatemala City.

The country gained independence from Spain in 1821, joined (1824) the United Provinces of Central America, and with the break-up of that entity in 1838, became an independent republic (1839). Internal struggles between liberals and conservatives and a series of border clashes with neighbours retarded development in the 19th century. By the early 20th century the conservatives had gained ascendancy and the presidency remained within a handful of élite families as if it were their personal patrimony. El Salvador's 20th-century history has been dominated by a series of military presidents. While some of them, such as Oscar Osorio (1950–56) and José M. Lemus (1956–60), appeared mildly sympathetic to badly needed social reform, they were held in check by their more conservative military colleagues in concert with the civilian oligarchy. Fidel *Castro's Cuban revolution and leftist guerrilla activity in other Central American countries pushed the Salvadoran army steadily to the right. Repressive measures and violations of human rights by the army during the 1970s and 1980s were documented by a number of international agencies, and posed a large refugee problem. Under President Felix Cristiani (elected 1989) negotiations began with the extreme left-wing guerrilla group Frente Farabundo Marti de Liberación (FMLN), and a peace agreement was reached in 1992. The FMLN was recognized as a political party and took part in the 1994 elections. The Alianza Republicana Nacionalista (ARENA), under President Armando Calderón Sol, won the majority of seats and held power for the next 15 years. In 1995 the government announced plans for economic reform. El Salvador was devastated by hurricanes in 1998 and 1999, and then by two earthquakes in 2001. The 2009 elections were won by the FMLN and Mauricio Funes was elected President.

emancipists Ex-convicts in early 19th-century Australia. In a narrow sense, the term referred only to those convicts who had been pardoned, conditionally or absolutely, by the governor. In a broader sense, it was applied to all ex-convicts who, having served their term of imprisonment or enforced servitude, had become free, and in some cases, wealthy. There was much conflict between emancipists and *exclusionists in New South Wales, Australia, especially during *Macquarie's governorship (1810–21). The term was also applied to members of a political group, consisting of emancipists and liberals, which campaigned for reforms during the 1820s, 1830s, and early 1840s. William Wentworth was the acknowledged leader of this political group for many years. In 1835, it founded the Australian Patriotic Association.

Emin Pasha (or **Mehmed Eduard Schnitzer**) (1840–92) German explorer and physician. He joined the Ottoman army in 1865, and in 1876 he served under General *Gordon in Khartoum. Gordon used him for administrative duties and diplomatic missions and in 1878 appointed him governor of the Upper Nile area of Equatoria, where he surveyed the region and suppressed slavery. Isolated when the *Mahdi controlled the Sudan, he was rescued in 1888 by H. M. *Stanley. In 1890 he was employed by the German government in East Africa. While engaged in exploration for Germany, Arab slave-raiders murdered him.

emirate A Muslim territory ruled by an emir (Arabic *amir*, 'lord' or 'prince'), often uniting civil and military authority. Depending on the strength of the caliphate, an emir might be either a diligent subordinate, subject to supervision and removal, as under the early *Abbasids, or a virtually independent princeling, able to defy his nominal master.

Emirates, Fulani *See* FULANI EMPIRE OF SOKOTO.

Emmet, Robert (1778–1803) Irish nationalist. Involved in the United Irishmen movement, during 1800–02 he visited France in an attempt to win support for Irish independence. Returning to Ireland in 1803 with a small band of followers, he began an insurrection in Dublin against British rule, which ended in disaster. Emmet escaped but was subsequently captured and executed. Gallant and reckless, he was to become a potent symbol in the cause of Irish nationalism.

Ems telegram (13 July 1870) A dispatch from the Prussian king *William I to his chancellor, *Bismarck, that precipitated the outbreak of the *Franco-Prussian War. A relative of the Prussian king, Prince Leopold of Hohenzollern-Sigmaringen, had accepted an offer to the Spanish throne. This alarmed the French, who feared Prussian influence south of the Pyrenees. Leopold withdrew his claim a few days later, but the French ambassador approached William at the German spa town of Ems, asking for an assurance that Leopold's candidacy would never be renewed. The king refused, politely but firmly, and he sent his chancellor a telegram to the effect that the crisis had passed. Bismarck, intent on provoking war with France, published a shortened version which turned the refusal into an insult. French public opinion was outraged and Napoleon III declared the Franco-Prussian War, whose consequences were to include the downfall of the French Second Empire and the creation of the *German Second empire.

Enabling Law The law passed in Germany in 1933 that granted Adolf *Hitler dictatorial powers.

enclosure An area of land formed as the result of enclosing (with fences, ditches, and hedges) what had usually been *common land so as to make it private property. In Tudor times enclosure was popularly seen as the conversion of the peasants' tilled land to grass on which a landowner's sheep would graze: the sheep were eating men, it was said, because the villagers were losing both their employment and their tillage. Enclosures became a national issue, but although they were denounced by the church (especially by Cardinal *Wolsey and Thomas *More) and were penalized by statutes and royal proclamations, and even provoked Kett's Rebellion (1549), their financial advantages were so strong that they continued to be carried out.

In the second half of the 18th century enclosure by private Act of Parliament increased dramatically, and the General Enclosure Act of 1801 standardized the procedure. Enclosures were less unpopular in the 18th century, as they enabled farmers to introduce improvements in crops and breeding without reference to their neighbours.

Encyclopédistes The '*philosophes*' and others who contributed to and otherwise supported the *Encyclopédie*, published in France in 35 volumes between 1751 and 1780, one of the great literary achievements of the 18th century. It was a complete review of the arts and sciences of the day, explaining the new physics and cosmology and proclaiming a new philosophy of humanism. It was edited by Denis Diderot (1713–84) and Jean le Rond d'Alembert (1717–83) with important articles contributed by

Voltaire (1694–1778), *Montesquieu, *Rousseau, and George Buffon (1707–88). A decree of 1752 suppressed the first volumes and in 1759 it was placed on the Index (of books forbidden to Roman Catholics), but it continued to circulate. The critical attitudes fostered by the *Encyclopédie* are believed to have contributed to the *French Revolution.

Engels, Friedrich (1820–95) German socialist and political philosopher, resident chiefly in England from 1842. The founder of modern communism with Karl Marx, he collaborated with him in the writing of the *Communist Manifesto* (1848). Engels also completed the second and third volumes of Marx's *Das Kapital* (1885; 1894). Engels's own writings include *The Condition of the Working Classes in England in 1844* (1845).

England The largest division of the United Kingdom. There were settlements in England from at least palaeolithic times, and considerable remains exist of neolithic and Bronze Age cultures. These were followed by the arrival of the Celtic peoples whose civilization spread over the whole country. The Romans under Julius Caesar raided the south of Britain in 55 and 54 BC, but full-scale invasion did not take place until a century later; the country was then administered as a Roman province until the Teutonic conquest of Gaul in the early 5th century and the subsequent withdrawal of the last Roman garrison. In the 3rd to 7th centuries Germanic-speaking tribes, traditionally known as Angles, Saxons, and Jutes, raided and then settled, establishing independent kingdoms, and when that of Wessex became dominant in the 9th century England emerged as a distinct political entity before being conquered by William, Duke of Normandy, in 1066. The neighbouring principality of Wales was gradually conquered during the Middle Ages and politically incorporated in the 16th century. During the period of Tudor rule (1485–1603) England emerged as a Protestant state with a strong stable monarchy and as a naval power. Scotland and England have been ruled by one monarch from 1603, and the two parliaments were formally united in 1707. In 1999 a separate Scottish parliament was established, with tax-raising powers and control over local affairs; however, Scottish MPs in the union parliament retained the right to vote on internal English affairs.

English Civil War (1642–49) The armed struggle between the supporters of the king (*Cavaliers) and Parliamentarians (*Roundheads), which erupted in 1642 and continued,

with an interruption, until 1648. It arose from constitutional, religious, and economic differences between *Charles I and the Members of the *Long Parliament. Of these the most decisive factor was religion, since the attempts of *Laud to impose liturgical uniformity had alienated substantial numbers of clergy, gentry, and craftsmen. All sections of society were affected, though many in the localities desired peace not war, and sometimes families were divided by conflicting allegiances.

The king's primary objective in 1642 was the capture of London, a Parliamentary stronghold. After an indecisive engagement at *Edgehill, he eventually had to take refuge in Oxford, which became his wartime capital. His plan in 1643 to bring together Cavalier armies from Oxford, Newcastle, and the south-west, followed by a march on London, was not realized. Meanwhile the balance was tipping toward the Roundheads, for by the *Solemn League and Covenant they secured Scottish assistance, of value in 1644 at *Marston Moor. Charles's attempt to march on London (1644) was frustrated at the battle of Newbury. With the formation of the *New Model Army, the Roundheads were able to inflict a crushing defeat on the Cavaliers at *Naseby (1645). Charles, having rejected terms previously offered him at the Uxbridge negotiations, eventually surrendered to the Scots near Newark (1646) after Oxford had fallen.

Charles's subsequent attempts to profit from divisions between the Parliamentary factions prevented a settlement from being reached in 1647. His escape to the Isle of Wight and 'Engagement' with the Scots sparked off the second phase of the war (1648). This consisted of unsuccessful Cavalier risings in Wales, Essex, and Kent, and a Scottish invasion which came to grief at *Preston. *Pride's Purge of Parliament then cleared the way for the trial and execution of the king and the establishment of the English *Commonwealth.

Enlightenment (or **Age of Reason**) The philosophical, scientific, and rational attitudes, the freedom from superstition, and the belief in religious tolerance of much of 18th-century Europe. In Germany the *Aufklärung* ('Enlightenment'), which extended from the middle of the 17th century to the beginning of the 19th century, was a literary and philosophical movement that included Gotthold Lessing (1729–81), J. W. von Goethe (1749–1823), and Friedrich Schiller (1759–1805), as well as Immanuel Kant (1724–1804). The Yiddish literature of Eastern Europe experienced a new dynamism, while a similarly invigorating freedom of ideas affected writers as far apart as Sweden, Russia, and Britain. In France the Enlightenment was associated with the *philosophes*, the literary men, scientists, and thinkers who were united in their belief in the supremacy of reason and their desire to see practical change to combat inequality and injustice. The movement against established beliefs and institutions gained momentum throughout the 18th century under Voltaire (1694–1778), *Rousseau, *Condorcet, and others. Through the publication of the *Encyclopédie* (1751–76) their attacks on the government, the church, and the judiciary provided the intellectual basis for the French Revolution.

The English Enlightenment owed its origin both to the political theories of John *Locke, and to the French example. Thomas *Paine, an admirer of the French, advocated American independence, and many writers and poets transmitted Enlightenment ideas. In Scotland an intellectual movement flourished in Edinburgh between 1750 and 1800; its outstanding philosophers were Hume and Adam Smith and important scientific advances were made in chemistry, geology and medicine. The *Encyclopaedia Britannica*, began in 1768–71 as a dictionary of the arts and sciences, was issued by a 'Society of gentlemen in Scotland'. In literature, some have seen a connection between the philosophy of the Enlightenment, the growth of literary realism, and the rise of the novel. It influenced the Romantic movement in the arts by releasing the more individualist attitudes in which this movement was based, and as the Romantics themselves reacted against the coldly scientific intellectualism which the Enlightenment represented.

enosis *See* EOKA.

Entebbe raid (July 3–4, 1976) The rescue of 103 hostages on a French aeroplane by an Israeli commando squad. The flight from Israel to France had been hijacked by Palestinian terrorists on June 27 and forced to land at Entebbe, Uganda. The hijackers freed 258 non-Israeli passengers but held the rest, demanding the release of 53 imprisoned terrorists. The squad of Israeli soldiers rescued most of the hostages within an hour of arriving in Entebbe and only three hostages, one soldier, and seven terrorists were killed. The success of the raid won Israel international acclaim.

entente cordiale (1904) Friendly understanding between Britain and France. It aimed to settle territorial disputes and to encourage cooperation against perceived German pressure. Britain was to be given a free hand in Egyptian affairs and France in Morocco. Germany, concerned over this *entente*, tested its strength by provoking a crisis in Morocco in 1905, leading to the Algeciras Conference (1906). The *entente* was extended in 1907 to include Russia and culminated in the formal alliance of Britain, France, and Russia in World War I against the Central Powers and the Ottoman empire.

Enver Pasha (1881–1922) Turkish political and military leader. A leader of the Young Turks in the revolution of 1908, he came to power as part of a ruling triumvirate following a coup d'état in 1913. He played a significant role in creating Turkey's alliance with Germany during World War I, and served as Minister of War (1914–18).

EOKA (National Organization of Cypriot Fighters) The militant wing of the **enosis** (Greek, 'union') movement in Cyprus. Colonel Georgios Grivas (1898–1974), commander of the Greek Cypriot national guard, was its most famous leader. During 1954 to 1959 guerrilla warfare and terrorist attacks were waged against the British forces. In 1956 *Makarios was exiled on the charge of being implicated with EOKA. After independence in 1960 the organization was revived as EOKA-B. Renewed demands for enosis in 1970 almost achieved success in 1974. In response Turkey invaded and partitioned the island to protect the Turkish minority.

Epicurus (341–270 BC) Greek philosopher. His physics (later expounded by the Roman writer Lucretius) is based on the theory of a materialist Universe, unregulated by divine providence, composed of indestructible atoms moving in a void. From this philosophy of Epicureanism, a restrained type of hedonism: mental pleasure was regarded more highly than physical and the ultimate pleasure was held to be freedom from anxiety and mental pain, especially that arising from needless fear of death and of gods.

Equatorial Guinea

Capital:	Malabo
Area:	28,051 sq km (10,831 sq miles)
Population:	704,001 (2013 est)
Currency:	1 CFA franc = 100 centimes
Religions:	Roman Catholic 87.0%; other Christian 6.0%; traditional beliefs 5.0%

Ethnic Groups:	Fang 85.7%; Bubi 6.5%; Mdowe 3.6%
Languages:	Spanish, French (both official); Fang, Bubi, and local languages
International Organizations:	UN; AU; Non-Aligned Movement; Franc Zone

A small country in equatorial West Africa on the Gulf of Guinea.

Physical Equatorial Guinea includes the plateau of Río Muni bounded by Cameroon and Gabon, and the more mountainous and fertile, but smaller, island of Bioko (Fernando Póo).

Economy The exploitation of offshore oil generated rapid economic growth in the early 2000s, and Equatorial Guinea's economy now relies on oil production and export. Subsistence farming is the main occupation, but the agricultural sector has been neglected. There are deposits of gold, iron ore, copper, manganese, uranium, silica, and titanium.

History Formerly a Spanish colony, it was a haunt of slave-traders and merchants. The mainland was not effectively occupied by Spain until 1926. Declared independent in 1968, a reign of terror followed until President Macias Nguema was overthrown and executed (1979) by his nephew, Obiang Nguema. The new regime pursued less repressive domestic policies with some degree of success. A referendum in November 1991 appeared to give overwhelming approval for multiparty politics, and in January 1992 an amnesty was granted by President Nguema to returning exiles; but in February a number of opposition leaders were arrested and some later died in prison. Multiparty elections were planned, but opposition parties claimed they were not allowed to campaign freely. Few people voted in the 1993 elections, which were reported as being unfair by international observers. Nguema's ruling party officially won and remained in power, as it has done in subsequent elections. In 1995 the UN reiterated its concern about serious violations of human rights in the country.

Erasmus, Desiderius (born **Gerhard Gerhards**) (c.1469–1536) Dutch humanist and scholar. During his lifetime he was the most famous scholar in Europe and the first to

achieve renown through the printed word. He published his own Greek edition of the New Testament (1516), followed by a Latin translation, and paved the way for the Reformation with his satires on the Church, including the *Colloquia Familiaria* (1518). However, he opposed the violence of the Protestant Reformation and condemned Luther in *De Libero Arbitrio* (1523).

Erastus (born **Thomas Lieber**, or **Liebler** or **Lüber**) (1524–83) Swiss theologian and physician. He was professor of medicine at Heidelberg University from 1558. A follower of Zwingli, he opposed the imposition of a Calvinistic system of church government in Heidelberg because of the Calvinists' excessive use of excommunication. The doctrine of Erastianism (that the state should have supremacy over the Church in ecclesiastical matters) was later attributed to him, although his views were less extreme.

Erhard, Ludwig (1897–1977) German economist and statesman, Chancellor of the German Federal Republic (1963–66). A Christian Democrat, he was Minister for Economic Affairs from 1949 to 1963, during which time he assisted in his country's "economic miracle" (German, *Wirtschaftswunder*), which trebled the gross national product in the post-war years.

Eric the Red (c.940–c.1010) Norse explorer. Exiled from Iceland for manslaughter in 982, he sailed in search of land to the west, exploring Greenland and establishing a Norse settlement there in 986.

Eritrea

Capital:	Asmara
Area:	117,600 sq km (45,406 sq miles)
Population:	6,233,682 (2013 est)
Currency:	1 nafka = 100 cents
Religions:	Muslim 50.0%; Eritrean Orthodox 24.0%; Roman Catholic 10.0%; other Christian 6.0%
Ethnic Groups:	Tigrinya 55.0%; Tigré 30.0%; Saho 4.0%
Languages:	Arabic, English, Tigrinya (all official); Tigré; minority languages
International Organizations:	UN; AU; Non-Aligned Movement

Ermine Street

A country in north-eastern Africa, on the Red Sea.

Physical Eritrea consists of a narrow coastal low-lying area and rises towards the Ethiopian plateau in the south. It is very hot and arid.

Economy The economy has been badly affected by the war of independence and subsequent conflicts with Ethiopia and Djibouti. Agricultural products include sorghum, lentils, and vegetables, and there are food-processing, textile, and clothing industries. Subsistence agriculture is the main economic activity. Remittances from expatriates are important.

History In 1869 Italy purchased the coastal town of Assab, and in 1885 began the occupation of the rest of Eritrea, which it declared a colony in 1889. It was from here that the Italians launched their disastrous campaign against *Ethiopia in 1896, ending in their defeat at *Adowa. Under British military administration (1941–52), a plan to join the Muslim west with the Sudan and the Christian centre with Ethiopia failed. Instead, the United Nations voted to make Eritrea a federal area subject to Ethiopia. In 1962 Emperor *Haile Selassie declared it a province of Ethiopia and the Eritrean People's Liberation Front (EPLF) then emerged, seeking secession. Fierce fighting between the EPLF and the Ethiopian regime continued through the 1980s. In February 1990 the EPLF captured Massawa, and in 1991, in an alliance with other Ethiopian rebel groups, the EPLF defeated the Ethiopian government's forces. A transitional Eritrean government was set up by the EPLF and a referendum was held in 1993. Independence was approved by the referendum and was achieved later that year. An intermittent border war was fought with Ethiopia between 1998 and 2000, and another with Djibouti in 2008.

Ermine Street 1. The Roman road between London and Lincoln via Huntingdon.

2. The Roman road connecting Silchester with Gloucester.

escutage *See* SCUTAGE.

Essex, Robert Devereux, 2nd Earl of
(1566–1601) English courtier, favourite of *Elizabeth I. He distinguished himself as a soldier during the *Dutch Revolt (1586), but earned the queen's displeasure by participating in the disastrous Lisbon expedition (1589) and by marrying Sir Philip Sidney's widow (1590). The love-hate relationship between queen and courtier continued throughout the 1590s. He commanded an English contingent during the *French Wars of Religion (1591–92) and shared in the capture of Cadiz (1596). Gradually, his rivalry with the *Cecil faction grew. In 1599 Elizabeth sent him as Lord Lieutenant of Ireland to put down *Tyrone's rebellion. He failed ignominiously and was stripped of his offices. His subsequent attempt to raise the London people in an anti-Cecil coup (1601) led to his trial and execution for treason.

Essex, Robert Devereux, 3rd Earl of
(1591–1646) English soldier, commander of the *Roundheads. Although he served *Charles I in 1625 he opposed him at the outbreak of the *English Civil War and in 1642 was appointed commander of the Roundhead forces, leading them at the Battle of *Edgehill. After a number of Roundhead defeats, the *New Model Army was organized in 1645 and Essex resigned his command.

Estates-General *See* STATES-GENERAL.

Estonia

Capital:	Tallinn
Area:	45,228 sq km (17,463 sq miles)
Population:	1,266,375 (2012 est)
Currency:	1 euro = 100 cents
Religions:	Eastern Orthodox 16.2%; Lutheran 9.9%; other Christian 2.2%
Ethnic Groups:	Estonian 68.7%; Russian 24.8%; Ukrainian 1.7%
Languages:	Estonian (official); Russian
International Organizations:	UN; OSCE; EU; NATO; Council of Europe; WTO; OECD

A country in the north of Europe, bounded on the north by the Gulf of Finland, on the east by Russia, on the south by Latvia, and on the west by the Baltic Sea.

Physical Two large islands and numerous small ones lie off the coast, which is occasionally ice-bound in winter although the summers are warm. The mainland comprises a limestone plateau in the north, and a low-lying plain on which are situated forests and lakes of glacial origin.

Economy Estonia has developed a successful market economy since the collapse of the Soviet Union. Its principal exports are machinery and electrical equipment, wood and wood products, metals, and furniture. It also has a significant information technology industry. The agricultural sector is small, its main products being grain, potatoes, and vegetables.

History Annexed by Russia in 1709, Estonia regained its independence in 1918, at the time of the Bolshevik revolution. Its history during the 1920s was of an agrarian revolution, whereby the great estates of the Baltic barons (mostly German) were broken up, creating a prosperous peasantry. An attempted communist uprising in 1924 was suppressed. Its economy was adversely affected by the Great Depression and from 1934 until 1939 it experienced a highly autocratic regime led by Konstantin Paets. His attempt to make a pact with Hitler was invalidated by the Nazi-Soviet Pact of August 1939. In September Soviet troops occupied key ports and in 1940 the whole country. It welcomed German troops in 1941, but its anti-Bolshevik Resistance forces could not prevent the Red Army from reoccupying it in 1944. It became a constituent republic of the Soviet Union. In February 1990 there were mass rallies in the capital Tallinn demanding independence, and in May its Supreme Soviet reinstated the constitution of 1920. Talks began with the Soviet Union, which recognized the Republic's independence in September 1991. The collapse of its markets in Russia during 1991 resulted in an economic crisis, with food and fuel rationing in January 1992, eased by trade agreements with the European Community and by IMF support. In 1992 a new constitution was adopted and Lennart Meri (1929–2006) was elected President. Russian residents were disturbed by a proposed law that would have denied them Estonian citizenship. The law was amended (1993) before it was passed, making citizenship available to residents who passed Estonian language tests. Two mainly Russian cities voted for autonomy (1993) but the government declared their referendums illegal. In 1994 the last Russian troops withdrew from Estonia. Estonia joined NATO and the *European Union in 2004; it adopted the euro as its currency in 2011.

Etaples, Treaty of (9 November 1492) A truce concluded between Charles VIII of France and Henry VII of England. The latter had revived claims from the *Hundred Years War and raised an army, but little fighting took place following an invasion and Henry was

bought off in return for a sum of 745,000 gold crowns paid in annual instalments. Charles was left free to proceed with his planned invasion of Italy.

Ethelred I (died 871) King of Wessex (866–71). His rule coincided with unremitting Danish raids that assumed the scale of an invasion. Assisted by his younger brother, *Alfred, Ethelred had some success against those Danes advancing into neighbouring Mercia (868), and into Wessex itself (870). However, three major battles, including a defeat near the Danish base at Reading and a notable victory at Ashdown, and numerous skirmishes, failed to give any advantage to Ethelred who died of wounds received in the Battle at Merton.

Ethelred II (the Unready) (c.968–1016) King of England (978–1016). He succeeded his stepbrother *Edward the Martyr, who had been murdered on instructions from Ethelred's mother Alfrida. This inauspicious beginning to the reign was compounded by further blunders which earned Ethelred the title "unready", meaning "devoid of counsel". Encouraged by his misfortunes the Danes renewed their invasions. Ethelred bought them off on five occasions (991, 994, 1002, 1007, 1012) with *Danegeld. His attempt (1002) to massacre all the Danes in his kingdom was answered (1013) by the invasion of the King of Denmark, *Sweyn I, who ruled England until his death (1014) when Ethelred was restored.

Ethiopia

Capital:	Addis Ababa
Area:	1,104,300 sq km (426,373 sq miles)
Population:	93,877,025 (2013 est)
Currency:	1 Ethiopian birr = 100 cents
Religions:	Ethiopian Orthodox 43.5%; Muslim 33.9%; Protestant 18.6%
Ethnic Groups:	Oromo 34.5%; Amhara 26.9%; Somali 6.2%; Tigray 6.1%; minority groups
Languages:	Amharic, English, Arabic (all official); Oromo; local languages
International Organizations:	UN; AU; Non-Aligned Movement

A country, formerly known as Abyssinia, in north-eastern Africa. Sudan is on its western border, Eritrea on its northern border, and Kenya on its southern, while Somalia reaches round it on the east.

Physical The low-lying Ogaden region in the east is very hot and arid; but the entire centre of the country is a group of volcanic mountain ranges with high plateaux where the air is mild and there is moderate summer rain. The Great Rift Valley runs through these, and the whole area is cut about with ravines and fertile valleys. In the north-west lies Lake Tana, the source of the Blue Nile, while in the south-west forests rise along the slopes of the mountain ranges.

Economy The Ethiopian economy was centrally planned and based on collectivized agriculture until 1991. Subsistence agriculture remains the mainstay of the economy, with all land owned by the state and long-term leases being granted to tenant farmers. Crops include cereals, pulses, and coffee, the major export. Other exports include khat, gold, and leather products. The principal industries are food processing, beverages, textiles, and leather.

History By the 2nd century AD the kingdom of *Aksum had a brisk trade with Egypt, Syria, Arabia, and India in gold, ivory, and incense, and minted a gold currency. In the 4th century the court became Christian. Aksum collapsed c.1000, and, after a time of confusion, the Zagwe dynasty emerged. In 1270 it was replaced by the Solomonic dynasty claiming lineal descent from Solomon and the Queen of Sheba, bringing the Amharas from the mountains of central Ethiopia to prominence. This may have been known to Europeans in the Middle Ages as the legendary kingdom of *Prester John. In the 16th century the Muslims of the lowlands attacked the Christian highlands, but were repulsed in 1542 with Portuguese artillery. When Jesuit missionaries came to Ethiopia Emperor Susenyos was converted to Roman Catholicism (1626). His son Fasilidas (1632–67), having forced him to abdicate, made Gondar the capital. Surrounded by Islam and torn by warring factions, the empire foundered. The only unifying force was the Ethiopian Coptic Church and the empire was not reunited until 1855, when Emperor Tewodros II was crowned, and this was continued during the reign of Menelik II.

Ethiopia successfully repelled Italian attempts at colonization by a decisive victory at *Adowa in 1896, but was conquered by *Mussolini in 1935–36. The Ethiopian emperor *Haile Selassie was restored in 1941 after the Abyssinian Campaigns and in the 1950s and 1960s Ethiopia emerged as a leading African neutralist state. Haile Selassie's failure to deal with severe social and economic problems led to his deposition by a group of radical army officers in 1974. A subsequent coup brought Colonel *Mengistu Haile Mariam to power in 1977, but his centralized Marxist state was confronted by a Somali-backed guerrilla war in *Eritrea. Famine broke out on a massive scale (1984–87), and despite Soviet and Cuban military assistance and an international relief effort to alleviate starvation, neither peace nor plenty returned. In May 1991 Mengistu was forced to flee the country by the Ethiopian People's Revolutionary Democratic Front (EPRDF) and their allies. Peace talks in London resulted in the recognition of an EPRDF government in Addis Ababa, which largely succeeded in restoring order. Eritrea voted to secede and became independent in 1993. A new constitution was adopted in 1994, which gave the regions considerable autonomy. The first multiparty elections (1995) were won by the EPRDF, under Meles Zenawi; they have been re-elected at all subsequent elections, although those of 2005 saw significant political violence. An intermittent border war was fought with Eritrea between 1998 and 2000. Zenawi remained Prime Minister until his death in 2012, when he was succeeded by Hailemariam Desalegn.

Etruscans The inhabitants of ancient Etruria (approximating to modern Tuscany, Italy), west of the Apennines and the River Tiber. Twelve independent cities including Vulci, Clusium, and Cortona were formed into a league and came to dominate central Italy in the 7th and 6th centuries BC. Tradition held that they came from Asia Minor in the 10th century BC, though it is now believed that they were native to Italy before that and only culturally influenced by the Greek colonies of south Italy. In the 6th century BC they were driven out of southern central Italy by the Greeks, Latins, and Samnites. In the following century their navy was defeated off Cumae. Traditionally, in 510 BC the last Etruscan king of Rome, *Tarquin, was expelled. In the 4th century they were driven out of Elba and Corsica, defeated by the Gauls in 390, and finally allied themselves with Rome after defeat in 283. From this time they came under Rome's control and began to lose their unique cultural identity.

Etruscan art reveals an aristocratic society in which women enjoyed an emancipated style of life. The Etruscan language has so far proved beyond translation; it was still spoken and written in the 1st century AD but no literature survives.

Eugène of Savoy (1663–1736) Prince of the House of Savoy. He was born in Paris; his mother, Olympe Mancini, was a niece of *Mazarin. When Vienna was besieged by the Turks in 1683 he entered the Austrian army and became one of the country's greatest generals. In 1697 he was given command of the Danube army and won a decisive victory over the Turks at Zente. In the War of the *Spanish Succession he was President of the Council of War, co-operated successfully with *Marlborough at *Blenheim and *Oudenarde, and won control of north Italy at the Battle of Turin in 1706. In 1716–17 he led another successful campaign against the Turks and recovered Belgrade.

Eugénie (born **Eugénia María de Montijo de Guzmán**) (1826–1920) Spanish empress of France 1853–71 and wife of Napoleon III. Throughout her husband's reign she contributed much to the brilliance of his court and was an important influence on his foreign policy. She acted as regent on three occasions (1859; 1865; 1870).

eunuch A castrated human male. Eunuchs were used as guardians of harems in ancient China and in the Persian empire of the Achaemenids and also at the courts of the Byzantine emperors and the Ottoman sultans. They became the friends and advisers of the rulers of these powers, as they did of Roman emperors. Castration was also imposed as a form of punishment (*Abelard suffered in this way); was practised voluntarily by some Christian sects (the most notable Christian eunuch being the theologian Origen); and was used to produce male adult sopranos in Italy—castrati—until Pope Leo XIII banned the practice in 1878.

Eureka Rebellion (1854) An armed conflict between diggers and authorities on the Ballarat gold fields of Australia. Gold had been found here in 1851; by 1853 over 20,000 diggers from around the world had crowded into Ballarat. Their grievances, which included the licence system and its administration, corruption among officials, lack of political representation, and limited access to land, culminated in an attack by soldiers and police on diggers who were in a stockade on the "Eureka lead". Thirteen diggers faced charges of high treason; one case was dropped and the others were acquitted. A royal commission led to reforms on the goldfields.

euro The currency of the *European Union, which is used in 19 of its member states (Austria, Belgium, Cyprus, Estonia, Finland, France, Germany, Greece, Ireland, Italy, Latvia, Lithuania, Luxembourg, Malta, the Netherlands, Portugal, Slovakia, Slovenia, and Spain). Introduced in 1999 as an accounting unit to which participating countries pegged their national currencies, the euro replaced these national currencies in 2002 when notes and coins were issued. The single monetary policy required for **European Monetary Union** is directed by the European Central Bank in Frankfurt-am-Main. The euro is also the official currency of Monaco, San Marino, and the Vatican City, and is used in Andorra, Kosovo, and Montenegro.

Europe The smallest continent of the northern hemisphere, stretching westward from the Ural Mountains in Russia and surrounded on three sides by sea.

Physical The structure of Europe is complex. In the north-west, mountains of old, hard rock occupy most of the Scandinavian Peninsula, the north-west of the British Isles, and Brittany in France; much of this area is covered by barren rocks and moorland. Most of it is separated by the shallow North and Baltic seas from the North European Plain, which spreads from England and France across the north of the continent to Finland and the Baltic states and down to the Black Sea. Southern Europe is hilly or mountainous, except for two plains: a triangular plain in northern Italy and the broad one of the middle Danube. From west to east is a curving chain of ranges—the Pyrenees, Alps, and Carpathians—while pointing southward are the Apennines and the parallel ranges of the Balkan Peninsula. They form barriers, yet are so cut by rivers and valleys that no part of Europe is completely isolated. The extreme south is volcanic, being close to the edge of the Eurasian plate.

History Throughout its history Europe has exerted an influence disproportionate to its size. Its most important ancient civilizations developed in the Mediterranean region. Greek civilization reached its zenith between c.500 and c.300 BC, to be succeeded by that of *Rome. *Christianity became the official religion of the Roman empire in the late 4th century, shortly before the empire's western section succumbed to Germanic invaders. The eastern section lived on as the *Byzantine empire, centred on Constantinople, which eventually fell to the *Ottoman Turks in 1453.

During the *Middle Ages a politically fragmented Europe underwent varying degrees of invasion and colonization from *Moors, *Vikings, *Magyars, and others. The attempt of the powerful *Franks to re-establish the Western Roman empire soon failed, but the year 962 marked the foundation of what later became the *Holy Roman Empire. The *Roman Catholic Church became the unifying force throughout the continent; but in the wake of the *Renaissance, the 16th century bought about a religious schism (the *Reformation) in western Christendom and ushered in an era of national and international politico-religious warfare.

Post-medieval Europe was characterized by the rise of strong individual nation-states such as Spain, France, England, the Netherlands, and eventually Russia. Their influence on the rest of the world was the result of their acquisition of vast empires outside Europe. Imperial expansion continued through the age of European revolutions, of which the *French Revolution was the most momentous. In the late 18th and early 19th centuries north-western Europe became the first region of the world to undergo industrialization (see INDUSTRIAL REVOLUTION).

The modern history of Europe is largely that of its constituent nations. In the 20th century European history has been dominated by *World War I and *World War II. Since the end of World War II the *European Community and its successor, the *European Union, have brought an altogether more hopeful era to the peoples of Europe.

European Community (EC) An organization of Western European countries, which came into being in 1967 when the executive bodies of the European Economic Community (Common Market or EEC), European Atomic Energy Community (EURATOM), and European Coal and Steel Community (ECSC), merged. Committed to economic and political integration as envisaged by the Treaties of Rome, in 1993 it was absorbed into the *European Union. It was abolished in 2009 by the *Lisbon Treaty.

European Economic Community (EEC or **Common Market**) An economic organization of European states set up by the Treaties of *Rome in March 1957. Its member states agreed to coordinate their economic policies, and to establish common policies for agriculture, transport, the movement of capital and labour, and the erection of common external tariffs, with the ultimate goal of political unification. The EEC provided an extension of the functional cooperation inaugurated by the European Coal and Steel Community (made up of Belgium, France, Federal Republic of Germany, Italy,

Luxembourg, and the Netherlands). It owed much to the campaigning initiative of Jean Monnet and to the detailed planning of Paul-Henri *Spaak. Preliminary meetings were held at Messina in 1955, which led to the Treaties of Rome in 1957 and the formal creation of the EEC in January 1958. Cooperation in the EEC was most organized in the area of *agriculture, and the Common Agricultural Policy (CAP) was the largest item in the EEC budget. The Institutions of the EEC merged with those of the European Atomic Energy Community (EURATOM) and the European Coal and Steel Community (ESCA) in 1967 to form the *European Community (EC).

European Parliament One of the constituent institutions of the *European Union (formerly the *European Community), meeting in Strasbourg or Luxembourg. Set up in 1952 under the terms of the treaty which established the European Steel and Coal Community (ECSC), the Parliament was replaced and extended in 1958 to serve two new communities, the *European Economic Community and the European Atomic Energy Community (EURATOM). From 1958 to 1979 it was composed of representatives drawn from the Assemblies of the member states. However, quinquennial direct elections have taken place since 1979, and it is now made up of 751 seats, distributed among member states according to the size of their populations. Its powers have steadily increased: originally purely consultative, it was given a greater say under the Single European Act (1987) and under the *Maastricht Treaty (1992) its powers were enhanced to include the right of veto on some bills, further budgetary control, and a say in the membership of the Commission. Following the *Lisbon Treaty (2009), most EU legislation must be approved by both the Parliament and the Council of the European Union (the member states' ministers).

European Union (EU) An organization now numbering 28 European countries that was established in 1993. The EU took over all the *European Community institutions, such as the *European Parliament, but also extended the scope of the EC according to the terms of the *Maastricht Treaty. The member countries agreed to add a shared foreign policy and commitment to cooperation on security matters, including justice and policing, to their economic and political links under the EC. These constituted the `three pillars' of the EU, one pillar being the EC, another pillar coordinating foreign and external security policies (originally designating the *Western European Union as the EU's defence wing), and the third pillar coordinating internal matters and justice (particularly on immigration and political asylum). Proposals concerning the creation of a single European currency were not acceptable to all members and there were also disagreements over social policies. However, in 1999 a European currency, the *euro, was launched. It is now the official currency of 18 European Union states. In 2009 the *Lisbon Treaty merged the three pillars into a single entity, provided for a permanent EU president and foreign minister, and made the EU's charter of rights legally binding.

In 1995 Austria, Finland, and Sweden joined the EU; in 2004 they were joined by Cyprus, the Czech Republic, Estonia, Hungary, Latvia, Lithuania, Malta, Poland, Slovakia, and Slovenia; in 2007, by Bulgaria and Romania; and in 2013, by Croatia. With the European Free Trade Association (EFTA), a free-trade area that includes a number of non-EU European states, the EU established a frontier-free zone in 1994, known as the European Economic Area (EEA).

Eurozone Crisis A series of financial crises in countries using the *euro from 2010. In the wake of the *Credit Crunch, the world financial markets lost confidence in the creditworthiness of *Ireland (2010), *Greece (2010), *Portugal (2011), *Italy (2011), *Spain (2012), and *Cyprus (2012). A common factor was that all had large public-sector debts. In Ireland and Spain this resulted from a banking crisis following the Credit Crunch, and in Cyprus from its banking sector's exposure to Greek debt; but in the other countries the main cause was long-standing public-sector deficits that had been fuelled by credit at the low interest rates available to eurozone members. When confidence evaporated, the interest rates at which they could borrow money on world markets to cover their deficits became prohibitively high; in most cases the gap was covered by loans, mainly from the International Monetary Fund and from fellow members of the eurozone. Although initially reluctant, the latter were driven by a fear that one or more of these countries would leave the euro, which would imperil both the project of monetary union and, perhaps, the *European Union itself. The lenders demanded economic and structural reforms to guard against the need for future loans. By the mid-2010s the crisis seemed to have been contained. It led to proposals for tighter integration between members of the eurozone, with central supervision of their budgets.

The Eurozone Crisis was preceded by similar crises in *Iceland (2008) and *Hungary (2009).

Evatt, Herbert Vere (1894–1965) Australian statesman. A federal politician (1925–30, 1940–60), he led the Labor Opposition (1951–60). Noted for his championship of the rights of the smaller nations, and for greater independence from Britain, Evatt presided over the UN General Assembly (1948–49).

Evelyn, John (1620–1706) English diarist and writer. He is remembered chiefly for his *Diary* (published posthumously in 1818), which covers most of his life, describing his travels abroad, his contemporaries, and such important historical events as the Great Plague and the Great Fire of London. He was also a pioneer of English forestry and gardening, and a founder member of the Royal Society.

Everest, Mount (Nepali **Sagarmatha**; Chinese **Qomolangma**) The highest mountain in the world (8848 m, 29028 feet), in the Himalayas on the border of Nepal and Tibet. It is named after Sir George Everest (1790–1866), surveyor-general of India, and its summit was first reached in 1953 by the New Zealand mountaineer and explorer (Sir) Edmund Hillary and the Sherpa mountaineer Tenzing Norgay.

Evesham, Battle of (4 August 1265) A crucial engagement in the second *Barons' War (1264–65) when Prince Edward defeated Simon de *Montfort and rescued his father Henry III. Simon's headless corpse was buried in the abbey at Evesham which subsequently became a place of pilgrimage.

Évian Agreements (1962) A series of agreements negotiated at Évian-les-Bains in France. Secret negotiations between the government of General *de Gaulle and representatives of the provisional government of the Algerian Republic of *Ben Bella began in Switzerland in December 1961 and continued in March 1962 at Évian. A ceasefire commission was set up and the French government, subject to certain safeguards, agreed to the establishment of an independent Algeria following a referendum. The agreements were ratified by the French National Assembly but were violently attacked by the extremist Organization de l'Armée Secrète (OAS).

evolution *See* EARLY HUMANS.

Exchequer A former English government department dealing with finance. The Normans created two departments dealing with finance.

One was the Treasury, which held money and other valuables on behalf of the monarch; the other was the Exchequer, which was itself divided into two parts, lower and upper. The lower Exchequer was an office for receiving and paying out money and was connected to the Treasury; the upper Exchequer was a court of law dealing with cases related to revenue, and was merged with the High Court of Justice in 1880.

excise See CUSTOMS AND EXCISE.

Exclusion crisis The attempt to exclude James, Duke of York, later *James II, from succeeding to the English throne because he was a Catholic. After the unmasking of the *Popish Plot the Whigs tried in three successive parliamentary sessions to force through a bill to alter the succession but all three attempts (1679, 1680, 1681) failed. The Whig opposition eventually triumphed at the *Glorious Revolution.

exclusionists (or **exclusives**) Australian settlers opposed to the emancipation of ex-convicts. The name was applied in New South Wales, during the period of convict transportation, to those people who opposed the restoration of civil rights to ex-convicts or *emancipists. The exclusives were composed for the most part of civil and military officials and of gentleman squatters and settlers who were called in derision "Pure Merinos".

Exile The captivity of the Jews in *Babylon (the "Babylonian Captivity"). In 597 BC the Babylonians captured *Jerusalem and took King Jehoiachin and many leaders of the Judaean community, including the prophet Ezekiel, into exile in Babylon. Following further revolt, they again attacked Jerusalem and, after a three-year siege captured and destroyed it in 586 BC. Many of those taken to Babylon were settled in communities, with the result that distinctive Jewish teaching, religion, and life could continue. In 539 BC Babylon fell to Persia and one year later *Cyrus II (the Great) gave permission for Jews who wished to do so to return home. The number returning was probably small and the return protracted over a long time.

exploration The investigation of undiscovered territories. The urge to travel is as old as humanity, with the first humans probably spreading out from Africa, and possibly Asia, across the globe. The Native Americans of both North and South America probably walked there over land-bridges from what is now Russia, some 30,000 years ago. For the early European explorers, travel was easier by sea than by land: *Phoenician traders frequently sailed to Galicia (in Spain) and Brittany, and perhaps even to Cornwall.

In the early Middle Ages the *Vikings sailed as far west as Greenland and to North America and curiosity about the "marvels of the east" led the Italian *Marco Polo overland to China (1271–95). Meanwhile, the Chinese Ming emperors supported the seven voyages of discovery of *Zheng He (1405–33) and Polynesian peoples discovered the Pacific Islands and New Zealand. Under the patronage of Prince *Henry the Navigator, the Portuguese in the 15th century sailed to the Indian Ocean, and in 1498 Vasco *da Gama crossed the South Atlantic; in 1516 the Portuguese reached China. Probably with the aim of reaching the East, Christopher *Columbus crossed the North Atlantic (1492) and Ferdinand *Magellan found the strait which enabled him to reach the Chinese coast (1521). The North American landmass was such a deterrent that searches were long made for a navigable passage to the north of it: the search for a north-west passage led *Cabot to what was probably Hudson Bay (1509) and *Cartier along the St Lawrence River (1534–41). North America's interior began to be explored in the 17th century, but it was not until about 1730 that the Rocky Mountains were discovered, and the continent was not crossed until 1793, when Mackenzie traversed Canada. The United States was first crossed by Lewis and Clark, in 1803. His previous scientific research helped Captain James *Cook secure backing from the Royal Society for his voyages to New Zealand and eastern Australia (1769–77). The exploration and mapping of the interiors of continents continued throughout the 19th century and often accompanied colonialism.

Fabians British socialists aiming at gradual social change through democratic means. The Fabian Society was founded in 1884 by a group of intellectuals who believed that new political pressures were needed to achieve social reforms. It was one of the socialist societies that helped found the Labour Representation Committee, the origin of the *Labour Party, in 1900. Trade Union militancy from 1910 to 1926, and the harshness of unemployment in the 1930s, weakened the appeal of Fabian gradualism but by 1939, with moderate leaders, such as Clement *Attlee, coming to the forefront, their influence revived.

Fabius Maximus Verrucosus, Quintus (known as **'Cunctator' ('the Delayer')**) (died 203 BC) Roman general and consul five times between 233 and 209. He was appointed dictator in 221 and again for a second time in 217 after the Battle of Trasimene, during the Second *Punic war. Appreciating that the Carthaginian forces were superior to his own, he declined to engage in pitched battles. His unspectacular tactics of slow harassment against Hannibal's army in Italy at first won little popular support, and the nickname *Cunctator* was intended as an insult. After the defeat at *Cannae (216) the feeling against his strategy waned and the insult became a title of approval. He opposed *Scipio Africanus's aggressive war against Carthage on the African mainland.

Factory Acts Laws to regulate conditions of employment of factory workers. In Britain two early Acts of Parliament in 1802 and 1819, which aimed to protect children and apprentices, failed because they could not be enforced. The Factory Act of 1833 banned the employment of children under 9, restricted working hours of older children, and provided for the appointment of factory inspectors. Legislation in Britain (1844 and 1847) extended protection of workers into mines and other industries and reduced the working day to ten hours. A Factory Act (1874) consolidated the ten-hour day and raised the

age of children in employment to 10, this being further raised to 12 in 1901 and 14 in 1920. In the 20th century a complicated structure of industrial law developed. It was to counter the problem of child labour and the exploitation of factory workers, particularly women, that the International Labour Organization (ILO) was formed by the League of Nations (1919). Despite such initiatives, the exploitation of Third World women and children in such trades as the garment industry remains a matter of serious concern. In Britain workers have been further protected by such legislation as the Employers' Liability (Compulsory Insurance) Act (1969), the Health and Safety at Work Act (1974), and the Employment Act (1989). The 'Social Chapter' of the *Maastricht Treaty (1992) harmonized labour laws throughout the EU; however, the UK opted out of this section of the treaty until 1997.

Fadden, Sir Arthur William (1895–1973) Australian accountant and politician, Prime Minister in 1941 for five weeks following the resignation of Robert Gordon *Menzies.

Faisal I (or **Feisal**) (1885–1933) King of Iraq (1921–33). The son of *Hussein Ibn Ali, he commanded the northern Arab army in Jordan, Palestine, and Syria in association with T. E. *Lawrence in the Arab Revolt of 1916–18. In 1920 Faisal was chosen King of Syria by the Syrian National Congress but was expelled by France, the mandatory power. He was then made King of Iraq by Britain, who held the mandate for that territory. As ruler of Iraq (1921–33) he demonstrated considerable political skill in building up the institutions of the new state.

Faisal ibn Abd al-Aziz (1905–75) King of Saudi Arabia (1964–75). Brother of King Saud ibn Abd al-Aziz, he became effective ruler of Saudi Arabia in 1958, dealing with the main consequences for Saudi Arabia of the immense increase of oil revenues. Pro-West, he worked in association with the USA while remaining inflexible in his opposition to Israel's ambitions and unyielding on Arab claims to Jerusalem. Faisal stood against the demands of radical Arab nationalism represented by Egypt under *Nasser. He was assassinated by a nephew.

Falange, the (Spanish, 'phalanx') A Spanish political party, the Falange Española. Founded in 1933 by José António Primo de Rivera, the son of General *Primo de Rivera, its members were equally opposed to the reactionary Right and the revolutionary Left. It proposed that Spain should become a syndicalist state on Italian fascist lines. During the *Spanish Civil War Franco saw the potential value of the Falange and adopted the movement in April 1937. After World War II it ceased to be identified with fascism and its influence waned. It was formally abolished in 1977.

Falkirk, Battles of Two battles fought at Falkirk, a town 16 km (10 miles) from Stirling in Scotland. The first (22 July 1298) resulted in victory for *Edward I of England over Sir William *Wallace, leader of the Scottish resistance to English sovereignty. The second (17 January 1746) was a victory for the Jacobite army of Prince Charles Edward Stuart over the government forces in the *Forty-Five rebellion.

Falklands War (Malvinas War) (2 April–14 June 1982) The Argentine–British war in the Falkland Islands, a UK Overseas Territory comprising a group of islands in the south Atlantic, about 480 km (300 miles) off the coast of Argentina. The islands were first occupied by the French in 1764. The British ousted the French settlers within a year but the French sold their claim to Spain. In 1820 Argentina claimed sovereignty as Spain's successor and have disputed Britain's claim to the islands since 1833. Repeated attempts at negotiation for the transfer of the islands from British to Argentine rule having failed, an Argentine warship was sent by General Leopoldo Galtieri's military junta to land a party of "scrap dealers" on South Georgia on 19 March 1982 with the intention of reclaiming the Falklands. This was followed on 2 April by a full-scale military invasion. Attempts by the UN, the USA, and Peru to secure a peaceful resolution to the conflict failed, and Britain sent a task force of 30 warships with supporting aircraft and auxiliary vessels across 13,000 km (8,000 miles) of sea to recover the islands. Although all but three Latin American nations supported Argentina, the USA, in a difficult position because of close ties to both countries, sided with the British. The ten-week conflict, which claimed the lives of nearly 1,000 British and Argentine servicemen and civilians,

ceased with the surrender of the Argentine forces on 14 June. The British victory contributed to the downfall of General Galtieri's government. Argentina officially declared a cessation of hostilities in 1989.

Fanti Confederation A loose association of small states along the Gold Coast (Ghana) in West Africa. Having migrated from the north in the 17th century, the Fanti served as middlemen between the slave and gold-producing states of the African interior and European traders along the coast. The coastal states were threatened by the rise of *Asante power in Kumasi in the 19th century, and they supported the British in the Asante Wars. The Fanti played a prominent role in the affairs of Ghana after independence in 1957.

farmers-general A group of some 40 to 60 financiers in 18th century France, who bought from the crown the right of collecting indirect taxes on wine, tobacco, and salt (a practice known as "farming" taxes). Employing inspectors to collect the money, they retained the difference between what they paid the crown for this right and what they actually extorted. The salt tax (*gabelle*) was especially harsh. The system was abolished in the French Revolution.

Farnese An Italian family which ruled the duchy of Parma from 1545 to 1731. Originating in the 11th century, its first outstanding member was **Alessandro** (1468–1549), who became Pope Paul III in 1534 and created the duchy of Parma and Piacenza. His grandson **Alessandro** (1520–89) was named a cardinal at the age of 14, and remained a powerful figure at the papal court for 50 years; he was a noted patron of the arts.

His nephew **Alessandro** (1545–92), Duke of Parma from 1586, was the family's most distinguished scion. After serving against the Ottomans at the Battle of *Lepanto (1571), he succeeded Don John of Austria as governor-general of the Netherlands and commander-in-chief of the Spanish forces which were dealing with the Dutch Revolts (1578). By subtle diplomacy he detached the southern provinces from the revolt (1579). Then he conducted a sequence of superbly planned military campaigns further north, including the capture of Antwerp (1585). In 1588 *Philip II diverted him from his campaigns in the north, ordering him to liaise with the *Spanish Armada. In 1590 he was diverted again, this time to intervene in the *French Wars of Religion, where he managed to relieve Paris (1590) and Rouen (1592), but was wounded and died.

Farouk (1920–65) King of Egypt (1936–52). On assuming power he dismissed Prime Minister Nahas Pasha, but was forced by the British government to reinstate him. Farouk's defeat in the Arab–Israeli conflict of 1948, together with the general corruption of his reign, led to a military coup in 1952, headed by General Neguib (1901–84) and masterminded by Nasser. Farouk was forced to abdicate in favour of his infant son, Fuad; he was sent into exile and eventually became a citizen of Monaco.

Farrakhan, Louis *See* NATION OF ISLAM.

fasces In ancient Rome, bundles of rods bound with thongs that symbolized regal or magisterial authority both within and outside Rome. After the expulsion of the *Etruscan kings, consuls had twelve fasces (a dictator 24), praetors six, lesser magistrates fewer. Originally axes were included in the bundle; but from the early republic the axe was removed in Rome, in deference to the ultimate power of the people in capital cases. In 1919 Musssolini used the symbol for his political party, which derived its name, *fascism, from this word.

fascism A political ideology of the first half of the 20th century, the central belief of which was that the individual should be subjugated to the needs of the state, which in turn should be directed by a strong leader embodying the will of the nation. It arose in opposition to *communism but adopted totalitarian styles of propaganda, organization, and violence. The word (from the Roman *fasces) was first used by the Fascio di Combattimento in Italy in 1919. *Mussolini shaped fascism into a potent political force in Italy and *Hitler developed a more racist brand of it in Germany. Similar movements, which adopted a paramilitary structure, sprang up in Spain (the *Falange), Portugal, Austria, the Balkan states, France, and South America. In Britain the National Union of Fascists under *Mosley was founded in 1932, and between 1934 and 1936 was violently anti-Semitic.

Once in power (in 1922 in Italy) fascists attempted to impose a military discipline on the whole of society at the expense of individual freedom (though, despite the socialist elements in fascist ideology, there was little interference with private ownership). Democratic institutions were replaced by the cult of the single leader, whose pronouncements were unchallengeable. Fascism was thus a form of *totalitarianism and was finally defeated only by military means in the course of World War II. Since then various extreme right-wing parties based on fascist principles have emerged in Europe and elsewhere, but are generally supported only by a tiny minority of the population.

Fashoda incident (18 September 1898) The culmination of a long series of clashes between Britain and France in the "scramble for Africa". The French objective, to occupy the sub-Saharan belt from west to east, countered the British aim of linking their possessions from the Cape to Cairo. Thus in 1896 the French dispatched a force under General Jean-Baptiste Marchand from *Gabon to occupy the *Sudan, at the same time that *Kitchener was moving up the Nile to recover Khartoum. Both reached Fashoda during the summer of 1898, and as neither side desired conflict, they agreed that both French and British flags should fly over the fort. The matter was referred to London and Paris, and for a while tension between the two countries was extreme. In December the French ordered Marchand to withdraw, and this enabled an agreement to be reached whereby the Nile and Congo watersheds should demarcate the respective spheres of influence by the two countries in Africa.

Fatah, al- (Arabic, 'victory') A militant Palestinian organization. It was founded (1962) in Kuwait to fight for the restoration of *Palestine to the Arabs. Al-Fatah assumed the leadership of the *Palestine Liberation Organization in 1969 and remained the dominant group within the PLO. Its guerrilla units were expelled from Jordan after the civil war in 1970, and it withdrew to southern Lebanon (Fatahland). Subsequently al-Fatah was drawn into the Lebanese imbroglio and became divided; a part was expelled from Lebanon after the Israeli invasion of 1982. Leadership remained in the hands of Yasser *Arafat, who had led al-Fatah from its foundation. Al-Fatah played a leading role in the achievement of the 1993 peace agreement with Israel. However, divisions within the organization over the progress of PLO–Israeli negotiations became apparent in 1995 with some factions no longer remaining loyal to Arafat. In 1996 al-Fatah won the first legislative elections for the Palestinian National Authority (PNA) and Arafat was elected President. A surprise defeat by *Hamas in the 2006 legislative elections led to a de facto division of the PNA, with al-Fatah controlling the West Bank and Hamas the Gaza Strip.

Fatimid (or **Fatimite**) A descendant or Arabian dynasty claiming descent from Fatima, the daughter of the Prophet Muhammad. The Fatimids ruled in parts of North Africa from 908 to

1171, and during some of that period in Egypt and Syria.

Faulkner of Downpatrick, Baron
(Arthur Brian Deane Faulkner) (1921–77) Northern Ireland statesman. A Unionist Member of Parliament at *Stormont (1949–73), he was Minister of Home Affairs (1959–63; 1971–72), and Prime Minister (1971–72). His negotiations with the Westminster government for constitutional changes in *Northern Ireland lost him support in his own party.

Fawcett, Dame Millicent Garrett (1847–1929) British feminist. Sister of Elizabeth Garrett *Anderson, she was a pioneer of the movement in Britain to secure equality for women in voting, education, and careers. She was strongly supported by her husband, Henry Fawcett, a Liberal politician and academic. In 1897 she became President of the National Union of Women's Suffrage Societies, whose policy was to gain votes for women without the militancy soon to be associated with the *suffragettes.

Fawkes, Guy (1570–1606) English conspirator. He was hanged for his part in the *Gunpowder Plot of 5 November 1605. The occasion is commemorated annually with fireworks, bonfires, and the burning of a guy.

Federal Bureau of Investigation (FBI)
The investigative branch of the US Department of Justice. Established by Attorney-General Charles J. Bonaparte (1851–1921) in 1908, it was at first called the Bureau of Investigation. It was reorganized in 1924 when J. Edgar *Hoover was appointed as director, giving it wider powers to investigate violations of federal laws. Hoover successfully led the 1930s drive against gangsters. During World War II the FBI began spying activities against Nazi sympathizers in the USA and Latin America. The later excesses of Hoover, in particular his harassment of political dissidents and radicals such as Martin Luther *King, brought its counter-intelligence activities into disrepute. It was roundly criticized by the Senate in investigations of the *Watergate scandal in 1975–76. From the 1990s the FBI's anti-terrorism activities expanded, particularly following the *September 11 attacks.

Federalist Party US political party. The first political party to emerge after the *Constitution of the USA became operative (1789), it took its name from the *Federalist Papers*, a collection of essays written by James *Madison, Alexander *Hamilton, and John *Jay to influence the ratification of the Constitution by New York. The party of George *Washington and John *Adams, it had support in New England and the northeast generally, both from commercial interests and wealthier landowners. It stood for strong central government and the firm enforcement of domestic laws, was pro-British in foreign affairs, and identified itself with the economic policies of Hamilton. The party's role, which would benefit "the wise, the good, and the rich", was exemplified in the military campaign in 1794 against the refusal of the *Whisky Rebels to pay excise duty. The emergence of new political issues, disagreements over commercial and foreign policy, and the narrowness of its popular appeal gradually undermined the Party, although it continued to elect members to Congress until it finally disappeared in 1825.

Federal Reserve System The central bank of the USA, established in 1913, that holds the US gold reserves and implements government financial policy. There are 12 Federal Reserve Districts in the USA and each has its own Federal Bank. The Federal Reserve System is controlled by the Federal Reserve Board, based in Washington, DC.

Federation of Rhodesia and Nyasaland
See CENTRAL AFRICAN FEDERATION.

Feisal I *See* FAISAL I.

feminism A broad-based movement concerning the social, political, and economic rights of women. Its advocates have for the most part demanded equal rights for both sexes, although some have asserted the right of women to separate development. Throughout the ages women had generally been subordinated to men and largely excluded from education, from the ownership of property, from economic independence, and from political representation. A recognizable movement to rectify woman's subordinate position began at the end of the 18th century, finding its British mouthpiece in Mary *Wollstonecraft, whose classic *A Vindication of the Rights of Woman* (1792) has remained a key work.

Contemporary feminism has its roots in such works as Simone de Beauvoir's *The Second Sex* (1949); *The Feminine Mystique* (1963) by the US feminist Betty Friedan; *Sexual Politics* (1969) by the US writer Kate Millett; *The Female Eunuch* (1970) by Germaine Greer; Adrienne Rich's *Of Woman Born* (1977); and *Gyn/Ecology* (1979) by Mary Daly. In particular, the later 1960s saw the advent of women's liberation (popularly known as Women's Lib), arguing that male domination is implicit in all personal and professional relationships. It demanded the improvement of women's status in society and was concerned with changing stereotypes of both sexes. Women's liberation was especially vocal and active as a movement in the USA; in 1966 the National Organization for Women (NOW) was formed in the USA and has remained active since. Practical demands were focused on the right to equal pay and opportunities. In Britain the Sex Discrimination Acts (1975 and 1986) and the creation of the Equal Opportunities Commission in 1975 gave legal effect to some demands, although some employment practices and financial rewards still fail to achieve equality.

During the 1970s women's liberation gave way to a broader feminist movement, which sponsored public campaigns on such issues as abortion, childcare provision, pornography, and domestic violence against women. Other aspects of the movement have aimed to integrate the interests of women who are not of the dominant culture (for example, women of colour, working-class women, and lesbians, who individually have contributed much to the movement) into mainstream feminism, while continuing to strive for gender equality in the workplace and at home.

In developing countries, feminists have been faced with a different order of problem. Women in such countries generally suffer from a greater degree of inequality than their counterparts in Western countries. Their participation in the paid labour force and their literacy rates tend to be lower, and their fertility rates and maternal mortality rates tend to be higher. Less access to education, combined with religious or social traditions, is responsible for women's limited role in economic, public, and political life. The revival of Islamic fundamentalism, with its enforced social isolation of women *Purdah*, has led to the establishment of segregated systems of banking, commerce, and education in Muslim communities. Nevertheless, in many countries women have tried to improve their status, for example by opposing divisive legal and seclusion codes, and by campaigning against genital mutilation (female circumcision). In Africa, development groups are now supporting women agriculturalists (who produce 70% of the continent's food) by giving women greater access to and control of technology.

Fenian Originally a member of a secret revolutionary society, named after the Fianna, the Irish armed force in legendary times. Founded as the Fenian Brotherhood in the USA by John O'Mahony and as the Irish Republican Brotherhood (IRB) by James Stephens in Ireland (1858), the name was later applied to supporters of Irish republicanism. Many of its early members had been actively involved in the *Young Ireland movement. Its military wing was known as the *Irish Republican Army (IRA). Their exploits drew attention to Irish discontent and helped to convince *Gladstone of the urgent need to find a solution to Ireland's problems. Several Fenians became Members of Parliament at Westminster during the *Home Rule period. In the latter part of the 1860s the Fenian Brotherhood split into three sections, each in theory supporting the IRB but in practice sharply divided by personalities and policies. The organization was superseded in the USA by Clan-na-Gael, a secret society headed by John Devoy, and by other open Irish-American organizations supporting Irish republicanism.

Ferdinand II ((1578–1637) Holy Roman Emperor (1619–37), king of Bohemia (1617–27) and of Hungary (1618–26). He was educated by the Jesuits and developed into a determined spokesman for *Counter-Reformation Catholicism. Before his election to the imperial throne, he used authoritarian measures against the Protestants of Inner Austria, with some success, but in 1619 the largely Protestant Bohemian Diet deposed him in favour of *Frederick V (the Winter King). This crisis was one of the opening moves in the catastrophic *Thirty Years War. The first ten years of the conflict did not go badly for Ferdinand. He reached his high point when he issued the Edict of Restitution (1629), which ordered the return of all Roman Catholic property seized since 1552. Subsequently he was seen as a threat to German liberty and opposed by both Catholic and Protestant princes. The interventions of Sweden and France finally turned the tide of the war against him, and he was forced to abandon his more extreme Catholic absolutist ambitions.

Ferdinand V (or **Ferdinand the Catholic**) (1452–1516) King of Castile and León (1474–1516), King of Aragon as **Ferdinand II** (1479–1516), King of Sicily (1468–1516), and King of Naples (1502–16). He was the son of John II of Aragon. In 1469 he married the future *Isabella Iof Castile, a significant step towards Spanish unification. He succeeded to the throne of Aragon in 1479, and in the same year helped Isabella to win the war of succession in Castile (1474–79). They began to rule jointly in both kingdoms in 1481, and in 1492 annexed the conquered territory of Granada to Castile. On

Isabella's death in 1504, he was recognized as Regent of Castile for his daughter *Joanna the Mad. He subsequently married Germaine de Foix (1506), and incorporated Navarre into Castile (1515), thus becoming personal monarch of all Spain from the Pyrenees to Gibraltar.

A ruthlessly realistic politician, he was especially successful in the conduct of foreign policy. He surrounded France with a network of allies and acquired Naples. At home he modernized Spain's governmental institutions, vested in himself the grand masterships of the wealthy military orders, and won important ecclesiastical concessions from the papacy, including the Bull of 1478 authorizing the *Spanish Inquisition, a powerful council to combat heresy, to be controlled by the crown.

Ferdinand VII (1784–1833) King of Spain (1808–33). He succeeded to the throne after the forced abdication of his father, Charles IV, and was in turn forced by the French to abdicate in favour of *Napoleon's brother, Joseph Bonaparte, spending the years of the *Peninsular War in prison in France. Known as 'The Desired One', he was released in 1814 and restored to the throne. He abolished the liberal constitution of 1812 and instituted his own absolutist rule, relying on the support of the Church and the army. The loss of the colonies in America (*Spanish–South American Wars of Independence) deprived the government of a major source of income, and his troops mutinied. The revolutionaries held him practically a prisoner until 1823, when French forces came to his aid. Restored to power, he carried out a bloody revenge on the insurgents.

Ferry, Jules François Camille (1832–93) French statesman. Prefect of the Seine (1870–71) during its siege in the *Franco-Prussian War, his narrow escape (18 March 1871) from the *Paris Commune left him with a strong dislike of extremist politics. After serving as French ambassador in Greece, he was elected to the French Chamber of Deputies (1876–89) and was in government from 1879 to 1885, twice as Prime Minister (1880–81; 1883–85). He was responsible for much liberal legislation, extending freedom of association and of the press and legalizing trade unions. He weakened the grip of the Roman Catholic Church on education, extended higher education, created lycées for girls, and made French elementary education non-clerical (March 1882), free, and compulsory. His ministries also saw wide French colonial development in Tunisia (1881), the Congo (1884), Madagascar (1885), and Indo-

China (1885). This latter lost him support and he fell from office. He narrowly failed to be elected President of the Republic in 1887.

Fertile Crescent The fertile land stretching from the Mediterranean coast of Syria, Lebanon, and Israel down the valley of the Tigris and Euphrates rivers to the Persian Gulf. The expression was coined by the archaeologist James H. Breasted to describe that part of the Middle East that formed the cradle of early civilizations such as the Assyrian, Sumerian, Phoenician, Babylonian, Hittite, and Hebrew. Archaeological evidence confirms the existence of agricultural communities in the area by 8000 BC.

feudal system A medieval European political and economic system based on the holding of lands on condition of homage or military service and labour. Feudalism probably originated in the Frankish kingdom in the 8th century and spread into northern Italy, Spain, and Germany. It was introduced by the *Normans into England, Ireland, Scotland, southern Italy, and Sicily. The nobility held lands from the crown and provided troops for the king in times of war. The knight was the tenant of the noble and a class of unfree peasants (*villein) lived on the land under the jurisdiction of their lord (*manorial system). Bishops and abbots were invested by secular lords with their livings in return for services and the church received produce and labour from the peasantry. It became a varied and complex system: lords built up their own military forces and power to the point where they became semi-independent of the king; from the 12th century payments (scutage) could be substituted for military duties. The system broke down in the 12th and 13th centuries as towns (*commune) and individuals achieved independence from their lords, though serfdom survived in some countries for much longer.

Fíanna Fáil (Gaelic, 'soldiers of destiny') Irish political party. Its main aim was to create a united republican Ireland, politically and economically independent of Britain. Eamon *de Valera founded the Party in 1926 from opponents of the Anglo-Irish Treaty (1921), which established the *Irish Free State. The Party won control of the government (1932). It dominated Irish politics for the following decades, being out of office only for short periods. In 1973 it lost to an alliance of the Fine Gael and the Labour Party, but returned to government in 1977 and has held power, either alone or in coalition, for most of the years since then (1977–81, 1982, 1987–94, and 1997–2011).

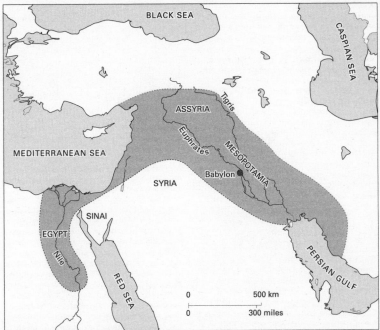

Fertile Crescent. Bounded by mountains in the north and desert in the south, by the Mediterranean in the west, and the Persian Gulf in the east, the Fertile Crescent is interrupted by desert in Mesopotamia, Syria, and Sinai. Archaeological research suggests that the development of primitive irrigation, made necessary by the dry summers, probably preceded the rise of the ancient civilizations of Babylon, Assyria, and Egypt.

fief The land held under the *feudal system by a *vassal from his lord. Fiefs ranged in size from vast duchies down to the area of land needed to support a single knight, called a knight's 'fee'. Large or small, they provided the agricultural produce which was the source of all wealth. During the early Middle Ages areas which had been forest or barren land came under cultivation and were incorporated into the system.

Field of the Cloth of Gold The site near Calais, where *Henry VIII of England met *Francis I of France in June 1520, in an attempt to forge a diplomatic alliance. Henry's retinue was made up of more than 5000 people. He wrestled, danced, jousted, and tilted with Francis for almost a fortnight, amid scenes of great festivity and pageantry. However, the two sovereigns retained their initial mutual suspicions, and within days of leaving Francis, Henry met

the French king's arch-rival, Emperor Charles V, at Gravelines.

Fifteen, the (1715) A *Jacobite rebellion aimed at removing the Hanoverian *George I from the British throne. Queen *Anne's sudden death in August 1714 had caught the Jacobites by surprise. Their lack of preparedness and their inability to win the English Tories to their cause delayed the rebellion until September 1715. A simultaneous rising in Scotland and England was planned, with Thomas Forster to lead the English northern rebels and the indecisive Earl of Mar to command the Scots. Forster was compelled to surrender his small force at Preston and Mar's inconclusive battle at Sheriffmuir virtually ended the rebellion.

Fifth-Monarchy Men An extreme Puritan sect in England in the mid-17th century. They believed that the rule of Jesus Christ and his saints was imminent, and that it would be the fifth monarchy to rule the world, succeeding those of Assyria, Persia, Greece, and Rome. They hoped that, through the *Barebones Parliament, the rule of the saints would become a reality, but *Cromwell's establishment of the Protectorate turned them against him. Their agitation became a nuisance, their leaders were arrested, and their abortive rebellions in 1657 and 1661 were suppressed.

Fiji

Capital:	Suva
Area:	18,274 sq km (7056 sq miles)
Population:	896,758 (2013 est)
Currency:	1 Fiji dollar = 100 cents
Religions:	Protestant 55.4%; Hindu 27.9%; Roman Catholic 9.1%; Muslim 6.3%
Ethnic Groups:	Fijian 57.3%; Indian 37.6%
Languages:	English, Fijian (both official); Hindi; local languages
International Organizations:	UN; Colombo Plan; Secretariat of the Pacific Community; Pacific Islands Forum; Commonwealth; WTO; Non-Aligned Movement

A country comprising a group of islands, in the Melanesian archipelago of the south-west Pacific Ocean.

Physical Fiji consists of mountainous volcanic islands. There are two main islands, Viti Levu and Vanua Levu, and over 800 smaller ones.

Economy The main economic activity is agriculture, with a large subsistence element and sugar as the principal cash crop and export. Other exports include clothing, gold, and timber. Tourism is the main industry.

History The islands first became known to Europeans when Tasman visited them in 1643. Captain Cook landed in 1774. In the 19th century Fuji was notorious for inter-tribal wars and cannibalism, a situation not assisted by an influx of deserting seamen, traders seeking sandalwood, and whalers. The islands became a British crown colony in 1874, the Western Pacific High Commission being set up for the pacification and control of the labour trade. By 1879 Indians began to be imported under the indenture system. By the 1950s Indians outnumbered Fijians and were dominating commercial life, while Fijians owned most of the land. The country became independent in 1970. The election of a government with an Indian majority (1987) brought ethnic tensions to a head, which led to two military coups to restore indigenous Fijian control. Civilian rule, under a new constitution that guaranteed a Melanesian parliamentary majority, was restored in 1990. Subsequent heavy Indian emigration resulted in a loss of skills and capital. Opposition parties attacked the new constitution as racist and there were threats of another military coup, but in 1992 the Fijian Political Party won the general election and Major General Sitiveni Rabuka, who had led the coups of 1987, became Prime Minister as head of a coalition. The government collapsed in 1994 but was re-elected with Rabuka's party increasing its majority. In 1997 the racist elements were removed from the constitution and in 1999 Mahendra Chaudry became Fiji's first ethnic Indian Prime Minister. However, in 2000 Chaudry and several members of parliament were taken hostage by indigenous Fijian rebels. They were soon freed, but in the meantime the military had taken control of the state; Laisenia Qarase, an ethnic Fijian, was installed as Prime Minister. He won elections held in 2001 and 2006, but was ousted in a military coup in 2006. The military leader, Voreqe Bainimarama, was installed as Prime Minister in 2007. Elections held in 2014 resulted in victory for Bainimarama and his party.

filibusters Originally piratical adventurers or freebooters who pillaged the Spanish colonies in the 17th century. Subsequently it was used of anyone who engaged in unauthorized war against foreign states. This meaning led to its use to describe speakers in the US Congress, British parliament, or any other assembly seeking to delay legislation by making long speeches to obstruct business.

Fillmore, Millard (1800–74) US Whig statesman, 13th President of the USA (1850–53). He succeeded to the presidency on the death of Zachary Taylor. Fillmore was an advocate of compromise on the slavery issue. However, his unpopular enforcement of the 1850 Fugitive Slave Act hastened the end of the Whig Party.

Fine Gael (Gaelic, 'United Ireland') Irish political party. Founded in 1922 as Cumann na nGaedheal, it changed its name in 1933. It originated among supporters of the Anglo-Irish Treaty that created the *Irish Free State. William *Cosgrave was its leader (1922–44). Fine Gael was in power as the dominant element in a coalition from 1948 to 1951, with John Costello as its leader. This government in 1949 declared Ireland to be a republic. Since then, Fine Gael has been intermittently in power, most recently from 2011, but has required coalition support to remain so. It has advocated the concept of a united Ireland achieved by peaceful means.

Finland (Finnish **Suomi**)

Capital:	Helsinki
Area:	338,145 sq km (130,559 sq miles)
Population:	5,266,114 (2013 est)
Currency:	1 euro = 100 cents
Religions:	Lutheran 82.5%; Eastern Orthodox 1.1%; other Christian 1.1%
Ethnic Groups:	Finnish 93.4%; Swedish 5.6%; Russian and other minorities
Languages:	Finnish, Swedish (both official); Russian and other minority languages
International Organizations:	UN; EU; OECD; Council of Europe; OSCE; Euro-Atlantic Partnership Council; WTO

A Baltic country, sometimes considered part of Scandinavia. It is bounded by Norway on the north, Sweden and the Gulf of Bothnia on the west, and Russia on the east.

Physical A long coastline round the west and south, studded with over 6000 Åland islands, thrusts into the Baltic Sea. Finland's 60,000 lakes are linked by short rivers, sounds, or canals to form busy waterways. A third of the country lies north of the Arctic Circle and is part of Lapland.

Economy Finland is an industrialized country with little agriculture. Industries include metals and metal products, electronics, machinery, and scientific instruments. The principal exports are electrical and optical equipment, machinery, and transport equipment; the products of Finland's extensive forests, such as paper, timber, and wood pulp, are also exported. The only significant mineral resources are chromium and copper.

History Occupied between 100 and 800 AD by Finno-Ugrian tribes who drove the original Lapp population into its northernmost regions, Finland was conquered and converted to Christianity by Eric IX of Sweden in the late 1150s, and throughout the Middle Ages found itself at the centre of Swedish-Russian rivalry in the Baltic area. In 1556 Gustavus Vasa made Finland into a separate duchy for his second son John, and following the latter's succession to the Swedish throne as John III in 1568 it was elevated to a grand duchy. Although still dominated by Sweden, Finland was allowed its own Diet and granted a degree of autonomy.

However, the Treaty of Tilsit (1807) between Tsar Alexander I and Napoleon led to the annexation of Finland as a grand duchy of Russia until 1917. Attempts to impose the Russian language and military conscription brought widespread discontent and the *Russian Revolution of 1917 offered opportunities for national assertion. Independence was achieved (1919) under Marshal Mannerheim, and a democratic, republican constitution introduced. In 1920 Finland joined the League of Nations, which achieved one of its few successes in resolving the dispute with Sweden over sovereignty of the Åland Islands in the Gulf of Bothnia. After the Nazi–Soviet Pact of 1939, Finland was invaded in the *Finnish-Russian War (1939–40). Finnish resistance excited international admiration but no practical help, and surrender entailed a considerable loss of territory (Karelia and Petsamo). When Germany invaded the Soviet Union in 1941 the Finns sought to regain these territories by fighting on the side of the *Axis Powers, but capitulated to the Soviet Union in 1944 and were burdened with a huge reparations bill. Since World War II Finland has accepted neutrality in international affairs. Finland's economy suffered from the collapse of eastern European markets following the end of the Soviet Union, and austerity measures were introduced in 1992. Finland joined the *European Union in 1995 and adopted the *euro as its currency in 2002. However, opposition to EU membership has grown following the *Eurozone Crisis.

Finnish–Russian War (or **Winter War**) (1939–40) A war fought between Finland and the Soviet Union. The Finnish government under General Mannerheim had rejected Soviet demands for bases and for frontier revisions similar to those accepted by the lesser Baltic states. Soviet armies attacked on three fronts, and at first the Finns' superior skill in manoeuvring on skis on the frozen lakes and across the Gulf of Finland, and in the forests of their country, kept the Soviet forces at bay. After 15 weeks of fierce fighting the Soviets breached the Mannerheim Line and Finland was forced to accept peace on Stalin's terms, ceding its eastern territories and the port of Viipuri (Viborg).

Fire of London A major fire that devastated London in September 1666. The fire began in a baker's shop and, fanned by an east wind, raged for four days, destroying 87 churches, including St Paul's, and more than 13,000 houses mostly built from wood. It was stopped by blowing up buildings in its path. There are eyewitness accounts in the diaries of Samuel *Pepys and John *Evelyn. Plans for a modern city with wide streets and squares were abandoned, but Sir Christopher Wren rebuilt St Paul's and a number of other churches and public buildings, and designed the Monument (1677), which commemorates the fire.

First World War See WORLD WAR I.

Fisher, Andrew (1862–1928) Australian statesman. He was a Member of the Queensland Legislative Assembly (1893–96, 1899–1901) and led the Labor Party (1907–15). He was federal Prime Minister and Treasurer (1908–09, 1910–13, 1914–15). His second government extended social welfare and established the Commonwealth Bank. Wartime stress, and conflict with W. M. *Hughes, led to his resignation, after which he was High Commissioner in London (1916–21).

Fitzgerald, Garret (1926–2011) Irish politician, Prime Minister of the Republic of Ireland (1981–82; 1982–87). He was leader of Fine Gael (1977–87) and negotiated the controversial Anglo-Irish agreement in 1985.

five members The five members of the English parliament that *Charles I attempted to arrest on 4 January 1642. Mounting opposition to the king, culminating in the *Grand Remonstrance (December 1641), had been led by *Pym, supported by *Hampden, Holles, Hesilrige, and Strode. Charles rashly decided to arrest and impeach them. He entered the House of Commons only to find that the members had fled into the City of London; they returned to the House of Commons a week later. This attempted use of force by the king hardened Parliamentary opposition against him and was a factor leading to the outbreak of the *English Civil War. No other monarch has since set foot in the House of Commons; its inde-

pendence from interference is fundamental to its existence.

Five Nations See IROQUOIS.

Flodden Field, Battle of (9 September 1513) An important battle that took place between the English and the Scots on the Scottish border; it resulted in a major English victory that gave *Henry VIII security in the north for many years. A large army led by *James IV was defeated by a somewhat smaller force of about 20,000 English soldiers under the command of Thomas Howard, Earl of Surrey. Long Scottish spears were no match for English bills and longbows, and the Scots lost perhaps as many as 10,000 dead, including James IV himself.

Foch, Ferdinand (1851–1929) French general. He strongly supported the use of offensive warfare, which resulted in many of his 20th Corps being killed by German machine guns in August 1914. He became Supreme Commander of all Allied Forces on the Western Front in early 1918, and served as the senior French representative at the Armistice negotiations.

Fontenoy, Battle of (11 May 1745) A battle in the War of the *Austrian Succession, fought at Fontenoy, a village in Hainault in south-west Belgium: it saw a major victory for the French over Austria and her allies. *Saxe, the French commander, had overrun the Austrian Netherlands. The British general, the Duke of *Cumberland, was advancing to the relief of Tournai with a British, Austrian, and Dutch force; he found a gap in the French line of fortifications but was driven back.

Forbes, George William (1869–1947) New Zealand statesman. A Member of Parliament for the Liberal (later United) Party, Forbes succeeded the Prime Minister, J. G. *Ward, in 1930. He attempted to meet the *Depression by balancing the budget and paying "the dole" only to men who worked on labour-intensive public works schemes. In 1931 Forbes, in coalition with the more dynamic J. G. *Coates, won the election on a policy of retrenchment, but in 1935 was swept out of office by Labour with its policy of economic expansion.

Force Acts Popular name for US Acts designed to enforce federal law. Such an Act was passed in 1833 and was designed to counteract *nullification: it empowered President Andrew *Jackson to use the army and navy, if necessary, to enforce the laws of Congress. Four Enforcement Acts of Congress (1870–75) were intended to compel recognition by the South of the *Civil

Rights Act of 1866, of the *Fourteenth Amendment and later, the Fifteenth Amendment: Congressional elections were placed under national control, and the acts of armed organizations such as the *Ku Klux Klan were declared tantamount to rebellion.

Ford, Gerald (Rudolph) (1913–2006) US Republican statesman, 38th President of the USA (1974–77). He became President on the resignation of Richard *Nixon in the wake of the Watergate affair. The free pardon he granted Nixon two months later aroused controversy.

Ford, Henry (1863–1947) US motor manufacturer. He was a pioneer of mass production and had a profound influence on the widespread use of motor vehicles. In 1909 Ford produced his famous Model T, of which 15 million were made over the next 19 years at gradually reducing prices due to large-scale manufacture, a succession of simple assembly tasks, and the use of a conveyor belt. He went on to produce a cheap and effective farm tractor, the Fordson, which had a great effect on agricultural mechanization. Control of the Ford Motor Company passed to his grandson, **Henry Ford II** (1917–87), in 1945 and is now a huge multinational corporation. Among the first Henry Ford's philanthropic legacies is the Ford Foundation (established 1936), a major charitable trust.

Formigny, Battle of (15 April 1450) A battle in the *Hundred Years War. English forces were intercepted by French troops on their way to reinforce the garrison at Caen. Despite successes won by their archers, the English were overcome when French reinforcements arrived. This French victory led to the fall of Caen two months later, and the English loss of Normandy soon after.

Forrest, John, 1st Baron (1847–1918) Australian explorer and statesman, Premier of Western Australia (1890–1901). From 1864, as colonial surveyor, he was one of the principal explorers of Western Australia. He did much to secure the colony's self-government and became its first Premier.

Fort Stanwix A colonial American military stronghold. Named after General John Stanwix, the fort was an important defence point and trading centre located between the Upper Mohawk River and Wood Creek. It fell into disrepair after 1763, but was rebuilt at the beginning of the War of Independence. Fort Stanwix is chiefly remembered as the site of the signing of two treaties with Native Americans in 1768 and 1784, in the second of which the *Iroquois ceded their territory in Pennsylvania to the US government.

Fort Sumter Military stronghold in Charleston harbour, USA. The Confederates, having seized Federal funds and property in the South, demanded the evacuation of the Federal Fort Sumter in Charleston Harbor. Major Robert Anderson, in command, refused and General Beauregard bombarded it (12–13 April 1861) just as relief for the Federalists approached. The fall of the fort marked the beginning of the *American Civil War.

Forty-Five, the (1745) A *Jacobite rebellion in England and Scotland. Its aim was the removal of the Hanoverian *George II from the throne and his replacement by James Edward *Stuart, the Old Pretender. Jacobite hopes centred on the facts that Britain was heavily engaged in the War of the *Austrian Succession, and that the Hanoverians had never been popular. The Pretender sent his 25-year-old son Charles Edward *Stuart (Bonnie Prince Charlie, the Young Pretender) to represent him. Most of Scotland was soon overrun and the Jacobite victory at Prestonpans was followed by the invasion of England. But the English armies of General Wade and the Duke of *Cumberland were closing in and, without any significant numbers of English recruits, Charles was advised by his commanders to return to Scotland. The Jacobites turned back at Derby when barely 160 km (100 miles) from London, where panic at their advance had caused a run on the Bank of England. The decision to retreat meant that the rebellion was doomed. The last Jacobite army was routed at the battle of *Culloden, which ended any serious Jacobite challenge to the Hanoverian succession.

forum An open public space in a town or city of the Roman empire. From the 6th century BC the Roman forum was a place for civic meetings and religious and military ceremonial. The Curia (Senate House) and *comitia were situated there, together with markets, libraries, and courts. War trophies were put on display, the most famous being the ram-beaks ("rostra") of Carthaginian galleys taken in the First *Punic war, which decorated the public platform or "rostra" outside the Senate House. Other forums were built in Rome by early emperors including *Augustus, *Vespasian, and *Trajan. The model was followed in virtually every town of the Roman empire.

Fosse Way An ancient Roman road in Britain, so called from the fosse or ditch on each side. It probably ran from Axminster to Lincoln, via Bath and Leicester (about 300 km, 200 miles), and marked the limit of the first stage of the Roman occupation (43 AD).

Foster, William Zebulon (1881–1961) US political leader. He joined the International Workers of the World in 1909, and after organizing the steelworkers' strike in the Chicago area in 1919, became a member of the newly formed US Communist Party. He ran as its presidential candidate in 1924, 1928, and 1932, and in 1945, after the discrediting of Earl Browder, the Party's war-time leader, became its chairman. He died in Moscow.

Fouché, Joseph, duc d'Otranto (c.1759–1820) French statesman. He was a leading member of the *Jacobin Club in Nantes in 1790. He supported their violent doctrines, demanded the execution of the king, and was used to crush revolts in the west. He helped initiate the atheistical movement which led him into conflict with *Robespierre and to his ejection from the Jacobin Club in 1794. During the next five years his skill and energy enabled him to play a successful part in the coups that overthrew Robespierre and the *Directory. As Minister of Police (1799–1802), and of the Interior under *Napoleon, he was one of the most powerful men in France until his resignation in 1815.

Founding Fathers The 55 delegates to the Constitutional Convention of 1787 that drafted the *Constitution of the USA. They included outstanding public officials, of whom the most respected were George *Washington and Benjamin *Franklin, while the leaders were James *Madison and George Mason of Virginia, Governor Morris and James Wilson of Pennsylvania, and Roger Sherman and Elbridge Gerry of Massachusetts. Of the 55 delegates, over half were lawyers, while planters and merchants, together with a few physicians and college professors, made up the rest. Washington was elected President of the Convention and William Jackson secretary. Jackson's notes were meagre, but a report of the debates was given in Madison's journal (and in notes made by other delegates), though, as the Convention was sworn to secrecy, Madison's notes were not published until 1840.

Four Modernizations Four key aspects of China's post-Mao development. The need to modernize agriculture, industry, national defence, and science and technology was implied in a speech by *Mao Zedong in 1963, but in the *Cultural Revolution ideology was considered to be more important than economic development. After *Deng Xiaoping came to power, the Four Modernizations began to take priority. Training of scientists, engineers, and managers, and the reform of agriculture by the "responsibility system" (the transfer of management power from the commune to the individual) are key examples.

Fourteen Points (8 January 1918) A US peace programme for a just settlement at the end of World War I contained in President Woodrow *Wilson's address to Congress. They comprised freedom of the seas, equality of trade conditions, reduction of armaments, adjustment of colonial claims, evacuation of Russian territory and of Belgium, the return to France of Alsace-Lorraine, recognition of nationalist aspirations in eastern and central Europe, freedom for subject peoples in the Turkish empire, independence for Poland, and the establishment of a 'general association of nations'. Accepted, with some reluctance, by the Allies, they became in large part the basis for the negotiations of the *Versailles Peace Settlement.

Fourteenth Amendment (1868) The most important of the three *American Civil War and Reconstruction amendments to the US Constitution. Drawn up in 1866 by the Joint Committee of Fifteen, the Fourteenth Amendment extended US citizenship to all persons born or naturalized in the USA (and thus, by including ex-slaves, reversed the *Dred Scott decision). It also prohibited the states from abridging the privileges and immunities of citizens or depriving any person of life, liberty, or property without due process of law, or denying any person the equal protection of the laws. Another clause reduced the representation in Congress of states that denied the vote to Black people. The Fourteenth Amendment has caused more legal controversy than any other part of the constitution. In the late 19th century, it was used as a device to protect big business from state regulation. In the 20th century it has been the main constitutional instrument of the *civil rights movement and, in more recent years, of the women's rights movement. (The Fifteenth Amendment, adopted in 1870, provided that the right to vote should not be denied on grounds of race, colour, or previous condition of servitude.)

Fox, Charles James (1749–1806) British Whig statesman. At the age of 19 he entered Parliament advocating American independence, and later welcomed the French

Revolution. After Lord North's resignation he became Secretary of State, collaborating with his former opponent North to form a government in 1783. The coalition was brought down the same year and Fox remained in opposition until the death of Pitt the Younger in 1806, when he took office again as Foreign Secretary and passed an anti-slavery bill through Parliament.

Fox, George (1624–91) English preacher and founder of the Society of Friends (Quakers). He began preaching in 1647, teaching that truth is the inner voice of God speaking to the soul, and rejecting priesthood and ritual. Despite repeated imprisonment, he established a society called the 'Friends of the Truth' (c.1650), which later became the Society of Friends.

France

Capital:	Paris
Area:	551,500 sq km (212,935 sq miles)
Population:	65,951,611 (2013 est)
Currency:	1 euro = 100 cents
Religions:	Roman Catholic: between 83.0% and 88.0%; Muslim: between 5.0% and 10.0%; Protestant: 2.0%
Ethnic Groups:	French 80%; other European, African, and Asian minorities
Languages:	French (official); minority languages
International Organizations:	UN; NATO; EU; OECD; Council of Europe; OSCE; Franc Zone; Secretariat of the Pacific Community; WTO

A country in western Europe, which is bounded on the north by the English Channel (la Manche), on the west by the Atlantic Ocean, on the south by the Pyrenees and the Mediterranean, and on the east by Belgium, Germany, Luxembourg, Switzerland, and Italy.

Physical France is Europe's second largest country after Russia. In the north-west the Brittany peninsula with its low granite hills, Normandy with its fertile uplands, the broad Loire valley, and the Seine Basin, all enjoy a temperate climate. In the north-east is agricultural land on chalk or limestone well drained by rivers. There are also deposits of coal. Southward the ground rises to the Massif Central. To the west lie the Bordeaux lowlands and the Gironde Estuary, to the south the plains of Languedoc, and to the east the Rhône valley. Extending from south to north along France's eastern border are the Jura Mountains, the Vosges, and the western Alps, falling away on their northern slopes to Alsace-Lorraine.

French overseas departments and dependencies include French Guiana, French Polynesia, Guadeloupe, Martinique, Mayotte, New Caledonia, and Réunion.

Economy France has a diverse economy and the fifth-largest GDP in the world. Industries include machinery, chemicals, vehicles, metallurgy, aircraft, and electronics, with machinery, transportation equipment, aircraft, plastics, and chemicals being the principal exports. Agriculture produces cereals, sugar beet, and potatoes; wine production remains important, although France's traditional dominance of this market has declined in recent years. Tourism is also important, with France being the most visited country in the world.

History Prehistoric remains, cave paintings, and megalithic monuments attest to a long history of human settlement. The area known as *Gaul to the Romans was conquered by the armies of Julius *Caesar, and its native inhabitants thoroughly Romanized by centuries of occupation. After 330 it was invaded by *Goths, *Franks, and Burgundians, and then ruled by Clovis (465–511), a *Merovingian king. It became part of the empire of *Charlemagne and, after repeated assaults from *Vikings and *Saracens, a *Capetian dynasty emerged in 987. Fierce competition with the rival rulers of Brittany, *Burgundy, and, after 1066, with the Norman and Plantagenet kings of England ensued, culminating in the *Hundred Years War. France did not emerge as a permanently unified state until the ejection of the English and the Burgundians at the end of the Middle Ages. Under the *Valois and *Bourbon dynasties France rose to contest European hegemony in the 16th to 18th centuries, notably in the wars of *Louis XIV. In the 18th century, weak government, expensive wars, and colonial rivalry with England wrecked the monarchy's finances, and mounting popular anger culminated in the *French Revolution (1789).

The First Republic (1792–1804), established after the fall of the Bourbon monarchy, lasted until the First Empire (1804–14) under *Napoleon I, when France became the dominant political power in Europe. After his fall the monarchy was restored (1814) and, with a brief interval in 1815, lasted until the abdication of Louis Philippe (1848). During this period, having lost influence in India and Canada, France began to create an overseas empire in North Africa. The Second Republic, established in 1848, lasted until 1852, when *Napoleon III proclaimed the Second Empire (1852–70). It saw further expansion of the French empire, particularly in south-east Asia and in the Pacific. The Third Republic (1870–1940) was established after the capture and exile of Napoleon III and France's defeat in the *Franco-Prussian War (1870). France took part in the Berlin Conference (1884) on Africa, and by 1914 ruled over Morocco, Tunis, Madagascar, and the huge areas of *French West Africa and *French Equatorial Africa. The Third Republic fell in 1940, following defeat by Nazi Germany. Northern France was occupied by the Germans, unoccupied France to the south was under the *Vichy government, and a *Free French government was proclaimed in London. The Fourth Republic (1946–58) was replaced by the Fifth Republic (1958–), under the strong presidency of Charles *de Gaulle (1959–69). Protracted and costly wars led to the decolonization of Indo-China (1954) and of Algeria (1962), while, from 1956, the rest of the African empire gained increasing independence. After 1945 France regained its position as a major European power and was a founder member of the *European Economic Community (1958). As a nuclear power it refused to sign the *Nuclear Test-Ban Treaty (1963) and withdrew formally from the military division of *NATO in 1966. President de Gaulle's successor, Georges *Pompidou, supported the extension of the *European Community (now the *European Union), and President *Mitterrand's referendum in 1992 narrowly endorsed the *Maastricht Treaty. Mitterrand did not contest the presidential elections in 1995 and the right-wing moderate Jacques *Chirac was elected. In 1997 a leftist government was elected, but the right returned to power in 2002. In the same year Chirac was re-elected and France adopted the *euro as its currency. In 2005 Paris and other French cities saw a wave of riots in their poorer suburbs with large Muslim populations. Chirac stood down as President in 2007 and the right-wing Nicolas *Sarkozy was elected. Unpopular economic policies, in particular austerity measures to reduce the budget deficit, contributed to his defeat in 2012 by the socialist François *Hollande. However, Hollande's pro-growth policies did not deliver the promised results and his popularity quickly declined.

Francia, José Gaspar Rodriguez de (1776–1840) Dictator of Paraguay. A leader of the Paraguayan movement for independence from Spain (1811), he dominated the post-independence period by establishing (1814) one of the most absolute dictatorships in 19th-century Latin American history. Dogmatic, anti-clerical, and xenophobic, he placed his country in almost complete isolation from the outside world. At home his autocratic rule earned him the name *El Supremo*. As time went on, he grew more arbitrary and despotic. The extravagances of his later years were considered symptomatic of his insanity, although he held office until his death in 1840.

Francis (born **Jorge Mario Bergoglio**) (1936–) Pope (2013–). Born in Buenos Aires, Argentina, he graduated as a chemical technician before training for the priesthood. He became a Jesuit novice in 1958 and a priest in 1969. Thereafter he served as Jesuit Provincial Superior for Argentina (1973–79), an auxiliary bishop of Buenos Aires (1992–98), and Archbishop of Buenos Aires (1998–2013). Theologically conservative, he became a strong advocate of the poor and gained a reputation for humility and simplicity. He was elected Pope (2013) following *Benedict XVI's resignation. He immediately emphasized spiritual renewal and the problems of the poor, and spurned tradition to adopt a simple lifestyle. Francis is the first South American and the first Jesuit to become Pope, and the first non-European for almost 1300 years.

Francis I (1494–1547) King of France (1515–47). He was in many respects an archetypal Renaissance prince, able, quick-witted, and licentious, and a patron of art and learning, but he developed into a cruel persecutor of Protestants, and devoted the best part of his reign to an inconclusive struggle with the *Habsburgs. He began by recovering the duchy of Milan (1515), but failed in his bid to be elected Holy Roman Emperor (1519). In 1520 he tried to secure the support of *Henry VIII of England against the successful candidate, *Charles V, at the *Field of the Cloth of Gold, and in 1521 he embarked on the first of four wars against the emperor, which ended with his capture at the Battle of *Pavia (1525). He gained his release from captivity in Spain by renouncing his claims in Italy, but hostilities were resumed and continued intermittently, with the recovery of Milan as a main object, until the Peace of Crespy in 1544. His foreign wars were ruinously expensive, and the prodigality of his court foreshadowed that of *Louis XIV. The palace of Fontainebleau was rebuilt during his reign, and the artists Leonardo da Vinci, Benvenuto Cellini, and Andrea del Sarto worked at his court.

Francis Ferdinand (1863–1914), Archduke of Austria and heir presumptive to Emperor *Francis Joseph. He aimed to transform *Austria-Hungary into a triple monarchy to include a Slavic kingdom. He was opposed by the Hungarians, who refused to make concessions to Slavs, and by extreme Slav nationalists (including Serbs), who saw no future for the emergent nations within the empire. On 28 June 1914, while on an inspection tour at Sarajevo, he and his wife were assassinated by Gavrilo Princip, a Serbian nationalist. The subsequent ultimatum by Austria to Serbia led directly to the outbreak of World War I.

Francis Joseph (1830–1916) Emperor of Austria (1848–1916), King of Hungary (1867–1916). He succeeded to the throne (aged 18) amid the *Revolutions of 1848. He suppressed all nationalist hopes until forced to meet Hungarian aspirations in the establishment of *Austria-Hungary (1867). His foreign policy lost Habsburg lands to Italy (1859 and 1866) and led to the loss of Austrian influence over German affairs and to the ascendancy of Prussia. Seeking compensation in the *Balkans, he aroused Slav opposition which ultimately resulted in World War I. His wife Elizabeth was assassinated by the Italian anarchist Lucheni. Opposed to social reform, Francis Joseph maintained administrative centralization and opposed the federalist aspirations of the Slavs.

Francis of Assisi, St (born **Giovanni di Bernardone**) (c.1181–1226) Italian monk, founder of the Franciscan order. Born into a wealthy family, he renounced his inheritance in favour of a life of poverty after experiencing a personal call to rebuild the semi-derelict church of San Damiano of Assisi. He soon attracted followers, founding the Franciscan order in 1209 and drawing up its original rule (based on complete poverty).

Franco, Francisco (**Francisco Franco Bahamonde**) (1892–1975) Spanish general and head of state. A monarchist, he rose rapidly in the army until 1931, when Alfonso XIII abdicated and was replaced by a republican government. He was temporarily out of favour, but by 1935 was chief of the General Staff. Elections in February 1936 returned a more left-wing government and the army prepared to revolt. At first he hesitated to join in the military

conspiracy but in July led troops from Morocco into Spain to attack Madrid and overthrow the republic. After three years of the savage *Spanish Civil War he was victorious and became dictator of Spain (1939). In 1937 Franco adopted the *Falange, expanding it into a Spanish fascist party and banning all political opposition. During World War II he remained neutral though sympathizing with Hitler and Mussolini. His government was ostracized by the new United Nations until, with the coming of the *Cold War, his hostility towards communism restored him to favour. His domestic policy became slightly more liberal, and in 1969 he named Prince Juan Carlos (1938–), grandson of Alfonso XIII, as his successor and heir to the reconstituted Spanish throne. On his death Spain returned to a democratic system of government under a constitutional monarchy.

Franco-Prussian War (1870–71) The war between France, under *Napoleon III, and Prussia. The war itself was provoked by *Bismarck, who had skilfully isolated the French, and altered an uncontroversial message from his king (the *Ems telegram). Prussian armies advanced into France; the French forces led by MacMahon were driven out of Alsace whilst a second French army was forced to retire to Metz. MacMahon, marching to relieve Metz, was comprehensively defeated by Moltke at Sedan. Napoleon was captured and, discredited in the eyes of the French, ceased to be emperor. Bismarck refused to make peace, and in September the siege of Paris began. Hopes of a French counterattack were dispelled when Bazaine surrendered at Metz and Paris finally gave way in January 1871. An armistice was granted by Bismarck, and a national assembly elected to ratify the peace, but the population of Paris refused to lay down arms and in March 1871 rose in revolt and set up the Commune of *Paris. The French government signed the Treaty of *Frankfurt in May and French prisoners-of-war were allowed through Prussian lines to suppress the Commune. For Prussia, the proclamation of the *German Second empire at Versailles in January was the climax of Bismarck's ambitions to unite Germany.

Frank, Anne (1929–45) German Jewish girl. Her diary, first published in 1947, records the experiences of her family living for two years in hiding from the Nazis in occupied Amsterdam. They were eventually betrayed and sent to concentration camps; Anne died in Belsen from typhoid. Her diary has been translated into more than 30 languages, including an English version, and has become a symbol of the suffering of European Jews at the hands of the Germans.

Frankfurt, Treaty of (10 May 1871) An agreement that ended the *Franco-Prussian War. By it France surrendered Strasburg, Alsace and part of Lorraine, together with the great fortresses of Metz to *Bismarck's Germany. An indemnity of five billion gold francs was imposed by Germany on France, and a German army of occupation was to remain until the indemnity had been paid. Bismarck's aim in this treaty was to ensure that France would be entirely cut off from the Rhine.

franklin English freeholder in the 13th and 14th centuries. Franklins paid a rent for their land and did not owe military service to their lord. Their status was above that of the free peasant but below the gentry. After the *Black Death (1349) the status of many franklins improved in the favourable economic climate. The newly rich and socially ambitious franklin was satirized by Chaucer in the Prologue to his *Canterbury Tales*.

Franklin, Benjamin (1706–90) US statesman, inventor, and scientist. A wealthy printer and publisher, he was one of the signatories to the peace between the USA and Great Britain after the War of American Independence. His main scientific achievements were the formulation of a theory of electricity, based on the concept of an electric fluid, which introduced (and arbitrarily defined) positive and negative electricity, and a demonstration of the electrical nature of lightning, which led to the invention of the lightning conductor. His inventions include the 'Franklin stove' (a kind of free-standing cast-iron heater) and bifocal spectacles.

frankpledge (or **peace-pledge**) A system for preserving law and order in English communities from the 10th century to the 14th, when it was superseded by the appointment of Justices of the Peace. Communities were grouped into associations of ten men (a tithing) under a headman (chief pledge or tithingman) and held responsible for the good behaviour of members. Twice a year, in the "view of frankpledge", sheriffs examined its effectiveness. Frankpledge was not applied to the aristocracy, to certain freeholders, or to vagrants, nor was it found in northern England where the alternative system of Serjeants of the Peace existed.

Franks A group of Germanic tribes who dominated Europe after the collapse of the Western

*Roman empire. They consisted of Salians from what is now Belgium and Ripuarians from the Lower Rhine. They settled in Gaul by the mid-4th century and ruled it by the following century when the Salians under *Clovis defeated the Romans at Soissons. Gaul became 'Francia', ruled from the old capital Lutetia Parisiorum (Paris) of the Parisii Gauls. The *Merovingian succession continued until 751. Power then passed from the kings to their palace mayors. In 751 Pepin, son of Charles Martel, became the first *Carolingian ruler of the Franks.

Franz Josef *See* FRANCIS JOSEPH.

Fraser, Malcolm (John Malcolm Fraser) (1930–) Australian Liberal statesman, Prime Minister (1975–83). He became the youngest-ever Australian MP in 1955 and was minister for the army, education and science, and defence before becoming leader of the Liberal Party in 1975. He was appointed Prime Minister with the dissolution of the previous administration by the Governor-General and was elected a month later. Unable to curb unemployment, his government was defeated in 1983. He resigned from the Liberal Party in 2009.

Fraser, Peter (1884–1950) New Zealand statesman. He was gaoled during World War I for opposing conscription, and upon his release joined the New Zealand Labour Party. Elected to Parliament in 1918, he became the party's deputy leader in 1933, and Prime Minister (1940–49). One of the architects of the United Nations (1945), he held a life-long commitment to equality in education, and the modern New Zealand education system is perhaps his most enduring monument.

Frederick I (or **Frederick Barbarossa**, 'Redbeard') (*c.*1123–90) King of Germany and Holy Roman emperor (1152–90). He made a sustained attempt to subdue Italy and the papacy, but was eventually defeated at the Battle of Legnano in 1176. He was drowned in Asia Minor while on his way to the Third Crusade.

Frederick I (1657–1713) Elector of Brandenburg from 1688, King of Prussia (1701–13). He lacked the ability of his father, *Frederick William, the Great Elector, and dissipated funds in display and extravagance. In 1700 he supported the Holy Roman Emperor Leopold I in the War of the *Spanish Succession and with his approval was able to proclaim himself king, taking his title from his territory of East *Prussia. In 1713 he acquired Upper Gelders. With his second wife Sophia Charlotte he developed Berlin and established the Academy of Science and the University of Halle.

Frederick II (1194–1250) Holy Roman Emperor (1220–50). The grandson of *Frederick I (Barbarossa), Frederick II was known as *Stupor Mundi* ('Wonder of the World') because of the breadth of his power and of his administrative, military, and intellectual abilities. He was crowned King of the Germans in 1215 and Holy Roman Emperor in 1220, but his reign was dominated by a long and ultimately unsuccessful struggle for power with the papacy. In 1228 he led a successful crusade to Jerusalem, obtaining, in 1229, Jerusalem, Nazareth, and Bethlehem for Christendom. Twice excommunicated by Pope Gregory IX, and opposed in Italy by the Lombard League, Frederick devolved a great deal of imperial power within Germany on the lay and clerical princes in an effort to maintain their support, and concentrated on building a power base in Sicily, a process completed by the Constitution of Melfi in 1231. He defeated the Lombard League at Cortenuova in 1237 and humiliated Gregory IX prior to the latter's death in 1241, but failed in his efforts to conciliate Innocent IV who appealed to Germany to revolt at the Synod of Lyons in 1245. Frederick's position was crumbling in the face of revolt, papal propaganda, and military defeat when he died in 1250, leaving an impossible situation for his heirs to solve. Many scholars and artists of his court migrated to north Italian cities, becoming precursors of the *Renaissance.

Frederick II (or **Frederick the Great**) (1712–86) King of Prussia (1740–86). On his succession Frederick promptly claimed Silesia, plunging Europe into the War of the Austrian Succession (1740–48). During the Seven Years War (1756–63), he joined with Britain and Hanover against a coalition of France, Russia, Austria, Spain, Sweden, and Saxony, and succeeded in considerably strengthening Prussia's position. By the end of his reign he had doubled the area of his country. He was a distinguished patron of the arts.

Frederick III (1415–93) King of Germany (1440–93), Holy Roman Emperor (1452–93). He inherited the *Habsburg domains as Archduke of Austria in 1424. He failed to assert family interest in Hungary, and was troubled by rival claimants to his own lands, and by Turkish attacks, which became more threatening after the fall of Constantinople in 1453. On good terms with the papacy, he was the last Holy Roman Emperor to be crowned by the pope at Rome.

He earned unpopularity by his efforts to suppress John *Huss's followers in Bohemia and Hungary. By arranging the marriage of his son Maximilian I to Mary, daughter of *Charles the Bold, he greatly extended the dynastic power of the Habsburgs.

Frederick V (the Winter King) (1596–1632) Elector Palatine (1610–20) and King of Bohemia (1619–20). In 1613 he married Elizabeth, daughter of *James I of England. He then assumed the leadership of the German Protestant Union, and accepted the Bohemian crown when it was offered, following the deposition of *Ferdinand II in November 1619. Thenceforth his fortunes followed the course of the *Thirty Years War, a struggle in which he took little personal part after his defeat at the Battle of the White Mountain (November 1620). He withdrew to The Hague, and forfeited the Palatinate. *George I of Great Britain (1660–1727) was his grandson.

Frederick William (known as **'the Great Elector'**) (1620–88) Elector of Brandenburg (1640–88). His programme of reconstruction and reorganization following the Thirty Years War, including the strengthening of the army and the development of the civil service, brought stability to his country and laid the basis for the expansion of Prussian power in the 18th century. In his foreign policy he sought to create a balance of power by the formation of shifting strategic alliances.

Frederick William I (1688–1740) King of Prussia (1713–40). He was the son of *Frederick I and was known as 'the royal drill-sergeant': he was a strict Calvinist, hardworking, violent tempered, and notorious for his ill-treatment of his son, *Frederick II. He left a model administration, a large revenue, and an efficient and well-disciplined army. He acquired Stettin in 1720.

Frederick William II (1744–97) King of Prussia (1787–97). He was the nephew of *Frederick II and a man of little ability, though a patron of the arts. He fought in the early campaigns against the French Revolutionary armies but became more concerned with Poland gaining land, including Warsaw, in the partitions of 1793 and 1795.

Frederick William III (1770–1840) King of Prussia (1797–1840). After his defeat at the Battle of *Jena he was forced by the Treaty of Tilsit (1807) to surrender half his dominions by the creation of the kingdom of Westphalia and the grand duchy of Warsaw. In 1811 he joined *Napoleon in the war against Russia but, following the retreat of Napoleon from Moscow, he signed a military alliance with Russia and Austria. From 1807 onwards he supported the efforts for reform made by Stein and Hardenberg, and at the Congress of *Vienna he won back for Prussia Westphalia and much of the Rhineland and of Saxony. He signed the *Holy Alliance, and became progressively more reactionary during the last years of his reign.

Frederick William IV (1795–1861) King of Prussia (1840–61). A patriarchal monarch by temperament, he was the champion of a united Germany, but could not accept the degree of democracy envisaged by the Frankfurt Parliament of 1848 (*see* REVOLUTIONS OF 1848). He therefore refused (1849) the offer of a constitutional monarchy for the German Confederation. For Prussia he promulgated a conservative constitution allowing for a parliament, but with a restricted franchise and limited powers. This remained in force until 1918.

Freedom Riders In the early 1960s, groups of non-violent Black and White protesters against racial discrimination in the US Southern states. They were mostly volunteers from the north who in 1961 began chartering buses and riding through the Southern states to challenge the segregation laws. Many Freedom Riders were arrested or brutally attacked by Southern White racists, but their actions did help to arouse public opinion in support of the *Civil Rights campaign.

Free French, the A World War II organization of Frenchmen and women in exile. Led by General *de Gaulle, it continued the war against the *Axis Powers after the surrender of *Vichy France in 1940. Its headquarters were in London, where, apart from organizing forces that participated in military campaigns and cooperating with the French *resistance movement, it constituted a pressure group that strove to represent French interests. In 1941 its French National Committee was formed and this eventually developed into a provisional government for liberated France. The Free French army in French Equatorial Africa, led by General Leclerc (Philippe, Vicomte de Hauteclocque), linked up with the British forces in Tripoli (1943), after completing an epic march of *c.*2400 km (1500 miles) from Lake Chad. A provisional Free French government was established in Algiers, moving to Paris in 1944.

Freemason A member of an international fraternity called `Free and Accepted Masons',

which declares itself to be based on brotherly love, faith, and charity, and is characterized by elaborate rituals and systems of secret signs, passwords, and handshakes. The rituals are based largely on Old Testament anecdotes and moralities and are illustrated by the tools of a mason, the square and compasses. The original `free masons' were probably skilled itinerant stonemasons who (in and after the 14th century) found work wherever important buildings were being erected, all of whom recognized their fellow craftsmen by secret signs. The 'accepted masons' were honorary members (originally supposed to be eminent for architectural or antiquarian learning) who began to be admitted early in the 17th century. The distinction of being an 'accepted mason' became a fashionable aspiration; before the end of the 17th century the purpose of the fraternities seems to have been chiefly social. In 1717 four of these societies or 'lodges' in London united to form a Grand Lodge, with a new constitution and ritual. The Masonic Order is forbidden to Roman Catholics, as the Church regards certain masonic principles as incompatible with its doctrines.

Free-Silver Movement A movement in the 19th century in the USA for an unlimited silver coinage. Following the *gold rushes of the 1850s and 1860s, large deposits of silver were discovered in the West. Silver miners wished to see unlimited production, but in 1873 Congress refused to include the silver dollar in its list of authorized coins. A protest movement resulted, and in 1878 the silver dollar became legal tender, the US Treasury agreeing to purchase silver to turn into coins. In 1890 the Sherman Silver Purchase Act doubled the agreed issue of silver, but following a stockmarket crisis in 1893 the Act was repealed. Eastern bankers were blamed for a depressed silver market, and the Democratic Party adopted the demand for unlimited free silver in the presidential campaign of 1896. Following the 1900 election, a Republican Congress passed the Gold Standard Act, which made gold the sole standard of currency. Franklin Delano *Roosevelt passed legislation securing guaranteed US Treasury purchases of silver for use in coins. Supplies of silver decreased during the 1960s and in 1970 the Treasury stopped using silver and sold its surplus stock.

free trade An economic policy advocating a free flow of goods between countries to encourage mutual economic development and international harmony by the commercial interdependence of trading nations. A policy of free trade prohibits both tariffs on imports and subsidies on exports designed to protect a country's industry. The doctrine's best early statement was by Adam Smith in his *Wealth of Nations* (1776). At a conference in Geneva in 1947 a first schedule for freer world trade was drawn up, the *General Agreement on Tariffs and Trade (GATT). For over a decade after World War II Britain also was a strong supporter of moves to restore freer trade. It was a founder member of the European Free Trade Association (EFTA) in 1958, but as adverse economic conditions developed in the 1960s Britain sought entry into the *European Economic Community (now the *European Union). In Eastern Europe a similar community, COMECON, was established in 1949; after 1987 COMECON sought cooperation with EEC countries. The highly successful growth of the Japanese economy after the war led many countries to seek tariffs against Japan. By the 1990s world economic policies were confused, some policies supporting free trade and others supporting trade protection measures. In 1993, at the conclusion of the Uruguay Round of GATT negotiations, the members of GATT agreed to further cuts in tariffs and to create the *World Trade Organization (WTO) as GATT's successor. In addition to tariffs, important related issues in the early 2000s were the use of export subsidies, which allow rich countries to 'dump' their exports on poor countries to the detriment of their economic development, and the fair access of poor countries to rich countries' markets.

Frei, Eduárdo (Eduárdo Frei Montalva) (1911–82) Chilean statesman, President of Chile (1964–70). The programmes he initiated, including agrarian reform and the 'Chileanization' of the copper industry (whose controlling interest had until then been held by US companies), were ambitious, but his failure to check inflation or to redistribute wealth turned many of his supporters against him. His son, Eduárdo Frei Ruiz-Tagle, was also President of Chile (1994–2000).

Frelimo War (1964–75) A war fought between *Mozambique nationalist groups united into the Mozambique Liberation Front (Frelimo) and Portuguese troops. The Portuguese failed to contain the conflict, and by 1968 Samora Machel claimed one-fifth of the country. Brutal Portuguese counter-terrorism made conciliation even more impossible and Portugal conceded independence in 1974. Frelimo became the dominant political force in the new People's Republic of Mozambique.

Frémont, John Charles (known as 'the Pathfinder') (1813–90) US explorer and politician. He was responsible for exploring several viable routes to the Pacific across the Rockies in the 1840s. He made an unsuccessful bid for the presidency in 1856, losing to James Buchanan.

French, John Denton Pinkstone, 1st Earl of Ypres (1852–1925) British field-marshal. Having distinguished himself in the Sudan and the Second *Boer War (1899), he was appointed commander-in-chief of the *British Expeditionary Force in France (1914). Under instructions from Lord *Kitchener he opposed the German advance through Belgium and Flanders. He and his armies were ill-equipped for the kind of *trench warfare in which they found themselves involved, and in December 1915 French resigned in favour of Sir Douglas *Haig. At the Irish *Easter Rising in 1916 French dispatched two divisions to suppress the uprising. He served as Lord Lieutenant of Ireland (1918–21) at a time when outrages and reprisals were widespread.

French and Indian wars (1689–1763) Anglo-French conflicts in North America, part of the international rivalry between the two nations, in which many Native Americans became embroiled. They consisted of King William's War (1689–97), Queen Anne's War (1703–13), King George's War (1744–48), and the French and Indian War (1755–63), the American part of the *Seven Years War. As a result of an alliance with Prussia, *Pitt was able to devote more British resources to America. In 1755 the British commander, General Braddock, led forces into Ohio but was defeated at Fort Duquesne. Other forces defeated the French at the Battle of Lake George, but no advantage was taken. The French claimed a number of victories in 1756 and 1757 against the British, already weakened by friction between the new commander, Lord Loudoun, and the states of Massachusetts and Virginia. In 1759, however, *Wolfe defeated the French at the Battle of the *Plains of Abraham. Quebec surrendered shortly thereafter, followed by Montreal one year later, all Canada then passing into British hands. By the Treaty of *Paris (1763) Britain gained Canada and Louisiana east of the Mississippi.

French Community A political union superseding the French Union, established by France in 1958 and comprising metropolitan France, its overseas departments and territories, and 12 French colonies in Africa, which were granted substantial autonomy as 'member states'. The Community quickly became defunct when all the member states became fully independent in 1960, but it was not formally abolished until 1995.

French East India Company A commercial organization, founded in 1664 to compete with the *Dutch and English *East India companies. Until the 1740s it was less successful than its rivals, but led by an ambitious governor, Dupleix, the Company then made a bid to challenge English influence in India, notably by alliances with local rulers in south India. Although a number of trading ports, including Pondicherry and Chandernagore, remained in French control until 1949, the Company itself collapsed during the French Revolutionary period.

French empire The colonial empire of France. France under the Valois family had come to approximate its modern boundaries by the end of the 15th century. Most of its colonial possessions were acquired during the 17th century, these included parts of America, Canada, India, and the Caribbean. In the 18th century a long rivalry with Britain ended with the loss of Quebec and recognition of British supremacy in India. By 1815 only some West Indian Islands, French Guiana, and Senegal and Gabon were left. However, the 19th century witnessed a rapid revival of the empire. The conquest of Algeria began (1830), while Far Eastern possessions—Cochin China, Cambodia, and New Caledonia—were added. In the 'Scramble for Africa', Tunisia became a protectorate (1881), and by 1912 *Morocco, *Madagascar, and French Somaliland (*Djibouti) had been added to *French Equatorial Africa and *French West Africa to make the African empire 20 times the size of France itself. Britain frustrated French aspirations in Egypt and the Sudan, and rivalry at Fashoda (1898) nearly caused war until the Entente Cordiale brought agreement. After World War I Togoland and the Cameroons, former German colonies, became French Mandates, as did Syria and Lebanon (1923). Defeat in World War II and short-lived post-war governments prevented urgent reforms, causing the loss of both Far Eastern and African empires. In Indo-China the communist leader, *Ho Chi Minh, established his Vietnamese republic (1945) which France refused to recognize. Open warfare (1946–54) ended with the French capitulation at *Dienbienphu and the consequent independence of Cambodia, Laos, and Vietnam. In Algeria almost the entire French army failed to quell an Arab rising (1954). By 1958 *de Gaulle realized that Algerian

independence was inevitable, and it followed in 1962. In 1946 the empire was formed into the French Union, which was replaced in 1958 by the *French Community; this quickly became defunct when other French colonies in Africa achieved independence in 1960.

French Equatorial Africa A federation of French colonies created in 1910 to consolidate French territories in west-central Africa. Originally called French Congo, its constituent territories were Gabon, Middle Congo, Chad, and Ubangi-Shari (now the Central African Republic). The federation was dissolved in 1958.

French Foreign Legion A French volunteer armed force consisting chiefly of foreigners. In 1831 *Louis Philippe reorganized a light infantry legion in Algeria as the *régiment étranger*, the foreign legion. It fought in numerous 19th-century wars and in both World Wars. Following Algeria's independence in 1962 the legion was transferred to France. No questions are asked about the origin or past of the recruits, whose oath binds them absolutely to the regiment whose unofficial motto is *legio patria nostra* ('the legion is our fatherland').

French Indo-China Former French colonial empire in south-east Asia. Having gained early influence in the area through assisting Gia-Long in establishing the Vietnamese empire in the early 19th century, the French colonized the area between the late 1850s and 1890s, using the term Indo-China to designate the final union of their colonies and dependencies within Annam, Cambodia, Cochin-China, Laos, and Tonkin. Nationalist movements aiming particularly at the formation of an independent and united Vietnam sprang up between the wars, and French influence in the area was fatally undermined in the early 1940s by the collaboration of the *Vichy colonial administration with the Japanese. The *Vietminh resistance movement became active during the war; having consolidated a peasant base, it resisted attempts by the French to reassert their control after 1945. French rule ended after the *French Indo-China War.

French Indo-China War (1946–54) A conflict fought between French colonial forces and *Vietminh forces largely in the Tonkin area of northern Vietnam. The Vietminh began active guerrilla operations during the Japanese occupation of World War II and in September 1945 their leader, *Ho Chi Minh, proclaimed a Vietnamese Republic in Hanoi. The French opposed independence, and launched a military offensive. Ho Chi Minh was forced to flee Hanoi and begin a guerrilla war in December 1946. By 1950, foreign communist aid had increased Vietminh strength to the point where the French were forced into defensive lines around the Red River delta, but Vietminh attempts to win the war failed in 1951. Guerrilla operations continued until an ill-advised French attempt to seek a decisive engagement led to the encirclement and defeat of their forces at *Dienbienphu in 1954. The war, and French rule in Indo-China, were formally terminated at the *Geneva Conference in April–July of that year.

French Revolution (1789) The political upheaval that ended with the overthrow of the Bourbon monarchy in France and marked a watershed in European history. Various groups in French society opposed the *ancien régime with its privileged Establishment and discredited monarchy. Its leaders were influenced by the American Revolution of the 1770s and had much popular support in the 1780s and 1790s. Social and economic unrest combined with urgent financial problems persuaded Louis XVI to summon the *States-General in 1789, an act which helped to set the Revolution in motion. From the States-General emerged the National Assembly and a new Constitution which abolished the *ancien régime*, nationalized the church's lands, and divided the country into departments to be ruled by elected assemblies. Fear of royal retaliation led to popular unrest, the storming of the *Bastille, and the capturing of the king by the National Guard. The National Assembly tried to create a monarchical system in which the king would share power with an elected assembly, but after the king's unsuccessful flight to Varennes and the mobilization of exiled royalists, the Revolutionaries faced increasing military threats from Austria and Prussia which led to war abroad and more radical policies at home. In 1792 the monarchy was abolished, a republic established, and the execution of the king was followed by a **Reign of Terror** (September 1793–July 1794). The Revolution failed to produce a stable form of republican government as several different factions (*Girondins, *Jacobins, Cordeliers, *Robespierre) fought for power. After several different forms of administration had been tried, the last, the Directory, was overthrown by *Napoleon in 1799.

French Wars of Religion A series of nine religious and political conflicts in France, which took place intermittently between 1562 and 1598. They revolved around the great noble families fighting for control of the expiring

*Valois dynasty, supported on one side by the Protestant *Huguenots and on the other by Catholic extremists. The wars were complicated and prolonged by interventions by Spain, Savoy, and Rome on the Catholic side and by England, the Netherlands, and the German princes on the Protestant side. After the turning-point of the *St Bartholomew's Day Massacre (1572), a third party of moderate Catholic "Politiques" emerged under the Montmorency family. However, its advocacy of mutual religious toleration was undermined in 1576 by the formation of the Catholic extremist *Holy League, which opposed *Henry III's tolerant settlement of the fifth war. The Guise-led League grew more militant after the *Bourbon Huguenot leader Henry of Navarre became heir to the French throne in 1584. The resulting War of the *Three Henrys (1585–89), ended with the assassination of Henry III. Henry of Navarre fought on, overcame the League, and drove its Spanish allies out of the country. He adopted Catholicism (1593), and as *Henry IV was able to establish religious toleration in France with the Edict of *Nantes (1598). At the Peace of Vervins (1598) he reached a settlement with Spain. Then he applied himself to providing the firm monarchical rule which had been so damagingly lacking since the death of Henry II in 1559.

French West Africa A former federation of eight French colonies created in 1895 to consolidate French territory in north and west Africa. Its constituent territories were Dahomey (now Benin), French Guinea, French Sudan, Ivory Coast (Côte d'Ivoire), Mauritania, Niger, Senegal, and Upper Volta (now Burkina Faso). The federation was dissolved in 1959.

Freyberg, Bernard Cyril, 1st Baron (1889–1963) New Zealand general. A professional soldier, he was appointed commander-in-chief of the New Zealand Expeditionary Forces (November 1939). He commanded the unsuccessful Commonwealth expedition to Greece and Crete (June 1941). He took an active part in the North African and Italian campaigns, where his New Zealand Division greatly distinguished itself, although suffering heavy losses. From 1945 until 1952 he was governor-general of New Zealand.

Friendly Islands *See* TONGA.

Frisians A Germanic seafaring people. In Roman times they occupied northern Holland and north-west Germany. Apart from records of their revolts against Rome between 12 BC and

69 AD, little is known about them. Some of them served in the Roman army in Britain in the 3rd century. By the 4th century they were under Saxon domination. The *Franks attempted to convert them to Christianity by force, though this was less successful than the missionary efforts of St Wilfred from England. They were part of the *Carolingian empire, and in the 16th century became part of the Habsburg empire of *Charles V. In 1579 they reluctantly joined the Union of *Utrecht against *Philip II. They continued their independent role in the new state, electing their own Statholder (or President) until 1747.

Froissart, Jean (c.1337–c.1410) Flemish poet and court historian. His four *Chroniques* provide a detailed, often eye-witness account of European events from 1325 to 1400. His first book copied the work of an earlier chronicler, Jean le Bel (c.1290–c.1370). The others, drawn from extensive travels, especially to the English court, provide an account of events during the *Hundred Years War.

Fronde (from French *fronde*, 'sling') Street fighting in Paris; the word was applied particularly to two revolts against the absolutism of the crown in France between 1648 and 1652 during the minority of *Louis XIV. The First Fronde began as a protest by the *Parlement* of Paris supported by the Paris mob against war taxation. Disaffected nobles joined in and intrigued with France's enemy, Spain. Peace was restored in March 1649. The Second Fronde began in 1651 with *Mazarin's arrest of the arrogant and overbearing *Condé. Throughout France nobles indulged in irresponsible and confused fighting in which certain great ladies played a conspiratorial role. Mazarin fled from France, but Condé and the mutinous nobles who supported him soon lost popularity. Mazarin was able to return, giving the command of the army to the Vicomte de Turenne, who had rejoined the royalist party and quickly recovered Paris for the king. The Fronde ended in Paris in October 1652.

Front de Libération nationale (FLN) Algerian radical Muslim independence movement. It was formed in 1954 as the political expression of the ALN (Armée de Libération Nationale) when the Algerian war of independence broke out. In spite of differences of opinion between military, political, and religious leaders, the movement hung together, and brought its military leader, *Ben Bella, to power successfully as the first President of Algeria in 1962 following President de Gaulle's successful national referendums on the *Évian Agreements. The principal policies of the party were independence, economic development in a socialist state, non-alignment, and brotherly relations with other Arab states. In 1989 Algeria's constitution was amended so that other political parties were legalized, but the FLN continued to hold all the seats in the National Assembly. Its incipient defeat by extreme Islamists in the 1992 elections led to a military coup. Since the restoration of multiparty elections in 1997, the FLN has been an important, but no longer the dominant, party.

Frontenac, Louis de Buade, comte de ((1622–98) Governor of New France (1672–82; 1689–98). He fought with distinction in the *Thirty Years War. During his first service in Canada, he strengthened the defences of the colony of New France and encouraged exploration, but clashed with Bishop Laval of Quebec and was recalled. Returning to Canada in 1689, he repulsed the New Englanders' attack on Quebec in 1690 and reimposed French authority against the Iroquois in 1696.

Fry, Elizabeth (Gurney) (1780–1845) British philanthropist and prison reformer. The wife of a London Quaker, Joseph Fry, she subsequently became recognized as a preacher in the Society of Friends. After a visit to Newgate prison in 1813, horrified by what she found there, she began to press for more humane treatment for women prisoners. Her unflagging determination resulted in eventual reform. She visited other European countries to advocate improvement in prison conditions and in the treatment of the insane. She also founded hostels for the homeless.

Fuchs, Klaus (Emil Klaus Julius Fuchs) (1911–88) German-born British physicist. Fuchs was a Communist who went to England to escape Nazi persecution. During the 1940s he passed to the USSR secret information acquired while working in the US, where he was involved in the development of the atom bomb, and in Britain, where he held a senior post in the Atomic Energy Research Establishment at Harwell. He was imprisoned from 1950 to 1959, and on his release he returned to East Germany.

Fugger A south German family of bankers and merchants, the creditors of many rulers in the Middle Ages. The family first achieved prominence under Jacob I (1410–69), head of the Augsburg weavers' guild. Ulrich (1441–1510) supplied cloth, and then lent money to the *Habsburgs. **Jacob II** (1459–1525), headed the family from 1510 and lent enormous sums to

*Maximilian I and *Charles V, financing Charles's candidacy as *Holy Roman Emperor in 1519. Resources came from silver and mercury mines in Germany and later from the Spanish empire in South America. The Fuggers were deeply involved in the finances of the *papacy, and in the sale of *indulgences. The family was ennobled and, in 1546 attained a peak of prosperity. Thereafter, Habsburg bankruptcies and the ravages of the *Thirty Years War damaged their position. They safeguarded their remaining wealth by shrewd management of their extensive estates.

Fugitive Slave Acts US legislation providing for the return of escaped slaves to their masters. After the abolition of slavery in the northern states of the USA, these "free states" became lax in enforcing the first Fugitive Slave Act of 1793. The second Act, part of the *Compromise of 1850, introduced more stringent regulations, specifically aimed at the *Underground Railroad. Unpopular in the North, it added fuel to the slavery controversy, and "liberty laws" passed by free states to thwart the Act drove the South further towards rebellion. Fugitive slave legislation was finally repealed in 1864.

Fujiwara A noble Japanese family whose members enjoyed the patronage of the Japanese emperors. In 858 Fujiwara Yoshifusa became the first non-imperial regent for a child emperor. Soon it was customary for every emperor to have a Fujiwara regent. For about three centuries they dominated the court of Kyoto, securing their power by marrying their daughters into the imperial family.

The Fujiwara period (late 9th to late 12th century) saw great artistic and literary development. A court lady, Lady Murasaki, wrote Japan's most famous classic novel *The Tale of Genji* (c.1001–15). But the central administration Prince *Shotoku had initiated in the 7th century was breaking down into a near feudal society. Tax-free estates proliferated and warrior families came to prominence. The establishment of the *Kamakura shogunate marked the end of Fujiwara ascendancy, though they acted as important court officials until the Meiji period in the 19th century.

Fulani empire of Sokoto West African Islamic empire. In the late 18th century the Fulani, a nomadic cattle-herding people, came into contact with the nominally Muslim Hausa states. One of their clerics, Uthman dan Fodio (1754–1817), had built up a community of scholars at Degel in the Hausa state of Gobir,

whose new sultan in 1802 enslaved Uthman's followers. A quarrel developed, Uthman was proclaimed 'commander of the faithful', and in the ensuing *jihad* (holy war) all the Hausa states collapsed. By 1810 Uthman had created a vast empire, to be administered by emirs in accordance with Koranic law. High standards of public morality replaced the corruption of the Hausa states and widespread education was achieved. In 1815 he retired, appointing his son Muhammed Bello his successor and suzerain over all the emirates. Bello had built the city of Sokoto, of which he became the sultan, and he considerably extended the empire, establishing control of west Bornu and pushing down into the *Yoruba empire of Oyo. Although losing some of its high ideals, the Fulani empire of Sokoto continued under Bello's successors. In the late 19th century British penetration of the empire increased. Kano and Sokoto were sacked in 1903, when the empire ended, although the emirates survived under the system of indirect rule instituted by the first High Commissioner, Frederick Lugard.

Fulbright, James William (1905–95) US politician. An early enemy of *isolationism, he was Chairman of the Senate Foreign Relations Committee from 1959 to 1974. He was an active critic of US foreign policy in the 1960s and 1970s, attacking particularly the US involvement in the *Vietnam War, and urging that Congress should have more control over the President's powers to make war. A Rhodes Scholar himself, in 1946 he sponsored the Fulbright Act, which provided funds for the exchange of students and teachers between the USA and other countries.

fundamentalism *See* CHRISTIANITY, ISLAM.

Funj A Sudanese kingdom founded, together with the city of Sennar, by Amara Dunkas in about 1504–05. Successive rulers expanded it over the Gezira and southern Kordofan, and fought two wars with Ethiopia. In the 17th century the monarchy was kept in power by a great army of slaves, and thereafter declined. When the Egyptians invaded it in 1821, the last king (whose state had been weakened by disunity) offered no resistance.

fusilier Originally a soldier armed with a "fusil" (an improved flintlock musket) in the 17th-century French army. The *fusiliers du roi* were an élite force and the first to be armed with bayonets. Later the name was given to various infantry regiments, including machine-gunners.

fyrd The military force of freemen available to the Anglo-Saxon kings. Military service was one of the three duties (the *trinoda necessitas*) required since the 7th century of all freemen—the other two duties being the maintenance of forts and the upkeep of roads and bridges. It was unusual for the fyrd to serve outside the shire in which it was raised. Modified by *Alfred the Great, it continued to be called even under the Norman kings. Henry II reorganized it in his Assize of Arms (1181) and Edward I in the Statute of Winchester (1285). It eventually became the *militia.

Gabon

Capital:	Libreville
Area:	267,667 sq km (103,347 sq miles)
Population:	1,640,286 (2013 est)
Currency:	1 CFA franc = 100 centimes
Religions:	Christian: between 55.0% and 75.0%; Muslim and traditional beliefs
Ethnic Groups:	Fang, Bapounou, Nzebi, Obamba, and other tribes
Languages:	French (official); Fang; Myene; Nzebi; Bapounou; Bandjabi
International Organizations:	UN; AU; Non-Aligned Movement; Franc Zone; WTO

An equatorial country on Africa's Atlantic coast, bounded inland by Equatorial Guinea, Cameroon, and Congo.

Physical Along the coast of Gabon are many lagoons, mangrove swamps, and large deposits of oil and natural gas. A broad plain covered by thick rainforest rises gradually to a plateau which surrounds a central river valley, and near the head this vegetation gives way to savannah.

Economy Oil discovered in the 1970s has made Gabon one of the wealthiest African countries, but with a wide disparity in income levels. Other exports include timber, manganese, and uranium. The government is attempting to attract investment to diversify the economy.

History In 1839 the French made it a naval base to suppress slave trade. Thus a French colony developed, exploiting the rare woods, gold, diamonds, other minerals, and oil. The country became autonomous within the French Community in 1958 and fully independent in 1960. Almost entirely on the basis of its natural resources it has had one of the fastest economic growth rates in Africa. After early years of political instability, Omar Bongo was elected President in 1967 and continued to rule until his death in 2009. Although multiparty politics was restored in 1990, Bongo and his Gabonese Democratic Party were repeatedly returned to power in elections widely seen as flawed. After Omar Bongo's death, his son Ali Bongo was elected President.

Gaddafi, Mu'ammar Muhammad al (or **Mu'ammar Muhammad al Qaddafi**) (1942–2011) Libyan colonel, head of state since 1970. After leading the coup which overthrew King Idris (1890–1983) in 1969, he gained power as chairman of the revolutionary council and established the Libyan Arab Republic. As self-appointed head of state Gaddafi pursued an anti-colonial policy at home, expelling foreigners from Libya and seeking to establish an Islamic Socialist regime. He was accused of supporting international terrorism and was involved in a number of conflicts with the West, as also with neighbouring Arab countries. However, in 2003–04 he reduced his hostility to the West and renounced Libya's plans to develop weapons of mass destruction. From 1979 he held no formal post, although he had the ceremonial title 'leader of the revolution'. Following the *Arab Spring uprisings in Tunisia and Egypt, popular protest against his regime began in February 2011, most effectively in Benghazi. With UN-approved NATO aerial protection, the protesters resisted military attack from the regime's troops. In August 2011 Tripoli fell and in October Gaddafi was killed, in disputed circumstances, as his final bastion of Sirte was overwhelmed.

Gadsden Purchase (1853–54) US acquisition of Mexican territory. Following the

*Mexican-American War and under pressure to construct a transcontinental railway across the south-west of the USA, the administration of President *Pierce sent Senator James Gadsden to negotiate the necessary redefinition of the Mexico–US border. In the resulting transaction, Mexico was paid $10 million for ceding a strip of territory 76,767 sq km (29,640 sq miles) in the Mesilla Valley, south of the Gila River. The area completed the present borders of the mainland USA.

Gage, Thomas (1721–87) British general, appointed British commander in America in 1763, after service in Flanders, at *Culloden, and in the *French and Indian wars. His responsibilities shifted from frontier defence to quelling unrest in such towns as New York and Boston. He was appointed governor of Massachusetts in 1774 to enforce the Coercive Acts, but he bungled Lexington and Concord, and resigned after *Bunker Hill.

Gaiseric *See* GENSERIC.

Gaitskell, Hugh Todd Naylor (1906–63) British politician. He entered Parliament in 1945, holding several government posts dealing with economic affairs (1945–51), including Chancellor of the Exchequer (1950–51). He became leader of the Labour Party (1955–63). He represented the moderate right-wing of his party and believed in the welfare legislation of 1944–51 and the need for a balance between private and state finance. Gaitskell was particularly vigorous in his opposition to the government over the *Suez War and in resisting the unilateralists within his own party.

galleon A sailing warship of the late 16th century. Galleons eventually replaced the less manoeuvrable carracks as the principal type of European trading ship. From the designs of Sir John *Hawkins, English galleons were the first to develop the characteristic beaked prow and modestly sized forecastle. These features were later incorporated in the great Spanish and Portuguese galleons which were used for overseas trade. In particular, 'plate fleets' of Spanish and Portuguese galleons brought large quantities of gold and silver from the Americas to Europe during the 16th and early 17th centuries. Spain continued to use galleons until the late 17th century.

galley A warship used principally in the Mediterranean from the 2nd millennium BC. The galley's major weapon was originally a ram

on the water-line, used to hole enemy ships or to smash their oars. It was propelled by oars in battle, and carried sails for use in favourable winds. The success of the galley as a warship was due to its great speed and manoeuvrability. This type of galley reached its furthest development in ancient Greece. The best-known type of Greek galley was the *trireme, with three banks (rows) of oars; a famous trireme battle took place between the Greek and Persian fleets at *Salamis in 480 BC. The Viking *longship was a small but durable type of galley. Galleys continued to be of military importance until the 16th century; *Lepanto (1571) was the last great naval battle involving large numbers of galleys. Galleys continued to be used as convict ships until the 18th century.

Gallic wars Julius *Caesar's campaigns (58–51 BC), which established Roman rule over central and northern Europe west of the River Rhine (*Gaul) (see map p. 237). Crossing into Transalpine Gaul, Caesar repelled German tribes in the south and east, Belgae in the north, and Veneti in the west. He even crossed the Rhine to demonstrate Roman control of that crucial natural frontier. With speed and ruthlessness and helped by inter-tribal disunity he subdued the northern and western coasts. He twice (55 and 54 BC) invaded Britain, which was regarded as a Belgic refuge and threat to Rome. In the winter of 53–52 BC, *Vercingetorix rallied the central Gallic tribes in unusual unity. In a long and bitter war, Caesar defeated him and his successors, and he was executed. Caesar's war dispatches, *De Bello Gallico*, supply most of the information about these events.

Gallipoli Campaign (1915–16) An unsuccessful Allied attempt to force a passage through the Dardanelles during *World War I. Its main aims were to force Turkey out of the war, and to open a safe sea route to Russia. A naval expedition, launched in February and March 1915, failed. A military expedition (relying mainly upon British, Australian, and New Zealand troops), with some naval support, was then attempted. The first landings, on the Gallipoli peninsula and on the Asian mainland opposite, were made in April 1915. Turkish resistance was strong and, although further landings were made, fighting on the peninsula reached a stalemate. The Australian casualties on Gallipoli were 8587 killed and 19,367 wounded. The Allied troops were withdrawn. Winston *Churchill, who was largely responsible for the campaign, was blamed for its failure.

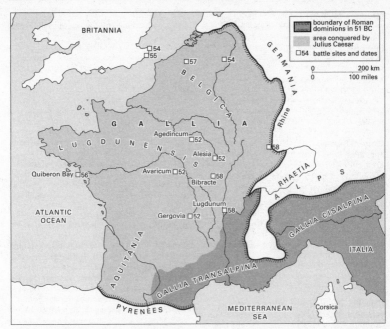

Gallic Wars. (58–51 BC) Julius Caesar was governor of Cisalpine Gaul when he embarked on the Gallic wars in 58 BC. His victory over the Helvetti at Bibracte was the first in a series of conquests in successive campaigning seasons. The Nervii, most powerful of the Belgic tribes, were defeated in 57, and a revolt by the Veneti was put down at Quiberon Bay in 56. These earlier victories were a tribute to the superior organization and generalship, but Caesar faced his greatest test in 52, when the Gauls united under Vercingetorix. The rebellion was broken by the siege of Alesia and Gaul was subsequently organized as a Roman province.

Gambia, the

Capital:	Banjul
Area:	11,295 sq km (4,361 sq miles)
Population:	1,883,051 (2013 est)
Currency:	1 dalasi = 100 butut
Religions:	Muslim 90.0%; Christian 8.0%; traditional beliefs 2.0%
Ethnic Groups:	Mandingo 42.0%; Fulani 18.0%; Wolof 16.0%; Dyola 10.0%; Serahuli 9.0%
Languages:	English (official); Mandingo; Wolof; Fulani; local languages
International Organizations:	UN; AU; ECOWAS; Non-Aligned Movement; WTO

A country on the West African coast.

Physical The Gambia runs west to east along the lower 320 km (nearly 200 miles) of the River Gambia, entirely surrounded inland by Senegal. Its territory on either bank is no more than about 24 km (15 miles) in width.

Economy The Gambian economy is heavily dependent on the growth, processing, and export of groundnuts, with fish, tourism, and remittances from expatriates also important.

History The beginning of the colony was the building of a fort by the British at Banjul in 1816, as a base against the slave trade. Renamed Bathurst, the new town was placed under

*Sierra Leone in 1821. Gambia became a British colony in 1843. The Soninki-Marabout Wars in neighbouring Senegal caused serious disturbances and were ended by Anglo-French intervention in 1889. A British Protectorate over the interior was proclaimed in 1893. Gambia became an independent member of the Commonwealth in 1965, and a republic in 1970, with Sir Dawda Kairaba Jawara as the country's first President. In 1982 the Gambia and Senegal formed a limited confederation, Senegambia, but this had lapsed by 1989. In 1994 Jawara was ousted in a military coup by Lieutenant Yahya Jammeh, who was elected President in 1996. He was re-elected in 2001, 2006, and 2011. The Gambia left the *Commonwealth of Nations in 2013.

Gamelin, Maurice Gustave (1872–1958) French general. As a staff officer in World War I he helped to plan the successful Battle of the *Marne (1914) and served with distinction through the war. In World War II as commander-in-chief of the Allied forces, he was unprepared for the German thrust through the Ardennes which resulted in disaster for his forces. In mid-May 1940 Gamelin was replaced by General *Weygand.

Gandhi, Indira (1917–84) Indian stateswoman, Prime Minister (1966–77; 1980–84). The daughter of Jawaharlal *Nehru, she had already served as President of the Indian National Congress (1959–60) and Minister of Information (1964) when she succeeded Lal Bahadur Shastri (1904–66) as Prime Minister. In her first term of office she sought to establish a secular state and to lead India out of poverty. However, in 1975 she introduced an unpopular state of emergency to deal with growing political unrest, and the Congress Party lost the 1977 election. Mrs Gandhi lost her seat and was unsuccessfully tried for corruption. Having formed a breakaway group from the Congress Party—known as the Indian National Congress (I)—in 1978, she was elected Prime Minister again in 1980. Her second period of office was marked by prolonged religious disturbance, during which she alienated many Sikhs by allowing troops to storm the Golden Temple at Amritsar; she was assassinated by her own Sikh bodyguards.

Gandhi, Mahatma (born **Mohandas Karamchand Gandhi**) (1869–1948) Indian nationalist and spiritual leader. After early civil-rights activities as a lawyer in South Africa, in 1914 Gandhi returned to India, where he became prominent in the opposition to British rule and was frequently imprisoned. The President of the Indian National Congress (1925–34), he never held government office, but was regarded as the country's supreme political and spiritual leader and the principal force in achieving India's independence. The Salt March to Dandi (1930) was followed by a campaign of civil disobedience until 1934, individual *satyagraha*, 1940–41, and the 'Quit India' campaign of 1942. As independence for India drew near, he cooperated with the British despite his opposition to the partition of the sub-continent. In political terms Gandhi's main achievement was to turn the small, upper-middle-class Indian National Congress movement into a mass movement. In intellectual terms his emphasis was upon the force of truth and non-violence (*ahimsa*) in the struggle against evil. His acceptance of partition and concern over the treatment of Muslims in India made him enemies among extremist Hindus. One such, Nathuram Godse, assassinated him in Delhi. Widely revered before and after his death, he was known as the Mahatma (Sanskrit, 'Great Soul').

Gandhi, Rajiv (1944–91) Indian statesman, Prime Minister (1984–89). The eldest son of Indira *Gandhi, he entered politics following the accidental death of his brother **Sanjay** (1946–80), becoming Prime Minister after his mother's assassination. His premiership, at the head of the Indian National Congress (I) party, was marked by continuing unrest and he resigned in 1989; he was assassinated during the election campaign of 1991. His widow, **Sonia Gandhi** (1946–), became leader of Congress (I) in 1998. The party headed a coalition government after the 2004 election, but she declined the post of Prime Minister.

Gang of Four Four radical Chinese leaders. Jiang Qing, *Mao Zedong's fourth wife, Wang Hongwen, Yao Wenyuan, and Zhang Chungqiao all rose to prominence during the *Cultural Revolution, with a power base in Shanghai. They occupied powerful positions in the Politburo after the Tenth Party Congress of 1973. After the death of Mao in 1976 they are alleged to have planned to seize power, and in 1980 were found guilty of plotting against the state. They have been blamed for the excesses of the Cultural Revolution.

Gao See SONGHAY.

Garcia Moreno, Gabriel (1821–75) President of Ecuador (1861–65; 1869–75). An extreme conservative, his goal was to convert Ecuador into the leading theocratic state of Latin America. His 1861 constitution, which accorded wide powers to the president, and his 1863 Concordat with the Vatican almost succeeded in doing so.

The Catholic Church enjoyed greater power and privilege during his two administrations than it ever had before. A sound administrator, he put Ecuador on a stable financial basis and introduced material reforms. He was assassinated in 1875.

Garcia y Iñigues, Calixto (1836–98) Cuban nationalist. He led his country's preliminary struggles for independence from Spain. A leader during the Ten Years' War (1868–78), and the Little War (1879–80), his military efforts enjoyed scant success and resulted in his prolonged imprisonment. Cuban troops under his command supported US forces during the Spanish-American War, but Garcia, shortly before his death, rejected his erstwhile allies, fearing that Cuba had simply exchanged one master for another.

Gardiner, Stephen (*c.*1490–1555) Bishop of Winchester (1531–51; 1553–55). A protégé of Thomas *Wolsey, he assisted in the negotiations to secure *Henry VIII's divorce from Catherine of Aragon. He defended the royal supremacy over the Church, most notably in *De Vera Obedientia* (1535), but was opposed to Protestantism. Under *Edward VI he was imprisoned (1548–53) and deprived of his see. *Mary I restored him to Winchester, made him Lord Chancellor, and relied on him until his death.

Garfield, James Abram (1831–81) US politician, 20th President (1881) of the USA. He served in the *American Civil War, retiring as a major-general, and then entered national politics as a Republican Congressman (1863–80). One of the politicians smeared with the Crédit Mobilier of America financial scandal, he was rescued by James G. *Blaine. During the Republicans' feud between the self-styled "Half Breeds" (members of that wing of the Republican Party that favoured a conciliatory policy towards the South, and advocated civil service reforms) and "Stalwarts" (their Republican opponents), he emerged as the compromise candidate to fight, and win, the presidential election of 1880. His assassination within months of taking office by a disappointed office-seeker sealed the fate of the Stalwarts and ensured support for civil service reform in the Pendleton Act (1883).

Garibaldi, Giuseppe (1807–82) Italian patriot and military leader. He was a hero of the Risorgimento (the movement for the unification and independence of Italy), who began his political activity as a member of the Young Italy Movement. After involvement in the early struggles against Austrian rule in the 1830s and 1840s he commanded a volunteer force on the Sardinian side in 1859, and successfully led his 'Red Shirts' to victory in Sicily and southern Italy in 1860–61, thus playing a vital part in the establishment of a united kingdom of Italy. He was less successful in his attempts to conquer the papal territories around French-held Rome in 1862 and 1867.

Garvey, Marcus Moziah (1887–1940) Jamaican Black leader. He organized the Universal Negro Improvement and Conservation Association (UNICA) in Jamaica in 1914 to encourage racial pride and Black unity with the slogan "Africa for the Africans at home and abroad". In 1916 he went to the USA, promising repatriation of Black Americans to a new African republic (to be created out of former German colonies). He established four branches of UNICA in South Africa in 1921, which encouraged the growth of Black movements there in the 1930s. Deeply resented by William *Du Bois, Garvey's followers clashed with more moderate Black people in the 1920s. Although personally honest and sincere, he mismanaged his movement's finances and was convicted (1923) of attempted fraud.

Gates, Horatio (1728–1806) American general, born in England. He fought under General Braddock and Baron *Amherst in the *French and Indian wars but thereafter supported the American cause in the War of Independence. His victory at *Saratoga (1777) led the Conway Cabal of New England officers to plot for him to replace George *Washington. His rout at *Camden (1780) ended his military career, though he later served under Washington.

GATT *See* GENERAL AGREEMENT ON TARIFFS AND TRADE.

gaucho A horseman of South America, often Indian or mestizo. Early in the 19th century the gauchos took part in the *Spanish–South American Wars of Independence, and later were prominent on the Argentine pampas in the development of the cattle industry. By the late 19th century the pastoral economy had given way to more intensive land cultivation in fenced-off estancias (estates), forcing many gauchos to become farmhands or peons.

Gaul An ancient region of Europe, corresponding to modern France, Belgium, the south Netherlands, south-west Germany, and northern Italy. The area was settled by groups of Celts, who had begun migration across the

Rhine in 900 BC, spreading further south beyond the Alps from 400 BC onwards and ousting the Etruscans. The area south of the Alps was conquered in 222 BC by the Romans, who called it **Cisalpine Gaul**. The area north of the Alps, known to the Romans as **Transalpine Gaul**, was taken by Julius Caesar between 58 and 51 BC, remaining under Roman rule until the 5th century AD. Within Transalpine Gaul the southern province, parts of which had fallen to the Romans in the previous century, became known as *Gallia Narbonensis*.

Gaulle, Charles de See DE GAULLE, CHARLES.

Gautama Siddhartha See BUDDHA.

gavelkind See PRIMOGENITURE.

Gaveston, Piers (*c.*1284–1312) Earl of Cornwall. A Gascon who was brought up in the English royal household as the foster-brother of the future *Edward II, he exploited the king's infatuation for him. Edward gave him the earldom of Cornwall in 1307, and appointed him Regent of England (1307–08). The enraged English barons called for his banishment; Edward twice complied (1308, 1311), but Gaveston returned and in 1312 was killed by the Earl of Warwick.

gay rights activism Political campaigning by homosexual men and women for an end to social and legal discrimination on the grounds of sexual preference. Concerted gay activism originated in the USA, where the 'Stonewall Riots', which took place in New York in 1969, saw the gay community react against sustained police brutality. The work of pressure groups and the liberalization of public opinion have ensured the decriminalization of consenting homosexual acts throughout the Western world. A US Supreme Court ruling of 1996 expressly precluded state and local administrations from denying basic civil-rights protection to homosexuals. The first nation to permit same-sex marriages was the Netherlands (2001); it has since been followed by 15 other countries, including England and Wales (2014), and several US states. However, other jurisdictions, including the majority of US states, have adopted legal bans on same-sex marriage. Discrimination is sometimes still enshrined in civil law, in such diverse matters as inheritance and insurance cover. Christian Fundamentalists, with their championing of the heterosexual couple as centre of the family, continue to challenge gay rights. Similarly, many traditionalist societies ranging from the Islamic states of the Arab world to socialist Zimbabwe remain hostile to homosexual people.

General Agreement on Tariffs and Trade (GATT) An international trade agreement. Established by the *United Nations Organization in 1948, and with a secretariat in Geneva, Switzerland, it had 125 member countries. The aim of its members (who together accounted for some 90% of all world trade) was to promote international trade by removing obstacles and trade barriers, to lay down maximum tariff rates, and to provide a forum for the discussion of trading policies. By the 1980s there were demands for modification of the GATT agreements. In 1986 the 'Uruguay Round' of talks (so called because they were held in the Uruguayan capital, Montevideo) undertook to resolve outstanding agricultural issues. The discussions, frequently deadlocked, continued into 1993 seeking a compromise agreement on farm subsidies, prior to talks in Geneva in 1994 for global trade deals. In April 1994 the Final Act of the Uruguay round was formally signed, concluding negotiations for broad cuts in tariffs and export subsidies and for the creation of the *World Trade Organization (WTO), which replaced GATT in 1996.

General Assembly See UNITED NATIONS GENERAL ASSEMBLY.

General Strike (UK) (1926) A British trade union strike. It was in support of the National Union of Mineworkers whose members were under threat from mine owners of longer hours and lower wages because of trading difficulties. The owners had locked out the miners from the pits to try to compel acceptance. The General Council of the Trades Union Congress responded by calling workers out on strike in certain key industries such as the railways, the docks, and electricity and gas supply. This began on 4 May 1926 and ended nine days later. Irresolute trade union leadership, skilful government handling of information to the public, and help by troops and volunteers to keep vital services running, all led to the collapse of the strike. It was followed in 1927 by a Trade Union Act, restricting trade union privileges.

Geneva Conference (1954) A conference held in Geneva, Switzerland, to negotiate an end to the *French Indo-China War. Planned by the wartime Allies to settle the future of *Korea and Indo-China, it made rapid progress on the latter after the French defeat at *Dienbienphu. The resulting armistice provided for the withdrawal of French troops and the partition of Vietnam, with the north under the control of *Ho Chi Minh's *Vietminh and the south under Saigon. Intended as a prelude to reunification through general elections, the Conference actually resulted in the emergence of two antagonistic regimes which were not to be united until Hanoi's victory in the *Vietnam War in 1975.

Geneva Conventions A series of international agreements on the treatment of victims of war, ratified in whole or partially by the majority of states and certain non-state organizations, such as the PLO (the Palestine Liberation Organization). The first Geneva Convention was established by the Swiss founder of the *Red Cross, Henri Dunant, in 1864, and concerned the treatment of the wounded in war and the protection of medical personnel. Subsequent Conventions in 1907, 1929, 1949, and 1977 covered the treatment of prisoners of war and the protection of civilians, forbidding such acts as deportation, torture, hostage-taking, collective punishment or reprisals, and the use of chemical and biological weapons. The 1977 Convention dealt with more extensive noncombatant protection, and covered problems arising from internal wars.

Genghis Khan (1162-1227) The founder of the Mongol empire. Originally named Temujin, he took the name Genghis Khan ('ruler of all') in 1206 after uniting the nomadic Mongol tribes under his command and becoming master of both eastern and western Mongolia. He then attacked China, capturing Beijing in 1215. When he died his empire extended from the shores of the Pacific to the northern shores of the Black Sea. His grandson Kublai Khan completed the conquest of China.

genocide The systematic policy of destruction of a group or nation on grounds of race or ethnic origin. Following the Nazi policy of genocide of the Jews and of ethnic groups such as gypsies, the Convention on the Prevention and Punishment of the Crime of Genocide was adopted by the UN in 1948. Since the signing of the Convention, many conflicts in the world have split groups along ethnic or tribal lines, and claims of genocide have been made. Examples include the Nigeria–Biafra conflict in 1969; Uganda in the 1970s; the Pol Pot regime in Kampuchea (Cambodia) (1976–79); Iraq's treatment of the Kurds (1986–91); the ethnic cleansing of Bosnian Muslims by Christian Serbs (1992–95); the massacre of Tutsis by Hutus in Rwanda (1994); and the attacks on Black Africans by Arab militias in the Darfur region of Sudan (2003–). The international community has failed in most cases to respond effectively to claims of genocide: firm evidence is hard to obtain and states are reluctant to intervene in the domestic affairs of another state on the grounds that this is a violation of national sovereignty.

Genseric (or **Gaiseric**) (c.390–477 AD) King of the *Vandals from 428. An *Arian Christian, he was ousted by the *Goths from his lands in Spain and took his entire nation of 80,000 across to North Africa in 429. He besieged Hippo just after the death of *Augustine of Hippo. Carthage fell ten years later and from there he declared an independent kingdom. Three times he defeated the Roman armies. With a fleet he took Sicily and Sardinia. Rome nicknamed the campaign the "Fourth *Punic war". In 455 he took Rome and indulged in a fortnight of looting. Fleets sent against the Vandals in 457 and 468 were defeated, and, at his death Genseric was in possession of all of his conquered territories.

Geoffrey of Monmouth (c.1100–55) Bishop of St Asaph in Wales and the author of a chronicle, the *Historia Regum Britanniae* ('The History of the Kings of Britain') (c.1136) In this work King *Arthur was projected as a national hero defending Britain from the Saxon raiders after the departure of the Roman armies.

geopolitics An approach to understanding international politics that seeks to explain the political behaviour of states in terms of geographical variables such as size or location. The term is particularly associated with the work of the Swede R. J. Kjellen (1864–1922) and the German Karl Haushofer (1869–1946). Haushofer's perception of geopolitics as involving the struggle between states to occupy the world was taken up by the Nazi Party in Germany to justify its expansionist goals, a connection which helped to bring the subject into disrepute. However, the term is still used to stress the interplay of geographical and political factors in international relations. It is considered particularly helpful in understanding the problems facing strategically sensitive areas of the world.

George I (1660-1727) Elector of Hanover (1692-1714) and King of Great Britain and Ireland (1714-27). His mother Sophia (1630-1714), a granddaughter of *James I, and her issue were recognized as heirs to the throne of England by the Act of *Settlement (1701), which excluded the Roman Catholic *Stuarts. He succeeded peaceably to the throne on Queen *Anne's death in 1714, and the *Jacobite rebellion a year later helped to unite the country behind him. He had little sympathy for British constitutionalism, the need to accept the limitations of Parliament and ministers, and he disliked England, spending as much time as possible in Hanover. But he developed a good command of English, despite his German accent, and his unswerving support for *Walpole from 1721 helped to consolidate the supremacy of the Whigs. He ruled without a queen, having divorced his wife, Sophia Dorothea, in 1694.

George II (1683-1760) King of Great Britain and Ireland (1727-60) and Elector of Hanover. He resented his father, *George I, because of his treatment of his mother, Sophia Dorothea. George's own marriage, to Princess *Caroline of Ansbach, was very successful, and through her he learned to accept *Walpole as his Prime Minister. He had a fiery temper and was intolerant in his dealings with others: he insisted on the execution of Admiral *Byng in 1757, and was always on bad terms with his son, Prince Frederick Louis. He was the last English king to lead his troops in battle, at Dettingen in 1743 in support of the Empress *Maria Theresa during the War of the *Austrian Succession. He disliked *Pitt the Elder and endeavoured to keep him out of office; his final acceptance of Pitt in 1757 paved the way for British success in the *Seven Years War.

George II (1890-1947) King of the Hellenes (1922-23; 1935-47). He came to the throne when General Palstiras deposed his father (1922), but the continuing unpopularity of the Greek royal family caused him to leave Greece (1923). In 1935 a plebiscite favouring the monarchy enabled him to return. His position was difficult, for real power lay with the dictatorial General *Metaxas. In April 1941 Hitler attacked Greece, driving him into exile again. With strong backing from Britain, the king returned to Greece in 1946, but the Greek communists who had resisted Hitler now waged civil war against the restoration of the monarchy. He died in 1947 and US support for his brother Paul brought the civil war to an end in 1949.

George III (1738-1820) King of Great Britain and Ireland and of dependencies overseas, King of Hanover (1760-1820). He was the first Hanoverian ruler to be born in Britain. The son of Frederick Louis, he succeeded to the throne on the death of his grandfather *George II, with strong convictions about a monarch's role acquired from Viscount *Bolingbroke and *Bute. He was a devoted family man and a keen patron of the arts, building up the royal art collection with impeccable taste. He disliked the domination of the government by a few powerful Whig

families and preferred to remain above politics, which was a major reason for the succession of weak ministries from 1760-1770. He was against making major concessions to the demands of the American colonists, and he shared with many Englishmen an abhorrence of the American aim of independence. He suffered from porphyria, a metabolic disease that causes mental disturbances; this manifested itself briefly in 1765, when plans were made for a regency council, and for several months in 1788-89, when his illness was so severe as to raise again the prospect of a regency. Although his political interventions were fewer than have often been alleged, his interference did bring down the Fox-North coalition in December 1783. Increasing reliance on *Pitt the Younger reduced his political influence, although Pitt always had to take it into account. When the King refused to consider *Catholic emancipation to offset the Act of *Union with Ireland, Pitt resigned (1801). In 1811 increasing senility and the onset of deafness and blindness brought about the *Regency of the profligate Prince of Wales, which lasted until he succeeded as *George IV.

George IV (1762-1830) King of Great Britain and Ireland and of dependencies overseas, King of Hanover (1820-30). As regent (1811-20) and later king, he led a dissolute life and was largely responsible for the decline in power and prestige of the British monarchy in the early 19th century. The eldest son of *George III, he cultivated the friendship of Charles James *Fox and other Whigs. In 1785 he secretly and illegally married a Roman Catholic widow, Maria Fitzherbert (1756-1837). Ten years later he reluctantly married Caroline of Brunswick, and separated from her immediately after the birth of their only child, Princess Charlotte. George III became increasingly senile at the end of 1810 and in the following year the prince was appointed regent. He gave his support to the Tories, but soon quarrelled with them too, leaving himself without a large personal following in Parliament. His reign saw the passage of the *Catholic emancipation Act (1829). His attempt to divorce Caroline for adultery in 1820 only increased his unpopularity. He was a leader of taste, fashion, and the arts, and gave his name to the *Regency period. He was succeeded by his brother *William IV.

George V (1865-1936) King of Great Britain and Ireland (from 1920, Northern Ireland) and dependencies overseas, Emperor of India (1910-36). The son of *Edward VII, he insisted that a general election should precede any reform of the House of *Lords (1911). He brought together party leaders at the Buckingham Palace Conference (1914) to discuss Irish *Home Rule. His acceptance of Ramsay *MacDonald as Prime Minister of a minority government in 1924, and of a *National government in 1931, contained an element of personal choice. He was succeeded by *Edward VIII.

George VI (1895–1952) King of Great Britain and Northern Ireland and dependencies overseas (1936–52), Emperor of India until 1947. He succeeded his brother, *Edward VIII, after the Abdication Crisis. His preference for Lord Halifax rather than Winston *Churchill as Prime Minister in 1940 had no effect, but he strongly supported Churchill throughout World War II. Likewise he gave his support to Clement *Attlee and his government (1945–50) in the policy of granting Indian independence. He and his wife, Elizabeth Bowes-Lyon, will be remembered for sustaining public morale during the German bombing offensive of British cities. He was succeeded by his elder daughter, *Elizabeth II.

Georgia

Capital:	Tbilisi
Area:	69,700 sq km (26,900 sq miles)
Population:	4,555,911 (2013 est)
Currency:	1 lari = 100 tetri
Religions:	Eastern Orthodox 83.9%; Muslim 9.9%; Armenian Apostolic 3.9%
Ethnic Groups:	Georgian 83.8%; Azeri 6.5%; Armenian 5.7%
Languages:	Georgian (official); Russian; Armenian; Azeri; Abkhaz (official in Abkhazia); minority languages
International Organizations:	UN; OSCE; Council of Europe; Euro-Atlantic Partnership Council; WTO

A mountainous country in west Asia. It is separated from Russia in the north by the Caucasus Mountains. It has a coast on the Black Sea, shares a border with Turkey to the west, and is bounded by Azerbaijan and Armenia to the east and south.

Physical About one-third of the land is forest. On the coastal plain and in the central valley fruit trees, palms, and eucalyptus flourish. By contrast, the east is treeless grassland, but rich in minerals.

Economy Georgia's mineral resources include coal, petroleum, manganese, copper, and gold, with mining of the last three being particularly important industries. Other industry includes beverages, metals, machinery, and chemicals. Principal agricultural products are citrus fruits, grapes, tea, hazelnuts, and vegetables.

History Georgia has been a distinctive state since the 4th century BC. In the 3rd century AD it became part of the *Sassanian empire but the Persians were expelled c.400. The 12th and 13th centuries saw territorial expansion and cultural achievement cut short by Mongol destruction. Revival was likewise curtailed by the ravages of *Tamerlane (1386–1403) and national decline was confirmed by the decision of Alexander I to split the kingdom between his three sons. After some two and a half centuries of partition, the western half being under *Ottoman rule, the eastern under Persian, the area was reunited by the Russian conquest of 1821–29.

Throughout the 19th century, Tsarist Russia continued to suppress Georgian nationalism. A strong Social Democrat Party of Mensheviks emerged in Georgia in the early 20th century, which formed a brief republic (1918–21), under British protection. In 1921 Georgia was conquered by the Red Army from Russia, and became part of the Transcaucasian Soviet Federal Socialist Republic with Azerbaijan and Armenia. A large-scale anti-communist uprising was suppressed in 1924 and in 1936 the Georgian Soviet Socialist Republic became a full member of the Soviet Union. Another uprising in the capital Tbilisi in 1956 was suppressed, and in April 1989 there were extensive riots, again brutally suppressed. In April 1991, however, it gained independence under President Zviad Gamsakhurdia. Opposition to Gamsakhurdia's 'dictatorial methods' led to his deposition, following the outbreak of civil conflict in December 1991. In March 1992 Eduard Shevardnadze (Soviet Foreign Minister 1985–91) became Chairman of the State Council and in September he was elected President. The civil conflict continued throughout 1992 and 1993 as forces loyal to Gamsakhurdia attempted to gain control. In November, however, with the aid of Russian troops, government forces routed the rebels. The country was also beset by other internal conflicts. In 1989 a rebellion erupted in South Ossetia, which demanded greater autonomy and secession from Georgia. A ceasefire was eventually agreed in mid-1992 and South Ossetia confirmed its intention to secede. In August 1992, following periodic unrest since 1989, conflict began over the region of Abkhazia's demands for independence. By September 1993 Georgian forces were defeated and expelled from the region. A provisional ceasefire was negotiated in April 1994, when Shevardnadze agreed to cede considerable autonomy to Abkhazia. In March 1995 Shevardnadze was re-elected as President. However, he was forced to resign in the *Rose Revolution (2003) and was replaced by Mikhail Saakashvili, the leader of the opposition. Saakashvili's popularity rapidly declined and more demonstrations led to early elections in 2008, which he narrowly won. Continued tensions over South Ossetia and Abkhazia led to a short war with Russia in 2008, which left Russia in occupation of the two regions; Russia subsequently recognized their independence. In 2012 the opposition Georgian Dream coalition won the parliamentary election, and in 2013 their candidate, Giorgi Margvelashvili, secured the Presidency.

Germain-en-Laye, St, Treaty of *See* VERSAILLES PEACE SETTLEMENT.

German Confederation (1815–66) An alliance of German sovereign states. At the Congress of *Vienna (1815) the 38 German states formed a loose grouping to protect themselves against French ambitions. Austria and Prussia lay partly within and partly outside the Confederation. The Austrian chancellor *Metternich was the architect of the Confederation and exercised a dominant influence in it through the Federal Diet at Frankfurt, whose members were instructed delegates of state governments. As the rival power to Austria in Germany, Prussia tried to increase its influence over other states by founding a federal customs union or *Zollverein. In the *Revolutions of 1848 a new constituent assembly was elected to Frankfurt, and tried to establish a constitutional German monarchy, but in 1849 the Austrian emperor refused the crown of a united Germany because it would loosen his authority in Hungary, while the Prussian king, *Frederick William IV, refused it because the constitution was too liberal. The pre-1848 Confederation was restored, with *Bismarck as one of Prussia's delegates. In 1866 Bismarck proposed that the German Confederation be reorganized to exclude Austria. When Austria opposed this, Bismarck declared the Confederation dissolved and went to war against Austria. In 1867, after Prussia's victory

over Austria in the *Austro-Prussian War (1866), the 21 secondary governments above the River Main federated into the North German Confederation (Norddeutscher Bund), with its capital in Berlin and its leadership vested in Prussia. Executive authority rested in a presidency in accordance with the hereditary rights of the rulers of Prussia. The federation's constitution was a model for that of the *German Second empire, which replaced it after the defeat of France in the *Franco-Prussian War (1871).

German Democratic Republic (or East Germany) A former eastern European country. It emerged in 1949 from the Soviet Zone of occupation of Germany. Its frontier with Poland on the Oder-Neisse line, agreed at the *Potsdam Conference, was confirmed by the Treaty of Zgorzelec in 1950. Its capital was East Berlin, but the status of West Berlin,—an enclave of the Federal Republic of *Germany 150 km (93 miles) inside East German territory, whose existence was guaranteed by the Four-Power Agreement between the victorious allied powers—caused serious problems (*see* BERLIN AIRLIFT). In the first five years the republic had to pay heavy *reparations to the Soviet Union, and Soviet troops were used to put down disorder in 1953. In 1954, however, the republic proclaimed itself a sovereign state and in the following year became a founder-member of the *Warsaw Pact. In 1956 the National People's Army was formed; this organization was instrumental in sealing the GDR's borders in August 1961 (including erecting the *Berlin Wall) to prevent large-scale emigration to West Germany. Walter Ulbricht (1893–1973) was General Secretary of the ruling Socialist Unity Party (1946–71) and Chairman of the Council of State (1960–71). In 1972 the German Federal Republic, as part of the policy of *Ostpolitik, established diplomatic relations with the republic. Admission to the UN followed in 1973, after which the republic was universally recognized. Although economic recovery from World War II was slower than in the west, East Germany, under Erich *Honecker (Chairman of the Council of State, 1976–89), succeeded in establishing a stronger industrial base than most of its fellow members of *COMECON. However, its highly bureaucratic, centralized system of control steadily atrophied, corruption spread from the top, and its secret police, the Stasi, became ever more ruthless. During 1989 a series of huge demonstrations took place, mostly in Berlin and Leipzig, with a new political grouping, New Forum, demanding democratic reforms. In November 1989 the Berlin Wall was opened and the communist monopoly of power collapsed. The first free elections since 1933 were held in March 1990, with the conservative Christian Democratic Union emerging victorious, and on 3 October 1990 the republic ceased to exist, being absorbed into the Federal Republic of Germany. Criminal proceedings were instituted against those who were deemed to have committed human rights abuses in the GDR regime, but few were punished. The case against Erich Honecker was dropped due to his ill-health. His successor, Egon Krenz, and several officials were found guilty of various crimes, notably ordering the shooting of refugees across the Berlin Wall.

German Second empire (or **Reich**) (1871–1918) A continental and overseas empire ruled by Prussia. The First Reich was the Holy Roman Empire, which ended in 1806. The Second empire replaced the *German Confederation and the short-lived North German Confederation (1866–70). It was created by *Bismarck following the *Franco-Prussian War, by the union of 25 German states under the Hohenzollern King of Prussia, now Emperor William I. An alliance was formed with *Austria-Hungary in 1879 and German economic investment took place in south-east Europe. In 1884 Bismarck presided over a conference of European colonial powers in Berlin, to allocate territories in Africa. In the same year Karl Peters founded the Society for German Colonization, and Bismarck was prepared to claim three areas of Africa: German South-West Africa, bordering on Cape Colony; the Cameroons and Togoland, where Britain had long monopolized the trade; and German East Africa, thus threatening British interests in Zanzibar. Northern New Guinea and the Bismarck Archipelago in the Pacific were also claimed. With the accession of William II (1888) colonial activity, especially in the Far East, increased. In 1898 Germany leased the Chinese province of Shandong and purchased the Caroline and Mariana Islands from Spain. In 1899 Samoa was partitioned between Germany and the USA. Potential friction with Britain was averted by a mutual agreement in 1900, following its intervention to crush the *Boxer Rising. In that year von *Bülow became Chancellor (1900–09). The growth of German industry had now made it the greatest industrial power in Europe, and inevitably the search for new markets led to tension with other colonial powers. The expansion of the German navy under *von Tirpitz led to rivalry with the British navy, while competition with France in Africa led to a crisis over *Morocco (1905). In a second Moroccan Crisis

(1911), an international war came close. The assassination at Sarajevo caught the empire unawares. After some debate it was decided that the 1879 alliance with Austria-Hungary must be honoured even if it meant war against Russia and France. During *World War I most German African territories were conquered and at the *Versailles Peace Settlement Germany was stripped of its overseas empire, which became mandated territories, administered by the victorious powers on behalf of the *League of Nations. At the end of the war the emperor abdicated and the *Weimar Republic was created.

Germantown, Battle of (4 October 1777) When the British occupied Philadelphia during the American War of *Independence the greater part of their army camped at Germantown, north of Philadelphia. After the defeat at *Brandywine and the British occupation of Philadelphia, George *Washington attempted a surprise counter-attack on the main British camp. Bad weather and bad coordination resulted in American defeat, heavy losses, and withdrawal to winter quarters at *Valley Forge.

Germany, Federal Republic of

Capital:	Berlin
Area:	357,022 sq km (137,847 sq miles)
Population:	81,147,265 (2013 est)
Currency:	1 euro = 100 cents
Religions:	Protestant 34.0%; Roman Catholic 34.0%; Muslim 3.7%
Ethnic Groups:	German 91.5%; Turkish 2.4%
Languages:	German (official)
International Organizations:	UN; EU; OECD; NATO; Council of Europe; OSCE; WTO

A central European country covering an area of almost 357,000 sq km (138,000 sq miles). In the west it extends across the Rhine valley, in the south it includes the central Alps, and in the east it is partially bounded by the River Oder. Germany has borders with Denmark, Poland, the Czech Republic, Austria, Switzerland, France, Luxembourg, Belgium, and the Netherlands.

Physical The whole of northern Germany is set in the North European Plain. The Rhine Basin encompasses some of the most beautiful landscape and best wine-growing regions in Europe. More than a quarter of Germany is covered with forest. In the west are the Ruhr coalfields, while in the east there are large lignite deposits. Southward the ground gradually rises to the Black Forest (Schwarzwald), and the Swabian Jura, with dense pine forests and moorland, and potash, salt, and other minerals. In Bavaria, further south, the land becomes rugged. Here are patches of mountain pasture and lakes; to the east is the deep Danube valley.

Economy Germany has a highly successful industrial economy which continues to be the dominant economic force in Europe. It also enjoys excellent labour relations and a high degree of worker participation in management. Industry includes iron, steel, coal, cement, chemicals, machinery, vehicles, machine tools, electronics, food and drink, shipbuilding, and textiles, with vehicles, machinery, chemicals, and computer and electronic products as the principal exports. Mineral resources include coal, lignite, salt, and some natural gas. Nuclear power formerly generated around one-quarter of Germany's electricity, but government policy is to phase it out in favour of renewable sources. The main agricultural crops are potatoes, sugar beet, wheat, and barley. Viticulture is most extensive in the Rhine and Mosel valleys in west Germany.

History Germany was originally occupied by Teutonic tribes who were driven back across the Rhine by Julius *Caesar in 58 BC. When the Roman empire collapsed, eight Germanic kingdoms were created, but in the 8th century *Charlemagne consolidated these kingdoms under the *Franks. The region became part of the *Holy Roman Empire in 962, and almost 200 years later was invaded by the Mongols. A period of unrest followed until 1438 when the long rule of the *Habsburgs began. The kingdom, now made up of hundreds of states, was torn apart during the *Thirty Years War; when this ended with the Peace of Westphalia in 1648, the Elector of Brandenburg-Prussia emerged as a force ready to challenge Austrian supremacy. By the end of the *Napoleonic Wars, the alliance of 400 separate German states that had existed within the Holy Roman Empire (962–1806) had been reduced to 38. At the Congress of *Vienna these were formed into a loose grouping, the *German Confederation, under Austrian leadership. The Confederation was dissolved as a result of the *Austro-Prussian War (1866), and

in 1867 all northern Germany formed a new North German Confederation under Prussian leadership. This was in turn dissolved in 1871, and the new *German Second empire proclaimed. After Germany's defeat in World War I, the *Weimar Republic was instituted, to be replaced in 1933 by the *Third Reich under Adolf *Hitler. After the end of World War II the country divided into the Federal Republic of Germany (**West Germany**) and the *German Democratic Republic (**East Germany**).

The Federal Republic was created in 1949 from the British, French, and US zones of occupation. It became a sovereign state in 1955, when ambassadors were exchanged with world powers, including the Soviet Union. Konrad *Adenauer, as Chancellor (1949–63), was determined to see eventual reunification of Germany and refused to recognize the legal existence of the German Democratic Republic. A crisis developed over Berlin in 1958, when the Soviet Union demanded the withdrawal of Western troops and, in 1961, when it authorized the erection of the *Berlin Wall. The Berlin situation began to ease in 1971, during the chancellorship of the social democrat Willy *Brandt (1969–74) with his policy of *Ostpolitik. This resulted in treaties with the Soviet Union (1970), Poland (1970), Czechoslovakia (1973), and one of mutual recognition and cooperation with the German Democratic Republic (1972), with membership of the UN following in 1973. Economic recovery was assisted after the war by the *Marshall Plan. The challenge of rebuilding shattered cities and of absorbing many millions of refugees from eastern Europe was successfully met, as was that of recreating systems of social welfare and health provision. The Federal Republic joined *NATO in 1955, when both army and air force were reconstituted; large numbers of US and British troops remained stationed there. In 1957 it signed the Treaty of *Rome, becoming a founder-member of the *European Economic Community in 1958. Although the pace of economic growth slackened, the economy remained one of the strongest in the world, under a stable democratic regime. In 1982 the social democrat coalition of Helmut *Schmidt collapsed and was replaced by the centre-right coalition under Helmut *Kohl.

Following economic and monetary union with the Democratic Republic in June 1990, a Treaty of Unification was signed in August and unification took place in October. Since then, the country has consisted of 16 *Länder* or states, each of which has wide powers over its domestic affairs. However, the economic problems of the five new eastern *Länder* were soon to produce a sense of disillusion, with unemployment rising to 17% and a resurgence of support for the former communists. The cost of restructuring the economy of the former GDR proved far higher than expected. Against a background of recession and political disillusionment in western Germany, further measures were taken in 1993 to fund the restructuring of the eastern German economy. Germany's liberal policies on asylum resulted in a large influx of migrants, with accompanying social problems. A resurgence of right-wing extremism in the form of attacks on Jews and foreigners led the government to ban four far-right organizations in 1992 and more in 1995. The ruling coalition under Helmut Kohl was defeated in elections in 1998 by the Social Democrats, led by Gerhard *Schröder. The federal government moved from Bonn to Berlin in 1999. Germany adopted the *euro as its currency in 2002. In 2005, an indecisive election led to the formation of a 'grand coalition' of the Christian Democrats and Social Democrats under Angela *Merkel. She remained in power after the 2009 election at the head of a coalition with the Free Democrat Party, and led another 'grand coalition' after 2013. Germany's pivotal role in the EU was enhanced from 2011 by the *Eurozone Crisis, in which Germany's wealth underpinned the emergency loans made to other EU member states.

Geronimo (*c.*1829–1909) Apache chief. He led his people in resistance to White encroachment on tribal reservations in Arizona, waging war against settlers and US troops in a series of raids, before surrendering in 1886.

Gestapo The Nazi secret police or *Geheime Staatspolizei*. In 1933 Hermann *Goering reorganized the Prussian plain-clothes political police as the Gestapo. In 1934 control of the force passed to *Himmler, who had restructured the police in the other German states, and headed the SS and *Schutzstaffel*. The Gestapo was effectively absorbed into the SS and in 1939 was merged with the SD or *Sicherheitsdienst* (Security Service), the intelligence branch of the SS, in a Reich Security Central Office under Reinhard *Heydrich. The powers of these organizations were vast: any person suspected of disloyalty to the regime could be summarily executed. The SS and the Gestapo controlled the *concentration camps and set up similar agencies in every occupied country.

Gettysburg, Battle of (1–3 July 1863) A battle in the *American Civil War. On 1 July elements of the Army of Northern Virginia under *Lee and the Union Army of the Potomac under Meade came into contact west of Gettysburg, Pennsylvania. Although early Confederate attacks were repulsed, the arrival of reinforcements forced the Union troops to retreat back through the town. By the following day, however, fresh Union troops in strong defensive positions on Cemetery Ridge repelled Confederate attacks. On the third day, Pickett's charge against the centre of the Union line was defeated with heavy losses, and Lee was forced to abandon his invasion of the North. He lost 20,000 men from a force of 70,000 and Meade 23,000 from one of 93,000. The retreat from Gettysburg, together with the simultaneous surrender of *Vicksburg in the west, marked the turning point of the war, although over a year and a half of heavy fighting would follow before Lee was finally forced to surrender.

Ghana

Capital:	Accra
Area:	238,533 sq km (92,098 sq miles)
Population:	25,199,609 (2013 est)
Currency:	1 cedi = 100 pesewas
Religions:	Christian 71.2%; Muslim 17.6%; traditional beliefs 5.2%
Ethnic Groups:	Akan 47.5%; Mole-Dagbon 16.6%; Ewe 13.9%; Ga-Dangme 7.4%; Gurma 5.7%
Languages:	English (official); Asante; Ewe; Fante local languages
International Organizations:	Commonwealth; ECOWAS; Non-Aligned Movement; AU; UN; WTO

A West African country with a south-facing coast, bounded by the Côte d'Ivoire on the west, Burkina Faso on the north, and Togo on the east.

Physical Ghana's flat and sandy coast is backed by a rolling plain of scrub and grass, except in the west, where moderate rains produce thick forest. The forest extends northward to the Ashanti plateau, which produces cocoa and tropical hardwoods, as well as manganese, bauxite, and gold.

Economy Offshore oil production began in 2010 and the industry is expanding rapidly; oil is now Ghana's principal export. Other mineral extraction includes gold, manganese, diamonds, and bauxite; all are exported, as is aluminium smelted from bauxite. Agriculture is still the principal occupation, with cocoa the main export crop. Hydraulic power accounts for most of the country's electricity production.

History The area now covered by Ghana was composed of several kingdoms in the middle ages. From the late 15th century, the Portuguese and other Europeans began trading with the area, which they called the Gold Coast. It became a centre of the slave trade from the 16th century onwards. British influence gradually predominated. In 1850 the British Colonial Office purchased residual Danish interests in the region and gave some protection to the *Fanti Confederation. Inland the area was dominated throughout the 19th century by the *Asante Confederation. Britain occupied the capital Kumasi after wars with the Ashanti in 1824 and 1874, when the colony of the Gold Coast was established. Further wars against the Ashanti followed in 1896 and 1900. After 1920 economic growth based on mining and the cocoa industry, combined with high standards of mission schooling, produced a sophisticated people demanding home rule. Following World War II, in which many Ghanaians served, there were serious riots in Accra (1948) leading to constitutional discussions. In 1957 the Gold Coast and British Togoland to the east were combined to become the independent Republic of Ghana, under the leadership of Kwame *Nkrumah, the first British African colony to be granted independence. Nkrumah transformed the country into a one-party state. Economic problems and resentment over political repression and mismanagement led to his overthrow by the army in 1966. Following his fall continuing economic and political problems unbalanced Ghana. After a succession of coups, a group of junior officers under Flight-Lieutenant Jerry Rawlings (1942–) took power in 1979, executed three former heads of state, and installed a civilian government. When this failed, Rawlings again seized power (December 1981), suspending the constitution and establishing a Provisional National Defence Council, with himself as Chairman. During the 1980s with IMF support it regained some economic and political stability. A new constitution was adopted in April 1992, legalizing political parties. In November 1992 Rawlings was victorious in multiparty presidential elections as candidate for the National Democratic Congress (NDC), but opposition parties contested the result. Rawlings was sworn in as President in 1993 and re-elected in 1996. He did not stand in 2000 and the opposition candidate, John Kufuor, was elected; he was re-elected in 2004. The NDC regained the Presidency in 2008 when John Mills was elected; on his death in office (2012) Vice-President John Mahama took office. Mahama was elected in his own right later that year.

Ghana, kingdom of An ancient kingdom in what is now east Senegal, south-west Mali, northern Guinea, and southern Mauritania. As early as *c*.800 al-Fazari called Ghana 'the land of gold'. According to tradition there were 22 princes ruling before Muhammad, and 23 after. In 990 the king of Ghana conquered Berber lands and took control of the gold, salt, and caravan trade. The kingdom fell to the *Almoravids in 1054. The name was adopted by the former British colony of the Gold Coast when it became independent in 1957.

Ghaznavid A Turkish dynasty whose founder, Sebuktegin, was appointed governor of Khurasan by the Persian Samanids and established his own power in Ghazna, Afghanistan, in 962. His successors extended their realm into Persia and the Punjab, but after the reign of Mahmud (969–1030) it fragmented under *Seljuk pressure, although the dynasty clung on in Lahore until 1186, when it was extinguished by the Ghurids, founders of the Delhi sultanate.

Ghent, Pacification of (1576) An alliance forged during the *Dutch Revolts. It enshrined the agreement of the Catholic and Calvinist Netherlands to oppose Spanish rule and to call for the removal of imperial troops. Ruled by Austria from 1714, Ghent was seized by the French in 1792, and was incorporated into the kingdom of Belgium in 1830.

Ghent, Treaty of (1814) A treaty ending the *War of 1812 between Britain and the USA. It did not address the issues that had caused the war, but provided for the release of all prisoners, restoration of all conquered territory, and the appointment of a commission to settle the north-eastern boundary dispute. Other questions, including naval forces on the Great Lakes and fishing rights, were left to future settlement.

ghost dance A *millenarian movement which spread among the Native American *Plains Peoples during the second half of the 19th century. The ghost dance, which involved dancing for days on end to induce a trancelike state, was said to presage the end of the world, when the White settlers would leave and the Native Americans would have their lands restored.

Giap, Vo Nguyen (1912–2013) Vietnamese military and political leader. As North Vietnamese Vice-Premier and Defence Minister, he was responsible for the strategy leading to the withdrawal of American forces from South Vietnam in 1973 and the subsequent reunification of the country in 1975. His book *People's War, People's Army* (1961) was an influential text for revolutionaries.

Gibbon, Edward (1737–94) British historian. While on a visit to Rome in 1764 he conceived the plan for what has become the most celebrated historical work in English literature, *The History of the Decline and Fall of the Roman Empire* (1776–88), a six-volume study that traces the connection of the ancient world with the modern, encompassing such subjects as the establishment of Christianity, the Teutonic tribes, the conquests of Islam, and the Crusades.

Gilbert, Sir Humphrey (*c.*1539–83) English explorer. After a distinguished career as a soldier, Gilbert led an unsuccessful attempt to colonize the New World (1578–79). On a second voyage in 1583 he claimed Newfoundland for Elizabeth I and established a colony at St John's, but was lost on the trip homewards when his ship foundered in a storm off Nova Scotia.

Gilbert Islands *See* KIRIBATI.

gild *See* GUILD.

Gildas (*c.*500–70) British monk and historian. He is best known as the author of a polemical work (*c.*550) *De excidio et conquestu Britanniae* ("The Ruin and Conquest of Britain") in which he attacked the British for their wickedness. In spite of its rhetorical tone and historical inaccuracies it is the only substantial written source for the condition of Britain during a crucial period. It contains an account of a British victory over the Saxons at Mount Badon, possibly a site in Dorset, around 500. *Nennius later claimed that King Arthur had fought at the battle.

Gillard, Julia (Eileen) (1961–) Australian Labor politician, Prime Minister (2010–13). First elected to parliament in 1998, she was promoted to the shadow cabinet in 2001 and became Labor Party deputy leader in 2006. Following the Labor victory in the 2007 general election she became Deputy Prime Minister and Minister for Education, Employment, and

Workplace Relations. In 2010 she successfully challenged Kevin *Rudd for the party leadership and became Australia's first woman Prime Minister. She continued in office as leader of a minority government after the 2010 general election, but, after much party infighting, was ousted by Rudd in 2013. She retired from politics at the 2013 election.

Giolitti, Giovanni (1842–1928) Italian statesman, Prime Minister five times between 1892 and 1921. A former lawyer, he was responsible for the introduction of a wide range of social reforms, including national insurance (1911) and universal male suffrage (1912).

Girondin A member of a French political party whose main exponents came from the Gironde region. The Girondins were closely associated with the *Jacobins in the early days of the *French Revolution. They held power at a critical time and were responsible for provoking the wars with France's enemies. The eventual failure of these wars led not only to the king's execution but also to the downfall of the party and the introduction of the Reign of Terror.

Giscard d'Estaing, Valéry (1926–) French statesman, President (1974–81). As Secretary of State for Finance (1959–62) and Finance Minister (1962–66) under President de Gaulle, he was responsible for the policies which formed the basis of France's economic growth. Dismissed following mounting opposition to his policies, he regained the finance portfolio under President Pompidou, whose death in 1974 paved the way for Giscard d'Estaing's own election to the presidency. However, French economic conditions worsened during his term of office and he was defeated by François Mitterrand. He was a member of the European Parliament (1989–93), and was leader of the centre-right Union pour la Démocratie Française (1988–96). In 2002–03 he chaired a convention that produced a draft EU constitution which became the basis of the *Lisbon Treaty.

gladiator (Latin 'swordsman') A slave or prisoner trained to fight other gladiators, wild beasts, or condemned criminals for the entertainment of the people in ancient Rome. Gladiators belonged to four categories: the Mirmillo, with a fish on his helmet, and the Sammite, both heavily armed with oblong shield, visored helmet, and short sword; the Retiarius, lightly clad, fighting with net and trident; and the Thracian, with round shield and curved scimitar. Thumbs up or down from the crowd spelt life or death for the loser. Formal combat degenerated into butchery watched by huge crowds.

Gladstone, William Ewart (1809–98) British Liberal statesman, Prime Minister (1868–74; 1880–85; 1886; 1892–94). After an early career as a Conservative minister, he joined the Liberal Party, becoming its leader in 1867. His ministries were notable for the introduction of a series of social and political reforms (including the introduction of elementary education, and the passing of the Irish Land Acts and the third Reform Act) and for his campaign in favour of Home Rule for Ireland, which led to the defection of the Unionists from the Liberal Party.

glasnost and perestroika The policies of 'openness' and 'restructuring' that led to major changes in Soviet society in the 1980s, as well as profoundly influencing East–West relations. Introduced into Soviet domestic politics by Mikhail *Gorbachev, who became Soviet leader in 1985, the concepts are described in his book *Perestroika* (1987). The twin processes aimed to reduce inefficiency and corruption in the former Soviet Union, and to encourage political liberalization. Internally the results of the 'Gorbachev doctrine' were mixed and contributed to growing unrest, provoked by nationalist demands and economic discontent, which in 1991 brought about the disintegration of the structure of the Soviet Union, the secession of the Baltic republics, the displacement of the Communist Party from its formerly dominant position, and the formation of a new *Commonwealth of Independent States.

glebe Land belonging to a parish church used to support its priest. The size of glebes varied enormously from 1 ha. (2 acres) to a few hundred hectares; priests might afford to engage labourers or be obliged to work the land themselves, and they could sub-lease part or all of the land. Since the glebe was a freeholding, the lord of the manor could not demand labour duties of the priest, although this immunity was not always observed.

Glencoe, Massacre of (13 February 1692) A massacre for political reasons of members of the Macdonald clan in Scotland. By failing to swear allegiance to *William III by 1 January 1692, the rebellious clan Macdonald was technically guilty of treason; their chief's delaying tactics had been compounded by bad weather, and his oath was six days late. The Campbells, hereditary enemies of the Macdonalds, undertook to destroy them, which they attempted after enjoying Macdonald hospitality for

12 days. The clan chief and more than 30 of his followers were murdered, but the rest (about 300) escaped. Although the king probably did not order the atrocity, he did little to punish the perpetrators.

Glendower, Owen (or **Owen Glyndwr**) (*c*.1354–*c*.1417) Welsh chief. A legendary symbol of Welsh nationalism, he was leader first of armed resistance to English overlordship and then of a national uprising against Henry IV. He proclaimed himself Prince of Wales and allied himself with Henry's English opponents, including Henry Percy ('Hotspur'); by 1404 this policy had proved sufficiently successful for Glendower to hold his own Parliament. Though suffering subsequent defeats, he continued fighting against the English until his death.

globalization The process by which the world increasingly functions as a single community, rather than as many widely separated communities. The term is used particularly to refer to the increasing integration of the world's national economies and the growth of multinational companies that bestride them. In this specific sense, globalization dates from the late 20th century and is largely a consequence of the increased speed and reduced cost of communications. Jet aircraft, introduced commercially in the 1950s, have made it possible for people and goods to be conveyed to the other side of the world in a single day; and 20th-century developments in telecommunications and broadcast media, notably the *Information Revolution of the 1980s and 1990s, have not only provided instant worldwide information but also made possible the establishment of global bodies of data and systems to access them. These technological innovations have been accompanied by the growth of international agreements and regulatory bodies since World War II, such as the *General Agreement on Tariffs and Trade (GATT), which sought to remove obstacles to international trade, and the *World Trade Organization (WTO), which extended GATT's role by regulating such matters as intellectual property rights. Many companies have benefited from these developments, which have enabled them to expand easily into overseas markets and to conduct their operations wherever in the world is most efficient and most profitable. However, these companies are almost exclusively based in the developed world, especially in the USA, and their increased power is seen in many quarters to benefit already rich countries at the expense of the developing world. A key issue is the removal of tariffs and other barriers to international trade: many countries, both developing and industrialized, argue that exposing their internal markets to unfettered foreign competition would undermine indigenous enterprises and damage their economies. Allied to this is a fear in some cases that the penetration of foreign products and mass media will corrode a country's traditional culture. Many of these concerns are expressed in the form of anti-Americanism: the USA and US-based corporations are perceived to be the principal economic beneficiaries of globalization, and elements of US culture have penetrated almost every country in the world.

global warming See CLIMATE CHANGE.

Glorious Revolution The bloodless English revolution of 1688–89 in which *James II was removed from the throne and was replaced by his daughter Mary and her husband *William III (of Orange). It marked the end of Stuart attempts at despotism, and the establishment of a constitutional form of government.

From his accession in 1685, James II's actions aroused both Whig and Tory concern. In defiance of the law he appointed Roman Catholics to important positions in the army, the church, the universities, and the government. He claimed the right to suspend or dispense with the laws as he pleased, and his two *Declarations of Indulgence suspended penal laws against Roman Catholics and dissenters. The birth of a son to the king in 1688 appeared to ensure the Roman Catholic succession and provoked leading politicians of both the main parties to invite the king's son-in-law William of Orange to England. William landed with a Dutch army in Devonshire in November. James's army refused to obey its Catholic officers, his daughters deserted him, and he was allowed to escape abroad. Parliament asked William and Mary to take over the vacant throne. James II landed in Ireland with French troops (March 1690), besieged Londonderry, and was defeated at the Battle of the *Boyne (July 1690). He returned to exile in France. The Act of *Settlement of 1701 provided for the Protestant succession.

Göbbels, Joseph See GOEBBELS.

Gobind Singh (1666–1708) The tenth and last of the Sikh Gurus. Gobind Singh encouraged the militarization of the Sikhs against the Mogul empire. During *Baisakhi* (the new year festival) in 1699, he called upon five Sikhs to give up their lives, but instead of killing the volunteers he rewarded their courage and loyalty by initiating them into the *Khalsa*, a newly formed army of soldier-saints.

Gobineau, Joseph Arthur, Comte de (1816–82) French diplomat and scholar, the intellectual founder of racism. His most famous book, *Essay on the Inequality of Human Races* (1853–55), put forward the thesis that the races are innately unequal and that the White Aryan race is not only the purest but also superior to all others. His writings had a sinister influence on the German *Nazi theorists, for whom they became a justification for *anti-Semitism.

Goderich, Frederick John Robinson, Viscount and 1st Earl of Ripon (1782–1859) British statesman, Prime Minister (1827–28). He first entered Parliament in 1806 and held a succession of offices, including those of President of the Board of Trade (1818–23), Chancellor of the Exchequer (1823–27), and Secretary for War and the Colonies (1827). As Viscount Goderich he succeeded George Canning as Prime Minister in August 1827, but, ill-suited to the task, resigned the following January. He was created Earl of Ripon in 1833.

Godfrey of Bouillon (or **Godefroi de Bouillon**) (c.1060–1100) French Crusader and ruler of *Jerusalem. He was a prominent leader of the First *Crusade and financed a large part of the expeditionary force. Having distinguished himself at the siege of Jerusalem, he was elected Advocate of the Holy Sepulchre—in effect, king—a position which his brother, *Baldwin I, was to assume on his death. His victories against the Muslims confirmed the Crusaders' hold on Palestine and were celebrated in the medieval song cycle, the *Chansons de Geste*.

Godolphin, Sydney, 1st Earl of (1645–1712) English statesman who gave loyal service to *Charles II, *James II, and Queen *Anne. Although he maintained close links with the Jacobites, he served *William III until he quarrelled with his colleagues in 1696. He was Queen Anne's Lord Treasurer for most of her reign, and in spite of being himself a Tory played an important part in excluding Tories from her government and in securing the Act of *Union with Scotland in 1707. Godolphin's fortunes were linked with *Marlborough's: he financed the duke's campaigns in the War of the *Spanish Succession, but when Marlborough lost favour and the Tories regained influence in 1710 his career ended.

Godunov, Boris See BORIS GODUNOV.

Godwin, Mary Wollstonecraft See WOLLSTONECRAFT (GODWIN), MARY.

Godwin, William (1756–1836) British social philosopher and novelist. At first a dissenting minister, he subsequently became an atheist and expounded theories of anarchic social organization based on a belief in the goodness of human reason and on his doctrine of extreme individualism. His ideological novel *Caleb Williams* (1794), which exposes the tyranny exercised by the ruling classes, was an early example of the crime and detection novel. In 1797 he married Mary *Wollstonecraft, who died after giving birth to their daughter who became Mary Shelley.

Goebbels, Joseph (Paul Joseph Goebbels or **Göbbels**) (1897–1945) German Nazi leader and politician. In 1933 he became Hitler's Minister of Propaganda, with control of the press, radio, and all aspects of culture. With a total disregard for the truth, he manipulated the media in order to further Nazi aims. A supporter of Hitler to the last, he committed suicide rather than surrender to the Allies.

Goering, Hermann Wilhelm (or **Hermann Wilhelm Göring**) (1893–1946) German Nazi leader and politician. In 1934 he became commander of the German air force, and was responsible for the German rearmament programme. Until 1936 Goering headed the Gestapo, which he had founded; from then until 1943 he directed the German economy. In that year he fell from favour, was deprived of all authority, and was finally dismissed in 1945 after unauthorized attempts to make peace with the Allies. Sentenced to death at the Nuremberg war trials, he committed suicide in his cell.

Gokhale, Gopal Krishna (1866–1915) Indian nationalist politician. The leader of the moderate faction in the Indian National *Congress, he became prominent in the Indian legislative Council established under the Morley–Minto Reforms in 1910, specializing in finance. He also founded in 1905 the Servants of India Society, an austere organization dedicated to the service of India.

Golden Horde The *Tartars of the Mongol *khanate of the Western Kipchaks (1242–1480). The word "horde" derives from the Mongol *ordo*, meaning a camp, while "golden" recalls the magnificence of Batu Khan's headquarters camp. In 1238 Batu, a grandson of *Genghis Khan, invaded Russia with a Mongol-Kipchak force. He burned Moscow and in 1240 took Kiev. After a sweep through eastern Europe he established his camp at Sarai on the Lower Volga. Khan of a region extending from Central Asia to the River Dnieper, he claimed sovereignty over all Russia but, apart from demanding tribute in money and military contingents, interfered little with the Russian princes, who in general avoided trouble by cooperating. The destruction of Kiev led to the rise of a more northerly, forest-based Russian civilization, and it was from Moscow that resistance to the Horde started.

Defeat by *Tamerlane in 1391 seriously weakened the Horde. Independent khanates emerged in the Crimea and Kazan. In 1480 the power of the Tartars was broken by *Ivan III (the Great).

gold rushes Sudden influxes of people to newly discovered gold fields. The most famous gold rush was to California, where in 1848 gold was found by a Swiss settler, J. A. Sutter. As news spread, adventurers from all over the world made for California. Hard-drinkers and gamblers, the 'forty-niners' created an archetypal saloon society, where more fortunes were made from speculation in land and goods than from gold. The second great rush was to Australia, where gold was first found near Bathurst in New South Wales in 1851 and later in Victoria at Bendigo and Ballarat, the richest alluvial gold field ever known. A ten-year boom brought diggers back across the Pacific from the declining California field, as well as from Britain, where Cornish tin-mining was declining. The population of Victoria rose from 97,000 to 540,000 in the years 1851–60. Later rushes were to New Zealand (1860), to North Australia, Alaska, Siberia, and South Africa (1880s), and to Klondike in Canada and Kalgoorlie in West Australia (1890s). The most important was probably to Witwatersrand, South Africa, in 1886, where the influx of loose-living miners (*Uitlanders or outlanders) precipitated political tensions, which led to the Second *Boer War.

Gómez, Juan Vicente (1864–1935) Venezuelan statesman. During his 27-year rule as President (1908–35) he established an absolute dictatorship. The foreign investment that he attracted to Venezuela enabled him to build extensive railways, highways, and other public works. Rich petroleum discoveries (1918) in the Lake Maracaibo basin provided a budgetary surplus which not only enabled Gómez to pay off the foreign debt but also assured him a favourable reputation abroad. Because of the brutal nature of the dictatorship, this reputation was not shared at home. When he died in office the city of Caracas marched in celebration.

Gomułka, Władysław (1905–82) Polish politician. He was Secretary-General during the crucial period 1943–1949 when the Polish United People's Party was being formed. Gomułka's attempted defiance of Stalinism led to his dismissal and imprisonment (1951). He was restored to power (1956) on the intervention of Khrushchev, after Polish and Soviet frontier troops had exchanged fire in the wake of serious rioting in Poznań. He helped to sustain a degree of post-Stalinist liberalism, but resigned in 1970 following popular disturbances against increases in food prices.

Gondomar, Diego Sarmiento de Acuña, Conde de (1567–1626) Spanish diplomat. He achieved notoriety as ambassador to England (1613–18; 1620–22), when he made himself one of the most influential members of *James I's court, much to the chagrin of zealous English Protestants. He was largely responsible for the execution of Sir Walter *Raleigh, and he tried to interest the king in a royal Spanish wife for the Prince of Wales. When his unpopularity in England reached its peak in 1622, he was recalled to Spain.

Good Friday Agreement *See* NORTHERN IRELAND.

Good Neighbor Policy The popular name for the Latin American policy of the early administration of President F. D. *Roosevelt. It was implemented by the withdrawal of US marines from Latin American countries and the abrogation of the Platt Amendment, which had given the US government a quasi-protectorate over Cuba. The Montevideo Conference (1933) declared that "no state has the right to intervene in the internal or external affairs of another".

Gorbachev, Mikhail (Sergeevich) (1931–) Russian statesman and Executive President of the Soviet Union (1990–91). A Communist Party member since 1952, he was elected to the General Committee in 1979 and to the Politburo in the following year. On the death of Konstantin Chernenko in March 1985 he became the Soviet leader, exercising control from his position as General Secretary of the Communist Party of the Soviet Union (CPSU). Gorbachev's efforts to carry out *perestroika* (*see* GLASNOST AND PERESTROIKA), the economic and social reform of Soviet society, led to a gradual process of liberalization and the introduction of high technology to the Soviet Union. Together with his foreign minister, Eduard *Shevardnadze, he negotiated (1987) an arms control (INF) treaty with the West to reduce nuclear forces in

Europe. On the domestic front he introduced stringent laws against alcohol abuse and encouraged a greater degree of *glasnost* in the face of inefficiency and corruption. He released many political dissidents from restraint, including Andrei Sakharov and, for the first time, the Russian people were told of the enormities of the crimes against humanity perpetrated by Stalin's regime. He initiated a number of constitutional changes, whereby the Congress of People's Deputies was directly elected, the Congress then duly electing him Executive President. He withdrew from Afghanistan, and in August 1990 negotiated with Chancellor *Kohl that a united Germany could remain in a reformed *NATO. He supported the United Nations policy leading to the *Gulf War; but he faced increasing resistance from a conservative, bureaucratic hierarchy, while the constituent republics of the Union sought ever-greater independence. Tensions during 1991 culminated in an attempted coup in August, which he survived, but only because of the support given him by his rival Boris *Yeltsin. He had by then accepted that the political monopoly of the Communist Party of the Soviet Union had ended, but still believed in his communist ideals, and that the Union could be reformed along evolutionary lines. As the Soviet command-economy disintegrated his power-base collapsed, as did the Union itself. He resigned in December 1991. Gorbachev made an unsuccessful attempt to regain power in the presidential election of 1996, but failed significantly to challenge Yeltsin.

Gordon, Charles George (1833–85) British general and colonial administrator. He went to China in 1860 while serving with the Royal Engineers, and became known as 'Chinese Gordon' after crushing the Taiping Rebellion (1863–64). In 1884 he was sent to rescue the Egyptian garrisons in Sudan from forces led by the Mahdi (Muhammad Ahmad of Dongola, 1843–85), but was trapped at Khartoum and killed before a relieving force could reach him.

Gordon riots Anti-Catholic riots in London in 1780. They were led by Lord George Gordon (1751–93), who objected to parliamentary moves towards *Catholic emancipation. His followers terrorized London for a fortnight. Prisons were broken open, property damaged, and people killed before order was restored. Gordon was acquitted of high treason, but was later convicted of libel and died in Newgate Prison.

Gore, Al (Albert Gore) (1948–) US Democratic politician, Vice-President of the USA (1993–2001). An editorial writer and land developer, he was senator for Tennessee from 1985–1993. In the 2000 presidential election, he received more votes than George W. *Bush but, after a protracted legal controversy that was only resolved by the Supreme Court, he lost to Bush in the electoral college. Since this defeat he has campaigned actively on *climate change. His documentary film on this subject, *An Inconvenient Truth*, won the Oscar for Best Documentary Feature in 2007; in the same year he shared the Nobel Peace Prize with the Intergovernmental Panel on Climate Change.

Göring, Hermann *See* GOERING.

Gorton, Sir John Grey (1911–2002) Australian Liberal politician, Prime Minister as head of a coalition (1968–71). Gorton, a former air-force pilot, maintained Australian troops in Vietnam and increased educational opportunities for Aborigines.

Goths Germanic tribes that overran the Western Roman empire. Originally from the Baltic area, by the 3rd century AD they had migrated to the northern Black Sea and the Lower Danube. The eastern group on the Black Sea were known as *Ostrogoths, the western settlers on the Danube in Dacia were known as *Visigoths.

Gottwald, Klement (1896–1953) Czechoslovak politician. He was a founder-member of the Czechoslovak Communist Party in 1921, becoming General Secretary in 1927. After the *Munich Pact (1938) Gottwald went to the Soviet Union. After World War II he returned to Czechoslovakia. He was Prime Minister in a coalition government (1946–48) and, after the communist coup in 1948, President (1948–53) in succession to *Beneš. He dominated the country through purges, forced labour camps, and show trials, culminating in the Slansky trial and the execution (1952) of leading communists. He acquiesced in Stalin's plan of reducing Czechoslovakia's industries to satellite status within *COMECON.

Gowon, Yakubu (1934–) Nigerian general and statesman, head of state (1966–75). He seized power in 1966, ousting the leader of an earlier military coup. Following the Biafran civil war (1967–70) he maintained a policy of 'no victor, no vanquished' that helped to reconcile the warring factions. Gowon was himself removed in a military coup in 1975.

Gracchus, Tiberius Sempronius (*c.*163–133 BC) Roman tribune. He and his brother, **Gaius Sempronius Gracchus** (*c.* 153–121BC), were responsible for radical social and economic legislation, passed against the wishes of the senatorial class. Tiberius was killed by his opponents after the passing of his agrarian bill (133 BC), which aimed at a redistribution of land to the poor. Gaius continued his brother's programme and instituted other reforms to relieve poverty, but was killed in a riot.

Graf Spee *See* PLATE, BATTLE OF THE RIVER.

Grafton, Augustus Henry Fitzroy, 3rd Duke of (1735–1811) British statesman, Prime Minister (1766–70). He was first Lord of the Treasury until *Pitt the Elder's resignation from office. Although he favoured a conciliatory policy towards the Americans, he was overruled in cabinet. He handled *Wilkes's return from exile badly, and was subjected to ferocious personal attacks by the satirical writer known as 'Junius'. He held office again under *North in 1771 and under *Shelburne in 1782, but played little part in politics thereafter.

Granby, John Manners, Marquis of (1721–70) British army officer. He became a hero during the *Seven Years War. He was made commander-in-chief of the British army in 1766, but was subjected to bitter political attacks. Unnerved by such savage criticism, and in declining health, he resigned most of his public offices in 1770, and died in debt.

Grand Alliance, War of the *See* NINE YEARS WAR.

Grand Remonstrance (1641) A document drawn up by opposition members of the English *Long Parliament, indicting the rule of Charles I since 1625 and containing drastic proposals for reform of church and state. Although it passed the *House of Commons by just eleven votes, and swords were first drawn in the Commons over the question of its printing, many saw it as a vote of no confidence in the king. It drove Charles into his disastrous attempt to arrest its prime movers, including John Pym, an act of force that further alienated opposition Members of Parliament.

Grand Siècle The age of *Louis XIV (1643–1715), the period of France's greatest magnificence, when it replaced Spain as the dominant power in Europe and established its cultural pre-eminence. The genius of *Richelieu as chief minister (1624–42) had established the authority of the monarchy and achieved a far greater degree of internal unity for France than was possessed by its rivals. Europe was impressed by the splendours of the court of Versailles. French military predominance was won by the brilliant victories of *Condé and Turenne and the creation of the first modern standing army. The splendour of the *Grand Siècle*, based as it was on heavy taxation of the poorest classes, and a commitment to expensive military campaigns, gave way after the king's death to the more turbulent climate of the 18th century.

Grand Tour A leisurely journey through Europe, often lasting several years, made by young Englishmen in the 18th and 19th centuries. The sons of the aristocracy, often accompanied by a tutor, completed their education by enriching their knowledge of classical art and of European society. The eventual destination was Italy, specifically Naples and Rome, where there were well-established colonies of expatriate painters, architects, and connoisseurs. As well as purchasing antique sculpture these patrons bought contemporary Italian paintings, including portraits of themselves, with which to adorn their houses. The wealth of Greek and Roman statuary and Italian drawings and paintings in the country houses and museums of Great Britain are the legacy of the Tour.

Granger Movement A movement begun in 1867 as a social and educational association of mid-western farmers in the USA. It was more properly known as the National Grange of the Patrons of Husbandry. It believed in the importance of the family farm and opposed what it saw as a drift towards economic monopolies, particularly the abuse of freight rates. It never formed a major political party, but its supporters in a number of states did produce local legislation to fix maximum railway rates. These were validated by the US Supreme Court, which accepted the important new presumption that public regulation of private property was legitimate if the property provided public service. After the mid-1870s the movement declined.

Grant, Ulysses Simpson (1822–85) US general and 18th President of the USA (1869–77). He entered the *American Civil War as a colonel of volunteers in support of the Union (Northern states), and success brought him rapid promotion. He was active in most of the early engagements in the western theatre, winning the nickname "Unconditional Surrender" for his capture of Fort Donelson (12 February 1862). As a major-general, he captured *Vicksburg in 1863 and was again successful at *Chattanooga before being promoted to the supreme command of all the Union forces in February 1864. Basing himself in Virginia, he maintained relentless pressure on *Lee in a bloody year-long campaign in which Lee was finally forced to abandon Richmond and surrender at *Appomattox, bringing the war to an end. Grant served briefly as Secretary of War (1867–68) before being twice elected as Republican President of the USA. His presidency saw the collapse of the *reconstruction programme in the South. One of the greatest of all US soldiers, Grant was also one of the least successful US presidents.

Grattan, Henry (1746–1820) Irish statesman, a champion of Irish independence. He was born and educated in Dublin, where he trained as a barrister and entered the Irish Parliament in 1775. A brilliant orator, he led the movement to repeal Poynings' Law, which made all Irish legislation subject to the approval of the British Parliament. After considerable agitation the British government yielded and repealed the Act (1782). He also strongly opposed the Act of *Union (1801), which merged the British and Irish parliaments. In 1806 he became member for Dublin in the British House of Commons and devoted the rest of his life to the cause of *Catholic emancipation.

Gravettian *See* PALAEOLITHIC.

Great Awakening An American revivalist movement, which was a response to the growing formalism of early 18th-century American Christianity. Though revivals began in New Jersey in 1719, the preaching of the Puritan scholar Jonathan Edwards (1703–58), and the resultant conversions in the 1730s gave it widespread recognition and influenced the founders of Methodism, the Wesleys. George Whitefield's mission (1739–41) won many converts from Pennsylvania to Maine, but his followers Gilbert Tennent and James Davenport precipitated schisms in both Congregational and Presbyterian Churches, which also affected colonial politics. In Virginia, Samuel Davies led revivals (1748–53) among the "New Side" Presbyterians. Baptists and Methodists also embraced the new movement. By questioning established authority, founding new colleges, and revivifying evangelical zeal, it helped to prepare the revolutionary generation in America.

Great Britain *See* BRITAIN.

Greater East Asia Co-Prosperity Sphere The pseudo-political and economic union of Japanese-dominated Asian and Pacific territories during World War II. In the aftermath of Japan's dramatic conquests of 1941–42, some nationalist leaders (for example, Indonesia's *Sukarno and Burma's *Aung San) collaborated with the Japanese for tactical reasons. However, the hardships wrought by the Japanese (principally through their requisitioning of supplies and use of forced labour) soon disabused the local populations about Japan's intentions. By the end of the war, the Co-Prosperity Sphere had become an object of hatred and ridicule.

Great Exhibition A major international trade exhibition held in London in 1851 under the sponsorship of Prince Albert. It was housed in the vast Crystal Palace, designed by Joseph Paxton (1801–65), built in London's Hyde Park entirely of glass and iron, except for the flooring and joists. The exhibition, which lasted 23 weeks, attracted 17,000 exhibitors and more than 6 million visitors. The profits were invested, and are still being used, to promote education and science. The Crystal Palace was dismantled and moved to the London suburb of Sydenham, where it burnt down in 1936.

Great Leap Forward (1958) Chinese drive for industrial and agricultural expansion through 'backyard' industries in the countryside and increased production quotas to be reached by the people's devotion to patriotic and socialist ideals. Massive increases in the quantity of production were announced, but quality and distribution posed serious problems. In agriculture, *communes became almost universal, but disastrous harvests resulting in famine with an estimated 13 million victims, together with poor products discredited the Leap. Its most important advocate, *Mao Zedong, took a back seat until the late 1960s. The *Cultural Revolution can be seen partly as his attempt to re-introduce radical policies.

Great Northern War *See* NORTHERN WAR.

Great Plague (1664–65) A disastrous epidemic, mainly confined to London and southeast England. Bubonic plague had recurred at intervals since the Middle Ages, but there had been no serious outbreak for thirty years and its violent reappearance was not expected. About a fifth of London's population of almost half a million died. Business in the city came to a standstill. The court and all those able to move into the countryside prudently did so, as the disease was less virulent there. At the height of the epidemic plague pits were dug to receive the dead, and hand-carts were taken from house to house, collecting the bodies. The *Fire of London in the following year destroyed many of the close-packed slums in which the plague flourished, and after 1665 the disease disappeared from London.

great power A state seen as playing a major role in international politics. A great power possesses economic, diplomatic, and military strength and influence, and its interests extend beyond its own borders. The term is usually associated with the emergence of Austria, Russia, Prussia, France, and Great Britain as great powers in Europe after the Congress of Vienna in 1815; they worked together under a loose agreement known as the Concert of Europe. After World War I, the USA grew in importance, while after World War II, the USA and the Soviet Union, through their industrial strength, global influence, and nuclear capabilities, attained the status of "superpowers", and world events became dominated by bipolarity. Since the collapse of the Soviet Union in 1991, the only superpower is the USA, though China's growing economic and military strength may assure it superpower status in the next few years. The UK and France have declined from their former great power status, although they are still recognized by the *United Nations Organization, together with the USA, Russia, and China, as permanent members of the *United Nations Security Council with power of veto. The number of great powers at any time is considered a key feature of the international system, important in determining the level and nature of war.

Great Schism Two breaches in the Christian Church. The Great or *East–West Schism (1054) marked the separation of the Eastern (Orthodox) and Western Christian churches. The Great Schism of 1378–1417 resulted from the removal of the papacy from Italy to France in 1309. Feuds among the Italian cardinals and their allies among the Italian nobility led to Pope Clement V (1305–14) moving the papal residence from Rome to Avignon in southern France. French interests came to dominate papal policy and the popes, notorious for their luxurious way of life, commanded scant respect. An attempt to return the papacy to Rome was followed by schism as two rival popes were elected by the cardinals, Urban VI by the Roman faction and Clement VII by the French faction. The period of popes and rival *antipopes lasted until the Council of *Constance (1417) elected Pope Martin V of the Roman party and deposed his French rival. The division of the papacy discredited the Church and was criticized by those demanding reform, notably *Wyclif.

Great Trek, the The movement northwards in the 1830s by Boers to escape from British administration in the Cape Colony. From 1835 onwards parties of Voortrekkers reached Natal, where in 1837 *Zulu resistance provoked them to kill some 3,000 Zulus at the Battle of *Blood River in revenge for the death of their leader, Piet Retief. Natal became a British colony in 1843 and migration continued northwards into the Orange River country and the Transvaal.

Great Wall of China A defensive wall in northern China, extending over a total distance of 6700 km (4200 miles) from the Jiayuguan Pass in Gansu province to Shanhaiguan on the Yellow Sea north of Beijing. Its origin dates from c.210 BC when the country was unified under one ruler (Qin Shi Huang), and the northern walls of existing rival states were linked to form a continuous protection against nomad invaders. It was rebuilt in medieval times largely against the Mongols, and the present wall dates from the Ming Dynasty (1368–1544). Although principally a defensive wall it served also as a means of communication, and is said to be the only man-made feature that would be visible from a space orbit.

Greece (Greek **Hellas**)

Capital:	Athens
Area:	131,957 sq km (50,949 sq miles)
Population:	10,772,967 (2013 est)
Currency:	1 euro = 100 cents
Religions:	Greek Orthodox 98.0%; Muslim 1.3%
Ethnic Groups:	Greek 93.0%
Languages:	Greek (official); minority languages
International Organizations:	UN; EU; NATO; OECD; Council of Europe; OSCE; WTO

A maritime, largely mountainous country in the south-east of Europe, bounded by Albania, Macedonia, and Bulgaria to the north, and by Turkey to the east. The many islands round its long coastline include Corfu, Crete, the Cyclades, and the Sporades. The peninsula is bounded by the Ionian, Mediterranean, and Aegean Seas.

Physical Thrace in the north-east is mainly low-lying, as are the river deltas of Macedonia. Most of the mainland, however, is a peninsula of mountains, the highest being Olympus. These continue southward beyond the Gulf of Corinth and its isthmus and on to the high Peloponnese peninsula. In winter the northern plateaux are cold and suitable only for sheep grazing. One-third of the country can be cultivated; in areas where the climate is truly Mediterranean, crops include tobacco, tomatoes, and vines.

Economy Both agriculture and industry are important to the Greek economy, and the manufacturing sector experienced large growth in the 1980s. However, tourism is the most important industry and a substantial earner of foreign exchange. Exports include food and drink, manufactured goods, oil products, chemicals, and textiles. However, the economy has contracted by over a quarter since the *Credit Crunch and the consequent financial crisis in Greece.

History Greek history begins c.2000–1700 BC with the arrival in the mainland of Greek-speaking peoples from the north. There followed the *Mycenaean civilization which flourished until overthrown by the *Dorians at the end of the 12th century BC. After an obscure period of history (the Greek 'Dark Ages') the city-state (polis) emerged.

In the early 5th century the Greeks repulsed Persian attempts to annex their land. *Athens and *Sparta were now the major sea and land powers respectively, and after a prolonged struggle it was Sparta who by 404 had crushed Athens and destroyed the Athenian empire in the *Peloponnesian War. In the 4th century Thebes toppled Sparta, but Greece as a whole was soon forced to bow before an outside conqueror—*Philip II of Macedonia. After the death of his son, *Alexander III (the Great), the Greek world was dominated by the Hellenistic kingdoms with the cities of Greece playing comparatively minor parts in the power struggle. Then Rome intervened in the *Macedonian wars, until the year 146 BC saw the defeat of the *Achaean League, the sacking of Corinth, and the final incorporation of Greece into the Roman empire. Later it was part of the *Byzantine empire, but fell under the control of the Ottoman Turks in 1460. It remained under Turkish jurisdiction, apart from a brief period in the late 17th and early 18th centuries when Venice controlled parts of the country, until independence in the early 19th century.

The *Greek War of Independence (1821–33) resulted in the establishment of an independent Greece, with Duke Otto of Bavaria as king. Otto was deposed in 1862 and a Danish prince, William, installed, taking the title George I of the Hellenes (1863–1913). A military coup established a republic (1924–35). *George II was restored in 1935 but fled into exile in 1941. After repulsing an attempted invasion by Italian forces in 1940, Greece was occupied by the Germans in World War II, and the country suffered bitter fighting between rival factions of communists and royalists. The monarchy was restored by the British in 1946, and civil war broke out, lasting until 1949, when the communists were defeated. With the help of aid from the USA, recovery and reconstruction began. In 1967 a military coup took place. King Constantine II fled and government by a military junta (the 'Colonels') lasted for seven years, the monarchy being abolished in 1973. A civilian republic was established in 1974 and in the 1981 general election Andreas Papandreou became the first socialist Prime Minister, remaining in office until 1989. Greece had joined the European Community in 1981, whose agricultural policies boosted its economy; but as tariff barriers were reduced, a balance-of-payments crisis developed. During 1992 strong opposition emerged against the name of the proposed republic of Macedonia, since Greece regards its own northern province as having sole right to the name. This issue and that of the ailing economy led ultimately to the fall of the right-wing government of Constantine Mitsotakis in June 1993. Andreas Papandreou was subsequently returned to power. A dispute over territorial waters in the Aegean threatened war with Turkey in late 1994. In 1996 Costas Simitis became Prime Minister after Papandreou resigned because of ill-health. He retained power until a Conservative victory in the 2004 elections, when he was replaced by Costas Karamanlis. Greece adopted the *euro as its currency in 2002.

In the early 2000s the Greek economy grew rapidly through increased consumer and government spending financed by the cheap credit available on global markets. The *Credit Crunch of 2008 removed this prop, and Greece's public finances deteriorated rapidly. The crisis was compounded by two factors: the revelation that Greece's published financial statistics were misleading; and the extreme political difficulty in implementing the harsh cuts to social benefits necessary to stabilize Greek public finances. In 2009–10 Greece's credit rating was progressively downgraded to "junk" status and it could no longer borrow from the bond markets. The possibility that Greece might default on its debts and be forced to withdraw from the euro precipitated the *Eurozone Crisis, and since 2010 two emergency loans have been made to Greece by the EU and IMF. In return Greece promised to introduce austerity measures to control its deficit. Although these did not meet the creditors' demands, their severity caused a severe economic contraction, political instability, and social unrest. Two elections in 2012 produced strong support for extremist parties that rejected the bailout terms, and the government continued to experience difficulties in implementing the measures demanded by Greece's creditors. However, by 2014 sufficient progress had been made for Greece to resume borrowing on the global bond markets.

Greek city-state *See* POLIS.

Greek-Persian wars Conflicts that dominated the history of the eastern Mediterranean in the first half of the 5th century BC. In 499 BC the Greek cities of Ionia in Asia Minor revolted from the Persian empire. With some short-lived support from Athens and Eretria, they captured and burnt the important city of Sardis, but gradually the Persians regained control, the Greek fleet being finally crushed at Lade in 494. In 490 a Persian expeditionary force sailed across the Aegean. The capture of Eretria—the first goal—was achieved after a week-long siege and with help from Eretrian traitors. The Persians then landed in Attica but after a defeat at *Marathon they were forced to withdraw to Persia.

In 480 a much larger invasion force threatened Greece, advancing along the northern and western shores of the Aegean. A small Greek army and a large Greek fleet were positioned respectively at *Thermopylae and Artemisium, but despite vigorous fighting on land and sea the Greeks were forced to withdraw to the Isthmus of Corinth. With central Greece lost, the Athenians evacuated their city, while the Greek fleet, at *Themistocles' urging, lured the Persians into battle off *Salamis. In these narrow waters the Greek warships had the advantage and won a decisive victory which caused the Persian king *Xerxes to withdraw to Asia. Mardonius, his second-in-command, remained to continue the campaign with the army. In 479 Greeks and Persians met at Plataea. The Greeks were eventually successful, the Spartans and their Tegean allies ensuring victory when they overcame the élite Immortals (the Persian royal bodyguards) and killed Mardonius. Meanwhile a Greek fleet was winning another great victory off Mycale in Asia Minor. Soon afterwards some of the Greeks formed the *Delian League to be the instrument by which they would continue the war against the Persians.

Greek religion The religion of the ancient Greek world. It was polytheistic, involving the worship of several gods and goddesses. The most important deities were the sky-god Zeus (ruler of Olympus), his wife Hera (goddess of marriage), Poseidon (god of sea and earthquakes), the virgin goddess Athene (learning and the arts), Apollo and his sister Artemis (Sun and Moon, the one patron of music and poetry, the other of chastity and hunting), Hephaestus (fire and metalwork), Aphrodite (love and beauty), Ares (war), Demeter (crops), Hestia (hearth and home), and Hermes, the messenger of the gods. Although all were revered, different cities had different individual gods as their special patrons.

Greek War of Independence (1821–32) The revolt by Greek subjects of the *Ottoman empire against Turkish domination. It had its origins in the nationalistic ideas of the Hetairia Philike ('Society of Friends'), who chose Alexander Ypsilanti, a Russian general, and son of the ruler of Wallachia, to lead the revolt. Links were established with Romanian peasants, Serb rebels, and Ali Pasha, the warlord of western Greece. Ypsilanti crossed into Turkish territory in March 1821, but only after his defeat in June did the Greeks rebel. Although atrocities took place on both sides, the revolt gained the popular support of the Christian world and many foreign volunteers (of whom Lord Byron, who went out in 1823, was the most celebrated) joined the Greek forces. By the end of 1821 the Greeks had achieved striking successes on land and sea and in January 1822 an assembly met to declare Greece independent. Four years later, however, Mehemet Ali of Egypt reconquered the Peloponnese and threatened to restore Turkish control. At the Treaty of London in 1827, Britain and Russia offered to mediate and secure an autonomous Greek state. When the Turks refused, Britain, Russia, and France sent a combined fleet which destroyed the Egyptian fleet at Navarino (1827). The following year the Russian army seized Adrianople and threatened Constantinople. The Turks agreed to make peace (1829), and the Conference of London (1832) confirmed Greek independence. The following year a Bavarian prince, Otto I, was crowned King of *Greece.

Greene, Nathanael (1742–86) American general who led his colony's troops at the Siege of Boston (1775–76) and fought at Long Island, Trenton, *Brandywine, *Germantown, and Monmouth. In command in the south (1780–81) he waged a brilliant hit-and-run campaign against *Cornwallis, eventually recapturing most of the region.

Green Mountain Boys An association of guerrilla fighters from Vermont, active in the American War of *Independence. They were originally organized in 1771 by Ethan *Allen to defend their settlements against New York claims. Named after Vermont's mountain chain, they came to support the patriot cause, assisting in the capture of *Ticonderoga (1775), the Battle of *Bennington, and Burgoyne's surrender at *Saratoga (1777).

Greensboro incident (1960) An incident in the US *Civil Rights campaign. Four young Black students staged a sit-in at a segregated lunch counter in Greensboro, North Carolina. This led to similar sit-ins in many other Southern towns and sparked off waves of protest against the segregation laws and practices.

Greenwich Mean Time (GMT) The mean solar time on the Greenwich Meridian of longitude, which was defined to pass through the Airy Transit Circle at Greenwich in England and was adopted internationally as the zero of longitude at a conference in Washington in 1884. Its acceptance was facilitated by the overwhelming use of the Greenwich Meridian in navigation and the adoption, in the USA and Canada, of time zones based on Greenwich. Originally different towns in Great Britain kept their own local time, varying according to longitude. In the mid-19th century Greenwich time was adopted by railways throughout Britain for the sake of uniformity. However, it was only in 1880 that Greenwich Mean Time became the legal time throughout Great Britain. The international reference time-scale for civil use is now based on atomic clocks but is subject to step adjustments (leap seconds) to keep it close to mean solar time on the Greenwich Meridian. The formal name of the time-scale is UTC (a language-independent abbreviation of coordinated universal time) but it is still widely known as Greenwich Mean Time.

Gregory I, St (or **Gregory the Great**) (540–604) Pope (590–604). When he became pope Italy was in a state of crisis, devastated by floods, famine, and Lombard invasions, and the position of the Church was threatened by the imperial power at Constantinople; it was owing to Gregory that many of these problems were overcome. He made a separate peace with the Lombards in 592–93, and (acting independently of the imperial authorities) appointed governors to the Italian cities, thus establishing the temporal power of the papacy. One of his greatest achievements was the conversion of England to Christianity, by St *Augustine of Canterbury. Throughout his papacy he effectively opposed the double assault on the Church from paganism and the *Arian heresy. His interest in music led to developments in the plain chant which bears his name—the Gregorian Chant.

Gregory VII, St (or **Hildebrand**) (*c.*1021–85) Pope (1073–85). He argued for the moral reform of the Church and that the Christian West should be united under the overall leadership of the papacy. The latter was opposed by many secular rulers and the prolonged struggles that followed have come to be known as the Investiture contests. His most formidable opponent was the Holy Roman Emperor Henry IV. When in 1077 he submitted to the pope at *Canossa papal supremacy seemed nearer. However, Henry's submission was merely a tactical one and he later attacked Rome itself, forcing the pope to retreat to Salerno in southern Italy, where he died. He urged celibacy of the clergy and opposed *simony.

Grenada

Capital:	St George's
Area:	344 sq km (133 sq miles)
Population:	109,590 (2013 est)
Currency:	1 East Caribbean dollar = 100 cents
Religions:	Roman Catholic 53.0%; Anglican 13.8%; other Protestant 33.2%
Ethnic Groups:	Black 82.0%; mixed 13.0%; European and East Indian 5.0%
Languages:	English (official)
International Organizations:	UN; OAS; CARICOM; Commonwealth; Non-Aligned Movement; WTO

A state comprising the southernmost of the Windward Islands in the Caribbean and several small islands, part of the Grenadines archipelago.

Physical The island of Grenada contains rugged and forested mountains, rising to Mount Saint Catherine at 838 m (2749 feet), with crater lakes and springs. The mountains are of volcanic origin and enclose valleys where bananas, spices, and sugar cane are grown.

Economy Tourism is Grenada's main earner of foreign exchange. The principal exports are agricultural products: nutmeg, bananas, cocoa, and fruit and vegetables. Industries include food and drink and textiles; an offshore finance sector is developing. Tourism and agriculture both suffered severely from hurricanes in 2004–05, and reconstruction has left a large legacy of debt.

History Grenada was discovered by Columbus in 1498. Colonized by the French governor of Martinique in 1650, it passed to the control of the French crown in 1674. The island was conquered by the British during the *Seven Years War and ceded to them by the Treaty of Paris (1763). An uprising in 1795 against British rule, supported by many slaves, was put down the following year, and Grenada remained a British colony for almost two centuries. Universal adult suffrage was granted in 1950 when the United Labour Party, led by Matthew Gairy, emerged. The Windward Islands were granted self-government in 1956 and became a member of the West Indies Federation (1958–62). Following the break-up of the federation, the various Windward Islands sought separate independence. This was gained by Grenada in 1974, when Gairy became Prime Minister. He was deposed in a bloodless coup (1979) by Maurice Bishop (1944–83), leader of a left-wing group, the New Jewel Movement, who proclaimed the People's Revolutionary Government (PRG). He encouraged closer relations with Cuba and the Soviet Union but, following a quarrel within the PRG, he was overthrown and killed by army troops led by General Austin in 1983. Military intervention by the USA prevented a Marxist revolutionary council from taking power. US troops left the island in December 1983, after democratic government was re-established. Under Prime Minister Herbert Blaise (1984–89) political stability was restored. By the end of the decade, however, difficulties with the economy led to an IMF austerity programme. In June 1995 a general election brought the New National Party (NNP) to power under Prime Minister Keith Mitchell. It was re-elected in 1999 and 2003 but defeated in 2008 by the New Democratic Congress. Mitchell and the NNP returned to power in 2013.

Grenville, George (1712–70) British statesman, Prime Minister (1763–65). As premier he was largely responsible for the government's mishandling of the *Wilkes affair and also for the effort to raise revenue in America that resulted in the *Stamp Act of 1765. George III came to dislike him and some of his fellow politicians objected to his authoritarianism, although his budgets were well-received by backbenchers in Parliament. His failures led to his dismissal from office in 1765.

Grenville, Sir Richard (1542–91) English naval commander. He became Member of Parliament for Cornwall (1571), led the unsuccessful expedition to colonize Roanoake planned by his cousin Sir Walter *Raleigh, and supplied three ships to the force assembled against the Spanish Armada. He died after an epic battle off the Azores, during which his ship *Revenge* held out for 15 hours against a powerful Spanish fleet.

Grenville, William Wyndham, Baron (1759–1834) British statesman, Prime Minister (1806–07). He entered the House of Commons in 1782 and served as Secretary of State for Foreign Affairs (1791–1801) under William Pitt the Younger. After Pitt's death he formed the so-called 'Ministry of all the Talents' (February 1806–March 1807). Attempts to end the *Napoleonic Wars failed, but a bill for the abolition of the British overseas slave trade succeeded, following a resolution introduced by Charles James *Fox. A bill to emancipate Roman Catholics, however, was rejected by George III, and Grenville resigned from politics.

Gresham, Sir Thomas (*c.*1519–79) English financier. He founded the Royal Exchange in 1566 and served as the chief financial adviser to the Elizabethan government. He founded Gresham College in 1579 as a venue for public lectures and the Royal Society grew from these meetings at Gresham's house. His fame rests on **Gresham's Law**, wrongly attributed to him in the 19th century, which states that 'bad money drives out good'. According to this law, if there are two coins in circulation with different ratios of face value to intrinsic value (in terms of the precious metal content of the coins), the coin with the higher intrinsic value will tend to be taken out of circulation for hoarding or melting down.

Grey, Charles, 2nd Earl (1764–1845) British statesman, Prime Minister (1830–34). He was an advocate of electoral reform and his government passed the first Reform Act (1832) as well as important factory legislation and the Act abolishing slavery throughout the British Empire.

Grey, Edward, Viscount Grey of Fallodon (1862–1933), British politician. He was Foreign Secretary from 1905–1916, negotiating the Triple Entente (1907), which brought Britain, France, and Russia together, and in 1914 persuading a reluctant British cabinet to go to war, because Germany had violated Belgian neutrality.

Grey, Sir George (1812–98) British colonial administrator. He served as governor of South Australia (1841–45) and of New Zealand (1845–53; 1861–68), where he oversaw the introduction of representative government and gained a reputation for suppressing rebellion and promoting the "amalgamation" of the *Maori people into settler society. After the onset of the *Taranaki War, he failed in negotiations with the quasi-nationalist *Kingitanga, and invaded the Waikato in 1863. He ended his governorship in disfavour with the Colonial Office, as the war dragged on.

Grey, Lady Jane (1537–54) The 'Nine Days Queen' of England in July 1553. As a descendant of *Henry VII's younger daughter Mary, she had some claim to the English throne, and her father-in-law, John *Dudley, persuaded *Edward VI to name her as his successor. *Mary I ousted her easily, and she was beheaded after her father had incriminated her further by participating in *Wyatt's Rebellion.

Griffith, Arthur (1872–1922) Irish nationalist leader and statesman, President of the *Irish Free State (1922) government. In 1905 he founded and became President of *Sinn Fein. Griffith was among those who established the unofficial Irish Parliament, the Dáil Éireann, in 1919, becoming Vice-President of the republic it declared in the same year. With Michael *Collins, he negotiated the Anglo-Irish Treaty (1921) that established the Irish Free State, becoming its head of government in 1922. He died in office several months later.

Grotius, Hugo (or **Huig de Groot**) (1583–1645) Dutch jurist and diplomat. His fame rests on the legal treatise *De Jure Belli et Pacis*, written in exile in Paris and published in 1625, which established the basis of modern international law.

Group of 8 (G8) An association of the world's eight largest industrial democracies. The Group was originally the **Group of 7** (G7) but became G8 in 1998 when Russia joined. The G7 was set up in 1975 with the aim of coordinating efforts to promote growth and stability in the world economy, and to bring the world's key exchange rates into line. The original five members (France, Japan, the UK, the USA, and West Germany) were joined in 1976 by Canada and Italy, with the EC acquiring observer status in 1977. The 1991 summit was marked by the invitation to the then Soviet President Mikhail Gorbachev to attend post-summit discussions on the Soviet economy's transition to a free market. The G8 has no permanent headquarters, but holds regular meetings between the finance ministers and the governors of the central banks of member countries. The annual meeting of the G8 heads of state is of growing importance, and has expanded to include discussion of key foreign policy issues. However, the G8 was suspended in 2014 following Russia's annexation of the Crimea.

Group of 20 (G20) An association of 20 of the world's largest industrial and emerging powers. Formed in 1999 to extend the concept of the *Group of 8 beyond the established industrial nations, its members are Argentina, Australia, Brazil, Canada, China, the EU, France, Germany, India, Indonesia, Italy, Japan, Mexico, Russia, Saudi Arabia, South Africa, South Korea, Turkey, the UK, and the USA. It came to prominence in 2008 when a special meeting was called to discuss a coordinated international response to the *Credit Crunch.

Guatemala

Capital:	Guatemala City
Area:	108,889 sq km (42,042 sq miles)
Population:	14,373,472 (2013 est)
Currency:	1 Guatemalan quetzal = 100 centavos
Religions:	Roman Catholic 65.0%; Protestant 43.0%
Ethnic Groups:	Mestizo and European 59.4%; K'iche 9.1%; Kaqchikel 8.4%; Mam 7.9%; Q'eqchi 6.1%; other Mayan 8.6%
Languages:	Spanish (official); Mayan languages
International Organizations:	UN; OAS; Non-Aligned Movement; WTO

A Central American country, bounded by Mexico on its north and west and by Honduras and El Salvador on its south-east. It has a southern coast on the Pacific Ocean and access to the Caribbean Sea on the east, where it is also bounded by Belize.

Physical A very high range of volcanic mountains crosses Guatemala from east to west and rivers water the lower slopes, which support crops of coffee. The plateaux have a mild climate, the lowlands a hot one. Earthquakes are frequent, the country lying near a junction of crustal plates.

Economy Guatemala has a primarily agricultural economy which employs almost 40% of the workforce. Important agricultural exports are coffee, sugar, bananas, and vegetables. Crude oil, discovered in the 1970s, is also exported. Industries include sugar processing, textiles, clothing, and furniture. Wealth distribution is very uneven, with over half the population living in poverty. Remittances from expatriates are important to the economy.

History In prehistory Guatemala was culturally linked to the Yucatán peninsula and witnessed the rise of pre-Maya and *Maya civilizations. The modern Guatemalan population is largely descended from Maya ancestors. In the northern and central lowlands arose the great, classic Maya cities such as Tikal, Uaxactún, Altar de Sacrificios, Piedras Negras, Yaxhá, and Seibal; in the southern highlands were the cities of Zacualpa, Kaminaljuyú, Cotzumalhuapa, and others. They had political and economic connections with each other, and with prehistoric cities in southern and central Mexico, such as Teotihuacán and Monte Albán (in Oaxaca). Spanish *conquistadores arrived in 1523, seeking new American conquests, and the region soon became the Audiencia (a high court with a political role) of Guatemala, under the viceroyalty of New Spain. For almost three hundred years, Guatemala remained under Spanish rule. In 1821 it declared itself independent from Spain and became part of the short-lived Mexican empire of Iturbide. When that collapsed (1823), Guatemala helped to found the United Provinces of Central America (1823–38). Strong opposition to federation, led by Rafael Carrera, resulted in its collapse, Guatemala declaring itself an independent republic with Carrera its first President (1839–65). His successors as President became increasingly despotic. A left-wing government under

Jacobo Arbenz (1951–54) instituted social reforms, before being forced to resign, following US intervention through the *Central Intelligence Agency. Ten years of disorder were followed by the peaceful election of Julio César Méndez Montenegro as President (1966) on a moderate platform. But military intervention recurred, and during the 1970s and early 1980s violent suppression through the violation of human rights occurred. In 1985 civilian elections were restored. Jorge Serrano Elias, who became President in 1991, opened negotiations with the left-wing guerrilla movement URNG, and began a purge against the military for its corruption and repressive measures. In September 1991 he ended the long dispute over *Belize, recognizing that country's existence. In May 1993 Serrano was ousted following attempts to acquire dictatorial powers. Ramiro de Léon Carpio was elected President in June. Peace talks between the government and URNG guerrillas were resumed. In 1995 Alvaro Arzu was elected President, retaining power in further elections in 1996, which also saw the achievement of a peace settlement with the URNG. Arzu was succeeded as President in turn by Alfonso Portillo (2000), Óscar Berger (2004), Álvaro Colom (2008), and Otto Pérez Molina (2012).

Guderian, Heinz (1888–1954) German general and tank expert. A proponent of the *Blitzkrieg tactics, he used tanks in large formations in the conquest of Poland (1939) and of France (1940). As commander-in-chief of the Panzer (tank) forces, he played a leading role in the German victories of 1940–41, but was dismissed when he disagreed with Hitler's order to stand fast in the 1941–42 Soviet counter-offensive outside Moscow. In 1944 he became chief-of-staff to the German Army High Command, but in March 1945 was again dismissed, this time for advocating peace with the Western Allies.

Guelph A member of a faction originating in the German Welf family, who were dukes of Saxony and Bavaria. The Welfs were the traditional opponents of the *Hohenstaufens in Germany and Italy (where they were known as Guelphs and the latter were known as the Ghibellines). In the 12th century the Guelph leader was Henry the Lion, Duke of Saxony and Bavaria, and he tended to support the papacy against the aspirations of the Holy Roman Emperors. Guelph support was in the major Italian towns and cities. Their rivals were the imperial party and their strength came mainly from the great aristocratic families. In local feuds, no

matter what the cause, the antagonists came to associate themselves with one or other of the opposing families whose names continued to be used for many years after the original disputes were forgotten.

Guernica (or **Guernica y Luno**) A town in the Basque Provinces of northern Spain, 25 km (16 miles) east of Bilbao. Formerly the seat of a Basque parliament, it was bombed in 1937, during the Spanish Civil War, by German planes in support of Franco, an event depicted in a famous painting by Picasso.

guerrilla (Spanish, 'little war') A person taking part in irregular fighting by small groups acting independently. The word was coined during the *Peninsular War (1807–14) to describe the Spanish partisans fighting the armies of Napoleon. From Spain the use of the word spread to South America and thence to the USA.

Guerrilla warfare avoids full-scale military confrontation while keeping the enemy under pressure with many small-scale skirmishes. The technique is suited to harsh terrain, particularly jungle and mountainous areas, and has been used effectively by materially weak forces against militarily strong opponents, where there are few opportunities for conventional military forces to use superior firepower. During *World War II guerrillas formed the basis of the *resistance movements that harassed the Japanese and German occupying forces. In post-war years they have become associated with such revolutionary movements as those in South America under Che *Guevara. *See also* TERRORISM.

Guesclin, Bertrand du (c.1320–80) French army commander and Constable of France from 1370. He attracted attention at the Siege of Rennes (1356–57) and was promoted by the regent, *Charles V, to the office of Constable of France. He fought in campaigns against the English, and, from 1366–1369 against Spain where he was defeated and captured at the Battle of Najera in 1367. It was his conduct of the war against the English which helped Charles recover his kingdom.

Guevara, Che (born **Ernesto Guevara de la Serna**) (1928–67) South American revolutionary and political leader. An Argentine by birth, he joined the pro-communist regime in Guatemala, and when this was overthrown (1954) he fled to Mexico. Here he met Fidel *Castro and helped him prepare the *guerrilla force which landed in Cuba in 1956. Shortly after Castro's victory Guevara was given a cabinet position and placed in charge of Cuban economic policy. He played a major role in the transfer of Cuba's traditional economic ties from the USA to the communist bloc. A guerrilla warfare strategist rather than an administrator, he moved to Bolivia (1967) in an attempt to persuade Bolivian peasants and tin-miners to take up arms against the military government. The attempt ended in failure as Guevara was captured and executed shortly thereafter. His remains were discovered in 1997 and returned to Cuba for a state funeral.

Guicciardini, Francesco (1483–1540) Italian statesman and historian. As Florentine ambassador to Aragon (1512–14), and then in the service of the papacy (1515–34), he showed outstanding administrative ability, and he also became a prolific political writer. In 1536, back in Florence, he began his monumental *Storia d'Italia* ("History of Italy"), which covered the years from 1494–1534. Although he died before completing the final revision, it stands as the most objective contemporary history of the country during the period of Italy's wars with France.

guild An association of townspeople formed to provide mutual protection of trading practices. Religious guilds, mainly devoted to devotional, charitable, and social activities, were important in English towns and parishes throughout the Middle Ages. From the early 11th century merchants and traders combined to regulate trade. The merchant guilds they formed controlled markets, weights and measures, and tolls, and negotiated charters granting their towns borough status. They maintained the charitable work of the earlier religious guilds. However, their monopolistic character forced the small crafts and trades to form their own associations, craft guilds, before the end of the 12th century. Each craft had its own guild which set quality standards and evolved a hierarchy consisting of master, journeymen, and apprentices (serving for up to twelve years). Guilds declined from the 16th century, being unable to adapt to the emergence of new markets.

guillotine The instrument used to inflict capital punishment by decapitation during the *French Revolution. A similar device had been used in Europe since the Middle Ages and had fallen into disuse when Dr Guillotin (1738–1814) suggested its reintroduction. After satisfactory tests on dead bodies it was erected on the Place de Grève in Paris in 1792. 'La Guillotine' was used extensively during the Reign of Terror, accounting for 1376 victims between 10 June and 27 July 1794.

Guinea

Capital:	Conakry
Area:	245,857 sq km (94,926 sq miles)
Population:	11,176,026 (2013 est)
Currency:	1 Guinean franc = 100 centimes
Religions:	Muslim 85.0%; Christian 8.0%; traditional beliefs 7.0%
Ethnic Groups:	Peuhl 40.0%; Malinke 30.0%; Soussou 20.0%
Languages:	French (official); local languages
International Organizations:	UN; AU; ECOWAS; Non-Aligned Movement; WTO

A West African country with an Atlantic coast, bounded on the north by Senegal, Guinea-Bissau, and Mali, on the east by Côte d'Ivoire, and on the south by Liberia and Sierra Leone.

Physical Inland from the marshy coast is a plain with large bauxite deposits. This rises to a sandstone plateau, the Fouta Djallon. Southward is the source of the Niger River; and further south still (the country bends like a hook) are large reserves of iron ore.

Economy Guinea is richly endowed with natural resources, and the major exports are bauxite, alumina, gold, and diamonds. Iron-ore mining is being developed. However, it is a poor country with over 75% of the population working in agriculture. Principal crops are rice, coffee (which is exported), pineapples, palm kernels, and cassava.

History From the 5th to the 8th centuries AD, the far north of modern Guinea formed part of the kingdom of *Ghana. This area of the country was incorporated in the Mali Empire in the 16th century. From 1849 onwards, French encroachment upon the region increased, leading to conflict with the empire of Samori Touré in eastern Guinea c.1879–91, when Guinea became a French colony. In 1895 Guinea was made part of the huge territory of French West Africa, and remained a French colony until 1958, when a popular vote rejected membership of the French Community, and Ahmed Sékou *Touré became first President.

His presidency was characterized by severe unrest and repression, and almost complete isolation from the outside world, although before his death in 1984 a degree of liberalization was introduced. This trend has continued under the military rule of President Lansana Conté. In 1990 Conté established a Transitional Committee for National Recovery, following a referendum that backed a new constitution. The slow pace of democratization, together with an IMF-imposed austerity programme, led to a general strike in 1991, after which the government introduced a multiparty system. In 1993, in the country's first multiparty elections, Conté was re-elected. He retained power until his death (2008), which was immediately followed by a military coup. Elections were not held until 2010, when Alpha Condé, an opposition politician, was elected President.

Guinea-Bissau

Capital:	Bissau
Area:	36,125 sq km (13,948 sq miles)
Population:	1,660,870 (2013 est)
Currency:	1 CFA Franc = 100 centimes
Religions:	Muslim 50.0%; traditional beliefs 40.0%; Christian 10.0%
Ethnic Groups:	Balanta 30.0%; Fula 20.0%; Manjaca 14.0%; Mandinga 13.0%; Papel 7.0%
Languages:	Portuguese (official); creole; local languages
International Organizations:	UN; AU; Non-Aligned Movement; ECOWAS; Franc Zone; WTO

A small tropical country on the coast of West Africa, bounded by Senegal on the north and Guinea on the south. Offshore is the Bijagós archipelago with a score of inhabitable marshy islands.

Physical The deeply indented coast of Guinea-Bissau, stretching for some 240 km (150 miles) from north to south, is marshy and contains the mouths of three major rivers. The interior, which extends eastward for some 300 km (185 miles), consists mainly of river valleys filled with rainforest; it rises to above 200 m (650 feet) only in the south.

Economy Guinea-Bissau is a poor country with a mainly agricultural economy whose significant exports are fish, cashews, groundnuts, and palm kernels.

History Portuguese explorers and traders were active around the coast from the mid-15th century, developing the area into a centre of the slave trade. First incorporated as part of the Portuguese Cape Verde Islands, it became the separate colony of Portuguese Guinea in 1879. Its boundaries were fixed by the 1886 convention with France. In the 1960s a movement for liberation from colonial rule emerged and grew under the leadership of Amilcar *Cabral, and in 1974 Portugal formally recognized its independence. In 1977 an unsuccessful attempt was made to unite with Cape Verde (a newly formed republic of islands to the west). In 1980 a military coup established a revolutionary council with João Vieira as President and a National Assembly elected from the ruling Marxist party, the PAIGC. In 1989 Vieira was re-elected and in 1991 the National Assembly agreed to the introduction of multiparty democracy. The country's first multiparty elections, in 1994, were won by the ruling party and Vieira was re-elected President. An attempted coup in 1998 was suppressed but violence continued and Vieira was overthrown by a military coup in 1999. Civilian rule was restored in 2000, but was ended by another coup in 2003. Presidential elections were held in 2005, when Vieira was returned to power; he was assassinated in 2009. The following years saw military unrest; there was at least one attempted coup and claims that more had been foiled. A coup succeeded in 2012, but after international pressure the civilian Manuel Serifo Nhamadjo was named President of a transitional government.

Guiscard, Robert (c.1015–85) Norman warrior. He was the son of Tancred de Hauteville, and with his brother Roger established himself in southern Italy. In 1053 they defeated the forces of Pope Leo IX, securing Apulia and Calabria. Pope Nicholas II, enlisting Norman aid against the *Byzantines, gave him Sicily, though it was not finally conquered till 1090. Excommunicated by Pope Gregory VII for his attack on Benevento, he nevertheless fought for him against the invading *Henry IV of Germany. The brothers sacked Rome in 1084, driving Henry out.

Guise A branch of the ducal house of Lorraine that rose to prominence in 16th-century France. **Claude de Lorraine** (1496–1550) was created duke in 1528; he had distinguished himself in a number of French military victories, including Marignano (1515). **Francis** (1519–63), his son and heir, became the most effective commander in the armies of Henry II. He was active throughout the 1550s, capturing Calais from the English (1558) and helping to bring about the Peace of Cateau-Cambrésis in 1559. His brother **Charles** (1524–74) became Cardinal of Lorraine in 1550, and his sister **Mary** (1515–60) married James V of Scotland and was the mother of *Mary, Queen of Scots.

In 1559, on the accession of Francis II, the Catholic Guise family was the most influential in France. Its dealings with the *Huguenots and *Bourbons (1559–62) led directly to the outbreak of the *French Wars of Religion. Francis was assassinated in 1563. His son **Henry** (1550–88), the third duke, fought in the third and fourth wars, and was one of the instigators of the *St Bartholomew's Day Massacre. In 1576 he took the lead in organizing the Holy League, but Henry III had him assassinated in 1588, when he was being put forward as a possible heir to the throne. His brother, **Charles** (1554–1611), kept the Guise and extremist Catholic causes alive until 1595, when he submitted to *Henry IV. The Guise ducal line died out in 1688.

Guizot, François Pierre Guillaume

(1787–1874) French historian and statesman. Entering official service in 1815, he lost office in 1822 and led the liberal opposition to *Charles X's government. Involved in the *July Revolution of 1830, he returned to official service and, in 1833, introduced a national system of primary education. For the next 18 years he served *Louis Philippe. A moderate monarchist, he succeeded *Thiers as leader of the government in 1840. His passive but immovable resistance to change finally led to his downfall in the *Revolution of 1848.

Gujral, Inder Kumar

(1919–2012) Indian politician. Having been a member of the Janata Dal party for 50 years and held numerous government posts Gujral became Prime Minister as the head of a fragile coalition in April 1997. He resigned in November that year after Congress (I) withdrew support from the coalition following allegations in a magazine linking one of the parties in the coalition to the murder of Rajiv *Gandhi.

Gulf War

(1991) An international conflict in the Gulf region of Kuwait and Iraq. Iraq, as the successor to the Ottoman empire, claimed Kuwait in 1961, claimed Kuwait in 1961, but the issue was not pressed and Kuwait later supported Iraq financially, especially during the Iran-Iraq war. However, in 1990 Saddam *Hussein claimed Kuwait was deliberately lowering oil prices by over-producing oil, costing Iraq money, and that Kuwait had seized Iraqi territory and oil. Kuwait denied the charges, but on 2 August 1990, Iraqi troops invaded Kuwait, Saddam Hussein demanding control of its large and valuable oilfields and declaring Kuwait the 19th province of Iraq. The UN Security Council imposed economic sanctions, and the US-led coalition of 29 countries was mobilized. Intense diplomatic activity failed, and on 17 January 1991 a massive air attack was launched. Strategic targets, some placed by Hussein in densely populated areas, were immobilized by electronically guided bombs. By 24 January Allied forces had established air supremacy, 'carpet bombing' Iraqi forces, which could not shelter in the deserts of southern Iraq. The land war, named by Hussein as 'the mother of all battles', and by the UN forces under their Commander-in-Chief, General Norman Schwarzkopf, as 'Operation Desert Sabre' lasted from 24 to 28 February, during which time the Iraqi forces were routed by a massive Allied tank advance. The Allied offensive by air was called 'Operation Desert Storm'. On the Allied side the war was fought with sophisticated electronic equipment and weapons systems, notably the F-117 Stealth Fighter, laser-guided bombs, and depleted uranium shells for penetrating armour. Iraq's defence system, which included chemical and biological warheads intended for delivery by Soviet SCUD ballistic missiles, had been rendered ineffective by Allied bombing. By the end of February 1991, Hussein, having set fire to over 700 Kuwaiti oil wells, accepted the UN ceasefire terms, but had openly flouted these by early 1993. Final casualties of the war numbered some 33,000 Kuwaitis killed or captured, 234 Allied dead, and between 85,000 and 100,000 Iraqi soldiers killed. UN sanctions imposed on Iraq remained in place and tension continued throughout the 1990s as Iraq refused to allow UN weapons inspections. This provoked several bombing raids by the USA and contributed, eventually, to the causes of the 2003 *Iraq War.

gunboat diplomacy

Diplomacy supported by the threatened use of force by one country in order to impose its will on another. The term is used specifically with reference to the 19th century when, in furtherance of their own interests, the great maritime nations, notably Britain, employed their naval power to coerce the rulers of small or weak countries. It was used by the British Foreign Secretary, Lord *Palmerston, during the *Opium Wars with China. In

Egypt in 1882 a British fleet bombarded Alexandria in order to crush a nationalist movement. During the *Boxer Rising in China in 1900 the European powers combined their forces in order to protect their interests and punish the rebels. Gunboat diplomacy was also employed by the USA in the Philippines in 1898 and has been used to enforce US policies in Latin America.

Gunpowder Plot A Catholic scheme to murder *James I of England and his Parliament at the state opening on 5 November 1605, to be followed by a national Catholic uprising and seizure of power. The plotters, recusants led by Robert Catesby, saw violent action as the only way to gain toleration for English Catholics. They were subsequently disowned by the majority of their fellow religionists, who had little sympathy for the conspiratorial tradition established by Roberto Ridolfi, Francis Throckmorton, and Anthony Babington. It has been suggested that Robert *Cecil manufactured the plot, in order to discredit the Catholic cause. Cecil learned of the plot through Lord Mounteagle, a Catholic peer. On the eve of the opening, Guy *Fawkes was discovered in the cellar under the House of Lords on guard over barrels of gunpowder. The other plotters were overcome in the Midlands after brief resistance. Fawkes and seven others, including Sir Everard Digby were tried before *Coke and executed in January 1606. Immediately afterwards, the penal laws against Catholics were stiffened, and an Oath of Allegiance imposed, but to the chagrin of many Puritans and Anglicans, enforcement of the new legislation soon became sporadic. Bonfires, fireworks, and the burning of 'guys' still mark 5 November in Britain.

Guomindang *See* KUOMINTANG.

Gupta A Hindu dynasty established in 320 by Chandra Gupta I in Bihar. The Gupta empire eventually stretched across most of northern India, but began to disintegrate towards the end of the 5th century, only north Bengal being left by the end of the 6th century.

Gustavus I (Vasa) (1496-1560) King of Sweden (1523-60) and founder of the Vasa dynasty. He fought against the Danes in 1517-18, but was successful only after 1520, thanks to financial and naval backing from the city of Lübeck. His election as king ended the 126-year-old Union of *Kalmar by which Sweden had been subordinated to Denmark. He created a national army of volunteers and built an efficient navy. He also modernized the economy, and in 1527 broke with the Roman Catholic Church for mainly political reasons. In 1544 the Swedish crown was made hereditary in the Vasa family.

Gustavus II (Adolphus) (1594-1632) King of Sweden (1611-32). He was the grandson of *Gustavus I and is generally recognized as Sweden's greatest ruler. His partnership with the Chancellor, *Oxenstierna, bore fruit in important reforms in the government, the armed forces, the economy, and education. His reign was notable for the absence of friction between crown and aristocracy.

Abroad he inherited three Baltic struggles: the Kalmar War with Denmark (1611-13); the Russian War (1611-17); and the intermittent conflict with Poland. The successes achieved by his mobile, highly motivated, and disciplined forces impressed Cardinal *Richelieu, who negotiated the Treaty of Altmark (1629) between Sweden and Poland, so that the Swedes could be released for action in the *Thirty Years War. Leaving the domestic government in the hands of Oxenstierna, Gustavus crossed to Germany in 1630 and proceeded to turn the tide of the war against the imperial forces. He was a devout Lutheran, and his war aims grew more ambitious as his invasion prospered. Originally intending to prevent the Catholic Habsburgs from dominating the Baltic, by 1632 he was pursuing grand imperial designs of his own. He was killed in action at *Lützen.

Gutenberg, Johannes (*c.*1400-68) German printer. He is remembered as the first in the West to print using movable type; he introduced typecasting using a matrix, and was the first to use a press. By *c.*1455 he had produced what later became known as the Gutenberg Bible, the first book to be printed from movable type and the oldest book still extant in the West.

Guyana

Capital:	Georgetown
Area:	214,969 sq km (83,000 sq miles)
Population:	739,903 (2013 est)
Currency:	1 Guyana dollar = 100 cents
Religions:	Protestant 30.5%; Hindu 28.4%; Roman Catholic 8.1%; other Christian 18.8%; Muslim 7.2%
Ethnic Groups:	East Indian 43.5%; Black 30.2%; Mixed 16.7%; Amerindian 9.1%

| Languages: | English (official); English creole; also Amerindian languages, Hindi, and Urdu |
| International Organizations: | UN; Commonwealth; CARICOM; Non-Aligned Movement; OAS; WTO |

A country on the north-east coast of South America, extending for 800 km (500 miles) from north to south and for 460 km (285 miles) from east to west.

Physical Guyana is bordered by the Atlantic Ocean to the north, Surinam to the east, Brazil to the south and south-west, and Venezuela to the west. Much of the country is covered with dense rainforest.

Economy The economy is based on agriculture and mining. Major exports are sugar (the province of Demerara gave its name to a type of sugar that originated there), gold, bauxite, shrimp, timber, and rice.

History The country was first settled by the Dutch in the 17th century. British rule was formally secured in 1831 when three colonies, Essequibo, Demerara, and Berbice (named from the three rivers) were consolidated to form the crown colony of British Guiana. Boundary problems with neighbours dominated the 19th century. During World War II the lease of military and naval bases to the USA proved useful to the Allied war effort. Britain granted independence to the colony in 1966 and Guyana became a nominally cooperative republic in 1970. Its Prime Minister, Forbes Burnham, became executive President (1980–86) with supreme authority under an authoritarian constitution. He was succeeded by Desmond Hoyte, who embarked on a policy of restoring good relations with the USA by a 'rolling back of cooperative socialism'. Hoyte survived an IMF-imposed austerity programme, but in December 1991 proclaimed a state of emergency, postponing a general election. In the general election of October 1992 a victory by the People's Progressive Party, under Cheddi Jagan, ended 28 years of rule by the People's National Congress. The new government pledged to follow the free market policies of the previous administration, while the country continued to experience a protracted economic crisis. In 1997 Jagan died and his widow Janet was elected President. She was succeeded in 1999 by Bharrat Jagdeo, who was re-elected in 2001 and 2006. Donald Ramotar was elected President in 2011.

Guzmán Blanco, Antonio (1829–99) Venezuelan statesman. Appointed to negotiate loans from London bankers in 1870, he seized power and two years later had himself elected President. He was absolute ruler of Venezuela (1870–89). He fostered railroad construction, public education, and free trade. An efficient administrator, he reformed the civil service and instituted public works. His extravagance gradually alienated the Venezuelan populace and in 1888, while visiting Paris, he was deposed by Juan Paúl.

Gwalior *See* SINDHIA.

Gwynn, Nell (full name **Eleanor Gwynn**) (1650–87) English actress. Originally an orange-seller, she became famous as a comedienne at the Theatre Royal, Drury Lane, London. She was a mistress of Charles II; one of her sons was later created Duke of St Albans.

Haakon IV (or **Haakonsson the Old**) (1204–63) King of Norway (*c.*1220–63). His reign was troubled by internal dissensions and he had Earl Skule executed in 1239. Iceland and Greenland were added to the Norwegian crown but control of the Hebrides was lost. This followed his defeat by *Alexander III of Scotland in the decisive battle at Largs in 1263.

Haakon VII (1872–1957) King of Norway (1905–57). Formerly Prince Charles of Denmark, he was elected by the Norwegian Storting (parliament) to the throne in 1905. In April 1940 he was driven out by the German invasion. Refusing the suggestion of the government of Vidkun *Quisling to abdicate, he continued the struggle from London. He returned to Norway in 1945. He dispensed with much of the regal pomp attached to the monarchy, and became known as the 'people's king'.

Habsburg The most prominent European royal dynasty from the 15th to the 20th century. Their name derives from Habichtsburg (Hawk's Castle) in Switzerland, built in 1020. The founder of the family power was Rudolf I, who was King of the Romans (1273–91) and conqueror of *Austria and Styria, beginning the family's rule over Austria. Habsburg domination of Europe resulted from the shrewd marriage policy of Maximilian I (1459–1519), whose own marriage gained The Netherlands, Luxembourg, and Burgundy and that of his son, Philip, which brought Castile, Aragon, and the Spanish New World possessions as well as Naples, Sicily, and Sardinia. Habsburgs also ruled Hungary and Bohemia from 1526 to 1918. Thus the zenith of Habsburg power came under Charles I, King of Spain and emperor (as Charles V, 1519–56) in the 16th century. In 1700 the Spanish line became extinct and in the subsequent War of the *Spanish Succession (1703–13) the Spanish inheritance passed to the Bourbons. The Austrian Habsburgs (after 1740 the House of Habsburg-Lorraine) flourished again under *Maria Theresa (1717–80) and her son Joseph II (1741–90).

The Habsburgs ended the Napoleonic wars with the loss of the Austrian Netherlands and the title Holy Roman Emperor, but continued to rule over Austria. Following the *Austro-Prussian War of 1866 they had to make concessions to Hungarian nationalism with the formation of *Austria-Hungary. The emperor *Francis Joseph came increasingly to clash with Russian ambitions in the *Balkans. Nationalist aspirations led eventually to the disintegration of his empire during World War I. The last Habsburg monarch, Emperor Charles I of Austria (Charles IV of Hungary), renounced his title in November 1918 and was later deposed.

hacienda A large estate with a dwelling-house, originally given by monarchs in Latin America as a reward for services done. Such estates are known as *estancias* in Argentina and *fazendas* in Brazil. The first major eruption of violence, calling for the break-up of the haciendas, occurred in Mexico in 1910. Most Latin American countries experienced similar demands during the 20th century, and they have remained a major political issue.

Hadrian (full name **Publius Aelius Hadrianus**) (76–138 AD) Roman emperor (117–38). He became emperor as the adopted successor of Trajan, and spent much of his reign touring the provinces of the Empire, promoting good government and loyalty to Rome, and securing the frontiers. The building of *Hadrian's Wall was begun after his visit to Britain in 122.

Hadrian's Wall A defensive fortification in northern Britain. It was built 122–26 AD after a visit to Britain by Emperor *Hadrian. It is 117 km (73 miles) long, a stone barricade with a turf section in the west. Large fortress bases, milecastles, and signal towers marked its length. A road ran along it to the south and defensive ditches accompanied it on both sides. The wall was damaged several times by the Picts and was finally abandoned in 383, but long stretches of the wall still stand.

Haganah A Jewish defence force in Palestine. It was established in 1920 first as an independent, armed organization and then under the control of the Histadrut to defend Jewish settlements. During the 1936–39 Arab rebellion it was considerably expanded. It gained a general staff and was put under control of the Jewish Agency, acquiring new duties of organizing illegal Jewish immigration and preparing for the fight against Britain, who held the mandate over Palestine. In 1941 the Palmah (assault platoons) were formed. In 1948 Háganah provided the nucleus of the Israeli Defence Force, formed to protect the newly created state of Israel.

Haig, Douglas, 1st Earl (1861–1928) British field-marshal. After being chief-of-staff in India (1909) he commanded the 1st Army Corps in Flanders at Ypres and Loos and succeeded Sir John French as commander-in-chief. His strategy of attrition created huge numbers of casualties on the *Somme (1916) and at *Passchendaele (1917) and was much criticized. His conduct of the final campaign (1918) ended the war more quickly than *Foch expected. After the war he devoted himself to working tirelessly for ex-servicemen, and instituted the "Poppy Day" appeal associated with his name.

Haile Selassie (born **Tafari Makonnen**) (1892–1975) Emperor of Ethiopia (1930–74). He lived in exile in Britain during the Italian occupation of Ethiopia (1936–41), but was restored to the throne by the Allies and ruled until deposed in a Communist military coup. As a statesman, he made his country a prominent force in Africa and helped establish the Organization of African Unity (now the *African Union) in the early 1960s. He was deposed by left-wing army officers in 1974 and assassinated the following year. He is revered by the Rastafarian religious sect, which is named after him.

Haiti

Capital:	Port-au-Prince
Area:	27,750 sq km (10,714 sq miles)
Population:	9,893,934 (2013 est)
Currency:	1 gourde = 100 centimes
Religions:	Roman Catholic 80.0%; Baptist 10.0%; Voodoo is also widely practised
Ethnic Groups:	Black 95.0%; Mulatto and White 5.0%
Languages:	Haitian (French) creole, French (both official)
International Organizations:	UN; OAS; CARICOM; WTO; Non-Aligned Movement

A Caribbean country that occupies the western third of the island of Hispaniola.

Physical The country is mainly mountainous with three main mountain ranges. Much of it is forested but the valleys support agriculture.

Economy Haiti is a very poor country with over three-quarters of the population living in poverty. Subsistence farming is widespread. The only important export is clothing, and remittances from expatriates are the main source of foreign exchange. The economy was badly damaged by an earthquake in 2010.

History Hispaniola was discovered by Columbus during his first voyage to the New World, and became a Spanish colony in the 16th century. French corsairs settled on the western part of the island in the 17th century and Spain recognized the French claims to the area in 1697 in the Treaty of Ryswick. Known as Saint Domingue in the 18th century, it became a rich source of sugar and coffee for the European market. African slaves replaced a decimated Indian population and by the end of the 18th century the population of Haiti was predominantly Black. French rule was challenged in 1791 by a slave insurrection led by *Toussaint L'Ouverture.

The country declared its independence (1804) and *Dessalines was proclaimed emperor. After his assassination (1806) a separate kingdom was set up in the north, while the south and west became republican. The country was re-united in 1820 as an independent republic. Haiti and the eastern part of the island (later the *Dominican Republic) were united from 1822 to 1844. In 1859 it became a republic on its own again, whose anarchic history has been exacerbated by the hostility between the Black and mixed race communities. The USA, fearing that its investments were jeopardized and that Germany might seize Haiti, landed its marines (1915) and did not withdraw them until 1934. The country was dominated by President François *Duvalier (1957–71), and by his son and successor, Jean Claude (1971–86). When the latter was exiled to France, a council assumed power. A new constitution and elections followed, but they in turn were followed by a series of military coups and violence under General Prosper Avril. Strikes and yet more violence ended his regime, and elections in December 1990 brought a dissident Roman Catholic priest, Jean-Bertrand Aristide, into office. In September 1991 rebel troops seized the President and civil violence flared up against a new military regime. Aristide fled to Venezuela and appealed to the *Organization of American States (OAS) for help. OAS and US diplomatic efforts at restoring Aristide to office eventually led to the appointment by Aristide of a new Prime Minister, Robert Malval, in August 1993. An upsurge in army- and police-sponsored violence, however, prevented Aristide's return, while international sanctions held the economy in a state of crisis. In September 1994 US troops landed on Haiti to oversee the transfer of power to Aristide, following an agreement with military leaders. Aristide returned in October and, in March 1995, military authority was transferred from the US-led multinational force to the UN Mission in Haiti (UNMIH). In mid-1995 the Lavalas Political Organization, endorsed by Aristide, won legislative elections marred by irregularities and violence. Presidential elections in 1995 were won by René Préval, an associate of Aristide. His presidency was dominated from 1997 by constitutional conflict with parliament and opposition parties, which was not resolved by the re-election of Aristide as President in 2000. Aristide was overthrown in 2004 by an insurrection and Boniface Alexandre became interim President. Préval was re-elected President in 2006; he was succeeded in 2011 by Michel Martelly. In 2010 Port-au-Prince was devastated by an earthquake that killed over 300,000 people and left over a million homeless.

Haldane, Richard Burdon, Viscount Haldane of Cloan (1856–1928) British politician. As Secretary for War (1905–12) he showed great organizational skill in his reforms of the British army. Recognizing the growing danger from German militarism, he used his knowledge of the German army to redevelop the military organization in Britain to meet the requirements of modern warfare. A small expeditionary force ready for instant action was formed with a Territorial Army as a reserve, and an Imperial General Staff to organize military planning on an improved basis. Haldane was sent on a mission to Berlin in 1912 to secure a reduction in naval armaments, but failed.

Halder, Franz (1884–1972) German general. As Nazi chief-of-staff from 1938 he was responsible for the planning of the *Blitzkrieg campaigns of World War II. He opposed Hitler's decision to strike against *Stalingrad in 1942,

and was dismissed. After the July Plot to assassinate Hitler, he was sent to a concentration camp. He was freed in 1945.

Halidon Hill, Battle of (19 July 1333) A battle fought near Berwick-on-Tweed, on the border between England and Scotland, which saw a major victory for Edward *Balliol over the nationalist Scots. Balliol had been crowned King of Scotland in 1332 but subsequently driven out of the kingdom: his victory at Halidon Hill, which was achieved with the help of English archers supplied to him by *Edward III, regained him his kingdom—at the price of doing homage for it to the English crown.

Halifax, Edward Frederick Lindley Wood, 1st Earl of (1881–1959), British Conservative politician. From 1925 to 1931 he was governor-general and viceroy of India (as Lord Irwin), and was involved in that country's struggle for independence. Halifax, who favoured *dominion status for the subcontinent, ordered the imprisonment of Mahatma *Gandhi after the *Salt March. As a member of *Chamberlain's government, he visited Germany and met Hitler. An advocate of *appeasement, Halifax accepted the post of Foreign Secretary in 1938 on *Eden's resignation. He accepted, de facto, the *Anschluss of Austria and the dismemberment of *Czechoslovakia after the *Munich Pact. Halifax refused an invitation to Moscow, thus losing the chance of agreement with the Soviet Union, and leaving the door open for Hitler and Stalin to draw up the *Nazi–Soviet pact. During World War II he was British ambassador to the USA.

Halsey, William Frederick (1882–1959) US admiral. In 1941, commanding the Pacific Fleet aircraft carriers, he and his fleet were out of harbour when the Japanese attacked *Pearl Harbor. In 1942 he led a spectacular raid against the Marshall and Gilbert Islands and during the campaign of the *Solomon Islands he took command of the South Pacific area. As commander of the 3rd Fleet at the Battle of *Leyte Gulf (1944), he sank a number of Japanese aircraft carriers and in 1945 led the seaborne bombing offensive against Japan.

Hamas The Islamic Resistance Movement founded in 1976 by Sheikh Yassin Ahmed (c.1938–2004), with the aim of creating an Islamic state in the former Palestine. Originally a non-militant organization, it became increasingly militant during the 1990s, launching terrorist attacks on Israeli targets. Opposed to the peace process between Israel and the *Palestine Liberation Organization (PLO), which it regarded as a capitulation to Israel, Hamas carried out a series of suicide bombings in Israel from 1996. Its influence grew during the second *intifada, during which Yassin was killed in an Israeli airstrike. In 2006 it won legislative elections for the Palestinian National Authority, replacing al-*Fatah as the governing party. A unity government was briefly established in 2007, but this broke down in fighting that split the Palestinian territories, with Hamas in control of the Gaza Strip and al-Fatah of the West Bank. An agreement to form another unity government was reached in 2014. Persistent Hamas rocket attacks against Israeli cities led Israel to launch air and ground operations against Gaza in 2014, causing the deaths of some 2000 civilians.

Hamilcar Barca (died *c.*229 BC) Carthaginian general and father of *Hannibal and *Hasdrubal. He commanded the Carthaginian forces in the later part of the first of the *Punic wars and negotiated the peace of 241 BC. When the mercenaries in Carthaginian service rebelled, Hamilcar, along with his rival Hanno, defeated them. In 237 he went to Spain, and brought the southern and eastern areas under Carthaginian control.

Hamilton, Alexander (*c.*1757–1804) US Federalist politician. He served under George Washington as First Secretary of the Treasury (1789–95) and established the US central banking system. Hamilton was a prime mover behind the Federalist Party's commitment to strong central government in the aftermath of American independence. He died from a gunshot wound after a duel with Aaron Burr.

Hamilton, James, 3rd Marquis and 1st Duke of (1606–49) Scottish nobleman, a supporter of the *Cavalier cause. *Charles I appointed him the king's commissioner in Scotland in 1638, but despite negotiating with the *Covenanters, he was unable to avert the *Bishops' Wars. Charles kept faith with him on the outbreak of the *English Civil War, but his negotiations in Scotland came to nothing in 1643, when he was expelled for refusing to sign the *Solemn League and Covenant. His attempt to revive the Cavalier cause in 1648 ended in defeat at *Preston, and his execution.

Hammarskjöld, Dag Hjalmar Agne Carl (1905–61) Swedish diplomat and Secretary-General of the *United Nations Organization (1953–61). In 1953 he was elected UN Secretary-General as successor to Trygve *Lie. He was re-elected in 1957. Under him, the UN established an emergency force to help maintain order in the Middle East after the *Suez War, and UN observation forces were sent to Laos and Lebanon. He initiated and directed (1960–61 the UN's involvement in the *Congo crisis, making controversial use of Article 99 of the UN Charter, which he believed allowed the Secretary-General to exercise initiative independent of the *United Nations Security Council or *United Nations General Assembly. While in the Congo he was killed in an aeroplane crash over Zambia.

Hammurabi (died 1750 BC) The sixth king of the first dynasty of Babylonia (1792–1750 BC). He made Babylon the capital of Babylonia and extended the Babylonian empire. He instituted one of the earliest known legal codes, which took the form of 282 case laws dealing with the economy and with family, criminal, and civil law.

Hampden, John (1594–1643) English politician, who played a leading part in the opposition to *Charles I's arbitrary government. In 1627 he was imprisoned for refusing to pay the "forced loan" imposed by Charles to finance his unpopular foreign campaigns. Ten years later he was prosecuted for refusing to pay *ship money. As a member of the *Long Parliament he was prominent in the impeachment of *Strafford, and a close ally of John *Pym. In 1642 he survived the king's attempt to arrest him (*five members), and was appointed to the Committee of Safety to organize the parliamentary *English Civil War effort. He died of wounds received in action.

Hampton Court Conference (1604) A meeting in which the new king of England, *James I, presided over an assembly of bishops and Puritans. The 'Millenary Petition' presented by the Puritans in 1602 had listed church practices offensive to them and had asked for reform in the Anglican Church. Most of their demands were refused, although it was agreed to produce a new translation of the *Bible, the Authorized Version of 1611.

Hampton Roads Conference (3 February 1865) An abortive conference to negotiate an end to the *American Civil War. At a meeting on a Union (Northern) steamer moored in Hampton Roads, Virginia, Confederate demands, put forward by the Southern President Jefferson *Davis, that the *Confederacy be treated as a sovereign state foundered on the refusal of President *Lincoln to negotiate on any other terms but reunion and abolition of slavery. The conference broke up without result, and the war carried on until the Confederate surrender two months later at *Appomattox.

Han The Chinese dynasty that ruled from 206 BC until 200 AD with only a brief interruption. During this period the territory was expanded, administration was in the hands of an organized civil service, Confucianism was recognized as the state philosophy, and detailed historical records were kept. The arts flourished, and technological advances included the invention of paper.

Hancock, John (1737–93) American Revolutionary leader. A radical Boston merchant who supplemented his inherited fortune by smuggling, he came into open conflict with British customs officers when his sloop *Liberty* was seized (1768). He was a generous backer of the patriot cause, helped to organize the *Boston Tea Party, and as President of the Second *Continental Congress was the first to sign the *Declaration of Independence. He was first governor of independent Massachusetts.

Hannibal (247–182 BC) Carthaginian general. He precipitated the second Punic War by attacking the town of Saguntum in Spain, an ally of Rome. In 218, in a pre-emptive move, he led an army of about 30,000 over the Alps into Italy. There he inflicted a series of defeats on the Romans (*see* CANNAE), campaigning for 16 years undefeated but failing to take Rome itself. After being recalled to Africa he was defeated at Zama by Scipio Africanus in 202.

Hanover, House of The family of sovereigns of Great Britain and Ireland from George I to Victoria (1714–1901). The dynasty was named after the city of Hanover, the capital of Lower Saxony in Germany. In 1658 Sophia, daughter of Elizabeth of Bohemia and granddaughter of James I of England married Ernest Augustus, Duke of Brunswick-Lüneburg, who subsequently became an Elector of Germany (1692), taking Hanover as his title and capital city. Their son became *George I, the first Hanoverian King of Great Britain in 1714. Hanover's territories included the important towns of Göttingen and Hildesheim and their defence was an

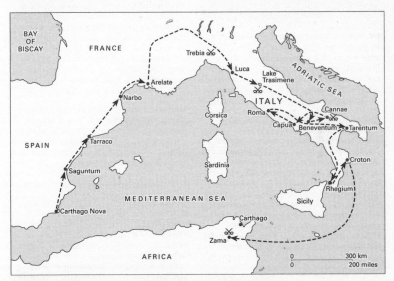

Hannibal. Hannibal marched north from Carthago Nova (Cartagena) into France in 218 BC and astounded the Romans by crossing the Alps with an army of troops and elephants and descending into Italy. The Alpine crossing, accomplished in a mere 15 days, is regarded as one of the greatest feats of ancient warfare. Despite several devastating victories over the Romans, Hannibal was not strong enough to attack Rome itself and his march on the city in 211 was merely a feint to divert the Romans from their siege of Capua. In 203 he was recalled to Carthago (Carthage). The Second Punic War ended in 201, following Hannibal's defeat at Zama (202).

important factor in British foreign policy in the 18th century.

Hanseatic League An association of north German cities (Hanse Towns), formed in 1241 as a trading alliance. Cologne, which had enjoyed special trading privileges with England, was joined by other traders following an agreement between Hamburg and Lübeck (1241) and a Diet of 1260. The towns of the League dealt mainly in wool, cloth, linen, and silver. In the later Middle Ages the League, with about 100 member towns, was an independent political power with its own army and navy. It began to collapse in the early 17th century and only three major cities (Hamburg, Bremen, and Lübeck) remained in the League until it was finally broken up in the 19th century.

Hapsburg See HABSBURG.

Hara Takashi (or **Hara Kei**) (1856–1921) Japanese statesman. Leader of the Seiyukai (Friends of Constitutional Government) Party and a strong advocate of government by political party rather than by interest groups, he became the first commoner to hold the post of Prime Minister (1918–22). Attempts to build links with the business community brought him under suspicion of corruption and he failed either to prevent the breakdown of civil order or stop military intervention in the *Russian Civil War. He planned to end the military administration of Taiwan and Korea but was assassinated by a right-wing fanatic.

Hardenberg, Karl August, Prince (1750–1822) Prussian statesman and reformer. In 1810 he was appointed Chancellor of Prussia and continued the domestic reforms inaugurated by *Stein. These included the improvement of Prussia's military system, the abolition of serfdom and of the privileges of the nobles, the encouragement of municipalities, the reform of education, and civic equality for Jews. In 1813 he persuaded *Frederick William III to join the coalition against Napoleon. He represented Prussia at the Congress of *Vienna where he achieved substantial gains for his country.

Hardie, Keir (**James Keir Hardie**) (1856–1915) Scottish Labour politician. He worked as a miner before entering Parliament in 1892, becoming the first leader of the Independent Labour Party the next year. In 1906 he became a co-founder and first leader of the Labour Party. His pacifist views prompted his withdrawal from Labour politics when the majority of his

party's MPs declared their support for British participation in World War I, although he remained an MP until his death.

Harding, Warren Gamaliel (1865–1923) US Republican statesman, 29th President of the USA (1921–23). He died suddenly in office, before the worst revelations of his administration's incompetence and corruption had been made.

Hardy, Thomas (1752–1832) Scottish radical leader, a champion of parliamentary reform. He moved to London in 1774, where he became a shoemaker. In 1792 he founded the London Corresponding Society, whose aim was to achieve universal manhood suffrage. The country was at war with Revolutionary France and the government became alarmed at the Society's growing influence. In 1794 Hardy was arrested on a charge of high treason but at the subsequent trial he was acquitted.

Harley, Robert, 1st Earl of Oxford and Mortimer (1661–1724) British statesman. He entered Parliament as a Whig, and during the early years of Queen *Anne's reign served variously as Speaker of the House of Commons and Secretary of State. He abandoned the Whigs and used the influence of his cousin Abigail Masham, a lady-in-waiting, to undermine *Marlborough's standing with the queen. In 1710 he headed the new Tory government whose greatest achievement was the Peace of *Utrecht (1713). In the subsequent power struggle among the Tories just before Anne's death in 1714 he lost to Viscount *Bolingbroke, and the Whig administration of *George I imprisoned him and began impeachment proceedings against him. He was released two years later, but took no further part in public affairs.

Harmensen, Jakob See ARMINIUS, JACOBUS.

Harmsworth, Alfred Charles William, 1st Viscount Northcliffe (1865–1922) British journalist and newspaper proprietor. In 1887 he used his savings to form a general publishing business with his brother, Harold Harmsworth (1868–1940). In 1894 the two brothers acquired the *Evening News* and two years later founded the *Daily Mail*. This opened a new epoch in Fleet Street by presenting news to the public in a concise, interesting style, using advertisements and competitions, and financing schemes of enterprise and exploration. In 1903 the *Daily Mirror* was founded, while in 1905 the *Observer* came under Harmsworth's control, and in 1908 he became chief proprietor of *The Times*. He was appointed to head the British War Mission to the USA in May 1917, soon after the USA entered World War I.

Harold I (*c*.850–933) First King of all Norway (872–933). A series of battles with minor kings culminated in his decisive victory at Hafrsfjord. He then succeeded in bringing the Orkney and Shetland islands, together with much of northern Scotland, into his kingdom and forced out many Vikings who went on to conquer Iceland and land in western Europe.

Harold II (*c*.1020–66) King of England (1066). He was the second son of Earl Godwin of Wessex, whom he succeeded in 1053. The Godwin family had great political ambition. Harold's sister Edith was married to *Edward the Confessor, and his brother Tostig was Earl of Northumbria (1055–65). Exiled after an abortive attempt to intimidate the king, Harold and his father returned (1052) to dominate political affairs in England. Harold succeeded Edward the Confessor in 1066, despite the Norman claim that Edward had designated Duke William of Normandy as his heir and that Harold had recognized William's right. Tostig, who had been dispossessed of his earldom, raided the south-east coast before joining the invasion by Harald Hardrada of Norway in northern England. Harold defeated them at *Stamford Bridge and then marched 402 km (250 miles) south to meet William's invasion at the Battle of *Hastings, where he died.

Harper, Stephen (Joseph) (1959–) Canadian statesman; Prime Minister (2006–). An MP from 1993 to 1997 and from 2002, he has championed the rights of Canada's provinces against the power of the federal government. He was elected leader of the newly formed Conservative Party of Canada in 2004 and formed a minority government after the 2006 general election, which continued after a further general election in 2008. The Conservative Party's victory in the 2011 election enabled Harper to form a majority government.

Harrison, Benjamin (1833–1901) US Republican statesman, 23rd President of the USA (1889–93). He was the grandson of William Henry *Harrison.

Harrison, William Henry (1773–1841) US Whig statesman, 9th President of the USA, 1841. He died of pneumonia one month after his inauguration. He was the grandfather of Benjamin *Harrison.

Harsha (*c*.590–647) Buddhist ruler of a large empire in north India (*c*. 606–47). He dominated the entire Gangetic plain, and also parts of the Punjab and Rajasthan, but was repulsed from the Deccan plateau. He allowed conquered rulers to keep their titles in return for tribute, and he is considered an enlightened and talented ruler. He organized Buddhist assemblies, established charitable institutions, and patronized learning, particularly poetry. His reign is well documented, notably by his celebrated court poet, Bana, and by a Chinese Buddhist pilgrim, Xuan Cang.

Hartford Convention (1814–15) US political conference, held by Federalist supporters to consider the problems of New England in the *War of 1812. Dominated by moderates rather than extremists, the Convention adopted the establishment of an inter-state defence machinery independent of federal government provision, the prohibition of all embargoes lasting more than 60 days, as well as a series of constitutional amendments. The Treaty of *Ghent brought an abrupt end to its deliberations, and the adverse publicity which it attracted accelerated the decline of the *Federalist Party.

Harun al-Rashid (literally, **"Aaron the rightly guided"**) (*c*. 763–809) The fifth *Abbasid caliph (786–809). Under him Baghdad reached its greatest brilliance, partly thanks to the ability of the Persian *viziers of the house of Barmak (until their fall in 803). He was a competent commander and a patron of learning and the arts. His court and capital provided the setting for many of the stories in the *Thousand and One Nights*. His division of the empire among his heirs led to conflict after his death (809–18). According to French chronicles, there was an exchange of embassies between Harun and *Charlemagne.

Hasan, Muhammad Abdille Sayyid (1864–1920) Somali nationalist leader, known to the British as the 'Mad Mullah'. He believed that Christian colonization was destructive of Islamic faith in Somaliland and in 1899 he proclaimed a *jihad* (holy war) on all colonial powers. Between 1900 and 1904 four major expeditions by the British, Italians, and Ethiopians failed to defeat him. After a truce (1904–20) he resumed war again and was routed and killed by a British attack in 1920.

Hasdrubal (died 207 BC) Carthaginian general. He was the son of Hamilcar and younger brother of Hannibal. At the start of the second

Punic War in 218 he was left in command of Carthaginian forces in Spain after Hannibal had departed for Italy. After a defeat, Hasdrubal campaigned with only moderate success before crossing the Alps with the aim of joining Hannibal, but was intercepted and killed in battle.

Hasidism *See* JUDAISM.

Hastings, Battle of (14 October 1066) A battle fought at Senlac, inland from Hastings (south-east England) between the English under *Harold II and an invading army under Duke William of Normandy (*William I). Harold heard the news of the Norman invasion after his defeat of Harald Hardrada at *Stamford Bridge, near York, and immediately marched southwards with his troops. The English resisted the Norman attack throughout a long day's fighting but the Norman cavalry and crossbowmen were superior to the English soldiers, fighting on foot and armed with axes. Harold was killed, traditionally by an arrow piercing his eye, and William, the victor, marched towards London.

Hastings, Warren (1732–1818) British colonial administrator. In 1774 he became Governor-General of Bengal, in effect the first Governor-General of India, and during his term of office introduced many of the administrative reforms vital to the successful maintenance of British rule in India. On his return to England in 1785 he was impeached for corruption; he was eventually acquitted in 1795 after a seven-year trial before the House of Lords.

Hatshepsut (*c.*1540–*c.*1481 BC) Egyptian ruler, the daughter of Thutmose I. After the death of her half-brother and husband, Thutmose II, the young *Thutmose III succeeded, but she soon replaced him as the effective ruler and reigned until her death 20 years later. As well as furthering her father's building programme at *Karnak, she had a magnificent temple constructed at Deir al-Bahri.

Haughey, Charles (1925–2006) Irish politician, Prime Minister of the Republic of Ireland (1979–81; 1982; 1987–92). He was President of Fianna Fáil from 1979 to 1992. He resigned as a result of a number of scandals.

Hausa The people of north-western Nigeria and southern Niger. The original Hausa states, which included Kano and Zaria, were for many years the vassals of Bornu (*see* KANEM-BORNU). Muslim missionaries seem to have come in the 14th century, but during the reign of Muhammad Rumfa of Kano (1463–99) the celebrated divine al-Maghili is said to have introduced the

sharia (the Muslim code of law), *Sufism, and a body of constitutional theory. The Hausa states were conquered by the *Songhay in 1513 and by the *Fulani in the early 19th century.

Their traditional trading activities contributed to the spread of the Hausa language as a lingua franca throughout most of West Africa. Their society is hierarchical, consisting of several hereditary classes.

Havel, Václav (1936–2011) Czech dramatist and statesman, President of Czechoslovakia (1989–92) and of the Czech Republic (1993–2003). Having written plays, such as *The Garden Party* (1963), which were critical of totalitarianism, in the 1970s he became the leading spokesman for Charter 77 and other human rights groups and was twice imprisoned as a dissident. Shortly after his release in 1989 he founded the opposition group Civic Forum and led a renewed campaign for political change; in December of that year he was elected President following the peaceful overthrow of Communism (the Velvet Revolution). He became President of the Czech Republic (1993–2003) after the partition of Czechoslovakia. Following his retirement he returned to playwriting with *Leaving* (2008).

Hawke, Bob (**Robert James Lee Hawke**) (1929–) Australian statesman; Labor Prime Minister (1983–91). Hawke was President of the Australian Council of Trade Unions (1970–80) before becoming President (1973–78) and leader (1983–91) of the Labor Party. In 1990 he proposed a radical and controversial privatization programme but nevertheless won a fourth election victory, resigning a year later after losing his party's support.

Hawkins, Sir John (or Sir John Hawkyns) (1532–95) English sailor. In the 1560s and early 1570s he became involved in the slave trade and participated in early privateering raids in the Spanish West Indies. He was appointed treasurer of the Elizabethan navy in 1573 and played an important part in building up the fleet which defeated the Spanish Armada in 1588. He died at sea during an unsuccessful expedition to the West Indies.

Hawkins, Sir Richard (or Sir Richard Hawkyns) (1560–1622) English sailor, son of Sir John *Hawkins. Commander in the Elizabethan navy serving against the *Spanish Armada (1588). In 1593 he left England with the intention of surveying eastern Asia, where he hoped to establish an English trading empire. On the way, he plundered Valparaiso in Spanish

America, and was held by the Spaniards until a ransom was paid in 1602.

Haya de la Torre, Victor Raúl (1895–1979) Peruvian statesman. He founded and led the Alianza Popular Revolucionaria Americana (APRA), known as the Aprista Party (1924), which became the spearhead of radical dissent in Peru. He advocated social and economic reform, nationalization of land and industry, and an end to US domination of South American economies. After the *Leguía regime fell he urged his APRA followers to overthrow the army-backed conservative oligarchy. He stood for President in 1931, but ballots were rigged and Colonel Sánchez Cerro was proclaimed victor. He was imprisoned 1931–33 and, after the latter's assassination, was in hiding in Peru (1935–45), becoming widely known through his writings. In 1945 the Aprista Party took the name Partido del Pueblo (People's Party) and supported José Luis Bustamante as President, but when he was overthrown in 1948 Haya took asylum in the Colombian Embassy in Lima until 1954, when he went into exile in Mexico until 1957. He contested the 1962 presidential election, but the army intervened and Terry *Belaúnde was declared the winner. In 1979 Haya de la Torre drafted the new constitution which restored parliamentary democracy, but he died before his party came to power.

Hayes, Rutherford Birchard (1822–93) US Republican statesman, 19th President of the USA (1877–81). His administration brought the Reconstruction era in the South to an end (*see* RECONSTRUCTION ACTS); power returned from Federal government to white southern leaders, who then introduced a policy of racial segregation.

Haymarket Square riot (1886) An outbreak of violence in Chicago, USA. A protest at the McCormick Harvester Works culminated in a riot in which 100 people were wounded and several died. Eight anarchists were convicted of incitement to murder, and four were hanged. The international sympathy aroused for the accused led Governor John P. Altgeld to pardon the survivors on the grounds of judicial prejudice and mass hysteria.

Hay Treaties (1901, 1903) US treaties concerning the construction of a Central American canal linking the Atlantic and the Pacific. Negotiated by US Secretary of State John Milton Hay, the Hay–Pauncefote Treaty (1901) nullified the Clayton–Bulwer Treaty of 1850, which had prevented British or US acquisition of territory in Central America. The Hay–Herrán Treaty of 1903 leased the USA a canal zone from Colombia. Agreement broke down and was followed by a revolt in *Panama (then a department of Colombia), undertaken with US connivance. Independence of Panama (1903) was followed by the Hay–Bunau–Varilla Treaty, a new treaty that granted the USA a larger zone in perpetuity. President Roosevelt (rather than Secretary Hay) has, however, been held more responsible for this treaty.

health services Provision of hospital, medical, and dental services. During the 19th century there was startling progress in medical science, but also an increased awareness of health hazards and the need for improved urban public health. In the mid-20th century the development of public health-service hospitals and clinics became one of the main provisions of the *welfare state, the British **National Health Service** being introduced in 1946. It provides a comprehensive, largely free, medical and surgical service for the whole UK population. Funded from national taxation, it is the largest employer in Europe. Although the founders expected costs to fall or remain constant as the health of the nation improved, in fact they have escalated as a result of medical advances making more therapeutic procedures available and a marked increase in longevity (largely as a result of the service), resulting in increased demands by the elderly. Successive governments have grappled with the problem of maintaining the standard of service within acceptable budgets, largely by reorganizing the way in which the service is managed and financed.

During the communist regimes of the former Soviet Union and east European republics, state health services alone were officially available, which is still the case in communist Cuba, while in Britain and many western countries health services through privately financed insurance schemes are an alternative to state services. In the USA, by contrast, most health facilities are privately funded, apart from Medicare and Medicaid, and there is widespread resistance to state intervention: reforms introduced by President *Obama (2010) to reduce health-care insurance cost and increase its accessibility and coverage proved controversial.

Hearst, William Randolph (1863–1951) US newspaper publisher and tycoon. He is noted for his introduction of large headlines, sensational crime reporting, and other features designed to increase circulation; his innovations revolutionized US journalism. At the peak of his fortunes in the mid-1930s he had acquired a number of newspapers and magazines, radio stations, and two film companies. He was the model for the central character of Orson Welles's film *Citizen Kane* (1941).

Heath, Sir Edward (Richard George) (1916–2005) British Conservative statesman, Prime Minister (1970–74). In 1973 his long-standing commitment to European cooperation was realized when Britain joined the European Economic Community. His premiership was marked by problems of inflation and balance of payments (exacerbated by a marked increase in oil prices in 1973); attempts to restrain wage rises led to widespread strikes. After a second national coal strike Heath called an election to strengthen his position, but was defeated.

Hébert, Jacques René (1757–94) French journalist and Revolutionary. He became a prominent member of the Cordeliers Club (an extreme Revolutionary club) in 1791. The following year he was a member of the Commune of Paris and was arrested in 1793 after his violent attacks on the *Girondins. Although he was always popular with the mob, he and his followers, the Hébertistes, came into conflict with *Robespierre when he organized "The Worship of Reason". This substitute for the worship of God led to his arrest and execution in March 1794.

Hegel, Georg Wilhelm Friedrich (1770–1831) German philosopher. He is especially known for his three-stage process of dialectical reasoning (set out in his *Science of Logic*, 1812–16), which underlies his idealist concepts of historical development and the evolution of ideas; Marx based his theory of dialectical materialism on this aspect of Hegel's work.

hegira (Arabic *hijra*, 'exodus', 'migration', or 'breaking of ties') *Muhammad's secret departure from *Mecca in 622, accompanied by *Abu Bakr, to live among the people of Yathrib, later called Medina, thus founding the first Muslim community. Under the second caliph, Umar, this key event in the history of Islam was chosen as the starting-point for the Muslim calendar.

Helena, St (*c.*255–*c.*330 AD) Roman empress and mother of Constantine the Great. She was a convert to Christianity and in 326 visited the Holy Land, where she founded basilicas on the Mount of Olives and at Bethlehem. Later tradition ascribes to her the finding of the cross on which Christ was crucified.

Hellenistic civilization The result of the adoption of the Greek language and culture by non-Greeks. (Hellas, an area of southern Thessaly, was synonymous with Greece from the 7th century BC.) It has come to refer specifically to the civilization that arose in the wake of the conquests of Alexander the Great. The many cities founded by him and his successors were the centres for a fusion of Greek and 'barbarian' ways of life, with *Alexandria in Egypt becoming the literary focus of the Mediterranean world.

Hellfire Club (1745–63) A notorious English society that met in the ruins of Medmenham Abbey in Buckinghamshire. It was founded by Sir Francis Dashwood in 1745, and its members reputedly indulged in debauchery and in the mocking of organized religion by the performance of blasphemous 'black masses'. Its membership included many politicians.

helot An inhabitant of ancient Greece forced into serfdom by conquering invaders. Helots were used as agricultural labourers and in domestic service. The Messenians, subjected by *Sparta, greatly outnumbered the Spartan citizens, and fear of their rebellion caused the city to keep them under ruthlessly tight military control.

Helsinki Conference (1973–75) Meetings at Helsinki and later Geneva, attended by leaders of 35 nations representing the entire membership of *NATO, the *Warsaw Pact, and the non-aligned countries, at which the Conference on Security and Cooperation in Europe (CSCE) was launched (1975). The conference produced the Helsinki Final Act containing a list of agreements concerning political freedom, mutual cooperation, and human rights; it can be considered the major achievement of *détente. The 34 heads of state also adopted the Charter of Paris for a New Europe. In 1992 the CSCE decided to create its own armed peacekeeping force; it was renamed the Organization for Security and Cooperation in Europe (OSCE) and now has 57 member states.

Helvetii Celts who migrated from southern Germany to south and west of the Rhine in the 2nd century BC. In 102 BC they joined the Cimbri and Teutones in invading Italy and were defeated by Emperor *Marius. Under pressure of Germanic migrations they attempted a mass migration into Roman *Gaul in 58 BC. Julius *Caesar drove them back. *Augustus incorporated their territory into Belgic *Gaul. Overrun in the 5th century by a succession of Alemanni, *Franks, Swabians, and Burgundians their name is preserved in the formal name for *Switzerland—the Helvetic Confederacy (or Helvetia).

Hengist and Horsa Jutish brothers, leaders of the first Anglo-Saxon invasion of England. According to *Bede, they were invited by King *Vortigern to help reinforce British resistance to the raiding Picts and Scots (c.449). The *Anglo-Saxon Chronicle claimed that Hengist and Horsa were joint kings of Kent and that when Horsa was killed (455) in battle, Aesc, the son of Hengist (died c.488), succeeded him.

Henrietta Maria (1609–69) Daughter of Henry IV of France, queen consort of Charles I of England (1625–49). Her Roman Catholicism heightened public anxieties about the court's religious sympathies and was a contributory cause of the English Civil War. From 1644 she lived mainly in France.

Henry I (or **Henry the Fowler**) (c.876–936) Duke of Saxony (912–36) and King of Germany (919–36). He was elected king by the Franks and Saxons in 919 and was the first king of the Ottonian dynasty. He developed a system of fortified defences against Hungarian invaders whom he defeated in 933 at the Battle of the Riade. Despite challenges from the nobility, he laid a strong foundation for his son *Otto I.

Henry I (1068–1135) King of England (1100–35). He was the fourth and youngest son of *William I. When his brother *William II died, Henry seized the treasury at Winchester and was crowned three days later in London, while his elder brother Robert was still on Crusade. Although Robert received the duchy of Normandy in compensation and exacted an annual pension of £2,000 (1101), Henry invaded Normandy in 1106. Robert was defeated at Tinchebrai and imprisoned at Cardiff Castle until his death in 1134. Louis VI of France exploited the situation in Normandy but in two campaigns (1111–13, 1116–20) he failed to take the duchy.

A determined ruler, Henry clashed with Archbishop *Anselm over his claim to appoint bishops (lay investiture). He improved royal administration, particularly in the *Exchequer, and extended and clarified the judicial systems. His law code, the *Leges Henrici Primi*, embodied much that had survived from Anglo-Saxon law. Unfortunately the death by drowning (1120) of his only legitimate son William whilst journeying to England from Normandy led to the accession of Henry's nephew *Stephen and a period of anarchy and civil war between Stephen and Henry's daughter, *Matilda.

Henry II (1133–89) King of England (1154–89). He succeeded King *Stephen, who by the Treaty of Winchester (1153) had recognized Henry as his heir. As the son of Geoffrey, Count of Anjou, Henry also inherited Normandy, Maine, Touraine, Brittany, and Anjou (this last title making him the first *Angevin king of England). His marriage to *Eleanor of Aquitaine (1152), the repudiated wife of Louis VII of France, brought Henry even greater estates in France so that his lands stretched from northern England down to the Pyrenees. These territorial gains were reinforced by the homage of Malcolm III of Scotland (1157) and by his recognition as overlord of Ireland (1171).

Henry's immediate task on becoming king was to end the anarchy of Stephen's reign. He dealt firmly with barons who had built castles without permission, and undertook the confirmation of *scutage (1157), an overhaul of military obligations in a review of feudal assessments (1166), and the introduction of a law that his subjects should equip themselves for military service (1181). He initiated a number of important legal reforms in the Assizes of *Clarendon (1166) and of Northampton (1176), and in his reign the land-law was developed to meet the needs of a more complex society. His reign, however, also saw rebellions led by his sons (1171–74) and the murder of the Archbishop of Canterbury, Thomas à *Becket (1170), a crime of which Henry was later absolved by Pope Alexander III (1172).

Henry III (1207–72) King of England (1216–72). He succeeded his father *John at the age of nine. During his minority (until 1227) England was managed by William Marshal, the first Earl of Pembroke, Peter des Roches, Bishop of Winchester, and Hubert de Burgh. Henry's personal rule soon proved his general incompetence as king, his preoccupation with aesthetic pursuits, including the rebuilding of Westminster Abbey, and his preference for foreign advisers and favourites. He received an early warning of baronial frustration when a rebellion broke out (1233–34) led by Richard Marshal, the third Earl of Pembroke. In 1258, one of the king's French favourites, Simon de *Montfort, led the English barons to draft a series of reforms (the Provisions of Oxford). While appearing to accept these, Henry sought to recover his independence. The ensuing civil war (1264–67) led to the temporary control of England by de Montfort following his victory at Lewes (1264). Although Henry recovered control after the Battle of Evesham (1265), where de Montfort was killed, he became increasingly dependent upon his son, the future *Edward I.

Henry IV (1366–1413) King of England (1399–1413). He was the only legitimate son of *John of Gaunt, and would have inherited vast estates on his father's death (in 1399) had *Richard II not banished him. He retaliated by invading England and forcing Richard to yield both the estates and the crown of England. Henry's position as king was not a strong one. He needed the support of the Church (which caused him to be a persecutor of *Lollards), the nobility (who dominated his councils), and the House of Commons (which resented his frequent requests for money). Until 1408 he had to deal with the rebellions of Owen *Glendower and the *Percys, and for the remaining five years of his short life he was in poor health.

Henry IV (or **Henry of Navarre**) (1553–1610) King of France (1589–1610). As king of Navarre, Henry was the leader of Huguenot forces in the latter stages of the French Wars of Religion, but on succeeding the Catholic Henry III he became Catholic himself in order to guarantee peace. He founded the Bourbon dynasty, established religious freedom with the Edict of Nantes (1598), and restored order after prolonged civil war. He was assassinated by a Catholic fanatic.

Henry V (1387–1422) King of England (1413–22), eldest son of *Henry IV. He was a skilful military leader, with experience gained in campaigning against Owen *Glendower, and took advantage of French weakness by claiming the French crown (1413) and then invading France (1415), where he won the magnificent victory of *Agincourt. In 1417 he invaded France again, and again fortune favoured him. He was able to conclude the very favourable Treaty of Troyes (1420), by which he was to succeed to the French crown at Charles VI's death and meantime to marry Charles's daughter, Katherine of Valois. However, he died only 15 months later. He was a popular hero, as celebrated in Shakespeare's play *Henry V*, and restored civil order in England in addition to his French campaigns.

Henry VI (1422–71) King of England (1422–61, 1470–71). He inherited the throne from his father *Henry V when only nine months old. During his minority, the court was divided by a power struggle between Humphrey, Duke of Gloucester, and the *Beauforts, which led to the Wars of the *Roses. A pious and withdrawn man, he suffered from insanity from 1453. His marriage to *Margaret of Anjou brought him a son, Edward, in 1453, who displaced Richard

Plantagenet, 3rd Duke of *York as heir to the throne. Richard claimed it for himself in 1460 and when he was killed at *Wakefield, his son Edward seized it in March 1461 and was crowned Edward IV. Henry was later captured, and spent the rest of his life in the Tower of London apart from the brief period when *Warwick restored him to the throne (1470–71), but Edward then defeated Warwick and reimprisoned Henry. When Henry's son, Prince Edward was killed at *Tewkesbury in 1471, Edward IV won back the throne and had Henry put to death.

Henry VII (1457–1509) King of England (1485–1509), the son of Edmund *Tudor and Margaret *Beaufort. Through his mother he was an illegitimate descendant of *John of Gaunt and so had a tenuous claim to the throne, but rivals' deaths in the Wars of the *Roses strengthened his position as the Lancastrian claimant and enabled him to oust *Richard III at the Battle of *Bosworth Field. He established the Tudor dynasty on firm foundations. The children of his marriage to Elizabeth of York were married to foreign royalty (his son Arthur to *Catherine of Aragon, and his daughter Margaret to James IV of Scotland), while he built up the crown's financial resources so that he was not dependent on Parliament and was able to leave a considerable fortune to his son, *Henry VIII.

Henry VIII (1491–1547) King of England (1509–47). The second son of *Henry VII and Elizabeth of York, he succeeded to the throne aged 18 and began his reign by executing Dudley and Empson, two of his father's financial officers. From 1513 to 1529 Thomas *Wolsey managed affairs of state and diplomacy while Henry played the part of the Renaissance prince, preferring hunting and dancing to government.

From 1525 he turned against his wife *Catherine of Aragon because of her failure to provide him with male heirs. The pope's refusal to annul his marriage led to England's break with the *Roman Catholic Church. With the assistance of Thomas *Cromwell and a compliant, anticlerical Parliament (1529–36), legislation was passed to sever the English Church from papal jurisdiction and Henry became Supreme Head of the English Church (1534). He exploited the Dissolution of the *Monasteries for his own profit and used the revenues from the dissolution to pay for his military campaigns of the 1540s. But he remained conservative in doctrine, believing in Catholicism without the pope and retaining the title "Defender of the Faith" granted him by the pope in 1521 for his treatise against *Luther. Meanwhile he married Anne *Boleyn and subsequently Jane *Seymour, *Anne of Cleves, Catherine *Howard and Catherine *Parr, of whom only Jane Seymour bore him a son, the future *Edward VI.

Little was achieved by his expensive wars with France and Scotland, but a powerful English navy was created. His attempts to capitalize on the struggles of *Francis I of France and *Charles V of Spain severely undermined the English economy.

Henry the Navigator (1394–1460) Portuguese prince, the third son of John I of Portugal and grandson of *John of Gaunt. He did not himself undertake any voyages of exploration, but was the patron of a succession of Portuguese seamen who made voyages of discovery among the Atlantic islands and down the west coast of Africa as far south as Cape Verde and the Azores, which led, after his death, to the discovery of the Cape of Good Hope and the sea route to India. With the aim of finding a new route to the Indies, as governor of the Algarve he established a school at which navigation, astronomy, and cartography were taught to his captains and pilots, and constructed the first observatory in Portugal.

Heraclius I (575–642) Byzantine emperor (610–41). He came to power having ousted the usurper Phocas, and set about the reorganization of the empire and its army, driving back the Persians in Asia Minor and securing a peace treaty. He then turned his attentions to the north, coming to terms with the invading Avars, who had invaded Europe from central Asia, and strengthening the frontier. He then devoted his energies to the study of religion, neglecting the empire and losing Syria and Egypt to the Muslims.

heraldry The study of coats of arms worn for individual identification, and of the accessories of crests, badges, mottoes, and flags that accompanied them. Its origins are military. Soldiers in armour and helmets could not easily be identified in battle and so the practice evolved of displaying a sign or device on the shield and on the linen surcoat worn over the armour (from which the terms 'coat-of-arms' and 'court armoury' derive). The first heraldic designs may have been worn by the Crusaders, but their use became widespread in Europe in the 12th century. A similar system also emerged in Japan during the 12th century.

By the 13th century heraldry had so developed that it had its own terminology, based on Old French. Its colours are called 'tinctures' of which there are two metals—gold (*or*) and silver (*argent*)—and five colours—blue (*azure*), black (*sable*), green (*vert*), purple (*purpure*), and red (*gules*). In England heralds were formed into the College of Arms (1484), which still controls the grant of arms. Scotland has its Court of the Lord Lyon (1592).

Herero Wars (1904–08) Campaigns by German colonialists against the Herero people in German South-West Africa (now Namibia). A Herero rebellion resulted in the deliberate near-extermination of the population by the Germans, their numbers falling from over 100,000 to 15,000. The survivors were resettled in the inhospitable desert land of contemporary Hereroland in Namibia. The Nama people, who also rebelled in 1904, suffered a similar fate. A United Nations report in 1985 classed the treatment of the Herero and Nama as genocide; the German government apologized in 2004.

heresy Belief in a doctrine held to be false by the Christian Church. During the Middle Ages it was believed to be necessary to follow the one 'true' religion, which provided the only guarantee of salvation and afterlife. Consequently those who came to believe that orthodox teaching was inadequate or wrong risked being declared heretics. Since the Church sought to maintain the unique validity of its declared doctrine conflict was inevitable.

The early Church condemned Gnostics in the 2nd century and *Arianism and the *Nestorians in the 4th century. The Iconoclasts were condemned at the Council of *Nicaea in 787. The condemnation of the *Cathars in southern Europe led to the *Albigensian Crusade. Later dissatisfaction with orthodox teaching led ultimately to the establishment of the *Protestant Church. The *Inquisition from its earliest days upheld the Church's doctrine and became responsible for the rooting out of unorthodoxy.

Hereward the Wake (11th century) Semi-legendary Anglo-Saxon rebel leader. Although little is known of Hereward's life beyond what can be found in literary accounts of dubious reliability, he is remembered as a leader of Anglo-Saxon resistance to William I's new Norman regime, and was apparently responsible for an uprising centred on the Isle of Ely in 1070.

Herod Four rulers of ancient Palestine. **Herod the Great** (*c.*74–4 BC) ruled from 37 to 4 BC. He built the palace of Masada and rebuilt the Temple in Jerusalem. Jesus is thought to have been born during his reign; according to the

New Testament (Matt. 2:16), he ordered the massacre of the innocents. **Herod Antipas** (22 BC–c.40 AD), son of Herod the Great, was tetrarch of Galilee and Peraea (4 BC–40 AD). He married Herodias and was responsible for the beheading of John the Baptist. According to the New Testament (Luke 23:7), Pilate sent Jesus to be questioned by him before the Crucifixion. **Herod Agrippa I** (10 BC–44 AD), grandson of Herod the Great, was king of Judaea (41–44 AD). He imprisoned St Peter and put St James the Great to death. **Herod Agrippa II** (27–c.93 AD), son of Herod Agrippa I, was king of various territories in northern Palestine (50–c.93 AD). He presided over the trial of St Paul (Acts 25:13 ff.).

Herodotus (known as 'the Father of History') (c.490–c.425 BC) Greek historian. His *History* tells of the Persian Wars of the early 5th century BC, with an account of the earlier history of the Persian empire and its relations with the Greeks to explain the origins of the conflict. He was the first historian to collect his materials systematically, test their accuracy to a certain extent, and arrange them in a well-constructed and vivid narrative.

Herrin massacre (22 June 1922) A clash between unionized strikers and non-unionized miners in the USA. It occurred in Herrin, Illinois, where the employers had attempted to break a strike by importing non-union men. Striking miners forced these to stop working, promised them safe-conduct, marched them from the mine, and then opened fire, killing around 25 men. A grand jury returned 214 indictments for murder and related offences, but local feeling prevented convictions.

Hertzog, J. B. M. (James Barry Munnik Hertzog) (1866–1942) South African politician, Prime Minister of the Union of South Africa (1924–39). He advocated the rights of Afrikaners and political separation of the British and Dutch communities. He founded the National Party (1914) and as Prime Minister he made Afrikaans an official language. He formed a coalition with Jan *Smuts in 1933 and in 1934 the National Party merged with the South African Party to form the United Party. He implemented policies to segregate White and Black people and disenfranchised the Cape Bantu. He advocated neutrality in World War II and resigned when this was rejected

Herzen, Alexander Ivanovich (1812–70) Russian author and revolutionary. He was exiled to Viatka in 1835 after being suspected of sympathy with the *Decembrists. He returned to Moscow in 1842, where he became a leader of the "Westernizers" who believed that Russia must adopt the free institutions and secular thought of western Europe in order to progress. Herzen left Russia in 1847. An exile in London, Geneva, and Paris, he wrote prolifically, supporting both moderate reform and radical revolution in turn and influencing Russian liberals and communists alike.

Herzl, Theodor (1860–1904) Hungarian-born journalist, dramatist, and Zionist leader. He worked for most of his life as a writer and journalist in Vienna, advocating the establishment of a Jewish state in Palestine; in 1897 he founded the Zionist movement, of which he was the most influential statesman.

Hess, Rudolf (Walther Richard Rudolf Hess) (1894–1987) German politician. He was deputy leader of the Nazi Party (1934–41) and a close friend of Hitler. In 1941, secretly and on his own initiative, he parachuted into Scotland to negotiate peace with Britain. He was imprisoned for the duration of the war, and after his conviction at the Nuremberg war trials was sentenced to life imprisonment in Spandau prison, where he died.

Hexham, Battle of (15 May 1464) A battle of the Wars of the *Roses in which a *Yorkist force led by John Neville, Earl of Montagu, captured Henry *Beaufort, 3rd Duke of Somerset, three miles from the town of Hexham, in Northumberland. Somerset was beheaded on the field of battle and many of his followers were executed soon afterwards, while Neville was rewarded with the estates of the *Percy family and the earldom of Northumberland.

Heydrich, Reinhard (1904–42) German police official. He joined the *SS in 1931, and in 1934 became deputy head of the *Gestapo. From 1941 he administered the Czech territory of Bohemia-Moravia, his inhumanity earning him the names the 'Hangman of Europe' and 'the beast'. He was assassinated by Czech nationalists in 1942. The Germans retaliated by indiscriminately executing hundreds of civilians including the entire male population of the villages of Lidice and Ležáky.

Hezekiah (died 687 BC) King of Judah (715–687 BC). When he came to power, Judah was a vassal state of the *Assyrian empire, and with the leaders of neighbouring states he was involved in a number of planned rebellions. The prophet *Isaiah spoke against these, but eventually Hezekiah did rebel and was heavily defeated in 701, when *Sennacherib invaded, the land was devastated, and only Jerusalem escaped destruction. The Bible describes his work of religious reform, destroying local shrines and various cult objects, and attempting to suppress the worship of local gods. The reform was short-lived, pagan practices being reintroduced after his death by his son and successor Manasseh.

Hidalgo y Costilla, Miguel (1753–1811) Mexican priest and freedom fighter. He inspired (16 September 1810) the Mexican War for Independence from Spain with his *Grito de Dolores* ("Cry of Dolores"), proclaimed from the pulpit of his parish church at Dolores. Within a few months he had amassed an army of almost 80,000, but lacking the military skill necessary to complement his well-developed social ideology, the movement was defeated after much bloodshed at the hands of the royalist army. Captured in 1811, he was tried by the Inquisition and referred to the secular authorities for execution.

Hideyoshi (1536–98) Japanese warrior. He continued *Oda Nobunaga's work of unifying the country that had been fragmented by the feuds between *daimyo. Between 1582 and 1591, by a mixture of military strategy and skilful diplomacy he broke their power. Mistrustful of the power of Buddhist monks, for a time he encouraged Catholic missionaries but later savagely persecuted Christians in Nagasaki. He built castles, carried out land surveys, and disarmed peasants. His ambition was to conquer China, and when in 1592 *Korea, a vassal state of China, refused passage to his troops, his army numbering 200,000 captured Seoul and advanced north until *Ming armies forced him to retreat. The Koreans routed him at sea. A second campaign was abandoned when Hideyoshi died. He appointed *Tokugawa Ieyasu a guardian of his son, Hideyori.

hieroglyphs The signs used for formal inscriptions in ancient *Egypt. They were devised in about 3000 BC and were used, mainly for religious and monumental purposes, until the late 3rd century AD. They were representational in design, and were held to have near-magic powers. For practical purposes the structure of the script, as well as its form, was much too clumsy, and even cursive or 'long-hand' versions, the hieratic and demotic scripts, required long professional training to learn. Hieroglyphs have played an important part of archaeological research (*Rosetta stone), extending written history by 2000 years beyond classical times. The term has been applied more loosely to

other complicated but ornamental scripts used by the *Minoan civilization, the *Hittites, and the *Maya. *See also* WRITING.

Highland Clearances The deliberate removal of Scottish "crofter" peasants by landlords during the 19th century. In the later 18th century, Scottish society in the Highlands suffered severely with the collapse of the system of chiefs and fighting clans. Subsistence farming could not sustain an increasing population and this was aggravated by the policy of many major landowners of clearing their land for sheep farming by expulsion of crofters and the burning of their cottages. The potato famine during the *Hungry Forties aggravated the problem and in the 1880s, after the arrival of the railway, sheep were replaced by deer. In 1882 there were outbreaks of violence, the "Crofters War", which was investigated by a Royal Commission. In 1885 the crofters voted for the first time in a general election, and an Act of Parliament in 1886 gave them some security of tenure. Yet depopulation steadily continued. Many Scottish Highlanders emigrated throughout the British empire.

highwaymen Robbers who plagued Britain's main roads during the 17th and 18th centuries. There had been thieves and footpads from Anglo-Saxon times, but improved roads, more frequent travelling, and the growth of coaching inns made rich pickings for mounted thieves who sometimes worked in gangs in collusion with innkeepers. They were in reality much less romantic than is generally shown in fiction; the fear of being identified made them only too willing to murder their victims. Some, such as Swift Nick Levison, hanged at York in 1684, Dick Turpin (1705–39), and Jack Sheppard (1702–24), became folk heroes, but in fact highwaymen were always dangerous, and their appearance in central London in broad daylight in the mid-18th century provoked vigorous efforts to stamp them out. By the early 19th century the menace of highwaymen had been largely overcome.

Hill, Sir Rowland (1795–1879) British educationist, administrator, and inventor. He was initially a teacher who introduced a system of self-government at his school in Birmingham and wrote on the challenges of mass education. In the 1830s he invented a rotary printing press. Hill is chiefly remembered for his introduction of the penny postage-stamp system in 1840; he later became Secretary to the Post Office (1854–64).

Himmler, Heinrich (1900–45) German leader, chief of the *SS (1929–45) and of the

Gestapo (1936–45). He established and oversaw the programme of systematic genocide of more than 6 million Jews and other disfavoured groups between 1941 and 1945. He was captured by British forces in 1945, and committed suicide by swallowing a cyanide capsule.

Hindenburg, Paul von (1847–1934) German general and statesman. He fought at the Battle of Königgratz (*Sadowa) and in the *Franco-Prussian War (1870–71) and retired in 1911. He was recalled to active service at the outbreak of *World War I and crushed the Russians at Tannenberg in east Prussia (August 1914). In 1916 he became chief of the general staff. After the failure of Germany's offensive (1918) he advised the need to sue for peace. After the war he came to tolerate the *Weimar Republic and in 1925 was elected as President in succession to Ebert. Re-elected (1932), he did not oppose the rise of *Hitler, but appointed him as Chancellor (January 1933) on the advice of Franz von *Papen.

Hinduism A system of religious beliefs and social customs, especially influential in India. As both a way of life and a rigorous system of religious law, Hinduism developed over a period of about 50 centuries. Unlike most religions, it requires no one belief regarding the nature of God: it embraces polytheism, monotheism, and monism. More important are the beliefs concerning the nature of the Universe and the structure of society. The former is described by the key concepts of *dharma*, the eternal law underlying the whole of existence; *karma*, the law of action by which each cause has its effect in an endless chain reaching from one life to the next; and *moshka*, liberation from this chain of birth, death, and rebirth. The latter is prescribed by the ideals of *varna*, the division of mankind into four classes or types, the forerunner of caste; *ashrama*, the four stages of life; and personal dharma, according to which ones religious duty is defined by birth and circumstance. There are an estimated 705 million Hindus in the world.

Hindu revivalism arose from Hindu encounters with western ideas in the 19th and 20th centuries. There are many thinkers and ideas associated with this process. Raja Ram Mohun *Roy (1772–1833) was the forerunner of new Hinduism; he learned English, located Hindu ideas in the context of Western ones in order to promote Hindu self-understanding, and founded the reform movement the Brahmo Samaj (Society of God). Debendranath Tagore (1817–1905) was his successor as leader of the Society; he explicitly questioned the infallibility of the Vedas and called for an experimental spirituality based on the aphorisms of the Upanishads. The most famous figure was Swami Vivekananda (1863–1902), who claimed that Vedanta was the Hindu exemplification of that oneness to which all religions aspired, and that the idea and practice of tolerance and universality were India's gift to the world; he admired Western self-confidence and scientific success, and formed a model of mutual influence in which the West taught its material skills to India, which reciprocated with its spiritual teachings. Dayanand Saraswati (1824–83), founder of the *Arya Samaj (Society of Aryans), tried to emphasize the global significance of Vedic teachings by discerning scientific and technological ideas in them.

The term "Hindu revivalism" is also used to describe an ideology of nationalism based on allegedly Hindu values that is professed by some groups (notably the BJP party) in contemporary Indian politics.

Hindu Mahasabha A Hindu communal organization. It was first established in the Punjab before 1914, and became active during the 1920s under the leadership of Pandit Mohan Malaviya (1861–1946) and Lala Rajpat Rai (1865–1928), when it campaigned for social reform and for the reconversion of Hindus from Islam. Its attitude towards Hindu–Muslim relations strained the relations of the Mahasabha with *Congress and in 1937 it broke away from Congress. After independence the party declined in importance as the Jana Sangh became the leading exponent of Hindu communal ideas.

hippodrome A course on which the ancient Greeks and Romans held chariot and horse races. The courses were U-shaped with a barrier down the centre. The competitors would race down one side and then back up the other. Spectators watched from tiered stands. *Olympia had an early example, and hippodromes were a typical feature of major Greek cities of classical and Hellenistic times. The one at Constantinople (now *Istanbul) held about 100,000 spectators and was the scene of fierce rivalry among partisan supporters. The Circus Maximus at Rome was modelled on the Greek hippodrome.

Hirohito (born **Michinomiya Hirohito**) (1901–89) Emperor of Japan (1926–89). Regarded as the 124th direct descendant of Jimmu, he ruled as a divinity and generally refrained from involvement in politics. In 1945, however, he was instrumental in obtaining his government's agreement to the unconditional surrender which ended World War II. He was obliged to renounce his divinity and become a constitutional monarch by the terms of the constitution established in 1946.

Hiroshima, Bombing of Hiroshima, a city in southern Honshu, Japan, became the target of the first atomic bomb attack on 6 August 1945, which resulted in the virtual obliteration of the city centre and the deaths of about one-third of the population of 300,000. The atomic bombing by the US of Hiroshima, together with that of *Nagasaki three days later, led directly to Japan's unconditional surrender and the end of World War II.

Hiss case (1949–50) A US legal case involving allegations that Alger Hiss (1904–96), a State Department official, committed espionage. In 1950 Hiss was found guilty of perjury for having denied on oath the charge that he had passed secret documents to Whittaker Chambers, a self-confessed Communist Party courier. Although Hiss maintained his innocence, and high government officials testified for him, he was sentenced to five years in prison. His controversial trial came to symbolize the fears and suspicions aroused by the *Cold War; although most Americans believed in his guilt, others alleged that the *Federal Bureau of Investigation had tampered with evidence so as to obtain his conviction. He was released in 1954 and spent the rest of his life in attempts to clear his name. Some experts feel that documents released by the Russians since the collapse of communism support the view that Hiss was guilty.

historiography The study and writing of history. The recording and interpretation of past events began with the retelling of legends handed down through oral traditions: the epic poems Homer (*fl. c.*800 BC) were an expression of oral history, while in the classical age of ancient Greece *Herodotus and *Thucydides wrote narrative histories of their own times. In China *Sima Qian (*c.*145–*c.*85 BC) is known as the "Father of Chinese History". The Roman historians, who include *Tacitus, *Livy, and *Suetonius, wrote works which served as models for later medieval and Renaissance historians. In the Arab world al-Tabaric (838–923) wrote the *Annals*, a history of the world from its creation to 915, and *Ibn Khaldun (1332–1406) the *Kitab al-'bar* (Book of Examples), a major history of Muslim north Africa and developed important theories of historical analysis. In medieval Europe history was written by the literate clergy (*Bede) and was mostly confined to

chronicles (*Anglo-Saxon Chronicle, *Froissart). In the 15th and 16th centuries the Italian historians *Machiavelli and *Guicciardini wrote political analyses of the state and its rulers. The 18th century *Enlightenment injected a considerable measure of rationalism and scepticism into historical writing, producing such masterpieces as *Gibbon's *The History of the Decline and Fall of the Roman Empire.*

In the early 19th century the German historians Barthold Georg Niebuhr (1776–1831) and Leopold von Ranke (1795–1886) transformed the writing of history. Seeking to explain "how it actually happened", Ranke set new standards of historical research based on primary evidence subjected to critical evaluation. Still narrowly nationalistic, this "scientific history" led to systematic collection and cataloguing of sources (for example, *Monumenta Germaniae Historicae*, 1825–1925), and to more rigorous academic teaching. This approach was slower to develop in Britain, where history was dominated by the literary Whig tradition of Thomas Babington *Macaulay. Another form of "scientific history", the positivist belief in underlying general laws, was pioneered by the French historian Auguste Comte (1798–1857). Karl *Marx, in his theory of dialectical materialism, presented one such general law—change through class struggle. Its focus on the economic infrastructure of society challenged narrow political interpretations. This challenge continued in the 20th century. The Annales approach, pioneered in the journal *Annales d'histoire économique et sociale* launched in 1929 by Lucien Febvre (1878–1956) and Marc Bloch (1836–1944) and developed in the work of Fernand Braudel (1902–1983, sought "total history", an understanding of the structures within which people act, and of "mentalities", drawing on psychology and other social sciences. With the development of computers, quantitative techniques have become important to economic, demographic, and social historians, although few share the supreme confidence in statistical theory of the "cliometricians", such as Robert W. Fogel (1926–2013), who claim mathematical objectivity for Clio, the muse of history. British Marxist historians, for example, Christopher Hill (1912–2003), Eric Hobsbawm (1917–2012), and E. P. Thompson (1924–93), rejecting rigid dogmas of an all-determining infrastructure, have applied Marxist ideas creatively to intellectual history and to "history from below". The study of the role of women, developed as part of mainstream historiography by the women's movement of the 1960s, has broadened to encompass the history of gender. Yet concern with political history has

h

remained strong, notably in the empirical approach of A. J. P. Taylor (1906–90) or Sir Geoffrey Elton (1921–94), who emphasized the role of individuals and the importance of the unexpected.

Hitler, Adolf (1889–1945) German dictator. He was born in Austria, the son of Alois Hitler and his wife Klara Poelzl. He volunteered for the Bavarian army at the start of World War I, becoming a corporal. After demobilization he joined a small nationalist group, the German Workers' Party, which later became the National Socialist German Workers (or *Nazi) Party. In Vienna, he had imbibed the prevailing *anti-Semitism and this, with tirades against the *Versailles Peace Settlement and against Marxism, he used as a basis for his oratory in winning over a Germany humiliated by defeat. In 1921 he became leader of the Nazis and in 1923 staged an abortive uprising, the Munich 'beer-hall putsch'. During the months shared in prison with Rudolph *Hess he dictated *Mein Kampf*, a political manifesto in which he spelt out Germany's need to rearm, strive for economic self-sufficiency, suppress trade unionism and communism, and exterminate its Jewish minority. The Great *Depression beginning in 1929 brought him a flood of adherents. After the failure of three successive Chancellors, President *Hindenburg reluctantly appointed Hitler head of the government (1933). As a result of the *Reichstag fire, Hitler established his one-party dictatorship, and the following year eliminated his rivals in the *Night of the Long Knives. On the death of Hindenburg he assumed the title of President and 'Führer of the German Reich'. He began rearmament in contravention of the Versailles Treaty, reoccupied the Rhineland in 1936, and took the first steps in his intended expansion of his *Third Reich: the *Anschluss with Austria in 1938 and the piecemeal acquisition of Czechoslovakia, beginning with the *Sudetenland. He concluded the Nazi–Soviet non-aggression pact with Stalin in order to invade Poland, but broke this when he attacked the Soviet Union in June 1941. His invasion of Poland had precipitated *World War II. Against the advice of his military experts he pursued 'intuitive' tactics and at first won massive victories; in 1941 he took direct military control of the armed forces. As the tide of war turned against him, he intensified the mass assassination that culminated in the Jewish *Holocaust. He escaped the July Plot to kill him (*see* STAUFFENBERG, CLAUS GRAF VON), and undertook a vicious purge of all involved. In 1945, as the Soviet army entered Berlin, he went through a marriage ceremony with his mistress, Eva Braun, with whom he committed suicide.

Hitler Youth A *Nazi agency to train young Germans. In 1931 Baldur von Schirach was appointed Youth Leader of the Nazi Party. In 1936 *Hitler outlawed all other youth organizations and announced that all young Germans should join the Jungvolk (Young Folk) at the age of 10, when they would be trained in out-of-school activities, including sports and camping, and receive Nazi indoctrination. At 14 the boys were to enter the Hitler Youth proper, where they would be subject to semi-military discipline, out-door activities, and Nazi propaganda, and girls the League of German Maidens, where they would learn motherhood and domestic duties. At 18 they would join the armed forces or the labour service. By 1936 3.6 million members had been recruited, and by 1938 7.7 million, but efforts to enrol young people were failing, so that in March 1939 a conscription order was issued.

Hittite A member of an ancient people of Asia Minor who gained control of central Anatolia *c*. 1800–1200 BC. The Hittite empire reached its zenith under the totalitarian rule of Suppiluliuma I (*c*.1380 BC), whose political influence extended from the capital, Hattusas, situated at Boğazköy (about 35 km (22 miles) east of Ankara in modern Turkey) west to the Mediterranean coast and south-east into northern Syria. In their struggle for power over Syria and Palestine the Hittites clashed with the troops of Rameses II of Egypt in a battle (1285 BC) at Kadesh on the River Orontes which seems to have ended indecisively. The subsequent decline and demise of Hittite power by 700 BC resulted from internal and external dissension, probably following an outbreak of famine.

Hobbes, Thomas (1588–1679) English philosopher. There were two key components in Hobbes's conception of humankind: he was a materialist, claiming that there was no more to the mind than the physical motions discovered by science, and a cynic, holding that human action was motivated entirely by selfish concerns, notably fear of death. His view of society was expressed in his most famous work, *Leviathan* (1651), in which he argued, by means of a version of a social contract theory, that simple rationality made social institutions and even absolute monarchy inevitable.

Ho Chi Minh (born **Nguyen That Thanh**) (1890–1969) Vietnamese Communist statesman, President of North Vietnam (1954–69).

He was a committed nationalist who was instrumental in gaining his country's independence from French rule. He founded the Indo-Chinese Communist Party in 1930, and led the Vietminh in guerrilla warfare against the Japanese during World War II. He then fought the French for eight years until their defeat in 1954, when Vietnam was divided into North Vietnam, of which he became President, and South Vietnam. Committed to the creation of a united Communist country, Ho Chi Minh then deployed his forces in the guerrilla struggle that became the Vietnam War.

Hohenstaufen A German royal house, members of which held the throne of the Holy Roman Empire (1138–1254), the rivals of the *Hohenzollerns. The emperor Henry IV (1084–1106) gave them the duchy of Swabia and in 1138 Duke Conrad became emperor as Conrad III. The family provided many emperors, including *Frederick I (Barbarossa) who attempted to build up German power in Italy. The relationship between the papacy and the Hohenstaufen was frequently acrimonious, resulting from their respective claims to land and personal powers. The empire grew to include Germany, northern Italy, and Sicily but proved too large to be managed in the face of papal and Lombard opposition, and the dynasty's last ruling member, Manfred of Sicily, was killed in battle in 1266.

Hohenzollern A powerful German princely family whose roots can be traced back to the 11th century. They took their name from a former Prussian province (now part of the state of Baden-Württemberg in Germany). From 1415 they ruled the electorate of *Brandenburg and the following century saw great expansion, Margrave Albert becoming grand master of the *Teutonic Knights in 1511. In 1614 the duchy of Cleves was acquired and in 1701 the Elector Frederick III of Brandenburg took the title of Frederick I of *Prussia. In 1871 William I of Prussia took the title Emperor William I of the German Empire. His grandson *William II abdicated in 1918. A member of a second branch, Prince Charles Hohenzollern-Sigmaringen, was elected Prince of *Romania in 1866, becoming King Carol in 1881. His brother Leopold was offered the throne of Spain in 1870 and turned it down, an incident that Bismarck used to provoke war with France by altering the Ems telegram.

Hojo A branch of a powerful Japanese family, the Taira. After Minamoto Yoritomo's death they provided regents for puppet shoguns,

nominated by themselves. From 1219 the regency was hereditary, and the country prospered under them until c.1300. They refused tribute to *Kublai Khan and executed his envoys. His two invasions, though failures, weakened Hojo power. Vassals the Hojo were unable to reward for their victories turned against them. From 1331 there was war between the regent's forces and those attempting to restore imperial rule under Go-Daigo. Their power ended (1333) when Ashikaga Takanji, a Hojo vassal, defected to the emperor and another vassal took Kamakura. The last regent and his family committed *seppuku* (ritual suicide).

Holkar An Indian *Maratha family of peasant origin that became rulers of one of the most powerful of the Maratha confederacy of states. The family's founder, Malhar Rao Holkar, rose through military service to the Peshwas to establish by 1766 virtually independent control of the Malwa region. The family's control was consolidated in the late 18th century, but succession disputes and quarrels with other Maratha chieftains offset the gains. During the reign of Jaswant Rao Holkar (1797–1811) British expansion destroyed Holkar claims in north India. After defeat in 1804 the Holkars had to accept British protection, remaining a Princely State until 1947.

Holland *See* NETHERLANDS, THE.

Holland, Sir Sidney George (1893–1961) New Zealand statesman. As leader of the National Party from 1940 and Prime Minister (1949–57), he was noted for his staunch support of private enterprise, for his vigorous handling of the 1951 waterfront strike, and for the abolition of the Legislative Council—the Upper House of the New Zealand Parliament. In the tradition of pragmatic conservatism Holland retained and even strengthened much of the welfare state and economic regulatory machinery put in place under Labour.

Hollande, François (Gérard Georges Nicolas) (1954–) French politician, President (2012–). Hollande joined the Socialist Party as a student; he became party leader in 1997, but resigned in 2008 after two successive election defeats. Known as 'Monsieur Normal' for his unflamboyant style, he emerged as the Socialist candidate for the 2012 presidential election, in which he defeated Nicolas *Sarkozy. His popularity quickly declined when his moderately left-wing policies failed to alleviate France's economic problems.

Holocaust, the The ordeal suffered by the Jews in Nazi Europe from 1933 to 1945. Conventionally it is divided into two periods, before and after 1941. In the first period various *anti-Semitic measures were taken in Germany, and later Austria. In Germany, after the Nuremberg Laws (1935) Jews lost citizenship rights, the right to hold public office, practise professions, inter-marry with Germans, or use public education. Their property and businesses were registered and sometimes sequestrated. Continual acts of violence were perpetrated against them, and official propaganda encouraged Germans to hate and fear them. As intended, the result was mass emigration, halving the half-million German and Austrian Jewish population by the start of World War II. The second phase, which occurred during World War II from 1941, spread to Nazi-occupied Europe, and involved forced labour, mass shootings, and *concentration camps, the latter being the basis of the Nazi 'final solution' (*Endlösung*) of the so-called Jewish problem through mass extermination in gas chambers. The last stages of the final solution were decided upon at the Nazi conference held at Wannsee in 1942. At this conference the grotesque plan and schedules were laid down, to be carried out by Adolf *Eichmann. During the Holocaust an estimated six million Jews died. Out of a population of three million Jews in Poland, less than half a million remained in 1945, while Romania, Hungary, and Lithuania also suffered grievously. The Holocaust has raised many problems concerning the nature of European civilization and the influence of Christianity (the Roman Catholic Church knew what was happening but failed to raise its voice in protest).

Holt, Harold Edward (1908–67) Australian statesman. He represented the United Australia Party and then the Liberal Party, holding a series of portfolios from 1939. After *Menzies retired in 1966, Holt became Prime Minister. His term of office coincided with Australia's increasing and controversial involvement in the *Vietnam War.

Holy Alliance (1815) A loose alliance of European powers pledged to uphold the

CONCENTRATION CAMPS

1 Auschwitz-Birkenau
2 Belzec
3 Bergen-Belsen
4 Buchenwald
5 Chelmno
6 Dachau
7 Flössenberg
8 Grossrosen
9 Maidanek
10 Mauthausen
11 Mittelbaudora
12 Natzweiler
13 Neuengamme
14 Plaszow
15 Ravensbrück
   (for women)
16 Sachsenhausen
17 Sobibor
18 Stutthof
19 Terezin
   (Theresienstadt)
20 Treblinka

1000   number of Jews killed, by country
-----   1937 frontiers

0   300 km
0   200 miles

NORWAY 1000
SWEDEN
FINLAND
ESTONIA 26,000
LATVIA 70,000
LITHUANIA 104,000
DENMARK 100
EAST PRUSSIA
SOVIET UNION 750,000
UNITED KINGDOM
IRELAND
NETHERLANDS 104,000
GERMANY 180,000
POLAND 2,600,000
BELGIUM 28,000
LUXEMBOURG 3000
CZECHOSLOVAKIA 60,000
AUSTRIA 60,000
HUNGARY 200,000
ROMANIA 750,000
SWITZERLAND
FRANCE 65,000
YUGOSLAVIA 58,000
ITALY 9000
BULGARIA 40,000
ALBANIA
GREECE 60,000
TURKEY
PORTUGAL
SPAIN

The Holocaust. The Nazi determination to rid Europe of Jews was rooted in the anti-Semitism of Central and Eastern Europe. From the earliest years of the Third Reich Jews were persecuted and from 1941 onwards a programme of extermination began, with certain camps in Eastern Europe equipped with gas-chambers for systematic slaughter. It is estimated that four million Jews died in these camps. Perhaps a further million died in ghettos by starvation and disease and over a million were shot by mobile killing squads (Einsatzgruppen).

principles of the Christian religion. It was proclaimed at the Congress of *Vienna (1815) by the emperors of Austria and Russia, and the king of Prussia. All other European leaders were invited to join, except the pope and the Ottoman sultan. The restored French king Louis XVIII did so, as did most others; Britain did not. As a diplomatic instrument it was short-lived and never effective and it became associated with repressive and autocratic regimes.

Holy Land *See* PALESTINE.

Holy League A name given to several European alliances formed during the 15th, 16th, and 17th centuries. The League of 1511–13 was directed against French ascendancy in Italy. The coalition was organized by Pope Pius II, and included England, Spain, Venice, the Holy Roman Empire, and Switzerland. It succeeded in its initial aims, but then there was squabbling over strategy and the hard-pressed French were able to conclude separate peace treaties with each member. The Holy League of 1526 was formed against emperor *Charles V by France, the papacy, England, Venice, and Milan. It achieved little in the subsequent war, and *Francis I of France made peace with Charles at Cambrai in 1529.

The French Holy League of 1576, also known as the Catholic League, was led by the *Guise faction during the *French Wars of Religion. Henry III ordered its dissolution in 1577, but it was revived in 1584 to play a major part in the War of the *Three Henrys (1585–89). Its power waned after *Henry IV accepted Catholicism in 1593.

The Holy (or Catholic) League of 1609 was a military alliance of the German Catholic princes, formed at the start of the War of the Jülich Succession (1606–14). During most of the *Thirty Years War its forces served the imperial cause, with *Tilly as its principal commander.

Holyoake, Sir Keith Jacka (1904–83) New Zealand statesman. A farmer active in agricultural organizations in the 1930s and 1940s, he entered Parliament in 1932, becoming leader of the National Party and Prime Minister (1957 and 1960–72). An able politician in the tradition of pragmatic conservatism, he led New Zealand skilfully in the decades of growing racial tension. He served a term as governor-general of New Zealand after his retirement from politics.

Holy Roman Empire The empire set up in western Europe following the coronation of Charlemagne as emperor, in the year 800. Of the emperors, after 1250 only five were crowned as such; the title was abolished by Napoleon in 1806. The empire lasted about 1000 years. The creation of the medieval popes has been called the emperors' greatest mistake; for whereas their intention was to appoint a powerful secular deputy to rule Christendom, in fact they generated a rival. No emperor ever ruled the whole of Christendom, nor was there any substantial machinery of imperial government. From Otto I's coronation (962) the Empire was always associated with the German Crown, even after it had become a Habsburg/Austrian preserve in the 15th century. Its somewhat mystical ideal was formal unity of government, based on coronation in Rome, memories of the old Roman Empire as well as Charlemagne, and devotion to the Roman Catholic Church.

Holy Roman Empire. *c.*1100 By the end of the 11th century the Holy Roman Emperor was the crowned ruler of Germany, Burgundy, and northern Italy, in addition to his imperial role as temporal leader of Christendom, and the empire was close to its height in terms of cohesion and extent. The degree of power he exercised varied, however, at different times. Within Germany there was constant rivalry between the emperor and the rulers of the margraviates, duchies, and kingdoms.

Home Guard A World War II military force raised in Britain. In 1908 the Territorial Force, a home defence organization, had been created, which became the Territorial Army in 1921. The Home Guard, known originally as the Local Defence Volunteers, existed from 1940 to 1944. In 1942 enrolment in the force became compulsory for sections of the civilian population. About a million men served in their spare time, and in its first vital year it possessed considerably more men than firearms. It never went into battle, but it did relieve the army of some duties and boosted morale, especially from 1940 to 1942.

Home Rule, Irish A movement for the reestablishment of an Irish parliament responsible for internal affairs. An association, founded in 1870 by Isaac Butt, sought to repeal the Act of *Union (1800) between Britain and Ireland. This became a serious possibility when Charles *Parnell persuaded the Liberals under *Gladstone to introduce Home Rule Bills. The first (1886) was defeated in the House of Commons. Gladstone's second Bill (1893) was also defeated. The third Bill (1912), introduced by Asquith, was passed by Parliament but its operation was postponed when war broke out in Europe in 1914. It left unresolved the question of how much of Ulster was to be excluded from the Act. When World War I ended the political situation in Ireland was greatly changed. The *Easter Rising in 1916 and the sweeping majority for *Sinn Fein in the 1918 general election were followed by unrest and guerrilla warfare. Lloyd George was Prime Minister when the fourth Home Rule Bill (1920) was introduced in the Westminster Parliament. The Bill provided for parliaments in Dublin and Belfast linked by a Federal Council of Ireland. The Northern Ireland Parliament, to govern the six north-eastern counties of Ulster, was set up in 1920. Following the Anglo-Irish treaty (1921) the *Irish Free State was set up and *Northern Ireland became a self-governing province within the UK. The 26-county Irish Free State had a vague *dominion status at odds with the independence claimed by Dáil Éireann in 1919. The Anglo-Irish treaty was approved by 64 votes to 57 in the Dáil. The majority group wanted peace and partial independence, the minority group, headed by Eamon *de Valera, desired the immediate independence of all Ireland and the setting up of a republic. The Irish Free State (called Éire from 1937 to 1949) left the Commonwealth in 1949 and became the Republic of *Ireland.

Homestead Act (1862) A US Act to encourage migration west. The Homestead Act gave any citizen who was head of a family and over 21 years of age 65 ha (160 acres) of surveyed public land for a nominal fee. Complete ownership could be attained after five years of continuous residence or by the payment of $1.25 per acre after a six-month period. While some 15,000 such homesteads were created during the *American Civil War years, speculation and the development of mechanized large-scale agriculture reduced the effectiveness of the Act in later years.

Homestead strike (1892) A US labour dispute. It was the bitter climax of deteriorating relations between the Carnegie Steel Company at Homestead, outside Pittsburgh, run by Henry Clay Frick, and the Amalgamated Association of Iron and Steel Workers, who had refused to accept a disadvantageous new contract and ordered a strike. When Frick imported 300 *Pinkerton detectives to protect the plant and the non-union workers, they were repulsed in an armed battle in which several people were killed. The state governor introduced state militia to restore order, and the strike failed. The union collapsed after the anarchist Alexander Berkman tried to kill Frick, and unionism in the industry was seriously weakened until the 1930s.

Homo *See* EARLY HUMANS.

Honduras

Capital:	Tegucigalpa
Area:	112,090 sq km (43,278 sq miles)
Population:	8,448,465 (2013 est)
Currency:	1 Honduran lempira = 100 centavos
Religions:	Roman Catholic 97.0%; Protestant 3.0%
Ethnic Groups:	Mestizo 90.0%; Amerindian 7.0%; Black 2.0%; White 1.0%
Languages:	Spanish (official); minority languages
International Organizations:	UN; OAS; Non-Aligned Movement; WTO

A country in Central America, bounded on the north and west by Guatemala and El Salvador and on the south by Nicaragua.

Physical Honduras has a long, north-east coast on

the Caribbean Sea and a short, south-west coast on the Pacific Ocean. Most of it is mountainous and heavily forested, and the soil is generally poor and acid.

Economy Honduras was formerly dependent on banana and coffee exports, but clothing and wiring harnesses for vehicles are now also important. Other crops include citrus fruit and cereals; other industries include sugar and wood products. Honduras is a very poor country with high levels of inequality. Over half the population live in poverty.

History The native inhabitants of Honduras are mestizo Indians. One of the lieutenants of Hernando *Cortés, Francisco de las Casas, founded the first settlement, the port of Trujillo, in 1523. Honduras was attached administratively to the captaincy-general of *Guatemala throughout the Spanish colonial period.

When independence came in 1821 it briefly became part of the empire of Agustin de Iturbide before joining the United Provinces of Central America (1825–38). Separate independent status dates from 1838, when the union broke up. An uninterrupted succession of *caudillos dominated the remainder of the 19th century. Improvement in the political process came slowly in the 20th century. Military dictators continued to be more prominent than civilian presidents, but the election in 1957 of Ramón Villeda Morales gave hope for the future. This optimism proved premature as the Honduran army overthrew him before he could implement the reform programme he had pushed through the congress. Military entrenchment was further solidified as Honduras fought a border war with El Salvador in 1969. In 1982 a new, US-backed, constitution aimed to increase democratic activity. As a condition for US support, however, the country provided a base for 'Contra' rebels from *Nicaragua. In 1985 a new President, José Azcona (1985–90) threatened to stop 'Contra' activity, as well as to reduce the power of the military. Honduras, however, remained economically dependent upon the USA, and in 1989 Rafael Callejas was elected President with US support. He faced economic turbulence, left-wing guerrilla activity, and security forces almost totally out of control. Despite assistance loans from the IMF and the World Bank, the government's economic structural adjustment plan, launched in 1990, provoked sustained hostility, causing social unrest and political instability in 1992. In September the long-standing border dispute with El Salvador was resolved by an International Court of Justice ruling. In the presidential elections of November 1993 Carlos Roberto Reina, who opposed Callejas, was elected. The declared priorities of the new government were the economy and the reduction of the military's role in politics. In 1998 the country was devastated by Hurricane Mitch. Reina was followed as President by Carlos Roberto Flores (1998–2002) and Ricardo Maduro Joest (2002–06). In 2009 Maduro's successor, José Manuel Zelaya Rosales, precipitated a constitutional crisis that culminated in his overthrow by a military coup. Following elections Porfirio Lobo Sosa became President in 2010. He was succeeded in 2014 by Juan Orlando Hernández.

Honecker, Erich (1912–94) East German Communist statesman, head of state (1976–89). He was appointed First Secretary of the Socialist Unity Party in 1971, becoming effective leader of East Germany in 1973, and head of state (Chairman of the Council of State) three years later. His repressive regime was marked by a close allegiance to the Soviet Union. Honecker was ousted in 1989 after a series of pro-democracy demonstrations. In 1992 he was arrested but proceedings against him for manslaughter and embezzlement were later dropped because of his ill health.

Hood, Samuel, 1st Viscount (1724–1816) British admiral. He served in the Seven Years War, the American War of Independence, and the French Revolutionary wars. He entered the navy in 1741, was promoted post-captain in 1756, and in 1759 captured a French frigate after a fierce action. In 1780, with the rank of rear-admiral, he went to the West Indies as second-in-command to Lord *Rodney. There he displayed masterly tactical skills and took a prominent part in the defeat of the French fleet near Dominica two years later. During the French Revolutionary wars he commanded the British fleet in the Mediterranean.

Hoover, Herbert Clark (1874–1964) US Republican statesman, 31st President of the USA (1929–33). He first gained prominence for his work in organizing food production and distribution in the USA and Europe during and after World War I. As President he was faced with the long-term problems of the Depression which followed the stock market crash of 1929. He returned to relief work after World War II as coordinator of food supplies to avert the threat of postwar famine.

Hoover, J. Edgar (John Edgar Hoover) (1895–1972) US lawyer and director of the FBI

(1924–72). Beginning his term of office with the fight against organized crime in the 1920s and 1930s, he went on to be instrumental in re-organizing the FBI into an efficient, scientific law-enforcement agency. However, he came under criticism for the organization's role during the McCarthy era and for its reactionary political stance in the 1960s.

Hopewell cultures A group of related cultures of the eastern USA (c.500 BC–500 AD). They are known for their conical burial mounds, most highly developed in Ohio, and often associated with earthworks in various shapes, the most famous being the Great Serpent Mound of Adams County, Ohio, 213 m (700 feet) in length.

hoplite A citizen-soldier of the cities of ancient Greece. Each man had to provide his own formidable armour (Greek, *hopla*)—2.7 m (9-feet) spear, short sword, large round shield, breastplate, and greaves (shin-pads). They fought in the close-packed phalanx formation, and were extremely effective when operating in the plains of Greece. However, over rough terrain they were vulnerable to fast-moving light infantry. The professional hoplites of *Sparta were pre-eminent in classical times until their defeat by the Thebans in 371 BC.

Horn, Filips van Montmorency, Graaf van (or **Hoorn Graaf van**) (c.1524–68) Flemish soldier and statesman. He had a long record of distinguished service to both Emperor *Charles V and *Philip II of Spain but, as a member of the regency council in the Netherlands (1561–65), he followed a similar opposition course to that of his colleague, Lamoral *Egmont. In 1566 he aligned himself with the Calvinists at Tournai, but then obeyed the regent's command to return to Brussels. Late in that year, he rejected *William I (the Silent)'s plan for armed resistance to the Spaniards, and withdrew to his home in Weert. In 1567 *Alba found him out, had him convicted of treason and heresy by the Council of Troubles, and he was beheaded.

Horthy de Nagybánya, Nikolaus (1868–1957) Regent of Hungary. He commanded the Austro-Hungarian fleet in World War I. In 1919 he was asked by the opposition to organize an army to overthrow Béla *Kun's communist regime. In January 1920 the Hungarian Parliament voted to restore the monarchy, electing Horthy regent. This post he retained, but thwarted all efforts of Charles IV, the deposed King of Hungary, to support the *Habsburg claim. He ruled virtually as dictator. He agreed to Hungary joining Germany in World War II

and declared war on the Soviet Union, but in 1944 he unsuccessfully sought a separate peace with the Allies. He was imprisoned by the Germans (1944) and released by the Allies (1945).

Hospitaller *See* KNIGHT HOSPITALLER.

Hotspur The nickname of Sir Henry Percy (*see* PERCY).

Houphouët-Boigny, Félix (1905–93) African statesman. In 1944 he was a co-founder of the Syndicat Agricole Africain, formed to protect Africans against European agriculturalists. He represented *Côte d'Ivoire (formerly the Ivory Coast) in the French Assembly (1945–59), and in 1946 formed the Parti Démocratique de la Côte d'Ivoire. At first allied with the Communist Party, he broke with it in 1950, and cooperated with the French to build up the economy of his country. When Côte d'Ivoire was offered independence in 1958, he campaigned successfully for self-government within the *French Community. He became President of Côte d'Ivoire in 1960 in a one-party state, and his international policies were recognizably moderate. He also maintained close links with France. In May 1990 opposition parties were allowed to function, and he was re-elected in presidential elections later that year. Following his death in 1993 he was succeeded as President by Henri Konan Bedie.

House of Commons (UK) The lower chamber of the British *Parliament. It began as an element of the Parliaments summoned by the king in the later 13th century: both knights of the shire and burgesses of *boroughs were summoned to Simon *de Montfort's Parliament in 1265. It took over 500 years for the Commons to become supreme in the tripartite division of power between it, the *House of Lords, and the monarchy. In the 14th century both Houses gained constitutional rights in relation to the monarchy; many of the struggles between *Richard II and his opponents were waged through the Commons—notably in the Merciless Parliament of 1388.

In the early 17th century, when differences between the monarchy and Parliament first surfaced, the Commons took the lead in, for instance, the *Petition of Right (1628), winning *Charles I's acceptance of the principle of no taxation without parliamentary assent. The *Long Parliament (1640–60 abolished the House of Lords and set up the *Commonwealth, and it was the Commons that was instrumental in inviting *Charles II to take up the throne, just as it promoted the *Bill of Rights (1689) and Act of

*Settlement (1701) that defined the relations between Commons, Lords, and the monarchy.

Although the Commons had gained considerable constitutional powers during the 17th century and had had some notable Prime Ministers, such as Robert Walpole and William Pitt, it was still, at the beginning of the 19th century, no more than an equal partner with the House of Lords. Extension of the franchise and the influence of such powerful members as Robert Peel, Lord Palmerston, Lord John Russell, and William Gladstone did much to extend its power, so that by the end of the century it was effectively regarded as the voice of the people. Following a series of *Reform Acts and other legislation (1832, 1867, 1884, 1918, 1928, 1948, 1969) members of the House of Commons are today elected by universal adult suffrage. By the Parliament Act of 1911, the maximum duration of a Parliament became five years.

The life of a Parliament is divided into sessions, usually of one year in length. As a rule, Bills likely to raise political controversy are introduced in the Commons before going to the Lords, and the Commons claim exclusive control in respect of national taxation and expenditure. Since 1911 Members have received payment.

Members of Parliament are elected from 650 single-member constituencies in plurality (first-past-the-post) elections. The presiding officer of the Commons is an elected Speaker, who has power to maintain order and functions in a strictly non-partisan way. The House of Commons is organized along adversarial lines, its proceedings normally controlled by a disciplined party majority. The exercise by the House of Commons of its powers in matters of legislation, finance, scrutiny, and enquiry are thus in practice largely party-dominated, subject to the rights conventionally accorded to the opposition. On the other hand, an increasing role is played by all-party committees, such as standing committees, which consider and amend bills, or select committees, which monitor the workings of government departments, taking evidence, questioning witnesses, and issuing reports. Following a general election, or a change of leadership, the leader of the party commanding an overall majority in the House of Commons is invited by the monarch to become Prime Minister and form a cabinet. When no party has an overall majority, the leader of the largest party usually becomes the Prime Minister of a single-party minority government that relies on other parties' support or abstention in crucial votes. The alternative is a formal coalition, such as that formed in 2010 between

the Conservative and Liberal Democrat parties; these are very rare in peacetime.

House of Lords (UK) The upper chamber of the British *Parliament. It derived from the medieval kings' Great Council. In the 13th and 14th centuries, as the councils gave way to parliaments, the Lords evolved into a separate body which, together with the *House of Commons, presented bills to the crown for enactment as statutes. The immense individual importance of many peers did not prevent them gradually losing to the Commons the right to levy taxes on the king's behalf. The House of Lords was abolished in 1649 and revived in 1660. It was put on what is still its constitutional basis vis-à-vis the crown and the House of Commons by the *Glorious Revolution (1688–89). Following the 1832 *Reform Act, its influence gradually declined as that of the House of Commons increased. The Parliament Act of 1911 reduced the Lords' powers to a "suspensory veto" of two years (further reduced to one year in 1949). By it bills can be delayed, but if passed again by the Commons, become law. The House of Lords has no power to revise or delay money bills. It still performs several useful parliamentary roles. These include the revision of bills from the Commons, the initiation of non-controversial legislation, scrutiny of the executive, and enquiry by select committee. Debate in the Lords is less raucously partisan and sometimes better informed than in the Commons.

The House of Lords currently consists of the Lords Spiritual (26 archbishops and bishops in order of seniority) and the Lords Temporal (approximately 670 life peers and 92 hereditary peers, with approximately 50 further members who are ineligible to participate in its proceedings). From the 16th century until 1999, the House was dominated by the hereditary peers, Lords Temporal whose titles, once created, descended to their heirs. Non-hereditary peers were introduced by the Life Peerage Act of 1958; and in 1999 hereditary peers were excluded from the House, except for 92 representatives. This hereditary remnant was intended as a transitional arrangement, pending further reform of the House. The House of Lords formerly acted as the highest court of appeal in the UK legal system, but this function was removed to a new Supreme Court in 2009.

House of Representatives The lower chamber of the two chambers of the US Congress, the other being the *Senate. The House of Representatives comprises 435 members, the number for each state being determined by population, though every state is entitled to at least one Representative. The size of the House increased with the USA's population until 1929 when the number of representatives was fixed. Seats are apportioned every ten years.

The House and the Senate have an equal voice in legislation; however, the right to originate finance bills is given to the House by the Constitution. The House also has the power to begin impeachment proceedings, through which the President, a judge, or other official can be removed from office for misbehaviour, if the resolution of the House to impeach is adopted by the Senate.

Houston, Samuel (1793–1863) US military leader and statesman. Houston lived for a time with the Cherokee and became a popular hero as a result of his exploits, while serving under Andrew *Jackson, against the Creek in 1814. In 1835–36, as military leader of the Texan insurgents, he defeated and captured *Santa Anna at the Battle of *San Jacinto, thus securing Texan independence. He was twice President of the Texan Republic (1836–38; 1841–44), and after Texas joined the United States served in the Senate from 1847 to 1859. In 1859 his popularity won him election as governor of his adopted state, but when Texas joined the *Confederacy in 1861, Houston was deposed.

Howard, Catherine (c.1521–42) Fifth wife of Henry VIII. She married Henry soon after his divorce from Anne of Cleves in 1540, probably at the instigation of her ambitious Howard relatives. She was accused of infidelity, confessed, and was beheaded in 1542.

Howard, John (1726–90) British philanthropist and prison reformer. In 1773 his sense of horror at conditions in Bedford jail led him to undertake a tour of British prisons; this culminated the following year in two Acts of Parliament setting down sanitary standards. His work *The State of Prisons in England and Wales* (1777) gave further impetus to the movement for improvements in the design and management of prisons.

Howard, John (Winston) (1939–) Australian Liberal statesman, Prime Minister from 1996. He was elected an MP in 1974 and held several posts in the Cabinet, including Federal Treasurer (1977–83). He was twice leader of the Liberal Party in opposition (1985–89, 1995–96) before becoming Prime Minister of a coalition government (1996–2007).

Hoxha, Enver (1908–85) Albanian statesman, Prime Minister (1944–54) and First Secretary of the Albanian Communist Party (1954–85). In 1941 he founded the Albanian Communist Party and led the fight for national independence. As Prime Minister and thereafter First Secretary of the Communist Party's Central Committee, he rigorously isolated Albania from Western influences and implemented a Stalinist programme of nationalization and collectivization.

Hoysala An Indian dynasty, first Jain and later Hindu, which ruled the south Deccan (c. 1006–1346), from a capital at Dwarasamudra (near Mysore in Karnataka state). Beginning as marauding hill chieftains, they finally established sway over a region corresponding to the later Mysore state.

Hsia *See* XIA.

Hsiung-nu *See* XIONGNU.

Hua Guofeng (or **Hua Kuo-feng**) (1920–2008) Chinese statesman. Hua won a succession of key posts between 1968 and 1975, becoming acting Premier after the death of *Zhou Enlai in 1976. He succeeded *Mao Zedong as chairman of the Central Committee, having defeated a challenge from the *Gang of Four. Hua resigned as Premier in 1980 and as chairman in 1981. He remained a member of the CCP Central Committee until 2002.

Hudson's Bay Company A company chartered in 1670 to Prince *Rupert and 17 others by Charles II to govern and trade in the vast area of the Canadian north-west, called Rupert's Land, which drained into Hudson Bay. Although huge profits accrued from the fur trade, the company was, until 1763, threatened by competition and military attack from the French. From 1787 there was occasionally murderous conflict with the North-West Company over control of the fur trade until the two companies amalgamated in 1821.

hue and cry The practice in medieval England whereby a person could call out loudly for help in pursuing a suspected criminal. All who heard the call were obliged by law to join in the chase; failure to do so would incur a heavy fine and any misuse of the hue and cry was also punishable. The system was regularized by Edward I in the Statute of Winchester (1285), which rationalized the policing of communities. The obligation on the public to assist the police in the arrest of a suspect has survived in principle to the present day.

Huerta, Victoriano (1854–1916) Mexican statesman and general. Appointed (1912) as commander of the federal forces, he became President of Mexico (1913–14) by leading a coup against Francisco *Madero. He instituted a ruthless dictatorship in which torture and assassination of his political opponents became commonplace. He was forced to resign under insurgent military pressure, supported not only by his Mexican opponents but also by the government of Woodrow *Wilson in the USA. An attempted return to power in 1915 ended unsuccessfully when he was arrested by US agents while attempting to cross the US–Mexican border.

Hughes, William Morris (1862–1952) Australian statesman. He became a Labor Member of the House of Representatives in 1901, where he served for over 50 years. He was Prime Minister of the Commonwealth of Australia (1915–23), and represented Labor until it split in 1916. In 1917 he helped to form the Nationalist Party, which he led until 1923, when the Country Party, now in coalition with the Nationalists, refused to serve with him. In 1929, he gave his support to the Labor Party over a matter of industrial relations and the Nationalists expelled him. The United Australia Party, which he led from 1941 until 1943, was transformed by *Menzies into the Liberal Party in 1944 and Hughes became a back-bench member.

Huguenot In the 16th and 17th centuries, a French Protestant who followed the beliefs of *Calvin. By 1561 there were 2000 Calvinist churches in France and the Huguenots had become a political faction that seemed to threaten the state. Persecution followed and during the *French Wars of Religion the Huguenots fought eight civil wars against the Catholic establishment and triumphed when, by the Edict of *Nantes in 1598, *Henry IV gave them liberty of worship and a 'state within a state'. Their numbers grew, especially among merchants and skilled artisans, until they were again persecuted. The centre of their resistance in 1627 was in the town of La Rochelle, which the *Richelieu government had to besiege for over a year before capturing it. In 1685 the Edict was revoked; many thousands of Huguenots fled to England, the Netherlands, Switzerland, and Brandenburg, some settling as far away as North America and the Cape of Good Hope. All these places were to benefit from their skill in craftmanship and trade, particularly as silk-weavers and silversmiths.

Hu Jintao (1942–) Chinese statesman; President (2003–). He joined the Chinese Communist Party in 1965 and served in the provinces of Guizhou and Tibet before becoming a member of the Politburo in 1992. He replaced *Jiang Zemin as General Secretary of the Communist Party (2002–12), as President of China (2003–13), and as Chairman of the Central Military Commission (2004–13). He was succeeded in all these offices by *Xi Jinping.

Hukbalahap Filipino peasant resistance movement with roots in the pre-war *barangay* (village) and tenant organizations in central Luzon. Led by Luis Taruc, the movement developed during World War II into the Anti-Japanese People's Army, a left-wing guerrilla organization which was as much opposed to the Filipino landlord élite and their US backers as to the Japanese. Active against the latter from 1943, the 'Huks' controlled most of central Luzon by the end of the war, but were denied parliamentary representation and went into open rebellion against the Manila government until all but destroyed by government forces between 1950 and 1954.

humanism An intellectual movement in which humans are regarded as the centre of the Universe. There is no systematic theory of humanism, but any world-view claiming that people alone supply the true measure of value, may be described as humanist. The relations between humanism and religious thought are complex, but humanism, by virtue of its belief in human perfectibility, contradicts the doctrine of original sin. In this way humanism also has connections with individualism, the notion that the goal for man includes the fulfilment of each person by the cultivation of his or her own individual nature, and with a belief in the possibility of social progress.

Historically, humanism was fully articulated for the first time in the 15th-century *Renaissance. Humanists were originally Christian scholars who studied and taught the humanities (grammar, rhetoric, history, poetry, and moral philosophy) by rediscovering classical Latin texts, and later also Greek and Hebrew texts. They came to reject medieval *scholasticism, and made classical antiquity the basis of western Europe's educational system and cultural outlook. They had no coherent philosophy, but shared an enthusiasm for the dignity of human values in place of religious dogma or abstract reasoning.

The invention of printing enabled the movement's ideas to spread from its birthplace in Italy to most of western Europe. Thomas *More, *Erasmus, and John Colet all contributed to the humanist tradition. Its spirit of sceptical enquiry prepared the way for both the *Reformation and some aspects of the *Counter-Reformation.

*Marx may be described as a humanist, and in the 20th century humanism was given expression, in both secular and religious forms, in the philosophy of existentialism.

Humayun (1508–56) The second *Mogul Emperor of India (1530–40, 1554–55). His name means 'fortunate', yet after ten years of precarious rule he was driven into exile in Persia, recovering his empire only shortly before his death in an accident.

Hume, David (1711–76) Scottish philosopher, economist, and historian. His philosophy rejected the possibility of certainty in knowledge, and he agreed with John Locke that there are no innate ideas, only a series of subjective sensations, and that all the data of reason stem from experience. His philosophical legacy is particularly evident in the work of 20th-century empiricist philosophers. In economics, he attacked mercantilism and anticipated the views of such economists as Adam Smith. Among his chief works are *A Treatise of Human Nature* (1739–40) and a five-volume *History of England* (1754–62).

Hume, John (1937–) Northern Irish politician, leader of the Social Democratic and Labour Party (1979–2001). He was awarded the Nobel Peace Prize in 1998 with David *Trimble for his role in negotiating peace in Northern Ireland.

hundred An administrative subdivision of an English *shire between the 10th century and the Local Government Act (1894), which established District Councils. Hundreds were probably based upon units of 100 hides. (A hide was a measure of land, calculated to be enough to support a family and its dependants, ranging from 25 to 50 ha. (60–120 acres) according to locality.) They did not exist in every shire. Their equivalents in the *Danelaw were wapentakes, in Kent lathes, in Yorkshire ridings, and in Sussex rapes. The hundred court of freeholders met once a month to deal with military defence, private pleas, tax levies, and to prepare indictments for the royal justices. The hundred bailiff served the sheriff's writs and the constable maintained law and order.

Hundred Days (20 March–28 June 1815) The period between *Napoleon's return from the island of Elba and the date of the second restoration of *Louis XVIII. Napoleon landed at Cannes on 1 March while the European powers were meeting at the Congress of *Vienna. He won great popular acclaim as he moved north through Grenoble and Lyons. He arrived in Paris on 20 March, less than 24 hours after Louis had fled. Napoleon's attempt to win over moderate royalist opinion to a more liberal conception of his empire failed. Moreover, he failed to persuade the Allies of his peaceful intentions, and had to prepare to defend France against a hastily reconstituted 'Grand Alliance'. By the end of April he had only raised a total strength of 105,000 troops, the Allies having a force of almost 130,000 men. Nevertheless, Napoleon took the offensive and forced the Prussians to retreat at Ligny. Two days later, on 18 June, Napoleon was defeated at *Waterloo. He returned to Paris and on 22 June abdicated for the second time. Six days later Louis XVIII was restored to power.

Hundred Days Reform (1898) Chinese reform campaign. Inspired by *Kang Youwei, and supported by Liang Qichao (1873–1921), it attempted to reform the *Qing state. Kang utilized official disenchantment with the measures of the *Self-Strengthening Movement and concern at renewed foreign intrusions in the wake of the *Sino-Japanese War of 1894–95 to have extensive reforms, based on Western thinking, adopted by Emperor Guangxu. These included a constitutional monarchy and modernization of the civil service. After a period of 103 days the reform programme was destroyed by a conservative backlash, the empress dowager *Cixi launching a palace coup in which the emperor was imprisoned, the reforms rescinded, and the reformers themselves exiled, dismissed, or put to death. Many of these reforms were finally implemented between the *Russo-Japanese War of 1904–05 and the Revolution of 1911.

Hundred Flowers Movement (1956–57) Chinese political and intellectual debate. The campaign, to encourage greater freedin of speech, was initiated by *Mao Zedong and others in the wake of Khrushchev's denunciation of Stalin. Mao argued that self-criticism would benefit China's development. After some hesitation, denunciation of the Communist Party and its institutions appeared in the press and there was social unrest. The party reacted by attacking its critics and exiling many to distant areas of the country in the Anti-Rightist Campaign.

Hundred Years War A war between France and England that lasted for more than a century between the 1340s and 1450s, not as one continuous conflict but rather a series of attempts by English kings to dominate France. The two key issues were the sovereignty of Gascony (the English king was Duke of Gascony and resented paying homage for it to the kings of France), and Edward III's claim, through his mother, to the French throne, following the death of the last *Capetian king. Rivalry over the lucrative Flanders wool trade and provocative French support for the Scots against England also contributed.

In 1328 Philip of Valois was crowned King of France and his subsequent confiscation of *Aquitaine (1337) provoked Edward's invasion of France (1338). The English won a naval battle at Sluys (1340) and major military victories at *Crécy (1346), Calais (1347), and *Poitiers (1356), where *Edward the Black Prince captured and later ransomed Philip's successor, John II. In 1360 the Treaty of Brétigny gave Edward considerable territories in France in return for abandoning his claims to the French throne. The French gradually improved their position and in the reign of Edward's successor, his grandson, *Richard II, hostilities ceased almost completely.

The English retention of Calais and Bordeaux, however, prevented permanent peace, and English claims to France were revived by *Henry V (invoking *Salic Law). He invaded Harfleur and won a crushing victory at *Agincourt (1415), followed by occupation of Normandy (1417–19) and much of northern France. The treaty of Troyes (1420) forced Charles VI of France to disinherit his son, the dauphin, in favour of the English kings. However, following Henry V's early death (1422) the regents of his ineffectual son *Henry VI gradually lost control of conquered territory to French forces. The English were defeated at Orleans (1429) by *Joan of Arc and by 1450 France had conquered Normandy and much of Gascony; Bordeaux, the last English stronghold, was captured in 1453. This effectively ended the war and thereafter the English retained only Calais (until 1558). The English never again made a serious attempt to conquer France, although their kings were styled 'King of France' until 1801. In France the virtual destruction of the nobility saw the *Valois monarchy emerge in a strong position.

Hungarian Revolution (23 October–4 November 1956) A revolt in Hungary. It was provoked by the presence in the country of Soviet troops, the repressive nature of the government led by Erno Gerö, and the general atmosphere of de-Stalinization created in February at the Twentieth Congress of the CPSU. Initial demonstrations in Budapest led to the arrival of Soviet tanks in the city, which served only to exacerbate discontent, Hungarian soldiers joining the uprising. Soviet forces were then withdrawn. Imre *Nagy became Prime Minister, appointed non-communists to his coalition, announced Hungary's withdrawal from the *Warsaw Pact, and sought a neutral status for the country. This was unacceptable to the Soviet Union. Powerful, mainly Soviet but some Hungarian, forces attacked Budapest. Resistance in the capital was soon overcome. Nagy was replaced by János *Kádár, while 190,000 Hungarians fled into exile. The Soviet Union reneged on its pledge of safe conduct, handing Nagy and other prominent figures over to the new Hungarian regime, which executed them in secret.

Hungary

Capital:	Budapest
Area:	93,028 sq km (35,918 sq miles)
Population:	9,939,470 (2013 est)
Currency:	1 forint = 100 filler
Religions:	Roman Catholic 37.2%; Calvinist 11.6%; Lutheran 2.2%
Ethnic Groups:	Magyar 92.3%; Roma 1.9%
Languages:	Hungarian (official); minority languages
International Organizations:	UN; OSCE; Council of Europe; NATO; EU; OECD; WTO

A country in central Europe, bounded by Slovakia on the north, Romania and Ukraine on the east, Slovenia, Croatia, and Serbia on the south, and Austria on the west.

Physical From north to south through the centre flows the Danube, in a broad plain (the puszta) which extends eastwards to the river Tisza across pastureland and areas suited to agriculture. West of the river is the Bakony Forest consisting of mainly deciduous trees, Lake Balaton (the largest and shallowest lake in central Europe), and a fertile plateau with granite hills.

Economy Machinery and equipment provide about half of Hungary's export earnings, with other manufacture providing about one-third and food products under one-tenth. The principal crops are cereals, sunflower seed, potatoes, and sugar beet; the principal industries are mining, metallurgy, and construction materials. Hungary has successfully made the transition from a centrally planned to a market economy

History The region comprising the Roman provinces of Pannonia and Dacia was overrun by Germanic tribes in the *Dark Ages and then conquered by *Charlemagne. By 896 elected *Magyar Arpad leaders ruled and Hungary emerged as the centre of a strong Magyar kingdom in the late Middle Ages. A Mongol invasion devastated the population in 1241 and the Arpad line ended in 1301. Thereafter, the crown was usually passed to a foreigner. The advance of the *Ottoman empire threatened, especially after the battle of Nicopolis in 1396, when Sigismund, King of Hungary, was defeated by the Turks. John Hunyadi (died 1456) and his son Matthias Corvinus brought revival, but in 1490 the Jagiellons gained the throne, and, in 1515, a *Habsburg claim arose. The disastrous defeat of the Hungarian king, Louis II, at Mohács (1526), led to the partition of Hungary between the Habsburgs and the Ottomans although Transylvania retained its independence. By 1711 all of Hungary had come under Habsburg rule and remained part of the Habsburg empire until 1919.

In the 19th century Magyar nationalism was antagonized by the repressive policies of *Metternich, leading to rebellion under *Kossuth in 1848. The Austrians, with Russian help, reasserted control. After defeat by *Prussia the Austrians compromised with the Magyars in 1867, setting up *Austria-Hungary, or the Dual Monarchy, which was first and foremost an alliance of Magyars and Austrian Germans against the Slav nationalities. Defeat in World War I led to revolution and independence, first under Károlyi's democratic republic, then briefly under Béla *Kun's communist regime. Dictatorship followed in 1920 under Horthy, and lasted until 1944. Allied to the *Axis Powers in World War II, defeat brought Soviet domination and a communist one-party system. This was resented and, briefly, in 1956, the *Hungarian Revolution saw resistance to the Soviet Union. Hungary experienced some degree of liberalization during the latter years of János *Kádár's regime (1956–88). Demonstrations in Budapest in 1988 resulted in multiparty politics being restored. Elections brought to power the Hungarian Democratic Forum (MDF) early in 1990; but after the collapse of *COMECON, trade fell and there was rising unemployment and popular discontent. Refugees from Romanian Transyl-

vania and from disintegrating Yugoslavia caused additional problems. A programme of ambitious reforms to revive the economy and introduce a free-market system were launched in 1990. However, continued economic recession and domestic political problems resulted, in the general election of May 1994, in the heavy defeat of the MDP. A new coalition, led by the Hungarian Socialist Party under Gyula Horn, took office. A small degree of economic growth was recorded in 1995, despite a sense of economic crisis in the country, which led to the introduction of economic austerity measures. In 1998 the reformist Fidesz movement won elections and Viktor Orban became Prime Minister; following the Socialist Party's victory in 2002, he was succeeded by Peter Medgyessy (2002–04) and Ferenc Gyurcsány (2004–06). Hungary joined NATO in 1999 and the *European Union in 2004. Austerity measures were again introduced in 2006 to control Hungary's budget deficit, but the *Credit Crunch created a crisis: Hungary was unable to borrow from the global financial markets to refinance its debt and in 2008 agreed to a bailout from the IMF, EU, and World Bank. Gyurcsány resigned in 2009 and a landslide Fidesz victory in the 2010 elections returned Orban as Prime Minister. Fidesz used its dominance to enact sweeping reforms, including a new constitution (2012) that attracted international criticism of its illiberal character. Fidesz was re-elected in 2014.

Hungry Forties A period in the early 1840s when Britain experienced an economic depression, causing much misery among the poor. In 1839 there was a serious slump in trade, leading to a steep increase in unemployment, accompanied by a bad harvest. The bad harvests were repeated in the two following years and the sufferings of the people, in a rapidly increasing population, were made worse by the fact that the *Corn Laws seemed to keep the price of bread artificially high. In 1845 potato blight appeared in England and Scotland, spreading to Ireland later in the year and ruining a large part of the crop. The potato blight returned in 1846, bringing the *Irish Famine.

Huns Pastoral nomads famed for their horsemanship, who in about 370 AD invaded southeastern Europe and conquered the *Ostrogoths. In 376 they drove the *Visigoths into Roman territory and early in the 4th century themselves advanced west, driving the *Vandals and others west into Gaul, Italy, and finally Spain. Under *Attila (434–53) they ravaged the Balkans and Greece, but a defeat was finally inflicted on them in 451 at the *Catalaunian Fields by the Romans and Visigoths under the command of Aetius. However that did not prevent them penetrating and plundering Italy the following year. Two years after the death of Attila they were decisively defeated near the unidentified River Nedao, and thereafter ceased to be of historical significance. The White Huns occupied Bactria and territory west towards the Caspian Sea. They vigorously attacked the power of the *Sassanians, defeating and killing Peroz in 484, but then moved south to establish an empire in northern India at the expense of the *Guptas.

Hunt, Henry (known as "Orator Hunt") (1773–1835) British political reformer. He advocated, among other things, full adult suffrage and secret ballots. An outstanding public speaker, in August 1819 he addressed the crowd at the great meeting at St Peter's Fields (*Peterloo massacre), Manchester. For this he was subsequently sentenced to two years' imprisonment. During 1830–33 he was Radical Member of Parliament for Preston.

Huron (or **Wyandot**) A confederation of five Iroquoian Indian groups living north-east of Lake Huron. Known to themselves as Wyandot or Wendat ('people of the peninsula') and surviving today in Quebec and Oklahoma, they were named Huron ('bristly-headed ruffian') by the French explorer Samuel de Champlain when he first encountered them in 1615.

Hurricane Katrina (2005) A hurricane that caused serious flooding in New Orleans. One of the strongest and largest hurricanes seen in the Gulf of Mexico, it caused extensive damage to the Gulf Coast of the USA; but its most serious effect was, on 29 August 2005, to breach the levees that protected the city of New Orleans, 80% of which lay below sea level. The consequent flooding exceeded the worst expectations. New Orleans ceased to function and had to be completely evacuated, amid chaotic scenes of suffering and lawlessness broadcast worldwide. Over 1600 people died, and the total cost of the physical and economic damage exceeded $100 billion. The administration of President George W. *Bush was held to have acted slowly and incompetently in response to the disaster.

Huss, John (or **Jan Hus**) (c.1372–1415) Bohemian religious reformer. A preacher in Prague and an enthusiastic supporter of *Wyclif's views, he aroused the hostility of the Church, was excommunicated (1411), tried (1414), and burnt at the stake. By his death he

was acclaimed a martyr and his followers (Hussites) took up arms against the *Holy Roman Empire and inflicted a series of dramatic defeats on the imperial army.

hussar A soldier of a light cavalry regiment. Hussars were originally mounted troops raised in 1485 by Matthias Corvinus, King of Hungary, to fight the Turks. As good light cavalry was scarce, other countries soon developed their own hussars: *Frederick II (the Great) proved the superiority of Prussian hussars over those of Austria during the War of the *Austrian Succession. Britain hired hussars from several German states in the 18th century, sending them to America where they were hated by the patriots.

Hussein, Saddam (or **Saddam Husain**; full name **Saddam bin Hussein al-Takriti**) (1937–2006) Iraqi President, Prime Minister, and head of the armed forces (1979–2003). In 1968 he played a leading role in the coup that returned the Baath Socialist Party to power. As President he suppressed opposing parties, built up the army and its weaponry, and made himself the object of an extensive personality cult. During his presidency Iraq fought a war with Iran (1980–88) and invaded Kuwait (1990), from which Iraqi forces were expelled in the Gulf War of 1991. Forced to accept the UN terms for a ceasefire, he failed to cooperate with UN inspectors and Britain and the US launched air strikes against Iraq. He also ordered punitive attacks on Kurdish rebels in the north of Iraq and on the Marsh Arabs in the south. Despite the suffering of the Iraqi people as a result of continued UN sanctions, Saddam maintained his grip on power during the 1990s. Arguing that Iraq was developing and stockpiling weapons of mass destruction, the USA and the UK launched the *Iraq War in 2003. This led to the swift collapse of the Baathist regime, and Saddam went into hiding. He was captured by US forces later that year and charged with genocide and crimes against humanity. A special Iraqi court convicted him of crimes against humanity in 2006 and he was sentenced to death. He was hanged on 30 December 2006.

Hussein ibn Ali (1856–1931) Arab political leader. A member of the Hashemite family, he was sharif of Mecca and leader of the 1916 Arab revolt. In 1916 he assumed the title of King of the Arab Countries, but the Allies only recognized him as King of the Hejaz territory. As ruler of the Hejaz (1916–24) he came into conflict in 1919 with Ibn *Saud, the Emir of Najd. He abdicated in favour of his son Ali in October 1924. His son Abdullah became ruler of TransJordan, and another son, *Faisal I, founded the royal line of Iraq.

Hussein ibn Talal (or Husain ibn Talal) (1935–99) King of Jordan (1953–99). Throughout his reign Hussein steered a middle course in his policies, seeking to maintain good relations both with the West and with other Arab nations. However, in 1967 he attacked Israel in the Six Day War, was defeated, and lost the West Bank and half the city of Jerusalem. After this defeat the Palestine Liberation Organization based itself in Jordan but after a short civil war in 1970 the Palestinians were expelled. In 1990 he acted as a mediator between the opposing sides following the Iraqi invasion of Kuwait, but in the subsequent Gulf War Jordan was the only Middle Eastern country to give open support to Iraq. More recently he has advocated peaceful relationships in the Middle East, gaining the support of President Clinton with whom he had talks in 1993. In 1994 he signed a treaty normalizing relations with Israel, and in the same year had talks with Itzhak *Rabin, at whose funeral in 1995 he spoke of continuing the peace process. He was succeeded by his son *Abdullah II.

Hyde, Edward *See* CLARENDON, EDWARD HYDE, EARL OF.

Hyder Ali (1722–82) Sultan of Mysore, south India (1761–1782. Born in relative obscurity, he managed to supplant the Hindu ruler of Mysore. However, he soon had to face the expanding *East India Company armies, aided by Indian allies. In wars with the Company (1767–69; 1780–84) he proved himself one of its most formidable obstacles, winning, with some French mercenary assistance, a series of remarkable victories. But heavy defeats in 1781 persuaded him that further struggle was pointless, and he urged his son, *Tipu Sultan, to seek terms with the Company.

Hyksos (from Egyptian, 'rulers of foreign lands') Invaders, probably from Palestine, who ruled Lower Egypt and part of Upper Egypt from c.1674 BC. Their power lasted until c.1550 BC, when they were overthrown by a rebellion started by the Egyptians of Thebes. The introduction of the horse and chariot was attributed to them. Egyptian remained the official language.

Ibarra, Francisco de (1539–75) Spanish explorer credited with the exploration and colonization of Nueva Vizcaya, the huge area of Mexico which today encompasses most of the states of Durango, Chihuahua, and part of Sonora. With funds provided by his uncle, who had made a fortune in the Zacatecas silver mines, Ibarra, as governor of Nueva Vizcaya, opened up much of the northern frontier of New Spain in the 1560s before returning to Mexico City.

Ibn Khaldun (1332–1406) Arab historian, one of the first historians to devise a nonreligious historiography. His masterpiece the *Muqaddimah* (Introduction to History) contains brilliant insights and social analyses, developing his concept of the science of culture. He also wrote an important history of Muslim north Africa (*Kitab al-'bar*).

IBRD *See* WORLD BANK.

Iceland

Capital:	Reykjavik
Area:	103,000 sq km (39,769 sq miles)
Population:	315,281 (2013 est)
Currency:	1 króna = 100 aurar
Religions:	Evangelical Lutheran 76.2%; Roman Catholic 3.4%; Christian and other minorities
Ethnic Groups:	Icelandic 94.0%
Languages:	Icelandic (official); English; Nordic languages; German
International Organizations:	UN; EFTA; OECD; NATO; Council of Europe; OSCE; WTO

An island country just south of the Arctic Circle in the north-eastern Atlantic Ocean.

Physical It is approximately 460 km (285 miles) long by 280 km (174 miles) wide; but only its coastal areas can be used for settlement and agriculture because the rest is a wasteland of ice, ash, and lava flows.

Economy Hydroelectric power stations provide over three-quarters of the country's electricity needs and geothermal energy is abundant. Six-sevenths of the land area is agriculturally unproductive. The fishing industry is of vital importance to the economy, accounting for 40% of export earnings; other exports are aluminium (produced from imported alumina) and ferro-silicon. The 2000s saw a rapid expansion of the banking sector followed by its collapse.

History Iceland was conquered by the *Vikings between 874 and 930. Its capital, Reykjavik, was founded, and the country was governed by some 36 chieftains, who met periodically in the Althing, an official assembly. A lawspeaker was appointed, and, in 1005, a Supreme Court. Authority, once derived from the pagan priests and temples, changed with conversion to Christianity in *c.*1000 to a partnership of Church and Althing. In 1262 Iceland passed to Norway and, in 1380, with Norway to the Danish crown. Under the rule of Denmark since 1380, a nationalist movement achieved the restoration of the Althing or parliament in 1845. Iceland acquired limited autonomy in 1874 and independence in 1918, although it shared its king with Denmark till 1943. It became an independent republic in 1944. An Allied base during *World War II, it joined the *United Nations Organization and *NATO (1949). It engaged in sometimes violent disputes with Britain over fishing limits, resulting in the 'Cod War' of 1972–76. In the late 1970s strong opposition to the presence of US bases developed, and Iceland became a nuclear-free zone in 1985. The country's worsening economic situation in 1992, caused by losses in the fishing industry, led the government to introduce emergency measures and to devalue the króna in 1993. From the late 1990s bank deregulation attracted global capital to Iceland's financial institutions, which expanded rapidly. By the mid-2000s this boom had left Iceland vulnerable to fluctuations in market sentiment, with its banks having liabilities over ten times the country's GDP. Iceland's banking structure imploded in the *Credit Crunch of 2008: investors lost confidence and withdrew capital, and Iceland's three largest banks collapsed. Threatened with national bankruptcy, Iceland favoured domestic customers of these banks for compensation over foreign investors—a policy that caused diplomatic disputes with the UK and the Netherlands. A loan from the IMF and unpopular austerity measures helped to stabilize the economy; but there was a severe recession until 2010 and work to restructure the economy continues.

Iceni A pre-Roman tribe of eastern England. By the time of the Roman invasion of 43 AD they were part-Romanized and had come under the rule of the dynasty of *Cymbeline. Their ruler Prasutagus was a treaty ally of Rome until his death in 60 AD. The treaty was broken by Rome and his widow *Boudicca led the tribe in a revolt, which was brutally suppressed.

Iconoclastic controversy (from Greek, 'breaking of images') A movement within the Eastern Christian Church in the 8th and 9th centuries that opposed the veneration of icons, both religious paintings and statues. Emperor Leo III banned such veneration in 726 and despite popular antagonism the decision was confirmed by Constantine V in 753. In the seventh ecumenical council of 787 at *Nicaea Empress Irene overturned the decrees but they were again enforced under the emperors Leo V, Michael II, and Theophilus. Veneration of icons was finally restored in 843 and the practice still survives in the Eastern Orthodox Church.

IDA See WORLD BANK.

Iguala, Plan of (1821) A set of constitutional guarantees for an independent Mexico proclaimed in the Mexican town of Iguala by the Creole leader *Iturbide, with the support of the guerrilla leader, Vincent Guerrero. The plan stated that Mexico would be organized as a constitutional monarchy under Ferdinand VII or another European prince, that Roman Catholicism would be the state religion, and that any person, regardless of race, could hold office. The Viceroy Apodaca was deposed and his successor confirmed the guarantees by the convention of Córdoba, but the Spanish government rejected them. The Plan was discarded when Iturbide proclaimed himself emperor (1822).

Ikeda Hayato (1899–1965) Japanese statesman. He entered the government tax service and rose by 1945 to become head of the National Tax Bureau. Having served as Vice-Minister of Finance in the *Yoshida Shigera cabinet of 1947, he was elected to the House of Representatives in 1949 and became successively Minister of Finance and Minister of International Trade. Serving in a succession of high ministerial posts throughout the 1950s, Ikeda became Prime Minister (1960–64) and devoted himself to sustaining Japanese economic growth through a broadening of international trading connections.

Ikhnaton See AKHENATEN.

Ilium See TROY.

Imhotep (*fl. c.*2700 BC) Egyptian architect and scholar. He is usually credited with designing the step pyramid built at Saqqara for the 3rd-dynasty pharaoh Djoser (*c.*2686–*c.*2613 BC) and, through this, with pioneering the use of hewn stone in building. He was later deified; in Egypt, he was worshipped as the patron of architects, scribes, and doctors, while in Greece he was identified with the god Asclepius.

imperialism The policy of extending a country's influence over less powerful states. Historically imperialism has existed in all periods: Greece, Rome, Ottoman Turkey, Spain, and Britain have all extended their respective domains by imperial rule. The *Industrial Revolution introduced a new form of imperialism as European countries competed throughout the world both for raw materials and for markets. In the late 19th century imperial ambitions were motivated in part by the need for commercial expansion, the desire for military glory, and diplomatic advantage. Imperialism generally assumed a racial, intellectual, and spiritual superiority on the part of the newcomers. The effects of imperialism, while in some measure beneficial to the subjected population, often meant the breakdown of traditional forms of life, the disruption of indigenous civilization, and the imposition of new religious beliefs and social values. The dreams of imperialism faded in the 1920s as anti-imperialist movements developed, and from the 1940s many colonies gained their independence.

Impressed ware culture See NEOLITHIC.

Inca The pre-Columbian Indian people of western South America. They comprised Quechua-speaking tribes around Cuzco (their capital), who formed a state contemporary to, and eventually superseding that of *Chimú. Sixteenth-century records indicate that the ruling dynasty was founded c.1200 AD by Manco Capac, but real expansion did not take place until 1438, forming an empire stretching from northern Ecuador, across Peru, to Bolivia and parts of northern Argentina and Chile by 1525 (some 3500 km, 2175 miles, north to south). Three important rulers carried out these conquests and the development of the imperial administration: Pachacuti (1438–71), Topa Inca (1471–93), and Huayna Capac (1493–1525). After Huayna Capac civil wars broke up the empire of his son *Atahualpa just before Spanish troops led by Francisco *Pizarro landed on the coast in 1532. Atahualpa was captured in 1533 and killed shortly thereafter. In the same year Pizarro captured Cuzco, and by 1537, after the defeat of Manco Capac, most of the empire had been subdued by Spain.

Inca technology was of a high standard and included specialized factories and workshops producing ceramics, textiles, and metal artefacts, with fine decoration, incorporating many regional styles. Architecture included accurately fitted stone masonry. Agriculture was based on systems of hillside terracing and included the potato, quinoa, and maize, and the guinea pig (for food), domestic dog, llama, and alpaca. Religion was centralized, local gods being respected but secondary to the Sun cult as the divine ancestor of the ruling dynasty and Viracocha, the creator god.

Incident of 26 February 1936 Attempted military coup in Japan. Young extremists of the Imperial Way faction (*Kodo-ha*) had been active within the Japanese army since the late 1920s, intent on using violent means to overthrow the conservative civilian government and set Japan on a course of military expansion, particularly in China. Their activities culminated in the attempted coup in which several prominent politicians were murdered (the Prime Minister Okada Keisuke only escaping through a case of mistaken identity) and much of central Tokyo seized. The revolt was put down on 29 February and most of its leaders executed, after which leadership of the military expansionist cause passed to the more moderate Control faction (*Tosei-ha*).

Independence, American War of (or **American Revolution**) (1776–83) The American revolution against British rule. It was triggered by colonial resentment at the commercial policies of Britain and by the lack of American participation in political decisions that affected their interests. Disturbances, such as the Boston

Tea Party (1773), developed into armed resistance in 1775 (for example at *Lexington and Concord and *Bunker Hill), and full-scale war, with the *Declaration of Independence in 1776. Britain, fighting 3000 miles from home, faced problems of supply, divided command, slow communications, a hostile population, and lack of experience in combating guerrilla tactics. America's disadvantages included few trained generals or troops, a weak central authority unable to provide finance, intercolonial

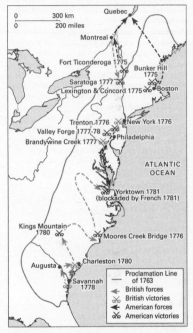

American War of Independence. 1776–83 The British strategy of attempting to break up the union of the colonies was initially successful, when Howe captured New York and forced Washington to retreat to Pennsylvania. However, Burgoyne's surrender at Saratoga raised American morale and persuaded the French to make an alliance with them. Having failed to cut off New England, the British began a southern campaign. Over 5,000 Americans surrendered at Charleston, but Cornwallis was trapped at Yorktown and, denied reinforcements by the French blockade, was forced to admit defeat.

rivalries, and lack of sea power. The French Alliance (1778) changed the nature of the war. Though France gave only modest aid to America, Britain was thereafter distracted by European, West Indian, and East Indian challenges.

The course of the war can be divided at 1778. The first, northern, phase saw the British capture of New York (1776), their campaign in the Hudson valley to isolate New England culminating in defeat at Saratoga Springs (1777), and the capture of Philadelphia (1777) after the victory of Brandywine. The second phase switched British attentions to the south, where large numbers of Loyalists could be recruited. Philadelphia was relinquished (1778) and George *Washington camped at West Point to threaten the British headquarters at New York. After Clinton's capture of Charleston (1780), *Cornwallis vainly chased the Southern Army under Greene before his own exhausted army surrendered at *Yorktown, Virginia (October 1781), effectively ending hostilities. Peace was concluded at *Paris (1783).

Despite frequent victories, the British did not destroy Washington's or Greene's armies and could not break the American will. America's success has been depicted as influencing the French Revolution (1789) and subsequent revolutions in Europe and South America.

Independent Labour Party (ILP) British socialist organization. It was founded at Bradford in 1893 under the leadership of Keir *Hardie. Its aim was to achieve equality in society by the application of socialist doctrines. The ILP was one of the constituent groups of the Labour Representation Committee (1900), which in 1906 became the *Labour Party. A split developed between the ILP and the Labour Party between the two World Wars. The sympathy of the ILP for communism, its pacifism, and its theoretical approach to politics were regarded as electoral liabilities by leading Labour politicians; from 1939 its influence declined.

India

Capital:	New Delhi
Area:	3,287,263 sq km (1,269,219 sq miles)
Population:	1,222,800,359 (2013 est)
Currency:	1 Indian rupee = 100 paisa
Religions:	Hindu 80.5%; Muslim 13.4%; Christian 2.3%; Sikh 1.9%
Ethnic Groups:	Indo-Aryan 72.0%; Dravidian 25.0%
Languages:	Hindi, Assamese, Bengali, Gujarati, Kannada, Kashmiri, Malayalam, Marathi, Oriya, Punjabi, Sanskrit, Sindhi, Tamil, Telugu, Urdu (all official); English
International Organizations:	UN; Commonwealth; Colombo Plan; Non-Aligned Movement; WTO

A South Asian country occupying most of the southward-pointing peninsula of the Indian subcontinent. It is bounded by Pakistan on the northwest, China, Nepal, and Bhutan on the north, and Myanmar (Burma) on the east.

Physical India is roughly triangular in shape, most of the northern frontier following the Himalayas, the world's highest mountains. The two southern sides are formed by a coastline on the Arabian Sea and another on the Bay of Bengal: they are backed by the ranges of the Western and Eastern Ghats. Across a northern belt of the Himalayas, are the Thar (or Great Indian) Desert, the central Punjab watershed with its fields of wheat, the Ganges floodplain, and Bengal. The land rises to the middle of the country, Madhya Pradesh, and the forested hills of Orissa. Extending southward is the Deccan plateau, terminating in the Nilgiri Hills. The southern coasts, Malabar and Coromandel, are famous for their paddy fields and citrus fruit.

Economy India's diverse economy ranges from subsistence agriculture to information technology. Historically the economy was highly regulated and virtually closed to imports and foreign investment, but liberalization since the 1990s has promoted growth. Important crops include rice, wheat, oilseed, cotton, jute, tea, and sugar cane; important industries are textiles, chemicals, food processing, steel, transportation equipment, cement, mining, oil, machinery, computer software, and pharmaceuticals. The service sector is expanding rapidly, especially in information-technology and business-outsourcing services. Exports include oil products, gems, machinery, iron and steel, chemicals, vehicles, and clothing. India now has the tenth-largest economy in the world and is expected to become a major power in the 21st century.

History Inhabited from an unknown date by Dravidian peoples, the *Indus civilization sites, dating from c.2500 BC, indicate one of the world's earliest urban cultures. It was destroyed c.1500 BC, possibly by the *Aryan invasions. The next 1000 years saw the evolution of the religious and social systems which remain characteristic of *Hinduism. Regional kingdoms rose and fell under Hindu, and later Buddhist, dynasties, but mastery over the entire subcontinent was rarely achieved. The *Mauryan empire (c.325–185 BC), was the first all-India empire, only the southern tip remaining outside its influence. After its disintegration, internecine struggles between local powers remained the characteristic pattern.

Waves of invasion from Central Asia from the 11th to the 16th century resulted in Muslim control over the north and the Deccan, and the evolution, through immigration and conversion, of India's largest minority. Only in a few areas, notably the *Rajput states and Vijayanagar, was Hindu political power maintained. Rule by the *Moguls (1526–1857), who claimed most of the subcontinent, marked the height of Indo-Muslim civilization. On their decline European trading powers were poised to take advantage of the power vacuum and the renewal of internecine struggle. Victorious over its French rival, the English *East India Company laid the basis in the 18th century for the subsequent hegemony of the *British Raj. Following the *Indian Mutiny control of India passed, via The Act for the Better Government of India (1858) from the English East India Company to the British Crown. The India Acts of the late 19th and early 20th century granted greater Indian involvement in government. The Indian National Congress, founded in 1885, conducted, under the leadership of M. K. *Gandhi, major campaigns for self-rule and independence. During 1945–47 Congress negotiated with Britain for independence, which was achieved in 1947 when Britain transferred power to the new states of India and *Pakistan.

The Republic (or Union) of India opted to remain within the *Commonwealth even though it adopted a republican constitution. The Princely States within the boundaries of the Indian Union plus *Kashmir all acceded to the Union, though pressure had to be used in some instances, especially Travancore-Cochin and Hyderabad. Eventually the Princely States were integrated or set up as separate states. The French voluntarily surrendered their few possessions in India, while the Portuguese territories agitating for accession were integrated through military action. The semi-autonomous state of Sikkim was absorbed into India through political pressure but without bloodshed. *Pakistan's claims over Kashmir, the bulk of which is formally integrated with India, remain a source of dispute. India is a federation of 25 states and 6 Union territories organized primarily on a linguistic basis. Since independence it has had three wars with Pakistan and one with China, and the relationship with *Sri Lanka is strained by the Indian Tamils' support for the Sri Lankan Tamils' movement for autonomy. The Sikh demand for autonomy and their terrorist action remain intractable problems in the Punjab. India's first Prime Minister was Jawaharlal *Nehru (1947–64), who initiated a policy of planned economic growth and non-alignment. Indira *Gandhi, his daughter, became Prime Minister in 1966. After splitting the Congress Party and experimenting with autocratic rule (1975–77) she suffered electoral defeat. She returned to power (1980) and adopted a firm approach to separatists in 1984 when she suppressed a militant Sikh movement that demanded autonomy for the Punjab. She was assassinated by a Sikh in the same year. Her son, Rajiv *Gandhi, succeeded her as Prime Minister (1984–89). Rajiv failed to win the 1989 election but, after his assassination by Tamil militants, the Congress (I) Party under Narasimha Rao regained political control with a minority government. In December 1992 Hindu extremists demolished the ancient Babri mosque at Ayodhya, which led to severe sectarian clashes in 1993. In 1996 Congress (I) was defeated in general elections by the Hindu nationalist Bharatiya Janata Party (BJP). A series of short-lived coalition governments followed until the 1999 election produced a stable majority for a BJP-led coalition with Atal Behari Vajpayee as Prime Minister. India carried out five underground nuclear tests in 1998. In December 2004 the Andaman and Nicobar Islands were devastated by the *Indian Ocean tsunami. The Congress (I) Party formed a coalition government following the 2004 general elections. The Prime Minister was Manmohan Singh, the Congress (I) leader, Sonia Gandhi (1946–), having declined the post. The coalition was re-elected in 2009 but the general election of 2014 saw a crushing defeat for Congress (I) and the BJP formed a government under Narendra Modi.

India Acts British parliamentary Acts for the government of India. The Act for the Better Government of India (1858) replaced rule by the English *East India Company by that of the crown. The viceroy would be assisted by a Council, which from 1861 was to have Indian as well as European members. The India Act (1909) allowed Indians a share in the work of legislative councils (*Morley-Minto Reforms). The Government of India Act (1919) following the *Montagu-Chelmsford Proposals, established a two-chamber legislature at the centre, enlarged provincial legislatures, and gave both an elected majority. Central government remained under the control of the viceroy's Executive Council, but in the provinces a measure of self-government was conceded through the system known as dyarchy. The Government of India Act (1935) separated Burma from India, and provided for provincial autonomy in British India, a federation of Indian princes, and for a dual system of government at the centre based on the principle of dyarchy. The provisions of this Act were never fully implemented.

Indian Mutiny (1857–58) An uprising against British rule in India. It began as a mutiny of Indian sepoys in the army of the English *East India Company, commencing at Meerut on 10 May 1857, and spreading rapidly to Delhi and including most regiments of the Bengal army as well as a large section of the civil population in Uttar Pradesh and Madhya Pradesh. The immediate cause was the soldiers' refusal to handle new cartridges apparently greased with pig and cow fat (an outrage to Muslims and Hindus respectively). The mutineers seized Delhi. The rebels restored the former Mogul Emperor Bahadur Shah II to his throne, whereupon the movement spread to *Lucknow, which was besieged, and to Cawnpore (now Kanpur), where the massacre of the British garrison is believed to have been instigated by Tantia Topi, a Maratha Brahman who became the military leader of the rebels. The recapture of Delhi by forces from the Punjab on 14 September 1857 broke the back of the mutiny. Following the restoration of British control, the East India Company's rule was replaced by that of the British Crown.

Indian National Congress *See* CONGRESS, INDIAN NATIONAL.

Indian Ocean tsunami A tsunami in the Indian Ocean on 26 December 2004 that killed an estimated 230,000 people. It was caused by an undersea earthquake measuring 9.0 on the Richter scale off the north-western coast of Sumatra. Tsunamis in the Indian Ocean are comparatively rare and there was no warning system in place; the 2004 tsunami therefore struck largely without warning on coastlines that had not been evacuated. Indonesia and Sri Lanka suffered the highest casualties, with probable death tolls of 168,000 and 35,000

respectively. The economic damage was equally severe: in Indonesia it amounted to about $4.5 billion and in Sri Lanka, about $1.5 billion. The 2004 tsunami was the most destructive tsunami on record and possibly the most destructive natural disaster of any kind.

Indian reservations Land set aside in the USA for the occupancy and use of *Native Americans. The Canadian equivalents are called reserves. The reservations were first created by a policy inaugurated in 1786. President Andrew *Jackson first practised removal to reservations on a large scale after Congress passed the Indian Removal Act of 1830. This sent the Creek, Seminole, Chickasaw, Choctaw, and *Cherokee tribes to an "Indian territory" in modern Oklahoma. In all some 200 reservations were set up in over 40 states. All but a handful were on poor quality land and proved economically unviable, so furthering the indigenous peoples' poverty.

Indian technology Technology derived from the ancient civilizations of the Indian subcontinent. Although far less closely studied, the Harappan civilization, which flourished in the Indus Valley (in modern Pakistan) around 4000 years ago, ranks with those of Egypt, Mesopotamia, and China. The ancient town of Mohenjo-Daro covered 85 ha (210 acres), and had an advanced town-planning scheme. In historic times Indian science and technology has made important contributions to Western civilization. Wootz steel (a type of crucible steel made in southern India) was prized by the Romans. The great 8-m (26-foot) iron pillar at Delhi (5th century AD) testifies to the skill of early Indian metalworkers. Early Hindu surgeons such as Susruta performed advanced eye operations and practised lithotomy (surgical removal of a stone from the urinary tract) and plastic surgery. Variolation (a form of immunization) was used for protection against smallpox from at least the 5th century AD. Indian philosophers were skilled in astronomy and mathematics—especially algebra and geometry—and their decimal notation found its way to the West via the Arab world.

Indo-Chinese War (20 October–22 November 1962) A border skirmish between India and China in the Himalayan region, which China claimed had been wrongly given to India by the *McMahon Line decision in 1914. Chinese forces began an offensive across the McMahon Line into India. Indian forces retreated and Assam appeared to be at the mercy of China, when the latter announced a ceasefire and withdrew to the Tibetan side of the Line, while retaining parts of Ladakh in Kashmir. Some of the border areas are still disputed.

Indo-Greek dynasties Rulers of parts of north-west India from the 3rd to the 1st century BC. In 326 BC Alexander the Great's army had invaded India and explored the Indus valley. His direct impact was slight, but in the next century Greek commanders, who already held Bactria in Central Asia again crossed the Indus, this time to establish power in the Punjab. Their successors were driven out of India after 200 years, but the 'Yavana' (Greek) rulers had an important impact on art and architecture, astrology and medicine. Evidence for Greek activity in India comes mainly from their inscribed coins.

Indonesia (formerly **Dutch East Indies**)

Capital:	Jakarta
Area:	1,904,569 sq km (735,358 sq miles)
Population:	251,160,124 (2013 est)
Currency:	1 Indonesian rupiah = 100 sen
Religions:	Muslim 86.1%; Protestant 5.7%; Roman Catholic 3.0%; Hindu 1.8%
Ethnic Groups:	Javanese 40.6%; Sundanese 15.0%; Madurese 3.3%; minority groups
Languages:	Bahasa Indonesian (official); English; Dutch; Javanese, Sundanese, and many other local languages
International Organizations:	UN; ASEAN; Non-Aligned Movement; Colombo Plan; WTO

A country composed of hundreds of tropical islands in south-east Asia, in the region where the Pacific and the Indian Oceans meet.

Physical Its east-west length is greater than the width of Australia or the USA, for among its larger islands are included parts of New Guinea (Irian Jaya) and Borneo (Kalimantan) and all of Sumatra, Java, and Sulawesi (once Celebes). Among its smaller islands are Bali, Timor, Flores, and the Moluccas. This vast area lies at the edge of the Eurasian plate. It contains over 70 volcanoes, some periodically active like Krakatoa; and it is subject to severe earthquakes. While many of the beaches are black with volcanic mud, others are coral, with very clear water.

Economy The principal exports are oil, natural gas, electrical goods, plywood, textiles, and rubber. Over one-third of the population work in agriculture, important products being rubber, palm oil, poultry, and beef. Industries include oil, natural gas, textiles, and vehicles.

History The Hindu Srivijaya Empire, based on Palembang, flourished between the 7th and 13th centuries AD. Towards the end of the 12th century the Majapahit kingdom, which was based on Java began to dominate the area of present-day Indonesia. During the 16th century the area was occupied by the Portuguese, the British, and the Dutch. The Dutch East India Company had acquired control of most of the islands of Indonesia by the end of the 17th century, with headquarters in present-day Jakarta (then Batavia).

The islands were formed into the Netherlands-Indies in 1914. By the 1920s, indigenous political movements were demanding complete independence. Prominent here was *Sukarno's Indonesian Nationalist Party (*Partai Nasionalis Indonesia*), banned by the Dutch in the 1930s. The Japanese occupation of 1942–45 strengthened nationalist sentiments, and, taking advantage of the Japanese defeat in 1945, Sukarno proclaimed Indonesian independence and set up a republican government. Dutch attempts to reassert control were met with popular opposition (the *Indonesian Revolution), which resulted in the transfer of power in 1949. By 1957 parliamentary democracy had given way to the semi-dictatorship or 'Guided Democracy' of President Sukarno, a regime based on the original 1945 constitution, with a strong executive and special powers reserved for the army and bureaucracy. Sukarno's popularity began to wane after 1963, with the army and right-wing Muslim landlords becoming increasingly concerned about the influence of communists in government. Rampant inflation and peasant unrest brought the country to the brink of collapse in 1965–66 when the army under General Suharto (1921–) took advantage of a bungled coup by leftist officers to carry out a bloody purge of the Communist Party (PKI) and depose Sukarno (1967). Despite his initial success in rebuilding the economy and restoring credit with its Western capitalist backers, Suharto's regime remained authoritarian and repressive, moving ruthlessly against domestic political opponents. In 1976 Indonesia annexed the former Portuguese colony of East Timor (*see* TIMOR-LESTE), causing thousands of civilian deaths. The United Nations (UN) disputed the action and conflict between the independence movement and government forces in East Timor continued. In 1999 a referendum, organized by the UN, showed overwhelming support for independence. Local militias then embarked on a campaign to kill the leading supporters of independence and thousands of people fled. A UN peacekeeping force was sent in and East Timor finally became independent, as Timor-Leste, in 2002. Conflict also erupted in the province of Irian Jaya, part of the island of New Guinea, where a rebellion was staged in support of unification with *Papua New Guinea. New border arrangements agreed between the two countries put a stop to fighting in 1979, but conflict broke out again in 1984, causing many refugees to flee from Irian Jaya to Papua New Guinea. Accords were signed by Indonesia and Papua New Guinea over security and trade issues in 1992, but further clashes between government troops and separatist rebels occurred in 1993. There was growing demand for greater democracy in Indonesia in the early 1990s. While Suharto appeared to accept these demands, the activities of new pro-democracy organizations were met with government repression. In 1990–91 a separatist rebellion in the province of Aceh (Sumatra) was crushed. The arrest of pro-democracy campaigners in 1996 resulted in demonstrations and civil unrest. In 1997 the country faced an economic crisis with the collapse of the rupiah, which led to food riots and civil disorder. The International Monetary Fund provided a financial rescue package. Suharto was elected for a seventh term of office in 1998 but resigned in favour of his deputy, B. J. Habibie, following mass protests and rioting. In 1999 Indonesia's first free elections for 45 years were won by the opposition Democratic Party. Abdurrahman Wahid became President later the same year, but in 2001 was impeached for corruption and succeeded by the Vice-President, Megawati Sukarnoputri. In 2004 Sukarnoputri was defeated in Indonesia's first direct presidential elections by Susilo Bambang Yudhoyono. At the end of that year, the *Indian Ocean tsunami killed over 160,000 people in Indonesia, mainly in northern Sumatra. Joko Widodo was elected President in 2014 and promised major reforms.

Indonesian Revolution (1945–49) Nationalist struggle for independence from Dutch rule in *Indonesia. In 1945, *Sukarno proclaimed Indonesia's independence. Attempts by the Dutch to re-establish their colonial administration led to fighting which was temporarily brought to an end by a compromise agreement (1946). This provided for the establishment of a United States of Indonesia tied to the Netherlands under a federal constitution. But the nationalists refused to accept this, forcing the Dutch to launch a new offensive which recaptured most of the estate areas and ended in a ceasefire in 1947. A second Dutch 'police action' a year later increased international pressure and forced the Dutch to convene a conference at The Hague in 1949. As a result, all of the Dutch East Indies, with the exception of western New Guinea, were transferred to the new state of Indonesia in 1949. Western New Guinea (now Irian Jaya) came under Indonesian administration in 1963.

Indo-Pakistan War (September 1965) A border conflict between India and Pakistan following an attempt by Pakistan to assist Muslim opponents of Indian rule in Kashmir. Fighting spread to the Punjab, but a UN ceasefire was accepted and by the Tashkent Declaration of 11 January 1966, a troop withdrawal was agreed. A renewal of frontier fighting occurred in 1971, at a time when *Bangladesh was seeking independence from Pakistan.

indulgence The cancelling by the Christian Church of the temporal punishment still owed for sins after they have been forgiven. The idea was found in various forms in the early Church, but as a widespread doctrine it dated from the 11th century, especially with the granting of indulgences to those who went on *Crusades. They could be obtained by saying certain prayers or by performing specified good works, such as helping the needy, taking part in a Crusade, or giving money to churches. It was through the connection with money payments that indulgences were most open to abuse, and that they became a focus for criticism by Martin *Luther and others during the Protestant *Reformation.

Indus civilization A highly developed urban civilization in the lower valley of the River Indus, in South Asia, which flourished from about 2500 to 1500 BC. Archaeological excavation, which began in the 1920s, is still being carried out and many important questions remain unanswered. City life seems to have ended abruptly *c*.1500 BC, possible causes being flooding, alteration of the course of the Indus, overpopulation, or an *Aryan invasion.

Among more than 70 sites now excavated, those at *Mohenjo-Daro, Harappa, Kalibangan,

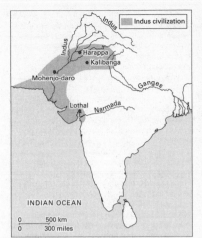

Indus civilization. Like other early civilizations in Egypt and Mesopotamia, the Indus civilization flourished in a region that despite low rainfall was irrigated by a great river. The civilization covered a very wide area and the discovery of new sites is constantly extending the known range of its cultural influence. The citadels of Mohenjo-daro and Harappa were both built on artificial mounds on riverside sites. Major buildings were substantial and the system of sanitation and drainage with extensive brick culverts, one of the hallmarks of the Indus civilization, implies careful planning under close state control.

and Lothal seem particularly important for revealing a civilization based on the use of bronze, copper, and stone tools, and also city planning, including granaries, baths, drains, and straight streets. There is evidence of contact with Mesopotamia, but the script, known by the discovery of seals which were probably used in trade, has not yet been deciphered. The nature of religious worship is also uncertain, although stone and terracotta figures, as well as motifs on the seals, suggest links between the Indus cults and later post-Aryan Hindu religious concepts. The civilization provides evidence of an important stage in India's past, and of one of the world's first highly developed urban communities.

industrialization The process of change from a basic agrarian economy to an industrialized one. It was first experienced by Britain in the *Industrial Revolution and at much the same time in the New England states of the USA,

from which it spread along the eastern seaboard and, after the American Civil War, across the continent. Belgium was the first continental European country to experience industrialization, which then spread to north-east France and, particularly after 1870, to Germany, where its growth was so rapid that by 1900 German industrial production had surpassed that of Britain. During those 30 years all industrialized nations saw rapid development and expansion in such heavy industries as iron and steel, chemicals, engineering, and shipbuilding. Japan was the first non-European power to become industrialized, which it had done by the end of the 19th century. The former Soviet Union saw industrialization on a massive scale under Stalin.

In many less developed countries, industrialization is equated with development, that is modernization, progress, and economic growth, a viewpoint often, though not always, justified by the circumstances of the individual countries. In recent decades there has been rapid industrialization in many developing countries, in particular those known as the newly industrializing countries; economic growth in these countries has generally exceeded that in those benefiting from ample natural resources, excepting certain oil-rich countries. Development plans favouring industrialization via import substitution have been superseded in many countries by policies of export promotion. Industrialization has been welcomed as providing employment for growing populations whom the land could no longer support; but since much industry is located in cities, there have been associated problems of massive urbanization and, often, pollution of the environment. The relationship between industrialization and development continues, therefore, to be debated. Since the latter decades of the 20th century, the phenomenon of deindustrialization has been witnessed in industrialized countries. This means that in these countries manufacturing employment accounts for a shrinking proportion of total employment, as a result of the growth both of manufacturing productivity and of tertiary employment.

Industrial Revolution The change in the organization of manufacturing industry that transformed Britain from a rural to an urban economy. The process began in England in the 18th century as a result of improved agricultural techniques, which freed workers from the land and made it possible to provide food for a large non-agricultural population. A combination of economic, political, and social factors, including internal peace, the availability of coal and iron ore, the availability of capital, and the development of steam power—and later the internal-combustion engine and electricity—led to the construction of factories, which were built for the mass production of manufactured goods. A new organization of work known as the factory system increased the division and specialization of labour. The textile industry was the prime example of industrialization and created a demand for machines, and for tools for their manufacture, which stimulated further mechanization. Improved transport became necessary and was provided by the expansion of the canal system and the subsequent development of railways and roads. The skills acquired during this period were exported to other countries and this helped to make Britain the richest and most powerful nation in the world by the middle of the 19th century. Simultaneously the process of industrialization radically changed the face of British society, leading to the growth of large industrial cities, particularly in the Midlands, the North, Scotland, and South Wales. As the population shifted from the countryside to the cities a series of social and economic problems arose, the result of such factors as low wages, slum housing, and the use of child labour. Similar changes followed in other European countries, in the USA, and in Japan during the 19th century, while in the 20th century Eastern Europe, China, India, and South-East Asia have undergone a similar industrialization process.

Information Revolution The radical changes wrought by computer technology on the storage of and access to information since the mid-1980s. Information previously stored on paper and manipulated manually is increasingly held on computer networks, which allow instant retrieval from anywhere in the world and sophisticated computerized processing in ways and at speeds that have not previously been possible. Also, using the same computer networks, individuals can easily communicate with each other worldwide and share information. Three factors have driven this Information Revolution. First, information-based occupations grew in importance throughout the 20th century (for example, nearly all office work deals with information), which produced a latent demand for more efficient storage and processing systems. These were provided by the second factor: the advent of cheap computing power in the 1980s and (especially) the 1990s that followed the development of the microprocessor in the 1970s. Previously, computer technology had been so

expensive that it could only be used by large organizations for special purposes; now, it was so cheap that its cost was no longer a significant issue. Also, the spread of cheap personal computers with user-friendly operating systems meant that computer use was no longer confined to the computer specialist, which enabled vastly more people to make direct and convenient use of computerized information. The third factor, which made a crucial contribution from the early 1990s, was the *Internet: a global computer network already in place that could be utilized to connect information providers and information consumers anywhere in the world. The Information Revolution has had major effects on both business and personal life. Organizations can make information readily available to staff via corporate intranets (private networks that work in the same way as the Internet); retailing companies hold less stock than formerly, relying on the instant availability of stock-control information from electronic point-of-sale terminals to allow just-in-time purchasing; many questions can be answered quickly by a search of the Internet, which is also used to buy products and services; and people can communicate worldwide via such Internet-based technologies as email and *social media. In the 21st century, developments in computing, telephony, and the Internet came together in such devices as tablets—truly portable computers—and smartphones—handheld computers that also function as telephones. These allow people to be always connected to their contacts and to the Internet, and a generation is growing up that regards such facilities as normal. Old skills have become redundant while new ones are in demand: jobs have declined in such areas as banking and printing, but new professions have been created, for example web designer and games developer. This has led to concerns over the potential for a growing economic and social divide between those people with the skills to take advantage of the Information Revolution and those without. There are also non-economic issues, in particular concerns over privacy and whether the large amount of personal information held in computer systems is adequately protected. The answers to these questions are currently unclear. The Information Revolution is still in its early stages and the full consequences of its opportunities and problems have yet to emerge.

Inkatha Freedom Party A South African Zulu political organization under the leadership of Chief Mangosuthu *Buthelezi. The party was founded as the Inkatha movement by Buthelezi in 1975 to counter the Xhosa-dominated *African National Congress (ANC). Unlike the ANC, which sought to overthrow the apartheid system through armed struggle, Inkatha was pledged to represent Zulu interests by working within the *Bantu homeland system established by the White regime. From the early 1980s onwards, increasingly violent clashes took place between supporters of the two groups, resulting in an estimated death toll of over 5000 people. The Inkatha movement became a political party in 1990 and changed its name to the Inkatha Freedom Party. In South Africa's first multiracial elections in 1994, Inkatha initially boycotted the poll but eventually participated. It won 43 seats in the new national assembly and Buthelezi was appointed home affairs minister. Inkatha's standing was damaged in the 1990s by revelations that it had been covertly funded and armed by the security forces in the 1980s, in an attempt to increase ethnic tension and destabilize the ANC. It lost ground to the ANC in the 1999, 2004, and 2009 elections, and went into opposition in 2004.

Innocent III (1160–1216) Pope (1198–1216). As pope he became an active and vigorous reformer of the Church. He reasserted control over the *Papal States and was acknowledged as the overlord of *Sicily. In Germany he asserted the pope's right to choose between two rival candidates for the imperial crown; he eventually supported *Frederick II's claims provided that he did homage for Sicily. He intervened in English affairs, excommunicating King *John for refusing to recognize Stephen *Langton as Archbishop of Canterbury and declaring *Magna Carta void; he also attempted to curb the independence of *Philip II of France.

Inönü, Ismet (1884–1973) Turkish soldier and statesman. He served against the Greeks during the Turkish war of independence (1919–22). He was chosen by *Atatürk as first Prime Minister of the Turkish republic (1923–37) and in 1938 succeeded him as President, remaining in power until the Democrat victory of 1950. Inönü remained leader of the Republican People's Party and served again as Prime Minister (1961–65) in the aftermath of the 1960 military coup.

Inquisition (or **Holy Office**) An ecclesiastical court established c.1232 for the detection and punishment of heretics, at a time when sectarian groups were threatening not only the orthodoxy of the Catholic religion but the stability of contemporary society. The Inquisition came into being when *Frederick II issued an edict entrusting the hunting-out of heretics to state inquisitors; Pope Gregory IX claimed it as a papal responsiblity and appointed inquisitors, mostly drawn from the Franciscan and Dominican orders. He had previously ordered the Dominicans to crush the *Albigensians (1223). Those accused of heresy who refused to confess were tried before an inquisitor and jury and punishments were harsh, including confiscation of goods, torture, and death. The Index (a list of books condemned by the Church) was issued by the Congregation of the Inquisition in 1557. The *Spanish Inquisition was a separate organization established in 1479 by the Spanish monarchy with papal approval. In 1965 the Holy Office was renamed the Sacred Congregation for the Doctrine of the Faith.

intelligence services Government organizations dedicated to the collection and evaluation of information, primarily about the intentions of other countries that are seen as adversaries. Such information can be economic, political, or military, and can relate either to general trends or to specific groups such as terrorists, individuals, and institutions. Much intelligence is gathered from public sources, but intelligence services have also developed extensive covert activities, designed to protect and enhance national security. They have also acquired functions in counter-intelligence, in order to safeguard their own operations and to manipulate those of adversaries. **MI5** and **MI6** are the Security Service and the Secret Intelligence Service in Britain. The sphere of MI5, founded in 1909, includes internal security and counter-intelligence on British territory while MI6, formed in 1912, covers all areas outside the UK. During World War II, MI6's successful cooperation with *resistance movements overseas contributed considerably to the outcome of the war. Since then, however, it has received adverse public exposure through disclosures that some of its employees, notably intellectuals recruited in Cambridge in the 1930s, such as Philby, Burgess, Maclean, and Blunt, were double agents whose final allegiance lay with the communist bloc. Strong evidence emerged in the 1980s of MI5's extra-constitutional role during the years of the Labour governments (1974–79), which it was seeking to destabilize. A campaign for more liberal legislation, which would reduce government powers to keep secret matters that should be publicly known, has so far largely failed. Although a Security Service Act of November 1989 placed MI5 and MI6 on a 'statutory basis', the accompanying Official Secrets Act increased government powers against 'unauthorized disclosures' of official information. Stella Rimington, director-general of MI5 from 1992 to 1995, was the first head of MI5 whose identity was officially confirmed. With the ending of the Cold War, MI5 and MI6 have sought a new role, and in 1995 plans to use them in the fight against organized crime were announced. Since *September 11, 2001, increased priority has been given to combating the threat of terrorism. The **Central Intelligence Agency** (CIA) is a US government agency. It was established by Congress in 1947 and is responsible to the President through the National Security Council. Its work consists of gathering and evaluating foreign intelligence, undertaking counter-intelligence operations overseas, and organizing secret political intervention and psychological warfare operations in foreign areas. The CIA has acquired immense power and influence, employing thousands of agents overseas, and it disposes of a large budget that is not subjected to Congressional scrutiny. During the 1980s it was actively involved in Nicaragua, Afghanistan, and Iran. In 1986 the CIA was criticized for its involvement in the Irangate scandal (*see* REAGAN, RONALD). During the 1990s it too sought to redefine its role following the end of the Cold War. The CIA was again criticized after the terrorist attacks of September 11, which it failed to anticipate; and for its role in events leading to the 2003 *Iraq War, the case for which was largely based on its inaccurate assessment of Iraq's ability to develop weapons of mass destruction.

intendant An agent of the French king under the *ancien régime. The office was developed as an emergency measure to counter disobedience during the 1630s, building on an earlier practice of sending royal officials from the central councils on tours of inspection in the provinces. Under *Richelieu and *Louis XIV their authority was extended into every sphere of administration, and they became the principal link between the central government and the provinces. They supervised local courts, oversaw the tax system, and kept the crown informed about the political and economic situation in their *généralités* (administrative units). The office was abolished at the Revolution, but many of the same functions were later performed by the *préfets*.

International Bank for Reconstruction and Development *See* WORLD BANK.

International Brigades International groups of volunteers in the *Spanish Civil War. They were largely communist, on the side of the republic against *Franco. At no time were there more than 20,000 in the Brigades. They fought mainly in the defence of Madrid (1936) and in the battle of the River Ebro (1938).

International Development Association *See* WORLD BANK.

Internationals Associations formed to unite socialist and communist organizations throughout the world. There were four Internationals. The First (1864), at which *Marx was a leading figure, met in London but was riven by disputes between Marxists and anarchists. By 1872 it had become clear that divisions were irreconcilable and it was disbanded (1876). The Second, or Socialist, International (1889) aimed at uniting the numerous new socialist parties that had sprung up in Europe. With headquarters in Brussels, it was better organized and by 1912 it contained representatives from all European countries and also from the USA, Canada, and Japan. It did not survive the outbreak of World War I, when its plan to prevent war by general strike and revolution was swamped by a wave of nationalism in all countries. The Third, usually known as the Communist International or *Comintern (1919), was founded by *Lenin and the *Bolsheviks to promote world revolution and a world communist state. It drew up the Twenty-One Points of pure communist doctrine to be accepted by all seeking membership. This resulted in splits between communist parties, which accepted the Points, and socialist parties, which did not. The Comintern increasingly became an instrument of the Soviet Union's foreign policy. In 1943 Stalin disbanded it. The Fourth International (1938), of comparatively little importance, was founded by *Trotsky and his followers in opposition to *Stalin. After Trotsky's assassination (1940) it was controlled by two Belgian communists, Pablo and Germain, whose bitter disagreements had by 1953 ended any effective action.

Internet A worldwide computer network. Technically, the Internet is an inter-network: a network that links many smaller networks into a uniform whole. The origins of the Internet are usually traced to ARPANET, the first multi-site network, which was established in 1969 under the auspices of the US Department of Defense to allow universities and other government-sponsored research institutions to exchange information. The Internet grew steadily and was genuinely global by the late 1980s, but was still largely restricted to specialist use. This changed in the 1990s because of two factors. First, in 1989 the **Worldwide Web** was introduced, which provided a simple technology for sharing information over the Internet in a user-friendly way. Second, the spread of personal computers (*see* INFORMATION REVOLUTION) vastly increased the number of people with potential access to such information. Business became aware of the possibilities of the Internet and drove its rapid expansion from the mid-1990s. Progress was not always smooth (*see* DOTCOM BUBBLE), but within ten years the Internet had transformed many aspects of life throughout the world. It is now assumed that an organization of any significance will have its own website, on which information about its activities can be found and products or services purchased; global email, *social media, and other Internet-based communication technologies have revolutionized the way people and companies communicate; and a generation has grown up for which life without the Internet and its facilities would be inconceivable.

intifada (Arabic, 'uprising') Two Palestinian uprisings against Israeli occupation of the West Bank and Gaza Strip. The **first intifada** lasted from 1987 to 1991 and was harshly repressed by Israel; however, it persuaded many people of the need for a political solution and contributed to secret Israeli–PLO negotiations. A framework for peace, the Declaration of Principles, was signed by the Israelis and Palestinians in 1993, but was not fully implemented. The **second intifada** began in 2000 in protest against the stalled peace process and continued Israeli occupation. Militant Palestinian suicide bombers targeted Israeli civilians, and the Israeli army reoccupied parts of the West Bank that had previously been relinquished. A ceasefire was established in 2005 following the death of Yasser *Arafat, whom Israel held responsible for failing to curb the insurgents.

Intolerable Acts *See* COERCIVE ACTS.

Inuit (or **Innuit**) A member of a North American people that inhabits Alaska, Nunavut region in northern Canada, Greenland, and eastern Siberia. A semi-nomadic hunting and gathering people, they were noted for their adaptation to a harsh environment and were sometimes called Eskimos. Their languages belong to the Inuit-Aleut family and are divided into two main branches: the Inupik or Inuk (spoken in Greenland, Labrador, the Arctic coast of Canada, and northern Alaska) and the Yupik or Yuk (spoken in southern Alaska and Siberia). There are approximately 50,000 Inuit in Greenland, 35,000 in Alaska, 50,000 in Canada, and several hundred in Siberia.

Invergordon mutiny (1931) A mutiny by sailors of the British Atlantic Fleet at the naval port on Cromarty Firth, Scotland. Severe pay cuts imposed by the *National government led the ratings to refuse to go on duty. The cuts were slightly revised but foreign holders of sterling were alarmed; an Act suspending the gold standard was rushed through Parliament, but the value of the pound fell by more than a quarter. The mutiny ended and the ratings' ringleaders were discharged from the navy.

Iqbal, Muhammad (1877–1938) Indian philosopher, poet, and political leader. He took an active part in politics in the Punjab and was President of the *Muslim League in 1930 when he advanced the idea of a separate Muslim state in north-west India, the beginning of the concept of Pakistan.

Iran (formerly **Persia**)

Capital:	Tehran
Area:	1,648,195 sq km (636,372 sq miles)
Population:	79,853,900 (2013 est)
Currency:	1 rial = 100 dinars
Religions:	Shia Muslim 90.0%; Sunni Muslim 9.0%
Ethnic Groups:	Persian 61.0%; Azeri 16.0%; Kurdish 10.0%; Luri 6.0%
Languages:	Persian (official); Azeri Turkish; Kurdish; minority languages
International Organizations:	UN; OPEC; Colombo Plan; Non-Aligned Movement

A country of the Middle East in central-west Asia. Bordering on Turkey and Iraq on the west, Turkmenistan on the north, and Afghanistan and Pakistan on the east, it has a northern coast on the Caspian Sea and a southern coast on the Gulf and Arabian Sea.

Physical Iran consists mostly of arid tableland surrounded by mountains (the Elburz in the north and the Zagros in the south-west) and containing extensive salt deserts: the Great Salt Desert or Dasht-e-Kavir in the north and the Dasht-e-Lut in the south-east.

Economy Iran's economy is dominated by an inefficient state-controlled sector, and potential growth is further limited by international sanctions. Crude-oil extraction is the main industry and provides over three-quarters of export earnings. Other industries include oil products, fertilizers, caustic soda, and textiles. Wheat, rice and other grains, and sugar are the principal agricultural crops. Substantial mineral deposits of coal, copper, and iron ore are relatively undeveloped.

History Early Persian dynasties included the *Achaemenids, whose rule ended with Alexander the Great's defeat of Darius III, and the *Sassanians who were overthrown by the Arabs. Since the fall of the Sassanian empire in 642, it has been under the rule of Islam. Persians were prominent in the empires of their Arab, Seljuk, and Mongol overlords for nine centuries, until Ismail I established a strong Persian state and converted the population to Shiite Islam. After *Abbas I Safavid power declined until the Qajar dynasty, founded by Agha Mohammad Khan and ruling from Tehran, took power in 1796.

Trade between Muslim countries and European powers had developed throughout the 19th century and both Russia and Britain were anxious to increase their influence over the Qajar dynasty in Iran. In 1906 Muzaffar al-Din granted a constitution; his successor sought to suppress the *Majlis* (Parliament) which had been granted, but was himself deposed. In 1901 oil concessions were granted to foreign companies to exploit what is estimated as one-tenth of the world's oil reserves. In 1909 the Anglo-Persian Oil Company (later BP) was founded and southern Iran came within Britain's sphere of influence, while Russia dominated northern Iran. Following the *Russian Revolution of 1917 British troops invaded Russia from Iran; at the end of this 'war of intervention' an Iranian officer, Reza Khan, emerged and seized power (1921), backed by the British. In 1925 he deposed the Qajar dynasty and proclaimed himself as *Reza Shah Pahlavi. In World War II Iran was occupied by British and Soviet forces and was used as a route for sending supplies to the Soviet Union. The Shah abdicated (1941) and was replaced by his son Muhammad Reza Shah *Pahlavi. It took him 20 years to establish political supremacy, during which time one of his Prime Ministers, Mussadegh, nationalized the Anglo-Iranian Oil Company (1951). In 1961 the Shah initiated a land-reform scheme and a programme of modernization, the so-called 'White Revolution' (1963–71). The secularization of the state led Islamic leaders such as *Khomeini into exile (1964), while popular

discontent with secular Western, especially US, influence was masked by ever-rising oil revenues, which financed military repression, as well as industrialization. Riots in 1978 were followed by the imposition of martial law. Khomeini coordinated a rebellion from his exile in France. The fall and exile of the Shah in 1979 was followed by the return of Khomeini and the establishment of an Islamic Republic. This proved strong enough to sustain the Iran Hostage Crisis of 1979–81 and to fight the long and costly *Iran–Iraq War (1980–88). Following the death of Khomeini in 1989 and a confused power struggle, Hashemi Rafsanjani was elected President. A moderate pragmatist, he achieved the restoration of good relations with Western states without unduly alienating Islamic fundamentalists. Rafsanjani's programme of social and economic reforms, however, caused discontent in Iran and serious rioting occurred in several major cities in mid-1992. Rafsanjani nevertheless secured a majority for his supporters in the *Majlis* following the 1992 general election; in 1993 he was re-elected President. In the early 1990s Iran's relations with the USA were strained by Iran's hostility to American interference in the region following the Gulf War and to the Israeli–PLO peace accord, signed in September 1993. The question of Iran's military expansion also caused friction. In 1995 the USA announced complete trade and investment sanctions against Iran in an attempt to halt the country's alleged involvement in international terrorism and its rumoured nuclear weapons programme. The Iranian leadership condemned the sanctions, while the country's economy continued to be beset with crises. In 1997 presidential elections were won by the moderate Mohammed Khatami, who was re-elected in 2001. US hostility increased from 2002, when President George W. *Bush accused Iran of developing weapons of mass destruction and of assisting terrorism. Legislative elections in 2004 produced a conservative majority, with many reformist candidates being disqualified by the clerical authorities, and in 2005 the hard-line Mahmoud Ahmadinejad was elected President. He was re-elected in controversial elections in 2009: the opposition candidate, Mir Hossein Mousavi, claimed victory, but after an enquiry Ahmadinejad was declared the winner and demonstrations supporting Mousavi were suppressed. Doubts about the peaceful purpose of Iran's nuclear research programme led to UN sanctions being imposed in 2006 and extended in 2009. Tensions began to ease with the election of the more moderate Hassan *Rouhani as President in 2013.

Irangate scandal *See* REAGAN, RONALD.

Iran Hostage Crisis (4 November 1979–20 January 1981) A prolonged crisis between *Iran and the USA. In the aftermath of Iran's Islamic Revolution, followers of the Ayatollah *Khomeini alleged US complicity in military plots to restore the Shah, *Muhammad Reza Shah Pahlavi, and seized the US Embassy in Teheran, taking 66 US citizens hostage. All efforts of President *Carter to free the hostages failed, including economic measures and an abortive rescue bid by US helicopters in April 1980. The crisis dragged on until 20 January 1981, when Algeria successfully mediated, and the hostages were freed. It seriously weakened Carter's bid for presidential re-election in November 1980, and he lost to Ronald *Reagan.

Iran–Iraq War (1980–88) A border dispute between *Iran and *Iraq, which developed into a major war. In 1980 President Saddam *Hussein of Iraq abrogated the 1975 agreement granting Iran some 518 sq km (200 sq miles) of border area to the north of the Shatt-al-Arab waterway in return for assurances by Iran to cease military assistance to the Kurdish minority in Iraq, which was fighting for independence. Calling for a revision of the agreement to the demarcation of the border along Shatt-al-Arab, a return to Arab ownership of the three islands in the Strait of Hormuz (seized by Iran in 1971), and for the granting of autonomy to minorities inside Iran, the Iraqi army engaged in a border skirmish in a disputed but relatively unimportant area, and followed this by an armoured assault into Iran's vital oil-producing region. The Iraqi offensive met strong Iranian resistance, and Iran recaptured territory from the Iraqis. In 1985 Iraqi planes destroyed a partially constructed nuclear power plant in Bushehr, followed by bombing of civilian targets which in turn led to Iranian shelling of Basra and Baghdad. The war entered a new phase in 1987 when Iran increased hostilities against commercial shipping in and around the Gulf, resulting in naval escorts being sent to the area by the USA and other nations. Senior officers of the Iranian army began to lose confidence as their troops suffered from shortages of arms and equipment, while Iraq continued to be supplied by the West. Early in 1988 the UN Security Council called for a ceasefire. Iraq agreed, but not Iran. Skilful negotiations by the UN Secretary-General, *Pérez de Cuéllar, however, achieved an armistice in July and a peace settlement in August. Nothing had been gained, but an estimated 1.5 million lives were lost.

Iraq

Capital:	Baghdad
Area:	438,317 sq km (169,235 sq miles)
Population:	31,858,481 (2013 est)
Currency:	1 New Iraqi dinar = 1000 fils
Religions:	Shia Muslim 63.0%; Sunni Muslim 34.0%; Christian or other 3.0%
Ethnic Groups:	Arab: between 75.0% and 80.0%; Kurdish: between 15.0% and 20.0%; Turkoman and Assyrian minorities
Languages:	Arabic, Kurdish (both official); minority languages
International Organizations:	UN; Arab League; Non-Aligned Movement; OAPEC; OPEC

A West Asian country bordering on Turkey on the north, Iran on the east, Syria and Jordan on the west, and Saudi Arabia and Kuwait on the south.

Physical A waterway, Shatt al-Arab, at the delta of the Euphrates, gives Iraq access to the Gulf in the south-east. The Euphrates and its tributary the Tigris traverse the whole country from north-west to south-east, bringing silt to a vast depression, which would be widely cultivable were it not for salinity and erosion. This land, once known as Mesopotamia, was the site of early civilizations. To the north are mountains and desert plateaux, to the west all is desert, and the climate is one of extremes.

Economy The economy is dependent on exports of oil, which constitute four-fifths of foreign exchange earnings. Other industries include chemicals, textiles, and leather; agriculture produces cereals, rice, vegetables, and livestock. Economic development is hampered by political and social instability following the *Iraq War, outdated infrastructure, and corruption.

History As *Mesopotamia, the area of present-day Iraq is known as 'the cradle of civilization'. It became a Muslim state in the 7th century AD following conquest by Arabia. It became a part of the Ottoman Empire in 1534, remaining such until the outbreak of World War I when the Turks were driven out by British forces. Following the British Mesopotamian Campaign in World War I, the country was occupied by Britain, who was then granted responsibility under a League of Nations mandate (1920–32). In 1921 Britain offered to recognize amir Ahd Allah Faisal, son of *Hussein ibn Ali, sharif of Mecca, as King Faisal. British influence remained strong until the fall of the monarchy in 1958. Further political rivalries ended with the 1968 coup, which led to rapid economic and social modernization paid for by oil revenues and guided by the general principles of the Ba'ath Socialist Party. A heterogeneous society, of many ethnic and religious groupings, Iraq has long been troubled by periodic struggles for independence by its *Kurds. It has often been isolated in Arab affairs by its assertiveness in foreign policy, though the long and bloody *Iran–Iraq War launched against Khomeini's Iran by President Saddam *Hussein in 1980 received financial support from formerly critical monarchist Arab states. During 1990 a frontier dispute with Kuwait was followed by the Iraqi invasion and an international crisis, leading to UN sanctions and to the *Gulf War. Following the end of the war, widespread uprisings among both Shia and Kurdish peoples were brutally suppressed. UN-imposed peace terms, a prerequisite to the lifting of sanctions, included the destruction of chemical and other weapons, acceptance of UN inspectors, and disclosure of Iraq's nuclear capability. Some progress was made, but in 1992 Iraq refused to accept a UN proposal that oil sales be resumed for humanitarian purposes pending resolution of outstanding differences. In mid-1992 Iraqi Kurds, who controlled an area of northern Iraq, elected their own national assembly. Renewed attacks by government forces on the Shia communities in southern Iraq in 1992–93 led to the establishment by Western powers of an exclusion zone over the area. Fighting between rival Kurdish groups broke out in northern Iraq in 1994 and continued in 1995–96. The United Nations continued to renew the period of economic sanctions on Iraq, while Iraq continued to reject the UN resolution to sell its oil to fund humanitarian efforts as a violation of its sovereignty. In 1996 government forces attacked Kurdish towns in the north of the country. In response, the USA bombed strategic targets in southern Iraq. Iraq's failure to cooperate with UN weapons inspectors led to recurrent crises and air strikes by Britain and the USA in 1998 and 2001. From late 2001 the USA adopted an

increasingly hard-line attitude to Iraq, which culminated in the *Iraq War of 2003 and the removal of Saddam's regime. The USA and its coalition partners—primarily the United Kingdom—acted as occupying powers and carried through a programme to establish a democratic successor regime: an interim government was established in 2004, and a transitional assembly was elected in January 2005. The assembly drafted a new democratic constitution, which was approved by referendum in October 2005; elections under its provisions were held in December and a government under Nuri al-Maliki was established in May 2006. However, Iraq's internal security was undermined by a terrorist insurgency, based in the Sunni community but with suspected *al-Qaeda support, and coalition forces remained in the country until 2011. In 2010 disputed elections led to an eight-month delay before a national unity coalition government was formed, again under al-Maliki. Continuing problems included the reconstruction of Iraq's infrastructure and economy, and the reconciliation of the formerly dominant but minority Sunni community to the newly powerful position of the more numerous Shias. From early 2014 the extreme Sunni jihadist group *Islamic State (IS) took control of large areas of northern and western Iraq, including the country's second city, Mosul , and imposed strict Islamic law. It also launched brutal attacks on the Christian and Yazidi communities. In August fears that Islamic State might capture the Kurdish capital of Irbil led to US air strikes. Al-Maliki resigned as Prime Minister and was replaced by Haider al-Abadi.

Iraq War (March–April 2003) A war between US-led forces and Iraq. In the context of the USA's ongoing *war on terrorism, in 2002 President George W. *Bush threatened military action to remove Saddam *Hussein's regime, which the USA claimed to be developing weapons of mass destruction. US forces, supported by small British and Australian contingents, invaded Iraq from Kuwait on 21 March 2003 on the grounds that Iraq had failed to cooperate with UN weapons inspectors; the UN itself, however, had not given explicit approval for such a course of action. The Iraqi army was no match for the invaders. Baghdad was taken by US forces on 9 April, and the fall of Tikrit on 14 April marked the end of the military campaign. The justice and legality of the invasion provoked much debate, not least in the participating countries, and subsequent events only increased this controversy. In particular, investigations in 2004 established that Saddam's regime had possessed neither weapons of mass destruction nor a current ability to produce them. More generally, the problems of establishing a peaceful, stable, and democratic successor regime in Iraq proved greater than anticipated, necessitating continued coalition involvement until 2011, which was increasingly unpopular. The coalition partners continued to justify the war on the grounds that it had removed a tyrant and spread democracy and freedom.

Ireland An island of the British Isles, lying west of Great Britain. Four-fifths of it is occupied by the Irish Republic (*see* IRELAND, REPUBLIC OF) and the remainder by *Northern Ireland, which is part of the United Kingdom. Settled by the Celts, the country became divided into independent tribal territories over which the lords of Tara exercised nominal suzerainty. Christianity reached Ireland, probably in the 4th century, to be consolidated by the work of St Patrick, and after the breakup of the Roman Empire the country became for a time a leading cultural centre, with the monasteries fostering learning and missionary work. English invasions began in the 12th century under Henry II, but the authority that he established was never secure and by the 16th century was confined to an area around Dublin (the English Pale) until the Tudors succeeded in extending it over the whole of the island. Revolts against English rule, and against the imposition of Protestantism (which met with unexpectedly stubborn resistance), resulted in the **plantation** of Ireland by English (and later Scottish) families on confiscated land in an attempt to anglicize the country and secure its allegiance. In Ulster in particular the descendants of such settlers retained a distinctive identity. After an unsuccessful rebellion in 1798, political union of Britain and Ireland followed in 1801. In spite of genuine efforts towards its success Ireland sank deeper into destitution. A share of Britain's industrial prosperity reached Protestant Ulster, but the rest of the island found its agricultural assets dropping in value. Unscrupulous *absentee landlords undermined the ability of the local population to make a living and at the failure of the potato crop (Ireland's staple) in the 1840s about a million people died in the famine, a million more fled abroad. The Home Rule movement, led by Parnell, failed to achieve its aims in the 19th century and implementation of a bill passed in 1914 was delayed by the outbreak of World War I. An armed uprising at Easter, 1916, was suppressed. Ireland was partitioned by the Anglo-Irish Treaty of 1921, which gave dominion status to Ireland with the exception of six of

the counties of Ulster (Northern Ireland), whose Protestant majority wished to preserve the Union and which remained part of the United Kingdom.

Ireland, Northern *See* NORTHERN IRELAND.

Ireland, Republic of

Capital:	Dublin
Area:	70,273 sq km (27,133 sq miles)
Population:	4,775,982 (2013 est)
Currency:	1 euro = 100 cents
Religions:	Roman Catholic 84.7%; Church of Ireland (Anglican) 2.7%; other Christian 2.7%
Ethnic Groups:	Irish 84.5%; other White 9.8%; Asian and Black minorities
Languages:	English, Irish (both official)
International Organizations:	EU; OECD; UN; Council of Europe; OSCE; Euro-Atlantic Partnership Council; WTO

A country in western Europe comprising four-fifths of the island of *Ireland, to the west of Great Britain.

Physical A flat and fertile plain surrounds a central lake, Lough Ree, and the basin of the River Shannon. It is surrounded by coastal areas of great beauty: the Wicklow Mountains in the south-east reach to nearly 1000 m (3300 feet); the Connemara Mountains in the west stand up above great lakes, while those of Kerry in the south-west reach to over 1000 m (3282 feet) and point like rugged fingers to the sea. Many islands, among them Aran, lie in the deep bays of the western coast, where there are sandy beaches among the rocks.

Economy Formerly dependent on agriculture, Ireland now has a diverse economy with industry and services predominant. Major exports include machinery and equipment, computers, chemicals, medical devices, pharmaceuticals, and food and animal products. A favourable tax regime has made Ireland the European base of several multinational corporations, especially in the information technology sector. A long boom from the 1990s was followed by a financial and economic crisis after 2008.

History After years of intermittent fighting, the Anglo-Irish Treaty of December 1921, concluded by Lloyd George with the *Sinn Fein leaders, gave separate *dominion status to Ireland (as the Irish Free State) with the exception of six of the counties of Ulster, which formed the state of *Northern Ireland. Irish republicans led by *de Valera rejected the agreement and fought a civil war against the Irish Free State forces, but were defeated in 1923. After the *Fíanna Fáil victory in the election of 1932, de Valera began to sever the Irish Free State's remaining connections with Great Britain. In 1937 a new constitution established it as a sovereign state with an elected president; the power of the British Crown was ended and the office of governor-general abolished. The title of Irish Free State was replaced by Ireland (in Irish, Eire). An agreement in 1938 ended the British occupation of certain naval bases in Ireland. Having remained neutral in World War II, Ireland left the *Commonwealth of Nations and was recognized as an independent republic in 1949. De Valera was elected President in 1959. He was succeeded as Taoiseach (Prime Minister) by Sean *Lemass (1959–66) and Jack *Lynch (1966–73). In 1973 Ireland joined the European Community (now the *European Union) and a *Fine Gael–Labour coalition led by Liam *Cosgrave came to power. Subsequent governments were controlled alternately by the Fíanna Fáil under Charles *Haughey (1979–81; 1982; 1987–92) and the Fine Gael–Labour coalition under Dr Garret *Fitzgerald (1981–82; 1982–87). In November 1985 Ireland signed the Anglo-Irish Accord (the Hillsborough Agreement) giving the republic a consultative role in the government of Northern Ireland. The election as President, in December 1990, of Mary *Robinson, of the Irish Labour Party, represented a move towards greater liberalism within Irish society. In 1992 Haughey was replaced by Albert *Reynolds, who resigned in 1994 following the collapse of his coalition. The Fine Gael leader, John *Bruton, became Prime Minister at the head of a new coalition. In December 1993 Albert Reynolds had joined the UK Prime Minister John *Major in issuing the *Downing Street Declaration, which set out general principles for the holding of future peace talks on Northern Ireland and represented a significant step towards peace in the province. The Republic was subsequently a party to the 1998 peace agreement (*see* NORTHERN IRELAND), by which it relinquished its constitutional claim to Northern Ireland. Ireland adopted the *euro as its currency in 2002. The *Credit Crunch led to a financial crisis in 2008, when Ireland's six domestic banks faced

insolvency. The state assumed their liabilities, but found them too great. Several savage austerity budgets and, in 2010, a loan from the IMF and the EU, were required to stabilize Ireland's finances (*see* EUROZONE CRISIS). In 2010 Pope *Benedict XVI apologized for many cases, spanning many decades, of sexual abuse of children by Roman Catholic clerics in Ireland.

Irene (*c*.752–803) Byzantine empress (780–802). After her husband Leo IV died (780) she ruled jointly with her son, Constantine VI, until 790 when he banished her. She soon returned, had him blinded and imprisoned and ruled as emperor (not empress) until again exiled (802) to Lesbos. She strongly opposed the iconoclasts (*Iconoclastic controversy). For her zeal in this cause she was canonized by the Greek Orthodox Church.

Irgun (Hebrew, in full *Irgun Zvai Leumi*, 'National Military Organization'; byname ETZEL) An underground *Zionist terrorist group dedicated to the foundation of a Jewish state, active (1937–48) in Palestine against Arabs and later Britons. Under the leadership of Menachem *Begin from 1944, it blew up the King David Hotel in Jerusalem (22 July 1946), with the loss of 91 lives. It was disbanded when its objectives were achieved with the creation of Israel.

Irigoyen, Hipólito (1850–1933) Argentine statesman. A leader of the Radical Party, he was elected to the presidency (1916–22). He actively supported organized labour until a series of strikes in 1918 and 1919 threatened economic paralysis. He then turned against the union movement with the same enthusiasm that he had shown in previously supporting it. Sitting out one term, Irigoyen was elected for a second time in 1928. It was an unstable period in Argentine history when corruption, continued labour unrest, and large budget deficits were all exacerbated by the Great *Depression. The Argentine military stepped in to overthrow Irigoyen in 1930.

Irish Famine (1845–51) A period of famine and unrest in Ireland. In 1845 blight affected the potato in Ireland and the crop failed, thus depriving the Irish people of their staple food. *Absentee landlords failed to prevent exploitation of tenants by their agents; farmers could not pay their rents; often they were evicted and their cottages destroyed. This exacerbated the blight by further reducing harvests. Committees to organize relief works for such unemployed persons, together with soup kitchens, were set up, and, especially in the western counties, large numbers sought refuge in workhouses. Deaths from starvation were aggravated by an epidemic of typhus, from which some 350,000 died in the year 1846–47. The corn harvest in 1847 was good and, although the blight recurred, the worst of the famine was over. It is estimated that one million people died in Ireland of starvation in the five years 1846–51 and another million emigrated to the USA or elsewhere.

Irish Free State The name for southern Ireland from 1921, when it gained dominion status on the partition of Ireland, until 1937, when it became the sovereign state of Eire, before becoming the Republic of *Ireland in 1949.

Irish Republican Army (IRA) Terrorist organization fighting for a unified republican Ireland. A development from the *Irish Republican Brotherhood and the *Fenian Brotherhood, it was organized by *Sinn Fein in 1919 as a nationalist armed force. Its first commander in Ireland was Michael *Collins. From 1919 to 1921 it fought an effective guerrilla campaign against British forces in Ireland. Following the establishment of the *Irish Free State a minority of the IRA continued to fight for a united sovereign Ireland. These forces were defeated by the Free State army in 1922–23 and the organization went underground. Bomb explosions for which the IRA was held responsible occurred in England in 1939 and hundreds of its members were imprisoned in Britain and Ireland during World War II. In 1956 violence erupted in *Northern Ireland and the IRA performed a series of border raids. Following the outbreak of the current 'Troubles' in Northern Ireland, the IRA split into Provisional and Official wings (1969). The Officials subsequently abandoned violence but the Provisionals and another group, the Irish National Liberation Army (INLA), staged assassinations and bombings in both Northern Ireland and Britain. These include the murder of Lord Mountbatten and the British MP Airey Neave in 1979, a bomb attack on the entire British cabinet in Brighton in 1984, a bombing in Enniskillen on Remembrance Day 1987, attacks on British military bases in England and Germany in 1989, the murder of Ian Gow MP in 1990, mortar attacks on Downing Street (1991) and on Heathrow Airport (1994), a bomb in the City of London (1992), and another in Warrington in 1993. In August 1994 the IRA announced a complete cessation of its military operations, following peace initiatives by the British and Irish governments and by Northern Ireland politicians. However, the issue of decommissioning IRA weapons became a stumbling block in the progress towards all-party

talks on a lasting peace settlement. The ceasefire broke down in 1995, with the resumption of IRA bombing campaigns in mainland Britain, notably in London Docklands and Manchester. After a further ceasefire, Sinn Fein was admitted to peace talks in 1997. In 1998 the *Good Friday agreement was signed but the issue of decommissioning continued to hinder the peace process. The IRA finally began the process of placing its weapons 'beyond use' in 2001 and announced the completion of this process and the end of its armed campaign in 2005.

Irish Republican Brotherhood (IRB) A secret organization founded in Dublin in 1858 by James Stephens (1824–1901) to secure the creation of an independent Irish republic. It was closely linked with the *Fenian Brotherhood in the USA and its members came to be called Fenians. The primary object of the IRB was to organize an uprising in Ireland; the Fenian Brotherhood worked to support the IRB with men, funds, and a secure base. The British government acted swiftly; IRB leaders including Stephens were arrested. The 1867 Fenian Rising, led by Thomas Kelly, was a failure. The *Home Rule League, the *Land League, the Irish Volunteers, and *Sinn Fein often appeared to supersede the IRB as political forces; but Fenians were active in all these organizations. The Home Rule Bills failed to satisfy them and in World War I the IRB, led by Pádraic Pearse, sought German help for the abortive *Easter Rising. The IRB was subsequently superseded by the *Irish Republican Army.

Iron Age The period of prehistory distinguished technologically by the use of iron. This was first mastered on a large scale by the *Hittites in Anatolia between 1500 and 1200 BC, and spread to the Aegean, and thence to south-east and central Europe and Italy. The spread was slow across Europe, as it only gradually replaced bronze. In Africa the Iron Age immediately followed the *Stone Age, bronze entering much later. In America, iron was not discovered before being introduced from Europe. The culture of the early European Iron Age (c.750–450 BC) is known as Hallstatt culture, after the site of a prehistoric cemetery near the town of Hallstatt in Austria. At first cremation was the rule, as were flat or low graves, though later the tumulus or raised barrow became standard. As iron became common, burial was used as well as cremation, and the quality of the characteristic geometric-style pottery degenerated. It was superseded by the late Iron Age Celtic La Tène culture, named after an archaeological site near

Lake Neuchâtel, Switzerland. La Tène culture began in *c*.450 BC, when the Celts came into contact with Greek and Etruscan civilization. It lasted, with various developments, until the 1st century BC, when most of the Celts came under the aegis of the Roman empire. A distinct artistic style developed, characterized by such devices as s-shapes, spirals, and circular patterns, which show that La Tène artists were influenced by Greek and Etruscan motifs. The finest examples of La Tène art display a remarkable mixture of abstract and figurative animal and vegetable representations. The society fragmented from about 400 BC but certain items including long iron swords, decorated scabbards, belts, shield bosses, hammers, sickles, and plough shares continued to be found throughout the area. Invaders from the north at first brought new artefacts and artistic devices, but the culture eventually disappeared.

Iron Curtain The colloquial name for the former frontier between East European countries dependent on the former Soviet Union and Western non-communist countries. Its application to countries within the Soviet sphere of influence originated in a leading article by *Goebbels in *Das Reich*, February 1945. This was reported in British newspapers, and the phrase was first used by Churchill: `I view with profound misgivings the descent of an iron curtain between us and everything to the eastward.' It was generally agreed to have gone by 1990, with the disintegration of Soviet influence in eastern Europe and the collapse of the Union itself in 1991.

Ironsides *See* NEW MODEL ARMY.

Iroquois The League of Five (later Six) Nations of North American Indian tribes (i.e. Huron, Mohawk, Oneida, Seneca, Onondaga, and Cayuga), speaking the Iroquoian languages, which joined in confederacy *c*.1570 by the efforts of the Huron prophet Deganawida and his disciple Hiawatha. A powerful force in early colonial history, the divisions in the confederacy occasioned by conflicting support of the various contestants in the War of American Independence saw the rapid decline of the Six Nations in the late 18th century, with half the League (i.e. the Cayugas, Mohawks, and Seneca) migrating north to Canada, where they accepted grants of land as allies of the defeated Loyalists and where they still continue to live. Traditional Iroquois society revolved around matrilineal residential and social organization.

Irredentism (derived from *Italia irredenta*, Italian, 'unredeemed Italy') An Italian patriotic

movement of the late 19th and early 20th centuries. Its members aimed at liberating all lands, mainly in the Alps and on the Adriatic, inhabited by Italians and still held by the Austro-Hungarian empire after 1866. Its activities were restrained when the Italian government entered into the *Triple Alliance with the Austro-Hungarian empire and Germany in 1882, but the movement headed the campaign for Italy's intervention in World War I in 1915. The Settlement of *Versailles satisfied most of its claims.

Irwin, Baron *See* HALIFAX, 1ST EARL OF.

Isabella I (known as **'Isabella the Catholic'**) (1451–1504) Queen of Castile (1474–1504). She united her kingdom with that of Aragon by her marriage with its king, *Ferdinand V, in 1469, retaining sole authority in Castilian affairs. She was noted for her Catholic piety, encouragement of the *Spanish Inquisition, and her intolerance towards Jews and Muslims. She patronized Spanish and Flemish artists, and supported the exploration of America.

Isabella II (1830–1904) Queen of Spain (1833–70). The daughter of *Ferdinand VII, her accession was contended by her uncle, Don Carlos, and this led to the Carlist Wars that raged until 1839. Her reign, after two unpopular regencies, was a succession of personal scandals, governmental changes, and conflicts between political factions. Isabella finally fled to France after an insurrection (1868), and was deposed. The crown, offered by the new constitutional Cortes to five successive candidates, was accepted by the sixth, the Duke of Aosta (1845–90), the second son of Victor Emanuel I of Italy. As Amadeus I he ruled from 1871 to 1873, when he abdicated and the first Spanish republic was declared.

Isabella of France (1292–1358) Daughter of Philip IV of France. She was queen consort of Edward II of England from 1308, but returned to France in 1325. She and her lover Roger de Mortimer organized an invasion of England in 1326, forcing Edward to abdicate in favour of his son, who was crowned Edward III after his father's murder in 1327. Isabella and Mortimer acted as regents for Edward III until 1330, after which Edward took control of the kingdom and Isabella was forced into retirement.

Isaiah (8th century BC) Hebrew prophet, who preached during the reigns of Jotham, Ahaz, and Hezekiah. Isaiah's message was that the safety of Judah was in God's hands and the king should trust him and not rely on foreign allies.

He advised Hezekiah to acknowledge Assyrian power and not ally with Egypt; when Judah was invaded by Israelites and Syrians in 735 BC, and by the Assyrians in 710 BC, and again in 703–701 BC, Isaiah promised that faith in God would guarantee the people's deliverance.

Isandhlwana, Battle of (22 January 1879) A battle fought between Zulu and British forces in South Africa. The *Zulu War had begun on 11 January when *Cetshwayo ignored the British ultimatum to disband his army of 30,000 Impis gathered in Ulundi. A British force, under Lord Chelmsford, of some 7000 regulars, with as many African levies, advanced on Ulundi. The British force was caught unawares at Isandhlwana, with 1600 killed in close-combat fighting. That night a force of Zulu warriors went on to attack a mission hospital at Rorke's Drift on the Buffalo River. Eighty defenders under Lieutenant Chard killed some 470 Zulus before being relieved by Chelmsford.

Islam The religion of the Muslims, a monotheistic faith founded by the Prophet Muhammad in the Arabian Peninsula in the 7th century AD and is now the professed religion of nearly 1000 million people worldwide. To become a Muslim means both to accept and affirm an individual surrender to God, and to live as a member of a social community. The Muslim performs prescribed acts of worship and strives to fulfil good works within the group; the Five Pillars of Islam include profession of the faith in a prescribed form, observance of ritual prayer (five obligatory prayer sequences each day as well as non-obligatory prayers), giving alms to the poor, fasting during the month of Ramadan, and performing the pilgrimage to Mecca. These ritual observances, as well as a code governing social behaviour, were given to Muhammad as a series of revelations, codified in the Koran and supplemented by the deeds and discourse of the Prophet. Islam is regarded by its adherents as the last of the revealed religions (following Judaism and Christianity), and Muhammad is seen as the last of the Prophets, building upon and perfecting the examples and teachings of Abraham, Moses, and Jesus. Islam carries three interrelated significations: the personal individual submission to Allah; the 'world of Islam' as a concrete historical reality comprising a variety of communities sharing not only a common religious outlook but also a common fund of cultural legacies; and finally, the concept of an 'ideal Muslim community', as set forth in the Koran and supporting sources. The two main branches of Islam are the *Shiites and the

*Sunni Muslims. **Sufism** is the mystical aspect of the religion that arose as a reaction to strict orthodoxy. Sufis seek personal union with God and there are many Sufi poets and scholars as well as organized orders and brotherhoods.

Islamic fundamentalism is the belief that the revitalization of Islamic society can only come about through a return to the fundamental principles and practices of early Islam. Fundamentalist movements have often been a response to political and economic decline, which is ascribed to spiritual and moral decay. In the 20th century, activist organizations, such as the Muslim Brotherhood, which was founded in Egypt in 1928 and other more radical groups, such as **Hizbullah** (or **Hezbollah**) (Party of God), became prominent. Such groups emphasize a literal interpretation of the Koran and *sharia*. Fundamentalists tend to stress the penal code and restrictions on women contained in the *sharia*, partly because such provisions have become symbols of cultural identity and opposition to westernization. Many Western observers date the resurgence in Islamic fundamentalism from the Iranian Revolution of 1979. *Al-Qaeda and *Islamic State are examples of contemporary terrorist groups inspired by Islamic fundamentalism.

Islamic modernism seeks to reinterpret Islam to meet the changing circumstances of contemporary life. By contrast with fundamentalism, Islamic modernism is a response to Western imperialism and economic dominance that attempts to reform legal, educational, and social structures. From the 19th century leading Muslim thinkers such as Jamal al-Din al-*Afghani and his followers in Egypt, Muhammad Abduh (1849–1905) and Rashid Rida (1865–1935), were concerned at the stagnation they perceived in Muslim intellectual, political, and social life. They advocated the reform of the *sharia* by reopening the door of *ijtihād*, or reinterpretation, which orthodox Sunni Muslims have regarded as closed since the 9th century. Western scientific advances should not be rejected as incompatible with Islam, but should be integrated into the structure of a religion that is essentially scientific. Abduh distinguished between an inner unchanging core of Islamic belief and practice, and outer layers of regulations that could be varied in accordance with contemporary social practice. The Egyptian modernists' concern with the establishment of a modern Muslim state was echoed in India, most influentially by the poet-philosopher, lawyer, and politician Muhammad *Iqbal. Influenced by his study of Western philosophers such as *Hegel, Fichte, and Nietzsche, Iqbal developed his own synthesis and interpretation of Islam. His view of the community as a religio-political state based on the supremacy of the *sharia* was influential in the establishment of *Pakistan in 1947. Islamic modernism has had widespread influence in most Muslim countries, but despite its emphasis on the reform of the *sharia*, no systematic reform has ever been undertaken. The two main branches of Islam are Shiite and Sunni Islam. Sufism emphasises the more mystical and ascetic aspects of the religion. Ismaili Muslims, a branch of Shiite Islam, recognize seven rather than twelve imams, believing Ismail to be the last imam and to return as the *Mahdi* (expected one). The movement split into subgroups, including the assassins and Druzes.

Islamic State (IS) A militant Sunni jihadist group that emerged in 2013 when elements of the *al-Qaeda operation in Iraq became involved in the insurgency against the Assad regime in Syria. It was known at first as the **Islamic State of Iraq and the Levant** (ISIL) or **Islamic State of Iraq and Syria** (ISIS). By January 2014 IS controlled much of northern Syria and it went on to occupy large areas of north-west Iraq, including the country's second city, Mosul. The group imposed strict Islamic law and declared a worldwide *caliphate, with its leader Abu Bakr al-Baghdadi as caliph. It also launched brutal attacks on Christians and other minority communities. The continuing unchecked expansion of IS prompted the US to begin air strikes against the group in August 2014. IS responded by murdering a number of Western hostages.

Ismail I Safavi (died 1524) First ruler of the Safavid dynasty in Persia (1501–24). His ancestor Safi ud-Din (1252–1334) was a Sufi holy man and founder of the Safaviyya, the mystic brotherhood after which the dynasty is named. Supported by Turcoman tribesmen, he established his rule over Persia, extending it into Kurdistan and driving the *Uzbeks from Khurasan in the north-east. His expansion was checked in the west by the *Ottoman sultan Selim I at Chaldiran in 1514. His most enduring achievement was to convert his realm from *Sunni to *Shia Islam.

isolationism An approach to US foreign policy that advocates non-participation in alliances or in the affairs of other nations. It derives its spirit from George Washington's proclamation of neutrality in 1793, and was further confirmed by the *Monroe Doctrine (1823). It foiled Woodrow Wilson in his attempt to take the USA into the *League of Nations (1919 and

1920), and it hindered Franklin D. Roosevelt's support for Britain, France, and China before and during World War II, by ensuring passage of restrictive Neutrality Acts (1935–37). Present-day isolationists favour political and military withdrawal from overseas bases as well as the establishment of a "fortress America" protected by an elaborate modern military system.

Isonzo A river in north-east Italy, the scene of fierce battles between Italian and Austrian forces following Italy's entry into World War I on the Allied side (1915). Some dozen battles, in which Italy had twice as many casualties as Austria, were fought along this front between May 1915 and October 1917, culminating in the Italian disaster at *Caporetto (1917).

Israel

Capital:	Jerusalem
Area:	20,770 sq km (8019 sq miles)
Population:	7,707,042 (2013 est)
Currency:	1 New Israeli shekel = 100 agorot
Religions:	Jewish 75.1%; Muslim 17.4%; Christian 2.0%; Druze 1.6%
Ethnic Groups:	Jewish 75.1%; Arab and others 24.9%
Languages:	Hebrew, Arabic (both official); English
International Organizations:	UN; WTO; OECD

A country of south-west Asia at the eastern end of the Mediterranean Sea. It is bounded on the north by Lebanon, on the east by Syria and Jordan, and on the south by Egypt.

Physical The coastal plain is very warm in summer and suited particularly to the growth of citrus fruits. The north includes the Sea of Galilee and part of the River Jordan, while the east extends to the Dead Sea with its deposits of potash and reserves of natural gas. Southward is a hot and arid rift valley (part of the Great Rift Valley system) running down the eastern side of the rocky Negev Desert. Massive irrigation programmes have brought large areas of former desert under cultivation.

Economy The Israeli economy has a well-developed manufacturing base, the main products being aviation, communications, and other high-technology products. Other exports include cut diamonds, pharmaceuticals, and computer software. However, high military expenditure and reliance on imported raw materials result in a large trade deficit; this is met by tourism, service exports, and foreign aid (principally from the USA). Agriculture has been successfully developed by irrigation and produces citrus fruits, vegetables, and cotton.

History The modern state of Israel has developed from the Zionist campaign for a Jewish state in *Palestine and the *Balfour Declaration (1917) in which the Jewish demand for a national home was supported by Britain. Under the British mandate (from 1922) in Palestine the Jewish community increased from about 10% of the population in 1918 to about 30% in 1936. In 1937 the Peel Commission recommended the partition of Palestine and the formation of Jewish and Arab states. Subsequently Britain abandoned the partition solution, but, after its referral of the Palestine problem to the United Nations in 1947, a United Nations Special Commission recommended partition and a resolution to that effect was passed by the General Assembly. The British mandate ended on 14 May 1948 and the independent Jewish state of Israel in Palestine was established. The creation of the state was opposed by the Palestinian Arabs supported by Syria, Lebanon, Jordan, and Egypt, but after a violent conflict Israel survived and considerably enlarged its territory at the expense of the proposed Arab state. A substantial Palestinian refugee problem was created as many Arabs fled from Israel-controlled territory. Further Israeli-Arab wars took place in 1956 (*Suez War), 1967 (*Six-Day War), 1973 (*Yom Kippur War), and 1982 (Lebanon War). As a result of these wars Israel extended its occupation to include all the territory of the former British mandate. After 1948 immigration into Israel took place from over 100 different nations, especially Jews from former communist and Arab countries, as well as from Europe, raising the population from about 700,000 in 1948 to 5.3 million by 1994. Despite a high inflation rate, the development of the economy has made Israel the most industrialized country in the region, greatly aided by funding from the USA and European powers. The right-wing leader of the Likud Party, Yitzhak *Shamir, led a government (1986–92) firmly opposed to any concessions over the Palestine problem. Under his successor as Prime Minister, the

Labour leader Yitzhak *Rabin, progress towards an eventual settlement began. Intense diplomatic efforts, led by the USA, during 1991–92 resulted in several sessions of Middle East peace talks. They were disrupted in late 1992 by violent clashes between Palestinians and Israeli security forces in the occupied territories and by the deportation of over 400 Palestinians, which caused the PLO to halt negotiations. Despite escalating violence, peace talks resumed in 1993 but remained deadlocked. An unexpected breakthrough in negotiations between Israel and the PLO, led by Yasser *Arafat, resulted in a declaration of principles on Palestinian self-rule in the occupied territories. Israel signed a peace treaty with Jordan in 1994 and had withdrawn its forces from all Jordanian territories by early 1995. The issue of Jewish settlement in the occupied West Bank, a long-standing source of dispute, sparked a crisis in the peace process in 1995; the assassination of Prime Minister Yitzhak Rabin in November by a Jewish extremist cast further doubt over the future. Shimon Peres succeeded Rabin and in 1996 *Hamas began a series of suicide bomb attacks on Israeli cities. In the elections of 1996 Peres lost to the hawkish Binyamin *Netanyahu and the peace process stalled. However, a further agreement was reached in 1998 and in 1999 elections were won by the Labour Party under Ehud *Barak. He attempted to reach a final peace agreement with Arafat in 2000, but the collapse of negotiations, together with the outbreak of the second Palestinian *intifada, led to Barak's defeat in the 2001 elections by Ariel *Sharon of Likud. Israel responded to the renewed Palestinian unrest and suicide bombings by reoccupying large parts of the West Bank (2001–02) and began to build a 'security fence', generally along its frontier with the West Bank but incorporating parts of the West Bank on the Israeli side. Sharon was re-elected in 2003 and in 2004 announced a unilateral withdrawal of all Israelis, including settlers, from Gaza. This was carried out against some opposition in 2005, and led Sharon to split with Likud and form a new party, Kadima, to fight the 2006 elections. These resulted in a Kadima–Labour coalition with Ehud *Olmert as Prime Minister, Sharon having suffered a serious stroke during the campaign. Later that year a month-long war in Lebanon against the Hezbollah paramilitary group ended in stalemate; and in 2008–09 Israel conducted a short campaign against the Hamas government of the Gaza Strip to stop rockets being fired into Israel. Corruption allegations obliged Olmert to resign the Kadima leadership in 2008, but he remained Prime Minister until the 2009 elections. These resulted in a Likud-led coalition under Netanyahu, who remained in power after the 2013 elections. In 2014 continuing Hamas rocket attacks led Israel to launch a fierce air and ground attack on the Gaza strip, resulting in some 2000 civilian deaths, as well as the destruction of many homes and much infrastructure.

Istanbul A great historic city, port, and the former capital (until 1923) of Turkey, situated on the Bosporus and partly in Europe, partly in Asia. Istanbul was founded c.660 BC by Dorian Greeks. Known as **Byzantium** until it became the second capital of the Roman Empire, it was renamed **Constantinople** in 330 AD by Constantine I. It was designed as a new Rome, straddling seven hills and divided into 14 districts. It was ruled by two emperors, until it was declared capital of the Eastern Roman Empire in 395. The city was largely rebuilt by Justinian (527–65). The capital of the *Byzantine empire, the city withstood siege by Goths, Persians, and Arabs but was looted after a horrifying attack by Western Crusaders in 1204. It finally fell to the Ottoman Turks in 1453 and became the capital of the *Ottoman empire. Most of its characteristic buildings, such as the Topkapi Palace, the Blue Mosque, and the Mosque of Suleiman the Magnificent, date from the Ottoman period (1453–1923).

Italian Campaign (July 1943–May 1945) The World War II military campaign in which Allied troops liberated Italy. Following the *North African Campaigns, *Montgomery and *Patton prepared British and US troops to invade Sicily. The landing was launched (July 1943) from Malta, and by the end of the month both the island's principal cities, Palermo and Catania, were captured: on the mainland *Mussolini was deposed and arrested. The German army under *Kesselring was withdrawn from Sicily and British and US forces landed in southern Italy (September 1943). An armistice was signed, ending hostilities between the Anglo-American forces and those of the new government of *Badoglio. A third surprise Allied landing on the "heel" of Italy captured the two ports of Taranto and Brindisi, and on 13 October 1943 Italy declared war on Germany. A large and well-organized partisan force now harassed the Germans, but reinforcements successfully reached Kesselring, who took a stand at Monte Cassino (late 1943), site of the ancient monastery of St Benedict. The Allies decided to by-pass this, landing 50,000 men at Anzio (January 1944), south of Rome, while also bombing the monastery, which was finally

captured (May 1944) by Polish troops. Rome fell (June 1944), and Florence was captured after bitter fighting (August 1944). The Germans consolidated in the River Po valley and fought a hard battle through the autumn of 1944. In April 1945 the Allied armies launched their final attacks, and on 2 May *Alexander accepted the surrender of the whole German army group serving in northern Italy and southern Austria.

Italy

Capital:	Rome
Area:	301,340 sq km (116,348 sq miles)
Population:	61,482,297 (2013 est)
Currency:	1 euro = 100 cents
Religions:	Christian 80.0% (overwhelmingly Roman Catholic)
Ethnic Groups:	Italian
Languages:	Italian (official); German; French; Slovene
International Organizations:	EU; NATO; OECD; UN; Council of Europe; OSCE; WTO

A country bounded on the north by France, Switzerland, Austria, and Slovenia, the mainland forming a peninsula in the Mediterranean Sea, and including the islands of Sardinia, Sicily, Ischia, and Capri.

Physical Among the southern foothills of the Alps in the north of the mainland are the Italian Lakes. Below them the River Po runs west–east across the fertile Lombardy Plain to the Adriatic Sea. The Apennines are the backbone of the peninsula itself. To their west are the hills and plains of Tuscany; further south the Tiber flows across the Pontine Marshes to the Tyrrhenian Sea. Further south still the coastal plain is enriched by the debris of Vesuvius and the climate becomes warmer. To the south is Calabria, where the mountains fall steeply to the sea and in summer the land bakes brown. Eastward, stretches a wide and arid limestone plain.

Economy With a developed industrial economy, Italy's main exports include engineering products, textiles, clothing, machinery, and vehicles. The public sector is significant, and industry is concentrated in north and central Italy with the south remaining predominantly agricultural and relatively poor. There are few large mineral deposits, excepting sulphur, mercury, and some oil in Sicily. The tourist industry is significant. The chief agricultural products are fruit, vegetables, grapes, potatoes, and sugar beet. Italy is a leading wine producer.

History Italy had come under *Etruscan, Greek, and Celtic influence before it was united in c.262 BC under Roman rule. In the 5th century it was overrun by the barbarian *Goths and Lombard tribes. In 775 *Charlemagne conquered the north and it became part of the Carolingian empire, while the south was disputed between the Byzantine empire and the Arab conquerors of Sicily. By the 12th century city-states had emerged in northern and central Italy and the south united under first Norman and then, in 1176, Spanish control. The 14th century was a time of great commercial activity, followed by the *Renaissance period. The country, now divided between five major rival states, came under first Spanish (1559–1700) and then, after the Treaty of *Utrecht in 1713, Austrian domination. In 1796–97 Italy, having been used to maintain the balance of power in Europe, was invaded by *Napoleon and hopes of independence and unification re-emerged. However, in 1815, the country reverted to a grouping consisting of Lombardy and Venetia, ruled by the *Habsburgs from Vienna; the kingdom of Piedmont Sardinia, which then consisted of most of Savoy, Piedmont, and the island of Sardinia; the Papal States, ruled by the popes in Rome; the duchies of Tuscany, Parma, and Modena, also ruled by the Habsburgs; and the Kingdom of the Two Sicilies, now ruled by restored Bourbons from Naples. France ruled part of Savoy and Corsica, but had lost Genoa to Piedmont. Revolutionary societies, such as the *Carbonari and *Young Italy, were formed. The new forces of the *Risorgimento created hopes of independence from Austrian and French rule. Under such leaders as *Cavour, *Mazzini, and *Garibaldi, unification of Italy was finally achieved, and in 1861 *Victor Emmanuel II was crowned king of Italy. In an effort to join the `scramble for Africa' the Italian Premier and Minister of Foreign Affairs, Francesco Crispi, claimed (1889) the colony of *Eritrea, but the abortive bid for *Ethiopia led to a decisive defeat (1896) at the battle of *Adowa. During the Turko-Italian War (1911–12), Italy conquered north Tripoli and by 1914 had occupied much of Libya, declaring it an integral part of the country in 1939. In World War I Italy supported the

Allies, regaining Trieste and part of the Tyrol. The fascist dictator *Mussolini, determined to establish an Italian empire, successfully invaded (1935) Ethiopia, combining it with Eritrea and Italian Somaliland to form Italian East Africa. In World War II Mussolini at first allied himself with Hitler, but by 1943 the country had lost its North African empire and in the same year declared war on Germany. In 1946 the king abdicated in favour of a republic. The immediate post-war period brought remarkable and sustained economic growth but also political instability, characterized by frequent changes of government. The Italian Communist Party successfully adjusted to democracy, but during the 1970s there were Red Brigade terrorist kidnappings and outrages. Governments of the republic have mostly been formed by elaborate coalitions, dominated by the Christian Democrats, but Italian politics became increasingly incompetent, with accusations of corruption. As a result, there were calls in 1991 by President Francesco Cossiga (1985–92) for constitutional reform. The early 1990s saw *Mafia violence escalate, which provoked public outrage at the authorities' inability to curb it. The government responded by increasing police and judiciary powers and key arrests were made. By 1994 official reports indicated a significant reduction in Mafia-related crimes. In 1992 President Cossiga resigned and was succeeded by Oscar Luigi Scalfaro (1992–99), while the government's economic reform policies led to large-scale anti-government protests. Allegations of corruption against ministers in 1993 further seriously undermined the authority of the government. That year the country's electoral process was changed from a proportional representation system to a first-past-the-post system. Under this system, the general election of 1994 brought to power a right-wing coalition government led by Forza Italia, a party formed by media magnate Silvio *Berlusconi, who became Prime Minister. However, conflicts of interest between Berlusconi's political and commercial interests led to his resignation in 1995. Following the 1996 general election a series of left-wing coalitions held power under Romano Prodi (1996–98), Massimo D'Alema (1998–2000), and Giuliano Amato (2000–01). Berlusconi was returned to power at the head of a right-wing coalition by the 2001 elections. However, he was narrowly defeated in 2006 by a left-wing coalition led by Prodi. Prodi's government fell in 2008 and Berlusconi returned to power after further elections. Following the *Credit Crunch, in 2011 the interest rates at which Italy could borrow money on global financial markets rose to prohibitive levels. Berlusconi's government enacted austerity measures and then resigned. It was replaced by a non-party administration headed by Mario *Monti, which in 2012 implemented more austerity measures and other reforms. These reassured the financial markets, but Monti lost the support of parliament in 2013. Indecisive elections were followed by a lengthy hiatus until a coalition was formed under the Democratic Party's Enrico Letta. Dissension within the party saw him replaced by Matteo Renzi in 2014.

Ito Hirobumi (1841–1909) Japanese statesman. As a young *samurai of the Choshu clan, he opposed Westernization before becoming aware of the benefits offered by modernization. He became one of the major political figures after the *Meiji Restoration (1868), travelling in Europe in search of a model for the *Meiji Constitution which he subsequently framed, and serving four times as Prime Minister, first in 1885. After the politics of the 1890s had shown the considerable veto power that political parties were able to exercise, and when *Yamagata Aritomo had given the armed services the power to break civilian governments, Ito formed (1901) the Seiyukai (Friends of Constitutional Government) Party. He retired from active politics soon after and exercised a moderating influence on imperial policy as first resident-general (1905–09) of the Korean protectorate. After his resignation he was assassinated by a Korean nationalist.

Iturbide, Agustín de (1783–1824) Mexican independence leader. A Creole officer in the Spanish royalist army, his decision to join the movement for independence from Spain and to proclaim the Plan of *Iguala was significant, as many other royalist officers followed his lead. With the defeat of the Spanish forces (1821) Iturbide managed to have himself proclaimed by his soldiers as Emperor Agustín I, and persuaded (1822) a hostile Congress to ratify the proclamation. On his accession he revoked the Plan of Iguala, refused to carry out his promised social reforms, and instituted a dictatorial government. A revolution led by *Santa Anna and Guadalupe Victoria overthrew the empire after 11 months. Iturbide left for Europe but when he returned in 1824 he was arrested, tried by the Congress of Tamaulipas, and executed.

Ivan III (Ivan the Great) (1440–1505) Grand Prince of Muscovy (1462). He was responsible for extending the territories of Muscovite Russia, becoming independent of the *Tartars, and subjecting the principalities of Livonia and Lithuania. Introducing a legal code in 1497, he claimed the title of "Ruler of all Russia", reorganized and reduced the independence of the nobility, and built up a class of new, loyal, dependent officials. Influenced by contemporary Italy and Byzantium, he claimed leadership of the *Eastern Orthodox Church. His authority subsequently declined as alcoholism, conspiracy, and succession problems diminished his effectiveness.

Ivan IV (Ivan the Terrible) (1530–84) Grand Prince of Muscovy (1533–84), the first ruler to assume the title of Tsar (Emperor) of Russia (1547). He had a violent and unpredictable nature, but his nickname (Russian, *grozny*) is better translated as "awe-inspiring" rather than "Terrible". From 1547 to 1563 he pushed through a series of legal and administrative reforms. He also continued to expand Russian territory although his campaigns against the Mongols and in Siberia were more successful than those in the west. In 1564 he entered on a reign of terror, caused partly by his deteriorating mental condition, and partly by his determination to wrest power from the *boyars. He used a special body of civil servants, the *oprichniki*, to break the power of the nobility. Shortly before his death, he precipitated further turmoil for Russia by killing in a fit of rage his gifted son and heir, Ivan: although another son, Fyodor, succeeded him, power soon fell into the hands of his favourite, *Boris Godunov.

Ivory Coast *See* CÔTE D'IVOIRE.

Izetbegović, Alija (1925–2003) Bosnian politician, President of Bosnia and Herzegovina (1992–96), and part of a rotating tripartite presidency (1996–2000). Izetbegović's championing of Islam brought him into conflict with the secular communist state of former Yugoslavia and he was imprisoned several times. In 1990, he formed the anti-communist Party of Democratic Action, which won power in the regional elections in Bosnia and Herzegovina; he was appointed President of a seven-member collective state presidency. When the republic declared its independence in 1992, a bloody civil war ensued, in which Izetbegović took a conciliatory line, attempting to keep the country intact with a constitution guaranteeing equal rights for all ethnic groups and religious toleration. After the secession of the Bosnian Serbs and violent acts of "ethnic cleansing", he eventually signed the *Dayton Accord in 1995, which formalized partition of the republic. He was the Muslim member of the resulting joint presidency and its chairman from 1996 to 1998.

Jackson, Andrew (1767–1845) US general and Democratic statesman, 7th President of the USA (1829–37). After waging several campaigns against American Indians, he defeated a British army at New Orleans (1815) and successfully invaded Florida (1818). As President, he replaced an estimated 20% of those in public office with Democrat supporters, a practice that became known as the spoils system.

Jackson, Thomas Jonathan (known as 'Stonewall Jackson') (1824–63) US general. During the American Civil War he made his mark as a commander at the first Battle of Bull Run in 1861; a successful defensive stand there earned him his nickname. As the deputy of Robert E. Lee, he played an important part in the Confederate victories in Virginia in the first two years of the war.

Jacobin Club The most famous of the political clubs of the *French Revolution. It had its origins in the Club Breton which was established after the opening of the *States-General in 1789, and acquired its new name from its headquarters in an old Jacobin (Dominican) monastery in Paris. Its membership grew steadily and its carefully prepared policies had great influence in the *National Assembly. By August 1791 it had numerous affiliated clubs and branches throughout the country. Its high subscription confined its membership to professional men who, at first, were not distinguished by extreme views. By 1792, however, *Robespierre had seized control and the moderates were expelled. The club became the focus of the Reign of Terror that began the following year, and was instrumental in the overthrow of the *Girondins (June 1793). Its success was based on sound organization and the support of the *sansculottes. It was closed after the fall of Robespierre and several attempts to reopen it were finally suppressed in 1799.

Jacobite A Scottish or English supporter of the exiled royal house of *Stuart. The Jacobites took their name from Jacobus, the Latin name for *James II, who had been deprived of his throne in 1688. Their strength lay among the Highland clans of Scotland, whose loyalty was personal; the weakness of Jacobitism was that it failed to win over the Tories in England, who might have made it a more powerful and dangerous movement. The Jacobites were politically important between 1688 and 1745. The *Fifteen and the *Forty-Five were their major rebellions, but neither succeeded and after 1745, with the government's suppression of the clans, Jacobitism ceased to have a firm political base.

Jacquerie A rebellion of French peasants in northern France (May–June 1358), named after "Jacques Bonhomme", the aristocrats' nickname for a French peasant. A leader, Guillaume Karle (or Cale) emerged, and a bourgeois revolt in Paris helped the movement. The *Black Death, the French defeat at *Poitiers, the ravages of brigands, feudal burdens, and governmental demands for extra fortification work were all contributory causes. Castles were demolished and looted; but the rebellion was short-lived, collapsing after the execution of Karle and the massacre of a mob at Meaux.

Jagiellon A Polish dynasty that reigned in Lithuania, Poland, Hungary, and Bohemia in the 14th, 15th, and 16th centuries. The family gained prominence under Jagiello, Grand Duke of Lithuania (c.1345–1434), who became King of Poland, as Ladislas I, in 1386. A descendant, Ladislas III, King of Poland (1434), governed Hungary as Lazlo I (1440) and was killed by the Turks at Varna in 1444. His brother, Casimir IV of Poland, fought the Teutonic Knights and gained the throne of Bohemia for his son, Ladislas II, and in 1490, as Lazlo II, of Hungary. His son was defeated and killed at the Battle of Mohács (1525). The line died out with Sigismund II Augustus, King of Poland (1548–72).

Jahangir (1569–1627) Emperor of India (1605–27), whose contribution to *Mogul greatness was artistic rather than military. His name means 'holder of the world', but control over the huge empire he inherited was threatened by court quarrels and by the dominance of his Persian wife, Nur Jahan.

He was criticized for addiction to alcohol and opium, but his own artistic interests encouraged a new naturalism in the work of his court painters.

Jaja of Opobo (died 1891) Nigerian merchant prince. A former slave, he became head of the Anna Pepple trading house at Bonny in the Niger Delta, acting as a middleman between the coastal markets and the Nigerian interior. He established (1869) his own state at Opobo on the Gulf of Guinea. From here he was able to prevent rival supplies from reaching the coast. In 1873 Jaja was recognized as King of Opobo. In the 1880s Jaja opposed increasing British influence in the area, and in 1887 was deported by Britain to the West Indies.

Jamaica

Capital:	Kingston
Area:	10,991 sq km (4244 sq miles)
Population:	2,909,714 (2013 est)
Currency:	1 Jamaican dollar = 100 cents
Religions:	Protestant 62.5%; Roman Catholic 2.6%
Ethnic Groups:	Black 91.2%; mixed 6.2%
Languages:	English (official); English creole
International Organizations:	CARICOM; Commonwealth; Non-Aligned Movement; OAS; UN; WTO

A Caribbean island country lying south of Cuba.

Physical Jamaica is about 235 km (146 miles) from west to east and 80 km (50 miles) from north to south at its widest point, the third largest island in the Caribbean. Along its spine is a range of limestone hills which rises to 2256 m (7400 feet) in the Blue Mountains in the east. Streams flow both north and south, the northern rivers reaching a coast which is very beautiful, with palm-fringed beaches and long, sandy bays.

Economy Jamaica is a major producer of bauxite; bauxite and alumina dominate exports. Other major exports include sugar, rum, and coffee. Tourism is the most important industry, and remittances from expatriates form almost one-sixth of GDP.

History Originally inhabited by Arawak Indians, Jamaica was discovered by Columbus in 1494 and settled by the Spanish in 1509. In 1655 it was captured by the British and prospered as a *buccaneer base. The importation of slaves to work on sugar cane plantations made Jamaica the leading sugar producer of the 18th century. When slavery was abolished (1834) its economy suffered. A Negro rebellion in 1865 was ruthlessly suppressed by Governor Eyre. In 1866 it became a crown colony, and representative government gradually developed from 1884.

In the 1930s there was widespread rioting, caused by racial tension and economic depression, and in 1944 self-government, based on universal adult suffrage, was granted. Economic recovery followed World War II. In 1958 Jamaica became a founding member of the Federation of the West Indies. When this collapsed, the Jamaican Labour Party (JLP) under William A. *Bustamante negotiated independence as a dominion in the *Commonwealth of Nations. Administrations have alternated between the JLP and PNP (People's National Party), whose leader Michael Manley introduced many social reforms in the 1970s. In 1980 the JLP returned to office under Edward Seaga, whose conservative economic policies failed to reverse economic decline. The PNP returned to power in 1989 under Michael Manley, an enthusiast for the *Caribbean Community and Common Market. Inheriting both high inflation and rising unemployment, his policy was to deregulate the economy. This resulted in protests that the PNP had betrayed its social democratic principles. In 1992 he was replaced as Prime Minister and as leader of the PNP by Percival J. Patterson, who despite his continuation of economic austerity policies, boosted the government's popularity. He was re-elected in 1993, 1997, and 2002 and succeeded by Portia Simpson-Miller in 2006. She lost the 2007 general election to the JLP's Bruce Golding, but returned to power in 2012 following a general election in December 2011.

James I (1394–1437) King of Scotland (1406–37). The third son of *Robert III, he was shipwrecked and held captive in England from 1406 until his ransom was arranged in 1423. His rule was firm and effective, particularly once he had arrested most of his opponents who had governed Scotland during his absence, but his policy of reducing the powers of the nobility and making more use of the Scottish Parliament ultimately led to a reaction. In February 1437 he was killed by Sir Robert Graham, leader of a conspiracy against him.

James I (1566–1625) King James VI of Scotland from 1567, King of England (1603–25). He succeeded *Elizabeth I of England, since she had never married and the *Tudor dynasty was ended. He was the son of *Mary, Queen of Scots and Henry, Lord *Darnley. As King of Scotland he survived several plots and assassination attempts, while he strengthened the power of the crown over Parliament, Kirk (Church of Scotland), and sectarian religious groups, and fostered good relations with England. As King of England, he lacked the shrewd judgement of his predecessor, his reign being marked by several errors of policy. He angered the Puritans by refusing to hear their demands at the *Hampton Court Conference and by his insistence on the maxim 'no bishop, no king' to counter their demands for the abolition of bishops, which put an end to their hopes of reform. His court was tainted by sexual and financial scandal and although *Cecil attempted reform, the king's promotion of *Buckingham from 1618 led him into costly and extravagant schemes that alienated Parliament. Although learned, he was tactless in his handling of Parliament, insisting repeatedly on his prerogatives as king. However the unsettled financial and religious position was his legacy from Elizabeth and it was an achievement that his reign was largely peaceful.

James II (1430–60) King of Scotland (1437–60), son and successor of *James I. During his minority successive earls of Douglas vied for power, and when he began to reign in his own right the Douglases remained a threat to his authority. He improved the courts of justice and regulated the coinage. He was killed by an accidental cannon blast while leading a siege against Roxburgh Castle, held by the English.

James II (1633–1701) King of England and Scotland (1685–88), the second son of *Charles I. As Duke of York he was Lord High Admiral in the second and third Anglo-Dutch Wars, during which the Dutch settlement of New Amsterdam was captured and renamed New York in his honour (1664). He became a Roman Catholic and married Mary of Modena, also a Roman Catholic, in 1673, resigning as admiral in that year under the *Test Act; attempts were made to exclude him from the succession during the years 1679–81, but on the death of *Charles II he ascended the throne without opposition. *Monmouth's rebellion came early in his reign, and the *Bloody Assizes that punished it were resented. Within three years of his accession he

had provoked the widespread opposition that culminated in the *Glorious Revolution, which replaced him on the throne by William and Mary. He died in exile in France.

James III (1452–88) King of Scotland (1460–88), son and successor of *James II. He came to the throne aged nine and after his mother died in 1463 his rule was challenged by members of his family and their supporters from the nobility. He did not take control of his kingdom until 1469. In 1479 he imprisoned his brother, Alexander Stuart, Duke of Albany, who later led a rebellion against him. He was defeated and killed in battle by his own nobility, supported by his son (who succeeded him as James IV), at Sauchieburn, close to Bannockburn.

James IV (1473–1513) King of Scotland (1488–1513). An able and popular king, he was successful in restoring order to Scotland, quelling an uprising of discontented nobles, and improving the prosperity of the kingdom. He made peace with England by the Treaty of Ayton (1497–98), and married *Henry VII's daughter Margaret Tudor, which brought the *Stuart line to the English throne in 1603. He led his country into a disastrous war with Henry VIII of England and was himself killed at *Flodden Field.

James V (1512–42) King of Scotland (1513–42). He succeeded his father James IV at the age of only two months. His mother, her husband, Archibald Angus, Earl of Douglas, and John Stuart, Duke of Albany, struggled for control of the kingdom during his minority. When he came to power he began to ally himself with France against his uncle *Henry VIII of England, and made diplomatic marriages to Madeleine, daughter of *Francis I of France (1536), and on her death to Mary of *Guise. His only child was a daughter, who succeeded him as *Mary, Queen of Scots.

Janata Party Indian political organization. A grouping of mostly right-wing Hindu political parties, it was based upon the Jana Sangh (People's Party, founded 1951). The so-called Janata Front was a broad coalition formed to oppose Indira *Gandhi in 1975. The Janata Party proper was formed in 1977 as a coalition under Morarji Desai; it won the 1977 election and formed a government that endured until the end of 1979. In 1989 an anti-Congress National Front, Janata Dal, was formed by V. P. Singh, who was briefly Prime Minister (1990); but the party split over the issue of the Untouchables (the people with the lowest status in the caste system) and the Congress (I) Party returned to power.

Janissaries (from Turkish *yeni cheri*, 'new troops') An élite corps of slave soldiers, bound to the service of the *Ottoman sultans. They were originally raised from prisoners of war, but from the time of *Bayezid I (1389–1403) they were largely recruited by means of the *devshirme* ('gathering'), a levy of the fittest youths among the sultan's non-Muslim subjects. Having been converted to Islam, most, after intensive training, served as foot soldiers, while the ablest passed into civil administration. Decimation in the great wars against Persia and Austria (1578–1606) lowered the traditionally high quality of the intake and opened the corps to Muslims. They exercised a powerful role in political life until their abolition in 1826.

Jansen, Cornelius Otto (1585–1638) Flemish Roman Catholic theologian and founder of Jansenism. A strong opponent of the Jesuits, he proposed a reform of Christianity through a return to St Augustine. To this end he produced his major work, *Augustinus* (1640), which was published by his followers after his death. The four-volume study followed St Augustine's teachings and formed the basis of Jansenism.

Japan (Japanese **Nihon** or **Nippon**)

Capital:	Tokyo
Area:	377,915 sq km (145,914 sq miles)
Population:	127,253,075 (2013 est)
Currency:	1 yen = 100 sen
Religions:	Shinto 83.9%; Buddhist 71.4%; Christian 2.0%. Many people follow both Shintoism and Buddhism.
Ethnic Groups:	Japanese 98.5%; Korean 0.5%; Chinese 0.4%
Languages:	Japanese (official)
International Organizations:	OECD; UN; Colombo Plan; WTO

A country occupying an archipelago off the coast of east Asia. It stretches about 2400 km (1500 miles) from Hokkaido in the north-east through Honshu, Shikoku, and Kyushu to the Ryukyu Islands in the south-west. Japan is separated from China to the south-west by the East China Sea, from Siberia and Korea to the west by the Sea of Japan, and from the islands of Sakhalin and the Kuriles to the north and north-east by the Sea of Okhotsk and the Nemuro Strait.

Physical The deeply indented coastlines are surrounded by many smaller islands, with the Inland Sea forming an important constituent of the country. The islands curve along the edge of the Eurasian plate, one of the Earth's geologically most active zones, creating almost perpetual earthquake and much volcanic activity. Mountains cover two-thirds of Japan's surface, and the rivers are generally unsuited for navigation. Generally the climate varies from the long Hokkaido winter of deep snow to subtropical conditions of the south, influenced by the Kuroshio and the Tsushima Currents. During the seasonal periods of heavy rainfall and typhoons, flooding becomes a major problem.

Economy The Japanese economy is the third-largest in the world, its success having been built on phenomenal export-led growth following World War II. However, the period since 1990 has seen relative decline, with persistent deflation and poor growth. Japan is among the world's largest producers of vehicles, electronic equipment, machine tools, metals, ships, chemicals, textiles, and processed food; principal exports include vehicles, semiconductors, and iron and steel products. There are gas fields around the main island of Honshu and some oil reserves, but Japan is short of mineral and energy resources and is the world's third-largest importer of oil. There is a substantial nuclear energy capacity, but its future is in doubt following a nuclear accident at Fukushima in 2011. Only one-sixth of Japan's land can be farmed or is habitable; agriculture is dominated by rice cultivation, in which Japan is self-sufficient, but over half of food needs must be met by imports.

History Originally inhabited by native Ainu, the Japanese themselves are thought to be descendants of people who migrated from various areas of mainland Asia. By the 5th century AD the *Yamato clan loosely controlled much of Japan and began to establish imperial rule. The developing state was much influenced by Chinese culture. *Buddhism was introduced in the 6th century and, after a brief conflict, coexisted with the Japanese religion, *Shinto. In the 7th century Prince Shotoku was partially successful in establishing an administrative system based on that of *Sui China. However, by the 9th century the *Fujiwara family had gained control over the imperial court and its power was undermined.

The growing strength of feudal lords and of Buddhist monasteries resulted in civil war for most of the 12th century, the ultimate victor being Minamoto Yoritomo, who in 1192 became the first shogun and established a military administration (*see* SHOGUNATE). From then effective power lay with the shogun rather than the emperor. Yoritomo's *Kamakura shogunate was replaced in 1333 by the Ashikaga shogunate, but its rule was one of prolonged civil strife. In the late 16th century three warriors, Oda Nobunaga, Hideyoshi, and *Tokugawa Ieyasu, broke the power of the feudal lords (daimyo), and Ieyasu's *Tokugawa shogunate provided stable but repressive rule until the restoration of the emperor in 1868.

Europeans had begun to trade with Japan in 1542 and Catholic missionaries, including Matteo Ricci, made numerous converts. The Tokugawa shogunate excluded all foreigners in 1639, except for a few Dutch and Chinese at Nagasaki, and proscribed Christianity. During the 18th and 19th centuries the wealth and power of merchants began to increase and Japan extended its influence over the northern island of Hokkaido.

In the first half of the 19th century Tokugawa power was gradually undermined by economic problems, insurrection, and the arrival of Western trading and naval expeditions, most notably those of the US Commodore Perry (1853–54). The shogunate's failure to resist foreign penetration served as the catalyst for armed opposition, which in 1868 finally succeeded in replacing the shogunate with a new regime led formally by the emperor Meiji Tenno (the *Meiji Restoration). In the succeeding decades feudalism was dismantled and a centralized state created which was dedicated to the rapid modernization of society and industrialization. Japan's new strength brought victory in the *Sino-Japanese War (1894–95) and the *Russo-Japanese War (1904–05), and established it as the dominant power in north-east Asia. Japan fought on the Allied side in World War I, but thereafter its expansionist tendencies led to a deterioration in its diplomatic position, most notably *vis-à-vis* the USA. In the inter-war period, expansionist-militarist interests gradually gained power within the country, and, after the occupation of Manchuria (1931) and the creation of *Manchukuo (1932), full-scale war with China was only a matter of time. The Sino-Japanese War finally broke out in 1937, and, having already allied itself with Germany and Italy in the *Anti-Comintern Pact, Japan finally entered World War II with a surprise attack on the US fleet at *Pearl Harbor in December 1941. Initially overrunning the colonial empires of south-east Asia at great speed, Jap-

anese forces were eventually held and gradually driven back (the Pacific Campaigns). In September 1945, after the dropping of two atomic bombs, Japan was forced to surrender and accept occupation. A new Japanese Constitution was introduced, and full independence was formally returned in 1952. Japan embarked on another period of rapid industrial development, to become one of the major economic powers in the world. Its relations with China and southeast Asian countries improved, but the large imbalance in its trade in its favour with Western nations (particularly the USA), resulted in economic instability. The Liberal Democratic Party (LDP) held office continually throughout these years, surviving numerous financial scandals. In the early 1990s Japan's economy suffered in the global recession. The government was defeated in a vote of no confidence in 1993 and a general election was called in which the LDP split and lost its overall majority. The opposition formed a seven-party coalition and ejected the LDP from office for the first time since its formation in 1955. The new government, led by Morihiro Hosokawa, introduced a system of single-seat constituencies and legislators elected by proportional representation; this was implemented by the end of 1994. Hosokawa resigned and coalition governments followed, during which the LDP gradually regained its leading role: it recovered the premiership in 1996 and its majority in the lower house of parliament in 1997. To mark the 50th anniversary of the end of the Pacific War, the government issued an official apology for Japan's actions during the conflict. A large economic stimulation package was also unveiled in an attempt to bring the Japanese economy out of its longest recession since 1945. However, Japan was affected by the financial crisis in the rest of south-east Asia in 1997–98 and economic stagnation continued into the 21st century. The reformist Junichiro Koizumi became Prime Minister in 2001 and limited structural reform followed. Koizumi retired in 2006 and his government was followed by several short-lived cabinets amid declining LDP popularity. The opposition Democratic Party of Japan (DPJ) won a decisive victory in the 2009 election, but was in turn swept out of power by the LDP in 2012. The new Prime Minister, Shinzō Abe, increased government spending and adopted other policies designed to stimulate economic growth. In 2011 tsunamis caused by an undersea earthquake off northern Honshu killed over 15,000 people and caused great damage, including significant radioactive leaks from the Fukushima Daiichi nuclear power station.

Japan, Occupation of (1945–52) The Allied occupation of Japan after World War II. After Japan's unconditional surrender on 2 September 1945, it came under the control of the Allied forces of occupation led by General Douglas *MacArthur in his capacity as Supreme Commander of the Allied Powers (SCAP). Although technically backed by an 11-nation Far Eastern Commission and a Four-Power Council (Britain, China, USA, and the Soviet Union), the military occupation was entirely dominated by the USA, with policy remaining in the hands of MacArthur and, after his removal in April 1951, of his successor General Matthew Ridgway. US occupation policy had two main goals, the demilitarization of Japan and the establishment of democratic institutions and ideals. The first objective was achieved through the complete demobilization of the army and navy and the destruction of their installations, backed up by the peace clause of the new *Japanese Constitution. The second was much more difficult, and although the new Constitution was in operation before the occupation was formally terminated in 1952, the real impact of US-inspired reforms on Japanese socio-political institutions has been questioned. Although a few *zaibatsu were dissolved, most survived. At the same time close links with the USA resulted in rapid economic recovery and expansion.

Japanese Constitution (1947) A constitution introduced during the Allied occupation after World War II, with the emphasis placed on the dismantling of militarism and the extension of individual liberties. Drafted under US influence, it was finally adopted on 3 may 1947. The constitution left the emperor as head of state but stripped him of governing power, vesting legislative authority in a bicameral Diet, the lower House of Representatives (originally 466, now 480 seats) being elected for four years and the upper House of Councillors (242 seats) for six (half at a time at three-year intervals). Executive power is vested in the cabinet, which is headed by a Prime Minister and is responsible to the Diet. The constitution specifically renounces war but has been interpreted as allowing self-defence: accordingly, Self Defence Forces have been created, although defence expenditure remains low by Western standards. In 1992 legislation was finally passed allowing Japan's Self Defence Forces to serve overseas in UN peacekeeping operations.

Japan-United States Security Treaty (1951) A defence agreement between Japan and the USA. Negotiated as part of the package of arrangements attending the formal return of Japanese independence after defeat in World War II, the treaty established the USA as the effective arbiter of Japan's defence interests, granting it a large military presence in Japanese territory. Renewal of the treaty in 1960, as a Mutual Security Treaty, with revised terms, produced a major political crisis in Japan: when renewal next became due in 1970, both countries agreed to a process of automatic extension on the condition that revocation could be achieved on one year's notice by either.

Jaurès, Jean (1859–1914) French socialist leader. Entering parliament (1885), his campaign on behalf of *Dreyfus and against *anti-Semitism strengthened socialist support in France. In 1905 he formed the United Socialist Party, which put pressure on the radical governments in order to achieve reforms for the working class. He opposed militarism, but tried to reconcile socialist internationalism and French patriotism. He was assassinated by a French nationalist in 1914.

Java man The human fossilized bones found at Trinil on the Solo River in Java. Originally classified as *Pithecanthropus erectus* ('erect ape-man'), these remains are now included within the species *Homo erectus*. Their date is uncertain but is probably 750,000–500,000 years ago. Subsequent finds of hominids, probably also *Homo erectus*, in Java were made at Sangiran and Modjokerto. Some of these may be rather older (up to 1.3 million years ago) than the Trinil remains.

Java War (1825–30) A war fought against the Dutch and their Javanese allies in central Java, led by *Diponegoro. The uprising proved difficult to suppress until the adoption by the Dutch of a system of rural strong points (*bèntèng*) and the use of mobile columns. Deprived of peasant support, Diponegoro was forced to negotiate with the Dutch and, when he refused to renounce his claim to the title of sultan and the status of Protector of Religion (*Panatagama*) in Java, he was arrested and banished. Thus ended the last and most serious challenge to the extension of Dutch rule in Java.

Jay, John (1745–1829) American statesman and jurist. He was a member of the first and second *Continental Congresses, became Chief Justice of New York, a member of Congress, Minister to Spain (1780–82), and a member of the delegation that negotiated peace with Britain (1783). A conservative Federalist, he was Secretary of Foreign Affairs (1784–90), before becoming Chief Justice of the USA (1789–95). As special envoy to England he negotiated the Jay Treaty (1794) to settle outstanding differences resulting from the War of Independence. It enforced the terms of the Peace of *Paris (1783) and ordered the British to leave their trading post in the north-west of the country. The British lost control of the lucrative fur trade and ceded a share in the trade with the West Indies to the Americans.

Jefferson, Thomas (1743–1826) US Democratic Republican statesman, 3rd President of the USA (1801–09). Jefferson was the principal drafter of the Declaration of Independence (1776) and played a key role in the American leadership during the War of Independence. He advocated decentralization and the restrained use of presidential power, in defiance of Alexander Hamilton. While President, Jefferson secured the Louisiana Purchase (1803), by which the western part of the Mississippi valley was sold to the USA by France.

Jeffreys of Wem, George Jeffreys, 1st Baron (1645–89) English judge and Lord Chief Justice. He presided at the trials of the *Rye House Plot conspirators, of those implicated in the *Popish Plot, and of Richard *Baxter, but he is chiefly associated with the *Bloody Assizes (1685) that followed *Monmouth's rebellion. Contemporary reports of his brutality may have been prejudiced, but he certainly browbeat witnesses and his sentencing of the 80-year-old Alice Lisle to be burnt for treason caused widespread revulsion. Following the *glorious revolution he was imprisoned, but died before proceedings could be taken against him.

Jehangir See JAHANGIR.

Jena, Battle of (14 October 1806) A battle between the Prussian army, led by Prince Hohenlohe, and *Napoleon's French forces, fought near the German town of that name. The Prussians underestimated the size of the French force and were comprehensively defeated. The defeat by *Davout of the Duke of Brunswick's main Prussian army at Auerstädt on the same day left the road to Berlin unprotected. After its double defeat Prussia embarked on a series of military, political, and social reforms in order to be able to challenge the French.

Jenkins's Ear, War of (1739–41) A war between Britain and Spain that broke out as a result of Britain's trade with South America. The Peace of *Utrecht, which gave the British South Sea Company a limited trade monopoly with the Spanish American colonies, caused general friction, but the main troublemakers were illicit traders who defied both the Company and the Spanish government. In 1737 British merchants were protesting at a tightening-up of Spanish control. The Spanish government and *Walpole both wanted peace but Walpole's enemies made it an excuse to attack him: a merchant captain named Jenkins was produced to tell a story of torture and the loss of an ear. Popular clamour was such that Walpole consented reluctantly to declare war. Admiral Vernon captured Porto Bello and France sent two squadrons to the West Indies. In 1740 the war merged into that of the *Austrian Succession.

Jericho An ancient city, now in the Palestinian-administered West Bank of the River Jordan. A well-watered oasis near the Jordan river-crossing at the head of the Dead Sea, it was of strategic importance, located at the junction of the trade routes of antiquity. It was occupied from *c.*9000 BC and is one of the oldest continuously inhabited cities in the world. Traces of a hunting society that developed into a settled agricultural community have been found. The principal mound, one of the best known of all Near Eastern tells (mounds of rubbish), accumulated over 15 m (50 feet) of deposit, even though the later occupation levels, from 2000 to 500BC, have been swept off the summit by erosion. The most interesting layers are of the pre-pottery *Neolithic period *c.*7000 BC, when Jericho was already a walled settlement of some 4 ha (10 acres). Little remains of the late Bronze Age period, the probable date of its destruction by Joshua recorded in the Old Testament of the Bible. Modern Jericho was granted Palestinian self-rule in 1994, as part of the 1993 peace agreement between Israel and the *Palestine Liberation Organization.

Jeroboam I (died *c.*901 BC) first king of the northern kingdom of *Israel (*c.*922–*c.*901 BC). After Solomon's death, his successor Rehoboam failed to gain the support of the northern part of Israel, which seceded under the leadership of Jeroboam. He then extended and strengthened the kingdom, taking advantage of Syrian and Assyrian weakness. He made the kingdom prosperous, but the prophet Amos spoke against his oppression and injustice. He was also criticized for encouraging the sanctuaries at Dan and Bethel to rival the Temple at Jerusalem.

Jerome, St (*c.*342–420) Doctor of the Church. Born in Dalmatia, he acted as secretary to Pope Damasus in Rome (382–85) before settling in

Bethlehem, where he ruled a newly founded monastery and devoted his life to study. He is chiefly known for his compilation of the Latin version of the Bible, the Vulgate.

Jerusalem A holy city to Jews, Christians, and Muslims. It was originally a Jebusite settlement, captured by *David c.1000 BC. Solomon's Temple, the central shrine of Judaism, destroyed by *Nebuchadnezzar in 586 BC, was rebuilt in 516 BC and even more magnificently by *Herod the Great. Jerusalem was razed by the Romans in 70 AD and the Temple destroyed: in 135 they built the city of Aelia Capitolina on its site. St *Paul regarded it as the home of the original Christian congregation, headed until his death in 62 by James, the apostle of *Jesus Christ. Constantine marked its significance by building the Church of the Holy Sepulchre (c.335) over the supposed tomb of Christ. Muslim rule from 637 was symbolized by the building of the Dome of the Rock, the city's holiest Muslim Shrine, in 691. The Christian knights of the *Crusades controlled the city from 1099 to 1187, when it fell to *Saladin. The Ottoman Turks conquered Jerusalem in 1516 and Suleiman the Magnificent built the walls still enclosing the old city in 1538. During World War I the British took over Jerusalem (1917) and held it under the Palestine mandate from 1922 to 1948. When the State of Israel was declared in 1948, Jerusalem was divided between Israel and Jordan. Jerusalem was declared the capital of Israel in 1950, although this is not internationally recognized. During the *Six-Day War in 1967, the Arab sector of Jerusalem was taken over by Israel, which has retained the entire city ever since, the status of occupied East Jerusalem remains a major issue in Israeli-Palestinian negotiations. The city's unique historical importance to three religions has made it a constant focus of religious and ethnic unrest.

Jervis, John, Earl St Vincent (1735–1823) British admiral. In 1795 he was put in command of the British fleet, and in 1797, with Nelson as his commodore, led his forces to victory over a Spanish fleet off Cape St Vincent; Jervis was created Earl St Vincent in recognition of this achievement.

Jesuit See ROMAN CATHOLIC CHURCH.

Jesus Christ (c.6 BC–c.30 AD) The central figure of *Christianity, believed by his followers to be the Son of God, of one essence with God the Father and God the Holy Spirit (the doctrine of the Trinity). The Gospels of the New Testament are the main sources of information about

Jesus. According to them, Jesus was born at Bethlehem to Mary, by tradition a virgin, in the reign of Augustus Caesar. He was brought up at Nazareth in Galilee and received a traditional Jewish education. He may have been a carpenter, the trade of Mary's husband, Joseph. About 27 AD he was baptized in the River Jordan by *John the Baptist and shortly thereafter started his public ministry of preaching and healing (with reported miracles). Through his popular style of preaching, with the use of parables and proverbs, he proclaimed the imminent approach of the Kingdom of God and the ethical and religious qualities demanded of those who were to enjoy it (summarized in the Sermon on the Mount). His interpretation of Jewish law did not reject ceremonial observances but regarded them as less important than the fundamental principles of charity, sincerity, and humility. From among his followers in Galilee he selected 12 disciples to be his personal companions and to teach his message. His preaching brought him into conflict with the Jewish authorities. Aware of this, he travelled to Jerusalem, where he was betrayed by Judas Iscariot, one of his disciples, and condemned to death by the Sanhedrin, the highest Jewish court. He then appeared before the Roman governor, Pontius Pilate, who sentenced Jesus to death by crucifixion. His followers claimed that three days after the sentence had been carried out the tomb in which his body had been placed was empty and that he had been seen alive. Belief in his resurrection from the dead spread among his followers, who saw in this proof that he was the Messiah or Christ. His followers started to form Christian communities around Jerusalem from which developed the Christian Church.

Jewish people A people claiming descent from the ancient Israelites of the Old Testament or who practise *Judaism. During the Exile from the land of Israel (597–538 BC) following the Babylonian conquest, their religion developed from a sacrificial temple cult into an elaborate code for daily living, which became the basis for communal identity. The revolt of the *Maccabees in 167 BC showed their determination to preserve that identity, which survived the Roman destruction of the Temple in 70 AD and of *Jerusalem in 135 AD.

Dispersed (see DIASPORA) throughout the Roman empire, they suffered much discrimination at the hands of its Christian successors and often welcomed *Arab conquests, which brought greater toleration. In Christendom, they were free to engage in usury, a sin for Christians, and were herded into ghettos.

Though they were tolerated for their usefulness, they suffered periodic persecution. The Jews who went to Spain and Portugal in the Diaspora are known as the Sephardim (from *Sepharad*, Hebrew for a region in the Bible thought to be modern Spain). Many of them held high rank in the Arab civil service. Having been expelled from Spain in 1492, the Sephardim, speaking Ladino, a Spanish dialect, found refuge in north Africa, the Levant, the Ottoman Empire, the Netherlands, and Italy. Jews who went to France and Germany in the early Middle Ages are known as Ashkenazim (from the biblical Ascanians of Phrygia, taken to be inhabitants of modern Germany). They spoke Yiddish, a variant of German, and established themselves in north-west and eastern Europe.

It is estimated that there are about 14 million Jews worldwide, with about 40% in each of the USA and *Israel and significant numbers in Argentina, Australia, Canada, France, Germany, Russia, and the UK.

Mainly city-dwellers in their recent history, many Jews are immigrants following massive population movements as a result of anti-Semitism, which found its most violent expression in the *Holocaust of World War II, when an estimated 6 million Jews were murdered by the Germans. More recently, large numbers of Soviet Jews have emigrated to Israel, following the relaxation of Soviet emigration laws. However, in most societies Jews are now more assimilated than ever before, while retaining a Jewish ethnic identity, although many have rejected the religion. They retain prominence far beyond their numerical significance in world political, cultural, and economic affairs.

Jewish Revolt A serious nationalist uprising led by the *Zealots against Roman rule (66–70 AD). In response *Vespasian invaded Palestine with 60,000 troops and by 68 the rebels were confined to the Jerusalem area. After Vespasian's deposition in the civil wars of 68–69, his son Titus besieged the city, which fell district by district, the Temple being destroyed. Prisoners were taken to Rome and used as slave labour to build the *Colosseum. The last insurgents held out at *Masada until 73. In 132–35 *Bar Cochba led another revolt, which ended with the sack of Bethar and Cochba's death.

Jiang Jiehi *See* CHIANG KAI-SHEK.

Jiangxi Soviet A Chinese communist rural base formed in 1931. Under *Kuomintang attack in 1927, some communists moved to the countryside, maintaining their strength through guerrilla warfare in remote mountain regions.

The group led by *Mao Zedong, which first established itself on the Hunan–Jiangxi border, merged with a group led by *Zhu De, and the First National Congress of the Chinese Soviet Republic was held in November 1931. Four nationalist "Encirclement Campaigns" were thwarted by guerrilla tactics between December 1930 and early 1933, but a fifth, beginning in October 1933, forced the evacuation of the Soviet and the commencement of the *Long March a year later. Many communist policies, including land reform, were first tried out in the Jiangxi Soviet which, at its height, had a population of some nine million.

Jiang Zemin (1926–) Chinese Communist politician, President of the People's Republic of China (1993–2003), Chairman of the Central Military Commission (1990–2005), and General Secretary of the Chinese Communist Party (1989–2002). Jiang Zemin studied as an engineer, worked in several factories, including a car plant in Moscow, and served as a diplomat before being appointed a member of the Politburo in 1967. An economic reformer, but conservative on questions of internal reform, he was appointed General Secretary of the Communist Party after his predecessor, the liberal Zhao Ziyang, had lost favour following the massacre of pro-democracy protesters in Tiananmen Square in 1989. He progressively relinquished his posts to *Hu Jintao between 2002 and 2005.

Jin (or **Chin**) (1126–1234) A dynasty that governed Manchuria, part of Mongolia, and much of northern China. It was founded by the Juchen, nomad huntsmen, who came from around the Amur and Sungari rivers. They were ancestors of the *Manchus. When the Northern *Song set out to overthrow the Liao, to whom they were tributary, they allied with the Juchen, hoping to play off one alien people against another. The latter, however, once having conquered the Liao, sacked the Song capital, Kaifeng, in 1126. The Song retreated south, establishing their new capital at Xingsai (Hangzhou).

The Juchen were in time tamed by their Chinese subjects, who far outnumbered them. Their frontier with Southern Song was stabilized. Jin emperors studied the Chinese classics and wrote poetry in Chinese. Their nomad vigour was sapped by a sedentary life. By 1214 much of their territory, including Beijing, their central capital, was in *Genghis Khan's hands. The dynasty survived, ruling from Kaifeng, until a final Mongol onslaught 20 years later.

Jin, Western See WESTERN JIN.

jingoism A mood of inflated patriotism. The term originated in 1878, when Russian successes in a war against the *Ottoman empire had created at the Treaty of San Stefano a Bulgaria that Britain regarded as a threat to its Eastern interests; a popular music-hall song of the time began with the lines: "We don't want to fight, but by Jingo if we do; We've got the ships, we've got the men, we've got the money too!" Strong anti-Russian feeling developed in Britain, where *Disraeli called up reserves for army service and war-fever gripped the country.

Jinnah, Muhammad Ali (1876–1948) Indian statesman and founder of Pakistan. He headed the Muslim League in its struggle with the Hindu-oriented Indian National Congress, and from 1928 onwards championed the rights of the Muslim minority at conferences on Indian independence. After 1937, when self-governing Hindu provinces began to be formed, his fear that Muslims would be excluded from office led him to campaign for a separate Muslim state. With the establishment of Pakistan in 1947 he became its first Governor-General.

Joanna the Mad (1479–1555) Nominal Queen of Castile (from 1504) and of Aragon (from 1516). She was the daughter of *Ferdinand V and *Isabella I of Spain and the wife of *Philip IV of Burgundy. After Philip's death in 1506 she became insane. In 1509 she retired to Tordesillas, accompanied by Philip's embalmed corpse. Her sons later became the emperors *Charles V and Ferdinand I.

Joan of Arc, St (known as 'the Maid of Orleans') (c.1412–31) French national heroine. Inspired by 'voices' of St Catherine and St Margaret, she led the French armies against the English in the Hundred Years War, relieving besieged Orleans (1429) and ensuring that Charles VII could be crowned in previously occupied Reims. Captured by the Burgundians in 1430, she was handed over to the English, convicted of heresy, and burnt at the stake in Rouen. She was canonized in 1920.

Jodl, Alfred (1890–1946) German Nazi general. Throughout World War II he was chief of the Armed Forces' Operations Staff, and was Hitler's closest adviser on strategic questions. His diaries reveal his complicity in many of Hitler's war crimes and he was condemned to death at the *Nuremberg Trials.

Joffre, Joseph Jacques Césaire (1852–1931) French Marshal. During World War I he was Commander-in-Chief of the French army on the Western Front (1914–16). Joffre was chiefly responsible for the Allied victory in the first Battle of the Marne, but resigned after the costly Battle of Verdun (1916).

John (known as **John 'Lackland'**) (1167–1216) King of England (1199–1216), son of Henry II. He lost Normandy and most of his French possessions to Philip II of France by 1205. His refusal to accept Stephen Langton as Archbishop of Canterbury caused an interdict to be placed on England in 1208, and led to his own excommunication the following year. In 1215 John was forced to sign Magna Carta by his barons. When he ignored its provisions, civil war broke out (the first Barons' War) and he died on campaign.

John I (or **John the Great**) (1357–1433) King of *Portugal (1385–1433), the illegitimate son of Pedro I. He led nationalist sympathizers against the Castilians, who supported Queen Eleanor, his rival. Defeating their invasion he went on to ally with England (through his marriage to Philippa, daughter of *John of Gaunt) and to encourage African and Western exploration. His reign was the start of Portugal's period of colonial and maritime expansion; his sons, including *Henry the Navigator, consolidated his achievements.

John II (or **John the Perfect**) (1455–95) King of Portugal (1481–95). He destroyed his rival, the Duke of Braganza in 1483, and crushed a conspiracy led by his brother-in-law in 1484. He sponsored African and American exploration, and negotiated the Treaty of *Tordesillas, which divided the lands of the New World between Spain and Portugal.

John III (or **John the Pious**) (1502–57) King of Portugal (1521–57). He encouraged Portuguese settlement in Brazil, claimed the Moluccas, and supported the *Inquisition.

John III (or **John Sobieski**) (1624–96) King of Poland (1674–96). He was elected king of Poland after a distinguished early career as a soldier. In 1683 he relieved Vienna when it was besieged by the Turks, becoming the hero of the Christian world.

John IV (or **John the Fortunate**) (1605–1656) King of Portugal (1640–56). The founder of the Braganza dynasty, he expelled a Spanish usurper and proclaimed himself king in 1640. He defeated the Spanish at Montijo in 1644, drove the Dutch out of Brazil in 1654, and generally restored Portugal's international position.

John V (1689–1750) King of Portugal (1706–50). He saw peace made with France (1713) and Spain (1715) after the War of the *Spanish Succession. His reign was prosperous but in his later years he became ill and dominance of his government by churchmen led to neglect of the country's affairs.

John VI (1769–1826) King of Portugal (1816–26). The son of Maria I and Peter III, he took over the control of the government in 1792 from his mother, who had become insane, and assumed the title of regent in 1799. A repressive monarch, he was submissive to Napoleon, who nevertheless forced him into exile in *Brazil in 1807. In 1816 he was recognized as King of Portugal but continued to live in Brazil until 1822, when he returned to accept the role of a "constitutional monarch". In the same year he overcame a rebellion by his son Dom Miguel. In 1825 he recognized his other son, Dom Pedro, as emperor of an independent Brazil.

John XXIII, St (born **Angelo Giuseppe Roncalli**) (1881–1963), Pope (1958–63). During his pontificate he made energetic efforts to liberalize *Roman Catholic policy, especially on social questions, such as the need to help the poor and the need for international peace. He was canonized in 2014.

John of Gaunt (1340–99) Fourth son of Edward III of England. Born in Ghent, he was created Duke of Lancaster in 1362. John of Gaunt headed the government during the final years of his father's reign and the minority of *Richard II, and was effective ruler of England in this period. His son Henry Bolingbroke later became King *Henry IV.

John Paul II, St (born **Karol Wojtyla**) (1920–2005) Pope (1978–2005). A Pole, he became the first non-Italian pope since the 16th century. He became the longest serving pope of the 20th century and travelled more widely on papal missions than any other pope. His term of office saw a slowing down of reforms advocated in the wake of the Second Vatican Council (1962–65), notably on the devolution of responsibility to the priesthood and laity. He maintained the Church's traditional opposition to the ordination of women, to artificial birth control, and to practising homosexuals. He was canonized in 2014.

Johnson, Andrew (1808–75) US politician; 17th President of the USA (1865–69). As the only southern senator to support the Union in the *American Civil War he was appointed military governor of Tennessee. Having been elected as Vice-President to Abraham *Lincoln in 1864, he became President as a result of Lincoln's assassination in April 1865. His reconstruction policy, which failed to protect the interests of former slaves in the ex-Confederate states, brought him into bitter conflict with the Republican majority in Congress: his vetoes of several reconstruction measures were overridden by two-thirds majorities in Congress. His dismissal of his Secretary of War, Edwin Stanton (in defiance of a Tenure of Office Act) led to his impeachment (a US legal procedure for removing officers of state before their term of office expires), and Johnson only survived by a single vote in the Senate (1868). He returned to the Senate in 1875 but died soon after.

Johnson, Lyndon B. (**Lyndon Baines Johnson**) (1908–73) US politician; 36th President of the USA (1963–68). A Democrat, Johnson represented Texas in Congress from 1937 to 1961, when he became Vice-President to John F. *Kennedy. When Kennedy was assassinated, he was immediately sworn in as President. Johnson acted decisively to restore confidence and pressed Congress to pass the former President's welfare legislation, especially the *civil rights proposals. He won a sweeping victory in the presidential election of 1964, with Hubert Humphrey as Vice-President. The administration introduced an ambitious programme of social and economic reform. It took his considerable negotiating skills to persuade Congress to support his measures, which included medical aid for the aged (Medicare) through a health insurance scheme, housing and urban development, increased spending on education, and federal projects for conservation. In spite of these achievements, urban tension increased. Martin Luther *King and *Malcolm X were assassinated and there were serious race riots in many cities. The USA's increasing involvement in the *Vietnam War overshadowed all domestic reforms, and led Johnson on an increasingly unpopular course involving conscription and high casualties. By 1968 this had forced Johnson to announce that he would not seek re-election.

Joinville, Jean de (1224–1317) French historian and courtier. He was a friend and confidant of *Louis IX, accompanying him on the Seventh *Crusade (1248–54). He advised against the Eighth Crusade and did not join it. His *Histoire de St Louis* was principally an account of the Seventh Crusade, written with humour and sincerity.

Jones, John Paul (1747–92) Scottish-born American naval officer. In 1775 he joined the American Continental Navy and carried out a daring series of attacks on shipping in British waters, his best-known exploit being his engagement and sinking of the naval frigate *Serapis* while in command of the *Bonhomme Richard* (1779). In 1788 he joined the Russian navy as a rear-admiral.

Jordan

Capital:	Amman
Area:	89,342 sq km (34,495 sq miles)
Population:	6,482,081 (2013 est)
Currency:	1 Jordanian dinar = 1000 fils
Religions:	Sunni Muslim 92.0%; Christian 6.0%
Ethnic Groups:	Arab 98.0%; Circassian 1.0%; Armenian 1.0%
Languages:	Arabic (official); English
International Organizations:	UN; Arab League; Non-Aligned Movement; WTO

A mainly inland Middle Eastern country, correctly the Hashemite Kingdom of Jordan, a part of historical Palestine. It borders on Syria in the north, Iraq in the east, Saudi Arabia in the south-east, and Israel in the west.

Physical Jordan's natural resources are meagre, and its only outlet to the sea is the port of Aqaba at the north-east end of the Red Sea. Most of the country is on a desert plateau which has only about 250 mm (10 inches) of rain a year; but in the west is the Jordan River valley (whose West Bank is occupied by Israel) where some crops can be grown.

Economy Jordan lacks natural resources and its economy is dependent on foreign aid. Important exports include clothing, fertilizers, potash, and phosphates. The small agricultural sector produces citrus and other fruit. Jordan's economic resources have been stretched by large influxes of refugees, most recently from Syria since 2012.

History The region was part of the *Ottoman empire until 1918, when it came under the government of King Faisal in Damascus. In 1920 Transjordan, as it was then called, was made part of the British mandate of Palestine. In 1921

Britain recognized Abdullah ibn Hussein as ruler of the territory and gave him British advisers, a subsidy, and assistance in creating a security force. In 1946 the country was given full independence as the Hashemite Kingdom of Jordan, with Abdullah ibn Hussein as king. In 1948–49 the state was considerably enlarged when Palestinian territories on the West Bank, including the Old City of Jerusalem, were added. As a result of the *Six-Day War in 1967, these West Bank territories passed under Israeli occupation. The king was assassinated in 1951, his son Talal was deposed in 1952 as mentally unstable. From 1953 until his death in 1999 Jordan was ruled by Talal's son, *Hussein. He was succeeded by his son, *Abdullah II. Palestinian refugees from territory under Israeli occupation established a commando force (*fedayeen*) in Jordan to raid Israel. Hostility from Palestinian refugees from the West Bank to the moderate policies of Hussein erupted in 1970 between the guerrillas and the government. The mainly Bedouin regiments loyal to the king broke up the military bases of al-*Fatah, and the *Palestine Liberation Organization moved its forces (1971) to Lebanon and Syria. During the *Yom Kippur War Jordan sent tanks to aid Syria, but there was no fighting along the Jordan frontier. In 1974 Jordan's relations with other Arab countries improved when it accepted that 'the PLO is the sole and legitimate representative of the Palestinian people'. It supported Iraq in the *Iran–Iraq War and suffered severely during the *Gulf War from the effects of UN sanctions against Iraq and the arrival of many thousands of expatriates from the Gulf. In June 1991 the 34-year ban on political parties was lifted. In 1993 the first multiparty election since 1956 was held, in which candidates loyal to the king were victorious. Despite the signing of the Israeli–PLO peace accord (1993), Jordan continued its own negotiations with Israel. In 1994 the two countries signed a declaration formally ending the state of conflict between them and agreed a peace treaty. In the early 21st century cautious political reform continued, particularly in 2011 following protests inspired by the *Arab Spring. At the same time Jordan has maintained a firm stance against militant Islamists.

Joseph II (1741–90) Holy Roman Emperor (1765–90). He was co-regent of Austria with his mother *Maria Theresa from 1765 and sole ruler from 1780 to 1790. Intelligent, dedicated to the principles of the *Enlightenment, and hoping to improve the lives of his subjects, he was nonetheless autocratic and too hasty. Attempts at major reforms brought many parts of the empire close to revolt. His most lasting achievements were the edicts in 1781 granting toleration to Jews and Protestants. He abolished serfdom and curtailed the privileges of the nobles. In German affairs he was outmanoeuvred by *Frederick II of Prussia and his alliance with *Catherine II (the Great) of Russia led to a disastrous war against the Turks.

Josephine (born **Marie Joséphine Rose Tascher de la Pagerie**) (1763–1814) Empress of France (1796–1809). Born in the West Indies, she was married to the Viscount de Beauharnais before marrying Napoleon in 1796. Their marriage proved childless and Josephine was divorced by Napoleon in 1809.

Josephus, Flavius (born **Joseph ben Matthias**) (c.37–c.100) Jewish historian, general, and Pharisee. A leader of the Jewish revolt against the Romans from 66, he was captured in 67; his life was spared when he prophesied that Vespasian would become emperor. He subsequently received Roman citizenship and a pension, and is remembered as the author of the *Jewish War*, an eyewitness account of the events leading up to the revolt, and of *Antiquities of the Jews*, a history running from the Creation to 66.

journeyman A qualified artisan working for someone else. Journeymen were workers (paid daily) who had served their apprenticeship and were not yet in a financial position to set up as masters. The late medieval craft *guilds, by restricting the number of masters without limiting the number of apprentices, created increasing numbers of discontented and sometimes unemployed journeymen: in the 16th century it was found necessary in England for Parliament to pass legislation to compel masters with apprentices to employ journeymen. This legislation was no longer enforced by the 18th century, if it ever had been, and the Industrial Revolution with its factory system and demand for unskilled labour spelled doom for the journeyman. Associations of journeymen were the earliest trade unions (as distinct from guilds) in both Britain and the USA, one of the longest-lived being the Federal Society of Journeymen Cordwainers in Philadelphia.

Juárez, Benito Pablo (1806–72) Mexican statesman, President (1861–64 and 1867–72). His refusal to repay Mexico's foreign debts led to the occupation of Mexico by Napoleon III and the establishment of Maximilian as emperor of Mexico in 1864. The withdrawal of the occupying French forces in 1867 prompted the execu-

tion of Maximilian and the rehabilitation of Juárez in the same year.

Judah Ha-Nasi (Judah the Prince) (135–c.220) Patriarch of Judaea. He is best remembered for organizing the compilation of the *Mishnah*, the first comprehensive statement of Jewish religious law. He won the favour of Roman emperors, forged closer links with the Jews of the *diaspora, and worked to raise the status of the Hebrew language.

Judaism The religion of the *Jewish people, with a belief in one God and a basis in Mosaic and rabbinical teachings. The Jews were called to reject polytheism and worship the one God, the Creator, whose will is revealed in the Torah, which comprises the first five books of the Bible (also known as the Pentateuch) and which contains the Ten Commandments. This monotheism, inherited by both Christianity and Islam, is the heart of Judaism. Jews believe that as a result of the covenant made by God with Abraham, they have a unique relationship with God (that they are the Chosen People). They also believe that an anointed person (the Messiah) will be sent by God to gather all of the peoples of Israel into the promised land and bring everlasting peace to Earth. Christians, but not Jews, believe that Jesus was the Messiah.

Orthodox Judaism teaches that the Torah (the five books of Moses) contains all the divine revelation that Jews require. Religious practice is strictly observed. When interpretation of the Torah is required, reference is made to the Talmud. Orthodox Jews maintain the separation of sexes in synagogue worship. There is only an Orthodox rabbinate in Israel, with the result that all official religion in that country is Orthodox controlled. While many Orthodox Jews support *Zionism, they deplore the secular origins of the movement and the fact that Israel is not a fully religious state. For example, the Orthodox recognize a person as Jewish only if he or she has a Jewish mother or undergoes an arduous process of conversion; whereas the Law of Return governing emigration to Israel accepts all those with a Jewish grandmother as potential Israeli citizens.

Liberal Judaism began in about 1780 in Germany, in response to the need to redefine the meaning and practical observance of the Torah in a changing society. Liberals saw the Torah's revelations as progressive rather than static, expressing God's teaching rather than God's law. This allowed for evolution in religious law and practice and resulted in dramatic changes in both diet and custom. In Europe the movement is also known as Progressive, and is roughly equivalent to US Reform Judaism.

Reform Judaism was founded in Germany by Zachariah Frankel (1801–75) in reaction to the perceived laxity of Liberal Judaism. Frankel questioned the wholly divine inspiration of the Torah, whilst retaining observance of some Jewish laws and traditions. In the UK, Reform Jews might be regarded as being on the 'right' of the Liberal or Progressive movement. In the USA, the term Reform Judaism refers to the whole of the Liberal tradition, brought across by German immigrants in the 19th century.

Hasidism (from Hebrew, 'pious') is a mystical movement that first found expression in 12th-century Germany. Modern Hasidism evolved in 18th-century Poland, where its leader, Ba'al Shem Tov (1700–60), taught a return to faith and piety. The movement advocated repeated prayer, song, chanting, and dance as joyous ways of perceiving God in all aspects of daily life. After rapid growth amongst the repressed Jewish communities of eastern Europe, the movement was curtailed by the rise of modernism. Today the largest groups of Hasidic Jews are to be found in the USA and Israel, where their leaders, *zaddikim* ('saints'), are in the forefront of the movement for religious legislation, and are determined defenders of Orthodox Judaism. Followers are distinguished by their black dress, reminiscent of clothes worn in Poland in the 17th–18th centuries, and curled side-locks, as well as by their acceptance of the Orthodox Jewish prohibition against cutting the beard, which probably originated in a wish to be distinguished from unbelievers.

Judas Maccabaeus (died *c.*161 BC) Jewish leader. He led a Jewish revolt in Judaea against the Seleucid king Antiochus IV Epiphanes from around 167, and succeeded in recovering Jerusalem, dedicating the Temple anew, and protecting Judaism from Hellenization. He also features in the Apocrypha as the hero of the Maccabees.

Jugurtha (died 104 BC) Joint king of Numidia (*c.*118–104). His attacks on his royal partners prompted intervention by Rome and led to the outbreak of the Jugurthine War (112–105). He was eventually captured by the Roman general Marius and executed in Rome.

Julian (or **Julian the Apostate;** full name **Flavius Claudius Julianus**) (*c.*331–63 AD) Roman emperor (360–63), nephew of Constantine. He restored paganism as the state cult in place of Christianity, but this move was reversed

after his death on campaign against the Persians.

Julius II (born **Giuliano della Rovere**) (1443–1513) Pope (1503–13) He strove to restore and extend the *Papal States and to establish a strong independent papacy. He crushed Cesare *Borgia and sponsored the League of *Cambrai and the Holy League against France in 1510. Before the end of 1512 the French were forced to leave Italy and several new territories were added to the papacy's holdings.

July Plot (20 July 1944) A plot to assassinate Adolf *Hitler. Disenchanted by the Nazi regime in Germany, an increasing number of senior army officers believed that Hitler had to be assassinated and an alternative government, prepared to negotiate peace terms with the Allies, established. Plans were made in late 1943 and there were a number of unsuccessful attempts before that of July 1944. The plot was carried out by Count **Berthold von Stauffenberg**, who left a bomb at Hitler's headquarters at Rastenburg. The bomb exploded, killing four people, but not Hitler. Stauffenberg, believing he had succeeded, flew to Berlin, where the plotters aimed to seize the Supreme Command headquarters. Before this was done, however, news came that Hitler had survived. A counter-move resulted in the arrest of some 200 plotters, including Stauffenberg himself, Generals Beck, Olbricht, von Tresckow, and later Friedrich Fromm. They were shot, hanged, or in some cases strangled. Field-Marshal *Rommel was implicated and obliged to commit suicide. The regime used the occasion to execute several prominent protesters such as Dietrich *Bonhoeffer.

July Revolution (1830) A revolt in France. It began when *Charles X issued his ordinances of 25 July, which suspended the liberty of the press, dissolved the new chamber, reduced the electorate, and allowed him to rule by decree. His opponents erected barricades in Paris and after five days of bitter street fighting Charles was forced to abdicate. The Duc d'Orléans, *Louis Philippe, was invited to become 'King of the French', a title which replaced the more traditional 'King of France'. His accession marked the victory of constitutional liberal forces over arbitrary and absolutist rule.

June War *See* SIX-DAY WAR.

Justinian I (482–565) Byzantine emperor (527–65). Throughout much of his reign his troops were engaged in a defensive struggle against Persia in the east and a successful war against the barbarians in the west. Believing that they had lost their initial vigour, he hoped to revive the old Roman empire. His general, *Belisarius, crushed the Vandals in Africa (533) and the Ostrogoths in Italy (535–53), making Ravenna the centre of government. His greater claim to fame lay in his domestic policy in which he was strongly influenced by his powerful wife, *Theodora. He reformed provincial administration and in his *Corpus Juris Civilis* he codified 4652 imperial ordinances (*Codex*), summarized the views of the best legal writers (*Digest*), and added a handbook for students (*Institutes*). A passionately orthodox Christian, he fought pagans and heretics. His lasting memorial is the Church of St Sophia in Constantinople.

Justo, Agustín Pedro (1876–1943) Argentine statesman. Justo participated in the conservative military coup that overthrew President Hipólito *Irigoyen in 1930 and was rewarded with the presidency (1932–38). Faced by the effects of revolution, high unemployment, and the economic decline that was caused by the Great *Depression, his regime was autocratic; for example, he outlawed the Communist Party in 1936. However, he supported *Pan-American cooperation and closer links with Britain. He was defeated in the 1937 presidential election by Roberto Ortiz, despite having been instrumental in ending the *Chaco War. A supporter of the Allies in World War II, he enlisted in the Brazilian army in 1942 and was killed.

Jute A Low-German tribe that invaded southern England (according to legend under Horsa and Hengist) in the 5th century and set up a kingdom in Kent.

Jutland, Battle of (31 may 1916) A naval battle between Britain and Germany, fought in the North Sea off the coast of Jutland. The only major battle fought at sea in World War I, it began between two forces of battle cruisers, the British under Admiral David Beatty (1871–1936) and the Germans under von Hipper. Suffering heavy losses, Beatty sailed to join the main British North Sea Fleet under Admiral John Jellicoe (1859–1935), which then engaged the German High Seas Fleet under *Scheer. Battle began at 6 p.m. at long range (approximately 14 km or 9 miles), but as the Germans headed for home in the night, they collided with the British fleet, several ships sinking in the ensuing chaos. Both sides claimed victory. The British lost 14 ships, including three battle cruisers; the Germans lost 11 ships, including one battleship and one battle cruiser; but the British retained control of the North Sea, the German fleet staying in port for the rest of the war.

Kabir (1440–1518) Indian mystic and poet, who preached the unity of all religions. There is uncertainty about his origins, but it is believed that he was adopted by a Muslim weaver after being abandoned by his Brahmin Hindu mother. His borrowings from both Hinduism and Islam resulted in the preaching of a new mystic path, the *Kabir panth*, and the founding, by one of his disciples, of the *Sikh religion. His mystical poems, stressing the oneness of God, together with his rejection of caste, have made Kabir one of the most popular religious figures in his country's history.

Kadafy, Moamar al *See* GADDAFI, MU'AMMAR.

Kádár, János (1912–89) Hungarian statesman, First Secretary of the Hungarian Socialist Workers' Party (1956–88) and Prime Minister (1956–58) and (1961–65). He replaced Imre Nagy as Premier after crushing the Hungarian uprising of 1956. Kádár consistently supported the Soviet Union, involving Hungarian troops in the 1968 invasion of Czechoslovakia, while retaining a degree of decentralization for the economy. His policy of 'consumer socialism' made Hungary the most affluent state in eastern Europe. He was removed as First Secretary following his resistance to the political reforms of the 1980s.

Kagame, Paul (1957–) Rwandan statesman, President (2000–). A Tutsi, Kagame grew up in Uganda after his parents fled *Rwanda in 1959 to escape Hutu-led ethnic purges. He became a follower of Yoweri Museveni (*see* UGANDA) and fought in his rebel army, rising to become head of military intelligence after Museveni became President of Uganda. Kagame joined the Rwandan Patriotic Front (FPR), a movement of Tutsi exiles, taking command of its army in 1990 after a failed invasion of Rwanda. Negotiations with the Hutu-dominated Rwandan government led to a ceasefire in 1993, but the genocide of 1994 provoked Kagame to lead a successful FPR invasion of Rwanda. He became Vice President and Minister of Defence in the new government but, as army commander, was de facto ruler of the country; he assumed the presidency in 2000. He decisively won multiparty presidential elections in 2003 and 2010, although irregularities were alleged on both occasions. As President he emphasized Rwandan unity and sought to rebuild the economy. Internationally, he intervened (1996–2002) in the Congo civil war (*see* CONGO, DEMOCRATIC REPUBLIC OF), initially to combat dissident Hutu forces, and cultivated relationships with Rwanda's East African neighbours, China, the USA, and the UK.

Kalinin, Mikhail Ivanovich (1875–1946) Soviet statesman, head of state of the USSR (1919–46). Born in Russia, he was a founder of the newspaper *Pravda* in 1912.

Kalmar, Union of (1397) The joining together of the crowns of Denmark, Sweden, and Norway. Margaret I (1353–1412), daughter of the King of Denmark and wife of Haakon VI of Norway (died 1387), defeated (1389) the King of Sweden and persuaded the Diets of Denmark, Norway, and Sweden to accept Eric of Pomerania, her grandnephew, as king. He was crowned (1397), the beginning of the Union of Kalmar, though Margaret herself ruled the three kingdoms until her death. The union was dissolved by Gustavus I of Sweden in 1523.

Kamakura shogunate The first feudal military *shogunate established by *Minamoto Yoritomo at the city of Kamakura, near Tokyo. The *Hojo family were shogun regents after Yoritomo's death. During the Kamakura shogunate (1192–1333) organized military power and the *samurai emerged.

Kamenev, Lev Borisovich (1883–1936) Soviet leader who joined the Social Democratic Party (1901) and sided with the *Bolshevik faction when the party split in 1903. He was exiled to Siberia for ordering Bolshevik deputies in the Duma to oppose World War I. In 1917 he presided over the Second All-Russian Congress of Soviets. On *Lenin's death in 1924 Kamenev,

*Zinoviev, and *Stalin formed a triumvirate to exclude Kamenev's brother-in-law, *Trotsky, from power. In 1936 he was accused of complicity in the murder of Kirov in the first public show trial of Stalin's great purge, and was shot.

kamikaze (Japanese, 'Divine Wind') Originally the fierce storms that twice saved Japan from Mongol invasion (in 1274 and 1281). In World War II a kamikaze was an aircraft laden with explosives and suicidally crashed by the pilot into an enemy ship. The Japanese naval command resorted to these desperate measures in 1944 in an attempt to halt the Allied advance across the Pacific. At first volunteers were used, but the practice soon became compulsory. Off Okinawa in 1945 over 300 kamikaze pilots died in one action.

Kampuchea See CAMBODIA.

Kanagawa, Treaty of (or **Perry Convention**) (31 March 1854) A treaty between Japan and the USA. After three years of negotiation, the US Commodore Perry came to an agreement with the Tokugawa *shogunate, opening two ports to US vessels, allowing the appointment of a consul, and guaranteeing better treatment for shipwrecked sailors. The Treaty of Kanagawa was followed within two years by similar agreements with Britain, Russia, and the Netherlands, and in 1858 by the more wide-ranging Treaty of *Edo with the USA, and marked the beginning of regular political and economic intercourse between Japan and the Western nations.

Kanaka A native Hawaiian, or more generally any Pacific Islander. Kanakas, mainly from the New Hebrides and the Solomon Islands, were brought to Australia between 1863 and 1904 as cheap labour. Theoretically, they voluntarily entered contracts for fixed terms. In practice, they were subjected to kidnap, slavery, and murder. Their entry to Australia was banned in 1904. Most of those in Australia were deported back to the islands from 1906 onwards, as part of the White Australia Policy.

Kanem-Bornu Two successive major African states in the Lake Chad region between the 11th and the 19th centuries. Ethnically and linguistically the peoples were mixed. They include Arab, Berber, and other African elements, and were mostly Muslims. An Islamic sultanate of Kanem, ruled by the Seyfawa family, existed by the 11th century, which, under Dunama (1221–59), came to extend from Fezzan and

Wadai to the Niger, and included Bornu. Following civil wars this empire collapsed in 1398, but a member of it created a new state of Bornu with N'gazargamu as capital, and Kanem as a province. Idris Aloma (ruled 1571–1603) was the most powerful of the Bornu rulers; he introduced firearms into the army and Bornu reached the peak of its power under his rule. A long period of stability followed until 1808, when the *Fulani sacked N'gazargamu. Muhammad al-Kanemi, a leading chief, restored the titular kings, retaining effective power himself. The last Mai, or titular king, was executed in 1846.

Kangxi (or **K'ang-hsi**) (1654–1722) The second *Qing Emperor of China (1662–1722). He extended the Qing empire by a series of military campaigns, subduing opposition to Manchu rule in southern China (1673–81), incorporating *Taiwan into China for the first time in 1683, and personally leading a campaign into Outer *Mongolia (1693). He opened certain ports to overseas traders and the Treaty of Nerchinsk (1689), established diplomatic contact with Russia. In 1692 he permitted Catholic missionaries to make converts and he employed Jesuits to teach astronomy and mathematics. He was renowned for his history of the Ming dynasty and an encyclopedia of literature.

Kang Youwei (or **K'ang Yu-wei**) (1858–1927) Chinese philosopher and political reformer. A scholar, whose utopian work *Da Tong Shu* (*One World Philosophy*, 1900) portrayed Confucius as a reformer, he believed that China's crisis could only be solved through the modernization of institutions along modified western lines. In 1898 he persuaded the emperor Guangxu to adopt his policies. The resulting Hundred Days Reform was brought to a premature end by the empress dowager *Cixi's conservative coup, and Kang spent the next 15 years in exile. He remained a monarchist and spent his last years trying unsuccessfully to engineer an imperial restoration.

Kansas–Nebraska Act (1854) An Act of the US Congress concerning slavery. Following the *Mexican–American War, the *Compromise of 1850 had allowed *squatters in New Mexico and Utah to decide by referendum whether they would enter the Union as "free" or "slave" states. This was contrary to the earlier *Missouri Compromise. The Act of 1854 declared that in Kansas and Nebraska a decision on slavery would also be allowed, by holding a referendum. Tensions erupted between pro-and anti-slavery groups, which in Kansas led to violence (1855–57). Those who deplored the Act formed a new political organization, the *Republican Party, pledged to oppose slavery in the Territories. Kansas was to be admitted as a free state in 1861, and Nebraska in 1867.

Kapp putsch (March 1920) The attempt by Wolfgang Kapp (1858–1922), a right-wing Prussian landowner and politician, to overthrow the *Weimar Republic and restore the German monarchy. Aided by elements in the army, including *Ludendorff, and the unofficial "free corps" which the new government was trying to disband, Kapp's forces seized Berlin, planning to set up a rival government with himself as Chancellor. The *putsch* was defeated by a general strike of the Berlin workers and the refusal of civil servants to obey his orders.

Karadžić, Radovan (1945–) Serbian political leader. He practised psychiatry in Sarajevo until 1990, when he helped found the Serbian Democratic Party. In 1992, when the Bosnian Serbs declared an independent state, the Republika Srpska, within *Bosnia and Herzegovina, Karadžić became its President. With the support of Serbian President Slobodan Milošević, he instituted a ruthless campaign (1992–95) to drive non-Serb Bosnians from the republic. In 1995, when Milošević withdrew support, Karadžić reluctantly signed the US-brokered Dayton peace accord. Twice that year he was indicted by the UN for war crimes, including 'ethnic cleansing'. He resigned as President of both the Republika Srpska and the Serbian Democratic Party in 1996 and went into hiding, successfully managing to evade arrest until 2008. His trial before the International Criminal Tribunal for the former Yugoslavia began in 2009.

Kara George, Petrović (1766–1817) Serbian revolutionary leader, founder of the dynasty of Karageorgević. The son of a peasant, in 1804 he became leader of a Serbian revolt against the Turkish army and played a major role in forcing the Turks out of *Serbia. Four years later he was proclaimed leader of Serbia but his ruthless and autocratic rule led to unrest. In 1813 his army was defeated by the Turks and he fled. He returned in 1817 only to be murdered, probably by his rival Milos *Obrenović. His son, Alexander, ruled Serbia as prince from 1843 to 1858, but was displaced by an Obrenović. Alexander's son, Peter, became King of Serbia in 1903; his grandson became *Alexander I of Yugoslavia.

Karelia A region on the frontier of Finland and Russia, which formed an independent Finnish state in medieval times and whose folk-tales were the source of the Finnish epic, the *Kalevala*. In the 16th century Karelia came under Swedish rule and in 1721 it was annexed by Russia. Following Finland's declaration of independence in 1917, part of Karelia became a region of Finland and part was subsequently designated an autonomous republic of the Soviet Union. After the Russian–Finnish War of 1939–40 the greater part of Finnish Karelia was ceded to the Soviet Union.

Karnak The religious centre of ancient Thebes, situated on the east bank of the Nile, where the great temple of Amun was constructed. This complex of buildings, the work of some 2000 years, includes the Hypostyle Hall with 134 columns each *c*.24 m (79 feet) high. It was begun by Ramesses I and completed by Seti I and *Ramesses II. A road lined with statues of sphinxes linked the site to nearby Luxor.

Károlyi, Mihály, Count (1875–1955) Hungarian statesman. A liberal, he favoured a less pro-German policy for *Austria–Hungary and supported equal rights for all nations within it. There was no hope of achieving this until the empire collapsed (November 1918), when Hungary proclaimed itself a republic with Károlyi as President. When in March 1920 he learned that Hungary must cede territory to Romania, Czechoslovakia, and Yugoslavia he resigned and was replaced by Béla *Kun's Communist regime.

Kasavubu, Joseph (1910–69) Congolese statesman. He became the first President (1960–65) of the Democratic Republic of Congo. He was a member of undercover nationalist associations to free the Congo of the Belgians. In 1955 he became President of Abako (Alliance des Bakongo), a cultural association of the Bakongo tribe, and turned it into a powerful political organization. On independence in 1960 he became Head of State. His Abako party formed a coalition with *Lumumba's party, and then ousted him as premier. In 1965 he himself was deposed from the Presidency by *Mobutu in a bloodless military coup.

Kashmir dispute The conflict between India and Pakistan over the region of Kashmir (now mostly part of the Indian state of Jammu-Kashmir) that erupted into war (1948–49) and remains unresolved, Kashmir, exposed successively to Hindu and Muslim rule, was annexed (1819) to the expanding Sikh kingdom. After the first *Sikh War the territory was acquired by Gulab Singh, then Hindu raja of the Jammu region. It was a Princely State for the rest of the British period. The Maharaja, a Hindu ruling over a predominantly Muslim population, initially hoped to remain independent in 1947, but eventually acceded to the Indian Union. The war between India and Pakistan (1948–49) over Kashmir ended when a United Nations peace-keeping force imposed a temporary ceasefire line which divided the Indian Union state of Jammu and Kashmir from Pakistan-backed Azad Kashmir. Kashmir remains divided by this 'line of control'. Conflicts between India and Pakistan over Kashmir flared up again in 1965 and 1971, together with demands for a UN-supervised plebiscite. In 1989 militant supporters of either Kashmiri independence or union with Pakistan intensified their campaign of violent civil unrest and Indian government troops were sent into the state. Direct rule by the President was imposed in 1990. Sporadic fighting continued, but a ceasefire agreed in 2004 was followed by improved relations across the line of control.

Kassites *See* BABYLON.

Kato Komei (or **Kato Takaaki**) (1860–1926) Japanese statesman who served as ambassador to Britain (1909) and Foreign Minister (1914–15), but was forced to resign after his presentation of the *Twenty-One Demands to China. He reorganized and led the conservative Kenseikai, and as Prime Minister (1924–25) pursued a moderate foreign policy while introducing universal manhood suffrage, cutting expenditure, and reducing the size of the army. He also introduced the stringent Peace Preservation Law to balance the possibly destabilizing effects of manhood suffrage. His cabinet was called the "Mitsubishi government" because both he and his foreign minister Shidehara Kijuro had marriage ties with the Mitsubishi *zaibatsu.

Katyn massacre A massacre in Katyn forest in the western USSR. In 1943 the German army claimed to have discovered a mass grave of some 4500 Polish officers, part of a group of 15,000 Poles who had disappeared from Soviet captivity in 1940 and whose fate remained unknown. Each victim had a bullet in the base of his skull. The Soviet Union denied involvement in the massacre until April 1990, when it was confirmed that the officers had been killed in the early days of close Nazi-Soviet collaboration, by order of Stalin.

Kaunda, Kenneth David (1924–) Zambian statesman. At first a schoolmaster, in 1949 he joined the *African National Congress (ANC). In 1959 he became its President and led opposition to the *Central African Federation, instituting a campaign of "positive non-violent action". For this he was imprisoned by the British, and the movement was banned. He was released in 1960 and was elected President of the newly formed United National Independence Party (UNIP). The UNIP became the leading party when independence was granted to Zambia in 1964 and Kaunda became the first President of the new republic. During his presidency education expanded and the government made efforts to diversify the economy to release Zambia from its dependence on copper. Ethnic differences, the Rhodesian and Angolan conflicts, and the collapse of copper prices engendered unrest and political violence, which led Kaunda to institute a one-party state (1973). Later, with the civil war in *Angola, he assumed emergency powers. Nevertheless, he was re-elected President in 1978, again in 1983, and in 1988. He legalized opposition parties in 1990, but was defeated by the trade-union leader Frederick Chiluba in the multiparty presidential election held in November 1991. In January 1992 he resigned as leader of the UNIP. He returned to politics in 1995, but was barred from standing in the 1996 presidential election; he finally resigned as UNIP president in 2000. In late 1997 he was arrested and accused of inciting a coup, but the charges were dropped in 1998. His Zambian citizenship was withdrawn in 1999 but restored in 2000. He was a staunch supporter of the *Commonwealth of Nations and took a strong line in demanding sanctions against South Africa for its policy of apartheid.

Kaunitz, Wenzel Anton, Count von (1711–94) Austrian diplomat and statesman. As Chancellor (1753–92) he controlled foreign policy under Empress *Maria Theresa and Emperor Joseph II. He was convinced that Prussia was Austria's most dangerous enemy and his main diplomatic feat was to reverse (1756–57) long-standing European alliances, but Britain remained opposed to France and Austria stayed allied to Russia. However, when Britain formed an alliance with its former enemy, Prussia, in order to protect Hanover, Kaunitz negotiated an alliance with France, thus isolating Prussia on the Continent. Although the ambitions of *Frederick II (the Great) were not fully checked, Kaunitz was a leading negotiator of the Treaty of Paris (1763).

k

Kazakhstan

Capital:	Astana
Area:	2,724,900 sq km (1,052,090 sq miles)
Population:	17,736,896 (2013 est)
Currency:	1 tenge = 100 tiyn
Religions:	Muslim 70.2%; Eastern Orthodox 23.9%; other Christian 2.3%
Ethnic Groups:	Kazakh 63.1%; Russian 23.7%; Uzbek 2.8%
Languages:	Kazakh, Russian (both official)
International Organizations:	UN; OSCE; Commonwealth of Independent States; Euro-Atlantic Partnership Council

A country of western central Asia, stretching for some 3200 km (2000 miles) from the Caspian Sea to Xinjiang. It is bounded by China on the east, Kyrgyzstan and Uzbekistan on the south, the Caspian Sea and Turkmenistan on the west, and Russia on the north.

Physical In the north a belt of fertile steppe with rich, black earth (chernozem) provides scope for cultivation. Southward, however, it becomes more arid, degenerating into the Kara-Kum desert. On the east Caspian coast, oil and natural gas are found. Further east, towards the Aral Sea, is a clay desert plateau; east and southeast of it, sand desert. To the east of this are the stony Kazakh uplands with huge coal deposits in their northern slopes and copper in their southern ones. Here is the extensive and partly saline Lake Balkhash, which is slowly evaporating.

Economy Kazakhstan has rich and varied mineral deposits, including oil, natural gas, tungsten, copper, lead, uranium, diamonds, coal, iron ore, and zinc. The mainstay of the economy is the exploitation of these resources, especially oil; however, the government is attempting to diversify the economy into other industries. Grain production and livestock-rearing dominate agriculture.

History For centuries, the steppelands of Kazakhstan were the home of nomadic Kazakh herdsmen, ruled by Mongol khans, whose territories were steadily annexed by Tsarist Russia during the 19th century, the *khanate being abolished in 1848. A nationalist movement developed in the early 20th century and there was a bloody anti-Tsarist revolt in 1916. In 1917 a national government was proclaimed in the capital Alma Ata; but this was suppressed by the Red Army, which occupied the country (1919–20), and large numbers of Russians and Ukrainians moved in. It became the Kazakh Autonomous Soviet Socialist Republic, which in 1936 became a full republic within the Soviet Union. Vast areas (some ten million acres) were developed for agriculture as state farms, while there was also heavy industrialization during the 1930s and 1940s. Large mineral deposits, including uranium, were discovered and exploited, particularly around Lake Balkhash. After 1941 Stalin's regime forcibly moved German, Greek, and Armenian deportees into the republic. In October 1990 it proclaimed its sovereignty, and in December 1991 its independence was recognized. The Communist-derived ruling party remained in power, under President Nursultan Nazarbayev. A new constitution was approved by referendum in 1995 and gave Nazarbayev ultimate power. He was re-elected in 1999 but observers condemned the elections as unfair. In December 1997 the capital was transferred from Almaty to Aqmola, which was renamed Astana. Nazarbayev was again re-elected in 2005 and 2011.

Keating, Paul (John) (1944–) Australian Labor statesman, Prime Minister (1991–96). He entered politics in 1969 when he became a member of the House of Representatives. He served as federal treasurer (1983–91) and deputy Prime Minister (1990–91) under Bob *Hawke, whom he replaced as Premier in 1991. His term of office was notable for a vociferous campaign to make Australia a republic as well as for measures to combat high unemployment.

Kefauver, Carey Estes (1903–63) US politician. A state Senator (1949–63), he came to national prominence in the early 1950s when, as chairman of a US Senate committee investigating organized crime, he exposed nationwide gambling and crime syndicates, which had infiltrated legitimate business and gained control of local politics. The evidence of corruption among federal tax officials led to several dismissals and the resignation of the commissioner of Internal Revenue. Kefauver won the Democratic Party's nomination for Vice-President

(1956), but President *Eisenhower (Republican) was re-elected.

Keitel, Wilhelm Bodewin Johann Gustav (1882–1946) German field-marshal. As chief-of-staff of the High Command of the German armed forces (1938–45), he handled the armistice negotiations with France in 1940 and ratified the unconditional surrender of Germany in 1945. He was a close adviser of *Hitler, and bore some of the responsibility for repressive measures taken by the army in occupied territory. He was hanged after trial at Nuremberg.

Kellogg-Briand Pact (or Pact of Paris) (1928) A multilateral agreement condemning war. It grew out of a proposal by the French Premier, Aristide *Briand, to the US government for a treaty outlawing war between the two countries. The US Secretary of State, Frank B. Kellogg, proposed a multilateral treaty of the same character. In August 1928 15 nations signed an agreement committing themselves to peace; the USA ratified it in 1929, followed by a further 46 nations. The failure of the Pact to provide measures of enforcement nullified its contribution to international order.

Kelly, Ned (1855–80) Australian outlaw. He was the leader of a band of horse and cattle thieves and bank raiders operating in Victoria. A bushranger from 1878, Kelly was eventually hanged in Melbourne.

Kelly, Petra (Karin) (1947–92) German political leader. Formerly a member of the German Social Democratic Party, she became disillusioned with their policies and in 1979 co-founded the Green Party, a broad alliance of environmentalists, feminists, and anti-nuclear activists. She became the Party's leading spokesperson and in 1983 was one of 17 Green Party members elected to the West German Parliament. The cause of her death remains a subject of controversy.

Kenilworth, Siege of (June–December 1266) An episode during the second Barons' War when *Henry III attacked Kenilworth Castle, refuge of the Montforts and their supporters. The Dictum of Kenilworth (31 October 1266) asserted the king's powers over the barons and offered inducements to peace by allowing them to recover their confiscated lands: the besieged earls finally surrendered in December.

Kennedy, John Fitzgerald (known as 'JFK') (1917–63) US Democratic statesman, 35th President of the USA (1961–63). A national war hero during World War II, Kennedy became, at 43, the youngest man ever to be elected President, as well as the first Catholic. He gained a popular reputation as an advocate of civil rights, although reforms were delayed by Congress until 1964. In foreign affairs he recovered from the fiasco of the Bay of Pigs invasion of Cuba to demand successfully the withdrawal of Soviet missiles from the country, and negotiated the Test-Ban Treaty of 1963 with the USSR and the UK. Kennedy was assassinated while riding in a motorcade through Dallas, Texas, in November 1963; Lee Harvey Oswald was charged with his murder, but was himself shot before he could stand trial. Oswald was said to be the sole gunman by the Warren Commission (1964), but the House of Representatives Assassinations Committee (1979) concluded that more than one gunman had been involved; the affair remains the focus for a number of conspiracy theories.

Kennedy, Robert Francis (1925–68) US Democratic statesman. The brother of John F. *Kennedy and Edward Kennedy, he worked closely with his brother John in domestic policy, serving as Attorney-General (1961–64), and was a champion of the civil-rights movement. Robert Kennedy stood as a prospective presidential candidate in 1968, but was assassinated during his campaign.

Kenneth I (MacAlpine) (died c.858) King of Scotland (c.843–58). He united the Scots and Picts to form the kingdom of Scotia (c.843), having succeeded in c.841 as King of Dalriada in the Highlands. In c.848 he moved the relics of St *Columba to Scone, where the kings of Scotland were crowned.

Kenneth II (died 995) King of Scotland (971–95). In return for recognizing the lordship of King *Edgar of England, Kenneth received Lothian two years after his accession in 971. He was murdered by Constantine III who, in turn, was killed by Kenneth III (died 1005), whose brief reign of civil wars from 997 ended with the accession of Malcolm II.

Kenny, Enda (1951–) Irish Fine Gael politician, Prime Minister of the Republic of Ireland (2011–). He became Prime Minister of a Fine Gael–Labour coalition following the 2011 general election. Later that year he publicly criticized the Roman Catholic Church in terms unprecedented in the Republic's history for its concealment of child sex abuse by clerics.

k

Kenya

Capital:	Nairobi
Area:	580,367 sq km (224,081 sq miles)
Population:	44,037,656 (2013 est)
Currency:	1 Kenya shilling = 100 cents
Religions:	Protestant 47.4%; Roman Catholic 23.3%; other Christian 11.8%; Muslim 11.1%
Ethnic Groups:	Kikuyu 22.0%; Luhya 14.0%; Luo 13.0%; Kalenjin 12.0%; Kamba 11.0%; Kisii 6.0%; Meru 6.0%; other African 15.0%
Languages:	Swahili, English (both official); local languages
International Organizations:	Non-Aligned Movement; AU; UN; Commonwealth; WTO

An equatorial country in east Africa, bounded inland by Somalia on the east, Ethiopia and Sudan on the north, Uganda on the west, and Tanzania on the south.

Physical In the south-east of Kenya is a hot, damp coast on the Indian Ocean, into which run two long rivers, the Tana and the Galana. They rise in the central highlands, a region containing Mount Kenya and cool slopes and plateaux suitable for farming of various kinds, particularly the cultivation of tea and coffee. The highlands are split by part of the Great Rift Valley, a region of lakes, and to the west fall away to the eastern shore of Lake Victoria. Northward is a rift-valley lake, Turkana, and to its east is a vast, hot, dry region with thorny scrub. In the south there is a smaller lake, Magadi, with major deposits of soda.

Economy Kenya has an agricultural economy with a developing industrial sector. The main exports are tea, coffee, horticultural products, and petroleum products (from imported crude oil). Agriculture employs three-quarters of the workforce and produces tea, coffee, cereals, sugar cane, fruit, and vegetables. Consumer goods, agricultural products, horticulture, and oil refining are the principal industries; tourism is also important. There are mineral deposits of soda ash, fluorspar, salt, and gold.

History In areas of the Great Rift Valley, such as Lake Turkana, palaeontologists have discovered some of the earliest fossil hominid remains. Arabs settled on the coast during the 7th century. During the 16th and 17th centuries, Portuguese traders operated in the region. The Maasai pastoral people came into the area in the 18th century from the north, but during the 19th century they were largely displaced by the agricultural Kikuyu, who steadily advanced from the south. British coastal trade began in the 1840s, and in 1887 the British East African Association (a trading company) secured a lease of coastal strip from the Sultan of Zanzibar. The British East Africa Protectorate was established in 1896, when thousands of Indians were brought in to build railways. The British crown colony of Kenya was created in 1920. By then a great area of the 'White Highlands' had been reserved for white settlement, while 'Native Reserves' were established to separate the two communities. During the 1920s there was considerable immigration from Britain, and a development of African political movements, demanding a greater share in the government of the country. Kikuyu nationalism developed steadily, led by Jomo *Kenyatta. From this tension grew the Kenya Africa Union, and the militant *Mau Mau movement (1952–57). An election in 1961 led to the two African political parties, the Kenya African National Union (KANU) and the Kenya African Democratic Union (KADU), joining the government. Independence was achieved in 1963, and in the following year Kenya became a republic with Kenyatta as President. Under him, Kenya remained generally stable, but after his death in 1978 opposition to his successor, Daniel arap Moi, mounted, culminating in a bloody attempted coup in 1982. Elections in 1983 saw the return of comparative stability with Moi still President, but of an increasingly corrupt and autocratic regime. In December 1991 Moi reluctantly agreed to end single-party politics. Multiparty elections, held in 1992 and 1997, were won by Moi amid allegations of electoral fraud. He did not stand for re-election in 2002, and the election was won by the opposition leader, Mwai Kibaki, who promised to end Kenya's by now endemic corruption. However, he failed to do so. The result of the 2007 election was disputed between Kibaki and Raila Odinga of the opposition Orange Democratic Movement. Kibaki was declared the winner by a narrow margin, but violence between their supporters, who in general divided along ethnic lines, resulted in over a thousand deaths. A power-sharing agreement was reached in 2008, but in 2012 the International Criminal Court indicted four prominent politicians – including Uhuru Kenyatta, son of Jomo Kenyatta – for instigating the violence. The next presidential elections, in 2013, were peaceful and resulted in victory for Kenyatta.

Kenyatta, Jomo (*c.*1891–1978) Kenyan statesman, Prime Minister of Kenya in 1963 and President (1964–78). He was imprisoned from 1952 to 1961 for alleged complicity in the Mau Mau uprising. On his release he was elected President of the Kenya African National Union and led his country to independence in 1963, subsequently serving as independent Kenya's first President. His son, **Uhuru Kenyatta**, became Kenya's fourth President in 2013.

Kerensky, Alexander Feodorovich (1881–1970) Russian revolutionary. He was a representative of the moderate Labour Party in the Fourth Duma (1912) and joined the Socialist Revolutionary Party during the *Russian Revolution. After the emperor's abdication in March (February, old style), he was made Minister of War in the Provisional Government of Prince Lvov, succeeding him as Premier four months later. Determined to continue the war against Germany, he failed to implement agrarian and economic reforms, and his government was overthrown by the *Bolsheviks in the October Revolution. He escaped to Paris, where he continued as an active propagandist against the Soviet regime.

Kesselring, Albrecht (1885–1960) German field-marshal. He commanded the *bombing offensive over Poland, the Netherlands, and France before commencing the Battle of *Britain, when he was hampered by interference from *Goering and *Hitler. Posted to the Mediterranean soon after, from 1943 to 1945 he commanded all German forces in Italy, and in 1945 in the West. Condemned to death as a war criminal in 1947, he had his sentence commuted to life imprisonment and was freed in 1952.

Kett's Rebellion (July–August 1549) An orderly English peasant protest against the profiteering and *enclosures of local Norfolk landlords. Led by Robert Kett, a well-to-do tradesman, 16,000 small farmers encamped outside Norwich, and eventually gained control of the city. By their disciplined self-government, the rebels aimed to impress the authorities and shame the local magnates. The rebellion was suppressed by forces under John Dudley (later Duke of *Northumberland) who routed the rebels at Dussindale on 27 August. Kett and his brother William were among those executed.

KGB (Russian abbreviation, Committee of State Security) Formed in 1953, the KGB was responsible for external espionage, internal counter-intelligence, and internal 'crimes against the state'. The most famous chairman of the KGB was Yuri Andropov (1967–82) who was Soviet leader (1982–84). He made KGB operations more sophisticated, especially against internal dissidents. In 1991 the KGB was dissolved, to be replaced by five separate bodies. These pledged themselves to work with Western Intelligence in the prevention of nuclear proliferation and the development of chemical and biological weapons, and to fight terrorism and drug trafficking.

Khalifa, Abdallah (or **Muhammad al-Ta'a'ishi**) (*c.*1846–99) The successor of the Sudanese *Mahdi. In 1883 the Mahdi made Khalifa commander of the army, and he was largely responsible for the victory over the British at Khartoum in 1885. When the Mahdi died Khalifa eliminated the remaining Egyptian garrisons, and waged war on *Ethiopia until 1889. After his defeat by *Kitchener at Omdurman he fled to Kordofan, where he died in battle.

Khalji A Muslim dynasty of Turkish origin which seized power in northern India in 1290. Its three kings successively ruled the Delhi sultanate for the next 30 years. Ala ud-Din (1296–1316), the second sultan, was the most successful. His armies held off Mongol threats, subdued large parts of Rajasthan and Gujarat, then carried Islam to Madurai in the extreme south of the subcontinent. Their object was pillage rather than permanent empire, yet Khalji expansion began a new era of Muslim penetration of Hindu southern India. On Ala ud-Din's assassination the dynasty declined, to be replaced in 1320 by the *Tughluq dynasty.

Khama, Sir Seretse (1921–80) Botswanan statesman, Prime Minister of Bechuanaland 1965 and President of Botswana (1966–80). An heir to the chieftainship of the ruling tribe in Bechuanaland, he was banished because of opposition to his marriage to an Englishwoman in 1948. He returned with his wife in 1956 and formed the Democratic Party in 1962, leading the party to a landslide victory in the elections of 1965; he became Botswana's first President the following year. A strong believer in multiracial democracy, he achieved nationwide free education.

k

khanate The region ruled by a **khan** (a Mongol or Turkic supreme tribal leader elevated by the support of his warriors). On *Genghis Khan's death in 1227 his empire was divided into four parts, each ruled by one of his descendants. By the mid-13th century the *Mongol empire consisted of four khanates; the khanate of the Western Kipchaks (the *Golden Horde); the khanate of Persia, whose ruler was called the Il-khan; the khanate of Turkistan (the White Horde of the Eastern Kipchaks), and the khanate of the Khakhan in East Asia. The three khans were subject to the Khakhan (the Great Khan), but were generally resentful in their relations with him. After the death of *Kublai Khan (1294) the Khakhan's authority was nominal. In 1368 the Mongols were driven out of China and by c.1500 all four khanates had disappeared. A number of lesser khanates emerged; the khanates of Kazan, Astrakhan, the Crimea, Khiva, Bukhara, Tashkent, Samarkand, and Kokand. These long presented a threat to the communities surrounding them. One by one all were absorbed by Russia. The last to fall was Kokand (1876).

Khilafat Movement An Indian Muslim movement. It aimed to rouse public opinion against the harsh treatment accorded to the Ottoman empire after World War I and specifically against the treatment of the Ottoman sultan and caliph (khalifa). The movement began in 1919 and, under the leadership of the Ali brothers, Muhammad Ali (1878–1931) and Shaukat Ali (1873–1938), assumed a mainly political character in alliance with the Indian National *Congress, adopting the non-cooperation programme in May 1920. The Khilafat movement had considerable support from Muslims but was extinguished in 1924 after the abolition of the caliphate by *Atatürk.

Khmer An ancient kingdom in south-east Asia, which reached the peak of its power in the 11th century, ruling over the entire Mekong valley from the capital at Angkor, and was destroyed by Siamese conquests in the 12th and 14th centuries.

Khmer Republic The former official name (1970–75) for *Cambodia.

Khmer Rouge Cambodian communist movement. Formed to resist the right-wing, US-backed regime of Lon Nol after the latter's military coup in 1970, the Khmer Rouge, with Vietnamese assistance, first dominated the countryside and then captured the capital Phnom Penh (1975). Under *Pol Pot it began a bloody purge, liquidating nearly the entire professional élite as well as most of the government officials and Buddhist monks. The majority of the urban population were relocated on worksites in the countryside where large numbers perished. The regime was responsible for an estimated 2 million deaths in *Cambodia (Kampuchea), and for the dislocation of the country's infrastructure. Frontier disputes with Vietnam provoked an invasion by the latter in 1978 which led to the overthrow of the Khmer Rouge regime, although its forces continued a guerrilla war against the Vietnamese-backed Heng Samrin regime from bases in Thailand. As the Party of Democratic Kampuchea, with its former leader Pol Pot still influential, it agreed to join the UN-backed Supreme National Council, following the peace agreement of October 1991. However, the Khmer Rouge refused to participate in multiparty elections in 1993 and continued to wage a guerrilla war against the elected government until 1998–99, when most of its members either joined or surrendered to the government forces.

Khomeini, Ruhollah (or Ayatollah Khomeini) (1900–89) Iranian Shiite Muslim leader. After 16 years in exile he returned to Iran in 1979 to lead an Islamic revolution which overthrew the shah. He established a fundamentalist Islamic republic, supported the seizure of the US embassy (1979) by Iranian students, and relentlessly pursued the Iran–Iraq War (1980–88). In 1989 he issued a *fatwa* condemning Salman Rushdie, author of *The Satanic Verses* and offering a reward for his murder, which provoked criticism from the West. The Iranian government withdrew its support from the *fatwa* in 1998.

Khosrau I (died 579 AD) King of Persia (531–79), whose reign, after a long period of turbulence, marked the highest point of the *Sassanian empire. Khosrau I restored royal authority over the army, bureaucracy, and lower nobility, reformed taxation, and restored defences and public works. He invaded Byzantine Syria in 540 and took Antioch. In 565, in alliance with the western Turks, he destroyed the Hephthalite empire on his eastern frontier. He also annexed *Yemen and died during negotiations with Byzantium over his invasion of Mesopotamia.

Khosrau II (died 628 AD) King of Persia (590–628) who succeeded to the throne after the deposition of his father, Hormidz. After being unseated by a coup, he accepted Byzantine aid to regain his throne in return for most of Armenia. He recovered his territory, with Edessa and Caesarea, in 610. In 611 *Jerusalem was taken and several thousand Christians massacred. In 616 Khosrau II simultaneously invaded Egypt, captured Ankara, and besieged Constantinople. A Byzantine counter-attack drove him back to Ctesiphon, where he was assassinated. He had overtaxed the resources of his empire, which fell to *Arab conquest within a decade of his death.

Khrushchev, Nikita (Sergeevich)

(1894–1971) Soviet statesman, Premier of the USSR (1958–64). Born in Ukraine, Khrushchev became First Secretary of the Communist Party of the USSR (1953–64) after the death of Stalin. He played a prominent part in the 'de-Stalinization' programme that began in 1956, denouncing the former leader in a historic speech, and went on to succeed Bulganin as Premier (Chairman of the Council of Ministers) in 1958. He came close to war with the USA over the Cuban Missile Crisis in 1962 and clashed with China over economic aid and borders. He was ousted two years later by Brezhnev and Kosygin, largely because of his antagonism to China.

Kiakhta, Treaty of (1727) A treaty between

Russia and China signed at Kiakhta, a town in Russia immediately north of the Mongolian frontier. A border was agreed between Siberia and Mongolia, China losing a large amount of peripheral land to Russia. Trade in Chinese silks, tea, and porcelain and Russian furs was permitted but limited to Kiakhta. The Russians were also allowed to send language students to Beijing and to build a church for them there.

kibbutz (Hebrew, 'gathering', 'collective')

An Israeli collective settlement, usually agricultural but sometimes also industrial. The land was originally held in the name of the Jewish people by the Jewish National Fund, and is now owned or leased at nominal fees by its members, who also manage it. The first kibbutz, Deganya, was founded in 1910 by Professor Franz Oppenheimer; they now number around 300 in Israel.

Kidd, William (or Captain Kidd) (1645–

1701) Scottish pirate. Sent to the Indian Ocean in 1695 in command of an anti-pirate expedition, Kidd became a pirate himself. In 1699 he went to Boston in the hope of obtaining a pardon, but was arrested in the same year and hanged in London.

Kiev Rus The historical nucleus of Russia.

Kiev, now in Ukraine, was probably founded in the 6th or 7th century, the centre of a feudal state ruled by the Rurik dynasty from the 9th to the 13th century. About 878 Igor advanced along the Dnieper River from Novgorod and made Kiev capital of the Varangarian–Russian principality. As the oldest established city it is known as 'the mother of Russian cities' and also 'the Jerusalem of Russia' as the first centre of the Greek Orthodox Church in Russia.

Killiecrankie, Battle of (27 July 1689) A

battle fought in a narrow densely wooded pass near Pitlochry in Scotland when John Graham of Claverhouse, Viscount Dundee, led the first *Jacobite attempt to restore *James II to the English and Scottish thrones. He overwhelmed the inexperienced forces of General Mackay, who lost 2000 dead and 500 taken prisoner, but Dundee was killed at the moment of victory. The Highlanders were subsequently unable to follow up their success.

Kim Il Sung (born Kim Song Ju) (1912–94)

Korean Communist statesman, first Premier of North Korea (1948–72) and President (1972–94). In the 1930s and 1940s he led the armed resistance to the Japanese domination of Korea; following the country's partition at the end of World War II he became Premier of the Democratic People's Republic of Korea (1948). He ordered his forces to invade South Korea in 1950, precipitating the Korean War (1950–53), and remained committed to the reunification of the country. He maintained a one-party state and created a personality cult around himself and his family; on his death he was quickly replaced in power by his son Kim Jong Il (1942–2011). In 2011 Kim Jong Il died and was succeeded by his youngest and little-known son Kim Jong Un (c.1983–)

King, Martin Luther (1929–68) US Baptist

minister and civil-rights leader. King opposed discrimination against Black Americans by organizing non-violent resistance and peaceful mass demonstrations, notably the year-long boycott of the local bus company in Montgomery, Alabama, in 1955 and the march on Washington involving 200,000 demonstrators in 1963. At the latter, King delivered his celebrated speech beginning 'I have a dream . . .'. He was awarded the Nobel Peace Prize in 1964. King was assassinated in Memphis in 1968.

King, William Lyon Mackenzie (1874–

1950) Canadian Liberal statesman, Prime Minister (1921–26; 1926–30; 1935–48). The grandson of William Lyon Mackenzie, he represented Canada at the imperial conferences in London

k

(1923; 1926; 1927), where he played an important role in establishing the status of the self-governing nations of the Commonwealth. He went on to strengthen ties with the UK and the USA and introduced a number of social reforms, including unemployment insurance (1940).

King George's War (1744–48) North American component of the War of the *Austrian Succession, which saw the capture of Louisburg on Cape Breton Island by a combined British Navy–New England force under William Pepperell in 1745. A subsequent campaign against the St Lawrence valley was abandoned. The fortress was returned to France in exchange for Madras in 1748.

Kingitanga A *Maori movement in New Zealand intended to unify the Maori under an hereditary kingship and restrain individual chiefs from selling land. In 1858, under the guidance of Wiremu Tamihana (the king-maker), Potatau, the first king, was recognized by tribes of central North Island. The Kingitanga sought to establish and enforce its own laws, but its more moderate leaders, including Tamihana, were willing to contemplate a defined authority under the British crown. Governor George *Grey was disinclined to recognize a movement which would hinder British authority and settlement. Independent-minded members of the Kingitanga such as Rewi Maniapoto became involved in the Taranaki war and gave Grey grounds for invading the Waikato in 1863. Even so, for many years, government authority did not run in 'the King Country'. In 1883, the King Country chiefs admitted settlement and King Tawhiao returned to his traditional land in lower Waikato. In the 20th century, largely under the influence of Te Puea, Tawhiao's niece, the King-itanga came to terms with government and became a focus for economic and cultural revival.

King Philip's War (1675–76) A Native American rising, which resulted from encroachments on Native lands in New England. It was led by Metacomet (or King Philip), chief of the Wampanoag, whose lands were in southern Massachusetts, but Mohawks of the *Iroquois Confederacy devastated frontier settlements in northern and western interior New England as well. Before Philip was betrayed and killed by Benjamin *Church in 1676 near Kingston, Rhode Island, Native Americans had raided within 32 km (20 miles) of Boston and one out of every ten adult males in Massachusetts had been killed.

King William's War (1689–97) A North American frontier war between the French and the English and their Native American allies, which was a colonial adjunct to the War of the League of Augsburg in Europe. The two main theatres were the northern coast and the Upper Hudson–Upper St Lawrence valleys. In 1690 Sir William Phipps's New England expedition sacked Port Royal in Acadia, but an intercolonial campaign against Quebec and Montreal ended in disaster. *Frontenac organized Abuski raids on English outposts in Maine and successfully intimidated the *Iroquois. Both sides lacked resources for full-scale war, and assistance from Europe was thwarted. The war was ended by the Treaty of Ryswick (1697) and a truce in Maine (1699).

Kinnock, Neil Gordon, Baron Kinnock of Bedwellty (1942–) British Labour politician and Leader of the Opposition (1983–92). Elected to Parliament in 1970, in 1978 he became a member of the National Executive Committee of the Labour Party, and after his party lost office in 1979, he was an effective opposition spokesman for Education. In 1983 he was elected leader of his Party and thus led the opposition to Margaret Thatcher's second and third administrations. Following Labour's electoral defeats in 1987 and 1992 Kinnock resigned. He was a European Commissioner from 1995 to 2004 and became a life peer in 2005.

Kiribati

Capital:	Tarawa
Area:	811 sq km (313 sq miles)
Population:	103,248 (2013 est)
Currency:	1 Australian dollar = 100 cents
Religions:	Roman Catholic 55.8%; Protestant 33.5%; Mormon 4.7%
Ethnic Groups:	I-Kiribati 89.5%; mixed 9.7%
Languages:	English (official); I-Kiribati
International Organizations:	UN; Commonwealth; Pacific Islands Forum; Secretariat of the Pacific Community

A country comprising a widely scattered archipelago of 33 islands in the Pacific Ocean, lying either side of the Equator and between longitudes 169° W and 147° E.

Physical Many of the islands are mere coral atolls not more than 1 km (0.5 mile) across. Kiribati comprises the 16 former Gilbert Islands, eight of the Line Islands, the eight Phoenix Islands, and Ocean Island (Banaba). The low-lying islands are at risk of being submerged completely if sea levels rise as a result of global warming.

Economy The economy of Kiribati is based on fishing and farming. The main resource is the coconut palm, from which copra is produced for export. Tourism is also important. The phosphate deposits on Ocean Island are now exhausted but proceeds from the industry were invested and remain a major source of revenue.

History Inhabited by Micronesians when sighted by the Spanish in the 16th century, the largest island group was named the Gilbert Islands in the 1820s by the Russian hydrographer Krusenstern. From 1837 European sperm whale hunters and traders began to inhabit the group, over which Britain declared a protectorate in 1892. In 1916 the group was named a crown colony, as the Gilbert and Ellice Islands. In 1942 Japanese naval forces occupied the islands, and in 1943 US marines landed and crushed Japanese resistance after fierce fighting. In 1974 the Ellice Islanders voted to secede from the colony, and the Ellice Islands became independent as *Tuvalu in 1978. The Gilbert Islands became the independent nation of Kiribati in 1979. Falling exports in copra and fish resulted in a trade deficit in 1990 of $24 million, with which the government of Teatao Teannaki (elected May 1991) had to contend. In 1994 Teannaki's government lost a vote of confidence and Teburoro Tito was elected President. In 1999 the country suffered a severe drought. Anote Tong was elected President in 2003 and re-elected in 2007 and 2012.

Kirk, Norman (1923–74) New Zealand statesman. A long-time Labour Party member, he entered Parliament in 1957 and successfully challenged A. H. Nordmeyer as parliamentary party leader in 1965. After two defeats, Kirk led the party to a landslide victory in 1972. As Prime Minister he embarked on a programme of social reform. After Kirk's death in 1974, his government swiftly lost popularity and was defeated in the 1975 general election.

Kirov, Sergei Mironovich (1886–1934) Russian-born revolutionary leader. A strong supporter of *Stalin, he began his revolutionary activities in Caucasia but moved to Leningrad (1928) and became a member of the *Politburo (1930). In 1934 he was assassinated by a young

party member, Leonid Nikolayev, possibly at Stalin's instigation. Stalin used Kirov's murder to launch the show trials and party purges of the late 1930s.

Kishi Nobusuke (1896–1987) Japanese statesman. A member of *Tojo Hideki's government, he was increasingly opposed to Japan's policies later in World War II. Imprisoned in 1945, he was released without trial. Elected to the Japanese House of Representatives (1953), he emerged as leader of the *Liberal Democratic Party, becoming Prime Minister in 1957. In foreign affairs he aimed to ease tensions with neighbouring Asian countries, while encouraging the US–Japanese link. His domestic policy was conservative, especially in education and over law and order. He resigned in 1960, following a riot within the Japanese Diet building, allegedly over his revised *Japan–United States Security Treaty.

Kissinger, Henry Alfred (1923–) US statesman. He acted as government consultant on defence (1955–68) and was appointed by President Nixon as head of the National Security Council (1969–75) and as Secretary of State (1973–77). He was largely responsible for improved relations (*détente*) with the Soviet Union, resulting in the *Strategic Arms Limitation Talks (SALT) of 1969. In addition, he helped to achieve a resolution of the Indo-Pakistan War (1971), rapprochement with communist China (1972), which the USA now recognized for the first time, and above all the resolution of the *Vietnam War. This he had at first accepted, supporting the bombing offensive against Cambodia (1969–70), but he changed his views and after prolonged negotiation he reached agreement for the withdrawal of US troops in January 1973. He was awarded the Nobel Peace Prize jointly with the Vietnamese representative Le Duc Tho, who refused the honour. Later in that year he helped to resolve the Arab–Israeli War and restored US diplomatic relations with Egypt. After the *Watergate scandal and President Nixon's resignation, he remained in office to advise President *Ford. He has since been a consultant and respected commentator on international affairs.

Kita Ikki (died 1937) Japanese revolutionary and political thinker. A former socialist and member of the nationalist Kokuryukai (Black Dragon Society), Kita played a key role in the upsurge in violent right-wing militarism in the 1930s, inspiring young dissidents with his call for a revolutionary regime, headed by the military, which would nationalize wealth, sweep away existing political forms, and prepare Japan to establish leadership over all of Asia. He was executed in 1937 for alleged involvement in the *Incident of 26 February 1936.

kitchen cabinet Unofficial advisers to a President or Prime Minister. The term was coined during the first years of Andrew *Jackson's presidency of the USA (1829–37). In his first years of office Jackson's official cabinet contained many strong but opposed personalities, including his first Vice-President, John Calhoun, and his Secretary for War, John Eaton. Thus while official cabinet meetings were held as seldom as possible Jackson took most of his advice from *Van Buren (later his second Vice-President and successor), John Eaton, Amos Kendall, Francis Blair (newspaper editors), and various personal friends appointed as minor government officials. After a cabinet reorganization in 1831 the President relied rather more on members of his official cabinet.

Kitchener, Herbert, 1st Earl Kitchener of Khartoum (Horatio Herbert Kitchener) (1850–1916) British soldier and statesman. After defeating the Mahdist forces at Omdurman and reconquering Sudan in 1898, he served as Chief of Staff (1900–02) in the Second Boer War and Commander-in-Chief (1902–09) in India. At the outbreak of World War I he was made Secretary of State for War, in which capacity he was responsible for organizing the large volunteer army that eventually fought the war on the Western Front. His commanding image appeared on recruiting posters urging 'Your country needs you!' He died when the ship taking him to Russia was sunk by a mine.

knighthood The special honour bestowed upon a man by dubbing (when he is invested with the right to bear arms) or by admission to one of the orders of chivalry. In England the emergence of knighthood was slow (the Anglo-Saxon word *cniht* means 'servant'). In the late 11th and early 12th centuries, knights were the lowest tier of those who held land in return for military service. During the 12th century their economic and social status improved, as society became more complex, and the market in free land developed. They became involved in local administration, and the new orders of knights, which emerged in Europe in the aftermath of the *Crusades, helped to give them a distinct identity. First to appear were the military orders of the *Knights Hospitallers (*c.*1070), the Knights of the Sepulchre (1113), and the *Knights Templars (1118). Their potential for

military colonization was best realized by the German Order of the *Teutonic Knights (1190), which pushed eastwards on the frontiers with Poland and acquired Prussia for itself. The Order of the Livonian Knights gained similar successes along the Baltic. The Order of the Garter (1348) was England's first and most important order of knighthood, followed by the Order of the Bath (1399). France created the Order of the Star (1352), and *Burgundy the Order of the Golden Fleece (1429).

Knight Hospitaller A member of a military religious order, formally the Knights Hospitallers of St John of Jerusalem, so called after the dedication of their headquarters in Jerusalem to St John the Baptist. From 1310 they were known as the Knights of Rhodes, from 1530 the Knights of Malta. They began in *c.*1070 with Muslim permission to run a hospital for sick pilgrims in Jerusalem, and were made a formal order when the city fell in 1099 to the First *Crusade. They adopted a black habit bearing a white eight-pointed (Maltese) cross. Under the first Master their function became primarily military and spread to Western Europe. They followed the Augustinian rule and were divided into three classes: knights, chaplains, and serving brothers. When they were driven out by *Saladin they went to Acre, only to be expelled a century later when Cyprus became their headquarters. In 1310 they captured the island of Rhodes and retained it till 1522. Given the island of Malta by Emperor Charles V they held it, having fought off the assaults of the Turks, until it finally fell to *Napoleon I. By this time the order had lost its former influence. Some members moved to Russia where Paul I was made Grand Master. His death in 1801 led to a period of confusion. The English branch of the order was revived in the 1830s and today cares for the sick.

Knights of Labor A US industrial trade union, founded in 1869 at a tailors' meeting in Philadelphia. By 1879 it was organized on a national basis, with membership open to all workers. Its goals were reformist rather than radical, and included the demand for an eight-hour day. Its growth was phenomenal. In 1882 the Knights helped push through Congress the Chinese Exclusion Act, prohibiting the entry into the USA of Chinese labourers. The union was at its height in 1886 under the leadership of Terence V. Powderly, with a membership of almost a million, but declined thereafter, partly due to involvement in unsuccessful strikes and to general antipathy to labour organizations after the *Haymarket Square riot. Factional disputes reduced its membership after the *American Federation of Labor was founded, and by 1900 it was virtually extinct.

Knight Templar A member of a military religious order properly called the Poor Knights of Christ and of the Temple of Solomon, founded in 1118 by Hugh de Payens, a knight of Champagne in France. He and eight companions vowed to protect pilgrims travelling on the public roads of the Holy Land (*Palestine). At the Council of Troyes (1128) approval was given to their version of the *Benedictine rule. They quickly became very influential, attracting many noble members and growing in wealth, acquiring property throughout Christendom. When Jerusalem fell in 1187 they moved to Acre together with the *Knights Hospitallers and great rivalry and hatred developed between the orders. In 1291 when Acre also fell, they retreated to Cyprus. In Cyprus their great wealth enabled them to act as bankers to the nobility of most of Europe and this affluence attracted much hostility, in particular that of *Philip IV of France. In 1307 they were charged with heresy and immorality. Though some of the charges may have been true, envy of their wealth seems to have been the reason for their persecution. They were condemned, their wealth confiscated, and the order suppressed. The Grand Master and many others were burned at the stake.

Knossos culture The culture based around the principal city of Minoan Crete, near the port of Heraklion. The area was occupied from neolithic times until c.1200 BC. Excavations by Sir Arthur Evans from 1900 onwards revealed remains of a luxurious and spectacular decorated complex of buildings which he named the Palace of Minos, with frescoes of landscapes, animal life, and the sport of bull-leaping. In c.1450 BC Crete was overrun by the Mycenaeans, but the palace was not finally destroyed until the 14th century or early 13th century BC, possibly by an earthquake. The city was destroyed by the Romans in 68–67 BC.

Knox, Henry (1750–1806) American general, who commanded the Continental Artillery during the War of *Independence. In 1775 he hauled the guns from Ticonderoga 124 km (200 miles) through the wilderness to Boston, forcing British evacuation. He was George *Washington's right-hand man throughout the War, and after it organized the Veterans' Society of the Cincinnati (1783). A Federalist, he was Secretary of War to the Confederation and under President Washington (1785–94), but his scheme for a national militia was thwarted.

Knox, John (c.1505–72) Scottish Protestant reformer. After early involvement in the Scottish Reformation he spent more than a decade preaching in Europe, during which time he stayed in Geneva and was influenced by Calvin. In 1559 he returned to Scotland and played a central part in the establishment of the Church of Scotland within a Scottish Protestant state. A fiery orator, he became the spokesman of the religious interests opposed to the Catholic Mary, Queen of Scots when she returned to rule in her own right in 1561.

Kohl, Helmut (1930–) German statesman, Chancellor of the Federal Republic of Germany (1982–90) and of Germany (1990–98). He became chairman of the Christian Democratic Party in 1973, and was leader of the opposition until 1982, becoming Chancellor of the Federal Republic of Germany when the ruling coalition collapsed. As Chancellor he showed a strong commitment to NATO and to closer European union within the European Community. In 1990 he presided over the reunification of East and West Germany and was elected Chancellor of the united country later the same year. The longest-serving postwar German leader, he won a fourth term in 1994 but in 1998 he was defeated in elections by Gerhard *Schröder. In 1999 it was revealed that the Christian Democrats had received illegal funding while he was leader.

Konfrontasi Diplomatic and military confrontation between *Indonesia and *Malaysia (1963–66). It centred on the formation of the Federation of Malaysia (1963), which President *Sukarno saw as a Western-inspired ploy to oppose anti-colonist forces in south-east Asia. Asserting that the Federation was part of a British plot against Indonesia, Sukarno launched a guerrilla war in Malaysia's Bornean territories, Sarawak and Sabah, in April 1963, hoping for support from local Chinese communist elements. His 'confrontation' policy, however, only served to increase support for the new federal arrangements within the Malaysian states (only *Brunei, with its massive oil reserves, remaining aloof). It led to increased disaffection in the Indonesian army which ultimately contributed to his downfall. With the guerrilla forces defeated by Malaysians with British, Australian, and New Zealand help, Sukarno's successor General Suharto ended Konfrontasi in 1966.

Kongo kingdom A kingdom in Central Africa, established south of the River Congo by 1300 which became one of the most powerful kingdoms in the region. The Kongo people traded over long distances, exploiting iron and

k

salt mines. On Loanda Island they had a monopoly of *nzimbu* shells, which provided a local currency. It was the first African kingdom after Ethiopia to be converted to Christianity, by Portuguese missionaries in the 16th century. The Portuguese also brought the slave trade, which encouraged civil wars and weakened the Kongo kingdom by the mid-17th century.

Königgrätz *See* SADOWA.

Konoe Fumimaro (1891–1945) Japanese statesman. He entered politics after World War I and as a member of the upper house emerged as a leading advocate of popularly based parliamentary democracy and an opponent of the military domination of government. As Prime Minister (1937–39, 1940–41), he strove unsuccessfully to control the political situation and prevent war with the USA, but in October 1941 was forced out of office by his War Minister, *Tojo Hideki. He committed suicide in December 1945 when summoned to answer charges of war crimes.

Köprülü An influential family of able administrators who through the office of *vizier dominated *Ottoman affairs for half a century. Muhammad (1656–61) crushed internal discord and bolstered the war effort against Venice. His son Ahmed (1661–76) ended the conflict successfully, acquiring Crete, and also won Podolia from Poland. Mustafa (1689–91) died in a counter-offensive in the lengthy war (1683–99) against Austria. Hüseyn (1697–1702) ended that conflict by the Peace of Carlowitz (1699), ceding many territories. By their energy the Köprülü had arrested the decay of the empire, but their demise saw it enter its long decline from greatness.

Koran (or **Qur'an**) The Holy Scripture of *Islam. Muslims believe the Koran to be the word and will of God, as revealed to his messenger Muhammad (570–632) through the angel Jibril or Gabriel over the period (610–32). Written in classical Arabic, it consists of 114 *sūras* (chapters) of varying length, each *sūra* being composed of a number of *āyas* (normally translated as verses because assonance is involved, although the Koran is a prose work). The first revelation on *Lailat al-Qadr*, the Night of Power, is commemorated during the month of Ramadan. The early revelations are highly charged and rhetorical, but the style becomes more relaxed with the passing of time. The contents are diverse, particularly prominent themes being the omnipotence of Allah, the duty to believe in Allah alone, descriptions of the Day of Judgement, heaven, and hell, stories of the Prophets, and, in the latest phase, social legislation. Since the Koran is regarded by Muslims as a literal transcription of God's revelations, for many years translations of the text were not permitted, and although today translations do exist, Muslims are taught to memorize and chant the original Arabic text. Calligraphic renditions of the text are a distinctive aid to worship in Islam.

Korea A region of eastern Asia forming a peninsula between the Sea of Japan and the Yellow Sea, now divided along the 38th parallel into South *Korea and North *Korea. Possessed of a distinct national and cultural identity and ruled from the 14th century by the Korean Yi dynasty, Korea has suffered from its position between Chinese and Japanese spheres of influence. Chinese domination was ended by the Sino-Japanese War (1894–95) and after the Russo-Japanese War a decade later the country was finally annexed by Japan in 1910. After the Japanese surrender at the end of World War II, the northern half of the country was occupied by the Soviets and the southern half by the Americans. Separate countries were created in 1948 and two years later the Northern invasion of the South resulted in the Korean War (1950–53). A 250 km-long demilitarized zone was established between the two countries at the end of hostilities but both North Korea and South Korea were some time in recovering from the devastation caused by military operations. While North Korea remains under Communist rule, South Korea is now a major industrial nation.

Korea, North (official name **Democratic People's Republic of Korea**)

Capital:	Pyongyang
Area:	120,538 sq km (46,540 sq miles)
Population:	24,720,407 (2013 est)
Currency:	1 North Korean won = 100 chon
Religions:	unknown. Official figures give small memberships for officially sponsored religious organizations, but many people are thought to worship in private.
Ethnic Groups:	Korean; small Chinese and Japanese minorities.
Languages:	Korean (official)
International Organizations:	UN; Non-Aligned Movement

A north-east Asian coun-
try. Consisting of the
northern half of the Korean
peninsula, mostly above
the 38th parallel, North
Korea was formed from the
zone occupied by the So-
viet Union at the end of
World War II. It borders to the south with South
Korea and to the north with the People's Republic of China.

Physical North Korea is largely mountainous
with narrow valleys, extensive forests, and rivers
which freeze in winter.

Economy North Korea is rich in metal deposits
such as iron ore, magnesite, phosphate,
sulphur, zinc, and copper; these are major exports, together with metallurgical products,
manufactures, and textiles. Agricultural products include rice, maize, potatoes, and soya
beans. North Korea has a centrally planned
economy, and its needs are subordinate to the
political requirements of the ruling communist
party. In the mid-1990s the economy suffered a
dramatic collapse owing to the ending of preferential trading terms with the Soviet Union and
China and severe floods that had a devastating
effect on agriculture; malnutrition is widespread
and mass starvation a constant threat.

History The Democratic People's Republic
was proclaimed an independent state on 1 May
1948. Intent on reuniting Korea, North Korea
launched a surprise attack on South *Korea in
June 1950, suffering considerable damage and
loss of life in the following three years of the
indecisive *Korean War. After the war, the ruling communist party of *Kim Il Sung (first
President of North Korea) undertook a programme of reconstruction, using the country's
mineral and power resources to finance economic development. From the early 1980s,
however, the economy was stagnant and then
in decline. This was a factor in the decision in
1985 to hold a series of economic talks with
South Korea. The result was a marked upturn
in trade between the two countries ($25 mil-
lion in 1990 to $192 million in 1991). Kim Il
Sung was re-elected in 1990; he supported a
policy of seeking 'normalization' with South
Korea, but not of reunification. An economic
agreement was signed in 1992. Tensions flared
again in the later 1990s, over allegations that
North Korea was building nuclear weapons
and a series of incursions into South Korean
territory. A mutual cooperation treaty between
the two Koreas was signed in 2000. Kim Jong Il
(1942–2011) succeeded his father as President

in 1995. Since 2006 North Korea has successfully
tested nuclear weapons and ballistic missiles. In
2011, Kim Jong Il died and was succeeded by his
youngest son, Kim Jong Un (*c.*1983–).

Korea, South (official name **Republic of
Korea**)

Capital:	Seoul
Area:	99,720 sq km (38,502 sq miles)
Population:	48,955,203 (2013 est)
Currency:	1 South Korean won = 100 jeon
Religions:	Buddhist 24.2%; Protestant 24.0%; Roman Catholic 7.6%
Ethnic Groups:	Korean; small Chinese minority
Languages:	Korean (official); English
International Organizations:	UN; Colombo Plan; OECD; WTO

A north-eastern Asian
country. Consisting of the
southern half of the Korean
peninsula, mostly beneath
the 38th parallel, South
Korea was formed from the
zone occupied by US forces
after World War II.

Physical The terrain of South Korea is made up
of low hills and wide valleys. Numerous small
islands in the sovereign territory of South Korea
lie off its western coast, in the Yellow Sea. The
climate is milder than in the north of the peninsula.

Economy South Korea has a mixed economy
with a successful export-based industrial sector,
and an agricultural sector which provides self-
sufficiency in food and high yields in rice production. The principal manufacturing industries
are electronics, telecommunications, vehicles,
chemicals, shipbuilding, and steel. The chief
exports are semiconductors, telecommunications equipment, vehicles, and computers.
There are few minerals except for large tungsten
deposits. Four decades of phenomenal economic growth ended in 1997, when South Korea
suffered an economic breakdown; the currency
collapsed and an IMF rescue plan had to be
implemented. Reforms were implemented and
growth resumed.

History The independent Republic of Korea
was proclaimed on 15 August 1948. Badly

damaged by the *Korean War (1950–53), the South Korean economy was initially restricted by its lack of industrial and power resources and by a severe post-war refugee problem. Unemployment and inflation damaged the reputation of the government of President Rhee, and its increasing brutality and corruption finally led to its overthrow in 1960. After a second civilian government had failed to restore the situation, the army, led by General Park Chung Hee, seized power in 1961. Park, who assumed the powers of a civilian President (1963–79) organized an extremely successful reconstruction campaign which saw South Korea emerge as a strong industrial power, but his repressive policies soon engendered serious unrest. Tension with North Korea remained high during this period, until an agreement between the two governments, signed in July 1972, laid foundations for possible future reunification. Park Chung Hee was assassinated by the head of the South Korean Central Intelligence Agency in a coup in 1979. His successor, General Chun Doo Hwan, continued his policies until forced partially to liberalize the political system after student unrest in 1987. A referendum was held and a new constitution proclaimed, under which Roh Tae Woo became President in 1988. Kim Young-Sam was elected President in 1992, the first civilian President for 32 years. A severe financial crisis in 1997 led to the election of former dissident Kim Dae Jung as President in 1998. A cooperation treaty with North Korea was signed in 2000 but relations have since worsened, notably with the North's sinking of a South Korean warship in 2010. Roh Moo-hyun was elected President in 2003 but his tenure proved troubled and he was succeeded by Lee Myung-bak of the Grand National Party in 2008. Roh later committed suicide (2009) after being implicated in a corruption scandal. In 2013 Park Geun-Hye became the first woman President of South Korea.

Korean War (1950–53) A war fought between North Korea and China on one side, and South Korea, the USA, and United Nations forces on the other. From the time of their foundation in 1948, relations between North and South Korea were soured by rival plans for unification, and on 25 June 1950 war finally broke out with a surprise North Korean attack that pushed US and South Korean forces far south towards Pusan by September. In the temporary absence of the Soviet representative, the Security Council asked members of the UN to furnish assistance to South Korea. On 15 September US and South Korean forces, under command of

General *MacArthur, launched a counter-offensive at Inchon, and by the end of October UN forces had pushed the North Koreans all the way back to the Yalu River, the frontier with the People's Republic of China. Chinese troops then entered the war on the northern side, driving south to recapture the South Korean capital of Seoul by January 1951. After months of fighting, the conflict stabilized in near-deadlock close to the original boundary line (the 38th parallel). Peace negotiations, undertaken in July 1951 by General M. B. Ridgway (who had succeeded MacArthur in April of that year), proved difficult, and it was not until 27 July 1953 that an armistice was signed at Panmunjom and the battle line was accepted as the boundary between North and South Korea.

Koryo A Korean kingdom that gave its name to the whole country. From 986 its kings ruled a united Korea from their Chinese-style capital, Kaesong. Chinese influence was strong in the administration of the kingdom and Buddhism flourished. A period of disorder in the 12th century was checked after 1196 by military families with powers similar to those of the Japanese *shogunate. Tributary to the *Song, Koryo also had to pay tribute to the Liao and *Jin. After 1231 the Mongols repeatedly invaded and despoiled Koryo, which later depended entirely on *Yuan support. After the overthrow of the Yuan, a Koryo general, Yi Song-gye, seized Kaesong and in 1392 established the Yi dynasty.

Kosciuszko, Tadeusz (or **Thaddeus**) (1746–1817) Polish soldier and patriot. A trained soldier, he fought for the American colonists during the War of American Independence, returning to Poland in 1784. Ten years later he led a nationalist uprising, defeating a large Russian force at Racławice. Captured and imprisoned by the Russians (1794–96), he eventually moved to France, where he devoted the rest of his life to the cause of Polish independence.

Kosovo

Capital:	Pristina
Area:	10,887 sq km (4203 sq miles)
Population:	1,847,708 (2013 est)
Currency:	1 euro = 100 cents
Religions:	Muslim; Eastern Orthodox; Roman Catholic
Ethnic Groups:	Albanian 92%; Serb and other minorities
Languages:	Albanian, Serbian (both official); minority languages

A small country of SE Europe, bordered by Serbia, Macedonia, Albania, and Montenegro. Kosovo's independence from Serbia is recognized by just over half the world's nations.

Physical Kosovo is largely mountainous; plains in the east and west are divided by a central region of hills.

Economy Kosovo is the poorest country in Europe and relies on remittances from expatriates and international aid. Subsistence farming is common, and cereals, berries, potatoes, peppers, and fruit are the main agricultural products. The principal industries are mining, construction materials, metals, leather, and machinery; exports include metals and metal products, leather products, and machinery.

History On 28 June 1389 **Kosovo Polje (the Field of Blackbirds)** was the site of a decisive battle in which the troops of the Serbs were defeated by an invading *Ottoman force. Although the Serbs enjoyed early success and Sultan *Murad I was killed, his son *Bayezid I took command and won the battle. Victory opened the way for Turkish invasion of central Europe. A second battle, between Hungarians and Turks, took place nearby in 1448 and saw *Murad II defeat the Hungarians. The Kosovo area was settled by Muslim Albanians during Ottoman rule.

After World War I Kosovo was absorbed into Yugoslavia; it became an autonomous region in 1945. In 1990 it declared independence, but in response Serbia removed its autonomous status. Conflict between Muslim Albanian separatists and Serbian troops continued until 1998, when Serbian forces succeeded in driving out and killing huge numbers of Albanians. This prompted NATO to launch air strikes against Serbia in 1999, which forced Serbia to withdraw its forces and to allow refugees to return. Kosovo was placed under UN administration, and elections were held in 2001. In 2008 it declared independence from Serbia, although the legality of this move was in doubt until a ruling of the International Court of Justice in 2010. The new country had difficulty imposing its authority on the Serb minority in the north. In 2013 they were granted some autonomy in return for Serbia's acquiescence in Kosovo's control of the area; but Serbia did not recognize Kosovo's independence, and a NATO-led peacekeeping force still enforces peace between Albanians and Serbs.

Kossuth, Lajos (1802–94) Hungarian statesman and patriot. Long an opponent of Habsburg domination of Hungary, he led the 1848 insurrection and was appointed governor of the country during the brief period of independence which followed. In 1849 he began a lifelong period of exile when the uprising was crushed, although he continued to strive for Hungarian independence.

Kosygin, Alexei Nikolayevich (1904–81) Soviet politician. He joined the Communist Party in 1927 and became an expert in economics and industry. He was Chairman of the Council of Ministers from 1964 to 1981. During his period in office he shared power with *Brezhnev, who came to overshadow him. Kosygin achieved a notable diplomatic success in bringing the 1965–66 *Indo-Pakistan War to an end.

Kremlin, the The citadel in Moscow, centre of administration of the Russian government and formerly of the Soviet Communist government. Covering an area of 28 hectares, its palaces, churches, and monuments are surrounded by a wall 2235 m (7333 feet) in length. The building of the Kremlin began in 1156 when Prince Yuri Dolgoruky ordered a wooden fort to be built on Borovitsky Hill. This later became the residence of the Grand Dukes of Moscow and the site where Russian emperors and empresses came to be crowned.

Kronstadt Mutiny (1921) Mutiny against the Bolshevik government of Russia. The Kronstadt naval garrison had enthusiastically supported the Bolsheviks in 1917, but in March 1921 the sailors rose against what they regarded as a Communist dictatorship, demanding political freedom and economic liberalism. The rising was brutally suppressed by Lenin, but the incident did cause a partial reassessment of economic planning along more progressive lines, with Lenin's New Economic Policy of 1922.

Kropotkin, Prince Peter (1842–1921) Russian anarchist. He was a geographer who carried out explorations of Siberia, Finland, and Manchuria before devoting his life to political activities. He became an influential exponent of anarchism and was imprisoned in 1874. He escaped abroad two years later and only returned to Russia after the Russian Revolution in 1917. His works include *Modern Science and Anarchism* (1903).

Kruger, Stephanus Johannes Paulus (known as **'Oom (uncle) Paul'**) (1825–1904) South African soldier and statesman. He led the

k

Afrikaners to victory in the First Boer War in 1881 and afterwards served as President of Transvaal from 1883 to 1899. His refusal to allow equal rights to non-Boer immigrants was one of the causes of the Second Boer War, during which Kruger was forced to flee the country. He died in exile in Switzerland.

Kubitschek, Juscelino (1902–76) Brazilian statesman. He was governor of the Province of Minas Gerais (1950–56), where he initiated a programme of industrial and agricultural development. He then served as President of Brazil (1956–61). Determined to diversify the economy and reduce unemployment, he embarked on a massive public works programme, including the creation of the new capital city of Brasília. Economic prosperity followed, but at the cost of high inflation. Brazil's national debt rose to $4 billion, while its population soared to over 60 million. He was forced into exile for three years by his successor Castel Branco.

Kublai Khan (1216–94) Mongol emperor of China, grandson of Genghis Khan. Between 1252 and 1259 he conquered southern China with his brother Mangu (then Mongol Khan). On Mangu's death in 1259 he was elected Khan himself, completing the conquest of China and founding the Yuan dynasty; he established his capital on the site of the modern Beijing. He successfully invaded Korea and Burma, but failed in attacks on Java and Japan.

Ku Klux Klan (KKK) A secret society founded (1866) in the southern USA after the *American Civil War to oppose reconstruction and to maintain White supremacy. Famous for its white robes and hoods, it spread fear among Black people to prevent them voting. Its use as a cover for petty persecution alienated public opinion and led to laws in 1870 and 1871 attempting to suppress it. The Klan reappeared in Georgia in 1915 and during the 1920s spread into the north and mid-west. It was responsible for some 1500 murders by lynching. At its height it boasted four million members and elected high federal and state officials, but it also aroused intense opposition. A series of scandals and internecine rivalries sent it into rapid decline. Klan activity increased during the 1950s and 1960s, as it violently opposed the civil rights movement. It survives at the local level in the southern states and during the early 1990s there was some concern that support for the Klan was increasing.

kulak (Russian, 'fist') Moneylenders, merchants, and anyone considered to be acquisitive. The term became specifically applied to wealthy peasants who, as a result of the agrarian reforms of *Stolypin (1906), acquired relatively large farms and were financially able to employ labour. As a new element in rural Russia they were intended to create a stable middle class and a conservative political force. During the period of Lenin's *New Economic Policy (1921) they increasingly appeared to be a potential threat to a communist state, and Stalin's *collectivization policy (1928) inevitably aroused their opposition. Between 1929 and 1934 the great majority of farms were collectivized and the kulaks annihilated.

Kulturkampf (German, 'conflict of cultures' or beliefs) The conflict between the German government headed by *Bismarck and the Roman Catholic Church (1872–87) for the control of schools and Church appointments. Bismarck, anxious to strengthen the central power of the *German Second empire in which southern Germany, Alsace-Lorraine, and the Polish provinces were predominantly Catholic, issued the May Decrees (1873), restricting the powers of the Catholic Church and providing for the punishment of any opponents. By 1876 1300 parishes had no priest: opponents had become martyrs. Needing Catholic support in the Reichstag, Bismarck repealed many of the anti-Church laws or let them lapse.

Kun, Béla (1886–1937) Hungarian communist leader. In World War I he was captured on the Russian front and joined the *Bolsheviks. He was sent back to Hungary to form a communist party and in March 1919 persuaded the Hungarian communists and Social Democrats to form a coalition government and to set up a communist state under his dictatorship. His Red Army overran Slovakia, but promised Soviet help was not forthcoming. In May 1919 he was defeated by a Romanian army of intervention. Kun fled the country and is assumed to have been liquidated in one of Stalin's purges.

Kuomintang (or **Guomindang; Chinese, 'National People's Party'**) Chinese political party. Originally a revolutionary league, it was organized in 1912 by Song Jiaoren and *Sun Yatsen as a republican party along democratic lines to replace the Revolutionary Alliance which had emerged from the overthrow of the *Qing dynasty. Suppressed in 1913 by Yuan Shikai, it was reformed in 1920 by Sun and reorganized with *Comintern assistance in 1923 in an arrangement that allowed individual communists to become members. At the party congress in 1924 it formally adopted the 'Three Principles of the People': nationalism, democracy, and 'people's livelihood'. In 1926 its rise to power began in earnest with the commencement of *Chiang Kai-shek's Northern Campaign. The communists were defeated in 1927 and the capture of Beijing in 1928 brought international recognition for its Nanjing-based Nationalist Government. It fought the *Chinese Civil War with the communists and retreated to Chongqing after the Japanese invasion of 1937. After World War II, the civil war recommenced, and by 1949 the Kuomintang's forces had been decisively defeated and forced to retreat to *Taiwan, where it formed the government until 2000.

Kurds A people who have maintained a distinct culture for over 3000 years despite never having been united under a single ruler. An Islamic pastoral people the Kurds inhabit an extensive plateau and mountainous region of the Middle East, south of the Caucasus, including large parts of Turkey, northern Iraq, western Iran, eastern Syria, Armenia, and Azerbaijan. The creation of a separate state of Kurdistan was proposed by the Allies after World War I, but this was abandoned in 1923 when Turkey reasserted its territorial authority in the region. The Kurds have suffered persecution in Turkey and Iraq.

Kursk, Battle of (5–15 July 1943) A fierce tank battle between the Red Army and German invasion forces around Kursk in the central European Soviet Union. Hitler had ordered the elimination of the important railway junction of Kursk. Under Field-Marshal Walter Model he concentrated 2700 tanks and assault guns on the city, supported by over 1000 aircraft. They were confronted by Marshal *Zhukov's Tank Army, backed by five infantry armies. Many of the large German tanks were mined and others became stuck in the mud. The Russians had more guns, tanks, and aircraft, and when they counter-attacked, the Germans were forced to retreat, losing some 70,000 men, 1500 tanks, and 1000 aircraft. The battle ensured that the German army would never regain the initiative on the Eastern Front.

Kush (or **Cush**) *See* NUBIANS.

Kut, Siege of (December 1915–April 1916) Successful siege of the town of Kut-al-Amara, now in Iraq, by Turkish troops in World War I. Kut-al-Amara is on the River Tigris and was garrisoned by a British imperial force under General Townshend, who had retreated there after his defeat by the Turks at Ctesiphon. Badly organized relief forces failed to break through and the garrison capitulated on 29 April 1916 after a four-month siege. 10,000 prisoners were marched across the desert, two-thirds dying on the way, while some 23,000 troops of the relieving force were also lost. The defeat severely weakened Britain's prestige as an imperial power although Kut-al-Amara was recaptured in February 1917.

Kutuzov, Mikhail Ilarionovich, Prince of Smolensk (1745–1813) Russian field-marshal. He distinguished himself in the Russo-Turkish War (1806–12), bringing Bessarabia into Russia. He commanded the Russian armies in the wars against Napoleon and was forced to retreat after the defeat of *Borodino (7 September 1812). Kutuzov's decision to disperse in the face of the advancing *grande armée* undermined Napoleon's plans for a swift victory, and forced him to retreat from Moscow before the severe Russian winter.

Kuwait

Capital:	Kuwait City
Area:	17,818 sq km (6880 sq miles)
Population:	2,695,316 (2013 est)
Currency:	1 Kuwaiti dinar = 1000 fils
Religions:	Sunni Muslim 59.5%; Shiite Muslim 25.5%
Ethnic Groups:	Kuwaiti Arab 45.0%; non-Kuwaiti Arab 35.0%; South Asian 9.0%
Languages:	Arabic (official); English
International Organizations:	UN; Arab League; GCC; OPEC; OAPEC; Non-Aligned Movement; WTO

A small country in the north-west corner of the Gulf, flanked by Iraq and Saudi Arabia.

Physical Kuwait is mainly low desert, very hot in summer but cool in winter, and extremely arid.

Economy With an estimated 6% of the world's petroleum reserves, Kuwait's economy is based on oil extraction, refining, and petrochemical industries. Oil constitutes nearly half of GDP and 95% of export earnings.

History Kuwait was founded in the early 18th century by members of the Utub section of the Anaiza tribe, and has been ruled since 1756 by the al-Sabah family. In 1899 the ruler, Muvarak, signed a treaty with Britain which established a *de facto* British protectorate over Kuwait, although it remained under nominal Ottoman suzerainty until 1914, when the protectorate was formalized. Kuwait became independent in 1961, when an Iraqi claim was warded off with British military assistance. Oil had been discovered in 1938; after World War II, Kuwait became one of the world's largest oil producers. The country's defensive pact with Britain lapsed in 1971, after which it tried to pursue a policy of neutrality. Its massive wealth was in part channelled into modernization programmes. But in 1990 Iraq revived the frontier dispute of 1961, and on 2 August 1990 began its seven-month occupation of Kuwait. In the period before liberation in the *Gulf War, thousands of Kuwaitis were killed. After the war, reconstruction costs were estimated at up to $100 billion, with serious environmental damage caused by Iraqi sabotage of 732 oil wells. In 1992 the first parliamentary elections in the country's history were held, in which only 13% of the population was eligible to vote. Even so, many opposition candidates were elected. In 2005 women were given the vote and allowed to stand for public office; four women were elected to Parliament in 2009. The 21st century has seen continued political conflict between the royal family and the increasingly assertive parliamentary opposition. In 2012 a revised electoral law considered favourable to government candidates led to popular protests and an opposition boycott of subsequent elections.

Kyoto Protocol An international agreement negotiated in 1993 that sought to limit emission levels of carbon dioxide and five other so-called greenhouse gases that are widely believed to contribute to *climate change. It committed 38 industrialized countries to reduce their emissions by 2012 to an average of 94.8% of their 1990 levels. A system of "carbon trading" was established by which those countries with emissions below their targets could sell their unused quota to other countries. The Protocol became a legally binding treaty in 2005. However, it did not seek to limit the emissions of developing countries, which was cited by the USA as a reason why it would not ratify what it regarded as a flawed treaty. In 2011 the parties to the Protocol agreed to finalize a more stringent successor treaty by 2015; however, in 2012 the Protocol was extended to 2020.

Kyrgyzstan (formerly Kirghizia)

Capital:	Bishkek
Area:	199,951 sq km (77,202 sq miles)
Population:	5,548,042 (2013 est)
Currency:	1 som = 100 tyiyn
Religions:	Muslim 75.0%; Eastern Orthodox 20.0%
Ethnic Groups:	Kirghiz 64.9%; Uzbek 13.8%; Russian 12.5%
Languages:	Kirghiz, Russian (both official); Uzbek; minority languages
International Organizations:	OSCE; UN; Commonwealth of Independent States; Euro-Atlantic Partnership Council; WTO

A country in central Asia bounded by Kazakhstan on the north and northwest, Uzbekistan on the south-west, and Tajikistan on the south.

Physical On the southeast the Tian Shan range of mountains, which rise to 7439 m (24,406 feet), span the border with China. Kyrgyzstan is a mountainous country with many snowfields, glaciers, and deep lakes. Its lower plains are exposed to hot desert winds. Its middle reaches are forested, while the lower slopes provide pasture for millions of sheep.

Economy Agriculture, the dominant economic activity, is based on livestock-raising and crops such as tobacco, cotton, vegetables, fruit, and berries. Kyrgyzstan has substantial mineral reserves, including gold and coal. Gold is the leading export, followed by cotton, wool, clothing, meat and tobacco. Remittances from expatriates are vital to the economy.

History Absorbed into the Russian empire during the 19th century, Kyrgyzstan became an autonomous province of the Soviet Union in 1924 and the Kirghiz Soviet Socialist Republic in 1936. In 1990 Askar Akayev, a supporter of reforms and of independence for Kyrgyzstan, was elected President. He survived an attempted coup in 1991 and resigned from the Communist Party of the Soviet Union. The Kirghiz Communist Party then dissolved itself and the country became independent as Kyrgyzstan.

New constitutions were adopted in 1993 and 1994 and the first multiparty elections were held in 1995. Akayev remained President and continued to introduce economic reforms; however, in 2005 he was forced out of office by popular demonstrations after disputed parliamentary elections. Kurmanbek Bakiyev, the leader of the opposition, was elected President by a large majority. He pursued increasingly authoritarian policies, and his apparent landslide victory in the 2009 presidential election was disputed. In 2010 he was overthrown following protests against rising prices; the subsequent instability featured Kirghiz–Uzbek ethnic violence in the south of the country. A new constitution was introduced, and the social democrat Almazbek Atambayev was elected President in 2011.

k

Labor Party (Australia) The oldest surviving political party in Australia. The title of the Labor groups founded in the 1880s and 1890s varied from state to state until 1918, when all adopted the name Australian Labor Party. The party formed minority federal governments in 1904 and 1908–09, and then a majority government after the 1910 election. It was replaced in 1916 by a Nationalist-Country Alliance, until the general election of 1929 returned it to power under J. H. Scullin (1929–31). Labor split again over policy differences during the Great *Depression. Some Labor followers combined with the Nationalist Party to form the United Australia Party under J. A. Lyons. Together with the Country Party it dominated federal and state politics until 1937, usually in coalition governments. The Labor Party was again in power from 1941 to 1949, but was then in opposition for 23 years. A breakaway Labor group emerged in 1955 over the attitude of the Party to communism, a group of federal Labor members forming the new Anti-Communist Labor Party, which later became the Democratic Labor Party. Since 1972 Labor has formed governments under Gough *Whitlam (1972–75), Bob *Hawke (1983–91), Paul *Keating (1991–96), Kevin *Rudd (2007–10; 2013), and Julia *Gillard (2010–13).

Labourers, Statute of (1351) A statute passed after a large part of the English population had died of the *Black Death. It followed an ordinance of 1349 in attempting to prevent labour, now so much scarcer, from becoming expensive. Everyone under the age of 60, except traders, craftsmen, and those with private means, had to work for wages which were set at their various pre-plague levels. It was made an offence for landless men to seek new masters or to be offered higher wages. The statute was vigorously enforced for several years and caused a great deal of resentment; it was specifically referred to in the *Peasants' Revolt of 1381.

Labour Party (Britain) A major political party in Britain. Following the third *Reform Act (1884), a movement developed for direct representation of labour interests in Parliament. In 1889 a Scottish Labour Party was formed, winning three seats in 1892, including one by Keir *Hardie, who in 1893 helped to form the *Independent Labour Party, advocating pacifism and *socialism. In 1900 a Labour Representative Committee was formed which in 1906 succeeded in winning 29 seats and changed its name to the Labour Party. In 1918 the Party adopted a constitution drawn up by the Fabian Sidney *Webb. Its main aims were a national minimum wage, democratic control of industry, a revolution in national finance, and surplus wealth for the common good. By 1920 Party membership was over four million. The Party now became a major force in British municipal politics, as well as gaining office with the Liberals in national elections in 1923 and 1929. The Party strongly supported war in 1939 and through such leaders as *Attlee, *Bevin, and *Morrison played a major role in Winston *Churchill's government (1940–45). In 1945 it gained office with an overall majority and continued the programme of *welfare state legislation begun during the war. It was in power 1964–70, when much social legislation was enacted, and 1974–79, when it faced grave financial and economic problems. During the 1970s and early 1980s left-wing activists pressed for a number of procedural changes, for example in the election of Party leader. From the right wing a group of senior party members split from the party in the 1980s to form the Social Democratic Party (see LIBERAL DEMOCRATS). After its defeat in 1987 it embarked, under its leader Neil *Kinnock (1983–92), on a major policy review which recommended more democratic processes and a less ideological approach to foreign affairs and economic problems. However, the party received only 34% of the vote in the general election of 1992. Tony *Blair, who became leader in 1994, supported private enterprise and promoted many reforms in the party, finally abandoning the ideological union-led principles of 'Old Labour' for a more popular and pragmatic approach, which gave Labour landslide victories in the 1997 and 2001 general elections. It was returned for a third term in 2005 with its majority much reduced. In 2007 Blair resigned and Gordon *Brown became leader; he resigned following defeat in the 2010 general election and was succeeded by Ed Miliband.

Labour Party (New Zealand) A major political party in New Zealand. It was formed in 1910 out of the trade union movement but was rivalled by the militant *Red Feds. Re-formed in 1916, the Party supported compulsory industrial arbitration and constitutional change. Its policies favoured nationalization of much industry and state leasehold of land, and these were further modified before it won office in 1935 under Michael *Savage. The first Labour government (1935–49) effected radical change, stimulating economic recovery through public works, state support for primary produce marketing, and minimum wages. It introduced social security, including free medical care. In World War II the Labour government declared war on Germany, introduced conscription for military service, and entered strongly into collective security arrangements. The Labour Party held office again (1957–60, 1972–75, 1984–90). Under its Prime Minister David Lange (1984–89) it carried its non-nuclear policy to the point of banning all nuclear-powered or nuclear-armed ships. The party was decisively defeated in the general election of October 1990, at a time of severe economic difficulty. It returned to power in 1999, 2002, and 2005 in coalition governments with Helen *Clark as Prime Minister. Since 2008 it has been in opposition.

Ladislaus I (canonized as **St Ladislaus**) (c.1040–95) King of Hungary (1077–95). He conquered Croatia and Bosnia and extended Hungarian power into Transylvania, as well as establishing order in his kingdom and advancing the spread of Christianity. He was canonized in 1192.

Ladislaus II (Polish name **Władysław**) (c.1351–1434) King of Poland (1386–1434). He was grand duke of Lithuania from 1377 to 1401, during which time he was known as Jogaila, and acceded to the Polish throne on his marriage to the Polish monarch, Queen Jadwiga (1374–99), thus uniting Lithuania and Poland. He converted Lithuania to Christianity and was the founder of the Jagiellon dynasty, which ruled the two states until 1572.

Ladysmith, Siege of A four-month siege by Boer forces during the Second Boer War of a town in eastern South Africa, in KwaZulu-Natal. It was founded in the early 19th century and named after the wife of the governor of Natal, Sir Harry Smith. Ladysmith was relieved on 28 February 1900 by Lord Roberts, who replaced General Sir Redvers Buller as commander of the British forces.

Lafayette, Marie Joseph Paul Yves Roch Gilbert du Motier, Marquis de (or **La Fayette**) (1757–1834) French soldier and statesman. In 1777 he went to America and became one of the leaders of the French Expeditionary Force, which fought alongside the American colonists in the War of Independence. On his return he played a crucial part in the early phase of the French Revolution, commanding the National Guard (1789–91) and advocating moderate policies. He became an opposition leader in the Chamber of Deputies (1825–30) and participated in the Revolution of 1830.

La Fontaine, Sir Louis-Hippolyte (1807–64) French-Canadian statesman. A member of the legislative assembly of Lower Canada (1830–37), he opposed *Papineau's Rebellion and was not in sympathy with *Mackenzie's Rebellion of 1837. An outspoken advocate of nationalism, he was arrested in 1838, but soon released, and, after the union of *Upper and Lower Canada (1841), assumed political leadership of the French-Canadian reformers. In partnership with Robert *Baldwin he twice formed the government of United Canada (1842–43, 1848–51), on the second occasion serving as Prime Minister in an administration which was notable for its reforms and its achievement of full parliamentary ("responsible") government in Canada. He left politics in 1851.

Lake Erie, Battle of (10 September 1813) A naval engagement in the *War of 1812. Control of Lake Erie was of critical importance to both the USA and the UK, and by the late summer of 1813 each had commissioned a locally built and manned squadron of warships. Ten US vessels under Commodore Oliver Hazard Perry met six British vessels under Captain James Barclay off Put-in-Bay. After hard fighting, Perry captured the entire British squadron. His victory opened the way for a renewed US attack on Canada.

Lake George, Battle of (8 September 1755) An engagement in the *French and Indian wars fought 80 km (50 miles) north of Albany, New York. New England and New York militia and

Iroquois commanded by William Johnson (1715–74) defeated a French force and halted their advance. This victory offset General Braddock's defeat of the summer.

Lally, Thomas Arthur, Comte de, Baron de Tollendal (1702–66) French general, the son of an Irish Jacobite, Sir Gerard O'Lally. From 1756 Lally was an able commander of the French army in India during the *Seven Years War. He had to give up the siege of Madras through lack of supplies, and surrendered Pondicherry after being defeated by the British commander Eyre Coote in January 1760. This put an end to the French empire in India, and on his return to France he was tried for treason and executed after two years imprisonment. The writer and philosopher Voltaire worked with Lally's son to obtain a posthumous vindication; the condemnation was declared unjust in 1778 and Voltaire, on his death-bed, recorded his pleasure that his efforts to clear Lally's name had succeeded.

Lambert, John (1619–83) English major-general. He rose to prominence as a *Roundhead officer during the *English Civil War. He accompanied *Cromwell as second-in-command on the invasion of Scotland (1650). He entertained high political ambitions and was chiefly responsible for drafting England's first written constitution, the *Instrument of Government* (1653). He supported Cromwell loyally (1653–57), but then resigned all his commissions when his own path to power seemed blocked. In 1662, after the *Restoration, he was tried for treason, and spent the rest of his life in captivity.

Lancastrian A descendant or supporter of *John of Gaunt, Duke of Lancaster. The Lancastrians held the throne of England as *Henry IV, *Henry V, and *Henry VI, (their badge was a red rose). In the Wars of the *Roses, a series of battles for the throne fought with the *Yorkists from 1455 onwards, the Lancastrians suffered a major reverse in the displacement of Henry by Edward IV in 1461; they took refuge in France, and under the leadership of *Margaret of Anjou invaded England and succeeded in restoring Henry to his kingdom in October 1470. Henry's rule was ended after a few months by the Yorkist victories at *Barnet and *Tewkesbury; most of the remaining Lancastrian leaders died in the latter battle. Yet the Lancastrian party was ultimately successful, for it then supported Henry Tudor, who in 1485, by his victory at *Bosworth Field, became king as *Henry VII.

Land League An agrarian organization in Ireland. It was founded in 1879 by an ex-*Fenian, Michael *Davitt, to secure reforms in the land-holding system. With Charles *Parnell as president, it initiated the boycotting of anyone replacing a tenant evicted because of non-payment of rent (*see* BOYCOTT, CHARLES CUNNINGHAM). The campaign for land reform was linked with parliamentary activity by the Irish *Home Rule Members of Parliament. The British government declared the Land League illegal and imprisoned Davitt and Parnell. Branches of the League were formed in Australia, the USA, and elsewhere. Between 1881 and 1903 British governments passed Land Acts to remove the worst features of the landlord system in Ireland.

land reform The changing of systems of land tenure, usually at government initiative. Systems of land tenure vary considerably, and have great importance for the social and political structure of a society. Land may be held corporately by lineages, in small individual plots, or by a tiny number of wealthy landowners. Land reform has varied purposes and takes different forms: it may aim to create a more equal society by abolishing feudalism, winning the support of peasants, and giving them a greater stake in society; it may also aim to increase economic efficiency by creating a pattern of landholding which maximizes investment and productivity; or it may seek to impose a socialist pattern of ownership, where individual land ownership is not in general permitted. Reforms have varied from the redistribution of land, to the imposition of land ceilings (so that no single owner controls more than a certain area), and from the complete abolition of private ownership, to attempts to alter the terms under which tenants work private owners' land, such as the terms of sharecropping agreements. In modern times, the first land redistribution was that in France following the Revolution (1789), which established the pattern of small family farms that continues today. In Britain there have not been any reforms initiated by the government, but the Enclosures movement (16th to 19th centuries) pushed many peasants off the land into the towns and led to the development of industry and of large-scale farming. In Russia, limited land reform giving the land to the peasants accompanied the emancipation of the serfs in 1861, but the land was taken away again from 1918 with the abolition of private ownership of land and extensive *collectivization. A similar process occurred in much of Eastern Europe after 1945 but the individual right to own land was reintroduced in the early 1990s.

In countries that espouse *communism, such as China, Cuba, and Vietnam, there has also been extensive collectivization, while in Mozambique and Ethiopia all land title was declared the nation's and the rights of the tillers of the land and their descendants guaranteed. Some land reforms in Asia have been very effective in increasing land ownership among peasants, including those in Taiwan, South Korea, and Malaysia, where a system of cooperative land settlement, resembling the Israeli use of kibbutzim, has been employed. In Latin America, attempts at reform have often been impeded by such factors as the high level of foreign ownership, prevalence of very large plantations, and opposition from politically powerful landowners. In the Middle East, a successful reform in Egypt in 1952 has been the model for reforms elsewhere, with varying degrees of success. State compensation to landowners whose land is expropriated often takes the form of state bonds; a noteworthy exception being in Taiwan, where shares in public industry were given in compensation. This illustrates the need for *industrialization to provide employment in countries where rapid population growth means that the land, however equitably distributed, cannot provide a living for all. The redistribution of land from large estates into small peasant farms has nearly always had the effect of raising productivity and reducing poverty; however, this is contradicted by the experience of Zimbabwe from 2000, where the expropriation of White-owned commercial farms contributed to a grave economic crisis. *See also* AGRICULTURE.

Lanfranc (*c.*1010–89) Scholar, teacher, and Archbishop of Canterbury (1070–89). He was born in Italy, and set up a school at Avranches, Normandy (1039). He studied as a monk at the abbey of Bec, Normandy (1042), becoming its prior (1046) and making it into one of the finest schools in Europe, whose pupils included *Anselm and Theobald, both future archbishops of Canterbury. Lanfranc's association with *William I began with his negotiation of papal approval for William's marriage while he was Duke of Normandy (1053) and continued after the conquest of England. Lanfranc sought to reform the English Church and to unite it under Canterbury, but he also recognized the king's right to intervene in Church affairs. He supported *William II in the rebellion of 1088.

Lange, David Russell (1942–2005) New Zealand politician; Labour Prime Minister (1984–89). Lange trained as a lawyer and became an MP in 1977. In 1979 he was appointed deputy leader of the opposition, becoming leader in 1983. He led his party to victory in the 1984 elections pledging a commitment to a nonnuclear defence policy. His banning of nuclear-armed and nuclear-powered ships from New Zealand's ports angered the USA. He introduced free-market reforms and reduced national spending.

Langton, Stephen (*c.*1150–1228) English prelate. His reputation rests mainly on his promotion of the interests of the English Church in the face of conflicting pressures from the papacy and the English throne. As Archbishop of Canterbury he defended the Church's interests against King John, was intermediary during the negotiations leading to the signing of Magna Carta, and protected the young Henry III against baronial domination.

Langtry, Lillie (born **Emilie Charlotte le Breton**) (1853–1929) British actress. Born in Jersey and the daughter of the dean of the island, she was noted for her beauty and became known as 'the Jersey Lily' from the title of a portrait of her painted by Sir John Millais. She made her stage début in 1881 and was one of the first actresses from an aristocratic background. She became the mistress of the Prince of Wales, later Edward VII.

Lansbury, George (1859–1940) British Labour politician and pacifist. As leader of Poplar Council in east London in 1921, he went to prison rather than reduce relief payments for the unemployed. Refusing to join the *National government in 1931, he became leader of the rump of the Labour Party (1931–35). His rejection of sanctions against Italy, following that country's invasion of Ethiopia in 1935, alienated his colleagues, and he resigned.

Lansdowne, Henry Charles Keith Petty-Fitzmaurice, 5th Marquis of (1845–1927) British statesman. As Foreign Secretary in the *Salisbury and then *Balfour governments (1900–05) Lansdowne negotiated the *Anglo-Japanese Alliance (1902) and the *entente cordiale (1904) with France. From 1906 Lansdowne led the Conservative Opposition in the House of Lords. His use of the veto on legislation from the House of Commons resulted in the Parliament Act (1911), which reduced the power of the *Lords to a two-year suspensory veto. He was the author of the Lansdowne letter of November 1917 in the *Daily Telegraph* advocating a negotiated peace with Germany.

Lansdowne, William Petty-Fitzmaurice
See SHELBURNE.

L'Anse aux Meadows An important archaeological site in northern Newfoundland, the
only confirmed *Viking settlement in the
Americas. Excavations have uncovered foundations of turf-walled houses unlike any dwellings
built by indigenous cultures, but identical to
Viking structures in Iceland and Greenland.
Norse construction is proved by associated finds,
including a spindle-whorl, a stone lamp, a bronze
ring-headed pin, iron nails, and a smith's hearth.
Radio-carbon datings from the structures range
from 700 to 1080 AD, concentrating in the late
10th century, which corresponds to the period of
Norse Vinland sagas. Identification with Leif
Ericsson, however, is purely speculative.

Laos

Capital:	Vientiane
Area:	236,800 sq km (91,400 sq miles)
Population:	6,695,166 (2013 est)
Currency:	1 kip = 100 at
Religions:	Buddhist 67.0%; Christian 2.5%
Ethnic Groups:	Lao 55.0%; Khmou 11.0%; Hmong 8.0%; minority groups
Languages:	Lao (official); French; English; minority languages
International Organizations:	UN; ASEAN; Colombo Plan; Non-Aligned Movement; WTO

A long, thin, landlocked
country in south-east Asia,
bordering China and
Myanmar (Burma) on the
north, Thailand on the west,
Cambodia on the south,
and Vietnam on the east.

Physical Laos is mostly
high and hilly, with evergreen forest, this terrain
also supporting maize. The Mekong River runs
through the north of the country, down the
western boundary, and through it again in the
south; and its wide valley, swept by a summer
monsoon, is ideal for rice growing.

Economy Agriculture employs three-quarters
of the population, with coffee being an export
crop. Other exports include wood products,

electricity (from hydroelectric plants), and tin
and other metals. Industries include mining,
timber, electricity generation, and food processing. The relaxation of central planning in
the late 1980s has led to fast economic growth,
but Laos is still one of the least developed
countries in the world.

History The Lao, originating in southern
China, were driven south by *Mongol pressure.
In 1354, following a period of Khmer rule, they
set up the Buddhist kingdom of Lanxang ('Million Elephants'), which for a time was very
powerful. Laos broke up into rival kingdoms in
the 18th century and gradually fell under Siamese (Thai) domination before Siam was forced
to yield its claim to France in 1893. Occupied by
the Japanese during World War II, it emerged
briefly as an independent constitutional monarchy (1947–53), but was undermined by guerrilla war as a result of the increasing influence of
the communist *Pathet Lao as a political force in
the mid-1950s. A coalition government was established under Prince *Souvanna Phouma in
1962, but fighting broke out again soon after,
continuing into the 1970s, with Laos suffering
badly as a result of involvement in the *Vietnam
War. A ceasefire was signed in 1973 and a year
later Souvanna Phouma agreed to share power
in a new coalition with the Pathet Lao leader, his
half-brother Prince Souphanouvong (1902–95);
but by 1975 the Pathet Lao were in almost
complete control of the country and on 3
December the monarchy was finally abolished
and the People's Democratic Republic of Laos
established, which, under Kaysone Phomvihane
(Prime Minister 1975–92), maintained close
links with Vietnam. In 1989 there began some
relaxation of his regime and moves to restructure the economy. A new constitution
was promulgated in 1991, which envisaged a
strong presidency, but no relaxation of control
by the Lao People's Revolutionary Party. In
1992 Kaysone was elected President, but died
later that year; he was succeeded by Nouhak
Phousavanh. The USA restored full diplomatic
relations in May 1992. There were border
clashes with Thailand throughout the 1990s.
Khamtay Siphandone became President in
1998; he was succeeded by Choummaly
Sayasone in 2006.

Laozi (or **Lao-tzu**; known as **'Master Lao'**)
A probably mythical Chinese philosopher, long
honoured in China as the founder of Daoism.
He is said to have beaten *Confucius, reputedly
his junior, in debate. The *Daodejing (Dao Te
Ching)*, which dates from about the 3rd century
BC (about 300 years after Confucius), was

attributed to him. The *Dao* is defined as the source of all being, in which life and death are the same. Daoists seek unity with the *Dao* through 'unmotivated action', allowing events to take their natural course. Daoists later claimed he was an immortal who left China for India, where he converted the *Buddha to Daoism.

Largo, Caballero Francisco (1869–1946) Spanish statesman. As a socialist he was imprisoned for life in 1917 for taking part in a general strike, but he was released on his election to Parliament in 1918. After the fall of *Primo de Rivera (1930) he joined the government of the Second Republic as Minister for Labour. After this collapsed he was imprisoned again (1934–35) for supporting an abortive rising, but was acquitted and released. He was leader of the Popular Front, which won the elections of February 1936, but did not become Prime Minister until September 1936, two months after the outbreak of the *Spanish Civil War, when he headed a coalition of socialists, republicans, and communists. He resigned following a communist take-over in Barcelona in May 1937.

La Salle, René-Robert Cavelier, sieur de (1643–87) French explorer in North America. He went to Canada in 1666 and in 1682, after exploring the Great Lakes, descended the Mississippi River to its mouth. He took possession of the whole valley, and named it Louisiana in honour of his king, *Louis XIV. On his return to Paris he was appointed Viceroy of North America and given authority to govern the whole region between Lake Michigan and the Gulf of Mexico. He set out with four ships for the Gulf but could not find the mouth of the Mississippi. The ships separated and he and his men landed on the Texas shore and attempted to find the way overland. Eventually the men became mutinous and murdered him. It was another twelve years before the French established a settlement in Louisiana.

Las Casas, Bartolomé de (1474–1566) Spanish missionary priest, the "Apostle of the Indies". He was a Dominican friar who criticized the conquest and exploitation of the Indians of the Spanish colonies. He had himself participated as a settler in Hispaniola in 1502 and as a member of the expedition to Cuba in 1511–12. His change of heart came in 1514, and for the next 50 years he travelled between the colonies and Spain advocating humanitarian reform, especially the abolition of Indian slavery, and writing books arguing the equality of Indians as subjects of the king. The most famous work was his *Brief History of the Indies* (1539). In 1542 his campaigning led to the New Laws to protect Indians in Spanish colonies. Their effectiveness, however, was limited by the opposition of the conquistadores.

La Tène *See* IRON AGE.

Lateran Council One of the synods or meetings of senior churchmen held at the Lateran Palace in Rome. The First in 1123 was to bring to an end the investiture contests and to specify which aspects of life should be governed by the church and which by the secular authorities. The Second was called in 1139 to clarify doctrine and to heal the schism which had been caused by the activities of the antipope Anacletus II. In 1179 the Third Council condemned *simony and regularized papal elections.

The Fourth Lateran Council (1215) is known as the "Great Council" and was called by Pope *Innocent III. It condemned the *Albigensian heresy and clarified church doctrine on the Trinity, the Incarnation, and transubstantiation. The Fifth Council from 1512 to 1517 condemned heresy and additionally revoked the *Pragmatic Sanction of Bourges by which Charles VI of France had claimed authority over the church.

Lateran Treaties (11 February 1929) Agreements between *Mussolini's government and Pius XI to regularize relations between the Vatican and the Italian government, strained since 1870 when the Papal States had been incorporated into a united Italy. By a treaty (*Concordat) and financial convention the *Vatican City was recognized as a fully independent state under papal sovereignty. The concordat recognized Roman Catholicism as the sole religion of the state. The Vatican received in cash and securities a large sum in settlement of claims against the state.

Latimer, Hugh (*c.*1485–1555) English Protestant prelate and martyr. He became one of Henry VIII's chief advisers when the king formally broke with the papacy in 1534, and was made bishop of Worcester in 1535. Latimer's opposition to Henry's moves to restrict the spread of Reformation doctrines and practices led to his resignation in 1539. Under Mary I he was imprisoned for heresy and burnt at the stake with Nicholas Ridley at Oxford.

Latin American Integration Association (LAIA; Spanish: Asociación Latinoamericana de Integración (ALADI)) An economic alliance of 13 Latin American countries. The permanent members of LAIA are Argentina, Bolivia, Brazil, Chile, Colombia, Cuba, Ecuador, Mexico, Panama, Paraguay, Peru, Uruguay, and Venezuela. The association was formed by the Treaty of Montevideo (1980) to replace the Latin American Free Trade Area (LAFTA); it began operations in 1981. LAFTA had been established in 1960 to increase trade between member countries and to promote their economic and social development. LAFTA, however, had only limited success, being considered overambitious and inflexible. LAIA was created by the members of LAFTA to continue LAFTA's policies, but without fixed timetables for the introduction of such measures as reductions in trade tariffs and with greater allowance for differences between member nations. *See also* ANDEAN COMMUNITY; MERCOSUR.

La Trobe, Charles Joseph (1801–75) British colonial administrator. He became superintendent of the newly settled Port Phillip District of New South Wales in Australia in 1839. When it was separated from New South Wales (and renamed *Victoria) in 1851, he became lieutenant-governor. Almost immediately he was confronted with the *gold rushes, when the population of Victoria rose in six months from 15,000 to 80,000. He introduced, among other measures, the licence system which later became a cause of the *Eureka Rebellion.

Latvia

Capital:	Riga
Area:	64,589 sq km (24,938 sq miles)
Population:	2,178,443 (2013 est)
Currency:	1 euro = 100 cents
Religions:	Lutheran 19.6%; Eastern Orthodox 15.3%: other Christian 1.0%
Ethnic Groups:	Latvian 61.1%; Russian 26.2%; Belarussian 3.5%; minority groups
Languages:	Latvian (official); Russian; minority languages
International Organizations:	UN; OSCE; EU; NATO; Council of Europe; WTO

A country lying on the shores of the Baltic Sea and the Gulf of Riga. It borders on Estonia to the north, Russia to the east, and Lithuania to the south.

Physical Latvia is generally flat, though hilly in the lakelands of the east and well forested with

fir, pine, birch, and oak. It has a modified continental climate.

Economy Mineral resources are limited, although there are unexplored reserves of oil. Manufacturing industry concentrates on processed foods, metals, and wood products as well as textiles. Agriculture specializes in dairy and meat production, grains, and vegetables. Exports include food and wood products, metals, machinery and equipment, and textiles.

History Originally inhabited by Lettish peoples, it was overrun by the Russians and Swedes during the 10th and 11th centuries, and settled by German merchants and Christian missionaries from 1158. In the 13th century the *Hanseatic League forged commercial links, while the *Teutonic Knights and German bishops imposed feudal overlordship. With Estonia it became part of Livonia in 1346, was partitioned under *Ivan IV (The Terrible) of Russia, and came under Lutheran influence in the *Reformation. It then fell to the Poles, and in the 17th century to the Swedes. Their rule lasted until 1721, when parts again reverted to Russia, the remainder succumbing in the partitions of *Poland. From the 1880s Tsarist governments imposed a policy of Russification to counteract growing demands for independence, which was proclaimed in April 1918. After a confused period of war between Latvians, Germans, and Bolshevik Russians, international recognition was gained in 1921 and the Constitution of the Republic agreed in 1922. During the years 1922–40 sea-ports and industry declined with the loss of Russian markets, but agriculture flourished, many of the great estates being broken up. In 1934 a neo-fascist regime was formed by Karlis Ulmanis, who vainly tried to win Hitler's support, but was sacrificed in the Nazi-Soviet Pact of 1939. The Red Army occupied it in June 1940, but German troops took Riga on 1 July 1941 and were welcomed. Re-occupied by the Red Army in October 1944, it became a constituent republic of the Soviet Union. Latvian nationalism never died however, and in May 1990 a newly elected Supreme Soviet passed a resolution demanding independence from the Soviet Union. Independence was recognized by the Soviet Union in September 1991. A new citizenship law excluded from political activity all who were not citizens of pre-war Latvia or their descendants, thus excluding 48.2% of the population, most of whom were Russians. In 1994 and 1998 the citizenship law was modified slightly but tensions between the Russian and Latvian communities continued. The last Russian troops were withdrawn from Latvia in August 1994. Latvia joined NATO and the European Union in 2004. Unsustainable economic growth in the mid-2000s was followed by a severe recession triggered by the *Credit Crunch in 2008–09. Assistance from the IMF, the EU, and other sources was secured at the price of austerity measures, which led to popular protests. There was further controversy in 2011–12 over the status of the Russian language. In 2014 Latvia adopted the euro as its currency and Laimdota Straujama became the country's first woman Prime Minister.

Laud, William (1573–1645) English prelate. In 1633 he was appointed Archbishop of Canterbury and set about the suppression of the prevailing Calvinism in England and Presbyterianism in Scotland. His moves to impose liturgical uniformity by restoring pre-Reformation practices aroused great hostility; they led to war in Scotland and were a contributory cause of the English Civil War. In 1640 Laud was impeached and imprisoned; he was later executed for treason.

Laurier, Sir Wilfrid (1841–1919) Canadian Liberal statesman, Prime Minister (1896–1911). He became the leader of the Liberal Party in 1891 and five years later was elected Canada's first French-Canadian and Roman Catholic Prime Minister. While in office he worked to achieve national unity in the face of cultural conflict; he also oversaw the building of a second transcontinental railway and the creation of the provinces of Alberta and Saskatchewan.

Lausanne, Treaty of *See* VERSAILLES PEACE SETTLEMENT.

Laval, Pierre (1883–1945) French politician. He trained as a lawyer before entering politics as a socialist. Gradually moving to the right, he was Prime Minister (1931–32 and 1935–36) but was best known as Foreign Minister (1934, 1935–36), when he was the co-author of the unsuccessful Hoare–Laval pact for the settlement of Mussolini's claims to Ethiopia. He fell from power soon after, but after France's defeat in 1940 he became chief minister in the *Vichy government. He advocated active support for Hitler, drafting labour for Germany, authorizing a French fascist militia, and instituting a rule of terror. In 1945 he was tried and executed in France.

Law, Bonar (Andrew Bonar Law) (1858–1923) British politician. He became leader of the Conservative Party in 1911, and supported Ulster's resistance to *Home Rule. A tariff reformer, in 1915 he joined *Asquith's coalition as Colonial Secretary and continued under *Lloyd George, serving as Chancellor of the Exchequer (1916–19) and Lord Privy Seal (1919–21). In 1922 the Conservatives rejected the coalition government of Lloyd George and he was appointed Prime Minister. He resigned the following May for reasons of ill health.

Law, John (1671–1729) Scottish financier based in France. He was an exiled Scotsman who believed that increased circulation of paper money and proper organization of credit would bring prosperity. The Regent of France, Philippe, Duc d'*Orléans, facing financial crisis, allowed him to set up a state bank and a trading company, the "Compagnie du Mississippi", to trade with Louisiana, and later gave it a monopoly of overseas trade. In January 1720 Law became Controller-General of Finance, but in December 1720 a wave of speculation brought his system to an end. The episode, which brought fortune to a few and ruin to many, is similar to the *South Sea Bubble.

Lawrence, T. E. (Thomas Edward Lawrence; known as **Lawrence of Arabia**) (1888–1935) British soldier and writer. From 1916 onwards he helped to organize and lead the Arab revolt against the Turks in the Middle East. His campaign of guerrilla raids contributed to General Allenby's eventual victory in Palestine in 1918; Lawrence described this period in *The Seven Pillars of Wisdom* (1926). In 1922 he enlisted in the RAF under an assumed name to avoid attention and remained in the ranks of that service for most of the rest of his life. He was killed in a motorcycle accident.

League of Nations An organization for international cooperation established in 1919 by the *Versailles Peace Settlement. A League covenant embodying the principles of collective security, arbitration of international disputes, reduction of armaments, and open diplomacy was formulated. Germany was admitted in 1926, but the US Congress failed to ratify the Treaty of Versailles, containing the covenant. Although the League, with its headquarters in Geneva, accomplished much of value in post-war economic reconstruction, it failed in its prime purpose as a result of the refusal of member nations to put international interests before national interests. The League was powerless in the face of Italian, German, and Japanese expansionism. In 1946 it was replaced by the *United Nations Organization.

Lebanon

Capital:	Beirut
Area:	10,400 sq km (4015 sq miles)
Population:	4,131,583 (2013 est)
Currency:	1 Lebanese pound = 100 piastres
Religions:	Muslim 59.7%; Christian 39.0%
Ethnic Groups:	Arab 95.0%; Armenian 4.0%
Languages:	Arabic (official); French; English; Armenian
International Organizations:	UN; Arab League; Non-Aligned Movement

A country of the Middle East at the eastern end of the Mediterranean Sea, bounded by Syria on the north and east and Israel on the south.

Physical Lebanon is some 200 km (125 miles) from north to south and 50–80 km (30–50 miles) from east to west. On the narrow coastal plain summers are sunny and warm; fruits of all kinds grow well. Inland the ground rises quickly, to two ranges of high mountains, where there is much winter frost and snow. Between them is the fertile Bekaa Valley, well suited to agriculture, while much of the eastern boundary resembles steppe.

Economy Lebanon is the financial centre for its region—a position it has worked hard to recover after the destruction of the 1975–90 civil war. Other industries include tourism, food processing, wine, and jewellery; the principal agricultural products are fruit and vegetables. Exports include jewellery, metals, chemicals, consumer goods, and fruit and vegetables.

History Much of present-day Lebanon formed part of Phoenicia, including the important trading towns of Tyre, Sidon, Byblos, and Arvad, which retained their importance under Roman rule. Mount Lebanon was a refuge for persecuted minorities such as the Christian Maronites, who settled there from the 7th century AD, and the Muslim Druze, who occupied the southern part of the mountain from the 11th century. After the Arab conquest during the 7th century Arab tribesmen settled in Lebanon. Successive governments in the region usually left the people of the mountain to manage their own affairs and contented themselves with exercising authority on the coastal plain. Part of the Ottoman empire from the 16th century, it became a French mandate after World War I. A Lebanese republic was set up in 1926. The country was occupied (1941–45) by *Free French forces, supported by Britain.

Independence was achieved in 1945. Growing disputes between Christians and Muslims, exacerbated by the presence of Palestinian refugees, undermined the stability of the republic. Hostility between the differing Christian and Muslim groups led to protracted civil war and to the armed intervention (1976) by Syria. The activities of the *Palestine Liberation Organization brought large-scale Israeli military invasion and led to Israeli occupation (1978) of a part of southern Lebanon. A UN peacekeeping force attempted unsuccessfully to set up a buffer zone. A full military invasion (1982) by Israel led to the evacuation of the Palestinians. A massacre by the Phalangist Christian militia in Israeli-occupied West Beirut of Muslim civilians in the Chabra and Chatila refugee camps brought a redeployment of UN peacekeeping forces. Syria again intervened in 1987. Israel established a South Lebanon Army (SLA), and there were 20 Israeli air raids during 1988. In March 1989 the Maronite Christian General Aoun launched an all-out war against Syrian troops. In October 1989 the Arab League successfully negotiated an accord in Taif, Saudi Arabia, whereby the Maronite dominance in government would be reduced. This was reluctantly accepted, and a frail peace established under continued Syrian protection, which was formalized by a treaty in May 1991. In 1992 the first general elections since 1972 were largely boycotted by Maronite Christian parties. Rafik Hariri became Prime Minister (1992–98; 2000–04) and began to implement a programme of economic reconstruction. Tension in southern Lebanon continued, with attacks by the radical, Iran-backed Hezbollah guerrillas against the Israeli-supported SLA. In 2005 Hariri was assassinated. Suspected Syrian involvement led to large demonstrations and the withdrawal of all Syrian troops from Lebanon. In 2006 a month-long Israeli military operation against Hezbollah caused economic damage in south Lebanon. Hezbollah used its enhanced prestige from this conflict to demand a greater role in Lebanon's government, which led to political stalemate. Armed clashes in Beirut between government and Hezbollah in 2008 resulted in Hezbollah being given a veto over government decisions.

Lebensraum (German, 'living-space') *Nazi political doctrine claiming a need to acquire more territory in order to accommodate the expanding German nation. First introduced as a political concept in the 1870s, the concept was given patriotic significance by *Hitler and *Goebbels. The corollary to *Lebensraum* was the *Drang nach Osten* (German, 'drive to the East'), which claimed large areas of eastern Europe for the *Third Reich to enable the so-called Nazi master race to subjugate and colonize the Slavic peoples.

Lebrun, Albert (1871–1950) French statesman, 17th and last President (1932–40) of the Third Republic. A moderate conservative, he pursued a respected but unspectacular parliamentary career (1920–32) until his election to the Presidency. He acquiesced in the French armistice (1940) that led to the *Vichy government of Marshal *Pétain. He was interned in Austria (1943–44) until the liberation of France, when he acknowledged *de Gaulle as head of the provisional government.

Lechfeld, Battle of (955) A major battle fought near Augsburg, in Germany, when the forces of the Holy Roman Emperor *Otto I defeated the *Magyars. This put an end to their westward expansion and the long period of harassment which they had inflicted on the German empire.

Lee, Robert E. (Robert Edward Lee) (1807–70) US general. He was the commander of the Confederate army of Northern Virginia, leading it for most of the American Civil War. Although he did much to prolong Confederate resistance against the Union's greater manpower and resources, his invasion of the North was repulsed by General Meade at the Battle of Gettysburg (1863) and he eventually surrendered to General Grant in 1865.

Lee Kuan Yew (1923–) Singapore statesman, Prime Minister (1959–90). In 1955 he formed the People's Action Party, a democratic socialist organization, which under his leadership dominated politics in Singapore from the late 1950s. He led Singapore as a component state of the newly formed Federation of *Malaysia in 1963, and then as a fully independent republic. His policies developed along increasingly authoritarian socialist lines. These centred on the establishment of a one-party rule and a free-market economy, tight government planning, and a hard-working population supported by an extensive social welfare system. The result was one of the world's most successful econ-

omies. He resigned as Prime Minister in 1990 but remained a senior minister in government.

Left (in politics) Ideas, movements, and parties of a radical or progressive character, usually associated with *socialism. Following the example of the representatives of the Third Estate at the time of the French Revolution (1789), members of legislative assemblies holding liberal, democratic, or egalitarian views have tended to sit on the left of their chambers. What counts as "Left" varies with time and place: classical Liberal views on economics, for instance, would count as "Right" nowadays, but were "Left" when first espoused in the late 18th century.

legion *See* ROMAN LEGION.

Leguía, Augusto Bernardino (1863–1932) Peruvian statesman. As leader of the Civilian Party Leguía was Prime Minister of Peru (1903–08) and President (1908–12, 1919–30). During his first term in office he settled frontier disputes with Bolivia and Brazil, introduced administrative reforms, and improved the public health system. He was reinstated as President by the army in 1919, introducing a new constitution in 1920. He chose largely to ignore this, governing by increasingly dictatorial methods. His second term saw rapid industrialization, but was adversely affected by the Great *Depression and fall in commodity prices. Criticized also for the *Tacna–Arica Settlement, he lost popularity and was forced from office by the military.

Leicester, Robert Dudley, 1st Earl of *See* DUDLEY, ROBERT.

Leif Ericsson *See* VIKINGS.

Leipzig, Battle of (also called the "Battle of the Nations", 16–19 October 1813) A decisive battle in the *Napoleonic Wars. It was fought just outside the city of Leipzig in Saxony, by an army under Napoleon of some 185,000 French, Saxon, and other allied German troops, against a force of some 350,000 troops from Austria, Prussia, Russia, and Sweden, under the overall command of *Schwarzenberg. Napoleon took up a defensive position and at first successfully resisted attacks by Schwarzenberg from the south and *Blücher from the north. The next day Russian and Swedish troops arrived, while Napoleon's Saxon troops deserted him. The battle raged for nine hours, but at midnight Napoleon ordered a retreat. This began in an orderly fashion until, early in the afternoon of 19 October, a bridge was mistakenly blown up, stranding the French rear-guard of 30,000 crack troops, who were captured. Following the battle French power east of the Rhine collapsed as more and more German princes deserted Napoleon, who abdicated in 1814.

Leisler, Jacob 1640–91) US rebel, who migrated from Germany to New Amsterdam in 1660. Leisler and other merchants resented English control of the colony from 1664. As a militia officer in the *Glorious Revolution in New York, he led the humbler residents against both *James II and the aristocratic patroons (lords of the manor) and assumed the governorship in 1689. When Governor Slaughter arrived from England in 1691 Leisler resisted and was captured; he was tried for treason and hanged. His execution precipitated factional conflict for a generation.

Lemass, Sean Francis (1899–1971) Irish Fianna Fáil politician, Prime Minister of the Republic of Ireland (1959–66). An IRA fighter when young, Lemass served under Eamon *de Valera in numerous government posts. As Prime Minister he advocated Irish membership of the *European Economic Community.

Lenclos, Ninon de (born **Anne de Lenclos**) (1620–1705) French courtesan. She was a famous wit and beauty and numbered many prominent writers and nobles among her lovers. She advocated a form of Epicureanism and defended her philosophy and lifestyle in her book *La Coquette vengée* (1659). In later life she presided over one of the most distinguished literary salons of the age.

Lend-Lease Act An arrangement (1941–45) according to which the USA supplied equipment to Britain and its Allies in World War II. It was formalized by an Act passed by the US Congress allowing President F. D. *Roosevelt to lend or lease equipment and supplies to any state whose defence was considered vital to the security of the USA. About 60% of the shipments went to Britain as a loan in return for British-owned military bases. About 20% went to the Soviet Union.

Lenin, Vladimir Ilich (born **Vladimir Ilich Ulyanov**) (1870–1924) The principal figure in the Russian Revolution and first Premier (Chairman of the Council of People's Commissars) of the Soviet Union (1918–24). Lenin was the first political leader to attempt to put Marxist principles into practice, though, like Marx, he saw the need for a transitional period to full communism, during which there would be a 'dictatorship of the proletariat'. The policies that

he pursued led ultimately to the establishment of Marxism-Leninism in the Soviet Union and, later, in China. Born in Russia, he lived in Switzerland from 1900, but was instrumental in the split between the Bolsheviks and Mensheviks in 1903, when he became leader of the more radical Bolsheviks. He returned to Russia in 1917, established Bolshevik control after the overthrow of the tsar, and in 1918 became head of state; he founded the Third International (or Comintern) the following year to further the cause of world revolution. With Trotsky's help he defeated counter-revolutionary forces in the Russian Civil War, but was forced to moderate his socio-economic policies to allow the country to recover from the effects of war and revolution. During the last years of his life he denounced, but was unable to prevent, the concentration of power in the hands of Stalin.

Leningrad, Siege of (September 1941– January 1944) The defence of Leningrad (now St Petersburg) against the Germans by the Soviet army in World War II. The German army had intended to capture Leningrad in the 1941 campaign but as a result of slow progress in the Baltic area and the reluctance of Germany's Finnish ally to assist, the city held out in a siege that lasted nearly 900 days.

Leo I, St (or **Leo the Great**) (*c*.390–461) Pope (440–61). He established the authority of the papacy by defending orthodoxy in regions far distant from his authority in Italy, most notably in Spain, Gaul, Africa, and the East. The Pelagian and Manichean sects in particular threatened papal control and authority. At *Chalcedon in 451 he obtained agreement between Eastern and Western churches on defining for Christian believers the relationship of God the Father to the Son. The following year he persuaded the barbarian *Attila to leave Italy. In 455 he saved Rome from *Vandal destruction.

Leo III (*c*.680–741) Byzantine emperor (717– 41). He repulsed several Muslim invasions and carried out an extensive series of financial, legal, administrative, and military reforms. In 726 he forbade the use of images in public worship; this policy, enforced by teams of iconoclasts, met with much popular opposition and a split with Rome.

Leo IX, St (1002–54) Pope (1048–54). An able church reformer, he enlisted like-minded churchmen to assist him including Hildebrand (later Pope *Gregory VII). His chief concerns were *simony and clerical celibacy; at the Easter synod of 1049 celibacy was enforced on all clergy. Attempting to establish papal control in southern Italy, Leo's forces were defeated by the Normans and he was made prisoner. His interference in south Italy in areas claimed by the *Byzantine empire led to the *East–West Schism of 1054 when the Patriarch of Constantinople was excommunicated. He died soon after being released from prison and, for his work in restoring the prestige of the papacy, was declared a saint.

Leonidas (died 480 BC) King of Sparta. He won immortal fame when he commanded a Greek force against the invading Persian army at the pass of *Thermopylae. He held the pass long enough to make possible the naval operation at Artemisium (*Greek-Persian wars). When counter-attacked he remained behind with 300 Spartans and 700 Thespians, and died fighting—an action which allowed his allies to escape.

Leopold I (1640–1705) Holy Roman Emperor (1658–1705). His long reign saw a major revival of Habsburg power, particularly after the *Ottoman attack on Vienna in 1683 was repulsed by an army led by King *John III (Sobieski) of Poland. The subsequent eastern campaigns brought the reconquest of Hungary, confirmed by the Peace of Carlowitz (1699). Increasing resentment at *Louis XIV's intervention in German affairs also allowed him to re-establish imperial leadership in Germany, an important contributory factor to the coalitions which inflicted heavy defeats on France between 1689 and 1713. After the removal of the Ottoman threat Vienna became a major European capital.

Leopold II (1835–1909) King of the Belgians (1865–1909). His reign saw considerable industrial and colonial expansion, due in large part to the wealth gleaned from the *Congo. The Berlin Colonial Conference (1884–85) had recognized Leopold as independent head of the newly created Congo Free State and he proceeded to amass great personal wealth from its rubber and ivory trade. Thanks to the report of an Englishman, Edmund Morel, his maltreatment of the Congo native population became an international scandal (1904) and he was forced to hand over the territory to his parliament in 1908.

Lepanto, Battle of (7 October 1571) A great sea-battle near the northern entrance to the Gulf of Corinth. On one side were the *Ottomans, who were seeking to drive the Venetians out of the eastern Mediterranean. On the other were the *Holy League forces of Venice, Spain, Genoa, and the papacy, under Don John of Austria. Despite the Ottomans' superior number of *galleys, the League won the battle. Lepanto was the last naval action fought between galleys manned by oarsmen and the first major Turkish defeat by the Christian powers, but it was not followed up, and had little long-term effect on Ottoman power.

Lesotho

Capital:	Maseru
Area:	30,355 sq km (11,720 sq miles)
Population:	1,936,181 (2013 est)
Currency:	1 loti = 100 lisente
Religions:	Christian 80.0%; traditional beliefs 20.0%
Ethnic Groups:	Sotho 99.7%
Languages:	Sesotho, English (both official); Zulu; Xhosa
International Organizations:	UN; AU; SADC; Commonwealth; Non-Aligned Movement; WTO

A small landlocked country entirely surrounded by the Republic of South Africa.

Physical Lesotho lies in the central and highest part of the Drakensberg Mountains, where summer rains cause severe soil erosion and in winter the temperature can be as low as –16°C (2°F). The Orange River rises here, in a terrain most suitable for grazing sheep and mountain goats, and only in its lower valley and to the west is there much scope for cultivation.

Economy South Africa dominates the economy of Lesotho, being the principal trading partner. Over one-third of Lesotho's adult male population work as migrant workers in South Africa, and their remittances are an important source of revenue. The remaining population mostly engages in subsistence agriculture, but Lesotho produces less than one-fifth of its food requirements—and production is declining because of soil erosion. Major exports are manufactures, wool and mohair, food, and livestock; diamonds, the chief mineral resource, are of growing importance. Limited industry includes food processing, textiles, clothing, handicrafts, construction, and tourism.

History Lesotho was founded as Basutoland in 1832 by Moshoeshoe I, who built a stronghold on Thaba Bosigo and unified the Sotho (Basuto). After fighting both Boers and British, Moshoeshoe put himself under British protection in 1868, and until 1880 Basutoland was administered from Cape Colony. In 1884 it was restored to the direct control of the British government with the Paramount Chief as titular head. When the Union of South Africa was formed in 1910, Basutoland came under the jurisdiction of the British High Commissioner in South Africa. It was re-named Lesotho and became independent in 1966 as a constitutional monarchy, with a National Assembly (1974) to work with hereditary chiefs. The National Assembly was disbanded in 1986 after a South African-backed military coup, by which the King was to rule through a Military Council. In November 1990 King Constantine Moshoeshoe II was deposed and replaced by his son, Letsie III. As chairman of the Military Council, Colonel Elias Ramaena held all effective power. He was ousted in a bloodless coup in 1991 by Major-General Justin Lekhanya, who established a democratic constitution. Multiparty elections were held in 1993 but tensions between the government and opposition parties led to a political crisis. Letsie III suspended the government and the constitution in 1994. After a negotiated settlement the government was restored and Letsie III abdicated in favour of his father (1995); but Moshoeshoe II was killed in a car accident in 1996 and Letsie III returned to the throne. Allegations of electoral fraud in 1998 led to an army uprising that was quelled by South African troops. A transitional body to organize electoral reform was established and elections under the new system were held in 2002. The country has one of the highest rates of AIDS and HIV infection in the world.

Lesseps, Ferdinand Marie, Vicomte de (1805–94) French diplomat. While in the consular service in Egypt he became aware of plans to link the Mediterranean and the Red Sea by means of a canal, and from 1854 onwards devoted himself to the project. Work began in 1859 and the Suez Canal was opened ten years later. In 1881 he embarked on the building of the Panama Canal, but had not anticipated the difficulties of this very different enterprise; the project was abandoned in 1889. The canal was not opened until 1914, after completion by US engineers.

Leticia dispute (1932–34) A border dispute between Colombia and Peru. The territory of Leticia on the upper Amazon River was ceded to Colombia by a treaty in 1924; it became an object of contention again in 1932 when Peru-

vian citizens seized the territory and executed Colombian officials. Colombia carried the dispute to the *League of Nations, which awarded Leticia to Colombia (1934). The active involvement of the USA with the League established a precedent, allowing the interference by an international body in territory protected by the *Monroe Doctrine. The successful reconciliation in the Leticia dispute was only one example of how the League of Nations was a striking success in Latin America.

Levellers English radicals of the mid-17th century. The Levellers were led by John Lilburne, William Walwyn, and John Wildman, and their early strength lay with the London poor. By 1647 they had won considerable support among the lower ranks of the *New Model Army. In that year Leveller 'Agitators' were elected from each regiment to participate in the Putney debates, with *Cromwell and the Army Grandees, in an attempt to resolve disagreements. Their political programme, embodied in such documents as the *Agreement of the People*, was less radical than that of the True Levellers or Diggers. It demanded the abolition of the monarchy and House of Lords, sovereignty for the people, manhood suffrage, social reform, liberty of conscience, and equality before the law. Exasperated by the conservatism of the Grandees and Parliament, they mutinied in 1647 and 1649. By May 1649 both the civilian and military wings of the movement had been broken.

Lewis and Clark expedition (1804–06) The most important transcontinental journey in US history. The expedition was commissioned by President *Jefferson to explore the vast area acquired as a result of the *Louisiana Purchase. Commanded by Meriwether Lewis and William Clark, it left St Louis in 1804 and sailed up the Missouri to winter in North Dakota before crossing Montana to the foothills of the Rockies. Crossing the Continental Divide at Lemhi Pass, Idaho, the expedition then moved north and in November 1805 reached the Pacific via the Clearwater, Snake, and Columbia rivers. In 1806, after crossing the Rockies, the expedition returned.

Lexington and Concord, Battle of (19 April 1775) The first engagement of the American War of *Independence. When General *Gage learnt that patriots were collecting military stores at Concord, 32 km (20 miles) north of Boston, he sent a force of about 800 men to confiscate them. Forewarned by Paul *Revere and others, the troops were met by

70 militia (the *minutemen) at Lexington. It is not known who fired the first shot, but in the ensuing skirmish eight minutemen were killed. The British marched on to Concord and confiscated some weapons, but retreated to Boston the same day, harried by patriots, who inflicted over 250 casualties on them.

Leyte Gulf, Battle of (October 1944) A naval battle off the Philippines. In the campaign to recover the Philippines, US forces landed on the island of Leyte. Four Japanese naval forces converged to attack US transports, but in a series of scattered engagements 40 Japanese ships were sunk, 46 were damaged, and 405 planes destroyed. The Japanese fleet, having failed to halt the invasion, withdrew from Philippine waters.

Liao (945–1125) A dynasty which ruled much of Manchuria and a small part of north-east China. It was founded by the Qidan (Khitan) tribesmen of Tungus stock, whose homeland was around the Liao River in Manchuria. From their name came the Russian *Kitai* and Marco Polo's Cathay. Qidan strength lay in cavalry. In 1004 their frontier with the Northern *Song was stabilized. Gradually they adopted Chinese habits, accepting the teachings of *Confucius, holding civil service examinations, and performing the customary Chinese rites. Overthrown by the Juchen, nomad huntsmen who founded the *Jin dynasty, some of them migrated westward to become the Kara Khitai of Central Asia.

Liaqat Ali Khan, Nawabzada (1895–1951) First Prime Minister of Pakistan (1947–51). He began his political career in British India as a Muslim leader in the United Provinces, and from 1933 became *Jinnah's right-hand man in the *Muslim League. In 1946 he became Finance Minister in the Interim Government. Between the death of Jinnah in 1948 and his own assassination in 1951 he was the most powerful politician in Pakistan, when he endeavoured to achieve a reconciliation with India via the Delhi Pact (1950).

Liberal Democratic Party (Japan) Japanese political party that has been the dominant party since World War II. Political alignments were slow to coalesce in post-war Japan, but in 1955 rival conservative groups combined to form the Liberal Democratic Party, which succeeded in holding power continuously until 1993. The Party's early leaders included *Kishi Nobusuke, his brother *Sato Eisaku, and *Tanaka Kakuei, who was forced to resign in 1974

as a result of a bribery scandal. Four leaders followed Kakuei in the space of eight years as the party's fortunes waned before some degree of recovery was achieved under the forceful leadership of *Nakasone Yasuhiro, who served as Prime Minister and LDP President from 1982 to 1987. The party developed close links with business and with interest groups such as fisheries and agriculture. A key feature has been its structure of internal factions, less concerned with policy than with patronage, electoral funding, and competition for party leadership. The party has also been involved in numerous financial and sexual scandals. Even so, it continued to appeal to a wide range of the electorate. The future of the party was threatened in 1992 by divisions arising from the uncovering of a further series of financial scandals. The LDP government lost a vote of confidence in 1993, lost the subsequent general election, and was ousted from office for the first time in its history. Two coalition governments collapsed and in 1994 the LDP joined the Social Democratic Party (SDP) of Japan and the Sakigake Party to form a coalition government. The SDP disbanded and the LDP formed a new coalition in 1996 and again in 1999, 2003, and 2005. Although heavily defeated in the 2009 general election, it returned to power in 2012 under Shinzo Abe (1954–).

Liberal Democrats A British political party that adopted this name in 1989. The party, which was formed in 1988, was formerly known as the Social and Liberal Democrats. The Social and Liberal Democrats were a merger of the **Social Democratic Party** (SDP) and the *Liberal Party. The SDP itself was established by four dissident members of the Labour Party (Roy Jenkins, David Owen, Shirley Williams, and William Rodgers), known as the 'gang of four'. As a new centre party, the SDP under David Owen's leadership, formed an alliance with the Liberal Party. However, after a poor showing in the 1987 election, the SDP voted to merge with the Liberal Party, to form the Social and Liberal Democrats. David Owen attempted to revive a reduced SDP in 1988 but wound it up in 1990.

Paddy Ashdown (1941–), leader of the Liberal Democrats from 1988 to 1999, managed to substantially increase the number of Liberal Democrat MPs in the 1997 election. Ashdown was succeeded as leader by Charles Kennedy (1959–), under whom further gains were made in the 2001 and 2005 elections. However, Kennedy was forced to resign in 2006 after admitting a problem with alcohol. He was succeeded by Sir Menzies Campbell (1941–), who in turn gave way to Nick *Clegg (1967–) in 2007. Following the 2010 general election the Liberal Democrats entered government for the first time, as junior partners in a coalition with the Conservative Party.

liberalism A political outlook attaching supreme importance to safeguarding the freedom of the individual within society. Liberal ideas first took shape in the struggle for religious toleration in the 16th and 17th centuries. The liberal view was that religion was a private matter; it was not the business of the state to enforce a particular creed. This later developed into a more general doctrine of the limited and constitutional state, whose boundaries were set by the natural rights of the individual (for instance in the political thought of *Locke). Around 1800 liberalism became associated with the doctrines of the free market and reducing the role of the state in the economic sphere. This tendency was reversed later in the 19th century with the arrival of 'New Liberalism', committed to social reform and welfare legislation. In contemporary debate both schools of thought are represented. Liberals unite in upholding the importance of personal liberty in the face of encroachment by the state, leading to demands for constitutional government, civil rights, and the protection of privacy.

Liberal Party (Australia) A major political party in Australia. The original party emerged in 1910 as an alliance of various groups opposed to the Australian *Labor Party, led by *Forrest. They were known for a while as the Fusion Party, adopting the title Liberal in 1913. The new Liberal Party was created in 1944 by Robert *Menzies, and a Liberal–Country coalition has alternated with Labor since then, being in office under Malcolm Fraser (1975–83), John *Howard (1996–2007), and Tony *Abbott (2013–).

Liberal Party (Britain) Formerly, a major political party in Britain. It emerged in the mid-19th century as the successor to the Whig Party and was the major alternative party to the *Conservatives until 1918, after which the *Labour Party supplanted it. Lord Palmerston's administration of 1854 is regarded as the first Liberal government. After World War II it was an opposition party of varying fortune, forming a Lib–Lab pact with the Labour government (1977–78), and then the Alliance (1983–87) with the Social Democratic Party, with which it merged in 1988 to form the Social and Liberal Democrats (later renamed the *Liberal Democrats).

Liberal Party (Canada) A major political party in Canada. Following the Confederation of Canada in 1867, a Liberal Party took shape as a major political force and remained so, forming a government (1873–78) under Alexander Mackenzie. The Liberal Party has had a strong appeal for French Canadians. With its power base in Quebec, the Party suffered from the *Québécois* secessionist demands, and failed to win federal office after 1984. It endorsed the all-party constitutional proposals of 1992 designed to prevent the break-up of the Canadian federation, although this in fact was rejected in a referendum in 1992. In 1993 the Liberal Party was re-elected and Jean *Chrétien, its leader since 1990, became Prime Minister. It held power until defeated in the 2006 general election.

Liberia

Capital:	Monrovia
Area:	111,369 sq km (43,000 sq miles)
Population:	3,989,703 (2013 est)
Currency:	1 Liberian dollar = 100 cents
Religions:	Christian 85.6%; Muslim 12.2%; traditional beliefs 0.2%
Ethnic Groups:	Kpelle 20.3%; Bassa 13.4%; Grebo 10.0%; Gio 8.0%; Mano 7.9%; Kru 6.0%; Lorma 5.1%
Languages:	English (official); indigenous languages
International Organizations:	UN; AU; ECOWAS; Non-Aligned Movement

A tropical country on the Atlantic coast of West Africa, flanked by Sierra Leone, Guinea, and Côte d'Ivoire.

Physical The climate is hot and very wet. Rainforest and swamp cover the coastal plain, which is traversed by several rivers flowing down from savannah-covered uplands.

Economy Liberia's economy was wrecked by the 1990–2005 civil war, but has since begun to recover under the stimulus of rubber, iron ore, timber, and diamond exports. Other important exports are cocoa and coffee. The large agricultural sector also produces rice, cassava, and palm oil, and most industry involves processing of agricultural products.

History Liberia is the oldest independent republic in Africa (1847). It owes its origin to the philanthropic American Colonization Society. US negotiations with local rulers for a settlement for the repatriation of freed slaves began in 1816. The first settlements were made in 1822, and the name Liberia was adopted in 1824. Independence was proclaimed by Joseph Jenkins Roberts, first President, in 1847. The real beginning of prosperity was in the 1920s, when the Firestone Rubber Company provided a permanent and stable market for rubber. W. V. S. *Tubman was President from 1944 until his death in 1971. With a decline in world rubber prices, the economy suffered in the 1970s and a bloody revolution in 1980 brought in the People's Redemption Council, a military government, under Master-Sergeant Samuel Doe. The latter was named President and Commander-in-Chief, and his ten-year autocratic rule was one of deep corruption, ending in 1990 with civil war. Two rebel groups, one led by Charles Taylor and a second by Prince Yormie Johnson, assailed the capital Monrovia. A peacekeeping force from ECOWAS intervened, Doe was murdered, and a ceasefire arranged in 1990. Peace agreements were made in 1991, 1993, and 1995 but did not end the fighting between rival factions. However, progress was made: a transitional legislature was set up in 1994, and Charles Taylor was elected President in 1997. Rebels forced him into exile in 2003, after which a multinational peacekeeping force was deployed and a transitional government established. Ellen Johnson Sirleaf was elected President in 2005, becoming Africa's first woman leader. Her government worked to rebuild Liberia's shattered economy and infrastructure, and a Truth and Reconciliation Commission was established in 2006. She was re-elected in 2011.

liberty An area or individual enjoying a special privilege of freedom from royal jurisdictions. Liberties of all kinds abounded in the Middle Ages: a ruler could grant privileges to people or places, and these would then be enforceable for ever, cutting across other laws and customs. In England the word "liberty" was usually taken to mean a territorial area held by some lay or ecclesiastical magnate; most of these liberties dated back to Anglo-Saxon times. The greatest liberties were the palatinate franchises of the bishops of Durham and the dukes of Lancaster.

Liberty, Statue of A statue on an island at the entrance to New York Harbour, a symbol of welcome to immigrants, representing a draped female figure carrying a book of laws in her left hand and holding aloft a torch in her right. Dedicated in 1886, it was the work of the French sculptor F. A. Bartholdi (who used his mother as a model) and was the gift of the French to the American people, commemorating the alliance of France and the USA during the War of American Independence and marking its centenary.

Libya

Capital:	Tripoli
Area:	1,759,540 sq km (679,362 sq miles)
Population:	5,853,000 (2013 est)
Currency:	1 Libyan dinar = 1000 dirhams
Religions:	Sunni Muslim 97.0%
Ethnic Groups:	Arab and Berber 97.0%
Languages:	Arabic (official); Italian; English; Berber
International Organizations:	UN; AU; OAPEC; OPEC; Maghreb Union; Arab League; Non-Aligned Movement

A country on the north coast of Africa, bounded by Tunisia and Algeria on the west, Niger and Chad on the south, and Sudan and Egypt on the east.

Physical The north-west region, Tripolitania, is cultivable near the coast, which has a Mediterranean climate; while inland the ground rises to a high desert of mainly limestone rocks. In Cyrenaica, the north-east region, some of the coast is high tableland, with light rain supporting forests. Southward the ground is low and sandy, though studded with oases. There are reserves of oil in huge quantities. The south of the country lies within the Sahara; but to the west, in the Fezzan region, there are a few large oases among the otherwise bare, stony plains and scrub-covered hills.

Economy The economy, exports, and industry are dominated by crude oil and oil products. Agriculture is limited by the arid nature of most of the country; principal crops include cereals, fruit, and vegetables.

History During most of its history Libya has been inhabited by Arab and *Berber nomads, only the coastlands and oases being settled. Greek colonies existed in ancient times, and later under the Romans; under the Arabs the cultivated area lapsed into desert. Administered by the Turks from the 16th century, Libya was annexed by Italy after a brief war in 1911–12. The Italians, however, like the Turks before them, never succeeded in asserting their full authority over the Sanussi tribesmen of the interior desert.

Heavily fought over during World War II, Libya was placed under a military government by the Allies before becoming an independent monarchy in 1951 under Emir Sayyid Idris al-Sanussi, who in 1954 granted the USA military and air bases. Idris was overthrown by radical Islamic army officers in 1969, and Libya emerged as a radical socialist state under the charismatic leadership of Colonel Muammar *Gaddafi. It used the wealth generated by exploitation of the country's rich oil resources to build up its military might and to interfere in the affairs of neighbouring states. Libyan involvement in Arab terrorist operations blighted its relations with western states and produced armed confrontations with US forces in the Mediterranean. In April 1986, there were US air strikes against Tripoli and Benghazi. President Gaddafi condemned the Iraqi occupation of Kuwait in 1990, taking a neutral stance. But Libya again clashed with the USA during 1992 over its refusal to extradite two Libyans accused of organizing the bombing of a PanAm aircraft over Lockerbie in Scotland in 1988. In April 1992 the UN Security Council imposed sanctions over this issue. In 1994 a peace settlement with Chad was agreed concerning the Aouzou Strip, in Northern Chad, which Libya had seized in 1973. Sanctions were lifted in 1999 when the Lockerbie suspects were handed over to the UN; and there was a further thaw in relations with the West in 2003 with the abandonment of Libya's nuclear weapons programme. The USA restored full diplomatic relations in 2006. Following the *Arab Spring uprisings in Tunisia and Egypt, popular protests against the Gaddafi regime began in February 2011 and quickly gained momentum. With UN-approved aerial protection from NATO, the protesters first resisted military attack from the regime's troops and then gained the upper hand. Tripoli fell in August 2011 and Gaddafi was killed in October as his final bastion of Sirte fell. A transitional government was formed and transferred power to an elected assembly in 2012. Although work continued to draft a new constitution, assert government authority, and overcome regional factionalism, the security situation deteriorated rapidly in 2014, with fighting between rival militia groups in several parts of the country. In September 2014 Islamist groups took over central Tripoli and established a rival government.

Lie, Trygve Halvdan (1896–1968) Norwegian Labour politician and first Secretary-General of the United Nations (1946–53).

Liebknecht, Wilhelm (1826–1900) German political leader. An early interest in *socialism led to his expulsion from Berlin in 1846 but, after the outbreak of the *Revolutions of 1848, he returned to Germany to help set up a republic in Baden. Forced to flee, he went to England, where he spent 13 years in close association with Karl *Marx. He returned to Germany in 1861 and in 1863 founded the League of German Workers' clubs with August Bebel. A pacifist, he refused to vote for war credits for the war with France in 1870, was convicted of treason, and spent two years in prison. In 1874 he returned to the Reichstag and in 1875, with the followers of the late Ferdinand Lassalle (1825–64), helped to form the German Social Democratic Labour Party, which became the German Social Democratic Party (SPD) in 1891.

Liechtenstein

Capital:	Vaduz
Area:	160 sq km (61.6 sq miles)
Population:	37,009 (2013 est)
Currency:	1 Swiss franc = 100 rappen (or centimes)
Religions:	Roman Catholic 75.9%; Protestant 7.6%; Muslim 5.4%
Ethnic Groups:	Liechtensteiner 65.6%
Languages:	German (official); Italian
International Organizations:	OSCE; EFTA; Council of Europe; WTO

In central Europe, one of the smallest countries in the world. It lies on the border between Austria and Switzerland, to the south of Lake Constance.

Physical The western section of Liechtenstein occupies part of the floodplain of the upper Rhine, while to the east it extends up the forested and then snow-covered slopes of the Rätikon Massif, part of the central Alps. Its mild climate is significantly affected by the warm Föhn wind from the south.

Economy The economy is based on financial services. Low tax rates and easy incorporation rules have attracted foreign holding companies, which provide 30% of state revenues. Light manufacturing, tourism, and agriculture also play a role. The main exports are machinery and metal and chemical products. There is a customs and monetary union with Switzerland.

History The principality of Liechtenstein was founded in 1719 when the two independent lordships of Schellenberg and Vaduz were united within the Holy Roman Empire. Liechtenstein remained part of the Empire until 1806, when it became part of the Rhine Federation. It joined the German Confederation in 1815 and became independent in 1866. A unicameral parliament was established by the 1921 constitution but the country has remained a monarchy, headed by the Prince. Any 900 persons or three communes may initiate legislation in the Diet (parliament). In 1989 Prince Hans-Adam II (1945–) succeeded his father, Prince Franz Joseph II (1906–89). Women were given the right to vote on national, but not local, issues in 1984. In 1992 a referendum approved Liechtenstein's entry into the European Economic Area. A constitutional row began to develop in 1996 following the stated intention of the government to remove certain powers from Prince Hans-Adam II, who announced that he would abandon the country unless he retained his full rights. In 2003 the Prince's powers were increased. In 2004 his heir, Prince Alois (1968–), became regent. The secrecy and opacity of Lichtenstein's banking and tax systems attracted criticism in the 2000s, especially after the *Credit Crunch. These issues were addressed by several bilateral information-sharing agreements with other countries in 2008–09.

Light Brigade, Charge of the *See* BALAK-LAVA.

Li Hongzhang (or **Li Hung-chang**) (1823–1901) Chinese statesman. He formed the regional Anhui army to help suppress the *Taiping Rebellion. In 1870 he became governor-general of Zhili (or Chihli) and High Commissioner for the Northern Ocean, becoming responsible for Chinese foreign affairs until 1895. Recognizing the superiority of foreign military technology, he

became the leader of the *Self-Strengthening Movement, establishing arsenals and factories and creating the Beiyang fleet (China's first modern navy). His reforms were piecemeal, however, and his prestige suffered when his forces were defeated in the *Sino-Japanese War.

Lilburne, John (*c.*1614–57) English political radical, the leader of the *Levellers. He was gaoled for smuggling Puritan pamphlets into England in 1638. Released by the Long Parliament, he fought as a *Roundhead in the English Civil War, rising to the position of lieutenant-colonel, but resigned in 1645 in opposition to the *Solemn League and Covenant. "Freeborn John" always spoke and wrote about the rights of the people, rather than those of kings or parliaments. He attacked in turn all constituted authorities, and suffered frequent imprisonment for his opinions. He became a member of the *Quakers shortly before he died.

Lin Biao (or **Lin Piao**) (1908–71) Chinese Communist statesman and general. After joining the Communists (1927) he became a commander of Mao Zedong's Red Army in the fight against the Kuomintang. He was appointed Minister of Defence (1959) and then Vice-Chairman under Mao (1966), later being nominated to become Mao's successor (1969). Having staged an unsuccessful coup in 1971, Lin Biao was reported to have been killed in an aeroplane crash while fleeing to the Soviet Union.

Lincoln, Abraham (1809–65) US Republican statesman, 16th President of the USA (1861–65). His election as President on an anti-slavery platform antipathetic to the interests of the southern states helped precipitate the American Civil War. He eventually managed to unite the Union side behind the anti-slavery cause and emancipation was formally proclaimed on New Year's Day, 1864. Lincoln won re-election in 1864, but was assassinated shortly after the surrender of the main Confederate army had ended the war. During his lifetime Lincoln was noted for his succinct, eloquent speeches, including the Gettysburg address of 1863.

Li Peng (1928–) Chinese communist politician, Prime Minister of the People's Republic of China (1987–98). Li Peng was born at Chengdu in Sechuan; his father, a writer, was executed in 1930 by the *Kuomintang for being a communist. Li Peng was looked after from 1939 by the wife of the veteran leader *Zhou Enlai. After working as a hydroelectric engineer, he became minister of water resources and electricity. In 1982 he joined the Central Committee of the

Communist Party, was appointed to the Polit-buro in 1985, as acting Prime Minister in 1987, and as Prime Minister in 1988. Early in his premiership, he adopted a hard line towards the pro-democracy student movement, and pre-sided over the Tiananmen Square massacre and subsequent mass arrests and executions. After retiring as Prime Minister in 1998, Li Peng was Chairman of the Standing Committee of the National People's Congress until 2003.

Lisbon Treaty A treaty signed by the 27 member states of the *European Union; it was agreed in December 2007, and came into effect on 1 December 2009. The treaty reformed the institutions of the EU, incorporating some of the provisions of the abortive European constitu-tion that had been rejected in 2004. The *Euro-pean Community, since 1993 a component of the EU, was abolished and its powers, struc-tures, and functions assumed directly by the EU. Two new EU officers were created: the President of the European Council and the High Repre-sentative for Foreign Affairs and Security Policy. The powers of the European Parliament were increased and the system of voting in the Council of Ministers revised. The treaty also gave legal force to the Charter of Fundamental Rights of the European Union, which guaran-tees various rights of EU citizens and residents.

Lithuania

Capital:	Vilnius
Area:	65,300 sq km (25,212 sq miles)
Population:	3,515,858 (2013 est)
Currency:	1 euro = 100 cents
Religions:	Roman Catholic 77.2%; Eastern Orthodox 4.1% ; Old Believer 0.8%
Ethnic Groups:	Lithuanian 84.1%; Polish 6.6%; Russian 5.8%
Languages:	Lithuanian (official); Russian; Polish; minority languages
International Organizations:	UN; OSCE; EU; NATO; Council of Europe; WTO

A Baltic country, lying be-tween Latvia to the north, Belarus to the east, and Poland to the south.

Physical Lithuania has just some 25 km (15 miles) of Baltic Sea coast, and is predominantly flat, though hilly in the east, where there are many lakes. The lowland plain is forested and fertile; it is drained by the Nemen and its tributaries.

Economy Lithuania is agriculturally self-sufficient, specializing in meat and milk pro-duction, but it depends on imports for supplies of energy and raw materials. There is some electricity production, but Lithuania relies on the unified grid of the Baltic region for much of its electricity supply. Mineral resources are var-ied, including various chemicals, iron ore, and oil. Lithuania's main industries are machinery, consumer appliances, oil refining, and ship-building. Tourism is of growing importance.

History Lithuania was a vast grand-duchy during the Middle Ages, stretching at one time from the Baltic to the Black Sea and almost to Moscow. By 1569 it had united with Poland and was absorbed into Russia in the Third Partition. After an uprising in 1863 the Lithu-anian language was forbidden, but nationalist and strong Social Democrat movements de-veloped from the 1880s. It was occupied by German troops (1915–18), and in March 1918 a German king was elected. He was deposed in November and a republic proclaimed. Bol-shevik troops now invaded from Russia and a short Russo-Lithuanian War ended in March 1920 with the Treaty of Moscow. This gave Lithuania German-speaking Memel, but it failed to gain Vilna (the present capital Vilnius), which went to Poland. At first a democratic republic, its politics polarized and a neo-Fascist dictator-ship under Antanas Smetona was established in 1926. In October 1939 a Soviet-Lithuanian Pact allowed Lithuania to claim Vilna, Memel having been lost to the Germans. In July 1940 the As-sembly voted for incorporation into the Soviet Union; but the country was occupied by the Germans (1941–44), when its large Jewish popu-lation was almost wiped out. Re-occupied by the Red Army in 1944, it became again a con-stituent Republic of the Soviet Union. In 1956 there were serious anti-Soviet riots, ruthlessly suppressed. In March 1990 a unilateral declar-ation of independence was made. The Soviet Union at first responded by an economic blockade, but in May it agreed to negotiate, and in September 1991 recognized Lithuania's in-dependence. In December citizenship was re-stricted to those with ten years' residence, a knowledge of the language and constitution, and a source of income. In 1992 a new consti-tution gave increased executive powers to the President; Algirdas Brazauskas, the former leader of the Lithuanian Communist Party, was elected. Valdas Adamkus, an independent, was elected President in 1998, but was defeated by Rolandas Paksas in 2003. However, Paksas was impeached for various criminal acts and removed from office; Adamkus was subsequently re-elected as President. Lithuania joined NATO and the *European Union in 2004. Economic problems led to violent protests in 2008. In 2009 Dalia Grybauskaitė was elected Lithuania's first woman President. The country adopted the euro at the end of 2014.

Little Big Horn, Battle of (25 June 1876) Scene of General *Custer's last stand in Montana when he and 266 men of the 7th Cavalry met their deaths at the hands of larger forces of Sioux. The battle was the final move in a well-planned strategy by the Sioux leader *Crazy Horse, following the invasion of the Sioux Black Hills by White *gold rush prospectors in violation of a treaty of 1868.

Little Entente (1920–38) Alliance of Czechoslovakia, Romania, and the new Kingdom of Serbs, Croats, and Slovenes (later termed Yugoslavia). It was created by the Czech Foreign Minister Edvard *Beneš, who in August 1920 concluded treaties (extended in 1922 and 1923) with both Romania and Yugoslavia. The principal aim of the Entente was to protect the territorial integrity and independence of its members by means of a common foreign policy, which would prevent both the extension of German influence and the restoration of the Habsburgs to the throne of Hungary. France supported the Entente, concluding treaties with each of its members. In 1929 the Entente pledged itself against both Bolshevik and Hungarian (Magyar) aggression in the Danube basin, while also seeking the promotion of Danube trade. In the 1930s, however, the members gradually grew apart. Romania under *Carol II (1930–40) leaned towards Hitler's *Third Reich, Czechoslovakia signed a non-aggression treaty with the Soviet Union (1935), while in February 1934 Romania and Yugoslavia joined Greece and Turkey to form the so-called Balkan Entente. In 1937 Yugoslavia and Romania were unwilling to give Czechoslovakia a pledge of military assistance against possible aggression from Germany and, when the *Sudetenland of Czechoslovakia was annexed (September 1938), the Entente collapsed.

Litvinov, Maxim Maximovich (1876–1951) Soviet revolutionary politician. He joined the *Bolsheviks (1903), and from 1917 to 1918 was Soviet envoy in London, having married an Engishwoman, Ivy Low in 1916. He headed delegations to the disarmament conference of the League of Nations (1927–29), signed the *Kellogg–Briand Pact (1928), and negotiated diplomatic relations with the USA (1933). An advocate of collective security against Germany, Italy, and Japan, he was Soviet foreign minister from 1930 until he was dismissed (1939), before *Stalin signed the Nazi-Soviet Pact.

Liu Shaoqi (or Liu Shao-ch'i) (1898–c.1974) Chinese statesman. He served as a communist trade union organizer in Guangzhou (Canton) and Shanghai before becoming a member of the Central Committee of the *Chinese Communist Party in 1927, and its chief theoretician. On the establishment of the People's Republic in 1949 he was appointed chief vice-chairman of the party. In 1959 he became chairman of the Republic, second only to *Mao Zedong in official standing, but during the *Cultural Revolution he was fiercely criticized by *Red Guards as a 'renegade, traitor, and scab', and in 1968 he was stripped of office; his death was announced in 1974. In 1980 he was posthumously rehabilitated.

Liverpool, Robert Banks Jenkinson, 2nd Earl of (1770–1828) British statesman. He was first elected to Parliament in 1790. He was appointed Foreign Secretary in 1801 and helped to negotiate the Peace of Amiens with France in the following year. He was Home Secretary during 1804–06 and declined the premiership on the death of William Pitt. He became Secretary for War and the Colonies in 1809, reluctantly taking office as Prime Minister (1812–27) after the assassination of Spencer *Perceval. After the *Napoleonic Wars his government used repressive measures to deal with popular discontent (*Peterloo massacre), opposing both parliamentary reform and *Catholic emancipation. Towards the end of his tenure the more liberal influences of men like Sir Robert *Peel and William Huskisson (1770–1830) led him to support the introduction of some important reforms.

livery company One of the London city companies that replaced the medieval craft *guilds, so called on account of the distinctive dress worn by their members. The liverymen constituted the freemen of the City of London, indirectly responsible for electing the mayor as well as the aldermen, while several of their companies, such as the Goldsmiths and Merchant Taylors, played an important role in the regulation of their trade and had monopoly powers within London. Since the 17th century there have been nearly 100 London livery companies but few have retained any importance other than as social and charitable institutions.

Livingstone, David (1813–73) Scottish missionary and explorer. He first went to Bechuanaland as a missionary in 1841; on his extensive travels in the interior he discovered Lake Ngami (1849), the Zambezi River (1851), and the Victoria Falls (1855). In 1866 he led an expedition into central Africa in search of the source of the Nile; after many hardships he was eventually found in poor health by the explorer Sir Henry Morton Stanley on the eastern shore of Lake Tanganyika in 1871.

Livy (Latin name **Titus Livius**) (59 BC–17AD) Roman historian. His history of Rome from its foundation to his own time contained 142 books, of which 35 survive (including the earliest history of the war with Hannibal). Livy is notable for his power of vivid historical reconstruction as he sought to give Rome a history that in conception and style might be worthy of her imperial rise and greatness.

Lloyd George, David, 1st Earl Lloyd George of Dwyfor (1863–1945) British Liberal statesman, Prime Minister (1916–22). As Chancellor of the Exchequer (1908–15) he introduced old-age pensions (1908) and national insurance (1911). His 'People's Budget' (1909), intended to finance reform by raised death duties and other taxes, was rejected by the Lords and led to a constitutional crisis which was eventually resolved by the Parliament Act of 1911. Supported by the Conservatives, he took over from Asquith as Prime Minister at the end of 1916 and led the coalition government for the remainder of World War I. In the postwar period his administration was threatened by increasing economic problems and trouble in Ireland; he resigned in 1922 after the Conservatives withdrew their support.

Llywelyn ap Gruffydd (or **Llewelyn II**) (died 1282) Prince of Gwynedd in North Wales. In 1258 he proclaimed himself prince of all Wales and four years later formed an alliance with Simon de Montfort, leader of the baronial opposition to Henry III. He later signed a treaty with Henry, which made him chief of the other Welsh princes but recognized Henry as his overlord (1265). His refusal to pay homage to Edward I led the latter to invade and subjugate Wales (1277–84); Llywelyn died in battle after raising a rebellion against Edward's rule.

Llywelyn ap Iorwerth (or **Llewelyn II**; known as **'Llywelyn the Great'**) (died 1240) Prince of Gwynedd (north Wales), the most powerful ruler in medieval Wales, his authority over other Welsh leaders being confirmed by the Treaty of Worcester (1218). Although married (1205) to Joan, the illegitimate daughter of King *John, Llywelyn took advantage of the political confusion in England to extend his influence over South Wales. He also had close ties with the marcher lords.

Lobengula (c.1836–94) Ndebele leader. The son of *Mzilikazi, he was the second and last *Ndebele king (1870–93). After his father's death there was civil war until 1870, when Lobengula acceded to the throne. He compromised Ndebele independence by land concessions to the British (1886) and in 1888 signed the concessions which gave mining rights to *Rhodes's British South Africa Company. Later, Lobengula tried to resist the expanding European settlement and influence in his country. In 1893 he went to war against the British, but was defeated. He died as he was escaping from Bulawayo, his capital.

Locarno, Treaties of (1 December 1925) A series of international agreements drawn up in Locarno, a health resort in Switzerland at the north end of Lake Maggiore. Their object was to ease tension by guaranteeing the common boundaries of Germany, Belgium, and France as specified in the *Versailles Peace Settlement in 1919. Gustav Stresemann, as German Foreign Minister, refused to accept Germany's eastern frontier with Poland and Czechoslovakia as unalterable, but agreed that alteration must come peacefully. In the 'spirit of Locarno' Germany was invited to join the *League of Nations. In 1936, denouncing the principal Locarno treaty, *Hitler sent his troops into the demilitarized Rhineland; in 1938 he annexed the *Sudetenland in Czechoslovakia, and in 1939 invaded Poland.

Locke, John (1632–1704) English philosopher, a founder of empiricism and political liberalism. Both his major works were published in 1690. In *Two Treatises of Government* he justified the Revolution of 1688 by arguing that, contrary to the theory of the divine right of kings, the authority of rulers has a human origin and is limited. In *An Essay Concerning Human Understanding* he denied that any ideas are innate, and argued instead for a central empiricist tenet that all knowledge is derived from sense-experience. He concluded that it is not possible to know everything of the world and that our limited knowledge must be reinforced by faith.

Lodi A family of Afghan origin whose rule over northern India (1451–1526) marked the last phase of the Delhi sultanate era. Their founder, Bahlul (1451–89), who already had a strong base in the Punjab, took advantage of *Sayyid weakness to seize power in Delhi. He and his two successors extended power eastwards through Jaunpur to the borders of Bengal and threatened Malwa to the south.

Sikander (1489–1517) consolidated his father's gains but was also renowned as a patron of poets, musicians, and other scholars. However, attempts by his successor, Ibrahim (1517–26), to secure greater centralization alienated many local governors. In retaliation, Daulat Khan, governor of the Punjab, invited the ruler of Kabul, the Mogul prince, *Babur, to invade India. His defeat of the Lodis in the ensuing battle at *Panipat (1526), resulted in the destruction of the dynasty and the establishment of the *Mogul empire.

Lollard Originally a follower of John *Wyclif, a Lollard was later anyone seriously critical of the Church. Lollards probably owed their name to the Dutch word *lollaerd*, meaning a mumbler (of prayers). Lollardy began in the 1370s as a set of beliefs held by Oxford-trained clerks who were keenly interested in Wyclif's teachings on papal and ecclesiastical authority; in an age unsettled by war and threatened by disease (especially the *Black Death), it also appealed to other educated sectors of society. They attacked clerical celibacy, *indulgences, and pilgrimages. *Richard II, who was himself an opponent of calls for ecclesiastical egalitarianism, none the less retained in his household some knights known to favour Lollardy. The nobility abandoned it only when *Henry IV came to the throne and backed Archbishop Arundel in a vigorous persecution of Lollards; further reaction against it, among the gentry, also resulted from the abortive Lollard uprising attempted by Sir John Oldcastle in January 1414. Thereafter, Lollardy's appeal seems to have been limited to craftsmen, artisans, and a few priests in the larger towns.

London Corresponding Society An organization founded in London in 1792 by Thomas *Hardy to agitate for universal manhood suffrage. It was the first real working-class political movement to appear in Britain—its members were mainly artisans of humble origin—and it rapidly established contact with similar societies in other towns, for example

the Sheffield Society of Constitutional Information. The aim of the societies was to circulate letters and pamphlets and to initiate orderly debates on reform proposals. *Paine's writings were a stimulus to the popular societies. When there was talk of a national convention the government, then at war with Revolutionary France, became alarmed. The London Corresponding Society was believed to have been involved in the *Nore mutiny: in 1798 all the Society's committee members were imprisoned without trial and in 1799 the Society itself was suppressed.

London Dockers' strike (1889) A successful strike, one of the major episodes in the history of British trade unionism. The London dockers, objecting to low pay and casual employment, went on strike to secure pay of sixpence an hour instead of fivepence, and a minimum working engagement of four hours. The episode signalled the beginning of "New Unionism", characterized by the increasingly effective use of strikes.

Long March (1934–35) The epic withdrawal of the Chinese communists from south-eastern to north-western China. By 1934 the Jiangxi Soviet was close to collapse after repeated attacks by the *Kuomintang army. In October a force of 100,000 evacuated the area. *Mao Zedong took over the leadership of the march in January 1935. For nine months it travelled through mountainous terrain cut by several major rivers. In October Mao and 6000 survivors reached Yan'an, having marched 9600 km (6000 miles). Other groups arrived later, in all about 20,000 surviving the journey. The march established Mao as the effective leader of the Chinese Communist Party, a position he consolidated in his ten years in Yan'an.

Long Parliament (1640–60) The English Parliament called by Charles I after the *Bishops' Wars had bankrupted him. Led by the Parliamentarian John *Pym, by August 1641 it had made a series of enactments depriving him of the powers that had aroused so much opposition since his accession. These reforms were intended to rule out absolutism for the future, and were eventually incorporated in the Restoration settlement, and again during the *Glorious Revolution. The Parliament was also responsible for the execution of the king's advisers William *Laud and Thomas Wentworth, Earl of *Strafford. Without its Cavalier members, the Long Parliament sat on throughout the *English Civil War, since it could be dissolved only with its own consent. Serious divisions emerged between the Presbyterian and Independent members, culminating in *Pride's Purge (1648). The remnant, the Rump Parliament, arranged the trial and execution of Charles I, and the establishment of the *Commonwealth (1649). *Cromwell ejected the Rump by force in 1653, but it was recalled after his son's failure as Lord Protector in 1659. In the next year General *Monck secured the reinstatement of those members 'secluded' by Pride. Arrangements for the Convention Parliament were made, and the Long Parliament dissolved itself in March 1660.

Long Parliament of the Restoration *See* CAVALIER PARLIAMENT.

Longshan *See* NEOLITHIC.

longship A *Viking ship, especially a warship. They were built usually of fir planks, and differed from the vessels of the Angles, Saxons, and Frisians in having a massive vertical keel of oak instead of a shallow horizontal one; this enabled them to carry a mast and sail. The clinker-built construction of overlapping planks secured by clench nails conferred great strength with flexibility, and the hulls were waterproofed with tar, seams between the planks being caulked with wool and hair. Later examples were over 46 m (150 feet) long and could carry hundreds of warriors who were also rowers. Longships were of extremely seaworthy design, and the addition of sails made very long voyages feasible, while the shallow draught meant that raiders could penetrate far inland by river. The violent expansion of the Norse peoples was dependent on the skilful use of such vessels.

López, Carlos Antonio (1792–1862) Paraguayan statesman, President of Paraguay (1844–62). His domestic policy, although authoritarian, promoted highway and railroad construction, reorganized the country's judicial system and its military, and attempted to strengthen the economy by creating government monopolies. He abandoned the isolationist foreign policy of his predecessor, but in the process involved his country in a series of disputes with the USA, the UK, Argentina, and Brazil.

López, Francisco Solano (1827–70) Paraguayan statesman. Son of Carlos Antonio *López, he became President (1862–70) on his father's death. He initiated grandiose building schemes and then led his country into a disastrous war with Brazil, Argentina, and Uruguay. This war (1865–70) was one of the fiercest and bloodiest ever fought in the New World. It

halved the population of Paraguay and left the country in a state of economic collapse; López himself was defeated and killed. Considered a cruel and dictatorial *caudillo in his lifetime, he afterwards came to be regarded as the champion of the rights of small countries against more powerful neighbours.

Lord Appellant One of five nobles who "appealed" (accused) certain of the leading friends of *Richard II of England of treason in November 1387. Thomas of Woodstock, Duke of Gloucester, Richard Fitzalan, Earl of Arundel, Thomas de Beauchamp, Earl of Warwick, Henry of Bolingbroke (*Henry IV), Earl of Derby, and Thomas Mowbray, 3rd Earl of Nottingham were opposed to the king's policy of peace with France. His position had been weakening for some months, and he was forced to summon a parliament to be held in February 1388; at this, the "Merciless Parliament", the Archbishop of York and others of his friends and their associates were accused of treason or were impeached. Four men, including a former Chief Justice, were executed. Richard II bided his time, gradually restoring his authority until in 1397 he was able to arrest the surviving Lords Appellant and have them accused of treason.

Lord Lieutenant An English magnate, originally commissioned to muster, administer, and command the militia of a specified district in times of emergency. *Henry VIII was the first to appoint them, and in 1551 during Edward VI's reign there were attempts to establish them on a permanent basis. From 1585 it became usual for every shire to have a lieutenant, and deputy lieutenants, and by the end of the 16th century they assumed additional roles, exercised on behalf of the sovereign, including the appointment of magistrates. They lost their military responsibilities in the army reforms of 1870–71, but still represent the crown in the counties.

Lord Ordainer A member of a committee chosen in March 1310 by the English lords who were opposed to *Edward II. They had forced Edward II to agree to the appointment of this committee of 21 lords, with full power to reform both his household and realm; he had infuriated many peers by his infatuation with *Gaveston, and they wished to make the crown's officials answerable to Parliament. The resultant ordinances were drawn up by August 1311, and the Ordainers enforced them until Edward II won the battle of Boroughbridge (1321) and at the Parliament of York in 1322 annulled all the ordinances and reasserted his authority.

Lords, House of See HOUSE OF LORDS.

Lorenzo the Magnificent See MEDICI, LORENZO DE.

Lorraine, House of See GUISE.

Louis I (or **Louis the Pious**) (778–840) King of the Franks, German emperor (813–40), a son of *Charlemagne. He administered the empire well but failed to organize his succession, thus jeopardizing the unity of the Frankish kingdom. He had four sons, the youngest by his second wife, and tried originally to settle the empire and its title on the oldest. This plan faltered as father and sons fought for control, causing Louis I to lose the throne briefly in 833.

Louis I (or **Louis the Great**) (1326–82) King of Hungary (1342–82) and of Poland (1370–82). He fought two successful wars against Venice (1357–58; 1378–81), and the rulers of Serbia, Wallachia, Moldavia, and Bulgaria became his vassals. Under his rule Hungary became a powerful state, though Poland was troubled by revolts.

Louis IX, St (1214–70) King of France (1226–70). He succeeded his father, Louis VIII, and worked effectively to stabilize the country and to come to terms with the English who maintained territorial claims in France. Henry III of England was forced to acknowledge French suzerainty in the disputed region of Guienne. He had a profoundly religious nature and built the Sainte-Chapelle in Paris, to house holy relics brought from Constantinople. Prompted by his recovery from a severe illness he raised the Seventh Crusade, which was directed against Egypt, and sailed in 1248. After initial successes he was captured by Sultan Turanshah and only released upon payment of a ransom in 1250. His involvement in the Crusades was recounted by *Joinville. He later mounted another Crusade to Tunis where he died. He was canonized by Pope Boniface VIII in 1297, his sanctity conferring immense prestige on the Capetian dynasty.

Louis XI (1423–83) King of France (1461–83). He was exiled for plotting against his father, Charles VII, but succeeded to the throne in 1461. As king he imposed new taxes, dismissed his father's ministers, and attempted to curb the powers of the nobility. They retaliated by forming a coalition against him which waged the "War of Common Weal". *Charles the Bold of Burgundy led a group including the Duke of Brittany, the Duke of Bourbon, and Louis XI's brother, Charles of France, supported by some lesser magnates, clergy, and a few towns. The

Battle of Montlhéry (July 1465) ended in stalemate, and Louis was able to gain the upper hand after Charles the Bold was defeated by the Swiss in 1477. He pursued a successful policy of territorial acquisition and centralization: by the time of his death only the duchy of Brittany remained largely independent.

Louis XI established firm government but nonetheless bequeathed a troubled legacy at his death. The minority of his son, Charles VIII, saw further outbreaks of discontent amongst the nobility and attempts by the dukes of Brittany to undermine the monarchy.

Louis XIV (1638–1715) King of France (1643–1715). On his father's death in 1643, his mother *Anne of Austria became regent and *Mazarin chief minister. Louis survived the *Fronde, was proclaimed of age in 1651, and married the Infanta Maria Theresa of Spain in 1660. He took over the government on Mazarin's death in 1661 and embarked on a long period of personal rule.

Domestic policy was aimed at creating and maintaining a system of absolute rule: the king ruled unhampered by challenges from representative institutions but with the aid of ministers and councils subject to his will. The States-General was not summoned, the *Parlement* largely ignored, the great nobles were generally excluded from political office, and loyal bourgeois office-holders were promoted. Jean-Baptiste *Colbert expanded the merchant marine and the navy, and encouraged manufacturing industries and trade, though he largely failed in his attempts to improve the tax system. In the provinces the *intendants established much firmer royal control. The French army became larger and more efficient; in his later years Louis was able to put between 300,000 and 400,000 men into the field. The greatest victories came in the earlier years, when the generals *Turenne and *Condé were available to take command. Victories were won in the War of *Devolution and the Dutch War, with the French frontiers strengthened by a series of strategic territorial gains, reinforced by the fortifications of Vauban. The *Nine Years War and the War of the Spanish Succession saw France hard-pressed as Europe united to curb Louis's aggressive policies; after 1700 France suffered a series of crushing defeats. The country was seriously impoverished by the burden of taxation.

Religious orthodoxy was strictly imposed, particularly after the Revocation of the Edict of *Nantes (1685) and the forced conversion of the *Huguenots, at least 200,000 of whom illegally fled the country. Within the Catholic church Jansenists, Quietists, and other deviants were also persecuted. On the positive side, the achievements of the reign in literature and the arts based on the court at Versailles have given it the name *Le Grand Siècle*. There was, however, a marked decline in these fields during the later part of the reign, and at his death Louis XIV left a series of political, economic, and religious problems of his great-grandson, *Louis XV.

Louis XV (1710–74) King of France (1715–74), a great grandson of *Louis XIV. During his minority Philippe, duc d'Orléans was regent, followed by Cardinal Fleury. After Fleury's death in 1743 Louis decided to rule without a chief minister, but he proved to be a weak king who reduced the prestige of the French monarchy both at home and abroad.

At the age of 15 Louis married Marie Leszczynska, daughter of the King of *Poland, and France intervened in the War of Polish Succession, gaining the duchy of Lorraine in 1766. In foreign affairs France was involved in almost continuous warfare; in the War of the Austrian Succession, in alliance with *Frederick II of Prussia until hostilities were concluded at *Aix-la-Chapelle. The *Seven Years War saw France and Austria fighting Prussia and Great Britain but with little success. The Treaty of *Paris (1763) marked the loss of most of France's overseas territories.

In domestic policy Louis XV was influenced by a succession of favourites and mistresses, including Madame *de Pompadour and Madame *du Barry, on whom he lavished enormous amounts of money. The extravagance of the court and the high cost of war absorbed all of France's resources and efforts to rationalize the tax system failed. The *Parlement* of Paris secured the suppression of the Jesuits in 1764 but otherwise failed to achieve reforms. The members of the *Parlement* were banished and a compliant *Parlement* appointed in their place in 1771. The reign saw the aristocracy and the wealthy bourgeoisie prosper, though the country was close to bankruptcy. The king's failure to solve his financial affairs left an insolvent government for his successor, *Louis XVI.

Louis XVI (1754–93) The last king of France (1774–92) before the *French Revolution. Weak and vacillating, unwisely advised by his Austrian wife, *Marie Antoinette, he could neither avert the Revolution by supporting the economic and social reforms proposed by *Necker and Turgot, nor, lacking all understanding of popular demands, become its popular leader. To meet the situation he summoned the largely aristocratic Assembly of Notables (1787), which achieved

nothing, and then (1789) the *States-General, which had not been called for 175 years. This marked the start of the Revolution. The royal family was forcibly brought back from Versailles to Paris (October 1789) and their attempt to flee the country ended when they reached *Varennes (1791). Thereafter they were virtually prisoners in the Tuileries Palace. The monarchy was abolished (September 1792) and Louis was guillotined in January 1793. His wife was executed six months later.

Louis XVIII (1755–1824) King of France (1795–1824). The brother of Louis XVI, he became titular regent after the death of the latter in 1793, and declared himself king on the death in prison of the ten-year-old Louis XVII. Known as the comte de Provence, he had fled to Koblenz, and then to England, where he led the counter-revolutionary movement. His exile ended in 1814 and with the help of *Talleyrand he returned to the throne of France and issued a constitutional charter. He appointed Marshal Soult (1769–1851) as his Minister of War, the latter going on to a long political career. Many of *Napoleon's reforms in the law, administration, church, and education were retained, but after the assassination (1820) of his nephew the duc de Berry, he replaced moderate ministers by reactionary ones. Civil liberties were curbed, a trend which continued under his younger brother and successor, *Charles X.

Louisiana Purchase (1803) US acquisition from France of over two million sq km (828,000 sq miles) of territory stretching north from the mouth of the Mississippi to its source and west to the Rockies. France had ceded Louisiana to Spain in 1762 but regained it by treaty in 1801. Concerned at the possible closure of the Mississippi to commerce and the related threat to US security, President *Jefferson sent James *Monroe to France in 1803 to help negotiate free navigation and the purchase of New Orleans and west Florida. At war again with Britain, Napoleon was anxious not to have extensive overseas territories to defend and sold the whole of Louisiana to the US for $15 million. Although the Constitution gave no authority to purchase new territory or promise it statehood, the Senate confirmed the agreement, increasing US territory by some 140% and transforming the USA into a continental nation.

Louis Philippe I (1773–1850) King of France (1830–48). The son of the duc d'Orléans he, along with his father, renounced his titles and assumed the surname Égalité. On the restoration of *Louis XVIII to the French throne he recovered his estates, and was elected King of the French, the 'citizen king', after the *July Revolution in 1830. During his reign political corruption, judicial malpractices, and limited parliamentary franchise united liberals and extremists in a cry for reform. After 1840, a series of disastrous foreign ventures and alliances with reactionary European monarchies alienated the liberal opinion on which his authority had been based. His rule ended in February 1848 when, after popular riots, he agreed to abdicate, and escaped to England as 'Mr Smith'.

Lovett, William (1800–77) British radical political reformer. He became involved in working-class radical groups, and in 1836, with Francis Place (1771–1854), set up the London Workingmen's Association. Lovett outlined a programme of political reform, which in 1838 was presented as the People's Charter. He was secretary of the first *Chartist Convention in 1839, but was imprisoned following violent incidents in Birmingham. He subsequently gave up all political activity.

Lowell, Francis Cabot (1775–1817) Founder of the US cotton industry. A Boston merchant, in 1814 he established the first US factory to use both spinning and weaving machinery (and the first in the world to manufacture cotton cloth using power machinery enclosed in a single building) at Waltham, Massachusetts. Lowell was singular among early US industrialists for the paternalistic concern he demonstrated for his workforce and for their living and working conditions.

Loyola, Ignatius, St (1491–1556) Spanish ecclesiastical reformer, founder and first general of the Society of Jesus (the Jesuits). Born into a noble family, he attached himself to the court of Ferdinand II of Aragon. His military career was ended by a leg wound received while fighting for Navarre against France (1521). During his convalescence he underwent a spiritual transformation. He spent almost a year in prayer and penance (1522–23) and wrote the first draft of his *Spiritual Exercises*, an ordered scheme of meditations on the life of Jesus Christ and the truths of the Christian faith. After a pilgrimage to Jerusalem in 1523 he attended the University of Paris (1528–35). There he collected a band of like-minded followers, who worked through the *Exercises*. In 1534 he and six others took vows of poverty, chastity, and obedience to the pope, and Pope Paul III recognized their "Society of Jesus" as an order of the Church in 1540. By the time of his death there were over 1000 Jesuits in

nine European provinces as well as those working in foreign missions.

Luba A Bantu kingdom founded c.1500, lying north of Lake Kisale in the Republic of Congo. The founders, the Balopwe clan, came from further north, and imposed their sovereignty over existing chiefdoms. Some of the Luba moved eastwards c.1600, and founded a kingdom among the Lunda; from there a large number of small chiefdoms proliferated stretching from eastern Angola to north-eastern Zambia, and making previously existing chiefdoms their vassals. The largest was the kingdom of Mwata Yamvo; others were the Bemba in north-eastern Zambia, Kazembe in the Luapula valley, and Kasanje in central Angola. They all paid tribute to the central kingdoms, but the organization was decentralized, and the kings served as settlers of disputes between communities. These were occupied not only by agriculture, but also in mining and trade in copper and salt against European goods obtained from the Portuguese. Kazembe was the richest and most important.

Lucknow, Siege of (1857–58) A siege of the British garrison during the *Indian Mutiny. The abolition by the British of the Kingdom of Oudh, whose capital Lucknow had been, became one of the causes of the Mutiny. On the outbreak of hostilities the British and Indian garrison, together with women and children, were confined to the Residency, and during the ensuing five-month siege they suffered heavy casualties. Lucknow was relieved first on 26 September by troops under Sir Henry Havelock. He was then besieged, and only relieved on 16 November by troops under Sir Colin Campbell. The city was not finally restored to British possession until 21 March 1858.

Luddite A member of a 19th-century protest group of British workers, who destroyed machinery, which they believed was depriving them of their livelihood. The movement began in Nottinghamshire in 1811, when framework knitters began wrecking the special type of 'wide frames' used to make poor-quality stockings, which were undercutting the wages of skilled craftsmen. The men involved claimed to be acting under the leadership of a certain 'Ned Ludd' or 'King Ludd', although it is doubtful whether such a person ever existed. The outbreaks of violence spread rapidly and by the early part of 1812 were affecting Yorkshire and Lancashire. Large groups of men stormed the cotton and woollen mills in order to attack the power looms. The government responded harshly by making machine-breaking an offence punishable by death. There were further sporadic outbreaks in 1816, but the movement subsequently died out.

Ludendorff, Erich (1865–1937) German general. Shortly after the outbreak of World War I he was appointed Chief of Staff to General von Hindenburg and they jointly directed the war effort until the final offensive failed (September 1918). Ludendorff later joined the Nazi Party and served as a member of the Reichstag (1924–28).

Lumumba, Patrice (Emergy) (1925–61) Congolese nationalist and politician. He founded the influential MNC (Mouvement National Congolais) in 1958 to bring together radical nationalists. He was accused of instigating public violence and was gaoled by the Belgians, but was released to participate in the Brussels Conference (January 1960) on the Congo. He became Prime Minister and Minister of Defence when the Congo became independent in June 1960. Sections of the army mutinied, the Belgian troops returned, and Katanga province declared its independence. Lumumba appealed to the United Nations, which sent a peacekeeping force. President Kasavubu, his rival in power, dismissed him and shortly afterwards he was put under arrest by Colonel Mobutu. He escaped, but was recaptured and killed.

Lusitania A British transatlantic liner (named after the ancient Roman province in the Iberian peninsula), torpedoed (7 May 1915) off the Irish coast without warning by a German submarine, with the loss of 1195 lives. The sinking, which took 128 US lives, created intense indignation throughout the USA, which until then had accepted Woodrow *Wilson's policy of neutrality. Germany refused to accept responsibility for the act, asserting (correctly) that the ship was carrying illegal munitions. Two years later (1917), following Germany's resumption of unrestricted submarine warfare, the USA severed diplomatic relations and entered the war on the side of the Allies.

Luther, Martin (1483–1546) German Protestant theologian, the principal figure of the German Reformation. From 1508 he taught at the University of Wittenberg, latterly as professor of scripture (1512–46). He began to preach the doctrine of justification by faith rather than by works; his attack on the sale of indulgences with his 95 theses (1517) was followed by further attacks on papal authority, and in 1521 Luther was condemned and

excommunicated at the Diet of Worms. At a meeting with Swiss theologians at Marburg (1529) he opposed Zwingli and gave a defence of the doctrine of consubstantiation (the presence in the Eucharist of the real substances of the body and blood of Christ); the next year he gave his approval to Melanchthon's Augsburg Confession, which laid down the Lutheran position. His translation of the Bible into High German (1522–34) contributed significantly to the spread of this form of the language and to the development of German literature in the vernacular.

Luthuli, Albert John (or Albert John Lutuli) (c.1898–1967) South African political leader. He inherited a Zulu chieftaincy in 1935 and was President of the African National Congress from 1952 to 1960. Luthuli's presidency was marked by the Defiance Campaign, his programme of civil disobedience. He was awarded the Nobel Peace Prize in 1960 for his commitment to non-violence as a means of opposing apartheid.

Lützen, Battle of (16 November 1632) A battle during the *Thirty Years War between the Protestant forces under *Gustavus II Adolphus and Bernard, Duke of Saxe-Weimar and imperial Catholic troops commanded by *Wallenstein. The Protestant attack was delayed by foggy conditions and the numerically superior imperial forces came close to victory. Gustavus was killed but Bernard eventually secured a victory for the Protestants.

Luxembourg, Grand Duchy of

Capital:	Luxembourg
Area:	2586 sq km (999 sq miles)
Population:	514,862 (2013 est)
Currency:	1 euro = 100 cents
Religions:	Roman Catholic 87.0%
Ethnic Groups:	Luxembourger 63.1%; Portuguese 13.3%; French 4.5%; Italian 4.3%
Languages:	Luxembourgish, French, German (all official)
International Organizations:	UN; EU; OECD; NATO; Council of Europe; OSCE; WTO

A small country in north-west Europe surrounded by Belgium to the west and north, Germany to the east, and France to the south.

Physical The climate is temperate continental and there are sizeable forests, but the ground is hilly and rocky with little fertile soil.

Economy Attractive conditions including banking secrecy have made international financial services the dominant industry; these now contribute over a quarter of GDP. Historically steel was the major industry (iron ore being abundant), but such areas as information technology, telecommunications, freight transport, food processing, and chemicals are now also significant. There is a small agricultural sector.

History Luxembourg was occupied by the Romans, then by the *Franks in the 5th century, passing to the counts of Luxembourg in the 11th century. The duchy of Luxembourg was created in 1354. Seized by *Burgundy in 1443, it passed to the *Habsburgs in 1477 and to *Spain in 1555. The French occupied it from 1684 until 1697. The first Count of Luxembourg was Conrad, who took the title in 1060. Luxembourg passed again to the Habsburgs after the War of the Spanish Succession (1701–14). In 1815 it was handed over to the Netherlands but joined the Belgians in the revolt of 1830; in 1831 Luxembourg was divided, the Walloon-speaking region becoming part of Belgium. The rest of Luxembourg remained within the Netherlands and became the Grand Duchy of Luxembourg in 1839 with its own government. In 1890 the King of the Netherlands died without a male heir and from then on the two countries were headed by different royal families. Grand Duke Jean (1921–) succeeded in 1964 when his mother, Grand Duchess Charlotte (1896–1985), abdicated in his favour. Luxembourg entered into an economic union with Belgium in 1921. The Netherlands joined this union in 1948, to form the Benelux Economic Union, which was the first free-trade area in Europe. Luxembourg was a founder member of the *European Economic Community (now the *European Union).

Grand Duke Jean abdicated in 2000 in favour of his son, Henri (1955–). Luxembourg adopted the *euro as its currency in 2002. Since World War II the centre-right Christian Social People's Party has been almost continuously in power as the leading partner in various coalitions; the exceptions are 1974–79 and from 2013, when a Democratic Party-led coalition was formed under Xavier Bettel.

Luxemburg, Rosa (1871–1919) Polish-born German revolutionary leader. She cofounded what became the Polish Communist Party (1893), before obtaining German citizenship in 1898. Imprisoned in 1915 for opposing World War I, she cofounded the revolutionary and pacifist group known as the Spartacus League (the Spartacists) in 1916 with the German socialist Karl Liebknecht (1871–1919). After her release from prison in 1918 she cofounded the German Communist Party; the following year she and Liebknecht were assassinated after organizing an abortive Communist uprising in Berlin.

Lynch, Jack (**John Mary Lynch**) (1917–99) Irish Fianna Fáil politician, Prime Minister of the Republic of Ireland (1966–73; 1977–79). He led Ireland into the European Community in 1973.

Lyons, Joseph Aloysius (1879–1939) Australian politician. He was a Labor politician in Tasmania from 1909 until 1929 and was Premier there from 1923 until 1928. He became a federal politician in 1929. When the Labor Party split in 1931, Lyons and others left, joining with the Nationalists to form the United Australia Party. Lyons led the Opposition from 1931 until 1932, when he became Prime Minister (1932–39), embarking on a programme of rearmament.

Lysander (died 395 BC) Spartan general. He commanded the Spartan fleet that defeated the Athenian navy in 405. Lysander captured Athens in 404, so bringing the Peloponnesian War to an end.

Maastricht Treaty A treaty signed by the 12 member states of the *European Union, agreed in February 1992, which came into effect on 1 November 1993. The treaty—officially known as the 'Treaty on European Union'—envisages political union, with the concept of 'union citizenship'; eventual monetary union under a European Central Bank; common policies on foreign affairs and security, with the *Western European Union becoming the military arm of the Community; greater cooperation on domestic and environmental matters; some strengthening of the European Parliament; and 'subsidiarity', that is, an effective level of demarcation between the powers and responsibilities of the EU institutions and individual member states. The ratification by the member states was complicated by disagreements over certain clauses of the treaty. Britain refused to accept the Social Charter in 1992, a section of the treaty that protects the rights of employees, but agreed to it in 1997. However, Britain secured the right to refuse to adopt the single European currency. Denmark at first rejected the treaty in a referendum, but agreed to ratify it in a second referendum, having negotiated the right to 'opt out' of various provisions.

MacArthur, Douglas (1880-1964) US general. He was in command of US (later Allied) forces in the SW Pacific during World War II. He formally accepted Japan's surrender in 1945, and administered that country during the Allied occupation that followed. In 1950 he was put in charge of UN forces in Korea, but was relieved of his command the following year.

Macaulay, Thomas Babington, 1st Baron (1800-59) British historian, essayist, and philanthropist. As a civil servant in India (1834-38) he established an English system of education and devised a new criminal code, before returning to Britain and devoting himself to literature and politics. Among his best-known works are *The Lays of Ancient Rome* (1842) and his *History of England* (1849-61), which covers the period from the accession of James II to the death of William III from a Whig standpoint.

Macbeth (*c.*1005-57) King of Scotland (1040-57). He came to the throne after killing his cousin Duncan I in battle, and was himself defeated and killed by Malcolm III. He is chiefly remembered as the subject of Shakespeare's tragedy *Macbeth*, in which the historical events are considerably embroidered.

Maccabees A Jewish dynasty founded by *Judas Maccabaeus (the Hammerer). In 167 BC the Syrian king Antiochus IV plundered the Temple in Jerusalem, set up an altar to the Greek god Zeus, and proscribed Jewish religious practices. A Jewish revolt began, led by Mattathias, an elderly priest, and guerrilla tactics were used against the Syrians. When Mattathias died in 166, his second son, Judas, assumed leadership. After a series of successful encounters with Syrian forces Judas retook the Temple area in 164 and cleansed the Temple in a ceremony that has from that time been commemorated annually as the feast of Hanukkah. Judas died in 160 and his brothers continued the struggle until independence from the Syrians was achieved, the third brother, Simon, becoming high priest, governor, and commander. The conquests and forced conversions of later rulers caused much discontent, and the dynasty ended with the arrival of the Romans in 63 BC.

McCarran Act (1951) A US Act that required the registration of communist organizations and individuals, prohibited the employment of communists in defence work, and denied US entry to anyone who had belonged to a communist or fascist organization. It arose out of the fear in the early 1950s of a communist conspiracy against the USA. In 1965 the Supreme Court ruled that individuals could refuse to admit being communists by claiming the constitutional privilege enshrined in the Fifth Amendment against self-incrimination.

McCarran–Walter Act (1952) A codification of US immigration laws. Passed over the President's veto, it maintained the quota system, whereby immigrant quotas were allocated by nationality, but it tightened up laws governing the admission and deportation of aliens, limited immigration from eastern and south-eastern Europe, removed the ban on the immigration of Asian and Pacific people, provided for selective immigration on the basis of skills, and imposed controls on US citizens abroad.

McCarthy, Joseph (Raymond) (1909–57) US Republican politician. Between 1950 and 1954, latterly as chairman of a government committee, he was the instigator of widespread investigations into alleged Communist infiltration in US public life. Although most of those accused during the period of 'McCarthyism' were not in fact members of the Communist Party, many of them were blacklisted, lost their jobs, or were otherwise discriminated against in a mood of hysteria, which abated only after the public censure of McCarthy in December 1954.

McClellan, George Brinton (1826–85) US general. Given command of the Department of Ohio at the beginning of the *American Civil War, McClellan secured a series of minor victories in West Virginia, and in November 1861 succeeded Winfield *Scott as general-in-chief of the Union (Northern) armies. While he lost this post in March 1862, he retained command of the Army of the Potomac. His attempt to capture Richmond in the Peninsular campaign proceeded too slowly and was then ruined by counter-attacks from forces of the *Confederacy in the Seven Days' battles. He checked *Lee at *Antietam, but missed the opportunity to destroy his opponent and bring the war to an end, and was subsequently removed from command. McClellan unsuccessfully ran as the Democrat presidential candidate against *Lincoln in 1864.

MacDonald, Flora (1722–90) Scottish Jacobite heroine. She aided Charles Edward *Stuart's escape from Scotland, after his defeat at Culloden in 1746, by smuggling him over to the Isle of Skye in a small boat under the eyes of government forces.

Macdonald, Sir John Alexander (1815–91) Canadian statesman. Elected a Tory member of the House of Assembly of United Canada in 1844, he was the leading figure in bringing about Confederation (1867) of the provinces of British North Canada as the Dominion of Canada after the passage of the *British North America Act. He became the first Prime Minister (1867–73) of the new Dominion of Canada. During his years in office, which continued from 1878 to 1891, Canada expanded territorially and experienced growth in its economy, its internal communications, and its sense of national purpose.

MacDonald, Ramsay (James Ramsay MacDonald) (1866–1937) British Labour statesman, Prime Minister (1924; 1929–31; 1931–35). In 1922 he became leader of the Labour Party, and served as Britain's first Labour Prime Minister in the short-lived Labour government of 1924; he was elected Prime Minister again in 1929, but without an overall majority. Faced with economic crisis, and weakened by splits in his own party, he formed a national government with some Conservatives and Liberals; this led to his being expelled from the Labour Party.

Macedonia (or **Macedon**) An ancient country in south-east Europe, at the northern end of the Greek peninsula, including the coastal plain around Salonica and the mountain ranges behind. In classical times it was a kingdom, which under Philip II and Alexander the Great became a world power. The region is now divided between Greece, Bulgaria, and the Republic of *Macedonia.

Macedonia, Republic of

Capital:	Skopje
Area:	25,713 sq km (9928 sq miles)
Population:	2,087,171 (2013 est)
Currency:	1 denar = 100 deni
Religions:	Eastern Orthodox 64.7%; Muslim 33.3%; other Christian 0.4%
Ethnic Groups:	Macedonian 64.2%; Albanian 25.2%; Turkish 3.9%; Serb and Roma minorities
Languages:	Macedonian, Albanian (both official); Turkish; minority languages
International Organizations:	UN; OSCE; Council of Europe; Euro-Atlantic Partnership Council; WTO

A landlocked country in the Balkan peninsula bordering Serbia in the north, Albania in the west, Greece in the south, and Bulgaria in the east; formerly a constituent republic of Yugoslavia.

Physical Most of the republic's territory is a plateau, from which rise forested mountain peaks.

Economy Mineral resources include iron ore, lead, zinc, and nickel. The chief crops are fruit, vegetables, and tobacco, with food processing, beverages, and textiles being important industries. Food, beverages, and tobacco are important exports. Macedonia has close economic links with the EU and its currency, the denar, is pegged to the euro.

History The country comprises part of the area of *Macedonia, which was divided in 1913 between Greece and Serbia. The Serbian part of Macedonia was known as southern Serbia from 1918 until 1947, when it became the Republic of Macedonia within the Federal Republic of Yugoslavia, with its own regional Parliament. Following elections in 1990 the anti-Communist Democratic Party was the largest in a hung Parliament. In January 1991 it declared the Republic of Macedonia 'sovereign and independent', while not at this stage rejecting membership of a Yugoslav Union of States. The declaration was overwhelmingly supported by a referendum. The country's independence was recognized by Bulgaria and Turkey, but Greece persuaded the EC to delay recognition, on the grounds that Greek Macedonia was the only region entitled to the name Macedonia. In 1993 Greece agreed to recognize the country on condition that it be known as the Former Yugoslav Republic of Macedonia (FYROM). Negotiations over the name and the use of symbols and emblems continued, and Macedonia agreed in 1995 to change its national flag. Although the issue has not yet been resolved, in the 2000s most of the world's nations recognized the name 'Republic of Macedonia'. Discontent within Macedonia's large Albanian minority flared into armed rebellion in 2001, and a NATO peacekeeping force was deployed. Constitutional changes made concessions to the Albanians.

Macedonian wars Conflicts fought between Rome and Macedonia in the 3rd and 2nd centuries BC. In the first war (211–205) Philip V was opposed by an alliance of Rome, Aetolia, and Pergamum, but with Rome also deeply involved in the second of the *Punic wars he was able to force Aetolia to accept terms, and then to agree favourable ones with Rome itself. But war broke out again (200) and this time Philip was defeated decisively at Cynoscephalae (197). Philip's son Perseus came to the throne in 179, and set about winning influence and friends in Greece.

This caused Roman suspicion, the outbreak of a third war, and another Roman victory, this time at Pydna in 168. Macedonia was divided into four republics. In 149–148 Andriscus, claiming to be a son of Perseus, attempted to set himself up as king but was defeated and Macedonia became a Roman province.

McGuinness, Martin (James Martin Pacelli McGuinness) (1950–) Irish politician, Deputy First Minister of Northern Ireland (2007–11, 2011–). Born in Londonderry, he joined the *Irish Republican Army about 1970 and is thought to have become one of its leaders. He was *Sinn Fein's chief negotiator in the talks that culminated in the Good Friday Agreement (*see* NORTHERN IRELAND). Elected to the new Northern Ireland Assembly, he became Northern Ireland Minister of Education (1999–2002) and subsequently Deputy First Minister in 2007 when Sinn Fein became the largest Nationalist party. In 2011 he stood down from this role to stand for election as President of the Republic of Ireland, but returned to it after he was defeated.

Machel, Samora Moises (1933–86) Mozambique statesman. He led the *Frelimo War against the Portuguese (1964–74) and became the first President (1975–86) of the People's Republic of Mozambique. A Marxist, he nationalized multinational companies; he also allowed his country to be used as a base for nationalist guerrilla forces operating in *Rhodesia and *South Africa. Nevertheless, his politics became increasingly pragmatic, accepting Portuguese aid and contact with South Africa. He died in an air crash, which some believe to have been deliberately caused.

Machiavelli, Niccolò di Bernardo dei (1469–1527) Italian statesman and political philosopher. After holding high office in Florence he was exiled by the Medicis on suspicion of conspiracy, but was subsequently restored to some degree of favour. His best-known work is *The Prince* (1532), a treatise on statecraft advising rulers that the acquisition and effective use of power may necessitate unethical methods that are not in themselves desirable. He is thus often regarded as the originator of a political pragmatism in which 'the end justifies the means'.

Mackenzie, Alexander (1822–92) Canadian statesman. After the creation of the Dominion of *Canada in 1867 he became leader of the Liberal opposition in the first House of Commons. One of the dominant figures of Canada's early days of nationhood, Mackenzie defeated the Conservatives under Sir John (Alexander) *Macdonald to become the country's first Liberal Prime Minister (1873–78). During his term in office voting by ballot was introduced, the Canadian Supreme Court formed, and the territorial government of the Northwest Territories successfully organized.

Mackenzie's Rebellion (1837) A popular uprising in Upper Canada (now part of Ontario). Growing pressure for democratic reform in Upper Canada could find no peaceful outlet after the defeat of the Reformers by the Tories in the election of 1836. The radical Reformers, led by the Scottish-born journalist and political agitator William Lyon Mackenzie (1795–1861), attempted an armed uprising on York (now Toronto) that was soon put down. Mackenzie fled to the USA where he set up a provisional government. In 1849 all those exiled as a result of this rebellion and *Papineau's Rebellion in Lower Canada, were pardoned, and in 1850 Mackenzie returned to Canada, settling in Toronto.

McKinley, William (1843–1901) US Republican statesman, 25th President of the USA (1897–1901). He supported US expansion into the Pacific, fighting the Spanish–American War of 1898 which resulted in the acquisition of Puerto Rico, Cuba, and the Philippines as well as the annexation of Hawaii. He was assassinated by an anarchist.

MacMahon, Marie Edme Patrice Maurice, Comte de (1808–93) French statesman. Of Irish descent, he fought successfully in the Crimea and at the battles of *Magenta and *Solferino in 1859. As a general in the *Franco-Prussian War he was defeated at Worth (1870) and, with *Napoleon III, capitulated at *Sedan, but he commanded the army that crushed the *Paris Commune in 1871. He had little sympathy with the new (Third) republic but did not support a royalist restoration and agreed to succeed *Thiers as President (1873–79). Dislike of the Chamber of Deputies as too republican led him to dissolve it, but the electorate returned an even more republican Chamber (1877). This incident established the principle of ministerial accountability to the Chamber rather than to the President.

McMahon, Sir William (1908–88) Australian politician, Liberal Prime Minister (1971–72). McMahon replaced Sir John *Gorton as party leader and Prime Minister but was defeated in the subsequent elections.

McMahon Line A boundary line dividing Tibet and India. It was marked out by the British representatives led by Sir Henry McMahon at the Simla Conference (1914) between Britain, Tibet, and China. The Chinese government refused to ratify the agreement, and after the reassertion of control by China over Tibet in 1951 boundary disputes arose between India and China culminating in the Indo-Chinese war of 1962.

Macmillan, Harold, 1st Earl of Stockton (Maurice Harold Macmillan) (1894–1986) British Conservative statesman, Prime Minister (1957–63). His term of office saw the signing of the Test-Ban Treaty (1963) with the USA and the USSR. He advocated the granting of independence to British colonies but his attempt to take Britain into the European Economic Community was blocked by the French President1 *de Gaulle (1963). Macmillan resigned on grounds of ill health shortly after the scandal surrounding the Secretary of State for War, John Profumo.

Macquarie, Lachlan (1762–1824) Scottish-born Australian colonial administrator. He served as governor of New South Wales (1809–21); the colony was chiefly populated by convicts, but during his term of office he improved its prosperity, expanded opportunities for former convicts, and promoted public works, further settlement, and exploration.

Madagascar

Capital:	Antananarivo
Area:	587,041 sq km (226,658 sq miles)
Population:	22,599,098 (2013 est)
Currency:	1 ariary = 5 iraimbilanja
Religions:	traditional beliefs 52.0%; Christian 41.0%; Muslim 7.0%
Ethnic Groups:	Malayo-Indonesian; Cotiers (mixed Malayo-Indonesian, African, and Arab); French, Indian, Creole, and Comoran minorities
Languages:	Malagasy, French (both official); English
International Organizations:	UN; AU; SADC; Non-Aligned Movement; WTO

A large island country lying 450–900 km (280–560 miles) distant from the south-east African coast, to which it runs parallel.

Physical A broad plain in the west rises to the Ankaratra Mountains, which slope steeply eastward to the Indian Ocean. The eastern coast is hot, very wet, subject to cyclones, and densely clad with rainforest. As a result of the island becoming separated from Africa during the period of continental drift, many of its plant and animal species, for example lemurs (prosimians), are unique.

Economy Economic activity in Madagascar is mainly agricultural, employing four-fifths of the population. Coffee, vanilla, shellfish, and sugar are major exports. Cattle breeding is extensive and meat processing is the principal industry; other industries include seafood, soap, and brewing. Chrome ore is mined and exported, and there are bauxite deposits. The 2009 coup and its aftermath led to international sanctions, a slowdown in investment, and a collapse of tourism.

History The Madagascan people are of Indo-Melanesian and Malay descent, mixed with some Bantu, Arabs, Indians, and Chinese. The time of arrival of different groups is controversial. Arab traders were probably visiting by the 10th century. In 1500 a Portuguese sea captain, Diego Dias, chanced on the island, calling it São Lourenço. However, Marco Polo had already named it Madagascar from hearsay knowledge, and this name endured. In the following centuries Dutch, English, and Portuguese vessels made frequent visits, and the French set up trading centres. Many of these were used as pirate bases. By the beginning of the 17th century a number of small Malagasy kingdoms emerged, and later the Sakalawa, from the west of the island, conquered northern and western Madagascar, but their kingdom disintegrated in the 18th century. The Merina people of the interior were later united under King Andrianampoinimerina (ruled 1787–1810), and became the dominant group on the island by the early 19th century.

In 1860 King Radama II gave concessions to a French trading company. This led in 1890 to a French Protectorate, although resistance lasted until 1895. After 1945 Madagascar became an Overseas Territory of the French Republic, sending Deputies to Paris. It became a republic in 1958, and regained its independence (1960) as the Malagasy Republic, changing its name

back to Madagascar in 1975. Severe social and economic problems caused recurrent unrest and frequent changes of government. Admiral Didier Ratsiraka was elected President in 1982 and again in 1989, working closely with a Supreme Revolutionary Council. A new multiparty constitution was adopted in 1992 and Albert Zafy became President following elections in 1993. In 1996 he was impeached, and later defeated in presidential elections by Ratsiraka. Marc Ravalomanana was narrowly victorious in 2001; however, Ratsiraka rejected the result, leading to a short period of chaos until he left the country. Instability continued and in 2009 Ravalomanana was overthrown by a military coup that installed Andry Rajoelina as President. Attempts to form a transitional unity government encompassing Ratsiraka, Zafy, Ravalomanana, and Rajoelina foundered; Rajoelina remained President and promulgated a new constitution in 2010. In 2013 Hery Rajaonarimampianina, a protégé of Rajoelina, was elected President.

Madero, Francisco Indalécio (1873–1913) Mexican statesman. President of Mexico (1911–13), he assumed leadership of the *Mexican Revolution of 1910. Thwarted in his attempt to unseat the dictator Porfirio *Díaz, he fled to the USA, from where he organized an armed movement that was unleashed on 20 November 1910. The Díaz dictatorship fell six months later and in the ensuing elections Madero won the Mexican presidency. After putting down five insurrections against him, Madero fell victim to the sixth led by General Victoriano *Huerta in 1913. He was murdered a few days after being deposed.

Madison, James (1751–1836) US Democratic Republican statesman, 4th President of the USA (1809–17). Before taking office, he played a leading part in drawing up the US Constitution (1787) and proposed the Bill of Rights (1791). His presidency saw the US emerge successfully from the War of 1812 against Britain.

Mafia An international secret society originating in Sicily. In its modern form the Mafia (Italian 'boldness') can be said to date from the period 1806–15, when, under British pressure, attempts were being made to break up the huge estates of the Sicilian feudal aristocracy. In the 1880s many Sicilians emigrated to the USA and the Mafia, as Cosa Nostra (Our Business), became established in New York and Chicago. In the 1920s the fascist government in Italy brought Mafia leaders to trial, but some escaped to the USA, where they were active during the *Prohibition era. After World War II, notably after the opening-up of the former Soviet bloc, Mafia activities spread worldwide, increasingly centred on the drug trade. The Mafia is also involved in organized prostitution, fraud, theft, and kidnapping. In the USA, the Mafia is notable also for its infiltration of legitimate business—for example, in transport, construction, gambling, and fast-food—and its use of these businesses for money-laundering. Mafia members are required to live by a code of silence and eschew all cooperation with legitimate authorities: any violation of this code is severely punished.

Magdalenian See PALAEOLITHIC.

Magellan, Ferdinand (Portuguese name **Fernão Magalhães**) (*c.*1480–1521) Portuguese explorer. In 1519, while in the service of Spain, he commanded five vessels on a voyage from Spain to the East Indies by the western route. He reached South America later that year, rounding the continent through the strait which now bears his name and emerging to become the first European to navigate the Pacific. He reached the Philippines in 1521, but soon after was killed in a skirmish on Cebu. The survivors, in the one remaining ship, sailed back to Spain round Africa, thereby completing the first circumnavigation of the globe (1522).

Magenta, Battle of (4 June 1859) A battle fought in Lombardy, between the French and the Sardinians on one side and the Austrians on the other. The Italian patriotic movement known as the *Risorgimento had been offered French military support at a meeting (1859) at Plombières between *Napoleon III and *Cavour. When war broke out, the French and Sardinian forces defeated the Austrians in a disorganized fight at Magenta, which opened the way to the occupation of Lombardy and Milan. Two weeks later it was followed by the decisive battle of *Solferino.

Maginot Line The line of defensive fortifications built along France's north-eastern frontier from Switzerland to Luxembourg, completed in 1936, in which the French placed excessive confidence. Partly because of objections from the Belgians, who were afraid they would be left in an exposed position, the line was not extended along the Franco-Belgian frontier to the coast. Consequently, although the defences proved impregnable to frontal assault, the line was easily outflanked when the Germans invaded France in the spring of 1940. It is named after the French Minister of War André Maginot (1877–1932).

Magna Carta (Latin, 'Great Charter') The document that the English barons, aided by Stephen *Langton, forced King *John to seal at Runnymede on 15 June 1215. It was a charter of 61 or 63 clauses (the final clause is sometimes subdivided into three) covering a wide range of issues, mainly limiting the power of the king. John sought and obtained papal condemnation of the charter on 24 August 1215, which led to the first *Barons' War four months later. Although the charter was often violated by medieval kings, it came to be seen as an important document defining the English Constitution.

Magyars A people who speak a Finno-Ugric language and whose ancestors came from an area round the River Volga in Russia. Under Prince Árpád, they entered what became *Hungary in the 9th century. They harassed the German kingdom but were finally defeated and repulsed by Otto I at the Battle of *Lechfeld. Pope Sylvester crowned Stephen as the first king of their country in 1000 and he established unity and introduced Christianity.

Mahdi In popular Muslim belief, a spiritual and temporal leader who will rule before the end of the world and restore religion and justice. The title has been claimed by various leaders; the most widely known of these was Muhammad Ahmad of Dongola in Sudan (1843–85), who proclaimed himself Mahdi in 1881 and launched a political and revolutionary movement which captured Khartoum and overthrew the Egyptian regime. For Shiite Muslims the title *Mahdi* refers to the twelfth imam.

Mahicans (or **Mohicans**) A Native American people who inhabited the Hudson River valley. They shared many traits with the *Iroquois to the west. European contact began when Henry Hudson sailed up the Hudson River in 1609. Beaver and other pelts were exchanged for beads and knives, and regular trade became centred round the Dutch Fort Orange (later Albany). As middlemen for other tribes they jealously kept the Mohawk Iroquois at bay until their control was finally broken in wars of 1662–69. Thereafter epidemics and dispersal by Dutch, then English and American, colonial pressures relegated them to an increasingly lesser role through the 18th century, and, like the *Delaware, they were eventually officially relocated to midwestern reservations in the 19th century.

Mahmud II (1784–1839) Ottoman Sultan (1808–39). He came to the throne on the deposition of his brother, Mustafa IV, and continued the reforming policies of his cousin, Selim III (1789–1807). He rid himself of the *Janissaries, the traditional military corps that had become unruly and inefficient, by having them massacred, and established a new, European-style army. He curbed the power of the religious classes, centralized government, and reduced provincial autonomy. He was attacked by *Mehemet Ali of Egypt, and his army defeated in the battle of Nizip (1839) in Syria.

Mahmud of Ghazna (969–1030) Muslim ruler of the Ghaznavid dynasty of Afghanistan and Khurasan (999–1030). He led 17 raids into northern India in the name of Islam. Sapping Hindu power in the process, he paved the way for Muslim conquest of the subcontinent. He also extended his power into Transoxania, Persia, and Mesopotamia.

Majapahit A Hindu empire based in the fertile valley of the Brantas River in eastern Java, which flourished between 1293 and the latter part of the 15th century. It experienced its 'golden age' under its last great ruler Hayam Wuruk (1350–89) whose reign is extolled in an epic poem, *Nagarakertagama* (1365). This poem claimed an empire for Majapahit covering much of peninsular Malaya, Sumatra, Borneo, Sulawesi (Celebes), Bali, and other islands, though its control in the more far-flung areas must have been weak. Its chief minister, Gajah Mada (died 1364), codified its laws and is said to have bequeathed a more centralized administration. After it was partitioned between Wuruk's sons there was decline. By c.1527 the last remnants of Majapahit's authority had been extinguished and many of its royal family had fled to Bali.

Maji-Maji A rebellion in German East Africa (1905–07) in the south and centre of present-day *Tanzania. The African warriors believed that magic water (*maji*) could make them immune to bullets. German settlers, missionaries, and traders were murdered, and the towns of Liwale and Kilosa sacked. The Germans adopted a scorched-earth policy, which ended the rebellion but greatly retarded economic development.

Major, Sir John (1943–) British Conservative statesman, Prime Minister (1990–97). He became Prime Minister following the resignation of Margaret Thatcher, and in 1992 he was returned for a further term. His premiership saw the joint *Downing Street Declaration of the UK and Irish governments, which initiated a new peace process in Northern Ireland, and the negotiations leading to the signing of the *Maastricht Treaty. Major survived a leadership challenge in 1995, but was faced with divisions within the Conservative Party over the degree to which Britain should integrate with Europe. He led the Conservatives to a dramatic defeat in the 1997 election.

Makarios III (born **Mihail Christodoulou Mouskos**) (1913–77) Greek Cypriot archbishop and statesman. Primate and archbishop of the Greek Orthodox Church in *Cyprus (1950–77), he reorganized the movement for enosis (the union of Cyprus with Greece). He was exiled (1956–59) by the British for allegedly supporting the *EOKA terrorist campaign of Colonel Grivas against the British and Turks. Makarios was elected President of Cyprus (1960–76). A coup by Greek officers in 1974 forced his brief exile to London, but he was reinstated in 1975 and continued in office until his death.

Malan, Daniel François (1874–1959) South African statesman. Rising to prominence in the National Party in Cape Province, he was elected to Parliament in 1918. His political thinking was dominated by desire for secession from Britain and republicanism. He was Prime Minister (1948–54), and initiated the racial separation laws known as *apartheid.

Malawi

Capital:	Lilongwe
Area:	118,484 sq km (45,747 sq miles)
Population:	16,777,547 (2013 est)
Currency:	1 kwacha = 100 tambala
Religions:	Christian 82.6%; Muslim 13.0%
Ethnic Groups:	Chewa 32.6%; Lomwe 17.6%; Yao 13.5%; Ngoni 11.5%; Tumbuka 8.8%; Nyanja 5.8%
Languages:	English (official); Chichewa; local languages
International Organizations:	UN; Commonwealth; Non-Aligned Movement; AU; SADC; WTO

A long, narrow, land-locked country running north to south in south-eastern Africa. Its eastern boundary includes much of Lake Malawi; Tanzania is to the north and Zambia to the west, while Mozambique almost encloses its southern half.

Physical Malawi lies at the southern end of the Great Rift Valley. The Shire River falling from Lake Malawi is flanked by high ground until it enters swampland, with three smaller lakes. To the north the ground rises westward from the lake to plateaux.

Economy The economy is mainly agricultural, exports being dominated by tobacco (which provides over half of export earnings), sugar, and tea. The main industries are the processing of these products. Cotton, maize, and potatoes are also grown. The only mineral resource is bauxite. Electricity is generated almost exclusively from hydroelectric sources.

History The area has been inhabited since at least 8000 BC, and several kingdoms had risen and fallen before Malawi was first explored by the Portuguese in the 17th century. Slave-traders from Zanzibar raided the area frequently in the 1840s, and its desolation is described by *Livingstone in 1859. In 1875 Scottish mission-aries settled, and for a while governed parts of the country. Colonial administration was insti-tuted when Sir H. H. Johnston proclaimed the Shire Highlands a British Protectorate in 1889. This became British Central Africa in 1891, then Nyasaland from 1907 until 1964. Unwillingly a member of the *Central African Federation (1953–63), it gained independence (1964) as Malawi, with Dr Hastings *Banda as first Prime Minister. When the country became a republic in 1966, he became President and was pro-claimed Life President in 1971. Malawi was a one-party state until the early 1990s, when op-position to this system increased and all non-humanitarian aid from the West was suspend-ed. Banda held a referendum on the issue in October 1992 and the adoption of a multiparty political system was approved. Elections in 1994 were won by the United Democratic Front (UDF), with Bakili Muluzi becoming President; he was succeeded in 2004 by Bingu wa Mutharika. After Mutharika was re-elected in 2009, he became increasingly autocratic, con-cerned more with maintaining power than tackling Malawi's serious economic problems. He died suddenly in 2012 and was succeeded by his deputy, Joyce Banda, with whom he had

fallen out. She became the first female southern African leader and established a reformist ad-ministration. However, elections in 2014 saw victory for Peter Mutharika, brother of the for-mer President Mutharika.

Malaya A former country in south-east Asia, consisting of the southern part of the Malay peninsula and some adjacent islands (originally including Singapore), now forming the western part of the Federation of *Malaysia, and known as West Malaysia. Malaya was domin-ated by the Buddhist kingdom of Srivijaya from the 9th to the 14th centuries and by the Hindu kingdom of Majaphit in the 14th century. Islam was introduced with the rise of the princely states, especially Malacca, in the 15th century. The area was opened up by the Dutch and Portuguese, and eventually Britain became dominant, investing heavily in rubber plant-ations using much immigrant labour from China and India. The several Malay states fed-erated under British control in 1896. Malaya was occupied by the Japanese from 1941 to 1945. After the war, Britain fought a successful twelve-year campaign against Communist guerrillas, mainly Chinese. The country became inde-pendent in 1957, the federation expanding into Malaysia in 1963.

Malayan Campaign (December 1941– August 1945) A military campaign in south-east Asia in World War II. After taking over military bases in Vietnam in July 1941 through an agreement with the *Vichy administration, and securing a free passage through Thailand, Jap-anese troops under General *Yamashita To-moyuki invaded northern Malaya in December 1941 while Japanese aircraft bombed Singapore. The British, Indian, and Australian troops re-treated southwards, where they were taken prisoner after the Fall of *Singapore in February 1942. During the retreat a small guerrilla resist-ance force was organized to conduct sabotage, operating behind Japanese lines. Known as the Malayan People's Anti-Japanese Army (MPAJA), it consisted largely of Chinese, most of whom were communists. In May 1944 Allied troops, advancing from Imphal, began the gradual re-conquest of Burma, and liberated Malaya in 1945.

Malayan Emergency A communist insur-gency in Malaya (1948–60). After World War II, minority Chinese resentment of Malay political dominance of the new Federation of Malaya was exploited by the (mainly Chinese) com-munist guerrillas who had fought against the Japanese. They initiated a series of attacks on planters and other estate owners, which between 1950 and 1953 flared up into a full-scale guerrilla war. Led by Chin Peng and supported by their own supply network (the Min Yuen), the communist guerrillas of the Malayan Races Liberation Army caused severe disruption in the early years of the campaign. However, during the time of *Templer's period in charge of British and Commonwealth forces (1952–54), the insurgents were gradually defeated through the use of new jungle tactics, and the disruption of their supply network. The loyalty of the Malay and Indian population to the British, and the skilful use by the British of local leaders in the government committees, facilitated the peaceful transition to independence in 1957. By then the insurrection had been all but beaten, although the emergency was not officially ended until 1960.

Malaysia

Capital:	Kuala Lumpur
Area:	329,847 sq km (127,355 sq miles)
Population:	29,628,392 (2013 est)
Currency:	1 ringgit = 100 sen
Religions:	Muslim 60.4%; Buddhist 19.2%; Christian 9.1%; Hindu 6.3%
Ethnic Groups:	Malay 50.4%; Chinese 23.7%; indigenous 11.0%; Indian 7.1%
Languages:	Malay (official); English; Chinese; Tamil; minority languages
International Organizations:	UN; Commonwealth; Non-Aligned Movement; Colombo Plan; ASEAN; WTO

A country in south-east Asia, having two parts, West and East, separated by the South China Sea.

Physical East Malaysia comprises Sarawak and Sabah in the north and north-west of the island of Borneo. West, or Peninsular, Malaysia comprises the former Federation of *Malaya and occupies the southern end of the Malay Peninsula, extending south from the south-east Asian mainland and bounded on the north by Thailand and on the south by Singapore; it has a south-western coast on the Strait of Malacca.

Economy Crude oil, gas, electronics, palm oil, and rubber are important exports, with Malaysia being a leading producer of rubber and palm oil. Other mineral resources include bauxite, iron ore, and copper. Malaysia has diversified its economy since the 1970s, when it was a raw-materials producer, and the government is encouraging further investment in the medical and pharmaceutical industries as well as high technology and financial services. The country is actively seeking to reduce its dependence on oil and gas, which provide about a third of government revenue.

History Established in 1963, the Federation of Malaysia originally included *Singapore but it was forced to secede in 1965 because of fears that its largely Chinese population would challenge Malay political dominance. *Brunei refused to join the Federation. The establishment of Malaysia was first suggested (1961) by Tunku *Abdul Rahman, who became its first Prime Minister (1963–70). The Federation aroused deep suspicion in Indonesia, and provoked President *Sukarno's policy of confrontation (*Konfrontasi), resulting in intermittent guerrilla war in Malaysia's Borneo territories, which was only defeated with Commonwealth military assistance (1963–66). In 1969, inequalities between the politically dominant Malays and economically dominant Chinese resulted in riots in Kuala Lumpur, and parliamentary government was suspended until 1971. As a result, there was a major restructuring of political and social institutions designed to ensure Malay predominance, the New Economic Policy being launched to increase the Malay (*bumiputra*) stake in the economy. The largest single political party remained the United Malays National Organization, which had been created by Tunku Rahman. Since 1971 this has ruled in uneasy alliance with the Malaysian Chinese Association and some other ten parties in a coalition, the National Front. Mahathir bin Mohamed became its leader and Prime Minister in 1981. A leading member of the *Association of South-East Asian Nations, Malaysia replaced the New Economic Policy in 1991 by a New Development Policy, whose aim was to diversify the economy. A financial and economic crisis in 1997–98 led the government to expel two million foreign workers. Mahathir bin Mohamed stepped down as Prime Minister in 2003 and was succeeded by Abdullah Ahmad Badawi. Badawi resigned in 2009 following criticism for failing to curb corruption and was succeeded by Najib Razak.

Malcolm III (Canmore) (*c.*1031–93) King of Scotland (1058–93). Malcolm was brought up at the English court of *Edward the Confessor after *Macbeth murdered his father, Duncan I. With English assistance he defeated Macbeth in 1054, and killed him in 1057. Malcolm married (1068) Margaret, the granddaughter of *Edmund II (Ironside). His support of Saxon exiles (including *Edgar the Aetheling) fleeing from the Normans, led to an invasion (1072) by *William I and Malcolm's homage to him. Tension continued, and Malcolm was killed at Alnwick while on his fifth invasion of England.

Malcolm X (born **Malcolm Little**) (1925–65) US political activist. He joined the Black Muslims (Nation of Islam) in 1946 and during the 1950s and early 1960s became a vigorous campaigner against the exploitation of blacks. He advocated the use of violence for self-protection and was opposed to the cooperative approach that characterized the rest of the civil-rights movement. In 1964, after converting to orthodox Islam, he broke away from the Black Muslims and moderated his views on black separatism; he was assassinated the following year.

Maldives

Capital:	Malé
Area:	298 sq km (115 sq miles)
Population:	393,988 (2013 est)
Currency:	1 Maldivian rufiyaa = 100 laaris
Religions:	Sunni Muslim
Ethnic Groups:	South Indian; Sinhalese; Arab
Languages:	Divehi (official); English
International Organizations:	UN; Commonwealth; Colombo Plan; Non-Aligned Movement; WTO

A country consisting of a chain of coral islands in the Indian Ocean some 650 km (400 miles) south-west of Sri Lanka.

Physical The islands comprise some 1800 small atolls and sandbanks built on the summits of old, submerged volcanoes.

Economy The economy of Maldives is based on tourism, which accounts for almost a third of GDP and almost two-thirds of foreign exchange receipts, and fish products, which are the only significant export. Ecological change threatens the future of the country, since many of its islands are a mere 1.8 m (6 feet) above sea level.

History From 1887 to 1952 the islands were a sultanate under British protection. Maldivian demands for constitutional reform began in the 1930s; internal self-government was achieved in 1948 and full independence in 1965. In 1968 the sultanate was abolished, and a republic declared. The Maldives became a full member of the *Commonwealth of Nations in 1985. In 1988, with Indian help, President Maumoun Abdul Gayoom (first elected 1978) suppressed an attempted coup. He was re-elected the following year, and again in 1993, 1998, and 2003. The Maldives suffered some damage and about 80 casualties from the *Indian Ocean tsunami. In 2008 a new, more democratic, constitution was adopted and the country's first multiparty presidential election gave victory to Mohamed Nasheed, a former political prisoner. His 2012 resignation—which he claimed to be involuntary—led to a period of political instability. In 2013 Nasheed was narrowly defeated in the presidential election by Abdulla Yameen Abdul Gayoom, half-brother of the former President Gayoom.

Maldon, Battle of (August 991) A major battle fought near Maldon in Essex between the East Saxons, under the leadership of Byrhtnoth, and Danish raiders, led by Anlaf. The battle is the subject of a short but moving poem written by an eyewitness, in which the heroism of the defeated East Saxons is celebrated.

Mali

Capital:	Bamako
Area:	1,240,192 sq km (478,841 sq miles)
Population:	15,968,882 (2013 est)
Currency:	1 CFA franc = 100 centimes
Religions:	Muslim 94.8%; Christian 2.4%; traditional beliefs 2.0%
Ethnic Groups:	Mande 50.0%; Peul 17.0%; Voltaic 12.0%; Tuareg and Moor 10.0%; Songhai 6.0%
Languages:	French (official); Bambara; local languages
International Organizations:	UN; AU; Franc Zone; ECOWAS; Non-Aligned Movement; WTO

A landlocked country in north-west Africa, sharing common boundaries with Mauritania, Algeria, Niger, Burkina Faso, Côte d'Ivoire, Guinea, and Senegal.

Physical The northern part of Mali is in the dry Sahara and its south is in the tropics. From the south-west, and through its centre flows the Niger, which provides fish. The Niger here has an inland delta which permits the seasonal growing of rice, while other areas contain sufficient pasture for cattle, sheep, and goats.

Economy Mali is amongst the world's poorest countries, with gold contributing four-fifths of export earnings. Agriculture employs four-fifths of the workforce, with livestock rearing predominant in the drought-ridden north and cotton cultivation in the southern savannah. Cotton and livestock are the other chief exports. Millet, maize, and rice are also important subsistence crops, and industry is based on food processing. Hydroelectric power contributes substantially to electricity supplies. In addition to gold, there are deposits of iron ore, marble, limestone, salt, and phosphates.

History The Mali empire in the upper Niger region of West Africa was established in the 13th century. The founder, Sundjata, conquered the remains of the empire of *Ghana c.1235–40 with his army of Malinke soldiers. Mali soon controlled the rich trade across the Sahara and became a major supplier of gold. The empire reached its peak in the early 14th century under Mansa Musa, who established an efficient administration. The Muslim traveller Ibn Battuta (1304–78) visited Mali in 1351–52 and gave a detailed account of the court and trade. However, by then the empire was beginning to decline. In 1335 *Songhay became independent of Mali and by the 15th century had conquered the rest of the empire. After the Moroccan invasion of 1591, the Songhai empire collapsed. Mali was only freed from Moroccan rule at the end of the 18th century, when it was divided among the Tuareg, Macina, and Ségou. France colonized it in the late 19th century. In 1946 it became an Overseas Territory of France. It was proclaimed the Sudanese Republic in 1958, an autonomous state within the *French Community. It united with Senegal as the Federation of Mali in 1959, but in 1960 Senegal withdrew and Mali became independent. A military government took over in 1968, under Lieutenant Moussa Traoré, who gradually re-introduced some degree of civilian

participation. In 1974, as General Traoré he was elected President, and re-elected in 1985. Pro-democracy rioting began in 1990, and in 1991 Traoré was arrested and a National Reconciliation Council took charge under Lieutenant Colonel Amadou Toumani Touré. The Alliance for Democracy in Mali won a majority in the general election of 1992, its leader Alpha Oumar Konaré being elected President. He was re-elected President in 1997 but did not stand in 2002, when Touré was elected. From 2006 northern Mali was increasingly unsettled by Tuareg rebels and an *al-Qaeda offshoot, al-Qaeda in the Islamic Maghreb. Their activity intensified in 2012, and government defeats led to a military coup that ousted Touré. In the succeeding instability rebels declared the north independent, and in 2013 Islamist forces moved into the government-held south; however, French intervention quickly re-established government control of the whole country. Later that year Ibrahim Boubacar Keïta was elected President.

Malplaquet, Battle of (11 September 1709) A battle fought in north-east France, close to the Belgian frontier, that saw *Marlborough's last victory over the French in the War of the *Spanish Succession. Marlborough's invasion of France in 1709 was an attempt to make *Louis XIV agree to the allies' harsh peace terms. Though Malplaquet was a victory, the losses of the combined forces of England and the Holy Roman Empire exceeded those of France and the invasion attempt was abandoned.

Malta

Capital:	Valletta
Area:	316 sq km (122 sq miles)
Population:	411,277 (2013 est)
Currency:	1 euro = 100 cents
Religions:	Roman Catholic 98.0%
Ethnic Groups:	Maltese (of Italian, British, and Phoenician origin)
Languages:	Maltese, English (both official)
International Organizations:	UN; Commonwealth; Council of Europe; OSCE; EU; Non-Aligned Movement; WTO

The largest of a group of three islands constituting a country of the same name in the central Mediterranean Sea between Tunisia and Sicily, the others being Gozo and the tiny Comino.

Physical The main island is some 27 km (17 miles) long by 14 km (9 miles) wide and rises to hills in the south-west. The climate is very warm and rather dry, with fierce winds, and the land is barren in appearance, with few trees and no rivers or streams.

Economy Formerly dependent on shipbuilding, Malta has evolved into a centre for tourism—the main industry—financial services, and freight trans-shipment. Major exports include machinery, mineral fuels, pharmaceuticals, and instruments. A small agricultural sector produces only one-fifth of Malta's food requirements.

History Malta was settled, possibly as long as six thousand years ago, during the *Neolithic era. In historic times it was a Carthaginian centre, falling to the Romans in 218 BC who named it Melita. The Byzantine empire controlled it until 870 when it was conquered by the Arabs. The *Normans annexed it to their kingdom of *Sicily, but, after having been retaken by Muslim forces, it finally fell to the Spanish kingdoms of Aragon and Castile and thence to Spain itself. Under Emperor Charles V it was given to the *Knights Hospitallers (1530), who defended it against Turkish attacks and fortified and enriched it. They were eventually expelled by Napoleon I of France (1798) and the island was taken by the British in 1800. The Treaty of Amiens (1802) returned Malta to the Knights Hospitallers but the Maltese people protested and requested British sovereignty, provided that Malta remained Roman Catholic and that the Maltese Declaration of Rights was honoured. Britain accepted these terms and the country was formally ceded to Britain by France in 1814. Malta developed as a strategic air and naval base and was awarded the George Cross for its resistance to German attack (1940–42). It gained full independence within the *Commonwealth of Nations in 1964 and in 1974 became a republic. Malta joined the European Union in 2004 and adopted the euro as its currency in 2008.

Malthus, Thomas Robert (1766–1834) English economist and clergyman. He was a pioneer of the science of political economy and is known for his theory, as expressed in *Essay on Population* (1798), that the rate of increase of the population tends to be out of proportion to the increase of its means of subsistence; controls on population (by sexual abstinence or birth control) are therefore necessary to prevent catastrophe.

Malvinas *See* FALKLANDS WAR.

Mameluke (from Arabic *mamluk*, 'possessed' or 'slave') Name of two Egyptian dynasties. Mamelukes or slave soldiers were a distinctive feature of Islamic armies from the 9th century. Captured in childhood, they were trained in every branch of warfare and had an exacting academic education. Turkish and Mongol slaves were bodyguards of the Ayyubid sultan al-Salih (1240–49). On his death a popular power struggle developed and the Bahri mameluke generals elected one of their number as sultan al-Malik al Muizz. In 1291 the last Franks were driven from Egypt. The Turkish Bahri sultans recruited Burji slaves as bodyguards, stationing them in Cairo's citadel. These were chiefly Circassian (from the Caucasus). In 1390 they too usurped the sultanate under al-Malik an-Nasir. The Burji ruled until 1517. Mameluke rule extended over Egypt and Syria (including the present Israel, Jordan, Lebanon, and western Arabia). There was an elaborate court, and a highly organized civil service and judiciary. Active encouragement of trade and commerce brought great prosperity throughout their dominions, as is witnessed by the splendid monuments which they built in Cairo and elsewhere. Their external trade reached across Africa as far as Mali and Guinea, and throughout the Indian Ocean as far as Java. In 1517 the Ottoman Turks captured Cairo and overthrew the Mamelukes. As Turkish power waned they re-established themselves as rulers. *Napoleon defeated them in 1798 and they were brought down by Muhammad Ali in 1811.

Manchester School A group of economists, businessmen, and politicians who became influential in Britain in the 1840s. Based in Manchester, the centre of the cotton industry, and led by such men as John *Bright and Richard *Cobden, the group followed the *laissez-faire* philosophy of Adam Smith and David *Ricardo. They supported *free trade and political and economic freedom, and opposed any interference by the state in industry and commerce. Their influence faded in the 1860s, when many European countries began to favour state intervention in economic matters.

Manchukuo Japanese puppet state in Manchuria (1932–45). Using the Mukden Incident as a pretext, the Japanese seized the city of Mukden in September 1931 and within five months had extended their power over all Manchuria. Japanese expansion to the west was halted by the Soviet army in 1939, but the Japanese remained in control of Manchukuo until the Chinese communists (with support from the Soviet Union, who removed large quantities of industrial equipment) took over at the end of World War II.

Manchus A nomadic people who conquered China and established the *Qing dynasty in the 17th century. Previously vassals of the *Ming, their base was north of the Liaodong Peninsula in Manchuria (north-east China). After 1582 their chief, Nurhachi (1559–1626), made alliances with neighbouring tribes, built a strong castle, and imported Chinese technicians and advisers. Everyone—tribesman, captive, serf, or slave—was registered under a distinctive banner, making possible an efficient system of taxation and military control. In 1616 Nurhachi took the title of emperor and in 1625 made Shenyang, renamed Mukden, his capital. When he died he had built his bannermen into a nation. His son, Abahai, campaigned extensively in Korea, Mongolia, and northern China. Twice he attacked Beijing. He ordered his people to call themselves Manchus, a name of obscure origin, and in 1636 proclaimed the Da Qing (Great Pure) dynasty. Eight years later Nurhachi's grandson became the first Qing emperor of China. While the Manchus adopted many aspects of Chinese life, they remained segregated from them, intermarriage with Chinese was forbidden, and they had separate quarters in all Chinese cities. During the 19th century segregation began to break down and in the 20th century they have merged into the mass of the Chinese people.

mandarin (Portuguese *mandarim*, from the Sanskrit *mantrin*, 'counsellor') A senior official in imperial China. From the Song dynasty (960 AD), officials were recruited predominantly by examination in the Confucian classics. (Since the *Han dynasty (206 BC) examinations had been used within the civil service.) There were nine grades of mandarin.

mandate A form of international trusteeship devised by the *League of Nations for the administration of former German and Ottoman colonies after World War I. In 1919 the League assigned a mandate for each territory to one of the Allied nations (principally, Britain and France). Marking an important innovation in international law, the mandated territories were neither colonies, nor independent countries, but were to be supervised by the League's Permanent Mandates Commission. The latter, however, had no means of enforcing its will on the mandatory power, which was responsible for the administration, welfare, and development of the native population until considered ready for self-government. Most mandated territories, with the important exceptions of Palestine and Namibia, had achieved independence by World War II. In 1946 the mandate system was replaced by the United Nations' trusteeship system for the remaining mandates.

Mandela, Nelson (Rolihlahla) (1918–2013) South African statesman, President (1994–99). From his twenties he was an activist for the African National Congress (ANC); he was first jailed in 1962 and was sentenced to life imprisonment in 1964. His authority as a moderate leader of black South Africans did not diminish while he was in detention, and he became a symbol of the struggle against apartheid. On his release in 1990 Mandela resumed his leadership of the ANC, and engaged in talks with President F. W. de Klerk on the introduction of majority rule. He shared the Nobel Peace Prize with President de Klerk in 1993, and in the country's first democratic elections was elected President the following year. He subsequently became a much loved and respected international statesman and was instrumental in founding the *Elders in 2007.

Manfred (1231–66) King of Sicily (1258–66). The illegitimate son of the Holy Roman Emperor *Frederick II, he ruled in Italy on behalf of Conradin, his half-brother, and with support from the Saracens took the Kingdom of the Two Sicilies (1257). He was excommunicated by Pope Alexander IV but invaded papal territories in Tuscany. He was again excommunicated by Pope Urban IV who gave his crown to Charles I of Anjou, and he was finally defeated and killed at the battle of Benevento.

Manhattan Project The code name for the secret project to develop the atomic bomb in the USA during World War II. When it became apparent in the late 1930s that it was feasible to build such a bomb Albert Einstein was persuaded by the physicist Leo Szilard to write to President Roosevelt, urging him to provide the resources to enable the USA, rather than Germany, to develop the atom bomb. Largely as a result of this initiative work was started on designing such a weapon at Los Alamos, New Mexico, under the direction of *Oppenheimer, who had the collaboration of the University of Chicago, where Enrico Fermi (1901–54) built the first atomic pile. Also involved were other physicists in US and UK universities. Uranium-235 was produced at Oak Ridge, Tennessee, and plutonium-239 at an atomic plant at Hanford, Washington state. The project culminated in the successful explosion of the first atomic bomb at Alamogordo, New Mexico, on 16 July 1945. After the war it became clear that the Germans, who had lost their mainly Jewish nuclear physicists, were many years behind the Americans.

manifest destiny A 19th-century US political doctrine advocating territorial expansion. It was proclaimed by John O'Sullivan as "Our manifest destiny to overspread the continent allotted by Providence for the free development of our yearly multiplying millions". A tenet of the Democratic Party, it gained support among Whig, and later Republican, interests, and played a significant part in raising popular support for the annexation of Texas (1845) and the *Mexican–American War (1846–48). It was later invoked by *Seward in the purchase of Alaska (1867), and re-emerged in the 1890s with the annexation of Hawaii and the acquisition of Spanish territories in the *Spanish–American War.

Manila Bay, Battle of (1 May 1898) Naval engagement during the *Spanish–American war in the Philippines, in which a US fleet under George *Dewey sank a Spanish fleet at dawn without losing a man. Dewey's objective had been to paralyse the Spanish fleet at the outset of the *Spanish–American War of 1898 over Cuba, but his overwhelming victory widened the scope of the war by opening the way for US expansion in the Pacific.

Mannerheim, Carl Gustav Emil, Baron von (1867–1951) Finnish military leader and statesman. Trained as an officer in the Tsarist army, he rose to the rank of general, and, defeating the Finnish Bolsheviks (1918), he expelled the Soviet forces from Finland. He was appointed chief of the National Defence Council (1930–39), and planned the "Mannerheim Line", a fortified line of defence across the Karelian Isthmus to block any potential aggression by the Soviet Union. When Soviet forces attacked (1939) he resisted in the *Finnish–Russian War, and in alliance with Germany renewed the war (1941–44). In 1944 he signed an armistice with the Soviet Union. The Finnish Parliament elected Mannerheim as President (1944–46). In March 1945 he brought Finland into the war against Germany.

manorial system The social, economic, and administrative system that emerged in Europe in the 5th century from the chaos and instability following the collapse of the Roman empire. Farmers sought the protection of powerful lords and in return surrendered certain rights and control over their lands. Gradually a system of obligations and service emerged, especially relating to manorial agrarian management, and set down in records called custumals.

The manor consisted of demesne land (private land of the lord) and tenants' holdings. Tenants were free or unfree (villeins), rank being determined by personal status or the status of their land. Not all manors had this balance of demesne, free land, and unfree land. In addition, meadow land for grazing livestock was available to all, and thus known as common land. Access to woodland for timber and grazing of pigs might be a further facility. The lord presided over the manorial court and received money or labour services from his tenants regularly (week work) or seasonally (boon work). A tendency in the 12th century for labour services to be commuted to cash rents was reversed after c.1200, when inflation encouraged landlords again to exact services in kind. Labour shortages following the *Black Death (1348), when Europe's population fell from 80 million to 55 million, enclosures, tenant unrest, and rebellions such as the *Peasants' Revolt (1381), effectively ended the manorial system in England by c.1500.

Mansa Musa (ruled 1307–37) The most celebrated of the rulers (kankans) of *Mali, chiefly because of his spectacular pilgrimage to *Mecca in 1324. He caused a sensation in Cairo with his 500 slaves and 80–100 camels carrying gold. In his absence one of his generals acquired Gao, the capital of the neighbouring *Songhay state for him. He returned from Mecca with the Andalusian poet-architect Es-Saheli, who built the palace and Great Mosque of Timbuktu. He greatly expanded the commerce and prosperity of Mali, and gave encouragement to Islamic learning and culture.

Manzikert, Battle of (1071) Battle fought at a site near Lake Van in Turkey. *Seljuk Turks, recent converts to *Islam, routed a Byzantine force, capturing its leader, Emperor Romanos Diogenes IV. Alp Arslan, the Seljuk leader released him, but the defeat left Anatolia open to Turkish invaders and the weakening of Byzantine control that was indirectly to provoke the First *Crusade.

Maori A member of the aboriginal people of New Zealand. Having arrived there first as part of a wave of migration from Tahiti, probably in the 9th century, by 1200 they had established settlements in various parts of the islands. The Maoris ceded all their rights and powers of sovereignty to the British Crown in 1840 with the signing of the Treaty of Waitangi. Maori Wars were fought intermittently in 1845–48 and 1860–72 between Maoris and the colonial government of New Zealand over the enforced sale of Maori lands to Europeans. In 1994 and 1995 the New Zealand government agreed to pay compensation to two tribal groups whose land had been seized illegally by settlers and to return traditional Maori lands in the government's possession. Many more Maori claims to land are under consideration. In 2001 about 600,000 New Zealanders were Maori or had Maori ancestry.

Mao Zedong (or **Mao Tse-tung**) (1893–1976) Chinese statesman, chairman of the Communist Party of the Chinese People's Republic (1949–76) and head of state (1949–59). After studying Marxism as a student he was among the founders of the Chinese Communist Party in 1921, becoming its effective leader following the Long March (the withdrawal of the Communists from SE to NW China, 1934–35). He eventually defeated both the occupying Japanese and rival Kuomintang nationalist forces to form the People's Republic of China, becoming its first head of state (1949). Although he initially adopted the Soviet Communist model, following Khrushchev's denunciation of Stalin (1956) Mao began to introduce his own measures, central to which were the concepts of permanent revolution, the importance of the peasantry, and agricultural collectivization. A brief period of freedom of expression (the Hundred Flowers) ended with the introduction of the economically disastrous Great Leap Forward (1958–60). Mao resigned as head of state in 1959 but retained his position as chairman of the Communist Party, and as such remained China's most powerful politician. He was the instigator of the Cultural Revolution (1966–68), which was intended to effect a return to revolutionary Maoist beliefs; during this time he became the focus of a powerful personality cult, which lasted until his death.

Maquis (from Corsican Italian *macchia*, 'thicket') French *resistance movement in World War II. After the fall of France in 1940, it carried on resistance to the Nazi occupation. Supported by the French Communist Party, but not centrally controlled, its membership rose in 1943–44, and constituted a considerable hindrance to the German rear when the Allies landed in France. Its various groups, often operating independently, were coordinated into the Forces Françaises de l'Interieur in 1944.

Marat, Jean Paul (1743–93) French revolutionary and journalist. The founder of a radical newspaper, he became prominent during the French Revolution as a virulent critic of the moderate Girondists and was instrumental (with Danton and Robespierre) in their fall from power in 1793. Suffering from a skin disease, he spent much of his time in later life in his bath, where he was murdered by the Girondist Charlotte *Corday. This was used as a pretext by Robespierre and the Jacobins to purge their Girondist rivals.

Maratha A Hindu warrior people of western India who in the 17th and 18th centuries led a military revival against Muslim expansion. They rose to prominence under the inspired leadership of *Shivaji, who, after victories against the *Moguls, established a Maratha kingdom in 1674. Their great age was the early 18th century when, after a temporary collapse, they benefited from Mogul decline to sweep over the north and central Deccan. They seemed poised for all-India mastery, but failure in 1761 of their bid to take Delhi (in the Battle of Panipat) was followed by increasing internal disunity and a failure to make a united stand against expanding British power.

Maratha Wars (1774–82; 1803–05; 1817–18) Wars between the *Maratha peoples of India and troops of the English *East India Company. By the late 18th century the Maratha Hindus, divided into over 90 clans, had formed an uneasy confederacy that became a significant force in northern and central India. Rivalries between chiefs were exploited by the British. In the Second War Sir Arthur Wellesley (later Duke of *Wellington) won the battles of Assaye and Argaon. The Charter of the East India Company was renewed in 1813, when no further British acquisitions were envisaged, but in 1817 Company troops under Lord Hastings invaded Maratha territory to put down *Pindari robber bands supported by Maratha princes, and finally made British power dominant within the subcontinent.

Marathon A plain in eastern Attica, Greece, scene of a battle in 490 BC in which the Greeks under Miltiades defeated a much larger Persian army. The non-stop run of a courier named Pheidippides bringing the news to Athens has given the name to the race.

marcher lord In the Middle Ages, a holder of land (a lordship) lying on the border (or march) between countries. The term applied to Italy (marche), Germany (mark), and in England along its borders with Scotland and Wales. The marcher lords on the Welsh border were particularly powerful. Between 1067 and 1070 three large marcher lordships were created, based on Chester, Shrewsbury, and Hereford. They extended their power into Wales despite Welsh resistance in the 12th century led by Owain Gwynedd and Rhys ap Gruffydd. About 140 lordships and sub-lordships were created, the most powerful being Glamorgan, Pembroke, and Wigmore. The crown sought to deal with them by first setting up the Council of the March in Wales (1472) and then abolishing them in the second Act of Union (1543). Their lands were attached to the six existing and the seven new Welsh shires and to the English border counties.

Marco Polo (*c.*1254–*c.*1324) Italian traveller. Between 1271 and 1275 he accompanied his father and uncle on a journey east from Acre into central Asia, eventually reaching China and the court of Kublai Khan. After service with the emperor and travelling widely in the empire for a decade and a half, Polo returned home (1292–95) via Sumatra, India, and Persia. His book recounting his travels gave considerable impetus to the European quest for the riches of the East.

Marcos, Ferdinand Edralin (1917–89) Filipino statesman, President (1965–86). A ruthless and corrupt politician, he initially achieved some success as a reformer and identified closely with the USA, but after his election to a second term he became increasingly involved in campaigns against nationalist and communist guerrilla groups, and in 1972–73 he first declared martial law and then assumed near dictatorial powers. Hostility to Marcos intensified after the murder of the opposition leader Benigno Aquino Jr in 1983. US support for his regime waned as a result of his failure to achieve consensus, and in February 1986 he was forced to leave the country. In 1988 he and his wife were indicted by US courts for fraud and embezzlement but he died before he could stand trial.

Marcus Aurelius *See* AURELIUS, MARCUS.

Margaret, Maid of Norway (*c.*1283–90) Queen of Scotland (1286–90). She was the daughter of Erik II, King of Norway, and the granddaughter of *Alexander III of Scotland. She

became Queen of Scotland at the age of three, although six guardians were appointed to govern the kingdom during her minority. Edward I of England proposed a marriage between Margaret and his son Edward, the first English Prince of Wales. Her death when crossing the North Sea from Norway to Scotland brought to an end the dynastic House of Canmore, which had ruled since 1057, and led to a dispute (1291–92) over the succession involving 13 claimants. Edward I of England judged in favour of John *Balliol.

Margaret, St (*c.*1046–93) Scottish queen, wife of Malcolm III. She exerted a strong influence over royal policy during her husband's reign, and was instrumental in the reform of the Scottish Church.

Margaret of Anjou (1430–82) Queen of England. Her marriage to *Henry VI in 1445 ensured a truce in the war between England and France. During the Wars of the *Roses Henry's weakness caused the *Lancastrian party to centre on his indomitable wife; in February 1461 she won the second Battle of St Albans but by her hesitation lost the chance to keep Henry on the throne, and she had to flee to Scotland and thence to France. Except for the few months that Henry regained the throne in 1470–71, she spent most of the rest of her life in her native Anjou.

margrave (German, *Markgraf,* "count of the mark") A governor appointed to protect vulnerable areas known as marks in the Holy Roman Empire. They were the equivalent of English marches (*marcher lord) and were usually frontier territories. Charlemagne introduced this office, which in the 12th century became hereditary, and the title came to rank equally with a prince of the empire.

Maria Theresa (1717–80) Archduchess of Austria, queen of Hungary and Bohemia (1740–80). The daughter of the Emperor Charles VI, Maria Theresa married the future Emperor Francis I in 1736 and succeeded to the Habsburg dominions in 1740 by virtue of the *Pragmatic Sanction (by which her father made provision for her to succeed him). Her accession triggered the War of the Austrian Succession (1740–48), during which Silesia was lost to Prussia. She attempted but failed to regain Silesia from the Prussians in the Seven Years War (1756–63). After the death of Francis I in 1765 she ruled in conjunction with her son, the Emperor Joseph II.

Marie Antoinette (1755–93) French queen, wife of Louis XVI. A daughter of Maria Theresa and the Emperor Francis I, she married the future Louis XVI of France in 1770, becoming queen four years later. She became a focus for opposition to reform and won widespread unpopularity through her extravagant lifestyle. Like her husband she was imprisoned during the French Revolution and eventually executed.

Maritime strike (1890) A shipping, mining, and shearing strike in Australia. It was a time of economic depression and workers were fighting for trade union recognition (including the "closed shop"), although other issues were also involved. The unions were defeated, some collapsing completely. This defeat has been seen as being a catalyst in the development of the labour movement and the formation of the Australian *Labor Party.

Marius, Gaius (c.157–86 BC) Roman general and politician. Consul for the first time in 107, he established his dominance by victories over Jugurtha and invading Germanic tribes. He was subsequently involved in a struggle for power with Sulla and was expelled from Italy, only to return and take Rome by force in 87. He was again elected consul in 86 but died soon afterwards.

Mark Antony (Latin name **Marcus Antonius**) (83–30 BC) Roman general. He had served with *Caesar at the end of the *Gallic wars. As tribune in 49 he defended Caesar's interest in the Senate as civil war loomed. He was present at Pharsalus, and represented Caesar in Italy. His offer of a crown to Caesar was refused. After Caesar's murder he took the political initiative against the assassins, and delivered the funeral speech. Octavian, however, was Caesar's designated heir and hostility arose between the two. During Antony's struggle for ascendancy over the Senate led by *Cicero, he was denounced in the 'Phillippic' orations and defeated at Mutina by the forces of the consuls and Octavian. He was then reconciled with Octavian, and together with Lepidus they formed the Second Triumvirate, disposed of enemies including Cicero and defeated the 'Liberators', Brutus and Cassius, at *Philippi in 42.

Antony received the government of the eastern Mediterranean and began (42) his liaison with Cleopatra. Although a powerful ally she cost him much support at Rome. Their marriage, Antony's fifth, was illegal in Roman law. In 34 he declared Caesarion (Cleopatra's son allegedly by Caesar) as Caesar's heir in Octavian's place and divided the east among his family. War followed. After the Battle of *Actium he committed suicide in Egypt.

Markiewicz, Constance *See* WOMEN'S SUFFRAGE.

Marlborough, John Churchill, 1st Duke of (1650–1722) English general. He was appointed commander of British and Dutch troops in the War of the Spanish Succession and won a series of victories over the French armies of Louis XIV, most notably *Blenheim (1704), *Ramillies (1706), *Oudenarde (1708), and *Malplaquet (1709), which effectively ended Louis's attempts to dominate Europe. The building of Blenheim Palace, Marlborough's seat at Woodstock in Oxfordshire, was funded by Queen Anne as a token of the nation's gratitude for his victory.

Marne, Battles of the (5–12 September 1914; 15 July–7 August 1918) Two battles along the River Marne in east central France in World War I. The first battle marked the climax and defeat of the German plan to destroy the French forces before Russian mobilization was complete. By September the Germans were within 24 km (15 miles) of Paris and the government moved to Bordeaux. *Joffre's successful counteroffensive has been hailed as one of the decisive battles in history. The retreating Germans dug themselves in north of the River Aisne, setting the pattern for *trench warfare on the *Western Front. The second battle ended *Ludendorff's final offensive, when, on 18 July, *Foch ordered a counter-attack.

Marprelate tracts Satirical English pamphlets signed by the pseudonymous "Martin Marprelate", which appeared in 1588–89. They featured scurrilous attacks on Anglican bishops, and were the work of Presbyterians who wished to discredit the episcopacy. *Elizabeth I, angered by them, prompted a search for the secret presses on which they were printed. Star Chamber prosecutions of leading ministers followed. Having appeared at a time when Presbyterian fortunes were already at a low ebb, the tracts probably served to discredit the movement still further with the public.

Marshall, George Catlett (1880–1959) US general and statesman. Serving as US Secretary of State (1947–49) he initiated the programme of economic aid to European countries known as the *Marshall Plan. He was awarded the Nobel Peace Prize in 1953.

Marshall Islands

Capital:	Majuro
Area:	181 sq km (70 sq miles)
Population:	69,747 (2013 est)
Currency:	1 US dollar = 100 cents
Religions:	Protestant 54.8%; Assembly of God 25.8%; Roman Catholic 8.4%
Ethnic Groups:	Marshallese 92.1%; mixed Marshallese 5.9%
Languages:	Marshallese, English (both official)
International Organizations:	UN; Pacific Islands Forum; Secretariat of the Pacific Community

A country consisting of a cluster of 29 low-lying atolls and five islands in the central Pacific.

Physical The archipelago comprises two parallel chains of islands, the Ratak (sunrise) chain to the east and the Ralik (sunset) chain to the west. The islands are coral caps over dome volcanoes and have a tropical climate.

Economy Farming and fishing are the main economic activities, and coconut oil and copra are exported. The Marshall Islands depend on US aid and lease payments for the US military base on Kwajalein Atoll.

History The islands were originally inhabited by Micronesians. They were sighted by European sailors in 1529 but were not exploited. The islands were named after a British captain who visited them in 1788. In 1886 the Marshall Islands became a German protectorate. After World War I the islands were administered by Japan, and after World War II they became a UN Trust Territory under US administration. From 1946 until 1958 the US used *Bikini and other atolls in the group for atomic bomb tests. In 1986 they were given semi-independence in a 'compact of free association' in which the USA maintained control over military activities. The Trusteeship was terminated in 1990 and the country joined the United Nations the following year. In 1992 the US government made the first payments to islanders of compensation for personal injury resulting from the testing of nuclear weapons.

Marshall Plan (or **European Recovery Program**) US aid programme. Passed by Congress in 1948 as the Foreign Assistance Act to aid European recovery after World War II, it was named after the Secretary of State, George *Marshall. It invited the European nations to outline their requirements for economic recovery in order that material and financial aid could be used most effectively. The Soviet Union refused to participate and put pressure on its East European satellites to do likewise. To administer the plan, the Organization for European Economic Cooperation was set up, and between 1948 and 1951 some $13.5 billion was distributed.

Marston Moor, Battle of (2 July 1644) A decisive victory for the *Roundheads and Scots during the *English Civil War. The *Cavalier general Prince Rupert had pursued them to Marston Moor, Yorkshire, after his relief of York. They attacked him unexpectedly in the evening, and Cromwell's disciplined cavalry routed the Royalist troops. The Cavaliers lost perhaps 3000 men through casualties, and 4500 prisoners. After the encounter few northern fortresses held out for the king.

Martin, Paul (Edgar Philippe) (1938–) Canadian statesman; Prime Minister (2003–06). A businessman, he entered parliament in 1988 as a Liberal MP and was Finance Minister (1993–2002) under Jean *Chrétien. He ousted Chrétien as leader of the Liberal Party in 2003 and became Prime Minister. Heading a minority government after the 2004 elections, Martin survived until a vote of no confidence forced elections in 2006, at which he was defeated by the Conservative Party under Stephen *Harper.

Martov, L. (born **Yuly Osipovich Tsederbaum**) (1873–1923) Russian revolutionary and leader of the Menshevik Party in opposition to *Lenin's *Bolsheviks. He had at first cooperated with Lenin as joint editor of *Iskra* ('The Spark'), but, at the meeting of the second Russian Social Democratic Party in London (1903), they disagreed over the degree of revolutionary class-consciousness in the labour movement and the extent to which it had to be controlled by a small party. Mensheviks favoured a mass labour party. After 1917 he supported Lenin against the "White" armies but continued to oppose his more dictatorial policies. He left the Soviet Union in 1920.

Marx, Karl (Heinrich) (1818–83) German political philosopher and economist, resident in England from 1849. The founder of modern communism, he collaborated with *Engels in the writing of the *Communist Manifesto* (1848). Thereafter Marx spent much of his time enlarging the theory of this pamphlet into a series of books, the most important being the three-volume *Das Kapital*. The first volume of this appeared in 1867 and the remainder was completed by Engels and published after Marx's death (1885; 1894). *See* MARXISM.

Marxism The system of economic and political ideas first developed by Karl *Marx and Friedrich *Engels and later developed by their followers together with dialectical materialism to form the basis for the theory and practice of *communism. At the heart of Marxism lies the materialist conception of history, according to which the development of all human societies is ultimately determined by the methods of production that people adopt to meet their needs. A particular technique of production determines a set of property relations to organize production (for instance slavery, feudalism, *capitalism), as well as the politics, religion, philosophy, and so on of a given society. The conflict between the particular social classes that emerged led to the next stage of social evolution. Feudalism had been followed by capitalism, which was destined to make way for socialism/communism. In this way Marx and Engels sought to establish the importance of the class struggle. Their attention was focused on capitalist societies, which they viewed as increasingly polarized between an exploiting capitalist class and an impoverished working class. Crucial to Marx's economic analysis of capitalism was his elaboration of the labour theory of value held by the classical economists *Smith and *Ricardo. Marx saw capitalists as expropriating the surplus value created by workers, and accumulating ever-increasing amounts of capital, as the workers (the proletariat) grew ever poorer. The development of industry would render capitalism obsolete, at which point the working class would be ready to overthrow the system by revolutionary means and establish a socialist society. Marx and Engels said little about the economics and politics of socialism; after their death, Lenin and his followers in the former Soviet Union and elsewhere used Marxist ideas to underpin communism, the ideology later being dubbed 'Marxism-Leninism', while other Marxists were critical of communist methods and regarded the Russian revolution (1917) as premature. Since then Marxists have had to grapple with the failure of the socialist societies to live up to the humanistic beliefs of Marx himself, and also with political developments, such as the rise of fascism, that appeared to

contradict historical materialism. Marxism-Leninism as practised in the USSR, and in other countries of the Soviet bloc, collapsed in the 1990s, when the command economy on which it was based was replaced by a market economy. In spite of this practical failure of Marxism, Marx's injunction that to understand a society we should first investigate its mode of production continues to influence many social scientists.

Mary I (1516–58) Queen of England and Ireland (1553–58), the only surviving child of *Henry VIII and Catherine of Aragon. During her parents' divorce proceedings, she was separated from her mother (1531), never to be reunited. She was banished from court, declared illegitimate, and barred from the throne before being restored to the succession in 1544.

During the reign of her half-brother *Edward VI she clung tenaciously to her Catholic faith. Then she outmanoeuvred Lady Jane *Grey to win the throne, and appeared to enjoy considerable public support, despite being the first ruling queen since *Matilda. Many people had remained loyal to the old Catholic religious forms, and there was little opposition to her reversal of Edward VI's Protestant legislation, but her projected marriage to the future *Philip II of Spain (1554) provoked *Wyatt's Rebellion. She proceeded with the marriage, which turned out to be unhappy and childless.

After 1554 she relied increasingly on Reginald *Pole for guidance in the reversal of Henry VIII's Reformation, except for the Dissolution of the *Monasteries, and the revival of severe heresy laws. Between 1555 and 1558 nearly 300 Protestants were executed including *Cranmer, Ridley, and *Latimer, earning her the name "Bloody Mary". She also lost popularity through her foreign policy. In 1557 Philip dragged England into the final phase of the European Habsburg-Valois struggle and England lost Calais, its last outpost on the Continent.

Mary II (1662–94) Queen of England, Scotland, and Ireland (1689–94), the daughter of *James II by his first wife Anne Hyde. She married William of Orange in 1677, and in 1688–89 supported her husband against her father during the *Glorious Revolution. She always deferred to her husband and refused to become queen in 1689 unless he was made king. Her popularity both in the *United Provinces and in England enabled *William III to trust her with the administration of England during his frequent absences abroad. Her lack of children and her quarrel with her sister *Anne, the successor to the throne, saddened her last years.

Mary, Queen of Scots (1542-87) Queen of Scotland (1542-67), the daughter of *James V of Scotland and Mary of *Guise. She was betrothed to the future *Edward VI of England in 1543 but Cardinal Beaton's veto of the marriage led to war with the English, and the Scottish defeat at *Pinkie (1547). Mary was then sent to the French court, where she received a Catholic upbringing under the supervision of her Guise uncles. She married the dauphin Francis (1558), who succeeded to the French throne in 1559 and died in 1560. By 1561 she had returned to Scotland, and had also proclaimed herself the rightful queen of England, as granddaughter of *Henry VIII's sister, Margaret Tudor.

She had to adapt to the anti-monarchical, anti-Catholic, anti-French atmosphere of Reformation Scotland. Her unpopular romantic marriage to *Darnley (1565), although it produced a son, the future James VI (*James I), was disastrous. Darnley murdered Mary's secretary *Rizzio and was then murdered himself. Soon after she married *Bothwell despite having been abducted by him. The subsequent rising of the Scottish lords resulted in her military defeat and flight to England. There she threw herself on the mercy of *Elizabeth I, who kept her confined in various strongholds until her death. Wittingly or not, she was involved in a number of Catholic conspiracies against Elizabeth, figuring in the scheming behind the *Northern Rising as well as the *Ridolfi and *Throckmorton Plots. Her implication in the *Babington Plot (1586) provided enough damaging evidence for a commission to find her guilty of treason. For years Elizabeth had turned a deaf ear to Protestant pleas to execute this fellow monarch. Even now she delayed signing the death warrant, and then disclaimed responsibility for the execution of Mary at Fotheringhay.

Masada The site, on a steep rocky hill on the south-west shore of the Dead Sea, of the ruins of a palace and fortification built by Herod the Great in the 1st century BC. It was a Jewish stronghold in the Zealots' revolt against the Romans (66-73 AD) and was the scene in 73 AD of a mass suicide by the Jewish defenders, when the Romans breached the citadel after a siege of nearly two years. The site is an Israeli national monument and tourist attraction.

Masaryk, Jan (1886-1948) Czechoslovak diplomat and statesman. The son of Tomáš *Masaryk, he helped in establishing the Czech republic and thereafter was mainly involved in foreign affairs. As ambassador to Britain (1925-38), he resigned in protest at his country's betrayal under the *Munich Pact (1938). On the liberation of Czechoslovakia by the Allies (1945) he became Foreign Minister, and was dismayed at the Soviet veto of Czechoslovak acceptance of US aid under the *Marshall Plan. At the request of President *Beneš, he remained in his post after the communist coup of February 1948, but he either committed suicide or was murdered three weeks later.

Masaryk, Tomáš Garrigue (1850-1937) Czechoslovak statesman. As a member of the Austrian Parliament (1891-93; 1907-14), he achieved fame by defending Slav and Semitic minorities. During World War I he worked with *Beneš in London for Czech independence and for his country's recognition by the Allies. By their efforts Czech independence was proclaimed in Prague (1918) and he was elected President. He favoured friendly relations with France, Germany, and Austria, and was a strong supporter of the League of Nations. He felt that the rising *Nazi menace required a younger President and he resigned (1935) in favour of Beneš.

Mason-Dixon Line (or **Mason and Dixon Line**) The boundary line between Pennsylvania and Maryland, which was laid out in 1763-67 by the English surveyors Charles Mason and Jeremiah Dixon. The name was later applied to the entire southern boundary of Pennsylvania, and in the years before the American Civil War it represented the division between the Northern states and the slave-owning states of the South.

Massey, William Ferguson (1856-1925) New Zealand statesman. He founded the Reform Party which campaigned for freehold tenure and free enterprise. As Prime Minister (1912-25) Massey also made extensive purchases of remaining *Maori land. He was challenged by militant unionists (*Red Feds) and broke the strikes of 1912-13, having enrolled farmers as special constables—'Massey's Cossacks'. He committed New Zealand manpower heavily in World War I, but his hold on domestic politics weakened with increasing urbanization.

mass production A system of industrial production involving the manufacture of a product or part in large quantities at comparatively low unit cost. It was in the car industry, initially in the US Ford Company in 1913, that the age of mass production was fully inaugurated. Standardized parts were brought together on a moving assembly line to turn out standardized cars at low cost, but with high wages and profits. At the same time, time-and-motion studies were undertaken to analyse and improve efficiency. Mass production methods thereafter were steadily introduced into other areas of manufacturing, for example in World War II in shipbuilding and aircraft manufacture.

Until recently, the high degree of mechanization and *automation involved in mass-production required the standardization of both the product and the raw materials used in its manufacture. However, the development of versatile manufacturing systems for product monitoring and control has led to improved flexibility. The development of mass-production methods for high-quality items, in particular electronic devices, has led to a shift in emphasis from quality control, in which sub-standard or damaged products are rejected at the end of the production process to quality assurance, in which the whole production process is designed to ensure that the products are of a high standard.

Matabeleland See ZIMBABWE.

Match Girls' strike (1888) A landmark industrial dispute in Britain. It involved the girls at the factory of Bryant and May in the East End of London, who complained about their low pay and the disfigurement of the jaw, nicknamed "phossy jaw", caused by the phosphorus used in match-making. Annie *Besant, a journalist and a *Fabian, organized their strike. Demonstrations, partly to show their disfigurement, won public sympathy. Their success in gaining an increase in pay was a small-scale prelude to the growing strength of *trade unionism.

Mather, Cotton (1663–1728) American Puritan clergyman. The son of Increase *Mather, he became his father's clerical colleague in 1685. Immensely learned, often pedantic, he published nearly 500 works on theology, history, political questions, science, medicine, social policy, and education. Although he did not support the *Salem witch trials, his *Memorable Providences relating to Witchcraft and Possessions* (1689) helped to stir emotions. After being passed over as President of Harvard, he helped found Yale University (1701), advocated Puritan involvement in social welfare, and championed smallpox inoculation. He was the first American-born scholar elected to the Royal Society.

Mather, Increase (1639–1723) American Puritan clergyman. The son of Richard Mather (1596–1669), who had helped define Congregational orthodoxy in 1648, he became a Boston minister in 1664 and married the daughter of John Cotton. He was a conservative President of Harvard College (1685–1701) but as colonial agent in London (1688–92) he negotiated a liberal royal charter for the state of Massachusetts. On his return he helped end the *Salem witch trials. He was a forceful preacher against "declension" (spiritual decline) as well as a prolific author, and was the foremost minister of his generation.

Matilda (or Maud; known as the **'Empress Matilda'**) (1102–67) English princess, daughter of Henry I. She was Henry's only legitimate child and was named his heir in 1127. In 1135 her father died and Matilda was forced to flee when his nephew Stephen seized the throne. Her claim was supported by King David I of Scotland, and she and her half-brother Robert, Earl of Gloucester (died 1147) invaded England in 1139. She waged an unsuccessful civil war against Stephen and eventually left England in 1148. Her son became Henry II.

Matteotti, Giacomo (1885–1924) Italian socialist leader. A member of the Italian Chamber of Deputies, he began in 1921 to organize the United Socialist Party. He openly accused *Mussolini and his *Blackshirts of winning the 1924 parliamentary election by force, giving examples of attacks on individuals and the smashing of the printing presses belonging to opposition newspapers. Within a week he was found murdered. How far Mussolini was personally responsible is uncertain, but in January 1925 he took full responsibility for the crime, and proceeded to tighten up the fascist regime.

Matthias I (Corvinus) (1443–90) King of Hungary (1458–90). He was the son of the Hungarian leader and hero John Hunyadi. He was 18 on his father's death and for the first few months of his reign he was under the control of a regent, his uncle. He had to repulse a military threat from Emperor Frederick III, and fight the Turks, before he was officially crowned in 1464. His reign saw almost continuous warfare; his military successes were based on army and fiscal reforms. In 1468 he accepted an overture from the papacy to lead a crusade to challenge the *Hussites in Bohemia; meanwhile he continued to wage war against the Turks who remained a constant threat. After the death of King George of Bohemia (1471) Matthias was successful over Bohemia, and the Peace of Olomuc (1478) granted him extensive territories and the (shared) title of King of Bohemia. In 1477 his armies moved into Austria and in 1485 he besieged and captured Vienna. As well as administrative reforms, he also codified the law, founded the University of Buda, and encouraged the arts and learning. At the time of his death his empire dominated south-central Europe but his successes were short-lived, as the *Jagiellon dynasty came to power.

Maud *See* MATILDA.

Mau Mau A militant nationalist movement in Kenya. Its origins can be traced back to the Kikuyu Central Association, founded in 1920, and it was initially confined to the area of the White Highlands which Kikuyu people regarded as having been stolen from them. It imposed fierce oaths on its followers. It was anti-Christian as well as anti-European. From 1952 it became more nationalist in aim and indulged in a campaign of violence, killing some 2000 Black Africans who failed to support its programme as well as some 230 Europeans. Jomo *Kenyatta was gaoled as an alleged Mau Mau leader in 1953. In a brutally effective counter-insurgency campaign the British placed more than 100,000 Kikuyu in detention camps. Widespread political and social reforms followed, leading to Kenyan independence in 1963.

Mauritania

Capital:	Nouakchott
Area:	1,030,700 sq km (398,000 sq miles)
Population:	3,437,610 (2013 est)
Currency:	1 ouguiya = 5 khoums
Religions:	Muslim 100.0%
Ethnic Groups:	black Moor 40.0%; white Moor 30.0%; black Africans 30%
Languages:	Arabic; Pulaar; Soninke; Wolof; French
International Organizations:	UN; AU; Arab League; Maghreb Union; Non-Aligned Movement; WTO

A coastal country in north-west Africa, bounded by Morocco and Algeria on the north and by Mali and Senegal on the east and south.

Physical Most of Mauritania lies in the Sahara. Except in the south-west corner it is arid, and everywhere it is hot. Inland from the Atlantic Ocean a region of smooth sand dunes slowly rises, over large deposits of copper and iron ore, to sandstone ridges and the granite highlands of the north-east of the country.

Economy Mauritania's exports are dominated by iron ore and fish; gold, copper, and crude oil are also exported. Agriculture, which employs half the population, includes the growing of millet, dates, sorghum, and rice. Nomadic livestock rearing has declined with periodic droughts and the expansion of mining. Apart from mining, industrial activity involves fish processing, and oil production. Other natural resources include gypsum, phosphates, sulphur, and uranium.

History Dominated from *c.*100 AD by nomadic Berber tribes (who still form one-quarter of its population), Mauritania was first sighted by Europeans in the 15th century. French penetration of the interior began in 1858, and in 1903 the country became a French protectorate. In 1920 Mauritania was made a territory of French West Africa. It became an autonomous republic within the *French Community in 1958, and fully independent in 1960. Following the Spanish withdrawal from Western Sahara in 1976 *Morocco and Mauritania divided between them the southern part of this territory, known as Tiris-el-Gherbia. Bitter war with the Polisario Front (who demanded Western Saharan independence) ensued, but in 1979 Mauritania relinquished all claims and withdrew, leaving Morocco to annex the formerly Mauritanian region. The country's first president, Moktar Ould Daddah, was replaced in 1978 by a military government. In 1991 a referendum voted overwhelmingly in support of a new constitution for what was to be an 'Islamic, African, and Arab republic' operating multiparty politics. In January 1992 Colonel Moaouia Ould Sidi Taya, who had seized control of the military regime and become President in 1984, was elected President under the new constitution. In 1989 some 40,000 Black Mauritanians were expelled to Senegal, following ethnic violence in both countries. A border war with Senegal lasted from 1989 until 1992. Ethnic tensions within Mauritania have continued. A series of unsuccessful coup attempts from 2003 culminated in a successful military takeover in 2005: Taya was deposed and a Military Council for Justice and Democracy, chaired by Colonel Ely Ould Mohamed Vall, took power. Presidential elections were held in 2007 and Sidi Ould Cheikh Abdallahi was victorious. However, in 2008 he too was ousted in a military coup, led by Mohamed Ould Abdel Aziz. Abdel Aziz was confirmed as President by elections in 2009.

Mauritius

Capital:	Port Louis
Area:	2040 sq km (788 sq miles)
Population:	1,322,238 (2013 est)
Currency:	1 Mauritian rupee = 100 cents
Religions:	Hindu 48.5%; Roman Catholic 26.3%; Muslim 17.3%; other Christian 6.4%
Ethnic Groups:	Indo-Mauritian 68.0%; Creole 27.0%; Sino-Mauritian 3.0%; Franco-Mauritian 2.0%
Languages:	English (official); Creole; Bhojpuri; French
International Organizations:	UN; Non-Aligned Movement; Commonwealth; AU; SADC; WTO

An island country lying in the southern Indian Ocean, about 800 km (500 miles) to the east of Madagascar; it is also the name of the principal island (the others are Rodriguez and the Agalega Islands).

Physical The main island, Mauritius itself, is volcanic in origin and nearly 2000 sq km (770 sq miles) in area, having steep hills and plains of lava, which have weathered into fertile soil. The slopes are forested, and the plains are green throughout the year with natural vegetation. Tropical cyclones frequently occur.

Economy The main exports of Mauritius are clothing, textiles, and sugar, which is grown on 90% of cultivated land. Tourism and financial services are also important economic activities, and the government is encouraging the growth in such new areas as fish processing and information and communications technology.

History Visited by the Arabs in the 10th century and discovered by the Portuguese in 1511, the island was held by the Dutch (1598–1710), and the French (1710–1810). The British took it in 1810, and under their rule massive Indian immigration took place. Mauritius became an independent state within the *Commonwealth of Nations in 1968. Sugar has always been the principal crop, and the fall of world prices in the 1980s resulted in a vigorous programme of

agricultural diversification. Politically it has maintained stability as a multicultural state, with the Mauritian Socialist Party, led by Sir Aneerood Jugnauth, dominating politics from 1982. In 1992 Mauritius became a republic. Caseem Uteem was elected to the largely ceremonial role of President in 1992. General elections were held in 1995 following the collapse of the government and the opposition alliance, led by Navin Ramgoolam, was elected. Jugnauth returned to power in 2000. President Uteem resigned in 2002 rather than approve a new anti-terrorism law. The law was eventually approved by one of a series of short-term presidents that lasted until Jugnauth assumed the post in 2003, being replaced as Prime Minister by Paul Raymond Bérenger. However, Bérenger was defeated in the 2005 general election by Ramgoolam, who was re-elected in 2010.

Mauryan empire (*c.*325–185 BC) The first empire in India to extend over most of the subcontinent. The dynasty was founded by *Chandragupta Maurya, who overthrew the Magadha kingdom in north-eastern India. He established his capital at Pataliputra, then expanded westwards across the River Indus, annexing some trans-Indus provinces deep into Afghanistan from Alexander the Great's Greek successors. His son, Bindusara (*c.*297–272 BC), moved south, annexing the Deccan as far as Mysore. Although the third emperor, *Asoka (*c.*265–238 BC) soon renounced militarism, his reign marked the high peak of Mauryan power, for his humane rule permitted the consolidation of his father's huge empire. On his death decline quickly set in, and the dynasty finally ended with the assassination of Birhadratha (185 BC) by the founder of the subsequent Sunga dynasty.

Maximilian (full name **Ferdinand Maximilian Joseph**) (1832–67) Emperor of Mexico (1864–67). Brother of the Austro-Hungarian emperor Franz Josef and Archduke of Austria, Maximilian was established as emperor of Mexico under French auspices in 1864. In 1867, however, Napoleon III was forced to withdraw his support as a result of US pressure, and Maximilian was confronted by a popular uprising led by Benito Juárez. His forces proved unable to resist the rebels and he was captured and executed.

Maximilian I (1459–1519) King of the Romans (1486–93) *Holy Roman Emperor (1493–1519). By marrying Mary, daughter and heiress of *Charles the Bold (1477), he added the duchy of Burgundy (which included the Netherlands) to the *Habsburg lands, thus earning the enmity of France. He defeated the French at the battle of Guinegate (1479) but the Habsburg–Valois rivalry continued in the Netherlands and Italy.

In 1490 he drove out the Hungarians, who, under *Matthias I (Corvinus), had seized much Austrian territory, and by the Treaty of Pressburg (1491) he was recognized as the future king of Bohemia and Hungary. After repulsing the Turks in 1493, he turned to Italy where war was waged between French and Habsburg troops until 1516. He was at a military disadvantage since the German princes refused to finance his campaigns and, despite allying with England against France, he was forced to cede Milan to France and Verona to the Venetians, and to sign the Treaty of Brussels with Francis I in 1516. He was also forced to grant the Swiss independence from the Holy Roman Empire in 1499.

Dynastically he had great success; his son Philip's marriage to the Infanta Joanna (daughter of *Ferdinand V and Isabella) united the Habsburgs and Spain, and his grandson's marriage to the daughter of the King of Bohemia and Hungary secured his inheritance to those lands. In Germany Maximilian's attempt to impose centralized rule on the princes and cities was resisted, since they were determined to remain self-governing. His achievements were in increasing Habsburg territory far beyond Germany, notably by linking it to Spain, and thus to Spain's empire in the Americas.

Maya An American Indian people of Yucatán and Central America who still maintain aspects of their ancient culture, which developed over an extensive area and reached its peak in the 4th–8th centuries, a period distinguished by a spectacular flowering of art and learning. Remains include stone temples built on pyramids and ornamented with sculptures. Among the most striking of the Maya achievements are a system of pictorial writing and a calendar system, more accurate than the Julian, that was still in use at the time of the Spanish conquest in the 16th century. The unexplained collapse of the early Mayan civilization with a population of as many as 16 million took place c.900–1500 but at least four million descendants still speak the Mayan language.

Mayflower *See* PILGRIM FATHERS.

May Fourth Movement Chinese nationalist movement that began on 4 May 1919 with the student protest in Beijing at the *Versailles Peace Settlement decision that Japan should

take over former German concessions in Shandong. In the New Culture Movement that emerged intellectuals grappled with Marxism and liberalism in their search for reforms. Socialist ideas became popular, and the movement played a major role in the revival of the *Kuomintang and the creation of the *Chinese Communist Party.

Mazarin, Jules (born **Giulio Mazzarino**) (1602–61) Italian-born French statesman. In 1634 he was sent to Paris as the Italian papal legate; he became a naturalized Frenchman and entered the service of Louis XIII in 1639. He was made a cardinal in 1641 and the following year succeeded Cardinal Richelieu as chief minister of France, which he governed during the minority of Louis XIV. His administration aroused such opposition as to provoke the civil wars of the *Fronde (1648–53).

Mazzini, Giuseppe (1805–72) Italian nationalist leader. While in exile in Marseilles he founded the patriotic movement Young Italy (1831) and thereafter worked for the independence and unification of Italy, becoming one of the Risorgimento's most committed leaders and planning attempted insurrections in a number of Italian cities during the 1850s. He continued to campaign for a republican Italy following the country's unification as a monarchy in 1861.

Mbeki, Thabo (1942–) South African politician, President (1999–2008). Mbeki was a student activist in the *African National Congress in the 1960s and was imprisoned by the Pretoria regime for his activities. He worked in the ANC's London information offices, undertook military training for its armed wing *Umkhonto We Sizwe* ("Spear of the Nation") in the Soviet Union, and represented the organization in other African countries in the late 1970s. He was elected ANC national chairman in 1989 and was a leading negotiator in CODESA (Commission for a Democratic South Africa), the body established by F. W. *de Klerk to oversee the transition from apartheid to multiparty democracy. Long regarded as the natural successor to Nelson *Mandela, he was elected executive Deputy President in the country's first free elections in 1994 and succeeded Mandela as leader of the ANC in 1997 and as President of South Africa after the 1999 election. Although he led the ANC to a further electoral victory in 2005, he lost the party leadership to Jacob *Zuma in 2007 and resigned as President the following year.

Mboya, Tom (1926–69) Kenyan political leader. In 1960, as leader of the Kenya Independence Movement, he attended a conference in London on the future of Kenya, and was instrumental in securing a constitution which would give Africans political supremacy. In 1960 he became Secretary-General of the newly formed Kenya African National Union. After Kenya gained its independence (1963) he served in various senior ministerial posts. He was assassinated in 1969.

Mecca A city in western Saudi Arabia, an oasis town located in the Red Sea region of Hejaz, east of Jiddah. The birthplace of the Prophet *Muhammad, it is the holiest city of Islam. Lying in a narrow valley in an arid region, it nevertheless prospered from trade and from the cult associated with its central shrine, the Kaaba. Muhammad's life was crowned by the incorporation of pilgrimage to the Kaaba into Islam. The city soon lost its commercial significance, its prosperity resting henceforth on the pilgrimage. It was sacked in 930 by the Qarmatians, a radical Ismaili sect, and fell under *Ottoman suzerainty in 1517. The centre of the Arab revolt against the Ottomans in World War I, it was briefly capital of an independent Kingdom of the Hejaz from 1916; but this was conquered by Abd al-Aziz ibn *Saud in 1925 and later formed part of Saudi Arabia.

Mečiar, Vladimir (1942–) Slovak politician; Prime Minister of the Slovak republic (1992–94; 1994–98). After serving the Communist regime of the former Czechoslovakia in a number of capacities, Mečiar was expelled as a dissident in 1970. He joined the Public Against Violence movement (the Slovak counterpart of the Czech Civic Forum) in 1989 as communism began to collapse in Eastern Europe. In the new Czech and Slovak Federative Republic, Mečiar, a populist nationalist, became premier of the Slovak region. He formed the Movement for a Democratic Slovakia (Slovak HZDS) to campaign for greater Slovak autonomy, which led to his dismissal. However, the following year, the HZDS won a resounding victory in assembly elections, hastening creation of a separate Slovak state in January 1993 with Mečiar as Prime Minister. He resigned following a vote of no confidence in March 1994, but won a general election in October. His party was unexpectedly defeated in elections in 1998. He stood unsuccessfully in the presidential elections of 1999 and 2004.

Mede A member of an ancient Indo-European people whose homeland, Media, lay south-west of the Caspian Sea. In the 7th–6th centuries BC they were masters of an empire that included most of modern Iran and extended to Cappadocia and Syria; it passed into Persian control after the defeat of King Astyages by Cyrus in 549 BC.

Medici, Catherine de (1519–89) Queen of France. The wife of Henry II of France, Catherine ruled as regent (1560–74) during the minority reigns of their three sons, Francis II (reigned 1559–60), Charles IX (reigned 1560–74), and Henry III (reigned 1574–89). She proved unable or unwilling to control the confused situation during the French Wars of Religion, and it was on her instigation that Huguenots were killed in the Massacre of St Bartholomew (1572).

Medici, Cosimo de (1389–1464) Florentine banker, the first member of the Medici family to rule Florence. In Florence the struggle for power between rival patrician families was intense and Cosimo was expelled from the city in 1433 before triumphing over his rivals in 1434. The basis of his wealth was the highly successful Medici bank. He was a keen patron of the arts.

Medici, Lorenzo de (known as 'Lorenzo the Magnificent') (1449–92) Aged 20 he became joint ruler of Florence with his brother Giuliano. In 1478 the brothers were the targets of a plot organized by the rival Pazzi family and the pope: Giuliano was killed but Lorenzo survived. His main concern was the promotion of his family, and he was rewarded by seeing his second son become Pope Leo X. He was a collector of antiquities and was Michelangelo's first patron.

Medina Sidonia, Alonso Pérez de Guzmán, Duke of (1550–1619) Spanish nobleman. He succeeded to his title in 1555. In 1588 *Philip II charged him with responsibility for commanding the *Spanish Armada against England. He begged to be relieved of the commission, on grounds of ill health and inexperience, but without success. He organized his fleet with great efficiency, and was by no means exclusively to blame for the Armada's eventual failure. He subsequently served Philip III.

Medvedev, Dmitri (Anatolyevich) (1965–) Russian politician, President (2008–12), Prime Minister (2012–). Born in Leningrad (now St Petersburg), he graduated in law from Leningrad State University in 1990. After working with Vladimir *Putin in the office of the mayor of St Petersburg, he ran Putin's successful campaign in the presidential election of 2000. He became Putin's chief of staff (2003) and then First Deputy Prime Minister (2005). Ineligible for a third consecutive term as President, Putin named Medvedev as his preferred successor, and he was elected with a large majority in 2008. The widespread assumption was that Medvedev was acting as a constitutional figurehead for Putin's continued power. Putin was indeed immediately appointed Prime Minister and maintained a high public profile during Medvedev's presidency. Medvedev did not contest the 2012 presidential election, becoming Prime Minister after Putin's re-election.

megalith Literally a large stone. The practice of building with large stones occurred in such diverse places as Inca Peru, ancient Egypt, and Easter Island. Megaliths usually consist of blocks built into tombs and other monuments in western Europe in the *Neolithic to *Bronze Age, c.4000–1500 BC. They were once thought to have been derived from a single source, but further study and close dating suggest that that is too simple a view, and that many areas were involved.

While many monuments consist of separate stones raised on end as menhirs, stone circles (as at *Stonehenge), and avenues (as seen at Carnac, in France), the same technique was often used in walling chambers. Roofs could be of horizontal capstones to make the so-called **dolmens**, or of oversailing courses of slabs, which are known as corbelled vaults. The largest block recorded is the capstone of the tomb at Browneshill, County Carlow, Ireland, estimated to weigh 100 tonnes. The movement, handling and dressing of such large stones, and, in some cases, their precise orientation, indicate that those responsible had considerable skill in mechanics, mathematics, and the organization of labour.

Mehemet Ali (c.1769–1849) Pasha (or viceroy) of *Egypt (1805–49). An Albanian by birth, he rose from the ranks to command an Ottoman army in an unsuccessful attempt to drive *Napoleon from Egypt. In 1801 he returned to Egypt in command of Albanian troops and by 1811 he had overthrown the *Mamelukes, who had ruled Egypt almost without interruption since 1250. Technically viceroy of the Ottoman sultan, *Mahmud II, he was effectively an independent ruler and reorganized the administration, agriculture, commerce, industry, education, and the army, employing chiefly French advisers, making Egypt the leading power in the eastern Mediterranean. He occupied the *Sudan (1821–23), and campaigned for the *Ottoman government in Arabia (1811–18) against the *Wahhabis, and in Greece (1822–28), when his fleet was destroyed by a combination of British, French, and Russian navies at the Battle of Navarino (1827). He took Syria (1831–33) and defeated the Ottoman troops at the battle of Nizip (1839). Threatened by united European opposition, he agreed to accept the suzerainty of the Ottoman sultan in 1841 and in return was granted a request that his family be hereditary pashas of Egypt.

Mehmed II (or Muhammad II, the Conqueror) (1430–81) *Ottoman sultan (1451–81). He was frustrated while ruling briefly (1444–46) during the retirement of his father, *Murad II, but on coming to power backed expansionist factions, and by 1453 had achieved the longstanding Ottoman objective of taking Constantinople and thus uniting the European and Asian parts of the empire. Ceaseless campaigns brought further gains in the Balkans, consolidated control of Asia Minor, and took Otranto in Apulia, but failed to wrest Rhodes from the Knights of St John. He modernized his forces by equipping them with firearms and artillery, and created the institutional framework of the developed Ottoman state.

Meighen, Arthur (1874–1960) Canadian Conservative politician, Prime Minister (1920–21; 1926). Meighen advocated a protective system of trade tariffs. His second term was curtailed by his party's defeat in the House of Commons and at the subsequent general election.

Meiji Constitution (1884–89) The constitution of the restored imperial Japanese state. Framed by *Ito Hirobumi and modelled on the existing German form, the Meiji Constitution was gradually developed from 1884 with the institution of a European-style peerage (1884), a cabinet system (1885), and a privy council (1888), and formally completed in 1889. It involved a bicameral system with an elected lower house and an upper house of peers, but effective power rested with the executive as representatives of the emperor, in whom ultimate power still resided. Although political leaders always experienced difficulties in controlling the lower house (which by 1925 was elected through universal manhood suffrage), policy in the earlier period was usually dominated by a group of highly influential senior statesmen, including such men as Ito

Hirobumi and *Yamagata Aritomo, and later fell under military influence. The old constitution was finally replaced by a new *Japanese Constitution, prepared under US supervision, on 3 May 1947.

Meiji Restoration The restoration of imperial rule in Japan, often defined as the overthrow of the Tokugawa *shogunate in 1868, but sometimes considered to stretch from that date to the formal institution of the new *Meiji Constitution in 1889. The Tokugawa shogunate was faced by increasingly severe internal problems in the first half of the 19th century, and its failure to deal effectively with foreign incursions into Japanese territory resulted in the uniting of opposition forces behind a policy of restoring the emperor to full power. Faced by a powerful alliance of regional forces, the last shogun formally surrendered his powers to the Meiji emperor Mutsuhito, who resumed formal imperial rule in January 1868, moving his capital to Tokyo a year later. Thereafter, the feudal *daimyo and *samurai systems were quickly dismantled, a Western-style constitution introduced, and a policy of government-sponsored industrial development implemented, which would transform Japan into a centralized modern state.

Meir, Golda (born **Goldie Mabovich**) (1898–1978) Israeli stateswoman, Prime Minister (1969–74). Born in Ukraine, she emigrated to the USA in 1907 and in 1921 moved to Palestine, where she became active in the Labour movement. Following Israel's independence she served in ministerial posts (1949–66); having left government in 1966 to build up the Labour Party from disparate socialist factions, she was elected Prime Minister in 1969, retaining her position through coalition rule until her retirement in 1974.

Melanchthon, Philipp (born **Philipp Schwarzerd**) (1497–1560) German Protestant reformer. In 1521 he succeeded Luther as leader of the Reformation movement in Germany. Professor of Greek at Wittenberg, he helped to systematize Martin Luther's teachings in the *Loci Communes* (1521) and drew up the Augsburg Confession (1530).

Melbourne, William Lamb, 2nd Viscount (1779–1848) British Whig statesman, Prime Minister (1834; 1835–41). He was appointed Home Secretary under Lord Grey in 1830, before becoming Premier in 1834. Out of office briefly that year, he subsequently became chief political adviser to Queen Victoria after her accession in 1837. His term was marked by

Chartist and anti-Corn Laws agitation. His wife, Lady Caroline Lamb (1785–1828), whom he married in 1805, had a notorious affair with Lord Byron, but the Lambs separated in 1825, before Lord Melbourne's premiership.

Memphis An ancient city of Egypt, whose ruins are situated on the Nile about 15 km (10 miles) south of Cairo. It is thought to have been founded as the capital of the Old Kingdom of Egypt in c.3100 BC by King Menes, the ruler of the Egyptian dynasty, who united the former kingdoms of Upper and Lower Egypt. Associated with the god Ptah, it remained one of Egypt's principal cities even after Thebes was made capital of the New Kingdom in c.1570 BC. It is the site of the pyramids of Saqqara and Giza and the great sphinx.

Mendès-France, Pierre (1907–82) French statesman. Elected as a Radical-Socialist Deputy in 1932, he was an economics minister in the government of Leon *Blum in 1938. He was imprisoned by the *Vichy government, escaped to London (1941), and joined the exiled Free French government of General *de Gaulle. He became Premier in May 1954, after the disaster of *Dienbienphu, promising that France would pull out of Indo-China. He resigned from the Radical Party in 1959, after which he never had an effective power-base, becoming increasingly opposed to the autocratic use of presidential power by de Gaulle.

Mendoza, Antonio de (c.1490–1552) Spanish colonial administrator. He served as the first viceroy of New Spain (which centred on present-day Mexico City) from 1535 to 1550, and did much to improve relations between Spaniards and American Indians, fostering economic development (especially in mining) and educational opportunities for both groups. From 1551 he was viceroy of Peru.

Menelik II (1844–1913) Emperor of Ethiopia (1889–1913). Originally ruler of Shoa (1863–89), with Italian support he seized the throne after Emperor John IV died. He made the Treaty of Ucciali (1889) with Italy, but when he learnt that the Italian wording of the treaty made Ethiopia a protectorate of Italy, he denounced the agreement. Italy's invasion and subsequent defeat at *Adowa greatly strengthened Menelik's position. He modernized Ethiopia, initiated public education, attempted to abolish slavery, and gave France a railway concession from *Djibouti, which opened up commerce. His conquests doubled the size of the country, and brought south Ethiopia into his domain.

Mengistu Haile Mariam (1937-) Ethiopian soldier and politician; President of Ethiopia (1987–91). An army officer, Mengistu first came to prominence in 1974, when the army staged a successful coup against the regime of Emperor *Haile Selassie. Appointed acting chairman of the provisional army council, he became head of state in a second coup in 1977. With aid from the Soviet Union and Cuba, he made Ethiopia into a Marxist–Leninist republic, ruthlessly suppressing all opposition. He imposed agricultural collectivization and mass deportations. He pursued the war against the breakaway province of *Eritrea, building his forces into the largest army in Africa. In 1984–85 his policies exacerbated one of the worst periods of famine and drought to affect the Horn of Africa, during which many thousands of Ethiopians died. In 1987 Mengistu introduced civilian rule; having banned all but his Workers' Party, he took the Presidency unopposed. After surviving one attempted coup in 1989, his downfall and exile came in May 1991, when a coalition of resistance movements from Eritrea and Tigray, which had made steady advances since the mid-1980s, overran Addis Ababa. In 1995 Mengistu was found guilty *in absentia* of genocide in his native country.

Menon, Krishna (Vengalil Krishnan Krishna Menon) (1896–1974) Indian politician. A prominent spokesman in Britain for the Indian nationalist cause, he served as India's High Commissioner in London (1947–52) as well as India's representative at the United Nations. As Minister of Defence (1957–62) he was heavily criticized for his autocratic decisions and for the defeat in the *Indo-Chinese War of 1962, and he was forced to resign.

Menshevik *See* BOLSHEVIK.

Menzies, Sir Robert Gordon (1894–1978) Australian Liberal statesman, Prime Minister (1939–41; 1949–66). Australia's longest-serving Prime Minister, he implemented policies resulting in fast industrial growth in the 1950s and gave impetus to the development of Australian universities. Menzies was noted for his anti-Communism, making an abortive attempt to abolish the Australian Communist Party in 1951 and actively supporting the USA in the Vietnam War.

mercantilism The 17th-century economic belief that aimed to exploit natural resources fully to promote exports and limit imports. Mercantilists believed that the possession of gold or 'bullion' was all-important and countries without a source of precious metal must obtain it by commerce; a nation's wealth was seen as chiefly dependent on its balance of trade. Trading was controlled by government-backed companies, tariffs were imposed, and trade wars, such as the *Anglo-Dutch Wars were fought. Later supporters of *free trade (laissez-faire) opposed the mercantilist theory that the volume of trade is fixed and that to increase one's share one must lessen that of others. In a celebrated essay of 1752, David *Hume contradicted the mercantilist view, arguing that a country's bullion reserves are essentially determined by the size of its economy and its consequential need for money as a circulating medium, and would not be permanently influenced either way by government interference with trade.

Merchant Adventurer Originally any English merchant who engaged in export trade. A trading company of Merchant Adventurers was incorporated in 1407 and flourished in the 15th and 16th centuries. It derived from loosely organized groups of merchants in the major English ports who sold cloth to continental Europe, especially the Netherlands. They acquired royal *charters in cities such as Bristol (1467) and London (1505) and in their European settlements. They became dominant in England's foreign trade, ousting their rivals, the German merchants of the *Hanseatic League. Until 1564 their principal continental market was in Antwerp, the commercial capital of north-western Europe; from 1611 they made Hamburg their foreign centre, but their main base had long been London. They were the forerunners of the great *chartered companies, and declined in importance in the 18th century.

Merchant Stapler (or member of the Company of the Merchants of the Staple) Any English merchant who traded in wool through the *wool staple at Calais, the fixed place for its marketing in continental Europe from the 13th to 16th century. The setting up of the Staple (which had between 26 and 38 members) had the effect of keeping down the price paid for wool in England, and thus of encouraging the rise of the English cloth industry and its merchants, such as the Clothworkers and *Merchant Adventurers. However, the Merchant Staplers were pre-eminent in English overseas trade well into the 16th century as a result of their monopoly in the trading of wool.

Mercia A former kingdom of central England. It was established by invading Angles in the 6th century AD in the border areas between the new Anglo-Saxon settlements in the east and the Celtic regions in the west. Becoming dominant in the 8th century under *Offa, it expanded to cover an area stretching from the Humber to the south coast. Its decline began after Offa's death in 796 and in 926, when *Athelstan became king of all England, it finally lost its separate identity. In modern times the name has been revived, for example, in the 'West Mercia Authority', an area of police administration covering the counties of Hereford and Worcester, and Shropshire.

Mercier, Honoré (1840–94) French-Canadian statesman. He opposed Confederation (1867) of the British North American provinces and founded (1871) the Parti National to represent the French element in Canada. He served in the Canadian House of Commons from 1872 to 1874. Elected to the legislative assembly of the province of Quebec in 1879, he became leader of the Liberal Party of Quebec in 1883, and in 1886, in the wake of the *Riel Rebellion, defeated the Conservatives to become Premier of Quebec. His immense popularity was eventually undermined by charges of corruption in connection with railroad subsidies, and in 1891 he was dismissed from office and defeated in the subsequent election. The new government acquitted Mercier of the charges.

Mercosur (Portuguese name **Mercosul**) A regional trade organization in South America, whose full title is the Southern Cone or South American Common Market. Founded in March 1991, with the aim of creating a common market in the area, Mercosur's member states were Argentina, Brazil, Paraguay, and Uruguay. Following protracted negotiations on tariffs, the final presidential accord to create the customs union was signed on 17 December 1994 and Mercosur was inaugurated on 1 January 1995. Chile joined as an associate member in 1996. Mercosur and the European Union signed a cooperation agreement in 1995 and pledged to open negotiations on the eventual creation of a Mercosur–EU free trade zone. In 2004 Mercosur concluded a cooperation agreement with the *Andean Community that aimed to merge the two organizations into a South American Community of Nations. As a result, most members of the Andean Community—Bolivia, Columbia, Ecuador, and Peru—became associate members of Mercosur; Venezuela, however, became a full member in 2005.

Meredith incident (1962) An episode in the US *civil rights struggle. Officials of the state of Mississippi defied a federal court order requiring the University of Mississippi to allow a Black man, James Meredith, to enrol as a student. The governor made defiant statements, thus encouraging thousands of segregationists to attack the federal marshals assigned to protect Meredith as he entered the university. President *Kennedy sent in national guardsmen and regular army troops to restore peace, enforce the court's orders, and secure the entry of Meredith as the university's first Black student.

Merkel, Angela (Dorothea) (1954–) German stateswoman; Chancellor (2005–). Born in Hamburg, Merkel was raised in East Germany. She entered politics during the collapse of communism in 1989 and served in East Germany's government in 1990 before being elected to the federal parliament on reunification as a Christian Democrat. She was a minister under Helmut *Kohl (1991–98) and became parliamentary leader of the Christian Democrats in 2002. Following the close elections of 2005, she became Chancellor in a "grand coalition" with the Social Democrats—the first woman and the first former East German to hold this post. She remained in office following further electoral victories in 2009 and 2013.

Merovingians A dynasty of kings of the *Franks, named after Mérovée (died 458), the grandfather of *Clovis. The Merovingians were warriors rather than administrators, few of them showing any interest in government. After the death of Dagobert I in 638, power passed from the kings to the 'mayors of the palace'. The mayor of the palace was originally the head of the royal household and came to represent royal authority in the country, administer the royal domains, and command the army in the king's absence. The most notable mayors of the palace were Pepin (ruled 687–714), *Charles Martel (ruled 714–41), famous for his victories over *Saracen invaders from Spain, and *Pepin, the father of *Charlemagne, who in 751 deposed the last of the Merovingian kings and usurped the throne.

Mesolithic The Middle Stone Age, a transitional period between the *Palaeolithic and *Neolithic ages. Its people were the hunting and gathering groups that existed about 10,000 years ago as the climate became warmer at the end of the last Ice Age. In western Europe, Mesolithic hunting societies continued to exist at the same time as Neolithic farming groups further east.

Mesopotamia An ancient region of southwest Asia in present-day Iraq, lying between the rivers Tigris and Euphrates. Its alluvial plains were the site of the ancient civilizations of Akkad, Sumer, Babylonia, and Assyria, now lying within Iraq.

Mesopotamia Campaign (World War I) A British military campaign against the Ottoman Turks in Mesopotamia (southern Iraq). In 1913 Britain had acquired the Abadan oilfield of Persia (now Iran), and when war broke out in 1914, it was concerned to protect both the oilfields and the route to India. When Turkey joined the war in October 1914, British and Indian troops occupied Basra in Mesopotamia. They began to advance towards Baghdad, but were halted and suffered the disaster of *Kut. General Sir Frederick Maude recaptured Kut in February 1917, entering Baghdad on 11 March. One contingent of British troops reached the oilfields of Baku (May 1918), which it occupied until September, when the Turks reoccupied the area. A further contingent moved up the River Euphrates to capture Ramadi (September 1917) and another up the River Tigris as far as Tikrit (July 1918), before advancing on Mosul. Meanwhile from Egypt General Sir Edmund *Allenby was driving north into Palestine and Syria, aided by Arab partisans organized and led by T. E. *Lawrence, a campaign that resulted in the military collapse of Turkey in October 1918. After the armistice of Mudros (30 October), British troops briefly reoccupied Baku (November 1918–August 1919), aiming to deprive the *Bolsheviks of its oil and to use it as a base in the *Russian Civil War. Britain had now occupied all Mesopotamia, and for a brief while considered the possibility of creating a single British dominion, consisting of Palestine, Jordan, Iraq, and Iran, linking Egypt with India and providing a bulwark against Bolshevism.

Mesopotamian technology See EGYPTIAN AND MESOPOTAMIAN TECHNOLOGY.

Metaxas, Ioannis (1871–1941) Greek general and statesman. He became chief of staff in the Greek army, but was exiled (1917) when Greece joined the Allies in World War I. He returned (1920), and, after leading a coup, was exiled again (1923–24). A strong monarchist, he held several ministerial posts from 1928 to 1936. With royal approval he dissolved Parliament

and became dictator of Greece (1936–41). Under him a united country successfully repelled an Italian invasion in 1940, but in 1941 Hitler's forces intervened and occupied Greece.

Methodism See PROTESTANTISM.

Metternich, Klemens Wenzel Nepomuk Lothar, Prince of Metternich-Winneburg-Beilstein (1773–1859) Austrian statesman. As Foreign Minister (1809–48), he was one of the organizers of the Congress of Vienna (1814–15), which devised the settlement of Europe after the Napoleonic Wars. He pursued policies that reflected his reactionary conservatism at home and abroad until forced to resign during the revolutions of 1848.

Mexican–American War (1846–48) A conflict between the USA and Mexico. Hostilities between the two countries began shortly after the USA annexed (1845) the Mexican state of Texas and sought to expand the boundaries of the state to include still more territory. In the ensuing war General Stephen Kearny took over the New Mexico territory and Captain John *Frémont annexed the California territory almost without a fight. In northern Mexico stiffer opposition was encountered as General Zachary *Taylor invaded Mexico across the Rio Grande and defeated General Antonio López de Santa Anna in the bloody Battle of Buena Vista (22–23 February 1847). The fiercest fighting occurred in central Mexico. General Winfield Scott's order of a mortar bombardment of Vera Cruz resulted in the deaths of hundreds of civilians. The US army then moved inland to Mexico City, where hotly contested engagements were fought at Molino del Rey, and Chapultepec Hill (12–13 September 1847). The US capture of the capital city (1847) occasioned the Mexican surrender. The Treaty of Guadalupe Hidalgo (1848) ended hostilities. By the terms of the treaty the USA confirmed its claim to Texas and gained control of the area, which would later become the states of New Mexico, Arizona, and California (where gold had recently been discovered). The USA agreed to pay Mexico 15 million dollars in return.

Mexican Revolution (1910–40) A period of political and social turmoil in *Mexico. The roots of the revolution can be traced to the demographic, economic, and social changes that occurred during the rule of President Porfirio *Díaz, known as the Porfiriato (1876–1911). The regime became increasingly centralized and authoritarian, favouring Mexico's traditional and newly emerging élites, but failing to incorporate growing urban middle-class and labour groups into national politics. In 1910 Francisco *Madero, the leader of the Anti-Re-electionist movement, received an enthusiastic response to his call to arms to overthrow the dictator. Although Díaz resigned in May 1911 and Madero was elected President, he failed to satisfy either his radical supporters or his Porfirian enemies, and was assassinated in a counter-revolutionary coup led by General Victoriano *Huerta in 1913. Huerta was defeated by an arms embargo, diplomatic hostility from the USA, and a coalition of revolutionary factions led by Emiliano *Zapata, Pancho *Villa, Venustiano *Carranza, and Alvaro Obregon. The victorious revolutionaries split into Constitutionalists (Carranza and Obregon), who sought to reform the 1857 Liberal Constitution, and Conventionists (Zapata and Villa) who wished to implement the radical proposals of the convention of Aguascalientes (1914). The civil war which ensued was protracted and bitter. In February 1917 the reformed Constitution was promulgated. However, the document was largely ignored, and Carranza's procrastination prompted his overthrow and assassination in 1920. Mexico's new revolutionary leaders faced the difficult tasks of economic regeneration and the reconstitution of central political authority, but were hampered by strong opposition from the Catholic Church. Tension culminated in the so-called War of the Cristeros (1928–30), in which thousands of Christian peasants arose in protest against the new "godless" state, and were finally defeated at the battle of Reforma (1930). When President Avila Camacho (1940–46) was elected, a period of consolidation and reconciliation began, marking the end of the revolution.

Mexico

Capital:	Mexico City
Area:	1,964,375 sq km (758,449 sq miles)
Population:	116,220,947 (2013 est)
Currency:	1 peso = 100 centavos
Religions:	Roman Catholic 82.7%; Pentecostal 1.6%; Jehovah's Witnesses 1.4%
Ethnic Groups:	Mestizo 60.0%; Amerindian 30.0%; White 9.0%
Languages:	Spanish (official); Amerindian languages
International Organizations:	UN; OAS; NAFTA; OECD; WTO

A country lying partly on the North American continent, bordering on the USA in the north, and partly in Central America, bordering on Guatemala and Belize in the south, with extensive coastlines on the Atlantic and Pacific Oceans.

Physical Geographically, Mexico divides into several distinct areas. The Isthmus of Tehuantepec, together with the curving eastern coastal plain and the north-eastward-thrusting Yucatán Peninsula, constitutes the main lowland area. In the far north-west, the splinter-like peninsula of Lower California, with its high sierras, is a southward extension of the Sierra Nevada. So also is the mountainous western Sierra Madre on the mainland, while the eastern Sierra Madre is an extension of the Rocky Mountains. The narrow coastal plain facing the Pacific Ocean in the west is largely covered by forests. Between the mountains lie high plateaux where, in the more temperate climate, cacti grow. There are several large lakes, saline in the north but fresh in the south, from which streams run in torrents through deeply cut canyons.

Economy Mexico is the tenth-largest world exporter of crude oil, and oil revenues have been used to develop an industrial base. Economic liberalization in the 1990s has also stimulated growth. Principal industries include food and drink, tobacco, chemicals, iron and steel, crude oil production, and mining; exports include manufactured goods, oil and oil products, and silver. The main food crop is maize, and export crops include fruit, vegetables, and coffee. Mexico concluded the *North American Free Trade Agreement with the USA and Canada in 1993, and its economy is closely tied to the USA. Despite Mexico's progress, poverty is widespread and large numbers of illegal emigrants enter the USA annually across the northern border in search of work.

History In prehistory Mexico formed the greater part of ancient Mesoamerica, within which arose a succession of related civilizations which shared many cultural traits: socio-political organization based on cities; ceremonial plazas of pyramids, platforms, and temples;

similar deities; calendrical systems; long-distance trading; and the ritual ball game. Some of these were the *Olmec (Gulf Coast), *Maya (Yucatán), Teotihuacán (Central Valley), Zapotec and Mixtec (Oaxaca), *Toltec (North Central), western cultures, and *Aztecs.

The conquest of the Aztec empire by *Cortés was complete by 1521, and New Spain became the first Spanish-American viceroyalty, eventually including all of ancient Mesoamerica, northern Mexico, the Caribbean, and most of the south-western USA. A rigid colonial administration, including repression and exploitation of the native population, lasted for the next 300 years. By the early 17th century, as many as 90% of the indigenous population had died of European-introduced diseases, and thereafter their numbers only slowly increased.

In the early 19th century, inspired by French revolutionary ideas, an independence movement developed, led by two priests, Miguel Hidalgo y Costilla and José Maria Morelos y Pavón, both of whom were captured and shot by the Spanish authorities (1810 and 1814). In 1821 Augustín de Iturbide briefly created an independent Mexican empire, which included the captaincy-general of *Guatemala. Following his exile (1823), the first Mexican constitution was proclaimed (1824), based on the US constitution. Two parties, the Federalist and the Centralists, quickly appeared, and in 1833 the liberal federalist Antonio López de Santa Anna emerged as President. He was not able to prevent the declaration of independence of *Texas (1836) nor the *Mexican–American War (1846–48), which resulted in the loss of huge territories, added to by the Gadsden Purchase of Arizona in 1853. A period of reform followed, and a new constitution (1857) was promulgated. But economic difficulties and French imperialist dreams resulted in the imposition by troops of *Napoleon III of the Habsburg prince *Maximilian as emperor (1864–67). When French troops were withdrawn, Maximilian was defeated, captured, and shot. There followed the long dictatorship of Porfirio *Díaz (1876–1910) and then the prolonged Mexican Revolution (1910–40). The Partido Revolucionario Institucional (PRI; the Institutional Revolutionary Party) monopolized political power from its foundation in 1929 until 2000. Under President Miguel Alemán (1946–52), the process of reconciliation begun by his predecessor, Avilo Camacho, continued. Since then democratic governments have continued to follow moderate policies, while seeking further to modernize the economy, bolstered by oil revenues. During the presidency of Miguel de la Madrid Hurtado

(1982–88) Mexico was faced by a fall in oil prices, a massive national debt, and one of the fastest growing birth-rates in the world. The 1988 elections were again won by the PRI with Carlos Salinas de Gortari as President. He continued the austerity programme initiated by his predecessor, but at the same time entered into discussions with Canada and the USA, leading to the North American Free Trade Agreement, which was ratified in 1993. In early 1995 there was an armed uprising in the poverty-stricken state of Chiapas, led by an Indian guerrilla group, the *Zapatista National Liberation Army, which demanded social and economic reforms. A peace agreement was reached in 1995 but some unrest continues. The PRI candidate, Ernesto Zedillo, was elected President in August 1994 amid allegations by the opposition of electoral fraud. In 2000 the opposition candidate, Vicente Fox Quesada, was elected President, ending the PRI's long political dominance. He was followed by Felipe Calderón in 2006 before the PRI regained the Presidency with Enrique Peña Nieto in 2012. The major challenge to Mexico in the 2000s was the increasing power and violence of gangs that trafficked illegal drugs into the USA, which in some areas overshadowed the power of the state. In 2006 Calderón deployed the Mexican army against the drug gangs, beginning the so-called 'Mexican Drug War'. This brutal conflict led to over 47,000 deaths by 2011 without a resolution.

Michael VIII Palaeologus (*c.*1225–82) Byzantine emperor (1259–82). He usurped the throne of the young emperor of *Nicaea, John IV, for whom he had been regent. He then recovered Constantinople and returned the Byzantine capital there, and was crowned Byzantine emperor. He attempted to reconcile the two branches of the church at Constantinople and Rome, though a voluntary union between them agreed at the Council of Lyons (1274) was for immediate political purposes and only lasted until 1289. His great rival was Charles I of Anjou and Naples; after the *Sicilian Vespers (1282) Angevin power was reduced and Michael's successor, Andronicus, withdrew from the union with Rome, no longer needing the pope as an ally.

Micronesia, Federated States of

Capital:	Palikir (on Pohnpei)
Area:	702 sq km (271 sq miles)
Population:	106,104 (2013 est)
Currency:	1 US dollar = 100 cents

Religions:	Roman Catholic 52.7%; Protestant 41.7%
Ethnic Groups:	Chuukese 48.8%; Pohnpeian 24.2%; Kosraean 6.2%; Yapese 5.2%
Languages:	English (official); Micronesian languages
International Organizations:	UN

A country in the west Pacific Ocean, comprising a group of islands divided into four states: Yap, Chuuk (formerly Truk), Pohnpei (formerly Ponape), and Kosrae.

Physical The Federated States of Micronesia forms part of the Caroline Islands group, one of the archipelagos east of the Philippines. The islands are low coral caps surmounting submerged extinct volcanoes. The climate is tropical, and the area is prone to typhoons.

Economy Economic activity is dominated by the government, which employs two-thirds of the labour force and is funded largely by US aid. Other principle activities are subsistence farming and fishing, with the main exports including fish, clothing, bananas, and black pepper. There is some tourism.

History The first settlers on the islands were probably Melanesians who arrived in about 1500 BC. Micronesia was colonized by Spain in the 17th century and was sold to Germany in 1898. The islands were occupied by Japan from 1914 until their capture by American forces in 1944. In 1947 Micronesia became part of the UN Trust Territory of the Pacific Islands, administered by the USA. From 1965 there were increasing demands for autonomy and Micronesia became independent in 1979. The US administration was not formally ended until 1986 and was not ratified by the UN until 1990. A compact of free association was signed with the USA in 1982, giving the USA responsibility for Micronesia's defence.

Middle Ages The period in Europe from c.700 to c.1500. The decline of the Roman empire in the West and the period of barbarian invasions in the 5th and 6th centuries (*Dark Ages) was followed by the emergence of separate kingdoms and the development of forms of government. The coronation of *Charlemagne in AD 800 is held to mark the end of anarchy and the revival of civilization and learning. England, under *Alfred, similarly saw the encouragement of learning and the establishment of monastic houses. Territorial expansion by *Vikings and *Normans throughout Europe in the 9th and 10th centuries, initially violent and disruptive, led to their assimilation into local populations. Trade and urban life revived.

The High Middle Ages (12th and 13th centuries) saw a growth in the power of the papacy, which led to clashes between the pope and secular rulers over their respective spheres of jurisdiction. The creation of new monastic orders encouraged scholarship and architecture. The obsession with pilgrimage to holy shrines was the impetus behind the *Crusades, in which thousands of Christian knights went to Palestine to fight the Muslims and convert them to Christianity. Society was organized on a military basis, the *feudal system, in which land was held in return for military service. But although war dominated this period, it also saw the growth of trade (notably the English wool trade), the foundation of universities, and the flowering of scholarship, notably in philosophy and theology (*scholasticism). Gothic art and architecture had its finest expression in the cathedrals built from the 12th century for the following 300–400 years.

During the 13th and 14th centuries various factors combined to cause social and economic unrest. The *Black Death, and the *Hundred Years War between France and England, resulted in a falling population and the beginnings of anticlericalism. In the 15th and 16th centuries the *Renaissance in Italy marked a new spirit of sceptical enquiry and the end of the medieval period.

Midlothian Campaigns (1879–80) A series of speeches by William *Gladstone to mass audiences in Britain, marking a new phase in party electioneering. Queen Victoria and *Disraeli, the Conservative Prime Minister, regarded these new tactics as unconstitutional, but it helped the Liberals to win a large majority in the general election of 1880. The campaigns recognized the importance of the new mass electorate created by the 1867 *Reform Act, and of the growing influence of newspaper reports of political speeches. Before setting out by train from London to the Edinburgh constituency of Midlothian, Gladstone addressed the crowds, repeating this at stations where the train stopped. The climax came in speeches at Edinburgh and other Scottish cities in which he strongly criticized the government. He gained the

Midlothian seat from the Conservative, Lord Dalkeith.

Mihailovich, Draza (1893–1946) Serbian army officer who, after the fall of Yugoslavia in World War II, organized royalist partisans against German forces. He structured his forces into bands (četa, prounced cheta), and these became known as chetniks. Their relations with the communist partisans of *Tito was uneasy. After Tito gained power, Mihailovich was tried and shot for collaboration with Germans and war crimes.

Miletus One of the leading Ionian cities of Asia Minor. It established a number of colonies on the Hellespont and Black Sea coasts in the 7th and 6th centuries BC, and traded widely. It continued to thrive even after coming within *Croesus' sphere of influence, and in 499 led the revolt of the Ionians against Persia. After its final defeat in 494 it was razed, and never thereafter recovered its former power. It revolted from the Athenian empire in 412, but then came under Persian control. The city's economic decline was hastened by the silting up of the harbour while it was part of the Roman empire.

militia A military force composed of citizens, enlisted or conscripted in times of emergency, usually for local defence. In England, it developed during the Middle Ages from the Anglo-Saxon fyrd. Its forces were usually raised by impressment (forcible recruiting), and until the 16th century it was supervised by the local sheriff. Then the Lord Lieutenants were given the responsibility until the later 19th century.

Modern militias fulfil a variety of roles. Although generally restricted to infantry or light-armoured roles on land, in certain cases (for example, the US National Guard), they are deployed in air and coastal defence. Such countries as Israel, Switzerland, the former Yugoslavia, and Sweden have based much of their defence planning on the use of militia units, and people's militias were a feature of former communist states, such as East Germany and Czechoslovakia. Militia forces can also play an important role in internal conflicts, where they may be raised and controlled by factions; in such cases, the dividing line between militia and *guerrilla forces can be blurred.

millenarianism (or **millennialism**) The belief in the imminent end of the present world order and the establishment of a new and radically different one. Millenarian movements, which are found all over the world in many different societies, usually occur at times of change and upheaval. The millenarian idea that divine intervention will bring about a reversal of worldly expectations resulting in an earthly paradise, tends to appeal to those who are dispossessed both culturally and economically. Much millenarianism has its roots in the Jewish expectation of the coming of the Messiah. It takes its name from the early Christians' anticipation of Christ's Second Coming, to be followed by a millennium, or thousand-year reign of peace and tranquillity. In Christianity, the early expectation of Christ's imminent return to this world was replaced by the theologian St *Augustine of Hippo's allegorical model of an other-worldly City of God. Millenarian Christian beliefs thereafter became associated with dissident sects, and are expressed today in the beliefs of sects such as the Jehovah's Witnesses, Seventh Day Adventists, Christadelphians, and *Mormons. In Islam, Shiite Muslims and sects such as the *Druse await the return of the hidden *imam* or *mahdi*; in the Islamic Republic of Iran, the spiritual leader, the *Walī Faqīh*, is stated to be the leader in the absence of the *mahdi*. The *Baha'i religion originates from a millenarian proclamation in 1844, the 1000th anniversary of the hidden *imam*'s disappearance. For many Jews, the establishment of the state of Israel was the fulfilment of millenarian beliefs (*see* ZIONISM), and the Afro-Caribbean *Rastafarian cult envisages the Black people's repatriation to Africa. Millenarian beliefs are less prominent in Buddhism, but in Hinduism, Kalki, the last avatar (incarnation) of Vishnu, is expected to destroy the degeneration of this age and instigate a new cosmic era.

Miloševic, Slobodan (1941–2006) Serbian politician; President of Serbia (1989–97) and of the Yugoslav Federal Republic (1997–2000). Miloševic trained as a lawyer and became director of the Belgrade Bank in 1978. He was elected as First Secretary of the Serbian Communist (later Socialist) Party in 1987 and won the presidential election in the republic two years later. A champion of Serbian hegemony over the constituent republics of the former *Yugoslavia, Miloševic organized the intervention of the Yugoslav federal army in Slovenia and Croatia (1991–92) and supported the secession of the Bosnian Serbs that began the war in *Bosnia and Herzegovina (1992–95), with its 'ethnic cleansing' policies. As a result he achieved isolation from the international community and the collapse of the Serbian economy. Serbia's subsequent policy of oppression, ethnic cleansing, and genocide against the majority Albanian population in the province of

Kosovo led NATO to unleash a devastating series of bombing raids against Yugoslavia from March to June 1999, when Serbia effectively capitulated. Defeated in the presidential elections of 2000, Milošević at first refused to relinquish power; however, he conceded defeat following massive demonstrations. He was arrested in 2001 on charges of corruption, but subsequently extradited to face war crimes charges before the International Criminal Tribunal for the former Yugoslavia at The Hague. His trial began in 2002 and was still in progress when he died.

Minamoto Yoritomo (1147–99) Japanese general, founder of the *Kamakura shogunate. His family, like their rivals, the Taira, had risen to prominence when imperial factions called for military support. In 1160 the Taira, having slain his father, placed him under the surveillance of their *Hojo kinsmen. Taira power reached its zenith in 1180 when Taira Kiyomori made his infant grandson, Antoku, emperor. However, by 1185 Yoritomo was master of Japan. The victories that swept him to power were won largely by his younger brother, Yoshitsune, later enshrined in history and legend as a tragic hero. After destroying the Taira's Inland Sea bases he annihilated their fleet on 25 April 1185 at Danno-ura at the southern tip of Honshu. Antoku was drowned.

In 1192 another child-emperor appointed Yoritomo as the first *shogun, whereupon he set up his military administration in Kamakura, which effectively became the central government of Japan. Yoshitsune and other Minamoto rivals had already been killed on Yoritomo's orders, but his supporters were given estates and were to become the basis of the *daimyo. On Yoritomo's death Hojo Tokimasa, whose daughter had married Yoritomo, made himself regent. By 1219 Yoritomo's own line was extinct.

Minden, Battle of (1 August 1759) A battle in the *Seven Years War. A French army seized the town of Minden, a German city guarding access to Hanover, but was surrounded by a large force of British, Hanoverian, and Hessian troops under Prince Ferdinand of Brunswick. On 1 August the French were severely defeated and Hanover was saved. This was the only pitched battle in which British troops were involved during the Seven Years War.

Mindszenty, József (born József Pehm) (1892–1975) Hungarian prelate. He was imprisoned by the Hungarian puppet government (1944–45) and was sentenced to penal servitude for life, commuted to house detention. Freed at the time of the *Hungarian Revolution, on the return of Soviet forces, he sought refuge in the US Legation in Budapest, staying there until 1971.

Ming The Chinese dynasty founded in 1368 by Chu Yuan-chang after the collapse of Mongol authority in China, and ruling until succeeded by the Manchus in 1644. It was a period of expansion and exploration, with lasting contact made in the 16th century between China and Europe, and a culturally productive period in which the arts flourished. The capital was established at Peking (Beijing) in 1421.

Minghuang (or **Xuanzong**) (684–762) *Tang Emperor of China (712–56). He came to the throne when the Tang were at their zenith. An army he dispatched to prevent the Tibetans joining with the Arabs crossed the Pamirs and reached the Hindu Kush. In 745 the emperor took as his consort Yang Guifei, formerly his son's concubine, and began to neglect his imperial duties. In 751 the Arabs defeated the Chinese at the Talas River, resulting in the loss of earlier Tang gains in Central Asia. In 755 An Lushan, a general Yang Guifei favoured, rebelled and took Luoyang. The court fled from Chang'an, Yang was executed, and the emperor abdicated. The revolt, which dragged on until 763, was suppressed only by calling in Uighur troops from Central Asia.

Minoan civilization The earliest civilization on European soil, centred on Crete (c.3000–1100 BC), it was first revealed by the excavations of Sir Arthur Evans, who gave it its name, based on the legendary King Minos. It had reached its zenith by the beginning of the late Bronze Age, extending over the islands of the south Aegean while its wares were exported to Cyprus, Syria, and Egypt. Urban centres were dominated by palaces such as those at Knossos, Mallia, Phaistos, and Zakro. Divided into two periods by a devastating earthquake that occurred c.1700 BC, the Minoan civilization was noted particularly for its Linear A script and distinctive palatial art and architecture. It greatly influenced the later Mycenacans, whose presence in Crete is attested from the 16th century BC and who succeeded the Minoans in control of the Aegean c.1400 BC.

minutemen American Revolutionary militiamen ready at a minute's notice to take up arms in defence of their property or country. Minutemen distinguished themselves in local short-term skirmishes and guerrilla actions such as *Lexington and Concord, but proved so unreliable in long campaigns and pitched battles that George *Washington turned to long-term recruits. The Second Amendment to the *Constitution of the USA, guaranteeing the right to bear arms, is said to owe its enactment to the "minuteman philosophy".

Mirabeau, Honoré Gabriel Riqueti, Comte de (1749–91) French revolutionary politician. Mirabeau rose to prominence in the early days of the French Revolution, when he became deputy of the Third Estate in the States General. His moderate political stance led him to press for a form of constitutional monarchy; he was made President of the National Assembly in 1791, but died shortly afterwards.

Miranda, Francisco de (1750–1816) South American revolutionary. He was a Creole born in Caracas, who received a commission in the Spanish army and fought against the British in Florida and the West Indies during the American Revolution. When that conflict ended with the independence of the 13 colonies he dedicated himself to the advancement of the same cause on the South American continent. From 1783 until his death he was the most active promoter of the idea of Spanish American independence. More successful as a political propagandist than as a military leader, he was ultimately captured by Spanish forces and died in a Cádiz prison.

Mississippi cultures A group of interrelated Native American cultures in the central and lower Mississippi valley from c.700 to 1700 AD. Three principal new features distinguish them from the preceding *Hopewell cultures. Most famous are the huge politico-religious centres of pyramidal, flat topped, earthen temple mounds, which were part of special religious practices, known as the Southern cult. They were surrounded by the wattle-and-daub houses of farmers. Inspiration for these ceremonial centres was ultimately derived from the cultures of Mexico (Mesoamerica), but exactly how is unclear. Famous sites include Cahokia (Illinois), Aztalan (Wisconsin), and Macon (Georgia), with vast mound complexes, the last two fortified. A second feature was the much decreased importance of burial mounds, and a third was the appearance of completely new pottery styles, also showing indirect Mesoamerican influence.

Missouri Compromise (1820–21) A series of measures passed by the US Congress to end controversy over the extension of slavery in the territories beyond existing state boundaries. It was agreed that Maine would enter the Union of the United States as a free state and Missouri as a slave state and that slavery would be prohibited elsewhere in the *Louisiana Purchase north of 36° 30′. This held out to the South the prospect of Florida and Arkansas being admitted as slave states, while securing the greater proportion of unsettled territory to the free North. The Compromise of 1820 temporarily laid the issue of slavery to rest, but the drawing of precise geographical lines between slave and non-slave areas led to fresh divisions.

Mitchel, John See YOUNG IRELAND.

Mithras The central figure of **Mithraism**, a cult popular among Roman soldiers of the later empire. Scholars are divided as to whether there is real continuity between this cult and the reverence for 'Mithra', an Indo-Iranian creator Sun-god, shown in much earlier scriptures of *Hinduism and Zoroastrianism. The Roman cult focused on secret rituals in cave sanctuaries devoted to sculptures of Mithras killing a cosmic bull. Initiates underwent severe tests, which demonstrated the cult's concern with the soldierly virtues of courage and fortitude. Women were excluded. Mithraism flourished along the empire's frontiers–the rivers Danube, and Rhine, and in Britain–but finally succumbed to the challenge of Christianity.

Mithridates VI (or **Mithradates VI**) (c.132–63 BC) King of Pontus (120–63). His expansionist policies led to a war with Rome (88–85), during which he occupied most of Asia Minor and much of Greece, until driven back by Sulla. Two further wars followed (83–82; 74–66); he was defeated by the Roman general Lucullus (c.110–c.57) and finally by Pompey.

Mitterrand, François (Maurice Marie) (1916–96) French statesman, President (1981–95). After working to strengthen the Left alliance, Mitterrand became First Secretary of the new Socialist Party in 1971. As President he initially moved to raise basic wages, increase social benefits, nationalize key industries, and decentralize government. After the Socialist Party lost its majority vote in the 1986 general election, Mitterrand asked the right-wing politician Jacques Chirac to serve as Prime Minister. Mitterrand was re-elected as President in 1988 and served until his retirement due to ill-health in 1995. He died the following year.

Mixtec A people of the mountainous regions of Oaxaca, Mexico. Several of their historical codices survive, from which their dynastic history can be traced back to 692 AD, including their famous king Eight-Dear-Tiger-Claw. By c.1000 AD they had formed a loose confederation of city-states and in the 14th century began to infiltrate the valley of Oaxaca where they sometimes fought, and sometimes mixed with, the Zapotec culture there.

Mizuno Tadakuni (1793–1851) Japanese statesman and reformer. As Chief Senior Councillor to the Tokugawa *shogunate, Mizuno responded to the crisis engendered by famine, insurrection, and foreign pressure in the 1830s by instituting a comprehensive programme of social, political, and economic measures known collectively as the Tempo reform. He introduced strict price controls, abolished restrictive merchant guilds, and attempted to bring outlying lands under direct government control through a land requisition scheme. Opposition to the last measure led to Mizuno being driven from office in 1845.

Mobutu, Sese Seko (full name **Mobutu Sese Seko Kuku Ngbendu Wa Za Banga**) (1930–97) Zaïrean statesman, President (1970–97). After seizing power in a military coup (1965), he changed his original name (Joseph-Désiré Mobutu) as part of his policy of Africanizing names; in 1971 he changed the name of his country (until then and since 1997 known as the Democratic Republic of Congo) to Zaïre. He remained in power despite opposition from tribal groups and small farmers until he was deposed by rebels led by Laurent Kabila in 1997.

Mochica (or **Moche**) A culture that developed (c.200–700 AD) in the Moche and Chicam valleys of *Peru. The earliest major civilization on the northern coast, it expanded into adjacent valleys, but was eventually eclipsed by the Huari culture to the south. Its rulers built huge pyramids of adobe bricks, known as Huaca del Sol (Temple of the Sun) and Huaca de la Luna (Temple of the Moon), south of Trujillo, which were painted with polychrome murals. They also constructed extensive irrigation works and fortifications round their ceremonial centres. Craftsmen mass-produced pottery bottles and bowls, including fine-quality water jars, painted with a variety of religious, military, and everyday scenes and its metal-smiths produced cast, alloyed, and gilded artefacts.

Model Parliament The English Parliament summoned by *Edward I (November 1295) and subsequently idealized as the model for all parliaments since it was supposed to be truly

representative of the people. In addition to earls (seven attended), barons (41), archbishops, bishops, abbots (70), heads of religious houses, two knights from each shire, two representatives from every city or borough, Edward called representatives of the lower clergy (one from each cathedral chapter, two from each diocese). The 'model' was hardly effective. Knights and burgesses did not attend regularly until the mid-14th century. Representatives of religious houses disappeared at the Reformation. The lower clergy preferred their own parliament, Convocation.

Moguls (or **Mughals**) A Muslim dynasty of mixed Mongol and Turkish descent, which invaded India in 1526, expanded over most of the subcontinent except the extreme south, and ruled in strength until the early 18th century. The first emperor was *Babur (1483–1530). He was succeeded by a line of remarkable emperors: *Humayun, *Akbar, *Jahangir, *Shah Jahan, and *Aurangzeb. They created a strong administration for the rapidly growing empire, and the official attitude of conciliation towards the majority Hindu population encouraged religious harmony. Culturally, the introduction of the Persian language and Persian artistic styles led to a distinctive Indo-Muslim style in miniature painting and architecture, the legacy remaining today in the tombs and palaces of Delhi, and Agra, and several other cities of India and Pakistan.

Internal and external pressure accelerated the weakening of central power during the 18th century. Rival court factions undermined the position of less capable rulers, allowing provincial governors to seize local power. The abandonment of conciliatory religious policies encouraged a resurgence of Hindu power, notably among the *Marathas. Hostile invasions from central Asia revealed the hollowness of the dynasty's claim to all-India hegemony, so that by 1803, when Delhi fell to the *East India Company, all real power had already been lost. For another half-century they enjoyed a 'twilight era' as nominal 'kings of Delhi', dependent on British goodwill, but in 1857 the last Mogul king was exiled and the title abolished.

Mohawk A subgroup of the Native American Iroquois tribe originally found in New York state and Canada.

Mohenjo-Daro An ancient city of the civilization of the Indus Valley (c.2600–1700 BC), now a major archaeological site in Pakistan, south-west of Sukkur. It was first excavated by the Indian Archaeological Survey under Sir John Marshall in 1922 and 1931.

Mohicans *See* MAHICANS.

Moi, Daniel arap (1924–) Kenyan states-man, President of Kenya (1978–2002). Originally a teacher, Moi was a founder of the Kenya Africa National Union (KANU). He oversaw the transition to multiparty politics in Kenya in the early 1990s and was twice re-elected.

Moldova

Capital:	Chisinau
Area:	33,851 sq km (13,070 sq miles)
Population:	3,619,925 (2013 est)
Currency:	1 leu = 100 bani
Religions:	Eastern Orthodox 98.0%; Jewish 1.5%
Ethnic Groups:	Moldovan (Romanian) 78.2%; Ukrainian 8.4%; Russian 5.8%
Languages:	Moldovan (Romanian; official); Russian; minority languages
International Organizations:	UN; OSCE; Commonwealth of Independent States; Euro-Atlantic Partnership Council; Council of Europe; WTO

A country in eastern Europe bounded on the north, east, and south by Ukraine, and on the west by Romania. Wider Moldova comprises lands between the Carpathian Mountains in the west and the Dneister River in the east, including the north-east of modern Romania.

Physical The Prut River waters the western part of Moldova, Bessarabia. Although landlocked, its proximity to the Black Sea gives it a mild climate. From the north into the centre runs a belt of hills with deep valleys in which vines and fruit trees flourish. Further south are low-lying steppes supporting grain, sugar beet, and to-bacco.

Economy Moldova's mineral resources are meagre, but the soil is fertile and agriculture prospers, with viticulture, fruits and vegetables,

and tobacco. Industry concentrates on food processing, machinery, domestic appliances, clothing, and textiles; food products, textiles, and machinery are the principle exports. Expatriate remittances are important.

History Moldova at one time formed part of Bessarabia, control over which was long disputed between Russians and Ottoman Turks, Russian occupation being confirmed in 1812. Although at first granted autonomy (1818–28), this was succeeded by a policy of Russification. A nationalist movement developed from 1905 and in November 1917 Bessarabia declared independence, voting in December 1918 for alliance with Romania. In June 1940 the Soviet Union demanded the return of Bessarabia and of northern Bukovina, and the Moldavian Soviet Socialist Republic was created. The northern region of Bukovina and the coastal plain from the Danube to the Dniester went to the Ukraine. Romania briefly reoccupied the area in 1941, but the 1940 situation was restored in 1947. In August 1991 the country declared its independence from the Soviet Union as the Republic of Moldova. The regions of Transdniestria and Gagauz also declared themselves to be separate republics, but their declarations were annulled by the Moldovan government. Ethnic violence broke out in Transdniestria and Russian troops were sent in to protect Russian residents. A strong movement for Moldovan unification with Romania increased interethnic tensions. However, Moldova's first multiparty elections, held in 1994, were won by supporters of Moldovan independence. A new constitution granted autonomous status to the Transdniestria and Gagauz regions but the situation remains unresolved, with Transdniestria being effectively an independent state beyond Moldovan control. Constitutional conflicts between the President and parliament from the late 1990s led to a reduction of presidential powers in 2000. The Communists returned to power in the 2001 elections and governed Moldova until 2009, when they were replaced by a four-party coalition.

Molly Maguires A secret US organization of Irish Americans (*c.*1865–75). Its name was based on an anti-landlord organization in Ireland. It dominated the eastern Pennsylvania coalfields, campaigning against anti-union mine-owners and managers. Resorting to murder and intimidation of the police, it was broken after infiltration by a *Pinkerton detective.

Molotov, Vyacheslav (Mikhailovich)
(born **Vyacheslav Mikhailovich**) (1890–1986)
Soviet statesman. Born in Russia, he was an
early member of the Bolsheviks and a staunch
supporter of Stalin after Lenin's death. As
Commissar (later Minister) for Foreign Affairs
(1939–49; 1953–56), he negotiated the non-aggression pact with Nazi Germany (1939) and
after 1945 represented the Soviet Union at
meetings of the United Nations, where his frequent exercise of the veto helped to prolong the
cold war. He was expelled from his party posts
in 1956 after quarrelling with Khrushchev.

Monaco

Capital:	Monaco
Area:	2 sq km (1 sq miles)
Population:	30,500 (2013 est)
Currency:	1 euro = 100 cents
Religions:	Roman Catholic 90.0%
Ethnic Groups:	French 47.0%; Monégasque 16.0%; Italian 16.0%
Languages:	French (official); English; Italian; Monégasque
International Organizations:	UN; OSCE; Council of Europe

A small principality lo-
cated in the south of
France in the hills above
the Mediterranean Sea.

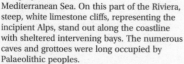

Physical The ancient
town and its fortress
perch on a rocky outcrop
that projects into the
Mediterranean Sea. On this part of the Riviera,
steep, white limestone cliffs, representing the
incipient Alps, stand out along the coastline
with sheltered intervening bays. The numerous
caves and grottoes were long occupied by
Palaeolithic peoples.

Economy Tourism and banking are Monaco's
major industries. Gambling is a major attraction;
the casino (built in 1861) has been state-run
since 1967. Low personal and business taxes
have made Monaco a tax haven. Mineral resources are lacking, and there is no agriculture.

History Monaco was held by the Genoese from
1191 until 1297, when it passed to the Grimaldi
family. The Grimaldis were allies of France,
except for a period of allegiance to Spain
(1524–1641), but Monaco was annexed by
France in 1793 under the French Revolutionary
Regime. The Congress of *Vienna returned the
principality to the Grimaldis but placed it under
the protection of Sardinia. In 1861 France restored Monaco's independence. Monaco
adopted its first constitution in 1911, formaliz-
ing its status as a hereditary principality. A more
democratic constitution was adopted in 1962,
but the monarchy was retained. Prince Rainier
III came to the throne in 1949 and was succeeded by his son, Prince Albert II, on his
death in 2005. In 1993 Monaco joined the
United Nations.

monarchy Rule, commonly hereditary, by
or in the name of a single individual.
Absolute monarchs wielding unlimited authority were once the norm throughout Europe,
but are now rare. Most contemporary
monarchs are constitutional rulers, with
severely limited or even purely ceremonial
powers. Succession to the position of monarch
is usually hereditary, though other methods,
including election, have been known. The association of monarchy with aristocracy and
privilege can be politically divisive, but constitutional monarchs can often provide a head of
state as a symbol of national unity without the
need to involve party politics in the election of a
president.

Monasteries, Dissolution of the (1536–
40) The systematic abolition of English monasticism and transfer of monastic property to the
Tudor monarchy, part of the English *Reformation. Thomas *Cromwell, *Henry VIII's vicar-
general, pointed the way ahead by commis-
sioning the *Valor Ecclesiasticus* (1535), a great
survey of church wealth, and by sending agents
to investigate standards within the religious
houses. An Act of Parliament (1536) dissolved
monasteries with annual revenues of under
£200. This provoked an uprising, the *Pilgrimage of Grace. In its aftermath, Cromwell forced
certain abbots to surrender larger houses to the
king. Another Act (1539) confirmed all surren-
ders that had been, and were to be, made, and
monastic lands passed to the Court of Aug-
mentations of the King's Revenue, a state department. Resistance was minimal. By 1540 all
800 or more English houses were closed. Eleven
thousand monks, nuns, and their dependants
were ejected from their communities, most with
little or no compensation.

The Dissolution had a number of consequences apart from the immediate wholesale
destruction of monastic buildings and the
despoliation of their libraries and treasures.

The nobility and gentry benefited financially from the distribution of former monastic lands, which were used to form the basis of new private estates, and the laity gained a monopoly of ecclesiastical patronage which survived for the next three centuries. The termination of monastic charity and the closure of monastery schools stimulated the introduction of the *Poor Law system and the foundation of grammar schools.

monastery A community of monks living by prayer and labour in secluded, often remote, locations. Such communities, which are meant to further the communal and individual practice of asceticism, are common to most religions. *Buddha founded a monastic order (sangha) and a code of discipline, which is still used and was spread by missionaries throughout Asia. In *Hinduism monasticism takes the form of ashrams, or retreats, where the influence of a guru or holy man and practices, such as yoga, are important. *Islam did not fully develop a monastic organization until the Sufis formed the Rifaite and Mawlawite brotherhoods in the 12th century. Although monasticism is not part of mainstream *Judaism, the Essenes, a messianic sect (2nd century BC) founded a remote community by the Dead Sea.

Christian monasticism evolved from the hermit communities founded in the 3rd century by men fleeing from Roman persecution to the Egyptian and Syrian deserts, where they sought union with God. Although St Antony (c.251–c.356) is usually regarded as the founder of Christian monasticism, it was St Pachomius (c.292–c.346) who founded the first organized community at Tabennisi in Egypt. Monasticism then spread rapidly in Eastern Europe through the Rule of St Basil (c.330–79), the first known Christian monastic rule, and in Western Europe through the Rule of Benedict of Nursia (c.480–c.550). In the *Roman Catholic Church, however, there are numerous orders whose members are often bound by vows of poverty, prayer, and meditation. Communities have both spiritual and practical functions, such as education and social work. From the 10th century the reformed Benedictine Order at *Cluny in France (founded 909) built a series of 'daughter houses' which extended throughout Europe, all under the direct control of the powerful abbot of Cluny. The Cistercians (founded 1098) also built monasteries in Europe and England, though these foundations enjoyed a semi-autonomous position and were only subject to the direct influence of the abbot of Citeaux at an annual council. The Cistercian Order follows the reformed Benedictine Rule; Cistercians of the Strict Observance (Trappist) form the largest contemplative order. Other orders were the Carthusians (1098), the Premonstratensians (1120), and the Gilbertines (1131). The Dominican Order, founded by St Dominic in 1220, and the Franciscan Order, founded by St *Francis of Assisi in 1209, were originally mendicant orders of friars, living from charity, although now most of their members are based in community houses.

Monasticism in the Anglican Communion has become more prominent since the 19th-century Anglo-Catholic movement, with the re-foundation of some ancient orders and the establishment of new orders, such as the Community of the Resurrection, founded in 1892. The ecumenical Taizé community in France, founded in 1940, is the best-known Protestant order. Although Christian monasticism is declining in Europe, it is expanding in the developing world, where it plays an important role in providing educational and other welfare services.

Monck, George, 1st Duke of Albemarle
(1608–70) English general, admiral, and statesman. He began his career as a Royalist and was taken prisoner during the *English Civil War; however, he was then given a command by Parliament and later completed the suppression of the Royalists in Scotland. In the first *Anglo-Dutch War he fought three naval battles before returning to Scotland in 1654. He was trusted by *Cromwell, but after the Protector's death he acted to secure the restoration of *Charles II in 1660, and he received many honours. Monck was placed in charge of London during the *Great Plague (1665) and *Fire of London (1666).

monetarism A school of economics that emerged mainly in the 1960s and 1970s, with US economist Milton Friedman (1912–2006) as its leading exponent. It is a revival of the classical (pre-Keynesian) approach to macroeconomics. Monetarist models assume that money, prices, and wages are flexible but that aggregate output and employment will automatically tend towards an optimal equilibrium. Therefore government policy should concentrate on achieving and maintaining the stability of the price level, which monetarists believe depends on proper management of the money supply mainly through monetary rather than fiscal policy.

money A medium of exchange allowing goods and services to be valued in terms of a legal tender consisting of objects with a high intrinsic value (gold) or a token value (banknotes), rather than traded directly as would occur in a barter economy. Coins of fixed values issued by a government first appeared in the 8th century BC both in Lydia, in Asia Minor, and in China. Britain's first coins, of silver and copper, appeared in the 1st century BC. Thereafter until recently most coins have been made of gold and silver, with copper and bronze used for coins of low value. Token money (such as banknotes) has an intrinsic value less than its face value. Banknotes were first issued by banks who undertook to pay the sum of money that appeared on the note from their deposits of gold. The *Bank of England issued notes from its foundation in 1694 and banknotes are now the principal form of money in circulation.

Mongkut (1804–68) King Rama IV of Siam (*Thailand) (1851–68). Mongkut remained a Buddhist monk for 27 years following the usurpation of the throne by his elder brother Pra Nang (Rama III) in 1824. After ascending the throne, he made a crucial contribution to the maintenance of Siamese independence at a time when the rest of South-East Asia was falling under European influence. His enlightened policies were continued by his successor, *Chulalongkorn.

Mongol empire An empire founded by *Genghis Khan early in the 13th century. Loosely related nomadic tribesmen who lived in felt huts (yurts) and subsisted on meat and milk—and fermented mares' milk (*koumiss*)—were united for the first time under his leadership. From Mongolia they swept out to Asia and eastern Europe. Splendid horsemen and archers, their onslaught was difficult to resist. Khakhans (Great Khans) elected from among Genghis's descendants continued his conquests. Central Russia, Poland, Hungary, Bulgaria, and Romania were overrun, but following the death of the Khakhan Ogodei in 1241 the Mongols withdrew to attend an election in their capital, Karakorum, in Mongolia. However, the *Golden Horde remained in control of Russia. In 1245 an advance towards *Mesopotamia began. In 1258 Hulagu, Genghis's grandson, sacked Baghdad, but was defeated by the *Mamelukes at Ain Jalut (1260). The conquest of China, begun under Genghis, was completed 65 years later under *Kublai Khan.

After Kublai moved the capital to Khanbaligh (now Beijing), it became increasingly difficult to maintain the Khakhan's authority over remote parts of the empire. Quarrels over succession, corrupt and incompetent administration, and revolts accelerated disintegration. After 1300 the *khanates were fully independent. By 1368 the Mongols were driven out of China and in 1372 a Chinese army burned Karakorum.

Mongolia

Capital:	Ulan Bator
Area:	1,564,116 sq km (603,909 sq miles)
Population:	3,226,516 (2013 est)
Currency:	1 tugrik = 100 mongo
Religions:	Buddhism 53.0%; Muslim 3.0%; Shamanist 2.9%; Christian 2.2%
Ethnic Groups:	Khalkha 81.9%; Kazakh 3.8%; Dorbed 2.7%
Languages:	Khalkha Mongolian (official); minority languages and dialects
International Organizations:	UN; Colombo Plan; Non-Aligned Movement; WTO; OSCE

A country in central Asia, bordered by Siberia, Russia on the north and China on the south. It was formerly known as Outer Mongolia (Inner Mongolia is now an autonomous region of China).

Physical Mainly a high, barren plateau, Mongolia has mountains and saline lakes in the north-west and the Gobi Desert in the south-east. In winter it is very cold, and rainfall is light. Even so, there are areas of steppe on which livestock can be supported, and some grain is grown.

Economy Mongolia's former dependence on aid and imports from the Soviet Union left a difficult economic legacy when the Soviet Union collapsed, but the country has succeeded in making the transition from a planned to a free-market economy. The traditional nomadic pastoral economy based on animal breeding is still significant, with livestock, meat, and other animal products being exported. However, Mongolia's considerable mineral resources are being exploited: copper, fluorspar, and coal are significant exports; and gold, molybdenum, uranium, tin, and tungsten have attracted investment.

History Although Mongolia is named after the Mongols, up to the 12th century they only controlled a small area near the sources of the Orkhon River, and other nomadic tribes, such as the Merkit and Naiman, held greater power in the Eastern steppes. In the 13th century, however, the Mongols swept out to create the *Mongol empire. In the 16th century they were converted to Lamaism. During the 17th century the *Manchus won control of Inner and then of Outer Mongolia.

Outer Mongolia remained part of the Chinese empire until the fall of the *Qing dynasty in 1911, although Russia mounted an increasingly strong challenge for the area in later years. While the neighbouring region of Inner Mongolia remained in Chinese hands, Outer Mongolia seized independence in 1911 and reasserted it after brief Chinese and White Russian occupations in 1919–21. Outer Mongolia became communist in 1924 as the Mongolian People's Republic and remained so, following a policy of alliance with the Soviet Union. In July 1990 it became a multiparty democracy, but the Communist Party, now the Mongolian People's Revolutionary Party (MPRP), retained power under Dashiyn Byambasuren. Trade with the former Soviet Union fell and, with price deregulation, an economic crisis developed, leading to rationing of basic foodstuffs. Mongolia adopted a new democratic constitution in 1992, which legalized private ownership. A general election, held in 1992, was again won by the MPRP. Punsalmaagiyn Ochirbat, first elected President in 1990, was re-elected in 1993, in the first direct presidential elections. In subsequent elections in 1996, the opposition Democratic Union coalition won a landslide victory and formed the first non-Communist administration for over 70 years. The Communists won the 2000 legislative elections and returned to power; however, they were obliged to rule in coalition after the indecisive 2004 elections. The following years saw a volatile political situation with a succession of short-lived governments.

Mongoloids One of the major human racial groups, distributed widely through Asia from the Caspian Sea eastwards. They are also found on many islands off the Asian mainland and, as Inuits and Aleuts, in northern Canada and in Greenland. The *Native Americans and Amerindians, the other indigenous peoples of America, were formerly sometimes grouped with the Mongoloids, but this is no longer considered accurate.

monks *See* MONASTERY.

Monmouth's Rebellion (1685) An insurrection in south-west England against *James II, led by the Duke of Monmouth, illegitimate son of Charles II. The Duke of Argyll led a revolt in Scotland against James and persuaded Monmouth to launch a rebellion in the south-west. He landed at Lyme Regis in Dorset, and was proclaimed king at Taunton, but could muster only limited support. He failed to take Bristol and, with forces inferior in training, experience, and equipment to the king's army, was routed at *Sedgemoor. Monmouth was captured a few days later and executed; his followers were harshly punished by the *Bloody Assizes.

Monomatapa *See* MWENE MUTAPA.

Monroe, James (1758–1831) US Democratic Republican statesman, 5th President of the USA (1817–25). In 1803, while minister to France under President Jefferson, he negotiated and ratified the Louisiana Purchase, by which territory formerly owned by France was sold to the USA. He is chiefly remembered, however, as the originator of the *Monroe Doctrine.

Monroe Doctrine US foreign policy declaration warning European powers against further colonization in the New World and against intervention in the governments of the American hemisphere; it also disclaimed any intention of the USA to take part in the political affairs of Europe. The background of the doctrine, spelt out in President James *Monroe's annual message to Congress in 1823, was the threat of intervention by the *Holy Alliance to restore Spain's South American colonies, and the aggressive attitude of Russia on the north-west coast of America. The doctrine was infrequently invoked in the 19th century, but after the development of territorial interests in Central America and the Caribbean it became a tenet of US foreign policy. During the early 20th century it developed into a policy whereby the USA regarded itself as responsible for the security of North and South America; this consistently complicated relations with Latin American countries.

Montagu-Chelmsford Proposals (1918) Constitutional proposals for British India. They were made in the Report on Indian Constitutional Reforms (1918) by Edwin Montagu (1879–1924), Secretary of State for India, and Frederick John Thesiger, 3rd Baron Chelmsford (1868–1933), governor-general of India (1916–21). They followed the promise of responsible government made in 1917, and envisaged a gradual progress towards devolution of power and

Indian self-government. In some ways the Government of India Act (1919) which followed can be seen as a measure to shore up imperial authority by containing opposition; it was regarded by Indian nationalists as inadequate and not a full implementation of the proposals.

Montcalm, Louis Joseph de Montcalm-Gozon, Marquis de (1712–59) French general. He defended Quebec against British troops under General Wolfe, but was defeated and mortally wounded in the battle on the Plains of Abraham.

Montenegro (Serbo-Croat **Crna Gora**)

Capital:	Podgorica
Area:	13,812 sq km (5387 sq miles)
Population:	653,474 (2013 est)
Currency:	1 euro = 100 cents
Religions:	Eastern Orthodox 72.1%; Muslim 19.1%; Roman Catholic 3.4%
Ethnic Groups:	Montenegrin 45.0%; Serbian 28.7%; Bosniak 8.7%; Albanian 4.9%
Languages:	Montenegrin (official); Serbian; Bosnian; Albanian; minority languages
International Organizations:	UN; OSCE; Council of Europe; Euro-Atlantic Partnership Council; WTO

A small republic in the Balkans, bordered by Serbia, Croatia, Bosnia and Herzegovina, and Albania.

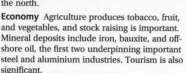

Physical Montenegro has a short Adriatic coastline. It is largely mountainous, with extensive forests in the north.

Economy Agriculture produces tobacco, fruit, and vegetables, and stock raising is important. Mineral deposits include iron, bauxite, and offshore oil, the first two underpinning important steel and aluminium industries. Tourism is also significant.

History Montenegro was absorbed into the Serbian empire in the 12th century but remained unsubdued when Serbia was conquered by the Turks in 1389. It was recognized as an independent nation in 1878. In 1918 it became part of the federation of Yugoslavia,

which came under communist control after World War II. When Yugoslavia disintegrated in 1989–1991, Montenegrins decided to maintain the federation with Serbia in a referendum (1992). Serbia and Montenegro declared themselves to be an independent country, the Federal Republic of Yugoslavia; this was replaced by the union of *Serbia and Montenegro, a much looser federation, in 2002. However, Montenegro's relations with Serbia remained uneasy and a referendum held in May 2006 resulted in a vote for independence. The union with Serbia was formally dissolved the following month. A priority since independence has been to gain EU membership.

Montespan, Françoise-Athénaïs de Rochechouart, Marquise de (1641–1707) French noblewoman. She was mistress of Louis XIV from 1667 to 1679, and had seven illegitimate children by him. She subsequently fell from favour when the king became attracted to their governess, Madame de Maintenon.

Montesquieu, Charles Louis de Secondat, Baron de La Brède et de (1689–1755) French political philosopher. A former advocate, he became known with the publication of his *Lettres Persanes* (1721), a satire of French society from the perspective of two Persian travellers visiting Paris. Montesquieu's reputation rests chiefly on *L'Esprit des lois* (1748), a comparative study of political systems in which he championed the separation of judicial, legislative, and executive powers as being most conducive to individual liberty, holding up the English state as a model. His theories were highly influential in Europe in the late 18th century, as they were in the drafting of the American Constitution.

Montezuma II (1466–1520) Aztec emperor (1502–20). The last ruler of the Aztec empire in Mexico, he was defeated and imprisoned by the Spanish conquistadors under Cortés in 1519. Montezuma was killed while trying to pacify some of his former subjects during the Aztec uprising against his captors.

Montfort, Simon de, Earl of Leicester (c.1208–65) English soldier, born in Normandy. He was the son of the French soldier Simon de Montfort. As leader of the baronial opposition to Henry III, he campaigned against royal encroachment on the privileges gained through Magna Carta, and defeated the king at Lewes, Sussex, in 1264. The following year he summoned a Parliament, which included not only barons, knights, and clergymen, but also two citizens from every borough in England. He was defeated and killed by reorganized royal forces under Henry's son (later Edward I) at Evesham.

Montgomery, Bernard Law, 1st Viscount Montgomery of Alamein (known as **'Monty'**) (1887–1976) British Field Marshal. In 1942 he commanded the 8th Army in the Western Desert, where his victory at El Alamein proved the first significant Allied success in World War II. He was later given command of the Allied ground forces in the invasion of Normandy in 1944 and accepted the German surrender on 7 May 1945.

Monti, Mario (1943–) Italian economist, Prime Minister (2011–13). Born in Varese, Monti graduated in economics and management in 1965 and became an academic economist. He served as an EU commissioner (1995–2004). In 2011, after the global financial markets had lost confidence in Italy's creditworthiness (*see* EUROZONE CRISIS), Monti was appointed Prime Minister of a technocratic non-party administration to reassure the markets and implement reforms. Acting also as finance minister, he sought to reduce Italy's public deficit by tax rises and other austerity measures, and also to remove restrictive practices in the labour market. In December 2012 Monti lost the support of parliament, which precipitated early elections in 2013. He led an alliance of centre parties, but did not win sufficient seats to continue as Prime Minister.

Montrose, James Graham, 1st Marquess of (1612–50) Scottish general. Montrose supported Charles I when Scotland entered the English Civil War and, commanding a small army of Irish and Scottish irregulars, inflicted a dramatic series of defeats on the stronger Covenanter forces in the north (1644–45) before being defeated at Philiphaugh. After several years in exile, he returned to Scotland in 1650 in a bid to restore the new king Charles II, but was betrayed to the Covenanters and hanged.

Montserrat An island in the Caribbean, one of the Leeward Islands. Visited by Columbus in 1493 and named after a Benedictine monastery on the mountain of Montserrat in Spain, it was colonized by Irish settlers in 1632. It was part of the British federal colony of the Leeward Islands from 1871 to 1956 when it became a separate UK Dependent Territory. In addition to offshore finance, it is a base for the production of light consumer goods, electronic components, and goods made from locally grown cotton. It is

governed by a Governor who presides over an Executive Council and a Legislative Council. Many of the islanders were evacuated in 1997 following a major volcanic eruption.

Moor A member of a Muslim people of mixed Berber and Arab descent, inhabiting north-west Africa and southern Spain from the 8th to the 15th centuries. Their name is derived from a Greek word (*Mauros*) for the inhabitants of ancient Mauretania. The Moorish period in Spain was the zenith of Islamic culture, especially in architecture. The Alhambra (in Granada) and the Great Mosque (in Cordoba) are among their most celebrated creations.

Moore, Sir John (1761–1809) British general. From 1808 he commanded the British army during the Peninsular War, conducting a successful 250-mile retreat to Corunna in midwinter before being mortally wounded by his French pursuers. His burial was the subject of a famous poem by the Irish poet Charles Wolfe (1791–1823).

Moravian Church *See* PROTESTANTISM.

More, Sir Thomas (canonized as **St Thomas More**) (1478–1535) English scholar and statesman, Lord Chancellor (1529–32). From the time of the accession of Henry VIII (1509), More held a series of public offices, but was forced to resign as Lord Chancellor when he opposed the king's divorce from Catherine of Aragon. He was imprisoned in 1534 after refusing to take the oath on the Act of Succession, sanctioning Henry's marriage to Anne Boleyn. After opposing the Act of Supremacy in the same year, More was beheaded. Regarded as one of the leading humanists of the Renaissance, he owed his reputation largely to his *Utopia* (1516), describing an ideal city-state.

Morelos y Pavón, José María (1765–1815) Mexican mestizo priest and leader of the revolution against Spain. Joining the insurrection in 1810, he led a successful campaign in the south, and assumed command of his country's struggle after the capture and execution (1810) of Miguel *Hidalgo y Costilla. From 1812 to 1815 he kept the royalist army on the run with guerrilla warfare. He sponsored the Congress of Chilpancingo (1813), which formally declared Mexican independence and adopted Mexico's first constitution with Morelos as head of government. Before its administrative, social, and fiscal reforms could be adopted, Morelos was captured by Spanish forces and shot.

Moreno, Mariano (1778–1811) Argentine revolutionary. His study of the Enlightenment thinkers led him to challenge Spanish mercantilist policies in the Rio de la Plata region. In his *Memorial of the Landowners*, he argued for free trade in terms similar to those of Adam Smith. Although trade restrictions were eased, Moreno became the secretary of the first revolutionary governing junta in 1810, which deposed the Spanish viceroy. Dispatched to Europe to secure assistance for the independence movement, he died aboard ship.

Morgan, Sir Henry (*c*.1635–88) Welsh *buccaneer, the scourge of Spanish settlements and shipping in the Caribbean between the 1660s and 1680s. Although he had semi-official employment as a privateer, he was little more than a pirate. Among his exploits were the capture and ransom of Porto Bello (1668), the sacking of Maracaibo (1669), and the taking of Chagres and Panama (1670–71). Although knighted and appointed lieutenant-governor of Jamaica in 1674, he continued to encourage piracy and lawlessness. He was disgraced in 1683 but restored just before his death.

Morínigo, Higinio (1897–1985) Paraguayan military dictator. He was an army officer during the *Chaco War and subsequently became Minister of War. When President José Félix Estigarríbia was killed in an air crash (1940), Morínigo became President (1940–48). He suspended the constitution and established a harsh military dictatorship. Housing and public health were improved during his tenure, and, in 1946, political exiles were brought into a more democratic cabinet. When these were ousted on suspicion of treason (1947), civil war broke out and a broadly based opposition, led by the Colorado Party, forced his retirement and exile to Argentina (1948).

Morley-Minto reforms (1909) Constitutional changes in British India, introduced to increase Indian participation in the legislature. They were embodied in the Indian Councils Act (1909) following discussions between John Morley, Secretary of State for India (1905–14), and Lord Minto, viceroy (1905–10). The reforms included the admission of Indians to the Secretary of State's council, to the viceroy's executive council, and to the executive councils of Bombay and Madras, and the introduction of an elected element into legislative councils with provision for separate electorates for Muslims. The reforms were regarded by Indian nationalists as too cautious, and the provision of separate electorates for Muslims was resented by Hindus.

Mormons Members of the Church of Jesus Christ of Latter-Day Saints, which was founded in New York in 1830 by Joseph Smith (1805–44). He claimed to have discovered, through divine revelation, the 'Book of Mormon', relating the history of a group of Hebrews who migrated to America *c*.600 BC. This work is accepted by Mormons as Scripture along with the Bible. A further revelation led him to institute polygamy, a practice that brought the Mormons into conflict with the Federal Government and was abandoned in 1890. Smith was succeeded as leader by Brigham Young (1801–77), who moved the Mormon headquarters to Salt Lake City, Utah, in 1847. Mormon teaching is strongly adventist; the movement has no professional clergy, self-help is emphasized, and tithing and missionary work are required of its members.

Moro, Aldo (1916–78) Italian statesman. He entered Parliament as a Christian Democrat in 1946. As Minister of Justice (1955–57) he reformed the prison system. He was Foreign Minister in several governments (1965–74), and Prime Minister (1963–68; 1974–76). Moro was kidnapped in 1978 by the *Red Brigades, who demanded the release of imprisoned terrorists for his return. The government's refusal to accede led to Moro's murder.

Morocco

Capital:	Rabat
Area:	446,550 sq km (172,414 sq miles)
Population:	32,649,130 (2013 est)
Currency:	1 dirham = 100 centimes
Religions:	Muslim 99.0%; Christian 1.0%
Ethnic Groups:	Arab–Berber 99.0%
Languages:	Arabic, Tamazight (both official); other Berber languages; French
International Organizations:	UN; Non-Aligned Movement; Arab League; Maghreb Union; WTO

A country in the north-west corner of Africa bounded inland by Algeria and Western Sahara and with coasts on both the Mediterranean Sea and the Atlantic Ocean.

Physical Much of Morocco consists of the Atlas Mountains, running from the south-west to the north-east. Near the coasts it is warm and wet; in the mountains, arid. South of the mountains begins the very hot and windy Sahara Desert. Rivers from the mountains water the coastal plains and permit a wide variety of crops.

Economy Formerly dependent on the extraction and export of phosphates, of which Morocco has the world's largest reserves, the economy has diversified, with agriculture and tourism now also important. Apart from phosphates, exports include clothing and textiles, electronic components, inorganic chemicals, oil products, and fruit and vegetables. Remittances from expatriates are important.

History By the 5th century BC *Phoenicians had stations on the Moroccan coast, when the Carthaginian admiral, Hanno, passed the Straits of Gibraltar, and perhaps reached the Gulf of Guinea. A kingdom of Mauritania was formed in northern Morocco in the 4th century BC; the Romans made it the province of Mauritania Tingitana, based on Tangier. Vandals from Spain occupied the region from 428, but the Berbers controlled the interior even after the Byzantines had recovered the coast in 533. It did not come under Arab control until Musa ibn Nusayr's conquest in c.705. Under Byzantium the puritanism of the Berber character had been manifested in the *Donatist heresy; under Islam a similarly austere movement, Kharijism, arose. True Arab domination was brief, and Berber dynasties emerged, Idrisids (788–974), *Fatimids (909–73), *Almoravids (1056–1147), *Almohads (1145–1257), Merinids (1248–1548), and finally the Sharifian dynasties from 1524 until the present. Having defeated the Portuguese at Al-cazarquivir (1578), Morocco itself attempted colonial expansion, defeating the *Songhay empire with the help of firearms in 1591, but ruling it inefficiently.

By the 19th century, Morocco had lapsed into endemic disorder and became the target for French and Spanish imperial ambitions. In the early 20th century, German opposition to French expansionism produced serious international crises in 1905 and 1911 which almost resulted in war. In 1912 it was divided between a French protectorate, a Spanish protectorate, and the international Zone of Tangier. Rif rebels under Abd *el-Krim fought the Spanish and French occupying powers in the 1920s, and Morocco became an independent monarchy under Muhammad V in 1956 when it absorbed Tangier. Muhammad was succeeded by his son

Hassan II in 1961, but opposition sparked the suspension of parliamentary government in 1965, and royal authority was maintained in the face of abortive military coups in the early 1970s and intermittent republican opposition. In 1980 a new constitution proclaimed the kingdom of Morocco to be a constitutional monarchy. From the mid-1970s Morocco was involved in an inconclusive desert war in the former Spanish Sahara. A convention was signed in 1976 dividing this mineral-rich area between Morocco and Mauritania; but the latter renounced its claims in 1979 in favour of a nationalist group, the Polisario Front. Morocco annexed the land from which Mauritania had withdrawn, despite violent resistance from the Polisario Front. Major battles were fought in 1979 and 1980, and Moroccan troops built a series of desert walls. A ceasefire was negotiated in 1991, but little progress has been made in negotiations to secure a permanent peace accord. A new constitution, adopted in 1992, increased the powers of the government while retaining the hereditary monarch as head of state. A programme of privatization was launched in 1993. Hassan II was succeeded by his son Mohammed VI in 1999. In 2011 the *Arab Spring inspired protests demanding further reform. Mohammed VI responded with a new constitution that again extended parliamentary and prime-ministerial powers but left the ultimate authority of the monarch intact. Elections in 2012 resulted in Morocco's first Islamist government.

Morrison of Lambeth, Herbert Stanley Morrison, Baron (1888–1965) British politician. As leader of the London County Council (1934–40), he unified the transport system under public ownership and created a "green belt" around the metropolis. Morrison was Minister of Supply and then Home Secretary in *Churchill's coalition government during World War II. He drafted the programme of nationalization and social services in the 1945 Labour manifesto. From 1945 he was Deputy Prime Minister under *Attlee, but he was defeated by *Gaitskell in the election for leadership of the Labour Party in 1955.

Morsi, Mohammed (Mohammed Mohammed Morsi 'Issa al- 'Ayyat) (1951–) Egyptian politician, President (2012–13). He studied engineering in Egypt and the USA and was professor of engineering at Zagazig University (1985–2010). Active in the Islamist Moslem Brotherhood organization, he was a member of Parliament (2000–05). Following *Mubarak's overthrow (2011) he won the 2012

presidential election as the Brotherhood's candidate. Soon after assuming office he asserted his authority over the army, which had sought to limit the new President's powers. However, a subsequent decree extending his powers and his support for an Islamist draft constitution (approved by referendum and implemented in December 2012) deepened Egypt's political divisions and led to mass demonstrations. In July 2013 he was overthrown by a military coup and imprisoned.

Mortimer, Roger de, 8th Baron of Wigmore and 1st Earl of March (c.1287–1330) English noble. In 1326 he invaded England with his lover Isabella of France, forcing her husband Edward II to abdicate in favour of her son, the future Edward III. Mortimer and Isabella acted as regents for the young Edward until 1330, when the monarch assumed royal power and had Mortimer executed.

Mortimer's Cross, Battle of (2 February 1461) An important battle in the Wars of the *Roses, which took place at a site near Wigmore in Herefordshire. The *Yorkist forces led by Edward, Earl of March, won a major victory over the Earl of Wiltshire's *Lancastrian army. It was not negated by the victory of Queen *Margaret of Anjou's army at St Albans less than a fortnight later, for Margaret could not win over the Londoners; on 4 March they acclaimed Edward as King *Edward IV.

Morton, John (c.1420–1500) English prelate and statesman. He rose to become Henry VII's chief adviser, being appointed Archbishop of Canterbury in 1486 and Chancellor a year later. He is traditionally associated with the Crown's stringent taxation policies, which made the regime in general and Morton in particular widely unpopular.

Mosley, Sir Oswald Ernald (1896–1980) British political leader. Mosley was a Member of Parliament successively as Conservative (1918–22), Independent (1922–24), and Labour (1925–31). Calling for a dictatorial system of government, he formed the National Union of Fascists in 1932. *Anti-Semitic and *fascist in character, the Union staged violent rallies in the East End of London. Mosley was interned during 1940–43. In 1948 he founded the 'Union Movement', whose theme was European unity.

mound-builders Native American tribes in Ohio and Illinois who, from c.1000 BC, erected richly furnished circular burial mounds, resembling the European barrows in shape and

function. In the Mississippi basin some centuries later (c.700 AD), larger and more complex mounds, presumably for ceremonial gatherings, were raised to support temples. Though most were rectangular, and frequently built in large groups as at Cahokia in Illinois, there are more bizarre ones, such as the 400 m (1300 feet) long snake mound in Adams County, Ohio. These may have been influenced from Mexico.

Mountain Men US fur trappers and traders, who explored and developed the Rocky Mountains between the 1820s and 1840s. They caught public attention through their exploits and occupy an important position in the frontier legend. Their living conditions were harsh, and only a handful, such as Kit *Carson, Jedediah *Smith, and Thomas Fitzpatrick, survived long enough to return to a more settled existence after a decline in beaverskin prices in the 1840s.

Mountbatten, Louis, 1st Earl Mountbatten of Burma (Louis Francis Albert Victor Nicholas Mountbatten) (1900–79) British admiral and administrator. A great-grandson of Queen Victoria, Mountbatten served in the Royal Navy before rising to become supreme Allied commander in SE Asia (1943–45). As the last viceroy (1947) and first Governor-General of India (1947–48), he oversaw the independence of India and Pakistan. He was killed by an IRA bomb while on his yacht in Ireland.

Mousterian See PALAEOLITHIC.

Mozambique (formerly **Portuguese East Africa**)

Capital:	Maputo
Area:	799,380 sq km (308,642 sq miles)
Population:	24,096,669 (2013 est)
Currency:	1 metical = 100 centavos
Religions:	Roman Catholic 28.4%; Protestant 27.7%; Muslim 17.9%
Ethnic Groups:	African 99.66%; Euro-Africans 0.2%; Europeans 0.06%
Languages:	Portuguese (official); Emakhuwa; Xichangana; Cisena; Elomwe; Echuwabo; local languages
International Organizations:	UN; AU; SADC; Commonwealth; Non-Aligned Movement; WTO

A country situated on the south-east coast of Africa, and bounded by Tanzania, Malawi, Zambia, Zimbabwe, South Africa, and Swaziland.

Physical The Zambezi flows across the middle of the country and the Limpopo across the south. The coastal plain is low and broad, with areas of sand between the marshy river valleys.

Economy Mozambique's mineral resources include large reserves of coal, iron ore, tantalite, and unknown reserves of natural gas and precious stones. The Cabora Bassa dam on the Zambezi River is one of Africa's largest hydroelectric dams, and electricity is exported to South Africa. Agriculture employs four-fifths of the workforce. The main export crops include cotton, cashew nuts, and sugar cane; shrimp are also important. The leading industry is aluminium production, which has boosted export earnings in recent years, followed by oil products, chemicals, and textiles. However, Mozambique remains a poor country; half the population lives in poverty and 40% of the budget consists of foreign aid.

History Mozambique was known to medieval Arab geographers as Musambih. According to the Arab historian al-Masudi it was already exporting gold from mines in the interior of what is now *Zimbabwe in the 10th century. Merchants from Mogadishu had a monopoly for a time, though it was taken over by Kilwa in the 12th century. The Portuguese sacked the port of Sofala in 1505, and built a new town as the seat of a captaincy to control the gold and other trade. Settlers also began to trade in slaves in the 16th century. The present city of Moçambique was begun with a fort in 1508 built by the Portuguese as a refreshment station on the way to Goa. The first inland settlements at Sena and Tete were Arab trading towns, from which they made contact with the Mwene Mutapa and other hinterland rulers until the 19th century.

The Portuguese gradually suppressed all indigenous resistance movements during the 19th century. In 1951, Mozambique became an overseas province of Portugal. In order to rid the country of colonial rule, in 1964 the Marxist–Leninist guerrilla group Frelimo was formed (*see* FRELIMO WAR). By the mid-1970s Portuguese authority had reached the point of collapse, and in 1975 an independent People's Republic was established under the Frelimo leader Samora Machel. Support for the guerrilla campaigns in Rhodesia and South Africa led to repeated military incursions by troops of those countries, and the establishment of a stable government within the framework of a one-party Marxist state was further hindered by the weak state of Mozambique's agricultural economy. In 1984 Mozambique and South Africa signed a non-aggression pact; but South African support of rebel groups, funded by Portuguese ex-colonists, continued. In 1989 there was a relaxation of its Marxist-Leninist line by Frelimo, and President Joaquim Chissano agreed to meet Afonso Dhlakama, leader of the rebel Mozambique National Resistance (RENAMO). There was heavy fighting early in 1990, but in November a new constitution took effect. This was accepted by RENAMO in October 1991. After a further year of negotiation a peace treaty was agreed in October 1992 and RENAMO became a legitimate political party. Mozambique's first multiparty elections were held in 1994 and Frelimo, under Chissano, was re-elected. In 1995 Mozambique was admitted to the *Commonwealth of Nations as a special case (it has no historical links with Britain). Chissano was succeeded as President by Armando Guebuza in 2005, who was re-elected in 2009.

Mubarak, Hosni (Muhammad Hosni Said Mubarak) (1928–) Egyptian statesman, President (1981–2011). Appointed head of the Egyptian air force in 1972, Mubarak became Vice-President in 1975 and succeeded President Sadat following the latter's assassination. Although he did much to establish closer links between Egypt and other Arab nations, including distancing himself from Israel when it invaded Lebanon in 1982, he risked division by aligning Egypt against Saddam Hussein in the Gulf War of 1991. After the resurgence of militant Islamic fundamentalism in Egypt in 1992, Mubarak's National Democratic Party government adopted extremely harsh measures to suppress activists. In 2011 large demonstrations inspired by the *Arab Spring led him to resign as president, and in 2012 he was sentenced to life imprisonment for complicity in the deaths of some demonstrators. However, a retrial was ordered in 2013 and Mubarak was released. In 2014 he was found guilty of embezzlement.

Mugabe, Robert (Gabriel) (1924–) Zimbabwean statesman, Prime Minister (1980–87) and President since 1987. In 1963 he co-founded the Zimbabwe African National Union (ZANU) and in 1975 became its leader; the following year he formed the Patriotic Front with the leader of the Zimbabwe African People's Union (ZAPU), Joshua Nkomo.

Mugabe was declared Prime Minister in 1980 after ZANU won a landslide victory in the country's first post-independence elections. In 1982 he ousted Nkomo from his Cabinet; ZANU and ZAPU agreed to merge in 1987 and Mugabe became President. He was re-elected in 1990, 1996, 2002, 2008, and 2013 in elections increasingly characterized by violence and electoral fraud. His corrupt and authoritarian rule and its disregard for human rights have impoverished Zimbabwe and led to international condemnation.

Mughals See MOGULS.

Muhammad (or **Mohammed**) (c.570–632) Arab prophet and founder of Islam. He was born in Mecca, where in c.610 he received the first of a series of revelations, which became the doctrinal and legislative basis of Islam and which were written down c.610–32 as the Koran. His sayings (the Hadith) and the accounts of his daily practice (the Sunna) constitute the other major sources of guidance for most Muslims. In the face of opposition to his preaching he and his small group of supporters were forced to flee to Medina in 622; this flight, known as the Hegira, is of great significance in Islam, and the Islamic calendar (which is based on lunar months) is dated from 622 AD (1 AH). After consolidation of the community in Medina, Muhammad led his followers into a series of battles, which resulted in the capitulation of Mecca in 630. He died two years later, having successfully united tribal factions of the Hejaz region into a force that would expand the frontiers of Islam. He was buried in Medina. Islam is now the professed faith of some 1600 million people.

Muhammad Ali (1769–1849) Ottoman viceroy and pasha of Egypt (1805–49), possibly of Albanian descent. As a commander in the Ottoman army he had overthrown the Mamelukes, Egypt's ruling military caste, by 1811. Although technically the viceroy of the Ottoman sultan, he was effectively an independent ruler and modernized Egypt's infrastructure, making it the leading power in the eastern Mediterranean. In 1841 he and his family were given the right to become hereditary rulers of Egypt, and the dynasty survived until 1952.

Muhammad Reza Shah Pahlavi (1919–1980) Shah of Iran (1941–79). The son of Reza *Pahlavi, he succeeded on the abdication of his father. After the fall of *Mussadegh in 1953 he gained supreme power and with the aid of greatly increased oil revenues, embarked upon a policy of rapid social reform and economic development, while maintaining a regime of harsh repression. In 1962 he introduced a land reform programme to break landlord power. In 1979 he was deposed by a revolution led by the Islamic clergy, notably Ayatollah *Khomeini, whose supporters were bitterly opposed to the pro-western regime of the Shah. He died in exile in Egypt.

Mujibur Rahman (known as **'Sheikh Mujib'**) (1920–75) Bangladeshi statesman, Prime Minister (1972–75) and President 1975. In 1949 he cofounded the Awami (People's) League, which advocated autonomy for East Pakistan. He led the party to victory in the 1970 elections, but was imprisoned in 1971 when civil war broke out. Released in 1972, he became the first Prime Minister of independent Bangladesh. After his failure to establish parliamentary democracy, he assumed dictatorial powers in 1975. He and his family were assassinated in a military coup.

Mukden incident (18 September 1931) Japanese seizure of the Manchurian city of Mukden (now Shenyang in NE China). A detachment of the Japanese Guandong army, stationed in Manchuria in accordance with treaty rights, used an allegedly Chinese-inspired explosion on the South Manchurian Railway as an excuse to occupy the city of Mukden. Acting without reference to their own government, and in the face of condemnation from the League of Nations, Japanese military authorities then went on to occupy all of Manchuria before the end of 1931, establishing the state of *Manchukuo. Japan, labelled an aggressor by the League of Nations, withdrew its membership.

Muldoon, Sir Robert (David) (1921–92) New Zealand statesman, Prime Minister (1975–84). He became a National Party MP in 1960, serving as deputy Prime Minister for a brief period in 1972 and as leader of the opposition from 1973 to 1974 before becoming Premier the following year. He was chairman of the board of governors for the IMF and World Bank (1979–80) and chairman of the ministerial council for the OECD (1982). His term of office was marked by domestic measures to tackle low economic growth and high inflation.

Mulroney, Brian (Martin Brian Mulroney) (1939–) Canadian Progressive Conservative statesman, Prime Minister (1984–93). After becoming leader of the Progressive Conservative Party in 1983, he won a landslide victory in the 1984 election. He was re-elected in 1988 on a ticket of free trade with the USA, but stood down in 1993 after the Canadian recession caused his popularity to slump in the opinion polls.

Munich 'beer-hall' putsch (8 November 1923) An abortive rebellion by German *Nazis. In a beer-hall in Munich a meeting of right-wing politicians, who had gathered to denounce the *Weimar Republic and to call for the restitution of the Bavarian monarchy, was interrupted by a group of Nazi Party members led by Adolf *Hitler. In a fierce speech Hitler won support for a plan to 'march on Berlin' and there install the right-wing military leader General *Ludendorff as dictator. With a unit of *Brownshirts (SA), he kidnapped the leader of the Bavarian government and declared a revolution. Next day a march on the centre of Munich by some 3,000 Nazis was met by police gunfire, 16 demonstrators and three policemen being killed in the riot that followed. Many were arrested. Ludendorff was released, but Hitler was sentenced to five years in prison, of which he served only nine months. During this period he dictated the first volume of his autobiography and manifesto *Mein Kampf* (1925) to his fellow prisoner, Rudolf *Hess.

Munich Pact (29 September 1938) The agreement between Britain, France, Germany, and Italy concerning Czechoslovakia. *Hitler had long demanded protection for the German-speaking *Sudetenland and shown readiness to risk war to attain his end. To avert conflict at all costs the British Prime Minister, *Chamberlain, had met Hitler at Berchtesgaden (15 September), and again at Bad Godesberg (23 September), by which time Hitler had extended his demands. He now stipulated the immediate annexation by Germany of the Bohemian Sudetenland and demanded that Germans elsewhere in Czechoslovakia should be given the right to join the *Third Reich. In a final effort Chamberlain appealed to *Mussolini, who organized a conference at Munich where he, Chamberlain, and Hitler were joined by Daladier, the French Premier. No Czech or Soviet representative was invited. Hitler gained most of what he wanted and on 1 October German troops entered the Sudentenland. As part of the agreement, Poland and Hungary occupied areas of Moravia, Slovakia, and Ruthenia. In March 1939 Bohemia and Moravia were occupied by German troops, and the rest of Slovakia became an independent client state; President *Beneš had resigned, and he left the country. Germany, which now dominated the entire Danubian area, emerged as the strongest power on the mainland of Europe.

Murad I (c.1326–89) *Ottoman sultan (c.1362–89). He consolidated his empire's hold on Asia Minor by marriage alliances and outright purchase and rapidly extended its Balkan territories, taking Adrianople in 1362, Macedonia after the battle of Cirnomen (1371), and Sofia and Nish in the 1380s. A Serbian counter-offensive was defeated at the first battle of *Kosovo, in which he was killed.

Murad II (c.1403–51) Ottoman sultan (1421–51). He overcame early opposition to his claim to the throne and, after significant reverses, routed a Hungarian-led "crusade" at the Battle of Varna and the second Battle of Kosovo (1448). He also made the *Janissaries a basic pillar of the Ottoman state.

Murat, Joachim (c.1767–1815) French general, king of Naples (1808–15). One of Napoleon's marshals, Murat made his name as a cavalry commander in the Italian campaign (1800). After he was made king of Naples by Napoleon, he made a bid to become king of all Italy in 1815, but was captured in Calabria and executed.

Muromachi *See* ASHIKAGA.

Museveni, Yoweri Kaguta *See* UGANDA.

Musharraf, Pervez (1943–) Pakistani general and statesman; President (2001–08). Musharraf was born in Delhi, but his family moved to Pakistan after the partition of India (1947). Joining the army in 1964, he rose to become army chief of staff in 1998. In 1999 he ousted the Prime Minister, Narwaz Sharif, in a bloodless coup following a dispute over policy towards Kashmir. Promising a return to democracy, he ruled as Chief Executive until 2001, when he declared himself President. A referendum in 2002 confirmed him in this office and the constitution was restored. Musharraf suspended it again in 2007, but restored it later the same year and was re-elected president. He resigned in 2008 following an opposition victory in parliamentary elections and subsequent moves to impeach him. He lived in exile until 2013, when he returned to Pakistan to contest the presidential election; however, his candidacy was ruled invalid and he was arrested on treason charges for his actions in 2007.

musketeer In the 16th and 17th centuries, a foot soldier armed with a musket, a large-calibre smooth-bore firearm that was aimed from the shoulder. Inefficient hand cannons had been used in Europe during the 14th century, and matchlock "arquebuses" were subsequently used, rather haphazardly, in battle. In the mid-16th century Spanish troops pioneered the use of the more powerful, more accurate *mosquete* (musket). They also evolved complementary battle tactics. Effective as these weapons were, infantrymen still needed forked stands as props for aiming and firing; and since they were slow to load, pikemen had to be included in battalions to protect musketeers from enemy cavalry charges. The 17th-century development of the bayonet eventually removed the need for pikemen. Wheel-lock and flintlock muskets also became practical for military use at this time.

Muskogee *See* CREEK.

Muslim League Political party founded in 1905 to represent the separate interests of the Indian Muslims, who felt threatened by the prospects of a Hindu majority in any future democratic system. The radical nationalist elements in the League forged a pact with the *Congress in 1916 on the basis of separate electorates and reserved seats in Muslim minority provinces. A section of the League allied itself to the Congress in the non-cooperation movement. In the provincial elections (1937), the League captured very few Muslim seats, but it succeeded in convincing the Muslim masses that the elected Congress ministries were oppressing Muslims. In 1940 it put forward the demand for an autonomous Muslim homeland, Pakistan, interpreted by its leader, M. A. *Jinnah, as an independent state during the transfer of power negotiations between the UK and India. He called for a Direct Action Day in August 1946. Mass rioting followed, whereupon the British and the Congress agreed to partition. The League was virtually wiped out at the first elections in Pakistan.

Muslims *See* ISLAM.

Mussadegh, Muhammad (1880–1967) Iranian political leader. An Iranian landowner and politician, in 1950 he led the democratic-nationalist opposition to the policies of Muhammad *Reza Shah Pahlavi in Parliament. A militant nationalist, he forced (1951) the nationalization of the Anglo-Iranian Oil Company, and after rioting in Abadan, was appointed Prime Minister (1951–53). He ruled with left-wing support until he was dismissed by the Shah in 1953.

Mussolini, Benito (Amilcaro Andrea) (known as **Il Duce, 'The Leader'**) (1883–1945) Italian Fascist statesman, Prime Minister (1922–43). Originally a socialist, Mussolini founded the Italian Fascist Party in 1919. Three years later he orchestrated the March on Rome by the Blackshirts and was created Prime Minister, proceeding to organize his government along dictatorial lines. He annexed Abyssinia in 1936 and entered World War II on Germany's side in 1940. Mussolini was forced to resign after the Allied invasion of Sicily in 1943; he was rescued from imprisonment by German paratroopers, but was captured and executed by Italian Communist partisans in 1945, a few weeks before the end of the war.

Mutesa I (died 1884) Kabaka (King) of Buganda (now in Uganda) (1857–84). An autocratic monarch, he furthered his country's wealth by opening up trade, often in slaves, with Arab merchants. He strengthened Buganda's army and improved its bureaucracy. He subdued Bunyoro, the leading state in south Uganda. Although a Muslim, he welcomed Christian missionaries. They were followed by the British East Africa Company, causing tensions that were unresolved when he died.

Mutesa II, Sir Edward Frederick (1924–69) The last Kabaka of Buganda (1939–63) and President of Uganda (1963–66). He assumed office after a regency, aged 18. Progressive in spirit, he nevertheless backed the protectorate government in suppressing Buganda nationalist risings in 1945 and 1949. In 1953, fearing the loss of Buganda's independence, he claimed the right of his kingdom to secede from the Ugandan protectorate. This was denied him by the Ugandan High Court, and he was deported by the British. In 1955 he returned as a constitutional monarch, and in 1963 was elected first President of Uganda. He disagreed with the left-wing policies of the Prime Minister, Dr Milton *Obote, who deposed him in 1966.

Mutiny Act (1689) English legislation concerning the enforcement of military discipline, primarily over mutineers and deserters. The Declaration of Rights (1689) had declared illegal a standing army without parliamentary consent. To strengthen parliamentary control of the army, the 1689 Mutiny Act was enforced for one year only, theoretically giving Parliament the right of an annual review. In fact there were years (1689–1701) when it was not in force and both army and navy long retained their close connection with the sovereign. Only when the crown ceased to pay for the upkeep of the army did Parliament's annual review become effective.

MVD (Ministry for Internal Affairs) A police organization of the former Soviet Union. Together with the MGB (Ministry of State Security), it replaced the NKVD (People's Commissariat of Internal Affairs) in 1946. The MVD controlled all police forces and administered forced prison camps. During the last years of *Stalin's rule it became a significant factor in the Soviet economy, one of its most notorious chiefs being Lavrenti *Beria. The powers of the MGB were extended to supervise and control police agencies throughout the Soviet bloc, and to eliminate all anti-Soviet, anti-communist opposition in the satellite countries. Both agencies were drastically reduced and decentralized between 1953 and 1960, when they were replaced by the *KGB.

Mwene Mutapa The title taken by Mutota, founder of the *Rozvi empire in East Africa. It has been translated as "master pillager" and as "lord of the conquered mines". The Portuguese corrupted it to Monomotapa, and used it as a name for the empire. The founder died c.1470, and was succeeded until 1480 by his son Matope, a great conqueror who took possession of the greater part of eastern Central Africa. On his death his son Changa seized most of the empire from the designated heir, proclaiming himself *Changamire. The dynasty lasted until the end of the 18th century.

Myall Creek massacre (1838) An incident in which, in retaliation for an alleged "outrage", White station hands killed 28 Aborigines at Myall Creek in New South Wales, Australia. As a result, 11 White men were tried for murder. They were acquitted, but seven of them were retried, found guilty, and hanged. There was much public protest. Although prosecution of White people for such an incident was unusual, the incident itself was not, and Aborigines continued to be indiscriminately killed as settlers moved into other parts of the continent.

Myanmar (formerly **Burma**)

Capital:	Naypyitaw
Area:	676,578 sq km (261,228 sq miles)
Population:	55,167,330 (2013 est)
Currency:	1 kyat = 100 pyas
Religions:	Buddhist 89.0%; Christian 4.0%; Muslim 4.0%
Ethnic Groups:	Burman 68.0%; Shan 9.0%; Karen 7.0%
Languages:	Burmese (official); minority languages
International Organizations:	UN; Colombo Plan; ASEAN; Non-Aligned Movement; WTO

A country in south-east Asia, with borders (on the west) with India and Bangladesh, on the north-east with China, on the east with Laos, and on the south-east and south with Thailand.

Physical Myanmar has a long, tropical western coast on the Indian Ocean and is cut off from the rest of Asia by mountains in the north and east. Between the mountains and down the centre of the country run the broad, cultivable valley of the Irrawaddy River and several tributary valleys. To the east is the valley of the Salween River.

Economy Myanmar has a mainly agricultural economy. Crops include rice, pulses, beans—all important exports—and sesame, groundnuts, and sugar cane. Other major exports include natural gas, wood products, fish, clothing, jade, and gems. Mineral resources include copper, zinc, lead, tin, and silver. The isolationist policy of the former military regime ended with the introduction of civilian government in 2011, and now Myanmar is seeking to attract international investment.

History There was a Mon kingdom, Prome, in Burma in the 5th century AD. After the arrival of the Burmans in the 9th century there was much hostility between them and the indigenous peoples. Following a period of Mon ascendancy the Burmans of Pagan unified the country for a time (c.849–1287). From the Mons an Indian script and Theravada *Buddhism spread to Pagan and thence throughout Burma. During the 16th century the country was re-united under the Toungoo, but wars against Thai kingdoms and *Laos exhausted it. The last dynasty, the Konbaung, founded by Alaungpaya in 1757, was constantly engaged in wars against Siam, which led to the fall of the Siamese state of Ayuthia in 1767. In 1770 Burma repelled a Chinese invasion. The conquest of the region of Arakan brought the Burmese border to the boundary of British India.

Burma was invaded by the British (1824–26; 1852; 1885). The first two *Anglo-Burmese Wars led to the cession of territory and the third resulted in the deposition of King Thibaw and the establishment of Upper Burma as a province of British India. In 1931 there was a two-year uprising by the peasantry against European companies, and the Dobama Asi-ayone (Thakin) Party demanded independence. In 1937 Burma became a Crown colony, with a large degree of autonomy, Ba Maw being elected Premier. When Japanese troops moved into Malaya in 1942, a Burma National Army formed under *Aung San, was at first ready to welcome the Japanese. This force however defected to the Allies during the later campaign of liberation. Full independence was gained in 1948, Burma electing to remain outside the Commonwealth of Nations. Civil war erupted, with challenges to central government by the Karens of the Irrawaddy Delta and the Chin, Kayah, and Kachin hill tribes. Unu's government succumbed to an army coup in 1962, led by *Ne Win. He established an authoritarian state based on quasi-socialist and Buddhist principles, maintaining a policy of strict neutrality. When he retired in 1986, U San Yu became chairman of the governing Burma Socialist Program Party, still faced by intransigent ethnic insurgent groups. In September 1988 General Saw Maung seized power, imposing martial law, and changing the country's name to Myanmar. Its social, economic, and political problems only worsened. During 1989, Aung San's daughter Daw *Aung San Suu Kyi emerged as a leader of the opposition, but was placed under house arrest. Her party, the National League for Democracy (NLD), won a two-thirds majority for a constituent assembly in elections in 1990. The military regime refused to allow the assembly to meet and arrested NLD leaders. By now various ethnic separatist guerrilla groups and private armies were roaming the country. Fighting in the Muslim majority border state of Rakhine between government forces and Rohingya rebels led to some 200,000 Rohingya Muslims fleeing to Bangladesh in 1992. In April 1992 Saw Maung was replaced by his deputy, General Than Shwe. Some degree of political liberalization followed, but the government's emergency powers remained in force. A national convention to coordinate the drafting of a new constitution was inaugurated in 1993, but few meetings were held. Aung San Suu Kyi agreed to hold meetings with military leaders and was released from house arrest in 1995. However,

the NLD boycotted the national convention, which it claimed was not committed to implementing democratic reform, and was then formally expelled from the convention by the military. By mid-1995 15 guerrilla groups had agreed to ceasefires, but the Karens and the Mong Tai Army continued to fight. Aung San Suu Kyi was again placed under house arrest from 2000 to 2002 and from 2003 to 2010. Significant reforms began in 2008 with the ratification of a new constitution, which came into force after parliamentary elections in 2010. In 2011 the military handed over power to a civilian government. International suspicions that these changes were a front for continued military control were largely allayed by a rapid series of liberal reforms, including the release of many political prisoners and the legalization of the NLD. Aung San Suu Kyi was elected to parliament in 2012. However, doubts remain about the genuineness and durability of the reforms: in particular, the military's exact role in the new regime is unclear.

Mycenaean civilization (or **Aegean civilization**) Greek culture that dominated mainland Greece from c.1580 BC to c.1120 BC, when the invading *Dorians destroyed the citadels of Mycenae and Tiryns. Another important Peloponnesian centre was Pylos, and Mycenaean influence spread as far north as southern Thessaly. In c.1450 Mycenaeans seem to have conquered *Knossos in Crete, and traders travelled widely to Asia Minor, Cyprus, and Syria. It seems that they also sacked Troy c.1200, though the duration and scale of the expedition was doubtless exaggerated by the poet Homer in his epic, the *Iliad*. Finds from the early period bear witness to considerable wealth and a high artistic skill.

Mzilikazi (c.1796–1868) *Ndebele leader. The first great ruler of the Ndebele, he united his people into a nation under his leadership. He became a war leader under *Shaka, King of the Zulu, but rebelled in 1822. He led his people away from Zululand to what was later the western Transvaal, and then settled with his subjects in the area of Bulawayo. In 1837 he fled north, subduing the Shona, and ruling the Ndebele until his death.

Nadir Shah (1688–1747) Ruler of Persia (1736–47) and scourge of central Asia and India. Of Turkish origin and until 1726 a bandit chieftain, he rose to prominence under the Safavid shahs of Persia, acting as king-maker during an era of disputed succession. In 1736 when the infant shah died he seized the throne and immediately embarked on expeditions against neighbouring states. In 1739 he attacked Delhi, capital of Mogul India, but retreated after slaughtering the citizens. Campaigns against Russia and Turkey followed but military adventures were by then at the price of Persia's economic stability. His own subjects suffered as much as his enemies from his ruthless methods, and he was assassinated by his own troops.

NAFTA *See* NORTH AMERICAN FREE TRADE AGREEMENT.

Nagasaki, bombing of The second target for an atomic bomb attack, three days after the Americans bombed *Hiroshima. A city and port in south-west Japan, on the west coast of the island of Kyushu, its population was 419,901 in 2002. Visited by the Portuguese in 1545, it was the first Japanese port to open up to western trade. The bomb fell on 9 August 1945. While the hilly terrain protected the population of 230,000 from the full effects of the explosion, 40,000 people were killed and tremendous destruction caused. On the following day Japan surrendered and the ceasefire began on 15 August, the official surrender finally being signed on 2 September. Nagasaki now specializes in shipbuilding and heavy engineering.

Nagy, Imre (1896–1958) Hungarian Communist statesman, Prime Minister (1953–55; 1956). During his first term in office he introduced liberal policies, pushing for greater availability of consumer goods and less collectivization, but was forced to resign. Back in power in 1956, he announced Hungary's withdrawal from the Warsaw Pact and sought a neutral status for his country. When the Red Army moved in later that year to crush the uprising Nagy was

removed from office and executed by the new regime under János Kádár.

Nakasone Yasuhiro (1918–) Japanese statesman. He was elected to the House of Representatives in 1947. Nakasone succeeded Suzuki as Prime Minister and President of the *Liberal Democratic Party in October 1982 and held power until his resignation in 1987, despite the damage done to his party by the involvement of Kakuei Tanaka in the Lockheed corruption scandal. His domestic policies were based on a package of administrative, fiscal, and educational reforms, while internationally he was committed to close ties with the USA and greater involvement in world affairs. He rejoined the party in 1991.

Namibia (formerly **South-West Africa**)

Capital:	Windhoek
Area:	824,292 sq km (317,818 sq miles)
Population:	2,182,852 (2013 est)
Currency:	1 Namibian dollar = 100 cents
Religions:	Christian: between 80.0% and 90.0%; traditional beliefs: between 10.0% and 20.%
Ethnic Groups:	Ovambo 50.0%; Kavango 9.0%; Herero 7.0%; Damara 7.0%; mixed 6.5%; White 6.0%; Nama 5.0%
Languages:	English (official); Afrikaans; German; local languages
International Organizations:	Commonwealth; UN; AU; SADC; Non-Aligned Movement; WTO

A country in southern Africa with borders on Angola in the north, Botswana in the east, and South Africa in the south.

Physical In the north-east of Namibia a long sliver of territory, the Caprivi Strip, reaches between Angola and Botswana to Zambia. In the west the Namib Desert stretches down the Atlantic Ocean coast; in the

east is the Kalahari. The higher land between is also hot and arid and has no permanent rivers.

Economy Mineral exports provide over half of foreign-exchange earnings. These are dominated by uranium and diamonds, followed by zinc, gold, copper, and lead. Tungsten, silver, and tin are also mined. Poor rainfall largely limits agriculture to livestock raising, although some crops are grown; cattle and processed fish are exported. There is a very unequal wealth distribution, with over half the population living in poverty.

History Namibia was occupied by Khoikhoin (Hottentot), San (Bushman), and Herero peoples when Portuguese navigators explored the coastal areas of the country in the late 15th century. German missionaries went there in the 19th century and in 1884 the German protectorate of South-West Africa was established. In 1915, during World War I, it was captured by South African forces, and in 1920 became a *League of Nations mandated territory under South Africa. In 1946 the United Nations refused to allow it to be incorporated into South Africa and ended the mandate (1964), renaming the territory Namibia. In 1971 the International Court of Justice at The Hague ruled that the continued occupation of Namibia by South Africa was illegal and the UN recognized the Black nationalist group, *SWAPO (South West Africa People's Organization), as the legitimate representative of the people of Namibia. A National Assembly for internal government was established by South Africa in 1979 but SWAPO guerrillas continued to operate from Angola, which South African troops invaded. In 1988 South Africa was persuaded by the UN to negotiate with the SWAPO leader Samuel Nujoma. A Geneva protocol was signed in August and SWAPO won elections in November 1989, with Nujoma becoming President. Namibia gained independence as a multiparty democracy in 1990. Walvis Bay, a major port, remained an enclave of South Africa until 1994, when it was returned to Namibia. Nujoma was succeeded as President in 2004 by Hifekepunye Pohamba, who was re-elected in 2009.

Nanak (or **Guru Nanak**) (1469–1539) Indian religious leader and founder of Sikhism. He was born into a Hindu family in a village near Lahore. Many Sikhs believe that he was in a state of enlightenment at birth and that he was destined from then to be God's messenger. He learned about both Hinduism and Islam as a child, and at the age of 30 he underwent a religious experience which prompted him to become a wandering preacher. He eventually settled in Kartarpur, in what is now Punjab province, Pakistan; there he built the first Sikh temple. Nanak sought neither to unite the Hindu and Muslim faiths nor to create a new religion, preaching rather that spiritual liberation could be achieved through practising an inward and disciplined meditation on the name of God. His teachings are contained in a number of hymns which form part of the principal sacred scripture of Sikhism, the Adi Granth.

Nana Sahib (or **Brahmin Dhundu Panth**) (c. 1820–59) Hindu leader. On the outbreak of the *Indian Mutiny in Cawnpore (now Kanpur) (1857), he reluctantly joined the rebels and accepted the surrender of the British garrison under Sir Hugh Wheeler, promising safe conduct to its people. A reluctant recruit to the Mutiny, he subsequently fled to Nepal and his fate is uncertain, but it is likely that he died in the jungle.

Nanjing, Treaty of (1842) The treaty between Britain and China that ended the First *Opium War. The first *Unequal Treaty, it ceded Hong Kong to Britain, broke the Chinese monopoly on trade, and opened the *treaty ports of Xiamen (Amoy), Guangzhou (Canton), Fuzhou (Foochow), Ningbo (Ningpo), and Shanghai to foreign trade. Further treaties extended trade and residence privileges to other nations and set up the framework for Western economic expansion in China.

Nanking, Rape of The sacking of the city of Nanking (Nanjing) by Japanese troops in 1937 during the Sino-Japanese War. Between 40,000 and 300,000 civilians were slaughtered.

Nansen, Fridtjof (1861–1930) Norwegian Arctic explorer. In 1888 he led the first expedition to cross the Greenland icefields. Five years later he sailed north of Siberia on board the *Fram*, intending to reach the North Pole by allowing the ship to become frozen in the ice and letting the current carry it towards Greenland. By 1895, it had drifted as far north as 84° 4′; Nansen then made for the Pole on foot, reaching a latitude of 86° 14′, the furthest north anyone had been at that time. Nansen became increasingly involved in affairs of state, serving as Norwegian minister in London (1906–08). In 1922 he was awarded the Nobel Peace Prize for organizing relief work among victims of the Russian famine.

Nantes, Edict of (1598) A decree promulgated by *Henry IV that terminated the *French Wars of Religion. It was signed at Nantes, a port on the Loire estuary in western France. The Edict defined the religious and civic rights of the *Huguenots, giving them freedom of worship and a state subsidy to support their troops and pastors. It virtually created a state within a state and was incompatible with the policies of *Richelieu and *Mazarin and of *Louis XIV. The fall of the Huguenot stronghold of La Rochelle to Richelieu's army in 1628 marked the end of these political privileges. After 1665 Louis XIV embarked on a policy of persecuting Protestants and in 1685 he revoked the Edict.

Naoroji, Dadabhai (1825–1917) Indian nationalist leader. He was the first Indian to be elected to the British House of Commons, serving as Liberal Member of Parliament for Central Finsbury (1892–95). His campaign against the drain of wealth from India to Britain, defined in his classic study *Poverty and Un-British Rule in India* (1901), stimulated economic nationalism in the subcontinent. Active in promoting Indian social and political causes, he was a founder of the Indian National *Congress, serving as its President (1886, 1893, and 1906).

Napier, Robert Cornelis, 1st Baron of Magdala (1810–90) British field-marshal and civil engineer. He served with distinction in the *Sikh Wars and during the *Indian Mutiny, but made his reputation as the engineer chiefly responsible for the programme of public works in the Punjab from 1849 to 1856. He led an expedition to Ethiopia in which he captured Magdala (1868) and compelled the release of British captives. In 1870 he became commander-in-chief in India.

Napoleon I (or **Napoléon Bonaparte**) (1769–1821) Emperor of the French (1804–14). Born in Ajaccio, he was a Corsican of Italian descent. By the age of 26 he was a general, and placed in supreme command of the campaign against Sardinia and Austria in Italy (1796–97). This provided him with some of the most spectacular victories of his military career and resulted in the creation of the French-controlled Cisalpine Republic in northern Italy. In 1798 he led an army to Egypt, intending to create a

French empire overseas and to threaten the British overland route to India. *Nelson, by destroying the French fleet at the Battle of the Nile (1798), prevented this plan. Bonaparte returned to France (1799) and, joining a conspiracy with Emmanuel Sièyes (1748–1836), overthrew the Directory and dissolved the First Republic. Elected First Consul for ten years, he became the supreme ruler of France. During the next four years he began his reorganization of the French legal system (*see* CODE NAPOLÉON), and education.

In 1804 Napoleon crowned himself Emperor of the French, and embarked on a series of campaigns known as the *Napoleonic Wars.

His ill-fated invasion of Russia (1812) and the set-backs of the *Peninsular War (1807–14) all contributed to Napoleon's decline. Following his defeat in the battle of *Leipzig and the proclamation by *Talleyrand of the deposition of the emperor, he abdicated in 1814. After a brief exile on Elba he returned, but defeat at the Battle of *Waterloo (1815) ended his rule after only a *Hundred Days. He spent the rest of his life in exile on St Helena. In 1796 he married *Josephine de Beauharnais, whose failure to give him a son led to their divorce. In 1810 Napoleon married the Austrian princess Marie-Louise. Their only child, Joseph-François-Charles, crowned as the Roi de Rome, died aged 21.

Napoleon III (or **Charles-Louis Napoléon Bonaparte**) (1808–73) Emperor of the French (1852–70). He was the third son of Hortense de Beauharnais stepdaughter of *Napoleon I and Louis Bonaparte (1778–1846), brother of Napoleon I and King of Holland (1806–10). After the fall of Napoleon I, Napoleon III began a long period of exile in Switzerland. On the death of Napoleon I's only son, the Roi de Rome, in 1832, he became Bonapartist pretender to the French throne and twice attempted to overthrow *Louis Philippe, as a result of which he was deported. In 1840 embarked upon the disastrous "Boulogne Conspiracy" to gather supporters. He was arrested and imprisoned in the fortress of Ham. He escaped to London (1846) disguised as a mason by the name of "Badinguet", which thereafter became his nickname. During the *Revolutions of 1848, he returned to France, and in December under the new constitution was elected President of the French Republic. In 1852, following a coup against Parliament, he had himself accepted as Emperor of the French. Napoleon III took part in the *Crimean War and presided over the Congress of *Paris (1856). His "Liberal Empire" (1860–70) widened the powers of the legislative assembly. Underestimating *Bismarck, he allowed the latter's belligerent *Ems telegram to provoke him into fighting the *Franco-Prussian War, the outcome of which brought ruin to the Second Empire. He was captured by the Prussians and deposed, spending the rest of his life in exile in England.

Napoleonic Wars The campaigns carried out between *Napoleon I and the European powers, including Britain (1796–1815). The first great Italian campaign (1796) under Napoleon I secured a series of decisive victories for the French over the Austrians in northern Italy. In 1798 he led an expedition to Egypt, but the British fleet under Admiral *Nelson destroyed the French fleet in Aboukir Bay. In 1799 Napoleon I led an army over the Alps to win the Battle of Marengo (1800) over the Austrians. Britain, apprehensive of Napoleon's threat in the Mediterranean and in continental Europe, was by 1803 once more at war with France. Nelson destroyed the combined Spanish and French fleets at *Trafalgar (1805), and in the same year Napoleon swung his *grande armée* towards Austria, which, with Russia and Sweden, joined Britain in the Third Coalition. Napoleon's forces encircled the Austrians at Ulm, forcing them to surrender without a battle. Napoleon fought and defeated the emperors of Austria and Russia at the Battle of *Austerlitz (1805) and forced Austria to sue for peace. In the following year Prussia joined the Third Coalition and, in a campaign that lasted 23 days, Napoleon broke the Prussian armies at *Jena and Auerstädt and accepted the surrender of Prussia. The Russian emperor *Alexander I concluded a treaty of friendship and alliance with Napoleon at *Tilsit in July 1807. In 1808 a revolt broke out in Spain, which by now was also under French rule. Napoleon sent a large force to quell it but was confronted by the British army under Sir Arthur Wellesley, later Duke of *Wellington. Britain won a series of victories in the *Peninsular War, which, though not conclusive, occupied 300,000 French soldiers when they were needed elsewhere. In 1812 Napoleon I defeated the Russians at *Borodino and occupied Moscow, but instead of suing for peace, Alexander I's forces withdrew further into the country. Napoleon I's *grande armée* was forced to retreat from Moscow in the severest winter conditions, which cost the lives of nearly half a million men. After a crushing defeat at *Leipzig the following year, Napoleon I abdicated and retired to Elba (1814). Next year he returned to France and was finally defeated by Wellington and Blücher at the Battle of *Waterloo (1815).

Narva, Battle of (30 November 1700) The crushing defeat of *Peter I (the Great) of Russia by *Charles XII of Sweden at the beginning of the *Northern War at the port of Narva, in Estonia. In 1704 Peter the Great recovered the town.

Narváez, Pánfilo de (*c.*1478–1528) Spanish conquistador. He gained a reputation as a ruthless soldier in the conquest of Cuba in 1511; later, as governor, he watched his men slaughter some 2500 unarmed Cubans. When he was sent to fetch the rebellious *Cortés in Mexico in 1520, most of his men deserted, and he lost an eye in the ensuing battle. Leading an expedition to Florida in 1528, he ignored advice from his lieutenant, *Cabeza de Vaca, divided his forces, and was lost at sea trying to return to Cuba in makeshift boats.

NASA (National Aeronautics and Space Administration) A civilian agency formed in 1958 to coordinate and direct the whole of aeronautical and space research in the USA. Its headquarters are in Washington, DC. As well as collaborating with industry and universities, NASA also maintains and develops its own installations. Among the latter are the Ames Research Center, California; the Goddard Space Flight Center, near Washington, DC; the Lyndon B. Johnson Space Center at Houston, Texas; and the Jet Propulsion Laboratory, California.

Naseby, Battle of (14 June 1645) A decisive victory for the Parliamentary forces during the *English Civil War. The battle took place near Naseby in Northamptonshire, after *Charles I's storming and sacking of Leicester. Led by Fairfax and Cromwell, the *New Model Army outnumbered the *Cavalier force by about one-third. Prince Rupert's cavalry squandered an early advantage, as at *Edgehill. After a bitter struggle the Roundhead forces proved superior, and the Cavaliers suffered extremely heavy losses.

Nash, Richard (or Beau Nash) (1674–1762) Welsh dandy. Master of Ceremonies in Bath from 1704, he established the city as the centre of fashionable society and was an arbiter of fashion and etiquette in the early Georgian age.

Nash, Sir Walter (1882–1968) New Zealand statesman. A life-long Christian Socialist, he joined the Labour Party, becoming the most important spokesman for its moderate wing. He (and Peter *Fraser) turned the Labour Party into a national organization and formulated the policies which led to the election of the first

Labour Government in 1935. He played a major role in piloting through Parliament in 1938 the great system of child allowances, and "free" medicine, which was the most extensive system of social security in the world at that time. He became leader of the Opposition in 1950. Nash led Labour to a narrow victory in the 1957 election, serving as Prime Minister until the party's defeat in 1960. During this period, despite financial stringency, he introduced further important social reforms.

Nasser, Gamal Abdel (1918–70) Egyptian colonel and statesman, Prime Minister (1954–56) and President (1956–70). He was the leader of a successful military coup to depose King Farouk in 1952, after which a republic was declared with Muhammad Neguib (1901–84) as its President. Nasser deposed Neguib in 1954, declaring himself Prime Minister; two years later he announced a new one-party constitution, becoming President shortly afterwards. His nationalization of the Suez Canal brought armed conflict with Britain, France, and Israel in 1956; he also led Egypt in two unsuccessful wars against Israel (1956 and 1967). With considerable Soviet aid he launched a programme of domestic modernization, including the building of the High Dam at Aswan. The lake created in 1960 after the building of the Aswan Dam is called **Lake Nasser**. It is 500 km (300 miles) long.

Natchez A Native American tribe of the Hokan-Natchez linguistic group, originally living in the lower Mississippi valley.

National Assembly The revolutionary assembly formed by members of the Third Estate on 17 June 1789 when they failed to gain the support of the whole of the French *States-General. Three days later the members signed the *Tennis Court Oath. The Assembly was accepted by *Louis XVI the following month, having added "Constituent" to its title. In August it agreed upon the influential declaration of the *Rights of Man and the Citizen and two years later its constitution was accepted by the king. Its reorganization of local government into departments, although long lasting, had less immediate success. Renamed the Legislative Assembly (1791) and the National Convention (1792), it was dominated by the *Girondins and the *Jacobins before being replaced by the *Directory in 1795.

National Federation of Labour *See* RED FEDS.

National governments The British coalition governments (1931–35). In August 1931 a financial crisis led to a split within the Labour government, nine ministers resigning rather than accepting cuts in unemployment benefits. The Liberal leader Herbert Samuel suggested that the Prime Minister, Ramsay *MacDonald, create a `government of national salvation', by inviting Conservatives and Liberals to replace them, and the first National government was formed on 24 August. An emergency budget was introduced, which increased taxes and proposed to reduce both benefits and public sector salaries. Britain abandoned the gold standard and free trade, adopting a policy of protection. The Labour Party split, supporters of the government being regarded as traitors to socialism. In October MacDonald won a general election and formed a second National government, but its balance was now strongly towards the Conservative Party. The governments of Stanley *Baldwin (1935–37) and Neville *Chamberlain (1937–40) retained the term National, but they were effectively Conservative governments.

National Health Service *See* HEALTH SERVICES.

National Party A South African political party. It was originally founded in 1913–15 by General J. B. M. *Hertzog after his secession from Botha's South African Party. In 1924 it became the Nationalist-Labour alliance under Hertzog, who joined *Smuts in the United Party in 1934. In the same year D. F. *Malan founded the Purified Nationalist Party, which was reunited in 1939 with Hertzog, emerging as the Afrikaner-dominated party of *apartheid. It held uninterrupted power from 1948 to 1994. Attempts by President P. W. Botha to meet the twin threats of domestic unrest and international condemnation of apartheid with a programme of mild reforms led to defections by supporters of apartheid to the Conservative Party and extreme right-wing Afrikaner groups. Under President *de Klerk it opened its ranks to all races in August 1990, winning, at the cost of further defections of right-wingers, some support from moderates among both the coloured and unenfranchised Black population. In South Africa's first multiracial elections in 1994 the National Assembly and de Klerk was appointed Second Deputy President by Nelson *Mandela. In 1996, following the ratification of a permanent constitution, the National Party withdrew from the government in order to become an opposition party. Renamed the New National

Party in 1998, its support declined rapidly. It voted to disband in 2005 and its Members of Parliament joined the *African National Congress.

National Party of Australia An Australian political party largely representing rural interests. Farmers' representatives were elected to colonial (later state) parliaments from the 1890s onwards. A number of farmers' candidates who had been elected to the Federal Parliament formed the Country Party of Australia in 1916. It has governed federally in coalition with the Nationalist Party (1923–29), the United Australia Party (1934–39; 1940–41), and the *Liberal Party (1949–72; 1975–83; 1996–2007; 2013–). Several of its parliamentary leaders have been Prime Ministers, albeit briefly. They were Earle Page (1939), Arthur William Fadden (1941), and John McEwen (1967–68). It has also governed (under various names), mostly in coalition with other parties, for periods in most states. The party's national name was changed to the National Country Party in 1975 and to the National Party of Australia in 1982.

National People's Party *See* KUOMINTANG.

Nation of Islam Splinter group of the *Black Muslim Movement, formed in 1985 by the radical African-American preacher **Louis Farrakhan** (1933–), who trained as a teacher and was converted to Islam by *Malcolm X. The Nation of Islam was the original name of the Black Muslims (disbanded in 1985 by the son of their founder Elijah Muhammad) and was adopted by Farrakhan to proclaim his group's adherence to the ideals of the movement, in

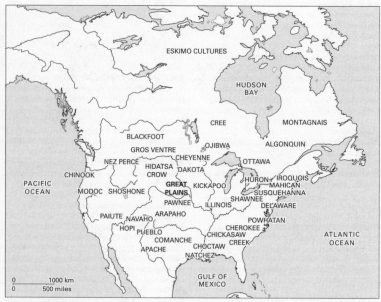

Native Americans. (tribal distribution in the late 15th century) When the first European settlers arrived in North America, the Native American population was scattered widely throughout the whole continent. There were numerous different tribes and an extraordinary diversity of languages and cultures. Some cultural similarities can, however, be found between tribes living in areas of similar geography and climate. For example, in the wooded north-west coastal area, with its hospitable climate and plentiful food supplies, tribes lived a settled life with a well-developed culture; on the central plains the majority of tribes were nomadic, living by hunting buffalo; while in the fertile south-east an agricultural and trading economy was firmly established by the 14th century.

particular Black separatism. In common with the original organization, the Nation of Islam has gained a reputation for instilling discipline and purpose in its members and working to rid the African-American community of exploitation through crime and drug abuse. In 1995, a "million-man" march on Washington, DC, was attended by around 400,000 supporters.

Farrakhan has been accused of fomenting racial hatred. In particular, his alleged *anti-Semitism led to him being banned from entering Britain in 1986 and from Israel in 1997.

Native Americans The original inhabitants of North America, who migrated from Asia from about 30,000 years ago. By the time of European colonization, the indigenous population was probably under 900,000, mostly living along the coasts rather than in the barren interior. They lived in small villages which, except in the south-west, were organized round hunting, with agriculture a secondary activity. The overall social organization was that of the tribe and warfare between tribes was endemic. British and French settlers in the north-east forced the Native Americans inland, as did the Spanish in the south-west. The acquisition of horses from Europeans increased the number of nomadic societies on the Great Plains. The major tribes are usually divided geographically, North-eastern Woodland (for example, Algonquin, Delaware, Iroquois, South-east (e.g. Cherokee, Choctaw, Creek, Great Plains (e.g. Blackfoot, Comanche, Dakota), Desert-west (e.g. Apache, Pueblo, Navaho), Far west (e.g. Paiute), Pacific North-west (e.g. Chinook), and Mountain or Plateau (e.g. Nez Percé). The Native people of Canada are the *Inuit and of Alaska are the Aleut. The indigenous people of Central and South America are usually called *Amerindians.

NATO *See* NORTH ATLANTIC TREATY ORGANIZATION.

Nauru

Capital:	Yaren (de facto; there is no official capital)
Area:	21 sq km (8.2 sq miles)
Population:	9,434 (2013 est)
Currency:	1 Australian dollar = 100 cents
Religions:	Protestant 45.8%; Roman Catholic 33.2%
Ethnic Groups:	Nauruan 58.0%; other Pacific Islander 26.0%; Chinese 8.0%; European 8.0%
Languages:	Nauruan (official); English
International Organizations:	UN; Commonwealth; Pacific Islands Forum; Secretariat of the Pacific Community

A tiny island country just south of the Equator in the south-western Pacific Ocean, between longitudes 166° and 167° E.

Physical Nauru is a coral island, with a band of fertile land around the coast rising to a central plateau.

Economy Nauru's wealth formerly lay in phosphate deposits. However, the supply of phosphates is almost exhausted and the trust funds into which phosphate revenues were paid have been dissipated. With 80% of the land rendered uninhabitable by phosphate extraction, Nauru faces grave economic problems and the economy and government are entirely dependent on Australian support.

History Nauru was settled by various Polynesian peoples who travelled there from other islands before being discovered by the British in 1798. In 1899 a British company, the Pacific Islands Company based in Sydney, found that the island comprised the world's richest deposits of phosphate of lime. The company began mining the deposits in 1906. From 1888 to 1914 the island was part of Germany's Marshall Islands protectorate. Thereafter, apart from three years of Japanese occupation during World War II, Nauru was a trust territory of Britain, Australia, and New Zealand, before achieving independence and a limited membership of the Commonwealth in 1968. In 1993 Australia, Britain, and New Zealand agreed to pay compensation for the damage done to the island by mining. From 2001 to 2008 a major source of employment and income was a holding centre for refugees and asylum seekers attempting to enter Australia. The centre was reopened in 2012.

Navaho A group of over 50 Native American clans, who were originally nomadic hunter-gatherers and, like the related *Apaches, originated in western Canada. They moved southwards to the "four corners" area of Utah, Colorado, Arizona, and New Mexico between the 11th and 15th centuries, displacing much of the native *Anasazi culture to the south by the end of the 13th century, and raiding the neighbouring Hohokam to the south. Spanish contact began in 1540–42, and from 1609 Spanish missions worked among them. The Navaho adopted horse-breeding and pastoralism from the Spanish, as well as learning Anasazi weaving skills and Spanish silver-working artistry.

The Navaho often engaged in sporadic warfare with the pueblo (village)-dwelling peoples, such as the Hopi. In the mid-19th century, the Navaho were resettled and most became sheep farmers. They are now the largest single Native grouping in the USA. Their kinship organization is based on extended matrilineal groups, in which women have a high status. Recent discoveries of oil and mineral reserves on their reservation have given them an extra source of material wealth.

Navigation Acts Legislation enacted by the English Parliament to prevent foreign merchant vessels competing on equal terms with English ships. The earliest Act goes back to the reign of Richard II, but the most important was that of 1651, requiring that goods entering England must be carried in either English ships or ships of the country where the goods originated. Its aim was to destroy the Dutch carrying trade and it provoked the *Anglo-Dutch Wars. The Acts applied to the colonies and despite the impetus they gave to New England shipping, they were widely resented in North America because of their increasingly strict measures against smugglers and against the colonial manufacture of certain goods that competed with English products. They were modified in 1823 and withdrawn in 1849.

navy A fleet of ships and its crew, organized for war at sea. In the 5th and 4th centuries Athens and Corinth relied on *triremes (galleys with three banks of oars) and high-speed manoeuvrable quinqueremes (five-banked galleys) were developed by the Macedonians. At the Battle of *Salamis an Athenian fleet won a decisive victory over the Persians, established Greek control over the eastern Mediterranean, and the fleet remained the crucial basis of Athenian supremacy. The Roman empire, though essentially a land-based power, fought Carthage at sea in the First *Punic War, and gained control of the Mediterranean.

Navies were needed to protect trading vessels against pirates: the *Byzantine empire maintained a defensive fleet to retain control over its vital trade arteries. In England, King *Alfred created a fleet in the 9th century in defence

against Scandinavian invasions. The *Cinque Ports supplied the English navy from the 11th to the 16th centuries and it was organized and enlarged under successive Tudor monarchs. The Italian city-states kept squadrons of galleys and adapted carracks (merchant ships) to defend their ports against the Ottoman Turks and the Battle of *Lepanto saw a Christian fleet decisively beat the Ottomans. The 17th century saw naval reorganization in England under *Pepys, and the Dutch and French also expanded their fleets as trade and colonial expansion accelerated in the 18th century.

From the early Middle Ages the warship altered from being a converted merchant ship, modified by the addition of 'castles', fortified with land artillery, and manned by knights, into a specially armed vessel. By the 14th century ships were being fitted with guns and by the 16th century special warships were being built with heavy armaments. Success or failure in battle, however, was determined by tactical skill as all sailing ships were at the mercy of the wind.

At the time of the *Napoleonic Wars, naval vessels were sailing ships, built of wood and armed with cannon that fired broadsides. They engaged at close quarters and ratings were armed with muskets and hand-grenades. Following the Battle of *Trafalgar (1805), the British navy dominated the oceans of the world for a century. Change came slowly. Steam power replaced sail only gradually, while in 1859 the French navy pioneered the protection of the wooden hull of a ship with iron plates (Ironclads). With the development of the iron and steel industry in the late 19th century, rapid advances were made in ship design and the armament of ships. At the same time the submarine, armed with torpedoes, emerged as a fighting vessel. When Germany challenged the supremacy of the British navy, the latter responded with the huge steel Dreadnought battleships (1906), equipped with guns with a range of over 32 km (20 miles). During World War I the German submarine (U-boat) fleet was checked by the *convoy system to protect Allied merchant shipping, but the major British and German fleets only engaged in the inconclusive Battle of *Jutland (1916). Between the wars aircraft were rapidly developed and naval warfare in World War II was increasingly fought by aircraft from aircraft carriers, particularly in the great naval battles of the Pacific Campaign. Since World War II, the development of submarines armed with long-range nuclear missiles has reduced the number of surface ships and revolutionized naval strategy as submarines are difficult to detect and destroy. Most countries retain fleets of small, fast vessels for coastal patrol. The USA and the former Soviet Union, however, competed in the size and armament of their navies. The *Falklands War (1982) revealed the extent to which there remained a place for a conventional navy, but also showed how exposed surface ships were to missile attack. During the *Gulf War and the *Iraq War the navies of the Allied forces played an important strategic role, with aircraft carriers providing launch sites from which air strikes against Iraqi ground targets were made.

Naxalite Movement An Indian revolutionary movement named after the village of Naxalbari in the Himalayan foothills in West Bengal, where it first began. The theoretician and founder of the movement, Charu Majumdar, a veteran communist, broke away from the Communist Party of India (Marxist) and established the Communist Party of India (Marxist-Leninist). The CPI (M-L) first organized several armed risings of landless agricultural labourers, especially in eastern India in 1967. It subsequently developed into an urban guerrilla movement, especially in Calcutta. Its programme of terror was suppressed with considerable violence. The CPI (M-L) eventually split up into several factions, one of which adopted a policy of participating in constitutional politics, but Naxalite activities continue.

Nazca (or **Nasca**) A culture developed on the southern Peruvian coast c.200 BC–600 AD, eventually eclipsed by the expansion of the Huari culture of central Peru in the 7th century. In the extremely dry environment its settlements and population remained modest, but its craftsmen produced a long sequence of pottery styles, with animal and human figures. It also produced large drawings of animals, abstract designs, and straight lines on the coastal plain (the Nazca Lines), by clearing and aligning the surface stones to expose the underlying sand; their purpose is uncertain, but may have been religious.

Nazi A member of the Nationalsozialistische Deutsche Arbeiterpartei or National Socialist German Workers' Party. It was founded in 1919 as the German Workers' Party by a Munich locksmith, Anton Drexler, adopted its new name in 1920, and was taken over by *Hitler in 1921. The Nazis dominated Germany from 1933 to 1945. In so far as the party had a coherent programme it consisted of opposition to democracy and a fascist belief in a one party

state. It claimed that a pure Aryan race existed and promulgated *anti-Semitism, allied itself to the old Prussian military tradition, and encouraged an extreme sense of nationalism, inflamed by hatred of the humiliating terms inflicted on Germany in the *Versailles Peace Settlement. The Nazi's declared their views were supported by the racist theories of the Comte de *Gobineau, the national fervour of Heinrich von Treitschke, and the superman theories of Friedrich Nietzsche. Nazi beliefs were given dogmatic expression in Hitler's *Mein Kampf* (1925). The success of the Nazis in dominating completely what had previously been regarded as a civilized country is to some extent explained by the widespread desperation of Germans over the failure of the *Weimar Republic governments to solve economic problems and by a growing fear of *Bolshevik power. Through Hitler's oratory, Germans in the 1930s appeared to accept his pronouncements, despite their lack of logic and rationality. Only after Hitler had obtained power by constitutional means was the *Third Reich established. Rival parties were banned, and the army, industry, and the banks supported Hitler in his mission to launch Germany on a war of conquest. By now virtually the whole German nation supported him, his few opponents were either murdered or frightened into acquiescence. Over six million Jews, Russians, Poles, gypsies, homosexuals, disabled people, and others were incarcerated and exterminated in German *concentration camps. The German Nazi Party was disbanded in 1945 after it had led Germany into a humiliating defeat, and its revival was officially forbidden by the Federal Republic of Germany. Worldwide revulsion at German policies of genocide and the enormous burden of guilt borne by the German people for their enthusiastic participation in Hitler's monstrous plans have ensured that Nazism has disappeared from mainstream politics, although occasional resurgences do occur in extreme right-wing fringes.

Nazi–Soviet Pact (23 August 1939) A military agreement signed in Moscow between Germany and the Soviet Union. It renounced warfare between the two countries and pledged neutrality by either party if the other were attacked by a third party. Each signatory promised not to join any grouping of powers that was "directly or indirectly aimed at the other party". The pact also contained secret protocols whereby the dictators agreed to divide *Poland between them and the Soviet

Union was given a free hand to deal with the Baltic states.

Ndebele A Bantu-speaking Zulu people, branches of which are found in Zimbabwe (where they are better known as **Matabele**) and in the Transvaal.

Neanderthals *See* EARLY HUMANS.

Nebuchadnezzar (*c.*630–562 BC) King of Babylon (605–562 BC). He rebuilt the city with massive fortification walls, a huge temple, and a ziggurat (a rectangular tiered tower), and extended his rule over ancient Palestine and neighbouring countries. In 586 BC he captured and destroyed Jerusalem and deported many Israelites from Palestine to Babylon (the Babylonian Captivity, which lasted until 539 BC).

Necker, Jacques (1732–1804) Swiss-born banker. He began work as a bank clerk in Switzerland, moving to his firm's headquarters in Paris in 1750. He rose to hold the office of director-general of French finances on two occasions. During Necker's first term (1777–81), his social and administrative reform programmes aroused the hostility of the court and led to his forced resignation. While in office for a second time (1788–89), he recommended summoning the States General, resulting in his dismissal on 11 July 1789. News of this angered the people and was one of the factors which resulted in the storming of the Bastille three days later.

Nefertiti (14th century BC) Wife and queen of *Akhenaten, Pharaoh of Egypt. She was a devoted worshipper of the Sun god Aten, whose cult was the only one permitted by her husband. She fell from favour, and was supplanted by one of her six daughters. She is known to posterity through inscriptions, reliefs, and above all a fine limestone bust which was found at ancient Akhetaton (modern Tell el-Amarna).

Negroids The indigenous peoples of Africa south of the Sahara and their descendants in other parts of the world. Bantu-speaking Negroid pastoralists and crop-growers are traditionally believed to have spread from western to eastern and southern Africa during the past few thousand years but recent evidence suggests that Negroids speaking other languages were in other parts of sub-Saharan Africa much earlier. They may indeed have originated in southern, not western Africa, but this is controversial. Unquestionably, though, they gained knowledge of agricultural techniques and domesticated animals from northern parts of the

continent. Negroids are extremely variable in appearance but they can be seen in their most typical form in West Africa; in the east, there has been much intermixing with Hamitic-speaking *Caucasoids (for example, Ethiopians and Egyptians); and in the south with the related hunting and gathering San (Bushmen) and the cattle-raising Khoikhoi (Hottentots). The pygmies of Central Africa are of Negroid stock.

Nehru, Jawaharlal (or **Pandit Nehru**) (1889–1964) Indian statesman, Prime Minister (1947–64). An early associate of Mahatma Gandhi, Nehru was elected leader of the Indian National Congress, succeeding his father Pandit Motilal Nehru (1861–1931), in 1929. Imprisoned nine times by the British for his nationalist campaigns during the 1930s and 1940s, he eventually played a major part in the negotiations preceding independence. Nehru subsequently became the first Prime Minister of independent India. He was the father of Indira Gandhi.

Nehru, Motilal (1861–1931) Indian political leader. Together with C. R. Das (1870–1925), he organized the Swaraj (Independence) Party in 1922. This set out to participate in the Indian legislative councils but aimed to oppose the British by wrecking the councils from within, as an alternative to Gandhi's *non-cooperation movement. In 1928 Nehru chaired the All Parties' Committee which produced the Nehru Report, setting out a proposed new Indian constitution with dominion status for India.

Nelson, Horatio, Viscount Nelson, Duke of Bronte (1758–1805) British admiral. Nelson's victories at sea during the early years of the *Napoleonic Wars made him a national hero. His unorthodox independent tactics (as a commodore under Admiral Jervis) led to the defeat of a Spanish fleet off Cape St Vincent in 1797. In 1798 Nelson virtually destroyed the French fleet in the Battle of Aboukir Bay; he began his notorious affair with Lady Hamilton, the wife of the British envoy to the court of Naples, shortly afterwards, while stationed in Naples. He proceeded to rout the Danes at Copenhagen in 1801, but is best known for his decisive victory over a combined French and Spanish fleet at the Battle of Trafalgar in 1805; Nelson was mortally wounded in the conflict.

Nennius (*fl. c.*800) Welsh chronicler. He is traditionally credited with the compilation or revision of the *Historia Britonum*, a collection of historical and geographical information about

Britain, including one of the earliest known accounts of King Arthur.

neoconservatism A school of political thought in the USA. Neoconservatism first emerged in the 1970s and is distinguished from other strands of *conservatism by its approach to foreign policy, which holds that security is best attained by using US power to spread freedom and democracy, if necessary by force and without international cooperation. Many early neoconservatives were former liberals converted to conservatism by the perceived failures of liberal and multilateral foreign policies: as Irving Kristol (1920–2009), a prominent neoconservative thinker, famously phrased it, a neoconservative is "a liberal mugged by reality". Neoconservatives were strong opponents of communism and supporters of the *Cold War and have exercised some influence during the administration of all Republican presidents since Ronald *Reagan. Their prominence grew after *September 11, 2001, when their views coincided with the perceived need for an assertive foreign policy to combat the terrorist threat to the USA. In particular, the invasion of Iraq (2003) and the subsequent attempt to establish a democratic regime there chimed closely with neoconservative ideals (*see* IRAQ WAR). Neoconservatism has been criticized on several grounds, including the charge that its definitions of "freedom" and "democracy" are essentially American and so cannot be imposed successfully on other countries and cultures.

Neolithic (New Stone Age) The later part of the *Stone Age, characterized by the Neolithic peoples' use of polished stone axes and simple pottery. The discovery of farming and the domestication of animals brought an end to the slow development of the hunting societies of the *Palaeolithic and *Mesolithic periods and initiated a time of rapid change that soon produced metalworking, cities, states, and empires. The term is thus best applied to the stone-using, farming populations of Asia and Europe, who used polished axes to clear the forests and cooked their grain in pottery vessels. The very first farmers, at sites like Jericho, had not discovered pottery, and are called pre-pottery Neolithic. In the Old World, agriculture began in the Near East by the 8th millennium BC and had spread to northern Europe by the 4th millennium BC.

Western Neolithic refers to the period after 4000 BC during which the indigenous hunting and gathering peoples living along the western coasts of Europe merged with incoming farmers from central Europe (related to the Bandkeramik culture, named after their characteristic pottery that was decorated with incised ribbon-like ornament) to form new groups of farmers with a basically similar material culture. Their simple round-based pottery has sometimes given them the name 'bowl cultures', but they are better known for the construction of monumental tombs out of large boulders or megaliths. The Bandkeramik peoples spread up from the Balkans c.5000 BC. They occupied small plots of land on fertile soil near rivers, where they built wooden longhouses for themselves and their livestock, and cultivated cereals, which they introduced to this area. They formed the basis of later Neolithic populations. An important Neolithic settlement is Çatal Hüyük, near Konya in south-central Turkey, which dates from c.6500 BC. Its small houses, built of mud bricks, were so close together that all access had to be by way of the flat roofs. A high proportion of rooms are believed to have been shrines, on the basis of numerous bulls' horns mounted in benches. There were also wall decorations, votive offerings, and richly furnished burials beneath the floors. Only part of the site has been excavated.

Impressed ware culture refers to the farming people who spread round virtually the whole coastline of the western Mediterranean from 6000 BC. Their characteristic pottery consists of round-bottomed bowls decorated with impressed designs, particularly using the crinkled edge of the cockle shell (the so-called Cardial ware). Material comes from both caves and open villages. By the 4th millennium the culture had split into many regional variants.

The **Yangshao** site in northern Henan province, China, has provided archaeological evidence of the Chinese Neolithic period. There were square and round houses of timber post construction with thatched roofs, in villages up to 5 ha (12 acres) in size. The red burnished pottery, often painted in black, was handmade but finished on a slow wheel. Polished stone axes and knives were in general use. The staple crop was millet, grown on terraces, and pigs and dogs were the commonest domestic animals. This culture was distributed over much of the middle Huang He (Yellow River) valley during the 4th and early 3rd millennia BC. This developed into the **Longshan** (Lung Shan) later Neolithic culture of the lower Huang He (Yellow River) valley, which flourished between 2500 and 1700 BC. Its economy was based primarily on millet, harvested with polished stone reaping knives, and on pigs, cows, and goats. Its distinctive pottery was the first in the Far East to be made on the fast wheel, and was kiln-fired to a uniform black colour.

Nepal

Capital:	Kathmandu
Area:	147,181 sq km (56,827 sq miles)
Population:	30,430,267 (2013 est)
Currency:	1 Nepalese rupee = 100 paisa (or pice)
Religions:	Hindu 81.3%; Buddhist 9.0%; Muslim 4.4%
Ethnic Groups:	Chhettri 16.6%; Brahman-Hill 12.2%; Magar 7.1%; Tharu 6.6%; Tamang 5.8%; Newar 5.0%; over 100 minority groups
Languages:	Nepali (official); over 100 other languages
International Organizations:	UN; Colombo Plan; Non-Aligned Movement; WTO

A south Asian country among the peaks and southern slopes of the Himalayas, sandwiched between China (Tibet) and India.

Physical Nepal contains the highest mountains in the world. The peaks are in the north; below the snow-line rivers run through turfy valleys and fine forests.

Economy Much of the land is not cultivable and deforestation is a major problem. However, the economy is primarily agrarian, with principal crops of pulses, rice, cereals, sugar cane, and jute. Industry is limited mainly to agricultural processing. Tourism is a major source of revenue and remittances from expatriates are important.

History Nepal's first era of centralized control was under the Licchavi dynasty, from about the 4th to the 10th centuries. During this period Buddhist influences were dominant, but under the Malla dynasty (10th–18th centuries) Hinduism was the dominant religion. In 1769 a successful Gurkha invasion brought to power the present ruling dynasty. From their capital at Kathmandu they wielded absolute power over the indigenous Nepalese tribes. Their incursion into north-west India led to a border war (1814–16) and to territorial concessions to the British (Treaty of Kathmandu, 1816). Effective rule then passed to a family of hereditary Prime Ministers, the Ranas, who cooperated closely with the British. Gurkhas were recruited to service in the British and Indian armies. Growing internal dissatisfaction led in 1950 to a coup, which reaffirmed royal powers under the king, Tribhuvan (1951–55). His successor, King Mahendra (1955–72), experimented with a more democratic form of government. This was replaced once more with monarchic rule (1960), which continued under his son, King Birendra Bir Bikram (1972–2001). Following pro-democracy demonstrations and mass arrests from 1989 onwards, the king agreed to legalize political parties, and granted a new constitution in November 1990, establishing a bicameral parliament; the first democratic election was held in May 1991. In 2001 the King and most of the royal family were murdered by the Crown Prince, Dipendra, who then committed suicide. Gyanendra, the late King's brother, took the throne. A Maoist guerrilla insurgency flared up in 2002, and in 2005 the King declared a state of emergency and assumed personal control of the government. However, popular protests forced him to restore parliamentary rule in 2006. Later that year he was stripped of his remaining powers and a ceasefire was agreed with the rebels. Negotiations for a final settlement and a new constitution soon became deadlocked, and a series of short-lived governments achieved little. However, in 2008 the monarchy was abolished and Nepal became a republic; Ram Baran Yadav became its first President.

Nerchinsk, Treaty of (1689) A treaty between Russia and China signed at Nerchinsk, a town in Russia. It was the first treaty China signed with a western power. Drawn up in Latin by Jesuits from the Chinese emperor *Kangxi's court, the treaty fixed the Sino-Russian frontier well to the north of the Amur River. Albazin, a fortress town the Russians had built on the Amur, was dismantled and rebuilt in the Western Hills near Beijing.

Nero, Claudius Caesar Drusus Germanicus (c.37–68 AD) Roman emperor (54–68 AD). He was adopted by *Claudius, who had married his own niece, Agrippina, Nero's mother. On Claudius' suspicious death in 54 AD Nero succeeded to the throne and poisoned Britannicus, Claudius' son by Messalina. Nero then had his mother murdered, compelled his boyhood tutor and state counsellor *Seneca to commit suicide, and had his own wife Octavia executed. Another wife, Poppaea, died as a result of Nero's violence towards her. He was the first emperor to persecute Christians, many of whom were put to death. Reputedly he set Rome alight in 64 AD, hoping to rebuild it in splendour. Revolt broke out in Palestine in 66 AD followed by an army rebellion in Gaul and he committed suicide.

Nestorian A member of the Nestorian Church, a sect of the Eastern Orthodox Church. Nestorians followed the teaching of the controversial Syrian Nestorius (died c.451), who was appointed Bishop of Constantinople in 428 and exiled to Egypt in 431. He taught that *Jesus Christ was a conjunction of two distinct persons, one divine and the other human, in whom the human and the divine were indivisible. The implication of this doctrine was that Mary was not the mother of God but simply of Jesus the man. This attack on the popular cult of the Virgin Mary led Nestorius' followers to establish a breakaway church in Edessa. They were expelled in 489 and settled in Persia until they were almost completely wiped out by the 14th-century Mongol invasions. A few Nestorian communities survived, mainly in Kurdistan. Missionaries had established other groups as far away as Sri Lanka and China. In 1551 some Nestorians joined the Roman Catholic Church and became Chaldeans. A small group joined the Russian Orthodox Church in 1898.

Netanyahu, Binyamin (1949–) Israeli Likud statesman, Prime Minister (1996–99; 2009–). Leader of the right-wing Likud coalition from 1993 to 1999, he narrowly defeated Shimon Peres in the elections of 1996. His attempts to maintain the impetus of the Middle-East peace process met with a number of obstacles and he was defeated by the Labour leader, Ehud Barak, in the general election of 1999. He resumed the leadership of Likud in 2005 and again became Prime Minister following the 2009 election.

Netherlands, the

Capital:	Amsterdam
Area:	41,863 sq km (16,163 sq miles)
Population:	16,805,037 (2013 est)
Currency:	1 euro = 100 cents
Religions:	Roman Catholic 30.0%; Dutch Reformed Church 11.0%; Calvinist 6.0%; Muslim 5.8%
Ethnic Groups:	Dutch 80.7%; EU 5.0%; Indonesian 2.4%
Languages:	Dutch, Frisian (both official)
International Organizations:	UN; OECD; NATO; EU; Council of Europe; OSCE; WTO

A European country on the North Sea. It is also known informally as Holland, although this properly refers only to two western provinces.

Physical Bounded by Germany on the east and Belgium on the south, the Netherlands is built up of sediment brought by the Rhine, Meuse, and other rivers. Everywhere, except for the extreme southern corner, is low and flat, much of the land being below sea level. The coast has several estuaries and a large lagoon, the IJsselmeer, partly reclaimed from the Zuider Zee. An ongoing programme of maritime land reclamation has increased total land area.

Economy Trade, banking, and shipping have traditionally been important and remain crucial to the economy, with Rotterdam being the largest port in Europe. A highly mechanized agricultural and market gardening sector produces grains, potatoes, sugar beet, fruit, vegetables, and livestock for food-processing industries and export. Other industries include metal and engineering products, electrical machinery and equipment, and chemicals.

History The area was conquered as far north as the River Rhine by the Romans; the Franks and Saxons moved in during the early 5th century. After the collapse of the Frankish empire in the mid-9th century, there was considerable political fragmentation. Consolidation began under the 14th- and 15th-century dukes of *Burgundy, and in 1477 the whole of the Low Countries passed to the House of *Habsburg. In 1568 the Dutch Revolts against Spanish Habsburg rule began. The independence of the United Provinces of the Netherlands (the northern provinces, which formed a self-governing federation) was finally acknowledged at the Peace of *Westphalia (1648). During the 17th century it was a formidable commercial power, and it acquired a sizeable *Dutch empire. It began to decline after the *Anglo-Dutch Wars and the protracted wars against *Louis XIV's France. From 1795 to 1814 the Netherlands came increasingly under the control of France. During those years Britain took over the colonies of Ceylon (now Sri Lanka) and Cape Colony in South Africa, important trading posts of the Dutch East India Company. At the settlement of the Congress of *Vienna the entire Low Countries formed the independent kingdom of the Netherlands (1815). Despite the secession in 1830 of *Belgium, the Netherlands flourished under the House of Orange, adopting in 1848 a constitution based on the British system. It remained neutral during World War I, suffered economic difficulties during the Great *Depression, and was occupied by the Germans during World War II, when many Jews were deported to *concentration camps. Until World War II it was the third largest colonial power, controlling the Dutch East Indies, various West Indian islands, and Guiana in South America. The Japanese invaded the East Indian islands in 1942 and installed *Sukarno in a puppet government for all *Indonesia. In 1945 he declared independence and four years of bitter war followed before the Netherlands transferred sovereignty. Guiana received self-government as *Surinam in 1954 and independence in 1975, but Curaçao and other Antilles islands remained linked to the Netherlands. Following the long reign of Queen *Wilhelmina (1890–1948) her daughter Juliana (1909–2004) became queen. She retired in 1980 and her daughter succeeded her as Queen Beatrix (1938–); she in turn abdicated in 2013 in favour of her son Willem-Alexander (1967–). The Netherlands was a founder member of the European Community, and of NATO. Since 1945 the Netherlands has been ruled by a succession of coalition governments. It adopted the *euro as its currency in 2002. In 2011 austerity measures to reduce the country's public deficit led to popular protests.

Neville's Cross, Battle of (17 October 1346) A major victory of the English over the Scots, near Durham. Edward III's army captured David II and obtained a large ransom for his release.

Nevilly, Treaty of See VERSAILLES PEACE SETTLEMENT.

New Australians Immigrants to Australia immediately after World War II. Before 1939 the population of the continent consisted of *Aborigines and people of predominantly British descent. The war greatly stimulated industrial production and a labour shortage was met by a programme of assisted immigration (£10 from London to Sydney). Of some 575,000 new arrivals between 1947 and 1952, over half were Polish, Austrian, Italian, Maltese, Dutch, Greek,

and Yugoslav, and they introduced cultural variety into Australia.

Newcastle, Thomas Pelham-Holles, 1st Duke of (1693–1768) British Whig statesman, Prime Minister (1754–56; 1757–62). Newcastle succeeded his brother Henry Pelham as Prime Minister on the latter's death in 1754. During his second term in office, he headed a coalition with William Pitt the Elder, until Pitt's resignation in 1761.

New Deal The programme of Franklin D. *Roosevelt (1933–38), in which he attempted to salvage the US economy and raise the Great *Depression. New Deal legislation was proposed by progressive politicians, administrators, and Roosevelt's 'brains trust'. It was passed by overwhelming majorities in Congress. The emergency legislation of 1933 ended the bank crisis and restored public confidence; the relief measures of the so-called first New Deal of 1933–35, such as the establishment of the Tennessee Valley Authority, stimulated productivity; and the Works Project Administration reduced unemployment. The failure of central government agencies provoked the so-called second New Deal of 1935–38, devoted to recovery by measures, such as the Revenue Act, the Wagner Acts, the Emergency Relief Appropriation Act, and the Social Security Act. Although the New Deal cannot be claimed to have pulled the USA out of the Depression, it was important for its revitalization of the nation's morale.

New Democratic Party A political party in Canada. It grew out of the Canadian Cooperative Commonwealth Federation (CCF), a political party of industrial workers and small farmers formed in 1932 during the Great *Depression. In 1956 a Canadian Labour Congress of Trade Unions was formed, and in 1961 this amalgamated with the CCF to form the New Democratic Party, a mildly socialist party, committed to a planned economy and extension of social benefits. Leaders of the NDP have been T. C. Douglas (1961–71), David Lewis (1971–75), Ed Broadbent (1975–89), Audrey McLaughlin (1989–95), Alexa McDonough (1995–2003), Jack Layton (2003–11), Nycole Turmel (2011–12), and Thomas Mulcair (2012–).

New Economic Policy A policy introduced into the Soviet Union by *Lenin in 1921. It represented a shift from his former "War Communism" policy, which had been adopted during the *Russian Civil War to supply the Red Army and the cities but had alienated the peasants. The NEP permitted private enterprise in agriculture, trade, and industry, encouraged foreign capitalists, and virtually recognized the previously abolished rights of private property. It met with success which Lenin did not live to see, but was ended (1929) by *Stalin's policy of five-year plans.

New France French possessions in North America discovered, explored, and settled from the 16th to the 18th centuries. Its centres were Quebec (founded in 1608) and Montreal (founded in 1642) on the St Lawrence River. In 1712 New France stretched from the Gulf of St Lawrence to beyond Lake Superior and included Newfoundland, Acadia (Nova Scotia), and the Mississippi valley as far south as the Gulf of Mexico. It began to disintegrate after the Peace of *Utrecht was signed in 1713, when France lost Acadia, Newfoundland, and Hudson Bay; it ceased to exist as a political entity in 1763 under the terms of the Treaty of *Paris. Louisiana, the last French colony on mainland North America, was sold to the USA in 1803.

New Granada A former Spanish viceroyalty in north-west South America that comprised present-day Colombia, Ecuador, Panama, and Venezuela.

Ne Win (1911–2002) Burmese general and socialist statesman, Prime Minister (1958–60), head of state (1962–74), and President (1974–81). An active nationalist in the 1930s, Ne Win was appointed Chief of Staff in Aung San's Burma National Army in 1943. He led a military coup in 1962, after which he established a military dictatorship and formed a one-party state, governed by the Burma Socialist Programme Party (BSPP). He stepped down from the presidency in 1981 and retired as leader of the BSPP after riots in Rangoon in 1988.

New International Economic Order (NIEO) A set of demands formulated by a group of *Third World countries at a special session of the *United Nations General Assembly in 1974. The NIEO envisaged a restructuring of the present international economic system to improve the position of the *developing countries (the South) with respect to the advanced industrialized countries (the North). The demands included increased control by developing countries over their own resources, the promotion of *industrialization, an increase in development assistance, and alleviation of debt problems. While the demand for an NIEO was in part a reflection of frustration at the inability to break out of the cycle of underdevelopment, it also drew inspiration from the experience of

OPEC in successfully raising world energy prices. By the 1990s the NIEO had not materialized, having met the joint obstacles of Western resistance, and lack of commitment and support from the developing countries themselves. (*See also* NORTH–SOUTH RELATIONS, BRANDT REPORT.)

New Left A movement of radical intellectuals in the 1960s, spanning the leading Western societies. The New *Left was socialist in inspiration but it was critical of orthodox *communism as practised in Eastern Europe at the time (as well as of existing socialist and communist parties in the West). Its members focused their attention on cultural factors, such as the mass media and the growth of consumer culture, which impeded revolutionary opposition to *capitalism. Seminal books were Raymond Williams's *Culture and Society* (1958) and Herbert Marcuse's *One-Dimensional Man* (1964). New Left ideas were influential mainly in such movements as that against the Vietnam War (1964–75) and played a large role in the student uprising in Paris in May 1968, which led to educational and administrative reforms.

Newman, John Henry (1801–90) British theologian. He was a leading figure in the Oxford Movement, a group of people who in the 1830s attempted to reform the Church of England by restoring the high-church traditions, and became a prominent convert (1845) to Roman Catholicism. The publication in 1841 of *Tract 90*, which argued that the Thirty-nine Articles of the Church of England could be reconciled with Roman Catholic doctrine, caused a major scandal. In 1846 he went to Rome, where he was ordained priest. A gifted writer, he published *Apologia pro Vita Sua* (1864), a justification of his spiritual evolution, and was created cardinal in 1879. He was beatified in 2010.

New Model Army The English *Roundhead force established by Parliamentary ordinance on 15 February 1645. A single army of 22,000 men, it was formed largely from the uncoordinated Roundhead forces of the first phase of the *English Civil War. Its first commander-in-chief was the Puritan Baron Thomas Fairfax, with Philip Skippon commanding the infantry and, after the Self-Denying Ordinance, Oliver *Cromwell in charge of the cavalry. Derided at first by the Cavaliers as the 'New Noddle Army', it consisted of regularly paid, well disciplined, and properly trained men, who became known as the Ironsides. Promotion was by merit. Resounding victories, such as *Naseby and *Preston won the war for the Roundheads. The army was inextricably involved in national

n

developments until the Restoration. Religious and political radicalism quickly permeated its ranks, with *Leveller influence particularly strong between 1647 and 1649. The army was responsible for *Pride's Purge (1648), and formed the basis of government in the following years.

New Orleans, Battle of (8 January 1815) A battle in the *War of 1812, fought outside the city of New Orleans. A numerically superior British attempt led by Sir Edward Pakenham to seize New Orleans was brilliantly repelled by US forces commanded by Andrew *Jackson. The battle proved of little military significance, the Treaty of *Ghent having formally ended the war two weeks earlier, but Jackson's triumph made him a national hero.

New Plymouth See PLYMOUTH COLONY.

Newport Rising (1839) A political insurrection which took place in Newport, Wales, in 1839, following the dissolution of the National Convention of the *Chartists. John Frost, a former mayor of Newport, planned to capture the town and release a Chartist leader, Henry Vincent, from gaol. However, the authorities were forewarned and soldiers ambushed the insurgents, killing several of them. Frost and others were arrested and received death sentences, later commuted to transportation.

New Right An intellectual movement of the 1970s and 1980s that sought to reformulate the basis of right-wing opposition to *social democracy and *socialism. New Right thinkers, whose influence was greatest in the USA and the UK, drew in varying proportions upon the ideas of libertarianism and *conservatism. The libertarian strain could be seen in their defence of the free market, and their belief that the role of government had been over-extended and now needed to be reduced. This meant, for example, the privatization of firms and industries owned by the state, monetarist policies, and a shift away from the *welfare state towards private insurance as a way of coping with ill health and old age. The conservative strain appeared in their strong commitment to law and order, and in their belief that the family unit needed to be strengthened.

New Spain Spain's colonial empire in north and Central America (*Spanish empire). The formation of the viceroyalty of New Spain began in 1518 with *Cortés's attack on the *Aztec empire in central Mexico. Following his destruction of Aztec power, Cortés erected a new capital at

Mexico City and was named governor and captain-general of New Spain (1522). He and his lieutenants extended Spanish authority south into Salvador, Guatemala, and Honduras, and north into the Mexican hinterland. New Spain grew to encompass California, the American south-west, and Florida, although Spanish settlement in many areas was very limited. In the 18th century Spain's involvement in European wars had affected its colonial possessions. In 1763 it ceded Florida to Britain and received Louisiana from France, regaining Florida in 1783, but being forced to return Louisiana to France in 1800.

New START See STRATEGIC ARMS REDUCTION TALKS.

New Zealand

Capital:	Wellington
Area:	267,710 sq km (103,363 sq miles)
Population:	4,365,113 (2013 est)
Currency:	1 New Zealand dollar = 100 cents
Religions:	Roman Catholic 11.6%; Anglican 10.8%; Presbyterian and Congregational 7.8%; other Christian 14.1%
Ethnic Groups:	European 71.2%; Maori 14.1%; Asian 11.3%; Pacific Island 7.6% (note: some people fall into more than one group)
Languages:	English, Maori, New Zealand Sign Language (all official)
International Organizations:	UN; Commonwealth; OECD; Pacific Islands Forum; Secretariat of the Pacific Community; Colombo Plan; WTO

A country situated over 1900 km (1180 miles) south-east of Australia, comprising the North Island and the South Island together with many smaller islands in the south-west Pacific Ocean.

Physical The two main islands, separated by the fairly narrow Cook Strait, together stretch north-east to south-west over a distance of some 1600 km (1000 miles).

Economy New Zealand's once mainly agrarian economy was affected by the loss of preferential treatment by the UK, then the chief trading partner, when the UK joined the EC in 1973. Since then the economy has diversified, although agriculture is still important: major exports include dairy products, meat, and fish, and food processing is an important industry. Major export industries include wood and wood products and machinery, with other industries including textiles, transport equipment, financial services, and tourism.

History First peopled by the Polynesian *Maori from about 800 AD, European contact began in 1642 with the exploration of the Dutch navigator Abel Tasman. Captain James Cook, in successive explorations from 1769, thoroughly charted the islands, and brought them within the British ambit. Commercial colonization began from New South Wales in Australia and from the New Zealand Association (later Company) (1837) of E. G. *Wakefield. Humanitarian pressures contributed to the decision formally to annexe the islands as the colony of New Zealand in 1840 on the basis that the rule of law was necessary to regulate Maori-settler relations (Treaty of *Waitangi). In 1846 the British government conferred a limited constitution (rescinded in 1848) on New Zealand, divided into the provinces of New Munster and New Ulster, and in 1852 granted the islands representative government. Responsible self-government came in 1856. Settlement of the South Island prospered, assisted by the *gold rushes of the 1860s. In the North Island, following the rapid acquisition of Maori land by settlers and by the government, the population was drawn into the disastrous *Anglo-Maori Wars, following which most Maori land was settled. Regulations of 1881 restricted the influx of Asians, who were resented as a threat to the ethnic purity of the New Zealand people. They were confirmed by the Immigration Restriction Act (1920), whose terms were gradually liberalized. The property qualification for voting was abolished and women were enfranchised in 1893. In 1931 New Zealand became an independent dominion, although it did not choose to ratify the Statute of *Westminster formally until 1947. In 1891–1911 (under the Liberal-Labour Party) and 1935–47 (under Labour) New Zealand won a world reputation for state socialist experiment, providing comprehensive welfare and education services. New Zealand actively supported the Allies in both World Wars, enjoying political stability and a high standard of living. After World War II it concentrated its defence policy on the Pacific and Far East, participating in *ANZUS (1951–86)

and sending a military force to Vietnam. Following British accession to the European Community (1973), New Zealand strengthened its trading links with Australia and its Pacific neighbours. When the *Labour Party returned to power in 1984 it adopted a non-nuclear policy leading to withdrawal from *ANZUS. The National Party under Jim *Bolger won the election of 1990 at a time of economic recession. It confirmed Labour's non-nuclear stance, but introduced stringent social welfare cuts, ending free state education and introducing health charges for all. The National Party was re-elected in 1993 and 1996 but lost its majority and Bolger formed coalition governments; Bolger resigned in 1997 and was succeeded by Jenny Shipley. Maori activists continued to demand compensation for land seized illegally by European settlers and the government agreed to pay compensation to the Waikato tribe in 1994 and to the Tainui tribal federation in 1995; in 1996 large tracts of South Island were granted to the Ngai Tahu tribe. In the 2000s Maori claims to own New Zealand's foreshore and seabed became a political issue. In 1999, 2002, and 2005 Labour-led coalition governments were elected with Helen *Clark as Prime Minister; these were followed by National Party-led coalitions under John Key in 2008 and 2011. In 2010 and 2011 two earthquakes on the South Island caused extensive damage in Christchurch.

New Zealand Company (originally **New Zealand Association**) An organization formed in 1837 by E. G. *Wakefield to colonize New Zealand. It was denied a charter by the British government, largely because of fears that it would come into conflict with the *Maori. Nevertheless, in May 1834 the company began sending out agents and settlers, buying land from the Maori. The establishment of the crown colony in 1840 led to a review of the company's grandiose land claims. This, and Maori resistance, prevented the settlements developing as planned and in 1843 a rash attempt at Wairau, near Nelson, to assert authority over the powerful Te Rauparaha resulted in the deaths of 23 settlers. By 1846 the Company had secured recognition from the Colonial Office, a loan, and a settlement of its land claims but it became commercially unviable and was dissolved in 1858.

Ney, Michel, Duc d'Elchingen (1769–1815) Marshal of France. The most famous and popular of *Napoleon's generals, he served Napoleon in the brilliant campaigns of 1794 and 1795, commanded the army of the Rhine (1799), and conquered the Tyrol. His support was decisive in Napoleon's victory at Friedland (14 June 1807). In the retreat from Moscow (1812) he commanded the defence of the *grande armée* against the Russians and was created Prince of Moscow by Napoleon in 1813. After the Battle of *Leipzig he urged Napoleon to abdicate (1814). He agreed to take the oath of allegiance to the restored monarchy, but, when sent to check Napoleon's advance (1815) during the *Hundred Days, he joined him instead, fighting heroically at *Waterloo, after which he was tried for treason and shot.

Ngo Dinh Diem (1901–63) South Vietnamese statesman, President (1955–63). He was exiled by the French in 1947 after forming the anti-French and anti-communist National Union Front. He returned to South Vietnam in 1954 with joint US and French support and, in the following year, became President of an anti-communist government of South Vietnam. He had commenced military resistance against the *Vietcong by 1960 and had achieved some degree of success with both social and economic reform. However, his harshly repressive regime, in which his brother, Ngo Dinh Nhu, earned particular notoriety as head of political police, aroused strong local resentment and he was killed in a military coup in 1963.

Nguni Several groups of ethnically related people in southern Africa. In the 1820s, the Zulu in the Natal area, under their king *Shaka, developed a superior military force, made up of regiments (or impis), which attacked neighbouring peoples in the Difagane Wars. Refugees from Shaka, copying the military discipline and strategy of their Zulu conquerors, established themselves in the *Ndebele state in Zimbabwe, the Gaza state in Mozambique, the Swazi state in Swaziland, and a group of Nguni states in Tanzania, Zambia, and Malawi. Nguni people came into conflict with European settlers: the British in the Cape Colony moved into the lands of the Xhosa, precipitating the *Xhosa Wars; Boer, and later British, settlers in Natal clashed with the Zulus. Urbanization during the 20th century was accompanied by the policy of *apartheid. The *Bantu homelands created in South Africa had little connection with original Nguni culture.

Nguyen Van Thieu (1923–2001) South Vietnamese statesman, President (1967–75). He participated in the post-war struggle against the French but left the *Vietminh because of its communist policies and thereafter became a general in the army of South Vietnam. He participated in the overthrow of *Ngo Dinh Diem's government in 1963 and together with another military strongman, Nguyen Cao Ky, dominated

the politics of his country. Elected President in 1967, and re-elected in 1971, he continued to press hard in the war against the *Vietcong and their North Vietnamese allies despite growing opposition to his dictatorial methods. In the early 1970s the war began to run against him and his US allies drastically reduced their support. In April 1975, with his army in ruins and enemy forces closing on Saigon, he finally resigned his office. He went to live in Taiwan, and later moved to Britain and the USA.

Nicaea, Councils of Two councils of the Christian Church, which took place in the city of Nicaea (now Iznik, Turkey). The first Council (325) was summoned by the Roman emperor *Constantine and issued a statement of orthodoxy against Arianism (the belief that Jesus Christ was not divine, but merely an exceptional human being), later known as the "Nicene Creed". The Second Council (787) was called by the Byzantine empress *Irene to end the *Iconoclastic controversy.

Nicaean empire (1204–61) A Byzantine principality comprising the territories centred on Nicaea (now Iznik, Turkey). The Nicaean empire was established by Theodore I (1175–1222) following the sack of Constantinople during the Fourth *Crusade; it adopted the institutions of the Byzantine empire, including emperors and patriarchs. Resisting the pressures of *Seljuks and Crusaders, Theodore I successfully annexed lands from the Komnenoi of Trebizond. His son-in-law John III sustained this miniature empire in exile but the early death of his son, Theodore II (1254–58), enabled *Michael VIII to dispossess and subsequently blind and imprison the infant heir, John IV Lascaris, after retaking Constantinople in 1261.

Nicaragua

Capital:	Managua
Area:	130,370 sq km (50,336 sq miles)
Population:	5,778,531 (2013 est)
Currency:	1 cordoba = 100 centavos
Religions:	Roman Catholic 58.5%; Protestant 23.2%
Ethnic Groups:	Mestizo 69.0%; White 17.0%; Black 9.0%; Amerindian 5.0%
Languages:	Spanish (official); Amerindian languages
International Organizations:	UN; OAS; Non-Aligned Movement; WTO

The largest country in Central America, bounded on the north by Honduras and on the south by Costa Rica.

Physical Nicaragua has a south-western-facing coast on the Pacific Ocean and a longer, eastward-facing one on the Caribbean Sea, the Mosquito Coast. In the west are fertile plains and volcanic mountains.

Economy The civil war of the 1980s devastated the economy, which also suffered from US attempts to enact a trade blockade and suspend foreign aid. Recovery was set back by severe damage caused by Hurricane Mitch in 1998; progress since has been slow, which has left Nicaragua one of the poorest American nations. Textiles and such agricultural products as coffee, beef, sugar, peanuts, and tobacco form nearly half of Nicaragua's exports. The principal industries include food processing, chemicals, machinery and metal products, and clothing.

History The first inhabitants of Nicaragua were Indians from South America who settled on the coast. From the 10th century AD peoples from Mexico began to immigrate into the region. The first Spanish colonization was undertaken by Francisco Hernándes de Córdoba, who founded the towns of Granada on Lake Nicaragua and León on Lake Managua in 1524. One of the main Indian tribes converted to Christianity, which enabled the Spanish to take control of the area with ease. Administratively part of the viceroyalty of New Spain and the captaincy-general of Guatemala, Nicaragua grew slowly. It depended upon agriculture, which developed substantially in the 18th century. The country achieved its independence from Spain in 1821. Nicaragua was briefly annexed into the Mexican empire of Agustín de Iturbide, and with the collapse of that experiment formed part of the United Province of Central America until becoming independent again in 1838. In 1848 the British seized San Juan del Norte, known as the Mosquito Coast, after a tribe of American Indians, the Miskito. In 1855 a US adventurer, William Walker, seized control of the country and made himself President (1856–57). His ousting helped unite the country, which made peace with Britain and recognized a separate Mosquito kingdom. The 20th century opened with the country under the vigorous control of the dictator José Santos Zelaya, who extended Nicaraguan authority over the Mosquito

kingdom. The USA, apprehensive of his financial dealings with Britain, supported the revolution which overthrew him in 1907. The US presence, including two occupations by the marines, dominated the country until 1933. In 1937 Nicaragua fell under the control of Anastasio *Somoza, who ruled until his assassination in 1956. He was succeeded by his son Luis (1957–63), and then by the latter's brother, General Anastasio Debayle Somoza (1967–72, 1974–79). In 1962 a guerrilla group, the Sandinista National Liberation Front, was formed. It gained increasing support from the landless peasantry and engaged in numerous clashes with the National Guard, ending in civil war (1976–79). Once established as a ruling party, the Sandinistas, led by Daniel Ortega, expropriated large estates for landless peasants and nationalized mines and forests. The dispossessed and exiled owners of the estates then organized opposition to the regime, recruiting a 'Contra' rebel army, funded and organized by the CIA. The *Reagan administration was seriously embarrassed by exposure in 1986–87 of illegal diversion of money to the Contras from US sale of arms to Iran. When President Bush took office in 1989 direct military funding to the Contras ended. Elections were held in 1990 with opposition groups generously funded by the USA. The Sandinistas lost to a coalition group led by Violeta Chamorro. Although she succeeded in winning a $300 million loan from the USA, severe economic recession followed. In 1992 there were violent clashes between re-armed Contras and Sandinista 're-Compas'. A ceasefire agreement was reached in 1994. In 1996 Chamorro resigned, and the conservative Arnaldo Alemán defeated Ortega in presidential elections. Enrique Bolaños became President in 2002. Ortega was returned to the Presidency in 2007 and was re-elected in 2011.

Nicholas I (1796–1855) Emperor of Russia (1825–55). The third son of Paul I, he succeeded his brother *Alexander I, having crushed a revolt by the *Decembrists, who favoured his elder brother Constantine. His rule was authoritarian and allowed for little social reform. Russia was ruled by the army bureaucracy and police, intellectual opposition only expressed itself in study circles and secret societies. These groups polarized into "Slavophiles", who held that Russian civilization should be preserved through the Orthodox Church and the village community, and "Westernizers" who wished to see western technology and liberal government introduced. Nicholas embarked on the *Russo-Turkish Wars and brutally suppressed the uprising (1830–31) in Poland. Religious minorities, including Jews, were persecuted. In the *Revolutions of 1848 he helped Austria crush the nationalists in Hungary, and his later attempts to dominate Turkey led to the *Crimean War (1853–56). He was succeeded by his son *Alexander II.

Nicholas II (1868–1918) Last Emperor of Russia (1894–1917). In 1894 he formalized the alliance with France but his Far Eastern ambitions led to disaster in the *Russo-Japanese War (1904–05), an important cause of the *Russian Revolution of 1905. He was forced to issue the October Manifesto promising a representative government and basic civil liberties. An elected Duma and an Upper Chamber were set up. Although Russia was prosperous under *Stolypin (1906–11) and Nicholas II won support for the war against Germany (1914), he unwisely took personal command of the armies, leaving the government to the empress Alexandra and *Rasputin. Mismanagement of the war and chaos in the government led to his abdication in February 1917 and later his imprisonment. On 16–17 July 1918 the *Bolsheviks, fearing the advance of counter-revolutionary forces, murdered him and his family at Ekaterinburg.

Nicopolis, Battle of (23 September 1396) A battle between Crusaders and Ottoman forces. The town of Nicopolis, on the River Danube was besieged by a force of Crusaders under *Sigismund of Hungary and John, son of Philip the Bold of Burgundy. A combined force of Hungarians and European knights had answered an appeal to relieve Constantinople from Turkish attack. After initial success, they were confronted by the *Turks under Sultan Bajazet I (ruled 1389–1402). The Crusaders were defeated and many of the knights were executed after the battle, although Sigismund himself escaped.

Niemöller, Martin (1892–1984) German Protestant churchman. A U-boat commander in World War I, he became a priest in 1924. In 1933 he founded the Pastors' Emergency League to help combat rising discrimination against Christians of Jewish background. His courageous opposition to the Nazification of the Church led to his confinement in a *concentration camp (1938–45). A pacifist, he became President of the World Council of Churches (1961–68).

Niger

Capital:	Niamey
Area:	1,267,000 sq km (489,062 sq miles)
Population:	16,899,327 (2013 est)
Currency:	1 CFA franc = 100 centimes
Religions:	Muslim 80.0%
Ethnic Groups:	Hausa 55.4%; Djerma Sonrai 21.0%; Tuareg 9.3%; Fulani 8.5%
Languages:	French (official); Hausa; Djerma; local languages
International Organizations:	UN; AU; Franc Zone; ECOWAS; Non-Aligned Movement; WTO

A large, landlocked West African country surrounded by Algeria, Libya, Chad, Nigeria, Benin, Burkina Faso, and Mali.

Physical The River Niger flows through the country in the extreme south-west, and the northern tip of Lake Chad lies in the extreme south-east. From these points the land rises to the high plateaux of the Sahara.

Economy Agriculture is the principal economic activity, employing nine-tenths of the workforce and concentrating on livestock and the cultivation of cowpeas, millet, groundnuts, sorghum, and other arable staples; cotton is also grown. Drought and desertification continue to be problems. Niger has large uranium deposits, and uranium ore is the principal export. Livestock and vegetables are also exported. Oil reserves are now being exploited, and other mineral deposits include gold and coal.

History Archaeological evidence shows that the area was inhabited in the *Palaeolithic period. The Tuaregs occupied parts of Niger in the 11th century AD and their kingdom of Agadès grew during the 15th century. In the 17th century the Zerma established an empire around the River Niger. The *Hausa, who had been moving into the area since the 14th century, expanded their territory during the 18th century, displacing the Tuaregs. In 1804 the *Fulani, ancient competitors for Hausa land, defeated the Hausa in a war and established the kingdom of Sokoto. The French first arrived in 1891, but the country was not fully colonized until 1914. A French colony (part of *French West Africa) from 1922, it became an autonomous republic within the *French Community in 1958 and fully independent in 1960, but there were special agreements with France, covering finance, defence, technical assistance, and cultural affairs. From 1974, it was governed by a Supreme Military Council, and all political associations were banned. Political activity was re-legalized in 1988. President Ali Saibou remained opposed to establishing multiparty democracy but strikes and demonstrations throughout 1990 prompted him to agree to implement reforms. Following a National Conference in 1991 a transitional government was formed. A multiparty constitution was approved by a referendum in 1992 and in 1993, following open elections, a coalition government took office and Mahamane Ousmane became President. In 1995 a peace agreement was made with ethnic Tuareg rebels, based in the north of Niger, who had been clashing with government forces since 1991. In January 1996 army officers staged a coup, throwing Ousmane out of office. After pressure from France a presidential election was held, which was won by the military leader Ibrahim Mainassara. His assassination in 1999 was followed by a brief period of military rule. Mamadou Tandja was elected President later that year and re-elected in 2004; but his attempts in 2009 to change the constitution so he could stand for a third term led to unrest and a military coup in 2010. Niger returned to civilian rule after presidential elections in 2011, which were won by Mahamadou Issoufou.

Nigeria

Capital:	Abuja
Area:	923,768 sq km (356,669 sq miles)
Population:	174,507,539 (2013 est)
Currency:	1 naira = 100 kobo
Religions:	Muslim 50.0%; Christian 40.0%; traditional beliefs 10.0%
Ethnic Groups:	Hausa and Fulani 29.0%; Yoruba 21.0%; Ibo 18.0%; Ijaw 10.0%; over 200 minority groups
Languages:	English (official); Hausa; Yoruba; Ibo; Fulani; over 500 local languages
International Organizations:	UN; Commonwealth; ECOWAS; AU; OPEC; Non-Aligned Movement; WTO

A large West African country consisting of a federation of 21 states, with the highest population (95 million) of any African country.

Physical Nigeria has a southward-facing coast and is bounded by Benin on the west, Niger and Chad on the north, and Cameroon on the east. The sandy coast is bordered by mangrove swamp, inland of which there is a low plain with tropical rainforest spreading up the valleys of the Niger to the north-west and the Benue to the east.

Economy Oil exports account for some 95% of Nigeria's foreign exchange earnings; other minerals include abundant supplies of natural gas, iron ore, coal, lead, and zinc. Agriculture employs about two-thirds of the workforce; principal crops include cocoa, groundnuts, cotton, palm oil, maize, and rice, and livestock are reared. Overdependence on oil and a massive foreign debt are problems that are being slowly addressed.

History The earliest known culture in Nigeria was the Nok culture, which existed from about the 6th century BC to the third century AD. Many different peoples have moved into the region; there are over 250 ethnic groups still living in Nigeria. The kingdom of *Kanem-Bornu rose during the 11th century and fell during the 14th century. Islam was introduced to the area during the 13th century. The Portuguese arrived in the 15th century and established a slave trade, supported by the people of the kingdom of *Benin. The British were involved in the slave trade by the 17th century. The *Hausa people broke away from the *Songhay kingdom and began to mingle with the nomadic *Fulani, some of whom settled in Hausa towns. In the early 19th century a Fulani empire emerged. The kingdom of Benin and the *Yoruba empire of Oyo occupied southern Nigeria.

The island of Lagos was a centre for the slave trade when this was banned by the British in 1807. The British had to use military force to stop the slave ships. In 1851 the British attacked and burnt the city of Lagos and ten years later bought it from King Dosunmu, administering it first from Freetown, Sierra Leone, and then from the Gold Coast (Ghana), until in 1886 a separate protectorate (later colony) of Lagos was formed. Explorers worked their way inland, but until the discovery of quinine (1854) to provide protection against malaria, the region

n

remained known as 'the white man's grave'. During the second half of the 19th century trading companies were established, forming the Royal Niger Company in 1886, which was then taken over by the British Colonial Office to become the Niger Coast protectorate in 1893. Following the conquest of the kingdom of Benin, this became the protectorate of Southern Nigeria (1900). The protectorate of Northern Nigeria was proclaimed in 1900. In 1906 the colony of Lagos was absorbed into the southern protectorate and in 1914 the two protectorates were merged to form the largest British colony in Africa, which, under its governor Frederick Lugard, was administered indirectly by retaining the powers of the chiefs and emirs of its 150 or more tribes. In Northern Nigeria Muslim chiefs of the Fulani tribes maintained a conservative rule over the majority of the country's Hausa population. In the West, the Yoruba dominated; the Ibo tribe was centred in the East.

Under the constitution of 1954 a federation of Nigeria was created, consisting of three regions: Northern, Eastern, and Western, together with the trust territory of Cameroons and the federal territory of Lagos. In 1960 the federation became an independent nation within the *Commonwealth of Nations, and in 1963 a republic. In 1967 the regions were replaced by twelve states, further divided in 1976 into nineteen states. Oil was discovered off Port Harcourt and a movement for Ibo independence began. In January 1966 a group of Ibo army majors murdered the federal Prime Minister, Sir Alhaji Abubakar Tafawa *Balewa, the Premiers of the Northern and Western regions, and many leading politicians. In July a group of northern officers retaliated and installed General *Gowon as Head of State. A massacre of several thousand Ibo living in the North followed. Attempts to work out constitutional provisions failed, and in May 1967 the military governor of the Eastern region, Colonel Ojukwe, announced his region's secession and the establishment of the republic of *Biafra. Civil war between the Hausa and Ibo peoples erupted, and Biafra collapsed in 1970. General Gowon was deposed in 1975. In 1979 the military government organized multiparty elections. Corruption and unrest precipitated more military takeovers, in 1983 and 1985, when General Ibrahim Babangida became Head of State. Political parties were re-legalized in 1989, but only two parties were allowed to register for elections, both having manifestos devised by the government. Open presidential elections in 1993 were annulled, which prompted serious social unrest. Babangida resigned and handed power over to another military government, promising that an elected civilian government would be installed in 1994. The social and political crisis continued and Sanni Abacha took over as head of state in November 1993. He reinstituted the 1979 military constitution, but continued to insist that a civilian government would eventually be installed. In 1995 the government lifted the ban on political activity. However, in October 1995 nine pro-democracy activists were charged with murder and executed. Following Abacha's death in 1998, General Abdulsalam Abubakar became President. He released the remaining political prisoners and restored democratic rule. In subsequent elections General Obasanjo was elected President. He was re-elected in 2003. Umaru Yar'Adua succeeded him in 2007, but power was transferred to Vice-President Goodluck Jonathan in 2010 because of Yar'Adua's ill health. Jonathan served the remainder of the term and was elected President in his own right in 2011. The early 21st century saw a rise in ethnic and religious conflict in Nigeria; in particular, the Islamist Boko Haram movement intensified attacks against state and Christian targets in the north from 2009, which led to government abuses of human rights in response.

Nigerian Civil War See BIAFRA.

Nightingale, Florence (1820–1910) British nurse and medical reformer. She became famous during the Crimean War for her attempts to publicize the state of the army's medical arrangements and improve the standard of care. In 1854 she took a party of nurses to the army hospital at Scutari, where she improved sanitation and medical procedures, thereby achieving a dramatic reduction in the mortality rate; she became known as `the Lady of the Lamp' for her nightly rounds. She returned to England in 1856 and devoted the rest of her life to attempts to improve public health and hospital care.

Night of the Long Knives (29–30 June 1934) The name coined by *Hitler for a weekend of murders throughout Germany. It followed a secret deal between himself and units of his personal bodyguard, the *SS. Precise details remain unknown, but the army is believed to have promised to support Hitler as head of state after *Hindenburg's death in return for destroying the older and more radical Nazi private army known as the SA (Sturmabteilung), or *Brownshirts, led by Ernst Röhm. Hitler announced that 77 people had been summarily executed for alleged conspiracy. Subsequent arrests by the SS all over Germany, usually followed by murder, numbered many hundreds, including some non-party figures, and the former Chancellor Schleicher.

nihilism The total rejection of authority as exercised by the church, the state, or the family. More specifically, the doctrine of a Russian extremist revolutionary party active in the late 19th and early 20th centuries. In their struggle against the conservative elements in Russian society, the nihilists justified violence, believing that by forcibly eliminating ignorance and oppression they would secure human freedom. The government of *Alexander II repressed the revolutionaries severely, and they sought vengeance by assassinating the emperor near his palace on 13 March 1881. After 1917 the small and diffuse cells of nihilists were themselves destroyed by better coordinated revolutionaries.

Nijmegen, Treaty of (1678) The Franco-Dutch War (1672–78) was terminated by the treaty signed at Nijmegen, in the Netherlands between France, the United Provinces, Spain, and the Holy Roman Empire; France gained substantially from the terms, which rationalized its frontiers.

Nile, Battle of the (1 August 1798) A naval battle fought at Aboukir Bay on the Mediterranean coast of Egypt, in which a British fleet defeated a French fleet. The French admiral had anchored his fleet of 13 vessels in the bay. He believed his ships to be safe from attack, but *Nelson, the British commander, was able partially to encircle the French fleet. Nine French ships were destroyed, including the flagship *L'Orient*. This conclusive victory established Nelson's prestige, destroyed *Napoleon's plans for Egypt, and encouraged the signing of the second coalition against France.

Nimeiri, Gaafar Muhammad al- (1930–2009) Sudanese statesman. He led campaigns against rebels in the southern Sudan in the 1950s and joined in leftist attempts to overthrow the civilian government. Following a coup, he became Prime Minister in 1969 and Chairman of the Revolutionary Command Council. President from 1971 to 1985, in 1972 he ended the civil war in the southern Sudan, granting it local autonomy. He switched from socialist economic policies to capitalism, to make the Sudan a major food producer. A devout Muslim, he proposed a new Islamic Constitution in December 1984 that made Islamic law apply to everyone. This was opposed in southern Sudan, where the majority of the population were not Muslim, and a military coup overthrew him in 1985. He returned to Sudan in 1999 and stood

unsuccessfully in the 2000 presidential elections.

Nimitz, Chester William (1885–1966) US admiral. After various surface ship commands and shore appointments, he took over command of the Pacific Fleet in 1941 following the Japanese attack on *Pearl Harbor. From his Hawaii headquarters, he deployed his forces to win the Battle of Midway, and subsequently supervised the moves in the *Pacific Campaigns, leading to successful actions off Guadalcanal and in the *Leyte Gulf. To a large extent he was responsible for making the Pacific Fleet, weakened by Pearl Harbor, the instrument of Japan's defeat. After the war he was briefly chief of naval operations.

Nineveh An ancient city located on the east bank of the Tigris, opposite the modern city of Mosul in northern Iraq. It was the oldest city of the ancient Assyrian empire and its capital during the reign of Sennacherib (704–681 BC) until it was destroyed by a coalition of Babylonians and Medes in 612 BC. A famous archaeological site, it was first excavated by the French in 1820 and later by the British; it is noted for its monumental Neo-Assyrian palace, library, and statuary and for its crucial sequence of prehistoric pottery.

Nine Years War (1688–97) Also known as the War of the Grand Alliance, a conflict that resulted from French aggression in the Rhineland, and that subsequently became a power struggle between *Louis XIV of France and *William III of Britain. In 1688 when French armies invaded Cologne and the Palatinate, the members of the League of Augsburg took up arms. Meanwhile William had driven *James II from the throne of England and in 1689 a Grand Alliance of England, the United Provinces, Austria, Spain, and Savoy was formed against France. The French withdrew from the Palatinate. James II, supported by French troops, was defeated in Ireland at the Battle of the *Boyne. In 1690 the French navy won a victory off Beachy Head, but in 1692 was defeated at La Hogue, though their privateers continued to damage allied commerce. The French campaigns in north Italy and Catalonia were successful, but the war in the Spanish Netherlands became a stalemate as one lengthy siege succeeded another. William's one success was the retaking of Namur. The war was a severe defeat for France, despite a good military performance, because its financial resources were not equal to those of Britain and the United Provinces. Peace was finally concluded by the Treaty of Ryswick.

n

Nixon, Richard (Milhous) (1913–94) US Republican statesman, 37th President of the USA (1969–74). He served as Vice-President under Eisenhower (1953–61), narrowly losing to John F. Kennedy in the 1960 presidential election. In his first term of office he sought to resolve the Vietnam War; the negotiations were brought to a successful conclusion by his Secretary of State, Henry Kissinger, in 1973. Nixon also restored Sino-American diplomatic relations by his visit to China in 1972. He was elected for a second term in November of that year, but it soon became clear that he was implicated in the *Watergate scandal, and in 1974 he became the first President to resign from office, taking this action shortly before impeachment proceedings began. He was granted a pardon by President Ford for any crimes he may have committed over Watergate. He returned to politics in 1981 as a Republican elder statesman.

Nizam Shahi Muslim dynasty of Ahmadnagar, based in the north-western Indian Deccan region, that flourished from 1490 to 1637. Its founder was Malik Ahmad who revolted against the *Bahmanis and set up an independent kingdom centred on a new capital, Ahmadnagar, which took its founder's name. His main achievement was the conquest of Daulatabad (1499). He and his successors then engaged in almost constant warfare. After abandoning an alliance with the Hindu kingdom of Vijayanagar, they participated in the final destruction of that city in 1565. The dynasty presented spirited resistance to subsequent Mogul encroachment into its territories but had lost all independent existence by 1637.

Nkomo, Joshua (Mqabuko Nyongolo) (1917–99) Zimbabwean statesman. In 1961 he became the leader of ZAPU; in 1976 he formed the Patriotic Front with Robert Mugabe, leader of ZANU, and was appointed to a Cabinet post in Mugabe's government of 1980. Dismissed from his post in 1982, he returned to the Cabinet in 1988, when ZANU and ZAPU agreed to merge, and was Vice-President (1990–96).

Nkrumah, Kwame (1909–72) Ghanaian statesman, Prime Minister (1957–60), President (1960–66). The leader of the non-violent struggle for the Gold Coast's independence, he became first Prime Minister of the country when it gained independence as Ghana in 1957. He declared Ghana a republic in 1960 and proclaimed himself President for life in 1964, banning all opposition parties; Nkrumah's dictatorial methods seriously damaged Ghana's economy and eventually led to his overthrow in a military coup.

NKVD (initial Russian letters for 'People's Commissariat for Internal Affairs') The Soviet secret police agency responsible from 1934 for internal security and the labour prison camps, having absorbed the functions of the former *OGPU. Mainly concerned with political offenders, it was especially used for *Stalin's purges. Its leaders were Yagoda (1934–36) Yezhov (1936–38), and *Beria until 1946, when it was merged with the MVD (Ministry of Interior). After Beria's fall in 1953 the Soviet secret police was placed under the *KGB (Committee of State Security).

Nok culture The people occupying northern Nigeria from c. 500 BC to 200 AD; this culture was important for two reasons. As the earliest known centre of iron-working south of the Sahara, it played a major part in passing on metallurgy and its distinctive terracotta figurines are considered ancestral to the later statuary of the city of Ife.

nomenklatura A practice of the former Soviet political system, by which the Communist Party exercised control over important appointments. It comprised a list of responsible posts, such as ministerial positions, newspaper editors, factory managers, heads of schools, and other institutions, together with a list of individuals approved by the Party to hold such positions. This created an élite within Soviet society with special rights and privileges, such as access to special shops, hospitals, or schools. Nomenklatura was one of the targets of Mikhail Gorbachev's programme of *glasnost and perestroika.

Non-Aligned Movement A grouping of 120 countries and liberation movements established in 1961 for the purpose of building closer political, economic, and cultural cooperation in the Third World.

Nonconformist (or **Dissenter**) A Protestant who did not conform to the disciplines or rites of the Anglican Church. Nonconformists include a number of groups. The *Puritans wished to purify the Church from within, while the Presbyterians were specific in their demands for the replacement of organization by bishops for a system of elected elders. The separatists under Robert *Browne left the Anglican Church entirely. All Nonconformists were subject to penalties; the *Pilgrim Fathers emigrated to escape persecution. During the

Civil War Nonconformists (especially *Congregationalists and Baptists) fought on the Parliamentary side and the Restoration Settlement (1660) enacted harsh measures against all Nonconformist groups. The 1662 Act of Uniformity deprived them of freedom of worship and subsequent persecution led to a further exodus to North America. In 1681 Pennsylvania was founded as a refuge for *Quakers. The Toleration Act (1689) brought some improvements in England, but until the 19th century Nonconformists were debarred from holding political office.

non-cooperation (in British India) A political campaign by the Indian National *Congress organized and led by M. K. *Gandhi (1920–22). Its aims were to force further concessions from the British government by organizing the boycotting of the legislative councils, courts and schools, and other symbolic acts. The movement, inspired by Gandhi's *satyagraha campaign, was intended to be non-violent but it degenerated into violence and was called off by Gandhi in February 1922 after the murder of a number of policemen by a mob at Chauri Chaura in the United Provinces. The movement failed to win enough support to paralyse government; its chief effect was to mobilize mass support for Congress and to consolidate Gandhi's position in the leadership of the national movement.

Nore mutiny (May 1797) A mutiny by sailors of the British navy stationed at the Nore anchorage in the Thames estuary. Encouraged by the earlier *Spithead mutiny, they demanded improvements in their conditions, the removal of unpopular officers, a greater share in prize money, and, under the influence of their ringleader, Richard Parker, certain radical political changes. This time the Admiralty would make no concessions and eventually the mutineers surrendered. About 19 men, including Parker, were hanged. Alarm at the mutiny probably contributed to the decisive defeat of Grey's parliamentary reform motion of May 1797.

Norman An inhabitant or native of Normandy, France, a descendant of a mixed Scandinavian ('Northmen') and Frankish people established there in early medieval times. The area, secured by Rollo in 912 from Charles III of France, was inadequate for settlement since inheritance laws left younger sons without territory; land hunger provided the impetus towards conquest and colonization. Under Duke William the Normans conquered England (*see* NORMAN CONQUEST), and later Wales, Ireland, and parts

of Scotland as well as large areas of the Mediterranean. Their expansion southwards, led by Robert Guiscard, was initially as mercenaries fighting the Muslims but they soon controlled much of Europe. In 1154, the year of Roger II of Sicily's death and *Henry II's accession to the English throne, Norman power was at its height, witnessed in the highly efficient governments of Sicily and England.

Norman Conquest The period beginning in 1066 with Duke William of Normandy's victory over the English at the Battle of *Hastings. As *William I (1066–87) he established a military superiority over the English, rebellions were crushed (1067–71), and about 5000 castles were constructed by the time of his death. England's frontiers were protected, first by marcher lords and then through conquest. Ruthless attention to detail characterized the Norman approach to government. English institutions were either retained and developed (such as the treasury, the king's council, the king's peace, sheriffs, and the shire system) or replaced with Norman versions. Not all changes were popular with the English, who had already lost heavily in terms of status, land holdings, and public office. Taxation was heavier, forest laws were harsh and outside the common law. Norman efficiency produced the unique survey recorded in *Domesday Book (1086), though it owed a great deal to existing English records. The language of government and of the court was Norman French. England prospered commercially: its towns grew, as did its population. Many of these developments would probably have arisen without Norman rule—as is also true of the reorganization of the English Church under Archbishop *Lanfranc—but the rapid nature of these changes owed most to the Norman Conquest. In architecture the Norman style, characterized by rounded arches and heavy pillars was introduced after the Conquest.

Normandy Campaign (June–August 1944) An Allied counter-offensive in Europe in World War II. A series of landings were made on the beaches of Normandy, France, beginning on 6 June 1944 (D-Day). Five beaches had been designated for the Allied invasion, code name 'Operation Overlord', for which General *Eisenhower was the supreme commander. British and Canadian troops fought across the eastern beaches, the US forces the western. Allied air forces destroyed most of the bridges over the Seine and the Loire, preventing the Germans from reinforcing their forward units. On D-Day plus 14 two vast steel-and-concrete

n

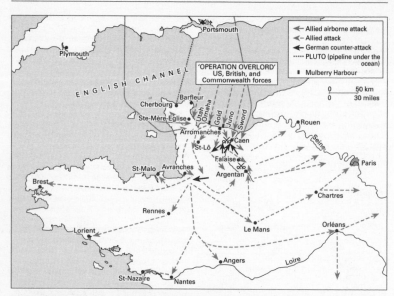

Normandy Campaign. The Allied plan 'Operation Overlord' succeeded in 1944 largely as a result of meticulous planning. U-boat bases in Brittany were captured in a lightning campaign by US troops, who then swung east. Other US forces, together with British and Commonwealth troops, defeated German defenders at the Battle of Falaise Gap. A swift drive through Normandy led to the capture of Rouen and Paris, and the advance into north-west Europe.

artificial harbours (code name 'Mulberry') were towed across the English Channel. One was sunk by a freak storm, but the second was established at Arromanches, providing the main harbour for the campaign. Meanwhile 20 oil pipelines (code name 'Pluto' – pipe line under the ocean) were laid across the Channel to supply the thousands of vehicles now being landed.

The US forces under General *Bradley had cut off the Cotentin Peninsula (18 June), and accepted the surrender of Cherbourg. The British army attacked towards Caen, securing it after heavy fighting (9 July) before advancing on Falaise. US troops broke through the German defences to capture the vital communications centre of Saint-Lô, cutting off the German force under *Rommel. The Germans launched a counter-attack but were caught between the US and British armies in the 'Falaise Gap' and lost 60,000 men in fierce fighting. Field-Marshal Model, transferred from the Eastern Front, was unable to stem Patton's advance, which now swept across France to Paris, while Montgomery moved his British army up the English Channel.

Paris was liberated by General Leclerc on 26 August, and Brussels on 3 September. By 5 September more than two million troops, four million tonnes of supplies, and 450,000 vehicles had been landed, at the cost of some 224,000 Allied casualties.

Norsemen See VIKINGS.

North, Frederick, Lord (1732–92) British Tory statesman, Prime Minister (1770–82). He sought to prevent the War of American Independence, but was regarded as responsible for the loss of the American colonies. This, together with allegations that his ministry was dominated by the influence of George III, led to his resignation in 1782.

North African Campaigns (June 1940– May 1943) A series of military campaigns in Africa in World War II. When Italy declared war in June 1940, General *Wavell in Cairo with 36,000 Commonwealth troops attacked first, the Italians giving up Sidi Barrani, Tobruk, and Benghazi between September 1940 and January 1941. In July 1940 the Italians had occupied parts of the Sudan and British Somaliland, but in January 1941 the British counter-attacked and on 6 April 1941 Ethiopia and all of Italian East Africa surrendered, thus opening the way for Allied supplies and reinforcements to reach the Army of the Nile. In March 1941 General *Rommel attacked, and the British withdrew, leaving *Tobruk besieged. Under General *Auchinleck, an offensive (Operation Crusader) was planned. At first successful, the campaign swung back and forth across the desert, both German and British tank casualties being high. Tobruk fell in June 1942 and the British took up a defensive position at El *Alamein in July. From there in October the reinforced 8th Army of 230,000 men and 1230 tanks now under General *Montgomery launched their attack, and Rommel fell back to Tunisia. Meanwhile 'Operation Torch' was launched, an amphibious landing of US and British troops (8 November) under General *Eisenhower near Casablanca on the Atlantic and at Oran and Algiers in the Mediterranean. It was hoped to link up with *Free French forces in West Africa. The Vichy French troops of General *Darlan at first resisted, but after three days acquiesced. From November 1942 to May 1943 German armies, although reinforced, were being squeezed between the 8th Army advancing from the east and the Allied forces advancing from the west. On 7 May Tunis surrendered. Some 250,000 prisoners were taken, although Rommel skilfully succeeded in withdrawing the best troops of his Afrika Korps to Sicily.

North American Free Trade Agreement (NAFTA) An economic pact permitting free trade between the USA, Canada, and Mexico. NAFTA extends a free trade agreement made between the USA and Canada in 1988. The treaty was signed in 1992, ratified in 1993, and took effect in 1994. It provides for the complete removal on all trade tariffs between the member countries, with tariffs on agricultural products to be phased out. Chile applied to join and in 1994 negotiations over its admittance began.

North American Indians *See* NATIVE AMERICANS.

North Atlantic Treaty Organization (NATO) An association of European and North American states, formed in 1949 for the defence of Europe and the North Atlantic against the perceived threat of Soviet aggression. Dominated by the USA, it identified in 1991 the disintegration of the USSR and instability in Eastern Europe as new dangers. Its headquar-

ters are in Brussels, Belgium. Since the collapse of the USSR, NATO has sought cooperation with Russia and the formerly communist nations of east Europe. In 1997 a treaty with Russia was signed and the Czech Republic, Hungary, and Poland joined NATO in 1999. They were followed in 2004 by Bulgaria, Estonia, Latvia, Lithuania, Romania, Slovakia, and Slovenia; and in 2009 by Albania and Croatia.

In 1995 NATO took its first aggressive action when it intervened in the war in Bosnia and Herzegovina, bombing Serb positions around the besieged city of Sarajevo; this developed into a peacekeeping operation that lasted until 2004. In 1999 it bombed Serbia in an attempt to end its policy of genocide in Kosovo. NATO has since operated in Afghanistan (2003–) and in air strikes against the *Gaddafi regime in Libya (2011).

North-east Passage A passage for ships eastwards along the northern coast of Europe and Asia, from the Atlantic to the Pacific via the Arctic Ocean, sought for many years as a possible trade route to the East. It was first navigated in 1878–79 by the Swedish Arctic explorer Baron Nordenskjöld (1832–1901).

Northern Expedition (1926–28) Military campaign in China waged by nationalist forces under the leadership of *Chiang Kai-shek to extend their power from their base in southern China to much of northern China by defeating local *warlord armies, initially with military assistance from the Soviet Union. Shanghai and Nanjing were captured in March 1927 and Beijing finally fell on 8 June 1928. A nationalist government was established in Nanjing from 1928 to 1932. The Northern Expedition was notable both for the final emergence of Chiang Kai-shek as the sole leader of the nationalist *Kuomintang and for his purge of the communists. This resulted in a series of unsuccessful communist risings in August 1927 and the first ten-year phase of the nationalist-communist civil war.

Northern Ireland A unit of the *United Kingdom comprising the six north-eastern counties of Ulster.

Physical Structurally, it is a south-westward extension of Scotland, separated by the North Channel of the Irish Sea. The central expanse of Lough Neagh is drained to the north by the River Bann, separating the Sperrin Mountains to the west and the Antrim Hills to the east. In the south-east are the Mourne Mountains, while in the south-west lies Lough Erne.

Economy The traditional linen and shipbuilding industries have declined but remain important, along with engineering and chemical industries. There is some mining. Many people are now employed in the service sector. Agricultural products include barley and potatoes; sheep and cattle are raised.

History Northern Ireland was established as a self-governing province of the United Kingdom by the Government of Ireland Act (1920) as a result of pressure from its predominantly Protestant population. Economic and electoral discrimination by the Protestant majority against the largely working-class Catholics (about one-third of the population) erupted in violence in the 1960s, heralding the decades of 'the Troubles' in Northern Ireland. Extremist Unionist reaction to protest marches organized by the civil rights movement (1968) led to riots, and violence escalated with paramilitary groupings such as the *Irish Republican Army (IRA) clashing with 'Loyalist' militant organizations, such as the Ulster Defence Association (UDA) and the Ulster Volunteer Force (UVF). In 1969 British soldiers were sent to the province to keep the peace, at the request of the *Stormont government, and have remained there ever since. The British government suspended (1972) the Northern Irish constitution and dissolved the Stormont government, imposing direct rule from London. In 1973 a power-sharing Northern Ireland Executive was established, responsible to a more representative Assembly. It collapsed in 1974, however, when Unionist leaders, such as the Reverend Ian Paisley, together with the Ulster Workers Council, organized a general strike that paralysed the province. After 1979 closer cooperation between the Republic of Ireland and Britain developed, leading to the Anglo-Irish Accord (the Hillsborough Agreement), signed in 1985, which gave the Republic a consultative role in the government of Northern Ireland. Sectarian terrorism continued, claiming over 3500 lives by the early 2000s. In 1991–92 talks were held with all major parties except *Sinn Fein, the political wing of the IRA; for the first time these included representatives from the Irish Republic. In 1993 the *Downing Street Declaration was signed by John *Major and Albert Reynolds, the Prime Minister of the Republic of Ireland, paving the way for negotiations with Sinn Fein (as well as other political groups) on condition that they commit themselves to peaceful and democratic means. In 1994 the IRA declared a 'complete cessation' of military activities, which was followed by similar declarations by Loyalist paramilitary

groups. However, little progress was made in peace negotiations during 1995 as a result of the UK government's refusal to negotiate with Sinn Fein until decommissioning of IRA weapons took place. In February 1996 the IRA broke the ceasefire by launching bomb attacks on London and Manchester. Sinn Fein was then excluded from the talks, which began in June 1996, but was admitted, following a new IRA ceasefire, in September 1997. In January 1998 the British and Irish governments issued, as a basis for negotiation, a joint document containing proposals for the future government of Northern Ireland, including: (1) a Northern Ireland Assembly to be elected by proportional representation, with a powersharing executive, (2) a north–south ministerial council linking the two parts of Ireland, and (3) an intergovernment council linking assemblies in Northern Ireland, Scotland, and Wales with representatives of the British and Irish governments.

In April 1998 a peace agreement based on these proposals, known as the **Good Friday Agreement**, was signed by the British and Irish Prime Ministers and the leaders of the negotiating parties. The agreement allowed for the phased release of paramilitary prisoners and required the decommissioning of terrorist weapons within two years. Following elections David Trimble became Northern Ireland's First Minister. However, the new political institutions have operated only intermittently, mostly because of the unionist parties' reluctance to engage with Sinn Fein in the absence of firm evidence of progress towards IRA disarmament. An executive that included Sinn Fein members was established in December 1999, but this and the assembly have operated only for two periods (December 1999–February 2000; May 2000–October 2002). Divisions seemed to harden in 2003 when elections for the still-suspended assembly made the hardline Democratic Unionists the largest party (and its leader, Ian *Paisley, the prospective First Minister) and Sinn Fein the largest nationalist party. However, prospects for progress improved in 2005 when the IRA announced that its 'war' was over and that it had completed decommissioning its weapons. After further Assembly elections in 2007, the Democratic Unionist Party and Sinn Fein agreed to a power-sharing executive, and devolved power returned to Northern Ireland in May 2007.

Northern Rising (November–December 1569) An English rebellion, led by the earls of Westmorland and Northumberland. Protesting loyalty to *Elizabeth I, the rebels aimed to remove "new men" like William *Cecil from power, preserve the Catholic religion, and have *Mary, Queen of Scots declared heir to the English throne. They ventured south and took Durham before government troops intervened and ended the rising. At the queen's insistence, around 400 rank-and-file rebels were executed. Meanwhile a number of the leaders fled abroad or were allowed to buy themselves pardons.

Northern War (1700–21) A conflict between Russia, Denmark, and Poland on one side, and Sweden opposing them, during which, in spite of the victories of *Charles XII, Sweden lost its empire and Russia under *Peter I became a major Baltic power. By the treaties of Stockholm (1719, 1720) Bremen and Verden were ceded to Hanover and most of Pomerania to Prussia. After further Russian naval successes, the Treaty of Nystadt, which ended the war, gave Russia Sweden's Baltic provinces.

Northern Wei (or **Toba Wei**) (386–535) One of the dynasties that ruled northern China after the empire disintegrated following the collapse of the *Western Jin in 311 AD. It was founded by a Mongol group, the Xianbi. Its rulers availed themselves of Chinese administrators and encouraged intermarriage with Chinese. Luoyang, once the Eastern Han capital, became their capital. Land reforms were instituted to build up a stable peasantry and an enduring system of collective responsibility. Its rule ended when tribal frontier garrisons, which were opposed to its policies, revolted.

North Korea See KOREA, NORTH.

North–South relations The relationship between the advanced industrialized countries (the North) and the *Third World, or *developing countries (the South). North–South relations became an issue in international politics following the process of decolonization, which brought a large number of new states into an international system in which they found themselves to be at a serious disadvantage, particularly in economic terms. The developing countries of the South tried through various means to reduce their dependence on the North. They were particularly active in the UN, notably in the *United Nations Conference on Trade and Development (UNCTAD) in 1964, where the framework was established for a set of demands for a new deal on world trade. The position of the South looked stronger by the late 1970s: *OPEC (the Organization of Petroleum Exporting Countries) had set an example to all developing countries by successfully raising world energy prices, the demand for a

*New International Economic Order had been presented to a UN General Assembly session in 1974, and the issue of North–South relations had been made the subject of an international commission which met from 1977 to 1979 under the chairmanship of Willy Brandt (1913–92; see BRANDT REPORT). The North–South wealth gap remained in the early 21st century, and such trends as *globalization were viewed in some quarters as reinforcing it. Some developing nations, such as China and India, had become major economic powers, but their resulting wealth was concentrated among relatively few people, with poverty still widespread and average GDP per head remaining low.

Northumberland, John Dudley, Earl of Warwick, Duke of (c.1502–53) Ruler of England on behalf of Edward VI (1551–53). He began his political career under *Henry VIII and was a member of Edward VI's Privy Council. As Earl of Warwick he sought to undermine *Somerset's power and was created Duke of Northumberland in 1551 shortly before ordering Somerset's imprisonment and execution. The new government was committed to radical Protestantism and produced a new Prayer Book (1552), supported by a new Act of Uniformity prescribing penalties for not attending Church services. In 1552 *Cranmer produced the Forty-Two Articles, a comprehensive statement of Protestant doctrine which formed the basis of the *Thirty-Nine Articles (1571). Though posthumous tradition condemned Northumberland as an evil schemer, his regime promoted stability. He terminated the unsuccessful wars against France and Scotland initiated by Somerset and introduced several important financial reforms. Northumberland brought about his own downfall by trying to ensure the succession of Lady Jane *Grey. He was executed and *Mary, Henry VIII's daughter, succeeded to the throne.

Northumbria An ancient Anglo-Saxon kingdom of north-east England and south-east Scotland extending from the Humber to the Forth. The name refers to persons living to the north of the Humber and has been revived in modern times by organizations, such as the 'Northumbria Authority', an area of police administration in north-east England.

North Vietnam See VIETNAM.

North-West Europe Campaign
(September 1944–May 1945) An Allied military campaign in World War II. Following the *Normandy Campaign, *Montgomery's forces

captured Antwerp (4 September) and crossed the Albert Canal. The US 1st Army captured Namur and Aachen, while the US 3rd Army moved east and reached the Moselle. Montgomery's attempt to seize the lower Rhine by dropping the 1st Airborne Division at *Arnhem ended in failure. In November the Germans consolidated and in December launched a counter-attack in the *Ardennes, the Battle of the Bulge. In January 1945 Montgomery's forces pushed forward to the Rhine. In March a massive bombardment at Wesel preceded a successful crossing of the lower Rhine by Montgomery's troops. The US 7th Army pushed east towards Munich, French forces moved up the upper Rhine to Lake Constance, and the US 3rd Army advanced to Leipzig and across the Austrian border into Czechoslovakia. On 11 April Montgomery reached the River Elbe. Following the capture of Berlin by the Red Army and the suicide of Hitler (30 April), Montgomery received the surrender of the German forces in north-west Europe on Lüneburg Heath on 4 May. Four days later (V-E Day), the war in Europe was declared at an end.

North-west Frontier Province A province of north-west Pakistan, in the Himalayas, the location of the strategic Khyber Pass to Afghanistan. Every great power in the region has sought to control the province, but its harsh terrain has allowed the inhabitants to remain semiautonomous.

North-west Passage The sea route between the Atlantic and Pacific Oceans along the north coast of North America. Long sought by explorers it was first traversed by Roald Amundsen (1903–06). Shrinkage of the Arctic ice sheet in the early 2000s made getting through the Passage easier, opening the possibility of its eventual commercial use.

North-west Territory (or **Old Northwest**) A region and former territory of the USA lying between the Mississippi and Ohio rivers and the Great Lakes. It was acquired in 1783 after the War of American Independence and now comprises the states of Indiana (1800), Ohio (1803), Michigan (1805), Illinois (1809), and Wisconsin (1836).

Norway

Capital:	Oslo
Area:	323,802 sq km (125,021 sq miles)
Population:	4,722,701 (2013 est)
Currency:	1 krone = 100 ore
Religions:	Church of Norway (Evangelical Lutheran) 82.1%; other Christian 5.7%; Muslim 2.3%
Ethnic Groups:	Norwegian 94.4%; other European 3.6%
Languages:	Bokmal Norwegian, Nynorsk Norwegian (both official); Sami; Finnish
International Organizations:	UN; NATO; EFTA; OECD; Council of Europe; OSCE; WTO

A country forming the north-western part of Scandinavia in northern Europe.

Physical Norway's extensive coast, fringed with innumerable small islands, stretches from the Arctic Ocean to the North Sea. Inland it borders on Sweden (a long boundary), Finland, and Russia. It is mountainous, rising to 2470 m (8104 feet) in the Jotunheimen range. Its warm climate is caused by the Gulf Stream, which usually keeps the fiords from freezing.

Economy Norway has one of the world's largest reserves of aluminium, though the main resource is North Sea oil and natural gas; in the north, in the Arctic, the Svalbard (Spitsbergen) archipelago contains rich deposits of coal. The extraction of North Sea oil and natural gas increased sharply in the 1970s and 1980s, and they make up about half of exports and provide a fifth of government revenue. Norway's economy is diverse, however, with other industries including food processing, shipbuilding, paper products, metals, chemicals, timber, mining, textiles, and fishing. Agriculture is limited, since only 3% of land area is cultivable. Norway invests some state oil revenues in the world's largest sovereign wealth fund.

History Norway was inhabited in prehistoric times by primitive hunting communities. Rivalry between chiefs, and the desire for land provoked excursions by the Norwegian *Vikings as far as England, Greenland, and Iceland. Political organization strengthened under Harald Fairhair (c.900) and under *Olaf I, who brought Christianity. *Olaf II furthered the work of Christian conversion, but was killed in a battle with the Danes. Danish rule (1028–35) followed, and thereafter civil war, and, in 1066, an

unsuccessful expedition to assert Harald Hardrada's claim to the English throne. The reign of
*Haakon IV brought order and, from 1254,
Norway traded with the *Hanseatic League. In
1397 the Union of *Kalmar brought Norway,
Sweden, and Denmark together under a single
monarch. Danish rule resulted in conversion to
the Lutheran Church. The Union was dissolved
in 1523, though Norway was ruled by Danish
governors until 1814 when it was ceded to
Sweden. The country had established its own
parliament (Storting) in 1807. A literary revival
and a new national consciousness brought demands for complete independence. Responsible government was granted in 1884, and
universal male suffrage in 1898. Finally, union
with Sweden was unilaterally declared dissolved
in June 1905, and Prince Charles of Denmark
elected as *Haakon VII. A Liberal Party government introduced women's suffrage and social
reform, and maintained neutrality during
*World War I. In *World War II, the Germans
invaded, defeating Norwegian and Anglo-
French forces at Narvik in 1940 and imposing a
puppet government under Vidkun *Quisling. In
1945 the monarchy, and a Labour government,
returned. Norway withdrew its application to
join the *European Economic Community
(1972) after a national referendum, while the
exploitation of North Sea oil in the 1970s gave a
great boost to the economy. Norwegians voted
against joining the European Union in a referendum held in 1994. In 1991 King Olav V (1957–
91) was succeeded by his son, Harald V. On 22
July 2011 a lone right-wing terrorist, Anders
Breivik, set off a bomb in Oslo and then shot
over 60 people dead at a Labour Party youth
camp on the island of Utøya.

Nostradamus (born **Michel de Nostre-
dame**) (1503–66) French astrologer and physician. His predictions, in the form of rhymed
quatrains, appeared in two collections (1555;
1558). Cryptic and apocalyptic in tone, they
were given extensive credence at the French
court, where Nostradamus was for a time personal physician to Charles IX. Condemned in
1781 by the Roman Catholic Inquisition, they
are no longer taken seriously.

Nubians A people who live chiefly in Egypt
and the Sudan, between the First and Fourth
Cataracts of the River Nile. Their recorded history begins with raids by Egyptians c.2613 BC,
when their country was called Kush. Then a
Nubian dynasty ruling at Napata from c.920 BC
conquered all Egypt. The Nubian Shabaka ruled
as King of Kush and Egypt with Thebes as his

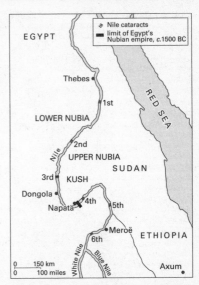

Nubians. The Romans gave the name Nubia to
the region of the Nile Valley extending
roughly from the First Cataract in Egypt to the
confluence of the Nile. In the 10th century BC
its rulers became pharaohs of Egypt, and
Napata, its capital, was briefly the centre of the
ancient world.

capital but Assyrians forced Taharka, his
successor, to withdraw (680–669 BC). After
several further struggles, the Nubians drew back
to Napata, and c.530 BC their capital moved to
Meroë. The dynasty continued until 350 AD,
when Aezanas of *Aksum destroyed it; its 300
pyramids remain. Nubia was converted to
Christianity in c.540 AD. Three Christian kingdoms emerged, but in 652 AD an Egyptian army
conquered that at Dongola, granting peace for
an annual tribute of slaves and at the end of
the 13th century *Mamelukes took the north.
The southern kingdom survived until the
16th century, when the *Funj kingdom of
Sennar absorbed it.

Nuclear Test-Ban Treaty (1963) An international agreement not to test nuclear weapons
in the atmosphere, in outer space, or under
water, signed by the USA, the Soviet Union, and
the UK (but not France). On 1 July 1968 the
UK, the USA, and the Soviet Union signed a
Non-Proliferation Treaty, which was endorsed
by 59 other states. China carried out

underground nuclear tests during 1994–95 and declared it would continue testing. France received international condemnation for carrying out a series of six tests in the south Pacific (1995–96) but then announced a permanent end of French tests. In 1996 member nations began signing a comprehensive test-ban treaty, which will not become legally binding unless all the nuclear nations sign.

nullification A US doctrine holding that a state had the right to nullify a federal law within its own territory. The Kentucky Resolutions of 1798–99 asserted the right of each state to judge whether acts of the federal government were constitutional. The nullification theory was fully developed in South Carolina, especially by John Calhoun, in response to the high protective tariffs of 1828 and 1832. South Carolina's Ordinance of Nullification in 1833 prohibited the collection of tariff duties in the state, and asserted that the use of force by the federal government would justify secession. Although this ordinance was repealed after the passing of new federal legislation in the same year, the sentiments behind nullification remained latent in Southern politics, and were to emerge again in the secession crisis prior to the *American Civil War.

Nupe A kingdom in West Africa, now part of Nigeria. According to tradition, Nupe was founded in the 16th century by Tsoede, who died in 1591 aged 120; he built Gbara and conquered a large amount of territory. Raba, the capital, became highly prosperous. Its wealth was largely dependent on wars to collect prisoners to sell as slaves. In the early 19th century the *Fulani asserted overlordship, leading to bitter struggles for independence.

Nuremberg Trials (1945–46) An international tribunal for Nazi war criminals. The trials were complex and controversial, there being few precedents for using international law relating to the conduct of states to judge the activities of individuals. The charges were: conspiracy against peace, crimes against peace,

violation of the laws and customs of war, crimes against humanity. As a result of the trials several Nazi organizations, such as the *Gestapo and the *SS, were declared to be criminal bodies. Individual judgements against the 24 war-time leaders included death sentences, imprisonment, and not guilty. Ten prisoners were executed, while *Goering and Ley committed suicide. Rudolf *Hess was sentenced to life-imprisonment.

Nyasaland The name of *Malawi until it gained independence in 1966.

Nye Committee (1934–36) A US Senate committee, chaired by Gerald P. Nye of North Dakota, to investigate the dealings of the munitions industry and bankers and their reputed profits from promoting foreign wars. The findings revealed high profits and a studied hostility to disarmament but no evidence to support the theory that President Woodrow *Wilson had at any time been influenced by the financial "stake" in his relations with Germany. However, so strong and widespread was the spirit of *isolationism that the Senate, in an effort to remain aloof from global problems, passed a series of Neutrality Acts (1935–39).

Nyerere, Julius Kambarage (1922–99) Tanzanian statesman, President of Tanganyika (1962–64) and of Tanzania (1964–85). He was an active campaigner for the nationalist movement in the 1950s, forming the Tanganyika African National Union (1954). He served as Prime Minister of Tanganyika following its independence in 1961 and became President a year later. In 1964 he successfully negotiated a union with Zanzibar and remained President of the new state of Tanzania until his retirement.

Nystad, Treaty of (1721) The final treaty of the *Northern War. It was signed at Nystad in south-west Finland. Under this treaty Sweden recognized *Peter I's title to Estonia, Livonia, Ingria, Kexholm, and part of Finland and so lost its Baltic empire.

OAS *See* ORGANIZATION DE L'ARMÉE SECRÈTE; ORGANIZATION OF AMERICAN STATES.

Oastler, Richard (1789–1861) British social reformer. He began his agitation in 1830 with the support of John Wood, a Bradford manufacturer, who revealed some of the worst abuses of child labour in factories. Oastler, a Tory radical, combined his attack on the factory system with a condemnation of the *Poor Law Amendment Act of 1834. He attained some of his objectives with the Ten Hours Act in 1847, which limited daily working hours.

Oates, Titus (1649–1705) English clergyman and conspirator. He is remembered as the fabricator of the *Popish Plot, a fictitious Jesuit plot that supposedly involved a plan to kill Charles II, massacre Protestants, and put the Catholic Duke of York on the English throne. Convicted of perjury in 1685, Oates was imprisoned in the same year, but was subsequently released and granted a pension.

Obama, Barack (Hussein) (1961–) US Democratic statesman, 44th President of the USA (2009–). The son of a Kenyan father and US mother, who divorced when he was a child, Obama was raised in Hawaii and Indonesia. He graduated in political science from Columbia University in 1983. A community organizer in Chicago from 1985 to 1988, he became active in the Democratic Party after graduating from Harvard Law School in 1991. He was elected to the Illinois Senate (1996) and then the US Senate (2004). In the 2008 presidential race he won a hard-fought primary campaign against Hillary *Clinton, and then defeated the Republican John McCain to become the USA's first Black president. Obama's campaign was characterized by inspiring oratory that raised great—perhaps unrealistic—hopes for his administration. In office Obama has been hampered by fiercely partisan Republican opposition in Congress. His significant domestic achievement has been the Patient Protection and Affordable Care Act (2010), which provided for health insurance for all US citizens; but this has proved a controversial change, viewed by opponents as unwarranted government interference in the liberty of Americans to regulate their private affairs. In foreign affairs he ended the US military presence in *Iraq (2011). In 2012 he defeated Mitt Romney to win re-election. He was awarded the Nobel Peace Prize in 2009.

Obote, Milton (Apollo Milton Obote) (1924–2005) Ugandan statesman, Prime Minister (1962–66), President (1966–71 and 1980–85). After founding the Uganda People's Congress in 1960, he became the first Prime Minister of independent Uganda. Overthrown by Idi Amin in 1971, he returned from exile nine years later and was re-elected President. Obote established a multiparty democracy, but was removed in a second military coup in 1985.

Obregón, Alvaro (1880–1928) Mexican general and statesman. President of Mexico (1920–24), he was elected after the most violent decade of the *Mexican Revolution. He succeeded in bringing about some measure of agrarian, educational, and labour reform, although peonage remained strong. His implementation of the revolutionary programme of 1917 brought him into bitter conflict with the Catholic Church. After turning the presidency over to his successor Plutarco Elías *Calles in 1924, he was elected to a second term in 1928 but was assassinated prior to taking office.

Obrenović Serbian dynasty (1817–1903). It was founded by a former cattle drover, Milos Obrenović I (1780–1860), who became a revolutionary fighting the Turks under *Kara George. After the murder (probably at his instigation) of Kara George, he persuaded the Turks to accept his election in 1817 as Prince of Serbia. His tyrannical rule led to his enforced abdication and the brief reign of Milan Obrenović II. Michael Obrenović III (1823–68) succeeded in 1840 but was forced into exile two years later.

Milos was reinstated in 1858 but died in 1860. Michael then resumed his rule, and proved an able and effective ruler. He was assassinated in 1868, and his cousin, Milan Obrenović IV (1854–1901), began 30 years of unpopular rule. He declared himself king of Serbia in 1882 but was forced to abdicate in favour of his son Alexander (1876–1903). Alexander's murder in June 1903 ended the dynasty, and the Karageorgević dynasty again came to power.

O'Brien, Smith *See* YOUNG IRELAND.

OCAS *See* ORGANIZATION OF CENTRAL AMERICAN STATES.

O'Connell, Daniel (known as **'the Liberator'**) (1775–1847) Irish nationalist leader and social reformer. His election to Parliament in 1828 forced the British government to grant Catholic Emancipation in order to enable him to take his seat in the House of Commons, for which Roman Catholics were previously ineligible. In 1839 he established the Repeal Association to abolish the union with Britain; O'Connell was arrested and briefly imprisoned for sedition in 1844.

O'Connor, Feargus Edward (1794–1855) Irish radical politician and Chartist leader. O'Connor was elected Member of Parliament for County Cork in 1832 as a supporter of Daniel *O'Connell but lost his seat in 1835. In 1837 he founded a radical newspaper the *Northern Star* in England, and it was largely through his tireless energy and his ability as an orator that *Chartism became a mass movement. After a term of imprisonment for seditious libel, he was elected Member of Parliament for Nottingham in 1847.

Octavian *See* AUGUSTUS.

October Revolution *See* RUSSIAN REVOLUTION (1917).

October War *See* YOM KIPPUR WAR.

Oda Nobunaga (1534–82) Japanese warrior, who overthrew many powerful *daimyo in an attempt to end the disorder of the *Ashikaga period. He was assisted by *Hideyoshi and *Tokugawa Ieyasu – and by the fact that many of his troops were armed with muskets, introduced by the Portuguese after 1542. In 1568 he entered Kyoto and in 1573 he drove out the *shogun. He began "sword hunts" to disarm much of the population and organized land surveys. By the time he was assassinated by one

of his followers, firm rule had replaced political chaos in most of central Japan.

Oder–Neisse Line The frontier, formed by these two rivers, established between Poland and Soviet-occupied Germany in 1945: it had once marked the frontier of medieval Poland. As a result of an agreement at the *Potsdam Conference, nearly one-fifth of Germany's territory in 1938 was reallocated, mainly to Poland. Germans were expelled from these eastern territories, which were resettled by Poles. The frontier, which became the eastern boundary of the German Democratic Republic, was later accepted by the Federal Republic (West Germany) as part of the policy of détente known as *Ostpolitik, and confirmed in 1990 when reunification took place.

Odoacer (433–93) Gothic chieftain who became the first Germanic ruler of Italy. He and his troops were part of the Roman army and when Romulus Augustus became emperor (476) he led an uprising and deposed him, making Ravenna his capital. This event marked the end of the Western *Roman empire. His troops later overran Dalmatia, threatening the power of Zeno, the Eastern emperor, who encouraged *Theodoric the Great, King of the Ostrogoths, to besiege Ravenna. Odoacer surrendered (493) on promise of retaining half of Italy but at a banquet was murdered by Theodoric, who became sole ruler.

OECD *See* ORGANIZATION FOR ECONOMIC CO-OPERATION AND DEVELOPMENT.

Offa (died 796) King of Mercia (757–96). After seizing power in Mercia in 757, he expanded his territory to become overlord of most of England south of the Humber. Offa is chiefly remembered for constructing the frontier earthworks called *Offa's Dyke.

Offa's Dyke A series of earthworks running the length of the Welsh border from near the mouth of the Wye to near the mouth of the Dee, built or repaired by *Offa (king of Mercia, 757–96) to mark the boundary established by his wars with the Welsh.

Oglethorpe, James Edward (1696–1785) British general, philanthropist, and founder of Georgia (USA). He entered Parliament (1722) after serving under Prince *Eugène of Savoy. Espousing the cause of imprisoned debtors, he led a group of philanthropists who became trustees of the new North American colony of

Georgia in 1732. He founded Savannah (1733) and governed the colony on paternalistic lines, encouraging immigration of persecuted Protestants from Europe and of former soldiers. His military preparedness saved the colony from Spanish attack in 1742, after which he returned to Britain, where he fought against the *Forty-Five rebellion.

OGPU (initial Russian letters for 'United State Political Administration') A security police agency established in 1922 as GPU and renamed after the formation of the *Soviet Union (1923). It existed to suppress counter-revolution, to uncover political dissidents, and, after 1928, to enforce *collectivization of farming. It had its own army and a vast network of spies. It was absorbed into the *NKVD in 1934.

O'Higgins, Bernardo (c.1778–1842) Chilean revolutionary leader and statesman, head of state (1817–23). The son of a Spanish officer of Irish origin, he was educated in England, where he first became involved in nationalist politics. On his return to Chile he led the independence movement and, with the help of José de San Martín, liberator of Argentina, led the army, which triumphed over Spanish forces in 1817, paving the way for Chilean independence the following year. For the next six years he was head of state (supreme director) of Chile, but then fell from power and lived in exile in Peru for the remainder of his life.

Ojibwa Native Americans who formerly inhabited the territory around Lake Superior in North America. The Ojibwa were hunters and fishers as well as subsistence farmers, and were constantly feuding with the Sioux. They also developed a unique form of picture-writing. During the 17th century they expanded their territory as far as North Dakota, and became one of the largest indigenous peoples of North America. Since the early 19th century they have been living on reservations in the states of North Dakota, Michigan, Minnesota, and Wisconsin.

Oklahoma Indian Territory An early Native American reservation in the western USA. Most of modern Oklahoma came to the USA by the *Louisiana Purchase, which stimulated President *Jefferson to think that one answer to relations between Whites and indigenous peoples would be to transfer the latter to these newly acquired lands. In 1817 some Cherokees made the journey west to join

original inhabitants like the Kiowa, Shawnee, Comanche, and Pawnee. After the Indian Removal Act of 1830 increasing numbers of indigenous peoples were transferred west and in 1867 the general Oklahoma Reservation was established. By the end of the 1880s many Whites had been persuaded that the land was not being used productively, and called for the opening of much of it to White settlement. In 1889 Congress authorized settlement, and in 1890 it organized the White-controlled areas into Oklahoma Territory, which became the 46th state in 1907.

Olaf I (or **Olaf Tryggvessön**) (969–1000) King of Norway (995–1000). Exiled when his father was killed, he was brought up in Novgorod in Russia. Viking expeditions took him to Iceland, England, and Ireland where he was converted to Christianity. In 995 he was accepted as King of Norway, and established the new religion. He was drowned at sea after a battle with the combined Danish and Swedish fleets.

Olaf II, St (or **Olaf Haraldsson**) (c.995–1028) King of Norway (1015–28). He was converted to Christianity and continued the work of conversion begun by *Olaf I but his attempts at reform provoked rebellion and he was killed in a battle with rebel and Danish forces. Canonized as a saint, he is honoured as Norway's national hero.

Oldenbarneveldt, Johan van (1547–1619) Dutch statesman and lawyer who played a key role in the *Dutch Revolts. A Calvinist and a keen supporter of *William I (the Silent), he helped to negotiate the Union of Utrecht (1579). After 1586, as leader of the Estates of Holland, he managed to impose unity on the diverse political, economic, and religious interests of the *United Provinces. He negotiated a twelve-year truce with Spain in 1609, but after this his political differences with Maurice of Nassau became part of a bitter internecine quarrel between two rival schools of Calvinism, and eventually Maurice had Oldenbarneveldt tried and executed on a charge of treason.

Oldowan The oldest tradition of human tool-making, named after the simple stone tools found at Olduvai Gorge, Tanzania but now known from many other early human occupation sites in Africa. The oldest certain stone tools, from the Hadar and Omo regions in Ethiopia and from the east of the Democratic Republic of Congo, were made between 2.5 and

2 million years ago, probably by *Homo habilis*. Usually, the toolmaker started with a large cobble, probably picked out of a stream bed, and flaked it with a hammerstone into the required shape. The detached flakes were also trimmed and put to use. Several distinct types of Oldowan tools were made and were probably used for different tasks. A more advanced tradition, Developed Oldowan, occurs also at Olduvai Gorge around 1.5 million years ago, the maker probably being *Homo erectus*.

Olmec 1. A member of a prehistoric people inhabiting the coast of Veracruz and western Tabasco on the Gulf of Mexico *c.* 1200–100 BC, who established what was probably the first developed civilization of Mesoamerica. They are noted for their sculptures, especially the massive stone-hewn heads with realistic features and round helmets, and small jade carvings featuring a jaguar.

2. A member of a Native American people living in the highlands of Mexico or migrating to the Gulf coast during the 12th century. Their name is derived from a Nahuatl word meaning 'people of the rubber(-tree) country'.

Olmert, Ehud (1945–) Israeli statesman; Prime Minister (2006–09). He was a Likud government minister from 1988 to 1992 and then Mayor of Jerusalem (1993–2003). He returned to government as Ariel *Sharon's Deputy Prime Minister and followed Sharon in splitting with Likud (2005) to found the Kadima party. After Sharon's incapacitation by a stroke (January 2006), Olmert became Acting Prime Minister and led Kadima in the 2006 elections. He emerged as Prime Minister of a Kadima–Labour coalition, but resigned as leader of Kadima in 2008 following allegations of corruption. He remained Prime Minister until elections in 2009. In 2012 he was convicted of breach of trust but acquitted on other charges; at a second trial in 2014 he was gaoled for accepting bribes.

Olympia A site in western Greece. It was the location of the most important shrine to the god Zeus. An oracle of Zeus was there and every four years a festival of competitive games was held in his honour. Archaeologists have recovered much, most notably many of the sculptures of the temple of Zeus (5th century BC), and also the workshop where the gold and ivory statue of Zeus was created by the Athenian Phidias probably in the 430s BC.

Oman (formerly known as **Muscat and Oman**)

Capital:	Muscat
Area:	309,500 sq km (119,499 sq miles)
Population:	3,154,134 (2013 est)
Currency:	1 Omani rial = 1000 baiza
Religions:	Ibadhi Muslim 75.0%; Shia Muslim 5.0%
Ethnic Groups:	Arab; Baluchi; Indo-Pakistani; African
Languages:	Arabic (official); English; Baluchi; Urdu
International Organizations:	UN; Arab League; GCC; Non-Aligned Movement; WTO

A country situated on the eastern corner of the Arabian peninsula.

Physical Oman has a coast on the Arabian Sea, and inland it borders on Saudi Arabia and Yemen. Mountains rise steeply from a narrow coastal plain to a plateau which merges into the desert of the 'empty quarter' or Rub al-Khali.

Economy Crude oil and natural gas are important export industries and sources of government revenue. The industrial base also includes construction and the production of cement, copper, steel, chemicals, and optical fibre. The coastal plain is fertile, producing fruit and vegetables. Oman is seeking to diversify its economy as its oil resources decline.

History Oman was a trading outpost of Mesopotamia, settled by Arabs in the 1st century AD. It was conquered for Islam in the 7th century. Expelling Portuguese incursions by 1650, the Omanis created a maritime empire with possessions as distant as Mombasa and the island of Zanzibar in East Africa and trade contacts with south-east Asia. By 1754 Ahmad ibn Said had expelled Turkish invaders and founded the sultanate that still rules Oman. Under Said ibn Sultan Sayyid Oman was the most powerful state in Arabia in the early 19th century, controlling Zanzibar and the coastal regions of Iran and Baluchistan (now mainly in Pakistan). Tension frequently erupted between the sultan of Oman and the interior tribes. Oil, now the country's major product, began to be exported in 1967. In 1970 the present ruler, Sultan

Qaboos bin Said (1940–), deposed his father Said bin Taimur in a palace coup. An uprising by left-wing guerrillas, the Popular Front for the Liberation of Oman, was defeated in 1975. A member of the Arab League, Oman managed to remain largely unaffected by both the *Iran–Iraq War and the *Gulf War. In 1996 Sultan Qaboos decreed Oman to be a hereditary absolute monarchy. However, the State Advisory Council was elected by universal suffrage in 2003. Demonstrations in 2011 inspired by the *Arab Spring resulted in some reforms but did not endanger Sultan Qaboos's regime.

OPEC *See* ORGANIZATION OF PETROLEUM EXPORTING COUNTRIES.

Opium Wars (1839–42; 1856–60) Two wars between Britain and China. In the early 19th century British traders were illegally importing opium from India to China and trying to increase trade in general. In 1839 the Chinese government confiscated some 20,000 chests of opium from British warehouses in Guangzhou (Canton). In 1840 the British Foreign Secretary, Lord *Palmerston, sent a force of 16 British warships, which besieged Guangzhou and threatened Nanjing and communications with the capital. It ended with the Treaty of *Nanjing (1842). In 1856 Chinese officials boarded and searched a British flagged ship, the *Arrow*. The French joined the British in launching a military attack in 1857, at the end of which they demanded that the Chinese agree to the Treaty of Tianjin in 1858. This opened further ports to Western trade and provided freedom of travel to European merchants and Christian missionaries inland. When the emperor refused to ratify the agreement, Beijing was occupied, after which, by the Beijing Convention (1860), the Tianjin Agreement was accepted. By 1900 the number of treaty ports had risen to over 50, with all European colonial powers, as well as the USA, being granted trading concessions.

Oppenheimer, Robert (Julius Robert Oppenheimer) (1904–67) US physicist. Oppenheimer was appointed in 1942 as Director of the *Manhattan Project, based at Los Alamos, New Mexico, which in 1945 made the first atomic bomb. In 1953, at the height of the witch-hunting campaign led by the US Senator Joseph *McCarthy, Oppenheimer was excluded from sensitive research on the grounds that he had Communist sympathies, but subsequently (1963) he was unreservedly rehabilitated.

Opus Dei *See* ROMAN CATHOLIC CHURCH.

oracle A place consulted for advice or prophecy. There were many oracles in the ancient Greek world, most notably at Delphi, Didyma on the coast of Asia Minor, Dodona in Epirus, and *Olympia. The most famous non-Greek oracle was that of the Egyptian Ammon at Siwah oasis in the Sahara, identified by the Greeks with Zeus and consulted by Alexander the Great in 331 BC. Apollo was the god most favoured as a giver of oracles though many other deities presided over oracular shrines. Consultations usually concerned religious matters but were also used by leaders seeking support for political or military actions.

Orange The ruling house (in full Orange-Châlons) of the principality centred on the small city of Orange, southern France. The city grew up around its Roman monuments, which include a semicircular theatre and a triumphal arch. In the 11th century it became an independent countship, and from the 12th century its rulers were vassals of the Holy Roman Emperor and came to style themselves 'princes'.

After 1530 the related house of Nassau-Châlons succeeded to the title, and in 1544 William of Nassau-Dillenburg (1533–84) became Prince of Orange and subsequently, as William I (the Silent), statholder in the Netherlands. His younger son, Maurice of Nassau (1567–1625), assumed the military leadership of the Dutch Revolts in 1584. Until the late 18th century the Orange dynasty continued to play a major part in the politics of the United Provinces. The principality itself was conquered by Louis XIV (1672) and incorporated into France by the Treaty of Utrecht (1713), but the title of Prince of Orange was retained by *William III, who became King of England, Scotland, and Ireland in 1689.

Orange, William of *See* WILLIAM III (OF ORANGE).

Orange Revolution (2004) A series of demonstrations in Kiev that led to a rerun of the 2004 Ukrainian presidential election. The original run-off poll, held on 21 November 2004, narrowly gave victory to the Prime Minister, Viktor Yanukovych, over the opposition candidate, Viktor Yushchenko. However, there were many reports of electoral fraud in favour of Yanukovych, and Yushchenko's supporters mounted a series of demonstrations and strikes in an attempt to overturn the result. Particularly prominent were the huge daily protests in Kiev, where demonstrators wore the orange colours of Yushchenko's party. The disputed poll was annulled and a fresh run-off made Yushchenko the winner; he was inaugurated as President on 23 January 2005. The Orange Revolution's wider significance hinged on the contrast between the generally pro-Russian policies advocated by Yanukovych and the pro-Western ones of Yushchenko. This also reflected an ethnic and geographical division: the predominantly Russian population of eastern Ukraine supported Yanukovych, while the Ukrainian west supported Yushchenko. The revolution was therefore seen as a move by Ukraine towards the West; but this was not a final resolution of the issues it raised (*see* UKRAINE).

ordeal A painful technique used in the early Middle Ages to determine the guilt or innocence of suspects by divine intervention, conducted and supervised by the Church. Ordeal by fire required suspects (usually freemen) to carry hot irons, or to walk blindfold and barefoot through red-hot ploughshares or over heated coals. If they emerged unhurt or their wounds healed within three days they were innocent. Immersion of a hand or arm in boiling water was another method. Suspects (often alleged witches) were thrown into cold water and deemed guilty if they floated. Trial by blessed bread was a test for priests, for it was assumed guilty clergy would choke on hallowed food. Ordeals were repudiated by the Church in 1215. They were not particular to Europe; tribes in east Africa and Madagascar practised similar tests.

Oregon Boundary dispute (1843–46) A territorial dispute between the USA and Britain. Since 1818, Britain and the USA had agreed on joint occupation of the Oregon country, an area west of the Rocky Mountains running down into the valley of the Columbia River. However, as settlers moved up the Oregon Trail, pressure mounted for the territory to become part of the USA. The settlers wanted their northern boundary with the British to be to the north of Vancouver Island on the 54° 40′. parallel, and in 1844 President *Polk used the slogan "54 40 or fight" in his victorious campaign. Discussions took place with the British, who at first insisted on the Columbia River as boundary. A compromise agreement between the British Foreign Secretary Lord *Aberdeen and President Polk was reached in 1846. This was to accept a line well to the south of Polk's original demands, extending the 49th parallel boundary to the Pacific, but excluding Vancouver Island. In 1848, Congress created the Oregon Territory. This was later split up into the state of Oregon (1859), the state of Washington (1889), the state of Idaho (1890), and parts of Montana and Wyoming.

Organization de l'Armée secrète (OAS) A French secret terrorist organization based in Algeria, formed in 1961. Its aim was the destruction of the French Fifth Republic in the interest of French colonial control of Algeria. It plotted an unsuccessful assassination attempt on President *de Gaulle in 1962. Its action had little effect on the French government, which by now was determined to grant independence to Algeria. Subsequent riots in Algiers were suppressed, and the OAS itself eliminated (1963) by the capture or exile of its leaders.

Organization for Economic Cooperation and Development (OECD) An organization of industrialized countries, established in 1961, and based in Paris, which seeks to promote coordination of economic and social policies among members, to make resources of capital and training available to developing countries, to contribute to the expansion of world trade, and to foster cooperation in fields such as education, energy, and transport. It was created as a replacement for the Organization for European Economic Cooperation, which had been formed in 1948 by those countries receiving aid under the *Marshall Plan. In 2014 its members were Australia, Austria, Belgium, Canada, Chile, the Czech Republic, Denmark, Estonia, Finland, France, Germany, Greece, Hungary, Iceland, Republic of Ireland, Israel, Italy, Japan, South Korea, Luxembourg, Mexico, the Netherlands, New Zealand, Norway, Poland, Portugal, Slovakia, Slovenia, Spain, Sweden, Switzerland, Turkey, the UK, and the USA. The OECD prepares an influential annual report on the economy of each member country.

Organization of African Unity *See* AFRICAN UNION.

Organization of American States (OAS) An association of 35 American and Caribbean states. Originally founded in 1890 for largely commercial purposes, it adopted its present name and charter in 1948. Its aims are to work for peace and prosperity in the region and to uphold the sovereignty of member-nations. Its General Secretariat is based in Washington, DC, USA.

Organization of Central American States (OCAS) (1951–60) A regional grouping comprising Costa Rica, El Salvador, Guatemala, Honduras, and Nicaragua. Established in 1951, its purpose was to establish the *Central

American Common Market. This goal was reached in 1960, but OCAS members cooperated on little else. The San Salvador Charter (1962) expanded the trade and fiscal provisions of the original treaty, envisaging permanent political, economic, and defence councils.

Organization of Petroleum Exporting Countries (OPEC) An international organization seeking to regulate the price of oil. The first moves to establish closer links between oil-producing countries were made by Venezuela, Iran, Iraq, Kuwait, and Saudi Arabia in 1949. In 1960, following a reduction in the oil price by the international oil companies, a conference was held in Baghdad of representatives from these countries, when it was decided to set up a permanent organization. This was formed in Caracas, Venezuela, the next year. Other countries later joined: Qatar (1961), Indonesia (1962), Libya (1962), United Arab Emirates (1967), Algeria (1969), Nigeria (1971), Ecuador (1973), Gabon (1975), and Angola (2007). Ecuador left OPEC in 1992 but re-joined in 2007, and Gabon (1994) and Indonesia (2009) have since withdrawn. OPEC's activities extend through all aspects of oil negotiations, including basic oil price, royalty rates, production quotas, and government profits.

The organization rose to prominence in the mid-1970s after it virtually quadrupled the price of oil over a three-month period at the end of 1973, and imposed an embargo on Western consumers who had supported Israel in the Arab-Israel (Yom Kippur) War. OPEC's successful use of the 'oil weapon' had important repercussions for *North–South relations, inspiring greater assertiveness among developing countries, and giving weight to their demands for a *New International Economic Order. Some Arab states made large profits from the sale of oil during this period. During the 1980s, however, the influence of OPEC on world oil prices declined slightly as Western industrialized countries, such as Norway and the UK, began to exploit their own oil resources, found alternative forms of fuel, or initiated programmes to cut the use of energy. The Organization of Arab Petroleum Exporting Countries (OAPEC), based in Kuwait, was established in 1968, to coordinate the different aspects of the Arab petroleum industry, and safeguard its members' interests.

Orlando, Vittorio Emanuele (1860–1952) Italian statesman and jurist. He had supported Italy's entry into World War I and after the *Caporetto disaster (1917) became Premier. At the *Versailles Peace Settlement he clashed with

President Woodrow *Wilson over what Wilson thought were excessive claims by Italy to former Austrian territory. In 1922 he at first supported *Mussolini, but after the murder of *Matteotti he resigned from Parliament in protest (1925) and fled the country. After the fall of Mussolini (1943) he became a leader of the Conservative Democratic Union.

Orléans, Duc d' A title borne by younger princes of the French royal family from the 14th century. Charles VI of France bestowed the duchy of Orléans on his brother Louis (1392). Louis's grandson became Louis XII of France. His great-grandson became *Francis I and the Valois-Orléans ended with the death of *Henry III in 1589. Philippe (1674–1723) of the second Bourbon-Orléans branch of the family became Regent of France in 1715 during the minority of *Louis XV. His great-grandson Louis Philippe Joseph ('Philippe Égalité') succeeded to the title in 1785. He was a supporter of the French Revolution from its beginnings, and in June 1789 he organized the 47 nobles who joined the Third Estate. In 1792 he voted for the death of the king but, with all the remaining Bourbons, was arrested, accused of conspiracy, and guillotined (1793).

Orsini, Felice (1819–58) Italian revolutionary. After being implicated in revolutionary plots, he was condemned in 1844 to life imprisonment. He was later pardoned by Pius IX but took part in Italy in the *Revolutions of 1848. In 1849 he joined *Mazzini in Rome and then went to Hungary, where he was arrested. After his escape in 1854 he formed a plot to assassinate *Napoleon III, seen as the principal obstacle to Italian independence. His attempt to blow up the imperial carriage failed (14 January 1858) and he was executed.

Ortega, Daniel See NICARAGUA; SANDINISTA LIBERATION FRONT.

Orthodox Church The Eastern or Greek Church, having the Patriarch of Constantinople as its head, and the national Churches of Russia, Romania, etc. in communion with it. Separation from the Western Church came in the 4th century, originally through cultural and political factors, focused from the 5th century onwards on differences of doctrine and ritual, and took formal effect in 1054 when the Pope and the Patriarch of Constantinople excommunicated each other. In the latter part of the 20th century the Orthodox Churches have taken an active part in the ecumenical movement; the mutual excommunication of 1054 was abolished in 1965.

Osborne judgement (1909) A British court decision concerning the use of trade-union funds for political purposes. It stemmed from an action brought by a Liberal trade unionist, W. V. Osborne, against the practice of using part of trade-union subscriptions to pay salaries to Labour Members of Parliament. The courts found in favour of Osborne. Up to this time Members of Parliament received no Parliamentary salary. This was remedied in 1911. The Trade Union Act (1913) authorized unions to have a political fund but subscriptions to it were optional, members being able to "contract out".

OSCE *See* HELSINKI CONFERENCE.

Osceola (*c.* 1800–39) Seminole chief. During the *Seminole War (1835–42), Osceola, an extremely capable military leader, held off US attempts to remove his tribe to the west for three years. Frustrated by his successful resistance in the Florida Everglades, General Jessup offered Osceola safe conduct to a peace conference, but treacherously imprisoned him at Fort Moultrie near Charleston, where he died.

Osman *See* UTHMAN.

Osman I (or **Othman**) (1259–1326) Turkish conqueror, founder of the Ottoman (Osmanli) dynasty and empire. After succeeding his father as leader of the Seljuk Turks in 1288, Osman reigned as sultan, conquering north-west Asia Minor. He assumed the title of emir in 1299.

Ostpolitik (German, 'eastern policy') The Federal Republic of *Germany's opening of relations with the Eastern bloc in the 1970s. It was a reversal of West Germany's refusal to recognize the legitimacy of the German Democratic Republic (East Germany), as propounded in the Hallstein Doctrine (1955). The policy of Ostpolitik was pursued with particular vigour by Willy *Brandt, as Chancellor of the Federal Republic. A General Relations Treaty (1972) normalized relations between the two Germanys, while treaties between West Germany and both the Soviet Union and Poland gave formal recognition to the Oder-Neisse frontier (1970–72).

ostracism A method of banishment in ancient *Athens. At a stated meeting each year, the Athenian assembly voted on whether it wanted an ostracism that year. If the vote was affirmative, an ostracism was held two months later. Every citizen who so wished then wrote a name on a sherd of pottery ("*ostrakon*"), and provided that at least 6000 valid "ostraka" were counted, the man with the most against him had to leave Attica for ten years, though he was allowed to enjoy any income from his property there while absent. A vote to ostracize often functioned as a sort of "general election", constituting a "vote of confidence" for the policies of the most powerful rival of the man thus named. Such trials of political strength were most notable in the ostracisms of Themistocles (*c.*471), Cimon (*c.*462), and Pericles' rival Thucydides (443). Ostracism was not resorted to after 417 or 416.

Ostrogoths The eastern *Goths on the northern shores of the Black Sea. They became vassals of the *Huns whose westward migration displaced them and under *Attila they could be defeated by Roman and barbarian allied armies on the *Catalaunian Fields, 451 AD. Forty years later *Theodoric the Great established a kingdom in Italy. After the murder in 533 of Theodoric's daughter, who was the regent of Italy, *Justinian's general *Belisarius twice invaded and defeated them, and the Ostrogothic kingdom was crushed by Narses in 552.

Oswald, Lee Harvey (1939–63) US alleged assassin of President *Kennedy at Dallas, Texas, in 1963. He was arrested but before he could be tried, he was himself killed by another civilian, Jack Ruby. Many theories have been aired that Oswald had accomplices, but the *Warren Commission concluded that he had acted on his own.

Oswald, St (*c.*605–42) King of the Northumbrian kingdom of Bernicia (*Northumbria) (633–42). He gained the kingdom after his victory near Hexham over the Welsh king *Cadwallon (633), who had in the previous year invaded Northumbria and killed Oswald's uncle Edwin. Following that invasion Oswald took refuge on Iona, where he became a Christian. On his return he arranged for missionaries from Iona, led by St Aidan, to convert his people (635). Oswald was killed in battle by the pagan king *Penda of Mercia.

Oswy (or **Oswiu**) (died 670) King of *Northumbria (651–70). He succeeded his brother Oswald as ruler of the Northumbrian kingdom of Bernicia in 642 and incorporated the other northern kingdom, Deira, after arranging the assassination of his cousin Oswin (651). Although initially Northumbria was still in the control of *Penda, king of the neighbouring Mercia, Oswy was able to defeat him (655) and establish himself as overlord of England. Oswy's support of St Wilfrid at the Synod of *Whitby (664), called to consider the rival claims of the Roman and Celtic forms of the Christian Church, was critical in gaining the decision in favour of Rome.

Ottawa Agreements (1932) A series of agreements on tariffs and trade between Britain and its *dominions. They were concluded at the Imperial Economic Conference, held at Ottawa, and constituted a system of imperial preference to counter the impact of the Great *Depression. They provided for quotas of meat, wheat, dairy goods, and fruit from the dominions to enter Britain free of duty. In return, tariff benefits would be granted by the dominions to imported British manufactured goods. The economic gains were helpful but not massive. After World War II the benefits were steadily eroded, and, with the prospect of British entry into the *European Economic Community, the agreements became increasingly dispensable: although seriously considered during the 1961–63 discussions, they played little part in the entry negotiations of 1971–72 apart from the question of New Zealand dairy products.

Otterburn, Battle of (5 August 1388) A victory for Scottish forces over the English at Otterburn, a village in northern England. Although the Earl of Douglas was himself killed, Henry *Percy the Younger (Hotspur) was captured and English control of the north was jeopardized for years to come. The event was immortalized in the *Ballad of Chevy Chase*.

Otto I (or **Otto the Great**) (912–73) King of the Germans (936–73), Holy Roman emperor (962–73). As king of the Germans he carried out a policy of eastward expansion from his Saxon homeland and defeated the invading Hungarians in 955. He was crowned Holy Roman emperor in 962 and began to establish a strong imperial presence in Italy to rival that of the papacy.

Otto III (980–1002) King of Germany (994–1002) and Holy Roman Emperor (996–1002). He had ambitions of recreating the glory and power of the old Roman empire with himself as leader of world Christianity aided by a subservient pope. His short life was torn between periods of intense religious devotion (he lived for a year in a monastery), and dreams of secular power wielded from Rome, where he lived in oriental seclusion in the palace that he had had built. To control the papacy he installed in turn his cousin Gregory VI (996–99) and his tutor Sylvester II (999–1003) as popes, but this did not prevent rebellions in Italy.

Ottoman empire The Muslim empire of the Turks (1299–1922), established in northern Anatolia by *Osman I and expanded by his successors to include all of Asia Minor and much of south-east Europe. Ottoman power received a severe check with the invasion of Tamerlane in 1401, but expansion resumed several decades later, resulting in the capture of Constantinople in 1453. The empire reached its zenith under Suleiman I (1520–66), dominating the eastern Mediterranean, including North Africa, and threatening central Europe, but thereafter it began to decline. Still powerful in the 17th century, it had, by the 19th century, become the 'sick man of Europe', eventually collapsing in the early 20th century.

Oudenarde, Battle of (1708) Military engagement during the War of the *Spanish Succession. At the Flemish city of Oudenarde *Marlborough and his Dutch and Austrian allies defeated the French army. It was Marlborough's third great victory and led to the capture of Lille. In 1745, during the War of the *Austrian Succession, the French took the town and dismantled the fortifications.

Outremer ("Beyond the Sea") The Frankish name given to the Latin Kingdom of *Jerusalem established in Palestine after the First *Crusade (1096–99). On Christmas Day 1100 *Baldwin I was crowned as its first king. He ruled over a narrow strip of coastal territory with no clear eastern boundaries, and the kingdom depended for its survival on sufficient settlers coming regularly from Europe. Muslims united against the invaders and Jerusalem fell to them in 1187.

Owen, Robert (1771–1858) Welsh social reformer and industrialist. A pioneer socialist thinker, he believed that character is a product of the social environment. He founded a model industrial community centred on his cotton mills at New Lanark in Scotland; this was organized on principles of mutual cooperation, with improved working conditions and housing together with educational institutions provided for workers and their families. He went on to found a series of other cooperative communities; although these did not always succeed, his ideas had an important long-term effect on the development of British socialist thought and on the practice of industrial relations.

Oxenstierna, Axel Gustaffson, Count (1583–1654) Swedish statesman. He entered the

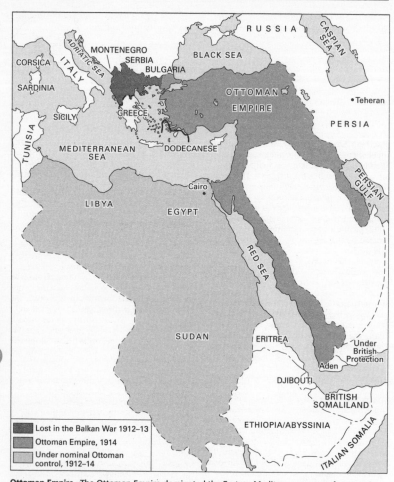

Ottoman Empire. The Ottoman Empire dominated the Eastern Mediterranean area for over six centuries but its decline in the early 20th century was rapid.

service of the Swedish state in 1602 and joined the Council of State in 1609. *Gustavus II (Adolphus) appointed him Chancellor in 1612, and for the next 22 years the two men worked together. An administrative reformer of note, Oxenstierna also made possible the reconciliation of the Swedish aristocracy to the monarchy. He negotiated the Truce of Altmark with Poland (1629), joined Gustavus in Germany in 1631, and after the king's death in 1632 was responsible for directing Swedish policy throughout the *Thirty Years War. He was also the effective ruler of Sweden from 1636 to 1644, when Queen *Christina reached her majority. His subsequent relations with her were not always harmonious. On his death, his son Erik succeeded him as Chancellor.

Oxford Movement *See* NEWMAN, JOHN HENRY.

Pacific Campaigns (1941–45) The naval and amphibious engagements in the Pacific during World War II. The war spread to the Pacific when Japanese aircraft attacked the US naval base of *Pearl Harbor in 1941. Japan was allied to Thailand and had bases in *Vichy-controlled Indo-China. Its landforces quickly occupied Hong Kong, Malaya, Singapore, and Burma. Other Japanese forces captured islands in the Pacific, while convoys sailed to occupy Borneo and the Dutch East Indies following the Japanese naval victory at the Battle of the Java Sea (27 February–1 March 1942). By April the Philippines were occupied, followed by northern New Guinea, and General *MacArthur withdrew to Australia, where he organized a counter-attack. The Battle of the Coral Sea (5–8 May) between Japanese and US aircraft carriers was strategically a US victory. It prevented Japanese landings on southern New Guinea and ended their threat to Australia. It was followed (3–6 June) by the decisive Battle of Midway Island, which, under Admiral *Nimitz, shifted the balance of naval power to the USA. In August 1942 US marines landed on Guadalcanal and Tulagi in the Solomon Islands, where fighting raged until February 1943. During 1943, the remaining Solomon Islands were recaptured by the USA; Bougainville was reclaimed from the Japanese in November, followed by New Britain early in 1944. In June 1943 MacArthur had launched his campaign to reoccupy New Guinea, and through 1944 US forces gradually moved back towards the Philippines. On 19 June 1944 the Japanese lost some 300 planes in the Battle of the Philippine Sea and in July the USA took the Mariana Islands, from which bombing raids on Tokyo were then organized. In October 1944 the Battle of *Leyte Gulf marked the effective end of Japanese naval power, while on the mainland the *Burma Campaign had reopened land communication with China and begun the process of reoccupation of the short-lived Japanese empire. Manila fell in March 1945, and in April US forces reoccupied Okinawa against fierce *kamikaze air raids, at the cost of very high casualties on both sides. Plans to invade Japan were ended by the decision to drop atomic bombs on *Hiroshima and *Nagasaki (6 and 9 August), which resulted in Japanese surrender.

Pacific scandal (1873) A Canadian political scandal. British Columbia had entered the dominion of *Canada in 1871 on the understanding that a trans-continental railway line would be built within ten years. In 1872 a contract for such a railway was awarded to a syndicate headed by Sir Hugh Alan, a banker, shipowner, and financial contributor to the Conservative Party. Following a general election in 1872, the defeated Liberals accused the Prime Minister, John *Macdonald, of having given the contract as a reward. Macdonald resigned and the contract was cancelled. The Conservatives were heavily defeated in a new election but the Canadian Pacific Railway was finally completed in 1885.

pacifism The belief that war is never justifiable, no matter how good the cause or how great the threat to one's country. Pacifism springs either from religious faith, as in the case of *Quakers, or from a humanist belief in the sanctity of life; the religious underpinning can be seen in works such as Tolstoy's *Christianity and Pacifism* (1883). In its purest form it prohibits all use of violence, even in self-defence. From the 20th century many states respected the beliefs of pacifists by recognizing conscientious objection as a ground for refusing conscription.

Páez, José Antonio (1790–1873) Venezuelan revolutionary and statesman. He was a leader of Venezuela's movement for independence, controlling (1810–19) a band of *Llaneros* (plainsmen) in guerrilla warfare against the Spanish. He led the separatist movement against *Bolívar's Colombian republic and became Venezuela's first President. During his first term (1831–35) he governed within the provisions of the Venezuelan constitution, but he became increasingly oligarchic in his subsequent terms of office (1839–46, 1861–63). He was exiled from 1850 to 1858 but returned in 1861 to become supreme dictator. In 1863 he again went into exile. He encouraged economic development, promotion of foreign immigration, and construction of schools.

Pahlavi, Reza *See* MUHAMMAD REZA SHAH PAHLAVI; REZA SHAH PAHLAVI.

Pai Marire (Maori, 'goodness and peace') A Maori political and religious movement. In 1862 Horopapera Te Ua of south Taranaki began teaching his people to worship the new Pai Marire god whom he saw as the Old Testament Jehovah. His followers danced around *niu* (decorated poles) seeking the gift of prophecy and powers to heal. Renewed war from 1865 saw the movement take a violent turn, becoming known as the Hau-hau. The ritual began to involve the exhibition of heads of White soldiers and missionaries and cannibalism was revived. The movement affected much of the North Island but gradually subsided after 1872.

Paine, Thomas (1737–1809) British political writer. After emigrating to America in 1774, he wrote the pamphlet *Common Sense* (1776), which called for American independence and laid the ground for the Declaration of Independence. On returning to England in 1787, he published *The Rights of Man* (1791), defending the French Revolution in response to Burke's *Reflections on the Revolution in France* (1790). His radical views prompted the British government to indict him for treason and he fled to France. There he supported the Revolution but opposed the execution of Louis XVI. He was imprisoned for a year, during which time he wrote *The Age of Reason* (1794), an attack on orthodox Christianity.

Paisley, Ian (Richard Kyle), Baron Bannside (1926–2014) Northern Irish clergyman; First Minister of Northern Ireland (2007–08). He became a minister in 1946, and then founded the Free Presbyterian Church in 1951; he remained its leader until 2008. Paisley first became politically active in the 1960s and was elected to the Northern Irish parliament (1970–72) and the House of Commons in London (1970–85; 1986–2010). A co-founder of the Ulster Democratic Unionist Party (1972), he was an outspoken defender of the Protestant Unionist position in Northern Ireland. Paisley was a Member of the European Parliament from 1979 to 2004. From 1998 he was a vocal opponent of most aspects of the Good Friday Agreement; however, he became a member of the Northern

Ireland Assembly it established. In 2007 he agreed to take his party into a power-sharing executive with Sinn Fein and became First Minister of Northern Ireland. He resigned in 2008.

Pakistan

Capital:	Islamabad
Area:	796,095 sq km (307,374 sq miles)
Population:	193,238,868 (2009 est)
Currency:	1 Pakistan rupee = 100 paisa
Religions:	Muslim 96.4%
Ethnic Groups:	Punjabi 44.7%; Pashto 15.4%; Sindhi 14.1%; Saraiki 8.4%; Muhajirs 7.6%
Languages:	Urdu, English (both official); Punjabi; Sindhi; Saraiki; Pashtu; minority languages
International Organizations:	UN; Commonwealth; Colombo Plan; Non-Aligned Movement; WTO

A country in the north-west of the Indian sub-continent, bounded by Iran on the west, Afghanistan on the north-west, China on the north-east, and India on the east.

Physical The Hindu Kush, Karakoram, and Himalaya mountain ranges ring the north of Pakistan. Other ranges sweep down its western side to the Arabian Sea. Below them is the long, broad valley of the Indus. The North-West Frontier Province, containing the strategically important Khyber Pass, is very high. To the south is the plateau of the Punjab, watered by the tributaries of the Indus. Wheat is grown here. To the east is the Thar Desert. Between the Sind Desert, which covers part of the Indus delta, and Baluchistan in the western hills, there are large reserves of natural gas and some oil, which is also present in the Punjab.

Economy Pakistan has a mainly agricultural economy, the most important crops being cotton, wheat, rice, and sugar cane. The output of the textile and clothing industries provides over half the country's export earnings. Other industry includes food processing, pharmaceuticals, and construction materials. Remittances from expatriates are important.

History Prior to 1947, Pakistan formed part of *India. Following the British withdrawal from the Indian sub-continent in 1947, Pakistan was created as a separate state, comprising the territory to the north-east and north-west of India in which the population was predominantly Muslim. The 'Partition' of the subcontinent of India led to unprecedented violence between Hindus and Muslims, costing the lives of more than a million people. Seven and a half million Muslim refugees fled to both parts of Pakistan from India, and ten million Hindus left Pakistan for India. Muhammad Ali *Jinnah, President of the *Muslim League, became the new state's first governor-general. The country's liberal constitution was opposed by the orthodox Muslim sector, and in 1951 the Prime Minister, Liaqat Ali Khan, was assassinated by an Afghan fanatic. In 1954 a state of emergency was declared and a new constitution adopted (1956). When attempts to adopt a multiparty system failed, Ayub Khan (1907–74) imposed martial law (1958). His decade of power produced economic growth, but also political resentment. The two wings of Pakistan were separated by a thousand miles of Indian territory. Allegations by the Bengalis in East Pakistan against West Pakistan's disproportionate share of the state's assets led to demands by the Awami League, led by *Mujibur Rahman, for regional autonomy. In the ensuing civil war (1971), the Bengali dissidents defeated a Pakistani army, with Indian help, and established the new state of *Bangladesh (1971). In 1970 the first ever general election brought to power Zulfikar Ali *Bhutto, leader of the Pakistan People's Party, who introduced constitutional, social, and economic reforms. In 1977 he was deposed, and later executed. The regime of General *Zia ul-Haq (1977–88) committed Pakistan to an Islamic code of laws. Although martial law was lifted in 1986, with the promise of a return to democracy, Zia's regime ended with his assassination. A general election in December 1988 brought back to power the Pakistan People's Party (PPP), led by Bhutto's daughter Benazir *Bhutto. For the next decade the PPP alternated in power with right-wing governments led by Mian Mohammad Nawaz Sharif. In 1998 Pakistan carried out a series of underground nuclear tests in response to similar tests by India. The military overthrew Sharif's government in 1999 and placed him under house arrest: General Pervez *Musharraf became Chief Executive, and then President in 2001. His rule was endorsed by a referendum in 2002. Musharraf suspended the constitution in 2007 but called for elections in 2008; Benazir Bhutto was assassinated while campaigning. After a delayed election, which his supporters lost, Musharraf was forced from office. In October 2008, he was replaced as president by Asif Ali Zardari, Benazir Bhutto's widower and leader of the Pakistan People's Party. Pakistan's cooperation with the USA's *war on terrorism after 2001 was controversial and, together with the influx of *Taliban and *al-Qaeda refugees from Afghanistan, led to a rise in Islamist activity in the country.

Pala A dynasty of Bihar and Bengal in north-eastern India that ruled from the 8th to the 12th century. Gopala, the founder, was chosen king by the great men of the region. The reign of his successor, Dharmapala (c. 770–810) marked the dynasty's apogee, after which power rose and fell intermittently until its final eclipse in the 12th century. The surviving Pala artefacts in both stone and metal are of a particularly fine decorative quality. An important development during their rule was the spread of *Buddhism to Tibet by missionaries from the University of Nalanda in Bihar, which received Pala patronage.

Palacký, František (1798–1876) Czech nationalist and historian. A leading figure in the Czech cultural and national revival, he presided over the *Pan-Slav Congress in Prague in 1848, advocating Czech autonomy within a federal Austria. After the suppression of the liberal and nationalist uprising of 1848, Palacký retired from active politics until 1861, when he became a deputy to the Austrian Reichstag. After the foundation of *Austria-Hungary in 1867, he advocated complete Czech independence. His influence on Czech political thought, and on later leaders such as Tomáš *Masaryk, was immense.

Palaeolithic (US **Paleolithic**) The earlier part of the *Stone Age, when primitive stone implements were used; a period, which extends from the first appearance of artefacts, some 2.5 million years ago, to the end of the last ice age c.10,000 BC. It has been divided into the **Lower Palaeolithic**, with the earliest forms of mankind and the presence of hand-axe industries, ending c.80,000 BC, the **Middle Palaeolithic** (or **Mousterian**), the era of Neanderthal man, ending c.33,000 BC, and the **Upper Palaeolithic**, which saw the development of *Homo sapiens* from c.50,000 years ago. Palaeolithic cultures include **Acheulian**, a culture characterized by handaxes, named after St Acheul near Amiens, France, but widely distributed across Africa, Europe, the Middle East, and parts of Asia. The handaxes were general-purpose stone tools produced from a cobble or large flake by trimming it to an oval or pear-shaped form. They lacked a handle but were nonetheless efficient slicing tools. They first appeared in Africa around 1.5 million years ago and continued to be made with little modification to the basic shape until 150,000 years ago. Sites with Acheulian tools have provided the earliest certain evidence of the control and use of fire by humans. The Lower Palaeolithic industries represented by the flint implements found at Clacton in Essex, south-east England, dated *c*.250,000–200,000 BC are known as **Clactonian**. The Palaeolithic industry of North Africa and southern Europe (*c*.8000–4500 BC) is noted for its microliths and called Capsian culture, taking its name from the town of Gafsa in Tunisia.

Mousterian culture is associated with Neanderthals in Europe. Tools of this type were named after the Neanderthal cave site of Le Moustier in the Dordogne, France, but have since been found throughout Europe. They date from *c*.130,000 years ago to *c*.30,000 years ago, disappearing with the emergence of anatomically modern humans and the start of the Upper Palaeolithic. They are also found in North Africa and the Near East. Characteristically, Mousterian tools were made from flint. Compared with the earlier Acheulian tools, there was a much greater emphasis on flakes, which allowed a larger range of tools to be produced. Small, neat handaxes and stone and bone projectile points were among other typical Mousterian tools. The **Upper Palaeolithic** occupies the second half of the last glaciation, ending 10,000 years ago. During the Upper Palaeolithic the early human population increased and formed larger communities, displaying a faster rate of cultural change than in the Middle Palaeolithic. Distinctive regional groups appeared for the first time. The most developed cultures were on the steppe and tundra belts south of the ice sheets, where there were plentiful herds of horses, reindeer, and mammoths. Several cultures, distinguished by their styles of toolmaking, can be distinguished in Europe: the earliest is **Aurignacian**, characterized by the first blade tools and a plentiful use of bone for missile heads. This was followed by the **Gravettian**, stretching from France to the Ukraine, featuring small pointed stone blades with one blunt edge, small female figurines are also associated with Gravettian culture. More localized traditions, such as the **Solutrian** and **Magdalenian**, were responsible for the cave art of south-western France and northern Spain. These cultures disappeared with the onset of warmer conditions at the end of the last Ice Age and the spread of forests, which displaced the large herds of game

animals. Magdalenian culture was named after the type-site at La Madeleine in the Dordogne region of France and dated to *c*.15,000–11,000 BC. It is characterized by a range of bone and horn tools, including elaborate bone harpoons; cave art reached a zenith during this period. The cave at **Lascaux** contains Palaeolithic drawings and paintings and is generally held to be the finest example of prehistoric art. It was discovered in 1940 in the Dordogne region of south-west-central France. Now closed for reasons of preservation, its artwork is reproduced in caves nearby (Lascaux II).

Palatinates Two regions in Germany that comprise the Upper Palatinate. *Frederick I bestowed the title of Count Palatine on his half-brother Conrad, who held lands east and west of the River Rhine (the Lower Palatinate). From 1214 these lands were ruled by the Bavarian Wittelsbach dynasty, whose own lands near Bohemia formed the Upper Palatinate. In 1356 the Counts Palatine were made Electors of the Holy Roman Empire.

The Rhenish (Lower) Palatinate became a centre of the Protestant *Reformation in the 16th century, but the choice of Elector *Frederick V as King of Bohemia led to clashes with Catholic Habsburg authority and the outbreak of the *Thirty Years War. After the Battle of the White Mountain (1621) the Palatinates were partitioned, with Bavaria annexing the Upper Palatinate and the Lower Palatinate passing to Frederick's heirs under the terms of the Treaty of *Westphalia. The Lower Palatinate was invaded and brutally devastated by *Louis XIV in 1688–89. In 1777 the two Palatinates were reunited. However, in the early 19th century, the Upper Palatinate was again absorbed into Bavaria, while the Lower Palatinate was divided between various German states and France. The modern German *Land* of Rhineland Palatinate (Rheinland-Pfalz) occupies a portion of the original Lower Palatinate's territory.

Palau (or **Belau**)

Capital:	Melekeok
Area:	459 sq km (177 sq miles)
Population:	21,108 (2013 est)
Currency:	1 US dollar = 100 cents
Religions:	Roman Catholic 49.4%; Protestant 30.9%; traditional beliefs 8.7%
Ethnic Groups:	Palauan 72.5%; Filipino 16.3%; Chinese 1.6%; Vietnamese 1.6%

| Languages: | Palauan, English (both official); Filipino |
| International Organizations: | UN; Pacific Islands Forum; Secretariat of the Pacific Community |

A republic comprising over 200 islands in the western Pacific, only eight of which are inhabited.

Physical The islands are geographically part of the Caroline Islands. The largest island is Babelthaup. Some of the islands are low-lying coral atolls but others are mountainous. The climate is tropical.

Economy The main economic activities are fishing, farming, and tourism. Palau depends on aid from the USA.

History Spain acquired the Caroline Islands in 1886 but sold them to Germany in 1899, having been defeated in the *Spanish–American War. Palau was occupied by Japan during World War I and remained under Japanese control until 1944, when it was captured by Allied forces. The islands were administered by the USA as part of the UN Trust Territory of the Pacific from 1947. The islanders voted against becoming part of the Federated States of *Micronesia in 1978 and became autonomous in 1981. Palau gained full independence and joined the United Nations in 1994. Under a compact of free association the USA controls the defence of Palau, and has nuclear storage facilities on the islands.

pale A distinct area of jurisdiction, often originally enclosed by a palisade or ditch. Pales existed in medieval times on the edges of English territory—around Calais (until its loss in 1558), in Scotland (in Tudor times), and, most importantly, as a large part of eastern Ireland (from *Henry II's time until the full conquest of Ireland under *Elizabeth I); the actual extent of the Irish pale depended on the strength of the English government in Dublin. *Catherine II (the Great) in 1792 made a Jewish pale in the lands she had annexed from Poland: Jews had to remain within this area, which ultimately included all of Russian Poland, Lithuania, Belorussia (now Belarus), and much of the Ukraine.

Palestine A historic area in the Middle East on the eastern coast of the Mediterranean Sea, also called the 'Holy Land' because of its links with Judaism, Christianity, and Islam. It has seen many changes of frontier and status in the course of history, and contains several places sacred to Christians, Jews, and Muslims. In biblical times Palestine comprised the kingdoms of Israel and Judaea. The land was controlled at various times by the Egyptian, Assyrian, Persian, and Roman empires before being conquered by the Muslims in 634 AD. It remained in Muslim hands, except for a brief period during the Crusades (1098–1197), until World War I, being part of the Ottoman Empire from 1516 to 1917, when Turkish and German forces were defeated by the British at Megiddo. The name 'Palestine' was used as the official political title for the land west of the Jordan mandated to Britain in 1920. Jewish immigration was encouraged by the Balfour Declaration of 1917, and increased greatly in 1948 when the State of *Israel was established. The name Palestine continues to be used, particularly in the context of the struggle for territory and political rights of Palestinian Arabs displaced when Israel was established. A Palestinian National Authority was established in the West Bank and Gaza Strip in 1993–95; Gaza has been under the control of the militant organization *Hamas since 2007.

Palestine Liberation Organization

(PLO) A political and military body formed in 1964 to unite various Palestinian Arab groups in opposition to the Israeli presence in the former territory of *Palestine. From 1967 the organization was dominated by al-*Fatah, led by Yasser *Arafat. The activities of its radical factions caused trouble with the host country, Jordan, and, following a brief civil war in 1970, it moved to Lebanon and Syria. In 1974 the organization was recognized by the Arab nations as the representative of all Palestinians. The Israeli invasion of Lebanon (1982) undermined its military power and organization, and it regrouped in Tunisia. Splinter groups of extremists, such as the 'Popular Front for the Liberation of Palestine' and the 'Black September' terrorists, have been responsible for kidnappings, hijackings, and killings both in and beyond the Middle East. In 1988 Arafat persuaded the movement to renounce violence, and its governing council recognized the State of Israel. Thereafter the PLO was accepted by an increasing number of states as being a government-in-exile. In 1993 Arafat became chair of the Palestinian National Authority, which administered the West Bank and the Gaza Strip from 1995. The PLO continued to be responsible for negotiations with

Israel, but these broke down in 2000. In 2004 Mahmoud Abbas became leader of the PLO following Arafat's death.

Pallava A south Indian dynasty that maintained a regional kingdom along the Carnatic coast between the 4th and 9th centuries. There is uncertainty about the origins and early history of the Pallava before their emergence to power from a previously subordinate role in the Deccan. They established their capital at Kanchi and traded in Sri Lanka and parts of south-east Asia. In the late 9th century they lost their territories to their own feudal vassals, the *Cholas. Their artistic legacy is important. Apart from patronage of music, painting, and literature, some of the greatest south Indian temples were built during their rule, including the 'Shore Temple', carved from solid rock on the coast at Mahabalipuram.

Palmerston, Henry John Temple, 3rd Viscount (1784–1865) British Whig statesman, Prime Minister (1855–58; 1859–65). He left the Tory Party in 1830 to serve with the Whigs as Foreign Secretary (1830–34; 1835–41; 1846–51). In his foreign policy Palmerston was singleminded in his promotion of British interests, declaring the second Opium War against China in 1856, and overseeing the successful conclusion of the Crimean War in 1856 and the suppression of the Indian Mutiny in 1858. He maintained British neutrality during the American Civil War.

Pan-Africanism A movement seeking unity within Africa. It became a positive force with the London Pan-African Conference of 1900. An international convention in the USA in 1920 was largely inspired by the Jamaican Marcus *Garvey. The invasion of Ethiopia by Italy in 1935 produced a strong reaction within Africa, stimulating anti-colonial nationalism. The Pan-African Congress in Manchester in 1945 was dominated by Jomo *Kenyatta and Kwame *Nkrumah, and by the 'father of Pan-Africanism', the American W. E. B. *Du Bois. In 1958 a conference of independent African states was held in Accra, followed by two further conferences in Monrovia in 1959 and 1961. In 1963 in Addis Ababa 32 independent African nations founded the Organization of African Unity (now the *African Union), by which time Pan-Africanism had moved from being an ideal into practical politics.

Pan-Africanist Congress South African political movement. A militant off-shoot of the *African National Congress (ANC), it was

formed in 1959 by Robert Sobukwe. He advocated forceful methods of political pressure and in 1960 sponsored the demonstration at *Sharpeville, in which 67 Black Africans were killed and 180 wounded by police. The South African government outlawed both the PAC and the ANC and imprisoned Sobukwe and other leaders. Some PAC members went into exile, continuing their campaign under the Secretary of the Party, Potlako Leballo. Although legalized in 1990 when it was moving away from its commitment to an armed struggle, the PAC at first refused to take part in the Convention for a Democratic South Africa (CODESA) which was set up in December 1991. The PAC participated in the first South African multiracial elections in 1994, winning five seats in the National Assembly, with 1.2% of the vote. Its support has since declined.

Panama

Capital:	Panama City
Area:	75,420 sq km (29,120 sq miles)
Population:	3,559,408 (2013 est)
Currency:	1 balboa = 100 centesimos (US$ also in circulation)
Religions:	Roman Catholic 85.0%; Protestant 15.0%
Ethnic Groups:	Mestizo 70.0%; Amerindian and mixed 14.0%; White 10.0%; Amerindian 6.0%
Languages:	Spanish (official); English
International Organizations:	UN; OAS; Non-Aligned Movement; WTO

A tropical country occupying the narrow isthmus linking Central and South America, bounded by Costa Rica to the west and Colombia to the east.

Physical Along the length of the country runs a range of hills, through the centre of which was cut the pass, for the *Panama Canal. The Canal gives access to shipping from the Caribbean in the north to the Pacific in the south. The land is fertile, supporting coffee on the higher ground and sugar cane on the coastal plains.

Economy The economy is dominated by international financial services, maritime services associated with the Panama Canal, ship registration, and tourism. In 2007 a project to widen the Canal began, which will allow it to accommodate larger ships and so more than double its capacity. The principal exports include gold, bananas and other fruit, shrimp from the coastal waters, sugar, and iron and steel waste.

History Panama was visited in 1501 by the Spaniard Rodrigo de Bastidas. It was explored more thoroughly in 1513 by Vasco Núñez de *Balboa, the first Spaniard to see the Pacific Ocean. Portobello on the Caribbean coast served as the principal port for the trade of the viceroyalty of Peru. In the 18th century, Panama became part of the viceroyalty of *New Granada. In 1821 the country gained independence from Spain as a province of Gran Colombia. Despite nationalist insurrections against Colombia in the 19th century, the area only became independent as the republic of Panama in 1903 as a protectorate of the USA. The latter had aided Panama's struggle in return for a Panamanian concession to build a canal across the isthmus and a lease of the zone around it to the USA. The volatile, élite-dominated politics which have characterized Panama during much of the 20th century have led to its occupation by US peacekeeping forces in 1908, 1912, 1918, and 1989. From 1968 to 1981, General Omar Torrijos controlled Panama, working to diversify the economy and reduce US sovereignty over the Canal Zone, an object of long-standing national resentment. In 1977 he signed the Panama Canal Treaties, but was killed in 1981. In 1988 General Manuel Noriega seized power. A US military invasion in December 1989 deposed him and installed Guillermo Endara as President, placing Noriega on trial in the USA for drug trafficking; he was convicted in 1992. Widespread strikes took place against Endara's government, which itself was accused of involvement with drug rings. In 1991 a new constitution abolished the armed forces. A general election in 1994 led to Ernesto Pérez Balladares becoming President and in 1999 Mireya Moscoso became Panama's first female President. At the end of that year Panama assumed control of the Panama Canal. Martín Torrijos was elected President in 2004; he was succeeded by Ricardo Martinelli in 2009.

Panama Canal A canal about 80 km (50 miles) long and 150 m (490 feet) wide, across the isthmus of Panama, connecting the Atlantic and Pacific Oceans. Its construction, begun by Ferdinand de Lesseps in 1881 but abandoned through bankruptcy in 1889, was completed by the USA between 1904 and 1914. The sur-

rounding territory, the Panama Canal Zone or Canal Zone, was administered by the USA until 1979, when it was returned to the control of Panama. Control of the canal itself remained with the USA until December 1999, when it passed to Panama.

Pan-Americanism The movement towards economic, military, political, and social cooperation among the 21 republics of South, Central, and North America. The first Pan-American conference was held in 1889 in Washington, DC, to encourage inter-American trade as well as the peaceful resolution of conflicts in the region. The seventh conference (Montevideo 1933) was important because the USA, in harmony with Franklin D. *Roosevelt's 'Good Neighbor' policy, finally adopted the long-espoused Latin American principle of non-intervention, while the conference at Buenos Aires in 1936 adopted a treaty for the peaceful resolution of conflicts between American states. The Conference at Chapultepec (1945) agreed on a united defence policy for the signatory nations. At the conference held in Bogotá in 1948, the *Organization of American States (OAS) was established, transforming the Pan-American system into a formal regional organization within the framework of the United Nations.

Pandya A Tamil dynasty which ruled in the extreme south of India from the 3rd century BC to the 16th century AD. Little is known about their early history during an era of frequent warfare among competing south Indian dynasties. Between the 7th and 14th centuries they expanded into Sri Lanka and Kerala, and northwards into *Chola and *Hoysala territories. They were at the height of their power during the reign of Jatavarman Sundara (1251–68). They were already weakened by family quarrels when their capital at Madurai was invaded in 1311 by the sultan of Delhi, Ala ud-Din *Khalji. Although they retained local power until the 16th century, they never again aspired to empire. *Marco Polo recorded the prosperity of their realm during its peak years in the late 13th century.

Panipat A town in Haryana state, north India, 70 km (43 miles) north-west of Delhi. It is historically important as the site of three battles which proved decisive for India's future. On each occasion armies moving out to defend the capital of Delhi clashed here with invaders approaching from the north-west. In the first Battle of Panipat (21 April 1526) the *Mogul invader, *Babur, defeated the Afghan sultan of Delhi. The second battle (5 November 1556) marked *Akbar's victory over the Sur Afghans who then held Delhi, and initiated the spread of strong Mogul power in India. In the third battle (14 June 1761) an invading Afghan army ended *Maratha ambitions to fill the power vacuum at Delhi caused by the decline of the Moguls.

Pankhurst, Mrs Emmeline (1858–1928) British suffragette. In 1903 Emmeline and her daughters Christabel (1880–1958) and (Estelle) Sylvia (1882–1960) founded the Women's Social and Political Union, with the motto 'Votes for Women'. Following the imprisonment of Christabel in 1905, Emmeline initiated the militant suffragette campaign and was responsible for keeping the suffragette cause in the public eye until the outbreak of World War I.

Pan-Slavism The movement intended to bring about the political unity of all Slavs. It should be distinguished from both Slavophilism, which was purely cultural and acted as a powerful stimulus towards the revival of Slavonic languages and literature, and from Austro-Slavism, which sought to improve the lot of Slavs within *Austria-Hungary. The aim of Pan-Slavism was to destroy the Austrian and *Ottoman empires in order to establish a federation of Slav peoples under the aegis of the Russian emperor. The ideology was developed in Russia, where it took on a militant and nationalistic form and helped provoke the *Russo-Turkish War (1877–78). Another manifestation was the Balkan League of 1912 by which Russia supported nationalist aspirations of the *Balkans against Austrian ambitions. This led to the crisis that precipitated *World War I. The Bolshevik government of the newly established Soviet Socialist Republic (1917) renounced Pan-Slavism, but during the *Cold War period the concept was revived as a justification for dominance by the Soviet Union in Eastern Europe.

Panth, Brahmin Dhundu See NANA SAHIB.

papacy The office of the pope (Bishop of Rome), derives its name from the Greek *papas* and Latin *papa*, which are familiar forms of 'father'. In early times many bishops and even priests were called popes, but in the Western Church the word gradually became a title restricted to the Bishop of Rome; Pope Gregory VII in 1073 forbade its use for anyone except the Bishop of Rome. The traditional enumeration lists 267 holders of the office, excluding *antipopes, beginning with St *Peter and reaching to the present holder, *Francis. The basis of papal authority derives from St Peter's position of leadership among the 12 Apostles, given him by

Jesus Christ, the early tradition that he came to Rome and was martyred there. The papal claim to extend its jurisdiction over all Christian Churches was a major cause of various Churches breaking with Rome, notably the *Orthodox Church definitively in 1054, and the Protestant Churches at the time of the *Reformation in the 16th century.

Papal States A part of central Italy held between 756 and 1870 by the Catholic Church, corresponding to the modern regions of Emilia-Romagna, Marche, Umbria, and Latium. Taken from the Lombards by the Frankish king Pepin III, the states were given to the papacy as a strategy to undermine Lombard expansionism. Greatly extended by Pope Innocent III in the early 13th century and by Pope Julius II in the 16th century, they were incorporated into the newly unified Italy in 1860 and 1870. Their annexation to Italy deprived the papacy of its temporal powers until the Lateran Treaty of 1929 recognized the sovereignty of the Vatican City.

Papen, Franz von (1879–1969) German politician. A member of the Catholic Centre Party, he had little popular following, and his appointment as Chancellor (1932) came as a surprise. To gain *Nazi support he lifted the ban on the *Brownshirts, but *Hitler remained an opponent. Attempts to undermine Nazi strength failed and he resigned. He persuaded *Hindenburg to appoint Hitler (January 1933) as his Chancellor, but as Vice-Chancellor he could not restrain him. He became ambassador to Austria (1934), working for its annexation (*Anschluss) in 1938, and to Turkey (1939–44). He was tried as a war criminal (1945) but released.

Papineau's Rebellion (1837–38) A French-Canadian uprising of those seeking democratic reforms and protesting against the proposed union of *Upper and Lower Canada. The Speaker of the Lower Canada Assembly, Louis-Joseph Papineau (1786–1871), led the reformist movement in French Canada (now Quebec) and in 1837 he agitated for armed insurrection against the British, but fled to the USA before fighting broke out. Clashes between a few hundred of his supporters and regular troops occurred at Saint Denis in November. The rebellion broke out again in 1838, but was suppressed, and 12 supporters were executed. Papineau received an amnesty in 1844 and returned to Canada in 1845, by which time the establishment of parliamentary "responsible" government had been achieved by such moderate reformers as Robert *Baldwin.

Papua New Guinea

Capital:	Port Moresby
Area:	462,840 sq km (178,704 sq miles)
Population:	6,431,902 (2013 est)
Currency:	1 kina = 100 toea
Religions:	Protestant 69.4%; Roman Catholic 27.0%; Baha'i 0.3%; traditional beliefs and other 3.3%
Ethnic Groups:	Melanesian, Papuan, Negrito, Micronesian, Polynesian
Languages:	English, Tok Pisin, Hiri Motu (all official); about 836 indigenous languages
International Organizations:	UN; Commonwealth; Colombo Plan; Pacific Islands Forum; Secretariat of the Pacific Community; WTO

A country consisting of the eastern half of the island of New Guinea north of Australia, together with the Bismarck Archipelago and other adjacent islands in the south-west Pacific Ocean. The western half of the island of New Guinea forms the province of Irian Jaya, part of *Indonesia.

Physical The mainland is divided by a central range of mountains rising to 4509 m (14,762 feet) at Mount Wilhelm. A low-lying plain is drained by the Fly River in the south-west, and there are active volcanoes in the east. The climate is tropical and monsoonal.

Economy Papua New Guinea exploits extensive copper, gold, and oil deposits, and together these account for almost two-thirds of the country's export earnings. About five-sixths of the workforce are engaged in agriculture; much of it is subsistence, but palm oil, coffee, and cocoa are exported. The predominant industries are food processing and mining.

History Contact with Europe goes back to the 16th century, when the Portuguese Jorge de Meneses named the island Ilhas dos Papuas (Malay, 'frizzy-haired') and the Spaniard Ortiz Retes christened it New Guinea because he was reminded of the Guinea coast of Africa. In 1828 the Dutch annexed the western half of the island, followed, in 1884, by the German and British division of the eastern half. In 1904 the British transferred their territory, now called Papua, to Australia, and at the outbreak of World War I an Australian expeditionary force seized German New Guinea (Kaiser-Wilhelmsland). During World War II Australian troops fought off a determined Japanese invasion. Formal administrative union of the area as Papua New Guinea was achieved in 1968. Self-government was attained in 1973 and in 1975 Papua New Guinea became an independent nation within the Commonwealth. Secessionist demands from some of the offshore islands, especially Bougainville, became a key issue facing the coalition government of Rabbie Namaliu (1990–92), troops being landed on Bougainville in May 1992. Namaliu's government was defeated in the 1992 general election and Paias Wingti was elected Prime Minister of another coalition government. During the early 1990s relations between Papua New Guinea and Indonesia, which had been strained throughout the 1980s over the conflict in Irian Jaya, improved. In 1994 Wingti was forced from office and replaced by Julius Chan. In 1997 the use of foreign mercenaries to suppress the rebellion on Bougainville led to a mutiny by the army and the resignation of Chan; Bill Skate replaced him as Prime Minister. In 1998 a permanent ceasefire was signed with the Bougainville Revolutionary Army. In 1999 Mekere Morauta became Prime Minister. However, his coalition government's proposed economic reforms led to widespread protest and its defeat in the 2002 election, after which Michael Somare became Prime Minister. He was re-elected in 2007 but in 2011 was removed from office because of ill health; his successor, Peter O'Neill, was confirmed in office by the 2012 elections. In 2013 Papua New Guinea agreed to host an Australian-funded detention centre for asylum seekers trying to enter Australia; those whose claims were accepted would be settled in Papua Guinea, not Australia.

Paraguay

Capital:	Asunción
Area:	406,752 sq km (157,048 sq miles)
Population:	6,623,252 (2013 est)
Currency:	1 guaraní = 100 céntimos
Religions:	Roman Catholic 89.6%; Protestant 6.2%
Ethnic Groups:	Mestizo 95.0%
Languages:	Spanish, Guaraní (both official)
International Organizations:	UN; OAS; Mercosur; WTO

A landlocked country in south-central South America, bordered by Bolivia and Brazil on the north and Argentina on the south.

Physical The navigable Paraguay River, running down the middle of the country, joins the Paraná and provides access to the sea. In the west the Gran Chaco provides rich pasture and hardwood forests. In the east, the land rises to a low range of forested hills, to the south of which there are swamps and palm-fringed, shallow lakes.

Economy Paraguay has a primarily agricultural economy, much of it subsistence, with cotton, soya beans, feed, meat, and edible oils being the principal exports. Cereals and cassava are also grown. Industries include textiles, food processing, cement, and electricity generation—the Itaipú dam, shared with Brazil, has the world's second-greatest hydroelectric capacity, and electricity is an important export.

History Paraguay was part of Spain's Rio de la Plata territory from the founding of the capital Asunción in 1537. It was only sparsely settled by Spaniards and was dominated by Jesuit mission villages among the Guaraní Indians until their suppression in 1767. The country achieved its independence (1811) when local Paraguayan military leaders led a bloodless revolt against the Spanish governor. The dictator José Gaspar Rodriguez de Francia ruled the new republic from 1813 to 1840, but the rest of the 19th century was dominated by corruption, coups, and chronic bankruptcy. Francisco Solano López led the country to disaster in the Paraguayan War (1864–70). Political turmoil continued into the 20th century with the exception of the presidency of the liberal Edvard Schaerer (1912–17), which was marked by foreign investment and economic improvements. In the *Chaco War (1932–35), Paraguay won from Bolivia the long-contested territory believed to have oil reserves. In 1954 General Alfredo Stroessner, supported by the USA, seized power. A massive hydroelectric scheme (the Itaipú dam) was begun and some progress made in settling landless peasants; but cattle exports to Europe fell, the economy declined, and the regime became increasingly brutal. Stroessner lost US support and was deposed in 1989. Elections brought General Andrés Rodríguez to office as President. Paraguay's first multiparty elections were held in 1993, with the civilian Juan Carlos Wasmosy being elected President. In 1998 Raul

Cubas Gran was elected President; however, following the pardon and release of his ally General Lino Oviedo—imprisoned for leading an attempted coup in 1996—parliament began impeachment proceedings the following year. Cubas's supporters assassinated his main rival, Vice President Luis Maria Argana in March 1999. Street violence began and Cubas fled the country to avoid arrest. González Macchi assumed the presidency for the rest of his term and was succeeded by Nícanor Duarte after elections in 2003. The victory of the centre-left Fernando Lugo in the 2008 presidential elections ended 62 years of Colorado Party rule. His policy of land redistribution proved controversial, and he was impeached and removed from office in 2012. In 2013 the Colorado Party regained the presidency with Horacio Cartes.

Paraguayan War (or **War of the Triple Alliance**) (1864–70) A conflict resulting from rivalries between Paraguay, Uruguay, Brazil, and Argentina. The Paraguayan President Francisco Solano *López, alarmed by Brazilian intervention in Uruguay and harbouring desires for Paraguayan territorial expansion and access to the sea, initiated hostilities against Brazil in 1864. Despite traditional rivalry between Brazil and Argentina, the latter joined Brazil and its puppet government in Uruguay in the Triple Alliance pact (May 1865) against Paraguay. Paraguay's well-trained army of 600,000 men did not prove equal to the task, and López's death in March 1870 ended one of the most destructive wars in Latin American history. In addition to losing more than half of its population, Paraguay was also stripped of considerable territory as a result of the war.

pardoners Agents of the Christian Church licensed to sell *indulgences. The rapid proliferation of pardoners in the 14th century meant that often they were not licensed. They might carry "holy" relics to assist sales and they exploited the gullibility of people for their own profit. Pope Boniface IX ordered an enquiry into these abuses (1390) and the abuse of indulgences was one of Martin *Luther's main quarrels with the Roman Catholic Church. The sale of indulgences was forbidden by the Council of Trent (1563).

Paris, Commune of (15 March–26 May 1871) A revolutionary government in Paris. It consisted of 92 members, who defied the provisional government of *Thiers and of the National Assembly. The Commune, which had no connection with communism, was an alliance between middle and working classes. Suspicious of royalist strength and opposing the armistice made with Prussia, the Communards wanted to continue the war and were determined that France should regain the principles of the First Republic. With the victorious German army encamped on the hills outside Paris, government troops were sent to remove all cannons from the city. They were bitterly resisted; Paris, demanding independence, broke into revolt. Thiers decided to suppress the revolt ruthlessly. For six weeks Paris was bombarded by government troops and its centre destroyed. Early in May its defences were breached and a week of bitter street fighting followed. Before surrendering, the Communards murdered their hostages, including the Archbishop of Paris. Over 20,000 people were massacred by the government forces, leaving France deeply divided.

Paris, Congress of (1856) A conference held to negotiate the peace after the *Crimean War, attended by Britain, Austria, Russia, Turkey, and Sardinia. It marked a defeat for Russia, which conceded part of Bessarabia to Moldavia and Wallachia in the Balkans. The revival of the Straits Convention of 1841 meant that the Black Sea was again closed to all warships and neutralized while navigation of the Danube was to be free. The *Ottoman empire was placed under joint guarantee of the West European powers and the sultan agreed to recognize the rights of his Christians. The decline of the Ottoman empire, however, was not halted and Russia, determined to retrieve its Balkan supremacy, was to break the Black Sea clause in 1870.

Paris, Pact of See KELLOGG-BRIAND PACT.

Paris, Peace of (1783) The treaty that concluded the American War of *Independence. It was mainly engineered by John Jay, Benjamin *Franklin, and the Earl of Shelburne, and was damaging to Spain, which regained only Florida. The peace recognized American independence, gave it north-eastern fishing rights, and attempted (unsuccessfully) to safeguard creditors, protect loyalists, and settle the frontier between Canada and the USA. These failures led to 30 years' friction, especially in the *Northwest territory, where Britain retained forts in retaliation, and led to the War of 1812.

Paris, Treaty of (1763) The treaty signed by Britain, France, and Spain which brought the *Seven Years War to an end. Britain did not fully exploit the worldwide successes it had enjoyed, as *Pitt had resigned and the Earl of Bute was

anxious for peace. Under the terms of the treaty Britain gained French Canada and all the territory France had claimed to the east of the Mississippi. France ceded some West Indian islands, including St Vincent and Tobago, but retained the islands of Guadeloupe and Martinique. In India, France retained its trading-stations but not its forts. Britain gained Senegal in West Africa and Florida from Spain; it also recovered Minorca in exchange for Belle Isle. Spain recovered Havana and Manila, and France's claims in Louisiana west of the Mississippi were ceded to Spain in compensation for Florida, which became British until 1783. Britain was supreme at sea and, for the time being, dominated the east coast of North America.

Paris Peace Settlement See VERSAILLES PEACE SETTLEMENT.

parish The smallest unit of ecclesiastical and administrative organization in England. In the 7th and 8th centuries regional churches ('minsters') were founded, staffed by teams of priests who served large 'parochiae' covering the area of perhaps five to 15 later parishes. These were broken up during the 10th to 12th centuries as landowners founded local churches for themselves and their tenants, though it was only in the 12th century that the territories which these served crystallized into a formal parochial system.

Park, Mungo (1771–1806) Scottish explorer. He undertook a series of explorations in West Africa (1795–97), among them being the navigation of the Niger. His experiences were recorded in his *Travels in the Interior of Africa* (1799). He drowned on a second expedition to the Niger (1805–06).

Parlement A sovereign judicial authority in France, the chief being in the capital, *Paris. First established in the 12th century, this functioned as a court of appeal, and as a source of final legal rulings. There were also provincial *Parlements*, those of Toulouse, Bordeaux, Rouen, Aix, Grenoble, Dijon, and Rennes. Political importance derived from their power to register royal edicts, and to remonstrate against them. This power could be overridden by the king, either by order or by *lit de Justice* (a personal intervention).

Parliament, British The supreme legislature in Great Britain and Northern Ireland, comprising the sovereign, as head of state, and the two chambers, the *House of Commons and the *House of Lords. Together, these chambers make up the Houses of Parliament, which occupy the Palace of Westminster.

Beginning in the 13th century as simply a formal meeting of the king and certain of his officials and principal lords, Parliament became partly representative, as in Simon de *Montfort's Parliament (1265), which contained commoners (knights of the shire and burgesses of the boroughs) who were elected in their locality, and in Edward I's *Model Parliament (1295).

Until the 16th century, both chambers grew in importance *vis-à-vis* the crown, as it came to be accepted that their approval was needed for grants of taxation; *Henry VIII effected the English *Reformation through the long-lived Reformation Parliament (1529–36). Kings such as Charles I tried to manage without summoning a parliament (1629–40), but by the 17th century the Commons had made themselves indispensable. Charles I had to call Parliament in 1640 in order to raise money, and Parliament, led by John Pym, led the opposition to him. The Parliamentary side won the *English Civil War, and at the end of the *Commonwealth period it was the members of the House of Commons who negotiated the *Restoration of Charles II (1660) and the accession of *William III and Mary (1688). The legislation enacted in the *Glorious Revolution of 1688–89 and the Act of *Settlement (1701) settled the relationship of crown, Lords, and Commons definitively and made clear the ultimate supremacy of the Commons.

Present-day workings of Parliament may be summarized as follows. The Prime Minister and the cabinet (a selected group of ministers from either House) are responsible for formulating the policy of the government. Acts of Parliament in draft form, known as Bills, each of which have to be 'read' (debated) three times in each House, are referred in the House of Commons (and occasionally in the House of Lords) for detailed consideration to parliamentary standing or select committees. The sovereign's powers of government are dependent on the advice of ministers, who in turn are responsible to Parliament. The monarch's prerogatives, exercised through the cabinet or the Privy Council, include the summoning and dissolution of Parliament.

In the 20th century the previous omnicompetence of Parliament was reduced. In Northern Ireland the subordinate *Stormont Parliament was established in 1921 to legislate on internal matters; it was suspended in 1972, with a new Northern Ireland Assembly being established in

1999. In Scotland and Wales devolved assemblies were likewise established in 1999. None of these assemblies challenged the ultimate sovereignty of Parliament; but the Treaty of Rome, which the UK accepted in 1972 prior to joining the *European Community (now the European Union), provided for a gradual development of Community institutions that took precedence over national sovereignty. Similarly, the European Convention on Human Rights, which came into force in 1953, made the rulings of its court regarding violations of the convention binding on member states. The view that these bodies posed an unacceptable challenge to UK parliamentary sovereignty became a matter of increased controversy in the early 21st century.

The British parliamentary system was adopted by many European countries and by most member countries of the *Commonwealth of Nations when they gained dominion status or independence.

Parnell, Charles Stewart (1846–91) Irish nationalist leader. Elected to Parliament in 1875, Parnell became leader of the Irish Home Rule faction in 1880, and, through his obstructive parliamentary tactics, successfully raised the profile of Irish affairs. In 1886 he supported Gladstone's Home Rule bill, following the latter's conversion to the cause. He was forced to retire from public life in 1890 after the public exposure of his adultery with Mrs Katherine ('Kitty') O'Shea (1840–1905).

Parr, Catherine (1512–48) Sixth and last wife of Henry VIII. Having married the king in 1543, she influenced his decision to restore the succession to his daughters Mary and Elizabeth (later Mary I and Elizabeth I). Soon after Henry's death in 1547 she married Thomas, Baron Seymour of Sudeley, but died after bearing his daughter.

Parthia An ancient Asian kingdom to the south-east of the Caspian Sea, which from c.250 BC to c.230 AD ruled an empire stretching from the Euphrates to the Indus, with Ecbatana as its capital. The Parthian culture contained a mixture of Greek and Iranian elements and the Parthians were superb horsemen, original and competent in warfare.

Parti Québécois A Canadian political party that advocates the independence of Quebec. Founded in 1968 by René Lévesque from a union of separatist movements, it has been elected the governing party of Quebec on several occasions (1976–85; 1994–2003; 2012–).

However, the people of Quebec have rejected independence in two referendums (1980, 1995).

Pašić, Nikola (1845–1926) Serbian statesman and a founder of *Yugoslavia. Suspicious of Croats on both political and religious grounds, his ideal was a "Greater Serbia", including much of Croatia and Dalmatia, with Serbs the master race. However, he signed the Corfu Pact (1917) which resulted in a union of Serbs, Croats, and Slovenes into a new kingdom which he represented at the *Versailles Peace Settlement (1919). He was twice Premier of the new kingdom (1921–24; 1924–26), which adopted the name Yugoslavia in 1929.

Passchendaele, Battle of (or **The Third Battle of Ypres**) (31 July–10 November 1917) A battle fought on the *Western Front in World War I. The name of this Belgian village has become notorious for the worst horrors of *trench warfare and failure to achieve any strategic gain for over 300,000 British casualties. *Haig, the British commander-in-chief, without French help, remained convinced, despite the *Somme, that frontal assaults in superior numbers must succeed. Torrential rain and preliminary bombardment reduced Flanders to a sea of mud, making advance impossible. Only on the final day did Canadians reach the ruined village of Passchendaele. Even this nominal gain was surrendered in the retreat before *Ludendorff's final offensive (April 1918).

passive resistance Non-violent opposition to a ruling authority or government. It frequently involves a refusal to cooperate with the authorities or a defiant breach of laws and regulations and has been a major weapon of many nationalist, resistance, and social movements in modern times. One of the most successful campaigns was that waged by Mahatma *Gandhi against British rule in India, when widespread civil disturbances and protests persuaded the British to make major concessions. Gandhi's example was an inspiration for the *Civil Rights movement in the USA from the 1950s, where passive resistance, large-scale demonstrations, and the deliberate breaking of segregation laws brought considerable improvements for the black population.

Patel, Sardar Vallabhbhai (1875–1950) Indian statesman. Deeply influenced by Mohandas *Gandhi, he became the principal organizer of many civil disobedience campaigns, suffering frequent imprisonment by the British. He was elected President of the Indian National *Congress in 1931. He played an important role in the negotiations that led to the partition of the subcontinent into India and Pakistan. As Deputy Prime Minister (1947–50) he initiated a purge of communists and with the assistance of V. P. *Menon, he integrated the *Princely States into the Indian Union.

Pathan A Pashto-speaking people inhabiting north-west Pakistan and south-east Afghanistan.

Pathet Lao Laotian communist movement. In the independence struggle after World War II, Pathet Lao forces cooperated with the *Vietminh against French colonial power. After the Geneva Agreement (1954), it emerged as a major political and military force within Laos, seeking the alignment of their country with communist China and North Vietnam. Between the mid-1950s and mid-1970s the Pathet Lao and its political wing, the Neo Lao Haksat (Patriotic Party of Laos) under the leadership of Prince Souphanouvong, waged a prolonged political and military struggle for power with non-communist government forces, eventually emerging triumphant with the formation of the People's Democratic Republic of Laos in 1975.

Patiño, Simon Iture (1860–1947) Bolivian capitalist. He pioneered the development of Bolivia's tin resources and died one of the world's richest men. Although his modest origins impeded his entry into the Bolivian social élite, by the 1900s Patiño controlled over half of the tin production in Bolivia and exerted considerable influence on his country's government. He is still criticized for not investing in the development of his own country.

patrician A privileged landed aristocrat of early republican Rome. The patricians (or 'fathers') gathered after the expulsion of *Tarquin to guide the state. Supported by revered tradition they were hereditary members of the *Roman Senate. They monopolized all magistracies and priesthoods but during the 'struggle of the Orders' with the plebeians they were forced to share power with them—in 367 BC the consulship was open to plebeians. Thereafter a 'plebeian nobility' arose, which together with the patricians formed the ruling class. Their ranks were thinned and their influence waned in the late republic but the ancient names still carried prestige.

Patrick, St (5th century) Apostle and patron saint of Ireland. His *Confession* is the chief source for the events of his life. Of Romano-British parentage, he was captured at the age of

16 by raiders and shipped to Ireland as a slave; there he experienced a religious conversion. Escaping after six years, probably to Gaul, he was ordained and returned to Ireland in about 432.

patronage system *See* SPOILS SYSTEM.

Patton, George Smith (1885–1945) US general. In World War II Patton commanded a corps in North Africa and then the 7th Army in Sicily. He lost his command in 1944 after a publicized incident in which he hit a soldier suffering from battle fatigue, but later led the 3rd Army in the *Normandy Campaign. His tendency to make rapid military advance, at times with no regard for supporting units or allies, became evident in 1944 in his spectacular sweep through France, across the Rhine, and into Czechoslovakia. As military governor of Bavaria, he was criticized for his leniency to Nazis. He was killed in a road accident while commanding the US 15th Army.

Paul, St (born **Saul of Tarsus**) (died *c*.64) Christian missionary to the Gentiles. Of Jewish descent, he was brought up as a Pharisee and at first opposed the followers of Jesus, assisting at the martyrdom of St Stephen. On a mission to Damascus, he was converted to Christianity after a vision and became one of the first major Christian missionaries and theologians. His missionary journeys are described in the Acts of the Apostles. Paul's radical understanding of the Christian message provoked hostility, and a riot against him on a visit to Jerusalem led to his arrest by the Roman authorities. He was eventually taken to Rome, where he is thought to have died a martyr's death. Several of Paul's letters to early Christian groups have been preserved in the New Testament. Through them his influence on Christian life and thought has been greater than that of any other of the first Christians.

Paul I (1754–1801) Emperor of Russia (1796–1801). He was the disturbed son of the empress *Catherine II and Peter III, and was greatly affected by the murder of his father during Catherine's *coup d'état* in 1762. After Catherine's death in 1796 he began a reign of frenzied despotism. He was obsessed by a fear of revolution and joined the coalitions against France. His attempts to violate the order of succession led to a conspiracy, which included his son, Alexander I, and in March 1801 resulted in his murder.

Paul VI (born **Giovanni Battista Montini**) (1897–1978) Pope (1963–78). He continued the work of his predecessor *John XXIII by reconvening the Second Vatican Council (1963–65) of the *Roman Catholic Church. Following the recommendations of the Council, he established important post-conciliar commissions. These investigated the need for reform of the liturgy and curia and ways to promote Christian unity and greater lay participation. A traditionalist by conviction, he was suspicious of any innovation that might undermine the authority of the Church, insisting on the necessity of priestly celibacy and condemning artificial methods of birth control.

Paulus, Friedrich von (1890–1957) German field-marshal. As deputy chief of staff he planned the German invasion of Russia (Operation Barbarossa) in World War II. In 1942 he failed to capture *Stalingrad, was cut off, and surrendered (February 1943). In captivity, he joined a Soviet-sponsored German organization and publicly advocated the overthrow of the Nazi dictatorship. He lived in East Germany until his death.

Pavia, Battle of (24 February 1525) An engagement in the Habsburg–Valois wars, which involved the papacy and England supporting *Charles V against *Francis I. In October 1524 the French invaded Italy and took Milan, and the Pope changed sides to join them. Then the city of Pavia, in Lombardy, saw a battle between the French and imperial armies. The imperial forces, numbering 23,000 defeated the French army even though it had 5,000 more soldiers, and Francis was taken prisoner. He was released in 1526 and the wars in Italy continued.

Pawnee A tribe of North American Indians of the Hokan-Caddoan linguistic group, originally occupying the plains and prairies of Nebraska.

Paxton Boys A group of American rebels in Pennsylvania, who were Scots-Irish frontiersmen from settlements round Paxton. In 1763, threatened by *Pontiac 's Rebellion and agitated by lack of colonial defence and political representation, they first massacred some Christian Native Americans and then marched on Philadelphia, where *Franklin managed to pacify them. They were symptomatic of a long-term antagonism between frontier and coastal settlers, having many similarities with *Bacon's Rebellion (1676) and the Carolina *Regulators (1768–71).

Paz Estenssoro, Victor (1907–2001) Bolivian statesman; President (1952–56; 1960–64; 1985–89). In 1941 he helped to form a left-wing political party, the Movimiento Nacionalista Revolucionario (MNR). In the same year he became Minister of Finance (1941–44), but then went into exile until 1951. In 1952, when the MNR came to power, he became President of Bolivia (1952–56). During this time the tin-mines were nationalized, adult suffrage introduced, and many large estates broken up and transferred to Indian peasants. He was re-elected President (1960–64), when he reached an understanding with international financiers for the re-organization of the tin industry. He was elected for a third time in 1964, but was overthrown by the army and went into exile until 1971. Military government ended in Bolivia in 1982 and in 1985 he was re-elected President in succession to Dr Herman Zuazo. In spite of a drop in world tin prices and consequential economic problems for Bolivia, his government survived until 1989, when he was succeeded by Jaime Paz Zamora.

Pazzi Conspiracy (1478) An unsuccessful plot to overthrow the *Medici rulers of Florence. Their rivals, the Pazzi family, backed by Pope Sixtus IV, conspired to murder Giuliano and Lorenzo de Medici at High Mass in Florence Cathedral and to seize power. Although Giuliano was murdered as planned, Lorenzo escaped. The mob rallied to the Medici and seized and murdered the main conspirators.

Peabody, George (1795–1869) US philanthropist. He established a prosperous trading business in the eastern USA before settling in London in 1837. He became one of the leading international bankers of his age, amassing a vast fortune, a substantial part of which he devoted to philanthropic ends, including the first educational foundation in the USA, the Peabody Education Fund, set up in 1867 to promote education in the South. He also gave large sums for slum clearance in Britain.

peace-pledge See FRANKPLEDGE.

Pearl Harbor A harbour on the Pacific island of Oahu, in Hawaii, the site of a major US naval base, where a surprise attack on 7 December 1941 by Japanese carrier-borne aircraft, inflicted heavy damage and brought the USA into World War II.

Pearson, Lester Bowles (1897–1972) Canadian diplomat and Liberal statesman, Prime Minister (1963–68). As Secretary of State for External Affairs (1948–57) he headed the Canadian delegation to the United Nations, served as chairman of NATO (1951), and acted as a mediator in the resolution of the Suez crisis (1956), for which he received the Nobel Peace Prize in 1957. Pearson became leader of the Liberal Party in 1958; he resigned as Prime Minister and Liberal Party leader in 1968.

Peary, Robert Edwin (1856–1920) US explorer. He made eight Arctic voyages before becoming the first person to reach the North Pole, on 6 April 1909.

Peasants' Revolt (1381) A social uprising in England. Widespread unrest caused by repressive legislation, such as the Statute of Labourers (1351) was brought to a head by the imposition of the *poll tax of 1380. The revolt drew support from artisans, *villeins, and the destitute. Men from Kent and Essex, led by Wat *Tyler and John *Ball, entered London, massacring some merchants and razing the palace of the Duke of Lancaster. The young king Richard II promised the men the abolition of serfdom, cheap land, and free trade. The rebels then occupied the Tower of London and beheaded the Archbishop and the king's Treasurer. The king persuaded the rebels to disperse, promising them further reforms. Tyler was murdered by the enraged Mayor of London, and the militant bishop of Norwich crushed the rebels in East Anglia. The government re-established control and reneged on the monarch's promise. The revolt succeeded only as a protest against the taxation of the poor and the further levying of the Poll Tax.

Peasants' War (1524–26) A mass revolt of the German lower classes during the *Reformation. It began in south-west Germany and spread down the River Rhine and into Austria. Frustrated by economic hardships, the rebels were encouraged by radical *Protestant preachers to expect a second coming of Jesus Christ and the establishment of social equality and justice. They raided and pillaged in uncoordinated bands, driving *Luther to condemn them in his fierce broadsheet *Against the thieving and murdering hordes of the peasants* (1525). Luther also supported the army of the Swabian League under Philip of Hesse, which helped to crush the main body of insurgents at Frankenhausen. Over 100,000 rebels were eventually slaughtered.

Pedro I (1798–1835) The first Emperor of Brazil (1822–31). The son of John VI of Portugal, he fled from Napoleon to Brazil. Recognizing that Brazilian independence from Portugal was inevitable, Pedro I led the revolt himself (1822) and then governed the new Brazilian monarchy under the executive powers of the constitution of 1824. Republican-inspired uprisings and nationalist resentment over his Portuguese connections undermined Pedro's rule; he abdicated (1831) in favour of his son *Pedro II.

Pedro II (1812–91) Emperor of Brazil (1831–89). The son of *Pedro I, he succeeded under a regency when his father abdicated (1831). The central government was unable to quell the uprisings at Balaiada (1838–41) and elsewhere until the General Assembly declared Pedro to be of age and confirmed (1840) his emperorship. Within 18 months he had established order throughout the country. A popular, moderate leader, he was dedicated to the economic progress of Brazil. After a long rule, with only occasional revolts and foreign conflicts, Pedro eventually alienated his military officers by his refusal to grant them privileges, and the planters by his gradual abolition of slavery (completed in 1888). The army and the Republican Party overthrew him in 1889 and he spent the rest of his life in exile in Europe.

Peel, Sir Robert (1788–1850) British Conservative statesman, Prime Minister (1834–35; 1841–46). During his second term as Home Secretary (1828–30) Peel established the Metropolitan Police (and gave his name to the nicknames *bobby* and *peeler*). As leader of the new Conservative Party he affirmed his belief in moderate electoral reform in the Tamworth Manifesto (1834). His repeal of the Corn Laws in 1846, however, split the Conservatives and forced his resignation. In the last years of his career he came to support the Whig policies of free trade.

Peisistratus *See* PISISTRATUS.

Peking Man The numerous remains of *Homo erectus pekinensis* (originally *Sinanthropus pekinensis*) found at *Zhoukoudian near Peking (now Beijing) in China since 1927. The term is often used for all *Homo erectus* fossils from China.

Pelagius (*c.*360–*c.*420) British or Irish monk. He denied the doctrines of original sin and predestination, defending innate human goodness and free will. His beliefs were opposed by St Augustine of Hippo and condemned as heretical by the Synod of Carthage in about 418.

Pelham, Henry (1696–1754) British Whig statesman, Prime Minister (1743–54). After serving in Sir Robert Walpole's Cabinet from 1721 onwards, he replaced him as Premier, and introduced a period of peace and prosperity by bringing to an end the War of the Austrian Succession (1740–48).

Peloponnesian War The war waged between Athens and Sparta and their respective allies between 431 and 404 BC. Sparta invaded Attica with its allies in 431, but *Pericles had persuaded the Athenians to withdraw behind the 'long walls', which linked Athens and its port of Piraeus, and avoid a land-battle with Sparta's superior army. Athens relied on its fleet of *triremes to raid the Peloponnese and guard its empire and trade-routes. It was struck a serious blow by an outbreak of plague in 430, which killed about a third of the population, including Pericles. Nevertheless the fleet performed well and a year's truce was made in 423 BC.

The Peace of Nicias was concluded in 421 BC, but Alcibiades orchestrated opposition to Sparta in the Peloponnese, though his hopes were dashed when Sparta won a victory at Mantinea in 418. He was also the main advocate of an expedition to Sicily (415–413), aimed at defeating Syracuse, that ended in complete disaster for Athens. War was formally resumed in 413 BC. Athenian fortunes revived, with naval victories at Cynossema (411), Cyzicus (410), and the recapture of Byzantium (408). There was a further victory at Arginusae in 406. From then on, Persian financial support for Sparta and the strategic and tactical skills of the Spartan *Lysander tilted the balance. Sparta's victory at Aegospotami and its control of the Hellespont starved Athens into surrender in April 404. An oligarchic coup followed immediately, supported by Sparta, and the reign of terror of the 'Thirty Tyrants', but democracy was restored in 403.

penal settlements, Australian Settlements in 19th-century Australia for convicts who had committed further crimes within the colonies. Newcastle, New South Wales was used as a penal settlement from 1804 to 1824, convicts there worked as coalminers, cedar cutters, and lime burners. Port Macquarie (1821–30) and Moreton Bay (1824–39) also were used as penal settlements. Norfolk Island, resettled in 1825 as a penal settlement, became notorious. It held an average of 1500 to 2000 convicts, considered to be of the worst type. Punishment was harsh and a number of mutinies occurred. The last convicts left Norfolk Island in 1856. Port Arthur, in Van Diemen's Land (modern Tasmania), begun in 1830, was finally closed in 1877.

Penda (died 655) King of *Mercia in the first half of the 7th century. He sought to establish the supremacy of Mercia over the other English kingdoms. He drove the King of Wessex into exile, killed the ruler of East Anglia in battle, and, in alliance with *Cadwallon, invaded *Northumbria. Edwin, its ruler, was defeated and killed in 633, as was his successor St *Oswald in 642. Although never a Christian, Penda allowed missionaries to preach in his kingdom. He was killed in battle by *Oswy, King of Northumbria.

Peninsular War (1807–14) One of the *Napoleonic Wars, fought in Spain and Portugal. War was caused by *Napoleon's invasion of Portugal (1807) in order to compel it to accept the *Continental System. In 1808 the conflict spread to Spain, whose king was forced to abdicate, Napoleon's brother Joseph Bonaparte being placed on the throne. In June the Spanish revolted and forced the French to surrender at Baylen, whereupon Joseph fled from Madrid. In August Wellesley (later the Duke of *Wellington) landed in Portugal and routed a French force at Vimeiro and expelled the French from Portugal. In November Napoleon personally went to Spain, winning a series of battles, including Burgos, and restoring Joseph to the throne. British hopes of pushing the French out of Spain were dashed in January 1809, after *Moore's retreat to Corunna. Despite his victory at Talavera, Wellesley withdrew to Lisbon. Here he built a strong defensive line, which he centred at Torres Vedras. In 1810 Napoleon sent Massena to reinforce Soult and drive the British into the sea. Massena attempted to lay siege to Torres Vedras, but after four months his army, starved and demoralized, was forced to retreat. Soult, jealous of Massena's command, was slow in coming to his support, but managed to capture Badajoz. Wellington, who had pursued Massena and defeated him at Almeida, withdrew from invading Spain and turned to face Soult. During 1812 Wellington recaptured Badajoz and after defeating Massena's replacement, Marmont, at Salamanca, entered Madrid. The following year he defeated Joseph at the decisive Battle of Vitoria. He went on to defeat Soult at Orthez and Toulouse (1814), having driven the French out of Spain.

Penn, William (1644–1718) English Quaker, founder of Pennsylvania. He was imprisoned in the Tower of London in 1668 for writing in defence of Quaker practices. Acquitted in 1670, he was granted a charter to land in North America by Charles II (1682), using it to found the colony of Pennsylvania as a sanctuary for Quakers and other Nonconformists in the same

year. In 1681 Penn also co-founded the city of Philadelphia.

penny post *See* HILL, SIR ROWLAND.

Pentagon Papers An official study of US defence policy commissioned in 1967 to examine US involvement in south-east Asia. Leaked by a former government employee, they revealed miscalculations, deceptions, and unauthorized military offensives. Their publication provoked demands for more open government.

Pentrich Rising (1817) A quasi-political insurrection which took place in Derbyshire, England. Led by Jeremiah Brandreth, a framework knitter, a group of about 200 men from Pentrich and other nearby villages, armed only with primitive weapons, began to march on Nottingham in a protest against the government. Brandreth had been tricked by a government spy into believing that they were taking part in a nationwide insurrection. They were dispersed by a troop of cavalry and Brandreth went into hiding. He was betrayed and later executed, together with two of his associates.

People's Party (USA) *See* POPULIST PARTY.

Pepin Three Frankish 'mayors of the palace' under *Merovingian rule who gave rise to the Carolingian dynasty. Pepin I of Landen was mayor of Austrasia, and his son Pepin II of both Austrasia and Neustria, the two most important parts of the Merovingian kingdom. Pepin III, the Short, was the grandson of the latter and son of *Charles Martel. He ousted the last Merovingian, Childeric III, in 751 and was crowned King of the Franks. A close ally of the papacy, he defended it from Lombard attacks and made the Donation of Pepin which was the basis for the *Papal States. He added Aquitaine and Septimania to his kingdom, which passed, on his death in 768, to *Charlemagne and Carloman.

Pepys, Samuel (1633–1703) English diarist and naval administrator. He is particularly remembered for his *Diary* (1660–69), an important record of contemporary events, such as the Great Plague (1665–66), the Fire of London (1666), and the sailing of the Dutch fleet up the Thames (1665–67). The *Diary* was written in code and was first deciphered in 1825. Pepys became secretary of the Admiralty in 1672 but was deprived of his post in 1679 and committed to the Tower for his alleged complicity in Titus Oates's fabricated Popish Plot. However, he was reappointed in 1684 and became President of the Royal Society in the same year.

Pequot War (1637) A war fought between Native Americans and White settlers in New England. The Pequot had lived peacefully alongside the mainly British settlers from 1620, but tensions increased on both sides. The British took over more and more land while the Pequot would only trade with the Dutch. In 1636 a trader was murdered, the Pequot were blamed, and the authorities destroyed Pequot villages. After several skirmishes, the Pequot camp at Mystic on the Connecticut coast near Rhode Island was surprised and set on fire, killing some 500 of the tribe, which did not recover. Poor colonist cooperation in this war led to the founding of the New England Confederation (1643).

Perceval, Spencer (1762–1812) British Tory statesman, Prime Minister (1809–12). He was shot dead in the lobby of the House of Commons by a bankrupt merchant who blamed the government for his insolvency.

Percy A family of marcher lords of medieval England with lands in Northumberland. Henry de Percy (1341–1408), 1st Earl of Northumberland, was the first of the family to be of major importance in the defence of England's northern frontier. The earl's son, Sir Henry Percy ('Hotspur') (1364–1403), was a hero at the Battle of Otterburn. When Henry of Bolingbroke landed in the north of England in 1399, the earl and Hotspur helped assure him of the crown; they were well rewarded, but within four years their greed for more offices or money led them into open rebellion. Hotspur and his uncle Thomas, Earl of Worcester, were killed at Shrewsbury in 1403. Five years later Earl Henry invaded England from Scotland, but he too was killed and his estates were forfeited.

Subsequently restored to their estates, later generations of the family resumed their role as guardians of the northern frontier and rivals of the Nevilles. The male line ended in 1670, but the earldom passed in the female line to Sir Hugh Smithson (1715–86) who took the name of Percy and in 1766 was created Duke of Northumberland.

Peres, Shimon (born Szymon Perski) (1923–) Israeli statesman, Prime Minister (1984–86; 1995–96); President (2007–14). Born in Poland, he emigrated to Palestine in 1934. Labour Party leader from 1977, Peres became head of a coalition government with the Likud Party in 1984, later serving as deputy to Yitzhak Shamir. As Foreign Minister from 1992 he played a major role in negotiating the PLO–Israeli peace accord (1993) and shared the 1994 Nobel Peace Prize with Yitzhak Rabin and Yasser Arafat. He replaced Rabin as Prime Minister after the latter's assassination, only to be narrowly defeated in the elections of 1996 by Binyamin Netanyahu. In 2005 he left the Labour Party to join the new Kadima Party formed by Ariel *Sharon. In 2007 he became President, standing down in 2014.

Pérez de Cuéllar, Javier (1920–) Peruvian diplomat. He served as Secretary-General of the United Nations (1982–91), and played a key role in the diplomatic aftermath of the Falklands War (1982) and in ending the Iran–Iraq War (1980–88). His efforts to avert the Gulf War in 1990 raised his international standing. He was an unsuccessful candidate in the 1995 Peruvian presidential election and was subsequently briefly Prime Minister (2000–01).

Pergamum An ancient city in what is now Turkey, some 20 km (12 miles) inland from the west coast of Asia Minor. It developed into a major power during the 3rd and 2nd centuries BC under the Attalid dynasty. In particular, Attalus I (ruled 241–197), inflicted a severe defeat on the Galatians and for a time wrested most of Asia Minor from the *Seleucids. He allied himself to Rome in the first two *Macedonian wars and his pro-Roman policy was followed by his successors. Thus Eumenes II (died c.160) helped to defeat Antiochus at Magnesia and in accordance with Attalus III's will the kingdom was bequeathed to Rome in 133 BC. It became a province of Asia, and was soon eclipsed by Ephesus as the chief city of the region.

Attalid Pergamum was a brilliant centre of Hellenistic civilization: its chief glories were its sculpture and its library, where parchment was developed in the 2nd century BC as a more durable material than papyrus for books.

Pericles (c.495–29 BC) Athenian statesman and general. A champion of Athenian democracy, he pursued an imperialist policy and masterminded Athenian strategy in the Peloponnesian War. He commissioned the building of the Parthenon in 447 and promoted the culture of Athens in a golden age that produced such figures as Aeschylus, Socrates, and Phidias. He died of the plague that struck Athens in 430.

Perón, Eva (full name **María Eva Duarte de Perón**; known as **'Evita Perón'**) (1919–52) Argentinian politician. After pursuing a successful career as a radio actress in the 1930s and 1940s, she married Juan *Perón and became de facto Minister of Health and of

Labour. Idolized by the poor, she organized female workers, secured the vote for women, and earmarked substantial government funds for social welfare. She was nominated for the vice-presidency in 1951, but was forced by the army to withdraw. She died the following year from cancer.

Perón, Juan Domingo (1895–1974) Argentinian soldier and statesman, President (1946–55; 1973–74). He participated in the military coup organized by pro-Fascist army officers in 1943, and was elected President in 1946, when he assumed dictatorial powers. He won popular support with his programme of social reform, but, after the death of his second wife, Eva *Perón, the faltering economy and his conflict with the Roman Catholic Church led to his removal and exile in 1955. Following a resurgence by the Peronist Party in the early 1970s, Perón returned to power in 1973, but died in office.

Perry, Matthew Calbraith (1794–1858) US naval officer and pioneer of Western contact with Japan. Perry served under his brother Oliver Perry during the *War of 1812. He headed an expedition to Japan in the fortified port of Uraga in 1853, and Edo (modern Tokyo) Bay in 1854. His display of Western technology, both military and civil, forced the *shogunate to open two Japanese ports to US trade in the Treaty of *Kanagawa. Perry's mission initiated the process which, within half a century, would transform Japan from an isolated feudal country to a highly industrialized world power.

Perry Convention *See* KANAGAWA, TREATY OF.

Persepolis The ceremonial capital of the *Achaemenid empire. A festival of tribute was held there each year, it was the burial place of the kings, and its treasury was a repository of enormous wealth. The city was captured, looted, and burnt in 331 BC by Alexander the Great's troops. Excavation of the palaces—built by *Darius I and *Xerxes—and other buildings, while confirming the destruction that took place, has also revealed some magnificent examples of Achaemenid art and architecture, particularly the bas-reliefs.

Pershing, John Joseph (known as 'Black Jack') (1860–1948) US general. He served in the *Spanish–American War and later in the Philippines. He led the US expedition against Mexico in 1916. In May 1917 he was appointed commander of the American Expeditionary Forces in France and his talent for organization was largely responsible for the moulding of

hastily trained US soldiers into well-integrated combat troops. In 1919 he became general of the armies of the USA and from 1921 to 1924 was army chief-of-staff.

Persia *See* IRAN.

Persian wars *See* GREEK–PERSIAN WARS.

Peru

Capital:	Lima
Area:	1,285,216 sq km (496,225 sq miles)
Population:	27,968,000 (2005)
Currency:	1 nuevo sol = 100 centimos
Religions:	Roman Catholic 86.2%; Protestant 5.2%
Ethnic Groups:	Quechua 47.0%; Mestizo 32.0%; European 12.0%; Aymara 5.0%
Languages:	Spanish, Quechua (both official); Aymara
International Organizations:	UN; OAS; Andean Community; Non-Aligned Movement; WTO

A country on the Pacific coast of South America, bounded by Ecuador and Colombia on the north, Brazil and Bolivia on the east, and Chile on the south.

Physical The north-east of the country is in the upper Amazon basin and comprises equatorial rainforest. The south-west half is occupied by the Andes mountain ranges, whose snow-capped peaks rise to over 6500 m (21,000 feet). Between the ranges are plateau areas, the high mountain lake, Titicaca, in the extreme south-east, and many valleys used for cultivation and the rearing of livestock. Minerals are found in rich profusion. The coastal plain is arid and mostly desert, cooled by the Peru Current.

Economy Exports include copper, zinc, lead, and silver. There is a wide range of agriculture, and Peru is almost self-sufficient in food. Llamas and sheep provide wool for export. One of the world's leading producers of fishmeal, Peru has a well-established manufacturing sector which includes petroleum products. There is widespread illegal cultivation of coca, processed in Colombia into cocaine.

History Peru was the site of a succession of complex cultures and states from *c*.1000 BC: Chavín in the central Highlands, Mochica on the northern coast, *Nazca on the southern coast, and Tiahuanaco round Lake Titicaca in the Andes. Between *c*.600 AD and 1000 Huari in the central Andes conquered a small 'empire', and the *Chimú state rose on the northern coast *c*.1000. The *Incas were another such group, based round Cuzco, who began their regional expansion *c*.1200 and eventually conquered a vast empire stretching from Chile to Ecuador during the 15th century. Spanish invader Francisco *Pizarro's defeat of *Atahualpa in 1532 was followed by rivalry for control and led eventually to direct rule by the Spanish crown. Inca revolts continued for nearly 50 years. The vice-royalty, with its capital at Lima, attempted to placate the various factions but was not in reasonable control until the mid-16th century. Further Inca insurrections occurred in 1780, led by Tupac Amarú, and in 1814.

In 1821 José de *San Martín captured Lima, proclaiming an independent republic and issuing a constitution (1823). In 1824 José de *Sucre won the Battle of Ayacucho, and Spanish troops were withdrawn. Political quarrels in the new republic led to an invitation to Simón *Bolívar to accept the powers of a dictator. He tried unsuccessfully to bring Peru into his state of Gran Colombia (which comprised present-day Colombia, Ecuador, and Venezuela). A long period of civil war followed, the situation stabilizing under President Ramón *Castilla (1844–62), who ended slavery, established an education system, and promoted the extraction of guano (natural nitrates and phosphates produced from sea-bird droppings), which brought immediate prosperity but was soon exhausted. The loss of nitrate revenue and the cost of the War of the Pacific (1879–84) led to national bankruptcy in 1889. Civilian politics had emerged in the 1870s with two parties, the Democrats and the Civilians, alternating in office. The latter, led by Augusto Leguia, held power (1908–30), introducing progressive legislation and settling the Tacna–Arica Dispute. After World War I a radical group, the Alianza Popular Revolucionaria Americana (APRA), led by Haya de la Torre, sought to obtain greater participation in politics by the Indians. President Manuel Prado, elected in 1939, aligned Peru with US policies in World War II. Terry Belaúnde gained office in 1963. In 1968 a left-wing military junta seized power, seeking to nationalize US-controlled industries. A more moderate junta succeeded in 1975, and in 1979 elections were again held. In 1980 Belaúnde was re-elected President, when a

new constitution was established. In the face of severe economic problems Belaúnde succeeded in re-democratizing the country, and in 1985 President Alan García was elected. Confronted by massive rescheduling requirements for Peru's foreign debts, his regime imposed an austerity programme and engaged in a guerrilla war against a strong ultra-left Maoist group, Sendero Luminoso ('Shining Path'). His APRA Party did badly in the 1990 elections, when the son of Japanese immigrants, Alberto Keinya Fujimori of the Cambio 90 Party, was elected President. The austerity measures which he continued resulted in protests, with strikes and guerrilla attacks across the country. In September 1992, however, his government captured and imprisoned Abimael Guzmán, who had founded and led Sendero Luminoso since 1970. Fujimori was re-elected in 1995 and again in 2000 but, amid allegations of corruption and electoral fraud, he resigned later in the year. Alejandro Toledo was elected President in 2001; he was succeeded by the former President Alan García, who was elected in 2006. Ollanta Humala was elected President in 2011.

Pétain, H. O. (Henri Philippe Omer Pétain) (1856–1951) French general and statesman, head of state (1940–42). He became a national hero in World War I for halting the German advance at Verdun (1916) and later became Commander-in-Chief of French forces (1917). In World War II he concluded an armistice with Nazi Germany after the collapse of French forces in 1940 and established the French government at Vichy (effectively a puppet regime for the Third Reich) until German occupation in 1942. After the war Pétain received a death sentence for collaboration, but this was commuted to life imprisonment.

Peter, St (died *c*.64 AD) Originally named Simon, the leader of the Apostles who followed *Jesus Christ. Jesus named him Cephas (Aramaic, 'rock'; Greek *petra*, 'rock') to signify his key role in establishing the early Christian Church. After the death of Jesus, Peter was the undisputed leader of the Church, preaching, and defending the new religious movement. He was the first to accept Gentiles (non-Jews) into the Church. It seems certain that Peter spent the last years of his life in Rome and was probably crucified during *Nero's persecution of 64. The *papacy traces its origins back to Peter and the *Roman Catholic Church identifies him as the founder and first bishop of the church of Rome.

Peter I (or **Peter the Great**) (1672–1725) Tsar of Russia (1682–1725). After the death of his half-brother Ivan in 1696 Peter I assumed sole authority and launched a policy of expansion along the Baltic coast. Modernizing his armed forces he waged the Great Northern War (1700–21) against Charles XII of Sweden, and went on to annex Estonia and Latvia, as well as parts of Finland, following the defeat of the Swedish monarch. Peter I's introduction of extensive government and administration reforms were instrumental in transforming Russia into a significant European power. In 1703 he made St Petersburg his capital.

Peterloo massacre (16 August 1819) A violent confrontation in Manchester, England, between civilians and government forces. A large but peaceable crowd of some 60,000 people had gathered in St Peter's Fields to hear the radical politician Henry 'Orator' *Hunt address them. After he had begun speaking the local magistrates sent in constables to arrest him. In the mistaken belief that the crowd was preventing the arrest, the magistrates ordered a body of cavalry to go to the assistance of the constables. In the ensuing riot 11 civilians were killed and over 500 injured.

Peter's pence A tax formerly paid annually to the papacy. First stated as compulsory in 787, it was levied in England from the 10th century at the rate of one penny per householder. It was revived by *William I as a single lump sum of £200 for the whole of England. It was abolished in England in 1534 during the Reformation.

Peter the Hermit (c.1050–1115) French monk. His preaching on the First Crusade was a rallying cry for thousands of peasants throughout Europe to journey to the Holy Land; most were massacred by the Turks in Asia Minor. Peter later became prior of an Augustinian monastery in Flanders.

Petition of Right (1628) A document drawn up by opposition members of the English Parliament, led by *Coke. It came at the time of Charles I's wars against France and Spain, and the lengthy quarrel over tunnage and poundage. It stated parliamentary grievances and forbade illegal unparliamentary taxation, the forced billeting of troops, the imposition of martial law, and arbitrary imprisonment. Charles did assent to the Petition but it was a limited parliamentary victory and did nothing to curb Charles's unconstitutional rule during the 11 years of government without Parliament.

petty sessions A court held by the sheriff of a *hundred in 16th-century England. They were mainly concerned with maintaining order and local economic regulations. More serious cases were referred to general or quarter sessions.

pharaoh A king of ancient *Egypt. The Egyptians themselves only used the term in this way from 950 BC onwards. The pharaoh was thought of as a god, the son of Osiris ruling on Earth, and acted as an intermediary between gods and men. He wielded immense power as the religious, civil, and military leader of the country.

Pharsalus, Battle of (48 BC) The battle in which *Pompey was defeated by Julius *Caesar. After Caesar crossed the *Rubicon, Pompey retired to Greece to rally his forces. Caesar crushed Pompey's supporters in Spain and then pursued him to northern Greece. Pompey's forces were routed in pitched battle, although he himself escaped.

Philip I (the Handsome) (1478–1506) King of Castile (1504–06). The son of *Maximilian I, Philip I inherited *Burgundy in 1482 and took over from his father's regency in 1494. His marriage to *Joanna (the Mad) of Spain in 1496 brought the *Habsburgs a dynastic link with Spain. When Queen *Isabella I died in 1504, the pair inherited Castile. His wife's increasing madness enabled Philip I to assume considerable power as king consort. He died of fever soon after his arrival at Castile, his claims passing to his son, who became *Charles V.

Philip II (382–336 BC) King of Macedonia (359–336 BC). Philip II transformed an ineffectual and divided *Macedonia into a power which dominated the Greek world. His success was based upon exploitation of Macedonia's natural advantages and the highly professional army which he created around a core of pike-armed infantrymen, the phalanx, and his excellent cavalry. He gradually extended his empire until, after the battle of *Chaeronea, it stretched from the Black Sea to the southern Peloponnese. When an assassin struck him down, he was preparing for the invasion of Persia, a project that his son *Alexander III inherited.

Philip II (Augustus) (1165–1223) King of France (1179–1223). One of the *Capetians, he succeeded his father Louis VII in 1180 and set about the restoration and expansion of his kingdom. Defeating the Count of Flanders and the Duke of Burgundy, he seized Artois and part of the valley of the Somme. He was obliged initially to accept the homage of King *John of England for Normandy, Aquitaine, and Anjou but later recovered Normandy, Anjou, Poitou,

p

and the Auvergne for the French crown. He defeated John and the Holy Roman Emperor jointly at the Battle of Bouvines (August 1214), leaving his country stronger and more united. After these military successes, he devoted his energy to reforming the law and building and fortifying Paris.

Philip II (1527–98) King of Spain, Naples, and Sicily (1556–98) and, as Philip I, of Portugal (1580–98). He was the only legitimate son of Emperor *Charles V. He was married four times: to Mary of Portugal (1543), to *Mary I of England (1554), to Isabella of France (1559), and to Anne of Austria (1570), whose son by him was his successor as Philip III of Spain. He ruled Spain and the *Spanish empire industriously during its 'golden age', not leaving the Iberian Peninsula at all after 1559. Although he generally subordinated his crusading zeal to more worldly considerations, his strongly Catholic religious policies helped to provoke the *Dutch Revolts (1568–1648) and the Revolt of the Moriscos within Spain (1568–70). His intermittent wars against the *Ottomans, his war with England (1585–1604), and his involvement in the *French Wars of Religion were all largely motivated by interests of state. His personal brand of absolute monarchy left the country economically crippled as a result of his military expenses.

Philip IV (the Fair) (1268–1314) King of France (1285–1314). He inherited the throne from his father and strengthened royal control over the nobility as well as improving the law. Pope Boniface VIII resisted his claim to the right to tax the clergy but was imprisoned by a royal agent and died soon afterwards. The next pope, Clement V, was under the king's control and acquiesced in the removal of the papacy from Rome to Avignon in France, the beginning of 70 years "captivity". Coveting the wealth of the *Knights Templar, he seized much of their property after Pope Clement suppressed their order by royal command in 1313. He also persecuted the Jews and had their property confiscated.

Philip V (1683–1746) King of Spain (1700–46). He was Philip of Anjou, the younger grandson of *Louis XIV, and succeeded under the terms of the will of the last Habsburg king, Charles II. It was Louis XIV's acceptance of this will that plunged Europe into the War of the *Spanish Succession. Philip's claim was confirmed at the Peace of *Utrecht. Catalonia was deprived of its liberties when Barcelona surrendered to him in 1714. For the rest of his reign he was dominated by his second wife, Elizabeth *Farnese, whose ambitions for her sons influenced Spanish foreign policy.

Philip VI (1293–1350) King of France (1328–50), the first of the *Valois kings. His right to the throne was challenged by *Edward III of England and the *Hundred Years War began in 1337. His ill-fated reign also witnessed the *Black Death and war with Flanders. Despite the ruinous expense of war and some disastrous military defeats, the government was strengthened during this period as an organized system of taxation evolved.

Philip of Hesse (1504–67) German prince. He played a leading role in establishing the *Protestant religion in Germany and in asserting German princely independence against Emperor *Charles V. After becoming converted to *Luther's doctrines (1524), Philip turned Hesse into a Protestant state. He was active at the Diet of Speyer (1529), a subscriber to the *Augsburg Confession (1530), and became a founder and leader of the Schmalkaldic League, an alliance of Protestant princes and cities (1531). He forfeited the loyalty of some of his followers by marrying bigamously (1540) and after his defeat in the *Schmalkaldic War he was imprisoned by Charles V. He lived to see Lutherans achieve equality with Catholics under the Peace of *Augsburg (1555).

Philippi, Battle of (42 BC) A battle fought at Philippi, a city in Macedonia in northern Greece, in which *Caesar's assassins under *Brutus were defeated by the armies of *Mark Antony and Octavian (*Augustus). Both Cassius and Brutus committed suicide after the defeat.

Philippines

Capital:	Manila
Area:	300,000 sq km (115,800 sq miles)
Population:	105,720,644 (2013 est)
Currency:	1 Philippine peso = 100 centavos
Religions:	Roman Catholic 80.9%; Muslim 5.0%; Protestant 2.8%
Ethnic Groups:	Tagalog 28.1%; Cebuano 13.1%; Ilocano 9.0%; Bisaya 7.6%; Hiligaynon Ilonggo 7.5%; Bicol 6.0%
Languages:	English, Pilipino (based on Tagalog) (both official);

| | Tagalog; Cebuano; Ilocano; Hiligaynon; Bicol; Waray; Pampango; Pangasinan |
| International Organizations: | UN; Colombo Plan; ASEAN; Non-Aligned Movement; WTO |

A country in south-eastern Asia comprising over 7000 islands between the Pacific Ocean and the South China Sea.

Physical Luzon and Mindanao are the largest islands; in the central Philippines, the islands of Leyte and Samar are linked by a 2162 m (7095 feet) long bridge. Being at a junction of crustal plates they contain volcanoes and are subject to earthquakes; and as they are in the path of two monsoons there is rain for most of the year. The climate is tropical throughout the year. Many of the islands are mountainous and heavily forested with teak, ebony, and sandalwood. Bamboo and coconut palms grow in profusion.

Economy Agriculture is the main economic activity, with sugar cane, coconuts, rice, maize, and fruit being important crops. Coconuts and fruit are exported, but other principal exports are all products of industry: semiconductors and other electronic products, transport equipment, clothing, and copper and oil products. Other mineral resources include coal, nickel ore, chromite, iron, silver, and gold. Remittances from expatriates are important.

History The original Negrito inhabitants of the Philippines were largely displaced by waves of Malay peoples migrating from Yunnan province in south-west China after *c.*2000 BC. By 1000 AD the islands were within the south-east Asian trade network. By the 16th century Islam was advancing from Mindanao and Sulu into the central islands and Luzon. After Spaniards under *Magellan visited the islands (1521), Spanish seamen discovered how to return eastbound across the Pacific to Mexico. In 1543 they named the islands after Prince Philip (later *Philip II of Spain). In 1564 Miguel de Legazpi, with 380 men, set out from Mexico to establish a settlement, Christianize the Filipinos, open up commerce with East Asia, and secure a share of trade in the Moluccas. A settlement was made in 1565 at Cebu in the western Visayas, but the Spaniards moved their headquarters to Manila

in 1571. Manila became the centre for a trade in Chinese silks with Mexico, in return for Mexican silver dollars. From there Spanish influence and control spread out through the Philippine island chain, particularly assisted by missionary activity. Christian outposts founded by Dominicans, Franciscans, and Augustinians grew into towns. Revolts against the harsh treatment of Filipinos by the Spanish were frequent, particularly in the 17th century. During the *Seven Years War the British occupied Manila for two years.

In 1896, a nationalist uprising against the Spanish colonial authorities broke out in Manila, led by José Rizal. After the outbreak of the Spanish–American War in 1898, General Emilio *Aguinaldo, acting with the support of the USA, declared the country's independence. After Spain's defeat, however, the nationalists found themselves opposed by the Americans, and after a brief war (1899–1901), the islands passed under US control. Internal self-government was granted in 1935, and, after the Japanese occupation during World War II, the Philippines became an independent republic in 1946 under the presidency of Manuel Roxas, with the USA continuing to maintain military bases. Successive administrations proved incapable of dealing with severe economic problems and regional unrest. In 1972, using the pretext of civil unrest, in particular the communist guerrilla insurgency conducted by the New People's Army in Luzon, and violent campaigns of Muslim separatists, the Moro National Liberation Front, in the southern Philippines, President *Marcos declared martial law, assuming dictatorial powers. While the Marcos regime achieved some success in dealing with both economic problems and guerrilla activities, the return to democratic government was never satisfactorily achieved and corruption was widespread, epitomized in the amassing of huge personal fortunes by the Marcos family. After the murder of the opposition leader, Benigno Aquino Jr, in 1983, resistance to the Marcos regime coalesced behind his widow Corazon *Aquino and the United Nationalist Democratic Organization. US support for the Marcos government waned and in 1986, after a disputed election and a popularly backed military revolt, Marcos fled, and Corazon Aquino became President in his place, restoring the country to a fragile democracy. There were no fewer than six attempted military coups against President Aquino, who refused to stand for re-election. She was succeeded in 1992 by her ex-Defence Secretary Fidel Ramos, who completed arrangements for the withdrawal of US forces from Subic Bay and other military and naval installations. In 1996 a peace agreement with Muslim rebels was made. Presidential elections in 1998 were won by the left-wing Joseph Estrada. He resigned in 2001 amid allegations of bribery and corruption. He was succeeded as President by Gloria Macapagal-Arroyo, the Vice-President, who was re-elected in 2004. Political instability, allegations of corruption, and her authoritarian style of government led to two attempted coups (2003 and 2006). Benigno Aquino III, son of Benigno Jr and Corazon, was elected President in 2010.

Philippines Campaign (1944–45) The US campaign that recaptured the Philippines in World War II. In the Battle of the Philippine Sea, fought in June 1944 by aircraft carriers while US forces were securing required bases in the Marianas, the Japanese naval air service suffered crippling losses. A further Japanese naval defeat was incurred at *Leyte Gulf on 25 October, following the landing of US forces on the island five days previously. Troops landed on Luzon in January 1945 and in July General *MacArthur announced that the whole territory was liberated. However, detached groups of Japanese, in accordance with their instructions to fight to the last man, were still at large after the war ended.

Philip the Bold (1342–1404) Duke of Burgundy (1363–1404). He was the fourth son of John the Good, King of France, and was created Duke of Burgundy in 1363. In 1369 he married Margaret, heiress of the Count of Flanders. In 1380 he helped to quell a revolt by the Flemish burghers against the count, which ended in 1382 with the massacre of 26,000 Flemings. On the death of the count in 1384 Philip inherited Flanders and proceeded to encourage commerce and the arts. During the minority of Charles VI (1380–88) Philip was virtual ruler of France and, when the king became insane (1392), Philip fought for power with Louis d'Orléans, the king's brother, a quarrel carried on after Philip's death by his son, John the Fearless.

Philip the Good (or **Philip III**) (1396–1467) Duke of Burgundy (1419–67). His first act as Duke of Burgundy was to forge an alliance with *Henry V of England, signing the Treaty of Troyes, in which Queen Isabella of France named Henry V as successor to the French throne. Philip was a powerful ally: by the early decades of the 15th century his territories included Namur (acquired 1421), Holland and Zeeland (1428), Brabant (1430), Luxembourg (1435) and the bishoprics of Liège, Cambrai,

and Utrecht were under Burgundian control. Some were his by inheritance, others had come through marriage, purchase, or conquest and they combined to constitute a formidable 'state'. The Treaty of Arras (1435) released Philip from the duty of doing homage to the French king and rendered him virtually independent of royal control. However, the king of France succeeded in breaking the alliance between France and England and from 1435 France and Burgundy joined forces to wage war on England. The imposition of taxes on the Burgundians provoked a rebellion, led by Ghent, but the rebels (of whom 20,000 were killed) were defeated (1454). Philip's court in Burgundy was the most prosperous and civilized in Europe. He founded an order of *chivalry, the Order of the Golden Fleece, and patronized Flemish painters.

Philistines A non-Semitic people, originally a group of the *Sea Peoples, who settled in southern *Palestine in the 12th century BC. Having established five cities—Ashdod, Askelon, Ekron, Gath, and Gaza—they gained control of land and sea routes and proved a formidable enemy to the Israelites, inflicting defeats on Samson and Saul. King *David, however, gained decisive revenge (c.1000 BC) and from then on Philistine power declined until they were assimilated with the *Canaanites.

Phoenicians A Semitic people of ancient Phoenicia in southern Syria, of unknown origin, but culturally descended from the Canaanites of the 2nd millennium BC, who occupied the coastal plain of modern Lebanon and Syria in the 1st millennium BC and derived their prosperity from trade and manufacturing industries in textiles, glass, metalware, carved ivory, wood, and jewellery. Their trading contacts extended throughout Asia, and reached westwards as far as Africa (where they founded Carthage), Spain, and possibly Britain. The Phoenicians continued to thrive under Assyrian and then Persian suzerainty until 322 BC, when the capital, Tyre, was sacked and the country incorporated in the Greek world by Alexander the Great.

Phoenix Park murders (1882) The assassination in Phoenix Park, Dublin, of the British Chief Secretary for Ireland, Lord Frederick Cavendish, and his Under-Secretary, T. H. Burke, by the "Invincibles", a terrorist splinter group of the *Fenians. In the subsequent climate of revulsion against terrorism, *Parnell was able to gain ascendancy over the Irish National League and strengthen the moderate *Home Rule Party.

Phrygia An ancient region of west-central Asia Minor, to the south of Bithynia. Centred on the city of Gordium west of present-day Ankara, it dominated Asia Minor after the decline of the Hittites in the 12th century BC, reaching the peak of its power in the 8th century under King Midas. Conquered by the Cimmerians *c.*760 BC, it was eventually absorbed into the kingdom of Lydia in the 6th century BC.

Pibul Songgram (1897–1964) Thai statesman. A career soldier, he took part in the bloodless coup which ended absolute rule by the Chakri dynasty in 1932. Emerging as the leader of militarist nationalist forces, he became head of state in 1938 and in January 1942 brought Thailand into World War II on the Japanese side. Overthrown in 1944, he returned to power in 1948 and controlled Thailand dictatorially until 1957, taking an anti-communist line, until overthrown after the corruption of his regime had aroused widespread resentment.

Pict A member of an ancient people, of disputed origin and ethnological affinities, who formerly inhabited parts of northern Britain. In Roman writings (*c.*300 AD) *Picti* ('painted people') was used to describe the hostile tribes occupying the area north of the Antonine Wall. According to chroniclers the Pictish kingdom was united with the Scottish under *Kenneth I in 843, and the name of the Picts as a distinct people gradually disappeared.

Pierce, Franklin (1804–69) US Democratic statesman, 14th President of the USA (1853–57). His presidency saw the rise of divisions within the country over slavery and the encouragement of settlement in the north-west. His support for the Kansas–Nebraska Act lost him the support of northern Democrats and any chance of renomination in 1856.

Pilgrimage of Grace (1536–37) A series of rebellions in the northern English counties, the most significant of which was led by Robert Aske, a lawyer. He managed, briefly, to weld together the disparate grievances of his socially diverse followers. The main causes of concern were the religious policies of Thomas *Cromwell, notably the Dissolution of the *Monasteries, although the rebels stressed their loyalty to *Henry VIII. Severe retribution followed, as Henry authorized the execution of about 200 of those involved, including Aske.

Pilgrim Fathers The 102 founders of the Plymouth plantation in America, who had travelled from Plymouth in England in the *May-flower* in 1620. Some of them had been persecuted as separatists from the Church of England, and the nucleus of them had fled from Scrooby in Nottinghamshire in 1608 to Holland. In 1618 they obtained backing from a syndicate of London merchants and permission to settle in Virginia. On the voyage, having no charter, they subscribed to a covenant for self-government, the Mayflower Compact. They landed at Cape Cod, Massachusetts, in December, where they decided to settle. Only half the party survived the first winter.

Piłsudski, Joseph Klemens (1867–1935) Polish general and statesman. His involvement in early revolutionary activity against Tsarist Russia had led to his imprisonment. In World War I he raised three Polish legions to fight Russia, but German refusal to guarantee the ultimate independence of Poland led him to withdraw his support of Germany. After the war, Poland was declared independent with Piłsudski as Chief of State (1918–22) and Chief of the Army Staff (1918–27). He successfully commanded the Poles in the war against the *Bolsheviks (1920–21). In 1926, after a military revolt, he assumed the office of Minister of Defence, establishing a virtual dictatorship, and tried to guarantee Poland's independence by signing non-aggression pacts with Germany and the Soviet Union in 1934. He died in office.

Piltdown Man Supposed fossil remains 'discovered' by Charles Dawson in 1908–13 in gravels in the hamlet of Piltdown in East Sussex, England. The association of a modern-looking skull, ape-like jaw, and extinct animal bones provided just the missing link in human evolution being keenly sought at the time. It was not until 1953 that '*Eoanthropus dawsoni*' was shown by scientific tests to be a forgery.

Pinckney, Charles Cotesworth (1746–1825) US statesman. He was appointed minister to France in 1796 and a year later participated in the unsuccessful diplomatic peace mission to avert a naval war with France, known as the *XYZ Affair. Pinckney ran with John *Adams for the *Federalist Party and was the unsuccessful Federalist candidate for President in 1804 and 1808. His brother Thomas (1750–1828) was also a diplomat and was responsible for negotiating the Treaty of San Lorenzo (popularly known as Pinckney's Treaty) with Spain in 1795, winning US trading rights at New Orleans, free navigation of the Mississippi River, and an agreed southern boundary between the USA and Florida.

Pindaris Groups of mounted marauders in central India, often in the service of the *Maratha princes, who raided *Mogul territory from the 17th century. The Pindaris were not paid but were allowed to forage and plunder freely. After 1807 they extended their depredations to British India, and under Lord Hastings (governor-general 1813–23) a major campaign (*Maratha Wars) was conducted (1817–18) to wipe out the Pindaris. A campaign led by Hastings and involving three British and Indian armies advanced into central India and successfully encircled and defeated some 30,000 Pindaris. Their extirpation confirmed British paramountcy in India.

Pinkerton, Allan (1819–84) Scottish-born US detective. He emigrated to the USA in 1842, and in 1850 he established the first US private detective agency (in Chicago), becoming famous after solving a series of train robberies. In the early years of the American Civil War (1861–62) he served as chief of the secret service for the Union side. His agency was later involved in anti-trade union activity, particularly in the coal industry (1877).

Pinkie, Battle of (10 September 1547) Military engagement between the Scots and English, sometimes known as Pinkie Cleuch, which was fought to the east of Edinburgh, Scotland. A large but poorly equipped Scottish army was defeated by an English expeditionary force under the Duke of *Somerset, but the expedition failed in its purpose of engineering a marriage between *Mary, Queen of Scots and *Edward VI of England and only drove the Scots closer towards alliance with France.

Pinochet Ugarto, Augusto (1915–2006) Chilean general and statesman, President (1974–90). He became Commander-in-Chief of Chile's armed forces in 1973 and in the same year masterminded the military coup that overthrew President Allende. He imposed a repressive military dictatorship until forced to call elections (December 1989), giving way to a democratically elected President in 1990. His regime has been accused of some 3000 political murders and other abuses of human rights. While recovering from an operation in London in 1998, he was arrested pending extradition to Spain to answer murder charges. He was released in 2000 on medical grounds. Following his return to Chile, he was charged with kidnapping and murder but subsequently declared mentally unfit to be tried.

pipe-roll The financial account presented to the Exchequer by the sheriffs of England. The earliest surviving roll dates from 1130 and there is an almost unbroken series from 1156 to 1832. The rolls were compiled by the clerks of the treasury and included details of rents, leases, and other royal revenues. Their name originated with the practice of enrolling the records on a rod, or "pipe".

Pisistratus (or **Peisistratus**) (c.600–c.527 BC) Tyrant of Athens. He seized power in 561 and after twice being expelled ruled continuously from 546 until his death. As ruler he reduced aristocratic power in rural Attica and promoted the financial prosperity and cultural pre-eminence of Athens.

Pitt, William, 1st Earl of Chatham (or **Pitt the Elder**) (1708–78) British Whig statesman. He was effectively Prime Minister 1756–61 (formally under *Newcastle) and headed a further coalition 1766–68. He brought the Seven Years War to an end in 1763 by using a successful maritime strategy to defeat France. He also masterminded the conquest of French possessions overseas, particularly in Canada and India. He was the father of Pitt the Younger.

Pitt, William (or **Pitt the Younger**) (1759–1806) British statesman, Prime Minister (1783–180; 1804–06). The son of Pitt the Elder, he became Prime Minister at the age of 24, the youngest ever to hold this office. He restored the authority of Parliament, introduced financial reforms, reduced the enormous national debt he had inherited, and reformed the administration of India. With Britain's entry into war against France (1793), Pitt became almost entirely occupied with the conduct of the war and with uniting European opposition to France. Having secured the Union of Great Britain and Ireland in 1800, he resigned in 1801 over the issue of Catholic Emancipation (which George III refused to accept). He returned as Premier in 1804 after hostilities with France had been resumed, and died in office.

Pius II (born **Aeneas Silvius Piccolomini**) (1405–64) Pope (1458–64). Born of an impoverished noble family, Pius II led a dissolute life as a poet but reformed, took holy orders in 1446, and became an outstanding *humanist. He became secretary to Felix V, the *antipope, from 1439, and an ecclesiastical diplomat, to be employed by Emperor *Frederick III as secretary and poet laureate. As pope he proclaimed a *Crusade against the *Ottoman Turks (October 1458) but a congress of Christian rulers summoned to Mantua in 1459 was a failure and despite repeated attempts to launch a Crusade the enterprise came to nothing. He had to face anti-papal movements in France and Germany and frequent quarrels with local rulers prevented him from carrying out his programme of reform. He died, bequeathing the problem of the *Hussite heresy and Turkish war to his successor.

Pius V, St (born **Antonio Ghislieri**) (1504–72) Pope (1566–72). Pius V was an austere Dominican, Bishop of Nepi and Sutri (1556), cardinal (1557), and Grand Inquisitor from 1558. As pope, he laboured to restore discipline and morality with a sometimes intransigent *Counter-Reformation zeal. His ill-timed Bull calling for the deposition of *Elizabeth I of England (1570) proved ineffectual, but he had more success in helping to organize the *Holy League, whose forces defeated the Turks at *Lepanto (1571). He was canonized in 1712.

Pius VII (born **Luigi Barnaba Chiaramonti**) (1740–1823) Pope (1800–23). His predecessor, Pope Pius VI, had seen the Papal States occupied by the French and died a prisoner in France in 1799. Pius VII restored papal fortunes by signing a *Concordat with Napoleon I in 1801, which re-established the Roman Catholic faith as the national religion of France. However, his attempts to increase papal influence by refusing to support the *Continental System against Britain led to the annexation of the Papal States in 1808–09. He, too, was imprisoned by Napoleon in France, but returned in triumph after Napoleon's downfall. He renounced his earlier liberalism, condemned revolution and secret societies, and re-established the Society of Jesus (Jesuits) in 1814.

Pius IX (born **Giovanni Maria Mastai-Ferretti**) (1792–1878), Pope (1846–78). Elected as a moderate progressive, he relaxed press censorship, freed political prisoners, set up a council of ministers which included laymen, and opened negotiations for an Italian customs union. After the *Revolutions of 1848 his Prime Minister was murdered and Pius himself fled in disguise. On the establishment of a Roman republic Pius appealed to the French to come to his aid, and, with their help, he re-entered Rome, which retained a French garrison until 1870. In that year Italian forces occupied Rome, which was then incorporated into the kingdom of Italy. Despite government assurances, Pius saw himself as a prisoner in a secular state, and never set foot outside the Vatican again. In 1854 he defined the doctrine of the Immaculate

Conception of the Virgin Mary (the Mother of Jesus Christ) and encouraged the Marian cult. He presided over the First Vatican Council (1869–70), which proclaimed the infallibility of the Pope when speaking *ex cathedra*.

Pius XII (born **Eugenio Pacelli**) (1876–1958) Pope (1939–58). He upheld the neutrality of the Roman Catholic Church during World War II, maintaining diplomatic relations with both Allied and Axis governments. After the war criticism of his failure to condemn Nazi atrocities and of his apparent indifference to the plight of European Jewry persuaded the Vatican to make a formal apology in 1997. Pius XII took steps to counter the rise of communism in postwar Italy, threatening to excommunicate its supporters.

Pizarro, Francisco (*c.*1478–1541) Spanish conquistador. In 1531 he set out from Panama to conquer the Inca empire in Peru. Crossing the mountains, he defeated the Incas and in 1533 executed their emperor Atahualpa (born 1502) setting up an Inca puppet monarchy at Cuzco and building his own capital at Lima (1535). He was assassinated in Lima by supporters of his rival Diego de Almagro (1475–1538).

Pizarro, Gonzalo (*c.*1506–08) Spanish conquistador and brother of Francisco *Pizarro. He assisted his brother in the conquest of the *Incas and defended Cuzco against the attacks of Manco Capac (1536–37). In 1538 he was appointed governor of Quito. The first viceroy of Peru, Blasco Núñez Vela, proclaimed the New Laws in 1542, drafted by *Las Casas, to protect Indian rights. Gonzalo became leader of conquistadores opposed to the New Laws and in the ensuing civil war defeated and executed the viceroy in 1546. He was offered a royal pardon by the new viceroy, but rejected it, and was beheaded in 1548 after his army had deserted him.

PKI (after 1924, Partai Kommunis Indonesia) Indonesian Communist Party. Formed in 1920, the PKI was active in trade-union activities, but Dutch repression and the abortive communist uprisings in Banten and West Sumatra in 1926–27 led to its eclipse until 1945. During the 1950s, the PKI became one of the largest communist parties outside China and the Soviet Union, winning 20% of the vote in the 1955 general elections. Rivalry with the army and communist-inspired actions against Muslim landlords in Java provoked the military to move against it after the abortive left-wing coup attempt of

1965. Up to one million PKI members were killed and the party was all but wiped out.

plague A number of epidemic diseases, particularly the infectious bubonic plague caused by bacteria in fleas carried by rodents. The form known as the *Black Death swept through Europe during 1346–50: England may have lost as much as half its population, with severe long-term consequences. In 1665 London was afflicted by the *Great Plague, which carried off at least 70,000 victims.

Plaid Cymru A political party devoted to the cause of Welsh nationalism. Founded in 1925 as Plaid Genedlaethol Cymru (Welsh Nationalist Party), it seeks to ensure independent recognition for *Wales in matters relating to its culture, language, and economy. It became active in the 1960s and 1970s, but its hope that Wales would be able to have a separate representative assembly was rejected by a referendum in Wales in 1979. In 1997 a further referendum led to the establishment of a representative assembly with limited powers. Plaid Cymru participated in a Labour-led coalition Welsh government from 2007 to 2011.

Plains of Abraham, Battle of the

(13 September 1759) A battle during the *French and Indian wars that took place on a plateau above the city of Quebec, Canada. *Wolfe ferried British troops up the St Lawrence past the French fort. Having tricked the sentries into believing them to be French, the British climbed the precipitous Heights of Abraham. In the ensuing battle, the French garrison under *Montcalm was routed and Quebec surrendered. Both commanders died but the British victory ended French rule in Canada.

Plains Peoples The original inhabitants of the Plains region of North America. Traditionally, there were two main groups, sedentary farmers and nomadic hunters. The introduction of the horse in the early 18th century had a profound effect, with many peoples, such as the Sioux and the *Cree, moving into the Plains area. These equestrian nomads became adept buffalo hunters. During the winter months, the tribes split into small groups. In many tribes, like the *Iroquois, women had a high status. Among men rank was not inherited but had to be achieved through warfare, as well as through generosity towards widows and orphans. The title of chief was largely a matter of prestige, as authority was exercised by the consensus of those of high status, who would act as arbiters in dispute resolution.

Plantagenet English dynasty descended from the counts of Anjou in France and rulers of England from 1154 to 1485, when the *Tudor line began. The unusual name arose from the sprig of broom plant, *Genista*, that Geoffrey (1113–51), Count of Anjou, wore on the side of his cap. It was Geoffrey's son Henry who became *Henry II (ruled 1154–89) of England and established the Plantagenet dynasty, although it is customary to refer to the first three monarchs Henry II, *Richard I (ruled 1189–99), and *John (ruled 1199–1216), as Angevins (descendants of the House of Anjou). The line was unbroken until 1399 when *Richard II was deposed and died without an heir. The throne was claimed by Henry Bolingbroke, Earl of Lancaster, Richard's cousin and the son of *John of Gaunt (Edward III's third son). In becoming king as *Henry IV he established the *Lancastrian branch of the dynasty which was continued by *Henry V (ruled 1413–22) and *Henry VI (ruled 1422–61; 1470–71).

The second branch of the family, the House of *York, claimed the throne through Anne Mortimer, the great-granddaughter of Lionel (Edward III's second son), who had married the father of Richard, Duke of York. The Yorkist claim succeeded when Edward, Richard's son, became *Edward IV (1461–70; 1471–83) and was in turn followed by *Edward V (ruled 1483) and Richard III (ruled 1483–85). In contending for the crown the Houses of Lancaster and York and their supporters resorted to civil war, known as the Wars of the *Roses (1455–83), and to murder (of Henry VI, the Duke of Clarence, and Edward V). The Plantagenet line was ousted by *Henry VII.

plantation A farming unit for the production of one of the staple crops in the southern colonies of North America and the British West Indies. Plantation farming may also refer to any tropical crops grown elsewhere, such as rubber, beverage crops, sisal, and oil palm. In North America plantation farming became widespread due to the success of tobacco production after 1614 along with the Virginia Company's emigration inducements of 20 ha (50 acre) "headright" land grants to each passage-paying settler and grants of private estates ("particular plantations") for investors and company officers. Between 1640 and 1660 Royalists emigrated to the Chesapeake and the Caribbean to grow tobacco and sugar. The Virginia Company's landholders and the Royalists formed the dominant colonial plantation aristocracy. The pattern was copied in South Carolina where rice and indigo were raised. Small profit margins after 1600, credit-worthiness in Britain, access to navigable rivers, and influence with colonial land officers ensured that a tightly knit group of families monopolized staple production. With the increased availability of slaves, after 1650 in the Caribbean and 1700 on the mainland, larger areas could be cultivated and, because tobacco was soil-exhaustive, planters acquired huge areas for future use. Robert "King" Carter of Nomini Hall, Virginia, owned over 12,000 ha (30,000 acres) in 1732. Successful West Indian sugar planters often returned to England, leaving their estates in the hands of overseers. The larger plantations resembled small towns, with warehouses, smithies, boatyards, coopers' shops, wharves, schools, burial grounds, and slave quarters near the big house of the landowner. Following the abolition of slavery most plantations were divided into small farms but some continue to be worked by low-paid labourers.

Plassey, Battle of (23 June 1757) The village of Plassey in West Bengal, India, was the site of Robert *Clive's victory over Nawab Siraj ud-Daula, which opened the way for the *East India Company's acquisition of Bengal. Clive had prepared Siraj's elimination by buying support from his enemies, notably by promising the nawabship to Mir Jafar, a rival. In the ensuing encounter, in which he was heavily outnumbered, Clive was aided both by good luck and by Mir Jafar's defection from Siraj. After the victory Mir Jafar was made nawab, with Clive as governor.

Plataea A city in southern Boeotia, in Greece. It was helped by Athens in 519 BC to defend itself against Thebes. Hence it alone of the Greek states helped the Athenians against the Persians at the Battle of *Marathon (490), the Spartans arrived too late to take part in the battle. In 479 Plataea was the site of the crucial land battle of the *Greek–Persian wars, when Mardonius was defeated. Its citizens were given refuge by Athens in 431 following a Theban attack, and a prolonged siege (429–427) led to the capture and the execution of the garrison who failed to escape.

Plate, Battle of the River (13 December 1939) A naval action between British and German forces in the South Atlantic. It was the first major naval surface engagement of World War II, in which the German battleship *Graf Spee*, which had sunk many cargo ships, was damaged by three British cruisers and forced into the harbour of Montevideo, from which she emerged only to be scuttled by her crew on Hitler's orders.

Plato (*c*.429–*c*.347 BC) Greek philosopher. He was a disciple of Socrates and the teacher of Aristotle, and he founded the Academy in Athens. His system of thought had a profound influence on Christian theology and Western philosophy. His philosophical writings, which cover metaphysics, politics, and ethics, are presented in the form of dialogues, with Socrates as the principal speaker; they include the *Symposium* and the *Phaedo*. An integral part of his thought is the theory of 'ideas' or 'forms', in which abstract entities or *universals* are contrasted with their objects or *particulars* in the material world. Plato's political theories appear in the *Republic*, in which he explored the nature and structure of a just society. He proposed a political system based on the division of the population into three classes, determined by education rather than birth or wealth: rulers, police and armed forces, and civilians.

plebs The common people of ancient Rome, including the poor and landless. In the early republic they were excluded from office and from intermarriage with *patricians. The political history of the early republic reflects largely their increasingly organized claim for greater political participation, which was rewarded by the concession of eligibility for the consulship in 367 BC. During the 'Struggle of the Orders' in the 5th and 4th centuries BC the office of *tribune became a watchdog over the activities of the traditional *Roman Senate.

Plekhanov, Georgi Valentinovich (1857–1918) Russian revolutionary and Marxist theorist. He became a leader of the populist Land and Liberty movement in 1877, but when this turned increasingly to terrorist methods, he formed an anti-terrorist splinter group to continue mass agitation. Exiled in Geneva, he became one of the founders of the League for the Liberation of Labour, the first Russian Marxist revolutionary organization (1883), which merged (1898) with the Russian Social Democratic Workers' Party. In the 1903 split with *Lenin he supported the Mensheviks but always tried to re-unite the party. He returned to Russia in 1917, but failed to prevent the *Bolsheviks from seizing power.

Pliny (or **Pliny the Elder**; full name **Gaius Plinius Secundus**) (23–79) Roman lawyer, historian, and naturalist. Of his many works only the 37 volumes of his *Natural History* survive, a valuable compendium of ancient scientific knowledge blended with folklore and anecdote. He died while leading a rescue (and research) party on the stricken coastline near *Pompeii, during the eruption of Vesuvius.

Pliny (or **Pliny the Younger**; full name **Gaius Plinius Caecilius Secundus**) (61–112) A senator and consul, nephew of the Elder *Pliny. A close friend of *Trajan and *Tacitus, he governed Bithynia (in present-day Turkey). His 'Letters', which are really essays, give a detailed picture of the lifestyle adopted by wealthy Romans of his class. Other letters, written after 100, provide the only detailed accounts of the eruption of Vesuvius in 79, in which his uncle perished, and the devastation of Campania of which he was a youthful eyewitness.

PLO *See* PALESTINE LIBERATION ORGANIZATION.

Plotinus (*c.* 205–70 AD) Philosopher, probably of Roman descent, who was the founder and leading exponent of Neoplatonism. Neoplatonism was a religious and philosophical system based on elements from Plato, Pythagoras, Aristotle, and the Stoics, with overtones of Eastern mysticism. It was the dominant philosophy of the pagan world from the mid-3rd century AD until the closing of the pagan schools by Justinian in 529, and also strongly influenced medieval and Renaissance thought. Plotinus studied in Alexandria and later Persia before finally settling in Rome in 244 and setting up a school of philosophy. His writings were published after his death by his pupil Porphyry.

'Plug' strikes (1842) A succession of strikes accompanied by rioting in the north of England. The agitation began as a protest by Staffordshire miners against cuts in wages, but spread to industries in other parts of the country. The men involved went from factory to factory, removing the boiler plugs from steam engines so that these could not be operated by anyone else. There were also attempts to use the strike as a weapon to compel the government to accept the *Chartist petition. Hundreds of strikers were arrested and the ringleaders were transported to Australia.

Plutarch (*c.*46–126 AD) Greek writer and philosopher of wide-ranging interests. His extant works include rhetorical pieces, philosophical treatises, and, most memorably, his *Parallel Lives*, paired biographies of famous Greeks and Romans. He was concerned to highlight the personal virtues (and sometimes vices) of his subjects, and the result has been an inspiration to later writers, most notably Shakespeare in his Roman plays.

Plymouth Colony The first permanent New England settlement, on the south-eastern Massachusetts coast in Cape Cod Bay. It was settled by the *Pilgrim Fathers in 1620 and grew slowly under the leadership of William *Bradford, profiting from the fur trade with the Native Americans. Overshadowed after 1630 by Massachusetts, it joined the New England Confederation in 1643. *King Philip's War (1675–76) began on its frontier. In 1691 it was incorporated into Massachusetts.

Pocahontas (*c.*1595–1617) Native American 'princess', the daughter of Powhatan, Chief of the Indians in the region of Virginia around Jamestown, the first permanent English settlement in America. Captain John Smith claimed that she saved him from torture and death in 1607. To cement Anglo-Indian relations, she was married to the colonist John Rolfe in 1614 with the Christian name of Rebecca. He took her to England, where she was presented at court, but she died of smallpox.

pocket borough A British Parliamentary borough effectively under the control of a single wealthy individual or family. Before the 1832 *Reform Act there was no uniform basis for the parliamentary franchise in towns and the right to vote tended to be limited to a small number of people. This made it easier for a local magnate to ensure the election of any candidate he chose to put forward. The borough was thus said to be "in his pocket". Such pressure on voters was not effectively ended until the introduction of secret ballots in 1872.

pogrom (Russian, 'riot' or 'devastation') A mob attack approved or condoned by authority, frequently against religious, racial, or national minorities – most often against Jews. The first occurred in the Ukraine following the assassination of *Alexander II (1881). Subsequently there were many pogroms throughout Russia, causing many Russian Jews to emigrate to the USA and western Europe, often giving their support to *Herzl's *Zionist campaign. After the revolution of 1905, *anti-Semitic persecutions increased. Conducted on a large scale in Germany and eastern Europe after Hitler came to power they led ultimately to the *Holocaust.

Poincaré, Raymond (1860–1934) French statesman. As President (1913–20) he strove to keep France united during *World War I and in 1919 supported stringent *reparations against Germany. When Germany defaulted, he ordered French troops to occupy the Ruhr (1923) until Germany paid. He could not sustain this policy and resigned in 1924. Reappointed Premier in 1926, he lessened an acute economic crisis by introducing a deflationary policy, balancing the budget, and in 1928 he secured the franc at one-fifth of its former value.

Point Four Program A US aid project, so called because it developed from the fourth point of a programme set forth in President *Truman's 1949 inaugural address, in which he undertook to make "the benefits of America's scientific and industrial progress available for the improvement and growth of under-developed areas". From 1950 Congress annually provided technical assistance for the long-term development of industries, agriculture, health and education in developing countries. The project also encouraged the flow of private investment capital to poorer nations. In 1953 it was merged with other foreign aid programmes.

Poitiers, Battle of (19 September 1356) A battle between the English and French during the *Hundred Years War. An English and Gascon force under *Edward the Black Prince was trapped by a superior French army while raiding. The English archers defeated the French and their king, John II, was captured. The *Jacquerie revolt followed soon after.

Poland

Capital:	Warsaw
Area:	312,685 sq km (120,728 sq miles)
Population:	38,383,809 (2005)
Currency:	1 złoty = 100 groszy
Religions:	Roman Catholic 89.8%; Eastern Orthodox 1.3%; Protestant 0.3%
Ethnic Groups:	Polish 96.9%; Silesian 1.1%; German 0.2%
Languages:	Polish (official); minority languages
International Organizations:	UN; OSCE; Council of Europe; NATO; EU; OECD; WTO

A country on the North European Plain with a Baltic Sea coast and bounded by Germany on the west, Russia, Lithuania, Belarus, and Ukraine on the east, and the Czech Republic and Slovakia on the south.

Physical The North European Plain is sandy in places, marshy in others and requires careful cultivation, although inland it is well drained by the Odra (Oder), Vistula, and other rivers. There are many small forests, which increase in size as the land rises through rolling hills and richer land to the Carpathian Mountains in the south-east.

Economy Since the collapse of communism, Poland has made the transition to a market economy, aided by EU membership since 2004. However, inefficiency and rigidity remain problems. Extensive mineral resources include coal, copper, iron, silver, sulphur, lead, and natural gas, and principal industries include machine building, iron and steel, coal, chemicals, and shipbuilding. The agricultural sector produces potatoes and other vegetables, fruit, wheat, meat, eggs, and dairy products. Machinery, transport equipment, manufactured goods, food, and animals are exported.

History Poland became an independent kingdom in the 9th century and was Christianized under Miezko I (962–92). Unity was imposed under Ladislas I (1305–33) and Casimir the Great, who improved the administration, and the country's defences, and encouraged trade and industry. Jagiellon rule (1386–1572) culminated in the brief ascendancy of Protestantism, and achievement in the arts and sciences. The 16th century saw Poland at its largest, after Lithuania was incorporated (1447, 1569), stretching from the Baltic to the Black Sea. However, the weakness of a hereditary monarchy took effect and despite the victories of John Casimir (1648–68) and John Sobieski (1674–96), internal decline and foreign attack undermined Polish independence, and much territory was ceded to Sweden and Russia. Ravaged by the Great Northern War and the War of the Polish Succession, it lost its independence in the 18th century. From 1697 the Electors of Saxony took the title of king and partition between Russia, Austria, and Prussia followed in 1772. Brief resistance under *Kosciuszko resulted in two further partitions in 1793 and 1795, mainly to the benefit of Catherine the Great's Russia, and Poland became effectively a protectorate of Russia.

Following the treaties of Tilsit in 1807 Napoleon created the Grand Duchy of Warsaw, under the King of Saxony, introducing the *Code Napoléon, but retaining serfdom and the feudal nobility. The duchy collapsed after the Battle of *Leipzig and at the Congress of *Vienna, when Poland was represented by Count Czartoryski, parts of the duchy reverted to Prussia and

Austria, but the bulk became the kingdom of Poland, which had its own administration but with the Russian emperor Alexander I as king. Revolutions took place in 1830, 1846–49, and 1863. Serfdom was ended in 1864, but policies of repression followed in both Russian and Prussian Poland. This did not, however, prevent the development of political parties demanding democratic government. After World War I in 1918 full independence was granted and Poland became a republic. War against Bolshevik Russia (1920–21) was followed by the dictatorship of Marshal Pilsudski. Poland was to have access to the port of Danzig (Gdańsk) via a *Polish Corridor. The status of Danzig and the existence of this corridor provided an excuse for the Nazi invasion in 1939, which precipitated World War II. As a result of the Nazi–Soviet Pact, Poland lost territory to both countries. After 1945 two million Germans left East Prussia (now in Poland) for the Federal Republic of Germany, and Poles, mainly from those Polish territories annexed by the Soviet Union, were re-settled in their place. Following the *Warsaw Uprising a provisional Polish government was established under Red Army protection, which cooperated with *Stalin to bring the country within the Soviet bloc. Political opposition was neutralized, and in 1952 a Soviet-style constitution was adopted. In 1956 Polish workers went on strike to protest against food shortages and other restrictions. Under Wladyslaw Gomulka (1956–70) rigid control by the government was maintained, leading to further strikes (1970). The election of a Polish pope, Karol Wojtyla, as John Paul II in 1978 strengthened the influence of the *Roman Catholic Church in the country. Strikes, organized by the Free Union of the Baltic Coast resulted in the formation of *Solidarity at Gdańsk. Martial law was imposed by Prime Minister General Wojciech Jaruzelski (1981–82), military tribunals continuing to operate after it officially ended. By 1987 the government was in crisis and put forward plans for limited decentralization of the economy; the ban on Solidarity was lifted, and round-table talks with all groups, including the Roman Catholic Church, began. A new constitution was agreed and multiparty politics were legalized in 1989; in December 1990 Lech *Wałęsa was elected President. In spite of recession, a private sector in the economy grew rapidly. The influence of Solidarity began to wane, and in June 1992 Wałęsa appointed his first non-Solidarity Prime Minister, Waldemar Pawlak, of the Polish Peasant Party. In 1993 the former Communist Party emerged as the largest single party in elections, forming a government under Józef Oleksy. The last Russian troops stationed in Poland left the country in 1994. Wałęsa was defeated by the former Communist Aleksander Kwasniewski in presidential elections in 1995. Solidarity won legislative elections in 1997 and headed a coalition government led by Jerzy Buzek. Poland joined NATO in 1999. In 2001 the former Communists won parliamentary elections and Leszek Miller became Prime Minister. Poland joined the *European Union in 2004, at which point Miller resigned and was succeeded by Marek Belka. He was in turn replaced by the right-wing nationalist Kazimierz Marcinkiewicz after the 2005 parliamentary elections. Also in 2005, Lech Kaczyński was elected President. His twin brother Jarosław become Prime Minister in 2006, but was replaced by Donald Tusk at the head of a more moderate centre-right coalition after early elections in 2007. Under Tusk's government Poland was relatively lightly affected by the 2009 global recession, and he was re-elected in 2011—the first time a Polish Prime Minister had served consecutive terms since the end of communism. In 2010 President Kaczyński and leading Polish figures were killed in a plane crash while visiting the site of the *Katyn massacre.

Pole, Reginald (1500–58) English cardinal and Archbishop of Canterbury. He held a *Yorkist claim to the throne of England through his mother, the Countess of Salisbury. This high birth, combined with his devotion to Roman Catholicism, made him very important in the eyes of foreign rulers during the English Protestant Reformation. After 1532 he lived abroad, disenchanted with *Henry VIII's marital and religious policies. He was made a cardinal (1536), and urged France and Spain to invade England in the name of Catholicism. Henry revenged himself on Pole's relatives, executing his brother and his aged mother. In 1554 he returned to England. His task was to assist the new queen, *Mary I, in her *Counter-Reformation programme. As Archbishop of Canterbury he began to lay the foundations of a revived Catholicism, although he seems to have disapproved of Mary's persecution of Protestants, and his work did not survive after his death.

police state A state in which a national police organization, often secret, is under the direct control of an authoritarian government, whose political purposes it serves, sometimes to the extent of becoming a state within a state. The inhabitants of a police state experience restrictions on their mobility, and on their freedom to express or communicate political or other views, which are subject to police monitoring or enforcement. In some cases, the exercise of police control is supported by systems, such as internal passports or internal exile, or by punishment camps. There is also often a strict system of censorship and extensive secrecy.

polis (plural *poleis*) The Ancient Greek city-state. The *polis* may have first emerged in the 8th century BC as a reaction to the rule of the early "kings". There were several hundred *poleis* in ancient Greece, many very small. Each consisted of a single walled town surrounded by countryside, which might include villages. At its centre was the *citadel and the agora (the marketplace). In the *Athenian democracy, which exemplified the *polis* in its highest form, power lay only in the hands of the citizen body, from which, for instance, women, resident foreigners, and slaves were excluded. Freedom, self-reliance, and autonomy were the ideals of the *polis*, but these aspirations were responsible for the innumerable wars between the Greek *poleis*. Even temporary unity in the face of a foreign invader, whether Persian or Macedonian, was very hard to achieve. The rise of the Hellenistic kingdoms at the end of the 4th century BC limited the power of the *polis*.

Polish Corridor A former region of Poland, which extended northwards to the Baltic coast and separated East Prussia from the rest of Germany. A part of Polish Pomerania in the 18th century, the area had since been subject to German colonization. It was granted to Poland after World War I to ensure Polish access to the coast. Its annexation by Germany in 1939, with the German occupation of the rest of Poland, precipitated World War II. After the war the area was restored to Poland.

Polish Succession, War of the (1733–38) A conflict between Russia and Poland on one side and France. It began after the death of *Augustus II the Strong: Austria, Russia, and Prussia supported the candidature of his son, while the French supported Stanislaus Leszczyński, the father-in-law of *Louis XV. Stanislaus was elected but was driven out by Russian troops and Augustus III became king (1733–63). There was fighting in Italy between Austria and Spain, supported by France, and Austria was driven from south Italy. Negotiations began in 1735, though the final treaty was not signed until 1738. Naples and Sicily went to the Spanish Bourbon, Don Carlos; Austria retained Milan and Mantua and acquired Parma; Francis, Duke of Lorraine became Duke of Tuscany, and Lorraine went to Stanislaus (it was to come to

France on his death); France accepted the *Pragmatic Sanction. The war, which began in Poland, chiefly affected Italy and France.

Politburo The highest policy-making committee of the former USSR and its satellites. The Soviet Politburo was founded, together with the Ogburo (Organizational Bureau), in 1917 by the *Bolsheviks to provide leadership during the *Russian Revolution. Both bureaux were later re-formed to control all aspects of Soviet life.

Polk, James Knox (1795–1849) US Democratic statesman, 11th President of the USA (1845–49). His term of office resulted in major territorial additions to the USA: Texas was admitted to the Union in 1845, and the successful outcome of the conflict with Mexico resulted in the annexation of California and the south-west two years later.

poll tax A tax levied on every poll (or head) of the population. Poll taxes were granted by the English House of Commons in 1377, 1379, and 1380. The third of these poll taxes, for one shilling from every man and woman, was acknowledged as a cause of the *Peasants' Revolt. The community charge (1988–93) was a poll tax replacing domestic rates. However, its unpopularity was a major cause of the downfall of Margaret Thatcher. In 1993 it was replaced by the council tax.

Pol Pot (born **Saloth Sar**) (*c.*1925–98) Cambodian Communist leader, Prime Minister (1976–79). From 1968 he led the Khmer Rouge, becoming Prime Minister soon after its seizure of power in 1975. During his regime the Khmer Rouge embarked on a brutal reconstruction programme in which more than 2 million Cambodians died. Overthrown by a Vietnamese invasion in 1979, Pol Pot led the Khmer Rouge in a guerrilla war against the new Vietnamese-backed government from his exile in Thailand. Following a split in the Khmer Rouge, he was captured by his former colleagues in 1997 and sentenced to life imprisonment: the cause of his death is unknown.

Poltava, Battle of (1709) The decisive victory of *Peter I (the Great) of Russia over *Charles XII of Sweden in the *Northern War. Aided by the support of the Cossack hetman (leader) Mazeppa (1644–1709) together with 5000 of his men, the Russians succeeded in defeating the Swedes at Poltava, near Kiev.

Polybius (*c.*200–*c.*118 BC) Greek historian. After an early political career in Greece, he was deported to Rome. His 40 books of *Universal*

History (only partially extant) chronicled the rise of the Roman Empire from 220 to 146 BC.

Polynesians Inhabitants of the islands of the eastern central Pacific, from Hawaii to Easter Island and New Zealand. They show close affinity in physical features, language, and culture, and probably spread from a focal centre in the area of Samoa and Tonga within the past 3000–2000 years. The principal immigration of *Maoris from the Marquesas into New Zealand is dated to about 1350 AD, though it was not the first. The origins of Polynesians are controversial. Some authorities, on the basis of their fair skin coloration, wavy hair, and stocky build relate them to the *Caucasoids; they have also been regarded as close to the Melanesians. Probably the widest held view is that they are a distant offshoot of a *Mongoloid population in south-east Asia.

Pombal, Sebastião José de Carvalho e Mello, Marquis of (1699–1782) Portuguese statesman. He was made Minister of Foreign Affairs and War in Portugal on the accession of José I in 1750; the king's indolence gave him control of the country. He regarded the dominance of the church as the chief reason for the retardation of Portugal. He suppressed the Jesuit missions established in South America (part of the *Portuguese empire), and in September 1759 expelled the Jesuits from Portugal. He also brought the *Inquisition under the control of the state. In 1755 when an earthquake devastated Lisbon, Pombal organized relief work and the rebuilding of the city. Although his reduction of ecclesiastical influence was held to be part of the *Enlightenment, Pombal had little interest in reform.

Pomerania A territory around the River Oder with the Baltic to the north. Its name derives from a Slav tribe that settled there in the 5th century. From 1062 to 1637 it enjoyed much independence, ruled by its dukes, but after the Peace of Westphalia in 1648 it was divided between Sweden and Brandenburg. In 1720 Prussia acquired most of Swedish Pomerania.

Pompadour, Jeanne Antoinette Poisson, Marquise de (1721–1764) Mistress of *Louis XV of France from 1745. She came from the world of wealthy officials and bankers, and was a lively witty woman, on friendly terms with the *philosophes* of the *Enlightenment. The people blamed her for the extravagance of the court and the disasters of the *Seven Years War, but her political influence has probably been exaggerated.

Pompeii An ancient city in western Italy, south-east of Naples. The life of the city came to an abrupt end following an eruption of Mount Vesuvius in 79 AD, as described by Pliny the Younger (and in which his uncle, the Elder Pliny, perished). The city lay buried for centuries beneath several metres of volcanic ash until excavations of the site began in 1748. The well-preserved remains of the city include not only buildings and mosaics but wall-paintings, furniture, graffiti, and the personal possessions of the inhabitants, providing an unusually vivid insight into the life, art, and architecture of the period.

Pompey (or **Pompey the Great**; full name **Gnaeus Pompeius Magnus**) (106–48 BC) Roman general and statesman. His greatest achievements were the suppression of the Mediterranean pirates (66), and the defeat of Mithridates in the east (63). He formed the First Triumvirate with Caesar and Crassus in 60, but disagreement with Caesar resulted in civil war. Pompey was defeated at the battle of Pharsalus, after which he fled to Egypt, where he was murdered.

Pompidou, Georges (Jean Raymond) (1911–74) French statesman. He served in the *resistance movement in World War II and, from 1944, became an aide and adviser to *de Gaulle. While the latter was President, Pompidou held the post of Prime Minister (1962–68) and played an important part in setting up the Evian Agreements. The strikes and riots of 1968 prompted de Gaulle's resignation (1969) and Pompidou was elected President. In a swift and decisive policy change he devalued the franc, introduced a price freeze, and lifted France's veto on Britain's membership of the *European Economic Community.

Ponce de León, Juan (*c.*1460–1521) Spanish explorer. He accompanied Columbus on his second voyage to the New World in 1493 and later became governor of Puerto Rico (1510–12). He landed on the coast of Florida in 1513, claiming the area for Spain and becoming its governor the following year.

Pontiac (*c.*1720–69) Leader of a Native American tribal confederacy, and chief of the Ottawa Indians, for many years allies of the French. After the French defeat in 1759 and British occupation of their forts, he managed to confederate many Algonquian tribes, fearful of British expansion and intransigence. Spurred by religious enthusiasm, Ottawa, Ojibwa, Potawatomi, Wyandot, Shawnee, and Delaware tribesmen rose in a concerted frontier attack from the Great Lakes to Virginia in May 1763. Only Detroit and Fort Pitt held out and 200 settlers were killed, many in western Pennsylvania. British punitive expeditions weakened the confederacy, and in 1766 Pontiac made peace. He was murdered in 1769 near St Louis by hired Indian assassins.

Pony Express (1860–61) Horse-borne mail delivery system in the 19th-century US west. It was founded in 1860 by the Missouri freight company of Russell, Majors, and Waddell to prove that there was a viable alternative to the southern route into California for the transportation of overland mail. It operated between St Joseph, Missouri, and Sacramento, California, using a relay of fresh ponies and riders, and took two weeks to cover the full distance of nearly 3200 km (2000 miles). High costs made the operation unprofitable, and the coming of the telegraph made it unnecessary.

Poor Laws Legislation that provided the basis for organized relief and welfare payments, originating in England in the 16th century. They gradually reduced the charitable obligations placed upon ecclesiastical institutions, guilds, and other private benefactors in the Middle Ages. With the Dissolution of the *Monasteries an important source of charity was abolished. Originally only those physically incapable were deemed worthy of charity and able-bodied beggars were dealt with harshly. However, a statute passed in 1576 recognized that men fit and willing to work might be genuinely unable to find employment and were in need of support. Three categories of poor were subsequently recognized: sturdy beggars or vagabonds, regarded as potential troublemakers, the infirm, and the deserving unemployed. In 1834 a Poor Law Amendment Act tried to end the giving of assistance outside the workhouse; it established the principle that all citizens should have the right to relief from destitution through accommodation. The workhouses were run by locally elected Boards of Guardians, who raised money through a poor-rate. The system proved inadequate in the growing cities, where the Guardians sometimes resorted to relief without the guarantee of accommodation. The Poor Law was gradually dismantled by social legislation of the 20th century, particularly that of the Liberal governments (1906–14) by important Acts in 1927, 1929 (when Boards of Guardians were abolished), 1930, 1934 (when Unemployment Assistance Boards were created), by social

security legislation following the *Beveridge Report (1942), and by the establishment of the *welfare state.

pope *See* PAPACY.

Popish Plot (1678) An alleged conspiracy by Roman Catholics to kill Charles II of England and replace him as king by his Roman Catholic brother, James, Duke of York. The plot was invented by Titus Oates, an Anglican priest, who asserted that a massacre of Protestants and the burning of London were imminent. The plot achieved credibility because of *Shaftesbury's willingness to use Oates as a means to secure James's exclusion from the throne. A nationwide panic ensued during which more than 80 innocent people were condemned before Oates was discredited. He was punished for perjury, but survived to receive a pension from *William III.

Popular Front A political coalition of left-wing parties in defence of democratic forms of government believed threatened by right-wing fascist attacks. Such coalitions were made possible by the strategy adopted by the *Comintern in 1934. In France such an alliance gained power after elections in 1936, under the leadership of Léon *Blum, who implemented a programme of radical social reforms. In Spain the Popular Front governments of Azaña, Caballero, and Negrín were in office from 1936 to 1939, and fought the *Spanish Civil War against *Franco and the Nationalists. A Popular Front government ruled in Chile (1938–47).

Populist Movement (Russia) A group of agrarian socialists in Russia devoted to radical reform and government by small economic units resembling village communes. The movement was active in the latter half of the 19th century, first under the name of Land and Liberty, when members such as *Herzen, *Bakunin, Lavrov, *Plekhanov, and Chernyshevsky advocated the overthrow of the Tsarist regime, being dissatisfied with government reforms; radicals were soon persecuted by the police. In 1879 the most radical wing of the Populist group re-formed under the name of the People's Will Movement and began to adopt terrorist tactics that culminated, two years later, in the assassination of *Alexander II.

Populist Party (USA) A US agrarian organization that began in 1889 as a grouping of southern and western interests seeking to remedy the lot of debtor farmers. It drew on the *Granger Movement, the Farmers' Alliances, the

Greenbacks, and other protest groups who met in Cincinnati to create the People's Party of the USA. Its members called for a flexible currency system under government control, a graduated income tax, and political reforms including direct election of US Senators. In 1892 its candidate for President, James B. Weaver, won over a million popular and 22 electoral votes. The movement then went into decline, largely because its objectives seemed more likely to be realized by other parties.

Portal, Charles Frederick Algernon, Viscount Portal of Hungerford (1893–1971)
British marshal of the Royal Air Force. In 1915 he joined the Royal Flying Corps and by 1937 he was an air vice-marshal and Director of Organization at the Air Ministry. In 1940 he was placed in charge of Bomber Command. The aircraft available had technical deficiencies, especially in navigation, but by carrying the *bombing offensive into Germany, they disrupted munitions factories, power plants, and railway junctions. While introducing technical improvements, he pressed for a policy of "area bombing" to replace that of specific targets. After the war he became Controller of Atomic Energy in Britain (1945–51).

Porteous Riots
A series of disturbances that took place in Edinburgh, Scotland, in 1736. Crowds had rioted during the hanging of a smuggler, and Captain John Porteous of the Edinburgh city guard tried to restore order by opening fire, killing several people. As a result he was condemned to death, but reprieved. An orderly crowd then attacked his prison, dragged him out, and lynched him on the day originally appointed for his execution; for this outrage Edinburgh was fined £2000 and the Lord Provost was removed from office.

Portsmouth, Treaty of (1905)
The treaty that ended the *Russo-Japanese War (1904–05). Although the Russians had been decisively defeated on land and at sea in 1904, it was the intervention of the US President Theodore *Roosevelt that finally brought a successful end to the Russo-Japanese War. The treaty, signed at Portsmouth, New Hampshire, allowed for the mutual evacuation of Manchuria but granted Japan railway rights in southern Manchuria, Russian acknowledgement of Japanese supremacy in Korea, and the ceding to Japan of the Liaodong Peninsula (including Port Arthur, now Lüshun) and the southern half of Sakhalin. Russian eastward expansion was thus halted and Japanese hegemony in north-east Asia confirmed.

Portugal

Capital:	Lisbon
Area:	92,090 sq km (35,556 sq miles)
Population:	10,799,270 (2013 est)
Currency:	1 euro = 100 cents
Religions:	Roman Catholic 81.0%; other Christian 3.3%
Ethnic Groups:	Portuguese; small African and East European minorities
Languages:	Portuguese, Mirandese (both official)
International Organizations:	UN; OECD; NATO; Council of Europe; EU; OSCE; WTO

A west European country on the Atlantic west coast of the Iberian peninsula, flanked by Spain on the north and east. The Atlantic archipelago of the Azores and Madeira are also part of Portugal.

Physical Half of the country lies on the edge of the high and ancient Iberian plateau, in a region of rugged hills, lakes, and deep gorges. Much of the region is covered with forests, and from it flow three great rivers—the Douro, Tagus, and Guadiana—which water the flat coastal plain, where vineyards, cereals, and citrus fruits flourish.

Economy One of the poorest countries in Western Europe, Portugal has a mixed economy with a large agricultural sector; fishing is also important. Principal crops include grain, potatoes, and fruit; livestock are also kept. Pyrites forms the country's main mineral resource, although there are also deposits of several other metallic ores. Industries include textiles and clothing, wood, cork (of which Portugal is the world's leading producer), paper, chemicals, vehicle components, base metals, food products, shipbuilding, and tourism. Exports include agricultural, food, oil, and chemical products, plastic, rubber, hides and leather, wood, and cork.

History Portugal was settled by Celtic tribes from c.500 BC, and during Roman domination was known as 'Lusitania'. Periods of Gothic and Moorish control followed the collapse of the Western Roman empire, and Portugal struggled to develop a distinct identity until the papacy recognized the kingship of Alfonso I in 1179. In 1249 the Portuguese completed the reconquest of their country from the *Moors. Then, after a series of unsuccessful wars against Castile, peace was at last concluded in 1411, and under the ruling house of Avis (1385–1580) the vast overseas Portuguese empire took shape. On the expiry of the Avis dynasty, *Philip II of Spain became king by force. The Spanish union lasted until 1640, when the native House of *Braganza was swept to power by a nationalist revolt. During the relatively peaceful and prosperous 18th century, close links were established with England. In the wake of the disastrous Lisbon earthquake (1755) the dynamic minister Pombal exercised the powers of an enlightened despot. During the *Napoleonic Wars the Prince Regent John (King John VI from 1816), together with the Braganza royal family, fled to Brazil. Here he met demands for political and economic freedom, Brazil emerging peacefully as an independent empire in 1822. Through most of the rest of the 19th century there was considerable political instability until 1910, when a republic was established. In 1926 there was a military coup which was followed in 1932 by the establishment of *Salazar as Prime Minister, Minister of Finance, and virtual dictator (1932–68), strongly supported by the Roman Catholic Church. Portugal supported the Allies in World War I and in World War II remained theoretically neutral while allowing the Allies naval and air bases. Goa, Diu, and Damao were lost to India in the 1960s, but Macao in South China was retained. Salazar's autocratic policies were continued by Marcello Caetano until a military coup in 1974. Increasingly bitter guerrilla warfare had developed in Portuguese Africa, especially in *Angola and *Mozambique. These gained independence in 1975, although both experienced civil war, while the state of *Guinea-Bissau was created in 1974. After two years of political instability at home, a more stable democracy began to emerge following the election of Antonio Eanes as President in 1976. Moderate coalition governments both left and right of centre have alternated, all struggling with severe economic problems. President Mario Soares was elected in 1986, having been Prime Minister since 1983. He was re-elected President in 1991, with Anibal Cavaço Silva of the Social Democrat Party as Prime Minister. Portugal joined the European Community in 1986. In the general election of 1995, the Socialist Party under António Guterres won power. He resigned in 2001 and, after elections in 2002, José Manuel Barroso of the Social Democrat Party became Prime Minister. Portugal adopted the *euro as

its currency in 2002. Barroso was succeeded in 2004 by Pedro Santana Lopes, who lost the 2005 election to the Socialist Party under José Sócrates. Despite increasing economic difficulties following the *Credit Crunch, the Socialists were re-elected as a minority government in 2009. However, Portugal's public debt—already large (see EUROZONE CRISIS)—expanded rapidly as the government tried to stimulate the economy; and in 2010 the global financial markets lost confidence in its sustainability and Portugal's credit rating was downgraded. The government introduced tax rises and spending cuts, but these were not sufficient to satisfy the markets. A proposed second round in 2011 was defeated in Parliament and Sócrates resigned. While awaiting elections his caretaker government negotiated a bailout package with the EU and IMF. The elections resulted in a centre-right coalition under Pedro Passos Coelho, which aimed to fulfil or even exceed the spending cuts and other structural reforms demanded by the bailout terms. These policies and the resulting increased unemployment led to popular protests in 2012. Thereafter the position improved slowly, with Portugal again able to borrow on the global financial markets in 2013.

Portuguese empire The overseas territories accruing to Portugal as a result of the country's leadership of the first phase of European overseas expansion, beginning in the 15th century. Portuguese imperialism was stimulated by a scientific interest in maritime exploration, a desire to profit from the spice trade of the Orient, and a determination to spread the Christian religion in non-Christian lands. By about 1530 the Portuguese empire included the islands of Cape Verde, Madeira, and the Azores, a large part of *Brazil, fortress settlements in East and West Africa, continuous stretches of the coastlines of Angola and *Mozambique, Indian Ocean bases like Ormuz, Goa, Calicut, and Colombo, and scattered Far Eastern posts including those in the Moluccas, Macao, the Celebes, Java, and Malacca.

The empire's wealth derived mainly from coastal entrepôts and its representatives often had to face highly developed Muslim civilizations. Thus, except in Brazil, there was little conquest or colonization along the lines of the contemporary *Spanish empire. The Portuguese crown was slower than the Spanish to establish a bureaucratic system of administration, but from 1643 the Overseas Council performed a similar role to that of the Spanish Council of the Indies. At the colonial level, however, the various viceroys, governors, and captains-general retained considerable freedom of action. The empire enriched Lisbon, the court, and an increasingly foreign merchant community, but little of the new wealth was reinvested in the mother country. During the 17th century the *Dutch empire in Asia was assembled largely at the expense of the Portuguese.

Potatau Te Wherowhero (died 1860) *Maori leader. Widely respected for his chiefly status, learning, and warrior prowess, Potatau was chosen in 1858 by Waikato and central North Island tribes as their first king in the hope of uniting all the Maori tribes. Potatau supported the *Kingitanga's moves to resist land selling and to secure recognition from the government of *rangatiratanga* (chieftainly authority). Up to his death he tried to avoid involving the Kingitanga directly in the *Taranaki war, which broke out in 1860. Potatau's lineal descendants still head the Kingitanga.

Potemkin, Gregory (1739–91) Russian soldier and favourite of *Catherine II. He was a man of great energy and an able administrator, who extended Russian rule in the south, carried out a series of army reforms, annexed the Crimea in 1783, and built a Black Sea fleet and a naval base at Sevastopol. In the war with the Turks he was made army commander and died in a year of Russian military victory. The battleship named after this soldier is famous for the mutiny that occurred on it in 1905. This incident persuaded the Emperor to agree to the election of a Duma.

potlatch A ritual based on gift exchange found among Native Americans of the north-west Pacific region. Potlatches were ritual feasts in which competitors for positions of status sought to outdo each other by giving ever more lavish gifts. The arrival of Europeans in the area during the 19th century, and the changes this brought to the local economy, caused a huge escalation in the scale of potlatches. Large quantities of European trade goods such as blankets were not only given away but were also publicly destroyed to force a rival to equal the gesture.

Potsdam Conference (17 July–2 August 1945) The last of the World War II summit conferences. Held in the former Hohenzollern palace at Potsdam, outside Berlin, the conference was attended by *Churchill (replaced by *Attlee during its course), *Stalin, and *Truman. It implicitly acknowledged Soviet predominance in eastern Europe by, among other things, accepting Polish and Soviet administration of certain German territories, and by agreeing to the transfer of the ten million or so German people in these territories and other parts of eastern Europe to Germany. It established a Council of Foreign Ministers to handle peace treaties, made plans to introduce representative and elective principles of government in Germany, discussed *reparations, outlawed the Nazi Party, de-monopolized much of German industry, and decentralized its economy. The final agreement, vaguely worded and tentative, was consistently breached in the aftermath of German surrender, as the communist and capitalist countries polarized into their respective blocs. The Potsdam Declaration (26 July 1945) demanded from Japan the choice between unconditional surrender or total destruction.

Potter, Beatrice *See* WEBB, SIDNEY.

Powhatan Chief of the Native American Algonquin tribes of central coastal Virginia in 1607, when the English settlers arrived to found Jamestown. Earlier contacts with the Algonquin had been made in 1570–71 and 1588 by the Spanish, and in 1584–86 by the English. During the early 17th century Powhatan's position was strengthened by wars of expansion. His daughter *Pocahontas intervened to save the captured John *Smith and was herself held hostage by the English to force their policy on her father.

Poynings' Law (1494) An act of the Irish Parliament, properly called the Statutes of Drogheda, named after Sir Edward Poynings, Lord Deputy of Ireland (1494–95). By its terms, the Parliament was to meet only with the English king's consent, and its legislative programme had to be approved in advance by the English king. It was intended to bolster English sovereignty and destroy Yorkist influence. It soon became a major grievance to Irish parliamentarians, but it was not until 1782 that Henry *Grattan managed to have it repealed.

Praemunire, Statute of (1353) English anti-papal legislation. Like the **Statute of Provisors** (1351), it resulted from a nationalism and anti-papalism that was widespread in later 14th-century England and was designed to protect rights claimed by the English crown against encroachment by the papacy. It was a powerful weapon for the English king; it was used, for instance, to prevent Bishop Henry *Beaufort from becoming papal legate in England and *Henry VIII several times resorted to it.

praetorian Originally a bodyguard for a Roman general or 'praetor'. In 27 BC *Augustus established nine cohorts of such troops in and near Rome. They were an élite, better paid than legionaries, serving shorter engagements and with many privileges. They also became 'king makers' since their support was essential for gaining high political office. At least four prefects became emperor before *Constantine abolished them early in the 4th century.

Pragmatic Sanction An imperial or royal ordinance issued as a fundamental law. The term was employed to denote an arrangement defining the limits of the sovereign power of a prince, especially in matters of the royal succession. The **Pragmatic Sanction of Bourges**, issued by the French clergy in July 1438, upheld the rights of the French church to administer its temporal property independently of the papacy and disallowed papal nominations to vacant benefices and church livings. In April 1713 the Habsburg emperor Charles VI promulgated a Pragmatic Sanction in an attempt to ensure that all his territories should pass undivided to his children. By 1720 it was clear that his daughter *Maria Theresa would be the heiress and Charles spent his last years in obtaining guarantees of support from his own territories and the major powers of Europe. On his death in 1740 the failure of most of these powers to keep their promises led to the War of the *Austrian Succession.

Prague, Defenestration of (1618) An act of rebellion by Bohemian Protestant nobles against Catholic *Habsburg rule. The Defenestration of Prague was the ejection of two imperial representatives and a Secretary from a window of the Hradčany Castle in Prague. It precipitated the beginning of the *Thirty Years War and, following the Habsburg victory at the Battle of White Mountain (1620), near Prague, the city underwent enforced Catholicization and Germanization. In 1635, during the Thirty Years War, the **Peace of Prague** reconciled the German princes to the emperor.

Prasad, Rajendra (1884–1963) Indian nationalist politician. A lawyer by profession, he began working with Mohandas *Gandhi in 1917. He was imprisoned by the British (1942–45) for supporting the *Congress opposition to the British war effort in World War II. He represented the conservative wing within Congress, of which he was President on four occasions between 1932 and 1947. Prasad became President of India (1950–62) when the republic was proclaimed.

prehistory The history of the time before written records were kept. The only source of evidence concerning early societies is archaeological. It thus covers an immense period that begins with the study of early hominids and the emergence of *Homo sapiens*. It is divided into the *Stone Age (*Palaeolithic, *Mesolithic, and *Neolithic), the *Bronze Age, and the *Iron Age. History, based on written records began c.3000 BC in Egypt and Mesopotamia.

Prempeh I (died 1931) African leader, Asantehene (Chief) of the *Asante. He was elected in 1888, but deposed by the British in 1896. In 1924 he was allowed to return to Kumasi and in 1926 was installed as Kumasihene, a simple divisional chief. On his death in 1931 his nephew, Prempeh II, was elected Kumasihene, and then Asantehene in 1935, when the Golden Stool, symbolic of Asante power, was returned by the British and the traditional Asante Confederacy was restored.

pressgang A detachment of sailors empowered to seize men for service in the British navy. The use of the pressgang had been sanctioned by law since medieval times but the practice was at its height in the 18th century. All able-bodied men were liable for impressment, although in fact the pressgangs confined their attention to the seaport towns, where they were able to find recruits with suitable experience. The navy continued to rely on the pressgangs until the 1830s, when improvements in pay and conditions provided sufficient volunteers. The system was also used to a lesser extent by the army but discontinued after 1815.

Prester John (from Greek *presbyter*, 'priest') A legendary Christian ruler to whom successive generations of Crusaders looked for help against the growing power of Islam. First mentioned in a 12th-century German chronicle, he was variously identified as a Chinese prince, the ruler of Ethiopia, and, in a papal appeal of 1177, as 'illustrious and magnificent King of the Indies'.

Preston, Battle of (17–19 August 1648) An encounter in Lancashire that effectively ended the second phase of the *English Civil War. On one side were the invading Scottish Engagers under the Duke of *Hamilton and on the other was Cromwell's *New Model Army. The raw Scottish recruits, although greatly superior in numbers, were no match for the English veterans. Cromwell caught up with them at Preston and dispersed them in a series of running battles.

Prestonpans, Battle of (21 September 1745) A military engagement during the *Forty-Five Rebellion on the Scottish coast 14.5 km (9 miles) east of Edinburgh. It resulted in a famous *Jacobite victory, when Bonnie Prince Charlie's untrained Scots met Sir John Cope's professional royalist forces and surprisingly routed them in little more than five minutes. The victory attracted many recruits to the Young *Pretender's standard and paved the way for his invasion of England.

pretender A person who puts themself forward as having a rightful claim to someone else's throne. False claims have been put forward by such pretenders as Lambert *Simnel and Perkin *Warbeck, who claimed the crown of *Henry VII of England, and *Pugachev during the reign of *Catherine II the Great of Russia.

In England the Stuart Pretenders were excluded from the throne because of their religion. The **Old Pretender**, James Edward Stuart (1688–1766), was the son of the exiled *James II and in the eyes of loyal *Jacobites became King of England on his father's death in 1701. He was a devout but unimaginative man who failed to win the affection even of his followers. Two Jacobite rebellions, the *Fifteen and the *Forty-Five, were organized by his supporters to accomplish his restoration, but he arrived in Scotland when the Fifteen was virtually over, and he entrusted the leadership in the Forty-Five Rebellion to his son Charles Edward, **the Young Pretender** (1720–88). Charles Edward (Bonnie Prince Charlie) had youth and charm, and aroused loyal devotion to his cause, but the Forty-Five was a failure, and Charles's career after his miraculous escape from Scotland was an anti-climax, marred by moral and physical decline.

Pretorius, Andries (Wilhelmus Jacobus) (1798–1853) Boer leader and general. After several frontier campaigns against the Xhosa he took part in the *Great Trek, and became commandant-general of the Boers after Piet Retief's murder (1838). He defeated the Zulu at the *Blood River (1838). In 1847 he organized protests against the British annexation of the land between the Orange and Vaal, but in 1848 he was defeated at Boomplaats by Sir Harry Smith, when the Orange River Sovereignty was established. In 1852 he was instrumental in negotiating the Sand River Convention, which recognized the land beyond the Vaal as the South African Republic.

Pretorius, Marthinus Wessel (1819–1901) Boer statesman. He was President of the South African Republic (1857–71), having followed his father, Andries *Pretorius, in the *Great Trek. After fighting the *Zulu, he became one of the four Transvaal commandant-generals, and was elected President. He was also elected President of the Orange Free State (1859–63). His claim to diamond fields (1867) on the Vaal River brought him into conflict with British interests. Following the annexation of the Transvaal by Britain in 1877 he was imprisoned. With the outbreak of the First *Boer War (1880–81) he proclaimed with *Kruger and Joubert a new Boer republic (January 1881). After the victory of Majuba Hill, he was a signatory of the Treaty of Pretoria, which re-established the independent states of Transvaal and Orange Free State.

Pride's Purge (6 December 1648) An English army coup in the aftermath of the *English Civil War, in which Members of Parliament (the exact number is uncertain but it was more than 100) who wished to reach an agreement with Charles I were forcibly excluded from the House of Commons by Colonel Thomas Pride, a Puritan army officer. The remaining members continued to sit in the Commons, forming the *Rump Parliament.

primary elections Elections for the selection of a political party's candidates for public office, most significantly for the US presidency. They are held by the state and the results are legally binding. There are both 'open' and 'closed' presidential primaries. In the former, any adult voter in a state may take part, regardless of his or her own party preference. In the latter, only those who are registered members of the party may vote.

Primo de Rivera, Miguel (1870–1930) Spanish general and statesman, head of state (1923–30). He came to power after leading a military coup in 1923, when he assumed dictatorial powers with the consent of Alfonso XIII. The decline of the economy contributed to his forced resignation in 1930. His son, José Antonio Primo de Rivera (1903–36), founded the Falange in 1933 and was executed by Republicans in the Spanish Civil War.

primogeniture The right of an eldest son to succeed to the estate of his father to the exclusion of all his siblings. It was developed in western Europe and introduced in England in the late 11th century by Norman lawyers as a means of preserving intact the landed wealth of the *barons, as the basis of their military service to the crown. As part of the *feudal system, primogeniture maintained the political and social status of the aristocracy. Although it was subsequently extended, it never applied to personal or movable property; where previous practice had been for lands to descend to females, then such lands continued to be divided equally amongst the children. Other exceptions to the practice of primogeniture included burghs and the county of Kent, where an alternative system of inheritance existed, known as **gavelkind**, under which land was divided equally between all sons. Despite the Statute of Wills (1540), which permitted the disinheriting of an oldest son, primogeniture survived in England until 1926 and in Scotland until 1964 and it continues to apply specifically to inheritances of the crown and of most peerages.

Primrose League An organization founded by Sir Drummond Wolf and Lord Randolph *Churchill in 1883, devoted to the cause of Tory democracy. The League used the emblem of *Disraeli's favourite flower to focus on his concept of Conservatism. This involved defence of traditional features of British life, but also a wish to broaden support for Conservatism by showing its capacity to improve living and working conditions for the masses.

Princely States More than 500 Indian kingdoms and principalities that existed during the *British Raj period (1858–1947). Although their rulers preserved some autonomy they were bound by treaty to the British. The states, although scattered, made up two-fifths of India's territory. Their princes were Hindu, Muslim, and a few Sikh and Buddhist, some, like those of Hyderabad and Kashmir, ruling majorities of other faiths. Most ruled autocratically, but a few, like Mysore, were regarded as progressive. Many princes had been forced to accept indirect British rule during the era of *East India Company expansion and paramountcy between 1757 and 1857. Mutual rivalries, historical, religious, and social, prevented coordinated resistance to British predominance. After 1857, when control of India passed to the crown, their collaboration was deliberately sought by confirmation of their internal autonomy. After 1877, when Queen Victoria was proclaimed Empress of India, they participated in imperial *Durbars. On British withdrawal in 1947, they came under pressure to join either India or Pakistan. In Kashmir, Hyderabad, and Junagadh crises occurred, but most acceded peacefully, hoping some of their privileges, particularly financial, would be upheld. Many of the smaller states were grouped together into unions, for example the United States of Rajasthan. Legislation in 1970 abolished the special privileges of their ruling families.

Princes in the Tower The young sons of Edward IV; Edward, Prince of Wales (born 1470) and Richard, Duke of York (born 1472), supposedly murdered in the Tower of London in or shortly after 1483. In 1483 Edward reigned briefly as Edward V on the death of his father but was not crowned; he and his brother were taken to the Tower of London by their uncle (the future Richard III). Richard was appointed Protector and the princes disappeared soon afterwards. They are generally assumed to have been murdered, but whether at the instigation of Richard III (as Tudor propagandists claimed) or of another is not known; two skeletons discovered in 1674 are thought to have been those of the princes.

Priscus, Lucius Tarquinius *See* TARQUIN.

prison camps, Soviet Punitive institutions for forced labour in the former Soviet Union. The tradition of exiling political protesters and reformers to Siberia was well-established in 19th-century Russia. By a decree of 1919 *Lenin maintained such punishment, operating through his police agency, the *CHEKA. During *Stalin's rule millions were arrested by the *MVD, including peasants who resisted *collectivization, Christians, Jews, intellectuals, and political protesters. The prisoners were passed to GULAG (acronym for the Main Administration of Corrective Labour Camps), which was established in 1930 and was responsible for administering the forced labour system. The camps were mostly situated in the east of the Soviet Union and were referred to metaphorically as the "Gulag archipelago". Estimates of numbers confined to Gulag camps in the years of Stalin vary, ranging between six and 15 million. After the worst years of the purges in the 1930s thousands continued to be sent to the camps. After the arrest and execution of *Beria (1953) and the de-Stalinization policy of *Khrushchev, there was a decline in the worst excesses of the camps, which were formally replaced in 1955 by Corrective Labour Colonies. Many distinguished Soviet citizens, including the writers Eugenia Ginzberg and Aleksandr Solzhenitsyn, were sent to prison camps; others were "exiled" to Siberia, placed in "psychiatric hospitals", or in other ways restrained. The physicist Andrei Sakharov and his wife Yelena Bonner were not allowed to leave Nizhny Novgorod (Gorky). In 1987 in the wake of a new policy of *glasnost* or openness, *Gorbachev ordered the release of some intellectual dissidents. All had allegedly been released by 1992.

Prithviraj III (died 1193) Hindu (Chauhan Rajput) King of Delhi, who died in a brave attempt to resist the establishment of Muslim power in northern India. Until the Muslim invasions, he was preoccupied with defending his territories in Ajmer and Delhi against rival Hindu kings. Although he was victorious in 1192, in his first encounter with the Turkish invader, Muhammad Ghuri, in 1193 he was defeated and killed thus opening the way for the founding of the Delhi sultanate. Prithviraj III has been immortalized in ballads and folk literature as a figure of romance and heroism.

privateers Licensed sea-raiders in time of war, who had government-issued letters of marque or reprisal allowing them to attack enemy shipping. Privateers were often employed in European wars in the 16th and 17th centuries by the English, French, and Dutch, and they later became common in the Caribbean, North America, and the Indian Ocean during imperial conflicts. The Americans resorted to widespread privateering during the Wars of Independence and 1812; the South followed this example during the Civil War. Privateers were internationally abolished by the Declaration of Paris (1856).

Proclamation Line (1763) A declaration that prohibited American settlement west of the Allegheny Mountains in an attempt by the British government to regularize relations between frontiersmen and Native Americans after the *French and Indian wars. The royal proclamation also established governments for captured territory and imposed royal control on Native American traders. It antagonized land speculators, pioneers, and war veterans who had been promised land in the west. It was partially amended by subsequent treaties with Native American tribes.

progress, royal A journey around the kingdom, regularly taken by monarchs and their courts in the days of personal rule. When communications were poor and regional control limited, progresses served to assert sovereignty and win loyalty. They also offered opportunities to hunt, to avoid the plagues that thrived in built-up cities, and to share the economic burden of maintaining the court among richer subjects. *Elizabeth I compelled her rich courtiers to entertain her and her retinue at their country houses. Emperor *Charles V, with his widely scattered dominions, was by necessity a "peripatetic monarch". Monarchs who refused to make progresses ran the risk of forfeiting their subjects' obedience, as was partly the case with *Philip II whose reclusive nature failed to inspire his subjects' loyalty.

Progressive Movement (US) (1890–1914) A US movement that sought to provide the basic political, social, and economic reforms necessary for the developing industrial economy. In both the Republican and Democratic parties Progressives were distinguished by a commitment to popular government, free trade, and control of competition-stifling trusts. To secure these ends they advocated direct *primary elections for the nomination of candidates, the popular election of Senators (secured in 1913), and *anti-trust laws. Social reforms were also demanded, for example legislation improving conditions of employment, and *Prohibition attracted much support. Under Progressive pressure, government extended its activity at municipal, state, and federal levels in the pursuit of equality, efficiency, and social harmony. In different ways, progressive policies were adapted by the Republican Theodore *Roosevelt and the Democrat Woodrow *Wilson.

Progressive Parties (US) (1912; 1924; 1948) Three US political organizations. In 1912 the first Progressive (the "Bull Moose") Party, led by the former President Theodore *Roosevelt, polled more votes in the presidential elections than the Republican candidate, President *Taft. By splitting the Republican vote, it allowed the Democrats to win on an equally progressive platform. In 1924 a revitalized Progressive Party, based on Wisconsin and other farm states, challenged the conservative outlook of both the Republican and Democratic parties. Although securing five million votes, the party carried only Wisconsin. In 1948 Henry A. Wallace (1888–1965), formerly Democratic Secretary of State for agriculture, campaigned for a more conciliatory policy towards the Soviet Union. His Progressive Party, however, appeared too sympathetic to communism, and failed to challenge either main party.

Prohibition era (1920–33) The period during which the manufacture, sale, and transportation of alcoholic drinks was prohibited in the USA. A culmination of the aspirations of the Temperance Movement, it began when the Eighteenth Amendment to the Constitution went into effect by the passing of the Volstead Act (1919). Despite the securing of some 300,000 court convictions between 1920 and 1930, drinking continued. Speakeasies (illegal bars) and bootlegging (illegal distilling of alcohol) flourished. The success of such gangsters as Al *Capone, who controlled the supply of illegal alcohol, led to corruption of police and city government. After the Wickersham Commission in 1931 reported that the prohibition laws were unenforceable and encouraged public disrespect for law in general, the Eighteenth Amendment was repealed by the Twenty-First Amendment. A number of states and counties retained full or partial prohibition, but by 1966 no state-wide prohibition laws existed.

propaganda The attempt to shape or manipulate people's beliefs or actions by means of information (true or false), arguments, or symbols. Propaganda may be printed, broadcast, or visual. All governments engage to some extent in propaganda activities, describing them in many cases as public information programmes, sometimes with a totally cynical disregard for the truth. In the 1930s, the German Nazis, led by Hitler's minister of propaganda, Joseph *Goebbels, conducted a highly skilful propaganda campaign that indoctrinated the German people with bogus racial theories, urged them to seek world domination, and excluded them from hearing what the rest of the world thought of them. The success of this campaign in persuading some 80 million Germans to embark on World War II may only have been possible because it reflected at least some aspects of their own aspirations. Culpability for the obscenities perpetrated by the Third Reich cannot, therefore, be laid exclusively at the feet of its leaders.

Protectorate, English (16 December 1653–25 May 1659) The rule of England established by Oliver *Cromwell. Unable to work with the *Barebones Parliament, Cromwell entrusted a council of army officers with the task of drawing up a new constitution. The resulting Instrument of Government made Cromwell Lord Protector, monarch in all but name, who would share power with a single House of Parliament elected by Puritans. Politically it was a failure. Cromwell could not work with his first Protectorate Parliament, so he divided England into 11 military districts ruled by army officers known as major-generals. This was so unpopular that he reverted to parliamentary rule through the second Parliament of the Protectorate in 1656. Although the Protectorate was successful in foreign policy and notable for religious toleration of all faiths other than Roman Catholicism, its stability depended on Cromwell's personal qualities. After his death in 1658 it did not take long for the army to remove Richard *Cromwell, his suc-

cessor, bringing the Protectorate to an end in 1659 in preparation for the *Restoration of Charles II.

Protestant A member or adherent of any of the Christian Churches that separated from the *Roman Catholic Church at the *Reformation. The term was coined after the imperial Diet summoned at Speyer in 1529 and derives from the 'Protestatio' of the reforming members against the decisions of the Catholic majority. These adherents of Martin *Luther were not merely registering objections: they were professing their commitment to the simple faith of the early Church, which they believed had been obscured by the unnecessary innovations of medieval Roman Catholicism.

All the early Protestants shared a conviction that the *Bible was the only source of revealed truth and it was made available to all in vernacular translations. They minimized the ceremonial aspects of Christianity and placed preaching and hearing the word of God before sacramental faith and practice. Numerous Protestant sects and churches were formed, largely because the principle of 'private judgement' in the interpretation of the scriptures led to many shades of doctrine and practice.

The established Church in England is the **Anglican Church**, recognized by the State and with the British monarch as titular head. Although Henry VIII broke with the Roman Catholic Church in 1533 and *Edward VI made moves to establish Protestant doctrines and practices, the formulation of distinctively Anglican principles dates from the reign of *Elizabeth I. The second Book of Common Prayer of Edward VI's reign was revised with modifications (1559) and its use enforced by an Act of *Uniformity. In 1563 the *Thirty-Nine Articles were issued by Convocation (the highest assembly of the Church) and finally adopted by the Church of England (1571) as a statement of its beliefs and practices. The aim was to set up a comprehensive, national, episcopal Church with the monarch as supreme governor. Those who refused to attend church services were fined. The *Puritans were dissatisfied with the Elizabethan religious settlement but the queen opposed all their attempts to modify her Anglican Church.

The 'Catholicization' of the Church in the 1630s under Archbishop *Laud exacerbated Puritan antipathy to the bishops, and religion was a crucial factor in the outbreak of the *English Civil War. Although Anglicanism was banned during the Commonwealth and Protectorate, it returned with vigour at the

Restoration (1660). The Clarendon Code and *Test Acts created a breach between establishment Anglicanism and *Nonconformists, and James II's pro-Catholic policies played a significant part in provoking the *Glorious Revolution. The *Toleration Act (1689) secured limited toleration for Nonconformists, although clergymen refusing to swear the oath of allegiance to William III were deprived of their office. (Catholics were not emancipated until 1829.)

The 18th century witnessed disputes between High Anglicans, who maintained Laud's conservatism, and Low Anglicans, or Latitudinarians, who were less concerned with forms of worship. The 19th century saw growing divergence between the 'High' Church tradition, which was revived by the Oxford Movement of the 1830s, led by John Henry *Newman, and the burgeoning evangelical movement. The former claimed historical continuity with the pre-Reformation Roman Catholic Church, stressing the authority of the bishops and priesthood, the doctrinal centrality of the seven sacraments, and the importance of ceremony in worship. By contrast, the Evangelicals were more Protestant in outlook, setting less store by the sacraments and tradition, and emphasizing the importance of the Bible as the basis of faith. In the 19th century the Evangelicals were particularly active in missionary work and social reform.

During the 20th century a third tradition, that of theological liberalism, has also been widely influential in its emphasis on the need for the Church to adapt to modern knowledge and conditions.

With over 80 million adherents worldwide, the **Lutheran** churches are the largest Protestant grouping. Lutherans derive their practice and doctrine from the teachings of Martin Luther, especially as set out in the Augsburg Confession of 1530. There is an emphasis on the preeminence of Scripture and on Luther's doctrine of justification by faith, but otherwise teaching varies widely. The Lutheran churches are particularly prominent in Germany, Scandinavia, and North America.

A more radical wing of the 16th-century Reformation was represented by **Anabaptism**, which centred on the belief that people baptized as infants must be rebaptized as adults. The Anabaptists originated mainly in Zürich in the 1520s, with the aim of restoring the spirit and institutions of the early Church. They managed to establish centres in Saxony, Austria, Moravia, Poland, the Lower Rhine, and the Netherlands, but made almost no headway in the French-speaking world. In the 17th century the Mennonites preserved some of the best of the Ana-

baptist traditions, which made a significant contribution to the religious history of modern Europe and America.

The modern **Baptist** movement dates its beginnings from the English church established in Amsterdam in 1609 by John Smyth (1554–1612) and the church in London under Thomas Helwys (1612). They were 'General' or Arminian Baptists, as opposed to 'Particular' or Calvinist Baptists, who evolved between 1633 and 1638. After the *Restoration they moved closer to the Presbyterians and Independents and were recognized as dissenters from the Anglican Church. America's first Baptist church was probably the one established at Providence, Rhode Island, with the help of Roger Williams (1639). From 1740, under the influence of the *Great Awakening, the movement made considerable headway, especially in the southern states.

In both Britain and the USA Baptist Churches grew in the late 18th century. Baptist missionaries first went to India in 1792 and in the 19th century were active all over the world including in Russia.

The **Methodist Church** was founded by John *Wesley in the 18th century. Stressing the individual believer's personal relationship with God, Wesley wished his followers to remain within the Anglican Church, but after his death Methodism's rejection of theological doctrine and traditional ecclesiastical authority led to its development as a distinct Church. In Wales the religious revival inspired by Howel Harris and Daniel Rowlands in the 18th century led to the establishment in 1811 of a dominant Calvinist form of Methodism. In the USA the Methodist Church divided into many groups, largely as a result of its over attitudes towards slavery.

Presbyterians subscribe to anti-episcopal theories of church government and usually to the doctrines of John *Calvin. Presbyterian churches oppose state intervention in religious affairs and advocate the primacy of the Bible as a rule of faith. The first American Presbyterian Church was founded in Philadelphia in 1706. The official Church of Scotland is one of the largest of the Presbyterian churches.

The first **Calvinist** Church to be organized on a national basis was in 16th-century France; its members became known as *Huguenots and they played a large part in provoking the French Wars of Religion. Reformed (Calvinist) congregations contributed to the *Dutch Revolt and once the Netherlands secured independence from Catholic Spain the Reformed Church became established there. Elsewhere in Europe, many congregations managed to survive the

*Counter-Reformation. In 1628 a Dutch Reformed Church was organized on Manhattan Island.

Proudhon, Pierre Joseph (1809–65) French social philosopher and journalist. His criticism of Napoleon III (Louis-Napoleon) and the Second Republic led to his imprisonment from 1849 to 1852; he later spent a period (1858–62) in exile in Belgium. His writings exercised considerable influence on the development of anarchism and socialism in Europe. He is chiefly remembered for his pamphlet *What is Property?* (1840), which argued that property, in the sense of the exploitation of one person's labour by another, is theft. His theories were developed by his disciple Bakunin.

Provisors, Statute of *See* PRAEMUNIRE, STATUTE OF.

Prussia A former kingdom of Germany, which grew from a small country on the south-east shores of the Baltic to an extensive domain covering much of modern north-east Germany and Poland. The forested area to the east of the Vistula, originally inhabited by a Baltic people known as the Prussians, was taken in the 13th century by the Teutonic Knights, and in the 16th century it became a duchy of the Hohenzollerns, passing in 1618 to the electors of Brandenburg. The kingdom of Prussia, proclaimed in 1701, with its capital at Berlin, grew in the 18th century under Frederick the Great to become a dominant power. After victory in the Franco-Prussian War of 1870–71, Prussia under Wilhelm I became the nucleus of the new German Empire created by Bismarck. With Germany's defeat in World War I, the Prussian monarchy was abolished and Prussia's supremacy came to an end.

Prynne, William (1600–69) English Puritan pamphleteer, a fearless campaigner on religious, moral, and political issues. His most famous pamphlet, *Histrio Mastix* (1632), was an attack on stage-plays; he was tried before the Star Chamber for its implied criticism of Queen *Henrietta Maria, who was a devotee of plays and masques. He was sentenced to life imprisonment and cropping of the ears (1634). He continued to write anti-episcopal pamphlets and in 1637 the remaining parts of his ears were removed. The *Long Parliament freed him in 1640. Elected to Parliament himself in 1648, he was expelled at *Pride's Purge, and eventually supported the *Restoration.

Ptolemies The Macedonian dynasty that ruled Egypt from 323 to 30 BC. **Ptolemy I** was an officer of Alexander the Great who, after the king's death, was appointed satrap of Egypt. He proclaimed himself king in 304, and by the time of his death in 283–82 he had established control over Cyprus, Palestine, and many cities in the Aegean and Asia Minor. The reigns of the Ptolemies who succeeded him were characterized externally by struggles with the *Seleucids for control of Syria, Asia Minor, and the Aegean; and internally by dissatisfaction and rebellion among the native Egyptians. Contact with the rising power of Rome came to a head during the reign of *Cleopatra VII, whose liaison with *Mark Antony led ultimately to defeat at Actium, suicide, and the annexation of Egypt by Octavian.

Pueblo A member of certain Native American peoples occupying a pueblo settlement. Their prehistoric period is known as the Anasazi (Pueblo) culture. The Chaco Culture National Historical Park in New Mexico, USA, embraces the remains of over 80 prehistoric communities of the Pueblo culture, which was centred at Chaco Canyon.

Puerto Rico

Capital:	San Juan
Area:	13,790 sq km (5324 sq miles)
Population:	3,674,209 (2013 est)
Currency:	1 US dollar = 100 cents
Religions:	Roman Catholic 85.0%; Protestant and other 15.0%
Ethnic Groups:	White 75.8%; Black 12.4%
Languages:	Spanish; English

An island commonwealth in the Caribbean, between Hispaniola and the Virgin Islands.

Physical The west-east length of Puerto Rico is some 180 km (112 miles), while its north-south width is about 60 km (37 miles) at the widest point. Its climate is tropical. The coast offers good harbours and the coastal plains are fertile, yielding sugarcane, sweet potatoes, and maize. In the interior highlands rise to 1220 m (4000 feet), coffee and tobacco are grown on their slopes.

Economy The mainstays of the Puerto Rican economy are tourism and manufacturing industry, the major products being pharmaceuticals, electronics, clothing, and food products. Principal exports, of which nine-tenths go to the USA, include chemicals, machinery and equipment, clothing, foodstuffs, and oil products. Agriculture is of declining importance. Mineral resources are scanty.

History Originally known as Boriquén, Puerto Rico was discovered by Columbus in 1493. Encouraged by tales of gold from the indigenous Arawak Indians, his companion, Juan *Ponce de León, was granted permission by the Spanish crown to colonize the island. In 1508 he founded the settlement of Caparra and in 1509 he was made governor. Caparra was abandoned and the settlement moved to nearby San Juan in 1521, to take better advantage of the bay for trading. By the end of the 16th century the Arawak were virtually extinct from European-introduced diseases and exploitation. In the 17th and 18th centuries the island remained important for its sugar and tobacco plantations, worked by imported black slaves, and as a key to Spain's defence of its trading interests in the Caribbean and Atlantic against France, Britain, and Holland.

Puerto Rico was maintained by Spain as a garrison protecting trade routes until the loss of Mexico in 1821 removed its strategic importance. In 1887 the Autonomist Party was founded to protect home rule under Spanish sovereignty. In 1898, during the Spanish–American War, the island came under US military rule and was ceded to the USA at the end of the war. In 1917 an Act of the US Congress (Jones Act) declared Puerto Rican inhabitants to be US citizens. Since the 1940s, with a decline in the sugar industry, there have been successful efforts at industrialization and diversification of the economy. Muñoz Marín (1898–1980) was the first elected governor (1948–64), being re-elected three times. In 1952 the Commonwealth of Puerto Rico was proclaimed, and ratified by a plebiscite. The party which has dominated politics since then, the Popular Democratic Party (PPD), has supported the status quo, while urging greater autonomy. Its rival, the New Progressive Party (PNP) would like the island to become the fifty-first state of the USA. There is also a small Independence Party, but the violent separatist organization, the FALN, has had little support on the island. The UN has regularly urged a plebiscite to decide the island's future. In 1993, Puerto Ricans voted to retain their country's status as a self-governing commonwealth, thereby rejecting both independence and US statehood. Another vote in 1998 produced the same result, but in 2012 a majority preferred US statehood.

Pugachev, Emelian Ivanovich (1726–75) *Cossack and leader of a massive popular uprising in 1773–74 against the rule of *Catherine II (the Great) of Russia. Deserting the army, he won the support of discontented serfs, cossacks, miners, and such recently conquered peoples as the Bashkirs and Tartars. He captured Kazan and established a court, claiming to be the assassinated Emperor Peter III. He promised the abolition of landlords, bureaucrats, serfdom, taxation, and military service and the restoration of traditional religion. His betrayal and execution were followed by the ruthless suppression of his followers.

Pullman strike (1894) A US labour dispute that began when the Pullman Palace Car Company of Chicago laid off men and cut wages, blaming the economic depression, and refused to discuss grievances with its employees. The cause of the workers was taken up by the powerful American Railway Union, led by Eugene V. *Debs. The strike threatened to paralyse the entire railway network unless Pullman went to arbitration. President *Cleveland's sympathies were with the company, and the federal circuit court at Chicago issued an injunction declaring the strike illegal. Rioting and bloodshed ensued, and Debs was gaoled in 1895. Injunctions were open to misuse until the Norris–La Guardia Anti-Injunction Act of 1932.

Punic wars The three wars fought in the 3rd and 2nd century BC between Rome and Carthage, so named from 'Poenicus' ('Dark skin' or 'Phoenician'). The contest was for control of the Mediterranean Sea. Rome emerged as victor from each war.

The First (264–241 BC) was fought largely at sea. Rome expanded its navy and took control of Sicily. Corsica and Sardinia were seized a few years later. *Hamilcar Barca, father of *Hannibal, led the defeated side. The Second (218–201) arose from Hannibal's invasion of Italy from Carthaginian bases in Spain via the Alps. He led a huge force including elephant squadrons. Rome suffered disastrous defeats, most notably in the mists by Lake Trasimene and at *Cannae. Italy was overrun by Hannibal but the Italian tribes did not rise against Rome. The strategy of the dictator *Fabius prevented further losses. In a long-drawn-out series of campaigns Hannibal's extended lines of supply were threatened by defeats in Sicily and Spain and the brilliant generalship of *Scipio Africanus. *Hasdrubal, Hannibal's brother, was defeated on the Italian mainland in 207. By 203 Hannibal, who had no effective siege engines, was summoned to withdraw to Africa to defend Carthage itself, now threatened by Scipio. Pursued by Scipio he was defeated at Zama in 202 and the Carthaginians were forced to accept humiliating terms the following year. Spain was acquired as a provincial territory by Rome.

In 149 BC at a peak of its territorial expansion and at the insistence of *Cato, Rome intervened in an African dispute to side with Numidia against Carthage. In the Third War (149–146) *Scipio Aemilianus besieged and destroyed Carthage utterly, sowed the site with symbolic salt, and declared Africa a Roman province.

Puritan A member of the more extreme English Protestants who were dissatisfied with the Anglican settlement and sought a further purification of the English Church from *Roman Catholic elements. Their theology was basically that of John *Calvin. At first they limited themselves to attacking 'popish' (Roman Catholic) practices – church ornaments, vestments, and organ music – but from 1570 extremists attacked the authority of bishops and government notably in the Marprelate tracts. However, James I resisted their attempts to change Anglican dogma, ritual, and organization, voiced at the *Hampton Court Conference. In the 1620s some emigrated to North America, but it was the policies of *Laud and Charles I in the 1630s that resurrected the Puritan opposition of the 1580s. The doctrine of Predestination (that God ordains in advance those who shall receive salvation) became a major source of contention between the Puritans, for whom it was a fundamental article of faith, and the Arminians who rejected it. Religion was a key factor leading to the outbreak of civil war in 1642. Puritanism was strong among the troops of the *New Model Army and in the 1640s and 1650s, with the encouragement of Cromwell, Puritan objectives were realized. After the Restoration they were mostly absorbed into the Anglican Church or into larger *Nonconformists groups and lost their distinctive identity.

Putin, Vladimir (Vladimirovich) (1952–) Russian statesman; President (2000–08), Prime Minister (2008–12), President (2012–). A former KGB colonel, he became deputy mayor of St Petersburg (1994–96) before joining Boris *Yeltsin's government. Appointed successively head of Russia's security services (1998) and Prime Minister (1999), he became Acting President on Yeltsin's resignation (31 December 1999) and was elected President in March 2000. His rule has been characterized by a reassertion of central government authority and an enhancement of presidential power. Putin's critics point to increasing government control of the media and a deteriorating human rights record as reasons to doubt his attachment to democracy. In foreign policy he has sought to reassert a Russian approach distinct from that of the West and to strengthen Russian influence over other former components of the Soviet Union. However, he suffered reverses in the Georgian *Rose Revolution (2003) and the Ukrainian *Orange Revolution (2004), both of which installed pro-Western governments. He was re-elected by a large majority in 2004, but a constitutional limit of two consecutive terms prevented him from contesting the presidency in 2008. He became Prime Minister under Dmitri *Medvedev but was widely regarded as still the centre of power. He was re-elected President in 2012. In 2014 Putin faced heavy criticism in the West for his response to the Ukrainian revolution of that year; this involved Russia's annexation of the Crimea region and the backing of armed separatist rebels in eastern Ukraine.

Puyi (or **P'u-i**) (1906–67) Last *Qing emperor of China (1908–12). Proclaimed emperor at the age of two by the empress dowager *Cixi (his great aunt), he reigned until the *Chinese Revolution forced his abdication in 1912. He continued to live in the imperial palace until forced to flee by a local warlord to Tianjin in 1924. After the Japanese seizure of Manchuria, Puyi was placed at the head of the puppet state of *Manchukuo. Captured by Soviet forces in 1945, he was later handed over to the communist Chinese, and allowed to live as a private citizen.

Pym, John (1584–1643) English politician. He entered Parliament in 1614, and by the 1620s was making his mark, especially as a manager of the impeachment of *Buckingham (1626), and as a supporter of the *Petition of Right (1628). In the *Long Parliament his debating and tactical skills brought him great influence and earned him the nickname "King Pym". He was the main architect of the reforming legislation of 1641, including the Acts of *Attainder against *Strafford and *Laud, and was responsible for having the *Grand Remonstrance printed and published. Pym was one of the *five Members of Parliament whom Charles I tried to arrest in 1642. Once the *English Civil War began, he played a role on the Committee of Safety (1642) and in 1643 engineered the *Solemn League and Covenant with the Scots.

pyramid A monumental structure especially characteristic of ancient Egypt, often built as a

royal tomb and usually made of stone, with a
square base and sloping sides meeting centrally
at an apex. At first the pharaohs were buried in
underground chambers over which were built
rectangular *mastabas*; these were stone structures housing the food and accoutrements the
pharaoh would need in the afterlife. Although all
the interior tombs were sealed, often with elaborate devices to prevent entry, all the pyramids
were robbed of their valuables in antiquity. The
first pyramid was that constructed for King Zoser
at Saqqara by *Imhotep *c.*2700 BC, the so-called
Step Pyramid which has six enormous steps and
is over 60 m (197 feet) high. Most of the best
known pyramids date from the Old Kingdom
(*c.* 2700–2200 BC), though some were built during
the eleventh and twelfth dynasties (*c.* 2050–1750
BC). The pyramids of Khufu, Khafre, and Men-
kaure at Giza are a spectacular illustration of the
skill of Egyptian architects – and of the state's
ability to organize a large work-force. The Great
Pyramid of Giza, constructed of stone blocks of
up to 200 tonnes in weight, is estimated to have
required some 84,000 people employed for 80
days a year for 20 years.

Stepped pyramids known as ziggurats survive
from the 3rd millennium BC in Mesopotamia.
Stepped-pyramid structures were also built as
bases for temples in pre-Columbian Central
America. These were erected by the *Mayas,
*Aztecs, and *Toltecs, for the most part between
250 AD and 1520. The Temple of the Sun in
Teotihuacán in Mexico is perhaps the most impressive.

Pyramids, Battle of the (21 July 1798)
The decisive battle fought near the pyramids of
Giza that gave *Napoleon control of Egypt.
He took Alexandria by storm on 2 July, and
then, with 40,000 men defeated a *Mameluke
army of 60,000 led by Murad Bey. The victory
enabled Napoleon to take Cairo and allowed
France to control Egypt until its withdrawal
in 1801.

Pyrrhus (*c.*318–272 BC) King of Epirus *c.*307–
272. After invading Italy in 280, he defeated the
Romans at Asculum in 279, but sustained heavy
losses; hence a **Pyrrhic victory** is one with an
excessive cost to the victor.

Q

Qaddafi *See* GADDAFI.

Qajar A Turkic tribe in north-east Iran that produced the Qajar dynasty, which ruled Persia (Iran) from 1794 to 1925. The dynasty was established by Agha Muhammad (1742–97), a eunuch who made Tehran his capital and was crowned Shah in 1796. He was succeeded by his nephew Fath Ali Shah (1797–1834), during whose reign Iran was forced to cede the Trans-Caucasian lands to Russia. The constitutional revolution of 1906 established a parliament. Muhammad Ali (1907–09) was deposed for attacking the constitution and after a lengthy regency, Muhammad Ali's son, Ahmad Shah (1914–25), became the last Qajar ruler, being deposed by an army officer, *Reza Shah Pahlavi, in 1925.

Qatar

Capital:	Doha
Area:	11,586 sq km (4373 sq miles)
Population:	2,042,444 (2013 est)
Currency:	1 Qatar riyal = 100 dirhams
Religions:	Muslim 77.5%; Christian 8.5%
Ethnic Groups:	Arab 40.0%; Indian 18.0%; Pakistani 18.0%; Iranian 10.0%
Languages:	Arabic (official); English
International Organizations:	UN; Arab League; OAPEC; OPEC; GCC; Non-Aligned Movement; WTO

A country of Arabia. It is bounded by Saudi Arabia inland and by *Bahrain to its west.

Physical Qatar is a hot arid country occupying a peninsula of desert on the southwest of the Persian Gulf.

Economy The economy and exports of Qatar are dominated by crude oil, which is present both on-shore and offshore. Oil and natural gas account for about half of GDP and five-sixths of export earnings.

Industries include oil-refining, gas liquefaction, ammonia, fertilizers, petrochemicals, cement, and steel. As a result of its oil wealth the country has the highest per capita incomes in the world.

History Historically linked with Bahrain, Qatar was under Bahraini suzerainty for much of the 19th century. In 1872 it came under Ottoman suzerainty, but the Ottomans renounced their rights in 1913. In 1916 Qatar made an agreement with Britain which created a *de facto* British protectorate. Oil was discovered in 1939 and exploited from 1949. The agreement with Britain was terminated in 1968 and Qatar became fully independent in 1971, under a constitution by which the Emir, Shaikh Khalifa bin Hamad al-Thani would govern as Prime Minister. Qatar provided bases for UN forces in the *Gulf War, after which it strengthened its links with Iran. In 1995 the Emir was overthrown in a bloodless coup by his son, Shaikh Hamad bin Khalifa al-Thani, who embarked on a programme of liberal reforms. This caused mounting tension with Bahrain and Saudi Arabia and led to an attempted coup in 1996. A new constitution in 2005 provided for an elected majority in the Advisory Council, whose members had previously been appointed by the Emir. In 2011 Qatar supported the rebellion in Libya against President *Gaddafi. Shaikh Hamad abdicated in 2013 in favour of his son Tamim bin Hamad al-Thani.

Qianlong (or **Ch'ien-lung**) (1710–99) *Qing Emperor of China (1735–95). During his rule China reached its greatest territorial extent with campaigns undertaken in the Turkistan (Xinjiang) region, Annam, Burma, and Nepal. In 1757 Qianlong restricted all foreign traders to

Guangzhou (Canton), where they could trade only from November to March. He rejected in 1793 the requests of a British delegation led by Lord Macartney for an expansion of trade and the establishment of diplomatic relations. Towards the end of his reign his administration was weakened by corruption, financial problems, and provincial uprisings, notably the *White Lotus Society in 1796. He gained a reputation as a philosopher-king, patronizing the arts, writing poetry, and overseeing the compilation of literary collections (in which anything thought critical of the Qing was expunged). Four years before his death he abdicated in favour of his son.

Qin (or **Ch'in**) (221–206 BC) China's first imperial dynasty. It was founded by Prince Zheng, ruler of the *Zhou vassal state of Qin. Unlike rival Chinese states, Qin used cavalry not chariots in battle and early adopted iron weaponry. It ensured a regular food supply by developing a system for land irrigation. Based in Shaanxi, it began to expand its territories c.350 BC. Under Zheng, it overthrew the Eastern Zhou and conquered (256–221 BC) all Zhou's former vassal states. Zheng then took the title Huangdi and is best known as Shi Huangdi (First Emperor). He died in 210 BC and his dynasty was overthrown four years later. From that time, though China was sometimes fragmented, the concept of a united empire prevailed. From Qin is derived the name China.

Qing (or **Ch'ing**) (1644–1912) The last dynasty to rule China. Its emperors were *Manchus. In 1644 a *Ming general, Wu Sangui, invited Manchu Bannermen massed at Shanhaiguan, the undefended eastern end of the Great Wall of China, to expel the bandit chieftain Li Zicheng from Beijing. The Bannermen occupied the city and proclaimed their child-emperor 'Son of Heaven'. Resistance continued for up to 30 years in south China. Chinese men were forced to braid their long hair into a queue or 'pigtail'. But Qing rule differed little from that of Chinese dynasties. It emphasized study of the Confucian classics and the Confucian basis of society (see CONFUCIANISM). The empire of China reached its widest extent, covering Taiwan, Manchuria, Mongolia, Tibet, and Turkistan. The Qing regarded all other peoples as barbarians and their rulers as subject to the 'Son of Heaven', and were blind to the growing pressure of the West. Under *Kangxi (1654–1722) and Qianlong (1736–96) China was powerful enough to treat the outside world with condescension.

Thereafter, however, the authority of the dynasty was reduced. Faced with major internal revolts, most notably the *Taiping Rebellion (1850–64) and a succession of Muslim uprisings in the far west, the Qing proved unable to contend simultaneously with increasing intrusions from western powers interested in the economic exploitation of China. Humiliating defeat in the *Sino-Japanese War (1894–95) and the *Boxer Rising (1900) weakened Qing power, and after the *Chinese Revolution of 1911, the last Qing emperor *Puyi was forced to abdicate in 1912.

Quadruple Alliance An alliance formed in 1813 by Britain, Prussia, Austria, and Russia that committed them to the defeat of Napoleon. At the Battle of *Leipzig (1813) Napoleon was decisively defeated.

Quakers (formal name **The Society of Friends**) A Christian body that rejects the formal structures of creed and sacraments and usually of clergy and liturgy, emphasizing instead the individual's search for 'inner light'. Founded by the Englishman George *Fox in the 17th century, the Quakers became convinced that their 'experimental' discovery of God – sometimes featuring trembling or quaking experiences during meetings – would lead to the purification of all Christendom. The name 'Quaker' was originally a term of contempt but is now widely used.

By 1660 there were more than 20,000 converts, and missionaries were at work in Ireland, Scotland, Wales, and the American colonies. They continued to grow in number, despite severe penalization from 1662 to 1689 for refusing to take oaths, attend Anglican services, or pay tithes. After considerable debate, they evolved their present form of organization, with regular monthly, quarterly, and annual meetings.

In 1681 William *Penn founded the American Quaker colony of Pennsylvania, and Quaker influence in the colony's politics remained paramount until the American War of Independence.

Quebec Liberation Front A French Canadian separatist movement. Set up in the early 1960s, it launched a terrorist and bombing campaign to secure the separation of Quebec Province from Canada. The Front de Libération du Québec (FLQ) was greatly encouraged when *de Gaulle used the separatist slogan *Vive le Québec Libre* (Long Live Free Quebec) while visiting Canada in 1967. But its terrorist activities proved unpopular; much more support was given to the constitutional *Parti Québécois.

Queen's War (1702–13) A war between Britain and France, part of the War of the *Spanish Succession, that was fought in North America. Frontier warfare in New England with savage French and Native American attacks on outlying settlements broke out again at the start of the 18th century (*see* FRENCH AND INDIAN WARS). In 1710 the French lost Port Royal in Acadia (known to the British as Nova Scotia), which came under British control. A British attempt to capture Quebec the next year was prevented by storms. In the south, a South Carolinian (British) expedition destroyed the Spanish city of St Augustine, Florida, in 1702 and a retaliatory French attack on Charleston (1706) was repulsed. In the Caribbean, St Christopher (St Kitts) was captured from the French in 1702, but Guadeloupe resisted British attacks in the following year. Thereafter only *privateers and *buccaneers remained active. The main British colonial gains at the Peace of *Utrecht were Nova Scotia, western Newfoundland, and St Christopher.

Queen's shilling (or **King's shilling**) A coin, which, if accepted from a recruiting officer obliged the recipient to serve in the British army. Recruiting sergeants in the 18th century would ply likely young men with drink and if they could persuade them to take the shilling, they were in fact accepting army pay. This ranked as a binding agreement from which escape was very difficult.

Quetzalcóatl One of the chief gods of ancient Mesoamerica (Mexico and northern Central America). The word literally means 'quetzalbird snake' and is usually translated as 'feathered serpent'. Quetzalcóatl was also the official title of the *Aztec high priest. As a god he was known throughout Mesoamerica and was called Kukulkán by the *Maya. Images and temples to him appear at early sites, such as Teotihuacán in Mexico, but he was especially revered during the period *c.* 700–1520.

Quezón, Manuel Luis (1878–1944) Filipino statesman, President (1935–44). He followed *Aguinaldo in the Philippine wars against Spain and the USA (1896–1901). Later he served in the Philippines Assembly and became resident commissioner for the Philippines in Washington (1909–16). His successful conduct in this post made him a national hero and he was elevated to the office of President of the Philippine Senate. In 1935 he became first President of the newly constituted Philippine Commonwealth and ruled his country dictatorially until forced into exile by the Japanese invasion in 1942. He headed a government in exile in the USA until his death, and was succeeded by his Vice-President, Sergio Osmena.

Quiberon Bay, Battle of (1759) A major British naval victory in the *Seven Years War that took place at Quiberon Bay on the west coast of Brittany in northern France. The French were planning to invade Britain. In 1759 Admiral *Hawke was blockading Brest, but in November the French admiral Conflans broke out during a storm. Hawke pursued the French fleet and when most of the ships took shelter in Quiberon Bay he came through the dangerous shoals in a gale. The French lost 11 ships and 25,000 men, and the British only two ships, ending the threat of a French invasion of Britain.

Quisling, Vidkun Abraham Lauritz Jonsson (1887–1945) Norwegian fascist leader. An army officer, he founded the fascist Nasjonal Samling (National Unity) Party, and in 1940 helped Hitler to prepare the conquest of Norway. He became head of a new pro-German government and was made Premier in 1942. He remained in power until 1945, when he was arrested and executed. By this time 'Quisling' had become a derogatory term to describe traitors who supported invaders of their countries.

Qu'ran *See* KORAN.

Rabin, Yitzhak (1922–95) Israeli general and statesman. Rabin was chief of staff of the Israeli army 1964–68, commanding the Israeli Defence Forces in the *Six-Day War of June 1967 against Israel's Arab neighbours. As leader of the Labour Party, he was Prime Minister from 1974 until 1977. He regained leadership of the party and the premiership in 1992, and in the following year signed a peace accord with Yasser *Arafat of the *Palestine Liberation Organization. This agreement brought Rabin the Nobel Peace Prize in 1994 (jointly with Arafat and Israeli Foreign Minister Shimon Peres). Arab and Jewish ultra-nationalists remained opposed to the settlement; while attending a peace rally in Tel Aviv in 1995, Rabin was assassinated by a Jewish right-wing extremist.

race A group, population, breed, or variety within a species, although because of difficulties in its definition race is rarely used in a scientific context.

Race is also sometimes used to divide humanity into different groups according to real or imagined common descent. Such divisions are usually based on physical characteristics, such as skin and hair colour, and shape of eyes and nose, which are related to the geographical origins of a particular group. In the 19th century, it was believed that human beings could be unambiguously classed as members of particular races, and that social and cultural differences could be explained on racial grounds. In the early 20th century the anthropologist Franz Boas claimed that racial typing on a physical basis was arbitrary and argued the cultural origin of psychological differences. His approach became generally accepted, though the Nazis, who produced entirely false theories of race, burned his book. Human variation continues to be studied but the notion of 'race' as a useful system of classification has largely been abandoned.

Racism is the spurious belief that human characteristics and abilities are determined by race or ethnic origin. Racism, like religious intolerance, has been the cause of much human strife and warfare throughout history. Imperialistic and militarily dominant peoples have usually justified their actions by believing themselves to be superior to the peoples they have conquered or enslaved. The Greek and Roman empires were built by the labour of slaves and the European empires, including the British Empire, also relied on *slavery and the destruction and dispossession of indigenous peoples. Within Europe the Jews were persecuted for centuries, in the 20th century suffering the *Holocaust. Six million Jews were exterminated by the Germans between 1939 and 1945 because the Germans had been indoctrinated to believe that they were racially superior to non-Aryans. Between 1948 and 1994 the policy of *apartheid attempted to separate Black and White people to prevent interbreeding in South Africa. In the second half of the century civil wars accompanied by genocide and 'ethnic cleansing' have cost thousands of lives in Bosnia and Herzegovina, Serbia, Rwanda, and Burundi.

In spite of the scientific disregard for the concept of race, racism continued throughout the 20th century to provide an ominous threat to many ethnic minorities. However, in Britain and elsewhere race-relations acts have outlawed blatant racial discrimination and encouraged a more tolerant attitude to differences in cultural and ethnic origins.

Race Relations Act (1976) British Act of Parliament. It repealed the Acts of 1965 and 1968, strengthened the law on racial discrimination, and extended the 1968 ban on discrimination to housing, employment, insurance, and credit facilities. The Act also established (1977) a permanent Race Relations Commission to eliminate discrimination and to promote equality of opportunity and good relations between different racial groups within Britain, which by then had become a multiracial society, with the immigration of large numbers of Asians and West Indians. The Public Order Act of 1986 contained six offences of inciting racial hatred, while the Criminal Justice Act (1994) included a provision against racial harassment in its offence dealing with threatening behaviour. Further amended in 2000 to promote active steps against discrimination, it was repealed in 2010 when the Equality Act consolidated and extended all existing anti-discrimination legislation.

Radhakrishnan, Sir Sarvepalli (1888–1975) Indian philosopher and statesman, President (1962–67). A teacher of philosophy at Mysore, Calcutta, and Oxford universities, he introduced some of the main ideas of classical Indian philosophy to the West. Major works include *Indian Philosophy* (1923–27) and *Eastern Religions and Western Thought* (1939). Radhakrishnan was Indian ambassador to the Soviet Union (1949–52) before returning to India in 1952 to become Vice-President under Nehru; he was elected President ten years later.

Raeder, Erich (1876–1960) German admiral. He was Admiral Hipper's chief of staff in World War I, and from 1928 was commander-in-chief of the German navy, secretly rebuilding it in violation of the *Versailles Peace Settlement. In the 1930s he elaborated his 'Z-Plan' for building a fleet capable of challenging Britain, but World War II began before this was achieved. He resigned and was replaced by Doenitz in January 1943, after Hitler became outraged by the poor performance of the surface fleet against Allied convoys. His part in unrestricted U-boat warfare led to his post-war imprisonment after trial at *Nuremberg.

Raffles, Sir Stamford (Thomas Stamford Raffles) (1781–1826) British colonial administrator. Born in Jamaica, he joined the East India Company in 1795, becoming Lieutenant General of Java in 1811. He later served as Lieutenant General of Sumatra (1818–23), during which time he persuaded the company to purchase the undeveloped island of Singapore (1819) and undertook much of the preliminary work for transforming it into an international port and centre of commerce.

Rafsanjani, Ali Akbar Hashemi (1934–) Iranian statesman and religious leader, President (1989–97). A supporter and former pupil of Ayatollah Khomeini, in 1978 he helped organize the mass demonstrations that led to the shah's overthrow the following year. In 1988 he helped to bring an end to the Iran–Iraq War, having persuaded Khomeini to accept the UN's peace terms. When Khomeini died in 1989 Rafsanjani emerged from the ensuing power struggle as

Iran's leader. He sought to improve Iran's relations with the West, and kept his country neutral during the Gulf War of 1991. He stood unsuccessfully in the 2005 presidential election and was barred from standing in 2013.

Raglan, FitzRoy James Henry Somerset, 1st Baron (1788–1855) British soldier. Joining the army in 1804, he served as aide-de-camp to Arthur Wellesley (Duke of *Wellington) during the *Peninsular War, and lost an arm at the Battle of Waterloo. Appointed to lead the British expeditionary force in the *Crimean War, he won a victory at Inkerman (5 November 1854) with French assistance, but was criticized for his general conduct of the campaign, and the disastrous cavalry charge at the Battle of *Balaklava.

Rahman *See* ABDUL RAHMAN, TUNKU.

railways, history of The advent of railways brought together the technology of the steam engine, developed in the early 18th century, and the horse- or human-powered wagon-ways used in mining since the 16th century. The British engineer Richard Trevithick (1771–1833) was the first to build a steam locomotive to run on such wagon-ways (1804); other steam locomotive pioneers, also British, were John Blenkinsop (1783–1831), William Hedley (1779–1843), and George Stephenson (1781–1848). Early locomotives were handicapped by the weakness of the available railway track: it was not until technical advances were made in track construction that the railway became truly practical.

    The Stockton and Darlington Railway (1825) was the first to carry both freight and passengers. In 1830 it was followed by the Liverpool and Manchester Railway, the line that heralded the beginning of the railway era using Stephenson's *Rocket* as locomotive. There followed a period of rapid expansion and development of railways throughout the world. By 1847, 250,000 navvies were employed in railway construction in the UK, and in the USA, where railroad companies were the main agents of westward expansion, nearly 34,000 km (21,100 miles) of railway were constructed between 1850 and 1860. By the end of the century railway networks covered Europe, the USA, Canada, and parts of imperial Russia. In Europe cheap and easy travel helped to break down provincial differences, while in Switzerland and the Mediterranean the holiday industry steadily developed. Railways were important for both sides in the American Civil War, for moving troops and supplies. The first electric locomotive was demonstrated in Berlin in 1879. Electric traction was commercially applied first on suburban and metropolitan lines, but was quickly adopted for underground railways. One of the earliest users of electric locomotives on main-line routes was Italy, where a line was opened in 1902.

The railways proved strategically important on all fronts in World War I. After the war many railway companies grouped together as national railway systems or large geographical concerns. In the late 1930s the steam locomotive reached its zenith, but electric locomotives were already in widespread use in Europe and Scandinavia, and main-line diesel locomotives were coming into service in the USA. In this period road and air transport began to challenge the railways.

Following World War II there was a period of reconstruction: new steam locomotives were introduced in the UK and mainland Europe, and new diesels were also under test. Steam locomotive production ended in the USA in the 1950s, and in Europe in the 1960s, and, as the competition from roads increased, there were major cutbacks in the rail network. In Japan in 1964, the high-speed *shinkansen* or 'bullet' trains began operation, running on specially developed track at speeds of up to 210 km/h (130 mph). At around the same period experiments began using ground guidance-systems other than conventional track.

In the last quarter of the 20th century, railway construction worldwide started to grow again, though in developed countries few new lines were built. In Europe, notably in France and more recently Germany, other high-speed trains have been developed. There has also been a considerable investment in commuter trains and light railway rapid-transit systems to ease congestion on roads and pollution. A new development in Jakarta, Indonesia, is the Aeromovel, a light, engineless train powered by compressed air blown through a duct below the track. New underground railways have been built in some of the newer large cities (for example, the Metro in Mexico City), while in China the railway network is growing at a rate of some 1000 km (600 miles) per year. The Channel Tunnel rail link between England and France began to operate in 1994. Following a model adopted by Sweden in the early 1990s, Britain privatized its rail network in the mid-1990s.

Rajagopalachariar, Chakravarti (1878–1972) Indian nationalist politician. He became a close associate of Mohandas *Gandhi and was imprisoned on several occasions for *non-cooperation with the British. Himself a Hindu,

he was tolerant of the right of Indian Muslims to demand special minority safeguards and of the creation of the separate state of Pakistan. He served as Governor-General of India (1948–50) and Chief Minister of the Madras government (1952–54). In 1959 he was one of the founders of the conservative Swatantra Party.

Rajput (Sanskrit, 'son of a king') The predominantly landowning class, also called Thakurs, living mainly in central and northern India, who claim descent from the Hindu Ksatriya (warrior) caste. Many leading clans are of royal lineage, but others include cultivators of Sudra (menial) caste. Their clans are divided into four lines: Solar, Lunar, Fire, and Snake.

Rakosi, Matyas (1892–1971) Hungarian politician. He played an important role in the Hungarian communist revolution led by Béla *Kun in 1919. After four years in Moscow (1920–24), Rakosi returned to Hungary but was later arrested, to be released only in 1940. In 1944 he became First Secretary of the Hungarian Communist Party and during this time established a ruthless Stalinist regime. He was Prime Minister (1952–53). Opposition to his Stalinist policies led to his resignation as Party Secretary and return to the Soviet Union in 1956. The brutality of his secret police contributed to the *Hungarian Revolution of 1956.

Raleigh, Sir Walter (or Sir Walter Ralegh) (c.1552–1618) English explorer, courtier, and writer. A favourite of Elizabeth I, he organized several voyages of exploration and colonization to the Americas, including an unsuccessful attempt to settle Virginia (1584–89) and a journey up the Orinoco River in search of gold (1595); from his travels he brought back potato and tobacco plants to England. Raleigh was imprisoned in 1603 by James I on a charge of conspiracy, but released in 1616 to lead a second expedition up the Orinoco in search of the fabled land of El Dorado. He returned empty-handed after a clash with some Spanish settlers, and was subsequently executed on the original charge.

Ramanuja (died 1137) Brahmin (member of the *Hindu priestly caste) from southern India, whose teachings inspired the *bhakti* devotional school. He identified Brahman (the supreme soul) with the god Vishnu, whose worship he then encouraged on pilgrimages throughout India. His preaching that the visible world is real and not illusory and that God should be worshipped devotedly, built a bridge between philosophy and popular *bhakti* religion.

Rambouillet, Catherine de Vivonne, Marquise de (1588–1665) French aristocrat

who presided over the first of the *salons* that dominated the intellectual life of 17th-century Paris. The Hôtel de Rambouillet was at the height of its influence between 1620 and 1645 and was frequented by such figures as the playwright Corneille, the writer Madame de Sévigné, and the clergyman Bossuet. The Marquise sought to promote philosophical conversation, refinement, and good taste, earning her the description *précieuse*, later mocked in Molière's comedy *Les Précieuses Ridicules*.

Ramesses II (or Ramesses the Great) Phar-

aoh of Egypt (ruled *c.*1304–1237 BC). When Ramesses II acceded to the throne Egypt was at war with the *Hittites. In the fifth year of his reign Ramesses II fought the Hittites at Kadesh where he managed to extricate himself from a perilous situation. In the 21st year of his reign the two powers concluded a peace treaty and Ramesses married a Hittite princess. He also undertook campaigns against the Libyans. His reign, which marked a high point in ancient Egyptian history, was one of considerable prosperity and he oversaw a substantial building programme, which included two temples cut out of the cliffs at Abu Simbel, the completion of his father Seti I's hypostyle hall at *Karnak, and temple at Abydos.

Ramesses III Pharaoh of Egypt (ruled *c.*1188–

1156 BC). Ramesses III successfully repelled three major invasions, two by the Libyans and one by the *Sea Peoples. Peace and prosperity followed, but the last years of his reign were marked by social unrest and an assassination attempt. He was the last Egyptian ruler to hold land in Palestine.

Ramillies, Battle of (23 May 1706) A battle

that took place in eastern Belgium between Namur and Louvain, *Marlborough's second great victory during the War of the *Spanish Succession over the French army under Villeroi. Marlborough duped his opponents into thinking his main attack was coming from the right and smashed through the French line from the left. The French losses were five times greater than Marlborough's. He went on to overrun much of Flanders and Brabant.

Randolph, Asa Philip (1889–1979) African-

American labour leader. He was prominent in many of the struggles for *civil rights. His threat of a march on Washington in 1941 contributed to the end of race restrictions on employment in the defence industries and his activities in 1948

helped to persuade President *Truman to end segregation in the armed forces. In 1957, as leader of the Brotherhood of Sleeping-Car Porters, he became a vice-president of the *American Federation of Labor. In 1963 he helped to organize the march on Washington for Jobs and Freedom, one of the largest civil rights demonstrations ever held in the USA.

Ranjit Singh (known as 'the Lion of the

Punjab') (1780–1839) Indian maharaja, founder of the Sikh state of Punjab. After succeeding his father as a Sikh ruler at the age of twelve, he seized Lahore from the Afghans in 1799 and proclaimed himself maharaja of Punjab in 1801. He proceeded to make the state the most powerful in India, securing the holy city of Amritsar (1802) and expanding his control north-west with the capture of Peshawar (1818) and Kashmir (1819). At the end of the Sikh Wars, following his death, most of his territory was annexed by Britain.

ransom A sum of money paid for the release of a prisoner or for the restitution of property. The demanding and paying of ransoms formed an accepted part of medieval warfare and diplomacy. Knights who were *vassals of a lord were obliged to pay for the release of their lord if he was captured in war, although in the late Middle Ages family and friends paid as well as a lord's estate. A suitable ransom would be negotiated and raised to secure eventual release. Needless massacre of prisoners, as after *Agincourt, aroused resentment among would-be captors. Notable ransom victims include John II of France and *Richard I of England.

Rapallo, Treaties of Two treaties signed at

Rapallo, a city in north Italy. The **First Treaty of Rapallo** (1920) established relations between Italy and the kingdom of Serbs, Croatians, and Slovenes (Yugoslavia). Italy obtained the Istrian peninsula while Dalmatia went to Yugoslavia. Fiume (Rijeka) became a free city. The **Second Treaty of Rapallo** (1922) was more important. It recorded an agreement between Germany and the Soviet Union. The two countries agreed to abandon any financial claims that each might bring against the other following *World War I. Secretly, in defiance of the *Versailles Peace Settlement, German soldiers were to be permitted to train in the Soviet Union.

Rashid Ali al-Ghailani (1892–1965) Iraqi

statesman. Member of a well-known religious family, he served as Prime Minister on four occasions. In April 1941 he seized power by a military coup that also deposed Abd al-Ilah, regent for the child-king, Faisal II. Believing the new government to be pro-Axis, Britain intervened to expel Rashid Ali in May 1941 and restored the regent.

Rasputin, Grigori (Efimovich) (1871–1916) Russian monk. Originally a Siberian peasant, he came to exert great influence over Tsar Nicholas II and his family during World War I by claiming miraculous powers to heal the heir to the throne, who suffered from haemophilia. His appropriation of ecclesiastical, political, and military powers, with the support of the Empress Alexandra during Nicholas's absence, combined with a reputation for debauchery, steadily discredited the imperial family and was one of the main causes of the Russian Revolution. Rasputin was eventually assassinated by a group loyal to the tsar.

Rastafarian A sect of Jamaican origin believing that African Americans are the chosen people, that the late Emperor Haile Selassie of Ethiopia was God Incarnate, and that he will secure their repatriation to their homeland in Africa. Ras Tafari (Amharic, *ras* chief) was the title by which Haile Selassie was known from 1916 until his accession in 1930.

Ratana, Tahupotiki Wiremu (1873–1939) Maori political and religious leader. A Methodist farmer, he founded the Ratana Church (1920), an interdenominational movement whose aim was to unite Maoris of all tribes. Its doctrine of faith-healing and many unorthodox rituals led to a rift with other Christian denominations in 1925. Politically Ratana struggled for Maori rights by pressing for full implementation of the Treaty of *Waitangi.

Rathenau, Walther (1867–1922) German industrialist and statesman. He was responsible for directing Germany's war economy (1916–18) and later became Minister of Reconstruction (1921) and Foreign Minister (1922) in the *Weimar Republic. He believed that Germany must fulfil its obligations under the *Versailles Peace Settlement, including payment of *reparations. Convinced of Germany's ability to gain ascendancy in Europe he negotiated the Second Treaty of *Rapallo (1922) with Russia, establishing military and trade links. He was assassinated by *anti-Semitic nationalists in 1922.

Rawlings, Jerry (John) (1947–) Ghanaian politician, President (1982–2001). Of mixed Ghanaian and Scottish parentage, Rawlings was born in Accra and educated in military academies. He won a commission in the country's

air force in 1969 and was promoted to flight-lieutenant in 1978. In the following year, he was at the head of a group of junior officers that overthrew the government and installed a civilian administration. In 1981, however, Rawlings staged a second coup and declared himself head of state.

Rawlings executed a number of politicians after the 1981 coup for alleged corruption and suspended constitutional rule for a period. In the later 1980s, however, he implemented an IMF/World Bank plan for Ghana's economic recovery and restored multiparty politics. In 1992, after promulgating a new constitution, he resigned and successfully contested the presidential elections as a civilian.

Reagan, Ronald (Wilson) (1911–2004) US Republican statesman, 40th President of the USA (1981–89). He was a Hollywood actor before entering politics and becoming governor of California (1966–74). In 1981, at the age of 69, he became the oldest-ever President of the USA. During his presidency military expenditure was increased, the Strategic Defense Initiative was launched, taxes and spending on social services were reduced, and the national budget deficit rose to record levels. An intermediate nuclear forces non-proliferation treaty with the USSR was signed in 1987.

Reason, Age of *See* ENLIGHTENMENT.

Rebecca riots (1839; 1842–43) A series of agrarian riots in south-west Wales. They were a protest against the toll-gates introduced by turnpike trusts. Bands of rioters disguised in women's clothes attacked and broke the gates. Each band was led by a "Rebecca" after the Old Testament story of Rebecca, "be thou the mother of millions, and let thy seed possess the gate of those which hate them". In 1843 a series of massed meetings took place. Troops and a contingent of the Metropolitan Police were sent from London, while a commission to investigate grievances took evidence. In 1844 an Act to "consolidate and amend the Laws relating to Turnpike Trusts in Wales" ended the protest.

Reconstruction Acts (1867–68) Legislation passed by the US Congress dealing with the reorganization of the South in the aftermath of the *American Civil War. The question of the treatment of the defeated *Confederacy raised conflicting priorities between reconciliation with white Southerners and justice for the freed slaves. In 1866 an impasse developed between President Andrew *Johnson, and the

Republican majorities in Congress. In 1867 Congress passed, over the President's veto, a Reconstruction Act that divided the South into military districts, and required the calling of a new constitutional convention in each state, elected by universal manhood suffrage. The new state governments were to provide for black suffrage and to ratify the Fourteenth Amendment as conditions for readmittance to the Union. Further Reconstruction Acts were passed in the following 12 months to counter Southern attempts to delay or circumvent the implementation of the first measure.

recusants The people, usually Roman Catholics, who refused to attend Anglican church services from the 16th century onward. Fines were imposed on them by Acts of Uniformity (1552 and 1559). Although *Nonconformists could be penalized for recusancy, the term was often used as an abbreviation of "Catholic Recusants", distinguishing them from "Church Papists", who were Catholics who attended Anglican services rather than pay the fines. The penal laws against Catholics were extended between 1571 and 1610, but were rarely enforced. They were systematically repealed in a series of Toleration Acts (see CATHOLIC EMANCIPATION).

Red Army Soviet army formed by *Trotsky as Commissar for War (1918–25) to save the *Bolshevik revolution during the *Russian Civil War. For trained officers, Trotsky had to rely on former officers of the Imperial Army. After *Hitler's invasion of the Soviet Union (1941) the Red Army became the largest in the world—reaching five million by 1945. Precise figures remain unknown, but Red Army casualties in World War II have been estimated as high as seven million men. The name fell into disuse shortly after World War II and was replaced by that of Soviet Armed Forces, which in turn adopted the titles of the independent republics after the breakup of the Soviet Union in 1991.

Red Brigades A grouping of Italian left-wing terrorists especially active in the period 1977–81. The security forces seemed powerless against them, although some arrests were eventually made. The Red Brigades were responsible for a number of incidents including the kidnapping and murder of the Italian statesman Aldo *Moro in 1978.

Red Cross International agency concerned with the alleviation of human suffering. Its founder, the Swiss philanthropist Henri Dunant (1828–1910), horrified by the suffering he saw at the Battle of Solferino, proposed the formation of voluntary aid societies for the relief of war victims. In 1863 the International Committee of the Red Cross was established and in the following year twelve governments signed the *Geneva Convention. This drew up the terms for the care of soldiers and was extended to include victims of naval warfare (1929), and, 20 years later, civilians. Its conventions have now been ratified by almost 150 nations. Its flag is a red cross on a white background. In Muslim countries the cross is replaced by a red crescent. The International Red Cross was awarded Nobel Peace Prizes in 1917 and 1944.

Red Feds The members of the **National Federation of Labour**, an association of militant unions formed in 1909 in New Zealand. Never winning the support of a majority of the country's unionists, the Federation briefly became an important force because of the presence of strong unions, such as the miners, in its ranks. In 1912 confrontation between government and Red Feds occurred at the Waihi gold-mine, when a strike resulted in violence and one death before the miners accepted defeat. The **United Federation of Labour** was formed, which was soon involved in a bitter strike, centred on the Wellington docks and again the government intervened. Thousands of mounted police were recruited and there were violent clashes, but this strike was also broken. The Red Feds and their methods of confrontation were permanently discredited. Since then the New Zealand trade unions have worked amicably through a process of arbitration and a series of Acts were passed to amend the basic Industrial and Conciliation Arbitration Act of 1894.

Red Guards Militant young supporters of *Mao Zedong during the Chinese *Cultural Revolution (1966–69). Taking their name from the army units organized by Mao in 1927, the Red Guards, numbering several million, provided the popular, paramilitary vanguard of the Cultural Revolution. As well as supposed reactionaries, they attacked the Communist Party establishment, China's cultural heritage, and all vestiges of Western influence, maintaining the momentum of the movement through mass demonstrations, a constant poster war, and violent attacks on people and property. Fighting between opposing Red Guard groups led to thousands of deaths. After the Cultural Revolution, many were sent into the countryside for forced 're-education'.

Redmond, John (Edward) (1856–1918) Irish politician. He succeeded Charles Parnell as leader of the Irish Nationalist Party in the House of Commons (1891–1918). The Home Rule Bill of 1912 was introduced with his support, although it was never implemented because of World War I.

Red River Settlement An early 19th-century agricultural colony in the Red River (now Manitoba) area of central Canada that was granted by the Hudson's Bay Company to Thomas Douglas, 5th Earl of Selkirk (1771–1820). Selkirk endeavoured to settle the dispossessed of Scotland and Northern Ireland there. His first group of settlers succumbed to North West Company pressure to abandon the area soon after their arrival in 1812. The colony was re-established in 1816, but 22 settlers were killed in a massacre at Seven Oaks, led by North West Company men and other attacks followed. Selkirk himself went bankrupt, but the publicity attracted by the affair led to the forced merger (1821) of the North West Company and Hudson's Bay Company and cleared the way for more successful settlement in the area.

Red Shirts Members of a nationalist organization in British India in the *North-West Frontier province. Formed in 1929 by Abdul Ghaffar Khan, a follower of Mahatma *Gandhi, it was correctly entitled Khudai Khidmatgar (Servants of God). It provided the main support for Ghaffar Khan's control of the province until 1946, during which time it was deployed in support of *Congress policies. Opposed to partition in 1947 Ghaffar Khan and the Red Shirts campaigned for a separate state of Pakhtunistan. The new government of Pakistan banned the Red Shirts and imprisoned Ghaffar Khan for 30 years.

reeve A local official in Anglo-Saxon and post-Conquest England. The most important were shire reeves (*sheriffs) who administered royal justice and collected royal revenues within their shire. Manorial reeves organized the peasant labour force on estates and their duties were considerable. They received a money wage, grants of grazing land, and remission of rent and feudal dues. Although often of *villein status those reeves who contrived through annual re-election to make their office hereditary had considerably improved their economic condition by the 14th century, when Chaucer wrote of them in *The Canterbury Tales*.

Reform Acts A series of legislative measures that extended the franchise in 19th- and 20th-century Britain. The Reform Act of 1832 eliminated many anomalies, such as *rotten boroughs, and enfranchised the new industrial towns,

which had hitherto been unrepresented. The Reform Act of 1867 doubled the size of the electorate and gave many urban working-class men the vote. However, agricultural labourers and domestic servants had to wait a further 17 years to be enfranchised: the Reform Act of 1884 increased the electorate to about five million. The Representation of the People Act (1918) gave the vote to all men over the age of 21 and conceded some of the demands of the *suffragettes by enfranchising women over 30, but on a property qualification. Universal adult suffrage for everyone over 21 was finally achieved in the UK in 1928, when women between the ages of 21 and 30 secured the right to vote and the property qualification was abolished. In 1969 the voting age was lowered to 18.

Reformation The 16th-century movement for reform of the doctrines and practices of the *Roman Catholic Church, ending in the establishment of *Protestant churches.

The starting point of the Reformation is often given as 1517, when the German theologian Martin *Luther launched his protest against the corruption of the papacy and the Roman Catholic Church, although he was breaking no new controversial ground. In fact, most of the Reformation movements laid stress, not on innovation, but on return to a primitive simplicity. Luther's theological reading led him to attack the central Catholic doctrines of transubstantiation, clerical celibacy, and papal supremacy. He also called for radical reform of the religious orders. By 1530 the rulers of Saxony, Hesse, Brandenburg, and Brunswick, as well as the kings of Sweden and Denmark had been won over to the reformed beliefs. They proceeded to break with the Roman Church, and set about regulating the churches in their territories according to Protestant principles.

In Switzerland, the Reformation was led first by Ulrich *Zwingli, who carried through anti-papal, antihierarchic, and antimonastic reforms in Zurich. After his death the leadership passed to *Calvin, in whose hands reforming opinion assumed a more explicitly doctrinal and revolutionary tone. Calvinism became the driving force of the movement in western Germany, France, the Netherlands, and Scotland, where in each case it was linked with a political struggle. Calvinism was also the main doctrinal influence within the Anglican Church. In Europe the reforming movement was increasingly checked and balanced by the *Counter-Reformation. The era of religious wars came to an end with the conclusion of the *Thirty Years War (1618–48).

Regency, the The period in Britain from 1811 to 1820 when the Prince of Wales, later *George IV, acted as regent for his father, *George III, who had become insane. Among the major events of the Regency were the *War of 1812 involving Britain and the USA, the successful conclusion of the *Napoleonic Wars, and the Congress of *Vienna (1814–15). In Britain the post-war period was marked by a slump in the economy, which caused much social unrest. The Tory government used severe measures to quell popular discontent, which culminated in the *Peterloo Massacre of 1819.

Regulators (1764–71) American rebels from inland North Carolina who felt aggrieved at the political control of the aristocrats over the coastal region. They turned to violence when legal action failed to increase their representation and reduce their taxation. "The Regulation", centred in Orange County, attacked magistrates and lawyers until it was overwhelmed by the militia under Governor Tryon at the Battle of the Alamance. Antagonisms between coastal and frontier settlers were not uncommon, as *Bacon's, *Culpeper's, and *Shays's rebellions demonstrated.

Reich *See* HOLY ROMAN EMPIRE.

Reichstag (German, 'imperial parliament') The legislature of the *German Second empire and of the Weimar Republic. Its role was confined to legislation, being forbidden to interfere in federal government affairs and having limited control over public spending. Under the Weimar Republic it enjoyed greater power as the government was made responsible to it. On the night of 27 February 1933 the **Reichstag fire** occurred. *Goering and *Goebbels allegedly planned to set fire to the building, subsequently claiming it as a communist plot. The arsonist was a half-crazed Dutch communist, Marinus van der Lubbe. The subsequent trial was an embarrassment as the accused German and Bulgarian communist leaders were acquitted of complicity and only van der Lubbe was executed. But the fire had served its political purpose. On 28 February a decree suspended all civil liberties and installed a state of emergency, which lasted until 1945. Elections to the Reichstag were held on 5 March 1933, but by the Enabling Act of 23 March 1933 the Reichstag effectively voted itself out of existence. Following German reunification in 1990 the Reichstag building in Berlin was restored; it has been the seat of the German parliament since 1999.

Reid, Sir George Houstoun (1845–1918) Australian statesman. Reid was Premier of New South Wales from 1894 until 1899. His ambivalent attitude towards *Australian federation resulted in his being dubbed "Yes–No" Reid. He led the Free Traders in the first federal parliament and was Prime Minister, leading a coalition of Free Traders and Protectionists (1904–05). After the defeat of his government, Reid led the Opposition until 1908. He was the first Australian High Commissioner in London (1910–16), after which he was elected to the British House of Commons.

Reith, John (Charles Walsham), 1st Baron (1889–1971) Scottish administrator and politician, the first general manager (1922–27) and first director-general (1927–38) of the BBC. He played a major part in the growth and developing ethos of the BBC, refusing to treat broadcasting simply as a means of entertainment and championing its moral and intellectual role in the community. Reith later served in various Cabinet posts during World War II. In 1948 the BBC established the **Reith Lectures**, broadcast annually, in his honour.

Religion, French Wars of *See* FRENCH WARS OF RELIGION.

Renaissance (French, 'rebirth') The intellectual and artistic flowering that began in Italy in the 14th century, culminated there in the 16th century, and greatly influenced other parts of Europe. The notion of a rebirth refers to a revival of the values of the classical world. The idea was brilliantly characterized by Alberti, himself an architect, painter, scientist, poet, and mathematician, and in Leonardo da Vinci. Brunelleschi is considered the first Renaissance architect; from his interest in Roman remains he created buildings that could be compared with the finest ancient examples. Other major architects included Bramante, regarded by his contemporaries as the most successful architect of the High Renaissance, and Palladio. In sculpture, it was Donatello in the early 15th century who assimilated the spirit of ancient sculpture. Ghiberti, Michelangelo, and others revealed new possibilities of expression that had been unknown to antiquity. In painting, fidelity to nature became a central concern to early Renaissance painters, such as Giotto and Masaccio, who brought scientific vigour to the problems of representation, while the invention of perspective assisted in the realistic portrayal of nature. Michelangelo, Raphael, Titian and others broke new ground by introducing the human figure, naturalistically depicted, into their paintings. Florence in the period around 1425 was the cradle of the Renaissance, but by the early 16th century—the 'High Renaissance'—Venice and Rome were equally important. The ideals and imagery of the Italian Renaissance did not generally begin to spread to the rest of Europe until about 1500. Dürer was the outstanding artist of the 'Northern Renaissance', making it his mission to transplant the new Italian ideas on to German soil. Out of the art of the High Renaissance there developed a style characterized by a sense of extreme elegance and grace, which became known as Mannerism.

In literature the Renaissance was led by humanist scholars and poets, notably Petrarch, Dante, and Boccaccio in Italy. Poetry and prose began to be written in the vernacular instead of Latin, and the invention of printing contributed to the spread of ideas. Among the notable writers of the Renaissance beyond Italy are Erasmus in the Netherlands; Montaigne and Rabelais, and the poets of the Pléiade in France; Lope de Vega and Cervantes in Spain; and Edmund Spenser, Sir Philip Sidney, Shakespeare, and Sir Francis Bacon in Britain. The Renaissance profoundly affected the presentation and content of theatrical production. Dramatists introduced classical form and restraint into their works, which were to be codified, notably in France, with greater severity than in classical times. The Renaissance had far-reaching consequences in many other fields. The impulse to explore the world led to the voyages of discovery of *Diaz de Novaes, *da Gama, and *Magellan. These in turn led to advances in geography and cartography and the colonization of new lands. The astronomers Copernicus, Kepler, and Galileo proposed new theories about the movement of the planets, and advances were made in biology, chemistry, physics, and medicine. The Flemish anatomist Vesalius wrote *De humani corporis fabrica* (1543), an influential anatomical treatise. The new spirit of enquiry also affected perception of the Church and paved the way for reform.

reparations Compensation payments for damage done in war by a defeated enemy. They were a condition of the armistice for World War I, and part of the *Versailles Peace Settlement. After World War II reparations took the form of Allied occupation of Germany and Japan. Britain, France, and the USA ended reparation collections in 1952. In the aftermath of the Gulf War (1991), the UN Compensation Commission obliged Iraq, whose invasion of Kuwait had precipitated the conflict, to pay reparations to war victims.

Representatives, US House of *See* HOUSE OF REPRESENTATIVES.

Republican Party A major political party in the USA. The present Republican Party was formed in 1854, being precipitated by the Kansas–Nebraska Act and by the agitation of the Free Soil Party; it brought together groups opposed to slavery but supporting a protective trade tariff. The party won its first presidential election with Abraham *Lincoln in 1860 and from then until 1932 lost only four such contests, two each to *Cleveland and Woodrow *Wilson. Under more recent Republican Presidents *Nixon, *Ford, and *Reagan, it became associated with military spending and a forceful assertion of US presence worldwide, especially in Central America. Strongly backed by corporate business, it nevertheless failed to maintain a grip on Congress, which usually had a Democratic majority even when the President was Republican. However, this trend was reversed in 1994, when the Republicans gained control of both the Senate and the House of Representatives for the first time in 40 years. Other important influences on the Republican Party in recent years have been the social and political conservatism of Christian fundamentalists and the radical ideas of *Neoconservatism. Both were prominent in the presidency of George W. *Bush. Since 2009 the Republican Party has been influenced by the *Tea Party Movement.

Repudiation Movement An attempt to set aside land purchase contracts in New Zealand. Ownership of *Maori land had been steadily proceeding through purchases from individual Maori, not tribal communities, ignoring the guarantees of the Treaty of *Waitangi (1840). In 1873 Henare Matua, a Maori chief, appealed to the Hawkes Bay Native Lands Alienation Commission to repudiate land purchase contracts drawn up in the Hawkes Bay area. He received some support from settler-politicians anxious to embarrass the large landed interests. The movement met with little success in overturning contracts, but it did contribute to the growing separatist movement among Maoris, the Kotahitanga.

resistance movements Underground movements that fought against Nazi Germany and Japan during World War II. Their activities involved publishing underground newspapers, helping Jews and prisoners-of-war to escape, conveying intelligence by secret radios, as well as committing acts of sabotage. In occupied Europe there were often deep divisions between communist and non-communist organizations, notably in France, where the *Maquis was active, as well as in Belgium, Yugoslavia, and Greece. Communist parties had at first remained passive, but following the German invasion of the Soviet Union (June 1941), they formed or joined underground groups. Dutch, Danish, and Norwegian resistance remained unified and worked closely with London, where in 1940 the British Special Operations Executive (SOE) was set up to coordinate all subversive activity, both in Europe and the Far East, and to supply arms and equipment by secret air-drops. In the Far East clandestine operations were carried out through British and US intelligence organizations. Much of their effort was devoted to intelligence gathering, psychological warfare, and prisoner-of-war recovery, while the actual sabotaging of selected installations and communication lines was conducted by native-born, nationalist, and often communist-inspired guerrillas.

Restoration (1660) The re-establishment in England, Scotland, and Ireland of the Stuart monarchy by placing Charles II, the exiled son of Charles I, on the throne. The Restoration was accompanied by the revival of the Church of England, the growth of Cavalier fortunes (although those who had sold their estates to pay fines could not get them back), and a flourishing cultural and social life. The Restoration did not restore the absolute authority of the Stuart monarchy, as Charles II was soon to discover.

Reuter, Paul Julius, Baron von (born **Israel Beer Josaphat**) (1816–99) German pioneer of telegraphy and news reporting. After establishing a service for sending commercial telegrams in Aachen (1849), he moved his headquarters to London, where he founded the news agency Reuters.

Revere, Paul (1735–1818) US patriot and silversmith. He was one of the demonstrators involved in the Boston Tea Party of 1773, the protest at the imposition of tax on tea by Britain. Two years later he made his famous midnight ride from Boston to Lexington to warn fellow American revolutionaries of the approach of British troops; the journey is immortalized in Longfellow's poem 'Paul Revere's Ride' (1863).

Revolutionary Wars (1792–1802) A series of wars in Europe following the *French Revolution. In 1791 Louis XVI attempted unsuccessfully to escape from France to Germany,

to win support from Austria and Prussia. In April 1792 France declared war on Austria, which then ruled Belgium (the Austrian Netherlands). A series of French defeats followed until, on 20 September, an invading Prussian army was defeated at Valmy. In February 1793 war was declared against Britain, Spain, and the United Provinces of the Netherlands. For a year a **Reign of Terror** operated in France, but, at the same time, under the skill of *Carnot, armies had been steadily raised and trained. At first the aim was to consolidate the frontiers of France along the 'natural frontiers' of the Rhine and the Alps, but from 1795, these armies were to conquer Europe. A number of brilliant young officers emerged, for example Bernadotte (later *Charles XIV of Sweden), Barthélemy Joubert (killed in battle 1799), and above all *Napoleon. All the Netherlands were conquered, Belgium being annexed, and the Republic of Batavia created from the United Provinces; French armies advanced across the Rhine and into South Germany. Switzerland was made into the Helvetic Republic (1798). In 1796–97 Napoleon took an army into Italy, defeated the Austrians at Arcola and occupied Venice, creating the Cisalpine and Ligurian Republics. In 1798 he led an expedition to Egypt, but the British fleet under *Nelson destroyed his fleet at Aboukir Bay, and Napoleon returned to Paris. Meanwhile Austrian and Russian troops had re-occupied Italy and in 1799 Napoleon again marched across the Alps to defeat the Austrians at Marengo. At the same time General Moreau won a second great victory at Hohenlinden. The peace treaties of Lunéville (1801 with Austria) and Amiens (1802 with Britain) were then negotiated, ending the Revolutionary Wars.

Revolutions of 1848 A series of revolutions in western and central Europe. Revolution erupted first in France, where supporters of universal suffrage and a socialist minority under Louis *Blanc caused the overthrow of the July monarchy of *Louis Philippe and established the Second Republic. In most German states there were popular demonstrations and uprisings, and a movement for an elected national parliament to draft a constitution for a united Germany. Rioting in Austria caused the flight of both *Metternich and the emperor, and the formation of a constituent assembly and the emancipation of the peasantry. A movement for Hungarian independence, headed by *Kossuth, led to a short-lived republican government from Budapest for all Hungarian lands; but Magyar refusal to consider independence for its own minorities resulted in an insurrection by Croat,

Serb, and Transylvanian forces and in Hungary's defeat by Austrian and Russian forces. In the Italian states there was a series of abortive revolutions which led to the temporary expulsion of the Austrians and the flight of Pope Pius IX from Rome, but the united, democratic republic dreamt of by *Mazzini did not come about. A Pan-Slav Congress in Prague inspired Czech nationalist demonstrations to demand autonomy within a federal Austria. By 1849 counter-revolutionary forces had restored order, but the concept of absolute monarchy and the feudal rights of a land-owning aristocracy had been tacitly abandoned.

Reynaud, Paul (1878–1966) French politician. He was Finance Minister (1938–40), and Prime Minister in the emergency of 1940, but, having appointed *Pétain and *Weygand, he was unable to carry on the war when these two proved defeatist. He resigned in mid-June 1940. After the war he was Finance Minister (1948) and Vice-Premier (1953) in the Fourth Republic. He assisted in the formation of the Fifth Republic, but later quarrelled with *de Gaulle.

Reynolds, Albert (1932–2014) Irish Fianna Fáil statesman, Taoiseach (Prime Minister) (1992–94). He was involved with John Major in drafting the *Downing Street Declaration (1993), intended as the basis of a peace initiative in Northern Ireland. He resigned in 1994 after losing the support of the Irish Labour Party.

Reza Shah Pahlavi (born **Reza Khan**) (1878–1944) Shah of Iran (1925–41). An officer of the Persian Cossack Brigade, he achieved power through an army coup (1921) and established a military dictatorship. He was successively Minister of War and Prime Minister before becoming Shah. He followed a policy of rapid modernization, constructing a national army, a modernized administrative system, new legal and educational systems, and economic development, notably through the Trans-Iranian Railway (1927–38). He crushed tribal and other opposition to his policies. In World War II his refusal to expel German nationals led to the invasion and occupation of Iran by Soviet and British forces. He was forced to abdicate in favour of his son, *Muhammad Reza Shah Pahlavi, and died in exile in South Africa.

Rhee, Syngman (1871–1965) Korean statesman. He was an early supporter of Korean independence from Japan and after a spell of imprisonment (1897–1904) for nationalist activities, he went to the USA and became President of a "government-in-exile" formed by a small group of his supporters. After World War II he returned to become leader of South *Korea during the US occupation and in 1948 he became the first President of the Republic of Korea, advocating the unification of Korea both before and after the *Korean War (1950–53). Rhee was re-elected in 1952 and 1956, but opposition to his corrupt and autocratic government grew more intense as economic conditions deteriorated and a third re-election in 1960 caused accusations of rigging and serious rioting, which forced Rhee into exile.

Rhodes, Cecil (John) (1853–1902) British-born South African statesman, Prime Minister of Cape Colony (1890–96). He went to South Africa in 1870, where he became a successful diamond prospector, and 20 years later owned 90% of the world's production of diamonds. Entering politics in 1881, he expanded British territory in southern Africa, annexing Bechuanaland (now Botswana) in 1884 and developing Rhodesia from 1889 onwards through the British South Africa Company, which he founded. While Premier, Rhodes was implicated in the Jameson Raid into Boer territory (1895) and forced to resign. In his will he established the system of Rhodes Scholarships to allow students from the British Empire (now the Commonwealth), the USA, and Germany to study at Oxford University.

Rhodesia 1. The former name of a large territory in central-southern Africa, divided into Northern Rhodesia (now Zambia) and Southern Rhodesia (now Zimbabwe). The region was developed by and named after Cecil *Rhodes, through the British South Africa Company, which administered it until Southern Rhodesia became a self-governing British colony in 1923 and Northern Rhodesia a British protectorate in 1924. From 1953 to 1963 Northern and Southern Rhodesia were united with Nyasaland (now Malawi) to form the federation of Rhodesia and Nyasaland (*see* CENTRAL AFRICAN FEDERATION).
 2. The name adopted by Southern Rhodesia when Northern Rhodesia left the Federation in 1963 to become the independent republic of Zambia.

Ribbentrop, Joachim von (1893–1946) German Nazi politician. A close associate of Hitler, Ribbentrop served as Foreign Minister (1938–45). During his ministry, he signed the non-aggression pact with the Soviet Union (1939). He was convicted as a war criminal at the Nuremberg trials and hanged.

Ricardo, David (1772–1823) British political economist who, with Adam Smith, founded British classical economics. In 1819–23 he was an MP, supporting *Free Trade, a return to the gold standard, and the repeal of the *Corn Laws. He is best remembered for his *Principles of Political Economy and Taxation* (1817), arguing that the value of a commodity is related to amount of labour required to make it—a premise later adopted by Karl *Marx. He also formulated the law of comparative advantage in international trade.

Ricci, Matteo (1552–1610) Italian Jesuit missionary. He was received at the court of the *Ming emperor Wanli in 1601, having arrived in southern China in 1583. He had made himself proficient in Chinese and always dressed in a Chinese scholar's robes. He interested the emperor in clocks brought from Europe, translated numerous books, among them the geometry of Euclid, into Chinese, and made a world map with China, the Middle Kingdom, at its centre. He established beyond doubt that China was Cathay, the land *Marco Polo had described. His tolerance and scholarship impressed influential Chinese, some of whom were converted. The emperor gave land for his tomb in Beijing.

Rice, Condoleezza (1954–) US political scientist and stateswoman. Born in Alabama, she graduated from Denver University, aged 19, in 1974. In 1981 she received her doctorate and immediately became a fellow of Stanford University. She served on the first President *Bush's National Security Council (1989–91) and then returned to Stanford, where she was the first Black woman provost (1993–99). After advising George W. *Bush on foreign affairs during his campaign for the presidency, she was appointed his National Security Advisor (2001–05) and then his Secretary of State (2005–09).

Richard I (the Lionheart) (1157–99) King of England (1189–99). Richard I was the third son of *Henry II and *Eleanor of Aquitaine. He was made Duke of Aquitaine at the age of twelve and in 1173 joined his brothers in their rebellion against Henry. Richard spent only six months of his life in England. Soon after his coronation he left with the Third *Crusade and in Palestine in 1191 he captured Acre and defeated *Saladin at Arsuf. The following year, after concluding a three-year truce with Saladin, he set out overland for England. He was imprisoned by Emperor Henry VI of Austria and, according to widespread legend, his whereabouts were discovered by the Minstrel Blondel. In 1194 England paid a ransom of £100,000 for his release.

During his absence his brother *John had allied himself with *Philip II of France against him. Within a few weeks of his return he began the military campaigns for the defence of Normandy against Philip that led eventually to his death whilst attacking the castle at Châlus. Richard's military exploits earned him the nickname *Coeur de Lion* (French, "Lionheart"). However, his absence abroad led to a growth in the power of the barons, a problem inherited by *John.

Richard II (1367–1400) King of England (1377–99). He was the only son of *Edward the Black Prince and the grandson of Edward III, whom he succeeded at the age of ten. In 1381 his courage helped prevent disaster in the *Peasants' Revolt, but in the next few years he had to face a more direct threat to his power from a group of magnates (Lords Appellant) led by his uncle Thomas of Woodstock, Duke of Gloucester. During the session of the Merciless Parliament (1388) they had Richard's chief supporters executed or imprisoned and it was only in 1397 that he was able to strike back at them by punishing the Lords Appellant. His attempt to impose his personal rule upon England alienated support and enabled Henry of Bolingbroke (*Henry IV) to seize the throne with comparative ease in 1399. Richard abdicated and died a few months later in prison. He was a sensitive man but temperamentally unbalanced and incapable of firm rule.

Richard III (1452–85) Duke of Gloucester (1461–85) and King of England (1483–85). He was a younger brother of *Edward IV and the eleventh child of Richard Plantagenet, Duke of *York. Tudor propaganda, notably the biography by Thomas *More and Shakespeare's plays *Henry VI, Part 3* and *Richard III*, portrayed him as a monster from birth, always a traitor to his own family; but as Duke of Gloucester he served Edward faithfully and was an able soldier and a capable administrator in northern England. Upon the accession of his young nephew *Edward V, he became Protector of England: the council over which he presided included his enemies, the Woodvilles, and he gained in popularity from striking at their power. His usurpation of the throne in June 1483 caused no outright hostility, but in all save the *Yorkist north of England there was revulsion when it came to be believed that he had had Edward V and his brother killed in the Tower of London. (When and how they died remains a mystery.) He had long expected a further invasion of England by the *Lancastrian Henry Tudor (*Henry VII), but when a battle was fought at *Bosworth

Field in August 1485 he was defeated and killed because he had lost the support of his army. His body was hurriedly buried at Leicester, but the precise location was subsequently forgotten. In 2012 an archaeological excavation at a likely site found a skeleton, which DNA tests proved to be Richard's remains. It showed he had suffered from scoliosis—curvature of the spine—which suggests that his portrayal by Shakespeare and others as a hunchback had some basis in fact.

Richard of York *See* YORK, RICHARD PLAN-TAGENET, 3RD DUKE OF.

Richelieu, Armand Jean du Plessis

(1585–1642) French cardinal and statesman. From 1624 to 1642 he was chief minister of Louis XIII, dominating French government. He destroyed the power base of the Huguenots in the late 1620s and set out to undermine the Habsburg empire by supporting the Swedish king Gustavus Adolphus in the Thirty Years War, involving France from 1635. In the same year, Richelieu was also responsible for establishing the Académie Française.

Richthofen, Manfred, Freiherr von

(known as 'the Red Baron') (1882–1918) German fighter pilot. In World War I he initially fought in the cavalry, but transferred to the flying corps, joining a fighter squadron in 1915 and flying a distinctive bright red aircraft. He was eventually shot down, probably by Allied infantrymen, after destroying 80 Allied planes.

Ridley, Nicholas (*c.*1500–55) English Protestant bishop and martyr. He became one of Thomas Cranmer's chaplains in 1537 and, during the reign of Edward VI, was appointed bishop of Rochester (1547) and then of London (1550). During this period, he emerged as one of the leaders of the Reformation, opposing the Catholic policies of Edward's sister and successor Mary I, for which he was later imprisoned (1553) and burnt at the stake in Oxford.

Ridolfi Plot (1571) An abortive international Catholic conspiracy, intended to put *Mary, Queen of Scots on the English throne in place of *Elizabeth I. It took its name from Roberto di Ridolfi (1531–1612), a well-connected Florentine banker who had settled in England. The English Catholics were to rise under Thomas Howard, 4th Duke of Norfolk. Then, with papal finance and Spanish military aid, Elizabeth was to be deposed in favour of Mary, who would marry Howard. Elizabeth's intelligence service uncovered the plot and its leading figures were arrested.

Riebeeck, Jan van (1610–77) Governor of Cape Town (1652–62) and the founder of European settlement in South Africa. He was sent by the Chamber of Amsterdam to found a refreshment station at Cape Town for Netherlands vessels sailing to the East Indies and arrived there on 6 April 1652 with 125 men. As commander he organized a simple government and ruled for ten years. He followed *Dutch East India Company policy in regarding the station as an opportunity for profit rather than for colonization. Growing corn and vines and rearing cattle were permitted, but he discouraged trade with Africans. In 1662 he was transferred to Malacca.

Riefenstahl, Leni (full name **Bertha Helene Amalie Riefenstahl**) (1902–2003) German film-maker and photographer. She is chiefly known for two films which she made during the 1930s; *Triumph of the Will* (1934) a powerful depiction of the 1934 Nuremberg Nazi Party rallies, and *Olympia* (1938), a two-part documentary of the 1936 Berlin Olympic Games. She was not a Nazi Party member and insisted on full control over these films, but outside Germany her work was regarded as Nazi propaganda.

Riel Rebellions (1869; 1885) Two uprisings of the métis or half-Indian population of Manitoba against the Canadian government, led by the French-Indian Louis Riel (1844–85). Expansion westwards led to the uprising in 1869 in which a provisional government under Riel was set up. Riel aroused outrage in the east by executing an Ontario settler, but the arrival of British and Canadian troops coincided with negotiations in Ottawa leading to the area's inclusion within the confederation, with all the local rights demanded by the métis. Riel escaped but increasing resentment of eastern domination and economic dislocation produced a second insurrection in 1885. Riel, who returned from the USA to lead it, was supported by several Native American tribes, but alienated most of the White population and was defeated by the Canadian militia. He was then tried and executed for treason.

Rienzo, Cola di (1313–54) Italian popular leader. As spokesman for the Roman populace he attempted to lead a revolution in 1347. Taking the title of tribune, he sought fiscal, political, and judicial reform. Rejected by the papacy and the powerful Orsini and Colonna lords, he was deposed in November 1347 and excommunicated. In 1350 he gained the support of the new pope, Innocent VI, who encouraged him to restore papal authority in Rome. He returned there in triumph in 1354 only to be killed by the mob. He was remembered in the 19th century as a symbol of Italian unity.

Right, the Political ideas, movements, and parties of a conservative or reactionary character. Following the example of the nobility at the time of the *French Revolution (1789), members of legislative assemblies holding authoritarian, anti-democratic, or anti-socialist views have tended to sit on the right of their chambers. As with *Left, the meaning of "Right" varies with context, denoting at different times conservative, liberal, or even *fascist outlooks. Recent trends have been called the *New Right.

Rights of Man and the Citizen A declaration of the guiding principles of the *French Revolution that was approved by the Constituent National Assembly in August 1789. *Jefferson, the US minister in Paris, was consulted and the Declaration was influenced by the US example as well as by the *Enlightenment. It set forth in clear language the principles of equality and individual liberty: "Men are born and remain free and equal in rights"; "No body of men, no individual, can exercise authority which does not issue expressly from the will of the nation". Civil and fiscal equality, freedom from arbitrary arrest, freedom of speech and the press, and the right to own private property were affirmed. Later the Revolution denied many of these rights, but the declaration ensured an initial welcome for the French Revolutionary armies in many European countries and was the charter of European liberals for the next half-century.

Riot Act An Act to prevent civil disorder passed by the British Parliament in 1715. The Act made it a serious crime for anyone to refuse to obey the command of lawful authority to disperse; thus the Act imposed upon the civil magistrates the dangerous duty of attending a riot, or a large meeting which might become riotous, and reading the Riot Act. Frequent use was made of the Act in the 18th century. Its use declined in the 19th century and it was repealed in 1911.

Ripon, George Frederick Samuel Robinson, 1st Marquess of (1827–1909) British statesman. He entered Parliament as a Liberal in 1853, supporting a scheme to provide working men with opportunities for education. He served as Secretary for War (1863–6), and Secretary for India (1866–68). As President of the Council (1868–73) he was responsible for the 1870 Education Bill, which his deputy, W. E. Forster carried through the House of Commons. In 1873 he became a Roman Catholic and resigned from public office. *Gladstone appointed him viceroy of India (1880–84) where he introduced a system of local self-government and ended restrictions on the freedom of the vernacular press. His Ilbert Bill (1883) gave qualified Indians jurisdiction over Europeans and established trial by a jury, of which half should be Europeans. On his return to Britain he again held ministerial office in Liberal governments.

Risorgimento (Italian, 'resurrection' or 'rebirth') (c.1831–61) A period of political unrest in *Italy, during which the united kingdom of Italy emerged. Much of Italy had experienced liberal reforms and an end to feudal and ecclesiastical privilege during the *Napoleonic Wars. The restoration of repressive regimes led to uprisings in Naples and Piedmont (1821), and in Bologna (1831), then part of the Papal States. Following the French *July Revolution in 1830, Italian nationalists began to support *Mazzini and the *Young Italy movement. In this they were encouraged by the liberal Charles Albert, who succeeded to the throne of Sardinia, and became ruler of Piedmont in 1831. In 1847 Count *Cavour started a newspaper, *Il Risorgimento*; this had a considerable influence on Charles Albert, who in 1848 tried to drive the Austrians out of Lombardy and Venetia. He was defeated at Custozza (1848) and Novara (1849) and abdicated. He was succeeded by his son *Victor Emmanuel II. During the *Revolutions of 1848 republicans held power briefly in Rome, Florence, Turin, and Venice and hoped to create a republic of Italy, but were also defeated. Under the guidance of Cavour, Prime Minister of Piedmont from 1852, the French emperor *Napoleon III was encouraged to ally with Piedmont, in return for promises of Nice and a part of the Alpine region of Savoy, and Austria was defeated in the battles of *Magenta and *Solferino in 1859. Austria evacuated Lombardy and much of central Italy. *Garibaldi liberated Sicily, marched north and almost reached Rome. Plebiscites were held and resulted in a vote to accept Victor Emanuel II as first King of Italy (1861).

Rizal, José (1861–96) Filipino nationalist. While training as a doctor in Spain he wrote two novels attacking Spanish repression in the *Philippines, marking him out as one of the leading spokesmen of the nationalist movement and of the publicity campaign known as the Propaganda Movement. An advocate of gradual change rather than a revolutionary, Rizal fell foul of the Spanish authorities when he established a reform society, the *Liga Filipina*, in 1892 and was exiled to Mindanao. Although not involved in the nationalist uprising of 1896, he was executed by the Spanish authorities for supposed complicity in the rebellion.

Rizzio, David (1533–66) Italian-born secretary and adviser to *Mary, Queen of Scots. He entered service at court in 1561 and by 1564 he had become her Secretary: he possibly arranged her marriage to his friend *Darnley. By March 1566 'Seigneur' David's arrogant monopoly of power, combined with fears of his being a papal agent, led to his assassination. Darnley, who suspected him of adultery with Mary, was involved in the plot.

Roanoke Island The first English colony in North America, in Albemarle Sound off the north coast of North Carolina. A group of settlers financed by *Raleigh landed there in 1585, but were evacuated, just before relief arrived from England, by *Drake returning from the Caribbean. A second colonizing group was sent in 1587 under John White, who then had to go back to England to obtain further supplies. His return from England was interrupted by the Spanish Armada, and in 1590 he found the settlement empty. The "lost colony" has been immortalized by White's paintings of local Native Americans and by Thomas Harriott's *Report* (1588).

Robert I (the Bruce) (1274–1329) King of Scotland (1306–29). Robert I had a successful reign, inheriting a contested throne in a country partly occupied by the English, and leaving a securely governed kingdom to his son, *David II. He was fortunate in that he was matched by an ineffectual English king, *Edward II, over whom he won an important victory at *Bannockburn in 1314. In 1322 Edward attempted a fresh invasion of Scotland, but Bruce outmanoeuvred him and then invaded England as far south as Yorkshire, nearly capturing Edward himself. In the Treaty of Edinburgh (1328), *Edward III recognized Bruce's title and Scotland's independence from England, although this was only a temporary lull in Anglo-Scottish hostilities.

Robert II (1316–90) King of Scotland (1371–90). Robert II inherited the throne from his uncle, *David II, fairly late in life; as Robert the Steward, he spent most of his active years in virtual opposition to David, leading the Scottish nationalists against the invading armies of *Edward III while David was in exile in France.

Shortly after his accession Robert successfully concluded a treaty with *Charles V (of France) that reaffirmed the Franco-Scottish alliance.

Robert III (*c*.1337–1406) King of Scotland (1390–1406). He was the eldest son of *Robert II and was christened John but assumed the name Robert on his succession. He had been severely injured by a horse-kick, so power was exercised by a regent—first his brother Robert, Earl of Fife and then his son David, Duke of Rothesay.

Robespierre, Maximilien François Marie Isidore de (1758–94) French revolutionary. Robespierre was the leader of the radical Jacobins in the National Assembly and, as such, backed the execution of Louis XVI and implemented a successful purge of the moderate Girondists (both 1793). Later the same year he consolidated his power with his election to the Committee of Public Safety (the revolutionary governing body 1793–94) and his appointment as President of the National Assembly. Robespierre was guillotined for his role in the Terror, although he had objected to the scale of the executions.

Robinson, Mary (Terese Winifred) (1944–) Irish Labour stateswoman, President (1990–97). She was called to the bar in 1967 and entered politics in 1969, when she became a member of the Irish Senate. In 1990 she became Ireland's first woman President. She was noted for her platform of religious toleration and for her liberal attitude to abortion, divorce, and homosexuality. From 1997 to 2002 she was UN Commissioner for Human Rights, and since 2007 she has been an active member of The *Elders.

Robinson, Peter (David) (1948–) Northern Irish politician, First Minister of Northern Ireland (2008–). A founder member of the Democratic Unionist Party (DUP) and Deputy Leader from 1980, he served as a member of the UK parliament (1979–85, 1986–2010) and became known as an uncompromising Unionist. In 1999, although he had strongly opposed the Good Friday Agreement (*see* NORTHERN IRELAND), he became a member of the new Northern Ireland Executive. In 2008 he succeeded Ian *Paisley as Leader of the DUP and as First Minister, working effectively with Martin *McGuinness of Sinn Fein as Deputy First Minister. He stepped down temporarily in 2010 following corruption allegations, resuming his role three weeks later.

Rob Roy (born **Robert Macgregor**) (1671–1734) Scottish outlaw. His escapades as a highland cattle thief and opponent of the government's agents on the eve of the Jacobite uprising of 1715 were popularized in Sir Walter Scott's novel *Rob Roy* (1817).

Rockefeller, John D. (**John Davison Rockefeller**) (1839–1937) US industrialist and philanthropist. One of the first to recognize the industrial possibilities of oil, Rockefeller established the Standard Oil Company (1870) and by the end of the decade exercised a virtual monopoly over oil refining in the USA. Early in the 20th century he handed over his business interests to his son, John D(avison) Rockefeller Jr. (1874–1960), and devoted his private fortune to numerous philanthropic projects, such as the establishment of the Rockefeller Foundation (1913). His son's many philanthropic institutions include the Rockefeller Center in New York (1939).

Rockingham, Charles Watson-Wentworth, 2nd Marquis of (1730–82) British statesman and leader of the political faction known as the Rockingham *Whigs. Most of his supporters were originally followers of the Duke of *Newcastle, but from the mid-1760s they transferred their allegiance to Rockingham. While Prime Minister (1765–66), his government repealed the American *Stamp Act and the controversial cider excise. He and his supporters strenuously opposed Lord *North and the American War of *Independence and argued for financial reforms, which the second Rockingham administration undertook in 1782. On his death in office the Rockingham Whigs split into further factions, of which the most important formed the basis of the new Whig party which was evolving at the end of the 18th century.

Rodney, George Brydges Rodney, 1st Baron (1719–92) British admiral. He gained his early naval expertise with *Hawke at Finisterre in 1747, and at Le Havre in 1759, where he destroyed the French flotilla in the *Seven Years War. His greatest victory was at the Battle of Les Saintes, 1782, in the West Indies, where he restored British supremacy at sea in the closing stages of the American War of *Independence.

Roger II (or **Roger Guiscard**) (*c.*1095–1154) King of *Sicily (1130–54). The *Norman expansion into southern Italy and Sicily was begun by the brothers Robert and Roger *Guiscard, initially in defiance of the pope, but subsequently with his grudging cooperation. The Treaty of Melfi (1059) empowered them to take south Italy from the Greeks and Sicily from the Muslims and by the time of Roger Guiscard's death, Sicily was in Norman hands. His son Roger II effectively ruled Sicily from 1113 but had to assert control over the anarchic Norman barons who threatened his rule, especially when backed by the pope in 1129. From 1130 Roger supported the *antipope's cause; despite excommunication by Pope Innocent II and internal revolt, he consolidated his power by 1140. He took Malta, Corfu, and many cities on the Greek mainland as well as controlling most of the land in North Africa between Tripoli and Tunis. In 1140 he issued a revised code of laws and in his later years he ruled one of the most sophisticated governments in Western Europe. His court at Palermo enjoyed a high artistic and scholarly reputation.

Rogers, Robert (1731–95) American frontier soldier. He formed the **Rogers Rangers**, a force of 600 New England frontiersmen who fought with great bravery in the *French and Indian wars at Lake George (1758) and the capture of Quebec (1759). He served in the relief of Detroit in *Pontiac's Rebellion. His loyalty to the Revolution was questioned and Washington had him arrested as a spy in 1776. Such treatment converted him into a loyalist and in 1780 he went to live in London.

Rokossovsky, Konstantin Konstantinovich (1896–1968) Polish-born Soviet field-marshal. Rokossovsky enlisted in the Tsarist army and joined the *Red Army in 1919. Arrested during *Stalin's purges, he was released from prison camp to become one of the outstanding generals of World War II, taking part in the battles of Moscow, *Stalingrad, *Kursk, and others. His Red Army troops stood by (August–September 1944) on the outskirts of Warsaw without helping in the *Warsaw Uprising against the German occupying forces. After the war he was transferred to the Polish army and became Deputy Premier and Minister of Defence under President Bierut. Rokossovsky led the army in a bloody suppression (June 1956) of Polish workers in Poznán, who were demonstrating for "bread and freedom". On 20 October Polish and Soviet troops exchanged fire; Rokossovsky's troops were recalled to Moscow, and *Gomułka's new nationalist government was able to claim some independence from interference by the Soviet Union.

Roland de la Platière, Marie-Jeanne Philipon (1754–93) French Revolutionary , whose *salon* became the centre of the *Girondin party. Through her political influence her husband, Jean-Marie Roland (1734–93), was appointed Minister of the Interior in 1792. She helped him write a letter, read out in the council, which criticized the actions of *Louis XVI. He was dismissed in July 1792 but returned to power in August following the overthrow of the monarchy. However, the following year he was forced to resign and, as the power of the Girondins weakened, Madame Roland was arrested. She was executed on 8 November 1793 and two days later her husband, hearing of her death, committed suicide.

Rollo (c.860–931) Leader of a band of *Vikings that invaded north-western France. In 912 as Duke Robert he accepted Normandy as a duchy from the French king Charles III and was baptized, but remained quite independent of French authority. He married a French princess, gave parcels of land in Normandy to his followers, and began the long chapter of *Norman influence on Europe.

Roman Britain (43–410 AD) The period during which most of Britain was part of the *Roman empire. Britain was first visited by the Romans under Julius *Caesar during the *Gallic wars. It was then the home of Gallic tribes and later a refuge for defeated allies of *Vercingetorix. *Claudius invaded Britain in 43 AD, attracted by the island's minerals and grain. At first the Belgic tribes were subdued as far north as the *Fosse Way. The frontier was then extended into native Celtic territories and established by the building of *Hadrian's Wall. Native culture absorbed many Roman ways: enlarged former tribal capitals adopted a Roman lifestyle. Army veterans settled there after discharge, as did traders, scholars, craftsmen, and soldiers from all parts of the Roman empire. Universally acknowledged Christian bishoprics were established. Roman villas, *Roman roads, and titles abounded, but little Latin was spoken and the people remained essentially Celtic. In 406 and 409 the Britons rebelled against Roman rule. The Romans withdrew from Britain in 410. The period of Roman decline and the early history of the Saxon kingdoms remains obscure.

Roman Catholic Church The Christian Church that acknowledges the pope as its head, especially as this has developed since the *Reformation. It has an elaborately organized hierarchy of bishops and priests. Popes are traditionally regarded as successors to St Peter, to whom Christ entrusted his power. In doctrine the Roman Catholic Church is characterized by strict adherence to tradition combined with acceptance of the living voice of the Church and belief in its infallibility. The classic definition of its position was made in response to the Reformation at the Council of Trent (1545–63). During this period the Catholic Church responded to the challenge of Protestantism by the movement known as the *Counter-Reformation, which brought about various reforms and a draconian tightening of Church discipline (see INQUISITION). During the Enlightenment the Church increasingly saw itself as an embattled defender of ancient truth, a belief that culminated in the proclamation of Papal Infallibility in matters of doctrine in 1870. The mid 20th century saw the Church become more open to the world, a change given effect in the decrees of the 2nd Vatican Council (1963–65). However, the pontificates of *John Paul II (1978–2005) and *Benedict XVI (2005–13) were marked by resistance to any change in the teaching of the Church on the controversial issues of contraception, abortion, divorce, homosexuality, and the celibacy of the priesthood. On all these issues, especially the first, the Church has maintained a position seriously at odds with liberal secular opinion.

A historically significant Catholic order is that of the **Jesuits** or the Society of Jesus, an order of priests founded in 1534 in Paris by Ignatius *Loyola, St Francis Xavier, and others. The Society became the spearhead of the Counter-Reformation, though originally intended as a missionary order. The success of Jesuits as missionaries, teachers, scholars, and spiritual directors—as well as the fear they have inspired—manifests how close they have been to their ideal of a disciplined force, effective in the cause of the Roman Church.

Another significant Catholic organization is **Opus Dei** (Latin, 'work of God'), which was founded in 1928 by the Spanish priest Josemaria Escrivá de Balaguer (1902–75). Members, of whom there are 90,000 worldwide, may be either priests or lay people, in which case they are encouraged to retain their social position and pursue their profession. Particularly active in General Franco's Spain (1939–75), the organization has exercised considerable, but controversial, influence on public affairs. There is a separate branch for women, segregation of the sexes being an important principle. Opus Dei emphasizes the austere and conservative aspects of Catholicism; members follow a range of ascetic and spiritual practices, which include daily 'mortification' in the form of brief self-flagellation, and celibacy is encouraged. Its secrecy and authoritarianism has been criticized, but Pope John Paul II was a supporter—he beatified de Balaguer in 1992.

Roman civil wars Conflicts that afflicted the last century of the Roman republic (88 BC–c.28 BC) and led to the inevitable institution of the unchallenged authority of one man, the Principate. Political life in Rome was unsettled from the period of *Sulla's dictatorship and the Catiline conspiracy (64–63 BC). Rivalry between the republican military leader Julius Caesar and *Pompey began after the collapse of their alliance. Caesar defeated the Pompeian army in Spain at Ilerda (49 BC) and Pompey himself at Pharsalus (48 BC); he won further victories in Asia and Africa. Cato's suicide in 46 BC signified the collapse of the republican cause. On his return to Rome, Caesar was made dictator and virtually sole ruler. His plans for safeguarding the empire by military expeditions against Dacia and Parthia were cut short by outraged republican traditionalists who murdered him in 44 BC. Further civil wars followed. Initially Octavian (*Augustus), supported by the republican party, struggled against *Mark Antony. In 43 BC Antony, Octavian, and Lepidus formed a coalition whose forces defeated the republicans led by Brutus and Cassius at *Philippi. Antony meanwhile joined forces with Cleopatra and was defeated by Octavian at *Actium. The Roman world was united under the sole leadership of Octavian, who annexed Egypt.

In 68 AD civil war broke out in the empire in the struggle for succession after *Nero's death. Galba was proclaimed emperor from Spain; he entered Rome in September but was murdered and succeeded by Otho; meanwhile Vitellius was proclaimed emperor in Germany and Otho committed suicide. *Vespasian then invaded Italy and took the throne, making 68–69 "the year of the four emperors". This crisis period was followed by the settled rule of Vespasian.

Roman empire The period when the Roman state and its overseas provinces were under the rule of an emperor, from the time of *Augustus (27 BC) until 476 AD. The Roman empire was divided in 375 AD by Emperor Theodosius into the Western and Eastern empires. The term is often used to refer to all Roman territories during both the republic and the empire.

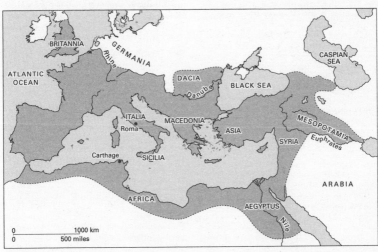

Roman empire. This map shows the expansion of the Roman empire at its greatest extent, in 117 AD. Rome expanded from a small settlement in the 6th century BC to rule most of the known European world by the early 2nd century AD. Having established control over Italy by c. 260 BC, Rome expanded to the east and west. By 133 BC all the territory formerly held by Carthage in the western Mediterranean and north Africa had been absorbed, together with Macedonia and Asia Minor in the east. Expansion continued for a further 150 years, the empire reaching its greatest extent in 117 AD, under Trajan. His successor, Hadrian, attempted to consolidate the empire behind fixed frontiers, drawing back to the Euphrates in the east and building the famous wall in Britain. However, less than 50 years later the decline of the empire had begun.

The city of Rome gradually gained power from the time of the Tarquins (6th century BC), subduing the Etruscans, Sabines, Samnites, and Greek settlers, and by the mid-3rd century BC, controlled Italy. It came into conflict with *Carthage in the western Mediterranean and with the Hellenistic world in the east. Success in the *Punic wars gave Rome its first overseas possessions in Sicily (241), Spain (201), and north Africa (146) and the Macedonian Wars eventually left Rome dominant in Macedonia, Greece, and parts of Asia Minor. Syria and Gaul from the Rhine to the Atlantic were added by the campaigns of *Pompey and Julius *Caesar and Egypt was annexed in 31 BC after the Battle of *Actium. *Augustus planned to consolidate the empire within natural boundaries, but in 43 AD *Claudius invaded Britain. *Trajan, in 106, made Dacia a province in response to raids across the Danube, although it was abandoned in 270. His annexation of Mesopotamia was very brief (114–117).

This vast empire was held together by secure communication and internal peace maintained by the *Roman legions. Fleets kept the sea safe for shipping and a network of *Roman roads, built to move troops quickly, facilitated trade, personal travel, and an imperial postal system. The development of a single legal system and the use of a common language (Latin in the west, Greek in the east) helped maintain unity. Roman cities flourished throughout the empire, assisted by efficient water and drainage systems. Roman influence and trade spread even further reaching India, Russia, south-east Asia, and through the *Silk Road, China.

The success of the empire also led to its downfall, its sheer size contributing to its collapse, exacerbated by power struggles and the invasion of land-hungry migrating tribes. Rome was sacked by the *Visigoths in 410, Carthage was conquered by the *Vandals in 455, and in 476 Romulus Augustulus, the last emperor of the Western empire was deposed. The Eastern empire (*Byzantine empire) lasted until 1453. *Gibbon's *The History of the Decline and Fall of the Roman Empire* (1776–81) is a classic account of the disintegration of imperial Rome.

Romania

Capital:	Bucharest
Area:	238,391 sq km (92,043 sq miles)
Population:	21,790,479 (2013 est)
Currency:	1 new leu = 100 bani

Religions:	Eastern Orthodox 81.9%; Protestant 6.4%; Roman Catholic 4.3%
Ethnic Groups:	Romanian 83.4%; Hungarian 6.3%; Romany 1.2%
Languages:	Romanian (official); Hungarian; Romany
International Organizations:	UN; OSCE; Council of Europe; NATO; WTO; EU

An east European country with its east coast on the Black Sea; it is bounded by Ukraine and the republic of Moldova on the north and east, Hungary and Serbia on the west, and Bulgaria on the south.

Physical Roughly half of Romania is mountainous. The Carpathians, curving from the north-west, meet the Transylvanian Alps in the centre of the country, where rainfall is heavy and there are large forests. The rest of the country is plain, much of it providing the richest soil in Europe. The Danube forms the southern border as it flows east to its delta on the Black Sea.

Economy Romania emerged from the repressive communist regime of Nicolae Ceausescu in 1989 with obsolete and unsuitable industry and widespread poverty. Progress towards a market economy only quickened after 2000, being encouraged from 2004 by the requirements of EU membership. However, one-fifth of the population still lives in poverty. Agriculture employs almost one-third of the workforce; principal crops are cereals, sugar beet, sunflower seeds, potatoes, and grapes. Mineral resources include coal, iron ore, petroleum, and natural gas. The principal export industries are machinery and equipment, metals and metal products, textiles, footwear, chemicals, minerals, and fuels; agricultural products are also exported.

History Although the regions known as Moldavia and Walachia were part of the *Ottoman empire from the 15th century onwards, Turkish domination was increasingly challenged by both Russia and Austria. In 1812 Russia gained control of north-east Moldavia (present-day Moldova). During the next 40 years Romanian nationalism precipitated many insurrections against the Turks. Following the *Crimean War, during which the region was occupied by Russia, Walachia and Moldavia proclaimed themselves independent principalities; in 1861 they united to form Romania, electing a local prince, Alexander Cuza, as ruler. On his deposition (1866) Prince Carol Hohenzollern-Sigmaringen was elected. At the Congress of *Berlin independence was recognized, and Prince Carol crowned king as *Carol I (1881–1914). His pro-German policy led in 1883 to Romania's joining the Triple Alliance of 1882 (Germany, Austria, and Italy). In World War I Romania remained neutral until, in 1916, it joined the Allies. At the *Versailles Peace Settlement the country was rewarded with the doubling of its territories, mainly by the addition of Transylvania from Hungary. Carol I was succeeded by Ferdinand I (1914–27) and then by *Carol II (1930–40), who imposed a fascist regime. He was forced to cede much territory to the *Axis powers in 1940. Romanian forces cooperated with the German armies in their offensives (1941–42), but after the Battle of *Stalingrad the Red Army advanced and Romania lost territory to the USSR and Bulgaria. A communist regime was established in 1948 and for the next 20 years the country became a Soviet satellite. A much greater degree of independence was restored during the presidency of Nicolae Ceausescu (1967–89), whose rule became increasingly brutal and autocratic. Stringent economic measures had to be enforced in 1987. During 1989 a movement towards democracy culminated in a violent revolution and the execution of the President and his wife on Christmas Day. A National Salvation Front (NSF) was formed, led by Ion Iliescu, who was elected President. He and many of his colleagues had been communists, and popular demonstrations against the government were brutally put down. Ethnic violence against Hungarians in Transylvania and against the large indigenous gypsy population increased. In spite of opposition from groups such as the Democratic Convention of Romania (CDR), Iliescu retained power in the 1992 presidential election, having secured a $748 million IMF loan. In 1995 the Chamber of Deputies enacted a Mass Privatization law affecting over 3000 businesses. In 1996 Iliescu was defeated in presidential elections by the CDR candidate, Emil Constantinescu. Social unrest and attacks on ethnic minorities continued. Iliescu was again President from 2000 to 2004, when the centre-right Traian Basescu was elected to succeed him. Romania joined NATO in 2004 and the EU in 2007. Basescu survived an attempted impeachment in 2007 and in 2009 was re-elected in a close-fought election. Following the *Credit Crunch Romania negotiated a bailout loan from the EU, IMF, and World Bank in 2009 to support its faltering economy (a second loan

facility was agreed in 2011 but not used). The loans' terms required austerity measures and privatizations; these increased political instability, with popular protests and another failed impeachment of Basescu in 2012.

Roman law The body of law developed in Rome between about 150 BC and 250 AD and codified by the Emperor *Justinian in 529 in his *Corpus Juris Civilis* ('Body of Civil Law'). Roman law re-emerged in the 11th century as a popular subject of study in the Italian universities; later it evolved into the common core of the civil law (or Romano-Germanic law) family of legal systems, which established itself in the lands of the Holy Roman Empire. The ideas of Roman law were dominant in the French *Code Napoléon, adopted in 1804, and in later civil codes adopted in Germany, Switzerland, and Austria. The codification movement appealed to the perceived higher rationality of Roman law as providing a logically consistent set of principles and rules for solving disputes.

Roman legion A division of the army in ancient Rome. Legions evolved from the citizen militia that equipped itself in times of crisis for defence of the state. During the Second *Punic War *Scipio Africanus reorganized the battle array and improved the army's tactics. Under *Marius, men of no property began to be recruited, a professional army appeared and new training methods were introduced. Ten cohorts, 6000 soldiers, with standards formed a named and numbered legion with an eagle standard. The cohorts, divided into six centuries (100 men in each century) commanded by a centurion, became the main tactical unit of the army. Cavalry and auxiliaries supported each regiment.

*Augustus established a standing army to man the frontiers of the empire. There appears to have been 28 permanent legions, each having a number and an honorific title. *Severus added three legions; *Constantine increased the number but limited them to 1000 men each to allow flexibility and to avoid mutiny. He also placed them under equestrian prefects instead of the traditional senatorial legates and placed a Christian symbol on their standards. On retirement a veteran in the early days earned a land grant in a "colony" where he continued to act as a Romanizing and pacifying influence throughout the empire, but from the time of Augustus it was more useful for him to receive money rather than land. Many nevertheless settled in the area where they had served, thus effectively "colonizing" it.

Romanov The ruling house of Russia from 1613 until the Revolution of 1917. After the Time of Troubles (1604–13), a period of civil war and anarchy, Michael Romanov was elected emperor and ruled until 1645, to be followed by Alexis (1645–76) and Fyodor (1676–82). Under these emperors Russia emerged as the major Slavic power. The next emperors established it as a great power in Europe: *Peter I (the Great) (1689–1725) and *Catherine II (the Great) (1762–96) were the most successful of these rulers.

Roman religion The religion of the Roman republic and empire. In its developed form it came to have much in common with *Greek religion, although it contained elements of Etruscan and other native Italian regional beliefs and practices. The Romans identified their gods with those of Greece: Jupiter = Zeus, Juno = Hera, Neptune = Poseidon, Minerva = Athene, Diana = Artemis, Mars = Ares, Mercury = Hermes, and so on; but it too had its array of minor deities. Romans also possessed domestic shrines of the spirits of the household (Lares and Penates). Although *Christianity became the official religion of the empire from the late 4th century AD, pagan beliefs and practices proved tenacious in many areas, especially away from the cities, and in many places the Christian Church had often to take over Roman festivals and hallowed shrines or sites under a new guise.

Roman republic (Latin *respublica*, 'common wealth') The political form of the Roman state for 400 years after the expulsion of *Tarquin. The rule of a sole monarch yielded to the power of a landed aristocracy, the *patricians, who ruled through two chief magistrates or consuls and an advisory body, the *Roman Senate.

The city of Rome could operate as a 'public concern' as long as the small landed aristocracy managed the state. But, with overseas expansion, generals had to be given power to deal with problems abroad. Their substantial independence threatened republican tradition with its corporate government and brief periods of high office for individuals in rotation. Eventually the generals simply ignored the law, which required generals to lay down their commands on returning to Italian soil. The last of these commanders-in-chief, Octavian, achieved a settlement that appeared to combine republican institutions with personal military power. The *Roman empire succeeded the republic.

Roman roads A systematic communications network originating in the Italian peninsula

joining Rome to its expanding empire. The *Appian Way was the first major stretch, leading into Samnite territory. The Via Flaminia, constructed in 220 BC was the great northern highway to Rimini. For travellers landing from Brindisi the Egnatian Way continued overland through Greece and on to Byzantium. By the 1st century AD three roads crossed the Alps and the Domitian Way went from the Rhône valley to Spain. Every province had such roads which served military and commercial purposes. In Britain major highways fanned out from Londinium (London), some now known by their Anglo-Saxon names: *Watling Street and *Ermine Street. Designed with several thick layers they were drained by side ditches, and maintained by engineers.

Roman Senate The assembly of the landed aristocracy and *patricians, which originated in the royal council of the kings of Rome. Entry widened to include those of plebeian origin by the late 4th century BC. A membership of 600 established by *Sulla was standard although it rose to 900 in *Caesar's time. This advisory body consisted of hereditary (patrician) and life (conscript) members, the latter being ex-magistrates. It was summoned by the consuls as chief magistrates and passed decrees, which were ratified by the people in assembly. It was expected that all magistrates would submit proposals to the Senate before putting them to the people. This procedure began to be flouted from the time of the Gracchi onwards. Its power was real but informal, based on prestige and wealth. Even the emperors made at least the token gesture of consulting the 'Fathers'. Until the 3rd century AD all bronze coinage carried the mark 'By Consultative Decree of the Senate'.

Rome, Treaties of (1957) Two international agreements signed in Rome by Belgium, France, Italy, Luxembourg, the Netherlands, and the Federal Republic of Germany. They established the *European Economic Community and Euratom (the European Atomic Energy Community). The treaties included provisions for the free movement of labour and capital between member countries, the abolition of customs barriers and cartels, and the fostering of common agricultural and trading policies. New members of the European Community are required to adhere to the terms of these treaties. The *Maastricht Treaty (1992), Amsterdam Treaty (1997), Treaty of Nice (2001), and *Lisbon Treaty (2007) were developments of the Rome Treaties.

Rommel, Erwin (known as **'the Desert Fox'**) (1891–1944) German Field Marshal. Rommel was posted to North Africa in 1941 after the collapse of the Italian offensive, and, as commander of the Afrika Korps, he deployed a series of surprise manoeuvres and succeeded in capturing Tobruk (1942). After being defeated by Montgomery at El Alamein (1942), he was ordered home the following year to serve as Inspector of Coastal Defences. He was forced to commit suicide after being implicated in the officers' conspiracy against Hitler in 1944.

Roosevelt, Franklin D. (Franklin Delano Roosevelt; known as **'FDR'**) (1882–1945) US Democratic statesman, 32nd President of the USA (1933–45). Roosevelt's early political career was curtailed by his contraction of polio in 1921; in spite of the disease, he resumed public life in a wheelchair in 1928 and received the Democratic presidential nomination in 1932. His New Deal package of economic measures (1933) helped to lift the USA out of the Great Depression, and after the American entry into World War II he played an important part in the co-ordination of the Allied war effort. In 1940 Roosevelt became the first US President to be elected for a third term in office, and he subsequently secured a fourth term. He was the joint author, with Winston Churchill, of the Atlantic Charter (1941), a declaration of eight common principles in international relations that was intended to guide a postwar peace settlement.

Roosevelt, Theodore (known as **'Teddy'**) (1858–1919) US Republican statesman, 26th President of the USA (1901–09). He was elected Vice-President in 1900, succeeding William McKinley in 1901 following the latter's assassination. At home Roosevelt was noted for his antitrust laws, while abroad he successfully engineered the US bid to build the Panama Canal (1904–14) and won the Nobel Peace Prize in 1906 for negotiating the end of the Russo-Japanese War.

Rosas, Juan Manuel de (1793–1877) Argentine dictator (1835–52). Reacting to the failure of the liberals, who dominated Argentina after independence, Rosas brutally repressed his political enemies and suppressed civil liberties. Often depicted as a *caudillo, he was a consummate politician who contributed to the establishment of national unity in Argentina and who stood up to foreign powers like Britain and France when they imposed two blockades (1838–40; 1845–50) as a result of disputes over Paraguay and Uruguay. In February 1852 Rosas was overthrown by another caudillo, Justo José de Urquiza, and fled to England.

Rosebery, Archibald Philip Primrose, 5th Earl of (1847–1929) British Liberal statesman, Prime Minister (1894–95). He succeeded Gladstone as Premier after the latter's retirement and subsequently alienated Liberal supporters as a result of his imperialist loyalties during the Second Boer War (1899–1902).

Rosenberg case (1953) A US espionage case in which Julius Rosenberg and his wife Ethel were convicted of obtaining information concerning atomic weapons and passing it on to Soviet agents between 1944 and 1945. They became the first US civilians to be sentenced to death for espionage by a US court. The only seriously incriminating evidence had come from a confessed spy and the lack of clemency shown to them was an example of the intense anti-communist feeling that gripped the USA in the 1950s. Evidence released since the fall of communism suggests that Julius, at least, was guilty of espionage.

Rose Revolution (2003) A series of demonstrations in Georgia that led to the overthrow of President Eduard *Shevardnadze. Parliamentary elections on 2 November 2003 were declared to have resulted in a majority for parties supporting the President; however, international observers reported widespread electoral fraud, and the opposition, led by Mikhail Saakashvili, claimed it should have been victorious. Large demonstrations in Tbilisi and other cities came to a head on 22 November, when the opening session of the new parliament was overrun by protesters (who carried roses, giving the revolution its name). Shevardnadze resigned on 23 November and the disputed elections were subsequently annulled. Saakashvili was elected President in January 2006, and fresh parliamentary elections in March gave him a large majority. The new government began to tackle the endemic corruption of the Shevardnadze era and to institute other reforms. The wider significance of the Rose Revolution was that it replaced a generally pro-Russian regime by a strongly pro-Western one, which subsequently led to friction with Russia.

Roses, Wars of the (1455–85) A protracted struggle for the throne of England, lasting for 30 years of sporadic fighting. These civil wars grew out of the bitter rivalry between two aspirants to the throne—Edmund *Beaufort (1406–55), Duke of Somerset, of the House of

Lancaster (whose badge was a red rose), and Richard, 3rd Duke of *York (whose badge was a white rose); the former was a close supporter of *Henry VI and *Margaret of Anjou, while Richard of York became their opponent. In 1455 Richard gained power by winning the first Battle of St Albans; a whole series of private enmities and disputes was now absorbed into a bitter and openly fought civil war. Richard of York was killed at the Battle of *Wakefield (1460), and Henry VI's supporters, the *Lancastrians, won a further victory at the second Battle of St Albans (February 1461), yet their hesitations allowed Richard's son Edward to gain the throne a month later as *Edward IV, the first *Yorkist king of England. In September 1470 a Lancastrian invasion restored Henry VI to the throne (although power was effectively exercised by 'the kingmaker', Richard Neville, Earl of *Warwick), but in April 1471 Edward regained it by the victory of *Barnet. Most of the remaining Lancastrian leaders were killed at *Tewkesbury in May 1471, but the struggle ended only in 1485 when Henry Tudor defeated *Richard III at *Bosworth Field. *Henry VII married Edward IV's eldest daughter, Elizabeth of York, in order to unite the two factions. The wars weakened the power of the nobility and after a bid for the throne from Lambert *Simnel in 1487, there were no serious challenges to the *Tudor dynasty.

Rosetta stone A piece of black basalt bearing inscriptions that provided the key to the deciphering of Egyptian *hieroglyphs. It was found in Rosetta (Rashid) near Alexandria in Egypt in 1799 by a French soldier during Napoleon's occupation of Egypt, and contained three inscriptions, in Greek, in Egyptian demotic, and in Egyptian hieroglyphics. Comparative study of the three texts, which date from 196 BC, was undertaken by Thomas Young and Jean-François Champollion, the latter finally unlocking the secrets of hieroglyphics in 1821–22. The stone is housed in the British Museum in London.

Rosicrucian A member of certain secret societies who venerated the emblems of the Rose and the Cross as symbols of Jesus Christ's resurrection and redemption. Rosicrucians claimed to possess secret wisdom passed down from the ancients, but their origin cannot be dated earlier than the 17th century. The anonymous *Account of the Brotherhood* published in Germany in 1614 may well have launched the movement. It narrated the tale of a mythical German knight of the 15th century, Christian

Rosenkreutz, who travelled extensively to learn the wisdom of the East, and then founded the secret order. Robert Fludd subsequently helped to spread Rosicrucian ideas. In later centuries many new societies were founded under this name.

Roskilde, Treaty of (1658) A treaty between Sweden and Denmark, named after a port in eastern Denmark. After the defeat of Frederick II of Denmark by Charles X of Sweden, this treaty expelled the Danes once and for all from the Swedish mainland: they surrendered Halland, Scania, Blekinge (provinces), and the island of Bornholm, as well as the Norwegian territories of Trondheim and Bohuslän. Bornholm was regained in 1660.

Ross, Sir John (1777–1856) British explorer. He led an expedition to Baffin Bay in 1818 and another in search of the North-west Passage between 1829 and 1833, during which he surveyed King William Land, the Boothia Peninsula, and the Gulf of Boothia.

Rothschild Family A Jewish banking family whose members exerted considerable influence on both economic and political affairs during the 19th and early 20th centuries. Mayer Amschel Rothschild of Frankfurt, who became financial adviser to the Landgrave of Hesse-Kassel, founded the Rothschild banking house in the 18th century. He and his five sons prospered in the years of the *Revolutionary and *Napoleonic Wars and moved to London in 1804. They loaned money for the raising of mercenary armies and negotiated means of bypassing Napoleon's *Continental System. After 1815 Rothschild houses were opened as a banking group in all the great cities of Europe. Of Mayer's sons, Anselm (1773–1855) became a member of the Prussian privy council, Salomon (1774–1855) became financial adviser to Metternich in Vienna, and Nathan (1777–1836) established a branch of the bank in London. His son, Lionel (1808–79), became the first Jew to sit in the British House of Commons (1858) and he lent the British government £4 million in 1875 to buy the *Suez Canal shares. His son **Nathan** (1840–1915) was the first British Jewish Peer and became regarded as the unofficial head of both French and British Jewish communities. It was to his son Lionel Walter (1868–1937), the second Baron and distinguished scientist and scholar, that the *Balfour Declaration was addressed in 1917. The Rothschilds are still prominent in banking and are notable patrons of the arts and sciences.

rotten borough A British Parliamentary borough whose population had virtually disappeared by 1832. At that time there were more than 50 such boroughs with two Members of Parliament. Among the most notorious were Old Sarum with a handful of electors and Dunwich, mostly submerged under the North Sea. They were abolished by the *Reform Act of 1832.

Rough Riders The 1st Regiment of US Cavalry Volunteers. They were largely recruited by Colonel Leonard Wood and Lieutenant-Colonel Theodore *Roosevelt for service in the *Spanish–American War of 1898. Comprising rangers, cowboys, Native Americans, and college students, their most notable exploit was the successful charge up San Juan Hill in Cuba, on foot as their horses had been left behind in Florida.

Rouhani, Hassan (1948–) Iranian cleric and politician, President (2013–). He trained as a cleric before graduating in law from Tehran University (1972). Active in the Islamic opposition to the government, he fled Iran in 1977 and joined Ayatollah *Khomeini, then exiled in France, in 1978. Following the Islamic Revolution Rouhani held a number of posts, including secretary of the Supreme National Security Council (1989–2005) and leader of Iran's delegation in negotiations about its nuclear programme (2003–05). He resigned his offices on the election of the hard-line Mahmoud Ahmadinejad as President (2005). In 2013 Rouhani stood as a moderate candidate in the presidential election and achieved a landslide victory. As President he quickly softened his predecessor's uncompromising diplomatic stance.

Roundheads Puritans and Parliamentarians during the *English Civil War. It originated as a term of abuse, referring to the Puritans' disapproval of long hair and their own close-cropped heads. Roundhead strength during the Civil War lay mainly in southern and eastern England.

Round Table Conferences The meetings held in London (1930–32) between Britain and Indian representatives to discuss Indian constitutional developments. The procedure was suggested by the viceroy, Lord Irwin, in 1929. *Congress boycotted the first session (November 1930–January 1931), but, following the Gandhi–Irwin Pact (March 1931), Mahatma *Gandhi attended the second session (September–December 1931). With the renewal of the *non-cooperation campaign, Gandhi was imprisoned and Congress took no part in the final session (November–December 1932). The constitutional discussions formed the basis of the

1935 Government of India Act, with its plan for a federal organization involving the Indian *Princely States.

Rousseau, Jean-Jacques (1712–78) French philosopher and writer, born in Switzerland. From 1750 he came to fame with a series of works highly critical of the existing social order; his philosophy is underpinned by a belief in the fundamental goodness of human nature, encapsulated in the concept of the 'noble savage', and the warping effects of civilization. In his novel *Émile* (1762) Rousseau formulated new educational principles giving the child full scope for individual development in natural surroundings, shielded from the corrupting influences of civilization. His *Social Contract* (1762) anticipated much of the thinking of the French Revolution. Rousseau is also noted for his *Confessions* (1782), one of the earliest autobiographies.

Rowlatt Act (1919) A piece of repressive legislation enacted in British India, following the report of a committee under Mr Justice Rowlatt. The report had recommended the continuation of special wartime powers for use against revolutionary conspiracy and terrorist activity. The Act aroused opposition among Indian nationalists and this was channelled by Mohandas *Gandhi into a nationwide *satyagraha, known as the Rowlatt agitation, which ended with the *Amritsar massacre.

Rowntree A family of English business entrepreneurs and philanthropists. Joseph (1801–59) a grocer, established several Quaker schools. His son Henry Isaac (1838–83) founded the family cocoa and chocolate manufacturing firm in York; Henry's brother Joseph (1836–1925) became a partner in 1869 and subsequently founded three Rowntree trusts (1904) to support research into social welfare and policy. The latter's son B(enjamin) Seebohm (1871–1954), chairman of the firm from 1925 to 1941, conducted surveys of poverty in York (1897–98; 1936).

Roy, Ram Mohan (1772–1833) Indian religious and social reformer. He devoted his life to reforming Indian society on the basis of a selective appeal to ancient Hindu tradition. He founded the Atmiya Sabha (Friendly Association) to serve as a platform for his liberal ideas. He evolved a monotheistic form of worship, adapting the ethical and humanitarian aspects of Christianity. He attacked idolatry and popular practices, including the burning of widows (suttee) and polygamy, discrimination against women, and the caste system. He also helped to found the Hindu College in Calcutta (1817) and several secondary schools in which English educational methods were employed. In 1828 he founded the Brahmo Samaj (Society of God), whose influence on Indian intellectual, social, and religious life has been profound.

Royal Progress *See* PROGRESS, ROYAL.

Rozvi empire An empire in East Africa named from a Karanga clan of the Shona, who established the authority of the *Mwene Mutapa in the 15th century. Probably originally spiritual leaders and then military rulers, by 1480 the Rozvi occupied all of present-day Zimbabwe and Mozambique. After about 1500 the central and southern provinces broke away under *Changamire, while the ports were subject to Kilwa. The Rozvi controlled gold-mining in the interior and for a time successfully warded off Portuguese attempts to conquer them, but in 1629 the Mwene Mutapa acknowledged Portuguese suzerainty. The empire was finally broken up by the Ndebele in the 1830s.

Ruanda-Urundi *See* BURUNDI.

Ruapekapeka (Maori, "the bats' nest") A strongly fortified village (*pa*) in New Zealand defended by the Maori chief Kawiti, an ally of Hone Heke, who, in 1844–45, challenged European sovereignty. The *pa* was attacked by about 1000 British troops, with artillery, and 500 Maori allies of the British. Kawiti and his people abandoned it, with few casualties, after about 24 hours' fighting.

Rubicon A small stream in north-east Italy near San Marino that flows into the Adriatic, marking the ancient boundary between Italy and Cisalpine Gaul. By taking his army across it (i.e. outside his own province) in 49 BC Julius Caesar committed himself to war against the Senate and Pompey.

Rudd, Kevin (Michael) (1957–) Australian Labor politician, Prime Minister (2007–10; 2013). Rudd had already joined the Labor party before he attended the Australian National University, where he graduated in Asian studies. He worked as a diplomat (1981–88) before becoming chief of staff to the Queensland Labor Party leader (1988–92) and then Director General of the Queensland Office of Cabinet (1992–96). When Labor lost power in Queensland he worked for the accountants KPMG before securing election to the federal parliament. A shadow minister from 2001, he was elected party leader in 2006 and became Prime Minister

following Labor's victory in the 2007 election; however, by 2010 his popularity had declined and he was ousted by Julia *Gillard. He served as Foreign Minister (2010–12) under Gillard but resigned as party infighting continued. He eventually ousted Gillard in June 2013 to become Prime Minister for the second time, but was defeated in a general election ten weeks later. He retired from politics later that year.

Rump Parliament The remnant of the English *Long Parliament, which continued to sit after *Pride's Purge (1648). In 1649 it ordered Charles I's execution, abolished both monarchy and House of Lords, and established the *Commonwealth. Its members were mostly gentlemen, motivated by self-interest, and its policies were generally unpopular. Oliver *Cromwell expelled the Rump in April 1653. Six years later it was recalled to mark the end of the *Protectorate; in 1660 the members excluded by Pride were readmitted, and the Long Parliament dissolved itself in preparation for the *Restoration of the monarchy.

Rum Rebellion (1808) A revolt in Australia, when colonists and officers of the New South Wales Corps (later known as the Rum Corps because of its involvement in the rum trade) overthrew Governor William *Bligh. It was fuelled by Bligh's drastic methods of limiting the rum traders' powers and his attempts to end the domination of the officer clique, while an immediate cause was the arrest of the sheep-breeder John Macarthur in his role as liquor merchant and distiller. The officers induced the commander, Major George Johnston, to arrest Bligh as unfit for office. When Governor *Macquarie took office in 1810, the Corps was recalled, George Johnston was court-martialled in England and cashiered in 1811. Bligh, although exonerated, was removed from office.

Rundstedt, Gerd von (Karl Rudolf Gerd von Rundstedt) (1875–1953) German field-marshal. He was called from retirement in 1939 to take command in the Polish and French campaigns of World War II. In 1941 he commanded the invasion of the Soviet Union but was dismissed after he had withdrawn from Rostov against Hitler's orders, in order to improve his chances of resisting a Soviet counter-offensive. From 1942 to 1945 he commanded the forces occupying France and launched the Battle of the Bulge in the *Ardennes Campaign in December 1944. Relieved of his command in March 1945, he was captured by US troops in May but released in 1949 on grounds of ill health.

Rupert, Prince (1619–82) English Royalist general, son of Frederick V, elector of the Palatinate, and nephew of Charles I. Born in Bohemia, he went to England and joined the Royalist side just before the outbreak of the Civil War in 1642. He made his name in the early years of the war as a leader of cavalry, but after a series of victorious engagements was defeated by Parliamentarian forces at Marston Moor (1644) and Naseby (1645). He later lived chiefly in France until the Restoration (1660), when he returned to England and commanded naval operations against the Dutch (1665–67 and 1672–74). In 1670 Rupert became the first governor of the Hudson's Bay Company in Canada. He was deeply interested in art and science, and was also responsible for the introduction of mezzotint engraving into England.

Russell, John, 1st Earl Russell (1792–1878) British Whig statesman, Prime Minister (1846–52; 1865–66). As a member of Lord Grey's government (1830–34), he was responsible for introducing the Reform Bill of 1832 into Parliament. He became Prime Minister when Sir Robert Peel was defeated (1846) and later served as Foreign Secretary in Lord Aberdeen's coalition government (1852–54); Russell's second premiership ended with his resignation when his attempt to extend the franchise again in a further Reform Bill was unsuccessful.

Russia (official name **Russian Federation**)

Capital:	Moscow
Area:	17,098,242 sq km (6,601,668 sq miles)
Population:	143,420,000 (2005)
Currency:	1 rouble = 100 kopeks
Religions:	Eastern Orthodox: between 15.0% and 20.0%; Muslim: between 10.0% and 15.0%; other Christian 2.0%
Ethnic Groups:	Russian 77.7%; Tatar 3.7%; Ukrainian 1.4%; minority groups
Languages:	Russian (official); minority languages
International Organizations:	UN; OSCE; Commonwealth of Independent States; Euro-Atlantic Partnership Council; Council of Europe; WTO

A country in northern Asia and eastern Europe. Its borders touch Norway and Finland in the north, Poland in the north-west, Estonia, Latvia, Lithuania, Belarus, and Ukraine in the west, Georgia, Azerbaijan, Kazakhstan, Mongolia, China, and Korea in the south; its maritime borders meet the Baltic Sea, Black Sea, the inland Caspian Sea, the Arctic, and the Pacific. It is separated from Alaska in the north-east by the Bering Strait.

Physical The largest country in the world, Russia extends from the Gulf of Finland in the west to the peaks of Kamchatka in the east, from the frozen islands of Novaya Zemlya in the north to the warm Black Sea, the Caucasus Mountains, and the Pamirs and other ranges bordering China and Mongolia in the south. The north–south Ural Mountains divide European from Asian Russia. The plateaus and plains of Siberia make up most of the area to the east. To the west of the Urals extends the North European Plain. Great rivers include the Volga flowing south to the Caspian Sea, the Ob, Yenisei, and Lena draining north into the Arctic Ocean, and the Amur entering the Pacific Ocean to the east. East of the Lena is an area of mountains stretching from the Verkhoyanska to the Anadyr Range. Lake Baikal is Eurasia's largest, and the world's deepest, lake. Across the country extend belts of tundra (in the far north), forest, steppe, and fertile areas.

Economy Following the collapse of communism and the end of the Soviet Union, Russia embarked on a difficult transition to a free-market economy by freeing prices and introducing measures for privatization and land reform. The 1990s saw chronic food shortages, hyperinflation, and a financial crisis, but more recent years have seen economic growth. Russia has rich mineral resources, potentially of enormous wealth, with huge deposits of coal, iron ore, gold, platinum, copper, diamonds, and other metals; and, in Siberia, the world's largest reserves of petroleum and natural gas, which constitute leading exports and have been used as diplomatic weapons in recent years. Other exports include such metals as steel and aluminium, wood and wood products, chemicals, and manufactured goods. These heavy industries dominate the economy.

The principal agricultural crops are grain, sunflower seeds, sugar beet, fruit, and vegetables.

History In the 9th century the house of Rurik began to dominate the eastern Slavs, establishing the first all-Russian state with its capital at *Kiev. This powerful state accepted Christianity in about 985. However, decline had set in long before the Mongols established their control over most of European Russia in the 13th century.

Following the collapse of Mongol rule in the late 14th century, the principality of Muscovy emerged as the pre-eminent state. Gradually it absorbed formerly independent principalities, such as Novgorod (1478), forming in the process an autocratic, centralized Russian state. *Ivan IV (the Terrible) was the first Muscovite ruler to assume the title of Tsar (Emperor) of all Russia (1547). During his reign the state continued its expansion to the south and into Siberia. After his death a period of confusion followed as *boyar families challenged the power of Theodore I (ruled 1584–98) and *Boris Godunov. During the upheavals of the Time of Troubles (1604–13), there were several rival candidates to the throne which ended with the restoration of firm rule by Michael Romanov. The *Romanov dynasty resumed the process of territorial expansion, and in 1649 established peasant serfdom. In the early 18th century *Peter I transformed the old Muscovite state into a partially Westernized empire, stretching from the Baltic to the Pacific.

From this time onward Russia played a major role in European affairs. Under the empresses *Elizabeth I and *Catherine II, it came to dominate *Poland, and won a series of victories against the Ottoman Turks. In 1798–99 the Russians joined Great Britain, Austria, Naples, Portugal, and the Ottoman empire to fight against *Napoleon. The Treaty of Tilsit (1807) enabled it to acquire Finland from Sweden, while the early Russo-Turkish Wars led to territorial acquisitions in Bessarabia and the Caucasus. Following Napoleon's defeat, the Treaty of *Vienna (1815) confirmed Russia and Austria as the leading powers on the continent of Europe. Attempts at liberal reform by the *Decembrists were ruthlessly suppressed, and Russia helped Austria to quell Hungarian nationalist aspirations in the *Revolutions of 1848. Rivalry of interests, especially in south-east Europe, between Russia and the Western powers led to the *Crimean War. Serfdom was abolished in 1861, and attempts at changes in local government, the judicial system, and education were partially successful, though they fell short of the demands made by the Populists and other radical reform groups. In the late 19th century Russian expansionism, curtailed by the Congress of *Berlin, led to its abandonment of the Three Emperors' League and, later, to a Triple Entente with Britain and France (1907). Defeat in the unpopular *Russo-Japanese War led to the *Russian Revolution of 1905. A *Duma (Parliament) was established, and its Prime Minister, Stolypin, attempted a partial agrarian reform. The beginning of the 20th century saw a rapid growth in Russian industry, mainly financed by foreign capital. It was among the urban concentration of industrial workers that the leftist Social Democratic Party won support, although it split after 1903 into *Bolsheviks and Mensheviks. Support for Balkan nationalism led Russia into *World War I. The hardship which the war brought on the people was increased by the inefficient government of *Nicholas II. A series of revolts culminating in the *Russian Revolution of 1917 led to the overthrow of the Romanov dynasty and to the *Russian Civil War, after which the *Soviet Union was established in 1922.

The Russian republic was by far the largest of the Soviet republics, with 70% of the population. In 1978 it received a new constitution as the Russian Soviet Federal Socialist Republic (RSFSR), consisting of six territories, 49 provinces, five autonomous regions, and 16 autonomous republics. The Communist Party of the Soviet Union maintained firm control over the federation until the late 1980s, when pressures developed for greater independence. In 1990 a new constitution created a Russian Congress of People's Republics and a Russian Supreme Soviet, of which Boris *Yeltsin was elected Chairman on a ticket of multiparty democracy and economic reform. In June 1991 he was elected President of the Federation by popular vote. Following the disintegration of the Soviet Union and the resignation of President *Gorbachev in December, Russia became an independent sovereign state. It took the leading role in forming a new body, the Commonwealth of Independent States (CIS), which most of the former Soviet republics joined. Problems facing Russia in the early 1990s included tensions between autonomous republics, ethnic conflicts, the re-deployment of military and naval forces and equipment, and of nuclear weapons, and a rapidly collapsing economy. Following endorsement of Yeltsin's economic reforms in a national referendum in 1993, communists staged an unsuccessful coup against his administration. Yeltsin suspended parliament and ruled by presidential decree. In December 1993, elections to the Federal Assembly saw the rise of the far-right Liberal Democratic Party of Russia under its nationalist leader Vladimir

Zhirinovsky. In 1994 serious unrest broke out in the Caucasian region of Chechnya, where Muslim Chechens declared an independent republic. Although invading Russian forces devastated the capital, Grozny, resistance continued; despite sporadic peace talks the status of Chechnya has not been resolved. In the mid-1990s, Yeltsin's position was further weakened by failing health and by the Communist Party's victory in parliamentary elections in 1995. Although he was re-elected President in 1996, the financial crisis of 1998 led to further power struggles between Yeltsin and parliament as a result of which Yeltsin sacked the entire government four times. Yeltsin unexpectedly resigned on the last day of 1999, Vladimir *Putin becoming Acting President. Putin was elected President in 2000 and re-elected in 2004. Limited to two consecutive terms, he stood down in favour of Dmitri *Medvedev in 2008, but became Prime Minister and was widely seen as still the dominant figure in Russia. He was re-elected President in 2012. His rule has been marked by increased authoritarianism and rehabilitation of the Soviet period at home together with renewed assertiveness abroad. In 2008 Russia fought a short war with Georgia which left it in control of South Ossetia and Abkhazia; and in 2014 it responded to instability in *Ukraine by annexing Crimea and backing separatist militias in the east of that country.

Russian Civil War (1918–21) A conflict fought in Russia between the anti-communist White Army supported by some Western powers, and the *Red Army of the Soviets in the aftermath of the *Russian Revolution of 1917. It is sometimes referred to as the War of Allied Intervention. Counter-revolutionary forces began organized resistance to the *Bolsheviks in December 1917, and clashed with an army hastily brought together by *Trotsky. In northern Russia a force made up of French, British, German, and US units landed at Murmansk and occupied Archangel (1918–20). Nationalist revolts in the Baltic States led to the secession of Lithuania, Estonia, Latvia, and Finland, while a Polish army, with French support, successfully advanced the Polish frontier to the Russian Ukraine, gaining an area not re-occupied by the Soviet Union until World War II. In Siberia, where US and Japanese forces landed, Admiral Kolchak acted as Minister of War in the anti-communist 'All Russian Government' and, with the aid of a Czech legion made up of released prisoners-of-war, gained control over sectors of the Trans-Siberian Railway. He, however, was betrayed by the Czechs and murdered, the

leadership passing to General *Denikin, who sought to establish (1918–20) a 'United Russia' purged of the *Bolsheviks. In the Ukraine Denikin mounted a major offensive in 1919, only to be driven back to the Caucasus, where he held out until March 1920. In the Crimea the war continued under General Wrangel until November 1920. A famine in that year caused further risings by the peasants against the communists, while a mutiny of sailors at Kronstadt was suppressed by the Red Army. To win the war, *Lenin imposed his ruthless policy of 'war communism'. Lack of cooperation between counter-revolutionary forces contributed to their final collapse and to the establishment of the *Soviet Union.

Russian Revolution (1905) A conflict in Russia between the government of *Nicholas II and industrial workers, peasants, and armed forces. Heavy taxation had brought mounting distress to the poor, and Russia's defeat in the *Russo-Japanese War aggravated discontent. A peaceful demonstration in St Petersburg was met with gunfire from the imperial troops. Mutiny broke out on the battleship *Potemkin*, and a soviet or council of workers' delegates was formed in St Petersburg. The emperor yielded to demands for reform, including a legislative *Duma. The *Social Democrats continued to fight for a total overthrow of the system, and were met with harsh reprisals. Democratic freedoms were curtailed and the government became increasingly reactionary.

Russian Revolution (1917) The overthrow of the government of *Nicholas II in Russia and its replacement by *Bolshevik rule under the leadership of *Lenin. It was completed in two stages—a liberal (Menshevik) revolution in March (February, old style), which overthrew the imperial government, and a socialist (Bolshevik) revolution in November (October, old style). A long period of repression and unrest, compounded with the reluctance of the Russian people to continue to fight in World War I, led to a series of violent confrontations aiming to overthrow the existing government. The revolutionaries were divided between the liberal intelligentsia, who sought the establishment of a democratic, Western-style republic, and the socialists, who were prepared to use extreme violence to establish a *Marxist proletarian state in Russia. In the March Revolution strikes and riots in Petrograd (St Petersburg), supported by imperial troops, led to the abdication of the emperor and thus to the end after more than 300 years of Romanov rule. A committee of the

*Duma (Parliament) appointed the liberal Provisional Government under Prince Lvov, who later handed over to the Socialist revolutionary *Kerensky. He faced rising opposition from the Petrograd Soviet of Workers' and Soldiers' Deputies. The October Revolution was carried through in a nearly bloodless coup by the Bolsheviks under the leadership of Lenin. Workers' Councils (*Soviets) took control in the major cities, and a ceasefire was arranged with the Germans. A Soviet constitution was proclaimed in July 1918 and Lenin transferred the government from Petrograd to Moscow. The *Russian Civil War continued for nearly three more years, ending in the supremacy of the Bolsheviks and in the establishment of the *Soviet Union.

Russo-Japanese War (1904–05) An important conflict over control of Manchuria and Korea. The Japanese launched a surprise attack on Russian warships at anchor in the naval base at Port Arthur (now Lüshun), Manchuria, without declaring war, after Russia had reneged on its agreement to withdraw its troops from Manchuria. Port Arthur fell to the Japanese, as did Mukden, the capital of Manchuria. The Russian Baltic fleet sailed 28,000 km (18,000 miles) from its base to the East China Sea, only to be destroyed in the Tsushima Straits by the Japanese fleet led by Admiral Togo Heihashiro (1846–1934). This was the first Japanese defeat of a Western power both on land and at sea. The war was ended by the Treaty of *Portsmouth. For Russia, it was a humiliating defeat, which contributed to the *Russian Revolution of 1905.

Russo-Turkish Wars (1806–12; 1828–29; 1853–56; 1877–78) A series of wars between Russia and the *Ottoman empire, fought in the Balkans, the Crimea, and the Caucasus for political domination of those territories. The wars enabled the Slavonic nations of *Romania, *Serbia, and *Bulgaria to emerge and stimulated nationalist aspirations throughout the area to develop. In 1806–12 a vigorous campaign under Marshal *Kutuzov in the Balkans compelled the Turks to make peace, recognizing the autonomy of Serbia and ceding Bessarabia to Russia. The war of 1828–29 was a result of the *Greek War of Independence as Russian ships fought at the Battle of Navarino in which the Turks were defeated, enabling Greece to gain independence. One Russian army invaded Wallachia and Moldavia and, advancing through the Balkans, threatened Constantinople; a second army crossed the Caucasus to reach the Upper Euphrates. The Treaty of Adrianople (1829), which ended the war, gave Wallachia and Moldavia

effective independence and granted Russia control over a part of *Armenia. Russia was opposed in the *Crimean War of 1853–56 by Britain and France as well as Austria and Turkey, and, at the Treaty of *Paris, ceded territories. In 1876 the Turks quelled an uprising in *Bulgaria, causing a European outcry against the "Bulgarian atrocities". Russian forces invaded in 1877, allegedly to protect Bulgarian Christians; they again threatened Constantinople. The Treaty of San Stefano (March 1878) (*Three Emperors' League) which ended the war, provoked criticism from Britain and Germany and was modified by the Congress of *Berlin (June 1878), as it was alleged to have given too much influence to Russia in the Balkans.

Ruyter, Michiel Adrianszoon de (1607–76) Dutch naval commander. He served under Maarten *Tromp in the First *Anglo-Dutch War and was the rival of Cornelius Tromp in the Second and Third wars. His most daring coup was in 1667 when, knowing that the English fleet was laid up for lack of money, he sailed up the rivers Thames and Medway, remained in the Chatham dockyard for two days destroying many ships, and made off with the *Royal Charles*, the English fleet's newest ship.

Rwanda

Capital:	Kigali
Area:	26,338 sq km (10,169 sq miles)
Population:	12,012,589 (2013 est)
Currency:	1 Rwanda franc = 100 centimes
Religions:	Roman Catholic 49.5%; Protestant 39.4%; other Christian 4.5%
Ethnic Groups:	Hutu 84.0%; Tutsi 15.0%; Twa 1.0%
Languages:	Kinyarwanda, French, English (all official); Swahili
International Organizations:	UN; AU; Non-Aligned Movement; WTO; Commonwealth

A small country in east central Africa. It is bounded in the west by the Democratic Republic of Congo and Lake Kivu, on the north by Uganda, on the east by Tanzania, and on the south by Burundi.

Physical Rwanda occupies a mountainous region where the equatorial climate is modified by the altitude. Set on the eastern edge of the Great Rift Valley, at the head of Lake Tanganyika, it is also volcanic.

Economy Rwanda is one of the poorest countries in the world. It has the highest population density in Africa, with the great majority engaged in subsistence agriculture. Coffee, tea, and hides are the main agricultural exports. The principal mineral resource is cassiterite (a tin ore), which is also exported. Other mineral resources include wolframite, gold and unexploited natural gas reserves. Limited manufacturing industry includes cement, agricultural products, beverages, and soap.

History Rwanda obtained its present boundaries in the late 19th century under pastoral Tutsi kings who ruled over the agriculturalist Bahutu (Hutu). In 1890 Germany claimed it as part of German East Africa. Belgian forces took it in 1916, and administered it under a League of Nations mandate. Following civil war (1959) between the Tutsi and Hutu tribes, Rwanda was declared a republic in 1961 and became independent in 1962. The now dominant Hutu forced large numbers of Tutsi into exile, but after the accession to power of President Juvénal Habyarimana in 1973 domestic stability improved. In 1975 Habyarimana's party, the National Revolutionary Movement for Development (MRND) declared itself the sole legal political organization; he was re-elected in 1978, 1983, and 1988. In October 1990 Uganda-based rebels of the Front Patriotique Rwandaise (FPR), many of whose members were Tutsi, invaded. Belgian and French forces helped to repel them, while the Organization of African Unity negotiated. In 1991 a new constitution legalized opposition parties, but the FPR refused to participate. In 1992 a coalition government was formed pending a general election, but Tutsi–Hutu tension persisted. In 1994 Habyarimana was assassinated and some 500,000 Tutsis were massacred by the Hutu-dominated army. The FPR, led by Paul *Kagame, emerged victorious in the ensuing civil war, but this provoked millions of Hutus to flee the country for fear of reprisals. Although a broad-based government was established, with Kagame as its dominant member, ethnic violence continued. By the late 1990s, however, some million refugees returned and the UN set up an international tribunal to prosecute those responsible for genocide. Kagame was elected President by the transitional National Assembly in 2000 and was re-elected in Rwanda's first multiparty elections after a new constitution came into force in 2003. In 2005 a Hutu rebel group announced its disarmament. Kagame was again re-elected in 2010 in elections characterized by repression and violence. Rwanda joined the *Commonwealth of Nations in 2009.

Rye House Plot (1683) A conspiracy of Whig extremists who planned to murder *Charles II of England and his brother James, Duke of York, after the failure of attempts to exclude James, a Roman Catholic, from the succession. The conspiracy takes its name from the house in Hertfordshire where the assassination was to have taken place. Of those accused of conspiracy, the Earl of Essex committed suicide and Lord Russell and Algernon Sidney were condemned to death on the flimsiest of evidence.

Ryswick, Treaty of (1697) The treaty that ended the *Nine Years War. *Louis XIV agreed to recognize *William III as King of England, give up his attempts to control Cologne and the Palatinate, end French occupation of Lorraine, and restore Luxembourg, Mons, Courtrai, and Barcelona to Spain. The Dutch were allowed to garrison a series of fortresses in the Spanish Netherlands as a barrier against France. Strasburg and some towns of Lower Alsace were the only acquisitions made since the Treaty of *Nijmegen that France retained.

SA *See* BROWNSHIRTS.

Sabines A tribe native to the foothills of the Apennines north-east of Rome. According to tradition they joined the earliest settlement of Rome in the 8th century BC. Legend relates how the Romans abducted the Sabine women during a festival; an army was raised to take revenge but the women appeared on the battlefield with new-born babies and the two sides were reconciled. They became Roman citizens only after conquest.

Sacco–Vanzetti Case The controversial US legal case (1920–27) in which two Italian immigrants, Nicola Sacco and Bertolomeo Vanzetti, were found guilty of murder. Many have alleged that their conviction resulted from prejudice against them as immigrants, *anarchists, and evaders of military service. Following the trial there were anti-US demonstrations in Rome, Lisbon, and Montevideo, and one in Paris, where a bomb killed 20 people. For six years efforts were made to obtain a retrial without success, although the judge was officially criticized for his conduct; the two men were electrocuted in August 1927. The affair helped to mobilize opinion against the prevailing *isolationism and conservatism of the post-war USA. Later evidence pointed to the crime having been committed by members of a gang led by Joe Morrelli.

Sacheverell, Henry (1674–1724) English divine and preacher. In 1709 he preached two sermons attacking the Whig government's policy of religious toleration, one of the principles of the *Glorious Revolution. The House of Commons condemned the sermons as seditious and Sacheverell was impeached. He attracted a popular following, with crowds shouting "High Church and Sacheverell" in his support. Although his sentence was a nominal one (a temporary suspension from preaching), the Sacheverell episode was important within a political context; the Tories used the message of "the Church in danger" to attract support from the conservative Anglican squirearchy against the Whigs, thereby crucially weakening the Whig ministry, which fell in 1710.

Sadat, (Muhammad) Anwar al- (1918–81) Egyptian statesman, President (1970–81). He broke with the foreign policies of his predecessor President Nasser, for example by dismissing the Soviet military mission to Egypt, removing the ban on political parties, and introducing measures to decentralize Egypt's political structure and diversify the economy. He later worked to achieve peace in the Middle East, visiting Israel (1977), and attending talks with Prime Minister Begin at Camp David in 1978, the year they shared the Nobel Peace Prize. Also in that year he founded the National Democratic Party, with himself as leader. He was assassinated by members of the Islamic Jihad.

Sadowa, Battle of (3 July 1866) A battle fought near the Bohemian town of Sadowa (Königgrätz), between the Prussian army under Field Marshal Moltke and Benedek's Austrian army. The Prussians were able to overcome Benedek by their superior mobility and weapons. This battle decided the Seven Weeks War (*see* AUSTRO-PRUSSIAN WAR) and marked the end of Austrian influence in Germany. Prussian domination in north Germany was confirmed.

Safavid *See* ISMAIL I.

Said ibn Sultan Sayyid (1791–1856) Ruler of Oman and Zanzibar (1806–56). In 1806 he became ruler (Sayyid) of *Oman, with his capital at Muscat on the Persian Gulf. In 1822, assisted by the British, he sent an expedition to Mombasa, whose rulers, the Mazrui family, owed him nominal allegiance, but who were seeking independence. He himself visited Mombasa in 1827 and in the next decade brought many East African ports under his control. In 1837 he ended Mazrui rule in Mombasa and signed commercial agreements with Britain, France, and the USA. He first visited Zanzibar in 1828, buying property and introducing clove production. In 1840 he took control of Zanzibar. Said sent trading caravans deep into Africa, seeking ivory and slaves, and Zanzibar became the commercial capital of the East African coast. Although an ally of the British, he was under constant pressure from them to end his trade in slaves, and he signed an agreement to do this in 1845. When he died, he divided the Asian and African parts of his empire between his two sons.

Saigo Takamori (1828–77) Japanese soldier and statesman. A member of a lowly but prestigious *samurai family, he played a central role in the overthrow of the *shogunate and the establishment of the *Meiji imperial state. Showered with the highest honours, he initially retired from public life, but in 1871 was persuaded to return to the government as commander of the Imperial Guard. Fearing for the decline of the samurai way of life in the face of the introduction of conscription, Saigo promoted a war of redemption against Korea, to be triggered by his own murder at Korean hands, but retired in 1873 when this plan was vetoed. Subsequently his private school at Kagoshima became a centre for samurai dissatisfaction, and in 1877 he was forced into rebellion by the actions of his followers. Defeated by government forces under *Yamagata, he had himself killed by one of his own men.

St Bartholomew's Day Massacre (23–24 August 1572) An event that marked a turning point in the *French Wars of Religion. The Catholic *Guise faction prevailed upon Catherine de Medici to authorize an assassination of about 200 of the principal *Huguenot leaders. Parisian Catholic mobs used these killings as a pretext for large-scale butchery, until some 3,000 Huguenots lay dead, and thousands more perished in the 12 provincial disturbances that followed.

Saintes, Les, Battle of (1782) A Caribbean naval battle fought off the coast of Dominica, between a British fleet under *Rodney and a French fleet under de Grasse. Five French ships were captured and one sunk. The engagement was notable because Rodney, taking advantage of the wind, broke the French line in two places, a manoeuvre later perfected by *Nelson. This victory somewhat offset the British defeat in the American War of Independence and re-established Britain's maritime supremacy.

St John, Order of *See* KNIGHT HOSPITALLER.

Saint-Just, Louis Antoine Léon Florelle de (1767–94) French Revolutionary leader. He was elected an officer in the National Guard when the *French Revolution began; his great loyalty to *Robespierre led to his appointment to the National Convention in 1792. In his first speech he condemned Louis XVI and he was subsequently instrumental in the overthrow of the *Girondins Jacques René Hébert and *Danton. He was the youngest member of the *Committee of Public Safety, organized the Reign of Terror of 1793–94 in which supposed enemies of the Revolution were executed without legal process, and carried out many missions to enforce discipline in the revolutionary armies. He was executed with Robespierre.

Saint Kitts and Nevis (or **Saint Christopher and Nevis**)

Capital:	Basseterre
Area:	261 sq km (101 sq miles)
Population:	51,134 (2013 est)
Currency:	1 East Caribbean dollar = 100 cents
Religions:	Anglican 50.0%; Roman Catholic 25.0%
Ethnic Groups:	Black; British, Portuguese, and Lebanese minorities
Languages:	English (official)
International Organizations:	UN; OAS; Commonwealth; CARICOM; WTO; Non-Aligned Movement

An island country in the Leeward Islands of the Caribbean.

Physical Saint Kitts is an oval-shaped volcanic island crossed by rugged mountains. In the south-east a narrow isthmus enlarges to a knot of salt ponds. Three kilometres (2 miles) to the south-east, Nevis, is a smaller island. Both have an equable, tropical climate. The tiny island, Sombrero, is included in the group.

Economy Tourism is the mainstay of the economy, having replaced sugar in the 1970s. The government is seeking to diversify the economy, and principal exports include machinery, food and drink, electronics, and tobacco. The sugar industry, dominant for more than

S

300 years, was closed down in 2005 after many years of losses.

History Originally inhabited by Caribs, the islands were visited by Christopher Columbus in 1493, who named the larger island Saint Christopher. English settlers in the early 17th century shortened the name to Saint Kitts; this was the first successful English colony in the Caribbean. The islands, together with Anguilla, were united as a single colony in 1882. In 1958, they joined the West Indies Federation. Anguilla became a separate British dependency in 1980, while Saint Kitts and Nevis gained independence within the British Commonwealth in 1983. Nevis has its own legislature and retains the right to secede from Saint Kitts at any time should it so choose. In 1998 a referendum was held in which 60% of the voters favoured secession, which fell short of the two-thirds majority required for independence.

St Laurent, Louis Stephen (1882–1973) French-Canadian lawyer and statesman. As Minister of Justice (1941–46) he upheld limited military conscription during World War II in the face of widespread French-Canadian opposition. In 1946 he became Secretary of State for External Affairs. Having succeeded Mackenzie *King as Prime Minister of Canada (1948–57), he played a significant part in setting up the *NATO alliance, and did much to raise the international reputation of Canada. Significant constitutional changes were also made during his administration, with the word "Dominion" being dropped from Canada's official name and Newfoundland becoming the tenth Province in 1949. After overwhelming victories in 1949 and 1953, he was defeated in the election of 1957. As only the second French-Canadian to become Prime Minister, St Laurent gave notable service in the promotion of good relations between English- and French-speaking Canadians.

Saint Lucia

Capital:	Castries
Area:	616 sq km (238 sq miles)
Population:	162,781 (2013 est)
Currency:	1 East Caribbean dollar = 100 cents
Religions:	Roman Catholic 61.5%; Seventh-day Adventist 10.4%; Pentecostal 8.9%

Ethnic Groups:	Black 85.3%; mixed 10.9%; East Indian 2.2%
Languages:	English (official); French patois
International Organizations:	UN; OAS; CARICOM; Commonwealth; Non-Aligned Movement; WTO

An island country, one of the Windward Islands of the Caribbean.

Physical Saint Lucia is 43 km (27 miles) in length and roughly oval-shaped. In the south-west is the dormant volcano Quali-bou. The twin peaks of the Pitons have fine volcanic cones. The fertile volcanic valleys and coastal plains are well watered. There is a fine harbour.

Economy Tourism generates almost two-thirds of GDP and is the main source of foreign exchange. Other industries include clothing, assembly of electronic components, and drinks; offshore banking is also important. Bananas, coconuts, fruit, vegetables, and cocoa are grown.

History The Arawak Indians, the earliest inhabitants of Saint Lucia, were driven out by Carib Indians before Europeans arrived. The British failed in their attempts to colonize the island in 1605 and 1638 and the French settled it, making a treaty with the Caribs in 1660. Saint Lucia changed hands several times before being ceded to Britain in 1814. A representative local government was established in 1924 and Saint Lucia was a member of the Federation of the West Indies from 1958 until 1962. Saint Lucia became an independent member of the British Commonwealth in 1979, after twelve years of internal self-government. Its economy was severely affected by the fall in prices for bananas (its then chief export) in the European market in 1993.

Saint-Simon, Claude-Henri de Rouvroy, Comte de (1760–1825) French social reformer and philosopher. In reaction to the chaos engendered by the French Revolution he developed a new theory of social organization and was later claimed to be the founder of French socialism. His central theory was that society should be organized in an industrial order, controlled by leaders of industry, and given spiritual direction by scientists.

Saint Vincent and the Grenadines

Capital:	Kingstown
Area:	389 sq km (150 sq miles)
Population:	103,220 (2013 est)
Currency:	1 East Caribbean dollar = 100 cents
Religions:	Anglican 47.0%; Methodist 28.0% ; Roman Catholic 13.0%
Ethnic Groups:	Black 66.0%; mixed 19.0%; East Indian 6.0%
Languages:	English (official); French patois
International Organizations:	UN; OAS; CARICOM; Commonwealth; WTO; Non-Aligned Movement

An island country in the Windward Islands of the Caribbean, consisting of the main island of Saint Vincent and two islets of the Grenadines.

Physical The main island, Saint Vincent, is 29 km (18 miles) long. Of volcanic origin, it has forested, rugged mountains rising to the active volcano of Mount Soufrière. There are picturesque valleys and fertile well-watered tracts. While the climate is tropical, there are hurricanes and occasional earthquakes.

Economy Tourism and banana production are the two most important economic activities. There is a small offshore banking sector, and remittances from expatriates are important.

History When Christopher *Columbus discovered the islands in 1498 they were inhabited by Carib Indians. Europeans did not colonize the islands until the 18th century when they made treaties with the Caribs. The islands changed hands several times but the British finally gained control in 1796. Most of the Caribs were deported and most of those remaining were killed in volcanic eruptions in 1812 and 1902. The British brought many African slaves to the islands, and after the abolition of slavery in 1834 many Portuguese and Asian labourers were brought in to work on sugar cane plantations. The country was a British colony from 1871 until 1956, when colonial rule was ended. Part of the Federation of the West Indies (1958–62), Saint Vincent and the Grenadines became fully independent in 1979. The country was governed from 1984–2001 by the right-wing New Democratic Party under Sir James Mitchell. However, the 2001, 2005, and 2010 elections were won by the Unity Labour Party, led by Ralph Gonsalves.

Sakharov, Andrei (Dmitrievich) (1921–89) Russian nuclear physicist. Having helped to develop the Soviet hydrogen bomb, he campaigned against nuclear proliferation and called for Soviet-American cooperation. He fought courageously for reform and human rights in the USSR, for which he was awarded the Nobel Peace Prize in 1975. His international reputation as a scientist kept him out of jail, but in 1980 he was banished to Gorky (Nizhni Novgorod) and kept under police surveillance. He was freed (1986) in the new spirit of glasnost, and at his death he was honoured in his own country as well as in the West.

Saladin (Arabic name **Salah-ad-Din Yusuf ibn-Ayyub**) (1137–93) Sultan of Egypt and Syria (1174–93). He invaded the Holy Land and reconquered Jerusalem from the Christians (1187), and, for a period, resisted the Third Crusade, the leaders of which included *Richard I (the Lionheart). He was later defeated by Richard at Arsuf (1191) and withdrew to Damascus, where he died.

Salamis, Battle of (480 BC) A naval battle fought in the Aegean Sea during the Greek-Persian wars. *Themistocles, the Greek commander, lured the Persian fleet of *Xerxes, the Persian king, into the narrow waters between the island of Salamis and the mainland. The outnumbered but nimbler and expertly handled Greek triremes took full advantage of the confusion engendered by the confined space to win a victory that offset the earlier reverses at *Thermopylae and Artemisium.

Salazar, Antonio de Oliveira (1889–1970) Portuguese statesman, Prime Minister (1932–68). While Finance Minister (1928–40), he formulated austere fiscal policies to effect Portugal's economic recovery. During his long premiership, he ruled the country as a virtual dictator, firmly suppressing opposition and enacting a new authoritarian constitution along Fascist lines. Salazar maintained Portugal's neutrality throughout the Spanish Civil War and World War II.

Salem witch trials (1692) The trial and execution of 19 supposed witches at Salem, Massachusetts. The hunt for witches began when girls in the minister's household believed themselves bewitched. Panic about devil worship and resultant accusations spread through surrounding towns until 50 people were afflicted and 200 had been accused. Increase *Mather and Governor Sir William Phips managed to halt the witch craze in October 1692.

Salic law The legal code of the Salian *Franks, which originated in 5th century Gaul. It was issued by *Clovis (465–511) and reissued under the *Carolingians. It contained both criminal and civil clauses and provided for penal fines for offenders. It also laid down that daughters could not inherit land and was later used in France and in some German principalities to prevent daughters succeeding to the throne.

Salisbury, Robert Arthur Talbot Gascoigne-Cecil, 3rd Marquess of (1830–1903) British Conservative statesman, Prime Minister (1885–86; 1886–92; 1895–1902). His main area of concern was foreign affairs; he was a firm defender of British imperial interests and supported the policies that resulted in the Second Boer War (1899–1902).

Sallust (full name **Gaius Sallustius Crispus**) (86–35 BC) Roman historian and politician. As a historian he was concerned with the political decline of Rome after the fall of Carthage in 146 BC, to which he accorded a simultaneous moral decline. His chief surviving works deal with the Catiline conspiracy and the Jugurthine War.

Salmond, Alex (Alexander Elliot Anderson Salmond) (1954–   ) Scottish politician, First Minister (2007–14). After graduating (1978) from St Andrews University, where he joined the *Scottish National Party (SNP), Salmond worked as a civil servant and in banking before being elected to the UK Parliament in 1987. He became SNP leader in 1990 and was prominent in the campaign to establish a devolved Scottish Parliament (1997). He became leader of the opposition in the first Scottish Parliament (1999), but resigned as SNP leader in 2000 following disputes within the party. From 2001 he was leader of the SNP MPs in the UK Parliament. He was re-elected as party leader in 2004 and to the Scottish Parliament in 2007, becoming First Minister of Scotland at the head of a minority SNP government. In 2011 he secured a second term when the SNP gained an absolute majority in the Scottish election. The SNP had promised a referendum on whether Scotland should become an independent country, and this took place in September 2014. Although Salmond led a vigorous campaign for a 'yes' vote, Scottish voters rejected independence by a margin of 10%. He subsequently resigned as First Minister and SNP leader.

Sālote Tupou III *See* TONGA.

SALT *See* STRATEGIC ARMS LIMITATION TALKS.

Salt March (12 March–6 April 1930) A march by Indian nationalists led by Mohandas

*Gandhi. The private manufacture of salt violated the salt tax system imposed by the British, and in a new campaign of civil disobedience Gandhi led his followers from his ashram at Sabarmati to make salt from the sea at Dandi, a distance of 320 km (200 miles). The government remained inactive until the protesters marched on a government salt depot. Gandhi was arrested on 5 May, but his followers continued the movement of civil disobedience.

Samaria The ancient capital of the northern kingdom of the Hebrews in central Palestine, now occupied by the village of Sabastiyah in the West Bank north-west of Nablus. Built in the 9th century BC, it was captured in 721 BC by the Assyrians and resettled with people from other parts of their empire (2 Kings 17,18). In New Testament times Samaria was rebuilt and greatly enlarged by Herod the Great. It is the alleged burial place of John the Baptist.

Samnite wars A succession of wars fought between the southern neighbours of Rome, the Samnites and the Latins. The first war (343–341 BC) was brief, but the second (326–304) was more protracted. Roman troops experienced the humiliation of having to walk like slaves under a yoke of spears after their defeat at the Caudine Forks. The *Appian Way was begun in 312 to assist communications between Rome and the war area. Gauls joined against Rome in the third of the wars (298–290), but were defeated. The Samnites were consistently hostile to Rome. They helped *Hannibal in the second *Punic War and revolted for the last time in the Social War of 90, after which they became allies of *Marius. *Sulla crushed them and devastated their homelands.

Samoa (formerly **Western Samoa**)

Capital:	Apia
Area:	2831 sq km (1093 sq miles)
Population:	195,476 (2013 est)
Currency:	1 tala = 100 sene
Religions:	Congregational 31.8%; Roman Catholic 19.4%; Mormon 15.2%; Methodist 13.7%; Assembly of God 8.0%
Ethnic Groups:	Samoan 92.6%; Euronesian 7.0%; European 0.4%
Languages:	Samoan (official); English
International Organizations:	UN; Commonwealth; Pacific Islands Forum; Secretariat of the Pacific Community; WTO

A country consisting of a group of nine islands in the south-west Pacific and forming part of the Samoan Archipelago.

Physical The country's two major islands, Upolu and Savai'i, are both volcanic and are fringed by coral reefs. The islands have evergreen rainforests and swamps.

Economy The economy of Samoa is based on agriculture and fishing, which employ two-thirds of the workforce and provide nine-tenths of exports. The main industry is food processing, and coconut cream, coconut oil, and copra are the principal exports. Tourism is expanding and contributes a quarter of GDP.

History The Samoan archipelago was first settled in about 1000 BC and was the centre of Polynesian migrations eastwards. Although sighted by the Dutch in 1722, the first European to set foot on the islands was Louis-Antoine de *Bougainville in 1768. Germany, Britain, and the USA competed for control of the archipelago until 1899 when the western part of Samoa passed to Germany and the eastern islands became American Samoa. Western Samoa remained a German protectorate until 1914; thereafter it was administered by New Zealand, initially (1920–46) under a League of Nations Mandate and then as a UN Trust Territory. It gained full independence in 1962 as Western Samoa and joined the *Commonwealth of Nations in 1970. Susuga Malietoa Tanumafili II became head of state in 1963. He is a constitutional monarch with the power to dissolve the legislative assembly, which is known as the *Fono*. In 1990 universal adult suffrage was introduced. In 1997 the country's official name was changed to Samoa. When Tanumafili died in 2007, Samoa became a republic with the new head of state, Tuiatua Tupua Tamasese Efi, being elected by the legislative assembly; he was re-elected in 2012.

Samori Touré (1830–1900) African military leader. A Muslim, he began to amass a personal following in the mid-1850s, establishing a military base on the Upper Niger. By 1870 his authority was acknowledged throughout the Kanaka region of the River Milo, in what is now eastern Guinea. By 1880 he ruled a vast Dyula empire, from the Upper Volta in the east to the Fouta Djallon in the west, over which he attempted to create a single Islamic administrative system. His imperial ambitions clashed with those of the French and there were sporadic battles between 1882 and 1886. His attempts to

impose Islam on all his people resulted in a revolt in 1888. A French invasion in 1891–92 forced him to move eastwards to the interior of the Ivory Coast, where he established himself in Bondoukon (1891–98). French forces, however, captured him and he was exiled to Gabon.

samurai (from Japanese, 'those who serve') Warrior retainers of Japan's daimyo (feudal lords). Prominent from the 12th century, they were not a separate class until Hideyoshi limited the right to bear arms to them, after which they became a hereditary caste. Their two swords were their badge. Their conduct was regulated by *Bushido* ('Warrior's Way'), a strict code that emphasized the qualities of loyalty, bravery, and endurance. Their training from childhood was spartan. Their ultimate duty when defeated or dishonoured was *seppuku*, ritual self-disembowelment.

sanctuary A sacred place recognized as a refuge for criminals. Such places existed in both Greek and Roman society and since 399 in the Christian world. In England a fugitive could claim refuge from immediate prosecution in a church or churchyard provided he agreed with the coroner to leave the realm by a specified port within 40 days. Failure to do so would result in prosecution. This right did not apply in cases of treason (1486). Towns having sanctuary privileges were restricted by Henry VIII to Derby, Launceston, Manchester, Northampton, Wells, Westminster, and York. In England criminals lost the right to sanctuary in 1623.

Sandinista Liberation Front *See* NICARAGUA.

Sandino, César Augusto (1893–1934) Nicaraguan revolutionary general. A guerrilla leader, he tenaciously resisted US intervention in Nicaragua from 1926–1933. His anti-imperialist stance attracted wide support in Latin America. After US marines withdrew, Sandino became leader of a cooperative farming scheme. Seen as a liberalizing influence, he was assassinated by Anastasio *Somoza's National Guard. The Sandinista Liberation Front, which defeated the Somoza dynasty in 1979, considered itself the spiritual heir of Sandino.

San Francisco Conference (1951) A conference held to agree a formal peace treaty between Japan and the nations against which she had fought in World War II. When the treaty came into force in April 1952, the period of occupation (*Japan, occupation of) was formally ended and Japanese sovereignty restored. Japan recognized the independence of Korea and renounced its rights to Taiwan, the Pescadores, the Kuriles, southern Sakhalin, and the Pacific islands mandated to it before the war by the League of Nations. The country was allowed the right of self-defence with the proviso that the USA would maintain its own forces in Japan until the Japanese were able to shoulder their own defensive responsibilities. The Soviet Union did not sign the treaty, but diplomatic relations were restored in 1956, while peace treaties with Asian nations conquered by the Japanese in the war were signed through the 1950s as individual problems with reparations were resolved.

Sanhedrin (from Greek *synedrion*, 'council') The supreme court of the *Jewish people, headed by the high priest, before the fall of *Jerusalem in 70 AD. It was probably founded around the 2nd century BC. Under the Romans its jurisdiction covered Palestinian Jews in civil and religious matters, though capital sentences required Roman confirmation.

San Jacinto, Battle of (21 April 1836) The last important battle of *Texas's brief struggle to establish an independent republic. Sam *Houston, with 800 Texans, defeated a Mexican force of 1400 at the San Jacinto River and captured the Mexican leader *Santa Anna. The armistice terms dictated by Houston established *de facto* independence for Texas, and Houston himself was installed as President.

Sankaracharya (*c.*700–50) Indian religious thinker who expounded and taught the Vedanta system, the most influential of the six recognized systems of Hindu thought. He was born in a Brahmin family in Kerala, south India, but renounced the world to travel all over India as a sannyasi (ascetic), having discussions with philosophers of various schools. His foundation of monasteries throughout India helped to spread his ideas, and he has remained one of the most influential teachers in the Hindu world. Within the Vedanta philosophy his teaching that Brahman (the supreme soul) and Atman (the human soul) are one, and that the visible world is *maya* (illusory), are the chief distinquishing marks of his school.

San Marino

Capital:	San Marino
Area:	61 sq km (24 sq miles)
Population:	32,448 (2013 est)
Currency:	1 euro = 100 cents

Religions:	Roman Catholic
Ethnic Groups:	Sammarinesi; Italian
Languages:	Italian (official)
International Organizations:	UN; OSCE; Council of Europe

A small landlocked country entirely surrounded by Italy.

Physical Situated on the slopes of the Apennine mountains, San Marino is dominated by Mount Titano.

Economy Tourism, banking, textiles, electronics, and ceramics are important industries.

History By tradition founded in 301, San Marino was recognized by the pope as an independent state in 1291. Its independence is guaranteed by a treaty made in 1862 with the newly united Italy.

San Martín, José de (1778–1850) Argentinian soldier and statesman. Having assisted in the liberation of his country from Spanish rule (1812–13) he went on to aid Bernardo *O'Higgins in the liberation of Chile (1817–18). He was also involved in gaining Peruvian independence, becoming Protector of Peru in 1821; he resigned a year later after differences with the other great liberator Simón *Bolívar.

sansculotte Originally, a member of the volunteer republican 'army' of the early *French Revolution. 'Sansculotte' ('without knee-breeches'), was chosen by the revolutionaries to describe the labourer's loose-fitting linen garment worn by their supporters. During the Reign of Terror public functionaries styled themselves *citoyens sansculottes*, with a distinctive costume: *pantalon* (long trousers), *carmagnole* (short-skirted coat), red cap of liberty, and *sabots* (wooden clogs).

Santa Anna, Antonio López de (1794–1876) Mexican military adventurer and statesman. He entered the Spanish colonial army and served as one of the Creole supporters of the Spanish government until 1821, when *Iturbide made him governor of Vera Cruz. At first a supporter of the Federal Party, he subsequently overthrew (1822) Iturbide and himself became (1833) President of Mexico. His policies led to the uprising at *Alamo, to his defeat and capture in the battle of *San Jacinto (1836), and to the secession of *Texas. He was released, and returned to Vera Cruz, where he defended the city against the French (1836–39). In his next presidential tenure during the early 1840s, he discarded the liberal constitution of 1824 and ruled as a dictator. Subsequently, despite defeat in the *Mexican–American War and the loss of half of Mexico's territory to the USA, Santa Anna was recalled to the presidency in 1853 by Mexican conservatives. In 1855 the liberal revolution of Ayutla deposed him.

São Tomé and Príncipe

Capital:	São Tomé
Area:	964 sq km (372 sq miles)
Population:	186,817 (2013 est)
Currency:	1 dobra = 100 centimos
Religions:	Roman Catholic 55.7%; Adventist 4.1%; Assembly of God 3.4%
Ethnic Groups:	Mixed; African; European
Languages:	Portuguese (official); Forro; minority languages
International Organizations:	UN; AU; Non-Aligned Movement

A country comprising two islands and several islets, lying on the Equator in the Gulf of Guinea, off the coast of West Africa.

Physical The two main islands are volcanic and both have coastal lowlands rising to central mountainous regions. The island of Príncipe lies about 144 km (90 miles) north of São Tomé. Tropical rainforests cover most of the islands.

Economy São Tomé and Príncipe is a very poor country with most of the population engaged in subsistence agriculture and two-thirds living in poverty. Cocoa accounts for four-fifths of exports, followed by copra, coffee, and palm oil. Tourism is expanding and offshore oil fields are being developed jointly with Nigeria.

History The islands were probably uninhabited when they were discovered by the Portuguese in 1471 and were annexed by Portugal in 1522. Independence was gained in 1975 with Manuel Pinto da Costa as President (1975–91). Multiparty democracy was instituted under a new constitution in 1990. In 1995 President Miguel Trovoada was deposed by Cuban-trained rebel forces but was swiftly restored to power. Tensions continued for the rest of Trovoada's

presidency and into that of his successor, Fradique de Menezes, who was elected in 2001 and re-elected in 2006. A coup in 2003 ended in a compromise between rebels and the de Menezes regime. Pinto da Costa was re-elected President in 2011.

Saracens Originally nomads belonging to tribes of the Syrian or Arabian deserts but at the time of the *Crusades the name used by Christians for all Muslims. In a surge of conquest Muslim Arabs swept into the Holy Land (western Palestine), north into the Byzantine territory of Asia Minor, and westward through North Africa during the 7th and 8th centuries. Spain was conquered (*Moors), together with most of the islands in the Mediterranean; they held Sicily from the 9th to the 11th century. Their expansion was halted by the Carolingians in France only with great difficulty. The Crusades against them, though initially effective, did not prove decisive in the long term, and they were not finally expelled from Spain until the 15th century.

Within their conquered territories they had a profound effect on cultural life, particularly in architecture, philosophy, mathematics, and religion. In religion they were often tolerant of local beliefs and customs. The lurid accounts of Saracen bloodshed must be offset by the financial advantages of their presence: Saracen gold, used to pay for European goods, invigorated the Frankish economy.

Saratoga campaign (1777) An operation devised by *Burgoyne to isolate New England from the other American colonies during the War of American *Independence. He advanced south from Montreal expecting to meet Howe from New York and St Leger from Oswego at Albany and thus secure the line of the Hudson valley. Thanks to bad coordination, however, Howe chose this time to embark on his Philadelphia campaign. Burgoyne captured Ticonderoga but his advance was slowed by unsuitable equipment, lack of supplies, and guerrilla attacks. Defeated at *Bennington and Freeman's Farm, with no help forthcoming from Howe, he was halted, and forced to surrender to *Gates. This British defeat encouraged France to enter the war in 1778 and was a vital tonic to the American cause.

Sarekat Islam An Indonesian Islamic political organization. Formed in 1911 as an association of Javanese batik traders to protect themselves against Chinese competition, it had developed, by the time of its first party congress in 1913, into a mass organization dedicated to self-government through constitutional means. Its leader H. Q. S.

Cokroaminoto (1882–1934), was viewed by many as a latter-day Messiah, but the organization was weakened from within by the political challenge posed by the emergent *PKI in the early 1920s; thereafter it gradually faded away as more radical nationalist parties, most prominently *Sukarno's PNI, were formed.

Sargon I *See* AKKAD.

Sargon II (died 705 BC) King of Assyria (721–705). He was probably a son of Tiglath-pileser III, and is thought to have been named after the semi-legendary King Sargon. He is famous for his conquest of a number of cities in Syria and Palestine; he also took ten of the tribes of Israel into a captivity from which they are believed never to have returned, becoming known as the Lost Tribes of Israel (2 Kings 17:6).

Sarkozy, Nicolas (1955–) French politician, President (2007–12). Born to Greek and Hungarian immigrant parents, Sarkozy studied law at university and then political science at the Institut d'Études Politiques (1979–81). He pursued a career on the right wing of French politics, being elected mayor of Neuilly-sur-Seine (1993–2002) and becoming Budget Minister under Édouard Balladur (1993–95). Differences with President Jacques Chirac kept him out of office until 2002, after which he served as Minister of the Interior (2002–04; 2005–07) and Minister of Finance (2004). He gained a high profile with his hard-line response to riots in 2005 and was elected President of France in 2007 on a platform of free-market reform. As President he implemented some of this programme and reintegrated France into *NATO's military structure (2009); he also played a leading role in the EU and in providing military support for Libyan opponents of the *Gaddafi regime (2011). However, his popularity declined as France's economic situation worsened and he was defeated in the 2012 presidential election by François *Hollande.

Saro-Wiwa, Ken(ule) Beeson (1941–95) Nigerian writer who spoke out in the early 1990s against the then military regime and the environmental damage being caused by the Anglo-Dutch petroleum company Shell. Along with eight fellow activists, he was executed by hanging, provoking international condemnation, suspension of Nigeria from the Commonwealth, and calls for sanctions.

Sassanian empire An empire that occupied much of south-west Asia from the 3rd to the 7th century. It was founded c.224 by Ardashir (ruled c.224–41), who overthrew Artabanus V, the last *Parthian king, in the name of vengeance for the last *Achaemenid king. The dynasty takes its name from his grandfather Sasan. Territorially the empire stretched from the Syrian desert, where Roman pressure was checked, to north-west India where the Kushan and Hephthalite empires, having restricted valuable trade routes, were eventually destroyed. Politically the empire fluctuated between centralization under strong monarchs like *Khosrau I (died 579), who were served by the army and bureaucracy, and local control by great nobles. The religious life of the empire was dominated by Zoroastrianism, established as the state cult in the 3rd century. Christians in Armenia and Transcaucasia survived persecution and, by breaking with the Byzantine Church in 424, threw off the suspicion of alien loyalties. The court at Ctesiphon (in modern Iraq) provided a focus for a brilliant culture, enriched by Graeco-Roman and eastern influences, in which such pastimes as chess and polo were played. The closing years of the dynasty were overshadowed for the masses, however, by lengthy wars, which may explain the empire's rapid disintegration before the *Arab conquest of 636–51.

Satavahana A dynasty that ruled the north-west Deccan of India, probably from the late 1st century BC until the 4th century AD. Its greatest king, Gautamiputra Satakarni (106–130 AD), consolidated his hold over the north-west Deccan, and extended his sway from coast to coast. Under his successors, Satavahana power gradually declined and had been entirely lost by the early 4th century.

Sato Eisaku (1901–75) Japanese statesman. As a supporter of *Yoshida Shigeru, he advocated cooperation with the USA in the immediate post-war period. Forced from the cabinet over allegations of corruption in 1954, he returned four years later and between 1964 and 1972 served as Prime Minister. He overcame a period of student violence, oversaw the extension of the revised United States Security Treaty (1970), negotiated with the USA for the return of Okinawa and the other Ryukyu islands, and normalized relations with South Korea. After leaving office he received a Nobel Peace Prize for his efforts to make Japan a nuclear-free zone.

satrap A provincial governor of the *Achaemenids, as first established by *Darius I (the Great) who divided his empire up into twenty satrapies. Although the satraps nominally owed allegiance to the king, the considerable power and autonomy vested in them fostered disloyalty and there were frequent uprisings, the most notable being that of 366–358 BC against *Artaxerxes II. Alexander the Great retained the system after his conquest, as did the Parthians, but under the *Sassanian empire the term "satrap" designated a less important figure.

satyagraha (Hindi, "holding to the truth") A policy of civil disobedience employing *passive resistance, developed by Mohandas *Gandhi in South Africa and widely used in India as a weapon against British rule. Frequently, campaigns of civil disobedience have degenerated into violence, but the method has had some success against liberal governments reluctant to use force. The technique continued to be employed in India and elsewhere after 1947, for example in Goa in 1955, when the satyagrahis were fired on and defeated.

Saud The ruling family of Saudi Arabia. Originally established at Dariyya in Wadi Hanifa, Nejd, in the 15th century, its fortunes grew after 1745 when Muhammad ibn Saud allied himself with the Islamic revivalist Abd al-Wahhab (*see* WAHHABISM), who later became the spiritual guide of the family. The first wave of Saudi expansion ended with defeat by Egypt in 1818, but Saudi fortunes revived under **Abd al-Aziz ibn Saud** (*c.*1880–1953), who captured Riyadh (1902), and other territories that formed the kingdom of *Saudi Arabia in 1932. Abd al-Aziz was succeeded by his sons Saud (1953–64), *Faisal ibn Abd al-Aziz (1964–75), Khalid (1975–82), Fahd (1982–2005), and Abdullah (2005–   ) as rulers of the richest oil state in the world.

Saudi Arabia

Capital:	Riyadh
Area:	2,149,690 sq km (830,000 sq miles)
Population:	26,939,583 (2013 est)
Currency:	1 Saudi riyal = 100 halalah
Religions:	Sunni Muslim 85.0%; Shia Muslim 10.0%
Ethnic Groups:	Arab 90.0%; Afro-Asian 10.0%
Languages:	Arabic (official)
International Organizations:	UN; Arab League; GCC; OAPEC; OPEC; Non-Aligned Movement; WTO; Colombo Plan

A country in south-west Asia occupying most of the peninsula of Arabia.

Physical Most of Saudi Arabia is set on a plateau of deserts, which rises to mountains in the south and falls away to a low plain in the east. The ground varies between rock, gravel, and bare sand, and little grows except in the oases and along the Red Sea coast, where slight seasonal rain makes possible the cultivation of dates and a few cereals.

Economy With one-sixth of the world's oil reserves, crude oil and oil products contribute almost half of GDP and nine-tenths of export earnings. The government is attempting to diversify the economy into such areas as power generation, telecommunications, natural gas, and petrochemicals. Foreign workers are important to the economy, whereas unemployment is a significant issue among less skilled Saudis.

History Saudi Arabia was formed from territories assembled by the *Saud family, who were followers of *Wahhabism, and proclaimed as the kingdom of Saudi Arabia in 1932. The early years of the kingdom were difficult, when revenues fell as a result of the declining Muslim pilgrim trade to Mecca and Medina. An oil concession was awarded to the US firm Standard of California in 1933 and oil was exported in 1938. In 1944 the oil company was re-formed as the Arabian American Oil Company (ARAMCO), and Saudi Arabia was recognized as having the world's largest reserves of oil. Since the death of Abd al-Aziz ibn Saud (1953) efforts have been made to modernize the administration by the passing of a series of new codes of conduct to conform both with Islamic tradition and 20th-century developments. The Saudi Arabian Minister for Petroleum and Natural Resources, Sheikh Ahmad Yemani, ably led the OPEC in controlling oil prices in the 1970s. King Fahd succeeded to the throne after the death (1982) of his half-brother, Khalid. There were various Saudi initiatives for peace in the Middle East in the 1980s, and that of 1989 finally resolved the crisis in *Lebanon by the Taif Accord. In 1990 the UN sent troops to protect Saudi oil fields from Iraqi invasion. The *Gulf War which followed had de-stabilizing social effects, with pro-democracy liberals and Islamic fundamentalists voicing criticism of the regime of King Fahd. In 1992 King Fahd announced the creation, by royal decree, of a Consultative Council, comprising 60 members chosen by the King

s

every four years. The council, inaugurated in 1993, was to have an advisory and not a legislative function, as the King expressed his view that democracy was not suited to the Gulf region. However, municipal elections were held in 2005. King Fahd also denounced the spread of Islamic fundamentalism. International concern has been raised over the abuse of human rights and the number of public executions in Saudi Arabia. Fahd was succeeded by Crown Prince Abdullah in 2005. His reign has seen limited political and economic reform while maintaining a firm stance on security.

Savage, Michael Joseph (1872–1940) New Zealand statesman. Settling in New Zealand in 1907, he joined the Labour Party on its foundation, entering Parliament in 1919, and becoming deputy-leader in 1923. He took over as leader in 1933 on the death of Harry Holland, and became Prime Minister in 1935 after Labour's landslide victory. Savage is best remembered for his insistent advocacy of the Social Security Act and was one of the most popular of the country's political leaders.

Savonarola, Girolamo (1452–98) Italian preacher and religious reformer. A Dominican monk and strict ascetic, in 1482 he moved to Florence, where he attracted great attention for his passionate preaching denouncing immorality, vanity, and corruption within the Church, and for his apocalyptic prophecies. He became virtual ruler of Florence (1494–95), but made many enemies, and in 1495 the pope forbade him to preach and summoned him to Rome. His refusal to comply with these orders led to his excommunication in 1497; he was hanged as a heretic.

Saxe, Maurice, Comte de (Count of Saxony) (1696–1750) Marshal of France and one of the best known military theorists of his age. He was an illegitimate son of *Augustus II the Strong, and was half-German and half-Swedish. In the War of the *Austrian Succession he won a series of victories, including *Fontenoy, and gained control of most of the Austrian Netherlands, which strengthened France's position at the Treaty of *Aix-la-Chapelle (1748).

Saxons Germanic tribes, possibly named from their single-edged *seax* ('sword'). Under pressure from the migrating *Franks they spread from their homelands on the Danish peninsula into Italy and the Frisian lands and engaged in piracy on the North Sea and English Channel between the 3rd and 5th centuries. They appear to have entered Britain, together with *Angles

and *Jutes as mercenaries in the late period of the Roman occupation. By the 5th century their settlements had marked the beginning of *Anglo-Saxon England. Their name survives in Wessex ('West Saxons'), Essex ('East Saxons'), and Sussex ('South Saxons') in England, as well as in Saxony in Germany.

Sayyid dynasty Muslim rulers of the Delhi sultanate in northern India (1414–51). They seized power from the Tughluqs, but never equalled their predecessors' imperial pretensions. Rival neighbours soon threatened their claims even in the north, and in 1448 their last sultan abandoned Delhi, to be replaced three years later by the Afghan Lodis.

scalawag A White supporter of the Republican Reconstruction programme in the American South in the early years after the *American Civil War. Like the *carpetbaggers with whom they associated, the scalawags were a diverse group including some profiteers, but also businessmen, reformers, former Southern Whigs, and poor yeoman farmers who supported the Republican regime.

Scanian War (1676–78) A struggle between Denmark and Sweden for the latter's southernmost province of Scania. For centuries it was controlled by Denmark but was gained by Charles X of Sweden at the Treaty of *Roskilde in 1658. Christian V of Denmark invaded Scania and was welcomed by the population. Charles XI of Sweden fought back in a harsh campaign and finally won a pitched battle at Lund (3 December 1676); the victory was acknowledged in the Treaty of Lund (1679), and Scania was ceded to Sweden.

Scapa Flow A stretch of sea in the Orkney Islands, Scotland. In May 1919 the terms of the *Versailles Peace Settlement were submitted to the Germans, who protested vigorously. As an act of defiance, orders were given under Admiral von Reuter to scuttle and sink the entire German High Seas Fleet, then interned at Scapa Flow. In October 1939 the defences of Scapa Flow were penetrated when a German U-boat sank HMS *Royal Oak*. The naval base was closed in 1957 but the anchorage at Flotta at the southern entrance to Scapa Flow became the centre of the oil industry in Orkney.

Schacht, Hjalmar (1877–1970) German financier. As Commissioner of Currency (1923) he applied a rigorous monetary policy to stabilize the mark after its collapse in that year. He took part in *reparations negotiations but rejected the *Young Plan (1929). Under *Hitler he became Minister of Economics (1934–37), responsible for Nazi programmes on unemployment and rearmament. Rivalry with *Goering caused his resignation. In 1944 he was imprisoned in a concentration camp for his alleged involvement in the July Plot to assassinate Hitler. At the *Nuremberg Trials (1946) he was acquitted.

Scheer, Reinhard (1863–1928) German admiral. After winning fame as a submarine expert, he commanded the High Seas Fleet during World War I (1916–18). His hopes of dividing and defeating the British Grand Fleet at *Jutland (1916) failed, but his brilliant manoeuvring saved his own fleet. In October 1918 the German fleet at Kiel mutinied under him, refusing to put out to sea. The mutiny spread rapidly to north-west Germany, and by November Germany had accepted an end to World War I.

Schengen Area The collective name for those countries that are party to the **Schengen Agreement**, which allows for uncontrolled cross-border movement of people between its members. The agreement was ratified in 1985 and came into force in 1995. The area now includes 26 countries: Austria, Belgium, Czech Republic, Denmark, Estonia, Finland, France, Germany, Greece, Hungary, Iceland, Italy, Latvia, Liechtenstein, Lithuania, Luxembourg, Malta, Netherlands, Norway, Poland, Portugal, Slovakia, Slovenia, Spain, Sweden, and Switzerland.

Schirach, Baldur von (1907–74) German Nazi youth leader. An enthusiastic Nazi while still a student, from 1933 to 1945 he led the *Hitler Youth. In 1940 he was appointed governor of Vienna, where he took part in plans to ship Vienna's Jews to *concentration camps. He was found guilty at the *Nuremberg Trials and sentenced to 20 years' imprisonment.

Schleswig–Holstein A state (*Land*) of northern Germany, formerly the subject of a long-running dispute involving Prussia, Austria, and Denmark (the **Schleswig–Holstein question**). Both Schleswig and Holstein were originally duchies owing allegiance to the Danish crown. At the Congress of *Vienna (1814) Holstein was incorporated into the Austrian-led *German Confederation. In 1848 Denmark incorporated Schleswig, but the German-speaking population gained support from the German Parliament at Frankfurt and Prussian troops invaded Denmark. Britain, Russia, and France intervened to oblige Prussia to agree to an armistice, and under the London Protocol of 1852 Denmark retained its traditional rights in the duchies. However, Denmark in 1864 again incorporated Schleswig, provoking Prussian and Austrian troops to invade and defeat the Danish army. In 1866, after the *Austro-Prussian War, Prussia annexed both duchies. Following World War I there were plebiscites and much of north Schleswig passed to Denmark as the province of South Jutland. Between the wars the existence of a German minority in the province created considerable tension. After World War II over three million refugees from East Germany crowded into Schleswig–Holstein and the area was reorganized to become a West German state.

Schmalkaldic War (1546–47) A brief and indecisive phase in the struggle between the Roman Catholic emperor *Charles V and the Protestant party within the *Holy Roman Empire. The defensive League of Schmalkalden was formed in the town of that name by Protestant states in 1531. It was led by *Philip of Hesse and John Frederick I of Saxony. The emperor was heavily committed elsewhere and did not come face to face with the League until 1546. Then he crushed the League with the help of Duke Maurice of Saxony, winning a notable victory at the battle of Mühlberg (24 April 1547).

Schmidt, Helmut (1918–) German statesman. A member of the Social Democratic Party, he was elected to the Bundestag (Parliament of the Federal Republic of Germany) in 1953. He was Minister of Defence (1969–72) and of Finance (1972–74). Elected federal Chancellor in 1974, following the resignation of Willy *Brandt, he served for a second period (1978–82), during which he increasingly lost the support of the left wing of his party and of the Green Party.

scholasticism The educational tradition of the medieval 'schools' (universities), which flourished in the 12th and 13th centuries. It was a method of philosophical and theological enquiry, which aimed at a better understanding of Christian doctrine by a process of definition and systematic argument.

The writings of Aristotle (translated from Greek into Latin by *Boethius) and of St *Augustine of Hippo played a crucial part in the development of scholastic thought. Scholastics did not always agree on points of theology; *Aquinas and *Duns Scotus argued from different standpoints. Scholasticism declined in the later Middle Ages; in the 14th century the writings of *William of Ockham challenged the scholastic position by stressing the opposition between faith and reason.

Schröder, Gerhard (1944–) German Social Democrat politician; Chancellor of Germany (1998–2005). He was Social Democrat Prime Minister of Lower Saxony from 1990 until he defeated Helmut *Kohl in the 1998 federal election. Re-elected in 2002, he declined a post in the grand coalition government that was formed after the inconclusive 2005 election.

Schuman Plan (9 May 1950) A proposal drafted by Jean Monnet and put forward by the French Foreign Minister Robert Schuman. It aimed initially to pool the coal and steel industries of France and the Federal Republic of Germany under a common authority, which other European nations might join. The Plan became effective in 1952 with the formation of the European Coal and Steel Community, to which Italy, Belgium, Holland, and Luxembourg as well as France and West Germany belonged. Britain declined to join. Its success ultimately led to the formation of the *European Economic Community.

Schuschnigg, Kurt von (1897–1977) Austrian statesman. He became Chancellor following the murder of *Dollfuss (1934). He considered his main task to be the prevention of German absorption of Austria. Although an Austro-German Agreement (July 1936) guaranteed Austrian independence, Hitler accused him of breaking it. In February 1938 Hitler obliged him to accept Nazis in his cabinet. His attempt to hold a plebiscite on Austrian independence was prevented and he was forced to resign. On 12 March German troops invaded Austria without resistance in the *Anschluss.

Schwarzenberg, Felix, Prince of (1800–52) Austrian statesman. A career diplomat, Schwarzenberg joined the army of Field-Marshal Joseph Radetzky on the outbreak of the *Revolutions of 1848. He persuaded the ageing Ferdinand I to abdicate in favour of his nephew, *Francis I. Opposed to granting autonomy to Austria's many states, Schwarzenberg drew up a constitution (1849) that transformed the Habsburg empire into a unitary, centralized, and absolutist state with strengthened imperial powers. The Hungarian nationalist uprising was crushed (1849) with Russian aid, and Habsburg supremacy was restored in northern Italy. He secured the revival of a strengthened *German Confederation, which maintained a precarious balance of power with *Prussia.

Schwarzenberg, Karl Philipp, Prince of (1771–1820) Austrian field-marshal. He entered the imperial cavalry in 1787. His courage at the Battles of Hohenlinden (1800) and Ulm (1805) saved many Austrian lives, and he was then appointed vice-president of the supreme imperial war cabinet in Vienna, where he was responsible for raising a popular militia to defend Austrian homelands. As general of cavalry he fought at the unsuccessful Battle of *Wagram (1809), after which Austria made peace with Napoleon in the Treaty of Schönbrunn. Schwarzenberg negotiated (1810) the marriage between Napoleon and Marie-Louise, daughter of the Austrian emperor, who in 1811 agreed to assist Napoleon in his forthcoming campaign against Russia. After Napoleon's failure to capture Moscow (1812) Schwarzenberg skilfully withdrew his troops back to Austria. Next year, when Austria joined Russia, Prussia, and Sweden to fight Napoleon (August 1813), he was appointed commander-in-chief of the Austrian Army and was the senior commander at the Battle of *Leipzig in October. He attended the Congress of *Vienna and then retired.

Scipio Aemilianus (full name **Publius Cornelius Scipio Aemilianus Africanus Minor**) (c.185–129 BC) Roman general and politician. He achieved distinction in the third Punic War, and blockaded and destroyed Carthage in 146. His successful campaign in Spain (133) ended organized resistance in that country. Returning to Rome in triumph, he initiated moves against the reforms introduced by his brother-in-law Tiberius Gracchus. Scipio's sudden death at the height of the crisis gave rise to the rumour that he had been murdered.

Scipio Africanus (full name **Publius Cornelius Scipio Africanus Major**) (c.236–184 BC) Roman general and politician. His aggressive tactics were successful in concluding the second Punic War, firstly by the defeat of the Carthaginians in Spain in 206 and then by the defeat of Hannibal in Africa in 202; his victories pointed the way to Roman hegemony in the Mediterranean. His son was the adoptive father of Scipio Aemilianus.

Scopes case (July 1925) The US legal case in which John T. Scopes, a biology teacher in Dayton, Tennessee, was charged with violating state law by teaching Darwin's theory of evolution. The state legislature had enacted (1925) that it was unlawful to teach any doctrine denying the literal truth of the account of the creation as presented in the Authorized (King James) Version of the Bible. The judge ruled out any discussion of constitutional legality, and since Scopes clearly had taught Darwin's theory of evolution he was convicted and fined $100. On appeal to the Supreme Court the constitutionality of the state's law was upheld, but Scopes was acquitted on the technicality that he had been "fined excessively". The law was repealed in 1967. However, Christian fundamentalists in the USA continue to campaign vigorously for a return to creationist teaching.

Scotland The northern part of Great Britain and of the United Kingdom. Sparsely populated until Celtic peoples arrived from the Continent during the Bronze and Early Iron Age, the inhabitants of Scotland were named the Picts by the Romans, who established a northerly line at the *Antonine Wall for about 40 years. An independent country in the Middle Ages, after the unification of various small Dark Age kingdoms of the Picts, Scots, Britons, and Angles between the 9th and 11th centuries, Scotland successfully resisted English attempts at domination but was amalgamated with her southern neighbour as a result of the union of the crowns in 1603 and of the parliaments in 1707. Broadly divided into Highland and Lowland regions, Scotland has a heavily indented west coast with numerous islands to the west (Inner and Outer Hebrides) and north (Orkney and Shetland Islands). The Highlands to the north and the Southern Uplands north of the English border are sparsely populated, the greater proportion of the Scottish population being concentrated in the Central Lowlands between the Firth of Clyde and the Firth of Forth. Oil and natural gas, agricultural produce, timber, textiles, whisky, paper, and high-tech electronic goods are amongst its chief industrial products. Scotland is divided into 32 administrative regions (unitary authorities). A referendum on devolution was held in 1997 in which the electorate overwhelmingly voted in favour of a measure of devolution. This included a Scottish parliament with 129 MPs elected by proportional representation in elections that took place in May 1999; power was transferred to the new body in July. The Scottish parliament initially had powers to make laws on most domestic matters and to vary the basic rate of income tax, with more powers being transferred over the next decade. The first two elections to the Scottish parliament resulted in Labour–Liberal Democrat coalition administrations, but the *Scottish National Party led by Alex *Salmond formed a minority administration in 2007 and gained an absolute majority in 2011. A referendum on whether Scotland should leave the United Kingdom took place in September 2014, and resulted in a clear majority (55% to 45%) for maintaining the Union. However, the leaders of all the main UK parties agreed in principle that additional powers should now be devolved to Edinburgh.

Scotland Yard The headquarters of the London Metropolitan Police, situated from 1829–1890 in Great Scotland Yard, a short street off Whitehall in London, from then until 1967 in New Scotland Yard on the Thames Embankment, and from 1967 in New Scotland Yard, Broadway, Westminster.

Scots (or **Dalriads**) Celtic Irish settlers, in what is now Scotland. In the early 6th century AD they settled Argyll (Ar Gael) after two centuries of raiding the coasts of Britain and Gaul. They overcame the northern *Picts in the Highlands and introduced the Celtic Gaelic language. The name 'Scotia' (Scotland), formerly a name for Hibernia (Ireland) passed to the land of Caledonia and the territories of all the Picts.

Scott, Sir Robert Falcon (1868–1912) British explorer and naval officer. As commander of the ship *Discovery* he led the National Antarctic Expedition (1900–04), surveying the interior of the continent and charting the Ross Sea. On a second expedition (1910–12) Scott and four companions made a journey to the South Pole by sled, arriving there in January 1912 to discover that the Norwegian explorer Amundsen had beaten them to their goal by a month. Scott and his companions died on the journey back to base, and their bodies and diaries were discovered by a search party eight months later. Scott, a national hero, was posthumously knighted. He was the father of the naturalist and artist Sir Peter Scott.

Scottish Martyrs A group of political reformers who were persecuted for their beliefs during the period of unrest in Scotland in the 1790s. In 1792 a Society for the Friends of the People was formed to promote parliamentary reform. The government reacted strongly and Thomas Muir, a member of the society, was convicted of treason. In October 1793 a meeting of the Society was broken up by force, three of its delegates being subsequently sentenced to long terms of transportation. A group of radical reformers calling themselves the United Scotsmen continued to meet in secret, but after further trials the movement broke up.

Scottish National Party (SNP) A Scottish political party, formed in 1934 from a merger of the National Party of Scotland and the Scottish

Party. The party gained its first parliamentary seat in 1945 at a by-election in Motherwell. In the October 1974 general election 11 of its candidates won parliamentary seats. In 1979 a referendum in Scotland on a Scottish representative assembly failed to elicit the required majority, and in the 1979 general election all but two of the candidates were defeated. Three were elected in 1987 and in 1992, six in 1997, five in 2001, and six in 2005. The SNP was not initially in favour of the Scottish parliament, but now sees it as a first step to full independence. From 1999 to 2007 it formed the main opposition in the Scottish parliament to the Labour–Liberal Democrat Scottish Executive, but in 2007 it formed a minority administration with Alex *Salmond as First Minister. The party achieved an absolute majority in the 2011 election and promised a referendum on whether Scotland should leave the United Kingdom. This was held in September 2014 and resulted in defeat for the independence proposal, which prompted Salmond to announce that he would resign as leader.

Scottsboro case (1931) A US legal case in which nine black youths were falsely accused by two white girls of multiple rape on a train near Scottsboro, Alabama. They were found guilty and sentenced to death or long-term imprisonment. The sensational case highlighted race relations in Alabama and across the USA. The intervention of the Supreme Court and a series of retrials returned a verdict of not proven and all the Scottsboro boys were released in the years 1937–50.

Scullin, James Henry (1876–1953) Australian statesman. He was a goldminer, shopkeeper, and organizer for the Australian Workers' Union before becoming a Labor Member of the House of Representatives (1910–13). He was re-elected in 1922, led the Opposition (1928–29), and in 1929 became Prime Minister. In the *Depression he faced deepening divisions within his own party, and deflationary measures brought electoral defeat. From 1932 he led the Opposition until his resignation as leader of the Labor Party in 1935.

scutage (or **escutage**; from Latin *scutum*, "shield") The payment (usually 20 shillings) made by a knight to the English king in lieu of military service. *Henry II raised seven scutages between 1157 and 1187. *Richard I was tempted (1198) to turn scutage into an annual tax not necessarily connected with military needs. The barons' opposition to John's annual scutages (1201–06) was a factor in their revolt (1214) and

was reflected in clause 12 of *Magna Carta (1215), which stated that the king was not to levy scutage without consent, except in recognized and reasonable cases.

Scythians A group of Indo-European tribes that briefly occupied part of Asia Minor in the 7th century BC before being driven out by the Medes. They subsequently established a kingdom in southern Russia and traded with the Greek cities of the Black Sea, but in about the 2nd century BC were compelled to move into the Crimea by the related Sarmatian tribe. They were a nomadic people, famed for their horsemanship and their skill as archers. When *Darius I (the Great) attempted to subdue them in c.512 BC, they successfully adopted a scorched-earth policy and c.325 BC they crushed a large detachment of Macedonian troops before making peace with Alexander the Great. The graves of Scythian kings and nobles have revealed many objects of gold and bronze, which bear witness to outstanding technical and artistic skill.

Sea Peoples (or **Peoples of the Sea**) Groups of people who encroached on the Levant and Egypt by land and by sea in the late 13th century. Their identity is still being debated. In the Levant they are associated with destruction; the Egyptians were successful in driving them away. Some, including the Philistines, settled in Palestine.

SEATO See SOUTH-EAST ASIA TREATY ORGANIZATION.

Second Front The opening of hostilities by US and UK forces on the mainland of Europe in World War II, when the Allies returned to confront the Germans after the fall of France. The First Front (a term not used) was that on which the Soviet Union fought the *Axis Powers in the east. From 1941 the Soviet government pressed for an early opening of the Second Front as a means of relieving heavy German pressure. The hope that it could be opened in 1942 was ended by Churchill's insistence that there was insufficient shipping. The disaster of the *Dieppe Raid (August 1942) confirmed this, although the Soviet and the US governments continued to criticize British hesitancy through 1943. When the successful *Normandy Campaign eventually opened the Second Front in June 1944 it was clear that the operation was an immense enterprise that could easily have failed had it been undertaken too hastily. In the event it led to the defeat of the German army.

Second Reich *See* GERMAN SECOND EMPIRE.

Security Council *See* UNITED NATIONS SECURITY COUNCIL.

Sedan, Battle of (1 September 1870) A battle fought on the River Meuse, near the Belgian frontier, between French and Prussian forces during the *Franco-Prussian War. The Prussians, discovering that *MacMahon's army had set out to relieve Metz, diverted two armies marching on Paris and encircled the army of *Napoleon III at Sedan. The French, under heavy shellfire, surrendered unconditionally. Napoleon III was taken prisoner, together with a large army. In World War II the Germans breached the *Maginot Line when they crossed the River Meuse at Sedan (1940).

Seddon, Richard John (1845–1906) New Zealand statesman. Arriving in New Zealand in 1866, he became the miners' advocate and was elected (1881) as parliamentary member for Kumara. He was Minister of Public Works in *Balance's first Liberal government and Premier from Ballance's death in 1893. Seddon oversaw the introduction of a range of radical legislation including low-interest credit for farmers, women's suffrage, the Industrial Conciliation and Arbitration Act, old age pensions, free places in secondary schools, and a State Fire Insurance Office.

Sedgemoor, Battle of (6 July 1685) The decisive battle of *Monmouth's Rebellion, fought near Westonzoyland in Somerset. Monmouth was blocked in his retreat from Bristol by the army of *James II, commanded by Lord Feversham and John Churchill (later Duke of *Marlborough). Monmouth attempted a night attack to give his raw recruits some advantage over the professional royalist army, but his plans miscarried and he suffered a crushing defeat. The battle proved to be the last fought on English soil.

Seku Ahmadu Lobbo (*c.*1775–1845) West African religious leader. A student of *Uthman dan Fodio, Ahmadu participated in Uthman's *jihad* (or holy war) before settling in the province of Macina (in Mali), where he founded an independent Muslim community. Expelled from Macina by the pagan king of Segu, he established a new capital at Hamdullahi and in 1818 proclaimed a *jihad*, capturing Macina, and extending his authority around it. He established a strictly theocratic Muslim Fulani state which survived until 1859, when it was absorbed in the Tukulor empire of *Umar ibn Said Tal.

Selden, John (1584–1654) English lawyer, historian, and antiquary. Although not a Puritan, he used his knowledge of the law on Parliament's behalf in its conflicts with Charles I, and was repeatedly imprisoned. A member of most of the Parliaments after 1621, he was active in the impeachment of *Buckingham (1626), and helped to draw up the *Petition of Right (1628).

selectors Small farmers in Australia during the second half of the 19th century. By the 1850s, *squatters had acquired much of the best agricultural land. Increasing demands were made, especially by those who had come during the gold rushes of the 1850s, for remaining land to be made available for small farms, at low cost. Selection before survey (hence the name "selectors") was introduced in all of the colonies between 1858 and 1872. Factors causing the failure of many selectors included the unsuitability of much Australian land for agriculture, lack of capital, and opposition from squatters.

Seleucid The Hellenistic dynasty founded by Seleucus I Nicator, one of the generals of Alexander the Great, ruling over Syria and a great part of western Asia 312–64 BC. Its capital was at Antioch.

Self-Denying Ordinance (3 April 1645) An English parliamentary regulation under which all Members of Parliament had to resign their military commands. Oliver *Cromwell was determined to create an efficient national army controlled and paid from Westminster, rather than by the counties. The House of Lords amended the Ordinance, so that it was possible for certain Members of Parliament to be reappointed to the *New Model Army, thereby enabling Cromwell to continue his military career as lieutenant-general under commander-in-chief Sir Thomas Fairfax.

Self-Strengthening Movement A Chinese military and political reform movement of the second half of the 19th century. Initiated in the early 1860s by Feng Guifen and supported by *Zeng Guofan, *Zuo Zongtang, *Li Hongzhang, and Prince Gong, the Self-Strengthening Movement attempted to adapt Western institutions and military innovations to Chinese needs. Prominent among the innovations introduced were the Zongli Yamen (1861), an imperial office established to manage relations with foreign countries, the Jiangnan Arsenal (1865), the Nanjing Arsenal (1867), the Beiyang fleet (1888) (China's first modern navy), and various government-sponsored modern industries. Such reforms, however, were superficial and failed to solve deep-seated institutional problems, as was made clear by China's humiliation in the *Sino-Japanese War of 1894–95.

Selim I (c.1470–1520) Ottoman sultan (1512–20) Recalled from Crimean exile after an aborted attempt to ensure his own succession, he defeated and killed his brother Ahmed in 1513. In 1514, responding to Safavid-inspired subversion in Asia Minor, he crushed a Persian army at Chaldiran. Turning against the *Mamelukes, he next conquered Syria and Egypt and took the titles of *caliph and protector of the holy cities of *Mecca and Medina.

Seljuk A Turkish dynasty that ruled Asia Minor in the 11th–13th centuries, successfully invading the Byzantine Empire and defending the Holy Land against the Crusaders.

Seminole Wars (1816–18; 1835–42) Two wars against Native American in the south-east US. Natives of Florida, the Seminole retaliated against US military forces sent into their area in search of escaped slaves. Andrew *Jackson's subsequent punitive expedition forced the Seminole south into the Everglades. In 1819 Spain ceded east Florida to the USA, and in 1832 the Seminole were forced to sign a treaty involving their removal to the Indian Territory west of the Mississippi (*Trail of Tears). A substantial part of the tribe under *Osceola refused to move and held out in the Everglades until Osceola was treacherously captured and most of his followers exterminated. General William T. Worth then ordered (1841) that the Seminoles' crops be burned and their villages destroyed. Starved into surrender, the Seminole signed a peace treaty (1842) and accepted their deportation westwards.

Semite Any of the peoples supposed to be descended from Shem, son of Noah, including especially the Jews, Arabs, Assyrians, and Phoenicians.

Senanayake, Don Stephen (1884–1952) Sinhalese statesman, Prime Minister of Ceylon (now Sri Lanka; 1947–52). In 1919 he cofounded the Ceylon National Congress, and during the 1920s and 1930s held ministerial positions on Ceylon's legislative and state councils. He became Prime Minister in 1947, and the following year presided over Ceylon's achievement of full dominion status within the Commonwealth.

Senate, Roman *See* ROMAN SENATE.

Senate, US The second, or upper, chamber of the US Congress, representing the 50 states of the union. The powers and composition of the Senate are set out in Article I of the US Constitution, and the Senate first met in 1789. Senators, two from each state, have six-year terms and were chosen by the state legislatures until 1913, when the Seventeenth Amendment provided for their direct election. The terms of one-third of the senators expire every two years. A senator must be at least 30 years old, must have been a US citizen for not less than nine years, and must be a resident of the state he or she represents. The Vice-President presides over the Senate, voting only in the case of a tie. The Senate must ratify all treaties, confirm important presidential appointments, and take a part in legislation. *See also* ROMAN SENATE.

Seneca, Marcus Annaeus (or **Seneca the Elder**) (c.55 BC–c.39 AD) Roman rhetorician, born in Spain. Seneca is best known for his works on rhetoric, only parts of which survive, including *Oratorum Sententiae Divisiones Colores* and *Suasoriae*. His son, **Lucius Annaeus Seneca** (or **Seneca the Younger**) (c.4 BC–65 AD) was a Roman statesman, philosopher, and dramatist. Born in Spain, he was banished to Corsica by Claudius in 41, charged with adultery; in 49 his sentence was repealed and he became tutor to Nero, through the influence of Nero's mother and Claudius' wife, Agrippina. Seneca was a dominant figure in the early years of Nero's reign and was appointed consul in 57; he retired in 62. His subsequent implication in a plot on Nero's life led to his forced suicide. As a philosopher, he expounded the ethics of Stoicism in such works as *Epistulae Morales*. Seneca also wrote nine plays.

Senegal

Capital:	Dakar
Area:	196,722 sq km (75,955 sq miles)
Population:	11,706,000 (2005)
Currency:	1 CFA franc = 100 centimes
Religions:	Muslim 94.0%; Christian 5.0%; traditional beliefs 1.0%
Ethnic Groups:	Wolof 43.3%; Fulani 23.8%; Serer 14.7%
Languages:	French (official); Wolof; Fula; minority languages
International Organizations:	UN; AU; Franc Zone; ECOWAS; Non-Aligned Movement; WTO

A West African country with an Atlantic coast.

Physical Senegal surrounds the Gambia and is itself bounded inland by Mauritania, Mali, Guinea, and Guinea-Bissau. Its most westerly point (and that of continental Africa) is Cape Verde, formed by a volcano. Inland there is savannah, sparser in the north than in the south; the south of the country has a marshy coast. In winter the drying harmattan wind blows from the interior.

Economy Senegal's principal exports are fish, groundnuts, oil products, phosphates, and cotton. Agriculture employs over three-quarters of the workforce, with other important crops including millet, maize, sorghum, rice, and vegetables. Industries include agricultural and fish processing, phosphate mining, fertilizers, and oil refining. Senegal is seeking to develop its iron ore reserves and is exploring for oil.

History Senegal has been part of several ancient empires, including those of *Ghana, *Mali, and *Songhay. The Tukulor, one of Senegal's seven main ethnic groups, converted to Islam in the 11th century, but animism remained widespread until the middle of the 19th century. Portuguese navigators explored the coast of Senegal in 1445. Founded by France in the 17th century, the colony of Senegal was disputed by Britain in the Napoleonic Wars. The interior was occupied by the French governor L. L. Faidherbe (1854–61); in 1871 the colony sent its first Deputy to the French Assembly. It became part of French West Africa in 1895, and in 1958 it was made an autonomous republic within the *French Community. It became part of the Federation of *Mali (1959–60). Under the leadership of Léopold Sédar *Senghor it became independent in 1960. It briefly federated with The *Gambia as Senegambia (1982–89). In 1980 Abdou Diouf succeeded Senghor as President within a multiparty system. Relations between Senegal and *Mauritania deteriorated sharply in 1989 following the killing of hundreds of Senegalese residents in Mauritania and the expulsion of thousands of thousands more. A virtual frontier war lasted through 1990, while both the Organization of African Unity and President Mubarak of Egypt tried to mediate. Faced with the problems arising from ethnic tension, President Diouf formed a power-sharing coalition government in 1991, which succeeded in restoring a degree of order; diplomatic relations were resumed with Mauritania in 1992. Meanwhile a separatist movement had developed within Casamance in southern Senegal, which continued into the 21st century. Diouf was re-elected in early 1993. Violence by the separatists marred the presidential election, but a ceasefire agreement was concluded later in the year. Despite French and IMF aid, the Senegalese economy was on the verge of bankruptcy; a currency devaluation took place early in 1994. Forty years of socialist rule ended in 2000 when Diouf was defeated by Abdoulaye Wade in the presidential election. Wade was re-elected in 2007 but defeated by Macky Sall in 2012.

Senghor, Léopold Sédar (1906–2001) Senegalese statesman and poet, President of *Senegal (1959–80). In 1946 he was elected to the French National Assembly as a Socialist Deputy and after Senegal became autonomous in 1958 he was elected President. Together with the writers Aimé Césaire and Léon Damas he formulated the concept of *négritude*, which he defined as "the sum total of cultural values of the Negro-African world". In 1960 he sought unsuccessfully to achieve federation among the former French West African colonies and in 1975 Senegal joined the West African Economic Community. His collections of lyrical poetry include *Chants d'ombre* (1945), *Nocturnes* (1961), and *Poèmes* (1984).

Sennacherib (died 681 BC) King of Assyria (705–681). The son of Sargon II, he devoted much of his reign to suppressing revolts in various parts of his empire, including Babylon, which he sacked in 689. In 701 he put down a Jewish rebellion, laying siege to Jerusalem but sparing it from destruction (according to 2 Kings 19:35) after an epidemic of illness amongst his forces. He rebuilt and extended the city of Nineveh and made it his capital, and also initiated irrigation schemes and other civil engineering projects.

separation of powers A classic doctrine of liberal government, usually associated with the French philosopher Montesquieu (1689–1755), although the tripartite division was earlier suggested by Aristotle and Locke. In *The Spirit of the Laws* (1748), Montesquieu set out that the three branches of government—the legislature, the executive, and the judiciary—should be constitutionally separate from each other, both in function and in persons. The doctrine is enshrined in the US Constitution, which provides a formal separation of Congress, President, and Supreme Court. The separation, however, is not total and some collaboration, especially between President and Congress, is necessary if the system is to work. In the UK, the executive,

S

formed from the majority in Parliament, dominates the legislature. The judiciary, however, is largely independent of legislative and executive processes, a separation that has become more pronounced in recent years: until 2005 the then head of the judiciary, the Lord Chancellor, was a member of the *cabinet (executive) as well as the presiding officer of the *House of Lords (legislature); and until 2009 the UK's highest court was in theory the full House of Lords and in practice its Appellate Committee.

September 11 (2001) The day on which *al-Qaeda terrorists struck at New York and Washington, killing over 3000 people. Four airliners were hijacked shortly after take-off by 19 suicidal terrorists: two were flown into the twin towers of New York's World Trade Center causing their collapse, one was crashed into the Pentagon in Washington, and one hit the ground near Pittsburgh, presumably after a struggle between the passengers and the hijackers. The outrage led the USA to launch its *war on terrorism.

Serbia

Capital:	Belgrade
Area:	77,474 sq km (29,913 sq miles)
Population:	7,243,007 (2013 est)
Currency:	1 dinar = 100 paras
Religions:	Eastern Orthodox 84.6%; Roman Catholic 5.0%; Muslim 3.1%
Ethnic Groups:	Serb 83.3%; Hungarian 3.5%; Romany 2.1%; Bosniak 2.0%
Languages:	Serbian (official), Hungarian, Bosnian, Romany
International Organizations:	UN; OSCE; Euro-Atlantic Partnership Council

A republic in SE Europe.

Physical It is mountainous in the south, descending to fertile plains in the north.

Economy The economy was badly damaged in the 1990s by mismanagement, civil war, international isolation, and NATO bombing in 1999. Recovery since has been slow, with gradual privatization of state-owned industries and reintegration into the international community. Agriculture employs a quarter of

the workforce, with the main crops being cereals, sunflowers, sugar beet, fruit, and vegetables. Principal industries include vehicles, metals, furniture, food processing, and machinery. Exports include iron and steel, rubber, clothing, wheat, fruit, and vegetables.

History An independent state as early as the 6th century, Serbia was conquered by the Turks in the 14th century. With the decline of Ottoman power in the 19th century, the Serbs successfully pressed for independence, finally winning nationhood in 1878. Subsequent Serbian ambitions to found a South Slav nation state brought the country into rivalry with the Austro-Hungarian empire and eventually contributed to the outbreak of World War I. Despite early successes against the Austrians, Serbia was occupied by the Central Powers and was, after the end of hostilities, absorbed into the new state of Yugoslavia. With the secession of four out of the six republics from the collective state in 1991–92, Serbia struggled to retain the viability of Yugoslavia and found itself internationally isolated as a result of armed conflict with neighbouring Slovenia and Croatia, involvement in the civil war in Bosnia, and the suppression of Albanian nationalism in the *Kosovo region. In 1992 Serbia and Montenegro formed a new Federal Republic of Yugoslavia. In late 1995 the governments of Serbia, Croatia, and Bosnia and Herzegovina accepted a US-brokered peace settlement. In 1997 Slobodan Milošević was appointed President of Yugoslavia and Milan Milutinović succeeded him as President of Serbia. In 1998 the Serbian army attempted to suppress ethnic Albanians in Kosovo, brutally destroying whole villages. After Serbia refused to accept an international peace plan in 1999, NATO began a campaign of airstrikes against Yugoslavia. The response of the Serbian army was to intensify its 'ethnic cleansing' of Albanians, some 1.5 million of whom were displaced. In June 1999 the Serbs surrendered in the face of intensified bombing and their army withdrew—to be replaced by an international peacekeeping force. Kosovo declared independence from Serbia in 2008. Milošević was deposed in a bloodless revolution in 2000 and Vojislav Kostunica took over. In 2002 Serbia joined with Montenegro in a looser federation, the union of Serbia and Montenegro. This was dissolved in 2006, when Montenegrins voted for complete independence in a referendum.

serf An unfree medieval peasant under the control of the lord whose lands he worked. As villeins or servants of a lord they represented the bottom tier of society. They were attached to the land and denied freedom of movement, freedom to marry without permission of their lord, and were obliged to work on their lord's fields, to contribute a proportion of their own produce, to surrender part of their land at death, and to submit to the justice and penalties administered by their lord in the manorial court in the case of wrongdoing. The lord had obligations to his serfs (unlike slaves), most notably to provide military protection and justice.

Serfdom originated in the 8th and 9th centuries in western Europe and subsequently became hereditary. In much of western Europe the system was undermined in the 14th century by the *Black Death and starvation resulting from war, which led to acute labour shortages. Commutation of their labour for cash meant that the lord became a rentier and the serf a tenant; in the *Peasants' Revolt in England (1381) the main demand was for the abolition of serfdom and the substitution of rent at 4 pence an acre for services. However, in the eastern regions of Germany and Muscovy, the increased power of the nobility led to consolidation of serfdom. It was formally abolished in France in 1789, but lingered in Austria and Hungary till 1848, and was abolished in Russia only in 1861.

Settlement, Act of One of several English Acts, that of 1701 being the most politically significant. It provided for the succession to the throne after the death of Queen *Anne's last surviving child, and was intended to prevent the Roman Catholic Stuarts from regaining the throne. It stipulated that the crown should go to James I's granddaughter, the Electress Sophia of Hanover, or her surviving Protestant heirs. The Act placed further limitations on royal power, and made the judiciary independent of crown and Parliament. On Anne's death in 1714, Sophia's son became Britain's first Hanoverian monarch as *George I.

Seven Weeks War *See* AUSTRO-PRUSSIAN WAR.

Seven Wonders of the World The seven most spectacular man-made structures of the ancient world. The earliest extant list of these dates from the 2nd century; traditionally they comprise (1) the pyramids of Egypt, especially those at Giza; (2) the Hanging Gardens of Babylon; (3) the Mausoleum of Halicarnassus; (4) the temple of Diana (Artemis) at Ephesus in Asia Minor, rebuilt in 356 BC; (5) the Colossus of Rhodes; (6) the huge ivory and gold statue of Zeus at Olympia in the Peloponnese, made by Phidias *c*.430 BC; (7) the lighthouse built by

Ptolemy II *c*.280 BC on the island of Pharos outside the harbour of Alexandria. Only the pyramids still exist.

Seven Years War (1756–63) A wide-ranging conflict involving Prussia, Britain, and Hanover fighting against Austria, France, Russia, Sweden, and Spain. It continued the disputes left undecided after the treaty of *Aix-la-Chapelle, and was concerned partly with colonial rivalry between Britain and France and partly with the struggle for supremacy in Germany between Austria and Prussia. Fighting had continued in North America with the Braddock expedition. Each side was dissatisfied with its former allies and in 1756 *Frederick II of Prussia concluded the Treaty of Westminster with Britain. This made it possible for *Maria Theresa of Austria and her minister Count von Kaunitz to obtain an alliance with France (known as the 'diplomatic revolution') by the two treaties of Versailles in 1756 and 1757; she was also allied with Elizabeth of Russia. At first the advantage was with the French and Austrians, but in July 1757 *Pitt the Elder came to power in England and conducted the war with skill and vigour. In November Frederick II won his great victory of Rossbach over the French, and in December he defeated the Austrians at Leuthen. Frederick was hard pressed in 1758, but he defeated the Russians at Zorndorf and Ferdinand of Brunswick protected his western flank with an Anglo-Hanoverian army. In 1759 *Wolfe captured Quebec, Ferdinand defeated the French army at *Minden, and *Hawke destroyed the French fleet at *Quiberon Bay. In India *Clive had won control of Bengal at Plassey, and in 1760 Montreal was taken. Admiral *Boscawen successfully attacked the French West Indies. In 1761 Spain entered the war and Pitt resigned. The death of Elizabeth of Russia eased the pressure on Frederick, as her successor Peter III reversed her policy. All were ready for peace, which was concluded by the Treaty of *Paris in 1763: overall England and Russia were victorious.

Seven Years War of the North (1563–70) A bitter conflict that resulted from a collision of the expansionist aims of Denmark and Sweden in the Baltic and became entangled with the contemporary war in Livonia. Frederick II of Denmark's troops achieved tactical successes on land, but the Swedes compensated with a series of victories at sea. In 1568 the insane Eric XIV of Sweden was deposed by an alliance of the nobility and replaced by John III. The new king swiftly sought peace from the equally exhausted Danes. By the Treaty of Stettin (1570) Denmark's

grip on the entrance to the Baltic remained unbroken, but Sweden retained Estonia. The contest
for the dominion of the whole Baltic was not resolved until the *Northern War of 1700–21.

Severus, Septimius (full name **Lucius Septimius Severus Pertinax**) (146–211) Roman
emperor (193–211). He was active in reforms of
the imperial administration and of the army,
which he recognized as the real basis of imperial power. In 208 he took an army to Britain to
suppress a rebellion in the north of the country,
and later died at York.

Sèvres, Treaty of (1920) A treaty, part of the
*Versailles Peace Settlement, signed between
the Allies and Turkey, effectively marking the
end of the *Ottoman empire. Adrianople and
most of the hinterland to Constantinople (now
Istanbul) passed to Greece; the Bosporus was
internationalized and demilitarized; a short-
lived independent *Armenia was created; Syria
became a French mandate; and Britain accepted the mandate for Iraq, Palestine, and Transjordan. The treaty was rejected by Mustafa
Kemal *Atatürk, who secured a redefinition of
Turkey's borders by the Treaty of Lausanne (*see*
VERSAILLES PEACE SETTLEMENT).

Seward, William Henry (1801–72) US
statesman. He served as Whig governor of New
York (1839–42) and then as Senator (1849–61). A
convinced opponent of slavery, he joined the
newly formed *Republican Party in 1855 and
served as Secretary of State under *Lincoln
during the *American Civil War. Wounded in a
separate attack at the time of Lincoln's assassination, Seward recovered and stayed in office
during the presidency of Andrew *Johnson,
generally supporting him against the radical
Republicans. Seward believed in the need for
the USA to expand its influence in the Pacific
and was responsible for the US purchase of
Alaska from Russia (1867). He advocated
friendly relations with China and pressed for the
annexation of Hawaii and other islands to act as
coaling stations for a US Pacific fleet.

Seychelles

Capital:	Victoria
Area:	455 sq km (176 sq miles)
Population:	90,846 (2013 est)
Currency:	1 Seychelles rupee = 100 cents
Religions:	Roman Catholic 76.2%; Anglican 6.1%; Hindu 2.4%
Ethnic Groups:	mixture of French, African, Indian, Chinese, and Arab
Languages:	Creole, English, French (all official)
International Organizations:	UN; Commonwealth; AU; Non-Aligned Movement; SADC

A country comprising an
archipelago in the Indian
Ocean.

Physical The Seychelles
consists of 92 islands lying
4°S of the Equator and
some 1500 km (930 miles)
from the east African coast.
One group, of which Mahé at 142 sq km (55 sq
miles) is the largest, is mainly hilly; another
outlying group is mostly flat. The climate is
warm and wet.

Economy Tourism is the mainstay of the
economy, employing a third of the workforce
and providing over two-thirds of foreign exchange earnings. Tuna fishing is also important.
The government is seeking to diversify the
economy by encouraging farming, fishing, and
manufacturing.

History The islands were uninhabited until
colonized by the French. They were discovered
in 1609 by an expedition of the British East India
Company and formally annexed to France in
1756. They were captured from the French by
Britain in 1810 during the Napoleonic Wars and
were administered from *Mauritius before becoming a separate crown colony in 1903.
The islands gained universal suffrage in 1970,
becoming an independent republic in 1975. In
1977 there was a coup, the Prime Minister,
France-Albert René proclaiming himself
President, and being re-elected in 1989.
In 1991 he ended his resistance to the
legalization of opposition parties. Multiparty
elections held in 1993 resulted in a landslide
victory for René's Seychelles People's
Progressive Front. Re-elected in 1998 and
2001, René retired in 2004; he was succeeded
by the Vice-President, James Michel. Michel
was elected in his own right in 2006 and
re-elected in 2011.

Seymour, Edward *See* SOMERSET, EDWARD
SEYMOUR, 1ST EARL OF HERTFORD AND DUKE OF.

Seymour, Jane (*c.*1509–37) Third wife of
Henry VIII and mother of Edward VI. She married Henry in 1536 and finally provided the king

with the male heir he wanted, although she died twelve days afterwards.

Seyss-Inquart, Arthur (1892–1946) Austrian Nazi leader. As Interior Minister in Vienna, he organized the *Anschluss with Germany in 1938, and was made governor of Austria by Hitler. He later became the Nazi commissioner in the occupied Netherlands, where he was responsible for thousands of executions and deportations to *concentration camps. He was sentenced to death at the *Nuremberg Trials.

Sforza An Italian family that rose to prominence in the 15th and 16th centuries. Muzio Attendolo (1369–1424) was one of the most powerful *condottieri of the period (his assumed name Sforza means "force"). His illegitimate son Francesco (1401–66) was also a successful condottiere, whose armies were involved in a three-way war with the Milanese republic and Venice, after which he entered Milan in triumph as duke (1450), and thereafter governed ably.

Ludovico (1451–1508), known as "Il Moro" (the Moor), usurped the Milanese government in 1480. He helped Charles VIII of France to invade Naples (1494), but he was subsequently driven out of his duchy by Louis XII (1499). In 1512 his son Massimiliano (1493–1530) was restored to Milan with Swiss aid; *Francis I of France defeated him at Marignano (1515), and forced him to cede his dominions, granting him a pension of 30,000 ducats. Massimiliano's brother Francesco II (1495–1535) was restored by Emperor *Charles V in 1522, but his death marked the end of the male ducal line.

Shackleton, Sir Ernest Henry (1874–1922) British explorer. A junior officer on Robert Falcon *Scott's National Antarctic Expedition (1900–04), he commanded his own expedition in 1909, getting within 155 km (97 miles) of the South Pole (the farthest south anyone had reached at that time). On a second Antarctic expedition (1914–16), Shackleton's ship *Endurance* was crushed in the ice. He and his crew eventually reached an island, from which he and five others set out in an open boat on a 1300-km (800-mile) voyage to South Georgia to find help. In 1920 he led a fourth expedition to the Antarctic, but died of a heart attack on South Georgia.

Shaftesbury, Anthony Ashley Cooper, 1st Earl of (1621–83) English statesman. He entered Parliament in 1640 as a royalist supporter, but changed sides in 1643, eventually becoming a member of *Cromwell's council of state. In 1660 he was one of the Commissioners of the Convention Parliament who invited Charles II to return, and Charles rewarded him with the Chancellorship of the Exchequer. After *Clarendon's fall he became one of the *cabal, but was dismissed in 1673 because of his support for the *Test Act and his unwavering opposition to Roman Catholicism. He became leader of the opposition, and used the *Popish Plot to try to exclude the Roman Catholic James, Duke of York, from the succession (the Exclusion Crisis), but his political failure led him to flee into exile in 1682.

Shaftesbury, Anthony Ashley Cooper, 7th Earl of (1801–85) British philanthropist and social reformer. He was a dominant figure of the 19th-century social reform movement, inspiring much of the legislation designed to improve conditions for the large working class created as a result of the Industrial Revolution. His reforms included the introduction of the ten-hour working day (1847); he was also actively involved in improving housing and education for the poor.

Shah Jahan (1592–1666) *Mogul Emperor of India (1628–58). He extended Mogul power, notably in the Deccan, and rebuilt the capital at Delhi. His buildings there and in Agra, notably the Taj Mahal, built as a shrine for his wife, mark the peak of Indo-Muslim architecture. His severe illness in 1657 caused a succession war between his four sons in which *Aurangzeb, the third son, killed his rivals, imprisoned his father in the Agra palace, and seized the throne. On his death Shah Jahan was buried with his wife in the Taj Mahal.

Shaka (or **Chaka**) (c.1787–1828) Zulu chief. After seizing the Zulu chieftaincy from his half-brother in 1816, he reorganized his own expedition and waged war against the Nguni clans in SE Africa, subjugating them and forming a Zulu empire in the region. Shaka's military campaigns led to a huge displacement of people and a lengthy spell of clan warfare in the early 1820s. He was subsequently assassinated by his two half-brothers.

Shamil (c.1798–1871) Leader of Muslim resistance to the Russian occupation of the Caucasus from 1834–1859. He became Imam of a branch of the Sufi Naqshbandi order known as Muridism which recommended strict adherence to Islamic law and preached *jihad* (holy war) against Russia. After the Crimean War Russia employed some 200,000 troops in the Caucasus to encircle and subdue Shamil and his followers. He was captured (1859), and imprisoned, but allowed to go on a pilgrimage to Mecca (1870), where he died.

Shamir, Yitzhak (born Yitzhak Jazernicki) (1915–2012) Israeli statesman, Prime Minister (1983–84; 1986–92). Born in Poland, he emigrated to Palestine in 1935 and became an active member of *Irgun and the *Stern Gang. On Menachem Begin's retirement in 1983, Shamir became Premier, but his Likud party was narrowly defeated in elections a year later. As Prime Minister of a coalition government with Labour, he sacked Shimon Peres in 1990 and formed a new government with a policy of conceding no land to a Palestinian state. Under his leadership Israel did not retaliate when attacked by Iraqi missiles during the Gulf War of 1991, thereby possibly averting the formation of a pro-Saddam Hussein Arab coalition. In 1992 his government fell when right-wing groups withdrew support as a protest against peace talks with Palestinians.

Shang A dynasty that ruled China during part of the 2nd millennium BC, probably 16th–11th centuries BC. The discovery of inscriptions on more than 100,000 tortoise shells confirmed literary references to the existence of the Shang dynasty, which witnessed the perfection of the wheel, the use of chariots in warfare, bronze casting, and the carving of jade and ivory.

Shankaracharya See SANKARACHARYA.

Shans A people of *Myanmar (Burma). They are akin to people in *Laos and *Thailand, and originated in Yunnan province in south-west China, entering Burma about the 13th century AD. Based in the hills east of the Irrawaddy River, they lived under chieftains thought to have divine powers. There was deep enmity between Burmans and Shans, though the latter, except in very remote areas, adopted Burman culture and Theravada *Buddhism. A kingdom founded by a Burmanized Shan prince at Ava had considerable power from about 1360 until the unification of Upper Burma under the first *Toungoo dynasty in the late 15th century.

Sharon, Ariel (1928–2014) Israeli soldier and statesman; Prime Minister (2001–06). He served in the Israeli army from the foundation of the state until 1973, playing a central role in the *Yom Kippur War. First elected to the Knesset in 1973, he became Minister of Agriculture in the Likud government in 1977. Throughout his political career Sharon was a controversial figure noted for his hardline stance on security issues. As Defence Minister from 1981 he was respon-

sible for the Israeli invasion of southern Lebanon in 1982, but was removed from office in 1983 following criticism over massacres of Palestinian refugees by Israel's Lebanese Christian allies. He subsequently served in a series of ministerial positions including Minister of Foreign Affairs (1998–99). He became leader of the Likud party after it lost the 1999 elections. In 2000 he visited the compound of the al-Aqsa mosque, a move that angered Palestinian opinion and sparked the second *intifada. In the subsequent crisis Likud won the 2001 elections and Sharon became Prime Minister. At first his government responded to the intifada with great severity, reoccupying large parts of the West Bank. However, in 2004 he announced plans for a complete Israeli withdrawal from the Gaza Strip as part of a unilateral attempt to impose a settlement. This was carried out in 2005, but strong opposition led Sharon to split with Likud and form a new party, Kadima, to contest the 2006 elections. However, in January 2006 he was incapacitated by a stroke that placed him in a long-term coma from which he never recovered consciousness. His functions were immediately taken over by Ehud *Olmert, although Sharon officially remained Prime Minister until the following April.

Sharpeville massacre (21 March 1960) An incident in the South African township of Sharpeville. The police opened fire on a demonstration against *apartheid laws, killing 67 Africans, and wounding 180. There was widespread international condemnation, and a state of emergency was declared in South Africa. 1700 persons were detained, and the political parties, the *African National Congress and Pan-Africanist Congress were banned. Three weeks later a White farmer attempted to assassinate the Prime Minister, *Verwoerd, and, as pressure from the Commonwealth against the apartheid policies mounted, South Africa became a republic and withdrew from the Commonwealth (1961).

Shastri, Lal Bahadur (1904–66) Indian statesman, Prime Minister (1964–66). Shastri had been a member of Mahatma *Gandhi's non-cooperation movement against British rule and was imprisoned several times. He served in regional government and was elected to the central legislature in 1952, becoming Minister of Home Affairs in 1961. In 1964 he succeeded Nehru as Prime Minister and was praised for his handling of the conflict in 1965 with Pakistan over Jammu and Kashmir. He died shortly after completing a peace agreement.

Shays's Rebellion (August 1786 to February 1787) An armed uprising in the USA led by Captain Daniel Shays (c.1747–1825), a Massachusetts war veteran. Shays led a group of destitute farmers from western Massachusetts against the creditor merchants and lawyers of the seaboard towns. The Rebellion was caused by the Massachusetts legislature adjourning without hearing the petitions of debt-ridden farmers for financial help. The rebellion prevented the sitting of the courts; the state militia routed Shays's force, but he escaped and was later pardoned. The uprising won concessions, but it also boosted the campaign for an effective constitution and central government for the USA.

Shearers' strikes (1891; 1894) Major strikes in Queensland and New South Wales, Australia. Sheep shearers were fighting for the principles of unionism and the "closed shop" (an establishment in which only trade-union members are employed), while sheep farmers were fighting for "freedom of contract" (the right to employ anyone). The strikes were marked by violence and bitterness on both sides. Non-union labour was used. Union leaders, including some from the Barcaldine shearers' camp of 1891, were arrested on charges such as conspiracy, seditious language, and riot. Some were gaoled. The unions were defeated.

Shelburne, William Petty-Fitzmaurice Lansdowne, 1st Marquis and 2nd Earl of (1737–1805) British statesman. He joined *Chatham's ministry in 1766, but failed to build up a political following and was regarded with distrust by many of his colleagues. His ideas were often regarded as impracticable, especially his conciliatory scheme of 1767 for settling the American question. He opposed the American policies of Lord *North and in 1782 succeeded Lord *Rockingham as Prime Minister. He was responsible for settling the main outlines of the peace treaty between Britain and America, but before these could be concluded he was brought down by a combination of the supporters of Charles James *Fox and North in 1783.

Shere Ali (1825–79) Amir (ruler) of Afghanistan (1863–79). He succeeded his father, *Dost Muhammad. During the early part of his reign Afghanistan experienced civil war and his authority was not confirmed until 1868, when he was given British assistance. Shere Ali introduced a number of reforms in Afghanistan including the establishment of a regular, European-style army. In 1878 he admitted a Russian mission to Kabul but refused to accept a British mission, resulting in the Second *Anglo-Afghan War. Shere Ali fled to northern Afghanistan seeking Russian support, and died.

Sheridan, Philip Henry (1831–88) US general. He emerged as the outstanding cavalry leader on the Union (Northern) side in the *American Civil War, distinguishing himself in Tennessee and in the *Chattanooga Campaign (November 1863) before being appointed in April 1864 to command the cavalry of the Army of the Potomac. His campaign in the Shenandoah Valley (September–October 1864) laid waste one of the south's most important supply regions, while his victory at Five Forks on 1 April 1865 effectively forced Robert E. *Lee to abandon Petersburg and Richmond. After the war Sheridan commanded the 5th military district in the South, and in 1884 he succeeded *Sherman as commander-in-chief of the US Army.

sheriff (from Old English, 'shire-reeve') The chief representative of the crown in the shires (counties) of England from the early 11th century, taking over many of the duties previously performed by ealdormen. Sheriffs assumed responsibility for the fyrd, royal taxes, royal estates, shire courts, and presided over their own court, the Tourn. They abused these powers, as an inquest of 1170 showed, when many were dismissed. However, by c.1550 the office had become purely civil, as a result of the proliferation of specialist royal officials (Coroners, 1170, Justices of the Peace, 1361, Lords Lieutenant, 1547).

Sheriffmuir, Battle of (13 November 1715) A battle fought in Scotland, the only major battle of the *Fifteen Rebellion. The *Jacobite army of 10,000 men, commanded by the Earl of Mar, met the much smaller loyalist force of the Duke of Argyll. Although the fighting was inconclusive, Mar was forced on to the defensive, and the chance of Jacobite success disappeared.

Sherman, William Tecumseh (1820–91) US general. He held various commands in the American Civil War at its outset in 1861, and in March 1864 succeeded Ulysses S. Grant as chief Union commander in the west. He set out with 60,000 men on a march through Georgia, during which he crushed Confederate forces and broke civilian morale with his policy of deliberate destruction of the South's sources of supply. In 1869 he was appointed commander of the US army, a post he held until his retirement in 1884.

S

Sher Shah Suri (c.1486–1545) Emperor of northern India (1540–45). His short-lived seizure of power from the second Mogul emperor, *Humayun, made an important impact on Indian administration. An Afghan of humble origins, he had risen through military service to be well placed to take advantage of temporary Mogul weakness. After defeating Humayun twice (1539 and 1540) he made himself Emperor of Delhi, extending his control to Gwalior and Malwa. Before his death in battle he carried out innovations in the land revenue system and the army that were subsequently built on by the great Mogul administrator, *Akbar.

Shevardnadze, Eduard (Amvrosievich) (1928–2014) Georgian statesman, head of state of Georgia (1992–2003). He became a candidate member of the Soviet Politburo in 1978 and a full member in 1985. In the same year Shevardnadze was appointed Minister of Foreign Affairs under Mikhail Gorbachev, a position he retained until his resignation in 1990. While in office, Shevardnadze supported Gorbachev's commitment to détente and played a key role in arms control negotiations with the West. In 1992 Shevardnadze was elected head of state of his native Georgia, following the toppling of President Zviad Gamsakhurdia (1939–94). He was re-elected in 1995 and 2000, but deposed in the *Rose Revolution (2003).

Shia (or **Shiah**) *See* ISLAM; SHIITES.

Shi Huangdi (Shih Huang-ti) (259–210 BC) First *Qin Emperor of China (221–210 BC). He became ruler of the state of Qin in 246 BC and declared himself emperor in 221 BC after overthrowing the *Zhou and their vassal states. He ordered that the frontier walls in northern China should be joined together and extended to make the *Great Wall of China and enlarged his empire into southern China. He could not accept the Confucian belief that an emperor should follow traditional rites, and so ordered the burning of all Confucian books, the banning of Confucian teaching, and the killing of scholars. In death as in life he was heavily guarded: close to his burial mound outside Xi'an stood an army of life-size pottery warriors and horses. The dynasty outlasted him by only three years, but he had imposed lasting unity on China by standardizing scripts, weights, and measures.

Shiites (from Arabic, 'sectarians') The minority division within *Islam, which consists of at most one-fifth of all Muslims. Shiites are in the majority in Iran (where Shia Islam is the state religion), southern Iraq, and parts of Yemen, and are also found in Syria, Lebanon, East Africa, northern India, and Pakistan. They originated as the Shiat Ali, the 'party of Ali', who was the cousin and son-in-law of *Muhammad. Ali and his descendants are regarded by Shiites as the only true heirs to Muhammad as leader of the faithful. Shiites now differ from *Sunni Muslims in a number of ways but primarily in the importance they attach to the continuing authority of the *imams*, who are the authentic interpreters of the *sunna* (customs), the code of conduct based on the *Koran and *hadith* (sayings and deeds of Muhammad). The suffering of the House of the Prophet, chiefly of Husain and his martyrdom in Karbala, and the *millenarian expectation of a future *imam* or *Mahdi who is currently hidden from the world, permeate much Shiite thinking, providing a set of beliefs in which oppression and injustice figure largely. The tenth day of the month of Muharram marks the martyrdom of Ali and his sons. Shiites also believe in an inner hidden meaning of the Koran. There are hundreds of different Shiite sects: the main ones are the Zaydis, Ismailis, and Ithna Ashariya (or Twelvers, who await the return of the hidden twelfth *imam*).

Shimonoseki, Treaty of (17 April 1895) The treaty between China and Japan that ended the *Sino-Japanese War (1894–95). With her navy destroyed and Beijing in danger of capture, China was forced to grant the independence of Korea, pay a large indemnity, grant favourable trade terms, and cede Taiwan, the Pescadores Islands, and the Liaodong peninsula (including the naval base at Port Arthur, now Lüshun). International pressure forced the return of Port Arthur and the abandonment of the claim to the Liaodong peninsula shortly afterwards, but Japanese domination over north China had been established.

Shining Path (Spanish, *Sendero Luminoso*) Peruvian left-wing terrorist group, active from the early 1970s to the early 1990s. The Shining Path gained notoriety for the violence of its campaign against the Peruvian government, which claimed some 28,000 lives. Founded in 1970 by a philosophy professor, Abimael Guzmán, the movement adopted the revolutionary principles of Mao Zedong; its many recruits came both from universities and from the disadvantaged Amerindian peoples of the Andes. From 1980 it attacked projects established by foreign aid agencies in rural areas, but later moved to the major cities. The emergency powers taken by President Alberto Fujimori in 1992, in an attempt to stem political violence, led in the first place to increased guerrilla activity, especially against local politicians, but resulted in the capture and sentencing of Guzmán to life imprisonment in September of that year. Following the arrest of their leader, who called for a cessation of fighting, some 6000 Shining Path members took advantage of a government amnesty and surrendered. Isolated pockets of resistance remain in more remote areas.

Shinto (Chinese/Japanese, 'the Way of the Spirits') A Japanese religion dating from prehistoric times, based on the worship of ancestors and nature-spirits. In early times each clan had its *kami*. With the supremacy of the *Yamato, its Sun-goddess, Amaterasu, enshrined at the temple at Ise, became paramount.

The name Shinto was adopted in the 6th century AD to distinguish it from Buddhist and Confucian cults. There is no official Shinto scripture, although the *Kojiki* (Records of Ancient Matters) and *Nihon-gi* (Chronicles of Japan), 8th-century compilations based on oral tradition, contain myths and stories about creation and the gods. During the 5th century AD, the spread of Confucianism introduced ancestor worship to Shinto, and in the 6th century Buddhist beliefs became incorporated into the ancient religion.

During the 19th century the rise of the unified Japanese state saw the development of state Shinto: the emperor came to be worshipped as a descendant of the Sun-goddess Amaterasu. State Shinto was not classed as a religion but as a code of conduct requiring loyalty and obedience to the divine emperor; it informed all public life and encouraged extreme nationalism, until it was rescinded by the emperor (under US pressure) in 1945. It was replaced by the older form, shrine Shinto, the worship of *kami* in shrines or sanctuaries, tended by priests. In the home, the *kami* are housed within a *kamidana*, or 'godshelf'. Personal worship involves purification rites and daily prayers to the *kami*. Shinto is regarded as the religion of life, while Buddhism is seen as that of death; marriages are therefore celebrated according to Shinto tradition, while people generally choose Buddhist rites for funerals.

Shipley, Jenny (1952–) New Zealand National Party politician, first female Prime Minister of New Zealand (1997–99).

ship money Originally, an occasional sum of money paid by English seaports to the crown to meet the cost of supplying a ship to the Royal Navy. Charles I revived the tax in 1634, while he was ruling without Parliament. From 1635 he extended it to the inland towns, and raised up to £200,000 a year as a result. In 1637 John Hampden was taken to court for refusing to pay and claimed that Charles needed Parliament's approval to levy such a regular tax. The judges decided by seven to five in Charles's favour, but the narrowness of the victory encouraged widespread refusal to pay tax afterwards. The *Long Parliament made ship money illegal in 1641.

shire Formerly, the main unit of local administration in England. Shires evolved as territorial units in Wessex in the 9th century, replacing the Roman system of provinces. They were extended over a wider area of England by *Alfred the Great and his heirs as administrative and political units. The English shire system reveals many different evolutionary processes. Some were based on former kingdoms (Kent, Sussex, Essex); others on tribal subdivisions within a kingdom (Norfolk and Suffolk); others were created during the 10th-century reconquest of the *Danelaw or as territories centred on towns (Oxfordshire, Warwickshire, Buckinghamshire, etc.). England north of the River Tees was not absorbed into the shire system until the Norman Conquest when shires were restyled 'counties'.

Shivaji (or **Sivaji**) (1627–80) Indian raja of the Marathas (1674–80). In 1659 he raised a Hindu revolt against Muslim rule in Bijapur, southern India, inflicting a crushing defeat on the army of the sultan of Bijapur. Shivaji was later captured by the Mogul emperor Aurangzeb, but escaped in 1666 and proceeded to expand Maratha territory. He had himself crowned raja in 1674; during his reign he enforced religious toleration throughout the Maratha empire and blocked Mogul expansionism by forming an alliance with the sultans in the south.

shogunate A Japanese institution under which government was in the hands of a *Sei-i dai-shogun* ('barbarian-conquering great general'). The shoguns exercised civil and military power in the name of emperors, who became figure-heads. The shogunate as a form of government originated with Minamoto Yoritomo's appointment without any limit to his authority (1192). After he died the *Hojo regents took control of affairs, but in theory they remained subject both to the emperor and the shogun. During the Ashikaga period the shoguns were independent of any other authority though their rule was ineffective. Under the *Tokugawa the power of the shogunate was decisive in national

S

politics. Japan had been effectively ruled by the Tokugawa since the beginning of the 17th century, but from the 1840s it was progressively undermined by political pressures unleashed by increasing foreign incursions into Japanese territory. Resistance to the shogunate's conservative policies coalesced around advocates of a return to full imperial rule, and between 1866 and 1869 the Tokugawa armies were gradually defeated by an alliance of provincial forces from Choshu, Satsuma, and Tosa acting for the Meiji emperor, who formally resumed imperial rule in January 1868.

Shotoku Taishi (574–622) Japanese prince. As regent for Empress Suiko, he set out at the age of 20 to convert a clan society into a centralized administration like that of China. He sent embassies to the *Sui, brought in Chinese artists and craftsmen, adopted the Chinese calendar, created a constitution, and instituted a bureaucracy based on merit. He promoted both *Buddhism and *Confucianism. After Shotoku's death, during the Taika ("Great Change") period (645–710), an imperial prince and a *Fujiwara initiated further reforms. Gradually, Chinese practices were adapted to Japanese conditions and a more centralized administration emerged.

Siam The name until 1939 of *Thailand.

Sicilian Vespers An uprising and massacre in Sicily in 1282, which began at the time of vespers (the evening church service). It marked the end of the rule of the *Angevins in the island and of their dynastic ambitions in Italy. Charles I of Anjou had received the Kingdom of the Two Sicilies from Pope Urban IV in 1266 and to claim it had defeated the Hohenstaufen *Manfred, son of the Holy Roman Emperor Frederick II. His rule was extremely harsh, enforcing heavy taxation, and the French occupation was generally hated. Within a month all the French had been killed or forced to flee and the crown was later given to Pedro III of Aragon, who thwarted Angevin attempts at reoccupation, and who passed the crown to his son Frederick III of Sicily.

Sicily (Italian **Sicilia**) A large triangular island in the Mediterranean Sea, separated from the 'toe' of Italy by the narrow Strait of Messina. It forms, with the neighbouring islands of Lipari, Egadi, Ustica, and Pantelleria, a region of Italy. Settled successively by Phoenicians, Greeks, and Carthaginians, it became a Roman province in 241 BC after the first Punic War. Sicily and southern Italy became a Norman kingdom towards the end of the 11th century. It was con-quered by Charles of Anjou in 1266, but the unpopularity of the Angevin regime led to the uprising known as the *Sicilian Vespers and the establishment in Sicily of the Spanish House of Aragon in its place; southern Italy remained under Angevin rule until reunited with Sicily in 1442. In 1816 the two areas were officially merged when the Spanish Bourbon Ferdinand styled himself King of the Two Sicilies. The island was liberated by Garibaldi in 1860 and finally incorporated into the new state of Italy.

Siegfried Line The line of defence constructed along the western frontier of Germany before World War II.

Sierra Leone

Capital:	Freetown
Area:	71,740 sq km (27,699 sq miles)
Population:	5,612,685 (2013 est)
Currency:	1 leone = 100 cents
Religions:	Muslim 60%; traditional beliefs 30.0%; Christian 10.0%
Ethnic Groups:	Temne 35.0%; Mende 31.0%; Limba 8.0%; Kono 5.0%
Languages:	English (official); Krio (English creole); Mende; Temne; other local languages
International Organizations:	UN; AU; ECOWAS; Commonwealth; Non-Aligned Movement; WTO

A tropical West African country with an Atlantic coast facing south-west and a fine natural harbour; it is surrounded inland by Guinea and Liberia.

Physical Swamps spread up river valleys, through a rainforested coastal plain to wooded savannah in the interior.

Economy Sierra Leone is still recovering from the civil war in the 1990s and early 2000s and is very poor; almost half the workforce is engaged in subsistence agriculture. Cocoa and coffee are the main cash crops and important exports; other crops include rice, palm kernels, palm oil, and groundnuts. Other principal exports are diamonds, rutile, and bauxite, and the main industry is mining.

History The Portuguese navigator Pedro de Cintra reached it in 1462, at about the time the Temne, its chief inhabitants, were reaching the coast. During the 16th and 17th centuries the slave trade and piracy attracted many Europeans, including English, so that the coast has a very mixed population. In 1772 Britain declared that any escaped slave who came to Britain would automatically become free. In 1787 the Anti-Slavery Society bought the coastal territory from the local ruler as a haven for slaves found destitute in Britain. British philanthropists organized their transport to Cape Sierra Leone, where Freetown was established. In 1791 Alexander Falconbridge formed a transport company, the Sierra Leone Company, landing the first colonists at Free-town in 1792. It became a crown colony in 1808. After 1815 British warships who captured slave ships brought freed captives there. During the 19th century the hinterland of Sierra Leone was gradually explored and in 1896 it became a British protectorate, which remained separate from the colony of Freetown until 1951. The country gained its independence under Prime Minister Sir Milton Margai (1895–1964) in 1961, but after his death electoral difficulties produced two military coups before some stability was restored by the establishment of a one-party state under Dr Siaka Stevens. Food shortages, corruption, and tribal tensions produced serious violence in the early 1980s, and in 1985 Stevens retired in favour of Major-General Joseph Saidu Momoh. As head of state, he retained a civilian cabinet with the All People's Congress (APC) the sole legal party; its rule was deeply corrupt. In April 1992 an army coup, led by Captain Valentine Strasser, ousted Saidu Momoh and formed a National Provisional Defence Council, committed to the elimination of corruption and the restoration of the economy. Although the ban on political parties imposed in 1992 was lifted in 1995, actions by rebel forces opposed to the government intensified. In 1996 Strasser was ousted by his deputy, Captain Julius Bio, who took over as head of state. In March 1996 democratic elections were won by Ahmad Tejan Kabbah (1932–2014), who became President of a civilian government. This government was overthrown in a military coup in 1997, but Nigerian forces retook the capital in 1998 and the President was reinstated. However, later in 1998 members of the deposed military regime joined by the left-wing Revolutionary United Front attacked Freetown causing considerable damage. The Nigerians returned to rout the rebels in January 1999. Despite the deployment of a UN peacekeeping force later that year, the civil war continued until a ceasefire was agreed in 2001. The UN established a special court in 2002 to try war crimes committed in the savage fighting; in 2012 it convicted Charles Taylor, the former President of Liberia, of war crimes and crimes against humanity. Kabbah won the presidential election in 2002 and in 2003 a truth and reconciliation commission was established. The UN peacekeeping force was withdrawn in 2005. Ernest Bai Koroma was elected President in 2007 and re-elected in 2012.

Sigismund (1368–1437) Holy Roman Emperor (1411–37), king of Hungary (1387–1437), Germany (1411–37), Bohemia (1419–37), and Lombardy (1431–37), the last emperor of the House of Luxemburg. In 1396 he was defeated by the Turks at Nicopolis but went on to acquire and secure a large number of territories and titles in a long and violent reign, which featured warfare with the *Hussites, Venetians, and rivals for the thrones of Hungary and Germany. An orthodox Catholic, he acted severely against the Hussites, and put pressure on the pope to call a council at *Constance to end the Hussite Schism; Sigismund promised Huss safe-conduct to attend the council, which subsequently ordered his death.

Sihanouk, Norodom (1922–2012) Cambodian king (1941–55; 1993–2004), Prime Minister (1955–60), and head of state (1960–70; 1975–76; 1991–93). Two years after Cambodian independence (1953) Sihanouk abdicated in order to become Premier, passing the throne to his father Prince Norodom Suramarit (died 1960). On his father's death, Prince Sihanouk proclaimed himself head of state, a position he retained until a US-backed military coup ten years later. Sihanouk was reinstated by the Khmer Rouge in 1975, only to be removed the following year. After serving as President of the government-in-exile (1982–89), he was appointed head of state by the provisional government and subsequently crowned for the second time (1993). In 2004 Sihanouk abdicated in favour of his son Norodom Sihamoni.

Sikhism A monotheistic religion founded in the Punjab in the 15th century by Guru *Nanak. It combines elements of Hinduism and Islam, accepting the Hindu concepts of karma and reincarnation but rejecting the caste system, and has one sacred scripture, the Adi Granth. The tenth and last of the series of gurus, Gobind Singh, prescribed the distinctive outward forms (the so-called five Ks)—long

S

hair (to be covered by a turban) and uncut beard (*kesh*), comb (*kangha*), short sword (*kirpan*), steel bangle (*kara*), and short trousers for horse-riding (*kaccha*). Originating as a religion, Sikhism became a militant political movement in the Punjab, where most of the world's 25 million Sikhs live.

Sikh Wars (1845–49) Two conflicts between the Sikhs of Lahore and the English *East India Company. The First Sikh War (1845–46) took place when Sikh troops crossed the Sutlej River into British India. After the drawn battles of Mudki and Firuzshah, the British defeated the Sikhs at Aliwal and Sobraon. By the Treaty of Lahore (1846) Britain obtained the cession of the Jullundar Doab, took Kashmir for Gulab Singh, and established control of the Lahore government through a Resident. Sikh discontent led to the Second Sikh War (1848–49); the bloody Battle of Chillianwallah was followed by the decisive British victory at Gujerat over an army of 60,000 Sikhs. The governor-general, Lord *Dalhousie, annexed the Punjab in 1849.

Sikorski, Władysław (1881–1943) Polish general and statesman. He commanded divisions against the *Bolsheviks (1919–20) and headed a non-parliamentary coalition government in Poland (1922–23). In 1939 he fled to France and organized a Polish army in exile that fought with the Allies in World War II. As head of the exiled Polish government in London he succeeded in maintaining tolerable relations with Moscow until news of the *Katyn massacre broke. During his ascendancy Polish prisoners-of-war in the Soviet Union were recruited to form the 'Polish Army in Russia' under General Władysław Anders to fight with the Allies. He was killed in an air crash.

Silk Road (or **Silk Route**) An ancient caravan route linking China with the West, used from Roman times onwards and taking its name from the silk that was a major Chinese export. By this route Christianity and (from India) Buddhism reached China. A 'North Road' skirted the northern edge of the Taklimakan Desert before heading westwards into Turkestan (and thence to the Levant), while a 'South Road' followed a more southerly route through the high passes of the Kunlun and Pamir mountains into India. A railway (completed in 1963) follows the northern route from Xian to Urumchi and into Kazakhstan.

Sima Qian (or **Ssu-ma Ch'ien**) (*c.*145–85 BC) Chinese historian, an official at the court of the *Han emperor Wudi. His *Historical Records* is a history of China from earliest times to the days of Wudi, and is a model for later dynastic histories. As well as recounting ancient myths, he provided much source material, quoting inscriptions from old bronzes and imperial decrees from the archives. One section of the

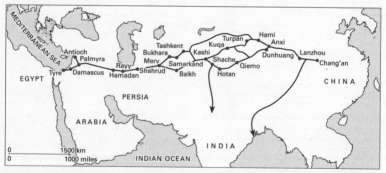

Silk road. Crossing Asia from eastern China to the Mediterranean, the Silk Road was pioneered by the Chinese in the 2nd century BC. Bactrian camels carried many goods besides silk on the Silk Road, but only a small proportion of the goods, and few merchants, ever travelled its whole length. The route began in the old capital, Chang'an (now Xi'an) and skirted the Taklimakan desert, in north-west China, north and south, before climbing into the Pamir Mountains from Kashi (Kashgar) and continuing through Persia to the Mediterranean. From Shache (Yarkand) another route led to India.

work, *Assorted Traditions*, has lively biographies of generals, poets, scoundrels, and court ladies. Angered by his defence of a general forced to surrender to the *Xiongnu, Wudi had him castrated. Although such punishment often led officials to commit suicide he decided to live on to complete his history.

Simnel, Lambert (*c*.1487–*c*.1525) English royal *pretender. Although he was actually a joiner's son certain *Yorkists pretended or believed that he was Edward of Warwick, son of the murdered George, Duke of *Clarence, and on 24 May 1487 he was crowned in Dublin as Edward VI. Next month he was brought to England, but the Yorkists were defeated and *Henry VII, showing mercy, gave him employment in the royal kitchens.

simony The buying and selling of spiritual or Church benefits. It is taken from the name of Simon Magus who, according to an account in the New Testament of the Bible, tried to buy spiritual powers from St Peter. It came to mean the purchase of any office or authority within the *Roman Catholic Church. The Church's policy that its benefices should not be sold for money was often jeopardized because many secular lords claimed that they were theirs to dispose of as they wished. Wealthy families bought offices for their members and used them as a form of patronage. Simony was one of the abuses criticized at the time of the *Reformation.

Simpson, Wallis (née **Warfield**) (1896– 1986) US wife of Edward, Duke of Windsor (*Edward VIII). Her relationship with the king caused the abdication crisis in 1936. She remained in France after her husband died and lived as a recluse until her death.

Sindhia A leading *Maratha family, based at Gwalior in northern India, which dominated the Maratha confederacy in the late 18th century. The founder of the family's fortunes, Ranoji Sindhia (died 1750), seized control of the Malwa region that he had been appointed to govern. A successor, Mahadaji Sindhia (ruled 1761–94), created a virtually independent kingdom in north India. He became the arbiter of power not only within the Maratha confederacy, but also at the *Mogul court at Delhi, and won victories against the **East India Company as well as the *Rajputs. His successors failed to stem British expansion in north India. Daulat Rao Sindhia was defeated in 1803, and in 1818 Gwalior became a Princely State under the Company's protection.

Singapore

Capital:	Singapore
Area:	697 sq km (269 sq miles)
Population:	5,460,302 (2013 est)
Currency:	1 Singapore dollar = 100 cents
Religions:	Buddhist 33.9%; Muslim 14.3%; Taoist 11.3%; Roman Catholic 7.1%; Hindu 5.2%
Ethnic Groups:	Chinese 74.2%; Malay 13.3%; Indian 9.2%
Languages:	Malay, Mandarin, Tamil, English (all official); Chinese dialects
International Organizations:	UN; Colombo Plan; Commonwealth; ASEAN; Non-Aligned Movement; WTO

A south-east Asian island state.

Physical Singapore comprises an island at the southern end of the Malay Peninsula, only 2° N of the Equator. The country comprises a large, low-lying island, about 40 km (25 miles) wide by 22 km (14 miles) from north to south, and many much smaller islands.

Economy The port of Singapore is one of the largest in the world and entrepôt trade has long been important. Manufacturing industry includes electronics, chemicals, oil drilling equipment, and oil refining. Singapore is also a leading financial centre. The principal exports are consumer electronics, IT products, and pharmaceuticals.

History The island of Singapore was formerly known as Tumasik or Temasek. It was inhabited mainly by fishermen and pirates before becoming part of the Sumatran empire of Srivijaya. It then passed to the Majapahit empire in the 14th century and then to the Ayutthaya empire of Siam. In the 15th century it became part of the Malacca empire, and subsequently came under Portuguese and then Dutch control.

The island was acquired for the English *East India Company by Sir Stamford *Raffles in 1819 from the sultan of Johore, and rapidly developed into an important trading port. In 1867 Singapore was removed from British Indian administration to form part of the new colony of the *Straits Settlements, its commercial development, dependent on Chinese immigrants, proceeding alongside its growth as a major naval base. In 1942 it fell to Japanese forces under General Yamashita and remained in Japanese hands until the end of World War II. The island became a separate colony in 1946 and enjoyed internal self-government from 1959 under the leadership of *Lee Kuan Yew. It joined the Federation of *Malaysia in 1963, but Malay fears that its predominantly Chinese population would discriminate in favour of the non-Malays led to its expulsion in 1965. A member of the *Commonwealth of Nations and the *Association of South-East Asian Nations, it has maintained close ties with Malaysia and Brunei. The People's Action Party has governed since 1965, with Lee Kuan Yew as the world's longest-serving Prime Minister (1965–90). Lee Kuan Yew resigned in 1990, filling the role of Senior Minister. He was succeeded as Prime Minister by Goh Chok Tung (1990–2004) and then by his son, Lee Hsien Loong (2004–).

Singh, Manmohan (1932–) Indian statesman; Prime Minister (2004–). An economist, he was a government advisor (1971–76), a director of the Reserve Bank of India (1976–80), and subsequently its governor (1982–85). From 1991–1996 he was Minister of Finance in the Congress government of P. V. Narasimha Rao and carried out a comprehensive programme of liberal market-oriented economic reforms. He unexpectedly became Prime Minister following the 2004 elections when Sonia *Gandhi, the leader of the Congress party, declined the position.

Singh, Vishwanath Pratap (1931–2008) Indian politician, Prime Minister of India (1989–90).

Sinn Fein (Gaelic, 'we ourselves') An Irish political party dedicated to the creation of a united Irish republic. Originally founded by Arthur *Griffith in 1902 as a cultural revival movement, it became politically active and supported the *Easter Rising in 1916. Having won a large majority of seats in Ireland in the 1918 general election, Sinn Fein Members of Parliament, instead of going to London, met in Dublin and proclaimed Irish independence in 1919. An independent parliament (Dáil Éireann) was set up, though many of its MPs were in prison or on the run. Guerrilla warfare against British troops and police followed. The setting up of the *Irish Free State (December 1921) and the partition of Ireland were rejected by a minority of Sinn Fein members, who kept the party

name. The party abstained from the Dáil and the Northern Ireland parliament for many years. In the late 1960s Sinn Fein re-emerged as the political wing of the Provisional *Irish Republican Army. In 1994, following a peace initiative by the Irish and British governments, Sinn Fein President Gerry Adams announced a complete IRA ceasefire. This was broken in February 1996, when Sinn Fein refused to commit the IRA to decommissioning weapons as a precondition to negotiation, and the party was excluded from talks on the future of Northern Ireland that began in June. They were admitted to the talks in 1997, following a further ceasefire, and in 1998 were parties to the Good Friday Agreement. Sinn Fein members participated in the assembly and executive established by this agreement. In the 2003 assembly elections Sinn Fein became the largest nationalist party, and in 2007 formed a power-sharing executive with Ian Paisley's Democratic Unionist Party.

Sino-French War (1884–85) A conflict between France and China over *Vietnam. China had assisted Vietnam in partial resistance to French expansion since the 1870s, first with irregular forces of the Black Flag Army and after 1883 with regular forces. In 1884, after both governments had rejected the compromise Li-Fournier agreement, war broke out. The Chinese were unable to resist the French navy, which attacked Taiwan and destroyed Fuzhou (Foochow) dockyard in south-east China, and the *Qing dynasty's reputation was weakened. In the treaty signed in 1885, France won control of Vietnam.

Sino-Japanese War (1894–95) War fought between China and Japan. After Korea was opened to Japanese trade in 1876, it rapidly became an arena for rivalry between the expanding Japanese state and neighbouring China, of which Korea had been a vassal state since the 17th century. A rebellion in 1894 provided a pretext for both sides to send troops to Korea, but the Chinese were rapidly overwhelmed by superior Japanese troops, organization, and equipment. After the Beiyang fleet, one of the most important projects of the *Self-Strengthening Movement, was defeated at the battle of the Yellow Sea and Port Arthur (now Lüshun) captured, the Chinese found their capital Beijing menaced by advancing Japanese forces. They were forced to sign the Treaty of *Shimonoseki, granting Korean independence and making a series of commercial and territorial concessions which opened the way for a

Japanese confrontation with Russia, the other expansionist power in north-east Asia.

Sino-Japanese War (1937–45) A conflict on the Chinese mainland between combined nationalist and communist Chinese forces and Japan. China had been the target of Japanese expansionism since the late 19th century, and after the *Mukden Incident of 1931 full-scale war was only a matter of time. Hostilities broke out, without any formal declaration of war by either side, after a clash near the Marco Polo bridge just west of Beijing in 1937. The Japanese overran northern China, penetrating up the Yangtze and along the railway lines, capturing Shanghai, Nanjing, Guangzhou, and Hankou by the end of 1938. In the 'Rape of Nanjing', over 100,000 civilians were massacred by Japanese troops. The invaders were resisted by both the *Kuomintang army of the nationalist leader *Chiang Kai-shek and the communist 8th Route Army, the former being supplied after 1941 by Britain and the USA. By the time the conflict had been absorbed into World War II, the Sino-Japanese War had reached a state of near stalemate, Japanese military and aerial superiority being insufficient to overcome tenacious Chinese resistance and the problems posed by massive distances and poor communications. The Chinese kept over a million Japanese troops tied down for the entire war, inflicting a heavy defeat upon them at Jiangxi in 1942 and successfully repelling a final series of offensives in 1944 and 1945. The Japanese finally surrendered to Chiang Kai-shek on 9 September 1945, leaving him to contest the control of China with *Mao Zedong's communist forces.

Sino–Soviet border dispute (March 1969) A brief conflict between China and the Soviet Union over possession of an island in the Ussuri River. The exact position of the border between north-east China and the Soviet Union had long been a subject of dispute. The disagreement turned into a military confrontation because of the ideological dispute between China and the Soviet Union after 1960 and the militant nationalism that was part of the *Cultural Revolution. In March 1969 two battles were fought for possession of the small island of Zhen Bao (also known as Damansky). The Chinese ultimately retained control of the island, and talks in September 1969 brought the crisis to an end.

Sioux (Siouan **Dakota**) A group of Native American tribes originally occupying the plains and prairies. With a population in the 19th

century of more than 30,000, it was one of the largest tribes in North America.

Sitting Bull (Sioux name **Tatanka Iyotake**) (c.1831–90) Sioux chief. As the main chief of the Sioux peoples from about 1867, he resisted the US government order of 1875 forcibly resettling the Sioux on reservations; when the US army opened hostilities in 1876, Sitting Bull led the Sioux in the fight to retain their lands, which resulted in the massacre of General *Custer and his men at Little Bighorn. In 1885 he appeared in Buffalo Bill's Wild West Show, but continued to lead his people; becoming an advocate of the *ghost dance cult, he was killed in an uprising.

Sivaji See SHIVAJI.

Six Acts (1819) Legislation in Britain aimed at checking what was regarded as dangerous radicalism, in an immediate response to public anger over the *Peterloo Massacre. It dealt with procedures for bringing cases to trial, the prohibition of meetings "for military exercises", the issue of warrants to search for arms, powers to seize seditious or blasphemous literature, the extension of a stamp-duty on newspapers and periodicals, and the regulation and control of all public meetings. The last three were particularly resented and regarded as a threat to freedom. The Acts proved counter-productive by provoking much opposition; three years later the government of Lord *Liverpool began to move towards more liberal policies.

Six-Day War (5–10 June 1967) Arab–Israeli war, known to the Arabs as the June War. The immediate causes of the war were the Egyptian request to the UN Emergency Force in Sinai to withdraw from the Israeli frontier, the increase of Egyptian forces in Sinai, and the closure of the Straits of Tiran (the Gulf of Aqaba) to Israeli shipping. An Egyptian, Syrian, and Jordanian military alliance was formed. The war was initiated by General Dayan as Israel's Minister of Defence, with a pre-emptive air strike, which was followed by the occupation of Sinai, Old Jerusalem, the West Bank, and the Golan Heights (9–10 June). The Arab–Israeli conflict erupted again in the *Yom Kippur War of 1973.

Slave Kings See MAMELUKE.

slavery The ownership of one person by another, who controls the slave's life and labour. Slaves are viewed by their owners as property, and are bought and sold accordingly. Slavery is closely associated with racial prejudice, the belief that one *race is superior to another.

Slavery has a history going back to the earliest civilizations. In ancient Greece much of the economy relied on slaves and the sacred island of Delos served as the main slave market of the Aegean. It was very often the practice amongst the peoples of the ancient world to enslave prisoners-of-war, and that was the major source of slaves. The expansion of the Roman empire created an enormous number of slaves, and although the coming of Christianity helped to improve the slave's lot, slavery proved persistent. Slavery was also commonplace in the Arab world (see SLAVE TRADE, ARAB).

One of the most significant periods of slavery was the use of African slave labour in the plantations of the Caribbean and the southern states of the USA during the 18th and early 19th centuries (see SLAVE TRADE, AFRICAN; SLAVE TRADE, ABOLITION OF).

During World War II the Germans made extensive use of slave labour. Able-bodied Jews, Russians, Slavs and others to whom the Germans believed themselves to be superior were forced to work as slaves. After the war, the word 'slave' was defined by the UN as anyone who cannot voluntarily withdraw his or her labour; the UN estimates that some 21 million such slaves exist, principally in Asia, Africa, and South America, where bonded labourers (persons who bind themselves over for a fixed period to pay off a debt or earn a fixed sum) and child slavery are widespread.

Slaves, US Proclamation for the Emancipation of (January 1863) The executive order abolishing slavery in the "rebel" (Confederate) states of the USA. The Proclamation, issued by President *Lincoln as commander-in-chief of the US Armed Forces, was partly a measure designed to win international support for the Union cause. It was of doubtful constitutional validity. Lincoln had issued a preliminary proclamation on 22 September 1862 advising that all slaves would be legally free as from 1 January 1863. This was now confirmed, to be enforced by military authority without compensation. After the war the US Congress passed (1865) the Thirteenth Amendment to the Constitution, abolishing slavery throughout the USA and thus confirming the constitutionality of the President's action.

slave trade, abolition of The slave trade reached its peak in the 18th century on the West African coast, where merchants from Europe

worked in cooperation with native chieftains and slave raiders who were willing to exchange slaves for Western commodities. Denmark made participation in the Atlantic slave trade illegal in 1792 and the USA did so in 1794. In Britain a group of humanitarian Christians, including Thomas *Clarkson and William *Wilberforce (members of the so-called Clapham Sect), argued that if the Atlantic slave trade were abolished, with its appalling cruelties, plantation owners would treat their slaves more humanely, as being more valuable. They succeeded in getting Parliament to pass a Bill abolishing the British trade in 1807 and at the Treaties of Ghent (1814) and Vienna (1815) Britain agreed to use the Royal Navy to try to suppress the trade, most European countries now supporting the abolition of slavery. However, for the next 40 years illegal smuggling continued, mainly from Africa. Even after slavery was abolished in the British West Indies (1834) trade in slaves between the southern US slave states and such places as Cuba, Costa Rica, Brazil continued. Within the US southern states the breeding, transport, and sale of slaves became highly profitable, there being some four million slaves on the plantations by the time of the Emancipation Proclamation (1863) (see SLAVES, US PROCLAMATION FOR THE EMANCIPATION OF). Slavery in the Caribbean did not cease until it was banned by such countries as Cuba (1886) and Brazil (1888). In the Muslim world the Arab slave trade from Africa operated from Morocco and Zanzibar and stretched throughout the Ottoman empire into Persia and India. In 1873 the Sultan of Zanzibar was finally persuaded by Britain and Germany to close his markets, while the Moroccan trade gradually dwindled with French and Spanish occupation. However, as late as 1935 there was still evidence of trade in slaves in Africa.

slave trade, African The trade in which Europeans captured people in Africa and transported them as slaves mainly to the Americas, where slave labour enabled colonists to establish *plantations. Following their 15th-century discoveries, the Portuguese began taking slaves from Senegambia and Guinea-Bissau: they went to Portugal, the Atlantic islands, and later to the Americas; by the 16th century they came also from Angola, and, occasionally, Mozambique. In the 17th century trading forts, stretching from Arguin (now in Mauritania) to Angola, had been established by slavers from Brandenburg, Denmark, Holland, Courland (on the eastern Baltic), England, France, Genoa, and Sweden. These forts could not have operated

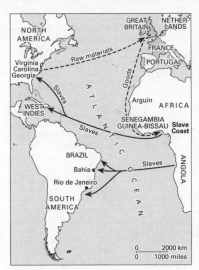

African slave trade. The African slave trade reached its height during the 17th and 18th centuries. Several hundred thousand Africans were transported across the Atlantic each year, to the plantations of the European colonies in the Americas. It was a triangular trade. A typical three-leg voyage set out from Europe to West Africa, carrying cotton goods, hardware, and, increasingly, guns. These goods were exchanged for slaves, who were taken to the West Indies and the southern colonies of North America. The ships returned to Europe with colonial produce, notably sugar.

without active African participation in supplying slaves for shipment to Brazil, and to British, French, Dutch, and Spanish colonies. It is thought that by the mid-19th century 9.5 million Africans had been transported to the New World, in addition to those who died while being captured or in transit. This figure does not include the Arab slave trade nor the flourishing trade in slaves within Africa. Disgust at this treatment of Africans led to demands for emancipation of the slaves and the abolition of the slave trade in the 19th century. (*See also* SLAVERY; SLAVES, US PROCLAMATION FOR THE EMANCIPATION OF; SLAVE TRADE, ABOLITION OF.)

slave trade, Arab A form of commerce in slaves that existed from earliest times in the Arabian peninsular. The Prophet *Muhammad forbade his followers to enslave Muslims, but did not free slave converts. His legislation

insisted on humane treatment and gave slaves rights against oppressive masters. In early Islam slaves were recruited from prisoners-of-war (including women and children) and were acquired by raiding and by purchase in Eastern and Southern Europe, Central Asia, and Central, East, and West Africa. Under the caliphs the trade was brisk. Slaves served a variety of purposes: agricultural, mining, domestic, and clerical, and for military service. Many slave women employed as concubines were given the rights of wives. Men and children often received vocational training after capture. Through international pressure, the trade was largely abolished during the 19th century. (*See also* SLAVERY.)

Slavs Peoples who occupied eastern Europe in ancient times and were known to the Romans as Sarmatians and Scythians. The name is believed to come from *slowo* ("well speaking"). After the collapse of the *Huns in the 5th century the Slavs migrated westwards to the Elbe, the Baltic, the Danube, the Adriatic, and the Black Sea. In the 9th century the missionaries Cyril and Methodius from Constantinople evangelized the Slovenes or southern Slavs.

Slim, William Joseph, 1st Viscount (1891–1970) British field-marshal. He commanded an Indian division in the 1941 conquest of the *Vichy French territory of Syria. In early 1942 he joined the *Burma Campaign, and in 1943 took command of the 14th Army. After the victory at Kohima he pushed down the Irrawaddy River to recapture Rangoon and most of Burma. After the war he became Chief of the Imperial General Staff (1948–52) and Governor-General of Australia (1953–60).

Slovakia

Capital:	Bratislava
Area:	49,035 sq km (18,928 sq miles)
Population:	5,488,339 (2013 est)
Currency:	1 euro = 100 cents
Religions:	Roman Catholic 62.0%; Protestant 8.2%; Greek Catholic 3.8%
Ethnic Groups:	Slovak 80.7%; Hungarian 8.5%; Roma 2.3%
Languages:	Slovak (official); Hungarian; Roma; other minority languages
International Organizations:	UN; OSCE; Council of Europe; EU; NATO; OECD; WTO

S

A central European republic, formerly part of *Czechoslovakia.

Physical Slovakia is surrounded by Poland to the north, Ukraine to the east, Hungary to the south, and Austria and the Czech Republic to the west. The Carpathian mountains dominate the country. Some steppe grasslands are to be found in the south-eastern lowlands; one third of the country is cultivated and two-fifths is covered in forest. The Danube briefly forms the border between Slovakia and Hungary flowing towards Bratislava and finally on to the Black Sea.

Economy Slovakia's transition from a Soviet-era centrally planned to a free-market economy is almost complete. Principal industries include metal and metal products, food and drink, energy, and chemicals; agricultural crops include grains, potatoes, sugar beet, hops, and fruit. The principal exports are machinery, electrical equipment, vehicles, base metals, chemicals, and minerals.

History A land belonging to the Hungarian crown since medieval times, Slovakia experienced an upsurge in nationalism in the late 18th and early 19th centuries. A final break with Hungary was made with the collapse of the Austro-Hungarian empire after World War I; Slovakia entered into union with the Czech lands. However, resentment at centralized control from Prague led to a declaration of autonomy within a federal Czecho-Slovak state on the eve of the Nazi annexation of Czechoslovakia in 1938; this was followed by nominal independence under German protection. With the end, in 1990, of the communist regime that had controlled Czechoslovakia since 1948, Slovak demands for independence grew and the Slovak Republic (with its capital at Bratislava) came into being on 1 January 1993 without conflict. Michal Kováč was elected President and the nationalist leader Vladimir Meciar became Prime Minister. He was, however, defeated in the 1998 elections, when a coalition was formed under Mikulas Dzarinda. Meciar was also defeated in the 1999 presidential election, when Rudolf Schuster was elected, and again in 2004, by Ivan Gašparovič. Problems have been experienced in restructuring the Slovak economy, which was geared to labour-intensive heavy industry under the influence of Stalinism in the 1950s. Tensions remain between the Slovak majority and the ethnic Hungarian minority population. Slovakia joined NATO and the European Union in 2004 and adopted the euro

as its currency in 2009. Gašparovič was re-elected as President in 2009, and Andrej Kiska was elected to succeed him in 2014.

Slovenia

Capital:	Ljubljana
Area:	20,273 sq km (7827 sq miles)
Population:	1,992,690 (2005)
Currency:	1 euro = 100 cents
Religions:	Roman Catholic 57.8%; Muslim 2.4%; Eastern Orthodox 2.3%
Ethnic Groups:	Slovene 83.1%; Serb 2.0%; Croat 1.8%
Languages:	Slovenian (official); Italian, Hungarian (official in some areas); Serbo-Croat
International Organizations:	UN; OSCE; EU; NATO; Council of Europe; WTO; OECD

A small country in south-east Europe.

Physical Slovenia is bordered by Austria to the north, Hungary to the east, Italy to the west, and Croatia to the south and east. It has an outlet to the Adriatic Sea. The country is largely mountainous and wooded, with fertile valleys; there are extensive mineral and coal reserves.

Economy Industries include iron and steel, aluminium products, lead and zinc smelting, electronics, and vehicles. Slovenia also has deposits of coal and mercury. Principal agricultural crops include potatoes, hops, cereals, sugar beet, and grapes. The main exports are manufactured goods, machinery and transport equipment, chemicals, and food.

History The Slovenes are a west Slavonic people, ruled by the Habsburgs from the 14th century until 1918. After World War I the majority of the Slovene people were incorporated into the new kingdom of Serbs, Croats, and Slovenes, later *Yugoslavia. In 1941 their lands were divided between Italy, Hungary, and the *Third Reich. In 1945, 1947, and 1954, areas of the Istrian peninsula, including parts of the Free Territory of Trieste, were incorporated into the Republic of Slovenia within the Federal Republic of Yugoslavia. The most economically and educationally advanced of the Slav republics,

Slovenes are predominantly Roman Catholic, with a strong Western heritage. During 1989 pressure began to mount for independence, and a coalition of six parties, the Democratic Opposition of Slovenia (DEMOS) emerged. In May 1990 it formed a non-communist government under President Milan Kučan, and in July declared independence, confirmed by a referendum in December. There was intermittent fighting between Slovene partisans and units of the Yugoslav army during 1990, before Serbia tacitly accepted the situation. In April 1992 DEMOS split, and the Liberal Democrats under Janez Drnovsek formed a government. A series of Liberal Democrat-led coalitions ruled Slovenia until 2004, with a brief conservative interlude in 2000. After 2004 centre-right and centre-left coalitions alternated in power. In 2004 Slovenia joined NATO and the European Union and in 2007 it adopted the euro as its currency. Unpopular austerity measures led to popular protests in 2012.

Sluys, Battle of (24 June 1340) A naval battle in the *Hundred Years War. A force of French, Genoese, and Castilian ships intercepted an English force but was defeated by massed archers. Both French commanders were killed and the victory gave the English control of the English Channel.

Smith, Ian (Douglas) (1919–2007) Rhodesian statesman, Prime Minister (1964–79). He founded the White supremacist Rhodesian Front (renamed the Republican Front in 1981) in 1962, becoming Prime Minister and head of the White minority government two years later. In 1965 he issued a unilateral declaration of independence (UDI) after Britain stipulated that it would only grant the country independence if Smith undertook to prepare for Black majority rule. He eventually conceded in 1979 and resigned to make way for majority rule; after the country became the independent state of Zimbabwe he remained active in politics, leading the Republican Front until 1987.

Smith, Jedediah Strong (1798–1831) US explorer. Born in New York state, he became one of the most famous of the *Mountain Men who opened up the American north-west. In 1824 he led the third expedition organized by fur-trader William Ashley (1778–1838) into Wyoming and in subsequent years made the first west–east crossing of the Sierra by a White man. Having opened more territory than any other explorer he was killed by a group of Comanche on the Santa Fe Trail.

Smith, John (1580–1631) Founder of Virginia and promoter of colonization in America. He was born in Lincolnshire and fought against Spain and the Turks (1596–1604). As one of the governing council of Virginia in 1607, his military discipline and firmness with the Native Americans saved the settlement of Jamestown from collapse. After being burnt in an explosion, he returned to England in 1609. Five years later he explored the New England coast. His optimistic *Description of New England* (1616) was a powerful encouragement to emigration there in the 1620s and 1630s. (*See* POCAHONTAS).

Smith, Joseph (1805–44) US religious leader and founder of the Church of Jesus Christ of Latter-Day Saints (the Mormons). In 1827, according to his own account, he was led by divine revelation to find the sacred texts written by the prophet Mormon, which he later translated and published as the Book of Mormon in 1830. He founded the Mormon Church in the same year and established a large community in Illinois, of which he became mayor. He was murdered by a mob while in prison awaiting trial for conspiracy.

Smuts, Jan Christiaan (1870–1950) South African statesman and soldier, Prime Minister (1919–24; 1939–48). He led Boer forces during the Second Boer War, but afterwards supported Louis Botha's policy of Anglo-Boer cooperation and was one of the founders of the Union of South Africa. During World War I he led Allied troops against the Germans in East Africa (1916); he later attended the peace conference at Versailles in 1919 and helped to found the League of Nations. He then succeeded Botha as Prime Minister. After World War II Smuts played a leading role in the formation of the United Nations and drafted the preamble to the UN charter.

Snowden, Philip, 1st Viscount (1864–1937) British politician. Permanently crippled in a bicycle accident, he became a socialist and worked for the *Independent Labour Party as a journalist. Elected to Parliament for Blackburn in 1906, he became known for his outspoken views, opposing British intervention in World War I, and advocating self-government for India. He served as Chancellor of the Exchequer in 1924 and 1929–31, and again in 1931–32 in the *National government. He did not support the *General Strike of 1926 and his cautious approach to welfare spending alienated many Labour supporters. His 1931 budget, which reduced unemployment benefits because of the alarming international financial crisis, further antagonized them. The abandonment of *free trade under the *Ottawa Agreements caused his resignation.

Sobieski, John *See* JOHN III.

socage In Anglo-Saxon and Norman England, a free tenure of land that did not require the tenant to perform military service. He might pay a rent in cash or in kind, and perform some ploughing on his lord's estates. He was liable to pay the three feudal dues—20 shillings when the lord's son came of age and when the lord's daughter married, and one year's rent to redeem his lord from captivity. In contrast to military tenure, no restrictions attached to the inheritance of the tenure nor to the marriage of the heir.

social credit A theory advanced by the social economist Clifford *Douglas, to eliminate the concentration of economic power. It became popular in Canada and New Zealand at the time of the Great *Depression. In Canada a Social Credit Party, led by William Aberhart, won an overwhelming victory in Alberta in 1935 and remained in power until 1971 without, however, implementing many of Douglas's ideas. In 1952 it won an election in British Colombia, but never gained more than a handful of federal seats in Ottawa, and largely disappeared after 1980. A New Zealand Social Credit Party was formed in 1953 and held up to two seats in the New Zealand Parliament until 1987. The party survives as the New Zealand Democratic Party for Social Credit.

social Darwinism A 19th-century theory of social and cultural evolution. Even before Charles Darwin published the *Origin of Species* (1859), the writer Herbert *Spencer had been inspired by current ideas of evolution to write the *Principles of Psychology* (1855), where he first applied the concept of evolution to the development of society. The theory, based on the belief that natural selection favoured the most competitive or aggressive individual (the "survival of the fittest"), was often used to support political conservatism. It justified inequality among individuals and races, and discouraged attempts to reform society as an interference with the natural processes of selection of the fittest. In the 20th century it has been used to justify racist ideologies as well as to explain the operations of the "free economy".

Social Democrat A member of a political party that supports social democracy. Wilhelm Liebknecht and August Bebel in Germany first used the term in founding the German Social Democratic Labour Party (1869). In 1875 it was fused with the German Workers' Association, founded (1863) by Ferdinand Lasalle, to form the Social Democratic Party (SDP) of Germany. Other parties followed, for example in Denmark (1878), Britain (1883; Henry Hyndman's Social Democratic Federation), Norway (1887), Austria (1889), the USA (1897), and Russia (1898), where a split came in 1903 into *Bolshevik and Menshevik factions. In other countries, for example France, Italy, and Spain, the term Socialist Party was more common. The German SDP was the largest party in the Weimar Republic, governing the country until 1933, when it was banned. It was reformed in West Germany after World War II, with a new constitution (1959), ending all Marxist connections. It has entered coalitions with the Christian Democrats (1966–69; 2005–09; 2013–), and headed coalitions with the Free Democrats (1969–82) and the Greens (1998–2005). In East Germany a revived SDP campaigned for office in 1990, following the collapse of the communist regime. In Sweden the SDP, socialist and constitutional in outlook, has been the dominant party since the 1930s, although it was out of office from 1976–1982 and from 1991–1994. In Britain four prominent members of the Labour Party resigned in 1981 to form a short-lived, moderate Social Democratic Party (*see* LIBERAL DEMOCRATS).

socialism A political theory of social organization advocating limits on the private ownership of industry. The word first appeared in France and Britain in the early 19th century. It covers a wide range of positions from *communism at one extreme to **social democracy at the other. Most socialists believe that the community as a whole should own and control the means of production, distribution, and exchange to ensure a more equitable division of a nation's wealth, either in the form of state ownership of industry, or in the form of ownership by the workers themselves. They have also often advocated replacing the market economy by some kind of planned economy. The aim of these measures is to make industry socially responsible, and to bring about a much greater degree of equality in living standards. In addition, socialists have argued for provision for those in need, as in the *welfare state. Socialism as a political ideal was revolutionized by Karl *Marx in the mid-19th century, who tried to demonstrate how *capitalist profit was derived from the exploitation of the worker, and argued that a socialist society could be achieved only by a mass movement of the workers themselves.

Both the methods by which this transformation was to be achieved and the manner in which the new society was to be run remained the subject of considerable disagreement and produced a wide variety of socialist parties.

These debates have been somewhat overshadowed in recent years by the question of whether socialism is viable at all as an alternative to capitalism. Most Western socialists now opt for social democracy, others for market socialism. It is only in certain developing countries that traditional socialist aims still attract support.

Socialist League A British political organization, set up in 1884 by the designer William Morris, to re-create society on socialist principles. The League published pamphlets, but its main activity took the form of processions and demonstrations, at times resulting in clashes with police and troops. Its membership, consisting partly of moderates seeking working-class progress through parliamentary methods, but partly, also, of revolutionary socialists and *anarchists, was too miscellaneous to endure. By 1890 most moderates had joined the *Fabians, leaving only an extremist and ineffective minority.

social media Applications of information and communication technology, especially using the World Wide Web (*see* INTERNET), that allow users to interact with each other. Such applications became very popular in the 2000s and now have billions of users worldwide. Users post material—text, pictures, films—on the application that other users can access. In a simple case, a person maintains a 'blog' (an online journal or 'web log') that is available on the Web and can be freely accessed and commented on. Other applications offer more sophisticated services. Facebook, founded in 2004 and the premier social-media application of the early 21st century, allows users to specify what content is visible to all users and what is visible only to a specified set of 'friends'; Twitter, founded in 2006, involves the posting of short messages ('tweets') that are received by all users who have chosen to 'follow' the sender. The application encourages users to make new contacts, and thereby build up social networks.

Such easy mass interaction, with a worldwide community of users, is an important phenomenon, but it is too new for its consequences to be assessed with certainty. In particular, it has been suggested that social media makes it harder for a repressive state to control its citizens. Social media has been credited with an important role in the *Arab Spring, when it enabled protesters to coordinate their activities; and, more generally, with enabling ordinary people to act as sources of information not controlled by the state. In all countries the number of social-media users and the speed with which information can be exchanged make them an increasingly important body of opinion. Likewise, social media is also a useful means for organizations to disseminate information to and interact with their customers, members, etc. Maintaining a presence on Facebook and Twitter for marketing purposes is considered important by many companies. However, concerns have been raised that social media's impact can be harmful and in extreme cases there have been suicides following campaigns of online bullying. Also, there are concerns about the amount of personal information that users are content to reveal.

Society of Friends *See* QUAKERS.

Socrates (469–399 BC) Greek philosopher. His interests lay not in the speculation about the natural world engaged in by earlier philosophers but in pursuing questions of ethics. He was the centre of a circle of friends and disciples in Athens and his method of inquiry (the *Socratic method*) was based on discourse with those around him; his careful questioning was designed to reveal truth and to expose error. Although he wrote nothing himself, he was immensely influential; he is known chiefly through his disciple Plato, who recorded Socrates' dialogues and teachings in, for example, the *Symposium* and the *Phaedo*. Charged with introducing strange gods and corrupting the young, Socrates was sentenced to death and condemned to take hemlock, which he did, spurning offers to help him escape into exile.

Solemn League and Covenant (1643) The agreement between the English Parliament and Scottish *Covenanters during the *English Civil War. It undertook that the Presbyterian Church of Scotland was to be preserved, and the Anglican Church was to be reformed. The Scots soon realized that Presbyterianism would not be imposed on England by the specially established Westminster Assembly of Divines. This put considerable strain upon the other aspect of the agreement: Scottish military aid for Parliament in return for £30,000 per month.

Solferino, Battle of (24 June 1859) A battle fought in Lombardy, between the armies of France and Piedmont on one side and Austria on the other. Piedmont, under the leadership of *Cavour, had persuaded France to give military support to the struggle against Austrian domination in Italy. The French and Piedmont-Sardinians had defeated the Austrians at *Magenta, and their armies, commanded by *Napoleon III, captured the elevated position at Solferino and successfully defended it after a fierce counter-attack by the Austrians. The latter, led by *Francis Joseph, began to retreat. A meeting between the two emperors took place shortly afterwards at *Villafranca di Verona, after which hostilities ceased.

Solidarity (Polish **Solidarność**) An independent trade-union movement in Poland. It emerged after a wave of strikes at Gdańsk in 1980 organized by the Free Union of the Baltic Coast. Demands included the right to a trade union independent of Communist Party control. Under its leader Lech *Wałęsa membership rose rapidly, as Poles began to demand political as well as economic concessions. In 1981 the Prime Minister, General Jaruzelski, proclaimed martial law and arrested the Solidarity leaders, outlawing the movement in 1982. In 1989 the government, under pressure from both Left and Right, sponsored round-table talks from which Solidarity emerged as the dominant political organization. In 1990 Wałęsa was elected President of the republic; but ideological differences soon emerged and the movement broke up into a number of separate political parties, only one, a minority party, retaining the name *Solidarność*. This party led a coalition government from 1997, but split in 2001. It did not win any seats in the 2001 election.

Solomon Islands

Capital:	Honiara
Area:	28,896 sq km (11,157 sq miles)
Population:	597,248 (2013 est)
Currency:	1 Solomon Islands dollar = 100 cents
Religions:	Protestant 73.4%; Roman Catholic 19.6%; other Christian 2.9%
Ethnic Groups:	Melanesian 95.3%; Polynesian 3.1%; Micronesian 1.2%
Languages:	English (official); Melanesian pidgin; minority languages
International Organizations:	UN; Commonwealth; South Pacific Forum; Secretariat of the Pacific Community; WTO

An island country in the south-west Pacific.

Physical The Solomon Islands form a large archipelago comprising a double chain of six large and many smaller islands, lying between 5° and 13° S of the Equator. The largest island, Bougainville, together with a few others in the north-west, is part of *Papua New Guinea; all the rest constitute a country in which the most important island is Guadalcanal. Lying at the edge of the Pacific plate, the region is subject to earthquakes; and there are volcanoes on the main islands.

Economy The economy collapsed during the ethnic violence of 1998–2003, but slowly recovered after order was restored. Agriculture employs three-quarters of the workforce, the principal crops being cocoa, coconuts, palm kernels, and rice; tuna fishing and timber are also important. Timber, fish, copra, palm oil, and cocoa are exported. The Solomon islands have extensive undeveloped mineral resources, such as lead, zinc, nickel, and gold.

History After some 3000 years of occupation, European missionaries and settlers arrived throughout the 18th and 19th centuries, and in 1885 the German New Guinea Company established control of the north Solomons. Britain declared a protectorate over the southern islands in 1893. During World War II the Solomons witnessed fierce battles between Japanese and Allied forces. The Solomon Islands became an independent member of the *Commonwealth of Nations on 7 July 1978. Solomon Mamaloni (Prime Minister since 1989) faced severe criticism during 1991 for allegedly ignoring the constitution and seeking to rule without a mandate. Following an election in 1993, the independent Francis Billy Hilly became Prime Minister. His short-lived administration ended in late 1994, when Mamaloni again won power. Relations with Papua New Guinea continued to be strained. After elections in 1997 a new government was formed, with Batholomew Ulufa'alu as Prime Minister. Ethnic violence broke out on Guadalcanal in 1998 between the indigenous population and the Malaitan community (from the neighbouring island of Malaita). This escalated until 2003, when an Australian-led peacekeeping force was deployed. Peace was thereafter gradually restored, but in 2006 there were anti-government disturbances and also tensions between the government and the peacekeeping force. The latter were resolved, and in 2014 the peacekeeping force was still present.

Solon (*c.*630–*c.*560 BC) Athenian statesman and lawgiver. One of the Seven Sages listed by Plato, he is notable for his economic, constitutional, and legal reforms, begun in about 594. He revised the existing code of laws established by Draco, making them less severe; for example, he abolished the punishment of slavery for debt and reserved the death penalty for murder. His division of the citizens into four classes based on wealth rather than birth with a corresponding division of political responsibility laid the foundations of Athenian democracy.

Somalia

Capital:	Mogadishu
Area:	637,657 sq km (246,201 sq miles)
Population:	10,251,568 (2013 est)
Currency:	1 Somali shilling = 100 cents
Religions:	Sunni Muslim
Ethnic Groups:	Somali 85.0%
Languages:	Somali, Arabic (official); English; Italian
International Organizations:	UN; AU; Arab League; Non-Aligned Movement; WTO

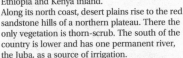

A country on the so-called 'horn' in the north-east of Africa.

Physical Somalia has north and south-east coasts on the Gulf of Aden and the Indian Ocean and borders Ethiopia and Kenya inland. Along its north coast, desert plains rise to the red sandstone hills of a northern plateau. There the only vegetation is thorn-scrub. The south of the country is lower and has one permanent river, the Juba, as a source of irrigation.

Economy One of Africa's poorest countries, Somalia has suffered from drought, flooding, famine, civil war, and high foreign debt in recent years. Agriculture, mainly nomadic pastoralism, employs over half the workforce and provides two-fifths of GDP and more than half of export earnings; principal exports are livestock, bananas, hides, and fish. There is little industry. Unexploited mineral resources include lead, gold, zircon, coal, uranium, and kyanite.

History The kingdom of Punt, mentioned in ancient Egyptian writings, probably occupied the area of Somalia's northern and eastern coastline. Muslim Arabs and Persians established trading routes in the area between the 7th and 10th centuries AD. Somali nomads had lived in the interior area from at least the 10th century AD and Galla peoples lived in the south and west of the country. After the British occupied Aden (now in Yemen) in 1839 European exploration of the region commenced. The area of the 'horn' of Africa was divided between British, French and Italian spheres of influence in the late 19th century. The modern Somali Republic is a result of the unification in 1960 of the former British Somaliland Protectorate and the Italian Trusteeship Territory of Somalia. From then onwards Somalia was involved in border disputes with Kenya and Ethiopia. In 1969 President Shermarke was assassinated in a left-wing coup and the Marxist Somali Revolutionary Socialist Party took power, renaming the country the Somali Democratic Republic under the dictatorship of General Muhammad Siyad Barrah (*c.*1911–95). There followed 21 years of one-man rule, with a sharply deteriorating economy and an escalating civil war. Fighting broke out in 1988 between government forces and rebel groups, the most important of these being the Somali National Movement (SNM). The country, already hit by drought, now descended into what has been described as the world's 'worst man-made disaster', as refugees fled the insurgents and famine and disease took their toll. Siyad Barrah fled office in January 1991, forming a breakaway grouping, the Somali National Front. The SNM proclaimed a Somaliland Republic in the north, reviving the republic that had briefly succeeded the former British Somaliland protectorate and repudiating a union with ex-Italian Somalia. It has become a stable *de facto* state, although its independence has not been recognized internationally. By mid-1992 some six million people were facing starvation, as UN troops were deployed against rival warlords throughout the country and relief agencies tried, in the face of the warlords' opposition, to alleviate the suffering. After UN peacekeeping forces, led by the USA, had failed to maintain a ceasefire, troops were withdrawn by March 1995. General Muhammad Aidid (1936–96) declared himself President in 1995, but this was not accepted by the international community. In 1996 he was killed in battle and was succeeded by his son, Hussein Aidid. Factional fighting continued despite several agreements and attempts to create a viable government. A transitional assembly was established in 2004, a President elected, and a government—the Transitional Federal Government (TFG)—

S

appointed (2005). However, these bodies were riven by faction and their authority was marginal. In 2006 violence flared up again when the Islamic Courts Union (ICU) routed rival warlords and seized Mogadishu, declaring its intention of creating a strict Islamic state. Ethiopia sent troops to assist the TFG and the ICU was expelled from Mogadishu in 2007; however, one faction, al-Shabaab, which was linked to *al-Qaeda, continued to wage a guerrilla campaign and captured towns in central and south Somalia. In 2009 the TFG was expanded to include a moderate Islamist faction and formed an alliance with other groups, including the ICU, against al-Shabaab. When the TFG's mandate expired in 2012, a provisional constitution was adopted and a parliament established with appointed members. This body elected Hassan Sheikh Mohamud as President of the Federal Government of Somalia. With international help the areas under government control gradually expanded as al-Shabaab was driven back.

Somerset, Edward Seymour, 1st Earl of Hertford and Duke of (c.1500–52) Protector of England and effective ruler of England on behalf of *Edward VI (1547–49). On the death of *Henry VIII in 1547 Edward Seymour (brother of Jane *Seymour) took the titles of Duke of Somerset and Lord Protector and won an immediate military success against Scotland at the Battle of Pinkie. His attempts to enforce the use of a Protestant English Prayer Book by Act of Uniformity (1549) sparked off the Western Rising. *Kett's Rebellion, coinciding with discontent among magnates grouped around his rival, the Earl of Warwick (later the Duke of *Northumberland), led to his downfall. He was overthrown in 1549 and executed on the orders of Northumberland in 1551.

Somme, Battle of the (July–November 1916) A major battle fought between British and German forces in northern France during World War I. The battle was planned by *Joffre and *Haig. Before it began the Germans attacked *Verdun, the defence of which nearly destroyed the French army. To relieve pressure on Verdun the brunt of the Somme offensive fell on the British. On 1 July the British advanced from their trenches almost shoulder to shoulder, presenting a perfect target for German machine gunners. The Germans fell back on the Hindenburg Line defences (a barrier of concrete pillboxes armed with machine guns; see SIEGFRIED LINE), while for the loss of some 600,000 men the Allies had gained a few kilometres of mud.

Somoza A family dynasty that dominated *Nicaragua from the 1930s until 1979. **Anastasio Somoza García** (1896–1956) engineered a successful coup against the liberal regime and took over the presidency in 1936, exercising dictatorial control until his assassination in 1956. Somoza family rule continued under his sons **Luis** and **Anastasio ('Tachito') Somoza Debayle** (1956–63, 1967–79, respectively). The Somozas used the National Guard to eliminate political opposition while they accumulated vast amounts of Nicaragua's agrarian and industrial resources. Military and economic assistance from the USA helped maintain the Somozas in power until 1979, when economic problems and world outcry against human rights abuses undermined Tachito's control and the Sandinista National Liberation Front took power.

Song (or **Sung**) A dynasty of Chinese emperors ruling from 960 to 1279, between the Tang and Yuan periods. During the Song Dynasty art and literature flourished and paper money was invented.

Songhay (or **Songhai, Songhoi**) A former West African empire on the Niger River and the name of the people and their language, which is spoken in Mali. Tradition claims that a Berber Christian, al-Yaman, founded Songhay in the 7th century AD on Kukiya Island, below Gao. The rulers became Muslim (c.1200) and transferred the capital to Gao. In 1325 the *Mali empire annexed Songhay, but in 1335 Sonni Ali Kolon, a descendant of al-Yaman made himself king. In about 1464 *Sonni Ali made Songhay independent and enlarged it greatly. However, his son, Bakari, was a weakling, and with him the line of al-Yaman failed. In 1493 the new dynasty founded by *Askia Muhammad I replaced him; he made Songhay the most important empire in western Africa, eclipsing Mali. In 1528 or 1529 Askia Muhammad was deposed by his son. He, and the seven other Askias who followed, were weak, cruel, and debauched, and the empire foundered. In 1591 it fell easy prey to a well disciplined and well armed force of Moroccans who defeated the Songhay army at Tondibi, near Gao. However, they could not control such a large area, and in the 17th century it broke up into a number of smaller states.

Sonni Ali (or **Ali-Ber, Ali the Great**) (died 1492) Ruler of *Songhay from 1464 or 1465, and the real founder of the Songhay empire. He made Songhay independent and then enlarged its boundaries. In 1469 he took Timbuktu, and in 1473 Jenné. Timbuktu chroniclers describe him as cruel, irreligious, and of immoral habits, and report that he persecuted men of religion, despite pretending to be a Muslim. He died by drowning, and was succeeded by his son Bakari, the last of his line.

Sons of Liberty American Revolutionary groups that sprang up in Massachusetts and New York in 1765 to organize colonial opposition to the *Stamp Act. In both colonies, serious riots, propaganda, and boycotts effectively nullified the measure. The organization then spread to other colonies and reactions to English "tyranny" were synchronized by committees of correspondence. Sons of Liberty were later responsible for the *Boston Tea Party (1773), the radicalization of the *Continental Congress (1774), and the tarring and feathering of pro-British loyalists.

Sophia (1630–1714) Electress of Hanover (1658–1714). The twelfth child of the Elector Frederick of the Palatinate and Elizabeth, daughter of *James I, she married Ernest Augustus of Brunswick-Lüneburg, who became Elector of Hanover. By the Act of *Settlement (1701), as the only surviving Protestant descendant of the *Stuarts, she was named as *Anne's successor on the British throne. She died a few weeks before Anne and her son became King *George I, the first Hanoverian king of England and Scotland. She was a cultured woman with a great interest in English affairs.

sophists (Greek *sophistēs*, "wise man") Itinerant professional teachers in Greece, the Greek colonies in Sicily, and southern Italy in the 5th century BC. Sophists offered instruction in a wide range of subjects and skills considered necessary for public life, especially rhetoric, in return for fees. Gorgias of Leontini (*c.*483–376 BC) specialized in teaching rhetoric, and his visit to Athens in 427 BC encouraged the development of oratory there. Young Athenian democrats needed rhetoric to persuade the democratic assemblies. By questioning the nature of gods, conventions, and morals, and by their alleged ability to train men "to make the weaker argument the stronger" through rhetoric, they aroused some opposition. Their readiness to argue either cause in a dispute brought them condemnation from Plato as self-interested imitators of wisdom lacking any concern for the truth. However, the most renowned sophists, such as Gorgias and Protagoras (*c.*485–415 BC) drew relativist or sceptical conclusions from the defensibility of opposed claims, indicating a seriousness of purpose that Plato failed to acknowledge.

During the Roman empire sophists were essentially teachers of rhetoric. The word sophistry, meaning quibbling or fallacious reasoning, reflects both Plato's view and the popular distrust of sophists.

SORT *See* STRATEGIC ARMS REDUCTION TALKS.

Sousa, Martim Afonso de (1500–64) Portuguese colonist, leader of an exploratory expedition to southern Brazil (1531–33). In 1532 he established the first permanent Portuguese colony in Brazil at São Vicente (near present-day Santos), where he introduced sugar cane. In his efforts to expel French intruders and to find precious metals he explored the coast south from Rio de Janeiro to the Rio de la Plata. In 1534 he was granted the hereditary captaincy of São Vicente but he never returned to Brazil, and later served as governor of India and as a member of the Council of State in Lisbon.

South Africa

Capital:	Pretoria (executive); Bloemfontein (judicial); Cape Town (legislative)
Area:	1,219,090 sq km (470,693 sq miles)
Population:	48,601,098 (2005)
Currency:	1 rand = 100 cents
Religions:	Protestant 36.6%; Roman Catholic 7.1%; other Christian 36.0%
Ethnic Groups:	Black African 79.2%; White 8.9%; Coloured 8.9%
Languages:	isiZulu, isiXhosa, Afrikaans, English, Sepedi, Setswana, Sesotho, Xitsonga, siSwati, Tshivenda, isiNdebele (all official)
International Organizations:	UN; AU; Commonwealth; SADC; Non-Aligned Movement; WTO

A country occupying most of the southern part of the African continent.

Physical The northern part of the country is bounded by Namibia, Botswana, Zimbabwe, Swaziland, and Mozambique. Southward, the Orange Free State region partly surrounds Lesotho, which forms an enclave. In the east are boundaries with Mozambique, Swaziland, and Lesotho. From Cape Agulhas in the extreme south to the Limpopo River in the extreme north-east is a distance of about 1600 km (1000 miles). Two great rivers, the Orange and its tributary the Vaal, traverse the country from the Drakensberg Mountains in the east to the Atlantic in the west, while many shorter rivers run south and east into the Indian Ocean. There are rolling grasslands, or veld, and deserts.

Economy The country has a wealth of minerals, including diamonds, gold, platinum, chromium, iron ore, lime, uranium, and coal. There are also reserves of natural gas. Gold, other metal products, and diamonds are the chief exports. Industry is highly developed, and includes mining, metals and metalworking, vehicles, machinery, textiles, chemicals, and foodstuffs. Agriculture is vulnerable to droughts; the main crops are cereals, sugar cane, and fruit, and livestock raising is also important. About one-third of the population, mostly Black South Africans, live in poverty and one-quarter are unemployed.

History South Africa was occupied by the San (Bushmen) and Khoikhoin (Hottentots) about 10,000 years ago. Bantu-speaking peoples had moved into the area and developed mining industries, trading along the east coast of Africa, by the time European exploration began in the 15th century. A Dutch colony was established in 1652; the settlers were at first known as *Boers and later as Afrikaners. At first the San and Khoikhoin associated and intermarried with the Boers, but later the Khoikhoin were displaced by the Boers and forced to become labourers on their farms. The San withdrew into mountainous areas. Some Boers known as *trekboers*, moved inland and encountered the Xhosa people, who had a settled, agricultural society. By the end of the 18th century frontier wars had broken out between the Xhosa and the Boers (the *Xhosa Wars).

Britain established a colony in 1806 and fought with the Bantu-speaking peoples. In the 1830s large numbers of Boers moved northwards in the *Great Trek. The Boers refused to form a federation with the British, leading to the *Boer Wars. The republics of Transvaal and Orange Free State were defeated by the British and were united with the British colonies of Cape and Natal in 1910 to form the Union of South Africa, a self-governing *dominion of the British crown. Politically dominated by its small White minority, South Africa supported Britain in the two World Wars, its troops fighting on a number

of fronts. After 1948 the right-wing Afrikaner-dominated National Party formed a government. It instituted a strict system of *apartheid, intensifying discrimination against the disenfranchised non-White majority. This policy entailed brutal repression of dissent (*see* SHARPEVILLE MASSACRE).

South Africa became a republic (1960) and left the Commonwealth (1961); the *African National Congress was banned and its leaders, including Nelson *Mandela, imprisoned. Although its economic strength allowed it to dominate the southern half of the continent, the rise of Black nationalism both at home and in the surrounding countries (including the former mandated territory of *Namibia) produced increasing violence and emphasized South Africa's isolation in the diplomatic world. In 1985 the regime of P. W. Botha began to make some attempts to ease tension by interpreting apartheid in a more liberal fashion. This failed, however, to satisfy either the increasingly militant non-White population or the extremist right-wing groups within the small White élite. In 1986 a state of emergency was proclaimed and several thousands imprisoned without trial. The domestic and international sides of the problem remained inseparable, with South African troops fighting against *SWAPO guerrillas in Namibia and Angola, and support by surrounding states for the forces of the outlawed African National Congress producing a series of cross-border incidents. In 1988 the US Congress voted to support the 'Front Line' African states in their demand for international sanctions. President Botha retired in 1989 and his successor President *de Klerk began the quest for racial reconciliation. Following the repeal of apartheid legislation in July 1990 sanctions were eased and South Africa re-admitted to international sport. In December 1991 delegations from the government, the National Party, the Democratic Party, the South African Communist Party, ANC, Inkatha, and from the Indian and Coloured communities, joined to form the Convention for a Democratic South Africa (CODESA). Its deliberations through 1992 were interrupted by a number of violent racial incidents, and it was fiercely attacked by the neofascist Afrikaner Resistance Movement. The government was replaced in 1993 by a multiparty Transitional Executive Council. The country's first multiracial elections were held in 1994, with the ANC emerging as clear victors. Nelson Mandela became President and de Klerk Deputy President, leading a coalition government of national unity. The same year, South Africa was admitted to the Organization of

African Unity (now the *African Union) and re-joined the Commonwealth. In 1996 a permanent multiracial democratic constitution was adopted. De Klerk and the National Party withdrew from the coalition government in order to form the official opposition. Mandela retired in 1999; in the same year the ANC won the elections and Thabo Mbeki became President. The ANC increased its majority in the 2004 elections. Mbeki resigned as President in 2008 at the request of the ANC, having lost the party leadership to Jacob *Zuma in 2007. The ANC maintained its dominance in the 2009 elections, after which Zuma became President.

South America The southern half of the American land mass, connected to North America by the Isthmus of Panama, bordered by the Atlantic Ocean to the east and the Pacific Ocean to the west. *Amerindian civilizations in South America included that of the *Chavin and the *Incas, who flourished before Europeans arrived. Colonized largely by the Spanish in the 16th century (although the British, Dutch, and Portuguese were particularly active in the north-east), much of the continent remained part of Spain's overseas empire until liberated under the leadership of Bolivar and San Martin in the 1820s. Both culturally and ethnically the continent is now a mixture of indigenous Indian and imported Hispanic influences, modified slightly by North European and North American penetration in the 19th and 20th centuries. Although many South American countries are still hampered by economic underdevelopment, a minority have emerged as world industrial powers in their own right.

South-East Asia Treaty Organization (SEATO) A defence alliance established in 1954 for countries of south-east Asia and part of the south-west Pacific, to further a US policy of containment of Communism. Its members were Australia, Britain, France, New Zealand, Pakistan, the Philippines, Thailand, and the US. The organization was dissolved in 1977.

South Korea *See* KOREA, SOUTH.

South Sea Bubble An English financial disaster in which the South Sea Company took over most of the National Debt in 1720 and needed a rise in the value of the shares of the Company. This was achieved not by past trading profits, but by rumours of future ones. Some politicians and even members of the court were bribed with cheap or free South Sea Company shares to promote the company's interests. The shares increased ten-fold in value, and expectations of high dividends rose accordingly. When confidence collapsed, the South Sea Company's shares fell to less than 10% of their peak value, and thousands of investors were ruined. Sir Robert *Walpole began his long period of office by saving the company and restoring financial stability.

South Sudan

South America. (*c.*1910) Investment, exports, and imports.

Capital:	Juba
Area:	644,329 sq km (248,777 sq miles)
Population:	11,090,104 (2013 est)
Currency:	1 Sudanese pound = 100 piastres
Religions:	traditional beliefs; Christian
Ethnic Groups:	Dinka 35.8%; Nuer 15.6%; minority groups
Languages:	English (official); Arabic; Dinka; Nuer; minority languages
International Organizations:	UN; AU

A country in north-east Africa, bordered by the Sudan, Ethiopia, Kenya, Uganda, the Democratic Republic of the Congo, and the Central African Republic.

Physical South Sudan is bisected by the White Nile, which forms the Sudd swamp—over 100,000 sq km in area—in the centre of the country. There are uplands on both sides on the river plain; these rise to significant mountains on the Ugandan border.

Economy South Sudan is poor and underdeveloped following decades of civil conflict when it was part of *Sudan. Subsistence agriculture occupies most of the population, with about half living in poverty. Principal crops include sorghum, maize, rice, millet, and wheat. The only significant industry is the production and export of crude oil, which provides almost all the government's revenue. South Sudan has not yet recovered from the suspension of oil production in 2012.

History South Sudan came into existence in 2011 after the ten southern provinces of *Sudan voted in a referendum to secede. This had been provided for in the peace agreement of 2005 that ended the Sudanese civil war between the Arabic Muslim north and the African Christian south, and the new state was immediately recognized. Its subsequent history has been turbulent. The previous regional government under President Salva Kiir Mayardit became the government of the new state and was not universally accepted. These political differences combined with ethnic tensions to produce a state of endemic violence in much of the new country. A number of disputes with Sudan remained unresolved, including the precise line of the border and how to share oil revenues, and these led to armed clashes. Oil production was shut down in 2012 for over a year following a dispute with Sudan over trans-shipment fees (all of South Sudan's oil is exported via a pipeline to Port Sudan). At the end of 2013 a power struggle between President Kiir and a former Vice-President, Riek Machar, led to ethnic fighting between Dinka and Nuer that killed several thousand people and displaced over a million. Peace talks began in 2014.

South Vietnam *See* VIETNAM.

South-West Africa *See* NAMIBIA.

South West Africa People's Organization *See* SWAPO.

South Yemen A former country on the south-west Arabian peninsula. It declared its independence in 1967 and, after long negotiations, amalgamated in 1989 with the Yemen Arab Republic to form *Yemen.

Souvanna Phouma, Prince (1901–84) Laotian statesman. A member of the post-war provisional government (1945–46), he opposed French recolonization and was elected Premier in 1951. During his first premiership (1951–54) civil war broke out between the government and the communist-led *Pathet Lao movement. He formed a brief coalition (1962–63) with the Pathet Lao (led by his half-brother, Prince Souphanouvong) and after the return of civil war, he continued as Premier. Although he tried to maintain a neutral policy during the Vietnam war, this proved impossible. In 1973 he signed a ceasefire agreement with the Pathet Lao and remained Premier until the People's Democratic Republic of Laos was declared in 1975.

Soviet (Russian, 'council') An elected governing council in the former Soviet Union. Russian Soviets gained their revolutionary connotation in 1905, when the St Petersburg Soviet of Workers' Deputies was formed to coordinate strikes and other anti-government activities in factories. Each factory sent its delegates, and for a time other cities were dominated by Soviets. Both *Bolsheviks and Mensheviks realized the potential importance of Soviets and duly appointed delegates. In 1917 a Soviet modelled on that of 1905, but now including deserting soldiers, was formed in Petrograd (previously St Petersburg), sufficiently powerful to dictate industrial action and to control the use of armed force. It did not at first try to overthrow *Kerensky's Provisional Government but grew increasingly powerful in its opposition to continuing Russian participation in World War I. Consisting of between 2000 and 3000 members, it was controlled by a powerful executive committee. Soviets were established in the provinces and in June 1917 the first All Russia Congress of Soviets met. The Bolsheviks gradually dominated policy, leading to their seizure of power in the *Russian Revolution (1917). During the *Russian Civil War village Soviets controlling local affairs and agriculture were common. The national Soviet was called the Supreme Soviet, comprising delegates from all the Soviet republics.

Soviet Union (official name **Union of Soviet Socialist Republics**) A former federation of 15 republics occupying the northern half of Asia and part of Eastern Europe, comprising Russia, Belorussia (Belarus), Ukraine, the Baltic States (Estonia, Latvia, and Lithuania), Georgia, Armenia, Moldova (Moldavia), Azerbaijan,

Kazakhstan, Kirghizia, Turkmenistan, Tajikistan, and Uzbekistan. Created as a Communist state after the 1917 revolution, the Soviet Union was the largest country in the world. Its agricultural and industrial production were increased, often by brutal means, until the devastation caused by World War II. In the postwar era it emerged as one of the two antagonistic superpowers, rivalling the USA, in the polarization of the Communist and non-Communist worlds. Attempts to reform its centrally planned economy during the 1980s led to a rise in nationalist feeling and unrest in the republics and some began to secede from the Union, which was finally dissolved in 1991.

Soweto A predominantly Black urban area, south-west of Johannesburg in South Africa. In January 1976 Black schoolchildren demonstrated against legislation proposing to make Afrikaans the compulsory language of instruction, and police broke up the demonstration, using guns and tear gas. This triggered off a wave of violence; by the end of 1976 some 500 Blacks and Coloureds, many of them children, had been killed by the police. The plans for compulsory teaching in Afrikaans were dropped. Thereafter, until the multiracial elections of 1994 that ended White minority rule, the anniversary of the demonstration was marked by further unrest.

Spaak, Paul-Henri (1899–1972) Belgian statesman. Entering Parliament as a socialist in 1932, he was Prime Minister (1938–39; 1947–49) and became the first President of the *United Nations General Assembly and of the consultative assembly of the *Council of Europe (1949–51). A firm supporter of a united Europe, he put forward proposals that formed the basis of the *European Economic Community.

space exploration In 1903 the Russian physicist Konstantin Tsiolkovsky was developing ideas for space rockets fuelled by liquefied gas and by 1926 Robert Goddard in the USA had successfully designed the first liquid-fuelled rocket. There followed considerable German research into rockets, culminating in the launch of the V-2 rocket in 1944. In 1957 the Soviet Union surprised the USA by putting the first artificial satellite, Sputnik I, in orbit; this was followed by the US Explorer I in 1958. Yuri Gagarin was the first man in space in 1961, followed by John Glenn in 1962. In 1961 President *Kennedy proposed the *Apollo programme to achieve a manned lunar landing by 1970, and in 1969 Neil Armstrong and Edwin ('Buzz') Aldrin landed on the Moon. The Soviet Union concentrated on unmanned flights, Luna

IX achieving a soft landing on the Moon in 1966. In the early 1970s space stations were launched by both the USA and the Soviet Union, and in 1975 an Apollo capsule linked up with a Soviet Soyuz capsule. Unmanned flights have been made to Venus and Mars, while the US probe, Voyager 2, launched in 1977, reached Neptune in 1989. Its companion, Voyager 1, also launched in 1977, studied Jupiter (1979) and Saturn (1980); it was still functioning in 2013, when it became the first artificial object to leave the Solar System and enter interstellar space. In 1981 the USA launched a space shuttle, the first reusable spacecraft. The shuttle fleet remained in use until 2011, although its commercial and scientific programme was twice interrupted (1986–88; 2003–05) following the loss of, respectively, the shuttles *Challenger* on lift-off and *Columbia* while returning to Earth. In 1986 the giant Soviet modular space station, Mir, was launched, with astronauts being ferried to the station by Soyuz spacecraft; this was followed in 1987 by the placing in space of the powerful Energiya station. The Hubble space telescope, which can produce images of other solar systems, was launched from a US shuttle in 1990. Its faulty mirror limited observations until it was repaired by astronauts in the space shuttle *Endeavour* in 1993. Construction of an international space station, conceived by the USA in 1984, began in 1998 and it has been crewed continuously since 2000. Space technology has resulted in numerous applications: telecommunication satellites have greatly improved global communications, meteorological satellites provide advance weather information, positioning satellites allow precise navigation, and reconnaissance satellites register the Earth's resources and military information.

Spain

Capital:	Madrid
Area:	505,370 sq km (195,124 sq miles)
Population:	47,370,542 (20013 est)
Currency:	1 euro = 100 cents
Religions:	Roman Catholic 94.0%
Ethnic Groups:	Spanish; Catalan; Galician; Basque; Aragonese
Languages:	Spanish (Castilian) (official); Catalan, Galician, Basque (all official in some areas)
International Organizations:	UN; EU; NATO; OECD; Council of Europe; OSCE; WTO

A country occupying most of the Iberian Peninsula in south-west Europe.

Physical Spain is bounded by France across the Pyrenees in the north-east and by Portugal on the west of the plateau, the Meseta, on which most of Spain lies. It has a rugged northern coast on the Atlantic Ocean and a gentler one on the Mediterranean Sea, where the Balearic Islands are found. In the Cantabrian Mountains to the north, iron ore is mined; and from here the Ebro flows eastward into Catalonia. Across the centre the Tagus runs westward to Portugal, while in the south the Guadalquivir flows through the broad valley of Seville. Andalusia and the southern coastal plains are famous for their terraced vineyards, above which rises the Sierra Nevada.

Economy Spain has a broadly based manufacturing sector; exports include machinery, vehicles, pharmaceuticals, medicines, and other consumer goods. Tourism makes a substantial contribution to the economy. Agriculture concentrates on grains, vegetables, fruit, and livestock raising. Mineral resources include iron ore, zinc, and lead.

History Spain has been inhabited for at least 20,000 years, and supported at least two early cultures. Celtic peoples began to migrate into Spain during the 9th century BC. Spain began to come under Roman control after 206 BC, after a period of Carthaginian domination. Roman rule was followed, after 415 AD, by that of the *Visigoths, who were themselves toppled by Muslim invaders from Morocco (711–18). Moorish Spain reached its zenith under the *Umayyad dynasty of al-Andalus (736–1031). During the subsequent political fragmentation, Christian kingdoms became consolidated where Muslim power was weakest, in the north: Aragon and Castile were the most significant of these. By 1248 Christian reconquest had been so successful that only Granada remained in Muslim hands. *Ferdinand II of Aragon and *Isabella I of Castile united their respective kingdoms in 1479, reconquered Granada in 1492, and went on to establish unified Spain as a power of European and world significance. (*See* SPANISH NETHERLANDS.) Under their rule the vast *Spanish empire overseas began to take shape, and under their 16th-century successors, *Charles V and *Philip II, Spain enjoyed its 'golden age'. Decline set in during the 17th century, the end of Habsburg rule came in 1700 when Philip V became the first Bourbon monarch. The accession of Philip V led to the War of the *Spanish Succession (1701–14), in which Spain lost many of its lands in Europe. In 1704 Gibraltar was captured by the British and formally ceded to Britain by the Treaty of Utrecht (1713). Spain has made many claims to have Gibraltar returned and there has been continued friction with Britain over the issue.

In the early 19th century Spain suffered as a result of the *Napoleonic Wars and briefly came under French control (1808–14). This defeat encouraged revolution in South America, resulting in the *Spanish–South American Wars of Independence, which led to the emergence as independent countries of Argentina, Bolivia, Peru, Venezuela, and Mexico. Spain subsequently remained peripheral and undeveloped in a Europe which was fast becoming industrialized. From 1814 the absolutist monarchy was involved in a struggle with the forces of liberalism, and from 1873–1875 there was a brief republican interlude. In 1898 the Spanish–American War resulted in the loss of Puerto Rico, the Philippines, and Guam, while Cuba, which had been more or less in revolt since 1868, became a US protectorate in 1903. In 1923 General Miguel *Primo de Rivera established a virtual dictatorship, which was followed by another republican interlude (1931–39), scarred by the savage *Spanish Civil War (1936–39). Nationalist victory resulted in the dictatorship of General Francisco *Franco (1939–75). His gradual liberalization of government during the late 1960s was continued by his successor Juan Carlos I, who established a democratic constitutional monarchy. Separatist agitation, often violent, by ETA, an organization seeking independence for the Basque provinces, continued throughout the period. Of its remaining colonies Spain granted independence to Spanish Sahara in 1976, which was divided between Morocco and Mauritania. King Juan Carlos survived attempted military coups in 1978 and 1981, and from 1982 a series of stable, left-of-centre governments were established under Prime Minister Felipe González. Spain joined the EC in 1986. Pressure for greater Catalan autonomy continued. González was defeated in elections in 1996 but the winning right-wing Popular Party gained no overall majority and formed a coalition government, led by José María Aznar. It was re-elected with a large majority in 2000. Spain adopted the *euro as its currency in 2002. Following an *al-Qaeda bomb attack in Madrid in March 2004, the Popular Party was defeated by the Socialists under José Luis Rodríguez Zapatero. By the time the Socialists were re-elected in 2008, Spain's economic outlook was worsening, and the *Credit Crunch precipitated a crisis: a property price bubble collapsed and the government had to support the weakened banking sector. The consequent rise in the public deficit led the global financial markets to reduce Spain's credit rating, and the government reacted with austerity measures. These failed to convince the markets while pushing Spain into a severe recession. There were extensive popular demonstrations in 2011 and the Socialists were heavily defeated in the general election by the Popular Party; Mariano Rajoy became Prime Minister. The new government intensified the austerity programme, but continued economic difficulties led to a loss of confidence in 2012 and Spain was unable to finance its deficit by borrowing on the global markets. A €100-million loan was negotiated with the EU to support the banking sector in return for banking reform (*see* EURO-ZONE CRISIS). Although the markets responded favourably and the crisis passed, the recession continued. In June 2014 Juan Carlos abdicated in favour of his son, who became King Felipe VI.

Spanish–American War (1898) A conflict between Spain and the USA. It had its roots in the struggle for independence of *Cuba, and in US economic and imperialist ambitions. Sympathetic to Cuban rebels whose second war of independence against Spain had begun in 1895, the USA used the mysterious blowing up of its battleship, the *Maine*, in Havana harbour as a pretext for declaring war. The Spanish navy suffered serious defeats in Cuba and the Philippines, and a US expeditionary force (which included the future President Theodore *Roosevelt and his *Rough Riders) defeated Spanish ground forces in Cuba and in Puerto Rico. Spain surrendered at the end of 1898, Puerto Rico being ceded to the USA and Cuba placed under US protection. The Pacific island of Guam was also ceded while the Philippines were bought by the USA for $20 million. The war signalled the emergence of the USA as an important world power as well as the dominant power in the Caribbean.

Spanish Armada A large naval and military force that *Philip II of Spain sent to invade England at the end of May 1588. It consisted of 130 ships, carrying about 8000 sailors and 19,000 infantrymen, under the command of the inexperienced Duke of *Medina Sidonia. The Spanish fleet was delayed by a storm off Corunna, and was first sighted by the English naval commanders on 19 July, then harassed by them with long-range guns, until it anchored off Calais. Unable to liaise with an additional force from the Low Countries led by *Farnese, its formation was wrecked by English fireships during the night and as it tried to escape it suffered a further pounding from the English fleet before a strong wind drove the remaining vessels into the North Sea and they were forced to make their way back to Spain round the north of Scotland and the west of Ireland. Barely half the original Armada returned to port.

Spanish Civil War (1936–39) A military struggle between left- and right-wing elements in Spain. After the fall of *Primo de Rivera in 1930 and the eclipse of the Spanish monarchy in 1931, Spain was split. On the one hand were such politically powerful groups as the monarchists and the *Falange, on the other were the Republicans, the Catalan and Basque separatists, socialists, communists, and anarchists. The elections of February 1936 gave power to a left-wing *Popular Front government, causing strikes, riots, and military plots. In July 1936 the generals José Sanjurjo and Francisco *Franco in Spanish Morocco led an unsuccessful coup against the republic, and civil war began. In 1937 Franco's Nationalists overran the Basque region, which supported the Republicans in the hope of ultimate independence. Franco then divided the Republican forces by conquering territory between Barcelona and Valencia (1938). The Republicans, weakened by internal intrigues and by the withdrawal of Soviet support, attempted a desperate counter-attack. It failed, and Barcelona fell to Franco (January 1939), quickly followed by Madrid. Franco became the head of the Spanish state and the Falange was made the sole legal party. The civil war inspired international support on both sides: the Soviet Union gave military supplies to the Republicans, while Italy and Germany supplied men to the Nationalists. Bombing of civilians by German pilots and the destruction of the Basque town of Guernica (1937) became the symbol of fascist ruthlessness and inspired one of Picasso's most famous paintings. As members of the *International Brigades, left-wing and communist volunteers from many countries fought for the Republican cause. The war cost about 750,000 Spanish lives.

Spanish empire The overseas territories which came under Spanish control from the late 15th century onwards. They included the Canaries, most of the West Indian islands, the whole of central America, large stretches of South America, and the Philippines. Christopher *Columbus laid the foundations of the empire with his four voyages (1492–1504) in search of a western route to the Orient. Then the *conquistadores followed, colonizing by force in *Mexico, *Peru, and elsewhere in the New World. As the wealth of these lands became apparent, private enterprise gradually gave way to direct rule by Spain. The gold and silver from the New World made 16th-century Spain the richest country in Europe, under Emperor Charles V. The colonies themselves were eventually divided into viceroyalties: New Spain (1535), Peru (1569), *New Granada (1717), and Rio de la Plata (1776). The Spanish empire ended in the first quarter of the 19th century with the *Spanish–South American War of Independence.

Spanish Inquisition A council authorized by Pope Sixtus IV in 1478 and organized under the Catholic monarchs *Ferdinand II and *Isabella I of Spain to combat heresy. Its main targets were converted Jews and Muslims, but it was also used against *witchcraft and against political enemies. The first Grand Inquisitor was *Torquemada. Its methods included the use of torture, confiscation, and burning at *autos-da-fé*. It ordered the expulsion of the Jews in 1492, the attack on the Moriscos (Muslims living in Spain who were baptized Christians but retained Islamic practices) in 1502, and, after the *Reformation attacked all forms of Protestantism. In the 16th century there were 14 Spanish branches and its jurisdiction was extended to the colonies of the New World, including Mexico and Peru, and to the Netherlands and Sicily. Its activities were enlarged in the reign of *Philip II, who favoured it as a *Counter-Reformation weapon. It was suppressed and finally abolished in the 19th century.

Spanish Netherlands The southern provinces of the Netherlands ceded to *Philip II of Spain in the Union of Arras (1579), during the Dutch Revolts. These lands originally included modern Belgium, Luxembourg, part of northern France, and what later became part of the United Provinces of the Netherlands. Although Philip II still intended to re-subjugate the rebellious northern provinces, he granted the sovereignty of the Spanish Netherlands to his daughter Isabella and her husband the Archduke Albert (1598). During the Twelve-Year Truce (1609–21) and the unsuccessful war against the United Provinces (1621–48), the region enjoyed only nominal independence from Spain. A great deal of territory was lost to *Louis XIV of France during the wars of the 17th century, including Artois and part of Flanders. On

the expiry of the Spanish Habsburg dynasty in 1700, the region came under French rule until 1706, when it was occupied by the British and Dutch. By the Peace of *Utrecht (1713) it passed under the sovereignty of the Austrian Habsburg Holy Roman Emperors.

Spanish–South American Wars of Independence (1810–25). The roots of the wars of independence are to be found in the attempts made by Spain after 1765 to re-establish imperial control over its American colonies (*see* SPANISH EMPIRE). This was resented by the Creoles (colonial descendants of Spanish settlers), whose political authority, economic prosperity, and sense of national identity were threatened. Creoles in Spanish America achieved *de facto* economic independence, and with the abdication of *Ferdinand VII (1808), political independence. In 1811 the first declarations of independence were made. Initially the movements were hampered by a counter-revolutionary drive by Spanish royalists. In 1816 Simón *Bolívar returned to Venezuela from exile and united with José Antonio Páez and the Ilaneros (plainsmen) of the interior. With the assistance of British mercenaries Bolívar crossed the Andes and won the battle of Boyacá, and proclaimed the United States of *Colombia (1819). The victories of Carabobo (1821) and Pichincha (1822) brought Venezuela and Ecuador into the Colombian Federation. Bolívar then linked up with the independence movement in the south under the leadership of *San Martín, who had crossed the Andes from the United Provinces of La Plata (Argentina) and won the battles of Chabuco (1817) and Maipo (1818) and liberated Chile. Both movements now closed in on the bastion of the Spanish empire, Peru. The battles of Junin and Ayacucho (1824) were the final victories in the liberation of the continent.

Spanish Succession, War of the (1701–13) A conflict that arose on the death of the childless Charles II of Spain in 1700. One of his sisters had married *Louis XIV, the other Emperor Leopold, so both the French *Bourbons and the Austrian *Habsburgs claimed the right to rule the Spanish empire, which included the southern Netherlands, Milan, Naples, and most of Central and South America. Before Charles II's death *William III took a leading part in negotiations to pre-empt the crisis, and a partition treaty was signed (1698) between *Louis XIV and William, that Spain and its possessions would be shared out between France, Austria, and Joseph Ferdinand, the 7-year old Elector of

Bavaria, grandson of Leopold. Charles II meanwhile left all of Spain's empire to Joseph Ferdinand. When he died, Louis and William signed a second partition (1699). However, Charles II left a will bequeathing his whole empire to Louis XIV's second grandson, the future Philip V. Louis accepted this will and, instead of allaying European fears of French domination, intervened in Spanish affairs, seized the Dutch barrier fortresses, recognized *James II's son as King of England, and refused to make it impossible for Philip also to inherit the French throne.

In 1701 William III formed a grand alliance of the English and Dutch with the Austrian emperor and most of the German princes to put the rival Austrian candidate, the Archduke Charles, on the throne; Savoy and Portugal later joined the alliance. William died in 1702 and the war therefore became Queen Anne's War. Fighting took place in the Netherlands, Italy, Germany, and Spain. France's only allies were Bavaria and the people of Castile, who supported Philip V while Catalonia declared for the Archduke Charles. *Marlborough and Eugène of Savoy won a series of brilliant victories, including *Blenheim. France was invaded in 1709 and the allies were stronger at sea, taking Gibraltar, in 1704. The war came to an end because Castile would not abandon Philip V and when Marlborough fell from power the new Tory government in England began the negotiations, which led to the Peace of *Utrecht (1713).

Sparta (Greek **Spartē**) A city in the southern Peloponnese in Greece. In ancient Greece, Sparta was a powerful city-state, capital of the state of Laconia. Invading Dorian Greeks occupied Laconia c.950 BC, and by about 700 BC the Spartans had emerged as the dominant element among them, with a large slave class of helots working on the land. Sparta had also, in the late 8th century, defeated and annexed the territory of Messenia, its western neighbour, reducing its population to helotry and dividing its land among the full Spartiate citizens. The stark austerity, militarism, and discipline of Spartan society were traditionally ascribed to a single great legislator, Lycurgus, variously dated c.900 and c.700 BC; it is likeliest that the fully developed Spartan system took shape somewhere between 700 and 600 BC.

From the 6th century, Sparta became the hub of an alliance comprising most of Peloponnesian and Isthmian states except its traditional rival, Argos; but many of these allies in the 'Peloponnesian League' were little more than puppets of Sparta. Sparta led the successful Greek resistance in the *Greek-Persian wars, but

later came into protracted conflict with *Athens in the *Peloponnesian War. Its final victory in 404 BC left it dominant in Greece and the Aegean; but after crushing defeats by Thebes at Leuctra (371) and Mantinea (362) and the loss of Messina it declined in importance.

Spartacus (died c.71 BC) Thracian slave and gladiator. He led a revolt against Rome in 73, increasing his army from some 70 gladiators at the outset to several thousand rebels. He was eventually defeated by Crassus in 71 and crucified.

Spartakist Movement A group of German radical socialists. Led by Karl Liebknecht and Rosa *Luxemburg, it was formed in 1915 in order to overthrow the German imperial government and replace it with a communist regime. Spartakist was a pseudonym used by Liebknecht in calling on the modern 'wage slave' to revolt like the Roman gladiator Spartacus. In December 1918 the Spartakists became the German Communist Party and attempted to seize power in Berlin. In January 1919, Gustav Noske, as leader of the armed forces, ordered the suppression of all radical uprisings throughout Germany. Within days, a second rebellion in Berlin was brutally crushed and the two leaders murdered without trial. There was a further Spartakist rising in the Ruhr in 1920.

Speer, Albert (1905–81) German Nazi leader. He was the official architect for the Nazi Party, designing the grandiose stadium at Nuremberg (1934). An efficient organizer, he became (1942) Minister for Armaments and was mainly responsible for the planning of Germany's war economy, marshalling conscripted and slave labour in his *Organization Todt* to build strategic roads and defence lines. He was imprisoned after the war.

Speke, John Hanning (1827–64) British explorer. From 1854–1858 he accompanied Sir Richard Burton on expeditions to trace the source of the Nile. They became the first Europeans to discover Lake Tanganyika (1858), after which Speke went on to reach a great lake which he identified as the 'source reservoir' of the Nile; he called it Lake Victoria in honour of the queen.

Spencer, Herbert (1820–1903) British philosopher and sociologist. He was an early adherent of evolutionary theory, which he set down in his *Principles of Psychology* (1855). Spencer embraced Darwin's theory of natural selection proposed four years later, coined the phrase the 'survival of the fittest' (1864), and advocated social and economic laissez-faire.

He later sought to synthesize the natural and social sciences in the *Programme of a System of Synthetic Philosophy* (1862–96).

Speransky, Mikhail Mikhailovich, Count (1772–1839) Russian statesman, chief adviser to *Alexander I. After the defeat of Russia by Napoleon and the Treaty of *Tilsit, he drew up, at the emperor's request, a constitution that proposed popular participation in legislation; this was only partially implemented. He increased the burden of taxation on the nobility and sought to educate the bureaucracy, establishing promotion on the basis of merit. In doing so he incurred the enmity of both the aristocracy and the bureaucrats, and was charged (1812) with treason and secret dealings with the French, and sent into exile. Reinstated four years later, he rejoined the council of state (1821) and spent his final years codifying Russian law.

Spithead mutiny A mutiny by sailors of the British navy based at Spithead, on the southern coast of Britain. In April 1797 the fleet refused to put to sea, calling for better pay and conditions, including the provision of edible food, improved medical services, and opportunities for shore leave. The Admiralty, acknowledging the justice of the sailors' grievances and fearing that the mutiny would spread further agreed to their demands and issued a royal pardon.

spoils system (or patronage system) In US politics, the convention whereby a victorious political party rewards its supporters with public appointments. The term was coined by Senator William Marcy of New York in 1832, in connection with appointments made by President Andrew *Jackson, who replaced 20% of federal office-holders by his political supporters during his two terms. A US President or state governor has considerable patronage at his disposal. After the American Civil War attempts were made to reduce patronage in the Civil Service, for example by the Pendleton Act (1883), which created the Civil Service Commission. The term "spoils system" is also used to refer to the award of contracts, especially defence contracts, to a state in return for the support of its representatives for presidential policies in Congress, and the granting of public contracts to party contributors on favourable terms.

Spurs, Battle of the Golden See COURTRAI, BATTLE OF.

squatter A person who takes unauthorized possession of unoccupied premises or land, usually to live there.

In the USA, from the late 18th century, a squatter was a settler having no normal or legal title to the land he occupied, particularly in a district not yet surveyed.

In New South Wales, Australia, the term was applied from the early 19th century to those, often ex-convicts, who occupied land without authority and stole stock. By the 1830s, its meaning had begun to broaden, often being applied to the many pastoralists settling beyond the official 1829 limits of settlement. They were mostly involved in the wool industry, and in 1836 were granted grazing rights for an annual licence fee. The squatters demanded security of tenure and pre-emptive rights, which they gained in 1847, securing the land most suitable for agricultural and pastoral purposes. Thereafter squatters became a very powerful group, socially, economically, and politically; they often struggled bitterly over land with *selectors during the second half of the 19th century. Squatters continued to be known by that name even after they acquired their land freehold. Eventually, the term was applied to all large pastoralists in Australia.

Squatting nowadays generally results from housing shortages, but whereas in rich countries squatters tend surreptitiously to take single buildings, in poorer ones the illegal occupation of land is on so great a scale that the authorities often condone it and sometimes grant squatters legal title.

squire (or esquire) Originally an apprentice *knight in medieval Europe. Usually young men, they served as the personal attendants of fully fledged knights. The title was then one of function rather than birth: it derives from the Latin "scutarius", referring to the shield-bearing role of the squire. In later medieval England the term came to be applied to all gentlemen entitled to bear arms. By the 17th century, "squire" had become synonymous with a district's leading landowner, perhaps even the lord of the manor. The considerable local influence, both political and ecclesiastical, of the "squirearchy" has since diminished.

Sri Lanka (formerly Ceylon)

Capital:	Colombo; Sri Jayewardenepura Kotte is the administrative capital
Area:	65,610 sq km (25,332 sq miles)
Population:	21,675,648 (2013 est)
Currency:	1 Sri Lankan rupee = 100 cents

Religions:	Buddhist 69.1%; Muslim 7.6%; Hindu 7.1%; Christian 6.2%
Ethnic Groups:	Sinhalese 73.8%; Moor 7.2%; Indian Tamil 4.6%; Sri Lankan Tamil 3.9%
Languages:	Sinhalese (official); Tamil; English
International Organizations:	UN; Commonwealth; Non-Aligned Movement; Colombo Plan; WTO

A pear-shaped island country in the Indian Ocean off the south-east coast of India.

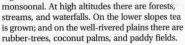

Physical Sri Lanka has very broad coastal plains which rise at the centre to highlands. The climate is monsoonal. At high altitudes there are forests, streams, and waterfalls. On the lower slopes tea is grown; and on the well-rivered plains there are rubber-trees, coconut palms, and paddy fields.

Economy The large agricultural sector produces rice, sugar cane, grains, pulses, oilseed, vegetables, fruit, tea, rubber, and coconuts; processing these products is an important industry, and tea, spices, and rubber and coconut products are important exports. Other export industries include textiles, clothing, precious stones, and fish. Important service industries include telecommunications, insurance, banking, tourism, and IT services.

History Sri Lanka's early history was shaped by Indian influences and its modern identity by three phases of European colonization. The origins of the dominant Sinhalese racial group go back to Indo-Aryan invaders from north India, whose successors dominated the north central plain from the 5th century BC until about 1200 AD. During the 2nd century BC *Buddhism spread, following the conversion of the reigning king. An outstanding ruler was Parakramabahu I (1153–86), who exercised strong military and administrative leadership and also reformed the quarrelling Buddhist sects. However, intermittent invasions from south India gradually created an enclave of Tamil Hindu power on the northern Jaffna peninsula and the north-eastern coast. The centre of Sinhalese and Buddhist civilization gradually shifted south-westwards, and political power was divided between a number of kingdoms.

European contacts began in the early 16th century when Portuguese merchants, profiting from the internal disunity, gained trading privileges on the west coast. Dutch traders gradually supplanted Portuguese influence in the 17th century, but were replaced by British forces in 1796. When the embattled interior kingdom of Kandy fell in 1815, the entire island came under the control of the British, who called it Ceylon. In the early 20th century the middle class was pressing for self-government. A new constitution was established in 1931, but racial tensions prevented its full implementation. The island, although now granted an element of self-government, remained a crown colony until 1948, when it was granted independence as a dominion within the *Commonwealth of Nations. A government was established by the United National Party under Don *Senanayake, who was succeeded (1952) by his son, Dudley Senanayake. The Socialist Sri Lanka Freedom Party was in power from 1956–1965, and Solomon *Bandaranaike was its dominant force until his death in 1959. His widow, Sirimavo Bandaranaike, succeeded him as Prime Minister (1960–65; 1970–77; 1994–2000). A new constitution in 1972 established the island as the Republic of Sri Lanka. Tensions have re-emerged between the majority Sinhalese, traditionally Buddhist, and the minority Tamil, chiefly Hindu, who had come from southern India and live in northern Sri Lanka. A ceasefire was arranged by the Indian government in 1987 between Tamil guerrilla groups and the Sri Lankan government, but a tense situation remained. During 1989–90 President Ranasinghe Premadasa initiated all-party talks to end civil strife, but these again failed and in 1991 the Defence Minister was assassinated. A state of emergency was declared, but violations of human rights by government forces led to suspension of UK aid. During the years 1990–91 civil strife claimed some 12,000 lives. Although peace talks were again initiated in April 1992, they made little progress. Meanwhile the Sri Lankan economy rapidly declined. President Premadasa was assassinated in 1993. Chandrika Kumaratunga, daughter of Solomon and Sirimavo Bandaranaike, was elected Prime Minister in 1994. Later in the same year, Kumaratunga became President and was succeeded as Prime Minister by her mother. Peace negotiations and a ceasefire between the Government and Tamil guerrillas in 1994 were abandoned, and renewed fighting erupted in 1995. Despite a successful assault by government forces on the Tamil guerrilla stronghold in the Jaffna peninsula in the north of the island, fighting continued until a ceasefire

S

was agreed in 2002. Peace talks began but were suspended in 2003. Sri Lanka was hit hard by the *Indian Ocean tsunami, with 35,000 people being killed. In 2005 President Kumaratunga was succeeded by Mahinda Rajapakse. The ceasefire with the Tamil guerrillas broke down in 2006 and the government secured a complete military victory in 2009. Rajapakse was re-elected in 2010.

SS (*Schutzstaffel*; German, 'protective echelon') The élite corps of the German Nazi Party. Founded (1925) by *Hitler as a personal bodyguard, the SS was schooled in absolute loyalty and obedience, and in total ruthlessness towards opponents. From 1929 until the dissolution of the *Third Reich in 1945 the SS was headed by Heinrich *Himmler, who divided it mainly into two groups: the Allgemeine SS (General SS), and the Waffen-SS (Armed SS). Subdivisions of the SS included the *Gestapo and the Sicherheitsdienst, in charge of foreign and domestic intelligence work. The Waffen-SS administered the *concentration camps. After the fall of the Third Reich, Himmler committed suicide and the whole corps was condemned by the court at the Nuremberg trials.

Stalin, Joseph (born Iosif Vissarionovich Dzhugashvili) (1879–1953) Soviet statesman, General Secretary of the Communist Party of the USSR (1922–53). Born in Georgia, he joined the Bolsheviks under Lenin in 1903 and co-founded the party's newspaper *Pravda* in 1912, adopting the name 'Stalin' (Russian, 'man of steel') by 1913; in the same year he was exiled to Siberia until just after the Russian Revolution. Following Lenin's death he became chairman of the Politburo and secured enough support within the party to eliminate *Trotsky as a contender for the leadership. By 1927 he was the uncontested leader of the party, and in the following year he launched a succession of five-year plans for the industrialization and collectivization of agriculture; as a result some 10 million peasants are thought to have died, either of famine or by execution. His purges of the intelligentsia in the 1930s along similarly punitive lines removed all opposition, while his direction of the armed forces led to victory over Hitler (1941–45). After 1945 he played a large part in the restructuring of postwar Europe and attempted to maintain a firm grip on other Communist states; he was later denounced by Khrushchev and the Eastern bloc countries.

Stalingrad, Battle of (1942–43) A long and bitter battle in World War II in which the German advance into the Soviet Union was turned back. During 1942 the German 6th Army under General von Paulus reached the key city of Stalingrad (now Volgograd) on the Volga. Soviet resistance continued, with grim and prolonged house-to-house fighting, while sufficient Soviet reserves were being assembled. The Germans were prevented from crossing the Volga and in November Stalin launched a winter offensive of six Soviet armies under Marshalls *Zhukov, Koniev, Petrov, and Malinovsky. By January 1943 the Germans were surrounded and von Paulus surrendered, losing some 330,000 troops killed or captured. This defeat marked the end of German success on the Eastern Front.

Stalwarts In the USA, a faction of conservative Republicans led by Roscoe Conkling (1829–88) during the presidency (1877–81) of Rutherford *Hayes. They supported the *spoils system, but opposed both the final ending of Reconstruction in the South (*Reconstruction Acts), symbolized by the withdrawal of Federal troops in 1877, and any reform of the Civil Service. In 1880 they sought a third term for former President *Grant, but failed. They dubbed their opponents, the anti-Grant wing of the Republican Party, the "Half-Breeds". Led in Congress by James *Blaine, the Half-Breeds succeeded in getting their candidate *Garfield elected in 1880. The nickname "Stalwart" was dropped after President Garfield was shot (July 1881) by a Stalwart who had been disappointed in his pursuit of office. A direct result of this tragedy was the Pendleton Act in 1883, which sought to make entry into the service dependent on merit rather than on reward.

Stamford Bridge, Battle of (25 September 1066) A battle at a village on the River Derwent in Yorkshire, north-east England, in which *Harold II of England defeated a large invading army under his exiled brother Tostig and the King of Norway, Harald Hardrada, both of whom were killed. Harold's army marched south from Stamford to face the Norman invasion and fight the Battle of *Hastings.

Stamp Act (1765) A British taxation measure, introduced by George *Grenville to cover part of the cost of defending the North American colonies. It required that all colonial legal documents, newspapers, and other items should bear a revenue stamp, as in England. Seen by the *Sons of Liberty and many other Americans as a first attempt at "taxation without representation", it was met with widespread resistance. In October 1765, nine colonial delegations met at the Stamp Act Congress in New York and petitioned for repeal. American boycotts of

British goods and civil disobedience induced *Rockingham to accede in 1766, though the Declaratory Act reasserted parliamentary power over the colonies. It helped initiate the campaign for American independence.

Stanislaus II (formerly **Count Stanislaus-Augustus Poniatowski**) (1732–98) The last King of Poland (1764–95). He was a lover of *Catherine II of Russia and her candidate for the Polish throne, which, as the country was under Russian control at that time, he gained. In the first partition of Poland in 1772, Russia, Austria, and Prussia all took slices of Polish territory. From 1773–1792 there was a period of national revival encouraged by Stanislaus. However, in 1793 he was forced to agree to the second partition of Poland, which left him with a truncated kingdom and made him almost a vassal of Russia. A rising led by General *Kosciuszko was crushed, and the third partition completed the destruction of Poland. In November 1795 Stanislaus was forced to abdicate.

Stanley, Sir Henry Morton (born **John Rowlands**) (1841–1904) British explorer. As a newspaper correspondent he was sent in 1869 to central Africa to find the Scottish missionary and explorer David *Livingstone; two years later he found him on the eastern shore of Lake Tanganyika. After Livingstone's death, Stanley continued his exploration, charting Lake Victoria (1874), tracing the course of the Congo (1874–77), mapping Lake Albert (1889), and becoming the first European to discover Lake Edward (1889). Stanley also helped establish the Congo Free State (now Zaire), with Belgian support, from 1879–1885.

Star Chamber An English court of civil and criminal jurisdiction primarily concerned with offences affecting crown interests, noted for its summary and arbitrary procedure. It was long thought to have had its origin in a statute of 1487; in fact, however, since the reign of *Edward IV the court of Star Chamber had been developing from the king's council acting in its judicial capacity into a regular court of law. It owed its name to the fact that it commonly sat in a room in the Palace of Westminster that had a ceiling covered with stars. Its judges specialized in cases involving public order, and particularly allegations of riot. Its association with the royal prerogative, and *Charles I's manipulation of legislative powers in the making of decrees during the period of his personal rule, made it unpopular in the 17th century and caused its abolition by the *Long Parliament in 1641.

START *See* STRATEGIC ARMS REDUCTION TALKS.

States-General (or **Estates-General**) Usually a gathering of representatives of the three estates of a realm: the Church; the nobility; and the commons (representatives of the corporations of towns). They met to advise a sovereign on matters of policy. The name was applied to the representative body of the United Provinces of the Netherlands in their struggle for independence from Spain in the 16th century.

In France, it began as an occasional advisory body, usually summoned to register specific support for controversial royal policy. It was developed by Philip IV, who held a meeting in 1302 to enlist support during a quarrel with the pope. Initially summoned quite frequently, it never established itself as a regular institution and its powers to grant taxation were eroded in the late 14th and 15th centuries. Thereafter it tended to be summoned only at times of crisis, most notably in 1789, when the meeting of the States-General—the first since 1614—marked the start of the *French Revolution.

states' rights A US political doctrine that upholds the rights of individual states against the power of the federal government. The framers of the *Constitution of the USA produced a federal system in which the delineation of power between the federal government and the states was open to interpretation, and from the very beginning divergent views on this issue have influenced US politics. In the early years of the USA Alexander *Hamilton and the *Federalist Party saw the Constitution as a sanction for strong central (federal) government, while *Jefferson and his followers believed that all powers not specifically granted to the federal government should be reserved to the states. The doctrine of states' rights lay behind the *Nullification Crisis of 1828–33 and provided the constitutional basis of the Southern case in the dispute leading up to the *American Civil War. In recent years the doctrine has been central to controversies over *civil rights and welfare expenditure.

statholders Provincial leaders in the Netherlands, as first appointed by the ruling dukes of *Burgundy in the 15th century. Their duties included presiding over the provincial state assemblies and commanding provincial armies. During the *Dutch Revolts (1568–1684), they were elected by the central States-General and subsequently by the provincial state assemblies. In the *United Provinces the House of Orange-Nassau came to dominate the statholderates. Within the province of Holland there was protracted dispute between the Orange statholders and the states for overall leadership. In 1795 the office of statholder ceased to exist.

Stauffenberg, Claus Graf von See JULY PLOT.

steam power The use of steam to power machinery, a major factor in the *Industrial Revolution. The earliest steam engine, developed by Thomas Newcomen (1663–1729) by 1712, was used to pump water from Cornish tin mines. Major improvements made by James Watt (1736–1819) greatly increased its efficiency and in 1781 he adapted a steam engine to drive factory machinery, thus providing a reliable source of industrial power. Before this many factories depended on water power and were therefore sited in the countryside near swiftly flowing streams, where transport was difficult; moreover, production was always dependent upon the weather. Although steam engines had none of these disadvantages, they were expensive and only large businesses could afford to install them. Factories were henceforth sited near coal mines and large towns grew up to house the factory workers. The use of steam engines in the textile industry and in other manufacturing processes led to a growth in the size of factories while their application in the 19th century to railways and steamships (thanks largely to the innovations of James Watt) led to both faster and cheaper travel and transport of goods. The steam-hammer (1808) enabled much larger pieces of metal to be worked, while such developments as the steam-driven threshing machine greatly accelerated the harvesting cycle and reduced farmers' reliance on wind- and water-mills. The direct use of steam engines began to decline in the early 20th century with the development of petrol and diesel engines and the use of steam-driven turbines to generate electricity, an energy source that can be applied more cleanly and easily in industry.

Stein, Heinrich Friedrich Karl, Baron vom und zum (1757–1831) Prussian statesman and reformer. After various diplomatic and administrative appointments he became Minister of Commerce in 1804. In 1807 he was dismissed by *Frederick William III for attempting to increase the responsibilities of the ministers of state. However, in the aftermath of the Prussian defeat at *Jena, Stein was recalled to begin his enlightened reforms. He persuaded the king to abolish the serf system, to end the restrictions on the sale to non-nobles of land owned by nobles, and to end the monopoly of the sons of the nobility in the Prussian officers corp. He

wanted the king to authorize a national insurrection against the French and mobilize patriotic energies by the grant of a "free constitution", but this alarmed Napoleon, who persuaded the king to dismiss him again (1808). His pleas for a united Germany were ignored at the Congress of *Vienna. Stein subsequently became chief counsellor to *Alexander I of Russia (1812–15).

Stephan Dushan (1308–55) King of *Serbia (1331–55). The greatest ruler of medieval Serbia, he deposed his father in 1331 and took the title of Emperor of the Serbs and Greeks in 1345. He also controlled Bulgaria as a result of a marriage alliance. He fought the Byzantine empire, and seized Macedonia, Albania, and much of Greece, and introduced a new code of laws. His achievements were shortlived as his son could not maintain the Serbo-Greek empire against *Ottoman invasion and regional challenges.

Stephen (*c.*1097–1154) Grandson of William the Conqueror, king of England (1135–54). Stephen seized the throne of England from *Matilda a few months after the death of her father Henry I. Having forced Matilda to flee the kingdom, Stephen was confronted with civil war following her invasion in 1139; although captured at Lincoln (1141) and temporarily deposed, he ultimately forced Matilda to withdraw from England in 1148. However, the year before he died Stephen was obliged to recognize Matilda's son, the future Henry II, as heir to the throne.

Stephen, St (*c.*977–1038) King and patron saint of Hungary, reigned (1000–38). The first king of Hungary, he united Pannonia and Dacia as one kingdom, and took steps to Christianize the country.

Stephenson, George (1781–1848) British engineer, the father of railways. He started as a colliery engineman, applied steam power to the haulage of coal wagons by cable, and built his first locomotive in 1814. He became engineer to the Stockton and Darlington Railway, and in 1825 drove the first train on it using a steam locomotive of his own design. His son **Robert Stephenson** (1803–59) assisted him in the building of engines and of the Liverpool to Manchester railway, for which they built the famous *Rocket* (1829)—the prototype for all future steam locomotives. Robert became famous also as a bridge designer, notably of major bridges at Menai Strait and Conwy in Wales, Berwick and Newcastle in northern England, Montreal in Canada, and in Egypt.

Stern Gang British name for a *Zionist terrorist group calling itself "Lohamei Herut Israel Lehi" (Fighters for the Freedom of Israel). It campaigned actively (1940–48) in British-administered Palestine for the creation of a Jewish state. Founded by Abraham Stern (1907–42), the Stern Gang numbered no more than a few hundred. They operated in small groups and concentrated on the assassination of government officials. Their victims included Lord Moyne, the British Minister for the Middle East (1944), and Count *Bernadotte, the United Nations mediator in Palestine (1948).

Stevenson, Adlai (Ewing) (1900–65) US statesman. He served in various government posts and in 1948 he was elected governor of Illinois with the largest majority in the state's history. Chosen as the Democratic candidate for the Presidency in the elections of 1952 and 1956, he was badly beaten on both occasions by Dwight D. *Eisenhower. A liberal reformer and internationalist, he was known for his brilliant and witty speeches. President *Kennedy appointed him US ambassador to the United Nations (1961–65) with cabinet rank.

Stewart See STUART.

Stilwell, Joseph Warren (1883–1946) US general. Popularly known as "Vinegar Joe" on account of his tactlessness, he served in China between the wars. In World War II, he commanded US and Chinese forces in south China and Burma, cooperating with the British in the *Burma Campaign. Technically, his authority was by virtue of his appointment as chief-of-staff in this region by *Chiang Kai-shek. Differences of opinion with Chiang led to his recall; he later commanded the US 10th Army at Okinawa.

Stimson, Henry Lewis (1867–1950) US statesman. He was Secretary of War for President *Taft (1911–13) and served in *World War I. While governor-general of the Philippines (1927–29) he pursued an enlightened policy of conciliation. As Secretary of State (1929–33) in the cabinet of President *Hoover, he promulgated the Stimson Doctrine (or Doctrine of Non-Recognition) in response to the Japanese invasion of Manchuria (1931): a refusal to grant diplomatic recognition to actions that threatened the territorial integrity of China or violated the *Kellogg-Briand Pact. He later served as Secretary of War (1940–45) under Franklin D. *Roosevelt and *Truman, in which post he made the recommendation to drop the atomic bomb.

Stock Market Crash (1929) A severe financial crisis in the USA, also known as the "Great Crash", the "Wall Street Crash", or the "Great Panic". During the first half of 1929 an unprecedented boom took place on the New York Stock Exchange. However, prices began to fall from late September and selling began. In less than a month there was a 40% drop in stock value, and this fall continued over the next three years. Its causes were numerous. Although the post-war US economy seemed to be booming, it was on a narrow base and there were fundamental flaws. The older basic industries, such as mining and textiles, were weak, agriculture was depressed, unemployment at four million was unacceptably high, and international loans were often poorly secured. A new rich class enjoyed a flamboyant lifestyle, which too many people tried to copy by means of credit and stock-market speculation, within an unsound banking system. Once the business cycle faltered, a panic set in. The effects of the crash were hugely to accelerate a downward spiral: real estate values collapsed, factories closed, and banks began to call in loans, precipitating the worldwide Great *Depression.

Stoic A member of a philosophical school founded by Zeno of Citium *c.*300 BC, who taught in the *Stoa Poikile* (painted colonnade in Athens (hence the name). Zeno's followers propounded various metaphysical systems, united chiefly by their ethical implications. All were variants on the pantheistic theme that the world constitutes a single, organically unified and benevolent whole, in which apparent evil results only from our limited view. Their philosophy had at its core the beliefs that virtue is based on knowledge; reason is the governing principle of nature; individuals should live in harmony with nature. The vicissitudes of life were viewed with equanimity: pleasure, pain, and even death were irrelevant to true happiness.

Stolypin, Piort Arkadevich (1862–1911) Russian statesman. The last effective statesman of the Russian empire, he was Premier (1906–11). He was hated for his ruthless punishment of activists in the *Russian Revolution of 1905, for his disregard of the *Dumas, and for his treatment of Jews. His constructive work lay in his agricultural reforms. Believing that a contented peasantry would check revolution, he allowed peasants (*kulaks) to have their land in one holding instead of strips that were periodically re-allocated within the peasant commune. Those taking advantage of this became prosperous, but were not powerful enough to stem the revolutionary tide. He was assassinated in a Kiev theatre.

Stone Ages Those periods of the past when metals were unknown and stone was used as the main material for missiles, as hammers, for making tools for such tasks as cutting and scraping and, later, as spear heads. Hard, fine-grained stone was the material most suitable for flaking. Although the best locally available would have been the material of first choice, stone needed for special purposes was occasionally brought from long distances, even by early toolmakers of up to 2 million years ago as at Olduvai Gorge and Koobi Fora in eastern Africa. Flint is popularly associated with flaked stone tools, especially in Europe, but in Africa, where flint is rare, quartz, chert, and volcanic rocks, such as basalt and obsidian (natural glass), were the materials worked long before early Europeans used flint. In Europe, three Stone Ages are recognized—the Old Stone Age (*Palaeolithic), the Middle Stone Age (*Mesolithic), and the New Stone Age (*Neolithic). In other parts of the world, different subdivisions are used. The Stone Ages are followed by the *Bronze and *Iron Ages. This division of prehistory into three chronological stages, defined by the main material used for tools (stone, bronze, and iron)—the Three Ages System—was first put to practical use for classifying archaeological material in Denmark in 1819. As it spread to other countries, it became necessary to subdivide the three ages. All human societies lived by hunting and gathering until the development of agriculture.

Stonehenge A unique megalithic monument on Salisbury Plain in Wiltshire, England. Its alleged connection with the Druids dates from the 17th century, when people's ideas about what constituted 'the past' were very vague. In the 12th century it was believed to be a monument over King Arthur's grave; other theories have attributed it to the Phoenicians, Romans, Vikings, and visitors from other worlds; modern theory inclines to the view that it was a temple. Scientific study and excavation have identified three main constructional phases between c.3000 BC and c.1500 BC, i.e. it was completed in the Bronze Age. The circular bank and ditch, double circle of 'bluestones' (spotted dolerite), and circle of sarsen stones (some with stone lintels), are concentric, and the main axis is aligned on the midsummer sunrise—an orientation that was probably for ritual rather than scientific purposes. It is believed that the 'bluestones' were transported from the Prescelly Hills, Pembrokeshire, Wales, a distance of 320 km (200 miles).

Stopes, Marie (Charlotte Carmichael) (1880–1958) British scientist and writer on parenthood and birth control. She was appointed lecturer in palaeobotany at Manchester University in 1904 and then taught at Imperial College in London. It was, however, her books, particularly *Married Love* (1918) and *Wise Parenthood* (1918), with her clear views on birth control, that made her famous. With her second husband, H. Verdon-Roe (1878–1949), she founded a clinic for birth control in London in 1921. Her activities roused opposition but also steadily increasing support among the medical profession and the general public.

Stormont A suburb of Belfast, seat of the Northern Ireland Assembly, and former seat of the parliament of *Northern Ireland. Created by the Government of Ireland Act (1920) as a subordinate body to Westminster, the Stormont Parliament was dominated by the *Ulster Unionist Party until, following the breakdown in law and order in the late 1960s, it was suspended in 1972. Direct rule from Westminster was imposed, to be administered by civil servants of the Northern Ireland Office based in Stormont Castle. The Northern Ireland Assembly has met there since 1999.

Strafford, Thomas Wentworth, 1st Earl of (1593–1641) English statesman. A Member of Parliament from 1614, he entered the service of *Charles I in 1628. Although he had previously opposed royal policies, he was a believer in firm government and accepted preferment in order to uphold the king's power. Thenceforth, as Lord President of the Council of the North (1628) and Lord Deputy of Ireland (1633), he was the principal exponent of the policy of "Thorough", putting the royal will into effect with the utmost authority. His autocratic style made him extremely unpopular, and most of his achievements in the north and Ireland turned out to be temporary. On the outbreak of the *Bishops' Wars he was recalled by Charles to England. Now at the centre of affairs for the first time, he could not avert the approaching *English Civil War. He was created Earl of Strafford in January 1640, but impeached for treason in the same year. Opposition members of the *Long Parliament claimed that Strafford was about to impose a Catholic dictatorship on England and he was executed under Act of *Attainder.

Straits Settlements Former British crown colony comprising territories bordering on the strategic Malacca Strait in south-east Asia. The three English East India colonies of Penang, Malacca, and *Singapore were combined in

1826 as the Straits Settlements. After 1858, they passed to British Indian control, and in 1867 became a crown colony, to which Labuan was added in 1912. The colony was dismantled in 1946, Singapore becoming a separate colony and Penang, Malacca, and Labuan joining the Malayan Union.

Strategic Arms Limitation Talks (SALT) Agreements between the USA and the Soviet Union, aimed at limiting the production and deployment of nuclear weapons. A first round of meetings (1969–72) produced the SALT I Agreement, which prevented the construction of comprehensive anti-ballistic missile (ABM) systems and placed limits on the construction of strategic (i.e. intercontinental) ballistic missiles (ICBM) for an initial period of five years. A SALT II Treaty, agreed in 1979, sought to set limits on the numbers and testing of new types of inter-continental missiles, but it was not ratified by the US Senate. New *Strategic Arms Reduction Talks (START) began in 1982.

Strategic Arms Reduction Talks (START) Discussions aimed at nuclear arms control between the USA and the Soviet Union (after 1991, between the USA and the four republics of the former Soviet Union that inherited nuclear weapons—Belarus, Ukraine, Russia, and Kazakhstan). START negotiations began in 1982, but were suspended by the Soviet Union at the end of 1983 in protest at US deployment of intermediate nuclear missiles in Western Europe. Resuming in 1985, the talks eventually led to the signing of the treaty known as **START I** in July 1991, which committed the USA and the Soviet Union to a 30% reduction in their nuclear weapons stockpiles. The four nuclear states that emerged from the break-up of the Soviet Union acceded to START I in November 1993. In the interim, Russia and the USA had signed **START II** in January 1993, which provided for the dismantling of two-thirds of each country's strategic nuclear warheads and in 1994 agreed to stop aiming their weapons permanently at each other's countries. However, ratification and implementation of START II stalled, as did negotiations for START III in the late 1990s. In 2002 START II was superseded by the more limited **SORT** (Strategic Offensive Reductions Treaty), an agreement for a two-thirds reduction in nuclear arsenals within 10 years. The more ambitious **New START**, which was signed in 2010, set a target for a further 30% reduction by 2018.

Strathclyde and Cumbria A Romano-British kingdom of north-west England and south-west Scotland: formed in the 2nd century AD, it survived until the 11th century, the last kingdom of the Britons to disappear. It survived invasions by Eadbert of Northumbria (750 and 756), plundering by the Danes (870), and the temporary loss of its independence (920) to *Edward the Elder of England. *Duncan I acquired Strathclyde in 1018 and united it with three other regions to found the kingdom of Scotland (1034).

Streicher, Julius (1885–1946) German Nazi leader and propagandist. Originally a schoolteacher, he expounded his anti-Semitic views in his periodical *Der Stürmer*. He was Party leader (*Gauleiter*) in Franconia (1933–40), and continued to function as a propagandist. He was sentenced to death at the *Nuremberg Trials and subsequently hanged.

Stresa Conference (April 1935) A conference between Britain, France, and Italy. Held at Stresa on Lake Maggiore in Italy, it proposed measures to counter *Hitler's open rearmament of Germany in defiance of the *Versailles Peace Settlement. Together these countries formed the "Stresa Front" against German aggression, but their decisions were never implemented. In June Britain negotiated unilaterally a naval agreement with Germany. In November 1936 *Mussolini proclaimed his alliance with Hitler in the Rome-Berlin *Axis.

Strijdom, Johannes Gerhardus (1893–1958) South African Nationalist politician, Prime Minister of the Union of South Africa (1954–58). A White supremacist, Strijdom advocated strict apartheid and altered the composition of the senate (1955) to ensure support for his policies.

Stroessner, Alfredo (1912–2006) Paraguayan military leader and President (1954–89). The son of a German immigrant, he fought in the *Chaco War (1932–35) against Bolivia. Having risen from the ranks to become commander-in-chief of the armed forces (1951–54), he was responsible for the overthrow of President Frederico Chavez in 1954. Basically supportive of the large landowners and international commercial interests, as President he used foreign aid to develop schools, hospitals, highways, and hydro-electric power. His regime remained strongly backed by the army and was essentially totalitarian in that, while allowing for some political dissent, it was guilty of harsh and repressive methods. Stroessner died in exile in Brazil.

Stuart (or **Stewart**) The family name of the Scottish monarchs from 1371–1714 and of the English monarchs from 1603–1714. The founder of the Stuart house was Walter Fitzalan (died 1177) who was steward (from which the name Stewart derives) to the King of Scotland. His descendant became the first Stewart king of Scotland as *Robert II (ruled 1371–90). The marriage of Margaret Tudor, daughter of *Henry VII, to *James IV linked the royal houses of Scotland and England, and on the death of *Elizabeth I without heirs in 1603, James VI of Scotland succeeded to the English throne as *James I. The Stuarts lost the throne temporarily with the execution of Charles I in 1649, regaining it with the *Restoration of Charles II in 1660. The *Glorious Revolution (1688) sent *James II into exile and the crown passed to his daughter Mary and her husband William, then to his second daughter *Anne. Her death without heirs in 1714 resulted in the replacement of the Stuart house by the house of *Hanover headed by George I. Supporters of the exiled house of Stuart were known as *Jacobites. After the failure of the *Fifteen and the *Forty-Five (1715 and 1745) rebellions the Stuart cause faded, and George III felt able to grant a pension to the last direct Stuart claimant, Henry, Cardinal York, who died in 1807.

Stuart, Charles Edward (or **the Young Pretender** or **'Bonnie Prince Charlie'**) *See* PRETENDER.

Stuart, James (Francis Edward) (or **the Old Pretender**) *See* PRETENDER.

Stuart, Mary *See* MARY, QUEEN OF SCOTS.

student revolts Social or political protests by student groups. Students have played an important part in almost every major revolution of the 19th and 20th centuries. In the early 19th century, the German universities produced student movements (*Burschenschaften*) supporting German nationalism and opposing the rule of *Metternich. In Tsarist Russia students who agitated for liberal reforms were imprisoned, exiled, or executed. In the period between the two World Wars the universities in Germany and Japan had movements supporting mainly right-wing causes and revolutions. After World War II universities in the developing countries often fostered strong nationalist and Marxist movements, while in the 1960s left-wing movements were predominant in many universities and colleges in Europe, the USA, and Japan. The protests at the University of California's Berkeley campus (1964) and the nationwide strike at approximately 200 US campuses (1970) challenged US policy in Vietnam. In Paris, French students and workers joined in the movement (1968) to challenge the *de Gaulle regime, while in Japan students acted militantly against the westernization of Japanese society.

Demonstrations by South Korean university students (1987) led to constitutional amendments and the release of political prisoners. Pro-democracy student rallies and hunger strikes in Beijing in 1989 were brutally suppressed by government forces in the Tiananmen Square massacre, which left an estimated 2600 dead and led to the arrest and execution of hundreds more. A series of student demonstrations in Prague in 1989 gained widespread support that led to the downfall of the Czechoslovak communist regime.

sturdy beggars Those classed in the English *Poor Law of 1531 as able-bodied persons who chose not to work. This presumed, wrongly, that there was enough work for everyone who wanted it. Those who took to the roads, seeking jobs or charity, were severely punished. This was because Tudor governments regarded them as threats to public order, especially returned soldiers who organized themselves into bands and robbed travellers. By the end of the century new poor laws made parishes provide work for the genuinely unemployed, while "incorrigible rogues" were to be whipped, returned to the parishes whence they had come, or even banished overseas for persistent offences.

Sucre, Antonio José de (1795–1830) Venezuelan revolutionary and statesman, President of Bolivia (1826–28). Sucre served as Simón *Bolívar's Chief of Staff, liberating Ecuador (1822), Peru (1824), and Bolivia (1825) from the Spanish. The first President of Bolivia, Sucre resigned following a Peruvian invasion in 1828; he was later assassinated. The Bolivian judicial capital Sucre is named after him.

Sudan, the

Capital:	Khartoum
Area:	1,861,484 sq km (718,723 sq miles)
Population:	34,847,710 (2013 est)
Currency:	Sudanese pound = 100 piastres
Religions:	Muslim 96.0%; Christian 3.0%
Ethnic Groups:	Arab 70.0%; Fur, Beja, Nuba, Fallata

| Languages: | Arabic, English (both official); Nubian; Ta Bedawie; Fur |
| International Organizations: | UN; AU; Arab League; Non-Aligned Movement |

A country in north-east Africa. Sudan takes its name from the great belt of open savannah crossing Africa south of the Sahara, from Ethiopia to Cape Verde.

Physical Sudan has Egypt on its northern boundary, a coast on the Red Sea, and boundaries also with Ethiopia, Eritrea, South Sudan, the Central African Republic, Chad, and Libya. The third-largest country on the African continent, it has equatorial forest in the south and the Nubian Desert in the north; its whole length is traversed from south to north by the River Nile. The mid-south contains the Sudd swamps, which are mainly covered with reeds and papyrus grass. There is a region of savannah, and near the junction of the Blue and White Niles cotton is grown under irrigation on the plains of the Gezira. Further north are areas covered with acacia bushes, the source of gum arabic. In the extreme north years may pass without rain, and the only cultivation is on the river's banks.

Economy Already devastated by the civil war, floods, and drought, Sudan's economy was further damaged by the loss of three-quarters of its oil production on the secession of *South Sudan in 2011 and then by the latter's suspension of oil production in 2012. The government is attempting to develop other industries, and gold is now the major export; however, oil exports are still important. Agriculture employs four-fifths of the workforce; cotton, sesame, livestock, groundnuts, gum arabic, and sugar are exported.

History Nubian culture was established in northern Sudan about 30,000 years ago. Most of Nubia gradually came under the control of Egypt from about 4000 BC. Nubia later formed part of the kingdom of Cush, which lasted from the 11th century BC to the 4th century AD. From about the 6th century AD missionaries established Christianity in the area. From the 13th century Arab nomads began immigrating into Sudan and eventually took control of the Christian areas.

By 1800 northern Sudan consisted of the Muslim empire of the Funji, where an Islamic revival was occurring. The Funji were then conquered by *Mehemet Ali from Egypt (1820–23). In 1874 Khedíve Ismail, viceroy of Egypt, offered the post of governor of the Egyptian Sudan to the Briton Charles *Gordon. His anti-slave administration was not popular. In 1881 Muhammad Ahmad declared himself *Mahdi and led an Islamic rebellion in the Sudan. Britain occupied Egypt in 1882 and invaded the Sudan where Gordon was killed (1885). The Mahdists resisted Anglo-Egyptian forces until Kitchener defeated them at Omdurman in 1898. Following the *Fashoda incident, an Anglo-Egyptian condominium was created for the whole Sudan (1899) under a British governor. A constitution was granted in 1948 but in 1951 King Farouk of Egypt proclaimed himself King of Sudan. After his fall, Egypt agreed to Sudan's right to independence; self-government was granted in 1953 and full independence in 1956. North–South political and religious tension undermined stability until General *Nimeiri achieved power in 1969 and negotiated an end to the civil war in the south (1972). However, the early 1980s saw the collapse of the economy, widespread starvation, and a renewal of separatist guerrilla activity in the south. Nimeiri was overthrown by the army in April 1985, and a brief civilian coalition government was formed under Sadiq al-Mahdi. But civil war continued; the Sudan People's Liberation Army (SPLA) militarized much of the south, while the Muslim Brotherhood's National Islamic Front (NIF) strengthened its hold in the north. A military coup by General Omar Hassan Ahmad al-Bashir in 1989 was followed by a ban on all political parties. The early 1990s saw an influx of several million refugees from Ethiopia and Chad. The continuing civil war, drought, and flooding led to large-scale destitution and famine. The strongly Islamic Bashir regime has been accused of sponsoring fundamentalist terrorism, particularly in neighbouring Egypt. The first presidential and parliamentary elections since the coup were held in March 1996, resulting in victory for Bashir and his supporters. In 1997 the SPLA made large gains in the south and east of the country. In 1999 Bashir announced that he would agree to the south seceding if this would end the civil war, and in 2004 a peace settlement granted virtual autonomy to the south with an option to secede after six years. Meanwhile, in 2003 a new conflict began in Darfur: a rebellion of Black Africans was followed by a campaign of savage ethnic cleansing conducted by Arab militias with government support. In a referendum in January 2011, the ten southern provinces voted overwhelmingly

S

for independence, and in July 2011 South Sudan became Africa's newest nation. Unresolved disputes, including the precise line of the border and how to share oil revenues, led to armed clashes.

Sudetenland An area of Bohemia in the Czech Republic adjacent to the German border, allocated to the new state of Czechoslovakia after World War I despite the presence of three million German-speaking inhabitants. The Sudetenland became the first object of German expansionist policies when the Nazis came to power; after war was threatened, it was ceded to Germany as a result of the Munich Agreement of September 1938. In 1945 the area was returned to Czechoslovakia, and the German inhabitants were expelled and replaced by Czechs.

Suetonius (full name **Gaius Suetonius Tranquillus**) (*c.*69–*c.*150 AD) Roman biographer and historian. His surviving works include *Lives of the Caesars*, covering Julius Caesar and the Roman emperors who followed him, up to Domitian.

Suez Canal A shipping canal 171 km (106 miles) long and without locks connecting the Mediterranean (at Port Said) with the Red Sea, constructed between 1859 and 1869 by Ferdinand de Lesseps. The canal, now important for Egypt's economy as providing the shortest route for international sea traffic travelling between Europe and Asia, came under British control after Britain acquired majority shares in it, at Disraeli's instigation, in 1875; after 1888 Britain acted as guarantor of its neutral status. It was nationalized by Egypt in 1956 and an Anglo-French attempt at intervention was called off after international protest (*see* SUEZ WAR). It has been enlarged to take ships of almost any draught.

Suez War (1956) A military conflict involving British, French, Israeli, and Egyptian forces. It arose from the nationalization of the *Suez Canal Company by Egypt in 1956. When attempts to establish an international authority to operate the Canal failed, Britain and France entered into a military agreement with Israel. The latter, concerned at the increasing number of *fedayeen* or guerrilla raids, was ready to attack Egypt. On 29 October Israel launched a surprise attack into Sinai, and Britain and France issued an ultimatum demanding that both Israel and Egypt should withdraw from the Canal. This was rejected by President *Nasser. British and French planes attacked Egyptian bases, and

troops were landed at Port Said. Under pressure from the USA, with the collapse of the value of sterling, and mounting criticism of most other nations, the Anglo-French operations were halted and their forces evacuated. A UN peacekeeping force was sent to the area. The US Secretary of State, J. F. Dulles, formulated the short-lived Eisenhower Doctrine (1957), offering US economic and military aid to Middle East governments whose independence was threatened. Israeli forces were withdrawn in March 1957 after agreement to install a UN Emergency Force in Sinai and to open the Straits of Tiran to Israeli shipping.

suffragette A member of a British militant feminist movement that campaigned for the right of adult British women to vote in general elections. The Women's Social and Political Union, which was founded by Emmeline *Pankhurst in 1903, gained rapid support, using as its weapons attacks on property, demonstrations, and refusal to pay taxes. There was strong opposition to giving women the vote at national level, partly from calculations of the electoral consequences of enfranchising women. Frustration over the defeat of Parliamentary bills to extend the vote led the suffragettes to adopt militant methods to press their cause; Parliamentary debates were interrupted, imprisoned suffragettes went on hunger strike, and one suffragette, flinging herself in front of the king's horse in the 1913 Derby horse-race, was killed. These tactics were abandoned when Britain declared war on Germany in 1914 and the WSPU directed its efforts to support the war effort. In 1918, subject to educational and property qualifications, British women over 30 were given the vote (the age restriction was partly to reduce the number of women in the electorate to match the reduction in the numbers of men, as so many had died in the war). In 1928 women over 21 gained the vote.

Sufi *See* ISLAM.

Suharto (1921–2008) Indonesian statesman and general. Having played a prominent role in the *Indonesian Revolution, he became chief-of-staff of the army in 1965. He crushed a communist coup attempt by the *PKI in 1965 and in 1966 President *Sukarno, who had been implicated in the coup, was forced to give him wide powers. Having united student and military opponents of the Sukarno regime, he became acting President in 1967, assuming full powers the following year. He ended the *Konfrontasi with Malaysia and revitalized the Indonesian economy, as well as restoring the country to the

Western capitalist fold. Increasingly dictatorial in the 1980s and 1990s, he faced considerable domestic opposition, most notably from the Islamic fundamentalist movement. The sudden collapse of Indonesia's economy in January 1998 prompted widespread civil disorder, which led to his resignation in favour of his deputy B. J. Habibie. Accused of corruption in 2000, he escaped trial because of ill health.

Sui A dynasty of emperors ruling China (589–618), between the period of The Three Kingdoms and the Tang Dynasty. Reuniting the country, the Sui emperors built the Grand Canal.

Sukarno, Achmad (1901–70) Indonesian statesman, President (1945–67). One of the founders of the Indonesian National Party (1927), he was Indonesian leader during the Japanese occupation (1942–45) and led the struggle for independence, which was granted by the Netherlands in 1949. From the mid-1950s his dictatorial tendencies aroused opposition. He was alleged to have taken part in the abortive Communist coup of 1965, after which he lost power to the army, being ousted two years later.

Suleiman I (or **Soliman, Solyman**) (c.1494–1566) Sultan of the Ottoman Empire (1520–66). The Ottoman Empire reached its fullest extent under his rule; his conquests included Belgrade (1521), Rhodes (1522), and Tripoli (1551), in addition to those in Iraq (1534) and Hungary (1562). This and the cultural achievements of the time earned him the nickname in Europe of 'Suleiman the Magnificent'. He was also a noted administrator, known to his subjects as 'Suleiman the Lawgiver'.

Sulla (full name **Lucius Cornelius Sulla Felix**) (138–78 BC) Roman general and politician. Having come to prominence as a result of military successes in Africa, Sulla became involved in a power struggle with Marius, and in 88 marched on Rome. After a victorious campaign against Mithridates VI Sulla invaded Italy in 83, ruthlessly suppressing his opponents. He was elected dictator in 82, after which he implemented constitutional reforms in favour of the Senate, resigning in 79.

sultanate A territory subject to sovereign independent Muslim rule. The word "sultan" is used in the *Koran and the traditions of the Prophet *Muhammad to mean "authority". *Mahmud of Ghazna was the first Muslim ruler to be addressed as sultan by his contemporaries. The term thereafter became a general title

for the effective holders of power, such as the *Seljuk or *Mameluke dynasties, though it was also used as a mark of respect under the *Ottomans for princes and princesses of the imperial house. The term "sultanate" was also used of a number of centres of Muslim power, such as the sultanate of Delhi (1206–1526), the predecessor of the *Mogul empire in India, and the Sulu sultanate, a trading empire in the southern Philippines, which flourished between the 16th and 19th centuries.

Sumerians A people living in southern Mesopotamia in the 4th and 3rd millennia BC. By 3000 BC a number of city states had developed in Sumer, such as *Uruk, Eridu, and *Ur. The Sumerians are credited with inventing the cuneiform system of writing, which was originally pictographic but gradually became stylized. Many simple inscriptions survive as evidence of this development; they also attest the increase in administration that accompanied urban growth. Their literature contains references to myths, hymns, and incantations. They developed a legal system, supported by complex political and economic organization. Their technological achievements included wheeled vehicles and potters' wheels, as well as such architectural features as columns, vaults, and domes.

The first great empire of Sumer was established by the people of *Akkad, who conquered the area in about 2350 under the leadership of Sargon. The dynasty founded by him was destroyed in about 2200, and after 2150 the kings of Ur not only re-established Sumerian sovereignty in Sumer but also conquered Akkad. This new empire lasted until roughly 2000 when pressure from the Elamites and Amorites reached its culmination with the capture and devastation of Ur. The Sumerians at this point disappear from history, but the influence of their culture on the subsequent civilizations of Mesopotamia was far-reaching.

summoner (or **apparitor**) In medieval England and Scotland a minor official (not a cleric), who summoned people before the ecclesiastical courts. Summoners acquired inquisitorial powers in cases that could incur excommunication, such as non-payment of tithes, heresy, usury, slander, and witchcraft. Over 10,000 excommunication writs survive from the 13th century. Summoners were condemned for extortion in the Council of London (1342), by Parliament (1378), and by writers including Chaucer in *The Canterbury Tales*.

Sundjata Keita Founder and ruler of the
*Mali empire (c.1235–55) in west Africa. He was
sickly as a child, but became a vigorous warrior.
In about 1235 he was called on to fight Sou-
mangourou, King of Sosso, and defeated him at
Krina. After further victories, he conquered
*Ghana and Walata, and then all the neigh-
bouring gold-bearing regions. After c.1240 he
devoted himself to administration. He died ac-
cidentally, either from an arrow shot at random
during a festival or by drowning in the Sankar-
ani River.

Sunni (from Arabic, *sunna*, 'tradition'), the
belief and practice of mainstream, as opposed
to Shia, *Islam (see SHIITES). Sunni Muslims,
constituting over 80% of all believers, follow the
sunna, a code of practice based on the *hadith*
collected in the *Sihah Satta*, six authentic Books
of Tradition about the prophet *Muhammad.
The *Sunna*, variously translated as 'custom',
'code', or 'usage', means whatever Muhammad,
by positive example or implicit approval, demonstrated as the ideal behaviour for a Muslim to
follow. It therefore complements the Koran as a
source of legal and ethical guidance.

　　Sunnis recognize the order of succession of
the first four *caliphs. They follow one of four
schools of law: the Hanafi, prevalent in the
Middle East and Pakistan; the Malikite, found in
western and northern Africa; the Shafite, found
in Egypt, East Africa, Malaysia, and Indonesia;
and the Hanbalite in Saudi Arabia.

Sun Yat-sen (or **Sun Yixian**) (1866–1925)
Chinese *Kuomintang statesman, provisional
President of the Republic of China (1911–12)
and President of the Southern Chinese Republic
(1923–25). Generally regarded in the West as the
father of the modern Chinese state, he spent the
period 1895–1911 in exile after an abortive attempt to overthrow the Manchus. During this
time he issued an early version of his influential
'Three Principles of the People' (nationalism,
democracy, and the people's livelihood) and set
up a revolutionary society, which became the
nucleus of the Kuomintang. He returned to
China to play a vital part in the revolution of
1911 in which the Manchu dynasty was overthrown. After being elected provisional President, Sun Yat-sen resigned in 1912 in response
to opposition from conservative members of the
government and established a secessionist government at Guangzhou. He reorganized the
Kuomintang along the lines of the Soviet Communist Party and began a period of uneasy cooperation with the Chinese Communists before
dying in office.

Superbus, Lucius Tarquinius *See* TARQUIN.

Supremacy, Acts of (1534 and 1559) Enactments of the English Parliament, confirming
respectively the supremacy of *Henry VIII and
*Elizabeth I over the Anglican Church. Henry
was styled "Supreme Head" of the Church but
Elizabeth, in an attempt to reduce opposition,
took the title "Supreme Governor". Under the
terms of both Acts the "Oath of Supremacy" was
demanded of suspected malcontents.

Surinam

Capital:	Paramaribo
Area:	163,820 sq km (63,251 sq miles)
Population:	566,846 (2013 est)
Currency:	1 Suriname dollar = 100 cents
Religions:	Hindu 27.4%; Protestant (mostly Moravian) 25.2%; Roman Catholic 22.8%; Muslim 19.6%
Ethnic Groups:	East Indian 37.0%; Creole 31.0%; Indonesian 15.0%; African 10.0%
Languages:	Dutch (official); English; Sranang Tongo; Caribbean Hindustani; Javanese
International Organizations:	UN; OAS; CARICOM; Non-Aligned Movement; WTO

A country on the north-
east coast of South Amer-
ica, known until 1948 as
Dutch Guiana.

Physical Surinam is sandwiched between Guyana
and French Guiana, with
Brazil to the south. The
climate is equatorial. Thick forest covers most of the
interior, which rises to highlands in the centre.
Rice and sugar cane can be grown on the coast.

Economy The extraction, processing, and export of alumina, gold, and oil dominate Surinam's economy, with these three commodities
accounting for five-sixths of exports. Lumber,
fish, rice, and bananas are also exported.

History Surinam's name is taken from the
name of its earliest inhabitants, the Surinen,
who had been driven out of the area by other
South American Indians by the time Europeans

arrived. Surinam was claimed by Spain in 1593 but was colonized by the Dutch from the beginning of the 17th century. The territory alternated between British and Dutch control until the Netherlands received it in a treaty settlement of 1815. In the 17th century African slaves had begun to be imported. By the late 19th century plantation labour was recruited from India and Java. The ethnic diversity of Surinam resulted in increasing racial and political strife after World War II. In 1954 Surinam became an equal partner in the Kingdom of the Netherlands, and full independence was granted in 1975. After several years of party strife the military took over in 1980 and Sergeant Desiré Bouterse became Surinam's de facto ruler. In 1986 an extended guerrilla protest by the Surinamese Liberation Army (SLA) was launched, organized from the jungle in neighbouring French Guyanne. In 1988 civilian rule was restored, following elections, but the military retained great influence. In 1990 a new military coup was staged, but in 1991 a coalition of opposition parties, the New Front for Democracy and Development, led by Ronald Venetiaan, won elections. A peace agreement with the SLA was made in 1992. Drug trafficking, gun-running, and money laundering all remained problems. After elections in 1996 a new coalition government led by the National Democratic Party was formed, and Jules Wijdenbosch was elected President. However, Venetiaan was again elected in 2000 and re-elected in 2005. In 2010 Bouterse was elected President, despite being on trial for murders committed by his military regime in 1982.

Sutton Hoo An estate in Suffolk, England, site of a group of barrows, one of which was found (1939) to cover the remains of a Saxon ship burial (or perhaps a cenotaph; no body was discovered) of the 7th century AD. The timbers had decayed and only their impression was left in the soil, with the iron bolts still in place, and in the centre was a magnificent collection of grave goods, including exotic jewellery, an iron standard, decorated shield, bronze helmet, and Merovingian gold coins.

Suvarov, Alexander Vasilevich, Count Rimniksky, Prince Italysky (1729–1800) Russian field marshal. His brilliant campaigns against the Poles (1769) and the Turks (1773–74) laid the foundations of his reputation. Further successes against the Turks 14 years later led *Catherine II to appoint him a count in 1788. In 1790 he was placed at the head of the army that subdued the Poles. He was dismissed by

the new emperor *Paul I in 1796, but was recalled to face the French in Italy three years later. After some early successes he was forced to retreat and returned to St Petersburg.

Swanscombe Man An early inhabitant of Britain, named after a village in Kent, England, where three skull bones were discovered in river gravels in 1935, 1936, and 1955. They are dated at around 250,000 years ago. The skull seems closely related to a skull from Steinheim in Germany; both probably represent late Neanderthals (*Homo neanderthalensis*) or *Homo heidelbergensis*.

SWAPO (South West Africa People's Organization) A nationalist organization formed in South West Africa (*Namibia) in 1964–66 as the South African government extended formal authority in the region. Driven from the country, SWAPO, under the presidency of Sam Nujoma, began a guerrilla campaign, operating largely from neighbouring Angola. Efforts by the United Nations failed to find an agreeable formula for Namibian independence and the guerrilla war continued until 1988. SWAPO won the first general election in November 1989. In the first post-independence elections in Namibia, in 1994, SWAPO secured a two-thirds majority in the National Assembly. It achieved similar results in 1999, 2004, and 2009.

swastika (from Sanskrit *svastika*, 'conducive to well-being') An emblem in the form of an even-length cross, with the arms bent at right angles, clockwise or anti-clockwise. A symbol of prosperity and good fortune, it was used in ancient Mesopotamia, in early Christian and Byzantine art, in South and Central America, and among the Hindus and Buddhists of India. In 1910 the German poet Guido von List proposed the swastika (German, *Hakenkreuz* 'hooked cross') as a symbol for all *anti-Semitic organizations in the mistaken belief that it was Teutonic in origin. The *Nazi Party adopted it in 1919, incorporated it (1935) into the national flag of the *Third Reich, and made it a symbol of German national depravity.

Swaziland

Capital:	Mbabane (administrative); Lobamba (royal and legislative)
Area:	17,364 sq km (6704 sq miles)
Population:	1,403,362 (2013 est)
Currency:	1 lilangeni = 100 cents

Religions:	African indigenous churches 40.0%; Roman Catholic 20.0%; Muslim 10%
Ethnic Groups:	African 97.0%; European 3.0%
Languages:	English, siSwati (both official)
International Organizations:	UN; AU; Commonwealth; SADC; Non-Aligned Movement; WTO

A small country of south-ern Africa.

Physical Swaziland is landlocked by South Africa on three sides and by Mo-zambique on the east. In the west are well-watered hills, rich in iron ore, from which run several rivers to the dry veld in the middle of the country. Here a variety of crops is grown, on the lower plains in the east there is livestock farming and cultivation of sugar cane.

Economy The economy is heavily dependent on South Africa, which is Swaziland's dominant trading partner; many Swazis find work in South African mines, and much of Swaziland's elec-tricity is imported from South Africa. The main export is sugar, with sugar cane being the principal crop. Other crops include cotton, maize, tobacco, rice, fruit, sorghum, and groundnuts. Industrial products include coal, wood pulp (formerly a leading export), soft drink concentrates, textiles, and clothing. About two-thirds of the population is employed in subsistence agriculture.

History Swaziland takes its name from the Swazis, who probably moved into the area dur-ing the 16th century. The name is thought to have been given to the people in 1836 when Mswati (Mswazi) II became king. A South African protectorate from 1894, Swaziland came under British rule in 1902 after the Second *Boer War, retaining its monarchy. In 1968 it became a fully independent kingdom under Sobhuza II (1921–82). Revisions of the constitution in 1973 in re-sponse to requests from its Parliament, and again in 1978, gave the monarchy wide powers. All pol-itical parties were banned under the 1978 consti-tution. As a result, King Mswati III, who succeeded in 1986, faced increasing demands (1991–92) for the introduction of democracy. Parliamentary elections were held on a non-party basis in 1993, but were widely held to be undemocratic. A new

constitution took effect in 2006, but left the King with near absolute power. HIV/AIDS was a major threat to Swaziland in the early 21st century: in 2012 a quarter of the population was infected, the highest rate in the world.

Sweden

Capital:	Stockholm
Area:	450,295 sq km (173,860 sq miles)
Population:	9,119,423 (2005)
Currency:	1 Swedish krona = 100 ore
Religions:	Lutheran 87.0%
Ethnic Groups:	Swedish; Finnish, Lapp, and other minorities
Languages:	Swedish (official); minority languages
International Organizations:	UN; EU; Council of Europe; OSCE; OECD; Euro-Atlantic Partnership Council; WTO

A country in northern Europe occupying the southern and eastern (the largest) part of the Scandi-navian peninsula.

Physical Sweden has a lengthy mountainous boundary with Norway on the north-west and a shorter one with Finland on the north-east. Its island-fringed coasts are on the Baltic Sea and the Kattegat, the channel to the North Sea. The northern part of the country is within the Arctic Circle. There are glaciers in the mountains, which are heavily forested with conifers. Parallel rivers fall to the Baltic Sea (Gulf of Bothnia) in rapids and falls, many of which have hydroelectric power stations. A region of hills and huge lakes lies to the south of the mountain range, and then the land rises again to a rocky, forested plat-eau. The southern coastal plain is extremely fertile.

Economy Sweden has an industrial economy based on the exploitation of abundant natural and mineral resources. Major exports include machinery, motor vehicles, paper, iron, and steel. A leading producer of iron ore, the coun-try also has deposits of copper, lead, and zinc. Commercial forestry is important. Electricity is generated mainly from nuclear and hydroelec-tric sources. The small agricultural sector pro-duces cereals, sugar beet, meat, and milk.

History The country's earliest history is shrouded in legend, but Suiones tribesmen are mentioned by Tacitus and were probably the founders of the first unified Swedish state. Swedish *Vikings were active in the Baltic area, and also ventured into Russia and the Arab caliphate of Baghdad. Christianity was introduced in the 9th century but the population was not converted until much later. In the 13th century parts of Finland and Karelia were occupied, but from 1397–1523 Sweden belonged to the Danish-dominated Union of *Kalmar. Gustavus Vasa led the revolt that ended in independence for Sweden, a national crown for himself and his dynasty, and the introduction of the Lutheran Church as the state religion. During the 16th and 17th centuries Sweden expanded territorially and achieved considerable political status, thanks largely to the efforts of *Gustavus II (Adolphus) and Axel Oxenstierna. The high point was reached after the Treaty of *Westphalia, during the reign of Charles X (1654–60), but the strains of maintaining a scattered empire began to tell during the reign of *Charles XII (1682–1718). After the *Northern War (1700–21) the empire was dismembered and parliamentary government prevailed until the coup of Gustavus III in 1771 who remained in power until 1792.

During the *Napoleonic Wars Sweden joined the Third Coalition against France (1805), but France defeated Russia, and the latter in turn took Finland from Sweden as compensation (1809). In that year the pro-French party in the Swedish estates overthrew the existing monarch, Gustav IV, and elected the aged and childless Charles XIII (1809–18). In 1810 they invited Jean-Baptiste Bernadotte to become crown prince. He subsequently ruled as *Charles XIV (1818–44), and his descendants have remained monarchs of Sweden ever since. From 1814–1905 Norway was united with Sweden. Pursuing a policy of non-alignment, Sweden kept out of both World Wars, and by the 1950s it had developed into one of the world's wealthiest and most socially progressive states with an extensive social welfare system. A long Social Democrat hegemony was challenged during the 1970s, but regained by Olof Palme (1982–86), until his assassination. Sweden has played a central role in UN peacekeeping missions. It hosted the conference in 1959 resulting in EFTA, but in 1991 it applied to join the *European Community and became a member of the European Union in 1995. The Moderate Unity Party under Carl Bildt came to power in 1991, committed to reduction in public expenditure on welfare provision. Social Democrat leader Ingvar Carlsson, who had succeeded Olof Palme as Prime Minister in 1986, regained power in 1994, but handed over power to Göran Persson in 1996. After elections in 1998 and 2002 further coalitions, led by the Social Democrats, were formed; but in 2006 a four-party centre-right coalition triumphed and Frederik Reinfeldt became Prime Minister. This coalition continued in power after the 2010 election as a minority government.

Sweyn I (or **Sven**; known as **'Sweyn Forkbeard'**) (died 1014) King of Denmark (c.985–1014). From 1003 he launched a series of attacks on England, finally driving the English king Ethelred the Unready to flee to Normandy in 1013. Sweyn then became king of England until his death five weeks later. His son Canute was later king of England, Denmark, and Norway.

Switzerland

Capital:	Berne
Area:	41,277 sq km (15,937 sq miles)
Population:	7,996,026 (2013 est)
Currency:	1 Swiss franc = 100 centimes
Religions:	Roman Catholic 38.2%; Protestant 26.9%; Muslim 4.9%
Ethnic Groups:	German 65.0%; French 18.0%; Italian 10.0%; Romansch 1.0%
Languages:	French, German, Italian, Romansch (all official); minority languages
International Organizations:	UN; OECD; EFTA; Council of Europe; OSCE; Euro-Atlantic Partnership Council; WTO

A country in central Europe, consisting of a Federation of 23 cantons; three cantons are subdivided making a total of 26 administrative units.

Physical Switzerland is surrounded by France, Germany, Italy, and the tiny country of Liechtenstein. It is Europe's loftiest country with the Alps stretching across the whole of its southern half. The rivers Rhône and Rhine rise here and form broad valleys. Below the forested mountain slopes, snow-covered all winter, the land is fertile and the summer temperature is warm. Northward the country stands on a hilly plateau which contains the Swiss Lakes and rises again in the north-west to the Jura Mountains.

Economy Switzerland is prosperous, with one of the highest GDPs per capita in the world. Major exports include machinery, chemicals, metals, watches, and agricultural products. Tourism and international banking and insurance are important. Agriculture produces grains, fruit, vegetables, meat, and eggs.

History Switzerland was occupied by the Celtic *Helvetii in the 2nd century BC. Its position astride vital Alpine passes caused the area to be invaded by the Romans, Alemanni, Burgundians, and Franks before it came under the control of the Holy Roman Empire in the 11th century. In 1291 the cantons (Swiss confederacies) of Uri, Schwyz, and Unterwalden declared their independence of their Habsburg overlords, and the alliance for mutual defence was later joined by Lucerne, Zürich, and Bern. During the 15th century this Swiss Confederation continued to expand, and it fought successfully against Burgundy, France, and the Holy Roman Empire, creating a great demand for its soldiers as mercenaries. During the *Reformation and *Counter-Reformation, its political stability was undermined by civil warfare, but in 1648 the Habsburgs acknowledged its independence in the Treaty of *Westphalia.

In 1798 French Revolutionary armies entered the country and established the Helvetic Republic. But at the Congress of *Vienna (1815) Swiss control was restored and the European powers guaranteed the confederation's neutrality. In 1847 a separate Roman Catholic league within the federation, the Sonderbund, was formed after radicals took power in one of the cantons. After a brief civil war, peace and stability were restored by the new, democratic, federal constitution of 1848. During World War I the country maintained its neutrality despite the contradictory affections of the French and German sections of its population. In World War II the Swiss again preserved their armed neutrality, and have continued since then to enjoy a high level of economic prosperity. In 1979 the 22 cantons of the confederation were joined by the new Canton of Jura. Women were not allowed to vote on a federal basis until 1971, and suffrage remains restricted in some cantons. Because of its long tradition of neutrality, the International Red Cross and the League of Nations were both based in Switzerland, as are many UN agencies. In 1992 it rejected by

referendum membership of the European Economic Area. In 1998, Ruth Dreifuss became its first female President. In this year, bowing to international pressure, the Swiss banks released $1.25 billion to the families of Jews murdered by the Germans in the Holocaust—money deposited by the victims before or during the war. In 2002 Switzerland joined the UN and in 2008 it joined the *Schengen Area.

Sykes–Picot Agreement (1916) A secret Anglo-French agreement on the partition of the Ottoman empire after World War I. It was negotiated by Sir Mark Sykes (1879–1919) and François Georges-Picot and provided for French control of coastal Syria, Lebanon, Cilicia, and Mosul, and for British control of Baghdad and Basra and northern Palestine. Palestine was to be under international administration and independent Arab states were to be created in the remaining Arab territories. The agreement reflected the British and French desire to compensate themselves for Russian gains under the secret Constantinople Agreement of 1915 between Russia, Britain, and France (in which the Dardanelles and the Bosporus were to be incorporated into the Tsarist empire in return for British and French influence in the Middle East). Embarrassment was caused to the Allies when the Bolsheviks revealed the terms of the Agreement in late 1917: its provisions appeared to clash with promises made to the Arabs by Sir Henry McMahon in 1915–16 and to the Zionists in the *Balfour Declaration, as well as the *Fourteen Points of President Wilson.

Syria

Capital:	Damascus
Area:	185,180 sq km (71,498 sq miles)
Population:	22,457,336 (2005)
Currency:	1 Syrian pound = 100 piastres
Religions:	Sunni Muslim 74.0%; Alawi, Ismaili, and Shia 13.0%; Christian 10.0%; Druze 3.0%
Ethnic Groups:	Arab 90.3%; Kurdish, Armenian, and other minorities
Languages:	Arabic (official); minority languages
International Organizations:	UN; Arab League; OAPEC; Non-Aligned Movement; WTO

A country in the Middle East at the eastern end of the Mediterranean Sea.

Physical Bounded on the north by Turkey, on the east by Iraq, on the south by Jordan, and on the south-west by Israel and Lebanon, Syria has a narrow coastal plain: citrus fruit and tobacco can be grown. Behind a range of hills the Asi (Orontes) River runs northward, along a rift valley; and beyond that the ground rises to a plateau. This merges into hot, dry desert, relieved only by the upper Euphrates, which runs across the country. In the extreme north-east there is oil.

Economy Exports include crude oil and oil products, minerals, agricultural produce, cotton fibre, textiles, and clothing. The principal agricultural crops are cereals, cotton, pulses, olives, and sugar beet. The economy has been badly damaged by the civil war since 2011.

History Syria was settled successively by the Akkadians, Arameans, and Canaanites, and formed a valuable province of successive empires, from the Phoenicians to the Byzantines. After the Arab conquest of the 630s, Damascus became the capital of the Arab caliphate under the *Umayyads from 661 to 750, but subsequently Syria became a province of other rulers, such as the *Fatimids and the *Mamelukes of Egypt. It became a province of the *Ottoman empire in 1516, and after the Turkish defeat in World War I Syria was mandated to France. Controlled by *Vichy France at the outbreak of World War II, the country was invaded and occupied by British and *Free French forces, and declared its independence in 1941. Political stability proved elusive, with three army-led coups in 1949 and others in 1951 and 1954. An abortive union with Egypt in the *United Arab Republic provided no solution and was terminated by a further army coup. A leading political grouping, the Ba'ath Socialist Party, remained split by personal and ideological rivalries, though one successful and two abortive coups in 1963 did see a swing to policies of nationalization. Further coups in 1966 and 1970 saw the eventual emergence of General Hafiz al-Assad as the leader of a new regime, capable not only of crushing internal opposition but also of asserting significant influence over neighbouring war-torn Lebanon. However, Syria suffered major reverses in the 1967 *Six-Day War and the *Yom Kippur War of 1973 against Israel. It was deeply involved in the civil war in *Lebanon (1975–89), and remained generally antagonistic towards Iraq, sending troops to defend Saudi Arabia in 1990 in the *Gulf War. In December 1991 a reconciliation took place with the PLO, when Yasser *Arafat visited Damascus. Relations with other Arab League states were improved and Syria took a cautious part in the Middle East peace negotiations of 1992. Unlike its former allies in the Six-Day War (Egypt and Jordan) Syria had not undertaken any rapprochement towards Israel. However, with the peace agreements between Israel and the PLO and Israel and Jordan (1993; 1994), President Assad made tentative moves to reach an accommodation with Israel. Assad died in 2000 and was succeeded as President by his son, Bashar al-Assad, who maintained his policies. Syria withdrew its troops from Lebanon in 2005 following accusations of involvement in the assassination of the former Lebanese Prime Minister Rafik Hariri. In 2011 popular protests inspired by the *Arab Spring were met with state repression and by 2012 the conflict had escalated into full civil war. By 2014 about 100,000 people had been killed and several million displaced from their homes. That same year a further conflict developed between moderate rebel forces and the Sunni jihadist group *Islamic State, which took control of large areas of northeast Syria.

S

Tacitus (full name **Publius**, or **Gaius, Cornelius Tacitus**) (*c.*56–*c.*120 AD) Roman historian. His major works on the history of the Roman Empire, only partially preserved, are the *Annals* (covering the years 14–68) and the *Histories* (69–96). They are written in a concise style, pervaded by a deep pessimism about the course of Roman history since the end of the Republic.

Tacna–Arica Conflict (1883–1929) A territorial dispute between Peru and Chile. The provinces of Tacna and Arica belonged to Peru at the time of its independence from Spain, but after the War of the Pacific (1879–84), Chile appropriated Arica and Tacna. In 1929 negotiations between Peru and Chile produced a settlement that returned Tacna to Peru with an indemnity of $6 million and left Arica under Chilean control.

Taff Vale case (1901) A British court action that established the principle that trade unions could be sued for damages. Following a strike by railwaymen employed by the Taff Vale Railway Company, the company sued the Amalgamated Society of Railway Servants for loss of revenue. The House of Lords, on appeal, awarded the company damages and costs. The resentment felt by workers at this contravention of the Trade Union Act of 1871, which had, they thought, established the immunity of union funds, was an important factor in the increased support given to the *Labour Party. The Trade Disputes Act, passed in 1906, effectively reversed the decision by exempting trade unions from this type of action; this remained the situation until the Trade Union Act of 1984, which permitted employers to seek redress if a strike was called without certain preconditions (such as a secret ballot) having been met.

Taft, William Howard (1857–1930) US Republican statesman, 27th President of the USA (1909–13). His presidency is remembered for its dollar diplomacy in foreign affairs and for its tariff laws, which were criticized as being too favourable to big business. Taft later served as Chief Justice of the Supreme Court (1921–30).

Taft–Hartley Act (1947) An act of the US Congress that curbed the power of trade unions. It banned the closed-shop and the secondary boycott, allowed employers to sue unions for breach of contract and for damages inflicted on them by strikes, empowered the President to order a 60-day "cooling-off period" before strike action, and required union leaders to take oaths stating that they were not communists. Despite protests from the unions, it has remained relatively unchanged.

taille *See* TALLAGE.

Taiping Rebellion (1850–64) Revolt against the Chinese *Qing dynasty. Led and inspired by Hong Xiuquan (1813–64), who claimed to be the younger brother of Jesus Christ, the Taiping Rebellion began in Guangxi province. It developed into the most serious challenge to the Qing, bringing most of the central and lower Yangtze region under rebel control, and costing 20 million lives. The rebels captured Nanjing in 1853 and established their capital there before launching an unsuccessful attack on Beijing. Taiping resistance was crushed with the capture of Nanjing in 1864, Hong Xiuquan having died in the siege, but the Qing regime never really recovered from the long civil war.

Taiwan (official name **Republic of China**)

Capital:	Taipei
Area:	35,980 sq km (13,892 sq miles)
Population:	23,299,716 (2013 est)
Currency:	1 New Taiwan dollar = 100 cents
Religions:	Buddhist–Daoist mixture 93.0%; Christian 4.5%
Ethnic Groups:	Taiwanese 84.0%; Mainland Chinese 14.0%; indigenous (Indonesian) 2.0%

| Languages: | Mandarin Chinese (official); Chinese dialects |
| International Organizations: | WTO |

A country (not recognized by most other countries and not a member of the UN) comprising a large island and several much smaller ones off the southeast coast of China.

Physical The main island is almost 370 km (230 miles) long from north to south and 130 km (81 miles) wide from west to east. High mountains running most of its length, richly forested with camphor, oak, cypress, and cedar, drop steeply eastward to the Pacific Ocean.

Economy Taiwan's industrial growth has been driven by exports, particularly of electronics (including IT equipment), machinery, and petrochemicals; other industries include textiles, iron and steel, vehicles, and consumer products. A small agricultural sector produces rice, vegetables, fruit, and tea.

History Portuguese explorers called it **Formosa** ('the Beautiful Island'). Sparsely populated by a non-Chinese people, it was long a Chinese and Japanese pirate base. In the 17th century the Dutch (1624) and the Spaniards (1626) established trading posts, the Dutch driving out the Spaniards in 1642. With the fall of the *Ming dynasty in 1644 opponents of the *Qing started to settle on the island and in 1661 'Koxinga' (Zheng Chenggong), a Ming patriot, expelled the Dutch. It was conquered by the Qing in 1683 and for the first time became part of China. Fighting continued between its original inhabitants and the Chinese settlers into the 19th century. Taiwan was occupied by Japan as a result of the Treaty of Shimonoseki in 1895 and remained under Japanese control until the end of World War II. The island was occupied by the Chinese forces of *Chiang Kai-shek in September 1945, but Taiwanese resentment at the administration of Chiang's governor Chen Yi produced a revolt which had to be put down by force of arms. When the *Chinese Civil War began to turn against the *Kuomintang in 1948, arrangements were made to transfer Chiang's government to Taiwan, a move completed in the following year, and by 1950 almost two million refugees from the mainland had also arrived on the island. Supported militarily by the USA, Taiwan maintained its independence from communist China, as the Republic of China, and, until expelled in 1971, sat as the sole representative of China in the United Nations. Chiang Kai-shek remained its President until his death in 1975, and was succeeded by his son, Chiang Ching-kuo. He died in 1988 and was succeeded by President Lee Teng-hui. Since the 1950s Taiwan has undergone dramatic industrialization, becoming one of the world's major industrial nations. In 1986 the creation of new political parties was legalized, but with strict regulations governing their policies. Martial law, in force since 1949, was replaced in 1987 by the slightly less severe National Security law. Pro-democracy demonstrations during the late 1980s and early 1990s led to further political reforms. The first full multiparty elections since 1949 were held in 1992 and were won by the Kuomintang. The Kuomintang has consistently opposed full independence for Taiwan and sought reunification with the mainland, but only if the mainland regime rejects communism. Negotiations between the two countries have been sporadic and generally unproductive, but in 1991 Taiwan officially ended its state of war with communist China. In 1993 a formal structure for further negotiations on economic and social issues was agreed but relations have remained tense. In 1996 Taiwan's first democratic presidential elections were won by the incumbent, Lee Teng-Hui. However, the Kuomintang's dominance ended in 2000 with the election of Chen Shui-bian, leader of the opposition Democratic Progressive Party, as President. He was narrowly re-elected in 2004, but the Kuomintang regained the presidency in 2008 with Ma Ying-jeou. In 2010 a trade agreement was signed with China

Taizong (or **T'ai-tsung**) (596–649) Second Tang Emperor of China (627–49). He was renowned for his military prowess, scholarship, and concern for people. He was a patron of Xuanzang, the Buddhist pilgrim who, in 645, brought back from India Buddhist scriptures, which he translated into Chinese.

Tajikistan

Capital:	Dushanbe
Area:	143,100 sq km (55,240 sq miles)
Population:	7,910,041 (2013 est)
Currency:	1 somoni = 100 dirams
Religions:	Sunni Muslim 85.0%; Shia Muslim 5.0%

Ethnic Groups:	Tajik 79.9%; Uzbek 15.3%; Russian 1.1%; Kyrgyz 1.1%
Languages:	Tajik (official); Russian
International Organizations:	UN; OSCE; Commonwealth of Independent States; Euro-Atlantic Partnership Council; WTO

A country bounded by China on the east and Afghanistan on the south; it occupies one of the highest regions of central Asia.

Physical The Pamir mountains occupy a third of Tajikistan while the Alai range stretches across its centre. Below the snow-line the slopes are generally great stretches of bare red and grey rocks, broken by alpine meadows.

Economy Tajikistan is the poorest of the former Soviet republics, despite considerable mineral resources that include gold, silver, uranium, and tungsten. Almost half the workforce is engaged in agriculture. The principal industries are aluminium production and hydroelectricity, and the principal agricultural crop is cotton. These three commodities are major exports. Remittances from expatriates are important.

History Tajiks were originally of Iranian stock, but were conquered by Arab people during the 7th and 8th centuries AD. Large numbers of Turkic people moved into the area, which came under the control of the Uzbek khanate of Bukhara from the 15th to the mid-18th century and was then conquered by the Afghans. By 1868 the whole area had been conquered by the Russians and proclaimed a protectorate. Following the Russian Revolution a Bukharan People's Soviet Republic was proclaimed in 1920. This however was conquered by the Red Army, and a confused situation lasted until 1929 when the Tajik Soviet Socialist Republic was formed, which in 1936 joined the Soviet Union. During 1990 opposition parties were legalized. In September 1991 independence was proclaimed and Tajikistan joined the *Commonwealth of Independent States (CIS). By 1992, polarization between a nationwide Islamic majority and a Russian minority based in the capital Dushanbe and the industrialized north had developed. There were armed skirmishes, with Russian troops still stationed in the country becoming involved. In that year President Rakhmon Nabiyev was removed from office by force. Fighting between government forces and Muslim rebels was halted by a ceasefire in 1994, but sporadic violence continued. A new constitution was approved in 1994 and Imamoli Rakhmanov (now Emomalii Rahmon), who had been acting head of state since 1992, was elected President. Legislative elections in 1995 resulted in victory for the ruling (formerly Communist) party. Subsequent elections have produced similar results. A further agreement with the rebels in 1997 led to constitutional changes and a reconciliation process.

Taliban (Pashto, 'seekers') An Islamic fundamentalist political and military grouping that controlled most of Afghanistan from 1996 until late 2001. The Taliban militia was formed in 1994 by Islamic theological students in the south of the country with the intention of unifying Afghanistan. Rival Mujaheddin factions had been fighting since the withdrawal of Soviet forces in 1989. After initial reverses, the Taliban captured the city of Herat in September 1995 and advanced to take Kabul in August 1996. A strict Islamic code of law was immediately imposed, which debarred women from paid work and education and proscribed television. In the late 1990s the Taliban consolidated its hold on power and took further territory from their main opponents, an alliance of forces concentrated in the north-east of Afghanistan. However, the regime remained internationally isolated and unrecognized, largely because of its support for international terrorism. Following the events of *September 11, 2001, the Taliban's links with *al-Qaeda provoked the USA to launch airstrikes on its command centres in Kabul and other cities (*see* WAR ON TERRORISM). The regime collapsed within weeks. The Taliban was expelled from the cities and severely weakened, but it continued to wage a guerrilla war in Afghanistan. Its strength and influence began to recover in the mid-2000s.

The Pakistani Taliban, a similar but separate group, has conducted an insurgency against the Pakistani state since 2007.

tallage A tax in medieval Europe that was generally imposed by an estate owner upon his unfree tenantry and its amount and frequency varied. In England it was a royal tax from the 12th century onward, levied on boroughs and royal lands. It was condemned by the barons in *Magna Carta in 1215 and became less important with the rise of parliamentary taxation, finally being abolished in 1340.

In France the "taille" was greatly extended in the 14th century to meet the expenses of the *Hundred Years War, although, because it was the monetary equivalent of feudal service, the nobility and clergy were exempted from payment. The main burden of the taille, by now the most important direct tax, lay upon the peasants until it was abolished in the *French Revolution.

Talleyrand (full name **Charles Maurice de Talleyrand-Périgord**) (1754–1838) French statesman. Foreign Minister under the *Directory from 1797, he was involved in the coup that brought Napoleon to power, and held the same position under the new leader (1799–1807); he then resigned office and engaged in secret negotiations to have Napoleon deposed. Talleyrand became head of the new government after the fall of Napoleon (1814) and recalled Louis XVIII to the throne. He was later instrumental in the overthrow of Charles X and the accession of Louis Philippe (1830).

Tamerlane (or **Tamburlaine**; born **Timur Lenk**, 'lame Timur') (1336–1405) Mongol ruler of Samarkand (1369–1405). Leading a force of Mongols and Turks, between about 1364 and 1405 he conquered a large area including Persia, northern India, and Syria and established his capital at Samarkand; he defeated the Ottomans near Ankara in 1402, but died during an invasion of China. He was an ancestor of the Mogul dynasty in India.

Tammany Hall Headquarters of a political organization in New York City. Founded in 1789, it was named after a late 17th-century Indian chief, and based its rites and ceremonies on pseudo-Indian forms. It acquired, under the control of Aaron *Burr, a political importance that endured until the 1950s. The word Tammany became synonymous with machine politics, graft, corruption, and other abuses in city politics.

Tamworth Manifesto (1834) The election address of Sir Robert *Peel to his constituents at Tamworth, Staffordshire. Peel promised to accept the Whig government's *Reform Act of 1832. He declared his adherence to a policy of moderate reform, while stressing the need to preserve what was most valuable from Britain's past. This concept of change, where necessary, within existing institutions marked the shift from the old, repressive Toryism to a new, more enlightened Conservatism.

Tanaka Kakuei (1918–93) Japanese statesman. First elected to the House of Representatives in 1947, his career was briefly interrupted by a bribery scandal soon after, but from 1957 he served successively as Minister of Communications, Minister of Finance (in three different cabinets) and Minister of International Trade. In 1972 he became Japan's youngest post-war Prime Minister (1972–74). He was forced to resign as a result of a bribery scandal in December 1974 and in 1976 had to face accusations of responsibility for the Lockheed scandal, relating to the corrupt sale of US military aircraft to Japan. During lengthy legal proceedings against him he remained a powerful force within the ruling *Liberal Democratic Party. He was sentenced to four years' imprisonment in 1983, but launched an appeal, which had reached the Supreme Court of Japan by October 1992. He was disabled by a severe stroke in 1985 and by 1987 his intra-party faction had disintegrated.

Tang The dynasty that ruled in China from 618 to c.906, a period noted for territorial conquest and great wealth; it is often regarded as the golden age of Chinese poetry and art.

Tanganyika *See* TANZANIA.

Tanzania

Capital:	Dodoma (many government offices remain in Dar es Salaam, the former capital)
Area:	947,300 sq km (365,755 sq miles)
Population:	48,261,942 (2013 est)
Currency:	1 Tanzanian shilling = 100 cents
Religions (mainland):	Christian 30.0%; Muslim 35.0%; traditional beliefs 35.0%. Zanzibar: more than 99.0% Muslim.
Ethnic Groups (mainland):	African (over 130 tribes) 99.0%. Zanzibar: Arab, African, and mixed race.
Languages:	Swahili, English (both official); Arabic (especially on Zanzibar); local languages
International Organizations:	UN; AU; Commonwealth; Non-Aligned Movement; SADC; WTO

A country in East Africa, consisting of the former republic of Tanganyika and the island of Zanzibar.

Physical Tanzania is bounded by Kenya and Uganda on the north, Rwanda, Burundi, and the Democratic Republic of Congo on the west, and Zambia, Malawi, and Mozambique on the south. It has a coast on the Indian Ocean and several islands; Pemba and Zanzibar islands both have a degree of autonomy. A hot, wet coastal plain rises through thick forest and areas planted with sisal to a warm plateau. In the north is Mount Kilimanjaro, below which the soil is volcanic and coffee can be grown. In the extreme north is Lake Victoria, round which cotton is cultivated; the Serengeti National Park is here. Lake Tanganyika along the western border and Lake Malawi in the south, both lie in the western arm of the Great Rift Valley.

Economy Formerly a socialist economy, Tanzania has almost completed its transition to free-market principles; however, despite recent growth it remains one of the poorest countries in the world. Agriculture is the mainstay of the economy: it employs four-fifths of the workforce and provides five-sixths of exports, principally coffee, cashew nuts, and cotton. Gold is another important export, and diamonds and iron are also mined. Other industries include agricultural processing.

History In the first millenium BC northern mainland Tanzania was inhabited by Caucasoid peoples, probably from Egypt. Bantu-speaking peoples from western Africa moved into the region and were established there by about 500 AD. Arab slave merchants settled along the coast, clashing occasionally with Portuguese explorers, who first arrived in the late 15th century. German missionaries went to Tanganyika (mainland Tanzania) in the 1840s and were followed by German colonists. By 1907 Germany had taken full control of the country. Tanganyika became a British mandate after World War I, and a trust territory, administered by Britain, after World War II. It became independent in 1961, followed by Zanzibar in 1963. The two countries united in 1964 to form the United Republic of Tanzania under its first President, Julius *Nyerere. In the Arusha Declaration of 1967 Nyerere stated his policy of equality and independence for Tanzania. In 1975 the Tan–Zam railway line was completed. Tanzania helped to restore democracy in Uganda in 1986 and gave strong support to political exiles from Zimbabwe, Angola, and Namibia. Nyerere was succeeded by President Ndugu Ali Hassan

Mwinyi, who was re-elected in 1990 and whose years in office saw a marked revival of the economy with its very considerable potential. In June 1992 he ended 27 years of one-party rule by the legalization of opposition parties. During 1994 and 1995, some 800,000 refugees from civil war and ethnic violence in the neighbouring countries of *Rwanda and *Burundi fled to Tanzania; some Tanzanian politicians called for their repatriation. Internal tensions also grew in this period, particularly in Zanzibar, where the ruling party encountered growing opposition from Islamic fundamentalists. Multiparty elections, held in November 1995, saw the Party for the Revolution retain power, with Benjamin Mkapa becoming the country's new President. He was re-elected in 2000 and succeeded in 2005 by Jakaya Kikwete, who was re-elected in 2010.

Tanzimat reforms (1839–71) A series of reforms in the *Ottoman empire. They were promulgated under sultans Abdülmecid I (1839–61) and Abdülaziz (1861–76) in response to western pressure. Under Mustafa Resid Pasha (1800–58) a programme of reform was steadily developed. The army was reorganized on the Prussian model and the slave trade was abolished. Abuses in the taxation system were to be eliminated and provincial representative assemblies were created. New codes of commercial, land, and criminal law, based on French models, were introduced, with new state courts, separate from the Islamic religious courts. In his last years sultan Abdülaziz lost interest in the Tanzimat and, from 1871, became increasingly autocratic.

Tara The ancient coronation and assembly place of the High Kings of *Ireland, in County Meath. Remains dating back to about 2000 BC have been found there and there is evidence of a network of halls, enclosures, and fortresses. The pillar stone may have been the inauguration stone of the kings of Tara. In the 4th century there were five tribal kingdoms: Ulster, Meath, Leinster, Munster, and Connaught, which nominally acknowledged the overlordship of the High King (the ruler of Tara). Conn was reputedly the first High King ("Ard Ri"). Niall of the Nine Hostages, possibly the son of a British prince, ruled there in about 400 and his son Leary received St Patrick there in 432. Tara appears to have been abandoned in the 6th century.

Taranaki Wars A major part of the *Anglo-Maori Wars in New Zealand. In 1859, Governor Browne accepted an offer of land on the Waitara

River from Teira (a Maori right-holder), despite the veto of the senior chief, Wiremu Kingi. When the survey was resisted, Browne sent troops to Waitara. Many Maori supported Kingi, believing the purchase to be a breach of the Treaty of *Waitangi. Fighting was inconclusive in 1860–61 and, after a two-year truce, resumed in 1863. Maori resistance on the coast was overcome and much land confiscated. Maori resistance in the interior, increasingly led by the *Pai Marire, continued through the 1860s.

tariff reform A British fiscal policy designed to end the nation's adherence to free trade by the use of protective duties on imported goods. Joseph *Chamberlain believed that the use of tariffs would strengthen Britain's revenue and its trading position; it would also strengthen links within the British empire by making possible a policy of imperial preference (the application of lower rates of duty between its member countries). Chamberlain's campaign (1897–1906) failed, it divided the Conservatives and was rejected by the Liberals. Tariff reform was rejected again in 1923 when Stanley *Baldwin and the Conservatives failed to secure an overall majority in an election primarily on that issue. However, the shock caused by the international financial crisis of 1929–31 and the intensification of nationalist political and economic rivalries made Britain's free trade policy even more of an anachronism. The adoption of protectionism by the MacDonald *National government from 1931 signalled the ultimate success of the tariff reform policy.

Tariq ibn Zaid (*fl.* 700–12) A freedman of Musa ibn Nusayr, *Umayyad governor of North Africa. In 711 he was sent to conquer Spain with 7000 men, landing near the famous rock that has immortalized his name, Jabal al-Tariq (Mount of Tariq), that is, Gibraltar. On 19 July 711 he defeated the Visigoth king Roderick and went on to conquer half of Spain. In 712 Musa crossed to Spain and, out of jealousy at Tariq's success, put him in chains. His subsequent fate is unknown.

Tarquin The fifth and the seventh Etruscan kings of Rome, **Priscus** (616–579 BC) and **Superbus** (534–510 BC), both subjects of legend and tradition. The stories were largely symbolic, contrasting the decadence of the monarchy with the idealism of the new *Roman republic. After this time the word 'king' was used by the Romans as a term of political abuse.

Tartars (or **Tatars**) A number of Central Asian peoples who, over the centuries, were a threat to civilized peoples in Asia and Europe. More specific names, for example Mongol, Turk, Kipchak, emerge for some of these peoples who were constantly moving, often over great distances, and who spoke a variety of related Turkic and Mongol languages. The name "Tartars" is applied specifically to tribesmen living south of the Amur who were defeated by the Ming emperor *Yongle in the early 15th century. Papal envoys (*c.*1250) to the Mongols consistently called them Tartars, probably by association with Tartarus, the place of punishment in the underworld of Greek mythology. The name was also applied to the *Golden Horde. Some of the Cossacks (originally Kahsaks, "free men") on the River Dnieper were Tartars. Later any people of Turkish stock in Russia were called Tartars. In the 15th century the Crimean Tartars formed an independent khanate, which was a tributary to the *Ottoman Turks until annexed by Russia in 1783. The khanates of the Volga Tartars came under Russian rule in the 16th century.

Tasman, Abel (Janszoon) (1603–*c.*1659) Dutch navigator. In 1642 he was sent by Anthony van Diemen (1593–1645, the Governor-General of the Dutch East Indies) to explore Australian waters; that year he reached Tasmania (which he named Van Diemen's Land) and New Zealand, and in 1643 arrived at Tonga and Fiji. On a second voyage in 1644 he also reached the Gulf of Carpentaria on the north coast of Australia.

Tata An Indian Parsi commercial and industrial family. It is one of the two (with the *Birlas) most important merchant families in modern India. The family began in Far East trade, but diversified their operations creating, under Jahangir Ratanji Dadabhai Tata (1904–93), an airline which later became Air India. His nephew, Ratan Tata (1937–), made the Tata Group a global business with major acquisitions in steel manufacture (Corus Group, 2007), vehicle manufacture (Jaguar Land Rover, 2008), and other areas.

Tawhiao Son of the Maori king *Potatau and head (1860–94) of the *Kingitanga movement. He led his people in the Second *Anglo-Maori War. Following a truce in 1868 an uneasy peace existed in the "King Country". When the government sought to build a railway, concessions were made to the Maoris. Tawhiao returned to Lower Waikato in 1883 and continued to press claims for the return of confiscated land and for recognition of Maori *rangatiratanga* (chieftainship).

Taylor, Zachary (1784–1850) US Whig statesman, 12th President of the USA (1849–50). He became a national hero after his victories in the war with Mexico (1846–48). As President, he came into conflict with Congress over his desire to admit California to the Union as a free state (without slavery). He died in office before the problem could be resolved.

Teamsters, International Brotherhood of A trade union in the USA. Formed in 1903, its members are workers in the transport industry. In the late 1950s its president, David Beck, was indicted for having links with criminals, and his successor, James R. Hoffa, was found guilty of attempting to influence a federal jury while on trial in 1964 for misusing union funds. The revelations of corruption did immense damage to the reputation of unions, and the Teamsters union was expelled from the AFL–CIO (*see* AFL) in 1957. It was readmitted in 1987, but left in 2005 to join the Change to Win alliance. From the 1980s its membership among transport workers declined but it diversified into other areas.

Tea Party Movement A US populist political movement that emerged in 2009. Taking its name from the Boston Tea Party (*see* BOSTON), it can be seen as standing in a long US tradition of suspicion of and hostility to government. With no central organization or formal agenda, Tea Party supporters' varied in their aims but at their core was a desire to reduce taxation, cut government spending, and reduce the size and scope of the federal government. Distrusting the political establishment to deliver such a radical change of political culture, they worked to secure the election of Tea Party supporters to Congress. The movement achieved some success in the 2010 Republican primaries, but the general election results were more mixed: while some Tea Party supporters were elected, in other cases Republican voters in winnable seats refused to support them and Democrats were elected. The Tea Party members of Congress became noted for their outspoken extreme views and unwillingness to compromise, and their influence exceeded their numbers: fearful of losing to Tea Party supporters in the next primary elections, other Republicans began to endorse the Tea Party agenda. The party lost ground in the 2012 elections, and Tea Party influence seemed to be declining. However, in 2013 the Tea Party was instrumental in a Republican attempt to remove funding from President Obama's health-care reforms, which led to a deadlock that temporarily shut down non-essential parts of the federal government. This tactic failed and cost the Republicans more support.

Teapot Dome scandal (1922–24) US fraud perpetrated by the "Ohio gang" surrounding President *Harding. It involved the siphoning of oil, intended for the US navy, from the oil reserves at Teapot Dome, Wyoming, to the Mammoth Oil Company. A second diversion allowed oil from Elk Hills, California, to be siphoned to the Pan-American Petroleum and Transportation Company. Harding died before the full extent of the involvement of the Secretary of the Interior, Albert B. Fall, was exposed by Senator Thomas J. Walsh of Montana in the years 1922–24. Fall was found guilty of accepting a $100,000 bribe and imprisoned (1929–32).

technology The techniques of engineering and applied science for commercial and industrial purposes. Many fundamental technologies—the smelting and working of metals, spinning and weaving of textiles, and the firing of clay, for example—were empirically developed at the dawn of civilization, long before any concept of science existed. With the advent, in about 3000 BC, of the first major civilizations in Egypt and Mesopotamia, many new technologies were developed—irrigation systems, road networks and wheeled vehicles, a pictographic form of writing, and new building techniques. Other civilizations subsequently became important technological centres, notably those of Greece and Rome, the Arab empire of the 7th to 10th centuries, and the Mayan, Aztec, and Toltec civilizations of the American continent. In the mid-16th century the focus of technological change shifted to Europe, with the beginning of the Scientific Revolution.

By the late 17th century, technology essentially meant engineering. During the 19th century science began to create many new technologies, such as electricity generation and supply and photography. The trend continued into the 20th century, especially with the development of road vehicles, the petrochemical industry, plastics, radio and television, sound recording and reproduction, synthetic fibres, a wide range of pharmaceutical products, nuclear power, and the advent of computers and information technology (*see* INFORMATION REVOLUTION). Since the 1970s pollution and the depletion of energy resources have caused increasing public concern. This has led to the growth of alternative technologies, with an emphasis on renewable energy sources, recycling of raw materials, and the conservation of energy. Recent areas of innovation are genetic engineering (the modification of plant or animal genes to produce a desired commodity or assist in an industrial process) and nanotechnology (manufacturing techniques that manipulate materials at an atomic scale).

Tecumseh (*c.*1768–1813) Native American Shawnee chief in the Ohio Valley. Tecumseh emerged as the most formidable opponent of the White westward expansion, believing that Native American land was a common inheritance, which could not be ceded piecemeal by individual tribes. Together with his half-brother, the Prophet **Tenskwatawa**, he formed a confederacy of tribes to negotiate a peaceful settlement with the settlers. This confederacy was defeated at the Battle of *Tippecanoe in 1811 and Tecumseh then sided with the British in the *War of 1812, but was killed at the Battle of the *Thames in 1813. This marked the end of Native American resistance in the Ohio Valley. Tenskwatawa retired to Canada with a British pension, but returned in 1826 and accompanied the Shawnee when they were moved, first to Missouri, and then to Kansas, where he died (*c.*1837).

Teheran Conference (28 November–1 December 1943) A meeting between *Churchill, *Roosevelt, and *Stalin in the Iranian capital. Here Stalin, invited for the first time to an inter-Allied conference, was told of the impending opening of a Second Front to coincide with a Soviet offensive against Germany. The three leaders discussed the establishment of the *United Nations after the war, and Stalin pressed for a future Soviet sphere of influence in the Baltic States and Eastern Europe, while guaranteeing the independence of Iran.

Te Kooti Rikirangi Te Turuki (*c.*1830–93) Maori spiritual leader. A member of the Aitanga-a-Mahaki tribe, he was accused in 1865 of complicity with the *Pai Marire and its militant offshoot, the Hau-hau, and was deported to the Chatham Islands. In exile he evolved a variation of Pai Marire ritual and belief, the Ringatu. In 1868 his group escaped, seized a government ship, and returned. Challenged by the military, he attacked the settlement at Poverty Bay, killing some Europeans and many more collaborating Maori. The subsequent pursuit and skirmishing lasted until 1872 when Te Kooti found sanctuary in the "King Country" until pardoned. The Ringatu church survives today.

Tel-el-Kebir, Battle of (12–13 September 1882) A battle between British and Egyptian forces, 83 km (52 miles) east of Cairo. British troops under Sir Garnet Wolseley defeated an Egyptian army led by *Arabi Pasha. Cairo fell on the following day, thus confirming the British conquest of Egypt.

Temple, William (1881–1944) British churchman and educationalist. He became a priest in 1909 and was Archbishop of Canterbury (1942–44). He worked with R. A. (later Lord) *Butler on his Education Bill, which became law in 1944. He also sought to secure a greater sense of common purpose between the different religious denominations and his work led to the foundation of the *World Council of Churches.

Templer, Sir Gerald (1898–1979) British field-marshal. Templer commanded the 6th Armoured Division in World War II and after the war served as vice-chief of the Imperial General Staff before being appointed high commissioner and commander-in-chief in Malaya (1952–54) at the peak of the *Malayan Emergency. Through a combination of military efficiency, adaptability to local circumstances, and fostering of good relations with village populations, Templer turned the tide of war decisively against the communist guerrillas.

Tennessee Valley Authority (TVA) An independent federal government agency in the USA. Created by Congress (1933) as part of the *New Deal proposals to offset unemployment by a programme of public works, it set out to provide for the development of the whole Tennessee River basin. It took over a project (begun in 1916) for extracting nitrate at Muscle Shoals, Alabama. In addition the TVA was authorized to construct new dams and improve existing ones, to control floods and generate cheap hydroelectric power, to check erosion, and to provide afforestation across seven states.

Tennis Court Oath A dramatic incident that took place at Versailles in the first stage of the *French Revolution. On 17 June 1789 the Third Estate of the *States-General under the presidency of Jean Bailly, a representative of Paris, declared themselves the *National Assembly, claiming that they were the only Estate properly accredited and that the First and Second Estates must join them. On 20 June they found their official meeting-place closed and moved to the Tennis Court, a large open hall nearby. The Oath bound them not to separate until they had given France a constitution.

Tenskwatawa *See* TECUMSEH.

Te Puea Herangi (or "Princess" **Te Puea**) (1883–1952) A niece of the Maori king, *Tawhiao. Thoroughly educated in *Maori language and culture, she took direction of the *Kingitanga movement. She built Turangawaewae, south of Auckland, as a leading *marae* (social, political, cultural, and spiritual centre) and secured recognition of the Kingitanga from the New Zealand government. Her leadership strengthened Maori values and institutions while fostering a controlled accommodation of European influences, including commercial farming and education.

Terror, Reign of A period of the *French Revolution that began in March 1793 when the Revolutionary government, known as the Convention, having executed the king, set about attacking opponents and anyone else considered a threat to the regime. A Revolutionary Tribunal was set up to bring "enemies of the state" to trial and the following month the *Committee of Public Safety was created. It began slowly but during the ruthless dictatorship that followed the defeat of the *Girondins at least 12,000 political prisoners, priests, and aristocrats were executed, including *Marie Antoinette and Madame *Roland de la Platière. The Terror was intensified in June 1794 after the execution of *Hébert and *Danton had left *Robespierre supreme. It ended the following month, after the arrest and execution of Robespierre.

terrorism The use of violent and intimidating acts, especially for political ends. Terrorism has been used most commonly by revolutionary groups, whose objective is the overthrow of a particular state authority, and by nationalist groups seeking national self-determination.

Techniques of terrorism involve bombing and shooting attacks against property and individuals, the assassination of significant persons associated with the established government or security forces, hostage-taking, and hijacking of aircraft, trains, ships, and buses. The major objectives of terrorism are: to keep a particular cause in the forefront of public consciousness; to pressure the political authorities to concede the terrorists' demands by inducing a state of public fear; and to induce a government to betray its own commitment to freedom and democracy by imposing illiberal security measures in order to contain such violence.

International collaboration against terrorism has not proved easy since it involves the close cooperation of legal and police authorities from many different states, which may have different international interests. The European Convention on the Suppression of Terrorism (1977), the 'Trevi system' of cooperation among EC members (1976), which has now spread to Council of Europe states, the Tokyo summit declaration on terrorism in 1986, and the participation of the former Soviet Union in anti-terrorist collaboration all helped to establish a climate of international cooperation in the late 20th century. Following the attacks of *September 11, 2001, the USA vigorously pursued a *war on terrorism that confronted not only terrorist organizations but also so-called state sponsors of terrorism. This interventionist and pre-emptive approach has proved controversial.

Tertullian (born **Quintus Septimius Florens Tertullianus**) (*c.*160–*c.*240) Early Christian theologian. Born in Carthage after the Roman conquest, he converted to Christianity *c.*195. His writings (in Latin) include Christian apologetics and attacks on pagan idolatry and Gnosticism. He later joined the millenarian heretics the Montanists, urging asceticism and venerating martyrs.

Test Acts Laws that made the holding of public office in Britain conditional upon subscribing to the established religion. Although Scotland imposed such a law in 1567, the harsh laws against recusants in England were sufficient in themselves to deter Roman Catholics and dissenters from putting themselves forward for office. But in 1661 membership of town corporations, and in 1673 all offices under the crown, were denied to those who refused to take communion in an Anglican church. In 1678 all Catholics except the Duke of York (the future *James II) were excluded from Parliament. In the 18th century religious tests in Scotland were not always enforced, except for university posts, and in England the test could be met by occasional communion, but this was not possible for Roman Catholics. The Test Acts were finally repealed in 1829, and university religious tests were abolished in the 1870s and 1880s.

Tet Offensive (29 January–25 February 1968) An offensive launched in the *Vietnam War by Vietcong and regular North Vietnamese army units against US and South Vietnamese forces. In a surprise attack timed to coincide with the first day of the Tet (Vietnamese Lunar New Year) holiday, North Vietnamese forces under General *Giap took the war from the countryside to the cities of South Vietnam. After initial successes, the attackers were repulsed with heavy losses on both sides, but the offensive seriously damaged South Vietnamese morale and shook US confidence in their ability to win the war and brought them to the conference table in Paris in 1969. This led to the Paris Peace Accords of 1973 and the withdrawal of US forces from Indochina.

Teutonic Knight A member of a military and religious order whose full title was the Order of the Knights of the Hospital of St Mary of the Teutons in Jerusalem. Founded in 1190 at Acre, it was made up of knights, priests, and lay brothers and was active in Palestine and Syria, though its members retreated to Venice when the Crusaders failed to contain the Muslims. The Holy Roman Emperor Frederick II employed the order as missionaries to overcome and convert the pagans beyond the north-eastern border of the empire and in this they were very successful, gaining Prussia in 1229.

In 1234, though in practice independent, they declared that they held the lands they had conquered as a fief from the pope. Joining with the Livonian Order, they continued to advance around the Baltic coast, amassing huge territories, but their progress was checked decisively when they were defeated at Tannenberg in 1410 by King Ladislas of Poland. In 1525 the Grand Master, Albert of Brandenburg, became a Lutheran, resigned his office, and the order was declared secular, and it remained an order under the control of the Electors of Brandenburg.

Teutons A Germanic tribe, believed to be from Holstein or Jutland, who migrated to southern Gaul and northern Italy with the Cimbri in the late 2nd century BC. In 102 they were defeated by *Marius at Aquae Sextiae (Aix-en-Provence). They disappeared from history but the name Teuton survived as a synonym for German.

Te Whiti Maori religious leader (c.1820–1907). In 1877, when British government officials began land surveys in South Taranaki without first creating reserves as guaranteed by the Treaty of *Waitangi, Te Whiti organized non-violent resistance. He prophesied success through continued non-violent resistance and 2000 people flocked to his settlement at Pari-haka. In 1881 government forces arrested Te Whiti and dispersed the settlement. After a year in custody Te Whiti rebuilt and modernized Parihaka, where his teachings were promoted for many decades.

Tewkesbury, Battle of (4 May 1471) A battle in the Wars of the *Roses fought between *Edward IV fresh from his victory as *Barnet and the Lancastrian forces of Margaret of Anjou.

Margaret's forces were defeated and her son, Prince Edward, was among those killed.

Texas, Republic of (1836–45) A short-lived independent republic in the south-west of the USA. Texas had only been lightly colonized by the Spanish and in 1821 the Mexican government granted Stephen Austin the right to bring US settlers into the region. Pressure began to build up for independence from Mexican control and a revolt broke out in 1835–36. After defeat at the *Alamo, Texan forces under *Houston captured the Mexican general *Santa Anna at *San Jacinto. An independent republic of Texas was proclaimed, which was recognized by the USA as the "Lone-Star" state. The republic lasted for almost a decade before it was admitted to the Union as the 28th state, an event that helped to precipitate the *Mexican–American War in the following year (1846).

Texas Rangers A paramilitary US police force. The Texas Rangers were first organized in the 1830s to protect US settlers in Texas against Mexican Indians. After the formation of the republic of *Texas (1836), they were built up by *Houston as a mounted border patrol of some 1600 picked men. They became renowned for their exploits against marauders and rustlers in the heyday of the great cattle drives after the *American Civil War.

Thailand (formerly **Siam**)

Capital:	Bangkok
Area:	513,120 sq km (198,117 sq miles)
Population:	67,448,120 (2013 est)
Currency:	1 baht = 100 satang
Religions:	Buddhist 93.6%; Muslim 4.9%; Christian 1.2%
Ethnic Groups:	Thai 95.9%; Burmese 2.0%
Languages:	Thai (official); Burmese; minority languages
International Organizations:	UN; ASEAN; Colombo Plan; Non-Aligned Movement; WTO

A country in south-east Asia bounded by Myanmar (Burma), Laos, and Cambodia, and, in the south, Malaysia.

Physical The country extends more than halfway

down the Malay Peninsula and its north–south length is over 1600 km (1000 miles). The north is hilly and covered with dense forest. In the centre is a great, low-lying plain threaded with rivers, which drain into the Gulf of Thailand. This is densely cultivated, with paddy fields, which yield fish as well as rice; further south, rubber is grown.

Economy Although the economy was dominated by agriculture until the late 20th century, almost half of Thailand's GDP is now contributed by industry. In recent years the country has experienced steady economic growth, based on exports of electronics, agricultural products, vehicles and parts, and processed foods. Other industries include tourism, textiles, and clothing. Rice, once the leading export, is still the most important crop.

History The Thais, akin to the Shans and Lao, originated in the Yunnan province of southwest China. Their name means 'free'. *Mongol pressure accelerated their southward movement from Yunnan. They set up kingdoms in Sukhotai and Chiengmai, formerly under *Khmer rule, became Theravada *Buddhists, and adopted an Indian script. About 1350 Ayuthia became the capital of a new Thai kingdom which, after prolonged fighting, captured *Angkor in 1431. Ayuthia ruled much of Cambodia and at times Tenasserim and nothern Malaya. Wars with Burma, whose kings coveted Ayuthia's sacred white elephants, brought no lasting loss of Thai territory.

Among Europeans who became active in Ayuthia the French were dominant. In 1684 Thai envoys presented *Louis XIV with elephants, rhinoceroses, and a letter engraved on gold. The Burmese finally destroyed Ayuthia in 1767. Under the leadership of General Taskin, the Burmese were expelled from Siam by about 1777. His successor, General Chakri (later Rama I) founded the Chakri dynasty and established Bangkok as his capital. The Chakri dominated much of *Laos and northern Malaya and succeeded in maintaining their country's independence through a policy of conciliation, ceding their vassal state in Laos and Cambodia to France in the late 19th and early 20th centuries. In the reigns of Mongkut (1851–68) and *Chulalongkorn (1868–1910) Thailand achieved substantial modernization in both the administrative and economic spheres. The middle class produced by the modernization process became intolerant of absolute royal rule, and an economic crisis in 1932 produced a bloodless coup which left the Chakri dynasty on the throne but transferred power to a constitutional government. Although technically allied to

Japan during World War II, Thailand retained western friendship because of prolonged guerrilla resistance to Japanese forces. Until the early 1970s the country was largely ruled by the army, Marshal Pibul Songgram maintaining near personal rule from 1946 to 1957. Severe rioting resulted in a partial move to civilian government in 1973 and the introduction of a democratic constitution in 1974, but the threat of communist aggression, particularly on its borders with Cambodia, allowed a pronounced military influence. Following a military coup in 1991 General Suchinda Kraprayoon was appointed Prime Minister and imposed a military crackdown. This resulted in riots, arrests, and the killing of demonstrators, before King Bhumibol (succeeded 1946) was able to restore stability; Suchinda resigned and civilian political parties were re-legalized. Elections in September 1992 were won by a coalition of pro-democracy parties and the leader of the Democrat Party, Chuan Leekpai, became Prime Minister. Following elections in 1996 Chavalat Yongchaiyudh became Prime Minister but Chuan Leekpai returned in the wake of the financial crisis of 1997. Taksin Shinawatra, a wealthy businessman, was elected Prime Minister in 2001 and 2005. However, accusations of abuse of power led him to call fresh elections in 2006, which were boycotted by the opposition parties and subsequently declared invalid. Taksin was ousted by a military coup later in 2006, and since that time Thai politics has been dominated by a struggle between his supporters and opponents, with both sides mobilizing mass demonstrations. In 2011 Taksin's sister, Yingluck Shinawatra, became prime minister. However, in 2014 the country's Constitutional Court ordered her to stand down for abuse of position. The military then took control and imposed martial law, insisting that this was only a temporary measure. Thailand was severely affected by the *Indian Ocean tsunami in 2004, with over 8000 people being killed.

Thames, Battle of the (5 October 1813) A military engagement in the *War of 1812, fought in present-day south-western Ontario, Canada. Following their abandonment of Detroit, British and Native American forces under General Proctor and *Tecumseh were overtaken and decisively defeated near Chatham on the Thames River by a US force under General William Henry *Harrison. The US victory, together with Tecumseh's death in the battle, destroyed the Native American confederacy and the British and Native American alliance and secured the US north-west frontier.

thane (or **thegn**) A nobleman of Anglo-Saxon England. Their status, as determined by their wergild, was usually 1200 shillings. In return for their services to the crown they received gifts of land, which became hereditary. The king's thanes, members of the royal household, were required to do military service, attend the *witan, and assist in government.

Thant, U (1909–74) Burmese statesman and third Secretary-General of the United Nations (1961–71). He entered the Burmese diplomatic service in 1948 and served at the United Nations from 1957. He succeeded Dag *Hammarskjöld as Secretary-General and filled the post with great distinction. His achievements included assistance in the resolution of the *Cuban Missile Crisis and the admission of communist China to full UN and Security Council membership in 1971.

Thatcher, Margaret (Hilda), Baroness Thatcher of Kesteven (1925–2013) British Conservative stateswoman, Prime Minister (1979–90). She became Conservative Party leader in 1975 and in 1979 was elected the country's first woman Prime Minister; she went on to become the longest-serving British Prime Minister of the 20th century, winning further election victories in 1983 and 1987. Her period in office was marked by an emphasis on monetarist policies and free enterprise, privatization of nationalized industries, and legislation to restrict the powers of trade unions. In international affairs she was a strong supporter of the policies of President Reagan. She was well known for determination and resolve (she had been dubbed 'the Iron Lady' as early as 1976), especially in her handling of the Falklands War of 1982. She resigned after a leadership challenge and was created a life peer in 1992.

thegn *See* THANE.

Themistocles (*c.*528–462 BC) Athenian statesman. He was instrumental in building up the Athenian fleet, which under his command defeated the Persian fleet at Salamis in 480. In the following years he lost influence, was ostracized in 470, and eventually fled to the Persians in Asia Minor, where he died.

Theodora (*c.*500–48) Byzantine empress, wife of Justinian. She is reputed (according to Procopius) to have led a dissolute life in her early years. She later became noted for her intellect and learning and, as Justinian's closest adviser, exercised a considerable influence on political affairs and the theological questions of the time.

Theodoric I (418–51 AD) King of the *Visigoths. He was defeated by the Romans at Toulouse in 439 after 15 years warfare. He joined Aetius as an ally against *Attila but was killed on the *Catalaunian Fields. His son Theodoric II ruled the Visigothic kingdom of Spain and parts of Gaul until 466.

Theodoric the Great (*c.*455–526) King of the Ostrogoths (475–526) and ruler of Italy from 493. He invaded Italy and established his capital at Ravenna. At its greatest extent his empire included not only the Italian mainland but Sicily, Dalmatia, and parts of Germany. An *Arian Christian, his reign brought a degree of authority and stability to the country, though the scholar *Boethius was executed on treason charges. His reign saw the beginning of a synthesis of Roman and Germanic cultures. He is a hero of German literature, figuring in the epic *Nibelungenlied*.

Theodosius, Flavius (or **Theodosius the Great**) (349–95 AD) Roman emperor in the East (379–94) and sole emperor (394–95). The son of a famous general, Count Theodosius, Gratian appointed him co-emperor in 378. After failing to defeat the *Goths he formed a treaty with them in 382. He was a champion of strict political and religious orthodoxy. His two sons, Arcadius and Honorius, succeeded him.

Thermopylae A pass in Greece, about 200 km (120 miles) north-west of Athens, originally narrow but now much widened by the recession of the sea. It was the scene of the heroic defence (480 BC) against the Persian army of Xerxes by 6000 Greeks including 300 Spartans under their commander Leonidas.

Thiers, Louis Adolphe (1797–1877) French statesman and historian. In the *Franco-Prussian War his diplomatic skill helped in the negotiations with *Bismarck that resulted in the Treaty of *Frankfurt. He ordered the ruthless destruction of the Commune of *Paris (1871). He was elected President of the Third Republic in 1871, for, although a monarchist, he believed that national unity demanded a republic. In 1873 he was overthrown by right-wing deputies.

Third Reich (1933–45) The period covering the *Nazi regime in *Germany.

Third World The undeveloped countries of the world. Of French origin (*le Tiers-Monde*), the expression formed part of a UN classification in which the developed capitalist countries were the First World and the developed Communist countries were the Second World. It is now more usual to refer to *developing countries.

Thirteen Colonies The British colonies in North America that ratified the *Declaration of Independence (1776) and thereby became founding states of the USA. They were, with dates of foundation or English colonial status: Virginia (1607), Massachusetts (1629), Mary-land (1632), Connecticut (1635), Rhode Island (1636), North Carolina (1663), South Carolina (1663), New York (1664), New Jersey (1664), Delaware (1664), New Hampshire (1679), Pennsylvania (1681), and Georgia (1732). By 1776 all were ruled by royal governors except Maryland, Pennsylvania, Delaware, Connecticut, and Rhode Island, and all had representative assemblies. Though there were major differences over such issues as slavery or religion and often quarrels between neighbouring colonies, they managed to sustain a fragile unity between 1776 and 1783. This improbable cohesion could be described as the greatest unsought achievement of *George III and his ministers, who, in *Franklin's words, "made thirteen clocks strike as one".

Thirteen Colonies. The Thirteen British colonies in North America, strung out along the eastern seaboard from Maine to Georgia, had even fewer ties to one another than to the mother country. However, they did share certain underlying interests, one of which was the potential and desire for westward expansion. The Royal Proclamation of 1763, which forbade settlement beyond the Appalachians, was therefore widely resented, particularly since it came at a time when economic recession made the land beyond the frontier especially attractive. The Proclamation was issued as an emergency measure designed to protect Native American lands, but it was widely ignored by the settlers.

Thirty-Nine Articles The set of doctrinal formulae first issued in 1563 and finally adopted by the Anglican Communion in 1571 as a statement of its position. Many of the articles allow a wide variety of interpretation. They had their origin in several previous definitions, required by the shifts and turns of the English Reformation. The Ten Articles (1536) and Six Articles (1539) upheld religious conservatism, but the Forty-Two Articles (1553), prepared by *Cranmer and Ridley, were of markedly Protestant character, and they provided the basis of the Thirty-Nine Articles.

Thirty Years War (1618–48) A series of conflicts, fought mainly in Germany, in which Protestant–Catholic rivalries and German constitutional issues were gradually subsumed in a European struggle. It began in 1618 with the Protestant Bohemian revolt against the future emperor *Ferdinand II; it embraced the last phase of the Dutch Revolts after 1621; and was concentrated in a Franco-Habsburg confrontation in the years after 1635.

By 1623 Ferdinand had emerged victorious in the Bohemian revolt, and with Spanish and Bavarian help had conquered the *Palatinate of *Frederick V. But his German ambitions and his Spanish alliance aroused the apprehensions of Europe's Protestant nations and also of France. In 1625 Christian IV of Denmark renewed the war against the Catholic imperialists, as the leader of an anti-Habsburg coalition organized by the Dutch. After suffering a series of defeats at the hands of Tilly and Wallenstein, Denmark withdrew from the struggle at the Treaty of Lübeck (1629), and the emperor reached the summit of his power.

Sweden's entry into the war under *Gustavus II (Adolphus) led to imperial reversals. After

Gustavus was killed at Lützen (1632), the Swedish Chancellor Oxenstierna financed the Heilbronn League of German Protestants (1633), which broke up after a heavy military defeat at Nördlingen in 1634. In 1635 the Treaty of Prague ended the civil war within Germany, but in the same year France, in alliance with Sweden and the United Provinces, went to war with the Habsburgs. Most of the issues were settled after five years of negotiation at the Treaty of *Westphalia in 1648, but the Franco-Spanish war continued until the Treaty of the Pyrenees in 1659.

Thistlewood, Arthur *See* CATO STREET CONSPIRACY.

Thompson, Sir John (Sparrow David) (1844–94) Canadian Liberal-Conservative politician, premier of Canada (1892–94).

Thrace (Greek **Thráki**) An ancient country lying west of Istanbul and the Black Sea and north of the Aegean, now part of modern Turkey, Greece, and Bulgaria. It extended as far west as the Adriatic but the Thracians retreated eastwards between the 13th and 5th centuries BC under pressure from the Illyrians and Macedonians. Conquered by Philip II of Macedon in 342 BC it later became a province of Rome. The region was ruled by the Ottoman Turks from the 15th century until the end of World War I, but northern Thrace was annexed by Bulgaria in 1885. In 1923 all of Thrace east of the Maritsa River was restored to Turkey.

Three Emperors' League (German, *Dreikaiserbund*) An alliance between Prussia, Austria, and Russia. In 1872, following the creation of the new *German Second empire, *Bismarck persuaded the emperors of Austria and Russia to join an unofficial alliance. It was strained by the Treaty of San Stefano (1878) which, in conclusion of the *Russo-Turkish Wars, assigned Russia the eastern part of *Armenia and created a large state of *Bulgaria. In June 1881, following the assassination of *Alexander II, the league was revived as a more formal alliance. Renewed in 1884, it finally expired three years later, as tension between Russia and Austria-Hungary mounted in the *Balkans.

Three Henrys, War of the (March 1585–August 1589) The eighth of the *French Wars of Religion. It was precipitated by the efforts of Duke Henry of *Guise to exclude the Huguenot Henry of Navarre from the succession to the French throne. Guise, backed by Spain and the Catholic League (*Holy League), forced Henry

III to capitulate in the Treaty of Nemours (1585) and to accept the Catholic Cardinal de Bourbon as his heir instead of Henry of Navarre. In the ensuing conflict, Henry III lost control of events and Guise acted as if he were king himself. In late 1588, Henry III had both Guise and the Cardinal de Bourbon murdered. When Henry III was murdered in turn (1589), most of France was in League or Huguenot hands, and Henry of Navarre became king as *Henry IV.

Three Kingdoms (220–280 AD) The period in China immediately following the end of the *Han dynasty. Three kingdoms, the Wei in the north, the Wu in the south-east, and the Shu Han in the west, rose and constantly fought each other for supremacy. The period ended when the Wei general Sima Yen seized power and unified China under the *Western Jin dynasty. Many events and legends of this period appear in one of the classics of Chinese literature, *The Romance of the Three Kingdoms.*

Three-Mile Island An island in the Susquehanna River in Pennsylvania, USA, the site of a potential nuclear disaster in March 1979. The core of the nuclear power station on the island underwent partial melt-down. Although many people in the area were evacuated, an official investigation found the levels of radiation in the vicinity (in milk, for example) to be little changed. However, the reactor was damaged beyond repair.

Throckmorton Plot (1583) An international Catholic conspiracy, in the manner of the *Ridolfi and *Babington plots, to place *Mary, Queen of Scots on the English throne. Francis Throckmorton (1554–84), a member of a leading English *recusant family, helped to contrive the plan. Henry of *Guise would invade England with a French Catholic force, financed by Spain and the *papacy, then the English Catholics would depose *Elizabeth I in favour of Mary. In late 1583 *Walsingham's agents uncovered the plan. Reprisals were moderate, but Throckmorton was tried and executed.

Thucydides (*c*.455–*c*.400 BC) Greek historian. He is remembered for his *History of the Peloponnesian War*, an account of a conflict in which he fought on the Athenian side. The work covers events up to about 411 and presents an analysis of the origins and course of the war, based on painstaking inquiry into what actually happened and including the reconstruction of political speeches of such figures as Pericles, whom he greatly admired.

thug (from Hindi *thag*, 'swindler') A devotee of the Hindu goddess Kali, who was worshipped through ritual murder and sacrifice of travellers. The thuggee centre was in remote central India, where victims were strangled. Eradication of the brotherhoods was difficult because of the secrecy of the cult. It was largely suppressed in the 1830s by the detective skills of William Sleeman, appointed to the task by Lord William *Bentinck. Indians welcomed the intervention, and there has been no revival, but the term passed into the English language.

Thutmose I (or **Tuthmosis I**) Pharaoh of Egypt (*c.*1525–1512 BC). He extended his domains deep into Nubia and later penetrated with his army as far as the River Euphrates. He made extensive improvements to the temple of Amun at *Karnak and was the first pharaoh to be buried in the *Valley of the Kings.

Thutmose III (or **Tuthmosis III**) Pharaoh of Egypt (*c.*1504–1450 BC). During the first 22 years of his reign Thutmose III was overshadowed by his aunt *Hatshepsut, wife of Thutmose II, who had herself declared regent in 1503. When she died in 1482, he promptly mobilized the army and defeated a coalition of Syrian and Palestinian enemies near Megiddo, gaining nearly all of Syria for his empire. Further successes followed, culminating in the defeat of the powerful Mitanni beyond the Euphrates. He extended Egyptian rule in Nubia, but generally he concentrated on the administration of his lands. The thriving prosperity of his reign was reflected in much new building at *Karnak.

Tiananmen Square *See* CHINA.

Tianjin, Treaty of (1858) *See* OPIUM WARS.

Tiberius (full name **Tiberius Julius Caesar Augustus**) (42 BC–37 AD) Roman emperor (14–37 AD). He was the adopted successor of his stepfather and father-in-law Augustus, under whom he had pursued a distinguished military career. As emperor he sought to continue his stepfather's policies but became increasingly tyrannical and his reign was marked by a growing number of treason trials and executions. In 26 he retired to Capri, never returning to Rome.

Tibet (Chinese **Xizang**) A mountainous region of Asia to the north of the Himalayas. Ruled by Buddhist lamas since the 7th century, Tibet was conquered by the Mongols in the 13th century and the Manchus in the 18th century. China extended its authority over Tibet in 1951 but only gained full control after crushing a revolt in 1959, during which the country's spiritual leader, the Dalai Lama, made his escape into India. Many of Tibet's monasteries and shrines were destroyed in an unsuccessful attempt to change national culture and consciousness. Almost completely surrounded by mountain ranges, Tibet is the source of some of Asia's largest rivers including the Yangtze, Salween, and Mekong. Separatist feeling has grown strongly since the 1980s, which has led to violent demonstrations against Chinese rule in 2008.

ticket-of-leave In Australia, a certificate that could be granted to a convict during the period of convict transportation. It allowed a convict to be excused from compulsory labour, to choose his or her own employer, and to work for wages. There were some restrictions and the ticket-of-leave could be withdrawn. It usually was granted for good conduct.

Ticonderoga A frontier fortress in New York, USA, commanding the Champlain-Hudson valley between Lake Champlain and Lake George. Built by the French as Fort Carillon in 1755, it held out against British attack in 1758, but the next year fell to *Amherst, who renamed it. In the War of Independence it was surprised by Benedict *Arnold and Ethan *Allen in 1775, recaptured by *Burgoyne in 1777, but recovered by the Americans after Saratoga (1777).

Tilak, Bel Gangadhar (1856–1920) Indian scholar and politician. Known as *Lokamanya* (revered by the people), he owned and edited *Kesari* (Lion), a weekly Marathi nationalist paper. He was imprisoned for sedition by the British (1897). Released in 1899, he continued to advocate radical policies within *Congress, playing an important role in the radical/moderate split of 1907. In 1914 with Annie *Besant he formed the Indian Home Rule League, but subsequently advocated more moderate, co-operative policies with Muslims in the Lucknow Pact (1916), which recognized separate electorates for Muslim minorities.

Tilly, Johannes Tserklaes, Count of (1559–1632) Flemish soldier. Tilly served under *Farnese in the Netherlands and then in the army of Emperor Rudolf II against the *Ottoman Turks (1594). In 1610 Duke Maximilian of Bavaria appointed him to create an army, which became the spearhead of the Catholic League during the *Thirty Years War. He was victorious at the Battle of the White Mountain (1620) and went on to dominate north-western Germany. He crushed the Danes at Lutter (1626) and, on *Wallenstein's dismissal, took command of imperial as well as League troops. His brutal destruction of the Protestant city of Magdeburg (1631) blackened his reputation. He was routed by *Gustavus II (Adolphus) at Breitenfeld (1631). Wounded at the battle of Rain (1632), he died two weeks later.

Tilsit, Treaties of (7 and 9 July 1807) Agreements between Russia and France, and Prussia and France. Napoleon I, having won the Battle of Friedland, agreed to meet *Alexander I on a raft on the River Niemen near the East Prussian town of Tilsit, now Sovetsk in Russia. Their negotiations, joined by *Frederick William III of Prussia, led to the two treaties. Prussia lost over a third of its possessions, had to pay heavy indemnities to France, and was forced to support a large French army on its soil. The Polish lands annexed by Prussia under the partitions were turned into a French puppet state, the Grand Duchy of Warsaw. Russia recognized the *Confederation of the Rhine and was forced to join the *Continental System. Prussia rescinded its treaty in 1813 when it deserted the French, following the latter's invasion of Russia and joined the Russian emperor in a campaign against Napoleon in Germany.

Timor-Leste (or East Timor)

Capital:	Dili
Area:	14,874 sq km (5743 sq miles)
Population:	1,172,390 (2013 est)
Currency:	1 US dollar = 100 cents
Religions:	Roman Catholic 96.9%; Protestant 2.2%; Muslim 0.3%
Ethnic Groups:	Austronesian; Papuan; Chinese minority
Languages:	Portuguese, Tetum (both official); Indonesian; English; minority languages
International Organizations:	UN; Non-Aligned Movement

An Asian country that occupies the eastern half of the island of Timor in the southern Malay Archipelago. The western half of the island is part of Indonesia.

Physical Timor-Leste is mainly mountainous and has a monsoon climate.

Economy The recent development of offshore oil and natural gas reserves has made oil the principal export, greatly increased government revenues, and led to high rates of economic growth. However, this specialized area has had little effect on the domestic economy: almost two-thirds of the workforce are employed in agriculture, two-fifths of the population live in poverty, and unemployment is high. Coffee, sandalwood, and marble are the other principal exports; other important crops include rice and maize. The oil revenues have financed increased government spending on electricity, roads, and other infrastructure projects.

History In colonial times Timor was divided into Dutch West Timor and Portuguese East Timor. In 1950 West Timor was absorbed into the newly formed Republic of Indonesia. In 1975, during the collapse of the Portuguese colonial empire, East Timor briefly declared itself independent from Portugal but was invaded and occupied by Indonesia. In 1976, against the wishes of the inhabitants, Indonesia formally annexed East Timor and administered it as the province of Timur Timur or Loro Sae. The independence movement was violently suppressed. A referendum in 1999, supervised by the UN, overwhelmingly supported independence from Indonesia. However, a pro-Indonesian militia murdered many of those who voted for independence and devastated the capital, Dili. Thousands of people fled or went into hiding. A UN administration and peacekeeping force was established to effect the transition to independence, which was achieved in May 2002 with the former guerrilla leader Xanana Gusmão as President. In 2006 there were violent protests involving former members of the security forces; UN forces were required to restore order, remaining until 2012. José Ramos-Horta was elected President in 2007 and survived an assassination attempt in 2008; he was succeeded by Taur Matan Ruak in 2012.

Timur *See* TAMERLANE.

Tippecanoe, Battle of (7 November 1811) A conflict between US forces and Shawnee, fought near the Wabash River 240 km (150 miles) north of Vincennes. Governor William Henry *Harrison of the Indiana Territory engineered a conflict with the British-supported Native American confederacy of the Shawnee chiefs *Tecumseh and his brother the Prophet Tenskwatawa in order to end Native American resistance to westward US expansion. In the resulting skirmish, Harrison sustained considerable losses but drove away the Native

Americans. Tippecanoe was hailed as a major victory, but the British and Native American threat to the north-west frontier was not destroyed until Tecumseh fell in the Battle of the *Thames two years later.

Tipu Sultan (*c*.1753–99) Sultan of Mysore (1782–99). He inherited the kingdom recently created by his father, *Hyder Ali and was a formidable enemy to both the British and neighbouring Indian states. Failure to secure active French support left him without allies in resisting the British. He was finally besieged in his own capital, Seringapatam, when unfounded rumours that he had secured an alliance with Revolutionary France gave the British the necessary pretext for a final assault. He was killed in the attack.

Tirpitz, Alfred von (1849–1930) German grand-admiral. As Secretary of State for the Navy (1897–1916) his first Navy Bill in 1898 began the expansion of the German navy and led to the naval race with Britain. In 1907 he began a large programme of Dreadnought-class battleship construction. During World War I he made full use of submarines, but following the sinking of the *Lusitania (1915), unrestricted submarine warfare was temporarily abandoned. The policy was resumed in 1917, resulting in US entry into the war.

tithe (Old English, 'tenth') A payment made by parishioners for the maintenance of the church and the support of its clergy. Levied by the early Hebrews and common in Europe after the synods of Tours (567) and Mâcon (585), tithes were enforced by law in England from the 10th century. They were divided into three categories—praedial (one-tenth of the produce of the soil), personal (one-tenth of the profits of labour and industry), and mixed (a combination of the produce of animals and labour). They were abolished finally in England in 1936.

Tito (born **Josip Broz**) (1892–1980) Yugoslav Marshal and statesman, Prime Minister (1945–53) and President (1953–80). Born in Croatia, he served in the Austro-Hungarian army during World War I and was captured by the Russians in 1915. After escaping, he fought with the Bolsheviks in the Russian Revolution and became an active Communist organizer on returning to his country in 1920. Tito responded to the German invasion of Yugoslavia (1941) by organizing a Communist resistance movement using guerrilla tactics. His success in resisting the Germans earned him Allied support and he emerged as head of the new government at the end of the war. Tito defied Stalin over policy in the Balkans in 1948, proceeding to establish Yugoslavia as a non-aligned Communist state with a federal constitution. As a result Yugoslavia was expelled from the *Cominform. On his death the office of President was to rotate between the six republics. However, by 1989 the country began to disintegrate into separate warring factions.

Toba Wei *See* NORTHERN WEI.

Tobruk, Siege of (1941–42) German siege of British and Commonwealth troops in Tobruk in North Africa in World War II. When General *Wavell's army captured Tobruk in January 1941 some 25,000 Italian troops were taken prisoner. The Afrika Korps of General *Rommel then arrived (April 1941) and the British withdrew east, leaving a largely Australian garrison to defend Tobruk, which was subjected to an eight-month siege and bombardment. In November 1941, after being reinforced by sea, the garrison broke out, capturing Rezegh and linking up with the 8th Army troops of General *Auchinleck. But the Germans counter-attacked and in June 1942, after heavy defeats, the British again withdrew leaving a garrison of two divisions, mostly South African and Australian, in Tobruk, which was then subjected to massed attack by German and Italian troops. On 20 June it capitulated, the garrison of 23,000 men surrendering, with vast quantities of stores. It was a major Allied defeat, but Tobruk was recaptured on 13 November 1942 by the troops of General *Montgomery.

Tocqueville, Alexis, Comte de (1805–59) French statesman and political analyst. Sent to the USA in 1831 to study its penal system, de Tocqueville carried out a systematic survey of US political and social institutions, publishing the results in *De la démocratie en Amerique* (1835 and 1840). The book immediately found a large readership and became one of the most influential political writings of the 19th century. It remains probably the greatest of all European commentaries on US politics and society.

Togliatti, Palmiro (1893–1964) Italian politician, Secretary of the Italian Communist Party (1926–64). After the fascist take-over Togliatti lived mainly in Moscow (1926–44) and became chief of the *Comintern in Spain during the *Spanish Civil War. After World War II he made the Italian Communist Party the largest in Western Europe. Togliatti was undogmatic in his communism: he recognized Roman Catholicism as the state religion of Italy and propounded the doctrine of "polycentrism", which advocates the existence of several ideologies within a political system. The Russian city of Stavropol on the Volga was renamed Togliatti in his honour in 1964.

Togo

Capital:	Lomé
Area:	56,785 sq km (21,925 sq miles)
Population:	7,154,237 (2013 est)
Currency:	1 CFA franc = 100 centimes
Religions:	Traditional beliefs 51.0%; Christian 29.0%; Muslim 20.0%
Ethnic Groups:	African (37 tribes) 99.0%
Languages:	French (official); Ewe; Mina; Kabye; Dagomba
International Organizations:	UN; AU; ECOWAS; Franc Zone; Non-Aligned Movement; WTO

A West African country lying between Ghana and Benin.

Physical Togo has a southern coastline on the Gulf of Guinea of only 56 km (35 miles) but extends inland for over 560 km (350 miles) to Burkina Faso. Northward the land rises to low mountains and a rolling sandstone plateau.

Economy Two-thirds of the labour force work in agriculture. The leading cash crops—cocoa, coffee, and especially cotton—provide two-fifths of Togo's export earnings. The main export industry is phosphate mining, and Togo is one of the world's leading producers of phosphate.

History Togo's earliest known inhabitants were Gur-speaking Voltaic peoples in the north and Kwa peoples in the south. The Ewé immigrated during the 14th–16th centuries and the Ane (Mina) entered the region in the 17th century. Part of Togo's slave coast was controlled by Denmark during the 18th century and the area formed a buffer zone between the Ashanti and *Dahomey kingdoms. Annexed by Germany in 1884 as a colony, Togoland was mandated between France and Britain after World War I. The western British section joined *Ghana on the latter's independence in 1957, and became known as the Volta region. The remainder of the area became a UN mandate under French administration after World War II and achieved independence, as Togo, in 1960. After two civilian regimes were overthrown in 1963 and 1967, Togo achieved stability under President Gnassingbe Eyadema, who in 1979 was elected executive President, as the sole candidate. Following violent demonstrations early in 1991, he agreed to legalize political parties. In 1993 Eyadema won the country's first multiparty presidential elections, but this result was widely considered a fraud and unrest continued. Early in 1994, fighting around the capital, Lomé, left 58 people dead. When Eyadema died in 2005, the army installed his son, Faure Gnassingbe, as President. He stood down after protests and international pressure, but was then returned to the presidency in the subsequent election. He was re-elected in 2010.

Tojo Hideki (1884–1948) Japanese general and statesman. He participated in the war against China in the 1930s, was leader of the militarist party from 1931 onwards, and became War Minister in 1940. He urged closer collaboration with Germany and Italy and persuaded *Vichy France to sanction Japanese occupation of strategic bases in Indo-China (July 1941). He succeeded *Konoe Fumimaro as Prime Minister (1941–44) and he gave the order to attack *Pearl Harbor, precipitating the USA into World War II. In 1942 he strengthened his position in Tokyo as War Minister and created a virtual military dictatorship. He resigned in 1944 after the loss of the Marianas to the USA. He was convicted at the *Tokyo Trials and hanged as a war criminal in 1948.

Tokugawa The last Japanese *shogunate (1603–1867). *Tokugawa Ieyasu, its founder, ensured supremacy by imposing severe restrictions on the daimyo (feudal lords). To avoid the effects of European intrusion, Christianity was proscribed in 1641 after the suppression of the Christian Shimabara rebellion and all foreigners except a few Dutch and Chinese traders at Nagasaki were excluded. Japanese were forbidden to go overseas. Interest in European science and medicine increased during the rule of *Tokugawa Yoshimune.

There followed 250 years of almost unbroken peace and economic growth. An economy based largely on barter became a money economy. An influential merchant class emerged whilst some daimyo and their *samurai were impoverished; some married into commercial families. The shogunate was faced with growing financial difficulties but under its rule educational standards improved dramatically.

Tokugawa Ieyasu (1542–1616) The founder of the *Tokugawa shogunate. His base was Edo (now Tokyo). In 1600, at Sekigahara, he defeated *daimyo loyal to *Hideyoshi's son Hideyori. Appointed *shogun in 1603, he abdicated two years later, but still controlled affairs. In 1615 Hideyori and his retainers, after a hard siege, committed suicide in their moated castle in Osaka. Ieyasu then executed Hideyoshi's grandson, Kunimatsu. Hideyoshi's line was extinct, Ieyasu's power complete.

Tokugawa Yoshimune (1684–1751) Japanese *shogun, the eighth *Tokugawa to hold that office (1716–45). He was extremely capable and, though conservative, was interested in science. In 1720 he allowed European books, hitherto excluded, to be imported by Dutch traders at Nagasaki. Religious books were still banned. He also had a Dutch–Japanese dictionary compiled. The introduction of *rangaku* (Dutch learning) had a profound effect on what had been a closed world. There was particular interest in medicine, cartography, and military science. Yoshimune worked to increase the shogun's authority and improve government finances.

Tokyo Trials The war crimes trials of Japanese leaders after World War II. Between May 1946 and November 1948, 27 Japanese leaders appeared before an international tribunal charged with crimes ranging from murder and atrocities to responsibility for causing the war. Seven, including the former Prime Minister *Tojo Hideki, were sentenced to death and 16 to life imprisonment (two others receiving shorter terms), but General *MacArthur refused to allow the Emperor *Hirohito to be tried for fear of undermining the post-war Japanese state.

Toleration Act (1689) The granting by the English Parliament of freedom of worship to dissenting Protestants, who could not accept the authority or teaching of the Anglican Church. Dissenters were allowed their own ministers, teachers, and places of worship subject to their taking oaths of allegiance and to their acceptance of most of the *Thirty-Nine Articles. The *Test Acts, which deprived dissenters of public office remained, but from 1727 annual indemnity acts allowed them to hold local offices. Roman Catholics were excluded from the scope of the Act, and had to rely on failure to enforce the penal laws.

Tolpuddle Martyrs Six English farmworkers who were charged in 1834 with taking illegal oaths, while establishing a local trade union

branch of the Friendly Society of Agricultural Labourers in the Dorset village of Tolpuddle with the aim of obtaining an increase in their wages (then seven shillings a week). The six were found guilty and condemned to seven years' transportation to Australia. The severity of the sentence provoked a storm of protest and mass demonstrations were held in London. After two years, in the face of continuing public hostility, the government was obliged to pardon the men.

Toltecs A northern Mexican tribe, who established a military state between the 10th and 12th centuries at Tula, *c.*80 km (*c.*50 miles) north of modern Mexico City. They played an important part in the downfall of the city of Teotihuacán and were themselves overrun in the mid-12th century by nomadic Chichimec tribes from the north. One of their kings was Topiltzín-*Quetzalcóatl, a religious leader who in their legendary history was driven from Tula by a military faction and sailed east into the Gulf of Mexico, vowing to return one day.

Tone, Wolfe (Theobald Wolfe Tone) (1763–98) Irish nationalist. In 1791 he helped found the Society of United Irishmen, which lobbied for parliamentary reform. In 1794 he went to France to induce a French invasion of Ireland to overthrow English rule. The invasion failed, and during the Irish insurrection in 1798 Tone obtained only limited French support. He was captured by the British and committed suicide in prison.

Tonga (or **Friendly Islands**)

Capital:	Nuku'alofa
Area:	747 sq km (288 sq miles)
Population:	106,322 (2013 est)
Currency:	1 pa'anga = 100 seniti
Religions:	Free Wesleyan 37.3%; Mormon 16.8%; Roman Catholic 15.6%; Free Church of Tonga 11.4%; Church of Tonga 7.2%
Ethnic Groups:	Tongan 96.6%
Languages:	Tongan, English (both official)
International Organizations:	UN; Commonwealth; Pacific Islands Forum; Secretariat of the Pacific Community; WTO

An island country bordering the Tonga Trench in the South Pacific Ocean.

Physical Tonga comprises over 150 islands, most of them too small for habitation and even the largest, Tongatapu, measuring a mere 40 km (25 miles) by 16 km (10 miles). Some are coral and some volcanic, with active craters.

Economy Tonga's main exports are agricultural: squash, fish, vanilla beans, and root crops. However, its main sources of foreign exchange are remittances from expatriates and tourism, which is the principal industry.

History Austronesian-speaking peoples inhabited the islands from at least 1000 BC. By the 13th century Tongans ruled islands as far flung as Hawaii. Named the Friendly Islands by Captain James Cook, who visited them in 1773, the country was soon receiving missionaries. King George Tupou I (1845–93) unified the nation and gave it a constitution. In 1900 his son signed a treaty, making the islands a self-governing British protectorate. During World War II Queen Sālote Tupou III (1900–65) placed the island's resources at the disposal of the Allies; she was succeeded by her son, Taufa'ahau Tupou IV, in 1965. In 1968 British controls were reduced, and in 1970 Tonga became independent within the *Commonwealth of Nations. Tonga's first political party was founded in 1994, with an agenda for democratic reform of the constitution. The government resisted the growing pressure for reform and there was little change before the death of Taufa'ahau Tupou IV in 2006. His son and successor, George Tupou V, moved to relinquish much royal power; following the 2010 elections a new Prime Minister, Lord Siale'ataongo Tu'ivakano, was elected by parliament. George Tupou V died in 2012 and was succeeded by his younger brother Tupou VI.

Tonkin Gulf Resolution (1964) A resolution by the US Congress, giving the President authority to take all necessary measures to repel any attack against the forces of the USA. The resolution was made in response to an alleged attack by North Vietnam patrol boats against the US destroyer *Maddox* in the Gulf of Tonkin. The US involvement in the fighting in the *Vietnam War followed. Subsequent investigation revealed that the intelligence information on which it was based was inaccurate and, following the war, the War Powers Act was passed in 1973. This restricts the time a President can commit US troops without Congressional approval to 60 days.

Tonypandy dispute (1910) A violent dispute over pay rates for miners in the former mining town in South Wales. Miners interfered with pit machinery and there was looting and disorder in the town. The local police requested government help and the Home Secretary, Winston *Churchill, sent 300 extra police from London and placed military detachments on stand-by. In a subsequent incident in Llanelli a year later troops mobilized by Churchill opened fire on strikers, killing four. Trade union hostility to Churchill was intense.

Tooke, John Horne (1736–1812) British radical politician and philologist. In 1769 Tooke founded the Society of Supporters of the *Bill of Rights, which was largely designed to pay John *Wilkes's debts and get him into Parliament. In 1771 he founded the Constitutional Society to agitate for British parliamentary reform and self-government for the American colonists. After the Battle of *Lexington and Concord, he associated himself with a denunciation of the British forces there as murderers, for which he was imprisoned. He supported the independent Whigs under William *Pitt the Younger against the rival Whig faction of Charles *Fox from 1783 until 1790, but the French Revolution led to public hostility to reformers, and as a leading member of the *London Corresponding Society he was tried for treason but was acquitted in 1794.

Topa Inca (died 1493) Inca emperor (1471–93), son of Pachacuti Inca (ruled 1438–71). While still heir-apparent to the throne he led his father's armies north, to conquer the powerful *Chimú state on the north coast of Peru. After his accession to the throne he extended the empire to the south, conquering the northern half of Chile and part of Argentina. He also built the great fortress of Sacsahuaman, overlooking the imperial city of Cuzco. His successor, Huayna Capac (1493–1525) extended the northern boundaries even further, conquering Ecuador and founding Quito as the second Inca capital.

Tordesillas, Treaty of (7 June 1494) An alliance between Spain and Portugal. It settled disputes about the ownership of lands discovered by *Columbus and others. Pope Alexander VI had (1493) approved a line of demarcation stretching between the poles 100 leagues (about 500 km) west of the Cape Verde islands. All to the west was Spanish, to the east Portuguese—an award disregarded by other nations. Portuguese dissatisfaction led to a meeting at Tordesillas in north-west Spain where it was agreed to move the papal line to 370 leagues (about 1850 km) west of Cape Verde. The pope sanctioned this in 1506. It was modified by the Treaty of Zaragossa (1529), which gave the Moluccas (Spice Islands) to the Portuguese.

Torquemada, Tomás de (1420–98) Spanish Dominican friar. He acted as the ruthlessly cruel first Grand Inquisitor of the *Spanish Inquisition. As such he was responsible for directing its early activities against Jews and Muslims in Spain, and in fashioning its methods, including the use of torture and burnings.

Tory A member of a British political party traditionally opposed to the *Whigs. In the political crisis of 1679 royalist supporters, who opposed the recall of Parliament and supported the Stuart succession, were labelled Tories (Irish Catholic brigands) by their opponents. In the reign of *James II many Tories preferred passive obedience to open defiance; they supported the royal prerogative, close links between church and state, and an isolationist foreign policy. The Tories had a brief revival under Robert Harley late in Queen Anne's reign, but were defeated in the 1715 general election and reduced to a 'country' party with about 120 Members of Parliament and no effective leaders. The Hanoverian succession dealt a severe blow to the Tories, as George I and George II preferred to trust the Whigs. The political power struggle in the 1760s was between rival Whig factions, despite pejorative accusations of Toryism levelled at *Bute, Grafton, and *North. William *Pitt the Younger, the independent Whig, fought the Foxite Whigs, and it was from the independent Whigs that the new Tory party of the 19th century emerged.

In colonial America loyalists to the crown were called Tories.

totalitarianism A political system in which all individual activities and social relationships are subject to surveillance and control by the state. The idea originated in the 1930s and 1940s, with Nazism under Hitler, *Fascism under Mussolini, and *communism under Stalin: one-party government headed by a single powerful individual; promotion of an official ideology; and extensive use of terror tactics by the secret police. A totalitarian regime is a specifically modern form of authoritarian state, requiring as it does an advanced technology of social control. Some observers, most notably the German-born US philospher Hannah Arendt (1906–75), have explained the emergence of such regimes with reference to the growth of

mass society: where the bonds of community break down, atomized individuals can be mobilized by the propaganda of political leaders. Features of totalitarianism are to be found in a number of developing countries governed by authoritarian regimes.

Toungoo (1539–1752) A Burman dynasty that brought unified rule after an interregnum following the state of Pagan's collapse. Its founder, **Tabinshweti** (1512–50), and his successor, Bayinnaung (*fl.c.*1570), subdued the *Shans and Mons, conquered Tenasserim, and overran Thai states in *Siam. However, the Thais broke free and in 1600 sacked Pegu, which, except for a brief period, was the Toungoo capital until 1634. From 1635 when Ava, two months' journey by river from the delta, became the capital, there was growing estrangement between the Toungoo and the Mons. Weakened by raids from Manipur, Toungoo fell when the Mons captured Ava.

Touré, Sékou (Ahmed Sékou Touré) (1922–84) African statesman, President of *Guinea (1958–84). In 1946, together with other African leaders, including *Houphouët-Boigny, he was a founder of the Rassemblement Démocratique Africain. He became Secretary-General of the CGT (Confédération générale du travail) for Africa in 1948. In 1955 he was elected Mayor of Conakry and took his seat in the French National Assembly in 1956. In 1957 he became Vice-President in the Guinea cabinet. He was elected President when Guinea became independent in 1958 and broke all links with the *French Community. A convinced Marxist, he received aid for Guinea from the Soviet bloc. Following his death in 1984 the armed forces staged a coup.

tourney (or **tournament**) An armed combat, usually under royal licence, between knights, designed to show their skills and valour. Tournaments were introduced into England from France in the 11th century. Early versions tended to be confused occasions of mock battles between groups of knights, but they were formalized in the 15th century. The elaborate ritual, in which *heraldry played an important part, included the issuing and accepting of challenges, conditions of engagement, and points scoring (according to the number of broken lances or blows sustained). Fighting could be on horseback with swords (tourney) or on foot. Simple mounted combat (jousting or tilting) with the two knights charging on either side of an anti-collision barrier (the tilt) was the most dramatic, but there were also mock sieges and assaults on defended places. Blunt weapons and padded armour reduced accidents, but deaths did occur, including that of *Henry II of France in 1559.

Toussaint L'Ouverture, François-Dominique (c.1743–1803) Haitian revolutionary leader. Brought up a slave in the western part of Hispaniola (now Haiti), in 1791 he became one of the leaders of a rebellion that succeeded in emancipating the island's slaves by 1793. In 1797 he was appointed Governor-General by the revolutionary government of France, and led the drive to expel the British and Spanish from western Hispaniola. In 1801 he took control of the whole island, establishing his own constitution, but the following year Napoleon (wishing to restore slavery) ordered his forces to regain the island; Toussaint was eventually taken to France, where he died in prison.

Townsend, Francis Everett (1867–1960) US physician and reformer. He is mainly remembered for his Old Age Revolving Pension scheme, known as the **Townsend Plan**, that was meant to help the elderly and assist the USA out of the Great *Depression. The plan called for payments of $200 a month to all aged 60 or more. The funds were to be provided by a federal tax on commercial transactions. The popularity of this and other programmes (he secured at least ten million signatures to his petitions) may have persuaded Franklin D. *Roosevelt to adopt more far-reaching social policies.

Townshend, Charles, 2nd Viscount (1674–1738) English politician and agriculturist. He became Secretary of State in 1714, but quarrelled with George I over foreign policy and was dismissed from the government in 1716. His brother-in-law *Walpole resigned in sympathy and Townshend was restored as Secretary of State when Walpole came to power in 1721. Walpole at first gave him a free hand in foreign affairs, but Townshend allowed a quarrel with Austria to get out of hand and frequent interference from Walpole led to his resignation in 1730. He retired from politics completely and went back to Norfolk to improve his family estate. He became famous as a pioneer of the *Agricultural Revolution, popularizing four-course rotation of crops, which enabled farmers to keep many more cattle alive during the winter and to grow more crops without having to keep one field in three fallow every year. He also introduced the widespread cultivation for winter fodder of the turnip, previously only a garden crop, which earned him the nickname "Turnip" Townshend.

Townshend Acts (1767) A British revenue measure, which was introduced after the failure to raise direct taxes in the American colonies by the *Stamp Act. Faced with a parliamentary revolt against his budget, the Chancellor of the Exchequer, **Charles Townshend**, grandson of Charles *Townshend, the agricultural reformer, sought revenue through taxes on American imports of paint, paper, glass, and tea. To enforce this trade tax, a new American Board of Customs Commissioners and Vice-Admiralty Courts without juries were established. The revenue was to be used to pay salaries of colonial officials, thus making them independent of the colonial assemblies. American resistance led to the repeal of the duties, except for that on tea, in 1770.

Towton, Battle of (29 March 1461) A desperate encounter near Tadcaster in Yorkshire in a snowstorm between the army of the newly crowned *Edward IV and the retreating Lancastrian forces of Queen *Margaret of Anjou and *Henry VI. The armies were large (the Lancastrians numbered over 22,000) and the losses on both sides were heavy, but in a late reverse the Lancastrians were routed and some of their ablest leaders killed.

Trades Union Congress (TUC) An organization of British trade unions. It was founded in 1868 with the purpose of holding national conferences on trade union activities. In 1871 it set up a Parliamentary Committee to advance the interests of unions with Members of Parliament. From 1889 onwards, it began to be more politically militant and in 1900 helped to found the Labour Representation Committee, known from 1906 as the *Labour Party, with whom it has had links ever since. The General Council, elected by trade union members, replaced the Parliamentary Committee in 1920. The Congress can urge support from other unions, when a union cannot reach a satisfactory settlement with an employer in an industrial dispute, but it has no powers of direction. After the *General Strike relations between the Congress and government (of whatever party) were cautiously conciliatory. It was closely involved in British industrial planning and management during World War II and under successive Labour and Conservative governments until 1979. In the 1980s it was faced with legislation designed by Margaret Thatcher's governments to weaken trade union power. Since then it has continued to be mainly on the defensive.

trade union An organized association of workers in a particular trade or profession.

Unions represent employees in negotiations with employers. In the USA they are referred to as labor unions. In Britain in the late 18th century groups and clubs of working-men in skilled trades developed, to regulate admission of apprentices and sometimes to bargain for better working conditions. During the wars with France (1793–1815) *Combination Acts suppressed any such activity, but on their repeal in 1824 limited trade union activity became possible in certain crafts. By 1861 a number of trade unions of skilled workers existed in Britain, forming the *Trades Union Congress (TUC) in 1868, gaining some legal status in 1871, and the right to picket peacefully in 1875. With the development of mass-production methods in the industrialized countries large numbers of semi-skilled and unskilled workers were recruited, and from the 1880s attempts were made to organize these into unions. These attempts were more successful in Britain and in Europe than in the USA, where cheap immigrant labour was for long available. Unions emerged in Australia and New Zealand and in other British dominions in the 19th century. As industrialization proceeded in other countries so trade unions developed, although in South Africa trade union activity among Black workers was illegal until 1980. In the former Soviet Union and communist Eastern Europe 90% of industrial workers belonged to government-controlled unions. Elsewhere, union membership fluctuates with political and economic vicissitudes, especially in developing countries.

Trade unions are funded by membership subscriptions and are usually run by an elected executive and full-time officials, and elected workplace representatives (shop stewards in Britain). Their main economic objectives are to attain good wages, good working conditions, and secure employment for their members. Trade unions aim to achieve their workplace industrial relations objectives through collective bargaining, supported when necessary by industrial action. A significant development since World War II was the increasing participation of trade unions in government and tripartite bodies at national or industry level. However, in such nations as the USA and UK union membership and influence declined in the late 20th century, especially in the private sector.

Trafalgar, Battle of (21 October 1805)
A naval engagement between the combined French and Spanish fleets, and the British, fought off Cape Trafalgar near the Spanish port of Cadiz. After failing to lure the British fleet away from Europe to enable *Napoleon to

transport his army to England, Admiral Villeneuve returned to Cadiz and the English Channel fleet, commanded by Cuthbert Collingwood (1748–1810) blockaded the port. On 29 September *Nelson arrived in his flagship, *Victory*, to take command. Villeneuve, 20 days later, was ordered by Napoleon to leave Cadiz and threatened with the loss of his command, finally put to sea but hoped to avoid a battle. Nelson, who had kept his main fleet out of sight, divided his fleet of 27 ships and signalled at the beginning of the battle that "England expects every man to do his duty". The British lost no ships but took 20 from the French and Spanish. Nelson was mortally wounded by a shot from the French ship *Redoubtable* but British naval supremacy was secured for the remainder of the 19th century.

Trail of Tears The route of enforced westward exile for many Native Americans. As more settlers moved into Georgia and to the states of Alabama, Mississippi, Louisiana, and Florida in the 1830s, it was US policy forcibly to expel the eastern tribes from their lands and move them to Oklahoma territory west of the Mississippi River. The peoples concerned were the *Cherokee, Creek, Choctaw, Chickasaw, and Seminole known as the Five Civilized Tribes. Bad weather, neglect, and limited supplies of food caused much suffering and death before the move was completed and the Trail of Tears closed in 1838. In time, even their new homeland became subject to White incursions.

trained band (or **trainband**) A unit of armed men based in one of the counties of England. The formation of these companies in 1573 was the result of a decision of *Elizabeth I's government that a selection of the most able *militia men in each county should be properly trained in the use of pikes and firearms. Freemen in each city were also selected. The bands multiplied in numbers and were extremely active in the early years of the *English Civil War. In the 18th century they were replaced by a standing army supported by militia.

Trajan (born **Marcus Ulpius Traianus**) (c.53–117 AD) Roman emperor (98–117). Born in Spain, he was adopted by Nerva as his successor. Trajan's reign is noted for the *Dacian wars (101–06), which ended in the annexation of Dacia as a province; the campaigns are illustrated on Trajan's Column in Rome. He was also an efficient administrator and many public works were undertaken during his reign.

Trans-Siberian Railway A railway built in 1891–1904 from Moscow east around the southern end of Lake Baikal to Vladivostok on the Sea of Japan, a distance of 9311 km (5786 miles). It opened up Siberia and advanced Russian interest in east Asia. A major extension to the north of Lake Baikal (the Baikal–Amur Mainline) was completed in 1984 and stretches 3102 km (1952 miles) from Ust-Kut in east Siberia to the Pacific coast.

treaty ports The Asian ports, especially Chinese and Japanese, that were opened to foreign trade and habitation as a result of a series of *Unequal Treaties in the 19th century. In China, the first five treaty ports were opened as a result of the Treaty of *Nanjing (1842), eleven more as a result of the Treaty of Tianjin (1858) and the Conventions of Beijing (1860), and approximately 35 more opened before the *Chinese Revolution of 1911, some on the Yangtze River. Foreigners living in their own concessions in treaty ports had the protection of their home governments and were not required to pay Chinese taxes or to be subject to Chinese laws. This was strongly resented by the nationalist government and all privileges were surrendered by 1943. In Japan, five treaty ports were established after the Treaty of Kanagawa (1858), but foreign powers were obliged to surrender their privileges in 1899.

Trenchard, Hugh Montague, 1st Viscount of Wolfeton (1873–1956) British Marshal of the RAF. He served in the army (1893–1912) before training as a pilot and becoming head of the Royal Flying Corps during World War I. As Chief of Staff (1918) then First Marshal (1927) of the RAF he built the force into the third major element of the British armed services. He was also Metropolitan Police Commissioner from 1931 to 1935.

trench warfare A form of fighting conducted from long, narrow ditches in which troops stood and were sheltered from the enemy's fire. At the beginning of World War I the belief that victory came from mass infantry charges dominated military thinking in spite of the introduction of rapid-firing small arms and artillery. After the first Battle of the *Marne thousands of miles of parallel trenches were dug along the Western Front, linked by intricate systems of communication trenches and protected by barbed wire. With such trenches stretching from the North Sea to Switzerland, a stalemate existed and to break it various new weapons were introduced, including hand-grenades, poison gas, trench mortars, and artillery barrages. Consequently

casualties hitherto undreamed of followed every mass infantry attack. Not until 1918, with an improved version of the tank (invented in 1915), was it possible to advance across the trenches. World War II by contrast was a war of movement with no comparable trench fighting. Slit trenches, manned by two or three machine gunners, replaced them. In the *Korean War and in *Vietnam fortified bunkers were used. Trench warfare was used by the protagonists in the *Iran-Iraq War of 1980–88.

Trent, Council of (1545–63) An ecumenical council of the Roman Catholic Church, which met in three sessions the city of Trento in northern Italy. It defined the doctrines of the Church in opposition to those of the *Reformation, reformed discipline, and strengthened the authority of the *papacy. Its first session (1545–47), produced a ruling against *Luther's doctrine of justification by faith alone. The brief second session (1551–52) included a rejection of the Lutheran and *Zwinglian positions on the Eucharist. By the third session (1562–63), any lingering hopes of reconciliation with the Protestants had disappeared. Various works recommended or initiated by the Council were handed over to the pope for completion, these included the revision of the Vulgate version of the Bible (finally completed in 1592). The Council thus provided the foundation for a revitalized Roman Catholic Church in the *Counter-Reformation.

Trent affair (November–December 1861) An incident between the USA and Britain during the *American Civil War. In November 1861 the US warship *San Jacinto* stopped the British mail packet *Trent* at sea and forcibly removed two Confederate (Southern) diplomats and their secretaries. News of the incident produced widespread demands in Britain for war against the Union (the North), but the crisis was averted partly through the intervention of Prince *Albert and by the decision of US Secretary of State William *Seward to release the diplomats on the grounds that the captain had erred in not bringing the *Trent* and its "personal contraband" to port.

Triad Societies Chinese secret societies, originally formed in the late 17th century to overthrow the Manchu *Qing dynasty and restore its Chinese Ming predecessor. The various societies forming the Triad shared a similar ritual and acted both as fraternal and criminal organizations. They grew in strength during the *Taiping Rebellion, and thereafter played an erratic and violent role in China. Some Triad branches assisted *Sun Yat-sen, while others exerted strong political influence in such cities as Shanghai. In recent years the Triad Societies have been involved in drug smuggling on a worldwide basis.

trial by ordeal *See* ORDEAL.

Trianon, Treaty of *See* VERSAILLES PEACE SETTLEMENT.

tribune In ancient Rome, ten tribunes were elected to protect *plebs from *patricians; they were empowered to veto decisions of magistrates and, later, the Senate's decrees. They could also propose legislation of their own. Roman emperors also took the title of tribune, which gave them the constitutional rights of tribunes and a popular image. Military tribunes were senior officers of legions, also elected. The Latin word *tribunus* was derived from *tribus*, tribe, indicating 'of the people'.

Trimble, David (William David Trimble) (1944–) Northern Irish politician, leader of the Ulster Unionist Party (1995–2005) and First Minister of the Northern Irish Assembly (1998–2002). He was awarded the Nobel peace prize in 1998 jointly with John *Hume for their roles in talks to establish peace in Northern Ireland. He resigned as leader of the UUP following its collapse in the 2005 general election.

Trinidad and Tobago

Capital:	Port of Spain
Area:	5,128 sq km (1980 sq miles)
Population:	1,225,225 (2013 est)
Currency:	1 Trinidad and Tobago dollar = 100 cents
Religions:	Protestant 32.1%; Roman Catholic 21.6%; Hindu 18.2%; Muslim 5.0%
Ethnic Groups:	East Indian 35.4%; Black 34.2%; mixed 21.0%
Languages:	English (official)
International Organizations:	UN; Commonwealth; OAS; CARICOM; Non-Aligned Movement; WTO

An island country in the south-east corner of the Caribbean Sea, the larger island, Trinidad, lying only 11 km (7 miles) off the northern coast of South America.

Physical Trinidad measures about 80 km (50 miles) by 60 km (37 miles). In the south-west is the great Pitch Lake, a basin of bitumen; and across the north is a range of low mountains. The densely forested hills of Tobago, to the north-east, are the ridge of an otherwise submerged mountain range.

Economy The economy is dominated by oil and gas, which constitute two-fifths of GDP and four-fifths of exports. Other export industries include methanol, ammonia, urea, steel products, and beverages. With declining oil and gas reserves, tourism, agriculture, information and communications technology, and shipping are being encouraged.

History The islands were originally inhabited by Arawak and Carib Indians. Trinidad was discovered by Columbus in 1498 during his third voyage. Trinidad was claimed by Spain but left to its indigenous *Caribs until 1532, when settlement was begun. As it lacked precious metals it remained largely ignored until 1595, when Sir Walter *Raleigh landed there for ship repairs and sacked the newly founded town of San José; the Dutch raided it in 1640, and the French in 1677 and 1690. Sugar and tobacco plantations were established in the 17th century, worked by imported African slaves. In 1797, during war between England and Spain, a British squadron entered the Gulf of Paria but met little resistance before the island surrendered. In 1802 it was officially ceded to Britain under the Treaty of Amiens. In 1962, the country became an independent member of the British Commonwealth and, in 1976, a republic. The first Prime Minister of the new republic was Eric Williams, founder of the People's National Movement (PNM). Trinidad's first President, Ellis Clarke, was succeeded in 1987 by Noor Mohammed Hassanali, who was in turn succeeded in 1997 by Arthur N. Robinson. In 2001 there was a constitutional crisis when elections produced a tie in parliament; the President appointed Patrick Manning of the PNM as Prime Minister. He was confirmed in office by another election in 2002 and re-elected in 2007. However, Manning's decision to call an early election in 2010 backfired: a centre-left coalition was victorious and Kamla Persad-Bissessar became Trinidad and Tobago's first woman Prime Minister.

Triple Alliance (1882) A secret alliance between Germany, Austria, and Italy signed in

May 1882 at the instigation of *Bismarck. The three powers agreed to support each other if attacked by either France or Russia. It was renewed at five-yearly intervals, but Italy reneged in 1914 by not coming to the support of the Central Powers.

Triple Alliance, War of the See PARA-GUAYAN WAR.

Tripolitan War (1800–15) A conflict between the USA and the Karamanli dynasty of Tripoli, which in 1796 had obtained from the USA the annual payment of $83,000 for the protection of its commerce from piracy. In 1801 the Bey of Tripoli demanded an increase; the USA declined and sent a naval force to blockade the port of Tripoli. In 1803 the Tripolitanians captured the US ship *Philadelphia*. US forces then captured the port of Derna and the Bey agreed to peace, which was concluded in 1805. The Bey received $60,000 as ransom for the *Philadelphia* and renounced all rights to levy tributes on US ships. In 1815, following breaches of the agreement, a US squadron under Captain Stephen Decatur again visited North Africa and compelled the Bey of Algiers to renounce payments for immunity.

trireme The principal warship of antiquity from the 6th to the late 4th century BC. A type of *galley with three banks of oars, it was lightly built for speed and manoeuvrability and unable to venture very far from land; each trireme carried a crew of some 200 men, the majority being rowers. They were probably seated three to a bench, the bench being angled so that each rower pulled a separate oar. A beak of metal and wood was set at the front of the galley, ramming being the principal aim of the steersman. Athens' fleet of triremes played a major part in the Greek victory at *Salamis and was instrumental in controlling the *Athenian empire.

Tromp, Maarten Harpertszoon (1597–1653) Dutch admiral, who was largely responsible for Dutch naval greatness in the 17th century. In 1639 Tromp completely defeated the Spanish fleet at the Battle of the Downs. In the First *Anglo-Dutch War he defeated *Blake off Dungeness in December 1652, fought magnificently but unsuccessfully to protect Dutch convoys in the English Channel, and was killed trying to break *Monck's blockade of the Dutch coast. His son Cornelius (1629–91), *Ruyter's rival, won victories in the Mediterranean in the Second and Third *Anglo-Dutch Wars and against Sweden at Gotland.

Trotsky, Leon (born **Lev Davidovich Bronstein**) (1879–1940) Russian revolutionary. Joining the Bolsheviks in 1917, he helped to organize the October Revolution with Lenin, and built up the Red Army that eventually defeated the White Russian forces in the Russian Civil War. After Lenin's death he alienated Stalin and others with his view that socialism within the Soviet Union could not come about until revolution had occurred in western Europe and worldwide. Trotsky was eventually defeated by Stalin in the struggle for power, being expelled from the party in 1927 and exiled in 1929. After settling in Mexico in 1937, he was murdered three years later by a Stalinist assassin.

troubadour A lyric poet or minstrel in the 11th century in southern France, particularly in Provence. Their poetry dealt with courtly love, *chivalry, religion, and politics, but usually the matter was heavily disguised in formal, decorative language. Much of it was heretical, and in the 13th century many of its devotees were persecuted.

Troy (Turkish **Truva**; Latin **Ilium**) In Homeric legend, the city of King Priam, which was besieged for ten years by the Greeks in their endeavour to recover Helen, wife of Menelaus, who had been abducted. It was believed to be a figment of Greek legend until a stronghold called by the Turks Hissarlik, in Asiatic Turkey near the Dardanelles, was identified as the site of Troy by the German archaeologist H. Schliemann, who in 1870 began excavations of the mound which proved to be composed of 46 strata, dating from the early Bronze Age to the Roman era. The stratum known as Troy VII, believed to be that of the Homeric city, was sacked $c.1210$ BC. Again destroyed $c.1100$ BC, the site was resettled by the Greeks $c.700$ BC and finally abandoned in the Roman period.

Trucial States See UNITED ARAB EMIRATES.

Truck Acts Measures passed by the British Parliament in the 19th century regarding the method of payment of wages. Certain employers paid their workmen in goods or in tokens, which could be exchanged only at shops owned by the employers—the so-called truck system. The Truck Act of 1831 listed many trades in which payment of wages must be made in coins. It was amended by an Act of 1887, which extended its provisions to cover virtually all manual workers. In 1896 a further Act regulated the amounts that could be deducted from wages for bad workmanship. The Payment of Wages Act of 1960 repealed certain sections of the Truck Acts to permit payment of wages by cheque.

Trudeau, Pierre (Elliott) (1919–2000)
Canadian Liberal statesman, Prime Minister of
Canada (1968–79; 1980–84). A committed federalist, Trudeau made both English and French
official languages of the Canadian government
(1969). During his second term, in 1980, a provincial referendum rejected independence for
Quebec; Trudeau also presided over the transfer
of residual constitutional powers from Britain to
Canada in 1982.

Trujillo, Rafael (born **Rafael Leónidas
Trujillo Molina**; known as 'Generalissimo')
(1891–1961) Dominican statesman, President of
the Dominican Republic (1930–38; 1942–52).
Although he was formally President for only two
periods, he wielded dictatorial powers from
1930 until his death. His dictatorship was
marked by some improvement in social services
and material benefits for the people, but also by
the deployment of a strong and ruthless police
force to crush all opposition. He was assassinated in 1961.

Truman, Harry S (1884–1972) US Democratic statesman, 33rd President of the USA
(1945–53). As Vice-President, he automatically
took office on Franklin Roosevelt's death in
1945. One of his first actions was to authorize
the use of the atom bomb against Hiroshima
and *Nagasaki in 1945 to end the war with
Japan. At home Truman put forward an extensive social programme, which was largely
blocked by Congress, although racial segregation in the armed forces and in federally funded
schools was ended. His expression in 1947 of
what became known as the *Truman Doctrine
(the principle that the USA should give support
to countries or peoples threatened by Soviet
forces or Communist insurrection) was seen by
the Communists as an open declaration of the
cold war. In 1948 his administration introduced
the Marshall Plan of emergency aid to war-
shattered European countries and helped to
establish NATO the following year. He later involved the USA in the Korean War.

Truman Doctrine (1947) A principle of US
foreign policy aimed at containing communism.
It was enunciated by President *Truman in a
message to Congress at a time when Greece and
Turkey were in danger of a communist take-
over. Truman pledged that the USA would
"support free peoples who are resisting attempted subjugation by armed minorities or by
outside pressures". Congress voted large sums
to provide military and economic aid to countries whose stability was threatened by communism. Seen by communists as an open

declaration of the *Cold War, it confirmed the
awakening of the USA to a new global responsibility.

Ts'ao Ts'ao *See* CAO CAO.

Tseng Kuo-fan *See* ZENG GUOFAN.

Tshaka *See* SHAKA.

Tshombe, Moise (Kapenda) (1920–69)
African leader in the Belgian Congo. He
founded the Conakat political party, which
advocated an independent but loosely federal
Congo. He took part in talks that led to
Congolese independence in 1960, but then
declared the province of Katanga independent
of the rest of the country. He maintained his
position as self-styled President of Katanga
(1960–63) with the help of white mercenaries
and the support of the Belgian mining company,
Union Minière. Briefly Prime Minister of the
Congo Republic (1964–65), he was accused of
the murder of *Lumumba, and of corruptly
rigging the elections of 1965, and fled the
country when General *Mobutu seized power.
In 1967 he was kidnapped and taken to Algeria,
where he died in prison.

Tso Tsung-tang *See* ZUO ZONGTANG.

Tubman, Harriet (*c.*1821–1913) Black
American abolitionist and social reformer. An
escaped Maryland slave, Tubman became one
of the most effective "conductors" on the
*Underground Railroad. During the *American
Civil War she served as a nurse and a Union
(Northern) spy behind *Confederacy lines. After
the conflict she worked in the cause of Black
education in North Carolina.

Tubman, William Vacanarat Shadrach
(1895–1971) Liberian statesman, President
(1944–71). A member of an Americo-Liberian
family, he was elected to the Liberian Senate in
1930 and became President in 1944. He encouraged economic development to remove
Liberia's financial dependence on the USA and
successfully integrated the inhabitants of the
country's interior into an administration.

TUC *See* TRADES UNION CONGRESS.

Tudjman, Franjo (1922–99) Croatian politician, President of Croatia as a federal republic
of Yugoslavia (1990–92) and as an independent
state (1992–99). Imprisoned in the 1970s and
1980s for his advocacy of Croatian independence, he led the Croatian forces in the fight
against the Serb-led Yugoslavian army (1991–
92) and involved Croatian forces in the civil war

in Bosnia and Herzegovina. He was re-elected President in 1997, although the election was criticized for his total control of the media.

Tudor The English royal house that began as a family of Welsh gentry. Its fortunes started to rise when *Henry V's widow, Katherine of Valois, married Owen Tudor (c.1400–61), her clerk of the wardrobe. He was executed after the *Yorkists' victory of Mortimer's Cross (1461) during the Wars of the Roses, but his son Edmund (c.1430–56), Earl of Richmond, married Margaret *Beaufort, and their son Henry was thus a descendant, though illegitimately, of the House of Lancaster. His claim to the throne became more acceptable after the death of *Henry VI's son Edward in 1471, and *Richard III's loss of the nobility's support paved the way for Henry's invasion of England and taking of the throne as *Henry VII in 1485.

Henry safeguarded his claim to the throne by marrying Elizabeth of York, the Yorkist heiress: she bore him eight children, although four died in infancy. Arthur died soon after marrying Catherine of Aragon, and it was his younger brother who succeeded to the throne, as *Henry VIII. Of his children, his only son, *Edward VI, died in his youth. His elder daughter *Mary died in 1558 after a childless marriage to Philip II of Spain, and *Elizabeth I never married. With Elizabeth's death (1603) the House of Tudor ended, and the throne passed to James VI of Scotland, of the House of *Stuart.

Tughluq A Muslim dynasty that ruled in India for almost a century (1320–1413). Seizure of power was followed by military campaigns that brought the sultanate of Delhi to its greatest territorial extent, including the extreme south of India. The chief architect of this success was the second sultan, **Muhammad ibn Tughluq** (1325–51). Some of his controversial actions are deemed to have undermined rather than strengthened the empire. Gifted and well intentioned, he nevertheless gained a reputation for extreme cruelty, which led to rebellions throughout his territories. The invasion of Timur in 1398, in which Delhi was devastated, increased the chaos and in 1413 the *Sayyids seized power from the Tughluqs.

Tuileries A French royal residence in Paris built in the 16th century. In June 1792 during the *French Revolution crowds forced their way into the palace, and on 10 August it was attacked, the Swiss Guard was massacred, and the royal family took refuge with the Assembly. The palace was burned down in the 19th century, but the formal gardens laid out in the 17th century remain.

tumulus *See* BARROW.

Tunisia

Capital:	Tunis
Area:	163,610 sq km (63,170 sq miles)
Population:	10,835,873 (2013 est)
Currency:	1 Tunisian dinar = 1000 millimes
Religions:	Sunni Muslim 99.1%
Ethnic Groups:	Arab 98.0%; European 1.0%
Languages:	Arabic (official); French; Berber
International Organizations:	UN; AU; Arab League; Maghreb Union; OAPEC; Non-Aligned Movement; WTO

A country on the North African coast, sandwiched between Algeria and Libya, which has its southern part in the Sahara.

Physical In the northwest of the country are hills, mostly covered in scrub though containing forests of cork oak. Salt marshes cover the central belt, where there are also large phosphate deposits. The south is sandy but contains oases.

Economy The principal industries include crude oil production, mining of phosphate and iron ore, tourism, textiles, and footwear. Agriculture produces olives and olive oil, grain, fruit, and sugar beet. Exports include oil and oil products, textiles and clothing, food products, chemicals, and phosphates. The economy, in particular the important tourist industry, was damaged by the revolution of 2011 and the subsequent political instability.

History Tunisia has been the strategic centre of the Mediterranean. *Phoenicians came first c.1000 BC; and, traditionally, *Carthage, seat of a sea-borne empire, was founded here in 814 BC. *Berber caravans came north to exchange produce for imports. Carthage fell in 146 BC, and, despite Berber resistance, Rome made the province of Africa Proconsularis rich in corn, olives, and vines. *Vandals from Spain took it in 429, but Byzantium recovered it in 533. The

Berbers, nevertheless, held the interior, giving way only when the Arabs built Kairouan as an inland base to control Africa. The caliphate was replaced by an independent local dynasty, the Aghlabids, in 800, until 909, when the *Fatimids took Kairouan. Another local dynasty, the Zirids, replaced them when they moved to Cairo in 969. In revenge, the Fatimids sent thousands of Arab tribesmen to lay waste the country. In the 12th century the Normans from Sicily held some towns, until the *Almohads expelled them. Then another local dynasty, the Hafsids (1228–1574) emerged, taking Algiers (1235) and Tlemcen (1242). In 1270 they repulsed the Crusaders under St *Louis IX. From 1574 until 1881 the Regency of Tunis owed nominal allegiance to the Ottomans, but after 1612 a dynasty of Beys established itself. The Bey of Tunis became increasingly independent and *corsairs operated from Tunis, leading to the Tripolitan War with the USA. A period of great prosperity ended when the corsairs and the slave trade were suppressed (1819). During the 19th century, the Bey's control weakened and, in 1881, France declared Tunisia a protectorate. The rise of nationalist activity led to fighting between the nationalists and the colonial government in the 1950s. Habib *Bourguiba, the nationalist leader, was imprisoned, but was released (1955) when the country achieved independence. The Bey of Tunis abdicated (1956) and the country became a republic led by Bourguiba and the neo-Destour Party. In the 1970s the government's refusal to allow the formation of other political parties caused serious unrest, while subsequent attempts at liberalization were interrupted by fresh outbreaks of rioting in 1984–85. Bourguiba was deposed (1987) and succeeded by President Zine el-Abidine Ben Ali, who introduced a multiparty system in 1988 and was re-elected in 1994, 1999, 2004, and 2009. However, the Islamic fundamentalist party al-Nahdah was suppressed in 1990, and there were recurring concerns over the country's human rights record. Popular discontent with poverty, high unemployment, and increasing government repression found a focus at the end of 2010: the public suicide of Mohammed Bouazizi, an unemployed fruit seller, on 17 December inspired mass protests. Attempts to suppress these only caused them to escalate, Ben Ali resigned as President in January 2011, and an interim unity government was formed. In October a Constituent Assembly was elected, which appointed the former dissident Moncef Marzouki as interim President; he was victorious in presidential elections held in early 2012. Tensions between Islamist and secular factions increased over the role of Islam in a new constitution, but agreement was reached in 2014. Tunisia's revolution sparked similar uprisings in other Arab countries that became known as the *Arab Spring.

Tupac Amarú (born **José Gabriel Condocanqui**) (*c.*1742–81) Leader of a widespread Indian revolt in the Peruvian highlands (1780–81). As the Indian chief of Tinta, south of Cuzco, Tupac Amarú used his links to the *Inca royal dynasty to develop an Indian base of support and his Spanish connections to attract Creole and Mestizo people to his reformist political movement that espoused Inca nationalism, fairer taxes, better courts, and a more open interregional economy. In 1780, reacting to economic abuses, Tupac Amarú plotted the execution of the local Spanish corregidor and then recruited a large indigenous army, led by non-Indian, middle-level, provincial leaders, which occupied much of the highland area, even threatening Cuzco. Although Tupac Amarú was defeated and executed in May 1781, the revolt spread into Upper Peru, becoming more hostile to non-Indians, and finally provoking severe repression that retarded the independence movement in Peru. His name has been used by revolutionary guerrilla groups in modern Peru and by the *Tupamaros in Uruguay.

Tupamaros Members of the *Movimento de Liberación Nacional* (National Liberation Movement) in Uruguay. An urban guerrilla organization, it was founded in Montevideo in 1963 and led by Raúl Sendic. It sought the violent overthrow of the Uruguayan government and the establishment of a socialist state. Its robberies, bombings, kidnappings and assassinations of officials continued until the early 1970s, when the movement was severely weakened by police and military repression. The Tupamaros derived their name from the 18th-century Inca revolutionary against Spanish rule, *Tupac Amarú.

Tupper, Sir Charles (1821–1915) Canadian statesman, who became Conservative Member of the Nova Scotia Assembly in 1855 and Premier in 1863. A Father of the Confederation, he entered the dominion Parliament in 1867 and served under John A. *MacDonald (1870–73; 1878–84). He became High Commissioner to Britain, holding the post, except for the years 1887–88, until 1896. Returning to Canadian politics, he was Prime Minister for a little over two months. He led the opposition until 1900, when he retired.

Turenne, Henri de la Tour d'Auvergne, vicomte de (1611–75) Marshal of France. A soldier of outstanding ability, he made his reputation on the battlefields of the *Thirty Years War. During the *Fronde he was briefly persuaded by *Condé's sister, Madame de Longueville, to join the antiroyalist faction, but finally supported *Mazarin in establishing order. He captured Dunkirk in 1658 and led the brilliant invasions of Flanders in 1667 and the United Provinces in 1672. In 1674, when *Louis XIV was threatened from all sides, he showed his supreme ability in deploying troops against superior forces in defending France's eastern frontier. He died on the battlefield.

Turin Shroud A cloth, preserved since 1578 in Turin Cathedral in Italy, which is venerated as the shroud in which *Jesus Christ was buried, although its history can be traced with certainty only to 1354. In 1988 radiocarbon dating indicated that it had been woven from 13th- or 14th-century flax, but the test results have since been disputed.

Turkey

Capital:	Ankara
Area:	783,562 sq km (302,535 sq miles)
Population:	80,694,485 (2013 est)
Currency:	1 New Turkish lira = 100 kurus
Religions:	Muslim (principally Sunni) 99.8%
Ethnic Groups:	Turkish: between 70.0% and 75.0%; Kurdish 18.0%
Languages:	Turkish (official); Kurdish; minority languages
International Organizations:	UN; OECD; NATO; Council of Europe; OSCE; WTO

A country partly in Asia and partly in Europe.

Physical The Asian and European parts of Turkey are separated by the Bosporus, the Sea of Marmara, and the channel of the Dardanelles. The smaller, European part is bounded by Bulgaria and Greece. The much larger Asian part comprises the whole of Asia Minor and is known as Anatolia. It has the Black Sea on the north, Georgia, Armenia, and Iran on the east, Iraq and Syria on the south, and coasts on the Mediterranean and Aegean seas. Its largest river, the Kizil Irmak, is saline for nearly half its course to the Black Sea. In the east rise the Tigris and Euphrates rivers.

The plateau is subject to devastating earthquakes, however, lying as it does at a junction of crustal plates.

Economy Turkey has a traditional agricultural sector, which employs a quarter of the workforce, and an expanding industrial sector. Important exports include clothing, textiles, foodstuffs, metal manufactures, and transport equipment. Turkey has rich mineral deposits of coal, antimony, copper, iron ore, sulphur, lead, and zinc. Tourism is important.

History Modern Turkey evolved from the *Ottoman empire, which was finally dissolved at the end of World War I. By the Treaty of *Sèvres at the Versailles Peace Conference parts of the east coast of the Aegean around the city of Izmir (Smyrna) were to go to Greece, and the Anatolian peninsula was to be partitioned, with a separate state of *Armenia created on the Black Sea. The settlement triggered off fierce national resistance, led by Mustafa Kemal. A Greek army marched inland from Izmir, but was defeated. The city was captured, Armenia occupied, and the new Treaty of Lausanne negotiated. This recognized the present frontiers, obliging some one and a half million Greeks and some half-million Armenians to leave the country (July 1923). In October 1923 the new Republic of Turkey was proclaimed, with Kemal as first President. His dramatic modernizing reforms won him the title of *Atatürk, 'Father of the Turks'. The one-party rule of his Republican People's Party continued under his lieutenant Ismel Inonu until 1950, when in the republic's first open elections, the free-enterprise opposition Democratic Party entered a decade of power, ending with an army coup. Civilian rule was resumed in 1961, but there was a further period of military rule (1971–73). Atatürk's neutralist policy had been abandoned in 1952 when Turkey joined NATO. Relations with allies, however, were strained by the invasion of *Cyprus (1974). A US trade embargo resulting from this was only lifted in 1978. Tension between left-wing and right-wing factions, hostility to Westernization by the minority Shiites, who seek to enforce Islamic puritanism, and fighting between Turks, Kurds, and Armenians, continued to trouble the country. A military coup, led by General Kenan Evren, overthrew the civilian government of Suleiman Demirel. Under Presidents Evren (1982–87) and Turgut Özal (1987–93) some political stability developed, with rather more concern for human rights. Martial law was lifted in 1987 and the state of emergency ended in 1988, some political parties having been legalized, including a neo-fascist Nationalist Workers' Party. The Kurdish Workers' Party, claiming to speak for Turkey's twelve million Kurds, continued its armed campaign for an independent Kurdistan. Civilian rule was resumed in 1991, with the re-election of Suleiman Demirel at the head of a coalition. 1993 saw the election of Tansu Çiller (1946–), Turkey's first woman Prime Minister, and Demirel became President. However, the secular nature of the Turkish state has been increasingly challenged by the rise of Islamic fundamentalism. In 1996 the pro-Islamist Welfare Party came to power as part of a coalition. This resigned in 1997 and a series of secularist coalitions followed. However, the 2002 election was won by the Islamist Justice and Development Party (AKP) and its leader, Recep Tayyip Erdogan, became Prime Minister the following year. The AKP was re-elected in 2007 and 2011, but in 2013 demonstrations sparked by a local issue in Istanbul became protests against the government's management of the economy and alleged authoritarianism. In 2014 Erdogan became Turkey's first directly elected President. In 1989 the European Community postponed consideration of Turkey's application for membership (1987), in part as a result of its human rights violations. Membership negotiations finally began in 2005 and constitutional changes were made in 2010 to meet EU democratic standards; nevertheless, some EU members remained opposed to Turkish membership and progress stalled.

Turkmenistan

Capital:	Ashgabat
Area:	488,100 sq km (186,400 sq miles)
Population:	4,833,000 (2005)
Currency:	1 manat = 100 tennesi
Religions:	Muslim 89.0%; Eastern Orthodox 9.0%
Ethnic Groups:	Turkmen 85.0%; Uzbek 5.0%; Russian 4.0%
Languages:	Turkmen (official); Russian; Uzbek; minority languages
International Organizations:	UN; OSCE; Commonwealth of Independent States; Euro-Atlantic Partnership Council; Non-Aligned Movement

A country lying east of the Caspian Sea and north of Iran.

Physical Turkmenistan is in an arid region; it contains the greater part of the Kara Kum desert, which has important mineral resources. The oases produce cotton and mulberry trees (for silkworms), while livestock roam the semi-desert areas. Oil and natural gas are found in the west, on the Caspian coastal plain.

Economy Turkmenistan has large reserves of oil and natural gas, and principal export industries include gas, crude oil, and petrochemicals. Agriculture employs almost half the workforce; the principal export crop is cotton, and wheat and melons are also grown.

History Turkmen never experienced political unity until conquered by the Russians in 1869. Even then fierce resistance lasted until 1881, and there was a rebellion in 1916. In 1918 a Social Revolutionary Transcaspian Republic was proclaimed. It was briefly supported by British troops until April 1919, after which it was conquered by the Red Army. In 1924 the Turkmen Soviet Socialist Republic was formed, and incorporated into the Soviet Union in 1925. It declared its sovereignty in August 1990 and its independence in October 1991. Turkmenistan joined the *Commonwealth of Independent States (CIS) in 1991. A new constitution in March 1992 increased the powers of its executive President Saparmuradi Niyazov, and allowed only ethnic Turkmen to work in state enterprises. The extension of President Niyazov's term of office was approved in a referendum in 1994, and in 1999 Niyazov became President for life. All seats in the legislative elections later that year were won by the former communists, renamed the Turkmen Democratic Party. The elections of 1999 and 2004 produced the same result. Niyazov died in 2006 and was succeeded by Gurbanguly Berdimuhammedov as Acting President. He won presidential elections held in 2007 and was re-elected in 2012.

Turks Originally nomads from the Turkistan region of central Asia. During the 6th century AD they controlled an empire stretching from Mongolia to the Caspian Sea. With the conquest of western Turkistan in the 7th century by the *Abbasids, many were converted to

Islam and moved westwards, retaining their distinctive language and culture. In the 11th century, under the *Seljuks they replaced the Arabs as rulers of the Levant and Mesopotamia, then expanded north-west at the expense of Byzantium. The rival house of Osman continued this trend, founding the *Ottoman empire, which endured for 600 years, and embraced most of the Middle East, North Africa, and the Balkans.

Turner, John Napier (1929–) Canadian Liberal politician, Prime Minister for four months in 1984. Turner succeeded *Trudeau as Prime Minister but was defeated in the subsequent general election.

Turner, Nat (1800–31) Black American leader of the Virginia slave revolt of 1831. Believing himself a divine instrument to guide his people out of bondage, Turner led about 60 slaves into revolt in Southampton County, Virginia, killing 57 White people before he, his followers, and a number of innocent slaves were killed. Turner's rebellion exacerbated Southern fears of insurrection and led to a tightening of police measures against slaves.

Tutankhamun (died *c*.1352 BC) Pharaoh of Egypt (*c*.1361–1352 BC). Little is known about his reign; his importance is largely that his tomb in the *Valley of the Kings escaped looting in antiquity. Hidden by rubble from the construction of a later tomb, it was found almost intact by the British archaeologist Howard Carter and his patron, Lord Carnarvon, in 1922. Tutankhamun's mummified body was inside three coffins, the inner one of solid gold; over his face was a magnificent gold funerary mask, and the burial chamber housed a unique collection of jewellery and weapons.

Tuthmosis I *See* THUTMOSE I.

Tuthmosis III *See* THUTMOSE III.

Tutu, Desmond (Mpilo) (1931–) South African clergyman. He served as General Secretary of the South African Council of Churches (1979–84), becoming a leading voice in the struggle against apartheid, calling for economic sanctions against South Africa and emphasizing non-violent action. He was awarded the Nobel Peace Prize in 1984, and in the following year he became Johannesburg's first Black Anglican bishop. He was archbishop of Cape Town (1986–96) and chaired South Africa's Truth and Reconciliation Commission (1995–2003).

Tuvalu

Capital:	Funafuti
Area:	26 sq km (10 sq miles)
Population:	10,698 (2013 est)
Currency:	1 Tuvalu dollar = 100 cents; Australian currency is also legal tender
Religions:	Church of Tuvalu 97.0%; Seventh-Day Adventist 1.4%; Baha'i 1.0%
Ethnic Groups:	Polynesian 96.0%; Micronesian 4.0%
Languages:	Tuvaluan, English (both official); Samoan; Kiribati
International Organizations:	UN; Commonwealth; Pacific Islands Forum; Secretariat of the Pacific Community

A country comprising a scattered archipelago of small islands between Kiribati and Fiji in the South Seas.

Physical Funafuti is the chief island in the group, which numbers nine, all of them coral atolls. Vegetation consists mainly of coconut palms.

Economy Tuvalu has few natural resources and the principal economic activities are subsistence farming and fishing. The only exports are copra and fish. The main sources of national income are remittances from expatriates, a trust fund, fishing licences, and leasing Tuvalu's national Internet suffix (.tv).

History The first settlers probably came from Samoa and Tonga in the 14th century AD. The islands were sighted by Spanish explorers in the 16th century. They were formerly called the Ellice Islands after a 19th-century British shipowner, Edward Ellice. In the 19th century whalers, traders, missionaries, and 'blackbirders' (*Kanaka catchers) for the Queensland sugar plantations began to take an interest in these atolls, which the British were to include in the Gilbert and Ellice Islands Protectorate in 1892. In 1974 the Ellice Islanders, who are of Polynesian descent, voted to separate from the Micronesian Gilbertese. They achieved independence in 1978, establishing a constitutional monarchy.

Tweed Ring A group of corrupt officials in New York City, USA. It revolved around William Marcy Tweed (1823–78), the New York city political "boss" and state senator who had built his power through the influence of *Tammany Hall. The ring, renowned for corrupt and dishonest dealing and for fraudulent city contracts and extortion, was exposed in the *New York Times* in 1871. Tweed was arrested and convicted but fled to Spain, from which he was extradited. He died in prison in 1878. The operations of the Tweed Ring were estimated to have cost New York City some $100 million.

Twentieth Congress (February 1956) The Congress of the Communist Party of the Soviet Union, noted for *Khrushchev's denunciation of *Stalin. After the first and open session of the Congress, Khrushchev, as First Secretary, made three significant doctrinal points, that peaceful co-existence between East and West was possible, that war between them was not inevitable, and that there were "different roads to socialism" besides the Soviet route. More dramatic was the speech he delivered in the secret session when he denounced the Stalinist cult of personality and Stalin's acts of terror. The speech was carefully constructed to emphasize Stalin's treatment of the Party rather than of the country at large. A fervour of de-Stalinization and demands for liberalization swept through Eastern Europe as well as the Soviet Union. Khrushchev's "secret" speech was an important contributory factor in prompting the uprisings in *Poland and *Hungary in 1956 and in the Sino-Soviet quarrel from 1960.

Twenty-One Demands The Japanese attempt to impose domination on China in January 1915. Taking advantage of its favourable international position after entering World War I on the Allied side and capturing the German base of Qingdao on the Chinese mainland, Japan attempted to impose virtual protectorate status on China, which was diplomatically isolated and torn by civil war. Although one group of demands dealing with the appointment of Japanese advisers throughout the Chinese government was not enforced, threat of war left China no choice but to concede the others, including extension of Japanese leases in Manchuria, takeover of former German concessions in Jiaozhou, substantial interests in Chinese mining concerns, and an embargo on future coastal territorial concessions to any other foreign power. The Twenty-One Demands greatly extended Japanese power in China, but provoked serious resentment within China and aroused US fears of Japanese expansionism.

Tyler, John (1790–1862) US Whig statesman, 10th President of the USA (1841–45). Successor to William Henry Harrison as President, he was noted for securing the annexation of Texas (1845). Throughout his political career Tyler advocated states' rights, and his alliance with Southern Democrats on this issue helped to accentuate the divide between North and South in the years leading up to the American Civil War.

Tyler, Wat (died 1381) English leader of the Peasants' Revolt of 1381. After capturing Canterbury, he led the rebels to Blackheath and took London. During a conference with the young king Richard II he put forward the rebels' demands (including the lifting of the newly imposed poll tax), to which Richard consented. At a later conference in Smithfield he was killed by the Lord Mayor of London and several other royal supporters.

Tyndale, William (c.1494–1536) English translator and Protestant martyr. Faced with ecclesiastical opposition to his project for translating the Bible into English, Tyndale went abroad in 1524, never to return to his own country; his translation of the New Testament (c.1525–26) was published in Germany. He then translated the Pentateuch (1530) and Jonah (1531), both of which were printed in Antwerp. Tyndale's translations later formed the basis of the Authorized Version. In 1535 he was arrested in Antwerp on a charge of heresy, and subsequently strangled and burnt at the stake.

Tyrone, Hugh O'Neill, 2nd Earl of (1540–1616) Ulster chieftain. Tyrone received his earldom from *Elizabeth I of England in 1585. He established himself as the most powerful chief in Ulster and with the support of other Catholic chiefs rebelled against Elizabeth and her religious policies in 1594. After a famous victory at the Yellow Ford (1598), the initiative slipped to the English, under Charles Blount, Lord Mountjoy. Spanish support for the rebels at Kinsale (1601) proved inadequate and in 1603 Tyrone surrendered. In 1607, after another abortive insurrection the earls of Tyrone and Tyrconnel and their households, fled to Flanders in the celebrated "flight of the earls", and Tyrone died in Rome.

Tz'u-hsi See CIXI.

Uganda

Capital:	Kampala
Area:	241,038 sq km (93,065 sq miles)
Population:	34,758,809 (2013 est)
Currency:	1 Uganda shilling = 100 cents
Religions:	Roman Catholic 41.9%; Anglican 35.9%; Muslim 12.1%; other Christian 6.1%
Ethnic Groups:	Baganda 16.9%; Banyakole 9.5%; Basoga 8.4%; Bakiga 6.9%; Iteso 6.4%; Langi 6.1%; minority groups
Languages:	English (official); Ganda; Swahili; Arabic; local languages
International Organizations:	UN; AU; Commonwealth; Non-Aligned Movement; WTO

A landlocked country in East Africa, bounded by Sudan on the north, Kenya on the east, Tanzania and Rwanda on the south, and the Democratic Republic of Congo on the west.

Physical Uganda's tropical climate is alleviated by its height, most of it being over 1000 m (3300 feet) above sea-level. Between lakes Victoria (the source of the Nile), Kyoga, and Albert in the southern half of the country are hills with richly fertile slopes and valleys. The savannah country in the north supports cotton and grain.

Economy Agriculture employs four-fifths of the workforce, and coffee accounts for the majority of export earnings. Other important exports are fish and fish products, tea, cotton, flowers, horticultural products, and gold. Industry concentrates on agricultural processing, textiles, cement, and steel. Oil reserves have been identified but not exploited.

History During the 18th and 19th centuries the kingdom of Buganda on Lake Victoria became the dominant power in the area under its kabaka (king) Mutesa I. He welcomed the explorers *Speke and *Stanley, hoping for protection against Arab slave and ivory traders. Following Mutesa's death tensions developed between Christians and Muslims, and also between British and German interests. In 1890 there was an Anglo-German agreement that the area be administered by the British, and the newly formed British East Africa Company placed Buganda and the western states Ankole and Toro under its protection. In 1896 the British government took over the protectorate. After World War II nationalist agitation for independence developed, with Mutesa II being deported. In 1962 internal self-government was granted. Uganda was to be a federation of the kingdoms of Ankole, Buganda, Bunyoro, Busoga, and Toro. In September the Prime Minister, Milton Obote, renounced this constitution and declared Uganda a republic. Mutesa II was elected first President, but in 1965 he was deposed by Milton Obote, who became President himself, only to be deposed in turn by General Idi *Amin (1971). Amin's rule was tyrannical and racist, including the expulsion of Uganda's Asian residents, an economically vital group of entrepreneurs. In 1980, after the invasion by Tanzanian forces and Ugandan exiles, Amin fled the country. Obote returned in 1981, but his failure to restore order led to a coup in 1985, the resulting military regime being overthrown by the National Resistance Army of Yoweri *Museveni, who became President in 1986. Under his presidency Uganda tried to recover from the disastrous years of 1971–80, which had ruined the economy and cost hundreds of thousands of lives. Extensive loans by the World Bank and IMF required demobilization of the armed forces. However, with growing insurgence in the north of Uganda during 1995–96 by the terrorist group, the Lord's Resistance Army, military strength has had to be increased once more. The ban on political parties, imposed when Museveni took power, was renewed in 1992 and enshrined in a new constitution in 1995. In 1994, non-party elections to the Constituent Assembly were won by Museveni's supporters. Museveni won the country's first presidential election in 1996 and was re-elected in 2001. Following a referendum on the issue in 2005, a multiparty system was introduced; Museveni was re-elected under the new system in 2006 and 2011.

Uitlanders (Afrikaans, "outsiders") The non-Boer immigrants into the Transvaal, who came after the discovery of gold (1886). They were denied citizenship, were heavily taxed, and excluded from government.

Ukraine

Capital:	Kiev
Area:	603,550 sq km (233,032 sq miles)
Population:	44,573,205 (2013 est)
Currency:	1 hryvnya = 100 kopiykas
Religions:	Eastern Orthodox; Ukrainian Catholic; other Christian
Ethnic Groups:	Ukrainian 77.8%; Russian 17.3%; Belarussian, Moldovan, Tatar, and other minorities
Languages:	Ukrainian (official); Russian; minority languages
International Organizations:	UN; OSCE; Commonwealth of Independent States; Council of Europe; Euro-Atlantic Partnership Council; WTO

A country comprising a large region of eastern Europe stretching from the Carpathian Mountains to the Donetz River and bounded on the south by the Black Sea. To the east are Poland, Slovakia, Hungary, Romania and Moldova; to the west, Russia.

Physical Northern Ukraine is a continuation of the low plains, woods, and marshes of Belarus.

To the south, and forming three-quarters of the region, is the treeless steppe. In the extreme south is the Crimea, a peninsula with a milder climate than the steppe.

Economy Mineral resources are abundant and varied. Export industries include iron, steel, and other metals, fuel, oil products, machinery, transport equipment, chemicals, and food processing; other important industries include coal mining. Grain, sugar beet, sunflower seeds, and vegetables are the most important agricultural crops.

History Originally inhabited by Neolithic settlers in the Dnieper and Dniester valleys, Ukraine was overrun by numerous invaders before Varangian adventurers founded a powerful Slav kingdom based on *Kiev in the 9th century. Mongol conquest in the 13th century was followed in the 14th century by Lithuanian overlordship until 1569, when Polish rule brought serfdom and religious persecution, which produced an exiled community of Cossacks who resisted both Polish and Russian domination. With the partition of Poland in 1795 the region, including the Crimea, under *Ottoman control from 1478, came under Russian control, a situation which lasted until the break-up of the Soviet Union in 1991. Yet Ukrainian nationalism, despite repression, remained strong. In 1918 independence was proclaimed, but by 1922 the area had been conquered by Soviet forces, to become the Ukrainian Soviet Socialist Republic. Stalin imposed *collectivization on the region, which suffered grievously from his purges. It was devastated during the German occupation of 1941 to 1944, although many nationalists welcomed the Germans. Territorial gains from Romania, eastern Poland, and Slovakia completed the union of all Ukrainian lands into one republic by 1945, the Crimea being added in 1954. By 1990 strong pressure had built up for independence from the Soviet Union, and the Ukraine Supreme Soviet formally declared independence in August 1991, with overwhelming support in a referendum. Multiparty elections followed, with Leonid Kravchuk elected President. The 20% Russian minority was placed under no pressure; at the same time, negotiations took place with Russia over naval and military armed forces, Ukraine declaring itself a nuclear-free zone. The Chernobyl nuclear power-station disaster of 1986 had left thousands of square kilometres of its countryside permanently contaminated; the plant was closed in 2000. Following independence, the largely Russian region of the Crimea declared itself an autonomous region in 1992. Ukraine formally joined the Commonwealth of

Independent States (CIS) in 1993. In elections to the Supreme Council, held in 1994, both communists and independent parties fared well. Later in the same year, the former Prime Minister Leonid Kuchma, who advocated economic reform and closer links with Russia, replaced Kravchuk as President; he was re-elected in 1999. Relations with Russia remained tense, as Ukraine continued to dispute the autonomy of Crimea. A new constitution abolishing Soviet-style institutions and consolidating democracy was adopted in June 1996. The 2004 presidential election was declared to have been won by the pro-Russian Prime Minister, Viktor Yanukovych. However, allegations of fraud quickly escalated into the *Orange Revolution: the election was re-run and the pro-Western opposition candidate, Viktor Yeshchenko, was elected. His presidency was characterized by disputes with Russia and factional splits among the supporters of the Revolution. His popularity collapsed and Yanukovych was elected President in 2010. A rapprochement with Russia followed, but progress towards closer association with the EU continued. Yanukovych's sudden rejection of the final agreement with the EU in 2013 provoked another crisis between pro-Western and pro-Russian Ukrainian factions. Anti-government protests broke out in Kiev, which escalated as the government attempted to suppress them. In February 2014 Yanukovych fled and the Chairman of Parliament, Oleksandr Turchynov of the pro-Western Fatherland Party, became Acting President. In March unmarked Russian forces moved into the largely Russian-speaking Crimea, which announced its secession from Ukraine and was integrated into the Russian Federation—a development not recognized by the USA or the EU. Petro Poroshenko was elected President in May 2014 but violence continued, with pro-Russian separatists seizing cities in the east, including Donetsk. In July a Malaysian Airlines passenger jet was shot down over eastern Ukraine, most likely by pro-Russian groups using Russian equipment, which caused the deaths of all 298 on board. Subsequent months saw a concerted counter-attack by the Ukrainian military as well as mounting evidence of direct Russian intervention in the region. A tentative ceasefire was agreed in September but sporadic fighting continued.

Ulster A former kingdom of *Ireland, lying in the north-east of the island. The kingdom of Ulster reached its zenith in the 5th century AD, at the beginning of the Christian era. During the Anglo-Norman conquest the de Lacey and de Burgh families held the earldom of Ulster from 1205 to 1333. By the 16th century, the O'Neill clan had reasserted its commanding position in the area, until the failure of the Earl of Tyrone's rebellion against *Elizabeth I and her unwelcome religious policy (1594–1601) marked the end of O'Neill supremacy. James I promoted the **plantation** in Ulster of thousands of Presbyterian Scots and Protestant English and many Catholics were forced off their land. These Protestants supported *William III in his campaign against *James II, which culminated in William's victory at the Battle of the *Boyne (1690). At the division of Ireland in 1920–21, six of the nine counties that originally comprised Ulster opted for self-governing status as *Northern Ireland, a province of the *United Kingdom. The remaining three counties of Cavan, Donegal, and Monaghan became part of the Irish Free State (later the Republic of Ireland).

Ulster Unionist Parties Political parties in *Northern Ireland supporting maintenance of the union with the UK. In 1886 Lord Hartington and Joseph *Chamberlain formed the Liberal Unionists, allying with the Conservatives and pledging to maintain the Union of Ireland with the rest of the United Kingdom. In 1920, with the division of Ireland, the majority party in Northern Ireland was the Unionist wing of the Conservative Party, now calling itself the Ulster Unionists, under Sir James Craig, who was Prime Minister (1921–40). The party, supported by a Protestant electorate, continued to rule under his successors, until the imposition of direct rule from Westminster in 1972. The increased violence between Nationalists and Unionists after the civil rights campaign of 1968 led to divisions in the party, and in 1969 it split into the Official Ulster Unionist Party and the Protestant Unionist Party. The latter, led by the Revd Ian *Paisley, was renamed in 1972 the Ulster Democratic Unionist Party (DUP), with policies more extreme than those of the Ulster Unionists (led from 1979 to 1995 by James Molyneaux, from 1995 to 2005 by David Trimble, and from 2005 by Sir Reg Empey). Support for the Ulster Unionists collapsed from 2005, which left the DUP as the leading unionist party.

Ulster Volunteers An Irish paramilitary organization, formed in 1912 to exclude Ulster from the *Home Rule Bill then about to go through Parliament. Its supporters pledged themselves 'to use all means' to resist this. They were given every encouragement by Sir Edward *Carson and several prominent English Conservatives. The Volunteers were drilled and armed: thousands of rifles were smuggled into Ireland for their use. A clash between these Volunteers and the nationalist Irish Volunteers (formed in Dublin in 1913) became probable but was averted by the start of World War I.

Umar ibn al-Khattab (*c.*581–644 AD) Second *caliph of Islam (634–44). He presided over the first major wave of *Arab conquests, which were the work of great captains such as Khalid ibn al-Walid. Hostile at first to *Muhammad, he became an ardent convert. The bond between them was strengthened by Muhammad's marriage to Umar's daughter Hafsa. His genius was administrative rather than military and his achievements included systematizing the rule of his vast territories, establishing the Islamic calendar, organizing state pensions, and upholding justice.

Umar ibn Said Tal (or **al-Hajj Umar** or **Umar Tal**) (*c.*1797–1864) Muslim ruler of a state in Mali (1848–64). Born among the Tukolor people, he established the Tukolor empire. He set out on the pilgrimage to Mecca *c.*1820, where he was designated caliph for Black Africa. He established himself in the Senegal River area and in 1854 proclaimed a *jihad* (holy war) against all pagans. He created a vast Tukolor empire, but failed to win many converts. He became a harsh ruler. In 1863 he captured Timbuktu but soon lost it to a combined force of Fulani and Tuaregs. He was killed in 1864 but the Tukolor empire survived until 1897, ruled by his son Ahmadu Seku.

Umayyad A Muslim dynasty, descended from the Quraish tribe to which the prophet Muhammad belonged, that ruled Islam from *c.*660 to 750 and later ruled Moorish Spain (756–1031).

UNCTAD See UNITED NATIONS CONFERENCE ON TRADE AND DEVELOPMENT.

Underground Railroad A secret network in the USA for aiding the escape of slaves from the South in the years before the *American Civil War. While the Railroad helped only a small number of slaves (perhaps 1000 per annum after 1850), it served as a valuable symbol for the abolitionist cause and was viewed in the South with far greater hostility than its actual size merited.

Unequal Treaties A number of treaties made between China and various Western powers in the 19th century. The *Qing dynasty was generally unable to resist foreign pressure for commercial and territorial concessions and in such

agreements as the Treaty of *Nanjing (1842) was forced to agree to Western demands.

UNESCO See UNITED NATIONS EDUCATIONAL, SCIENTIFIC AND CULTURAL ORGANIZATION.

UNGA See UNITED NATIONS GENERAL ASSEMBLY.

UNHCR See UNITED NATIONS HIGH COMMISSIONER FOR REFUGEES.

Unification Church A religious movement founded by Sun Myung Moon (1920–2012) in South Korea in 1954. Members are popularly known as the 'Moonies'. Its theology, found in the *Divine Principle*, claims that a sinless man (often thought to be Moon himself) could save the world and form the kingdom of God on Earth. There are said to be 3 million members. The movement has attracted controversy through its business practices and accusations that it brainwashes new recruits into absolute obedience.

Uniformity, Acts of A series of English laws intended to secure the legal and doctrinal basis of the Anglican Communion. The first (1549) made the Book of Common Prayer compulsory in church services, with severe penalties on non-compliant clergymen. The second (1552) imposed a revised Prayer Book, which was more Protestant in tone, and laid down punishments for recusants. *Mary I had both Acts repealed, but the third (1559) introduced a third Book of Common Prayer and weekly fines for non-attendance at church. The fourth (1662) presented a further revised, compulsory Book. Under its terms some 2000 non-compliant clergymen lost their benefices, creating the Anglican-*Nonconformist breach.

Union, Acts of Laws that cemented the political union of Great Britain and Ireland. Following the complete subjugation of Wales by 1284, the Statute of Rhuddlan, never submitted to a formal Parliament, sanctioned the English system of administration there. Not until 1536 was an Act passed by *Henry VIII, which incorporated Wales with England, and granted for the first time Welsh representation in Parliament. The Stuarts united the thrones but not the governments of England and Scotland in 1603. In 1707 an Act of Union between England and Scotland gave the Scots free trade with England, but in return for representation at Westminster they had to give up their own Parliament. The Protestant Irish Parliament enjoyed independence from 1782 to 1800, when legislation (1 August 1800) was introduced to establish the

*United Kingdom of Great Britain and Ireland (1 January 1801).

Union of Soviet Socialist Republics See SOVIET UNION.

United Arab Emirates (UAE)

Capital:	Abu Dhabi
Area:	83,600 sq km (32,278 sq miles)
Population:	5,473,972 (2013 est)
Currency:	1 UAE dirham = 100 fils
Religions:	Muslim 76.0%; Christian 9.0%
Ethnic Groups:	South Asian 50.0%; non-UAE Arab and Iranian 23.0%; UAE Arab 19.0%
Languages:	Arabic (official); Persian; English; Hindi; Urdu
International Organizations:	UN; GCC; Arab League; OAPEC; OPEC; WTO

A federation of seven sheikhdoms (emirates) occupying the southern (Arabian) coast of the Gulf between Qatar and Oman, together with its offshore islands.

Physical Abu Dhabi in the west is the largest emirate and also the richest in oil and natural gas. Dubai to the east is the second largest emirate and has oil offshore, as has Sharjah. Further east, Ras al-Khaimah and Fujairah are predominantly agricultural, while Ajman and Umm al-Qaiwain are very small.

Economy The economy of the UAE is based largely on crude oil, which, with natural gas, dominates exports. In addition, Dubai has a substantial entrepôt trade. However, recent government efforts have diversified the economy, reducing the oil and gas GDP contribution to one-quarter. Apart from oil and gas, industries include petroleum products, fishing, aluminium, cement, and fertilizers. Agricultural crops include dates, which are exported, vegetables, and watermelons. There is a large immigrant workforce, mainly of Pakistanis, Indians, and Iranians.

History The sheikhdoms concluded several treaties with Britain from 1820 onwards. In 1892, they accepted British military protection, becoming known thereafter as the Trucial States. (The name derived from a maritime

truce they made with Britain in 1836). The emirates came together as an independent state when they ended their individual special treaty relationships with the British government, and signed a Treaty of Friendship with Britain in 1971. The large oil resources of Abu Dhabi were first discovered in 1958. Each of the rulers of the seven constituent emirates has autonomy in his own state. Sheikh Zayed bin Sultan al-Nahayan of Abu Dhabi was President of the Federation from 1979 until his death in 2004; he was succeeded by his son, Sheikh Khalifa bin Zayid al-Nurhayyan. In 2006 limited elections, based on a restricted franchise, were held. From 2008 the UAE, and particularly the booming Dubai property market, suffered from the *Credit Crunch. Several pro-democracy activists were arrested in 2011 and 2012 following the *Arab Spring.

United Arab Republic A political union that existed between Egypt and Syria from 1958 until 1961. It was seen as the first step towards the creation of a pan-Arab union in the Middle East.

United Democratic Front (UDF) A South African non-racial political organization. It was formed in 1983 in response to the South African government's proposal to give the Coloured and Indian communities a limited role in government, as part of its campaign to defuse the country's political crisis. The UDF opposed this compromise, demanding full enfranchisement of all ethnic groups. By 1985 it had become a significant opposition group, with an affiliated membership of about 2.5 million. Its activities were banned in the same year.

United Empire Loyalists Some 50,000 Americans who were loyal to the British king George III and who emigrated to Canada during the War of *Independence. By 1784 about 35,000 had settled in Nova Scotia and some 10,000 in the Upper St Lawrence valley and round Lake Ontario, an area designated Upper Canada (later Ontario) in 1791. They came mainly from New England and New York and among them were several distinguished loyalists, or Tories as they were called, as well as thousands of farmers and artisans. In 1789 the governor-general ordained that all who had arrived by 1783 could put "UE" for United Empire Loyalist after their and their descendants' names—later arrivals were called "Late Loyalists". These "marks of honour" were treasured throughout the 19th century.

United Federation of Labour See RED FEDS.

United Irishmen A society established in Belfast in 1791 by Wolfe *Tone and others with the aim of bringing about religious equality and parliamentary reform in Ireland. Inspired by the ideals of the French Revolution, it drew its support from both Catholics and Presbyterians. The British government took steps to remove some grievances, notably with the Catholic Relief Act of 1793. However, after the dismissal of Earl Fitzwilliam, the Lord Lieutenant, who sympathized with the demands for religious equality, the society began to advocate violent revolution in order to overthrow British rule and establish an Irish republic. It sought military assistance from France, but a French expedition which set forth in 1796 to invade Ireland was scattered by storms. Repression of its members followed. In May 1798 sporadic risings occurred, especially in County Wexford, but two months later another French force was intercepted and Tone captured. Thereafter the society went into decline.

United Kingdom (UK)

Capital:	London
Area:	243,610 sq km (94,058 sq miles)
Population:	63,047,162 (2011 est)
Currency:	1 pound sterling = 100 pence
Religions:	Christian 59.5%; Muslim 4.4%; Hindu 1.3%
Ethnic Groups:	White 87.1%; Black: 3.0%; Indian 2.3%; Pakistani 1.9%
Languages:	English (official); Welsh (official in Wales); Scots; Scottish Gaelic; Irish; Cornish
International Organizations:	UN; EU; Commonwealth; OECD; NATO; Council of Europe; OSCE; WTO

A country in NW Europe consisting of *England, *Wales, and *Scotland, and the province of *Northern Ireland. The Channel Islands and the Isle of Man are British Crown dependencies but are not an integral part of the United Kingdom.

Physical The United Kingdom consists of Great Britain, a large island off Europe's north-west coast containing England, Scotland, and Wales, and the north-east corner of the neighbouring island of Ireland. Of its mountains, which lie in the north and west, few are higher than 1000 m (3300 feet), while of its rivers none is longer than the Severn at 354 km (220 miles). The south of the country has hills of chalk and flint or limestone rising to 300 m (less than 1000 feet). Here the valleys are broad, with sandy soil or clay supporting oak, ash, beech, and chestnut trees. In the east, which is lower and flatter, river gravels and alluvium from the North Sea have produced dark, rich soils. Its principal river, the Thames, flows into the North Sea.

Economy The United Kingdom's economy is dominated by service industries, with the formerly dominant manufacturing sector now accounting for only one-tenth of GDP. Economic growth is driven by banking and other financial services, and London is one of the world's premier financial centres. Industry is wide-ranging, including machine tools, all types of transport equipment, electronics, metals, chemicals, and consumer goods. Oil production has declined as the resources in the North Sea are depleted, and the UK became a net energy importer in 2005. The intensive agriculture sector produces almost two-thirds of the UK's food requirements; principal crops include cereals, oilseed, and vegetables. The UK was seriously affected by the *Credit Crunch.

History *Wales was incorporated into England in the reign of *Henry VIII. In 1604 *James I was proclaimed 'King of Great Britain', but although his accession to the English throne (1603) had joined the two crowns of *England and *Scotland the countries were not formally united. In the aftermath of the English Civil War, Oliver Cromwell effected a temporary union between England and Scotland, but it did not survive the *Restoration. The countries were joined by the Act of *Union (1707) which left unchanged the Scottish judicial system and the Presbyterian church. *Ireland was incorporated into the United Kingdom in 1800 but became independent (except for Northern Ireland) in 1921.

Britain was the first country in Europe to become fully industrialized, developing a predominantly urban, rather than a rural, society by the mid-19th century. A series of parliamentary reform acts, beginning with the *Reform Act of 1832, steadily increased the power of the *House of Commons compared to that of the monarch and the *House of Lords. Under Queen *Victoria, colonial expansion of the *British empire reached its height. However, growing pressure for independence from peoples within the empire meant that during the 20th century British dominions and colonies gradually gained independence; most of them elected to join the *Commonwealth of Nations, established in 1931. During *World War I and *World War II Britain fought against Germany and its allies, emerging from both conflicts on the victorious side. A period of austerity, which began to ease in the 1950s, followed World War II. Since 1967 gas and oil from offshore wells have been commercially produced, creating a major impact on the nation's economy. In 1973 Britain became a member of the European Economic Community, subsequently the *European Union. In 1982 Britain fought the *Falklands War with Argentina, in 1991 sent troops to support the US-led coalition in the *Gulf War, strongly supported the USA's *war on terrorism from 2001, and in 2003 was the USA's principal partner in the *Iraq War.

The main political parties in Britain are the *Conservative Party, the *Labour Party, and the *Liberal Democrats (*see also* LIBERAL PARTY). The Liberals have not been in power since the resignation of *Lloyd George in 1922. During World War II a coalition government under Winston *Churchill was formed. The postwar Labour *Attlee ministries saw the introduction of the National Health Service and the *welfare state, largely on the lines of the *Beveridge Report. Labour governments have traditionally been supported by *trade unions and legislated to nationalize service industries. Subsequent Conservative governments, notably those of Margaret *Thatcher and John *Major, reversed the procedure by privatizing many publicly owned companies; they also passed laws to restrict the power of the trade unions and restricted public spending. The Labour Party led by Tony *Blair won the general election of 1997 and formed a new government, which was re-elected in 2001 and 2005; in 2007 Blair was succeeded as Prime Minister by Gordon *Brown after several years of political infighting. This 'New Labour' regime abandoned such traditional Labour policies as nationalization and emphasized raising standards in education and combating poverty through the tax system while maintaining economic growth and avoiding excessive public borrowing. From 2007 there was a crisis in the financial services sector, with the Northern Rock bank suffering the first run on a British bank since the 1860s. In order to maintain confidence in the banking system, the British government nationalized Northern Rock rather than allow it to go bankrupt. The same strategy was followed as the crisis intensified in 2008, with the government taking significant stakes in the Royal Bank of Scotland Group and

Lloyds Banking Group. These investments, together with other measures to stimulate the economy and minimize the effects of recession, massively increased the UK's public deficit. Following the indecisive 2010 election a Conservative–Liberal Democrat coalition government was formed with David *Cameron (Conservative) as Prime Minister and Nick *Clegg (Liberal Democrat) as his deputy. This government believed the deficit had reached levels that threatened confidence in the UK's national solvency and embarked on a programme of spending cuts, tax rises, and other reforms to bring it under control and, eventually, eliminate it.

Progress has been made towards resolving the problem of Northern Ireland, which has seen recurrent conflict between Catholic supporters of a united Ireland and Protestant supporters of union with Britain. Peace talks involving all the main Northern Irish political parties began in 1996 and concluded in 1998 with the signing of a peace agreement by the British and Irish governments and the leaders of most of the Northern Irish parties. A separate Scottish Parliament and a Welsh Assembly, with limited powers, were established in 1999. In September 2014 a referendum asking Scottish voters whether Scotland should become an independent country resulted in defeat (45%–55%) for the proposal. Multiparty talks about a new constitutional settlement for the whole of the United Kingdom were promised.

United Malays National Organization

(UMNO) Malaysian political party. Formed by Dato Onn bin Jaafar, then Prime Minister of Johore, in 1946 in response to British attempts to form the Union of Malaya, UMNO's aim was to fight for national independence and protect the interests of the indigenous population. Since independence in 1957 UMNO has been the dominant party in *Malaysia, forming the cornerstone of successive electoral alliances, notably the Alliance Party of the 1960s and its successor, the National Front.

United Nations Conference on Trade and Development (UNCTAD) A permanent agency of the *United Nations Organization, with its headquarters in Geneva. It was established in 1964 to promote international trade and economic growth. The Conference, which meets every four years, called for discrimination in favour of the developing countries, since their industrial products are often subject to quotas and tariffs. UNCTAD has played an important role in devising economic measures to secure

advantageous prices for primary commodities and to ensure preferential tariff treatment for developing countries' manufactured goods. In 1968 it proposed that developed countries should give 1% of their gross national product in aid to developing countries, but the gap between rich and poor countries continued to widen (*Brandt Report), aggravated by a steady decline in the price of many basic world commodities, which the developing countries produce. Representatives from 150 countries attended its eighth full session in 1992, when it was agreed that increased emphasis in developing countries on domestic policy reforms and efficiency was needed in a changed international climate.

United Nations Convention on the Rights of the Child

An international treaty, adopted in 1989. The rights apply to all persons under 18 except in countries where the age of majority is lower. The Convention declares the family to be the natural environment for children and states that in all actions concerning children account should be taken of their best interests. It promulgates the child's right to a name and nationality, to privacy, freedom of association, thought, conscience, and religion. The obligations of others, especially parents and the state, are documented. The state, for example, must provide childcare for those with working parents, education, health care, and protection from child sexual exploitation, child abuse and neglect, drug abuse, and child labour. The treaty indicates the special protection required by vulnerable children, such as the victims of armed conflict, handicapped and refugee children, and the children of minorities. It is binding on states that ratify it, but there is no mechanism for enforcement.

United Nations Educational, Scientific and Cultural Organization

(UNESCO) A specialized agency of the United Nations, founded in 1946 and based in Paris, which promotes international collaboration in education, science, culture, and communication. In education, it supports the spread of literacy, continuing education, and universal primary education; and in science, assists developing countries, and international interchange between scientists. It encourages the preservation of monuments and sites, and of other aspects of culture such as oral traditions, music, and dance. By 1989 UNESCO's 'World Heritage List', designed to protect landmarks of 'outstanding universal value', comprised 315 sites in 67 countries. In the field of communication,

UNESCO is committed to the free flow of information. In 1980 its supreme governing body approved a New World Information and Communication Order despite opposition from those who believed it threatened press freedom. In 1984 the USA (which had been due to supply about a quarter of UNESCO's budget) and in 1985 the UK and Singapore withdrew, alleging financial mismanagement and political bias against Western countries. Following reforms, the UK re-joined in 1997 and the USA in 2003.

United Nations General Assembly

(UNGA) The main deliberative organ of the *United Nations Organization, where representatives of every member country sit and have a vote. The Assembly, based at UN headquarters in New York, can discuss and make recommendations on all questions which fall within the scope of the UN Charter; it is also responsible for the UN budget. It first met in January 1946 and meets for three months annually in regular session, although both special and emergency sessions can also be convened. Such sessions have been held to discuss issues of particular importance, such as the *Suez War in 1956, *Palestine, disarmament, or the sanctioning of the US-led war against Iraq in 1991. It may also meet when the *United Nations Security Council has failed to agree on a course of action in an international dispute, such as occurred in Afghanistan (1980), Namibia (1981), and the Israeli-occupied Arab territories (1982). Decisions on important questions require a two-thirds majority, otherwise a simple majority is sufficient. In the UN's early years, the USA could normally command a majority in the General Assembly, but with the dramatic increase in new members following decolonization, the balance shifted to favour the developing countries, who were often unwilling to endorse the policies of either superpower, preferring to adopt a non-aligned stance (see NON-ALIGNED MOVEMENT). Since the fall of communism in the Soviet Union and eastern Europe, the General Assembly's numbers have been further swelled by newly independent republics. In 2014 there were 193 member states.

United Nations High Commissioner for Refugees, Office of the

(UNHCR) A United Nations body established in 1951 to replace the International Refugee Organization. The UNHCR has two primary functions: to extend international protection to refugees under the terms of the 1951 UN Convention relating to the Status of Refugees, and, specifically, to ensure refugees obtain political asylum and are not forcibly returned to a territory where they fear persecution. The UNHCR also seeks to provide refugees with emergency relief, such as food, shelter, and medical assistance, and, in the long term, to assist in their voluntary repatriation or resettlement into a new community.

United Nations Organization (UN) An international organization established in 1945 as successor to the *League of Nations with the goal of working for peace, security, and co-operation among the nations of the world. Its permanent headquarters are in New York. The term "United Nations" was first used in a Declaration of the United Nations in January 1942, when representatives of 26 Allied nations pledged their governments to continue fighting together against the Axis powers, but it was only after further conferences held at Dumbarton Oaks, Washington, in 1944, and San Francisco in 1945 that representatives of 50 Allied countries signed the document, known as the Charter, setting up the new organization. The UN grew rapidly as former colonial territories became independent nations and applied for membership. In 2014 the organization had 193 members, most of the countries of the world.

In order to carry out its many functions, the UN is served by a wide range of organs and institutions. The six principal organs of the UN are the *United Nations General Assembly (UNGA), the *United Nations Security Council, the International Court of Justice, the Economic and Social Council (which deals with international economic, social, cultural, educational, health and related matters), the Trusteeship Council (which administers those territories held in trust by the UN), and the Secretariat, which is responsible for the general administration of the UN. The Secretariat is headed by the Secretary-General, who is appointed for a five-year renewable term by the General Assembly. There have been eight Secretary-Generals since the UN was founded: Trygve *Lie (Norway), (1946–53); Dag *Hammarskjöld (Sweden), (1953–61); U *Thant (Burma), (1961–71); Kurt *Waldheim (Austria), (1971–81); Javier *Pérez de Cuéllar (Peru), (1981–92); Boutros *Boutros-Ghali (Egypt), (1992–97); Kofi *Annan (Ghana), (1997–2007); and *Ban Ki-moon (South Korea) from 2007. The UN is also served by 15 intergovernmental agencies known as the specialized agencies, dealing with economic and social questions. They include the International Monetary Fund (IMF), the *United Nations Educational, Scientific and Cultural Organization (UNESCO), and the *World Health Organization (WHO). Other organs which are

part of the UN system include the *United Nations Conference on Trade and Development (UNCTAD), and the Office of the *United Nations High Commissioner for Refugees (UNHCR).

United Nations Security Council One of the six principal organs of the United Nations, based at UN headquarters in New York, whose prime responsibility is to maintain world peace and security. The Security Council, which first met in January 1946, consists of five permanent members (the USA, Russia, China, France, and the UK), and ten non-permanent members elected by the United Nations General Assembly for two-year terms on a rotating basis. The Security Council can investigate any international dispute, and recommend ways of achieving a settlement, including 'enforcement measures', such as sanctions, or the use of force by UN members (as, for example, in Somalia in 1992). It is also responsible for peacekeeping forces. Decisions taken by the Security Council require a majority of nine, including all five permanent members. This rule of great power unanimity, usually referred to as the right of veto, had been the cause of controversy. The effectiveness of the Council was improved after the collapse of the Soviet bloc in 1991. Since the 1990s the composition of the Security Council has been questioned. In particular, there have been proposals to increase the number of permanent members to reflect the changes in the economic and political balance of power since the UN's foundation. Brazil, Germany, India, Japan, and one Arab or African country have been suggested as appropriate candidates.

United Provinces of the Netherlands (or **Dutch Republic**) The historic state that lasted from 1579 to 1795 and comprised most of the area of the present kingdom of the Netherlands. It was recognized as an independent state by Spain at the conclusion of the *Dutch Revolts (1648) and power was subsequently shared between the Holland and Zeeland patricians and the *statholder princes of *Orange. During its "golden age" before 1700, the United Provinces developed the vast *Dutch empire, Dutch merchants traded throughout the world, and the arts flourished. The United Provinces gave refuge to religious refugees, especially Portuguese and Spanish Jews and French *Huguenots, who made a notable contribution to the country's prosperity. A series of wars was fought against England and France in the 18th century. The commercial and military fortunes of the Netherlands declined as those of England and France improved. When between 1794 and 1795 France overran the country during the French Revolutionary wars, there was a Dutch popular movement, inspired by the ideas of the *Enlightenment, that was ready to overthrow the ruler, William V of Orange, and to set up a Batavian Republic (1795–1806) under French protection in place of the United Provinces.

United States of America (USA)

Capital:	Washington DC
Area:	9,826,675 sq km (3,794,100 sq miles)
Population:	316,668,567 (2013 est)
Currency:	1 dollar = 100 cents
Religions:	Protestant 51.3%; Roman Catholic 23.9%; Jewish 1.7%; Mormon 1.7%
Ethnic Groups:	White (including Hispanic) 81.7%; Black 12.9%; Asian 4.2%; Amerindian and Alaska native 1.0%
Languages:	English; Spanish; numerous minority or immigrant languages
International Organizations:	UN; OAS; NATO; OECD; Colombo Plan; ANZUS Pact; OSCE; NAFTA; Secretariat of the Pacific Community; WTO

The world's fourth largest country, comprising the central belt of North America together with Alaska, Hawaii, Puerto Rico, and many small Pacific Ocean islands. Mainland USA is bounded by Canada on the north, generally along latitude 49° N and the Great Lakes, and by Mexico on the south, generally at about 32° N and along the Rio Grande.

Physical The West Coast is a series of mountain ranges with attendant valleys and plateaux running roughly parallel to the Pacific coast. In the north, the Cascade Range is cut by the valley of the Columbia River. In California, the reverse slopes of the Coast Range descend to the Sacramento and San Joaquin valleys, which are fringed inland by the snow-capped peaks of the Sierra Nevada. From here the Great Basin of Nevada and parts of Oregon, Idaho, Utah, and California extend eastward to the Rocky Moun-

tains. The Rockies are the 'Great Divide', the main watershed of the country. Out of their massive ranges in Montana, Wyoming, Colorado, and New Mexico (the Mountain States), emerge the westward-running Snake and Colorado rivers, and the eastward-flowing tributaries of the Mississippi. The Great Plains, occupied by the Dakotas, Nebraska, Kansas, Oklahoma, and Texas, are cut through by the eastward flows and have become a great prairie supporting cattle ranching and wheat cultivation. The prairies extend through the Middle West (including Minnesota, Iowa, Missouri, and north-west Arkansas) to the basin of the Mississippi. In the southern states of Louisiana, Mississippi, Tennessee, Alabama, and Georgia, the main crops are cotton, rice, tobacco, and sugar cane. In this region also there are oilfields which extend into the Gulf of Mexico. The south-eastern coastal plain, occupied by Virginia, the Carolinas, and eastern Georgia, is drained by the rivers of the Appalachian Mountains and supports much mixed farming. Mountainous New England, the north-eastern region, experiences harsh winters but contains rich pastures. Inland, the Great Lakes form a great transport artery and provide hydroelectric power for the northern states.

Economy The US economy is the world's largest and a leader in most economic sectors. It benefits from abundant natural resources and a large internal market; mineral resources include coal, oil, and many metals. Industry, which accounts for one-fifth of GDP, is widely diversified and includes oil, steel, vehicles, aerospace, telecommunications, chemicals, electronics, food processing, consumer goods, lumber, and mining. The main agricultural crops are maize, wheat, and other grains, fruit, vegetables, and cotton. Fishing, forestry, and livestock are also substantial. The USA is the home of many multinational companies, and New York is a leading global financial centre.

History The indigenous peoples of North America probably came from Asia across the Bering land bridge over 30,000 years ago. From the territory now occupied by Alaska, they spread out to populate the entire continent (and South America). By 1600 AD, it is estimated that there were around 1.5 million *Native Americans in what are now Canada and the USA. European colonization of the eastern seaboard of North America began in the early 17th century, gaining momentum as the rival nations, most notably the British and French, struggled for control of the new territory. The Treaty of *Paris (1763) marked the final triumph of Britain, but by that time the British colonies,

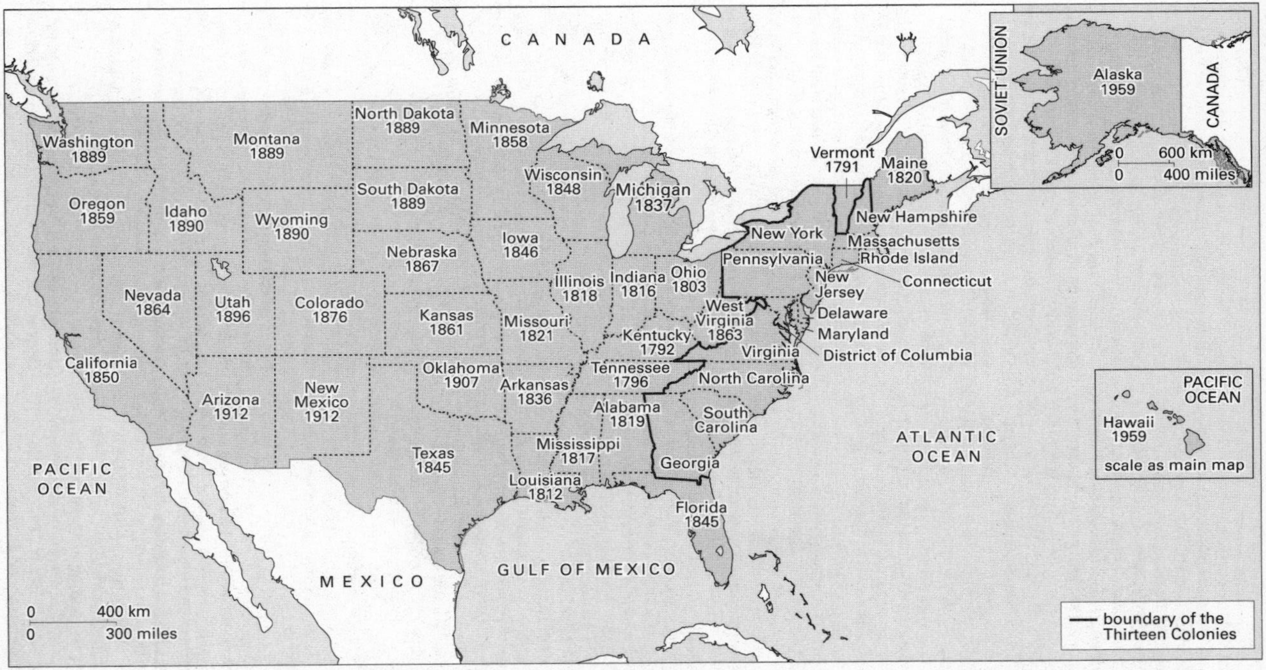
CANADA
Washington 1889
Oregon 1859
California 1850
Nevada 1864
Idaho 1890
Montana 1889
Wyoming 1890
Utah 1896
Colorado 1876
Arizona 1912
New Mexico 1912
North Dakota 1889
South Dakota 1889
Nebraska 1867
Kansas 1861
Oklahoma 1907
Texas 1845
Minnesota 1858
Iowa 1846
Missouri 1821
Arkansas 1836
Louisiana 1812
Wisconsin 1848
Illinois 1818
Michigan 1837
Indiana 1816
Ohio 1803
Kentucky 1792
Tennessee 1796
Mississippi 1817
Alabama 1819
Georgia
Florida 1845
South Carolina
North Carolina
Virginia
West Virginia 1863
Pennsylvania
New York
Vermont 1791
Maine 1820
New Hampshire
Massachusetts
Rhode Island
Connecticut
New Jersey
Delaware
Maryland
District of Columbia
PACIFIC OCEAN
ATLANTIC OCEAN
GULF OF MEXICO
MEXICO
0 400 km
0 300 miles
SOVIET UNION
Alaska 1959
CANADA
0 600 km
0 400 miles
PACIFIC OCEAN
Hawaii 1959
scale as main map
boundary of the Thirteen Colonies

United States of America. An Ordinance of 1787 laid down that when a US territory area reached a population of 60,000 free inhabitants it could petition Congress for admission to the Union as a state. Vermont and Kentucky were early admissions and many western states followed during the 19th century.

stretching from New England in the north to Georgia in the south, had become accustomed to a considerable measure of independence. British attempts to reassert central authority produced first discontent and then open resistance. The First *Continental Congress met in 1774 to consider action to regain lost rights, and the first armed encounters at Lexington and Concord in April 1775 led directly to full-scale revolt and to the formal proclamation of the separation of the Thirteen Colonies from Britain, as the United States of America, in the *Declaration of Independence (4 July 1776). In the American War of *Independence, which lasted until 1783, the American cause was assisted by France and Spain. The war ended with the Peace of *Paris (1783), which recognized US independence.

A structure of government for the new country was set out in the Constitution of 1787, which established a federal system, dividing power between central government and the constituent states, with an executive President, a legislature made up of two houses, the *Senate and the *House of Representatives, and an independent judiciary headed by the Supreme Court (*see also* CONGRESS). Territorial expansion followed with the *Louisiana Purchase of 1803, the acquisition of Florida between 1810 and 1819, and of *Texas, California, and the southwest following the *Mexican–American War of 1846 to 1848. The western lands of the Louisiana Purchase and those seized from Mexico were at first territories of the USA, administered by officers of the federal government. When the population reached some 60,000 an area of territory negotiated to be admitted to the Union as a new state. The mid-19th century was dominated by a political crisis over slavery and states' rights, leading to the secession of the Southern states and their reconquest in the *American Civil War of 1861 to 1865. The final decades of the century saw the westward expansion of European settlement, the purchase of Alaska (1867), and the acquisition of Spanish overseas territories after the Spanish–American War of 1898. In the 20th century the USA has participated in the two World Wars and has gradually emerged from isolationism to become a world power, a process accelerated by the *Cold War division. After the disintegration of the Soviet Union in 1991 US foreign policy concentrated on the resolution of major regional disputes and on providing military support for UN peace-keeping operations around the world. This changed with the election of George W. *Bush as President in 2000 and the terrorist attacks on New York of *September 11 2001. The USA launched a *war on terrorism that involved a

policy of confrontation with states whose regimes it considered to be sponsors of terrorism. In some cases this led to military intervention and forcible "regime change", which was also influenced by a belief in the benefits of spreading democracy and freedom (*see* NEOCONSERVATISM). Thus, the USA waged war on and deposed the *Taliban in Afghanistan (2001) and Saddam *Hussein in Iraq (2003) and established democratic regimes in their places. In 2008, the Democrat Barack *Obama was elected president, the first African American to hold the office. He swiftly intervened in the US economy to help cushion the worst effects of the global economic crisis resulting from the *Credit Crunch but soon faced strong opposition to his health-care reforms. In 2010 the Democrats lost control of the House of Representatives to the increasingly right-wing Republicans. With his own supporters disillusioned over what he had been able to achieve, Obama's campaign for re-election in 2012 against the Republican Mitt Romney was closely fought. Obama won the contest more easily than expected, however, to give him a second term as President.

Universal Declaration of Human Rights

An international declaration, adopted in 1948 by the General Assembly of the UN (with Saudi Arabia, South Africa, and the six Soviet members, Belarussian SSR, Ukrainian SSR, Russia, Poland, Czechoslovakia, and Yugoslavia, abstaining). It declares that all human beings are born free and equal in dignity and rights and are entitled to the rights and freedoms set out in the Declaration without discrimination on the grounds of race, colour, sex, language, political opinion, or religion. The rights enumerated include *civil rights, such as freedom of expression, conscience, movement, peaceful assembly, and association, and economic and social rights such as those to work, to an adequate standard of living, to education, and to participation in cultural life. The exercise of an individual's rights and freedoms is limited only by respect for the rights and freedoms of others. The Declaration is not legally binding but it has underpinned the activities of the UN, affected national and international law, and influenced debates on human rights. In 1966 the General Assembly adopted the International Covenant on Civil and Political Rights and the International Covenant on Economic, Social, and Cultural Rights, which embody the rights in the Declaration and have legal force.

Unrepresented Nations' and Peoples' Organization

(UNPO) An international organization, modelled on the *United Nations

Organization, that was established in 1991 to represent ethnic or minority groups aspiring to nationhood. Representatives from *Tibet, which has been occupied by Chinese troops since 1951 and made into a province of China, were prominent in the founding of the association. Other members include Australian *Aborigines, the Lakota Sioux people of North America, and many peoples of the former Soviet Union (including the Caucasian republics of Chechnya and Ingushetia, seeking independence from Russia, and Abkhazia, hoping to secede from Georgia).

Upper and Lower Canada Two British North American colonies or provinces (1791–1841). Following the American War of *Independence (1775–83) many loyalists to the British crown came north into the British colony of Quebec. Pressure developed among the settlers in the west for separate status, which was granted by the Constitutional Act of 1791. Quebec was divided along the Ottawa River: the eastern area, with its predominantly French population was known as Lower Canada (now Quebec); the western part was called Upper Canada (now Ontario) and adopted English common law and freehold land tenure. Government in both provinces remained in the hands of a governor appointed by the British crown, advised by an appointed executive council and a legislature consisting of an appointed upper house and a lower assembly of elected representatives, who in fact wielded little power. In both provinces movements for reform developed in the 1830s and, on the accession of Queen Victoria in 1837, two abortive rebellions took place led by Louis Joseph Papineau (*see* PAPINEAU'S REBELLION) in Lower Canada and William Lyon *Mackenzie in Upper Canada. In the wake of the Durham Report of 1838, an Act of Union was passed (1840) by the British Parliament and the two provinces united to form United Canada, with a legislature in which Canada West and Canada East enjoyed equal representation. Cabinet government directly responsible to the legislature was achieved in 1848, under Lord *Elgin.

Upper Palaeolithic See PALAEOLITHIC.

Ur A city of the *Sumerians. It was occupied from the 5th millennium BC, and was at one point damaged by a severe flood. By 3000 BC it was one of a number of sizeable Sumerian cities. It was subject to the rule of *Akkad, but emerged c.2150 as the capital of a new Sumerian empire, under the third dynasty established by Ur-Nammu. The city was captured by the Elamites c.2000, but thrived under the Chaldean

kings of Babylon. It was finally abandoned in the 4th century BC.

Urban II (born **Odo of Lagery**, c.1042–99) Pope (1088–99). A Cluniac monk, he was made Bishop of Ostia near Rome in 1078 and then a cardinal by Pope Gregory VII. At the Council of Clermont in 1095 he preached for the sending of the First *Crusade to recover *Palestine, which had fallen to the Muslims, hoping to unite the Christian West, then torn by strife between rival rulers. He continued Gregory's work of church reform and his councils condemned *simony, lay investiture, and clerical marriage.

Urban VIII (born **Maffeo Barberini**) (1568–1644) Pope (1623–44). He became a cardinal in 1606, and Bishop of Spoleto in 1608. As pope, he canonized Philip Neri and Ignatius *Loyola, condemned Galileo and *Jansenism, and approved a number of new religious orders. In diplomacy, his fears of Habsburg domination in Italy led him to favour France during the *Thirty Years War. He also extensively fortified the *Papal States, and fought the War of Castro (1642–44) against the north Italian Farnese Duke of Parma. The result was a humiliating defeat which crippled the papal finances and made him unpopular with the Roman people.

urbanization The increase in the proportion of a population living in urban areas and the process by which an area loses its rural character and way of life. Urbanization is a consequence mainly of rural–urban migration. This process began in Europe in the 19th century. Although large cities existed before 1800, the vast majority of the world's population lived in small, often self-sufficient village communities. Industrialization and population growth in Europe in the 19th century resulted in radical change: sometimes the excess peasant population moved to towns to seek paid work, often having to live in unhygienic slums and dying of infectious diseases.

Urbanization in the 20th century has proceeded at an unprecedented rate. In 1900 the UK became the first country to be predominantly urban. In 1920 only about 14% of the world's population lived in urban areas but by 1950 the proportion had reached 25%; by 1990, 43%; and by 2008, 50%. The population of such megacities as Tokyo, Guangzhou, Shanghai, Jakarta, and Seoul now exceeds 25 million; and formerly distinct towns and cities are effectively merging into megalopolises (clusters of urban areas so closely interlinked that they effectively function as one urban unit despite intervening rural land or other boundaries), for example the Pearl River Delta in China.

Uruguay

Capital:	Montevideo
Area:	176,215 sq km (68,037 sq miles)
Population:	3,324,460 (2013 est)
Currency:	1 Uruguayan peso = 100 centésimos
Religions:	Roman Catholic 47.1%; other Christian 11.1%: Jewish 0.3%
Ethnic Groups:	White 88.0%; Mestizo 8.0%; Black 4.0%
Languages:	Spanish (official), Portunol
International Organizations:	UN; OAS; Mercosur; WTO

A country in south-east-central South America with a coast on the Atlantic bounded by Argentina on the west and Brazil on the north-east.

Physical Uruguay has a coast on the estuary of the River Plate, and the Uruguay River flowing down its western boundary is navigable for some 320 km (200 miles). Tributaries flow westward across the country, which is mainly warm, grassy plain (pampas) supporting cattle and sheep. In the centre and north-east the plain is broken by occasional rocky ridges.

Economy Uruguay's major exports are agricultural products: beef, soya beans, cellulose, rice, wheat, wood, dairy products, and wool. Food processing is the principal industry; other industries include electrical machinery, transportation equipment, and oil products.

History Uruguay was inhabited by various indigenous peoples, such as the Chaná and Charnía, prior to the arrival of Spanish and Portuguese colonists in the 16th century. During the colonial period, it was known as the Banda Oriental and became a part of the Spanish viceroyalty of Rio de la Plata. In 1814 the leaders of the Banda Oriental, notably *Artigas, broke with the military junta in *Argentina and led a struggle for Uruguayan independence until occupied by Brazil in 1820. In 1825 an independent republic of Uruguay was declared, which was recognized by the treaty between Argentina and Brazil, signed at Rio de Janeiro in 1828. Under a republican constitution, the liberals (*Colorados*, redshirts) and the clerical conservatives (*Blancos*, whites) struggled violently throughout the 19th century for political control. In 1872 the Colorado Party began a period of 86 years in office. During the first three decades of the 20th century, José *Batlle y Ordóñez, while in and out of the presidency, helped mould Uruguay into South America's first welfare state. Numerous measures for promoting governmental social services and a state-dominated economy were enacted. In 1958 the elections were won by the Blanco Party. Economic and political unrest plagued the nation throughout the 1960s and saw the emergence of the Marxist terrorist group, the Tupamaros. The military took over in the 1970s, and a return to civilian rule took place in 1985, when Julio Sanguinetti became President. After a long campaign he won a referendum in 1989 in support of an Amnesty Law for political prisoners from the military regime of 1973 to 1985. In 1990 Luis Alberto Lacalle Herrera of the Blanco Party succeeded him, forming a coalition government with the Colorado Party. Sanguinetti was re-elected in 1995 and was succeeded by Jorge Battle in 2000. In 2005 Tabaré Vázquez became the country's first left-wing President; he was succeeded in 2010 by José Mujica, a former Tupamaros guerrilla. Uruguay has emerged as one of the most prosperous and literate nations in South America, despite suffering in 1999–2002 from the economic problems of Argentina and Brazil.

Uruk One of the leading cities of the *Sumerians. A community occupied the site as early as 5000 BC and in the 3rd millennium BC the city was surrounded by a 9.5-km (6-mile) wall. Excavation has revealed ziggurats dedicated to the two main gods, Anu and Inanna. It continued to be inhabited into Parthian times.

USSR See SOVIET UNION.

Uthman (or **Osman**) (*c.*574–656) Third *caliph of Islam (644–56). He restored representatives of the old Meccan aristocracy to positions of influence, creating considerable discontent. His personal weakness led to rivalry to his authority from Aisha, the youngest wife of *Muhammad, from Ali, his cousin and son-in-law, and others. He was murdered by mutinous troops from Egypt. His lasting memorial was the authorized version of the *Koran, compiled at his order.

Uthman dan Fodio (or **Usuman dan Fodio**) (1754–1817) West African religious and political leader. A Muslim Fulani, he began teaching in about 1775 among the Hausa and established the Emirates of Northern Nigeria (1804–08) after waging a *jihad* (holy war). He conceived the latter as a primary duty, not only against infidels, but against any departure, public or private, from the original and austere ideals of Islam. Under his rule as caliph, and that of his son, Muhammad Bello (died 1837), Muslim culture flourished in the *Fulani empire.

utilitarianism An ethical doctrine expounded by Jeremy Bentham and refined by John Stuart Mill. In his *Introduction to the Principles of Morals and Legislation* (1789), Bentham identified the goal of morality as 'the greatest happiness of the greatest number', and claimed that an action is right in so far as it tends to promote that goal. Acting as a pressure group on both Conservative and Liberal governments, they often gave a lead to public opinion. Mill's essay, *Utilitarianism* (1863), gave clear expression to the doctrine.

As a philosophical proposition, utilitarianism is hampered by the fundamental difficulty of comparing quantitatively the happiness of one person with that of another. Nevertheless, it has proved a remarkably persistent doctrine that continues to attract adherents.

Utrecht, Peace of (1713) The treaty that ended the War of the *Spanish Succession. After negotiations between the English and French, a Congress met at Utrecht without Austria and signed the treaties. The Austrian emperor Charles VI found he could not carry on without allies and accepted the terms at Rastadt and Baden in 1714. *Philip V remained King of Spain but renounced his claim to the French throne and lost Spain's European empire. The southern Netherlands, Milan, Naples, and Sardinia went to Austria. Britain kept Gibraltar and Minorca and obtained the right to supply the Spanish American colonies with Negro slaves (*see* ASIENTO DE NEGROS). From France it gained Newfoundland, Hudson Bay, St Kitts, and recognition of the Hanoverian succession. France returned recent conquests, but kept everything acquired up to the Peace of *Nijmegen in 1679 and also the city of Strasbourg. The Duke of Savoy gained Sicily and improved frontiers in northern Italy. The Dutch secured Austrian recognition for their right to garrison "barrier" fortresses in the southern Netherlands. French domination had been checked. Britain made significant naval, commercial, and colonial gains and thereafter assumed a much greater role in world affairs.

Uzbekistan

Capital:	Tashkent
Area:	447,400 sq km (172,741 sq miles)
Population:	28,661,637 (2013 est)
Currency:	1 som = 100 tiyins
Religions:	Muslim 88.0%; Eastern Orthodox 9.0%
Ethnic Groups:	Uzbek 80.0%; Russian 5.5%; Tajik 5.0%; minority groups
Languages:	Uzbek (official); Russian; Tajik; minority languages
International Organizations:	UN; Commonwealth of Independent States; OSCE; Euro-Atlantic Partnership Council; WTO

A country in central Asia situated south of Kazakhstan; to the south and east are Turkmenistan, Afghanistan, Tajikistan, and Kyrgyzstan.

Physical Uzbekistan extends south-east from the deserts of the Aral Sea to the Alai Mountains on the border with Afghanistan. At the foot of these lie the fertile Fergana valley and several large oases. The Amu Darya (Oxus) flows north-west to the Aral Sea, providing a second fertile belt, between the Kara Kum sand desert and the Kyzyl Kum desert of stony clay.

Economy Uzbekistan's principal mineral resources are natural gas, petroleum, coal, and metal ores. Natural gas and other energy products are the principal exports; cotton and gold are also significant. Agriculture is dominated by cotton, of which Uzbekistan is the world's sixth-largest producer. Industries include textiles, food processing, machine building, metallurgy, and mining. Unlike most other former Soviet republics, Uzbekistan's economy remains centrally planned.

History Uzbekistan was the centre of the empire of Genghis Khan, and its two ancient cities of Samarkand and Tashkent flourished with the silk caravan trade. Divided into three khanates, Bukhara, Khiva, and Kokand, it was repeatedly attacked by Russia from 1717 until its annexation in 1876. Its Sunni Muslim Uzbeks were excluded from office by the Russians, and in 1918 staged a rebellion.

This was suppressed by the Red Army, and a Soviet Socialist Republic was formed in 1929, which joined the Soviet Union in 1936. After 1989 the republic pressed for independence. The former Communist Party of Uzbekistan, renamed the People's Democratic Party, retained power in the country's parliament following elections in 1990. Uzbekistan declared independence from the Soviet Union in August 1991 with Islam Karimov, the former Communist leader, as President—a position he has retained in all subsequent elections. Uzbekistan joined the Commonwealth of Independent States in 1991, but dissatisfaction at Russian dominance of this body led Uzbekistan to form an alternative economic union with Kazakhstan and Kyrgyzstan in 1994. Opponents of the ruling regime have become increasingly violent, and in the 21st century President Karimov's regime came under increasing international criticism for violations of human rights.

Uzbeks A Turkish-speaking people, Mongol by descent and *Sunni Muslim by religion. They moved through Kazakhstan to Turkistan and Transoxania between the 14th and 16th centuries to trouble the Shiite Safavid rulers of Persia. Initially ruled by the Shaybanids and then the Janids, they later split into dynasties based on Bukhara, Khiva, and Kokand.

Vajpayee, Atal Behari (1924–) Indian politician, Prime Minister for 13 days in 1996 and again from 1998 to 2004 as head of a Bharatiya Janata Party-led coalition. During this time India provoked international concern by conducting nuclear weapons tests.

Valley Forge (1777–78) An American Revolutionary winter camp 32 km (20 miles) northwest of Philadelphia that was occupied by George *Washington's army after it had been defeated at *Brandywine and *Germantown and the British had occupied Philadelphia. A bitter winter and lack of supplies came close to destroying the Continental Army of 11,000 men. The Valley Forge winter was the low point in the American Revolutionary struggle; it hardened the survivors and became a symbol of endurance.

Valley of the Kings A narrow gorge in western Thebes containing the tombs of at least 60 pharaohs of the 18th to 20th dynasties (c.1550–1050 BC), beginning with Thutmose I. It was a rich hunting-ground for robbers in antiquity, and of those tombs discovered only that of *Tutankhamun had not been plundered.

Valmy, Battle of (1792) The first important engagement of the French Revolutionary wars. Near a small village on the road between Verdun and Paris the French commander-in-chief, Charles-François Dumouriez, with the belated assistance of Marshal François Christophe Kellermann, defeated the Duke of Brunswick's German troops. The French, whose morale was low after a series of defeats, were at first obliged to withdraw, but rallied the next day and forced Brunswick to retreat.

Valois The name of the French royal family from the time of Philip VI (1328) to the death of Henry III (1589), when the throne passed to the Bourbons.

Van Buren, Martin (1782–1862) US Democratic statesman, 8th President of the USA (1837–41). He was appointed Andrew Jackson's Vice-President in 1832 and became President five years later. His measure of placing government funds, previously held in private banks, in an independent treasury caused many Democrats to join the Whig party.

Vandals A Germanic tribe that migrated from the Baltic coast in the 1st century BC. After taking Pannonia in the 4th century they were driven further west by the *Huns. With the Suebi and Alemanni they crossed the Rhine into Gaul and Spain, where the name Andalusia ('Vandalitia') commemorates them. They were then ousted by the Goths. Taking ship to North Africa under Genseric, they set up an independent kingdom after the capture of Carthage. In 455 they returned to Italy and sacked Rome. *Belisarius finally subjected them in 534.

Vanderbilt, Cornelius (1794–1877) US businessman and philanthropist. Vanderbilt amassed a fortune from shipping and railroads, and from this made an endowment to found Vanderbilt University in Nashville, Tennessee (1873). Subsequent generations of his family, including his son William Henry Vanderbilt (1821–85), increased the family wealth and continued his philanthropy.

Van Diemen's Land The former name of Tasmania, Australia. Its name commemorates Anthony van Diemen (1593–1645), Dutch governor of Java, who sent *Tasman on his voyage of exploration.

Vane, Sir Henry (the Younger) (1613–62) Leading Parliamentarian, son of Sir Henry Vane (the Elder). He served briefly as governor of Massachusetts (1636–37) then played a leading role in the English *Long Parliament until 1660. A promoter of the *Solemn League and Covenant and the *Self-Denying Ordinance, from 1643 to 1653 he was the civil leader of the Parliamentary cause, while *Cromwell directed the army. He opposed the trial and execution of *Charles I and in 1653 disagreed with Cromwell over the expulsion of the Rump Parliament. After a period out of politics, he helped to bring about the recall of the Rump (1659). At the *Restoration he was arrested and executed for treason.

Vanuatu (formerly New Hebrides)

Capital:	Port Vila
Area:	12,189 sq km (4,706 sq miles)
Population:	261,565 (2013 est)
Religions:	Presbyterian 27.9%; Anglican 15.1%; Seventh Day Adventist 12.5%; Roman Catholic 12.4%
Ethnic Groups:	Ni-Vanuatu 97.6%
Languages:	Bislama, French, English (all official); local languages
International Organizations:	UN; Commonwealth; Pacific Islands Forum; Secretariat of the Pacific Community; Non-Aligned Movement; WTO

A country comprising a double chain of over 80 south-west Pacific Ocean islands between latitudes 13° and 21°S and longitudes 167° and 170°E.

Physical Only a dozen of Vanuatu's islands are suitable for settlement, the largest being Espíritu Santo, Efate, Malekula, Maewo, Pentecost, Ambrim, Erromanga, and Tanna. Of volcanic origin, they are very hilly. South-east trade winds moderate the heat from May to October.

Economy Small-scale agriculture employs about two-thirds of the workforce and provides Vanuatu's principal exports: copra, beef, cocoa, timber, kava, and coffee. Fishing, financial services, and tourism are also important.

History During the 19th century, thousands of the indigenous people of Vanuatu—*Kanakas—were taken to work on sugar plantations in Queensland, Australia. The population was decimated and took many years to recover. The islands were placed under an Anglo-French naval commission in 1887. In World War II they served as a major Allied base. They became an independent republic and member of the Commonwealth of Nations in 1980.

Varennes, Flight to (20 June 1791) The unsuccessful attempt by *Louis XVI to escape from France and join the exiled royalists. He had been prevented from leaving Paris in April 1791 and elaborate plans for an escape were made. On the night of 20 June the royal party, disguised and with forged passports, left Paris. They were recognized by a postmaster, pursued, and stopped at Varennes. The fugitives were returned and became virtual prisoners in the Tuileries.

Vargas, Getúlio Dornelles (1883–1954) Brazilian statesman, President (1930–45; 1951–54). Although defeated in the presidential elections of 1930, Vargas seized power in the ensuing revolution, overthrowing the republic and ruling as a virtual dictator for the next 15 years. He furthered Brazil's modernization by the introduction of fiscal, educational, electoral, and land reforms, but his regime was totalitarian and repressive. He was overthrown in a coup in 1945 but returned to power after elections in 1951. After widespread calls for his resignation, he committed suicide.

vassal A holder of land by contract from a lord. This tenurial arrangement was one of the essential components of the *feudal system. The land received was known as a *fief and the contract was confirmed when the recipient knelt and placed his hands between those of his lord.

Vatican City An independent papal state in Rome, the seat of the Roman Catholic Church. Following the *Risorgimento, the Papal States (the modern Italian provinces of Lazio, Umbria, Le Marche, and parts of Emilia-Romagna) became incorporated into a unified Italy in 1870 while, by the Law of Guarantees (1871), the Vatican was granted extraterritoriality. The temporal power of the pope was suspended until the Lateran Treaty of 1929, signed between Pope Pius XI and *Mussolini, which recognized the full and independent sovereignty of the Holy See in the City of the Vatican. It covers an area of 44 hectares (109 acres) and has its own police force, diplomatic service, postal service, railway station, coinage, and radio station. It has about 850 inhabitants.

Veneti An Italic tribe with their own distinctive language who inhabited north-east Italy from the 1st millennium BC. Always in need of protection against major invasions of Italy by the Gauls and by Hannibal, they remained loyal to the Roman empire. Under the later Roman empire their territory became the province of

Venetia. Their geographical position put their cities (for example, Aquileia and Padua) in the path of *Goth and *Hun invasions of Italy. A gradual migration took place towards the barely inhabited islands, marshes, and sandbanks of the coastal estuaries. The area grew in prosperity largely through trade. In the 9th century, the Republic of St Mark, better known as Venice, was established.

Venezuela

Capital:	Caracas
Area:	912,050 sq km (352,144 sq miles)
Population:	28,459,085 (2013 est)
Currency:	1 bolívar fuerte = 100 centimos
Religions:	Roman Catholic 96.0%; Protestant 2.0%
Ethnic Groups:	Spanish; Italian; Portuguese; Arab; German; African; indigenous
Languages:	Spanish (official); Amerindian languages
International Organizations:	UN; OAS; OPEC; Mercosur; Non-Aligned Movement; WTO

A country on the north coast of South America, with a coastline on the Caribbean Sea. It is bounded by Colombia on the west, Brazil on the south, and Guyana on the east.

Physical The island-fringed coast of Venezuela is tropical, with lagoons. Much oil is found here, notably around the shallow Lake Maracaibo. At the eastern end of the coast is the swampy delta of the Orinoco River. Inland are the Llanos and the maritime Andes. The Guyana Highlands lie in the south of the country and rise to nearly 2750 m (9000 feet), being cut by the valleys of the Orinoco's tributaries and containing the Angel Falls, the highest in the world.

Economy The Venezuelan economy is dominated by state-owned oil production, which provides one-eighth of GDP but almost all export earnings. Other export industries include bauxite, aluminium, minerals, chemicals, and agricultural products. Principal agricultural products include maize, sorghum, sugar cane, rice, bananas, vegetables, and coffee.

History Venezuela was visited in 1499 by the explorer Amerigo Vespucci, who gave it its name ('Little Venice') after sighting native houses built on stilts on Lake Maracaibo. It was subsequently colonized by the Spanish. By the mid-18th century wealthy Creoles (Spaniards born in the colony) were protesting against trade restrictions imposed by Madrid. It was in its capital Caracas that the Colombian Independence Movement began (1806), resulting in the creation by Simón *Bolívar of Gran Colombia. When this collapsed (1829), Venezuela proclaimed itself a republic under its first President, General José Antonio Páez (1830–43), who, while preserving the great estates, provided a strong administration, allowed a free press, and kept the army under control. The period that followed (1843–70) was politically chaotic and violent. Under President Guzmán *Blanco (1870–88) moves were made towards democracy, with the first election in 1881, and there was growth in economic activity. Despotic government returned under the *Caudillos Cipriano Castro (1899–1908) and Juan Vicente *Gómez (1909–35). Oil was discovered before World War I, and by 1920 Venezuela was the world's leading exporter of oil. Military juntas continued to dominate until Rómulo Betancourt completed a full term as a civilian President (1959–64), to be peacefully succeeded by Dr Raul Leoni (1964–69). Since then, democratic politics have continued to operate, with two parties, Accion Democratica and Christian Democrat, alternating in power, even though extremists of left and right have harassed them with terrorism. A postwar oil boom brought considerable prosperity, but rising population and inflation caused many problems for President Dr Jaime Lusinchi (1983–88). Falling oil prices and increased drug trafficking were additional problems for his successor Carlos Andrés Pérez, who faced serious riots in 1989 for his austerity measures, and two unsuccessful military coup attempts in 1992. In 1993 Pérez was removed from office and charged with corruption. Elections in December of that year saw Rafael Caldera Rodríguez accede to the presidency. In 1998 presidential elections were won by the left-wing populist Lt Col Hugo Chávez Frias, leader of one of the coup attempts in 1992. He was re-elected in 2000, following constitutional changes in 1999, and subsequently survived an attempted coup (2002) and a referendum seeking to remove him from office (2004). Following re-election in 2006 Chavez nationalized the oil industry (2007). He was again re-elected in 2012, but died the next year; Vice President Nicolás Maduro was elected to succeed him.

Economic problems led to violent demonstrations against the Maduro government in 2014.

Venizélos, Eleuthérios (1864–1936) Greek statesman. He became Premier (1910), modernizing Greek political institutions and joining the Balkan League against Turkey. In 1914 his wish to join the Allies was thwarted by the pro-German King Constantine, who later abdicated, thus enabling Greek troops to fight Germany. At the *Versailles Peace Settlement he negotiated promises of considerable territorial gains—the Dodecanese, western Thrace, Adrianople, and Smyrna in Asia Minor. In the event, following the challenge of *Atatürk's army only western Thrace was gained, and he resigned. Greece alternated between monarchy and republic and his periods as Premier alternated with periods in exile.

Vercingetorix (died 46 BC) King of the tribe of the Averni in Gaul. Towards the end of the *Gallic wars in 52 BC he revolted against Roman occupation and was acclaimed king of the united Gauls. Defeated and captured, he was finally marched through Rome as a trophy in *Caesar's triumph (46 BC) and then executed.

Verdun, Treaty of (843) The peace made between the Frankish kings Lothar, Louis, and Charles, the grandsons of *Charlemagne, who had been fighting a civil war. When their father, Louis the Pious, died in 840 he bequeathed them the united *Carolingian empire, but the brothers could not agree on how to divide the inheritance and they fought until 842. Long negotiations then culminated in the meeting in Verdun where the empire was divided into three kingdoms. Charles and Louis received West and East Francia (roughly, present-day France and Germany), while Lothar held the middle kingdom, a long strip of territory stretching from the North Sea over the Alps to Rome and bordered in the west by the rivers Scheldt, Meuse, and Saône and in the east by the Rhine. The treaty was not governed by geographical factors but was an attempt to satisfy the claims of each brother for a share in the Carolingian family estates, many of which were in the fertile lands of the middle kingdom, Lotharingia. Lotharingia soon lost its own identity and became a battleground for the embryonic kingdoms of France and Germany.

Vereeniging, Treaty of (31 May 1902) The peace treaty that ended the Second *Boer War. It provided for the acceptance by Boers of British sovereignty, the use of Afrikaans in schools and law courts, a civil administration leading to

self-government, a repatriation commission, and compensation of £3 million for the destruction inflicted during the war on Boer farms.

Vernon, Edward (1684–1757) English admiral. In 1739 he was sent to fight against the Spanish in the Caribbean. He captured Porto Bello (now in Panama) in the opening phase of the War of *Jenkins's Ear in 1739, but failed disastrously at Cartagena (now in Colombia) in 1741. His boat-cloak of grogram (a mixture of silk, mohair, and wool) gave him the nickname "Old Grog". "Grog" became the name of the naval rum ration when diluted with three parts of water, as Vernon was in the habit of issuing to his own sailors. He was removed from the active list in 1746 because he was thought to be the author of anonymous pamphlets attacking the Admiralty.

Verrazzano, Giovanni da (c.1485–c.1528) Italian (Florentine) navigator in the service of France. He led three expeditions in search of a westward passage into the Pacific and thus to the East. In 1524 he explored the North American coast from North Carolina to New York Bay and continued north to Newfoundland before returning to Dieppe. In 1527 he took a second expedition across the Atlantic and reached Brazil. He set out once more in 1528 but was met in the Antilles by cannibal *Caribs who killed and ate him.

Versailles Peace Settlement (1919–23) Sometimes referred to as the Paris Peace Settlement, a collection of peace treaties between the Central Powers and the Allied powers ending World War I. The main treaty was that of **Versailles** (June 1919) between the Allied powers (except for the USA, which refused to ratify the treaty) and Germany, whose representatives were required to sign it without negotiation.

Another treaty, that of St Germain-en-Laye (September 1919), was between the Allied powers and the new republic of *Austria. A third treaty, that of **Trianon** (June 1920), was with the new republic of *Hungary, in which some three-quarters of its old territories (i.e., all non-Magyar lands) were lost to Czechoslovakia, Romania, and Yugoslavia, and the principle of reparations again accepted. The treaty of **Neuilly** (November 1919) was with *Bulgaria, in which some territory was lost to Yugoslavia and Greece, but some also gained from Turkey; a figure of £100 million reparations was agreed, but never paid. These four treaties were ratified in Paris during 1920. A fifth treaty, that of **Sèvres** (August 1920), between the Allies and the old *Ottoman empire, was never implemented as it was followed by the final disintegration of the empire and the creation by Mustafa Kemal *Atatürk of the new republic of Turkey. The treaty was replaced by the Treaty of **Lausanne** (July 1923), in which Palestine, Transjordan, and Iraq were to be mandated to Britain, and Syria to France. Italy was accepted as possessing the Dodecanese Islands, while Turkey regained Smyrna from Greece.

Verwoerd, Hendrik Frensch (1901–66) South African statesman. As Minister of Native Affairs (1950–58) he was responsible for establishing the policy of *apartheid. He became Nationalist Party leader and Prime Minister (1958–66). During his government, in the aftermath of the *Sharpeville massacre, South Africa became a republic and left the Commonwealth. Harsh measures were taken to silence Black opposition, including the banning of the *African National Congress. He was assassinated in Parliament.

Vesey, Denmark (born **Telemaque Vesey**) (c.1767–1822) Leader of a planned American slave revolt. A slave who had educated himself and purchased his freedom having won a street lottery, Vesey in 1822 inspired a group of slaves with the idea of seizing the arsenals of Charleston, South Carolina, as a prelude to a mass escape to the West Indies. However, the plan was betrayed by a house servant and Vesey and about 130 of his followers were arrested, 32 were exiled and 35, including Vesey, were hanged. The authorities responded by tightening the restrictive "black codes" as a means of controlling the slave population.

Vespasian (full name **Titus Flavius Vespasianus**) (9–79 AD) Roman emperor (69–79) and founder of the Flavian dynasty. A distinguished general, he was acclaimed emperor by the legions in Egypt during the civil wars that followed the death of Nero and gained control of Italy after the defeat of Vitellius. His reign saw the restoration of financial and military order and the initiation of a public building programme, which included the rebuilding of the Capitol and the beginning of the construction of the Colosseum (75).

Vespucci, Amerigo (1451–1512) Italian merchant, navigator, and explorer. While in the service of the king of Portugal, Vespucci made several voyages to the New World and claimed, on dubious authority, to have been the first to sight the mainland of South America (1497). The name America is derived from his first name.

Vestal virgin An attendant of Vesta, goddess of fire, hearth, and home. The virgins numbered six, chosen by lot from a short list of aristocratic girls. Under vows of chastity they served for 30 years, dressed as brides, cleaning Vesta's shrine and tending the fire. Unchaste Vestals were buried alive. They lived in the House of the Vestals in the Forum at Rome, and wills were deposited with them for safekeeping.

Vichy government (1940–45) The pro-German French puppet government established after the Franco-German armistice in World War II. The Germans having occupied Paris, it was set up under Marshal *Pétain in Vichy by the French National Assembly (1940) to administer unoccupied France and the colonies. Having dissolved the Third Republic, it issued a new constitution establishing an autocratic state. The Vichy government was never recognized by the Allies. In 1941 it granted Japan right of access and air bases in Indo-China, from which it was to launch its Malaya and Burma campaigns. It was dominated first by *Laval, as Pétain's deputy (1940), then by *Darlan (1941–42) in collaboration with Hitler, and once more (1942–44) by Laval as Pétain's successor after German forces moved in to the unoccupied portions of France. After the Allied liberation of France (1944), the Vichy government established itself under Pétain at Sigmaringen in Germany, where it collapsed when Germany surrendered in 1945 and France was reunited.

Vicksburg Campaign (November 1862–July 1863) A military campaign in the *American Civil War. By the autumn of 1862 the stronghold of the *Confederacy forces at Vicksburg in western Mississippi was the last remaining obstacle to Union (Northern) control of the Mississippi River. In late 1862 advances by Generals *Grant and *Sherman failed to capture the city. In May 1863 Grant started a siege of the city. After six weeks of resistance, Vicksburg surrendered on 4 July. With its capture, the Confederacy was effectively split in half. The Union success at Vicksburg and *Gettysburg in July 1863 marked a major turning-point in the Civil War.

Victor Emmanuel II (1820–78) Ruler of the kingdom of Sardinia (1849–61) and king of Italy (1861–78). His appointment of Cavour as Premier in 1852 hastened the drive towards Italian unification. In 1859 Victor Emmanuel led his Piedmontese army to victory against the Austrians at the battles of *Magenta and *Solferino, and in 1860 entered the papal territories around French-held Rome to join his forces with those of Garibaldi. After being crowned first king of a united Italy in Turin in 1861, Victor Emmanuel continued to add to his kingdom, acquiring Venetia in 1866 and Rome in 1870.

Victor Emmanuel III (1869–1947) King of Italy (1900–46). He succeeded to the throne after his father's assassination. Under Mussolini, whom he had invited to form a government in 1922 in order to forestall civil war, Victor Emmanuel lost all political power. However, during World War II, after the loss of Sicily to the Allies (1943), he acted to dismiss Mussolini and conclude an armistice. Victor Emmanuel abdicated in favour of his son in 1946, but a republic was established the same year by popular vote and both he and his son went into exile.

Victoria (1819–1901) Queen of Great Britain and Ireland (1837–1901) and empress of India (1876–1901). She succeeded to the throne on the death of her uncle, William IV, and married her cousin Prince Albert in 1840; they had nine children. As queen she took an active interest in the policies of her ministers, although she did not align the Crown with any one political party. She largely retired from public life after Albert's death in 1861, but lived to achieve the longest reign in British history. During her reign Britain's power and prosperity grew enormously. Her golden jubilee (1887) and diamond jubilee (1897) were marked with popular celebration.

Victoria and Albert Museum A prestigious museum of applied arts founded in 1853 in Marlborough House in London, to house many of the articles displayed in the Great Exhibition of 1851. When Queen Victoria laid the foundation stone of the present building in South Kensington in 1899, she asked for it to be given its present name.

Vienna, Congress of (1814–15) An international peace conference that settled the affairs of Europe after the defeat of *Napoleon. It continued to meet through the *Hundred Days of Napoleon's return to France (March–June 1815). The dominant powers were Austria, represented by *Metternich, Britain, represented by *Castlereagh, Prussia, represented by *Frederick William III, and Russia, represented by *Alexander I. *Talleyrand attended as the representative of Louis XVIII of France. The Congress agreed to the absorption by the new kingdom of the Netherlands of the territory known as the Austrian Netherlands (now Belgium). Otherwise the Habsburgs regained control of all their domains, including Lombardy, Venetia, Tuscany, Parma, and Tyrol. Prussia gained parts of Saxony as well as regaining much of Westphalia and the Rhineland. Denmark, which had allied itself with France, lost Norway to Sweden. In Italy the pope was restored to the Vatican and the Papal States, and the Bourbons were reestablished in the Kingdom of the Two Sicilies. The German Confederation was established, and Napoleon's Grand Duchy of Warsaw was to be replaced by a restored Kingdom of Poland, but as part of the Russian empire with the Russian emperor also king of Poland. The Congress restored political stability to Europe.

Vietcong Communist guerrilla organization operating in South Vietnam (1960–75). Opposition to the Saigon-based regime of Ngo Dinh Diem had already produced widespread guerrilla activity in South Vietnam when communist interests founded the National Front for the Liberation of South Vietnam (known to its opponents as the Vietcong) in 1960. As US military support for the Saigon government broadened into the full-scale *Vietnam War so Vietcong forces were supplied with arms and supported by North Vietnamese forces brought to the south via the Ho Chi Minh Trail, which passed through neighbouring Laos and Cambodia. They maintained intensive guerrilla operations, and occasionally fought large set-piece battles. They finally undermined both US support for the war and the morale of the South Vietnamese army and opened the way for communist triumph and the reunification of Vietnam in 1975.

Vietminh Vietnamese communist guerrilla movement. Founded in 1941 in south China by *Ho Chi Minh and other exiled Vietnamese members of the Indo-Chinese Communist Party with the aim of expelling both the French and the Japanese from Vietnam, the Vietminh began operations, with assistance from the USA, against the Japanese (1943–45) under the military leadership of Vo Nguyen Giap. After the end of World War II, it resisted the returning French, building up its strength and organization through incessant guerrilla operations and finally winning a decisive set-piece engagement at *Dienbienphu in 1954. This forced the French to end the war and grant independence to Vietnam, partitioned into two states, North and South.

Vietnam

Capital:	Hanoi
Area:	331,210 sq km (127,881 sq miles)
Population:	8,628,000 (2005)
Currency:	1 dong = 10 hao = 100 xu

Religions:	Buddhist 9.3%; Roman Catholic 6.7%; Hoa Hao 1.5%
Ethnic Groups:	Vietnamese (Kinh) 85.7%; Tai 1.9%; Thai 1.8%
Languages:	Vietnamese (official); English; minority languages
International Organizations:	UN; ASEAN; Colombo Plan; Non-Aligned Movement; WTO

A country in south-east Asia, shaped like an 'S', bordering on China on the north and Laos and Cambodia on the west, and having long east and south coasts on the South China Sea.

Physical In the north of Vietnam the Red and Black rivers flow from forested mountains across wet lowlands spread with paddy fields. The south is even wetter, with rice being cultivated down the coastal strip and in the Mekong delta. Rubber and other crops are grown in areas where the ground rises to the central highlands.

Economy Vietnam had a centrally planned communist economy until 1986, when it adopted free-market reforms; state-owned enterprises now contribute about two-fifths of GDP. Industry has been promoted in recent years and the agricultural sector has correspondingly declined in importance; however, it still employs almost half the workforce. Seafood, rice, and coffee are exported; other agricultural products include rubber, tea, pepper, and soya beans. Industrial exports include clothes, shoes, electronics, oil, wooden products, and machinery. There are large reserves of oil, coal, iron ore, and other minerals.

History In 1802 the two states of *Annam and Tonkin were reunited by the Annamese general Nguyen Anh, who became emperor Gia-Long. Gia-Long was given French assistance and French influence increased in the 19th century. By 1883 Vietnam was part of *French Indo-China, although a weak monarchy was allowed to remain. In World War II the Japanese occupied it but allowed *Vichy France to administer it until March 1945. In September 1945 *Ho Chi Minh declared its independence, but this was

followed by French reoccupation and the French Indo-Chinese War. The Geneva Conference (1954), convened to seek a solution to the Indochina conflict, partitioned Vietnam along the 17th parallel, leaving a communist Democratic Republic with its capital at Hanoi in the north, and, after the deposition of the former emperor *Bao Dai in 1955, a non-communist republic with its capital at Saigon in the south. Ho Chi Minh, the North Vietnamese leader, remained committed to a united communist country, and by the time the South Vietnamese President Ngo Dinh Diem was overthrown by the military in 1963, communist insurgents of the *Vietcong were already active in the south. Communist attempts to take advantage of the political confusion in the south were accelerated by the infusion of massive US military assistance, and in the late 1960s and early 1970s, the *Vietnam War raged throughout the area, with the heavy use of US airpower failing to crush growing communist strength. Domestic pressures helped accelerate a US withdrawal and, after abortive peace negotiations, the North Vietnamese and their Vietcong allies finally took Saigon in April 1975; a united Socialist Republic of Vietnam was proclaimed in the following year. Despite the severe damage done to the economy, Vietnam adopted an aggressively pro-Soviet foreign policy, dominating Laos, invading Cambodia to overthrow the *Khmer Rouge regime (1975–79), and suffering heavily in a brief border war with China (1979). In 1989, Vietnamese troops withdrew from Cambodia. Attempts to reorder society in the south of the country produced a flood of refugees, damaging Vietnam's international standing and increasing its dependence on the Soviet Union. Many of these refugees were from the Chinese minority; known as the 'Boat People,' they fled Vietnam in small boats on the South China Sea. With the disintegration of the Soviet Union in 1991, Vietnam was prompted to normalize relations with China and the USA. A new constitution was adopted in 1992, incorporating major economic and political reforms. However, the Communist Party of Vietnam retained its position as the sole political party. Relations with the USA continued to improve during 1993–94, with joint investigations taking place into the whereabouts of US servicemen missing in action during the Vietnam War. Economic links were forged with the USA and other countries (e.g. Japan and Britain), notably to exploit oil and natural gas fields in the country's territorial waters. Vetted non-Communist candidates were allowed to stand in legislative elections from 1997. In 2001, following popular demonstrations, the Party leadership acted to curb corruption and galvanize economic development. Vietnam joined the World Trade Organization in 2007.

Vietnam War (1964–75) The civil war in Vietnam after the commencement of large-scale US military involvement in 1964. Guerrilla activity in South Vietnam had become widespread by 1961, in which year President *Ngo Dinh Diem proclaimed a state of emergency. Continued communist activity against a country perceived in the USA as a bastion against the spread of communism in south-east Asia led to increasing US concern, and after an alleged North Vietnamese attack on US warships in the Gulf of Tonkin in 1964, President Johnson was given congressional approval (Tonkin Gulf Resolution) to take military action. By the summer of 1965 a US army of 125,000 men was serving in the country, and by 1967 the figure had risen to 400,000, while US aircraft carried out an intensive bombing campaign against North Vietnam. Contingents from South Korea, Australia, New Zealand, and Thailand fought with the US troops. Although communist forces were held temporarily in check, the war provoked widespread opposition within the USA, and after the Tet Offensive of February 1968 had shaken official belief in the possibility of victory, the bombing campaign was halted and attempts to find a formula for peace talks started. US policy now began to emphasize the 'Vietnamization' of the war, and as increasing efforts were made to arm and train the South Vietnamese army, so US troops were gradually withdrawn. Nevertheless, US forces were still caught up in heavy fighting in the early 1970s and the bombing campaign was briefly resumed on several occasions. US troops were finally withdrawn after the Paris Peace Accords of January 1973, but no lasting settlement between North and South proved possible, and in early 1975 North Vietnamese forces finally triumphed, capturing Saigon (the capital of South Vietnam; renamed Ho Chi Minh City in 1976) on 30 April 1975. The war did enormous damage to the socio-economic fabric of the Indochinese states, devastating Vietnam and destabilizing neighbouring Cambodia (Kampuchea) and Laos.

Vikings Scandinavian traders and pirates of the 8th to 12th centuries. In the 8th century the Vikings began one of the most remarkable periods of expansion in history. Setting sail from Denmark and Norway, they voyaged westward in longships through the Shetlands, Iceland, and Greenland, as far as Vinland (modern Newfoundland), which was reached by Leif

Ericsson in the 11th century. They attacked Britain and Ireland, ravaged the coast of continental Europe as far as Gibraltar, and entered the Mediterranean, where they fought Arabs as well as Europeans. From the Baltic they sailed down the rivers of western Russia to a point from which they threatened Constantinople. In Europe they were able to strike far inland, sailing up the Rhine, Loire, and other rivers. Local rulers often preferred to buy them off, rather than resist.

The Vikings were also traders and farmers in the areas they settled, including Normandy, the north of England, and the area around Dublin in Ireland. They were skilled wood- and metal-workers and manufactured superb jewellery. They had a powerful oral poetic tradition, manifest in their sagas. They were an extremely adaptable people, able to absorb the cultures which they encountered while retaining their own vital qualities. This adaptability was perhaps forced upon them because they were greatly outnumbered by the native populations; it was easier to modify existing forms than to impose their own. They adopted languages and quickly modified fighting styles to suit land-based operations. The *Normans were descendants of the Viking *Rollo's settlement in Normandy, they became a powerful element in Europe, the *Crusades, and throughout the Mediterranean.

Viking ship The type of vessel used by the *Vikings for trade and warfare c.850–1200 AD. Viking warships were long, open, oared vessels, clinker-built and rowed by 40–80 men. They had a short mast carrying a single square sail that could be braced to allow some measure of travel into the wind. The larger vessels had a part-deck fore and aft. Viking trading ships ('knorrs') were broader in beam and relied on sails much more than on oar power. The Vikings sailed in such vessels as far as Vinland (Newfoundland) to the west; northern Africa to the south; and the Black Sea to the east.

Villa, Pancho (born **Doroteo Arango**) (1878–1923) Mexican revolutionary. He played a prominent role in the revolution of 1910–11 led by Francisco Madero (1873–1913), and together with Venustiano Carranza (1859–1920) overthrew the dictatorial regime of General Victoriano Huerta (1854–1916) in 1914. Later that year, however, he and Emiliano Zapata rebelled against Carranza and fled to the north of the country after suffering a series of defeats. Villa invaded the USA in 1916 but was forced back into Mexico by the US army. He continued to oppose Carranza's regime until the latter's overthrow in 1920. Villa was eventually assassinated.

Villafranca di Verona, Treaty of (1859) An agreement between France and Austria. After the battles of *Magenta and *Solferino, *Napoleon III and *Francis Joseph met at Villafranca, where the Austrians agreed to an armistice. Austria handed Lombardy over to France, who later passed it to Sardinia (Piedmont) but retained Venetia. The rulers of the central Italian duchies were restored. Piedmont acquiesced and *Cavour resigned.

Villehardouin, Geoffroi de (*c.*1150–1217) French historian and Marshal of Champagne. He took part in the disastrous Fourth *Crusade and became Marshal of the Eastern empire. His work *Conquête de Constantinople* described and justified the Fourth Crusade and is one of the earliest examples of French prose.

villein (from Latin *villanus*, 'villager') A medieval peasant entirely subject to a lord or attached to a manor, similar to a *serf. Both groups were part of the *manorial system which dominated Europe between the 4th and 13th centuries. Villeins provided labour services to the lord (in return for tilling their own strips of land). By the 13th century villeins in England had become unfree tenants. In Europe they had fewer duties and remained essentially free peasants, creating a significant difference in rank to the serfs. By the 15th century, even in England, social and economic changes had blurred the distinctions between free and unfree peasants, leading to a single enlarged class of peasants.

Villiers *See* BUCKINGHAM, GEORGE VILLIERS, 1ST DUKE OF.

Vimy Ridge, Battle of (9 April 1917) An Allied attack on a German position in World War I, near Arras in France. One of the key points on the *Western Front, it had long resisted Allied attacks. Canadian troops under General Byng and commanded by General Horne launched an offensive. In 15 minutes, despite heavy casualties, most of Vimy Ridge was captured and 4000 prisoners taken. The Allied offensive was unsuccessful elsewhere and by 5 May had ground to a halt.

Virginia Campaigns (July 1861–65) A series of engagements and campaigns in the *American Civil War. The first engagement of the Civil War was fought on 21 July 1861 at the first Battle of Bull Run. In a confused mêlée the *Confederacy was saved from defeat by the brigade of Thomas "Stonewall" *Jackson. In the Peninsula Campaign of April–June 1862 Union (Northern) forces under General *McClellan attempted to advance up the peninsula between the James and York rivers to capture Richmond, but in the Seven Days Battle (26 June–2 July) he was forced to withdraw by the Southern commander, General Robert E. *Lee. At the same time in the Shenandoah Valley a brilliant campaign by "Stonewall" Jackson pinned down Union forces. The second Battle of Bull Run followed (29–31 August), when Lee forced the Union army to retreat to Washington. The way was open for an invasion of the North, but it ended in defeat at the Battle of *Antietam (17 September). Following the Confederate army's escape back to Virginia, the new Union commander, General Ambrose Burnside, launched an assault on Lee's positions above Fredericksburg (13 December 1862). Burnside withdrew, the reverse severely shaking the Union war effort. In the spring of 1863 a reinforced Union army under General Joseph Hooker resumed the offensive in the Battle of Chancellorsville (2–4 May 1863). Lee withstood the assault, but suffered heavy casualties, including the death of Jackson. Lee now invaded Pennsylvania, but suffered the major defeat of *Gettysburg, after which he was on the defensive for the rest of the war. A series of engagements was fought in May and June 1864 in the "wilderness" region of Virginia, when General *Grant was defeated three times before retreating across the River James, to renew his attacks in the Petersburg Campaign. This last campaign was launched in June 1864 and continued into 1865. Three assaults on Richmond by Grant were repelled by Lee, after which Union forces besieged the Confederate capital through the winter. Lee was thus prevented from sending reinforcements south to repel *Sherman's advance through Georgia and on 1 April he was defeated at Five Forks and forced to abandon both Richmond and Petersburg. All but surrounded, he surrendered at *Appomattox on 9 April, bringing the campaign, and the war, to an end.

Virginius incident (1873) The capture of an arms-running ship fraudulently flying the US flag during the Cuban rebellion against Spain (1868–78). Seized off the coast of Jamaica by a Spanish gunboat, the *Virginius* was taken to Santiago de Cuba. Subsequently her commander, Captain Fry, a US citizen, and 52 others, including British and American citizens, were executed by the Spanish as *filibusters (persons engaged in unauthorized warfare against a foreign state). Despite the angry reaction of the USA the dispute was resolved by compromise and Spain paid the families of the executed Americans compensation totalling $80,000. The families of the British victims were also paid compensation.

Visigoths (or **western Goths**) A people originating in the Baltic area. Migrations in search of farmland took them to the Danube delta and the western Black Sea by the 3rd century AD. They raided Greece and threatened the eastern Mediterranean but were temporarily repulsed by Claudius II "Gothicus". *Aurelian conceded Dacia and the Danube to them. Competition over land with the migrating *Huns drove them south in 376 and they defeated the Roman emperor Valens at Adrianople. A treaty of alliance followed but on the death of *Theodosius they ravaged the empire and Rome itself under the leadership of *Alaric I. They occupied parts of Gaul and Spain (Languedoc and Catalonia), assisting Rome against other barbarians, notably against the Huns at the *Catalaunian Fields in 451. Frankish and Muslim invaders defeated and absorbed the Visigoths in the following two centuries.

Vitoria, Battle of (21 June 1813) A battle fought between the French and the British near the *Basque city of Vitoria, during the *Peninsular War. *Wellington decisively defeated the French under Joseph Bonaparte and Jourdan. News of this victory inspired Austria, Russia, and Prussia to renew their plans to attack France and they declared war on *Napoleon on 13 August.

Vittorio Veneto, Battle of (October 1918) The scene of a decisive victory in World War I by the Italians over the Austrians. A town in northeast Italy, it is named after *Victor Emmanuel II, in whose reign Venetia was regained from Austria after the Six Weeks War (1866). Italian forces under General Diaz avenged the *Caporetto disaster (1917) by routing the Austro-Hungarian army, which resulted in an Austrian request for an armistice.

vizier (Arabic, *wazir*) A leading court official of a traditional Islamic regime. Viziers were frequently the power behind nominal rulers. At times the office became hereditary, under the early *Abbasids falling into the hands of the Barmakids and under the *Ottomans in the late 17th century held by the *Köprülü family.

Vladimir I, St (956–1015) Grand Duke of *Kiev (978–1015). He was converted to Christianity and married the sister of the Byzantine emperor. By inviting missionaries from Greece into his territories he initiated the Russian branch of the Eastern *Orthodox Church, which was rapidly established. He was canonized and became the patron saint of Russia.

Vogel, Sir Julius (1835–99) New Zealand statesman. He came to Otago with the gold rushes and soon dominated provincial politics. He entered national politics in 1863 and, as Colonial Treasurer from 1869 and Premier (1872–74), was responsible for a bold and successful policy of borrowing to promote immigration, road and railway building, and land development. He was responsible for the establishment of the Government Life Insurance Office and the Public Trust, thus launching a tradition of state involvement for which New Zealand is noted. He served as Treasurer again (1884–87).

Volstead Act (1919) US federal *Prohibition Act, enforcing the Eighteenth Amendment, banning the manufacture, distribution, and sale of alcohol. The Act was devised by the Anti-Saloon League counsel Wayne Wheeler but named after Congressman Andrew Volstead of Minnesota. It proscribed beer and wine as well as distilled spirits, to the surprise of those moderate prohibitionists who wanted the prohibition of spirits only. It became void by the passage of the Twenty-first Amendment in 1933.

Voortrekkers *See* GREAT TREK.

Vorster, John (born **Balthazar Johannes Vorster**) (1915–83) South African Nationalist politician, Prime Minister (1966–78). An admirer of the Nazi regime and enthusiastic enforcer of apartheid, Vorster won the support of the Dutch Reformed Church and was chosen as Hendrik *Verwoerd's successor in 1966. He was elected President in 1978 but resigned the following year when it was revealed that he had helped to conceal the theft of huge sums of government money and various abuses of power.

Vortigern A legendary 5th-century Romano-British king said by *Bede to have invited *Hengist and Horsa to Britain as mercenaries in an attempt to withstand the raids by the *Picts and the *Scots. The plan rebounded on Vortigern when Hengist and Horsa turned against him (455) and seized lands in Kent. He was blamed by Gildas for his misjudgement and also for the loss of Britain.

Wafd (in full **Wafd al-Misri**; Arabic, 'Egyptian Delegation') Egyptian nationalist party. Under the leadership of Zaghlul Pasha it demanded freedom from British rule. When Egypt won nominal independence in 1922, the Wafd demanded full autonomy and control of the *Sudan and the *Suez Canal. After 1924 there were frequent Wafdist governments, in conflict with the monarchy. In 1930 the constitution was suspended and Egypt became a royal dictatorship until the Wafdists succeeded in restoring the constitution in 1935. In 1950 the Wafd formed a one-party cabinet and the struggle between King *Farouk and his government intensified. The monarchy fell in 1952 and the new Revolutionary Command Council under Colonel Gamal *Nasser dissolved all political parties.

Wagner–Connery Act (official name **National Labor Relations Act**) (1935) A US labour Act, introduced by Senator Robert Wagner of New York, that intended to outlaw employer-dominated trade unions and to provide for enforcement of the right of free collective bargaining. It established a National Labor Relations Board, with powers to supervise and conduct elections in which workers would select the union to represent them. The Board survived various attempts to secure a Supreme Court ruling of its unconstitutionality and it served to increase trade-union membership.

Wagram, Battle of (5–6 July 1809) A battle in the *Napoleonic Wars fought between the combined French and Italian forces led by *Napoleon, and the Austrians under the Archduke Charles, at the village of Wagram, near Vienna. Napoleon, determined to offset earlier setbacks, ordered a massive attack on the well-chosen Austrian position. The French, who had been close to defeat, claimed the victory, but their losses outnumbered those of the Austrians. It was followed by the Treaty of Schönbrunn, in which Austria lost territory and agreed to join the *Continental System against Britain.

Wahhabism The doctrine of an Islamic reform movement founded by Muhammad ibn 'Abd al-Wahhab (1703–92) in Nejd, Saudi Arabia. It is based on the *Sunni teachings of Ibn Hanbal (780–855), involving puritanism, monotheism and rejection of popular cults, such as the Sufi veneration of saints and tombs, on the grounds that these constitute idolatry. Under the *Saud family, the Wahhabis raided into the Hejaz, Iraq, and Syria, capturing Mecca in 1806. They were crushed by Ottoman forces in a series of campaigns (1812–18), but the Saud family gradually consolidated its power within the peninsula. The cult was revived by Abd al-Aziz ibn Saud in his bid for power after World War I, but later crushed, as too fanatical, with British help in 1929 at the Battle of Sibilla. Sunni Wahhabism revived after World War II, with the growth of Islamic fundamentalism, and Wahhabi Mujahidin were fierce participants in the Afghan civil war of 1979–89.

Waitangi, Treaty of (6 February 1840) A treaty between *Maori chiefs and the British government signed at Waitangi, New Zealand. Some 500 local Maori chiefs of the North Island were present and 46 Head Chiefs signed the document drawn up by the governor, recognizing Queen Victoria's sovereignty over New Zealand in return for recognition of the Maori's *rangatiratanga* (chieftainship) and land rights, and their rights as British subjects. The treaty cleared the way for a declaration of sovereignty on 21 May 1840. Subsequent encroachment on their lands led to the *Anglo-Maori Wars of 1860–72, in which Maori independence was overcome. Since its recognition by New Zealand statutes the treaty has since 1975 assumed new importance as a basis of relations between Maori and non-Maori New Zealanders. The Waitangi Tribunal was reconvened in 1975 to consider Maori land claims and in 1985 was given authority to settle claims dating from 1840. In 1994 and 1995 the government agreed to pay compensation to certain Maori tribes whose land was seized illegally by settlers.

Wakefield, Battle of (30 December 1460) A battle in the Wars of the *Roses fought in Yorkshire. The *Lancastrians defeated and killed the *Yorkist claimant to the throne, Richard, 3rd Duke of York.

Wakefield, Edward Gibbon (1796–1862) British colonial reformer and writer. In 1829 he published his *Letter from Sydney* using information he had obtained while serving a sentence in Newgate gaol in London. Concerned that Australian settlements were failing because land could be acquired so easily, he proposed a 'sufficient price' for land, which would finance the regulated emigration of labourers and oblige them to work to buy their own land. This would give a balanced colonial society and provide some relief to unemployment in Britain. His ideas were taken up and implemented from 1831, with some 70,000 migrants travelling to Australia in the next ten years. In 1837 Wakefield founded the New Zealand Association (later Company). He was largely responsible for the succession of systematic settlements in New Zealand. He wrestled for years for self-government for the colonists, emigrating to New Zealand in 1853.

Waldheim, Kurt (1918–2007) Austrian diplomat and statesman, President (1986–92). He was Secretary-General of the United Nations (1972–81) and, five years later, he stood as the right-wing People's Party candidate for the presidency of Austria; this he secured after a run-off election. During the campaign he denied allegations that as an army intelligence officer he had direct knowledge of Nazi atrocities during World War II; he was subsequently cleared in court of charges relating to his war record.

Wales (Welsh **Cymru**) The western part of Great Britain and a country within the *United Kingdom. Wales measures roughly 225 km (140 miles) from north to south and between 60 and 160 km from west to east, where it borders England. This border region, the Marches, is a stretch of pastureland much broken by hills, woods, and twisting rivers. It rises to the Cambrian Mountains, which stretch down the centre of the country. In the south-east are the Brecon Beacons and coalfields, and in the south-west the Pembroke Peninsula with its rocky coasts. Snowdonia is in the north-west. There are deposits of coal and slate and water is an important Welsh resource. Coalmining and steel production were the main economic activities in Wales until the 1980s, when depletion of the coal seams led to closure of most of the mines.

South Wales is now a major centre for the manufacture of electronic goods. Petrochemical industries have concentrated in South Wales around the deep-water port of Milford Haven. Forestry and farming, especially the rearing of sheep and cattle, remain important. The population of Wales, which is Celtic in origin, resisted the Romans (who penetrated as far as Anglesey in a campaign against the *Druids), and after the departure of the Romans was increased in size by British refugees from the *Saxon invaders (c.400). By the 7th century Wales was isolated from the other Celtic lands of Cornwall and Scotland. Christianity was gradually spread throughout Wales by such missionaries as St Illtud and St *David, but politically the land remained disunited, having many different tribes, kingdoms, and jurisdictions; Gwynedd, Deheubarth, Powys, and Dyfed emerged as the largest kingdoms, one notable ruler being Hwyel Dda (the Good), traditionally associated with an important code of laws.

From the 11th century the Normans colonized and feudalized much of Wales and Romanized the Church, but the native Welsh retained their own laws and tribal organization. There were several uprisings but as each revolt was crushed the English kings tightened their grip. Although *Llywelyn ap Iorwerth (the Great) (ruled 1194–1240) recovered a measure of independence, *Edward I's invasion in 1277 ended hopes of a Welsh state: Llywelyn II was killed in 1282, and in 1301 Edward of Caernavon (*Edward II) was made Prince of Wales. Thereafter Wales was divided between the Principality, royal lands, and virtually independent marcher lordships. The unsuccessful revolt of Owen *Glendower in the early 15th century revived Welsh aspirations, but *Henry VIII, the son of the Welsh *Henry VII, united Wales with England in 1536, bringing it within the English legal and parliamentary systems. Welsh culture was eroded as the gentry and Church became Anglicized, although most of the population spoke only Welsh, given a standard form in the Bible of 1588, until the 19th century. The strong hold of the *Nonconformists, especially of the Baptists and Methodists, made the formal position of the Anglican Church there the dominant question of Welsh politics in the later 19th century, leading to the disestablishment of the Church from 1920. The social unrest of rural Wales, voiced in the Rebecca riots, resulted in significant emigration. The *Industrial Revolution brought prosperity to South Wales but during the Great *Depression in the 1930s many people lost their jobs. Unemployment was exacerbated by the closure of most of the coalfields by the 1980s and remains a problem despite the introduction of a more diversified industry. Political, cultural, and linguistic nationalism survive, and have manifested themselves in the *Plaid Cymru party, the National Eisteddfod, and Welsh-language campaigns. A Welsh referendum in 1979 voted against partial devolution from the United Kingdom. A second referendum in 1997 reversed this decision by a small majority and a Welsh Assembly was established in 1999.

Wales, Prince of *See* CHARLES, PRINCE.

Wałęsa, Lech (1943–) Polish statesman, President (1990–95). A shipyard worker from Gdańsk, he founded the independent trade union movement *Solidarity after a wave of strikes in 1980. Further political agitation led to a total industrial stoppage along the Baltic seaboard, and the government under General Jaruzelski was forced to concede the right to organize themselves independently. In 1981 Solidarity was outlawed and Wałęsa imprisoned. Released in 1982, he forged close links with Pope John Paul II. In 1989 Solidarity was legalized, and in 1990 he was re-elected its chairman. Increasingly on the right wing of the movement and with the full power of the Church behind him, he defeated Tadeusz Mazowiecki in the presidential election of November 1990. Throughout Wałęsa's term of office, his governments grappled with the economic challenge of moving towards a free-market economy. In December 1995, Wałęsa was defeated in presidential elections by the former communist Aleksander Kwasniewski. He retired from politics after the presidential elections of 2000, in which he was crushingly defeated.

Wallace, Sir William (*c.*1270–1305) Scottish national hero. He was a leader of Scottish resistance to Edward I, defeating the English army at Stirling in 1297. In the same year he mounted military campaigns against the north of England and was appointed Guardian of the Realm of Scotland. After Edward's second invasion of Scotland in 1298, Wallace was defeated at the Battle of Falkirk; he was subsequently captured and executed by the English.

Wallenberg, Raoul (1912–47) Swedish diplomat. While working as a businessman in Budapest in 1944, he was entrusted by the Swedish government with the protection of Hungarian Jews from the Nazis. Wallenberg helped some 95,000 Jews to escape death by issuing them with Swedish passports. When Soviet forces took control of Budapest in 1945 he was arrested, taken to Moscow, and imprisoned. Although the Soviet authorities stated that Wallenberg had died in prison in 1947, his fate remains uncertain and there were claims that he was still alive in the 1970s.

Wallenstein, Albrecht Wenzel Eusebius von (1583–1634) Duke of Friedland (1625), Duke of Mecklenburg (1629), Czech magnate and military entrepreneur. At the outbreak of the *Thirty Years War he remained loyal to Emperor Ferdinand II and in 1621 was made governor of Bohemia, a position from which he profited enormously. He served as commander-in-chief of the emperor's Catholic forces (1625–30), but after driving the Danes from north Germany, he tried to establish his own empire on the Baltic, and the German princes prevailed upon the emperor to dismiss him. He was subsequently recalled as imperial general (1632–34) to deal with the ascendant Swedes and Saxons. Having become embittered by his earlier dismissal, he was determined to build up his personal power and his secret negotiations with the enemy were discovered. Ferdinand again removed him from command and shortly afterwards connived at his assassination.

Walpole, Sir Robert, 1st Earl of Orford (1676–1745) English statesman. He entered Parliament in 1701 and briefly held the offices of Secretary of War and Treasurer of the Navy until he was dismissed with his *Whig colleagues in 1710. The *Tories impeached him for corruption in 1711 and expelled him from Parliament, making him a martyr for the Whig cause. On the accession of George I in 1714 he became Paymaster of the Forces and Chancellor of the Exchequer in 1715, but resigned in sympathy with his brother-in-law *Townshend in 1717. The *South Sea Bubble crisis brought Walpole to power in 1721 and he remained in office as leading minister (effectively the first Prime Minister) until 1742.

During his long period of power he strove for peace abroad and also did his best to avoid political controversy at home, especially on such contentious issues as religion; he strengthened the economy and by his mastery of the House of Commons and use of patronage he maintained political stability. He regularly presided over *cabinet meetings and was thus generally regarded as the first effective Prime Minister; he insisted on cabinet loyalty and moved a long way towards the idea of the collective responsibility of the cabinet. In 1733 his unpopular attempts to impose excise duties on wine and tobacco were defeated in Parliament, but he placed a heavy duty on molasses imported into America, which became a major American grievance. He then faced an increasingly powerful opposition from within his own party in Parliament and lost an important patron when Queen Caroline died in 1737. After reluctantly going to war with Spain in 1739 and seeing Britain increasingly involved in the War of the *Austrian Succession, he accepted a peerage and resigned in 1742.

Walsingham, Sir Francis (*c.*1530–90) English politician. From 1573 to 1590 he served as Secretary of State to Queen Elizabeth I. He developed a domestic and foreign spy network that led to the detection of numerous Catholic plots against Elizabeth I and the gathering of intelligence about the Spanish Armada. In 1586 Walsingham uncovered a plot against Elizabeth involving Mary, Queen of Scots; he subsequently exerted his power to have Mary executed.

Walter, Hubert (died 1205) English cleric and statesman. After studying law at the University of Bologna he served first under *Henry II and then went with *Richard I on the Third *Crusade. On his return in 1193 he was made Archbishop of Canterbury and Justiciar, or Regent, of England. He was appointed papal legate in 1195. Walter's legal and administrative skills were recognized by both Richard I (whose £100,000 ransom he organized) and *John (whose accession he secured) who made him Chancellor. During Richard's frequent absences abroad he was virtually the ruler of England. Extensive financial and judicial reforms were made, including improvements to the enforcement of law and order (1195). He was Lord Chancellor from 1199.

Wandewash, Battle of (22 January 1760) One of the last great battles between the English and French East India Companies in south India, fought at the coastal fortress of Wandewash, in South India. Although the French commander, the comte *de Lally, had the advantage of numbers, he was hampered by dissensions among his forces. His attack was repulsed by the able British commander, Eyre Coote. The fall of Pondicherry followed.

Wang Anshi (1021–86) Chinese statesman, chief councillor to the *Song (1069–76). He introduced major financial and administrative reforms and reorganized local policing and the militia, known collectively as the "New Policies". The prices of commodities were stabilized

and farmers benefited from reduced land tax, low-interest state loans, and a reduction in the levy that replaced forced labour. There was much opposition to his reforms, particularly from officials and landowners, and he was dismissed in 1076. Many of his reforms were reversed shortly thereafter.

Warbeck, Perkin (1474–99) Flemish claimant to the English throne. Encouraged by Yorkists in England and on the Continent, he claimed to be Edward IV's son Richard, Duke of York (who had disappeared in 1483—*see* PRINCES IN THE TOWER), in an attempt to overthrow Henry VII. After a series of attempts to enter the country and begin a revolt he was captured and imprisoned in the Tower of London in 1497; he was later executed.

war crimes Certain activities in war that violate the established rules of warfare, as set out in the Hague and *Geneva Conventions. In most societies, such activities as the killing of prisoners, their torture or enslavement, hostage-taking, and the deportation and killing of civilians are deemed to be war crimes. Present-day attitudes to war crimes have been influenced by the trials at *Nuremberg and *Tokyo in 1945–46 of German and Japanese wartime leaders. In the course of these proceedings, it was made clear that an individual was to be held responsible for his or her actions even if carrying out the orders of a higher authority. During the *Vietnam War (1964–75), US soldiers were indicted on charges of killing civilians; and Iraq's hostage-taking and maltreatment of prisoners during its occupation of Kuwait (1990–91) also led to calls for those responsible to be tried for war crimes. A war crimes tribunal of the International Court of Justice, the principal judicial organ of the United Nations, was convened in 1993 to try people accused of 'ethnic cleansing' during the conflict in *Bosnia and Herzegovina. Several successful prosecutions followed. In 1999 this tribunal indicted the Yugoslav president, Slobodan *Milošević, of war crimes; his trial began in 2002 but was not completed before he died (2006). The trial of Radovan Karadžić, leader of the Bosnian Serbs, began in 2009. A similar tribunal was established in 1994 to prosecute those responsible for the genocide in Rwanda.

Ward, Sir Joseph George (1856–1930) New Zealand statesman. A minister of the first and successive Liberal cabinets, he provided low-interest credit to farmers. As Prime Minister (1906–12) and in coalition with William Massey (1915–19) he supported empire unity. He won office as Prime Minister again in 1928 as head of the United Party, partly on his reputation as a 'financial wizard', but failed to solve the crises brought on by the Great *Depression.

Wardrobe A department in the household of the English kings, who found the *Exchequer's methods of collecting revenues too cumbersome to meet their financial needs, particularly when travelling. King John had used another household department, the Chamber, but under Henry III the Wardrobe was developed and Edward I treated it virtually as his war treasury to supply military expenditure. By the late 15th century, however, the Chamber had become the main financial department.

warlords Chinese regional military rulers of the first half of the 20th century. Following the death of *Yuan Shikai in 1916, China was divided among many local rulers who derived their power from control of personal armies. In origin, the warlords were mostly former soldiers of the imperial and republican armies, bandits, or local officials. They depended on revenue from towns and agricultural areas in their own spheres of influence to feed the well-equipped troops with which they sought to establish their primacy over local rivals. The most successful warlords generally controlled easily defended areas and the largest of the many wars between rival cliques witnessed the mobilization of hundreds of thousands of soldiers. *Chiang Kai-shek's Nanjing government (1928–37) reestablished central authority over most warlord areas, but military rulers persisted in the far west of China into the 1940s.

War of 1812 (1812–15) A war between Britain and the USA. US frustration at the trade restrictions imposed by Britain in retaliation for Napoleon's *Continental System, together with a desire to remove British and Canadian obstacles to US westward expansion, led the US Congress to declare war on Britain (June 1812). The USA–British North American (Canadian) border was the main theatre of war. In July, the US General, William Hull, advanced into Upper Canada, but in early August withdrew to Detroit, which was soon after captured by Major-General Isaac Brock. In October 1812 a second invading US force crossed the Niagara River and stormed Queenston Heights, but it too was driven back by a British force, under Brock, who was killed. In October 1813 another US army under General William Harrison won the Battle of the *Thames, in south-western Ontario. In November US troops were defeated by a much smaller British force at Crysler's Farm on the St Lawrence. In July 1814, at the Battle of Lundy's Lane,

a US force under General Jacob Brown briefly fought at night a British force under General Drummond and then withdrew, after which no more attempts were made to invade Canada. On Lake Erie in September 1813 a US force captured a British squadron of six ships, while the following year (September 1814), in a similar victory on Lake Champlain, a British squadron of 16 ships was forced to surrender. At sea US warships won a series of single-ship engagements, but they were unable to disrupt the British naval blockade, which by 1814 was doing considerable harm to the US economy. In June 1814 a British expeditionary force landed in Chesapeake Bay, Virginia, marching north and burning the new city of Washington. War-weariness now brought the two sides to the conference table and in December 1814 the Treaty of *Ghent was signed, restoring all conquered territories to their original owners.

war on terrorism The war launched by President George W. *Bush in the aftermath of the outrage of *September 11, 2001, when he vowed that the USA would use its armed might to destroy terrorist organizations and any regimes that harbour them. In October 2001 the USA attacked Afghanistan, using air strikes to destroy the command centres of the *al-Qaeda movement and to bring down the anti-Western *Taliban regime. Subsequently, the focus shifted to so-called "rogue states" such as Saddam *Hussein's Iraq, which was invaded and occupied by US-led forces in 2003 (*see* IRAQ WAR).

Warren, Earl (1891–1974) US judge. During his time as Chief Justice of the US Supreme Court (1953–69) he did much to promote civil liberties, achieving the prohibition of segregation in US schools in 1954. He is also remembered for heading the commission of inquiry (known as the **Warren Commission**) held in 1964 into the assassination of President Kennedy; the commission found that Lee Harvey Oswald was the sole gunman, a decision that has since been much disputed.

Warsaw Pact A treaty of mutual defence and military aid signed in Warsaw on 14 May 1955 by Communist states of Eastern Europe under Soviet leadership. Established during the era of the Cold War in response to the creation of NATO, it began to break up in 1968 when Albania left and was finally dissolved in February 1991 following the collapse of the Communist system in the Soviet Union and Eastern Europe.

Warsaw Uprising 1. (February 1943) An uprising against the occupying German troops staged by 60,000–100,000 survivors of the Warsaw Ghetto (established in 1940 for 400,000 Jews). Although the Jewish survivors were poorly armed it took the heavily armed German garrison over one month to defeat and massacre them.

2. (August 1944) The Polish insurrection in Warsaw in World War II, in which Poles tried to expel the German Army before Soviet forces occupied the city. As the Red Army advanced, Soviet contacts in Warsaw encouraged the underground Home Army, supported by the exiled Polish government in London, to stage an uprising. Polish *Resistance Movement troops led by General Tadeusz Komorowski gained control of the city against a weak German garrison. Heavy German air-raids lasting 63 days preceded a strong German counter-attack. The Soviet Army under the Polish-born General *Rokossovsky reached a suburb of the city but failed to help the insurgents or to allow the western Allies to use Soviet air bases to airlift supplies to the hard-pressed Poles. Supplies ran out and on 2 October the Poles surrendered. The Germans then systematically deported Warsaw's population and destroyed the city itself. The main body of Poles that supported the Polish government in exile was thus destroyed and an organized alternative to Soviet political domination of the country was eliminated. As the Red Army resumed its advance into Poland the Soviet-sponsored Polish Committee of National Liberation was able to impose on Poland a Communist Provisional Government on 1 January 1945 without resistance.

Wars of Religion, French *See* FRENCH WARS OF RELIGION.

Warwick, Richard Neville, Earl of (known as 'the Kingmaker') (1428–71) English statesman. During the Wars of the *Roses he fought first on the Yorkist side, helping Edward IV to gain the throne in 1461. Having lost influence at court he then fought on the Lancastrian side, briefly restoring Henry VI to the throne in 1470. Warwick was killed at the Battle of Barnet.

Washakie (c.1804–1900) Native American (Shoshone) chief. He became the leader of the eastern band of his tribe in the 1840s. He chose to ally with White settlers in the Native American wars of the 1870s and was accorded a commission in the US army and a tomb in Fort Washakie.

Washington, Booker T. (Booker Taliaferro Washington) (1856–1915) US educationist. An emancipated slave, he pursued a

career in teaching and was appointed head in 1881 of the newly founded Tuskegee Institute in Alabama for the training of Black teachers. Washington emerged as a leading commentator for Black Americans at the turn of the century and published his influential autobiography, *Up from Slavery*, in 1901. His emphasis on vocational skills and financial independence for Blacks rather than on intellectual development or political rights, combined with his support for segregation, brought criticism from other Black leaders.

Washington, George (1732–99) US soldier and statesman, 1st President of the USA (1789–97). After serving as a soldier (1754–59) in the war against the French, Washington took part in two of the three Continental Congresses held by the American colonies in revolt against British rule (1774 and 1775), and in 1775 was chosen as commander of the army raised by the colonists, the Continental Army. He served in that capacity throughout the War of Independence, bringing about the eventual American victory by keeping the army together through the bitter winter of 1777 to 1778 at *Valley Forge and winning a decisive battle at *Yorktown (1781). Washington chaired the convention at Philadelphia (1787) that drew up the American Constitution, and two years later he was unanimously elected President, initially remaining unaligned to any of the newly emerging political parties but later joining the Federalist Party. He served two terms, following a policy of neutrality in international affairs, before declining a third term and retiring to private life.

Washington Conference The conference held in the USA between November 1921 and February 1922 to discuss political stability in the Far East and naval disarmament. Summoned on US initiative, the conference was attended by Belgium, Britain, China, France, Holland, Italy, Japan, Portugal, and the USA and resulted in a series of treaties including a Nine-Power Treaty guaranteeing China's independence and territorial integrity, a Japanese undertaking to return the region around Qingdao to Chinese possession, and an Anglo-French-Japanese-US agreement to guarantee each other's existing Pacific territories. Naval discussions resulted in a ten-year moratorium on capital-ship construction. The Washington Conference successfully placed restraints on both the naval arms race and Japanese expansionism, but by the 1930s both problems broke out afresh.

watch and ward The system developed in 13th century England to preserve the peace in local communities. Guards were appointed and the duties of the constables at night (watch) and in daytime (ward) were defined. Town gates remained closed from dusk to dawn, strangers had to produce sureties to prove their identity and business, up to 16 men maintained the watch in cities, twelve in boroughs, and four in smaller communities. Modifications to the system were eventually incorporated in the Statute of Winchester of 1285, a collection of regulations aimed at keeping the peace.

Watergate A building in Washington, DC, housing the offices of the Democratic Party, the scene of a bungled bugging attempt by Republicans during the US election campaign of 1972. The attempted cover-up and subsequent enquiry caused a massive political scandal, gravely weakened the prestige of the government, and finally led to the resignation of President Richard *Nixon in August 1974 to avoid impeachment (he was subsequently pardoned by the new President, Gerald *Ford).

Waterloo, Battle of (18 June 1815) A decisive battle between French and British and Prussian forces near the Belgian village of Waterloo. It was fought during the *Hundred Days of *Napoleon between his hastily recruited army of 72,000 men and *Wellington's Allied army of 68,000 men (with British, Dutch, Belgian, and German units) before the Prussians (45,000 men) arrived. There had been a violent storm in the night and Napoleon postponed his attack until midday to allow the ground to dry. By 2 p.m. a first contingent of Prussians arrived and attacked Napoleon on the right. At 6 p.m. Marshal *Ney ordered a coordinated attack and captured La Haye Sainte, a farmhouse in the centre of the Allied line. The French artillery then began attacking the Allies from the centre. At 7 p.m. Napoleon launched his famous Garde Impériale in a bid to break Wellington's now weakened infantry. At this point, however, *Blücher appeared with the main Prussian forces, taking Napoleon in the flank, and Wellington ordered a general advance. The French were routed, with the exception of the Garde, who resisted to the end. In Wellington's words, the outcome of the battle was "the nearest run thing you ever saw in your life". On 22 June, Napoleon signed his second and final abdication.

Watling Street A north-westerly Roman road of Britain that ran from Dubris (Dover), via Londinium (London) and Verulamium (St Albans), to Deva (Chester). Much of it was built c.60–70AD for the advance north of the *Fosse

Way. Its name derives from the Anglo-Saxon name for Verulamium ('Waeclingacaester').

Watson, John Christian (1867–1941) Australian politician, the first Labor Prime Minister of Australia (1904). Having been active in the labour movement, Watson became the leader of the Labor party. He formed the first Labor ministry but his party did not have a majority and after four months he was forced to form a coalition with the Liberal party.

Wavell, Archibald Percival, 1st Earl (1883–1950) British field-marshal and viceroy of India. In World War I he served in France (where he lost an eye) and in 1937–39 he commanded the British forces in Palestine. In 1939 he became commander-in-chief in the Middle East and won the victory of Sidi Barrani (1940) over the Italians. In 1941, forced to divert some of his forces to Greece, and facing new German formations, he had to retreat in North Africa and was dismissed by Churchill. He then served in India, first as commander-in-chief from 1941, then as viceroy (1943–47), where he made it his main task to prepare India for independence.

Wayne, Anthony (1745–96) American Revolutionary general, who led a Pennsylvanian regiment in the abortive invasion of Canada (1776). He displayed conspicuous initiative in such actions as Brandywine, Germantown, and Monmouth. In 1779 his brilliantly planned and executed night attack on Stony Point, a British-held fort on the Hudson, won him the nickname of "Mad Anthony". In 1794 he commanded the western army, which defeated the Native Americans at the Battle of Fallen Timbers and opened up the *North-west Territory to settlement.

Webb, Sidney, Baron Passfield (James Sidney Webb) (1859–1947) British socialist, economist, and historian. He and his wife, **(Martha) Beatrice Webb** (née Potter) (1858–1943), whom he married in 1892, were prominent members of the Fabian Society, and helped to establish the London School of Economics (1895). They wrote several important books on socio-political theory and history, including *The History of Trade Unionism* (1894) and *Industrial Democracy* (1897), as well as founding the weekly magazine the *New Statesman* (1913). Sidney Webb became a Labour MP in 1922 and served in the first two Labour governments.

Webster–Ashburton Treaty (1842) An agreement between Britain and the USA settling the present Maine–New Brunswick border. Negotiated by the US Secretary of State Daniel Webster (1782–1852) and the British minister Lord Ashburton, the treaty settled the disputed boundaries in the north-east, awarding the USA more than 18,000 sq km (7000 sq miles) of the 31,000 sq km (12,000 sq miles) disputed area and opening the St John River to free navigation. The treaty also fixed the Canadian–US boundary in the Great Lakes region and served as a precedent for the successful settlement of other 19th-century border disputes between Britain and the USA.

Weimar Republic (1919–33) The republic of Germany formed after the end of World War I. On 9 November 1918 a republic was proclaimed in Berlin under the moderate socialist Friedrich Ebert. An elected National Assembly met in January 1919 in the city of Weimar and agreed on a constitution. Ebert was elected first President (1919–25), succeeded by *Hindenburg (1925–34). The new republic had almost at once to face the *Versailles Peace Settlement, involving the loss of continental territory and of all overseas colonies and the likelihood of a vast reparations debt, the terms being so unpopular as to provoke a brief right-wing revolt, the Kapp putsch. The country was unable to meet reparation costs, and the mark collapsed, whereupon France and Belgium occupied the Ruhr in 1923, while in Bavaria right-wing extremists (including *Hitler and *Ludendorff) unsuccessfully tried to restore the monarchy. Gustav Stresemann succeeded in restoring confidence and in persuading the USA to act as mediator. The Dawes Plan adjusted reparation payments, and France withdrew from the Ruhr. It was followed in 1929 by the Young Plan. Discontented financial and industrial groups in the German National Party allied with Hitler's *Nazi Party to form a powerful opposition. As unemployment developed, support for this alliance grew, perceived as the only alternative to communism. In the presidential elections of 1932 Hitler gained some 13 million votes, exploiting anti-communist fears and anti-Semitic prejudice, although Hindenburg was himself re-elected. In 1933 he was persuaded to accept Hitler as Chancellor. Shortly after the *Reichstag fire, Hitler declared a state of emergency (28 February 1933) and, on Hindenburg's death in 1934, made himself President and proclaimed the *Third Reich.

Weizmann, Chaim (Azriel) (1874–1952) Israeli statesman, President (1949–52). Born in Russia, he became a British citizen in 1910.

A supporter of Zionism from the early 1900s, Weizmann participated in the negotiations that led to the Balfour Declaration (1917), which outlined British support for a Jewish homeland in Palestine. He later served as President of the World Zionist Organization (1920–31; 1935–46), facilitating Jewish immigration into Palestine in the 1930s. Weizmann also played an important role in persuading the US government to recognize the new state of Israel (1948) and became its first President in 1949.

Welensky, Sir Roy (Roland) (1907–91) Rhodesian statesman. He entered politics in 1938, and founded the Federal Party in 1953, dedicated to 'racial partnership'. The *Central African Federation, was created largely as a result of his negotiations. He was Prime Minister of the Federation (1956–63). When the Federation was dissolved (1963) Welensky lost the support of the White Rhodesians, who gave their allegiance to the Rhodesian Front of Ian *Smith.

welfare state A country with a comprehensive system of social welfare funded both by taxation and national insurance. The emergence of the strong secular state in 19th-century Europe was characterized by the development of state involvement in education, public health, and housing. Public education systems were first introduced in France and Prussia early in the 19th century, while the need for housing and public health measures accelerated as urbanization increased in Europe. A scheme of social insurance against unemployment, sickness, and old age was pioneered in Germany under *Bismarck, and other European states soon followed. In Britain a similar scheme, together with other social welfare measures, began to be introduced under the Liberal governments (1906–14). Between the wars significant developments towards its establishment took place in New Zealand under the *Labour Party, while F. D. Roosevelt's *New Deal in the USA created a series of federal social welfare agencies. In 1942 a report by William *Beveridge proposed a comprehensive British system of national social insurance. His proposals were implemented by Clement *Attlee's Labour government after World War II, which also introduced the National *Health Service. In the Soviet Union and East European states welfare provision became an official part of the fabric of society. In the USA, the concept of social welfare support is regarded as being fundamentally at odds with the free market economy and so remains highly selective. Sweden is usually taken as the purest example of a welfare state, because of its interventionist labour market policy and integrated health care system, but Belgium and The Netherlands have more generous social security. In a welfare state, the proportion of GNP allocated to social expenditure can rise as high as 40%. In Britain, the heavy public expenditure required to distribute social benefits was increasingly challenged and a revision of the NHS and the social security system took place in the 1980s and 1990s under the Conservatives; further reforms were initiated by the Labour government of 1997–2010. More radical reforms under the Conservative–led coalition government from 2010 sought not only to reduce costs but also to simplify the benefits system and target it at those most in need.

Wellington, Arthur Wellesley, 1st Duke of (known as **'the Iron Duke'**) (1769–1852) British soldier and Tory statesman, Prime Minister (1828–30; 1834). Born in Ireland, he served as commander of British forces in the *Peninsular War, winning a series of victories against the French and finally driving them across the Pyrenees into southern France (1814). The following year Wellington defeated Napoleon at the Battle of *Waterloo, ending the Napoleonic Wars. During his first term as Prime Minister he granted Catholic Emancipation under pressure from Daniel *O'Connell.

Wells, Fargo and Company US transport organization, founded by Henry Wells, William C. Fargo, and associates in 1852 to operate between New York and California. Wells and Fargo established a monopoly west of the Mississippi within a decade, succeeding the *Pony Express as the agency for transporting bullion to eastern markets, and for 20 years dominated the postal service in the West. In 1918 it merged with a number of other concerns to become the American Railway Express Company.

Welsh Nationalist Party *See* PLAID CYMRU.

Wenceslas, St (or **St Wenceslaus**; known as **'Good King Wenceslas'**) (*c.*907–29) Duke of Bohemia and patron saint of the Czech Republic. He worked to Christianize the people of Bohemia but was murdered by his brother Boleslaus; he later became venerated as a martyr and hero of Bohemia. The story told in the Christmas carol 'Good King Wenceslas', by J. M. Neale (1818–66), appears to have no basis in fact.

Wenceslas IV (1361–1419) King of Bohemia (1376–1419), King of Germany (1378–1400),

and Holy Roman Emperor (1378–1400). A weak king, he was overcome by the ambitions of the imperial princes, the town leagues, and by his brother *Sigismund. A Bohemian revolt, starting in 1394, deposed him in favour of Sigismund in 1402. He lost the German throne in 1400 in favour of Rupert Wittelsbach, although he regained it in 1404. Much of his reign was disturbed by the Hussite movement; Wenceslas supported *Huss and tried to prevent his execution, which was ordered by Sigismund.

Wentworth, Thomas *See* STRAFFORD.

wergild (or "man-price") The compensation that had to be paid by a murderer to the kinsmen of the victim in Anglo-Saxon England. The amount of an individual's wergild was fixed in law and varied according to his rank in society. An ordinary freeman (ceorl) was valued at 200 shillings, a nobleman (earl) at 1200 shillings, and the king at 7200 shillings. Although the unfree had no wergild, compensation for their murder was paid to their owners.

Wesley, John (1703–91) British preacher and co-founder of Methodism. He became the leader of a small group in Oxford, which had been formed in 1729 by his brother **Charles** (1707–88); its members were nicknamed the 'Methodists'. In 1738 John Wesley experienced a spiritual conversion as a result of a reading of Luther's preface to the Epistle to the Romans. He resolved to devote his life to evangelistic work; however, when Anglican opposition caused the churches to be closed to him, he and his followers began preaching out of doors. Wesley subsequently travelled throughout Britain winning many working-class converts. Despite his wish for Methodism to remain within the Church of England, his practice of ordaining his missionaries himself (since the Church refused to do so) brought him increasing opposition from the Anglican establishment and eventual exclusion; the Methodists formally separated from the Church of England in 1791.

Wessex The kingdom of the West Saxons, established in Hampshire in the early 6th century and gradually extended by conquest to include much of southern England. Under Alfred the Great and his successors it formed the nucleus for the Anglo-Saxon kingdom of England. The name was revived by Thomas Hardy to designate the south-western counties of England (especially Dorset) in which his novels are set, and is used in the titles of certain present-day regional authorities.

Western European Union (WEU) A West European defence organization founded in 1955 by Belgium, France, the UK, Luxembourg, the Netherlands, West Germany, and Italy. The WEU came into being as a successor to the Brussels Treaty organization, after France had refused to ratify the treaty providing for a European Defence Community; its primary function was to supervise the rearmament and accession to *NATO of West Germany. The Union formally ended the occupation of West Germany and Italy by the Allies. The social and cultural activities initially envisaged by its founders were transferred to the *Council of Europe in 1960, leaving the Union with the task of improving defence cooperation among the countries of Western Europe. Reactivated in 1984, it was involved from 1987 in arms control, and was joined by Spain and Portugal in 1989 and by the former East Germany after German reunification in 1990. The WEU helped to coordinate Europe's contribution to the anti-Iraq coalition in the Gulf War in 1991. In 1993, the Eurocorps rapid reaction unit was founded, comprising land-based forces from France, Germany, and Belgium. In 1994, several former Soviet satellite states of Eastern Europe (e.g. Bulgaria, Poland, Romania) were granted associate member status. The WEU was abolished in 2011 after its obligation for mutual defence had been transferred to the *European Union by the *Lisbon Treaty (2009).

Western Front The line of fighting in *World War I that stretched from the Vosges mountains through Amiens in France to Ostend in Belgium. Fighting in World War I began in August 1914 when German forces, adopting the Schlieffen Plan to fight on two fronts by first swiftly neutralizing France, were checked in the first Battle of the *Marne. The subsequent German attempt to reach the Channel ports was defeated in the first Battle of Ypres (12 October–11 November). Thereafter both sides settled down to *trench warfare, the distinctive feature of fighting on this front. The year 1915 saw inconclusive battles with heavy casualties: Neuve Chapelle (March), the second Battle of Ypres (April/May), when poison gas was used for the first time, and Loos (September). In 1916 Germany's heavy attack on Verdun nearly destroyed the French army but failed to secure a breakthrough. To relieve pressure on the French, the British bore the brunt of the *Somme offensive (July), gaining little ground and suffering appalling casualties. Early in 1917 the Germans withdrew to a new set of prepared trenches, the *Siegfried Line (or Hindenburg

Line), and in 1917 the Canadians captured *Vimy Ridge. In November the British launched yet another major offensive, the Battle of *Passchendaele (or third Battle of Ypres), and lost 300,000. The entry of the USA into the war (1917) meant that the Allies could draw on its considerable resources. US troops commanded by General Pershing landed in France in June 1917. In March 1918 *Ludendorff's final offensive began, with his troops again reaching the Marne before being stemmed by US forces at Château-Thierry. *Foch, now Allied commander-in-chief, began the counter-offensive with the third Battle of the Marne (July). British troops broke the Siegfried Line near St Quentin, while the Americans attacked through the Argonne region. By October Germany's resources were exhausted and on 11 November Germany signed the armistice that marked the end of World War I.

westernization The process by which a country or society adopts the customs and institutions that are said to characterize the Western world. For some governments and élites in *developing countries, westernization has been seen as synonymous with modernization and development and therefore as a desirable goal. Another more recent tendency, however, is to regard westernization as a pernicious process equated with the negative aspects of *capitalism and *globalization, which undermine local customs and values and which should therefore be strongly opposed. The Iranian Revolution of 1979 was, at least in part, a reaction to the westernizing policies of *Muhammad Reza Shah Pahlavi (1919–80), which neglected the traditional, particularly religious, values in Iranian society, and the anti-Western theme has, to a greater or lesser degree, been taken up by Islamic fundamentalist movements throughout the Muslim world.

Western Jin (or **Western Chin**) (265–316) A dynasty that briefly unified China after the period of the *Three Kingdoms. It was established by Sima Yan, a general of the Wei kingdom. He attempted to curb the power of the dominant families but after his death in 290, Sima princes feuded with each other and the central government collapsed. In the resulting chaos, a *Xiongnu invasion occurred and Luoyang (311) and Chang'an (316) were sacked. One Sima prince in the south-eastern kingdom of Wu established the Eastern Jin dynasty (317–420), but it too lacked strong central government. During this period, the colonization of southern China by *Han Chinese greatly increased.

Western Neolithic *See* NEOLITHIC.

Western Rising (July–August 1549) An English rebellion in Cornwall and Devon, at the same time as *Kett's Rebellion in Norfolk. The West Country rebels' main grievance was the imposition, by Act of *Uniformity, of the first Book of Common Prayer in English. Demanding that no such religious changes should be made until *Edward VI came of age, they laid siege to Exeter on 2 July. It was not until mid-August that government troops under Lord Russell scattered them, killing some 4000. The leaders were executed in London; lesser rebels were hanged throughout the West Country.

Western Samoa Name until 1997 of *Samoa.

West Indian independence A movement towards independence among the British West Indian colonies in the Caribbean. Pressure towards greater participation in the government of British West Indian colonies developed in the 19th century. A Black uprising in *Jamaica had been ruthlessly suppressed in 1865, but following a Jamaican deputation to London in 1884, elected legislatures, on a limited franchise to advise governors, were steadily introduced throughout the islands. After World War I there were further moves towards more representative government, for example, in *Trinidad in 1923. By 1940 the British government, aware of the strategic importance of the area, established a Commission for Development and Welfare in the West Indies, substantial financial aid was given and the principle of self-government was accepted. This policy did not, however, prevent large-scale unrest after World War II. Britain believed that individual islands could never be viable as independent states, hence the concept of federation and the attempt to form the **West Indies Federation** (1958–62). When this failed, Jamaica and Trinidad and Tobago were granted full independence in 1962 and *Barbados in 1966. New attempts to create a Federation of the East Caribbean also failed (1967), when many smaller islands temporarily became "associated states of the United Kingdom". Since then six new member states of the *Commonwealth of Nations have emerged: *Grenada 1974; *Dominica 1978; *Saint Vincent and the Grenadines 1979; *Saint Lucia 1979; *Antigua and Barbuda 1981; and *Saint Kitts and Nevis 1983. The island of Anguilla was first associated with Saint Kitts and Nevis, but unilaterally seceded from the association in 1967. The UK intervened and Anguilla was obliged to resume the status of an independent territory of the UK in 1969; it became a separate British dependency in 1980.

West Indies The islands of the Caribbean. *Columbus, who in 1492 was the first European to reach the islands, called them the West Indies because he believed he had arrived near India by travelling westward. The islands were opened up by the Spanish in the 16th century and thereafter were the theatre of rivalry between the European colonial powers. Cultivation of sugar was introduced and the population was transformed by the mass importation of West African slaves to work the agricultural plantations; their descendants form the largest group in the population.

Westminster, Statute of (1931) Legislation on the status of British *dominions. At the 1926 and 1930 Imperial Conferences pressure was exerted by the dominions of Canada, New Zealand, the Commonwealth of Australia, the Union of South Africa, Eire, and Newfoundland for full autonomy within the British *Commonwealth. The result was the Statute of Westminster, accepted by each dominion Parliament, which recognized the right of each dominion to control its own domestic and foreign affairs, to establish a diplomatic corps, and to be represented at the League of Nations. It still left unresolved certain legal and constitutional questions—not least the status of the British crown. The Consequential Provisions Act (1949) allowed republics such as India to remain members of the Commonwealth.

Westphalia, Treaty of (1648) The treaty signed at Münster and Osnabrück, which brought the *Thirty Years War to a conclusion. By its terms, the Habsburgs acknowledged the independence of Switzerland and the separation of the *United Provinces from the *Spanish Netherlands, France secured undefined rights in Alsace and retained the bishoprics of Metz, Toul, and Verdun, Sweden acquired West Pomerania and the bishoprics of Bremen and Verden, and Brandenburg acquired East Pomerania and the succession to the archbishopric of Magdeburg. The full sovereignty of the German states was recognized, thus marking the failure of the Holy Roman Emperor to turn Germany into a Catholic monarchy.

Weygand, Maxime (1867–1965) French general. He was *Foch's chief of staff in World War I, and in 1920 was sent by the French government to aid the Poles in their ultimately successful defence against the advancing Soviet *Red Army. In the military crisis of May 1940 Weygand was recalled to assume command of the French armies attempting to stem the German *Blitzkrieg attack. Advising capitulation, he later commanded the *Vichy forces in North Africa, was dismissed at the request of the Germans, arrested by the Gestapo, and then freed by the Allies. He was tried and acquitted under the *de Gaulle regime on a charge of collaboration with the Germans.

Whig A member of the British political party traditionally opposed to the Tories. The Whigs owed their name, like the Tories, to the *exclusion crisis of Charles II's reign. Those who petitioned for the recall of Parliament in 1679 were named Whigs (Scottish Covenanting brigands) by their Tory opponents. The Whigs suffered defeat in Charles's reign, but joined with the Tories in inviting *William III (of Orange) to England, and they alternated with the Tories in power until 1714. Their principles were to maintain the power and privileges of Parliament, to show sympathy with religious dissent, keeping links between Church and state to a minimum, and to play an active role in Europe.

From the accession of *George I the Hanoverian kings placed their trust in the Whigs, and there followed the long period of Whig supremacy. From the mid-1720s there were Whigs in opposition to *Walpole and the development of factions within the party became increasingly acute by the mid-century, bringing political instability in the 1760s. The Rockingham faction, which formed the core of Charles *Fox's followers, became the basis of the new Whig party in the late 18th century. The changed political and social conditions of the 19th century caused the break-up of the Whig party. Many of its members, however, formed the core of the *Liberal Party.

Whig Party A US political party of the second quarter of the 19th century. The Whig Party was formed in the mid-1830s by those who opposed what was perceived as the executive tyranny of President Andrew *Jackson. Dominated by Henry *Clay and Daniel Webster, the Party elected William Henry *Harrison to the White House in 1840 and *Taylor in 1848, but disunity on free-soil and slavery issues weakened it severely and it broke up.

Whisky Rebellion (1794) A rising of farmers in western Pennsylvania, USA, in protest at Secretary of the Treasury Alexander *Hamilton's excise tax of 1791. The frontiersmen who made whisky considered the tax discriminatory. President George *Washington called out 15,000 troops to quell the rioting, proving the federal government's power to enforce the country's laws and earning the frontiersmen's hatred of the *Federalists' policies.

Whitby, Synod of (664) A church council that resolved the differences between the Celtic and Roman forms of Christian worship in England, particularly the method used for calculating the date of Easter. The Celtic Church had its own method of fixing the date of Easter; this was a matter of dispute after the arrival of St *Augustine of Canterbury's mission. The Celtic case was presented by St Colman, Bishop of Lindisfarne. The Roman case was put forward by St Wilfrid of Ripon, whose arguments were finally accepted by King *Oswy of Northumbria. This decision was crucial, severing the connection with the Irish church and allowing for the organization of the English church under Roman discipline. Theodore, Archbishop of Canterbury, summoned an assembly of the whole English church at Hertford in 672.

White Australia policy A restrictive immigration policy pursued in Australia. In the mid-19th century there was a shortage of labour and *squatters brought in Chinese and *Kanakas (Pacific Islanders) as labour. By the 1880s developing trade unions were calling for a policy to protect the "White working man". By 1890 all states had legislation to preserve the purity of White Australia, Alfred *Deakin being one of its strongest advocates. The new Commonwealth government legislated to exclude non-Europeans (Immigration Restriction Act, 1901). The main device used was to be a dictation test in any European language (any "prescribed" language from 1905), the language being chosen to ensure failure. This policy of exclusion continued until the 1950s. The Labor administration of Gough *Whitlam repudiated the policy in the early 1970s. Since then, immigration from southeast Asia has grown considerably.

White Lotus Society (or **Incense Smelling Society**) A Chinese secret society. It had religious affiliations, tracing its origins to a Buddhist monk of the 4th century AD. The lotus, springing unsullied from the mud, is a Buddhist symbol. In times of trouble, its leaders preached of the coming of the Buddha and of the establishment of a new dynasty. Its supporters, bound by blood ceremonies and claiming magic powers, came from an impoverished peasantry. Major risings occurred in the mid-14th century during the decline of the *Yuan dynasty, and from 1796 to 1804, when they successfully opposed Manchu troops in southern Shaanxi province. This setback weakened Chinese belief in the invincibility of the Manchu troops and the authority of the *Qing dynasty.

White Russians 1. Those who fought against the Soviet *Red Army in the *Russian Civil War (1918–21). The name was derived from the royalist opponents of the French Revolution, known as Whites, because they adopted the white flag of the French Bourbon dynasty. The White Army, though smaller than the Red, was better equipped and had an abundance of Tsarist officers, some of whom offered to serve as ordinary soldiers. Its two main bases were in the south, where the army was successively led by Kornilov, Denikin, and Wrangel, and in Siberia where Kolchak was nominally head of a provisional government at Omsk. The White Russians were ultimately defeated by their own internal quarrels and by their refusal to grant land reforms in the areas under their control.
2. Citizens of the Republic of Belarus.

Whitlam, Gough (Edward Gough Whitlam) (1916–2014) Australian Labor statesman, Prime Minister (1972–75). While in office he ended compulsory military service in Australia and relaxed the laws for Asian and African immigrants. When, in 1975, the opposition blocked finance bills in the Senate, he refused to call a general election and was dismissed by the Governor-General Sir John Kerr, the first occasion in 200 years that the British Crown had removed an elected Prime Minister. The crisis was resolved when Malcolm Fraser, the Leader of the Opposition who had been appointed Prime Minister by Sir John Kerr, advised Kerr to dissolve both houses. The finance bills were then passed and Fraser's Liberal–National Country Party coalition secured majorities in both houses at the subsequent election. Whitlam remained leader of the Labor Party until 1977. He was subsequently Australia's ambassador to UNESCO (1983–86).

WHO *See* WORLD HEALTH ORGANIZATION.

Wilberforce, William (1759–1833) British politician and social reformer. An MP and close associate of Pitt the Younger, he was a prominent campaigner for the abolition of the slave trade, successfully promoting a bill outlawing its practice in the British West Indies (1807). Later he pushed for the abolition of slavery throughout the British Empire, his efforts resulting in the 1833 Slavery Abolition Act.

Wilderness Road A frontier trail in North America opened by Daniel *Boone in 1775 across the Allegheny Mountains. It ran for nearly 482 km (300 miles) from western Virginia through the Cumberland Gap to the upper Kentucky River at Boonesborough. It was commissioned by the Transylvania Company, an association of land speculators, to encourage settlement in Kentucky, Tennessee, and the Ohio valley. For 50 years it was a major route into the eastern Mississippi valley.

Wilhelmina (1880–1962) Queen of the Netherlands (1890–1948). Wilhelmina became queen as a child, with her mother as regent until 1898. During World War II she maintained a government in exile in London, and through frequent radio broadcasts became a symbol of resistance to the Dutch people. She returned to the Netherlands in 1945, but three years later abdicated in favour of her daughter Juliana.

Wilkes, John (1727–97) British journalist and politician. Wilkes was hailed in both Britain and America as a champion of liberty. In 1763 in issue 45 of his paper the *North Briton* he attacked George III's ministers and by implication the king himself, but when arrested for seditious libel he claimed the privileges of a Member of Parliament to contest the legality of his arrest, which had been made under a general warrant, not specifying him by name. The government then managed to expel him from Parliament on grounds of obscenity, particularly for the publication of his *Essay on Woman*, an obscene spoof on Alexander Pope's *Essay on Man*, and Wilkes fled to France in 1764. He returned in 1768 to fight the general election and to serve a 22-month sentence for his earlier offences. Controversy raged when Parliament refused to let him take his seat, even though he was elected Member of Parliament for Middlesex on four consecutive occasions. He was at last allowed back into Parliament in 1774 and sat for Middlesex until 1790. He supported the parliamentary reform movement and declared an interest in and sympathy for the American cause. All this time he enjoyed the support of the populace and a mob could always be called out to rally to his cause. In 1780, after some hesitation, he supported the action being taken to suppress the *Gordon riots and he was considered to have become respectable when he opposed the French Revolution.

Wilkins, Roy (1901–81) US social reformer and civil rights leader. The grandson of a slave, he worked for Black newspapers before he joined the National Association for the Advancement of Colored People (NAACP) in 1931. He was an active leader of the *civil rights movement to improve the status of the Black population. He held high executive office in the NAACP from 1955 to 1977, but came under increasing criticism from Black militants towards the end of his life, for his commitment to non-violence.

Wilkinson, James (1757–1825) US general and adventurer. He distinguished himself in the early days of the War of Independence. Moving to Kentucky, he became a principal figure in the confused politics of the developing south-west. He re-entered the army in 1791 and went on to serve as governor of the Louisiana Territory (1805–06). While there he became involved with Aaron *Burr's conspiracy, but betrayed the latter and acted as prosecution witness in the subsequent treason trial. The failure of his campaign to capture Montreal in the early stages of the *War of 1812 led to his removal from command.

Willard, Emma (1787–1870) US educational reformer. A pioneer of women's education, she founded a boarding-school in Vermont (1814) to teach subjects not then available to women (such as mathematics and philosophy). Willard moved the school to Troy, New York (1821), where it became known as the Troy Female Seminary; the college education that it offered served as a model for subsequent women's colleges in the USA and Europe.

William I (the Conqueror) (or **William the Bastard**) (1028–87) The first Norman King of England (1066–87). The illegitimate son of Robert I, Duke of Normandy, he succeeded to the dukedom as a child in 1035. His early life was fraught with danger—three of his closest advisers were murdered and an attempt was made on his own life. Twice he faced major rebellions. In 1047 he was saved only by the intervention of the French king, Henry I, who helped him in battle. Between 1053 and 1054 Henry failed to seize Normandy for himself. William's claim to the English throne was based on the promise allegedly given to him in 1051 by *Edward the Confessor. With papal backing he landed in England and defeated *Harold II at the Battle of *Hastings (1066). While the English leaders considered their next move William laid waste parts of Sussex, Surrey, and Hertfordshire. He was crowned on Christmas Day at Westminster Abbey.

The period 1067 to 1071 was characterized by a number of rebellions against his rule in Northumbria, Wessex, Mercia, and the Isle of Ely. His suppression of them was ruthlessly effective. Much of his later life he spent in Normandy fighting against the French king Philip I but before his death he initiated the *Domesday Book (1086). He died after being wounded on the battlefield, fighting Philip I of France.

William I (the Lion) (1143–1214) King of Scotland (1165–1214), succeeding his brother Malcolm IV. He helped to establish the independence of the Church of Scotland (1188), formulated the first major alliance between his country and France (1168), and stimulated Scotland's urban development. Initially loyal to *Henry II of England, he was determined to recover the earldom of Northumberland and supported Henry's three sons in a disastrous civil war. This resulted in William's capture at Alnwick (1175), the acknowledgement of Henry as his feudal superior by the Treaty of Falaise, and, in 1189, the payment of 10,000 marks to *Richard I to recover his independence.

William I (the Silent) (1533–84) Prince of *Orange and Count of Nassau-Dillenburg. William I is regarded as the founding father of the *United Provinces of the Netherlands. He was trusted by Emperor *Charles V and initially by *Philip II of Spain, who made him *statholder of Holland, Zeeland, and Utrecht (1559) and then of Franche-Comté (1561). Nevertheless he emerged in the 1560s as the leader of the aristocratic opposition to Philip's centralizing absolutism. On *Alba's arrival in the Netherlands (1567) he became the key figure in the first phase of the *Dutch Revolts. He was never a great general in the field, but his strengths lay in negotiating financial and military aid from abroad and in providing leadership in a country often torn by rivalries. He was recognized as statholder by the Estates of Holland (1572) and joined the Calvinist church (1573). His dream of a united Netherlands under a national government seemed close to realization with the signature of the Pacification of *Ghent (1576); he was powerless to prevent the permanent north–south division of 1579. In 1580 he was outlawed by Philip II and four years later he was assassinated by a Catholic fanatic.

William I (1797–1888) King of Prussia (1861–88) and German Emperor (1871–88). He devoted himself to the welfare of the Prussian army, assuming personal command in suppressing the *Revolution of 1848 in Baden. When he succeeded to the Prussian throne in 1861 he proclaimed a new 'era of liberalism', but this did not last for long. In 1862 he invited Otto *von Bismarck to become his Minister-President and from then on relied increasingly on Bismarck's policies, giving his approval to the growing influence of Prussia. During the *Franco-Prussian War he took command of troops, receiving the surrender of Napoleon III at *Sedan (September 1870). In January 1871 he was invited by the princes of Germany, at Bismarck's instigation, to become their emperor, thus creating the *German Second empire. Two unsuccessful assassination attempts strengthened his popularity, but also offered a pretext to suppress socialists.

William II (or **William Rufus**, 'red-faced') (c.1056–1100) King of England (1087–1100). William II was the second son of *William I (the Conqueror) and Matilda. His succession was challenged by some Norman barons led by his uncle, Bishop Odo of Bayeux, who preferred his elder brother Robert, Duke of Normandy. This rebellion (1088) was crushed as was a second revolt in 1095. Robert's departure on the First *Crusade (1096) gave William the opportunity to secure Normandy for himself. His successes there against the French king and in neighbouring Maine did much to secure the boundaries of Normandy. William's resistance to *Anselm's appointment as Archbishop of Canterbury contributed to his unpopular image with the chroniclers. His death from an arrow when hunting in the New Forest may have been arranged by his younger brother, who succeeded him as *Henry I.

William II (known as **Kaiser Bill**) (1859–1941) King of Prussia and Emperor of Germany (1888–1918). A grandson of Queen Victoria and of William I of Prussia, in 1890 he forced *Bismarck's resignation and embarked on a personal 'new course' policy that was regarded abroad as warmongering. He supported *Tirpitz in building a navy to rival that of Britain. On the failure (1896) of the privately financed raid on the Transvaal led by a British colonial administrator, Dr. Jameson, he sent a congratulatory telegram to the Boer leader, *Kruger, which offended public opinion in Britain. He made friendly overtures to Turkey and dangerously provoked France in the *Morocco crises of 1905 and 1911. His support of *Austria-Hungary against *Serbia (1914) led to World War I, although his personal responsibility for the war is less than was once thought. He played little direct part in the war and in 1918 was forced to abdicate.

William III (of Orange) (1650–1702) King of England, Ireland, and Scotland (1689–1702). William III was *statholder of Holland and took over effective rule of the **United Provinces (1672–1702) after the crisis of the French invasion in 1672. In 1677 he married his cousin, *Mary of England, and was invited in 1688 by seven leading English politicians to save

England from his Roman Catholic father-in-law, *James II. In what became known as the *Glorious Revolution, he landed at Torbay, met with virtually no resistance, and in 1689 jointly with Mary accepted from Parliament the crown of England. He defeated James II's efforts to establish a base in Ireland by the victory of the *Boyne and suppressed the Highlanders of Scotland. He commanded the Dutch army in the Netherlands and although he scored only one victory, at Namur in 1695, he was able to win a favourable peace at *Ryswick two years later. He was never popular in England and relied heavily on Dutch favourites, such as the soldier Arnold Keppel, 1st Earl of Albemarle (1669–1718). Although he preferred the *Whigs to the *Tories, he tried to avoid one-party government. His reputation was affected by his failure to honour the Treaty of Limerick (1691), in which William guaranteed political and religious freedom to Irish Catholics, and the massacre of *Glencoe (1692).

William IV (1765–1837) King of Great Britain and Ireland and dependencies overseas, King of Hanover (1830–37). The third son of George III, his reign marked a decline in the political influence of the crown. He joined the navy as an able seaman in 1779, subsequently becoming a close friend of Horatio *Nelson. In 1790 he set up house with an actress, Dorothea Jordan, who bore him ten children. In order to secure the succession to the throne, in 1818 he married Adelaide of Saxe-Meiningen and had two daughters, who both died in infancy. Becoming king on the death of his brother, *George IV, in 1830, he overcame his natural conservatism sufficiently to help ensure the passage of the *Reform Act of 1832.

William, Prince (full name **William Arthur Philip Louis, Duke of Cambridge**) (1982–) Second in line to the British throne. The son of Prince *Charles and *Diana, Princess of Wales, he was educated at Eton and the University of St Andrews. He trained as an army officer (2006) and then spent periods with the Royal Navy and RAF. Between 2010 and 2013 he served as a helicopter pilot with the RAF Search and Rescue Force. In 2011 he married Catherine Middleton; they have one son, Prince George Alexander Louis (2013–).

William of Malmesbury (c.1095–c.1143) Historian of 12th-century England. A librarian at the Benedictine abbey of St Aldhelm in Malmesbury, Wiltshire, he was the author of a history of the English church to 1125 (*Gesta Pontificum Anglorum*). He is best known for his other historical work the *Gesta Regum Anglorum* (Acts of the English Kings), dealing with the period from *Bede to 1120, and the *Historia Novella* (Modern History), which continues the account to 1142. His work is notable for its attempt to understand and interpret events rather than record them in an uncritical fashion.

William of Ockham (or **William of Occam**) (*c*.1290–*c*.1347) English theologian and scholastic philosopher. He was a Franciscan friar who developed an anti-papal theory of the state, denying the pope secular authority and was excommunicated in 1328, living thereafter in Munich under Emperor Louis IV's protection. His form of nominalist philosophy saw God as beyond human powers of reasoning, and things as provable only by experience or by (unprovable) scriptural authority. Hence his famous maxim, 'Ockham's razor', that the fewest possible assumptions should be made in explaining a thing.

Williams, Eric (Eustace) (1911–81) Trinidadian statesman. In 1955 Williams founded the People's National Movement (PNM), which won a landslide victory in the national elections of 1961. In 1962 he led his country to independence, becoming the first Prime Minister (1961–81) of the colony and then of the republic of *Trinidad and Tobago. An "empirical" socialist, Williams attracted foreign capital through tax incentives and, by skilful use of foreign aid, made Trinidad and Tobago the wealthiest Commonwealth nation in the Caribbean. He faced increasing militant opposition to his government before his death in 1981.

Williams, Roger (*c*.1603–83) English founder of the North American colony of Rhode Island. He emigrated to Massachusetts in 1631 and, as a minister at Salem, he soon quarrelled with John Cotton and Governor John Winthrop. In 1635 he was banished. He founded Providence, Rhode Island, where he developed friendly relations with local Native Americans and established the Baptist Church. He obtained a parliamentary charter for Rhode Island in 1644. Although free of religious persecution, the colony was beset by feuding for most of Williams's life.

Wilmington, Spencer Compton, Earl of (*c*.1673–1743) British politician, nominal Prime Minister (1742–43), as a compromise candidate while the Duke of *Newcastle and John Carteret (Earl Granville) effectively led the government.

Wilson, Harold, Baron Wilson of Rievaulx (James Harold Wilson) (1916–95) British Labour statesman, Prime Minister (1964–70; 1974–76). During both terms of office he faced severe economic problems; repeated sterling crises led to devaluation in 1967, while he attempted unsuccessfully to deal with high inflation in 1974–76 by seeking an agreement with trade unions over limiting pay increases. His government introduced a number of social reforms, including reducing the voting age to 18, liberalizing the laws on divorce, homosexuality, and abortion, and introducing comprehensive schooling. Overseas, he was unable to persuade the regime of Ian Smith in Rhodesia (Zimbabwe) to back down over its declaration of independence (1965), and therefore introduced economic sanctions against Rhodesia. In 1974 Wilson renegotiated Britain's terms of entry into the European Economic Community, confirming British membership after a referendum in 1975. He resigned as leader of the Labour Party the following year and was replaced as Prime Minister by James *Callaghan.

Wilson, Woodrow (Thomas Woodrow Wilson) (1856–1924) US Democratic statesman, 28th President of the USA (1913–21). He was a prominent academic in the field of law and political economy prior to his election victory. As President he carried out a series of successful administrative and fiscal reforms. He initially kept the USA out of World War I, but, following the German reintroduction of unrestricted submarine warfare, entered the war on the Allied side in April 1917. Wilson's conditions for a peace treaty, as set out in his 'Fourteen Points' speech (1918), and his plan for the formation of the League of Nations were crucial in the international negotiations surrounding the end of the war, and he was awarded the Nobel Peace Prize in 1919. However, he was unable to obtain the Senate's ratification of the Treaty of Versailles, his health collapsed, and he retired from politics.

window tax An English tax on any window or window-like opening, which was in force from 1695 to 1851. It was originally imposed to pay for the losses of the great recoinage of 1695 and was increased six times in the 18th century, particularly by *Pitt the Younger. The tax was eventually applied to all windows in excess of six in a building and windows bricked up to avoid the tax can still be seen in older houses throughout Britain.

Windsor, House of The official designation of the British royal family since 1917. Anti-German feeling during World War I was sufficiently strong for George V to feel that it would be an appropriate gesture to remove all references to the German titles of Saxe-Coburg, derived originally from the marriage of Queen Victoria to Prince Albert of Saxe-Coburg-Gotha. 'Windsor' was adopted because Windsor Castle, Berkshire, has long been a home of British monarchs.

Wingate, Orde Charles (1903–44) British major-general. A brilliant exponent of guerrilla warfare, in the 1930s he helped to establish and train Jewish irregular forces operating against Arabs in Palestine, and in 1941 he organized Sudanese and Abyssinian irregulars to fight the Italian occupiers and restore Emperor Haile Selassie to the throne. He created and led the *chindits*, a Burmese guerrilla group that operated behind Japanese lines. He died in an air crash in 1944 at the outset of his second, and greatly enlarged, *chindit* operation.

Winstanley, Gerrard (*c.*1609–after 1660) English radical Puritan. He was the leader of the *Diggers, who cultivated common land in Surrey in 1649–50, when food prices had risen sharply, and were then forced off their land by the authorities. Winstanley later became prominent as a pamphleteer with communistic ideas. In dedicating his most famous pamphlet, *The Law of Freedom in a Platform*, to *Cromwell in 1652, he showed surprising naïvety in thinking that Cromwell would approve the thesis that the *English Civil War had been fought against all who were enemies of the poor, including landlords and priests.

witan (from Old English *witenagemot*, 'moot', or meeting, of the king's councillors) The council summoned by the Anglo-Saxon kings. The meetings of the witan in the 10th and 11th centuries were a formalization of the primitive councils that existed in the early Saxon kingdoms of the 7th century. These formal gatherings of *aldermen, *thanes, and bishops discussed royal grants of land, church benefices, charters, aspects of taxation, defence and foreign policy, customary law, and the prosecution of traitors. The succession of a king had usually to be acknowledged by the witan.

witchcraft The malevolent exercise of supposed supernatural powers, especially by women, attributed to a connection with the devil or evil spirits. The witch's male counterpart is wizard, sorcerer, or warlock. There are accounts of witchcraft in ancient Greek and Roman texts, for example Medea, who uses sorcery to help Jason win the Golden Fleece. In the Old Testament King Saul consults the Witch of Endor. In the early Middle Ages popular superstition began to associate witchcraft with demonic possession and the rejection of God. By the late 13th century the *Inquisition dealt with cases of witchcraft involving heresy, and secular courts, especially in Germany, punished these supposed crimes with characteristic cruelty. Mass persecutions began to take place in the 15th century, and the publication of *Malleus Maleficarum* ('Hammer of Witches') in 1487, describing witches' sabbaths, night-flying, intercourse with the devil, transformation into animals, and malicious spells cast on men and cattle, greatly increased superstition and persecution. Witches were popularly depicted with a black cat (the 'familiar') and a broomstick. The 16th-century Reformers further contributed to the persecution of witches, as did the unrest stirred up by the religious wars. The last trials for witchcraft in England were in 1712, and on the Continent (in Prussia) in 1793. In America the belief in witchcraft was rife but the *Salem witch trials (1692) caused a general revulsion. In the 17th century better education led to rejection of belief in witchcraft, but popular superstition survived much longer. In the 20th century, in Europe and the USA, a new kind of witchcraft, claiming to be a revival of pre-Christian pagan religion, has been practised by a small number of adherents and has been associated with allegations of animal sacrifice and child sexual abuse.

Witt, Jan de (1625–72) Dutch statesman, an opponent of William II of Orange. He was the effective leader of the United Provinces during the minority of *William III, dominating the other provinces by his political skill and his knowledge of foreign affairs. The republican party sought to limit the powers of the Orange family and in 1654 members were excluded from state offices. In 1668 he signed the defensive Triple Alliance with England and Sweden to thwart *Louis XIV's designs on The Netherlands. When Louis invaded in 1672 de Witt was caught unprepared and William proved himself an able commander of the Dutch forces. De Witt's power was undermined and he and his brother Cornelius, a naval officer, were killed by a mob in 1672.

Witte, Sergei Yulyevich, Count (1849–1915) Russian statesman. As Finance Minister (1892–1903) and Premier (1905–06), he believed that if Russia was to become the equal of western industrial nations both government investment and foreign capital were essential. New railways linked the Donetz coalmines with

St Petersburg and Moscow and the Trans-Siberian railway was built. He encouraged the start of steel production and sufficient petroleum was produced to satisfy Russia's need and for export. Thus on the eve of political revolution Russia underwent a remarkable industrial revolution. Although Witte's ideal was economic modernization combined with authoritarian rule, during the *Russian Revolution of 1905 he urged *Nicholas II to issue the October Manifesto granting Russia a constitution and to summon the *Duma. Nicholas disliked him and dismissed him.

Wittelsbach A German family which formed a ruling dynasty in Bavaria between 1180 and 1918. By a marriage of 1214, the Rhenish Palatinate was added to the family holdings. **Duke Louis II** (c.1283–1347) was elected Holy Roman Emperor, and divided the Wittelsbach succession between a younger branch (which received Bavaria) and a senior one (which inherited the Rhenish and Upper Palatinate and was given an electoral title in 1356). During the *Reformation, the Bavarian branch remained staunchly Catholic. The Palatinate branch espoused the new Protestant faith and during the *Thirty Years War forfeited both its electoral vote and the Upper Palatinate to Bavaria. By the Treaty of *Westphalia (1648) a new electoral vote was created for the Rhenish Palatinate. The Elector Charles Albert of Bavaria (1697–1745) became Holy Roman Emperor (1742–45).

Wolfe, James (1727–59) British general. As one of the leaders of the expedition sent to seize French Canada, he played a vital role in the capture of Louisbourg on Cape Breton Island in 1758. The following year he commanded the attack on the French capital, the city of Quebec. He was fatally wounded while leading his troops to victory on the Plains of Abraham, the scene of the battle that was to lead to British control of Canada.

Wollstonecraft, Mary (1759–97) British writer and feminist, of Irish descent. She was associated with a radical circle known as the 'English Jacobins', whose members included Thomas *Paine and William *Godwin. In 1790 she published *A Vindication of the Rights of Man* in reply to Edmund Burke's *Reflections on the Revolution in France*. Her best-known work, *A Vindication of the Rights of Woman* (1792), defied Jean-Jacques *Rousseau's assumptions about male superiority and championed educational equality for women. In 1797 she married Godwin and died shortly after giving birth

to their daughter Mary, who became the wife of the poet Percy Bysshe Shelley.

Wolsey, Thomas (known as **'Cardinal Wolsey'**) (c.1474–1530) English prelate and statesman. Favoured by Henry VIII, he dominated foreign and domestic policy in the early part of Henry's reign and held positions as Archbishop of York (1514–30), cardinal (1515–30), and Lord Chancellor (1515–29). His main interest was foreign politics, in which he sought to increase England's influence in European affairs by holding the balance of power between the Holy Roman Empire and France. Wolsey incurred royal displeasure through his failure to secure the papal dispensation for Henry's divorce from Catherine of Aragon; he was arrested on a charge of treason and died on his way to trial in London.

women's liberation *See* FEMINISM.

women's movement *See* FEMINISM.

women's suffrage The right of women to take part in political life and to vote in an election. Women's suffrage was advocated by Mary *Wollstonecraft in *A Vindication of the Rights of Woman* (1792), and throughout the 19th century, in Britain and the USA, calls were made for voting rights for women. These were first attained at a national level in New Zealand (1893). The state of Wyoming, USA, introduced women's suffrage in 1869 and by 1920 all women over 21 were given the vote in the USA. The first European nation to grant female suffrage was Finland in 1906, with Norway following in 1913, and Germany in 1919. In Britain, as a result of agitation by the Women's Social and Political Union, led by Emmeline Pankhurst and her daughter Christabel (*see* SUFFRAGETTES), the vote was granted in 1918 to those over 30 and in 1928 to women over 21. In the years following World War I, women were granted the vote in many countries, including Germany, Poland, Austria, and Sweden (1919), and the USA (1920). The Roman Catholic Church was reluctant to support women's suffrage and in many Catholic countries it was not gained until after World War II; in France it was granted in 1944, in Belgium in 1948, while in Switzerland not until 1971. In Russia women gained the right to vote with the Revolution (1917), and women's suffrage was extended to the Soviet Union from 1922. In developing countries, women's suffrage was usually obtained with independence, and in most Muslim countries women now have the vote. Women still do not have the vote in certain absolute monarchies, such as Saudi Arabia. *See also* FEMINISM.

wool staple One of the towns in England, Wales, Ireland, or in Continental Europe, through which wool merchants traded. They were set up by *Edward III of England as a means of controlling the principal English export, wool, so that he could be guaranteed the tax due on it at the customs point. By the Ordinance of the Staple (1353) 15 British staple towns were established, but in 1363 Calais was made the wool staple through which all wool exports had to pass; a very profitable monopoly in the wool trade was given to the *Merchant Staplers. A continental staple existed until the ban on exports of wool in 1617.

workhouse A public institution in which people unable to support themselves were housed and (if able-bodied) made to work. The 1601 *Poor Law Act made parishes responsible for their own workhouses, but often they were hard to distinguish from the houses of correction, set up to discipline vagrants. The 1723 Workhouse Act denied relief to able-bodied paupers who refused to enter workhouses.

Works Project Administration (or **Works Progress Administration**) (WPA) A US federal relief measure for the unemployed. An agency of the *New Deal, it was established by the Emergency Relief Appropriation Act of 1935. The initiators were Harold Ickes and Harry Hopkins; they wanted the (estimated) 3.5 million unemployed but able-bodied to be given work and not a dole. Thus, through their wages, they would have money to spend and thereby help business to revive. The WPA employed about two million at one time and by 1941 eight million (20% of the labour force) were engaged in public works. It built roads, bridges, playgrounds, airport landing fields, school buildings and hospitals, and ran a campaign against adult illiteracy. It was also, as even its friends had to admit, a useful source of employment for Democratic Party workers.

World Bank An international financial organization. The **International Bank for Reconstruction and Development** (IBRD) was set up by the United Nations in 1945 to promote the economic development of member nations by facilitating the investment of capital for productive purposes, encouraging private foreign investment, and if necessary lending money from its own funds. It was complemented in 1960 by the establishment of the **International Development Association** (IDA) to make loans and grants to the world's poorest countries. The IBRD and the IDA have the same staff and headquarters (in Washington, DC); together

they are known as the 'World Bank'. The **World Bank Group** consists of the IBRD, the IDA, the International Finance Corporation (IFC), the Multilateral Investment Guarantee Agency (MIGA), and the International Centre for Settlement of Investment Disputes (ICSID).

World Council of Churches An interdenominational organization of Christian Churches, created in 1948. Apart from the *Roman Catholic Church and the Unitarians, the Council includes all the major and many minor denominations and nearly all the Eastern Orthodox Churches. Since 1961 the Roman Catholic Church has sent accredited observers. The World Council of Churches is the most important of a number of ecumenical movements advocating greater unity amongst the Christian Churches. Most of the work of the Council is advisory, but it also has a number of administrative units; the largest of these is the division of Inter-Church Aid, Refugee, and World Service.

World Economic Forum An international foundation that aims to improve the state of the world by encouraging and facilitating partnership between significant organizations. Founded in 1971 and based in Geneva, its members are, in principle, the world's 1000 leading companies. It is noted for its annual meetings, usually held at Davos in Switzerland, where leading figures from world business and politics confer in an informal atmosphere. Its supporters maintain that only good can come of such meetings. However, critics view the World Economic Forum as an elite club of the rich, dominated by the developed world. Its meetings have been targets for anti-capitalist and anti-*globalization protests.

World Health Organization (WHO) A United Nations specialized agency established in 1948 with the broad aim of attaining the highest level of health for all people, and supported by 194 member states. Its head office is in Geneva, Switzerland. WHO does not conduct its own research but promotes biomedical and health research in some 500 collaborating centres worldwide, arranging international medical conferences and the exchange and training of research workers. WHO compiles the *International Pharmacopoeia*, monitors epidemics, evaluates new drugs, and advises on biological standards. It publishes monthly an international journal of health development, the *Bulletin of the World Health Organization*. A notable success of WHO has been the global eradication of smallpox; in 2012 it declared the eradication of polio to be an urgent global health priority.

WHO advocates a number of public health measures to provide safe drinking water and adequate sanitation, the immunization of all children against major communicable diseases, and the reduction of malnutrition. In addition, it has intensified efforts to prevent and combat endemic diseases, such as malaria and tuberculosis, and to give access to essential drugs and to family planning services.

World Trade Organization (WTO) An international economic body, inaugurated on 1 January 1995 as the successor to the *General Agreement on Tariffs and Trade (GATT). The WTO has a wider role than GATT, covering commercial activities beyond the remit of the latter body, such as intellectual property rights and trade in services. It has 159 members.

World War I (1914–18) A war fought between the Allied Powers—Britain, France, Russia, Japan, and Serbia—who were joined in the course of the war by Italy (1915), Portugal and Romania (1916), the USA and Greece (1917)—against the Central Powers: Germany, the Austro-Hungarian empire, Ottoman Turkey, and Bulgaria (from 1915). The war's two principal causes were fear of Germany's colonial ambitions and European tensions arising from shifting diplomatic divisions and nationalist agitation, especially in the *Balkans. It was fought in six main theatres of war. On the *Western Front fighting was characterized by trench warfare, both sides believing that superiority in numbers would ultimately prevail despite the greater power of mechanized defence. Aerial warfare developed from reconnaissance into bombing and the use of fighter aircraft in air-to-air combat. On the Eastern Front the initial Russian advance was defeated at Tannenberg (1914). With Turkey also attacking Russia, the Dardanelles expedition (1915) was planned in order to provide relief, but it failed. Temporary Russian success against Austria-Hungary was followed (1917) by military disaster and the *Russian Revolution. The Mesopotamian Campaign was prompted by Britain's desire to protect oil installations and to conquer outlying parts of the Ottoman empire. A British advance in 1917 against the Turks in Palestine, aided by an Arab revolt, succeeded. In north-east Italy a long and disastrous campaign after Italy had joined the Allies was waged against Austria-Hungary, with success only coming late in 1918. Campaigns against Germany's colonial possessions in Africa and the Pacific were less

demanding. At sea there was only one major encounter, the inconclusive Battle of *Jutland (1916). A conservative estimate of casualties of the war gives 10 million killed and 20 million wounded. An armistice was signed and peace terms agreed in the *Versailles Peace Settlement.

World War II (1939–45) A war fought between the *Axis Powers and the Allies, including Britain, the Soviet Union, and *the USA. Having secretly rearmed Germany, *Hitler occupied (1936) the Rhineland, in contravention of the *Versailles Peace Settlement. In the same year the Italian fascist dictator, Benito *Mussolini, joined Hitler in a Berlin-Rome axis, and in 1937 Italy pledged support for the *Anti-Comintern Pact between Germany and Japan. In the 1938 *Anschluss, Germany annexed Austria into the *Third Reich, and in the same year invaded Czechoslovak *Sudetenland. Hitler, having secured the *Munich Pact with *Chamberlain in 1938, signed the Nazi–Soviet Pact with *Stalin in August 1939. Germany then felt free to invade the *Polish Corridor and divide Poland between itself and the Soviet Union. Britain, which until 1939 had followed a policy of *appeasement, now delivered an ultimatum to Germany demanding its withdrawal from Poland. Failure to do so would result in war. As a consequence of Germany's refusal to withdraw Britain declared war on Germany on 3 September. In 1940 Chamberlain resigned and Winston *Churchill became head of a coalition government. The Soviet Union occupied the Baltic States and attacked Finland. Denmark, parts of Norway, Belgium, the Netherlands, and three-fifths of France fell to Germany in rapid succession, while the rest of France was established as a neutral state with its government at *Vichy. A massive *bombing offensive was launched against Britain, but the planned invasion of the country was postponed indefinitely after Germany failed to gain air superiority in the Battle of *Britain. Pro-Nazi governments in Hungary, Romania, Bulgaria and Slovakia now joined the Axis Powers, and Greece and Yugoslavia were overrun in March–April 1941. Hitler, breaking his pact with Stalin, invaded the Soviet Union, where his forces reached the outskirts of Moscow. Without declaring war, Japan attacked the US fleet at *Pearl Harbor in December 1941, provoking the USA to enter into the war on the side of Britain. In 1942 the first Allied counter-offensive began against *Rommel in North Africa (*see* NORTH AFRICAN CAMPAIGNS), and in 1943 Allied troops began an invasion of the Italian mainland, resulting in the overthrow of

Mussolini's government a month later. On the Eastern Front the decisive battles around *Kursk and *Stalingrad broke the German hold. The Allied invasion of western Europe was launched in the *Normandy Campaign in June 1944 and Germany surrendered, after Hitler's suicide in Berlin, in May 1945. The Pacific Campaigns had eliminated the Japanese navy, and the heavy strategic bombing of Japan by the USA, culminating in the atomic bombing of Hiroshima and Nagasaki on 6 and 9 August 1945, induced Japan's surrender a month later.

The dead in World War II have been estimated at 15 million military, of which up to 2 million were Soviet prisoners-of-war. An estimated 35 million civilians died, with some 6 million Jews perishing in Nazi *concentration camps, in mass murders in Eastern Europe. Refugees from the Soviet Union and Eastern Europe numbered many millions. The long-term results of the war in Europe were the division of Germany, the restoration to the Soviet Union of lands lost between 1919 and 1921, together with the creation of communist buffer states along the Soviet frontier. Britain had accumulated a $20 billion debt, while in the Far East nationalist resistance forces were to ensure the decolonization of south-east Asian countries. The USA and the Soviet Union emerged as the two largest global powers. Their wartime alliance collapsed within three years and each embarked on a programme of rearmament with nuclear capability, as the *Cold War developed.

Worms, Diet of (1521) A meeting between *Luther and *Charles V that took place in the city of Worms, on the River Rhine, in Germany. Luther committed himself to the cause of Protestant reform and on the last day of the Diet his teaching was formally condemned in the **Edict of Worms**.

Wounded Knee, Battle of (1890) The last major battle between the US army and the Sioux people of the Great Plains. The site is a creek on Pine Ridge reservation, South Dakota, where, after the killing of *Sitting Bull, the 7th US Cavalry surrounded a band of Sioux. These were followers of the Native American *ghost dance religion, evolved around 1888 among the Paiute by *Wovoka, who preached the coming of a Native American messiah who would restore the country to the Native Americans and reunite the living with the dead. In 1890 a Ghost Dance uprising in South Dakota culminated at Wounded Knee, when US troops massacred some 200 Teton Sioux.

In 1973 the massacre was recalled when members of the American Indian Movement occupied the site. They were surrounded by a force of federal marshals; two Native Americans were killed, and one marshal seriously wounded. They agreed to evacuate the area in exchange for negotiation on Native American grievances.

Wovoka (or **Jack Wilson**) (*c.*1865–1932) A Native American (Paiute) prophet, who instigated the *ghost dance, a *millenarian movement in the late 19th century that promised beleaguered Native Americans redemption and freedom from oppression. In 1888 Wovoka experienced a vision in which he claimed the "Great Spirit" had assured him that the White invaders, who had overrun traditional lands and slaughtered the bison on which the Plains peoples depended, would be put to flight if the Native Americans united in performing the ghost dance. Wovoka's messianic movement failed to help the Native Americans. In 1890 the charismatic Hunkpapa (Dakota) Sioux leader *Sitting Bull, who supported the dance, was killed while resisting arrest and shortly afterwards a group of dancers, believing that their ritual garb made them immune to bullets, were massacred by US troops at the Battle of *Wounded Knee.

writing A system of inscribed signs replacing or recording spoken language. Various writing systems worldwide have developed independently. Writing is closely associated with the appearance of civilization, since in simple societies speech and memory were sufficient and there was no need for writing. It was essential, however, for the administration on which civilized states depend. The *quipus* of the *Incas, which were bundles of variously knotted strings, were a simple form of recording information that served the purposes of accounting but lacked the flexibility of other writing systems, whether carved, painted, scratched, impressed, or printed.

People had probably attempted writing by 6000 BC and it developed independently in such places as Egypt, Mesopotamia, China, and South America. The earliest forms of writing used simple pictorial signs to represent objects. The *Sumerians had developed a pictographical system of writing by about 3400 BC. The Sumerians and Egyptians also used symbols to represent spoken sounds, such as syllables and words.

The first complete alphabet, comprising symbols representing all the vowels and consonants of a language, was devised by the ancient Greeks. They based their alphabet on earlier sound-based partial alphabets, such as that used by the *Phoenicians. Chinese writing uses a system of symbols to represent words or concepts rather than sounds and is not directly linked to pronunciation.

The history of writing has been influenced by technological developments, such as the invention of paper and printing, and by increased literacy due to the expansion of formal education.

Wuchang Uprising (10 October 1911) A revolt in the city of Wuchang that started the *Chinese Revolution of 1911. An accidental explosion forced republican revolutionaries to begin a planned uprising earlier than intended, but on the next day army units that had been won over to the rebel cause seized the city. The Qing government failed to respond swiftly to the uprising and further provincial uprisings followed, leading to the formation of a Provisional Republican Government on 1 January 1912.

Wyatt's Rebellion (February 1554) A protest in England against *Mary I's projected marriage to the future *Philip II of Spain. Its leader was a Kentish landowner, Sir Thomas Wyatt (1521–54). Convinced that the marriage would turn England into 'a cockleboat towed by a Spanish galleon', he led 3000 Kentishmen in a march on London. The rebellion's ultimate aims are uncertain, as is the involvement of Mary's half-sister, Princess Elizabeth, but it led to the execution of Lady Jane *Grey. Wyatt found most Londoners' loyalty to Mary stronger than their antipathy to Spain. He surrendered, and was executed with 100 others.

Wyclif, John (or **John Wycliffe**) (c.1330–84) English religious reformer. He was a lecturer at Oxford (1361–82) and a prolific writer, whose attacks on medieval theocracy are regarded as precursors of the Reformation. He criticized the wealth and power of the Church, upheld the Bible as the sole guide for doctrine, and questioned the scriptural basis of the papacy; his teachings were disseminated by itinerant preachers. In accordance with his belief that such texts should be accessible to ordinary people, he instituted the first English translation of the Bible. He was compelled to retire from Oxford after his attack on the doctrine of transubstantiation and after the Peasants' Revolt (1381), which was blamed on his teaching. His followers were known as Lollards.

w

Xenophon (*c*.435–*c*.354 BC) Greek historian, writer, and military leader. He was born in Athens and became a disciple and friend of Socrates. In 401 he joined the campaign of the Persian prince *Cyrus the Younger against Artaxerxes II; when Cyrus was killed north of Babylon, Xenophon led an army of 10,000 Greek mercenaries in their retreat to the Black Sea, a journey of about 1500 km (900 miles). His historical works include the *Anabasis*, an account of the campaign with Cyrus and its aftermath, and the *Hellenica*, a history of Greece. Among his other writings are three works concerning the life and teachings of Socrates, and the *Cyropaedia*, a historical romance about the education of Cyrus the Younger.

Xerxes I (or **Xerxes the Great**) Ruler of the Achaemenid Persian empire 486–465 BC. He personally led the great expedition against Greece, but after watching his fleet being defeated at *Salamis in 480 BC, he withdrew, leaving behind Mardonius under whose command the army was defeated at Plataea in 479. The subsequent activities of the *Delian League deprived him of many Greek cities in Asia Minor. The latter part of his reign was marked by intrigues, one of which led to his murder.

Xhosa Wars (1779–1879) The wars between the Xhosa people and Dutch and British colonists along the east coast of Cape Colony, between the Great Fish and Great Kei rivers. From 1811 the policy of clearing the land of Xhosa people to make way for Europeans began and, following a year of fighting (1818–19), some 4000 British colonists were installed along the great Fish river. As they pushed the frontier east, however, the colonists met greater resistance, cattle raids resulting in retaliation. The war of 1834 to 1835 yielded 60,000 head of cattle to the colonists and was followed by the longer struggle of 1846 to 1853. The war of 1877 to 1879, which yielded 15,000 cattle and 20,000 sheep, was vainly fought by tribesmen returning from

the diamond fields in a last bid to regain their land. Afterwards all Xhosa territory was incorporated as European farmland within Cape Colony.

Xia (or **Hsia**) (*c*.21st century–*c*.16th century BC) The first dynasty to rule in China, according to tradition. It was reputedly founded by Yu the Great, a model ruler, who is said to have attempted to control flooding by irrigation schemes. As yet no evidence authenticates the Xia, but it is possible such evidence will be found, as the existence of China's second dynasty, the *Shang, was not verified until the 1920s.

Xi'an incident (December 1936) The kidnapping of the Chinese leader *Chiang Kai-shek while visiting disaffected Manchurian troops at Xi'an. Chiang was captured by conspirators headed by Zhang Xueliang, who attempted to force him to give up his campaign against the communists and lead a national war against the Japanese, who had occupied Manchuria in 1931. After Chiang had refused to accede to their demands, the communists, headed by *Zhou Enlai, also became involved in the negotiations and eventually Chiang was released, having promised to take a more active role against the Japanese and to allow local autonomy to the communists. Zhang Xueliang was imprisoned by Chiang, but the incident led to limited cooperation between the communists and the *Kuomintang against the Japanese.

Xi Jinping (1953–) Chinese politician, President (2013–). The son of a senior Communist Party official, he grew up in Beijing. However, his father was purged in the *Cultural Revolution and Xi was sent to work as a manual labourer in Shaanxi (1969–75), where he joined the Communist Party (1974). In 1979 he graduated in chemical engineering from Tsinghua University, Beijing, and thereafter worked for the Party and government in Beijing, Hebei, Fujian, Zhejiang, and Shanghai. In 2007 he was appointed to the standing committee of the Communist Party Politburo, and in 2012 he succeeded *Hu Jintao as Party General Secretary. He became President of China in 2013.

Xiongnu Nomad horsemen who began harrying northern Chinese states c.300 BC. Their homelands were in southern Siberia and Mongolia. It was to fend off their incursions that some Chinese states built walls, later joined together to form the *Great Wall of China. The most serious attacks came under the early *Han, after the Xiongnu had formed a league under their Shan Yu (Heavenly Ruler). In the confusion following the Han's collapse, claiming descent from Chinese princesses, they set up ephemeral dynasties in northern China. Thereafter Chinese records make no reference to them. The Eastern Turks, who submitted to the Tang emperor *Taizong, are thought to be their descendants.

Xuanzong See MINGHUANG.

XYZ Affair An episode (1797–98) in US–French diplomatic relations. A three-man mission was sent to France to resolve a dispute caused by the USA's unwillingness to aid France in the French Revolutionary wars in spite of treaty obligations made in 1778. *Talleyrand refused to see the delegation and indirect suggestions of loans and bribes to France came through Mme de Villette, a friend of Talleyrand. Negotiations were carried on through her with X (Jean Conrad Hottinguer), Y (a Mr Bellamy, a US banker in Hamburg), and Z (Lucien Hauteval). A proposal that the Americans should pay Talleyrand $250,000 created outrage in the USA. President *Adams, however, ignored calls for war and reached agreement with the French at the Convention of Mortefontaine (30 September 1800).

Yalta Conference (4–11 February 1945) A meeting between the Allied leaders *Stalin, *Churchill, and Franklin D. *Roosevelt at Yalta in the Soviet Union. They discussed the final stages of World War II, as well as the subsequent division of Germany. Stalin obtained agreement that the Ukraine and Outer Mongolia should be admitted as full members to the United Nations, whose founding conference was to be convened in San Francisco two months later. Stalin also gave a secret undertaking to enter the war against Japan after the unconditional surrender of Germany and was promised the Kurile Islands and an occupation zone in Korea. The meeting between the Allied heads of state was followed five months later by the *Potsdam Conference.

Yamagata Aritomo (1838–1922) Japanese soldier and statesman. A member of a samurai family, he was an early opponent of the westernization of Japan, but, having experienced western military supremacy, he became a strong advocate of the modernization of the recently created *Meiji state. Serving in a succession of senior posts, he was the prime architect of the modern Japanese army, shaping a mass conscript army organized on the principle of unswerving loyalty to the emperor. He served as the first Prime Minister (1889–91) after the introduction of the parliamentary system and held the post again (1898–1900). Serving also as chief of the general staff during the *Russo-Japanese War he exercised great influence and power, largely behind the scenes, in the years leading up to World War I.

Yamashita Tomoyuki (known as 'The Tiger of Malaya') (1888–1946) Japanese general. In World War II he led his forces in a lightning series of successes, capturing Malaya (1941–42), *Singapore (1942), and Burma. In 1944 he assumed control of the *Philippines Campaign. He surrendered to the Allies under *MacArthur in 1945, was tried before a military commission for atrocities committed by his soldiers, and hanged.

Yamato The clan from which all the emperors of Japan are descended. Claiming the Sun-goddess as ancestress, they had their chief shrine at Ise. Gradually they established control over rival clans and by the 5th century AD much of Japan was subject to them. They were influenced by Chinese culture, initially learning of China through southern Korea. *Buddhism and the study of Chinese language and literature were introduced in the 7th century and Prince Shotuku produced administrative systems based on *Sui China. The Yamato chief assumed the title emperor and built capitals based on *Tang Chinese designs first at Nara then at Kyoto. By the 9th century the Fujiwara family controlled the imperial court and during the period of the shoguns the imperial family had little power.

Yangshao *See* NEOLITHIC.

Yeltsin, Boris (Nikolaevich) (1931–2007) Russian statesman, President of the Russian Federation (1991–9). At first a supporter of Mikhail Gorbachev's reform programme, he soon became its leading radical opponent. In 1990 Yeltsin was elected President of the Russian Soviet Federative Socialist Republic; shortly afterwards he and his supporters resigned from the Communist Party. He emerged with new stature after an attempted coup in 1991, during which he rallied support for Gorbachev; on the breakup of the USSR at the end of that year he became President of the independent Russian Federation. He survived another attempted coup in 1993. Despite criticism over his handling of the conflict in Chechnya, a heart attack in 1995, and a subsequent coronary bypass operation, he was re-elected in the presidential elections of 1996. Concern over his health continued. During 1998 to 1999 he sacked the entire government four times but an attempt to impeach him failed. He resigned unexpectedly at the end of 1999.

Yemen, Republic of

Capital:	Sana'a
Area:	527,968 sq km (203,850 sq miles)
Population:	25,408,288 (2013 est)
Currency:	1 Yemeni rial = 100 fils
Religions:	Sunni Muslim 64.4%; Shiite Muslim 34.7%
Ethnic Groups:	Arab 92.8%; minority groups
Languages:	Arabic (official)
International Organizations:	UN; Arab League; Non-Aligned Movement

A country in the south of the Arabian peninsula, bordering Saudi Arabia and Oman on the north.

Physical Behind the western, Red Sea, coast are high mountains. The lower-lying eastern part has a coast on the Gulf of Aden. Mostly hot desert, these are areas where cotton can be grown.

Economy The production and export of oil, a declining resource, contributes one-quarter of GDP. Other exports include coffee, dried and salted fish, and liquefied natural gas. Industry is limited but includes textiles, leather goods, food processing, and handicrafts. Most of the work-force is employed in agriculture or livestock herding. In addition to coffee, principal crops include grain, fruit, vegetables, pulses, qat, and cotton.

History From *c.*950 to 115 BC Yemen was a flourishing region called Saba—the site of the kingdom of the biblical queen of Sheba. Because of its summer rains it was known to Rome as Arabia Felix ('Happy Arabia'), but it declined with its irrigation system around the 6th century AD. It was converted to *Islam in the 7th century and came under the rule of the Muslim caliphate. Much of it was under the rule of the Ottomans (1517–1918), although the British established the colony of Aden in 1839. In 1918, with British support, the territory (excluding Aden) was proclaimed a kingdom under Imam Yahya, its borders with both Aden and Saudi Arabia for long being matters of dispute. Yahya was assassinated in 1948, and his son Ahmad ruled until 1962. On his death the army under General Abdullah al-Sallal proclaimed the Yemen Arab Republic (North Yemen),

backed by both Egypt and Syria. Saudi Arabia supported those tribes who gave their loyalty to Ahmad's son Imam Muhammad al-Badr. Civil war lasted until 1967, when Nasser withdrew Egyptian troops, after the defeat of the Six-Day War. Sallal resigned and a more moderate government was formed. In April 1970 there was a general pacification, but in 1979 a month-long war broke out with the neighbouring People's Republic of Yemen (South Yemen, formed from Aden and neighbouring emirates when British rule ended in 1967). Intermittent talks to unify North Yemen and South Yemen followed, with a draft constitution agreed in December 1989. The unified state was proclaimed in May 1990, its political capital being Sana'a and commercial capital Aden. A five-member Council was headed by President Ali Abdullah Saleh. The new republic was welcomed to the UN and found itself a member of the Security Council at the time of the Gulf Crisis, when its decision to oppose the US-dominated intervention, leading to the *Gulf War, had strong popular support. Yet it resulted in economic reprisals by the Gulf States, by Europe, and by the USA, while some 800,000 migrant workers were expelled from Saudi Arabia. The latter also gave 'substantial financial support' to anti-government Islamic fundamentalists, who had a strong following among the conservative tribes of the interior. Political tensions, focusing on the distribution of oil revenues, culminated in the southern Yemeni leaders declaring secession, which prompted a three-month civil war in 1994. The war ended when forces from northern Yemen captured Aden. A peace settlement was made and the constitution was amended, the ruling Council being replaced by a directly elected President. Multiparty legislative elections were held in 1997 and presidential elections, in which Saleh was victorious, in 1999. Challenges to the regime grew in the 2000s: a rebellion in the north by Shia Muslims from 2004; disturbances in the former South Yemen from 2007; and *al-Qaeda-inspired terrorism in 2008. The inspiration of the *Arab Spring led to large demonstrations in Sana'a and other cities from January 2011, demanding reform and Saleh's resignation. The regime countered with increasing violence but, after complex political manoeuvres, in November Saleh agreed to transfer power to Vice President Abd Rabbuh Mansur Hadi, who would form a unity government and oversee constitutional reforms. Hadi was confirmed as President by an election in 2012 in which he was the only candidate. A National Dialogue Conference was held to discuss reform (2013–14) and reached agreement on some, but not all, issues.

yeoman A person in late Medieval England qualified by possessing free land of an annual value of 40 shillings to serve on juries, vote for knights of the shire, and exercise other rights. In the 13th and 14th centuries yeomen in England were freehold peasants, but by 1400, as many peasants became richer, all prosperous peasants, whether freeholders or not, as well as franklins (freehold farmers), were called yeomen. In the 15th century some yeoman farmers, leasehold as well as freehold, entered the ranks of the gentry.

Yom Kippur War (1973) The Israeli name for the Arab–Israeli war called by the Arabs the October War. The war began on 6 October, the Feast of Yom Kippur, Israel's most important holy day, when Egyptian forces crossed the Suez Canal and breached the Israeli Bar Lev Line. Syrian troops threw back Israeli forces on the Golan Heights, occupied by the latter since the *Six-Day War. The war lasted three weeks, in which time Israel pushed Syrian forces back into Syria and crossed the Canal, encircling an Egyptian army. In the aftermath, disengagement agreements were signed by Israel with Syria in 1974 and with Egypt in 1974 and 1975. The Israeli withdrawal from Sinai was completed in 1982 after the 1978 Israeli–Egyptian peace treaty.

Yongle (or **Yung-lo**) (1359–1424) *Ming Emperor of China (1403–24). Yongle was a usurper who seized the throne when the second Ming emperor, his young nephew, disappeared in a mysterious palace fire. A man of great enterprise, he obliged Japan to pay tribute and extended the empire by campaigns in the steppes and in *Annam. He and his successor sent *Zheng He on prestigious voyages as far as the east coast of Africa. In 1421 he transferred the main capital from Nanjing to Beijing, his power base, and assured its food supplies by restoring the Grand Canal, linking it to the Huang He and Yangtze rivers. He built the great halls and palaces of the Forbidden City in Beijing and arranged for the preparation of definitive editions of the Confucian classics.

York, Richard Plantagenet, 3rd Duke of (1411–60) The son of Richard, Earl of Cambridge, and Anne Mortimer. Until 1453 he was heir to the throne of England and led the opposition to *Henry VI, especially after the death of Humphrey, Duke of Gloucester in 1447. In 1455 he captured Henry at the first Battle of St Albans and became Protector of the kingdom. In October 1460 he claimed the English throne, but two months later he was defeated and killed by *Lancastrian forces in the Battle of *Wakefield. The *Yorkist party survived him, and triumphed at the second Battle of St Albans.

Yorkist A descendant, or a supporter of the descendants, of Edmund of Langley (1341–1402), fifth son of Edward III and (from 1385) 1st Duke of York. Adherents of his grandson Richard, 3rd Duke of *York, adopted a white rose as their badge. Despite Richard's death at the Battle of *Wakefield (1460), his party was soon afterwards successful against the *Lancastrians and his son Edward became king as *Edward IV. The House of York continued on the throne with *Edward V, and then with Edward IV's younger brother, *Richard III, until *Henry VII began the *Tudor dynasty after his victory at *Bosworth Field in 1485. Henry prudently married the Yorkist heiress, Edward IV's eldest daughter, Elizabeth of York.

Yorktown An American Revolutionary battlefield on the peninsula between the York and James rivers, in Virginia, USA. In August 1781 the British General *Cornwallis, his southern army exhausted after the vain pursuit of Nathanael *Greene, seized and fortified the area for winter quarters. Thanks to the promise of French naval support from the Caribbean, George *Washington was persuaded by the French to march from the Hudson and concentrate all his forces on a siege. With relief by sea cut off by 36 French warships, Cornwallis was forced to surrender on 19 October and American independence was assured.

Yoruba empire of Oyo A loose confederation of Yoruba kingdoms in West Africa. By the early 19th century the Yoruba empire of Oyo was beginning to disintegrate, a process accelerated by the decline of the slave trade and the rise of the *Fulani empire in the north. The Fulani destroyed the old city of Oyo, creating the Muslim emirate of Ilorin. Alafin Atiba, the new ruler of the Oyo empire (1836–59), built a capital, Ago Oja, and allied his empire with Ibadan, but on his death civil war developed. At the same time the influence of the spiritual leader of the Yoruba people, the Oni of Ife, began to decline with the arrival of Christian missionaries. In 1888 a treaty was made with the then Alafin of Oyo, whereby all the Yoruba kingdoms were brought under British protection. In 1900 the empire was incorporated into the protectorate of Southern Nigeria.

y

Yoshida Shigeru (1878–1967) Japanese statesman. A liberal-conservative politician whose appointment as Foreign Minister had been blocked in 1936 by militarist interests, he was imprisoned for advocating surrender in the closing stages of World War II. He emerged after the war as the leader of the Liberal party. As Prime Minister (1946–47; 1949–54), Yoshida was a major architect of Japan's political rehabilitation and socio-economic recovery, working closely with *MacArthur and espousing pro-Western policies.

Young, Brigham (1801–77) US *Mormon leader. After Joseph *Smith's death in Illinois in 1844, Young became the dominant figure of Mormonism, leading the migration west to Salt Lake City, ruling over the new community with autocratic firmness, and turning a desert waste into a flourishing and expanding city.

Young England A British political movement of young Tory aristocrats in the early 1840s. It aimed at ending the political dominance of the middle classes by an alliance between the aristocracy and the working classes, which would carry out all necessary social reforms. The romantic ideas of its members were given some substance by Benjamin *Disraeli, who defined its principles in his novel *Coningsby* (1844). The movement broke up in 1845 over the issue of *free trade and the disputed grant to Maynooth College, the principal institution in Ireland for training Roman Catholic clergy.

Young Ireland An Irish nationalist movement of the 1840s. Led by young Protestants, including Smith O'Brien (1803–64) and John Mitchel (1815–75), who, inspired by Mazzini's *Young Italy, set up their own newspaper, the *Nation*. It called for a revival of Ireland's cultural heritage. At first the members of Young Ireland were associated with Daniel *O'Connell in his campaign to repeal the Act of *Union, but later they turned to more radical solutions. In 1848 they attempted a rebellion, which was easily suppressed, O'Brien and Mitchel being sentenced to transportation.

Young Italy An Italian patriotic society. Formed in 1831 by Giuseppe *Mazzini and 40 other Italian exiles in Marseilles, it set out to replace earlier secret societies, such as the *Carbonari as a prime force in the *Risorgimento. Its significance lay in the kindling of national consciousness and thus contributed towards Italian unification.

Young Plan The programme for the settlement of German *reparations payments after World War I. The plan was embodied in the recommendations of a committee that met in Paris (February 1929) under the chairmanship of a US financier, Owen D. Young, to revise the *Dawes Plan (1924). The total sum due from Germany was reduced by 75% to 121 billion Reichsmark, to be paid in 59 annual instalments. Foreign controls on Germany's economy were lifted. The first instalment was paid in 1930, but further payments lapsed until *Hitler repudiated all reparations debts in 1933.

Young Turks A number of late 19th- and early 20th-century reformers in the *Ottoman empire who carried out the Revolution of 1908. The most prominent party was the Committee of Union and Progress, which seized power in 1913 and (under the triumvirate of *Enver Pasha, Talat Pasha, and Jamal Pasha) ruled the Ottoman empire until 1918, supporting the Central Powers in World War I.

Ypres *See* WESTERN FRONT.

Ypsilanti, Alexander (1792–1828) Greek nationalist leader. Ypsilanti served as a general in the Russian army and was elected leader of the *Philike Hetairia*, a secret organization that sought Greek independence from the *Ottoman empire. In 1821 he raised a revolt in Moldavia, proclaiming the independence of Greece, but he lacked the support of Russia or Romania and was defeated by the Turks and imprisoned in Austria. Together with the successful Greek rebellion in the Peloponnese, his uprising marked the beginning of the *Greek War of Independence.

Yuan A Mongol dynasty of emperors in China founded in 1271 by Kublai Khan. Described by Marco Polo, the elaborate court of the Yuan Dynasty lasted until it was overthrown in 1368 and replaced by the Ming Dynasty.

Yuan Shikai (or **Yuan Shih-k'ai**) (1859–1916) Chinese soldier and statesman, who established his military reputation in Korea and returned to China to undertake a programme of army reform. Yuan Shikai supported the empress dowager *Cixi in her suppression of the *Hundred Days Reform. Dismissed from office after her death (1908), he retired to his old power base in northern China. He was recalled by the court when the *Chinese Revolution of 1911 began, but he temporarily sided with the republicans and advised the emperor to abdicate. In 1912 he became President of the

y

republic. Initially successful in restoring central control, his suppression of *Sun Yat-sen's *Kuomintang, dissolution of Parliament, and his submission to Japan's *Twenty-One Demands provoked a second revolution in the Yangtze region. He had himself proclaimed emperor in 1916, but died shortly afterwards, leaving China divided between rival *warlords.

Yugoslavia A former country in south-east Europe. At the end of World War I it was formed as the Kingdom of the Serbs, Croats, and Slovenes, from the former Slavic provinces of *Austria-Hungary (Slovenia, Croatia, Bosnia and Herzegovina), together with Serbia and Montenegro, and with Macedonian lands ceded from Bulgaria. The monarch of Serbia, Peter I, was to rule the new kingdom and was succeeded by his son *Alexander I. At first the Serbian Premier Nikola Pasic (1921–26) held the rival nations together, but after his death political turmoil caused the new king to establish a royal dictatorship, renaming the country Yugoslavia (January 1929). Moves towards democracy ended with his assassination (1934). During World War II Yugoslavia was overrun by German forces (1941), aided by Bulgarian, Hungarian, and Italian armies. The king fled to London and dismemberment of the country followed, with thousands of Serbs being massacred and the puppet state of *Croatia established under Ante Pavelić. A guerrilla war began, waged by two groups, supporters of the Chetnik *Mihailovich and *Tito's Communist partisans. In 1945 Tito, supported by the Soviet Union, proclaimed the Socialist Federal Republic of Yugoslavia consisting of the republics of *Bosnia and Herzegovina, *Croatia, *Macedonia, *Montenegro, *Serbia, and *Slovenia, and two autonomous Serbian provinces, *Kosovo and Vojvodina. Expelled by Stalin from the Soviet bloc in 1948, Yugoslavia became a leader of the non-aligned nations and the champion of 'positive neutrality'. Improved relations with the West followed and, after Stalin's death, diplomatic and economic ties with the Soviet Union were renewed (1955).

On Tito's death in 1980 his presidency was replaced by an eight-man Collective State Presidency, with the office of President rotating annually. In 1989, multiparty systems were introduced in Croatia and Slovenia, and demands for independence soon followed. In 1990 a rebellion by Croatia's 12% Serb population was supported by Serbia, while in the same year Serbia, under its President, Slobodan *Milošević, brutally suppressed the 90% Albanian majority in the province of Kosovo. Croatia and Slovenia declared independence in 1991, provoking a full-scale military conflict with the Serb-led Yugoslav army. Atrocities were committed by both Croatian and Serb forces, creating large-scale refugee problems. The Belgrade leadership having failed to crush nationalism in Croatia and Slovenia, both states were recognized as independent in January 1991. Bosnia and Herzegovina was also recognized as independent in 1992, although its subsequent civil war – in which Belgrade supported the Bosnian Serbs – lasted until 1995. The independence of Macedonia was generally recognized in 1993.

A new Federal Republic of Yugoslavia, comprising Serbia and Montenegro only, was proclaimed in 1992. Because of its actions in the other successor states and in Kosovo, it was internationally isolated and denied recognition until the fall of Milošević in 2000. Tensions between Serbia and Montenegro, and in particular a strong demand in the latter for complete independence, led in 2003 to a new and much looser federation, the Union of Serbia and Montenegro. Finally, in 2006, Montenegrins voted in a referendum for complete independence; the union with Serbia was dissolved, making the break-up of Yugoslavia into its original constituents complete. In 2008 Kosovo declared independence; by 2013 this was recognized by about half of the world's nations.

y

Z

Zagwe (or **Zague**) An *Ethiopian dynasty founded in 1137 that derives its name from its founder. Zagwe and his successors are reckoned as usurpers because they were of Agau origin from Lasta, and not descended from the Solomonic kings of Ethiopia. There are few records of their emergence, but they claimed to have been descendants of the last king of *Aksum. The first five Zagwe kings are said to have been Jewish, the later kings Christian. They fought rebels in the south of the country and were powerful enough to stop Egypt attempting to convert the country to Islam. They organized the building of many rock churches and founded the holy city of Lalibela. At the end of the 13th century the Zagwe were overthrown by a faction claiming to be the true heirs of the Axumite kings.

zaibatsu Japanese business conglomerates. The zaibatsu (literally 'financial clique') were large business concerns, with ownership concentrated in the hands of a single family, which grew up in the industrialization of late 19th-century Japan. They had their origins in the activities of the seisho ('political merchants'), who made their fortunes by exploiting business links with the newly restored Meiji government. The five major zaibatsu (Mitsubishi, Mitsui, Okura, Sumitomo, Yasuda) controlled much of Japanese industry and trade up to World War II. In 1948 a decree limited the influence of the traditional zaibatsu families, and prevented members of these families from continuing to hold official positions in zaibatsu companies. The influence of the zaibatsu therefore declined. They are now more usually known in Japan as keiretsu.

Zaïre The former name (1971–97) of the Democratic Republic of *Congo.

Zambia

Capital:	Lusaka
Area:	752,618 sq km (290,587 sq miles)
Population:	14,222,233 (2012 est)
Currency:	1 Zambian kwacha = 100 ngwee
Religions:	Protestant 75.3%; Roman Catholic 20.2%
Ethnic Groups:	Bemba 21.0%; Tonga 13.6%; Chewa 7.4%; Lozi 5.7%; Nsenga 5.3%; many minority groups
Languages:	English (official); Bemba; Nyanja; Tonga; local languages
International Organizations:	UN; Commonwealth; SADC; AU; Non-Aligned Movement; WTO

A landlocked country lying on a plateau in central Africa, surrounded by Angola, the Democratic Republic of Congo, Tanzania, Malawi, Mozambique, Zimbabwe, and Namibia (the Caprivi Strip).

Physical The Zambezi and its tributaries the Kafue and Luangwa run through Zambia, while in the north the Chambeshi drains into swampy areas round Lake Bangweulu. In the south-west there are forests of teak.

Economy Zambia has rich mineral resources, including copper, coal, lead, zinc, manganese, cobalt, and gemstones. Exports are dominated by copper, followed by cobalt and electricity (from hydroelectric plants on the Zambezi and other rivers). Other industries include emerald mining, construction, food and drink, and chemicals. However, about five-sixths of the workforce is engaged in agriculture, mostly at a subsistence level, and almost two-thirds of the population lives in poverty. The importance of such cash crops as tobacco and sugar cane has declined. Tobacco, flowers, and cotton are significant exports; other crops include maize, sorghum, rice, groundnuts, sunflower seeds, vegetables, sugar cane, cassava, and coffee.

History Zambia was settled by Nguni people in flight from Zululand in 1835, but was also subject throughout much of the 19th century to Arab slave-traders. Agents from Cecil *Rhodes entered the country (known at this time as Barotseland) in 1890. Rhodes's British South Africa Company had been granted responsibility for it in its charter of 1889 and it began to open up the rich deposits of Broken Hill from 1902. The country was named Northern Rhodesia in 1911. It became a British protectorate in 1924 and between 1953 and 1963 was federated with Southern Rhodesia and Nyasaland, before becoming the independent republic of Zambia under President Kenneth *Kaunda in 1964. Dependent on its large copper-mining industry, Zambia has experienced persistent economic difficulties due to its lack of a coastline and port facilities and to low copper prices. It suffered from economic sanctions against Rhodesia (1965–80), but was assisted by the construction of the Tan-Zam railway. It gave refuge to political exiles from its neighbours Rhodesia (Zimbabwe), Angola, Namibia, and Mozambique, as well as from the ANC. In September 1990 Kaunda yielded to pressure to hold a referendum on the introduction of a multiparty system, and in November 1991 Frederick Chiluba was elected President. He inherited both severe economic problems and an inefficient and corrupt civil service, but was helped by promises that Zambia's international debt-loan would be eased. Chiluba's programme of economic reform was hampered by the drought that swept southern Africa in 1992–93. A state of emergency was declared (1997–98) following an attempted coup. Levy Mwanawasa was elected President in 2001. He was re-elected in 2006 but died in office in August 2008 to be succeeded by Rupiah Banda. Former President Chiluba was charged with corruption in 2003 and went on trial in 2006. He was surprisingly acquitted in 2009 (he had been found guilty of the theft of state funds in a case brought in London in 2007). Michael Sata was elected President in 2011.

zamindar A tax collector or landlord in India under the Mogul empire. The landlord system formed the basis of a system of land-settlement developed in India under British rule. It fell into two distinct groups. In Lower Bengal, the government of Lord *Cornwallis fixed the land revenue payable by the zamindars in perpetuity in 1793 in the hope of stabilizing the revenue, providing an incentive for improvement, and creating a class of loyal landlords. The effect was to create a privileged group of large and wealthy landlords. In the North Western Provinces, the government made a settlement during the 1830s, with much smaller landlords for 30-year periods, in the hope of creating a class of small yeoman farmers and retaining a larger revenue for government.

Zapata, Emiliano (1879–1919) Mexican revolutionary. In 1911 he participated in the revolution led by Francisco Madero (1873–1913); when Madero failed to redistribute land to the peasants, Zapata intitiated his own programme of agrarian reform and attempted to implement this by means of guerrilla warfare. He later joined forces with Pancho *Villa and others, overthrowing General *Huerta in 1914; from 1914 to 1919 he and Villa fought against the regime of Venustiano *Carranza. Zapata was ambushed and killed by Carranza's soldiers in 1919.

Zapatista National Liberation Army (EZLN) A Mexican guerrilla movement that arose in 1994 in the poor south-eastern province of Chiapas. The *Zapatistas*, named after the revolutionary leader Emiliano *Zapata, embarked on an armed struggle to fight discrimination against Maya Indian people in the allocation of land and jobs. Their grievances were fuelled by the *North American Free Trade Agreement concluded between Mexico, the USA, and Canada in 1993, which they claimed would benefit only the rich. The initial rebellion of 1994 left the EZLN in control of some territory and drew world attention to its cause. In 1996 it signed the San Andrés Accords with the Mexican government; these recognized the rights of indigenous peoples and promised greater autonomy. However the government subsequently rejected them and periodic violence continued. In the late 1990s the EZLN emphasized political action over armed conflict and, after further abortive negotiations, in 2003 unilaterally implemented the Accords in communities under its control. The EZLN continues to hold some territory in Chiapas.

Zarathustra (or Zoroaster) (7th–6th century BC) Persian religious reformer, the founder of Zoroastrianism. Born in an aristocratic family, and probably a priest, he is said to have received a vision from Ahura Mazda ('the Wise Lord'), one of many gods then worshipped, urging belief in one god. After King Vishtaspa's conversion (c.588 BC) the religion spread. It is difficult to distinguish between his actual teachings and later legends, for the details of his life cannot be

z

reconstructed with accuracy. He brought Ahura Mazda, the creator, to the centre of worship as the principle of 'good', but retained the ancient fire cult, while abolishing orgiastic sacrificial practices. The *Gathas* (hymns) contain his teachings, but they are unauthenticated.

Zealots The party of revolt among the Jews of Roman Palestine known for their fanaticism. Also known as Canaans after the early inhabitants of Palestine, they have been identified with the 'Daggermen' ('Sicarii') of the Jewish Revolt of 66 to 70 AD and the defenders of *Masada. Simon, one of the disciples of *Jesus Christ, was also known as 'the Zealot', meaning either that he was a member of the party, or equally likely, that he was of a 'zealous' disposition.

Zeebrugge raid (23 April 1918) A raid on a German U-boat base in Belgium during World War I. During the night of 22–23 April 1918 a force led by Admiral Keyes attacked the base sinking three blockships in the channel and almost closing it. More effective but less dramatic was the line of deep mines that he laid across the Straits of Dover.

Zen *See* BUDDHISM.

Zeng Guofan (or **Tseng Kuo-fan**) (1811–72) Chinese soldier and statesman. An imperial official and scholar, critical of the emperor's behaviour and the government's financial policies, in 1852 he reluctantly agreed to organize imperial resistance to the *Taiping Rebellion, raising the Hunan Army, and played a key role in wearing down resistance. With the crucial help of purchased modern European weapons, foreign military containment of the rebels along the eastern coast, and the capture of Nanjing in 1864, he finally broke their power. He became Governor-General of Liang-Jiang, which gave him considerable powers in east-central China. In the 1860s and 1870s he supported the *Self-Strengthening Movement and developed the Jiangnan Arsenal for the manufacture of modern arms and the study of Western technical literature and Western languages.

Zenobia (3rd century AD) Queen of Palmyra (*c.*267–72). She succeeded her murdered husband as ruler and then conquered Egypt and much of Asia Minor. When she proclaimed her son emperor, the Roman emperor Aurelian marched against her and eventually defeated and captured her. She was later given a pension and a villa in Italy.

Zheng He (or **Cheng Ho**) (died *c.*1433) Chinese admiral and explorer, a Muslim court *eunuch from Yunnan province. He commanded seven remarkable voyages (1405–33) undertaken by order of the Ming emperor *Yongle and his successor. His first voyage in 1405–07, consisting of 62 ships, called in at Malacca and reached India. Subsequent voyages went to the Persian Gulf and his last voyage in 1431–33 reached the coast of East Africa. His voyages were made possible by the use of the compass and by Chinese advances in navigation and shipbuilding. The purpose of the voyages is unclear, however, as they were used neither to develop trade nor political influence with the countries visited, although Zheng He did return with tribute in the form of gifts to the emperor, including giraffes, ostriches, and zebras from the city of Mogadishu in East Africa.

Zhou A dynasty of emperors in early China, ruling territory to the north of the Yangtze River from 1122–221 BC. Their capital moved from Hao to Luoyang *c.*700 BC and during the Zhou Dynasty multiplication tables and iron casting were developed.

Zhou Enlai (or **Chou En-lai**) (1898–1976) Chinese Communist statesman, Prime Minister of China (1949–76). One of the founders of the Chinese Communist Party, he joined *Sun Yat-sen in 1924. In 1927 he organized a Communist workers' revolt in Shanghai in support of the *Kuomintang forces surrounding the city. In the early 1930s he formed a partnership with *Mao Zedong, supporting his rise to power within the Communist Party in 1935. On the formation of the People's Republic of China in 1949 Zhou became Premier and also served as Foreign Minister (1949–58). During the 1960s he continued to keep open communication channels with the USA, and he presided over the moves towards détente in 1972–73. He was also a moderating influence during the Cultural Revolution.

Zhoukoudian (or **Choukoutien**) A cave complex south-west of Beijing, made famous by fossils of *Peking Man. The fossils are believed to represent a Chinese variant of *Homo erectus* (*Homo erectus pekinensis*). More than 40 male and female *Homo erectus* individuals are now known from the caves. Added to this hominid collection are many tens of thousands of simple flaked stone tools as well as fossilized bones of more than 100 animal species and so-called ash layers that were once interpreted as cooking hearths. The caves were occupied by Peking Man from about 500,000 to 250,000 years ago.

Zhu De (or **Chu The**) (1886–1976) Chinese revolutionary and soldier. He served as an officer in the imperial army and in the republican force that succeeded it. He became a communist in 1925, presenting his inherited wealth to the party. With *Mao Zedong he organized and trained early units of the People's Liberation Army (1931) in Jiangxi and served as its commander-in-chief until 1954. He was a leader of the *Long March of 1934–35 and commanded the 8th Route Army against the Japanese between 1939 and 1945 before overseeing the communist victory in the *Chinese Civil War. He became marshal in 1955 and remained influential until purged during the *Cultural Revolution. He was restored to favour in 1967 and lived out his life in honoured retirement.

Zhukov, Georgi (Konstantinovich) (1896–1974) Soviet military leader, born in Russia. He was responsible for much of the planning of the Soviet Union's campaigns in World War II. He defeated the Germans at Stalingrad (1943), lifted the Siege of Leningrad (1944), led the final assault on Germany and the capture of Berlin (1945), and became commander of the Soviet zone in occupied Germany after the war.

Zia ul-Haq, Muhammad (1924–88) Pakistani general and statesman, President (1978–88). As Chief of Staff he led the bloodless coup which deposed President Zulfikar Bhutto in 1977. After being sworn in as President in 1978, he banned all political parties and began to introduce strict Islamic laws. Re-appointed President in 1984, Zia ul-Haq lifted martial law but continued to maintain strict political control. He died in an air crash, possibly as the result of sabotage.

Zimbabwe

Capital:	Harare
Area:	390,757 sq km (150,872 sq miles)
Population:	13,182,908 (2013 est)
Currency:	US dollar, South African rand, Botswanan pula, and other currencies. The Zimbabwean dollar was suspended in 2009.
Religions:	mixed Christian and traditional beliefs 50.0%; Christian 25.0%; traditional beliefs 24.0%

Ethnic Groups:	Shona 82.0%; Ndebele 14.0%; other African 2.0%
Languages:	English (official); Shona; Ndebele
International Organizations:	UN; AU; SADC; Non-Aligned Movement; WTO

A landlocked country in southern Africa, surrounded by Zambia, Mozambique, South Africa, and Botswana

Physical On the northwest boundary of Zimbabwe with Zambia are the Victoria Falls and Lake Kariba on the Zambezi, and on the boundary with South Africa is the Limpopo. The country stands mainly on a plateau drained by tributaries of these and other rivers.

Economy Zimbabwe's economic health has declined greatly since 2000, with the main causes being inefficient and corrupt central planning; the financial strain of involvement in the civil war in the Democratic Republic of Congo (1998–2000); the expropriation of White-owned farms—the backbone of the commercial agricultural sector—from 2000; and hyperinflation in the 2000s. The economy began to grow again after the adoption of the US dollar and other currencies in 2009 put an end to hyperinflation, but two-thirds of the population live in poverty and unemployment remains high. The main exports are platinum, cotton, tobacco, gold, ferroalloys, textiles, and clothing. Other mineral resources include nickel, copper, tin, diamonds, and coal; mining and steel production are the principal industries. Agriculture produces cereals, cotton, tobacco, coffee, sugar cane, and groundnuts.

History Zimbabwe is named after the ancient palace city of Great Zimbabwe, a 24-ha (64-acre) site, that dates from the 11th to the 15th centuries. Gold and copper were exported from more than 1000 mines by the 10th century AD, the trade passing through Sofala, in Mozambique, to Arab hands. In the early 15th century the region's riches enabled the rise of the Shona (Karanga) empire, with the stone-built city as its capital. The sovereign had an elaborate court and constitution, and trade links with both sides of Africa; but after Portuguese incursions in the 16th century, Zimbabwe's fortunes steadily declined. In 1629 an attempt to expel the Portuguese resulted in the installation of a puppet

z

ruler. After 1693 the territory was absorbed by the Rozvi empire. In the early 19th century, the Ndebele, under their leader *Mzilikazi, invaded the country from the south. He created a kingdom of **Matabeleland**, which for the next 50 years was to be in a state of permanent tension with the Shona to the north, in what came to be called Mashonaland. When Mzilikazi died he had obtained a peace treaty with the new Transvaal Republic, and he was succeeded by his son Lobengula. In 1889 the British South Africa Company of Cecil *Rhodes was founded, and in 1890 his Pioneer Column marched into Mashonaland. Following the Jameson Raid and the Matabele War of 1893, Mashonaland and Matabeleland were united. Rebellion erupted in 1896–97, but it was ruthlessly suppressed. Rapid economic development followed, the country becoming the crown colony of Southern Rhodesia in 1911 and a self-governing colony in 1923.

After the victory of the right-wing Rhodesian Front in 1962, the colony sought independence but refused British demands for Black political participation in government and, under Prime Minister Ian Smith, issued the Unilateral Declaration of Independence (UDI) in 1965, renouncing colonial status and declaring Rhodesian independence. Subsequent British-sponsored attempts at negotiating a political compromise failed and nationalist forces waged an increasingly successful guerrilla campaign. Military pressure finally forced Smith to concede the principle of Black majority rule, but the regime of the moderate Bishop Muzorewa could not come to an accommodation with the guerrilla leaders of the Patriotic Front, Robert *Mugabe and Joshua *Nkomo. Following the Lancaster House Conference (1979) Robert Mugabe was elected Prime Minister, and Rhodesia became the republic of Zimbabwe in 1980.

The decade of the 1980s saw a revival of tension between Shona and Ndebele, personified by Mugabe and Nkomo. The new constitution of 1987 not only eased this, by merging the two parties of which Mugabe and Nkomo were leaders, but also ended racial representation and created the office of executive President. With internal domestic tensions eased, Zimbabwe played a leading role in the politics of southern Africa, while its five-year plan (1986–90) did much to expand the economy. The state of emergency of 1965 was finally ended in July 1990. Controversial land redistribution plans were enacted during 1993–94. In April 1995, the Zimbabwe African National Union-Patriotic Front (ZANU-PF), which had ruled the country

since the inception of black majority rule, won its fourth successive election victory with an increased majority. The leader of the only opposition party to win seats, the Revd Ndabaningi Sithole of ZANU-Ndonga, was arrested on charges of conspiracy to assassinate President Mugabe later the same year. In March 1996 Mugabe was re-elected as President; turnout at the polls was lower than 40% of the electorate. From 1997 Mugabe's regime responded with authoritarian measures to protests over food prices, corruption, and the lack of political reform, and from 2000 he colluded in the violent seizure of White-owned farms by squatters as part of a land reform programme. The 2000 parliamentary elections resulted in large gains for the opposition despite widespread intimidation. Mugabe was re-elected President in 2002 in a poll considered by foreign observers to be fraudulent; state violence during the campaign led to Zimbabwe's suspension from the Commonwealth (it withdrew from membership in 2003). ZANU-PF won the 2005 parliamentary elections. Its economic position continued to deteriorate, with annual inflation running at about 13,000 per cent in September 2007.

Presidential and parliamentary elections were held in March 2008. The Movement for Democratic Change (MDC) won a majority in parliament and its leader, Morgan Tsvangirai, won the first round of the presidential election. However, it was deemed that he had not won by a sufficient margin, requiring a run off. With MDC supporters suffering violent attacks from ZANU-PF, Tsvangirai withdrew and Mugabe was re-elected in June. Under pressure from South Africa, in September he agreed to share power with Tsvangirai; after further disputes Tsvangirai became Prime Minister in 2009. Meanwhile the economy declined further, with inflation running at 231 million per cent. There were food shortages and a major cholera outbreak that collapsing health services could not prevent. The power-sharing government lasted until 2013, but it quickly became clear that ZANU-PF and Mugabe had retained the real power. In 2009 the worthless Zimbabwean dollar was suspended in favour of the US dollar and other currencies, which ended hyperinflation and allowed economic recovery to begin. A new constitution was introduced in 2013; under its terms, Mugabe was re-elected President and ZANU-PF achieved a large parliamentary majority in relatively peaceful but flawed elections. MDC attempts to overturn the results were rejected.

Zimmermann note (19 January 1917) A German secret telegram, containing a coded message from the German Foreign Secretary, Alfred Zimmermann, to the German minister in Mexico City. This instructed the minister to propose an alliance with Mexico, offering Mexico the territories lost in 1848 to the USA. The British intercepted the message and gave a copy to the US ambassador. The US State Department released the text on 1 March 1917, even as US–German relationships were deteriorating fast over submarine warfare. With the possibility of a German-supported attack by Mexico, the *isolationists lost ground and on 6 April 1917 Congress entered *World War I against Germany.

Zinoviev, Grigori Yevseyevich (1883–1936) Soviet communist leader. Despite originally opposing the *Russian Revolution, he became chairman of the *Comintern (1919–26). In 1924 a letter apparently signed by him (known as the **Zinoviev letter**) was sent to the British Communist Party, urging revolutionary activity within the army and in Ireland. Published in British Conservative newspapers four days before the general election, it may have swung the middle-class vote away from the Labour Party, who claimed (correctly) that it was a forgery. On *Lenin's death Zinoviev, with *Stalin and Kamenev, formed a triumvirate, but he lost power and was executed after Stalin's first show trial.

Zionism A movement advocating the return of Jews to *Palestine founded in 1897 under the leadership of Theodore *Herzl. Originally a secular movement, Zionism has its foundation in the *millenarian belief that the Jews, the chosen people of God, will be reunited from diaspora (dispersion or exile) in their rightful homeland. After the Russian *pogroms of 1881, Leo Pinsker wrote a pamphlet, *Auto-Emanzipation*, appealing for the establishment of a Jewish colony in Palestine. Zionism assumed a political character, notably through Herzl's *Der Judenstaat* (1896). The issue of the *Balfour Declaration in 1917 and the grant of a mandate for Palestine to Britain gave impetus to the movement. During the mandate period (1920–48) under Chaim *Weizmann the World Zionist Organization played a major part in the development of the Jewish community in Palestine by facilitating immigration, by investment (especially in land), and through the Jewish Agency. The movement was further strengthened by the persecution and annihilation of the Jewish people in World War II (the *Holocaust). Zionist activities in the USA were influential in winning the support of Congress and the Presidency (1946–48) for the creation of the state of Israel.

Zionism remains an important issue in Israeli domestic politics and in the politics of the Middle East, since the question of the existence of the state of Israel and its claim to all the biblical territory of Israel has not been satisfactorily reconciled with the rights of the Palestinians. The continuing right of all Jews worldwide, whatever their nationality, to emigrate to Israel and to take Israeli citizenship, is a fundamental principle of Zionism, and the World Zionist Congress, an independent body, exists to support Jewish emigration to Israel.

Zog I (full name **Ahmed Bey Zogu**) (1895–1961) Albanian statesman and ruler, Prime Minister (1922–24), President (1925–28), and king (1928–39). A leader of the reformist Popular Party, he headed a republican government as Premier and later President, ultimately proclaiming himself king in 1928. Zog's autocratic rule resulted in a period of relative political stability, but the close links he had cultivated with Italy from 1925 onwards led to increasing Italian domination of Albania, and when the country was invaded by Italy in 1939, Zog went into exile. He abdicated in 1946 after Albania became a Communist state, and died in France.

Zollverein (German, 'customs union') A customs union to abolish trade and economic barriers between the German states. The Prussian Zollverein was founded in 1833 by merging the North German Zollverein with smaller customs unions, thus increasing Prussian influence. After the Austro-Prussian War (1866) the newly formed North German Confederation entered the Zollverein, and by 1888 the union, which excluded Austria, had largely achieved the economic unification of Germany.

Zulu A South African Bantu people inhabiting the north-eastern part of Natal and speaking a language of the Niger-Congo group of languages.

Zulu Inkatha Movement *See* INKATHA FREEDOM PARTY.

Zulu War (1879) A war fought between Britain and Zululand. Until he occupied the Transvaal in 1877, the policy of the Natal Secretary for Native Affairs, Theophilus Shepstone, had been to protect the Zulu empire of *Cetshwayo against Afrikaner aggression. After the annexation, he reversed this policy to placate the Afrikaner population, and a scheme was prepared to seize Zululand. Frontier incidents provided opportunities, and the British High Commissioner ordered the disbandment of the Zulu army within 30 days. However, Cetshwayo did not comply, and war began on 11 January 1879. On 22 January the British suffered disaster at Isandhlwana, but with reinforcements the Zulu capital, Ulundi, was burnt, Cetshwayo was captured (28 August), and the war ceased on 1 September.

Zuma, Jacob (Gedleyihlekisa) (1942–) South African politician, President (2009–). Zuma joined the outlawed African National Congress in 1959 and was imprisoned in 1963 for 10 years. He continued to work for the ANC after his release, going into exile in 1975 and working his way up the organization to join the National Executive Committee in 1977. In 1990 Zuma returned to South Africa when the ban on the ANC was lifted. He was appointed Deputy President by Thabo *Mbeki in 1999. The expectation that he would succeed Mbeki as President of South Africa was thrown into doubt in 2005 when he was dismissed on suspicion of corruption. Although subsequently charged with corruption and (separately) rape, he was acquitted on both counts in 2006. Despite continued corruption allegations, Zuma's popularity with the ANC membership enabled him to defeat Mbeki for the party presidency in 2007. He became President of South Africa following the ANC's victory in the 2009 election.

Zuo Zongtang (or **Tso Tsung-t'ang**) (1812–85) Chinese soldier and statesman. He rose to military prominence, assisting *Zeng Guofan in suppressing the *Taiping Rebellion and was appointed governor-general of Zhejiang province (1862). He supported the *Self-Strengthening Movement, in 1877 recapturing Xinjiang from Yakub Beg, and making possible its incorporation as a Chinese province.

Zwingli, Ulrich (1484–1531) Swiss Protestant reformer, the principal figure of the Swiss Reformation. He was minister of Zurich from 1518, where he sought to carry through his political and religious reforms and met with strong local support. From 1522 he published articles advocating the liberation of believers from the control of the papacy and bishops, and upholding the Gospel as the sole basis of truth. He attacked the idea of purgatory, the invocation of saints, monasticism, and other orthodox doctrines. His beliefs differed most markedly from Martin *Luther's in his rejection of the latter's doctrine of consubstantiation. The spread of Zwingli's ideas in Switzerland met with fierce resistance and Zwingli was killed in the resulting civil war.

General Links for this Work

SEE WEB LINKS

History World

- Comprehensive, coherent history site with a range of unique resources and material from blue-chip contributors.

SEE WEB LINKS

History Channel: Audio and Video

- This is an archive of video and audio clips from the History Channel. Here, you can view a video clip from 'this day in history', or listen to 'words that changed the world' in the extensive collection of audio speeches.

SEE WEB LINKS

CELT: Irish History, Literature and Politics

- University College Cork's CELT site is a collection of electronic texts on Irish history, literature, and politics. Texts are accompanied by introductions, bibliographies, and, where possible, translations from the Irish, Hiberno-Norman French, or Latin. Many also have images, including line-drawings and maps. The 'Resources' page lists relevant journals, bibliographies, and libraries, as well as providing a general overview of current electronic text projects worldwide.

SEE WEB LINKS

BBC History Online

- Something for everyone, everywhere!

SEE WEB LINKS

History

- This UK-based history portal is funded by JISC (Joint Information Systems Committee), and is aimed at scholars and students. With a useful search engine covering publications and research, and a comprehensive set of links to international resources, this is the pre-eminent history portal in the UK.

SEE WEB LINKS

World History database

- This is a truly international resource, with timelines, overviews of the great events, and portraits of major leaders in all nations. It also has a genealogy database to fit family stories into the wider events of world history!

SEE WEB LINKS

World History Compass

- This classy site has excellent design. It's aimed at teachers, students, and historians, and provides categorized links to world wide sites, including useful site reviews. A fantastic resource!

SEE WEB LINKS

National Archives of Australia

- This collection constitutes the archives of the Australian government - a vast and rich resource for the study of Australian history, Australian society, and the Australian people.

SEE WEB LINKS

Spartacus Educational

- A website providing information about historical figures and periods, run by Spartacus Educational Publishers Ltd.

SEE WEB LINKS

Middle East Network Information Center

- From the University of Texas at Austin, this site is easily navigable, with categorized links and resources or specific country searches.

SEE WEB LINKS

Russian Empire 1905–1915

- Sergei Mikhailovich Prokudin-Gorskii photographed the Russian Empire between 1905 and 1915, using an early colour process, producing about 1,900 glass-plate negatives, all of which have been digitized by the US Library of Congress and can be seen on this site.